Romanticism

Romanticism

AN OXFORD GUIDE

Edited by

Nicholas Roe

OXFORD
UNIVERSITY PRESS

OXFORD

UNIVERSITY PRESS

Great Clarendon Street, Oxford OX2 6DP

Oxford University Press is a department of the University of Oxford.
It furthers the University's objective of excellence in research, scholarship,
and education by publishing worldwide in

Oxford New York

Auckland Cape Town Dar es Salaam Hong Kong Karachi
Kuala Lumpur Madrid Melbourne Mexico City Nairobi
New Delhi Shanghai Taipei Toronto

With offices in

Argentina Austria Brazil Chile Czech Republic France Greece
Guatemala Hungary Italy Japan South Korea Poland Portugal
Singapore Switzerland Thailand Turkey Ukraine Vietnam

Oxford is a registered trade mark of Oxford University Press
in the UK and in certain other countries

Published in the United States
by Oxford University Press Inc., New York

A catalogue record for this book is available from the British Library

Library of Congress Cataloging in Publication Data

Romanticism : an oxford guide / edited by Nicholas Roe.
    p. cm.
  Includes bibliographical references and index.
  ISBN 0-19-925840-6 (alk. paper)
  1. English literature–19th century–History and criticism–Handbooks, manuals, etc.
  2. English literature–18th century–History and criticism–Handbooks, manuals, etc.
  3. Romanticism–Great Britain–Handbooks, manuals, etc. I. Roe, Nicholas
  PR457.R4575 2005
  820.9'145–dc22
                                                                        2004025235

ISBN 0–19–925840–6 (Pbk)

10 9 8 7 6 5 4 3 2 1

Typeset by RefineCatch Limited, Bungay, Suffolk
Printed in Great Britain by
Antony Rowe Ltd, Chippenham, Wiltshire

Preface

This book offers students and other readers a series of informed and accessible essays on Romantic literature and culture. The chapters cover a wide range of topics, and the volume has been prepared so that individual essays may be read on their own or in conjunction with others. Essays have been cross-referenced within the book, and there are helpful pointers to relevant material in Iain McCalman's *Oxford Companion to the Romantic Age* (Oxford: Oxford University Press, 1999). In the sections on 'Reading Romanticism' and 'Romantic Forms' each essay is followed by a practical reading that demonstrates the method discussed or analyses appropriate examples of a form or genre. All of the essays conclude with a list of further reading to encourage readers to explore more widely.

I am grateful to Fiona Kinnear, who commissioned this book, and to Ruth Anderson for her advice and assistance on editorial matters. My particular thanks go to all of the contributors for making the book's preparation a pleasure.

Nicholas Roe, March 2004

Outline contents

Carrie Jarrell Hest

Detailed contents

List of illustrations

List of contributors

Simon Bainbridge Lancaster University

John Barnard University of Leeds

Stephen C. Behrendt University of Nebraska

Andrew Bennett University of Bristol

Christoph Bode Ludwig-Maximilians-Universität München

Julie A. Carlson University of California, Santa Barbara

William Christie University of Sydney

Deirdre Coleman University of Sydney

Richard Cronin University of Glasgow

Nichola Deane University of St Andrews

David Fairer University of Leeds

Tim Fulford Nottingham Trent University

Marilyn Gaull New York University

Bruce E. Graver Providence College, Rhode Island

Alan Gregory Episcopal Theological Seminary of the Southwest, Austin, Texas

Anthony Harding University of Saskatchewan

Michael Herbert University of St Andrews

Jerrold E. Hogle University of Arizona

Kenneth R. Johnston University of Indiana, Bloomington

Steven E. Jones Loyola University, Chicago

Peter J. Kitson University of Dundee

Greg Kucich Notre Dame University

Edward Larrissy University of Leeds

Nigel Leask University of Glasgow

Debbie Lee Washington State University

Susan Manning University of Edinburgh

James C. McKusick University of Maryland

Anne K. Mellor University of California, Los Angeles

David S. Miall University of Alberta

Timothy Morton University of California, Davis

Michael O'Neill University of Durham

Judith Pascoe University of Iowa

Seamus Perry University of Oxford

Adela Pinch University of Michigan

Lynda Pratt University of Nottingham

Andrew Michael Roberts University of Dundee

Nicholas Roe University of St Andrews

Corinna Russell University of Cambridge

Charles J. Rzepka Boston University

Paul D. Sheats University of California, Los Angeles

Jane Stabler University of St Andrews

Fiona Stafford University of Oxford

Sophie Thomas University of Sussex

Carl Thompson Nottingham Trent University

Nicola Trott University of Glasgow

Peter Vassallo University of Malta

John Whale University of Leeds

Introduction

Nicholas Roe

The writers, painters, and musicians in the *Oxford Guide to Romanticism* include Jane Austen, Anna Laetitia Barbauld, William Blake, Samuel Taylor Coleridge, John Constable, Franz Josef Haydn, Leigh Hunt, John Keats, Mary Shelley, Charlotte Smith, J. M. W. Turner, Mary Wollstonecraft, and William Wordsworth. None of them thought of themselves or their age as 'Romantic', and the word 'Romanticism' did not become current until the mid-nineteenth century, long after most of them were dead. In Europe the meaning of 'Romantic' has varied from country to country, while the historical period of 'Romanticism' is a matter of continuing debate. In the *Oxford Guide to Romanticism*, leading scholars and critics provide accessible approaches to this immensely rewarding if sometimes daunting cultural field. First, we need to find out more about those words 'Romantic' and 'Romanticism'.

Events

'What an eventful period is this! I am thankful I have lived to it.' So the French Revolution of 1789 was greeted by an admirer in London. In Paris the prison of the Bastille had fallen. Tyranny had been overthrown. Thomas Paine, author of *The Rights of Man* (1791–2), was jubilant. His pamphlet *Common Sense* (1776) had urged the American colonies to break with the 'mother country' Britain, and he had helped to draft the Constitution enshrining American independence. As he watched liberty kindling in Europe, he was convinced it was 'an age of Revolutions in which everything may be looked for'.[1] The feminist Mary Wollstonecraft looked to the 'pure flame of patriotism' to transform relations between the sexes. For the poet Helen Maria Williams, the French Revolution was 'the triumph of humankind':

it was man asserting the noblest privileges of his nature; and it required but the common feelings of humanity to become in that moment a citizen of the world. For myself, I acknowledge that my heart caught with enthusiasm the general sympathy; and I shall never forget the sensations of that day.[2]

This surge of optimism would reverberate through European and American culture for decades afterwards. The poet William Wordsworth visited France twice during the early years of the revolution (in 1790 and 1791–2) and he too could not forget the sensations of that time. He recalled his visits in his autobiographical poem, *The Prelude*:

> a glorious time,
> A happy time that was. Triumphant looks
> Were then the common language of all eyes;
> As if awaked from sleep, the Nations hailed
> Their great expectancy . .
>
> (1805, VI. 681–5)

The human form of that 'glorious time' is seen in William Blake's radiant figure, 'Glad Day', arms spread wide with joy. Its musical signature is heard in Beethoven's exultant third symphony, the 'Eroica', composed in honour of his hero Napoleon. Shelley said that the French Revolution 'may be called the master theme of the epoch', and its influence continues to the present in ideas of democracy and human rights. We too like to think of ourselves as 'citizens of the world'.

But not everyone was happy. The politician Edmund Burke, for example, denounced the revolution in France as 'evil' and predicted that it would lead to bloodshed. When war broke out three years later, he seemed to have been proved right. The Church of England minister Isaac Hunt (a British loyalist at Philadelphia during the American Revolution) warned that the 'sovereign-deposing, bishop-kicking, title-levelling' Thomas Paine planned to revolutionize 'the government of England on the models of those in France and America'. That meant a 'mob assembly'.[3] While Burke and his kind were drawn to an idealized past of nurturing customs and traditions ('the age of chivalry'), Paine, Wollstonecraft, Williams, and others of like mind gazed with wild surmise into a glorious, liberated future. This was an age as enthralled by memory as it was magnetized by the future, and its art grew from vital tensions between tradition and experiment.

Then and now

Once the great debate about the French Revolution was underway, its repercussions would be felt in all areas of contemporary life. In Britain, men and women were imprisoned without trial for their ideas. Others were banished to Botany Bay in Australia. In France hundreds were dragged to the guillotine. Liberty and rights were contentious issues.

That 'eventful period' two centuries ago echoes through our own times. We too live in an age of revolutions, and the impact of '9/11' has proved no less potent than the American Revolution, the fall of the Bastille, or Napoleon's relentless conquests in Europe and the Mediterranean. Then as now, events seemed to have extraordinary, apocalyptic force, and people looked for meaning and pattern within them. Events were associated with millenarian excitement at the turn of the nineteenth century.

Some believed that a new age was at hand; others looked for the return of Christ, and the last days of the world. A few, like Anna Laetitia Barbauld in her poem 'Eighteen Hundred and Eleven', predicted the downfall of Britain, the ruin of London, and the rise of America as an imperial power. Any attempt to identify the particular character of our own era, post '9/11', is sure to provoke bitter argument divided by politics, race, and religion. Likewise, the age of revolutions leading up to the defeat of Napoleon at the Battle of Waterloo (1815) polarized opinions and was subject to conflicting interpretations (see for example the reading of Keats's *Hyperion* in the chapter on 'Epic').

While no one alive at the time thought of their age in terms of 'Romanticism', there was agreement that the momentous scenes on the world stage were as fantastic as the plot of a romance. Wordsworth, for example, thought of the 'events | Of that great change' in terms of 'an old Romance or Tale | Of Fairy' (1805 *Prelude*, IX. 305–8). On hearing news of Napoleon's astonishing escape from Elba early in 1815, the journalist Leigh Hunt observed: 'We want nothing now, to finish the romantic history of the present times, but a visit from the Man in the Moon.'[4]

To Wordsworth and Hunt the words 'romantic' and 'romance' were synonymous, and referred to the allegorical fictions and fabulous events of medieval and Elizabethan poetry (see further in the chapter on 'Romance'). Coleridge used 'romantic' in that sense to describe his poems 'The Rime of the Ancient Mariner', 'Kubla Khan', and 'Christabel'. But no one living at the time thought of him or herself as a 'Romantic' poet, painter, or musician. Writers who might otherwise have little in common were perceived to belong to various 'schools' such as the Lake School (Wordsworth, Coleridge, and Robert Southey lived in the English Lake District), the Cockney School (Leigh Hunt, Keats, and other Londoners), the Radcliffe school (imitators of novelist Anne Radcliffe's Gothic style). Blake, who is now recognized as a major poet and visual artist, was dismissed by many contemporaries as a 'harmless lunatic'. Benjamin West and Benjamin Haydon thought of themselves as being in the great tradition of historical painters whose canvasses depicted momentous events of past and present. Except for Walter Scott, Lord Byron, and Robert Bloomfield, none of the male poets sold well. Women writers, however, were conspicuously successful in the literary market-place: as Anne Mellor points out, from 1790 to 1830 Charlotte Smith, Anna Laetitia Barbauld, Anna Seward, Hannah More, Mary Tighe, Mary Robinson, Felicia Hemans, and Letitia Landon made up 30 per cent of the poetry market; the dramatists Hannah More, Elizabeth Inchbald, Hannah Cowley, and Joanna Baillie were among the most successful (see the chapter on 'Feminism').

One person, however, had noticed that some contemporary poetry was excitingly different from anything that had gone before. In the *Examiner* newspaper in December 1816, Leigh Hunt published an article, 'Young Poets', announcing 'a new school of poetry rising of late'. Hunt singled out 'three young writers': Percy Bysshe Shelley, John Hamilton Reynolds, and 'youngest of them all, and just of age', John Keats. By 1816 the revolutionary spirit was stirring again in England, and Hunt's three young poets represented reviving life and 'other pulses' in contemporary poetry. These were poets who think, feel, promise, aspire and energetically 'grapple with Nature'. Their poetry gazes into the world to come, Hunt argues,

> like stout CORTEZ, when with eagle eyes
> He stared at the Pacific,—and all his men
> Looked at each other with a wild surmise,—
> Silent, upon a peak in Darien.

Hunt places this quotation from Keats's 'Chapman's Homer' sonnet strategically, so that the close of his 'Young Poets' article stands on the threshold of a boundless prospect. He did not describe Shelley, Reynolds, or Keats as *Romantic* poets, although the modern associations of the word were already present in their feeling, promise, and aspiration. It would take another century for those threads to entwine to form Romanticism as the 'cultural fabric' of an entire age.[5]

Romantic history to Romantic literature

In the 1780s William Blake produced an odd, hybrid composition in prose and verse, *An Island in the Moon.* Blake used a topsy-turvy lunar scene to satirize two intellectual giants of the preceding century, the scientist Isaac Newton and the poet, critic, and lexicographer Samuel Johnson (see further, p. 313). While breaking away from the past, Blake also announced his own arrival by including poems like 'Upon a Holy Thursday' which later appeared in his *Songs of Innocence* (1789–90). The nursery rhyme verses of Blake's *Songs of Innocence and of Experience* (1794) juxtaposed childish and adult perspectives, to reveal the 'mind-forged manacles' of tyranny. Blake used the image of a slave's iron fetters to suggest how the human mind can be manipulated. Consciousness itself becomes an agent of oppression, Blake suggests: because we can think in no other ways, we do not notice our mental enslavement to ideas and systems imposed by others. By proclaiming the liberating force of the imagination, Blake struck an appropriate keynote for poetry in a time of 'romantic history'. That same note was heard when William Wordsworth's Preface to *Lyrical Ballads* (1800) argued that the 'great national events . . . daily taking place' must be answered in poetry that challenges 'pre-established codes of decision' (compare Blake's 'mental warfare' with prejudice). The critic William Hazlitt was quick to see that in *Lyrical Ballads* Wordsworth had announced a revolution in poetry, modelled on the 'levelling' principles of the French. Mary Wollstonecraft seized the moment to argue that women should 'share the advantages of education and government with man'.[6] Painters like J. M. W. Turner and John Constable, William Blake and Samuel Palmer, were making daring experiments with effects of colour and light. Mozart had perfected the musical ideals of the eighteenth century, while Beethoven and, later, Berlioz broke with eighteenth-century precedents and made vital innovations in symphonic form.

As yet, however, no one perceived these developments in terms of a broad cultural phenomenon called Romanticism. Thomas McFarland has argued that Jean-Jacques Rousseau's *Confessions* (1782, 1789) repeatedly used the word 'romanesque' with the 'full valence' of the modern word 'Romantic'.[7] In 1809 the German critic A. W. Schlegel had described 'the peculiar spirit of *modern* art' as '*romantic*', to differentiate it from 'the *antique* or *classical*' (although Schlegel's 'modern' meant medieval and Renaissance literature). Twelve years later, Lord Byron was aware that Schlegel and Madame de Staël had endeavoured to 'reduce poetry to two systems, classical and romantic', and added that 'the effect' of this division was 'only beginning'.[8] By the mid-nineteenth century its long-term consequence became apparent when the French critic and historian Hippolyte Taine identified in his *Histoire de la littérature anglaise* (1863) a 'Romantic School' comprising Wordsworth, Coleridge, and Southey. Byron had viewed all three of those poets with contempt, and Taine's improved estimate of them alerts us to the fact that the emergence of Romanticism was connected with the rise and fall of reputations, and the gradual reshaping of literary canons.

The leading Victorian critics and literary historians (for example Matthew Arnold and Walter Pater; Margaret Oliphant and George Saintsbury) may not have recognized a Romantic movement in literature, but they did discern a 'new spirit' in writing dating from the end of the eighteenth century.[9] Associated with this new spirit were a 'return to nature' and a 'new sympathy with man', both of which had been ideals of the French Revolution. By the beginning of the twentieth century, Leigh Hunt's era of 'romantic history' and 'young poets' had been transformed into 'the far-reaching and many-sided revival of imaginative power commonly known as Romanticism'.[10] Aspects of that Romantic reawakening included a creative interest in ideas and themes that expressed the character of the age: imagination, egotism, the particular, the remote, Greek antiquity, the primitive, the medieval, the East, irrational experiences (including dreams and drugs), an awareness of process and current (which extended to new 'organic' conceptions of art), and a longing for the infinite encountered through intense experiences of sublime nature (storms, mountains, the ocean).[11]

Writing in 1924, the French critic Émile Legouis argued that Romanticism could be 'defined only in terms of pure psychology'. For Legouis the 'events' of Romanticism took place in the inner sphere of thoughts and feelings, and Romantic writing was correspondingly introspective and focused on the self (Keats's description of the 'wordsworthian or egotistical sublime' captures this version of Romantic sensibility). Charlotte Smith said that her popular *Elegiac Sonnets* (1784) were written to relieve 'some very melancholy moments' by 'expressing in verse the sensations those moments brought', and Coleridge greatly admired the skill with which her sonnets combined 'a development of some lonely feeling' in relation to 'the scenery of Nature' (see for example David Fairer's discussion of Smith's Sonnet XII. 'Written on the Sea Shore— October, 1784'). The phrase 'some lonely feeling' describes what each individual feels, thinks, and experiences separately from any other person. For Coleridge, modern poetry begins in that centre of 'lonely feeling', and he argues daringly that different poetic forms such as Epigram, Elegy, Odes, Songs, and Inscriptions may be variations on the sonnet form (for more on experiments with genre, see the chapters 'Romantic forms: an introduction', 'Gothic', and 'Fragments'). The Epigram is a fore-shortened, fragmentary sonnet; an Elegy is a sonnet in which 'some lonely feeling' has overflowed the sonnet's fourteen lines to voice a prolonged 'effusion' of feeling. In Coleridge's 'Dejection: An Ode', for example, the poet's 'stifling, drowsy, unimpassion'd Grief' is reluctantly 'woo'd' towards 'other thoughts'. Wordsworth's auto-biographical poem *The Prelude* traces 'the growth of a poet's mind', and as we read this epic development of 'lonely feeling' we find that the 'eventful period' of the French Revolution is significant only for its effect on the poet. In *The Prelude*, the age of revolutionary events that inspired Paine and others has been reduced to an episode in the history of the poet's development; in *The Prelude* Wordsworth, not the French Revolution, has become the epoch's 'master theme'.

Chronology

If we refer to an eighteenth-century writer, we understand that he or she was alive in the period 1701–99, and we have no trouble in identifying a Victorian artist with the queen's reign, 1837–1901. The Romantic period has proved more difficult to fix chronologically, although there have been many attempts to pinpoint significant dates and works as markers of the 'beginning' and 'end' of Romanticism. The period 1789 to 1832, the year of the Great Reform Act, has often been cited in readers, anthologies, and course packs, although those dates (like all others) are arbitrary, and alternatives abound. The publication of Rousseau's *Confessions* (1782) marks another plausible 'beginning' for Romanticism, in that its sensational revelations scandalized Europe and initiated a wave of 'confessional' autobiographies such as Wordsworth's *Prelude* (1799, 1805, 1850), De Quincey's *Confessions of an English Opium-Eater* (1821), Hazlitt's *Liber Amoris* (1823), and Hunt's *Lord Byron and some of his Contemporaries* (1828). Goethe's novel of suicidal sensibility *The Sorrows of Young Werther* (1774) was another cult book that inspired numerous imitators (see the chapter on 'Sensibility'). Perhaps *Werther* was another Romantic beginning? Earlier still, Thomas Percy's *Reliques of Ancient English Poetry* (1765) initiated the English ballad revival often associated with Romanticism and which some would argue continues today (see the chapter on 'Narrative poetry'). Surely the *Reliques* was a Romantic starting-point too? What about the birth of William Blake in 1757? Some of Shakespeare's characters are embodiments of a Romantic sensibility: Coleridge detected a 'smack' of Hamlet in his own personality.

As Blake reminds us, the creative lives of many British Romantic writers extended far beyond the 'age of revolutions'. Edmund Burke, the author of the polemical *Reflections on the Revolution in France* (1790), was born more than sixty years earlier in 1729.

William Wordsworth's poetry in *Lyrical Ballads* (1798) grew out of the poet's pro-revolutionary sympathies, yet he continued active as a writer more than half a century later and long after the 1830s—the decade which for many critics marks a faltering of the Romantic impulse. In 1843 Wordsworth was appointed Poet Laureate to Queen Victoria, and *The Prelude* was published a few months after his death in 1850. Burke was a man of the eighteenth century. Wordsworth became an eminent Victorian. Yet both men are also bright stars on Romantic courses and in anthologies of Romantic writing. Assigning specific dates for the 'beginning' and 'end' of Romanticism has proved to be a difficult and haphazard enterprise, and part of the reason is that 'Romanticism' was (and is) a retrospective interpretation of cultural history. So perhaps we should look more closely at the emergence of a unified concept of 'Romanticism' during the nineteenth century.

Wordsworth takes over

While Wordsworth was writing *The Prelude* in the years 1799–1805, Charlotte Smith was one of the most popular and admired poets. Coleridge had placed her firmly in the poetic avant-garde. Wordsworth, by comparison, was virtually unknown. Yet by the start of the twentieth century Smith had been all but forgotten, and, thanks to his revaluation by Victorian critics such as Matthew Arnold, Wordsworth stood as the 'most original and commanding figure' of the new, Romantic canon. From that vantage point many claimed that the 'new age in literature' had been inaugurated by the publication of Wordsworth's and Coleridge's *Lyrical Ballads* in 1798.[12] But this emphasis could only make sense when numerous writers contemporary with Wordsworth had been overlooked, and then forgotten.

When *Lyrical Ballads* was published anonymously at Bristol in September 1798 it made little impact. The reading public was drawn to rival publications such as Matthew 'Monk' Lewis's Gothic novel *The Monk* (1796), his sensational play *The Castle Spectre* (performed 1797, published 1798), and Robert Bloomfield's best-selling *Farmer's Boy* (1801) which presented an English 'peasant poet' who resembled Robert Burns.

In subsequent years, however, *Lyrical Ballads* and 1798 were frequently invoked to define English Romanticism (and, in so doing, to obscure Burns's achievement). Writing in 1898, the critic Edmund Gosse was unshakeably confident about the book's place in literary history: 'In a little russet volume published at Bristol', he wrote, 'the old order of things literary was finally and completely changed. The romantic school began, the classic school disappeared, in the autumn of 1798.'[13] Gosse's almost millenarian conviction was widely echoed. '[*Lyrical Ballads*] initiated the higher Romanticism in England' (David Rannie, in 1907); 'with *Lyrical Ballads* the Romantic movement in poetry came into full existence' (Hamilton Thompson, 1917); 'The volume is epoch-making, for it is the prelude to the Romantic movement proper' (Edward Albert, 1932); 'The association of . . . intensely brilliant and inflammatory minds at what we call the psychological moment, produced full-blown and perfect the exquisite new flower of romantic poetry' (Edmund Gosse again).[14] Romanticism was now 'the Age of Wordsworth'.

Romantic inheritances

The idea that Romanticism emerged 'full-blown' in a single book one day in 1798 is evidently absurd. As David Fairer points out in his chapter on Sonnets, Romanticism was in many ways an eighteenth-century invention. Key Romantic preoccupations such as genius, the imagination, the sublime, and the primitive had grown from earlier, eighteenth-century discoveries. Coleridge's and Keats's experiments with sonnets, for example, developed from eighteenth-century sonnets by W. L. Bowles, Charlotte Smith, Thomas Warton, and Thomas Gray. By the same token, Romantic influences extended far into the nineteenth and twentieth centuries. To the Brontë sisters Byron was a God. Tennyson's great elegy *In Memoriam* (1850) learned from Wordsworth. The colloquial pizzazz of Robert Browning's dramatic monologues emulated Leigh Hunt. In the twentieth century, Ezra Pound's modernist slogan 'make it new' was a Romantic idea, updated from the Preface to *Lyrical Ballads*; James Joyce's 'epiphanies' in *Dubliners* and *A Portrait of the Artist as a Young Man* resembled the 'spots of time' on which Wordsworth's *Prelude* was structured. W. B. Yeats modelled his symbolic poetry on William Blake's. Seamus Heaney's poems about childhood such as 'Death of a Naturalist' and 'Personal Helicon' are thoroughly Wordsworthian in manner.

Hooking Romanticism on to key works and dates has not established its historical location with any precision, and as a European phenomenon it takes on different emphases and periodizations. The chapter on European Romanticism in this book shows that in Germany Romanticism began early, in France much later. The nature of Romanticism has proved altogether diverse, protean, amorphous—and fruitfully so.

Everything and nothing

By the 1920s ideas of Romanticism had so proliferated that some critics doubted whether the word had any meaning at all. A. O. Lovejoy argued in his famous essay 'On the Discrimination of Romanticisms' (1924) that there was no corresponding entity for the term 'Romanticism'. How could the same word refer to the vernacular lyrics of Burns's *Poems Written in the Scottish Dialect* (1786), and the ironic sophistication of Byron's *Don Juan* (1818–24)? If Romanticism was in some ways about a revolutionary break with the past, why were Benjamin Haydon (a painter) and John Keats (a poet) so fascinated by classical Greek sculpture? Romantic poets like Wordsworth and John Clare wrote about the natural world; Romantic prose writers like Hunt and Charles Lamb were inspired by the city. Women poets, supposedly confined to domestic life, in fact confidently tackled themes supposedly reserved for the men. Anna Laetitia Barbauld, author of 'Washing-Day', also composed in 1773 the visionary tour of the 'trackless deeps' of the universe in a 'A Summer Evening's Meditation',

> From the green Borders of the peopled Earth
>
> .   .   .   .
>
> To the dim Verge, the Suburbs of the System,
> Where cheerless Saturn, midst his watery Moons,
> Girt with a lucid Zone, majestic sits
> In gloomy grandeur . . .

When applied in so many contradictory directions, the word 'Romantic' no longer meant anything in particular. Lovejoy thought it would be prudent to refer to Romanticisms in the plural, or to abandon the word altogether.

Vanishings

In 1924 Legouis had included dozens of writers—male and female, poets, novelists, and playwrights—in his survey of Romanticism. By the mid-twentieth century, however, British Romanticism had shrunk to just five poets—Wordsworth, Coleridge, Byron, Shelley, and Keats. Blake remained on the margins until the 1950s, when the American critics Northrop Frye and David Erdman restored him to prominence. Mary Shelley's *Frankenstein* was the stuff of horror movies. Essayists such as Hazlitt and Lamb fell into obscurity. Burns was a northern delicacy. These years of Romantic diminishment coincided with the New Critical emphasis on the text. Authorial personality, biography, and history were deemed irrelevant to the close understanding of poetry or prose considered as a verbal artefact. As the New Critical tide retreated in the 1960s, Romanticism re-emerged as a form of secular religion, or 'natural supernaturalism', in which ideas of hope and redemption were transferred from a supernatural to a natural frame of reference.[15] The English Romantic poets were now seen as a 'visionary company' of male poet-prophets whose imagination transfigured the world to display 'the infinite which was hid' (Blake's words). Wordsworth's 'Tintern Abbey' invokes the mysterious presence of 'something far more deeply interfused'; Shelley's 'Mont Blanc' meditates on the 'still and solemn Power' inhabiting the sublime landscape of the Alps. In both of those poems the surge of quasi-religious expectation that accompanied an 'age of revolutions' was displaced into an idealistic quest for 'something evermore about to be'. Charlotte Smith, John Clare, Mary Shelley, Robert

Bloomfield, and countless other writers had vanished. So had the world of astonishing 'events'.

Changes

While the visionary company continued rapt by 'the human mind's imaginings' (Shelley's words), in the 1980s the critical scene was changing. Jerome McGann's polemical book, *The Romantic Ideology* (1983) argued from a broadly Marxist, materialist standpoint that Romantic poetry characteristically evades its contexts (the world of 'events') and substitutes instead the idealized universe of Romantic Ideology (for more, see the chapter on 'New Historicism'). McGann saw in Romantic poetry a powerful denial of context and a wish to credit its own compensating alternatives, which he described as 'fundamental illusions'. Romantic poems, seen from this perspective, became strategies of escape in which history is 'displaced', 'repressed', 'erased', 'obscured', or 'denied' by the imagination. Wordsworth, for example, writes in 'Tintern Abbey' of 'something far more deeply interfused' as a way of not writing about the failure of the French Revolution or poverty in the Wye valley. The task facing literary critics, McGann argued, was to return poetry 'to a human form—to see that what we read and study are poetic works produced and reproduced by numbers of specific men and women'.[16] So began the New Historicist project of restoring history and humanity as the 'displaced' contexts on which Romantic idealism was culpably dependent. The sublime claims of the visionary company were read now as admissions of guilt; Romanticism was a code word for betrayal and dereliction. Critical attention turned in the 1980s and 1990s to the wider scene of writing in the late eighteenth and early nineteenth centuries, readmitting a diverse literary society that had long been excluded: women, black writers, pamphleteers, lecturers, 'peasant' and 'worker' poets, playwrights, and forgers.

Now and then

Today, anyone approaching Romanticism for the first time will be confronted by scores of authors and hundreds of works (as David Miall shows in his chapter, 'Romanticism in the electronic age,' computers have been the means of restoring many of them to the attention of readers and scholars). Romantic music, theatre, painting, and sculpture are comparably energetic, noisy, and colourful arenas. Can this astonishingly rich cultural scene somehow be accommodated by the single word 'Romanticism' which, until recently, meant just six male poets? As the critic David Perkins points out, 'we must perceive a past age as relatively unified if we are to write literary history; we must perceive it as highly diverse if what we write is to represent it plausibly'.[17] For most of the twentieth century British Romanticism was perceived as a tiny cohort of male poets more or less unified under the banner of Romantic idealism (although Byron did not rally willingly to this flag). The last two decades, however, have opened a highly diversified field, and as we investigate it ever more closely we may (like critic A. O. Lovejoy) become less satisfied with terms like 'Romanticism' and 'Romantic'. Can we speak meaningfully of a 'Romantic period' or a 'Romantic age' in literature or any other art form? Themes of revolution, war, the sublime, women's rights, slavery, nature, politics, religion, and imagination have all been highlighted as 'Romantic', and yet those themes also preoccupied writers of the eighteenth century and the Victorian era. Painters have always experimented with light. Once again, 'Romantic' seems to mean so many things that, as A. O. Lovejoy found some eighty years ago, the word 'has ceased to perform the function of a verbal sign'.[18] One way to begin to resolve these problems at the start of the twenty-first century might be to understand the word Romanticism as singular *and plural in reference*, registering the paradoxical unity of 'an age . . . in which every thing may be looked for'.

The *Oxford Guide to Romanticism* introduces readers to this complex, contradictory period and its extraordinary outpouring of works of art. The Romanticism it represents is highly diversified, reflecting the subject as it is studied in universities and colleges now. Revolutionary models of Romanticism as 'making new' are discussed in some of the chapters, as well as emergent organic ideas of Romanticism: James McKusick's chapter on 'Ecology', for example, shows us how British Romantic poetry was the first to anticipate modern biological conceptions, and that poets such as Wordsworth, Coleridge, and Percy Bysshe Shelley were 'proto-ecological' in their intellectual orientation. Contemporary fears of environmental crisis are encouraging reassessments of nature in Romantic poetry, a nature no longer seen as the escapist resort of Romantic ideology but as the precursor of modern ecological thought. Equally, the 'romantic history' observed by Leigh Hunt continues to unfold in the present. Understanding Romanticism may help us come to terms with the extraordinary events and wild surmises of our own eventful period.

NOTES

1. Richard Price, *A Discourse on the Love of our Country* (1789), p. 49; *Rights of Man*, ed. Henry Collins (1791; Harmondsworth: Penguin, 1969), p. 168.
2. *Letters Written in France, in the Summer 1790* (London, 1790), p. 14.
3. *Rights of Englishmen. An Antidote to the Poison now Vending by the Transatlantic Republican Thomas Paine* (London, 1791), pp. 6, 8.
4. Leigh Hunt, 'Bonaparte in France Again', in *Examiner* (12 Mar. 1815), pp. 161–2.
5. Thomas McFarland, *Romanticism and the Heritage of Rousseau* (Oxford: Clarendon Press, 1995), p. 16.
6. *A Vindication of the Rights of Woman* (London: Johnson, 1792), ch. 12.
7. *Romanticism and the Heritage of Rousseau*, p. 16.

8. *Course of Lectures on Dramatic Art and Literature, by August William Schlegel*, trans. John Black, 2 vols. (London, 1815), i. 8; 'Letter to John Murray Esqre', in *Lord Byron: The Complete Miscellaneous Prose*, ed. Andrew Nicholson (Oxford: Clarendon Press, 1991), p. 142.

9. David Perkins, *Is Literary History Possible?* (Baltimore and London: Johns Hopkins University Press, 1992), p. 97.

10. C. H. Herford, *The Age of Wordsworth* (London: George Bell, 1897; 1928), p. xx.

11. Thomas McFarland, *Romantic Cruxes: The English Essayists and the Spirit of the Age* (Oxford: Clarendon Press, 1987), pp. 3, 13.

12. Herford, *Age of Wordsworth*, p. xiii; Emile Legouis and Louis Cazamian, *A History of English Literature* (1924; London and Toronto: Dent, 1930), p. 1026.

13. Edmund Gosse, *A Short History of Modern English Literature* (London: Heinemann, 1898), p. 279.

14. David Watson Rannie, *Wordsworth and his Circle* (London: Methuen, 1907), p. 79; *Selections from the Poems of William Wordsworth*, ed. A. Hamilton Thompson (Cambridge: Cambridge University Press, 1917), p. xix; Edward Albert, *A History of English Literature* (London: Harrap, 1932), p. 10; Gosse, *A Short History*, p. 279.

15. See M. H. Abrams, *Natural Supernaturalism: Tradition and Revolution in Romantic Literature* (New York: W. W. Norton, 1971).

16. Jerome J. McGann, *The Romantic Ideology: A Critical Investigation* (Chicago and London: Chicago University Press, 1983), p. 160.

17. Perkins, *Is Literary History Possible?*, p. 27.

18. A. O. Lovejoy, 'On the Discrimination of Romanticisms' (1924), in *Essays in the History of Ideas* (Baltimore and London: Johns Hopkins University Press, 1948).

Part I

Romantic orientations

1 | The historical context

Simon Bainbridge

The period from the American Declaration of Independence in 1776 to the passing of the Great Reform Bill in 1832 was one of the most dramatic in British history. It is often characterized as 'the age of revolution', in reference to events in America and France, to the rise of democracy, and to the various developments known collectively as the 'industrial revolution'. However, while many historians have emphasized the extent to which Britain was transformed politically, economically, and socially during these years, some have argued that these transformations were produced in what might better be thought of as an 'age of counter-revolution' as the nation responded to the serious challenges posed by revolution and war (see *Oxford Companion to the Romantic Age*, pp. 3–4).

The extraordinary historical context of the Romantic period is inextricably linked to the rich and diverse body of writing produced during it, though critics continue to debate the precise nature of this relationship. Certainly, writers took historical and political events for their subjects, producing works on the fall of the Bastille in 1789, the war with France that began in 1793 and culminated at Waterloo in 1815, the campaign to abolish the slave trade, and the Peterloo massacre of 1819. But the historical context also profoundly influenced the major literary modes and forms of the period; as the essayist William Hazlitt wrote of William Wordsworth's poetry: 'It partakes of, and is carried along with, the revolutionary movement of our age'.[1] Moreover, writers of the Romantic period rarely saw themselves as simply reacting to, or passively reflecting, historical events. Rather, writing in a highly politicized climate, they conceived their roles as crucial to the ways in which history was understood and to how it would be enacted in the future, an idea most famously articulated by the poet Percy Shelley at the conclusion of his essay 'A Defence of Poetry' (1821) when he declared that 'Poets are the unacknowledged legislators of the World'.[2]

Revolution

For many of those living during the period, there was no doubt that the most significant historical event of the age was the French Revolution, described by Percy

Shelley in 1816 as the 'master theme of the epoch in which we live'.[3] Often symbolized by the storming of the Bastille prison in Paris on 14 July 1789, the revolution was widely welcomed in Britain and immediately recognized as enormously important. The politician Charles James Fox commented: 'How much the greatest event it is that ever happened in the world! and how much the best!'[4] For many, such as Fox, the revolution in France was the next stage in the spread of liberty across the globe, and followed the American Revolution and War of Independence (1775–83) during which the thirteen colonies had broken away from British control, establishing America as a symbol of freedom for writers such as Blake, Coleridge, and Byron (see *Oxford Companion to the Romantic Age*, p. 405). While for some British supporters of the revolution, France appeared to have adopted the English model of a balanced constitution established by the 'Glorious Revolution' of 1688, to others it appeared as if the revolution was creating a new age of freedom in line with their wildest dreams. The poet Robert Southey commented that: 'a visionary world seemed to open upon those who were just entering it. Old things seemed passing away, and nothing was dreamt of but the regeneration of the human race.'[5] William Wordsworth, who was in France in 1790, captured both the sense of excitement generated by the revolution and its promise of a new beginning in his epic poem *The Prelude*, famously exclaiming: 'Bliss was it in that dawn to be alive, | But to be young was very heaven!'[6]

For many, the promise of the revolution was called into question and ultimately shown to be illusory by the increasingly violent and extreme nature of events in France, which included: the overthrow of King Louis XVI in August 1792 and his execution in 1793 (followed later in the year by the execution of Queen Marie Antoinette); the massacre of prisoners in September 1792; the outbreak of war between Britain and France in February 1793; the Jacobin 'reign of terror' presided over by Maximilien Robespierre from 1793 until his overthrow in 1794; the increasingly imperial nature of French foreign policy, seen particularly in its invasions of Italy in 1796–8 and Switzerland in 1798; and Napoleon Bonaparte's rise to power, culminating in his military coup of 1799 (see *Oxford Companion to the Romantic Age*, pp. 513–14). Many of the most interesting poems of this period, such as Coleridge's 'France: an Ode'(1798) and Wordsworth's *The Prelude* (begun 1798–9), show their authors wrestling with these international events and seeking to realign their political allegiances in various ways. A number of influential accounts of Romanticism have seen the disappointment at the failure of the revolution as producing a turn away from history, with writers internalizing their political hopes and seeking to realize them in the realm of the imagination. Other, more recent accounts have argued that the Romantic focus on the self and on nature represents a denial or displacement of historical and political issues in the wake of the revolution's failure. However, a third set of critics have emphasized the writers' continuing engagement with European political events and stressed the extent to which they saw themselves as playing an active role in them.

The French Revolution stimulated an intense political debate in Britain, important both because it addressed fundamental political issues and because it involved a much greater proportion of the population than had ever participated in such a debate before (in part a result of rising literacy levels). The central volumes in this revolution controversy were Edmund Burke's *Reflections on the Revolution in France* and Thomas Paine's *Rights of Man* which polarized political debate along conservative and radical lines and influenced political thinking for generations to come. Burke's *Reflections* was published in November 1790, at a time when the revolution was still broadly supported by the British public, but Burke's tremendously influential volume did much to turn public opinion against the revolution, gaining increasing authority from the way in which it seemed to anticipate the increasingly violent nature of events in France. Invoking the language and values of chivalry and romance, Burke presented highly theatrical descriptions of the main events of the revolution (most famously of the mob confronting Queen Marie Antoinette in her bedchamber) and argued for an organic model of the nation, passed down by previous generations and held in trust for future ones. For him, the revolution was potentially disastrous because it threatened to sweep away France's traditional institutions, leaving the nation without any solid foundation for government. Burke's conservative arguments and his attack on the revolution provoked over one hundred responses in favour of the events in France and the possibilities of political change, most importantly Thomas Paine's *Rights of Man* (published in two parts in 1791 and 1792), which ridiculed Burke's melodramatic descriptions of the revolution, defended the concept of the natural rights of man, and asserted the prerogative of the living to change their forms of government. Other important contributions to the radical side of the argument include Mary Wollstonecraft's feminist *A Vindication of the Rights of Woman* (1792) and William Godwin's claims for the rational perfectibility of humankind in *Political Justice* (1793).

The debate was a battle of styles as well as ideas; Paine answered Burke's highly rhetorical and figurative prose with a plain style designed to appeal to a wide number of readers. The huge sales of these volumes (see *Oxford Companion to the Romantic Age*, p. 20) emphasizes not only the importance of the debate over the French Revolution in Britain but also the extent to which it involved a large proportion of the population (though Mary Wollstonecraft's writing highlighted the frequent exclusion of women from the debate). While the literary writing of the 1790s needs to be understood within the context of the politically charged atmosphere created by this debate, the issues at stake can also be seen profoundly to influence texts produced in later decades such as Jane Austen's novels, with their interest in the social order, which have increasingly been read as part of the revolution controversy (see also the chapter on 'Non-fictional prose').

War

When William Wordsworth referred to 'the great national events which are daily taking place' in his discussion of the condition of contemporary literature in his Preface to

Fig. 1 'The Plumb-pudding in danger;—or—State Epicures taking un Petit Souper', by James Gillray, 1805. Presenting the British Prime Minister William Pitt and the French Emperor Napoleon Bonaparte dividing the world between themselves, Gillray's caricature brilliantly illustrates the global nature of the struggle between Britain and France that dominated the period and emphasizes Britain's colonial ambitions.

Lyrical Ballads, he was identifying the war with France as one of the crucial contexts of the Romantic period.[7] Britain (in a series of coalitions with other European powers) was at war with France from February 1793 until the Duke of Wellington's victory over Napoleon Bonaparte at Waterloo in June 1815. During this twenty-two-year period there were only two short passages of peace: the first of these, the Peace of Amiens, lasted from March 1802 to May 1803, and is conventionally used as the marker that divides the revolutionary and the Napoleonic wars. The second peace followed Napoleon's abdication in April 1814 and lasted until his return from exile on Elba in March 1815.

The Revolutionary and Napoleonic wars were unprecedented in scale and intensity and have been seen by many historians as a new kind of war altogether, a 'war of ideas' that was 'total' rather than 'limited' and involving the entire populations of nations rather than the small armies of professional soldiers that characterized warfare in the eighteenth century. There has been much debate about the validity of this argument (see *Oxford Companion to the Romantic Age*, pp. 26–34), and important elements of the wars were certainly anticipated by the American War of Independence, including the figure of the politically motivated citizen soldier fighting on behalf of his country rather than for territorial gain. Nevertheless, the French creation of the 'nation in arms' in response to the threatened invasions by Austria and Prussia in 1793 had a profound effect on the nature of war over the following two decades. While the size of armies grew considerably (the British army expanded from 40,000 men in 1793 to 250,000 in 1813[8]), the military success of the Revolutionary army in the 1790s compelled other European powers to adopt the French approach of appealing to the nation as a whole. In Britain, the government was forced to rely upon civilian volunteer units for the defence of the country against the threat of French invasion. It has been estimated that between 1797 and 1805, when this invasion threat was at its greatest (and felt to be very real), as many as one in five of the British adult male population participated in some branch of the nation's armed forces.[9] The length and scale of the wars placed a huge strain on manpower and resources in Britain, and while historians often disagree about the impact of the conflict on the nation's economy, many poems testify to the conflict's human cost with their focus on wounded and discharged soldiers, war widows and orphans (see, for example, William Wordsworth's *Salisbury Plain* of 1793–4). However, much of the writing of the period also constituted a call to arms, especially during the various invasion scares such as those of 1797–8 (the subject of Coleridge's 'Fears in Solitude') and 1803–5 (the context for a series of sonnets by Wordsworth, including 'To the Men of Kent') (see *Oxford Companion to the Romantic Age*, p. 559).

While there was some opposition to Britain's involvement in the war against France in the 1790s (especially on the part of those who believed it was a reactionary war fought to crush the French republican state), there was a much greater sense of unanimity in support of the conflict following the resumption of hostilities in May 1803. By now, France was under the control of Napoleon Bonaparte, the former general who had become First Consul for Life in 1802 and whose coronation as Emperor in December 1804 symbolized for many France's return to absolute monarchy (powerfully described by Wordsworth in *The Prelude* as 'the dog | Returning to his vomit'[10]. In many ways the central figure of the Romantic period, and crucial to its political and cultural debates, Napoleon became the focus of British propaganda which represented him as either a terrifying monster (the Corsican Ogre, the French Bugaboo, the Beast of the Apocalypse) or as a ridiculous overreacher as in the cartoonist James Gillray's caricatures of 'Little Boney', the diminutive and tantrum-prone Frenchman in an oversized hat (see *Oxford Companion to the Romantic Age*, pp. 616–17). Many writers wrote about Napoleon in the period (perhaps most interestingly Lord Byron, who declared himself 'The grand Napoleon of the realms of rhyme'[11]), and his dominating influence can also be detected in several of the most famous representations of political figures in the period, from Coleridge's 'Kubla Khan' (written in the late 1790s) with its juxtaposition of political and poetic creators, to Percy Shelley's portrait of the hubris of a fallen dictator in 'Ozymandias', written in 1817, two years after Napoleon's defeat at Waterloo.

Wellington's victory over Napoleon at Waterloo in June 1815 was celebrated by many in Britain as a triumph of good over evil, the inevitable conclusion of a conflict which had become increasingly represented as a holy war or crusade. The outcome of two decades of conflict appeared to confirm Britain's role as the most important world power and a leading imperial nation. But for some observers, such as Byron or the radical Hazlitt, the restoration of monarchical powers that followed the Congress of Vienna (1814–15) appeared a retrograde step that returned the world to the political situation pre-1789. Combined with a period of economic hardship that followed the conclusion of the war, this sense of political reaction and stagnation characterized the atmosphere of the years after Waterloo. Byron described this post-Waterloo period as the *Age of Bronze* in a poem published in 1822, while Percy Shelley analysed it in his sonnet 'England in 1819', savagely criticizing the corruption and exhaustion of the British institutions of power, from the mad monarch George III and his sons to the government, army, and church.

Nationalism

The American and French Revolutions and the wars that followed played crucial parts in the growth of nationalism into one of the most powerful ideologies and emotions of the nineteenth and twentieth centuries. A complex and much debated term, in the context of these events nationalism can be understood as referring to the individual's loyalty to the nation state and to the belief that the people of a nation should be free from any external influence to determine the management of their own economic, social, political, and cultural conditions. One of the distinctive elements of the American conflict to many British observers was that it was fought by a people asserting a demand for a greater role in their own government. Similarly, in the early stages of the Revolutionary war, many with radical sympathies saw the French republic as a united people battling for survival and natural rights against oppressive monarchical powers. It was allied aggression, some argued, that was responsible for France becoming the 'armed nation' that found its ultimate form in the imperialism of Napoleon's military machine (see *Oxford Companion to the Romantic Age*, p. 28). As this might suggest, war itself can have a nation-making effect, and it has been influentially argued that it was the long period of conflict with France, culminating in the Revolutionary and Napoleonic wars, that forged British national identity.

If the military success of the French army in the 1790s appeared to symbolize the power of nationalism, the increasing resistance to Napoleonic rule throughout Europe in the following decade was celebrated by many as a result of the same spirit of 'National Independence and Liberty' (a phrase Wordsworth later used to describe his sonnets on the events and heroes of this resistance[12]). The Spanish revolts in 1808 against the French-imposed government and the subsequent Peninsular war, in which the British army assisted the Spanish and Portuguese, confirmed for many this reversal in France's role. Napoleon was now seen as an aggressor fighting against a 'people' rather than against monarchical dynasties (an argument made forcefully by Wordsworth in his pamphlet on the Convention of Cintra, published in 1809). British interest in the Peninsular war was heightened by its large commitment of troops, under the leadership of the Duke of Wellington, until the French were finally driven from Spain in 1814. Britain's involvement, combined with the interpretation of the war as a nationalistic and religious struggle, helped elevate the conflict with France into a battle of good against evil. For Wordsworth, Coleridge, and Southey the Peninsular war was an opportunity to realign their enthusiasm for liberty with their sense of patriotism. The conflict also became an important subject for younger writers such as Felicia Hemans who published a youthful poem entitled *England and Spain; or, Valour and Patriotism* (1808), and Lord Byron, whose enormously popular *Childe Harold's Pilgrimage* (1812) celebrated Spanish resistance while attacking both British policy and British representations of the war.

The version of nationalism that came to be held by writers such as Wordsworth and Coleridge in the later stages of the war was essentially conservative and local; the influence of Burke has often been detected in Wordsworth's treatment of nature and his portrayal of local communities. That espoused by the younger poets Byron and Shelley was more cosmopolitan and linked to a desire for political change. In the years after Waterloo, the two main focuses for nationalist sentiment became Italy, again under the control of Austria, and Greece, which continued to be dominated by Turkey. The widespread enthusiasm for these national causes is seen not only in the works written directly about them (Felicia Hemans, *The Restoration of the Works of Art to Italy* (1816) and *Modern Greece* (1817); Shelley, 'Ode to Liberty' (1820) and *Hellas* (published 1822); Byron, 'Ode on Venice' (published 1819) and *Childe Harold's Pilgrimage* (1812)) but also in the wider interest in the literary and cultural heritages of the two countries. The Romantic commitment to the idea of national independence was most famously embodied in Lord Byron, who stored arms for Italian nationalists (the Carbonari) during their uprising against the Austrians in 1821, and whose death of fever at Missolonghi, Greece, in 1824 while contributing to the struggle against Turkey gained much support for the Greek cause.

[handwritten margin note: → Byron for everyone's freedom, not one country or people over other (did he support the poor, the workers?)]

Empire and slavery

[handwritten margin note, vertical left: for Byron Freedom = Poor for Habit!]

While the Revolutionary and Napoleonic wars have often been seen as a new kind of war fought for political and ideological reasons, for Britain they were also a continuation of the eighteenth-century colonial wars for territory. Though the loss of the thirteen colonies at the conclusion of the American War of Independence was a severe blow to the nation's imperial identity, Britain had maintained and strengthened its control of its other colonies in the Caribbean, Canada, and India. By the end of the Napoleonic wars, Britain had emerged as the world's most important and influential imperial power, expanding its dominion in India and the Caribbean and acquiring further territory in the Mediterranean, South Africa, and Australia. The conclusion of the wars has also been seen as marking a shift of focus in Britain's imperial ambitions from the west to the east and particularly towards India which was to become the 'jewel' in the imperial crown. Considerable debate has focused on the transformation from a colonial system based primarily upon economic motives, to an imperial one incorporating moral, political, and religious aspirations—a transformation which is now often located during the Romantic period (see *Oxford Companion to the Romantic Age*, pp. 51–8).[13]

The development of Britain's empire was in part a result of the transformations in the nation's trading system in the eighteenth century. Britain had increasingly become an exporter of manufactured goods and an importer of raw materials such as sugar from the Caribbean colonies, tobacco from America, and tea from India. Crucial to the British North Atlantic trading system was slavery, which saw the transportation of huge numbers of slaves from Africa to the Americas and particularly to the Caribbean sugar islands to undertake a variety of types of punishing work, most usually some form of labouring. One estimate is that 3.5 million slaves were shipped by British merchants between 1660 and 1807, a journey undertaken in horrific conditions with mortality rates as high as 20 per cent.[14]

Slavery and the welfare of slaves became issues of considerable public and parliamentary concern in Britain (see *Oxford Companion to the Romantic Age*, pp. 58–65). The movement for abolition gained increasing support in the late 1780s and early 1790s, drawing strength from the progressive political spirit of these years, from evangelical Christianity, and from the cult of sensibility (the ability to experience imaginatively the sufferings of others). Many writers produced anti-slavery poems, including Blake, Southey, and Coleridge, and Wordsworth criticized Napoleon's reimposition of slavery in France's colonies in his sonnets of 1802. The abolitionist movement was one in which women played a significant part. In 1787 the educator Hannah More wrote of 'the great object I have so much at heart, —the project to abolish the slave trade in Africa'.[15] In 1788 she celebrated one of the early pieces of anti-slavery legislation in *Slavery: A Poem*, and the same year also saw Anne Yearsley's 'A Poem on the Inhumanity of the Slave-Trade' and Helen Maria Williams's 'A Poem on the Bill Lately Passed for Regulating the Slave-Trade'. While commercial considerations and the political anxieties prompted by the French Revolution caused further legislation to stall temporarily, the slave trade was abolished by Act of Parliament in 1807 and slaves emancipated in 1833–8.

Issues of colonialism, empire, and slavery are central to the writing of the Romantic period, whether dealt with directly (as in Jane Austen's *Mansfield Park* (1814) in which Sir Thomas Bertram has to return to his sugar plantations in Antigua, the source of the family's wealth) or through examinations of earlier historical periods (as in Byron's *Sardanapalus* (1821) which uses the figure of the last king of the Assyrians to investigate the motivations for empire-building and to explore the arguments against it). They are also related to the sense of the age as one of discovery and exploration, exemplified by Captain James Cook's voyages (1768–80) which have been seen as partly inspiring many of the literary travel narratives of the period, from the Ancient Mariner's journey towards the South Pole in Coleridge's poem to Captain Walton's expedition to 'unvisited regions' that provides the narrative frame in Mary Shelley's novel *Frankenstein* (1818).[16] As the disastrous outcomes of both these fictional expeditions suggest, there was considerable anxiety about the motivations for such voyages of discovery (which could be seen to be implicated within the imperial project) and about the effects that they might have on the cultures they encountered.

Democracy, protest, and reform

The American Declaration of Independence of 1776 and the Great Reform Act of 1832, the events that define the historical period covered by this book, might appear to offer powerful symbols of political progress and the rise of democracy. Yet the age was one of counter-revolution as much as revolution, of reaction as well as rebellion, seen in both the repressive measures of the British government and the political development of many of the era's most famous writers. Though a period of unprecedented popular involvement in political activity, some historians have argued that this agitation produced no significant political or social reform (see *Oxford Companion to the Romantic Age*, pp. 34–42).

While there were various groupings active in the cause of social and political reform prior to the American Revolution and in the years after it, the French Revolution and the subsequent controversy over it stimulated the involvement of a much greater proportion of the population in political debate. One form of this involvement was the growth of corresponding societies (see *Oxford Companion to the Romantic Age*, pp. 467–8), such as the London Corresponding Society, which formed to discuss the political issues of the day and to correspond with other groups both in Britain and abroad. While the nature of these societies varied in terms of the sections of society from which they drew their membership and the extent of their aims, their existence and activities provoked considerable anxiety and even fear of revolution from the establishment. In the mid-1790s, the government under the leadership of William Pitt the Younger responded to the perceived threat of 'Jacobinism' (a term derived from one of the factions in the French Republican government, and used loosely to condemn those with liberal sympathies in Britain) with a number of high-profile treason trials and with repressive legislation known as the 'gagging acts' (see *Oxford Companion to the Romantic Age*, p. 516). These measures, together with developments in the war against France and the growth of loyalist and patriotic sentiment and propaganda, contributed to a decline in radical and reformist activity until the period of its resurgence after Waterloo.

In economic and social terms, the Romantic period was one of enormous change, seen most strikingly in the growth of population (between 1771 and 1831 England increased from 6.4 million people to 13 million, see *Oxford Companion to the Romantic Age*, p. 654) and the increasing proportion of people living in towns and cities, factors central to the series of developments known as the industrial revolution. Though the war years have often been presented as an era of growth, stimulated by the demands of the wartime economy and supported by the British monopoly on overseas markets, they were also characterized by a series of economic crises caused by high taxation, poor harvests, inflation, and industrial depression. The 1790s witnessed a number of popular protests including food riots in 1794–6 and 1799–1801, militia riots in 1795, and naval mutinies at Nore and Spithead in 1797 (see *Oxford Companion to the Romantic Age*, pp. 677–8) while the period of economic depression from 1808 to 1812 led to widespread calls for peace. One response to the process of industrialization was seen in the destruction of machinery in 1811–12 by rioting Luddites (named after the mythical frame-breaker, General Nedd Ludd (see *Oxford Companion to the Romantic Age*, pp. 588–9)). The government responded by making frame-breaking punishable by death, a measure against which Byron spoke in the House of Lords.

The end of the war with France in 1815 and a series of bad harvests plunged Britain into an economic recession that lasted into the early 1820s. These years saw a resurgence of social unrest and political agitation that culminated in the Peterloo massacre of 1819, one of the most notorious events of the Romantic period when a crowd campaigning for reform at St Peter's Field in Manchester were dispersed by the yeoman cavalry, resulting in at least ten dead and several hundred injured. While the immediate response of the government to Peterloo and similar protests was further legislation designed to control radical agitation, Peterloo has been seen as a crucial event in the move towards political reform, influencing several of the politicians who helped pass the Reform Act of 1832 (see *Oxford Companion to the Romantic Age*, p. 643). Although this Act introduced only limited reform (70–80 per cent of adult males remained without the vote, for example), it can be seen as one outcome of the various movements for reform and as symbolizing the advent of modern democracy (see *Oxford Companion to the Romantic Age*, p. 671).

[handwritten margin note: Scopes monkey trial didn't allow for evolution to be taught, but it warned those opposed that it WAS coming & fighting it was useless.
↳ Don't Ask, Don't Tell was a small step toward gradual freedom for sexuality/genders]

FURTHER READING

Abrams, M. H., 'English Romanticism: The Spirit of the Age', in *The Correspondent Breeze: Essays on English Romanticism* (New York and London: W. W. Norton, 1984), pp. 44–75. Stresses the importance of the French Revolution to Romanticism, and establishes the model of Romanticism as shaped by a turn away from history and politics as writers sought to establish their utopias internally through the power of imagination.

Bainbridge, Simon, *Napoleon and English Romanticism* (Cambridge: Cambridge University Press, 1995). Argues that Napoleon occupied a central place in the consciousness of many British writers of the Romantic period, and examines different literary representations of Napoleon in their political and cultural contexts.

—— *British Poetry and the Revolutionary and Napoleonic Wars: Visions of Conflict* (Oxford: Oxford University Press, 2003). Examines a wide range of British poetry written in response to the Revolutionary and Napoleonic wars, and argues that while poetry contributed to the ways in which people thought about the wars, the conflict with France also influenced ideas about the role of poetry.

Butler, Marilyn, *Romantics, Rebels and Reactionaries: English Literature and its Background 1760–1830* (Oxford: Oxford University Press, 1981). Offers a wide-ranging account of the historical, literary, and cultural contexts of Romanticism.

Christie, Ian R., *Wars and Revolutions: Britain 1760–1815* (London: Edward Arnold, 1982). Detailed, wide-ranging, and very readable history of the period.

Colley, Linda, *Britons: Forging the Nation 1707–1837* (London: Vintage, 1996). An influential account of the formation of British national identity, particularly as a result of the wars with France.

Cronin, Richard, *The Politics of Romantic Poetry: In Search of the Pure Commonwealth* (Basingstoke and New York: Macmillan and St Martin's Press, 2000). A wide-ranging and perceptive account of poetic responses to the historical and political events of the period.

Everest, Kelvin, *English Romantic Poetry: An Introduction to the Historical Context and the Literary Scene* (Milton Keynes: Open University Press, 1990). A helpful survey with sections on the historical context, social relations of the Romantic poets, and the literary scene.

Fulford, Tim, and Kitson, Peter J. (eds.), *Romanticism and Colonialism: Writing and Empire, 1780–1830* (Cambridge: Cambridge University Press, 1998). Essays illustrating different ways in which critics have seen the issues of colonialism and empire as influencing writing of the Romantic period.

McGann, Jerome J., *The Romantic Ideology: A Critical Investigation* (Chicago: University of Chicago Press, 1983). Influential New Historicist account of Romanticism, arguing that in its focus on the imagination, nature, and the self, much of the best-known writing of the period seeks to deny history.

NOTES

1. William Hazlitt, *Selected Writings*, ed. Jon Cook (Oxford: Oxford World's Classics, 1991), p. 348.

2. Percy Bysshe Shelley, *The Major Works*, ed. Zachary Leader and Michael O'Neill (Oxford: Oxford World's Classics, 2003), p. 701.

3. Percy Shelley, *The Letters of Percy Bysshe Shelley*, ed. Frederick L. Jones, 2 vols. (Oxford: Clarendon Press, 1964), i. 504.

4. Quoted in M. H. Abrams, 'English Romanticism: The Spirit of the Age', in *The Correspondent Breeze: Essays on English Romanticism* (New York and London: W. W. Norton, 1984), p. 48.

5. Ibid. 47.

6. William Wordsworth, *The Major Works*, ed. Stephen Gill (Oxford: Oxford World's Classics, 2000), p. 550.

7. Ibid. 599.

8. David Gates, 'The Transformation of the Army 1783–1815', in David Chandler and Ian Beckett (eds.), *The Oxford Illustrated History of the British Army* (Oxford: Oxford University Press, 1994), p. 133.

9. Ian R. Christie, 'Conservatism and Stability in British Society', in Mark Philp (ed.), *The French Revolution and British Popular Politics* (Cambridge: Cambridge University Press, 1991), p. 170.

10. Wordsworth, *The Major Works*, p. 556.

11. Lord Byron, *The Major Works*, ed. Jerome J. McGann (Oxford: Oxford World's Classics, 2000), p. 734.

12. *The Poetical Works of William Wordsworth*, ed. E. de Selincourt and Helen Darbishire, 5 vols. (Oxford: Clarendon Press, 1940–9), iii. 109.

13. Tim Fulford and Peter J. Kitson, 'Romanticism and Colonialism: Texts, Contexts, Issues', in Tim Fulford and Peter J. Kitson (eds.), *Romanticism and Colonialism: Writing and Empire, 1780–1830* (Cambridge: Cambridge University Press, 1998), p. 3.

14. *Cassell's Companion to Eighteenth-Century Britain*, ed. Stephen Brumwell and W. A. Speck (London: Cassell, 2001), p. 352.

15. William Roberts, *Memoirs of the Life and Correspondence of Mrs Hannah More*, 4 vols. (London: R. B. Seeley and W. Burnside, 1834), ii. 70.

16. Peter J. Kitson, 'Romanticism and Colonialism: Races, Places, Peoples, 1785–1800', in Fulford and Kitson, (eds.), *Romanticism and Colonialism* pp. 13–14.

2 | The literary background

Jane Stabler

In 'The Tables Turned' (*Lyrical Ballads*, 1798) William Wordsworth counters the view that books are a 'light bequeath'd' from generation to generation with the one that books are 'a dull and endless strife'. Dorothy Wordsworth's journal for 6 December 1801 notes that William was translating Chaucer and that she read Chaucer aloud, and her sister-in-law, Mary, read the first canto of Spenser's *The Faerie Queene*. However much the playful voice of *Lyrical Ballads* might call on readers to 'quit your books', the Wordsworth household clearly spent a lot of time in the company of old authors. Another dedicated student of literature, Mary Shelley, kept lists of the authors she and Percy Shelley read for the years 1814–18. Many of the texts they covered together were ancient Greek or Latin; increasingly, however, during this period, men and women who were not admitted to the public school system would place themselves in a native English rather than a classical literary tradition.

[handwritten margin note: classics were for rich ppl, largely by rich people, preaching their right, by divinity or birth, or both, to be above others not wealthy.]

The sublime

In 1712 the essayist Joseph Addison wrote a series of articles on the imagination. He identified distinct pleasures in reading about terror and encountering vastness and silence; he also located sublimity in the experience of reading Milton's epic *Paradise Lost* (1667–74). After the Restoration, Milton (who had supported Cromwell) envisaged himself as a lone voice singing of universal truths in a benighted age. His prophetic persona and dramatic depiction of Satan as vanquished leader caught the imagination of many Romantic-period writers who saw themselves as political or cultural outsiders. Shelley's Preface to *Prometheus Unbound* reminds readers that 'the sacred Milton was, let it ever be remembered, a republican, and a bold inquirer into morals and religion'.[1]

[handwritten margin note: – (who did the work in Hitler's world, where only pure white class existed!)?]

Miltonic sublimity was cosmic in scope and form. Literally inspired in that it takes huge breaths to speak aloud, Milton's blank verse sweeps the reader along, differing from the interlocking *terza rima* verses of Dante's epic *The Divine Comedy* which offer a more intricately patterned rendering of sin and redemption. As Wordsworth's 'Tintern Abbey' reaches its climax it enfolds a memory of Milton's isolation 'fallen on evil days ... and evil tongues ... with dangers compassed round'.[2] Other echoes of

[handwritten margin note: Dante seems more influential to the poet, who did Milton inspire?]

Milton reverberate through Wordsworth's *The Prelude*, Ann Radcliffe's brooding villains, Montoni and Schedoni, the cosmic flight of Anna Barbauld's poem 'A Summer Evening's Meditation', Keats's bid for independence in *Hyperion*, Anna Seward's 'Colebrook Dale' (part industrial, part volcanic sublime), Coleridge's 'Religious Musings', and Blake's satanic mythology in *The Marriage of Heaven and Hell* and *Milton*.

In his Dedication to *Don Juan* Byron joked that 'the word "Miltonic" means *sublime*' (st. 10). Milton was all-pervasive but he was not the exclusive source of literary sublimity for the Romantics. Old Testament prophecies and the apocalyptic Book of Revelation offered stirring cadences and vistas of terror, vastness, height, depth, and awe-inspiring power. Biblical language echoed throughout the religious poetry of the seventeenth and eighteenth centuries and was engrained on people's memories through church attendance and school education. Writers such as Abraham Cowley and Matthew Prior urged their contemporaries to rediscover the psalmist's power of transporting the soul towards God. The nonconformist tradition of English hymns culminating in those by John and Charles Wesley (see *Oxford Companion to the Romantic Age*, p. 552) blends with classical and pagan influences to shape the expressive dynamics of the Romantic lyric. Shelley's atheistical 'Hymn to Intellectual Beauty' borrows a Christian apprehension of God's sublimity in order to overturn it, although this arguably diminishes his poem's message.

During the eighteenth century transcendent imagery spread from orthodox religious forms into literary depictions of the natural world, especially those of mountains, the sea, and storms. James Thomson's poem *The Seasons* (1730) turned the intensity of Milton's blank verse on to earthly landscapes. His 'Winter' narrates the psychological effect of violent storms, snow and ice on the 'Disastered' human subject, caught in liminal space: 'Where, undissolving from the first of time, | Snows swell on snows amazing to the sky.' Thomson's indeterminate mass is a pale version of Milton's Death in *Paradise Lost*, the shape 'that shape had none' (II. 667). In *A Philosophical Enquiry into the Origin of our Ideas of the Sublime and Beautiful* (1757) Edmund Burke made Milton's personification of Death a touchstone for the literary sublime where 'all is dark, uncertain, confused, terrible and sublime to the last degree'.[3]

The perceptual and imaginative challenge of the Alps can be traced through the travelogues of the eighteenth century into descriptions such as Wordsworth's 'Simplon Pass' passage in Book VI of *The Prelude* (1805) where the poet's memory of a daunting physical landscape is surpassed by his realization of imaginative power. The relationship between divine grandeur and the human mind was the subject of Mark Akenside's *The Pleasures of Imagination* (1744) in which Miltonic blank verse unites the mind's aspirations 'to embrace | Majestic forms' with its 'ardor . . . to be free'.[4] Akenside's highborn soul 'soars | The blue profound' (I. 190–1) using run-on lines to re-create the resistless forward impulse of imagination, outdoing the radiance of Lucifer because it is a quest for truth and virtue. Particularly inspiring to Blake was Edward Young's *Night Thoughts* (1742) in which spectacular vistas of eternal life are conjured up to quell fears raised by the prospect of death: 'I gaze, and as I gaze, my mounting Soul | Catches strange Fire, Eternity! at thee.'[5] Blake's illustrations to Young's poem illuminate the poem's dramatic hold on its first readers.

Two of the greatest poets of the eighteenth century, William Collins and Thomas Gray, used Celtic mythology to explore the creative potential of the human imagination. In Gray's ode 'The Bard' (c.1755–7; again illustrated by Blake), the last survivor of the ancient bardic race prophesies ruin for the troops invading Wales before hurling himself into an abyss: 'He spoke, and headlong from the mountain's height | Deep in the roaring tide he plunged to endless night.'[6] Collins's 'An Ode on the Popular Superstitions of the Highlands of Scotland' dwells on 'dreary dreams' or 'moody madness' (ll. 57; 68), identifying the sublime in ragged cliffs, deep forests, and dark caves, but simultaneously projecting a force that can only be realized by human consciousness. Collins's ode was unfinished, but its fragmentary nature contributed to the effect of impressive obscurity. Anna Barbauld commented that the reader 'is not ill pleased to find his faculties put upon the stretch in the search of those sublime ideas which are apt, from their shadowy nature, to elude the grasp of the mind'.[7]

Sensibility

Following the sixteenth and seventeenth century's interest in the encyclopaedic range of human experience (explored in Montaigne's essays, Browne's *Pseudodoxia Epidemica*, Burton's *Anatomy of Melancholy*, and Locke's philosophy) the growth of the mind became the object of fascinated enquiry for eighteenth-century moral philosophers. Eighteenth-century novels and essays in the *Spectator* and *Rambler* transmitted the discussions of Shaftesbury, Hume, and Hutchinson about social relationships through to a wider audience. A new style of writing evolved, focusing on human emotions and subjectivity; it became known as the literature of sensibility (see also the chapter on 'Sensibility').

Mary Shelley's monster in *Frankenstein* reads Plutarch's *Lives* and Milton's *Paradise Lost*, and instructs himself in human history with the help of Johann Wolfgang von Goethe's *The Sorrows of Young Werther* (1774; first English translation 1779). In a series of letters and journal entries, Goethe's novel tells of the passion of the sensitive, idealistic Werther for Lotte and his decision to commit suicide to escape the anguish of unrequited love. The book sparked a cult across Europe and was alleged to have inspired a number of suicides. The influence of Goethe's *Werther* and Rousseau's *Émile* (1762; first English translation 1762–3), a study of how to foster the natural goodness of men away from the corrupting effects of society, led social commentators to connect sensibility with revolutionary fervour. Goethe's hero and Rousseau's natural man question the ties which bind individuals into civil society and assert a natural democracy of feeling. Spontaneous responses such as sighing, blushing, weeping, and fainting were revered as physical embodiments of this innate moral sense. Samuel Richardson's epistolary novel *Clarissa* (1747–8) keeps a finger on the pulse of the heroine through the compulsive correspondence Richardson called 'writing to the moment'. Clarissa's confessional intimacy allowed middle-class subjectivity to assume centre stage for the first time. While virtuous sensitivity was often perceived as a feminine trait, Richardson's *Sir Charles Grandison* (1753–4), Oliver Goldsmith's *The Vicar of Wakefield* (1766), and MacKenzie's *The Man of Feeling* (1771) all portrayed male characters vibrating with sympathetic impulses.

Laurence Sterne's *The Life and Opinions of Tristram Shandy* (1760–7) was another cult novel which drew readers into the labyrinths of human consciousness. Sterne's digressive particularity was borrowed by Coleridge when he wanted to give an account of his own intellectual journey in *Biographia Literaria*; Byron, too, would embrace Sterne's conversational, self-reflexive mode of narration for *Don Juan* which he called his poetical *Tristram Shandy*. In the later eighteenth century Sterne was read selectively and morally cautious editors cut out his bawdy humour. Like satire, sensibility assumed the moral high ground, and aimed to improve its readers; the two modes competed with each other throughout the second half of the eighteenth century when the satirical voices of Gray, Thomas Chatterton, and Shakespeare's Jacques were all silenced to accommodate the growing middle-class taste for tenderness. No one could say for certain whether sensibility would lead to greater social connection or solipsism (a question later explored in Jane Austen's *Sense and Sensibility*). Sensibility's anti-social extreme was, however, evident in a burgeoning poetry of emotional vulnerability and mournful retreat.

Following the voice of Milton's *Il Penseroso* (1645) and Anne Finch's 'Nocturnal Reverie' (1713) where 'silent Musings urge the Mind to seek | Something, too high for Syllables to speak',[8] the erudite and sociable Thomas Warton courted silence and private vision in 'The Pleasures of Melancholy' (1747), a poem that influenced the *Elegiac Sonnets* of Charlotte Smith (1784), the sonnets of William Lisle Bowles (1789), and, in their footsteps, Coleridge's effusions of 'lonely feeling' (see also the chapter on 'The Sonnet'). Warton's fascination with civilization on the verge of oblivion invests imaginative faith in the figure of the solitary poet-scholar who could connect the past with the present and understand the significance of 'mouldering names'. Gray's 'Elegy Written in a Country Churchyard' (*c*.1751) contemplates lives that pass into obscurity, conjuring up a melancholy youth who wanders through the countryside 'smiling as in scorn | Muttering his wayward fancies' (ll. 105–6); in 'Ode on a Distant Prospect of Eton College' (1747) Gray imagines 'little victims', destined for 'Sorrow's piercing dart' and doomed to inherit an adult consciousness that 'would destroy their paradise' (ll. 52, 70, 98). Wrapped in the mantle of Gray's 'lonely anguish', Charlotte Smith offers herself as a 'willing victim' of his 'Grim-visaged comfortless Despair'.[9]

The question of how the human memory could salvage something of value from what the poet William Cowper called 'Lamented change' is a continual concern in eighteenth-century literature from the moralizing of Samuel Johnson's essays to the scandalous revelations of Rousseau's *Confessions* (1781).[10] Samuel Rogers's *The Pleasures of Memory* (1792) drew on Oliver Goldsmith's reminiscent mode in 'The Traveller' (1764) and 'The Deserted Village' (1770). These poems lament lost pastoral innocence ('Sunk are thy bowers in shapeless ruin all | And the long grass o'ertops the mouldering wall' (ll. 47–8)), through the voice of painful, adult experience. Intense interest in the action of memory modified the seventeenth-century tradition of moralized verse scenes into a poetry of landscape revisited and infused with the viewer's feelings or memories. Ideas about the strength of local attachment and family love (explored in Adam Smith's social theory) found a more political edge in Cowper's and Hannah More's anti-slavery poems where universal love of home exposes the slave trade as a violation of nature. Sensibility was expressed in novels, quivering melodramas, sonnets, epistolary modes, and effusions but it is perhaps best represented by a supple blank verse that could re-create the incremental progress of the mind as in Cowper's conversational poem *The Task* (1785). The self-professed 'desultory' poems of the 1790s are part of the earlier eighteenth century's conviction that the unmethodical private stream of consciousness was as important as the ringing declarations of the public prophet.

Shakespeare

Nahum Tate's 1681 reworking of *King Lear* with a happy ending is one of many Restoration adaptations of Shakespeare. The sense that Shakespeare was good in parts, but needed tidying up continued well into the eighteenth century. As well as full-scale reworkings, significant cuts were made to make performances accord with the new audience expectation of sentimental entertainment. 'It is not every scene that may be found in Shakespear, which illustrates Shakepear', Barbauld wrote.[11]

Corrected versions of Shakespearean plays continued to attract huge audiences throughout the eighteenth century and a series of brilliant, charismatic actors re-created Shakespeare for an age of sensibility. In the domain of literary criticism, Nicholas Rowe's, John Dryden's, and Johnson's measured assessments began to be challenged by 'Bardolatry'. Charles Lamb argued famously that 'the Lear of Shakespeare cannot be acted' but could only be appreciated through dedicated private reading.[12] The very things that had been classified as Shakespearean flaws by previous critics (use of primitive superstition, ruggedness, unevenness, digressiveness, abrupt contrasts) began to be revered as evidence of Shakespeare's truth to nature, psychological penetration, and imaginative sublimity. In Henry Fielding's *Tom Jones* (1749) the servant, Partridge, sees a performance of *Hamlet* and is comically terrified by the ghost. Ann Radcliffe, however, used Shakespearean epigraphs such as 'I could a tale unfold' in *A Sicilian Romance* to heighten suspense and terror for her readers.

The *Hamlet* Samuel Pepys enjoyed in 1661 had been revised to make its hero more purposeful. By the later eighteenth century, however, Hamlet's pensive consciousness came to be valued as an expression of profound philosophy: 'The basis of Hamlet's character seems to be extreme sensibility of mind' Henry MacKenzie wrote in 1777.[13] Hazlitt saw Hamlet as 'the prince of philosophical speculators', above 'the common rules of life' and 'amenable only to the tribunal of his own thoughts'.[14] Hamlet stands behind Byron's gloomy aristocratic Manfred as he contemplates self-annihilation to escape his 'continuance of enduring thought' (1.1.4). Both Hamlet and Lear are used as ciphers for the period's fascination with madness and death. The poet and painter Benjamin Robert Haydon left a quotation from *King Lear* in place of a suicide note: 'Stretch me no longer on this tough World.'

In an age without psychologists, but with a keen interest in the disorderly human mind, Shakespeare's verbal complexity and superabundance no longer seemed chaotic or redundant, but offered a mode of apprehension for dealing with irrational extremity. Many of the young radicals who had supported the overthrow of the French monarch but were then appalled at the bloodletting of Robespierre's Terror, were haunted by Shakespeare's *Macbeth* and *Richard III*. Barbauld's 'Ode to Remorse' imagines such guilt as a continuation of the fall, 'And, never, since that fatal hour, | May man, of woman born, expect to escape thy power.'[15] Describing his return to Paris in the wake of the September massacres, Wordsworth 'seemed to hear a voice that cried | To the whole city, "Sleep no more!"' (*The Prelude*, 1805, IX. 76–7). In a play which reverberates with echoes of Shakespearean tragedy, Shelley's tyrannous count in *The Cenci* summons the night to cover the rape of his daughter, Beatrice, using Lady Macbeth's words 'Come, darkness!' (2.1.181). Beatrice's suffering reconfigures Lear's words. 'I shall go mad. Aye, something must be done; | What, yet I know not . . .' (3.1.86–7).

Shakespeare's politics were less obvious than those of the openly republican Milton. Hazlitt suspected that Shakespeare was a monarchist ('Shakespear himself seems to have had a leaning to the arbitrary side of the question'[16]), but that did not stop radical sympathizers such as Leigh Hunt from nominating a democratic tradition that originated with King Alfred, and gathered Chaucer, Spenser, Shakespeare, and Milton into one liberal pantheon. In the winter of 1817–18 Leigh Hunt's journalism about the afflictions of the poor in a harsh climate under an uncaring political regime deliberately echoed the language of *King Lear* and he frequently enlisted the 'readers of Shakespeare' to campaign for political reform. Hunt and his circle shared books and made a habit of annotating the margins of their own and each other's copies. This spirit of collaborative reading informs Keats's 'On Sitting Down to Read *King Lear* Once Again'. In an elaborate part Spenserian–part Shakespearean sonnet, Keats bids farewell to Spenser and reaches for the 'bitter-sweet' intensity of Shakespearean tragedy.

Shakespeare could salve as well as sear the imagination and his history plays were often used to buttress a sense of national identity. Smith's 'The Emigrants' alludes to the 'Famine and Sword and Fire' of *Henry V* to depict war-torn Europe and illuminate the haven that might exist in free England; Seward deploys the Shakespearean word 'umber'd' from *Henry V* (meaning 'shaded') to suggest the awesome industrial transformation of the landscape in 'Colebrook Dale'; Felicia Hemans's Troubadour sings to rouse the imprisoned English king's spirits with thoughts of England reminiscent of John of Gaunt's speech in *Richard II*. Connected with this quest for home was Shakespeare's sympathetic treatment of women's resourcefulness in a masculine world. In an age that was slow to recognize Mary Wollstonecraft's arguments for women as rational beings, Shakespeare provided an enlightened vision of female independence and strength of character. Maddalo's daughter in Shelley's 'Julian and Maddalo' is described 'Like one of Shakespeare's women' (l. 592). Anna Jameson's *Characteristics of Women* uses Shakespeare's 'consistent preservation of the feminine character' to argue that women are political beings with intellectual powers held back by masculine prejudice and the present system of education.[17]

Satire

During the years between the French Revolution and the first Reform Act in 1832 anti-establishment satire flourished alongside satire by Tories such as Thomas Mathias, William Gifford, and the editors of *The Anti-Jacobin* who attacked women writers, radicals, and Jacobin sensibility. The legacy of formal 'Augustan' verse satire predominated, but satire was also a pan-European mode: Byron's pen-name for *The Vision of Judgment*, Quevedo Redivivus, invoked an almost forgotten Spanish satirist whose prose visions of the Last Judgement exposed the hypocrisy and corruption he perceived to be rampant in his time. English writers who would haughtily defend Shakespeare from French neoclassical criticism would happily borrow the mock heroic discipline of Nicholas Boileau or the urbane detachment of Voltaire to lash their opponents.

The ancient tradition of flyting—excoriating personal abuse—has been a much-needed resource for every generation and Leigh Hunt's *Ultra-Crepidarius* and William Hazlitt's 'A half-length' vent their fury at William Gifford and John Wilson Croker, voices of the *Quarterly Review* and arch-enemies of the reform movement. Occasionally satires were taken as models of expression regardless of their content: Coleridge turned to the satires of John Donne when he wanted to locate a vigorous, conversational verse rhythm in English. Samuel Butler's *Hudibrastics* (1662–78) were satirical verse sketches directed against Puritanism, but they gave their name to the vehicle of the octosyllabic couplet and comic triple rhyme. In the later eighteenth and nineteenth centuries, 'hudibrastic' became a pejorative term for any verse deemed to be mildly scurrilous. By then, philosophers and conduct guides doubted the moral efficacy of satire which could degenerate into personal invective (especially in pamphlet broadsides) and thus become un-Christian and unsuitable for polite society—especially for women readers or writers. Conservative writers often paraphrased the Roman satirist Juvenal: using a tragic or angry speaker railing in heroic couplets to counter what they saw as spurious fashions threatening cultural integrity. By contrast the Roman satirist Horace took a more comic view of human foibles, was more open in form and more liberal in outlook. During the eighteenth century, Jonathan Swift and Johnson epitomized the Juvenalian voice and Sterne and Fielding the Horatian one. Many writers combined the two modes (Mary Robinson signed herself 'Horace Juvenal'), and the anti-establishment satire of Byron, Shelley, Moore, and Hunt used playful hybrid forms to evade prosecution. Just as many of the English Romantics identified themselves with Milton's Satan, the role of the lone satirist was adopted by those who felt excluded from, or oppressed by, their contemporary culture. Byron visited and lay down on the grave of Charles Churchill before leaving England in 1816. Churchill's satires also seem to have been enjoyed by Dorothy Wordsworth.

Eighteenth-century satire often used extended classical allusions to point out the unheroic squalor of contemporary existence. Swift's 'A Description of a City Shower' (1710) describes different sorts of refuse washing out of each street: 'Dung, Guts and Blood' and 'Dead cats and turnep-Tops'.[18] Johnson's *London* (1738) imitates Juvenal to describe a mercantile capital where crime flourishes and everyone is a slave to gold. Tones of despair and anger at metropolitan corruption re-emerge in Barbauld's apocalyptic vision of a ruined London and the end of the British empire in *Eighteen Hundred and Eleven* and Percy Shelley's acidic 'Peter Bell the Third': 'Hell is a city much like London' (l. 147). The exciting vitality of London society, however criminal or decadent, energized the satirical panoramas of Fielding and John Gay's *The Beggar's Opera* (1728) which feed into the critiques of superficiality and greed in Jane Austen's fiction and Byron's London cantos in *Don Juan*.

Satire thrives as a form of piracy, circulating in unauthorized forms and hijacking and redeploying the resources of the literary tradition. Parodic satire goes back at least as far as Chaucer's *Rime of Sir Thopas* in *The Canterbury Tales* which uses ornate minstrelsy to mock the pretensions of the bourgeoisie. Cervantes's *Don Quixote* (1605–15) parodies medieval romance to forward a disillusioned view of society. Pulci's Italianate mock heroic of the fifteenth century would find its way into English in Hookham Frere's *The Monks and the Giants* (1817–18) from where the *ottava rima* stanza form was seized by Byron. Dryden borrowed the cadences of Virgil's *Aeneid* and the Bible for his mock heroic *Absalom and Achitophel* (1681–2) and *MacFlecknoe* (1682), both aimed at contemporary politicians. Alexander Pope's *The Rape of the Lock* (1712) and *The Dunciad* (1728–43) exemplify the range of the mock heroic from light-hearted topical satire to dark prophecy of cultural disintegration. Dryden, Pope, and Swift were usually co-opted as anti-Jacobin satiric models in the Romantic period, but Byron's championing of the 'little Queen Anne's man' in the Pope–Bowles controversy reclaimed him for the liberal side of the question while Leigh Hunt's *Examiner* was published under a banner from Pope (initially attributed to Swift): 'Party is the madness of the many for the gain of a few.' In the battle for political and cultural authority, the satirical tradition itself became contested ground (for further discussion, see the chapter on 'Satire').

The south

The myth of the warm south has its roots in the genial communities and holiday atmosphere of Shakespeare's comedies. Italy and Greece were the birthplaces of ancient pagan cultures which appealed to the Romantic period writers as counters to the repressive established Church of England. The imaginative liberty of classical literature was seen to have continued in Dante, Boccaccio, and Ariosto even when, politically, Greece and Italy had lost their republican freedoms. Dante's pity in the *Inferno* for the illicit lovers Paolo and Francesca was a moment of humane sympathy to which Hunt, Keats, and Byron all responded. The romance tradition of Boccaccio and Ariosto was familiar to educated readers in the original Italian and through English Elizabethans such as Edmund Spenser and George Chapman whose verse translation of Homer would prove a ground-breaking experience for Keats (see also the chapter on 'Narrative poetry'). In the late eighteenth and early nineteenth centuries Italy's political abjection coupled with its legacy of aesthetic riches offered a 'Paradise of exiles' for many British and European liberals. Byron, Shelley, and Hunt gave their new radical journal, *The Liberal*, the subtitle, *Verse and Prose from the South*. Madame de Staël, Mary Robinson, Felicia Hemans, and Letitia Landon turned to southern figures of the improvisatrice, Sappho, and the troubadours to define a free-flowing woman's poetic.

Spenserian revivals in the eighteenth century used Spenser's stanza and his meandering, decorative quests through faery-land. This was the meaning of 'romantic' literature for the writers we now think of as Romantic. In the late eighteenth century romance became a vehicle for nostalgic images of a lost courtly, chivalric world. Richard Hurd and Thomas Warton explored this imaginative terrain in prose while poems like Thomas Beattie's *The Minstrel* (1771–4) popularized the image of the poet as an isolated survivor from a vanishing era—the progenitor of Byron's *Childe Harold's Pilgrimage*. With the image of the wandering romance hero, a southern ideal meets the northern legend of the Celtic bard created in James Macpherson's 'translations' of the Ossian poems (1760–3). A different literary interest in the south is apparent in eighteenth-century historiography: Gibbon's *Decline and Fall of the Roman Empire* (1776–88) disseminated a sceptical (sometimes satiric) account of Christianity, anticipating the radical thrust of Volney's *Ruins of Empire* (1791). As the home of Catholicism, Italy and other southern Mediterranean countries would supply the backdrop for many Gothic novels. Picturesque details of religious observance were culled from an abundant eighteenth-century literature of travel and historical research. For Romantic-period writers these observations on an alien faith and artistic tradition were transformed into meditations on the human capacity for sublimity (St Peter's in *Childe Harold Canto IV*), or sensibility (Samuel Rogers's gazing at a nun in *Italy*).

Critical debates about the origins of Romanticism shadow the contested views about the state of the English nation in the 1790s when Thomas Paine advocated a new beginning while Edmund Burke believed in working gradually to improve the legacy of the past. Romantic literature was once seen as a new dawn, but scholarly recovery of other writers from the period has taught us that what we ought to be asking is not 'was Romantic period writing something new?', but 'what is the quality of its relationship with the old?' A brief survey can only suggest the range of possibilities here, but it is clear that, amongst many other currents, Romanticism is a way of reading which emerged long before the Romantic period and extends into our own time.

FURTHER READING

Amarasinghe, Upali, *Dryden and Pope in the Early Nineteenth Century: A Study of Changing Literary Taste, 1800–1830* (Cambridge: Cambridge University Press, 1962). A comprehensive account of complex Romantic-period responses to Dryden and Pope.

Bate, Jonathan, *Shakespeare and the English Romantic Imagination* (Oxford: Clarendon Press, 1986). Summarizes the ways in which Blake, Wordsworth, Coleridge, Byron, Shelley, Keats, and Hazlitt used Shakespearean drama.

Fairer, David, *English Poetry of the Eighteenth Century 1700–1789* (Harlow and London: Pearson Education, 2003). A full discussion of the different currents of eighteenth-century poetry.

Kucich, Gregory P., *Keats, Shelley, and Romantic Spenserianism* (University Park, Pa.: Pennsylvania State University Press, 1991). Discusses the appropriation of Spenser by the English Romantic poets, especially Keats and Shelley.

McFarland, Thomas, *Romanticism and the Heritage of Rousseau* (Oxford: Clarendon Press, 1995). A provocative study of the relationship between Rousseau and the English Romantic tradition.

Mullan, John, *Sentiment and Sociality: The Language of Feeling in the Eighteenth Century* (Oxford: Clarendon Press, 1998). Traces the interdisciplinary strands of sensibility in philosophy, literature, and medical discourse.

Newlyn, Lucy, *'Paradise Lost' and the Romantic Reader* (Oxford: Clarendon Press, 1993). Examines the intertextual relationships between Milton and Blake, Wordsworth, Coleridge, the Shelleys, and Keats.

Note: Quotations from Romantic-period poetry are from *Romanticism: An Anthology*, ed. Duncan Wu, 2nd edn. (Oxford: Blackwell, 1998) unless otherwise stated.

NOTES

1. *Percy Bysshe Shelley: The Major Works*, ed. Zachary Leader and Michael O'Neill (Oxford: Oxford University Press, 2003), p. 231.

2. John Milton, *Paradise Lost*, ed. Alastair Fowler (Harlow: Longman, 1971), VII. 25–7. See 'Tintern Abbey', ll. 129–30.

3. James Thomson, *The Seasons and the Castle of Indolence*, ed. James Sambrook (Oxford: Clarendon Press, 1984), ll. 904–5; Edmund Burke, *A Philosophical Enquiry into the Origin of our Ideas of the Sublime and Beautiful*, ed. Adam Phillips (Oxford: Oxford University Press, 1990), p. 55.

4. Mark Akenside, *The Pleasures of Imagination to which is prefixed a Critical Essay on the Poem by Mrs Barbauld* (London: T. Cadell and W. Davies, 1795), I. 170–1.

5. Edward Young, *Night Thoughts*, ed. Stephen Cornford (Cambridge: Cambridge University Press, 1989), IV. 499–500.

6. *The Poems of Gray, Collins and Goldsmith*, ed. Roger Lonsdale (London: Longman, 1976), ll. 143–4.

7. *The Poetical Works of Mr William Collins With a Prefatory essay by Mrs Barbauld* (London: T. Cadell and W. Davies, 1797), p. vii.

8. *Eighteenth-Century Poetry: An Annotated Anthology*, ed. David Fairer and Christine Gerrard (Oxford: Blackwell, 1999), ll. 41–2.

9. 'Ode to Despair', ll. 6–7, in *The Poems of Charlotte Smith*, ed. Stuart Curran (New York: Oxford University Press, 1993).

10. *The Task*, IV. 576, in *The Works of William Cowper*, ed. Robert Southey, 8 vols. (London: Bohn, 1853), vi. p. 92.

11. *Poetical works of Mr William Collins*, p. x.

12. Jonathan Bate (ed.), *The Romantics on Shakespeare* (London: Penguin, 1992), p. 123.

13. *The Mirror*, 99 (18 Apr. 1777), 394.

14. Bate (ed.), *Romantics*, pp. 325–6.

15. *The Poems of Anna Letitia Barbauld*, ed. William McCarthy and Elizabeth Kraft (Athens, Ga.: University of Georgia Press, 1994), ll. 16–17.

16. Bate (ed.), *Romantics*, p. 282.

17. Anna Jameson, *Characteristics of Women, Moral, Poetical and Historical*, 2 vols. (London: Sanders and Otley, 1832), pp. xxv–vi.

18. *Eighteenth-Century Poetry*, ed. Fairer and Gerrard, ll. 61; 63.

3 | Classical inheritances

Bruce E. Graver

Literary historians have traditionally drawn sharp boundaries between Romanticism and the neoclassical era that preceded it. In the neoclassical era, writers looked to ancient Greek and Roman models and derived from them precise formal rules of composition to which they attempted to adhere in their literary works. Romantic writers, on the other hand, looked directly to nature, or to the light of their own genius, for their inspiration and created their works without the mediation of books, or the need of neoclassical rules. Or so the story went: a story that bears little relation to the historical evidence, but none the less has had a profound effect on the ways that literary works from both eras have been read. When we read a passage from Alexander Pope, for instance, we look instinctively to Horace or Virgil or Homer and compare the achievement of the English poet with his classical predecessors. When we read a passage from William Wordsworth, however, we usually do not—even when his verse is modelled on the very same Greek and Roman writers. Yet in Wordsworth's day, as in Pope's, to be educated meant to be learned in the languages and literature of classical antiquity: schoolboys of the privileged classes began their formal studies with Latin, acquired Greek by their early teens, and their university education at Oxford and Cambridge almost entirely consisted of intensive training in classical authors.[1] Moreover, the Romantic era was a time of immense vitality in classical studies: the rise of historical criticism reshaped the ways in which ancient authors were understood; there was a revival of Greek studies at the British universities; archaeological discoveries, especially at Pompeii and Herculaneum, supplied new information about the ways the ancients lived, and Greco-Roman antiquities were brought back to England from all over the Mediterranean and put on display, for the first time, in public museums. All this fired the imaginations of Romantic writers, whether it was John Keats viewing the Elgin marbles, Felicia Hemans reading of the excavations at Pompeii, or Samuel Taylor Coleridge studying classical philology at the University of Göttingen.

In the chapter which follows, I will look at three ways in which Romantic writers are indebted to the literature of ancient Greece and Rome. I will first discuss the new historical criticism, which had profound effects on the ways in which classical authors were read and understood. I will then consider what has been called 'Romantic Hellenism', that is, the fascination with ancient Greece that arose during the first decades of the nineteenth century. And I will close by considering how Romantic writers transformed that most classical of literary genres, the pastoral.

The rise of historical criticism

One of the most important scholarly contributions of the eighteenth century was the development of a precise historical methodology for the understanding of ancient texts. This methodology was developed largely in German universities, where scholars such as Johann Michaelis began to examine the Bible, not as the inspired, authoritative word of God, but as the expression of particular people who wrote in response to specific social and historical circumstances. To understand the Gospels, for instance, one must begin by understanding precisely who the Gospel writers were—their nationality, their social class, and their ethnic and religious predispositions—and the events of the historical era in which they lived. This understanding can then be used as the key for interpreting the contents of their narratives. A similar historical method-ology was applied to ancient secular texts, especially to the epics of Homer. But here the main impetus came not from Germany, but from Great Britain. In *An Enquiry into the Life and Writings of Homer* (1735), the Scottish scholar Thomas Blackwell treated Homer, not as a divinely inspired genius, but as an itinerant minstrel (Blackwell's phrase is 'stroling Bard', a translation of the Greek word *aoidos*), whose excellence derived from his acute observation of contemporary society, and his improvisatory skill when performing his works in noble households. Forty years later, Robert Wood refined and extended Blackwell's argument, in his *Essay upon the Original Genius and Writings of Homer* (1775). First, he demonstrated that alphabetical writing did not exist in the Greece of Homer's day, and thus the poet could not have written his poems down, nor could anyone read them if he had. Instead, Homer composed orally, and did so, Wood argued, in detachable units rather like ballads, of suitable length for an evening's performance. The ballad-like units were preserved for several centuries in the memories of Ionian rhapsodes, professional singers who performed the works of the *aoidoi* who preceded them. Finally, the Homeric fragments were collected, written down, and arranged by a later editor. For Wood, as for Blackwell, these circumstances help to account for the power of Homeric verse: because of the simpler state of ancient Greek society, and because of the peculiar demands of oral performance, the Homeric poems have an immediacy and power that later poets have been unable to equal.

Wood and Blackwell's arguments laid the foundation for a critical re-evaluation of the British poetic tradition. If Homer's poems, universally recognized as the greatest poems in the Western tradition, were the product of a preliterate oral culture, might there not be similar poems of similar worth in the British tradition, preserved orally in remote parts of the island, or transcribed by a later editor in an as yet undiscovered manuscript? If the Homeric epics were more like a collection of thematically related

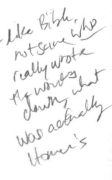

ballads than a single unified work with a unitary author, might there not be an epic still surviving in the collective memory of native folk culture, which could take its place as the great national poem? And what if contemporary poets were to turn to such works as their poetic models? The Scottish Highlander James Macpherson, who studied at Blackwell's college in Aberdeen, was among the first to confront these questions directly and produce a significant response. In the late 1750s, he began collecting fragments of what he called ancient Gaelic poetry, the supposed work of a third-century bard named Ossian. Macpherson published prose translations of these fragments in 1759, and then, with the encouragement and support of Scottish intellectuals, knitted these and other fragments together into two Ossianic epics, *Fingal* and *Temora*, published in 1762 and 1763, respectively. Within months, Ossian became a household word all over the British isles, and the poems spread quickly through Europe. Following Macpherson's lead, Thomas Percy began collecting manuscripts containing old English ballads. These ballads, he asserted, were the work of ancient minstrels, whom Percy described as itinerant entertainers at noble households during the later Middle Ages: they were, in short, the medieval British equivalent of Blackwell's Homer. Percy published his three-volume work in 1765, calling it *Reliques of Ancient English Poetry*; it was the first significant collection of medieval English ballads ever produced, containing such works as 'The Ballad of Chevy Chace', 'Edward, Edward', and 'Sir Patrick Spens'. As a result of the work of Percy and Macpherson, Ossian, Homer, and the ancient minstrel became, for readers throughout Europe, roughly interchangeable proofs of the power of primitive verse.

It is in this context that we need to understand the ballad revival of the late eighteenth century. With very few exceptions, the ballad had been considered a lower-class poetic form, the product of folk culture, and not the kind of thing a serious poet ought to aspire to write. But the Homeric scholarship of Blackwell and Wood and the researches of Macpherson and Percy gave a classical legitimacy to folk forms. As a result, contemporary poets felt free to experiment with these forms, especially with the ballad, in their own writing. In Germany, for instance, Wood, Percy, and Macpherson were widely read, and contemporary critics, such as Johann Herder, began to encourage poets to turn to Ossian and Percy's *Reliques*, and to the new historical understanding of Homer, to find models for their own works. And the poets listened: Goethe and Bürger wrote many modern ballads in imitation of Percy's *Reliques*, and their ballads were subsequently translated into English and published in prominent British periodicals, where British authors read them and began to produce imitations of their own. Among the translators was the young Scottish lawyer, Walter Scott. Among the authors who admired Scott's translations were two young friends who lived within a few miles of each other in Somerset, Samuel Taylor Coleridge and William Wordsworth.

In 1798, 'as an experiment', Wordsworth and Coleridge began to assemble into a single volume of poems a group of original ballads they had recently composed. This volume, which they called *Lyrical Ballads, with a few other poems*, was published in the early autumn of 1798, and has been regarded ever since as one of the most important publications in British literary history, marking the undisputed beginning of the Romantic movement in England. *Lyrical Ballads* opens with Coleridge's 'The Rime of the Ancyent Marinere', a work that masquerades as a late medieval ballad, roughly contemporary with the best of Percy's *Reliques*. Coleridge employed a quick-moving ballad stanza, often with internal rhyme in the first and third lines, and varying in length from four lines to as many as six. The metre is complemented by extensive use of archaic diction, much of it from northern or Scottish dialects ('kirk' for 'church' is a good example), and, especially in the first edition, there is much archaic spelling as well. The ancient mariner himself is an odd Coleridgean adaptation of Percy's idea of the minstrel: he stops a wedding guest on his way to a feast, holds him 'with his glittering eye', and relates his 'ghastly aventure'—a tale he has told repeatedly in his wanderings 'from land to land' (ll. 13, 584, 586). Wordsworth's ballad contributions are of a different sort. Rather than writing in imitation of elder poets, he sets his poems in contemporary England, intent on finding, in his own historical moment, the kinds of impulses that gave rise to folk poetry. These he finds in the sufferings of the lower classes, the subject-matter of poems as diverse as 'The Thorn', 'The Idiot Boy', and 'The Last of the Flock'. Wordsworth seems to designate himself as their poetical spokesman, a latter-day minstrel who will 'sing' their tales to the modern reading public. In Wordsworth and Coleridge's own day, these poems were read as a rejection of neo-classical poetic subjects and style. But the historical scholarship of Blackwell and Wood had radically redefined what constituted the classical. If simplicity and directness of language characterize Homeric style, and if the Homeric poems are themselves edited collections of ballad-like poems, then the *Lyrical Ballads* could very well be seen as exemplifying a kind of classicism, albeit a classicism of a different sort from what we normally associate with the term.

Romantic Hellenism

Along with the rise of historical criticism, the Romantic era was marked by a renewed interest in the art and literature of ancient Greece; indeed, it was during this period that ancient Greek culture began to displace ancient Rome as the chief model for modern writers, artists, and thinkers. Much of this interest was spurred by the scholarly work of Richard Porson, Regius Professor of Greek at Cambridge, and continued by his students after his death. They prepared meticulous editions of Greek authors, especially of Greek dramatists, which made it possible for their students and the educated élite to have a new appreciation for the achievements of ancient Greek theatre. At the same time, Greek artefacts were being excavated and brought back to England in unprecedented numbers, and Greek painting and sculpture were being re-evaluated, largely under the influence of the German Hellenist, Johann Joachim Winckelmann. Winckelmann believed that ancient Greek art, more so than that of any other nation, was characterized by 'stille Grösse, edle Einfalt' ('quiet grandeur, noble simplicity'), which to him were the highest ends the artist could achieve. Thus for Winckelmann and his followers (including the Anglo-Swiss artist Henry Fuseli, who translated Winckelmann's works into English, and John Flaxman, who produced impressive sets of engraved illustrations to classical Greek poems), modern artists should look to Greece as the principal inspiration for their works. Archaeological excavations at Pompeii, Herculaneum, and various sites in Sicily, uncovered new evidence to support Winckelmann's claims, and wealthy British sponsors, such as the Duke of Portland and the Prince of Wales, made sure that artefacts were brought back to Britain and put on public display. When these discoveries included a library of papyrus scrolls at Herculaneum, the hope was that lost works of Sophocles and Simonides might be found. In late 1819, Wordsworth celebrated this hope in a lyric poem:

> O ye who patiently explore
> The wreck of Herculaneum lore
> What rapture could ye seize
> Some Theban fragment, or unroll
> One precious, tender-hearted scroll
> Of pure Simonides!
>
> That were, indeed, a genuine birth
> Of poesy; a bursting forth
> Of Genius from the dust . . .
> ('Upon the same occasion', ll. 49–57)

The effects on British writers of what has been called Romantic Hellenism were diverse and complex. The self-educated William Blake, who angrily rejected classical models for poetic composition and, in his darker moods, dismissed Greek sculpture as mere mathematical reasoning, none the less modelled his drawings of human figures after classical statuary, championed nudity in art, and happily accepted commissions from Flaxman to engrave his illustrations to Homer and Hesiod. Lord Byron, on the other hand, warmly embraced Greek culture, both ancient and modern. Having received a strong classical education at Harrow and Cambridge, Byron travelled extensively in Greece and Turkey as a young man, turned his travels into verse in *Childe Harold's Pilgrimage* and in Cantos II and III of *Don Juan*, a poem which includes the celebrated lyric, 'The Isles of Greece'. In the 1820s he returned to Greece as a champion of Greek independence from Turkish rule, used his fortune to fund one faction of the Greek resistance movement, and died in Missolonghi in 1824, a Greek national hero. A poet like Wordsworth represents a kind of middle ground: although trained in Greek, his command of the language was never firm, and when he thought about classical antiquity he tended to focus almost exclusively on Rome. Yet his brother, Christopher, who became Master of Trinity College, Cambridge (Porson's college), was instrumental in the revival of Greek studies in English schools, and through him the poet kept in touch with many of the leading Hellenists of the day. But of all the major

Romantic writers, Percy Bysshe Shelley and John Keats best illustrate the powerful new attraction of ancient Greek culture.

Percy Shelley came from a privileged background, and at Eton and Oxford University received excellent training in the classical languages. In his studies of classical antiquity, as well as in his poems, he turned instinctively to the Greeks, rather than the Romans, for his models. At a time when the study of classical philosophy meant Cicero, Seneca, and sometimes Aristotle, Shelley preferred Plato. And not only did he read his works, but he translated, without blush or apology, the homoerotic *Symposium*, a work which remains one of the finest translations of Plato in our language. His 'Discourse on the Manners of the Ancient Greeks Relative to the Subject of Love', written as an introduction to this translation, is especially remarkable. Proclaiming that Periclean Athens was 'undoubtedly . . . the most memorable [period] in the history of the world', Shelley considers 'the combination of moral and political circumstances which produced so unparalleled a progress during that short period in literature and the arts'. And the moral circumstance he concentrates on is Athenian homosexuality, a practice he considers 'one of the chief distinctions between the manners of ancient Greece and modern Europe'. Without going so far as to say that the flowering of Greek culture is attributable to their homosociality, Shelley gives a balanced account of their sexual practices, especially as these affected Greek concepts of beauty, and he contrasts the brutality and obscenity of later erotic writers with the refined sentimentality of the Greeks. His duty, he concludes, is 'to overstep the jealous limits between what the learned and the unlearned know of the Greeks; and to indicate a system of reasoning which may enable the reader to form a liberal, consistent, and just judgement of the peculiarities of their domestic manners'.[2] Shelley's treatment of love in his own poetry, especially the idealized heterosexual love between spiritual and intellectual equals celebrated in *Epipsychidion*, *Prometheus Unbound*, and elsewhere, is thoroughly informed by his understanding of Greek homoerotic love.

Besides his interest in Plato and Platonic love, Shelley was deeply influenced by the Greek tragedians, especially Aeschylus, and attempted two verse dramas based on Aeschylean models: *Prometheus Unbound* and *Hellas*. In his *Prometheus*, Shelley completely reworks the fable of Aeschylus' lost tragedy, not 'to restore' it, but to give contemporary expression to his understanding of Prometheus' character, whom he regards as 'the type of highest perfection of moral and intellectual nature, impelled by the purest and the truest motives to the best and noblest ends'. Consequently, he celebrates not the reconciliation of Prometheus with Jupiter, 'the Oppressor of mankind', but Jupiter's final overthrow and the coming of a new cosmic harmony, generated by the renewed love of Prometheus and Asia. *Hellas* is a more topical tragedy, based on Aeschylus' *Persae*, but set in contemporary Constantinople, and intended to inspire 'the rulers of the civilized world' to come to the aid of the Greek independence movement. 'We are all Greeks', Shelley proclaims in his preface to the play, and we owe to them 'our laws, our literature, our religion, our arts'. Hence we have a moral duty to liberate 'the descendant of those glorious beings' from the oppression of 'the Turkish tyrant'. In both these plays, ancient Greece is, for Shelley, both a specific historical site and a staging ground for the vast drama of imaginative and political reform that was his lifelong project.

John Keats was just as fascinated with classical Greece as Shelley, but the terms of his engagement were dramatically different. Unlike Shelley and Byron, Keats did not receive a privileged education. Son of a successful London hostler, Keats attended Enfield Academy as a boy, a school which gave as much emphasis to the sciences and modern history and literature as it did to the ancient classics. Latin was taught there, but Greek was not, and thus Enfield students would have had difficulty gaining entrance to Oxford and Cambridge. When his parents died, Keats himself was forced to leave the school. As a result, throughout his life he had to rely on the mediation of translations and secondary works, such as Lemprière's *Classical Dictionary*, for his understanding of classical antiquity. His ambiguous relationship to the ancient classics is dramatized in the early sonnet 'On First Looking into Chapman's Homer'.

> Much have I travell'd in the realms of gold,
>   And many goodly states and kingdoms seen;
>   Round many western islands have I been
> Which bards in fealty to Apollo hold.
> Oft of one wide expanse had I been told
>   That deep-brow'd Homer ruled as his demesne;
>   Yet never did I breathe its pure serene
> Till I heard Chapman speak out loud and bold:
> Then felt I like some watcher of the skies
>   When a new planet swims into his ken;
> Or like stout Cortez when with eagle eyes
>   He star'd at the Pacific—and all his men
> Look'd at each other with a wild surmise—
>   Silent, upon a peak in Darien.

Here Keats allegorizes the Homeric poems as a 'wide expanse', whose 'pure serene' he had never breathed, until he read Homer, not in Greek, but in the seventeenth-century translation of the dramatist George Chapman. Chapman's translation, he claims, gives a truer sense of Homer's power than the carefully turned couplets of Alexander Pope, whose Homeric translations were the standard in Keats's day. The elder translation becomes something like a telescope: a means by which, 'like some watcher of the skies', the young poet can view 'a new planet'. Keats has in mind the discovery of Uranus by William Herschel in 1781. But just as Herschel could barely make out the outlines of Uranus through his telescope, so Keats's simile stresses the vast distance between himself and Homer, and the uncertainty of his understanding.

Keats's ambiguous relation to the arts of ancient Greece can also be seen in his poems about Greek sculpture: his sonnets on the Elgin marbles and 'Ode on a Grecian Urn'. In 1808, Lord Elgin shipped from Athens to London a set of marble sculptures that he had removed from the Parthenon; these sculptures, he believed, were the work of the celebrated Greek sculptor, Phidias. After much debate about their authenticity (Richard

Payne Knight, the art connoisseur, doubted it; Benjamin Robert Haydon, the historical painter, championed it; Lord Byron thought it a crime they had been taken from Greece), the marbles were purchased by the British nation, and put on permanent display in the British Museum. There Keats saw them, in the company of his friend Haydon, and marvelled at their 'Grecian grandeur' in his sonnet 'On First seeing the Elgin Marbles'. Yet even when viewing Greek art face to face, Keats's understanding is highly mediated: he sees them largely through Haydon's eyes, as monuments of Winckelmann's 'quiet grandeur'. 'I cannot speak | Definitively of such things', he writes to Haydon, and hence he relies on the better-educated expert to guide his perceptions. In 'Ode on a Grecian Urn' Keats again dramatizes the problem of how to approach Greek art. His speaker cannot interpret the urn's 'leaf-fringed legend', and thus can only ask it questions that, in the poem, remain unanswered: 'What men or gods are these?'; 'What pipes and timbrels?'; 'Who are these coming to the sacrifice?'; 'What wild ecstasy?' For Keats, these questions are a central part of the aesthetic pleasure the urn provides: it 'tease[s] us out of thought | as doth eternity', he concludes, and all we can finally know of the urn is the famous dictum 'Beauty is truth, truth beauty'. Here, at the end of the poem, Keats seems to suggest, paradoxically, that those lacking a classical education, those who do not know too much, may very well be the most insightful critics of Grecian art.

Romantic pastoral

Romantic attitudes towards classical antiquity are clearly illustrated by the ways different authors approach that most conventional of literary genres, pastoral poetry. Apparently invented by the Hellenistic poet, Theocritus, in the third century BC and codified as a genre by Virgil in his *Eclogues* (37 BCE), pastoral poetry had remained nearly unchanged in form and subject-matter for some two thousand years, and, since the Renaissance, almost all aspiring poets wrote it. Typically, pastoral poems depicted idealized shepherds, named Menalcas, Damon, or Thyrsis, singing at leisure about their beloveds (Amaryllis, Phoebe, or Aminta), having singing contests with each other, or lamenting the death of one of their friends. Some of these poems were enriched with thinly veiled political allegory. By the late eighteenth century, the genre had become so hackneyed that Samuel Johnson could dismiss Milton's 'Lycidas' just for being a pastoral poem: 'its form is pastoral', he wrote in his *Life of Milton*, 'easy, vulgar, and therefore disgusting'. In *The Village*, George Crabbe, attacked the pastoral on different grounds:

> On Mincio's banks, in Cæsar's bounteous reign,
> If Tityrus found the Golden Age again,
> Must sleepy bards the flattering dream prolong,
> Mechanic echoes of the Mantuan song?

From Truth and Nature shall we widely stray,
Where Virgil, not where Fancy, leads the way?
Yes, thus the Muses sing of happy swains,
Because the Muses never knew their pains.

(ll. 15–22)

The challenge for Romantic writers was how to restore to the pastoral the vigour of the original Theocritean or Virgilian impulse.

William Wordsworth apparently took Crabbe's criticism to heart. Rather than depicting idle singers, far removed from the realities of rural life, he peopled his pastorals with the hard-working shepherds he knew from his boyhood in the English Lake District. As he put it in Book VIII of *The Prelude*:

Shepherds were the men that pleased me first.
Not such as, in Arcadian Fastnesses
Sequestered, handed down among themselves,
So ancient Poets sing, the golden Age;

.   .   .   .

But images of danger, and distress
And suffering, these took deepest hold of me,
Man suffering among awful Powers, and Forms.

(ll. 182–5, 211–13)

To depict such men in his pastoral poems, Wordsworth turned to another classical model: the Virgilian *Georgic*. Virgil's *Georgics* are about farming and emphasize the arduousness of rural labour, as well as its tremendous cultural benefits. Wordsworth's pastoral poems employ industrious shepherds from the georgic tradition, to re-enact, in a contemporary English setting, traditional pastoral themes. In 'Michael', for instance, he reworks the Virgilian theme of pastoral dispossession, in a story of a shepherd who, for all his labour, cannot preserve his patrimonial land. 'The Idle Shepherd-Boys' re-imagines the singing contests of the pastoral tradition as a childish game that keeps two shepherd lads from attending to their duty. 'The Brothers', a poem which Coleridge praised as 'that model of English pastoral',[3] is one of Wordsworth's many reworkings of pastoral elegy—in this case, of Milton's 'Lycidas'. In 'Lycidas', a young shepherd laments the premature death of a shepherd friend who left his native hills for an ocean voyage and drowned at sea. 'The Brothers' reverses this situation: Leonard Ewbank has returned from the sea to the pastoral mountains of his birth, to find that his younger brother, James, is dead. For Milton, the conventions of classical pastoral are employed allegorically, as a way of idealizing both himself and his deceased Cambridge classmate, Edward King. Wordsworth avoids most of these conventions, choosing instead to present a starkly realistic portrait of rural life, emphasizing the ways in which historical and economic forces impinge upon it. And whereas, in 'Lycidas', we are called upon to weep for the fallen shepherd, from the first line of the poem, in 'The Brothers' lamentation is suppressed, and we must infer Leonard's grief by power of sympathy, as he stands before the unmarked grave and hears the story of his brother's death.

Shelley's *Adonais*, his elegy on the death of John Keats, represents a different approach to the pastoral. Rather than depicting realistically drawn shepherds in an English setting, Shelley returns to the classical, modelling his poem after two Greek pastoral elegies: Bion's 'Epitaph for Adonis', and Moschus's 'Epitaph for Bion'. But this is not the hackneyed pastoral that Samuel Johnson deplored. Instead, Shelley comes to the pastoral with genuine scholarly learning, and in the poem attempts to unite pagan, biblical, and neo-Platonic ideas into a syncretic vision of death and immortality. Shelley's syncretism is evident in the poem's title: 'Adonais' refers both to the Adonis, the mortal lover of Aphrodite who was worshipped in Greek fertility cults, and to 'Adonai', the Hebrew word for 'Lord', used to address Yahweh. The poem itself moves from lamentation for Adonais, 'the youngest, dearest . . . nursling' (ll. 46–7) of the epic Muse, Urania, to a recognition that 'He is a portion of the loveliness | Which once he made more lovely' (ll. 379–80); rather than dying, Adonais 'hath awakened from the dream of life' (l. 344) and is now 'one with Nature' (l. 370). Thus we should not mourn his death, but rejoice that he is now united to the neo-Platonic one:

> The One remains, the many change and pass;
> Heaven's light forever shines, Earth's shadows fly;
> Life, like a dome of many-coloured glass,
> Stains the white radiance of Eternity,
> Until Death tramples it to fragments.
>
> (ll. 460–4)

In an ironic inversion of the Anglican marriage liturgy, Shelley proclaims 'No more let Life divide what Death can join together' (l. 477). The poem ends with the speaker adrift in his 'spirit's bark', 'borne darkly, fearfully afar', yet guided by 'The soul of Adonais', whose light burns 'through the inmost veil of Heaven', and 'like a star, | Beacons from the abode where the Eternal are' (ll. 488–95). For Shelley, the idealizing power of the classical pastoral becomes the means by which he lifts the historical John Keats out of time, to become an eternal emblem of poetic power.

For Romantic writers, then, the classical tradition is a rich cultural inheritance which they drew upon variously in their own imaginative works. The classical past, especially ancient Greece, represented a cultural ideal which they might strive to understand and approach, or which might provide the model for a programme of cultural reform. The new historical understanding of the classical past, supplemented by contemporary archaeological research, made the ancient world and its authors intelligible to Romantic writers in ways that were unavailable to their predecessors. They used this understanding to find, in their own historical present, new ways to explore classical themes and poetic genres.

FURTHER READING

Clancey, Richard, *Wordsworth's Classical Undersong* (New York: St Martin's Press, 1999). Provides a comprehensive description of the curriculum of a typical English grammar school in the later eighteenth century.

Curran, Stuart, *Poetic Form and British Romanticism* (Oxford: Oxford University Press, 1986). Surveys the ways in which British Romantic writers experimented with traditional poetic genres and forms.

Foerster, Donald, *Homer in English Criticism: The Historical Approach in the Eighteenth Century* (New Haven: Yale University Press, 1947). Gives an account of Homeric criticism in the eighteenth century.

Graver, Bruce E., 'Wordsworth's Georgic Pastoral: *Otium* and *Labor* in *Michael*', *European Romantic Review*, 1 (1990–1), 119–34. Describes how Wordsworth draws on classical models to reshape his pastoral poetry.

Groom, Nick, *The Making of Percy's Reliques* (New York and Oxford: Oxford University Press, 1999). Traces the genesis of Percy's *Reliques of Ancient English Poetry*.

Holmes, Richard (ed.) *Shelley on Love* (Berkeley: University of California Press, 1980). Provides texts of Shelley's prose works on love, including his translation of Plato's *Symposium*.

Magnuson, Paul, *Reading Public Romanticism* (Princeton: Princeton University Press, 1998). The chapter on Keats discusses 'Ode on a Grecian Urn' and its cultural context.

Phinney, A. W., 'Keats in the Museum: Between Aesthetics and History', *Journal of English and Germanic Philology*, 90 (1991), 208–29. Looks at the importance of the public museum for Keats and his understanding of Greek art.

St Clair, William, *Lord Elgin and the Marbles* (3rd edn., Oxford: Oxford University Press, 1998). A comprehensive account of the Elgin marbles controversy.

Webb, Timothy, 'Romantic Hellenism', in Stuart Curran (ed.), *The Cambridge Companion to British Romanticism* (Cambridge: Cambridge University Press, 1993), pp. 177–95. Provides an overview of Romantic interest in ancient Greek culture.

NOTES

1. Education for privileged girls, however, almost always lacked training in Greek and included only limited training in Latin. There were a few, such as Elizabeth Carter, the translator of Epictetus, and Anne Wakefield Aikin, daughter of the scholar Gilbert Wakefield, who were given a full classical education by their fathers. But they were the exceptions. Indeed, when in 1811 Lucy Aikin dedicates her *Epistles on Women* to Anne Wakefield Aikin, it is precisely because of her unusual education, which makes her (in Lucy Aikin's eyes) the model for what womankind should become.

2. Richard Holmes (ed.), *Shelley on Love* (Berkeley: University of California Press, 1980), pp. 101–12.

3. Samuel Taylor Coleridge, *Biographia Litereria*, ed. James Engell and W. Jackson Bate, in *Collected Works of Samuel Taylor Coleridge VII*, 2 vols. (Princeton: Princeton University Press, 1983), ii. 80.

4 | Sensibility

Adela Pinch

'Sensibility' refers to one of the most fascinating literary and cultural movements of all time. It spread across Europe and Euro-America in the middle of the eighteenth century, and its effects persisted until the middle of the nineteenth century, and indeed have endured, in some ways, into our own era. Its epicentre, however, was late eighteenth-century England. The *Encylopaedia Britannica* of 1797 defined 'sensibility' as 'a nice and delicate perception of pleasure or pain, beauty or deformity' which 'seems to depend upon the organization of the nervous system'. Sensibility as a literary movement consists of texts from that era which glorify and elicit such sensitive emotional reactions. For example, when one of the heroes of Thomas Bridge's popular novel of Sensibility, *Adventures of a Bank-Note* (1770–1), Mr Villiers, encounters a beautiful, sad, young lady, he is so moved that his own face becomes 'a striking picture of sorrow and despair':

He remained speechless for a considerable time, whilst strong convulsions seemed to shake his whole frame. At last, the woman's part of his composition came to his aid, and tears gave relief to those convulsive emotions, which else must certainly have been fatal; tears coursed each other down his manly cheeks, and form'd a rapid current o'er his garments.[2]

This demonstration of Sensibility seems utterly ridiculous to modern readers. The empathy with a perfect stranger so intense it is almost fatal; a man who is said to cry like a woman; the torrential tears: all these features strike us as outrageous. Yet such displays of extravagant emotion were common in the poetry, plays, and fiction of the late eighteenth century, and the qualities we see as 'sentimental' in a negative sense struck late eighteenth-century readers as 'sentimental' in a wholly positive sense: possessed of the finest, most morally and aesthetically right feelings.[3] The intriguing challenge of studying Sensibility is to understand these serious, positive meanings.

The connection between Sensibility and Romanticism is close and complex, and the chronological relation between them is vexing. Literary historians used to see Sensibility (flourishing roughly between 1740 and 1798) as the literary movement that *preceded* Romanticism (flourishing roughly 1798 to 1832). The job of the literary historian—and of the student—was to tell a convincing story about when, exactly, literary writers left off the silliness of Sensibility and began writing the more sophisticated, great works of Romanticism. Their job was also to explain what, exactly, the Romantics may have learned from Sensibility and what, more importantly, they left *behind.* It was usually assumed that Romanticism was an improvement on Sensibility. The literature of Sensibility—full of weeping men and women, trembling poets, sob stories, and exclamation points—often seems to modern readers more superficial, more clichéd than the deep and original achievements of the Romantics. Most of the writers associated with Sensibility have been largely forgotten, except perhaps as embarrassing precursors to the Romantics.

However, placing emphasis on the *differences* between Sensibility and Romanticism—and attempting to pinpoint the transition between them on a timeline—can be a frustrating exercise. First, so many of the features of Romantic literature—an emphasis on passion, on the centrality of subjective experience and expression—are strikingly similar to some of the features of Sensibility. Second, Sensibility was parodied and criticized from the outset, long before Coleridge and others reacted against it. And third, some of the most extravagant and sophisticated features of the literature of Sensibility persisted right through the Romantic age. It may be more accurate to see Sensibility as a literary movement that preceded, enabled, *and* coexisted with Romanticism. And perhaps Romanticism ought to be seen as simply one phase of a longer Era of Sensibility. Writers of the Romantic era, from Jane Austen to Byron, did indeed often try to distance themselves from Sensibility. But whether embraced or rejected, praised or blamed, the powers of 'Sweet Sensibility' were always close at hand.

Cultural change

Sensibility was not just a literary movement; it was a cultural phenomenon that affected the lives of men and women across Europe and America. What could make a culture place such a high value on extravagant emotional sensitivity both in literature and in life? It is very difficult to provide firm historical explanations for changes in people's emotional lives. But one possibility is that Sensibility arose in response to the vast social changes of the eighteenth century, in particular the changing economies of Europe and its colonies. Due to the increased volume of trade within and between nations, and the vast influx of goods—sugars, spices, cloth, other luxury items—from Europe's overseas conquests in Asia, Africa, and the Americas—eighteenth-century Europe was increasingly a consumer society (see *Oxford Companion to the Romantic Age*, pp. 51–8, 181–7). The increasing affluence of middle-class families, in England in particular, brought a new emphasis on leisure, on culture, refinement, and all the good things in life, as well as a new self-consciousness about the gulf that separated the prosperous livers of the good life from the poor. The language of Sensibility had a crucial place in this new society. Though social rank and status remained important throughout the eighteenth and nineteenth centuries, the new consumer society valued individuals not only according to their place in a traditional hierarchy, but also according to the inherent qualities—a good heart, good taste—he or she brought to an ever-expanding public world of market-places and recreations. An exquisite Sensibility was a badge of social distinction.

This newly affluent society also witnessed the creation of new gender roles for both men and women, and here again Sensibility was part of the shift. As middle-class families grew more comfortable, they sought to create a social place for their wives and daughters similar to that of aristocratic women: a feminine world of leisure and beauty. Throughout the second half of the eighteenth century, massive numbers of treatises on 'the fair sex' depicted women as inherently sensitive creatures whose tears and blushes demonstrated their domestic virtue and their feeling hearts (see *Oxford Companion to the Romantic Age*, pp. 42–51, 125–33). Meanwhile, the culture of Sensibility transformed the understanding of masculinity for almost a hundred years, elevating an ideal not of the hard, stoical man, but of the 'man of feeling' full of civic, sociable emotions (see *Oxford Companion to the Romantic Age*, pp. 102–14).

Attitudes to religion also changed. The later eighteenth century saw the rise of Protestant movements (such as Methodism and Evangelicalism) that emphasized the individual's personal, emotional experience of faith (see *Oxford Companion to the Romantic Age*, pp. 93–101). One of the key words connecting religion and literature during the era of Sensibility was 'enthusiasm', which could refer to a fervent state of either religious devotion *or* literary inspiration. While earlier eighteenth-century writers saw 'enthusiasm' negatively, as a dangerous religious fanaticism, writers of the age of Sensibility and Romanticism tended to use the word positively. Coleridge wrote enthusiastically in his journal *The Friend* (1808–10) about restoring to the people 'the true Christian enthusiasm'.[4] The Romantics—Coleridge included—brought a similar enthusiasm to poetry.

Philosophy and science

Sensibility, both as a social and as a literary movement, was supported by new understandings of the human mind and body. In his *Essay on Human Understanding* (1689), Locke famously argued that all of our ideas originate in the impressions of external sensations upon the mind. A common heritage in Lockean philosophy, and a common belief in the importance of sensory impressions, is one of the shared features of Sensibility and Romanticism. We can hear it in Keats's famous exclamation, 'O for a Life of Sensations rather than of Thoughts'.[5]

The Lockean revolution in understanding mind as formed via sensation gave new importance to the role of emotion in mental and social life. No longer seen, as they often were in medieval and early modern Europe, as irrational humours that interfered with reason and society, emotions could now be seen as the origin of thought and as a positive social force. Locke's more radical successor, David Hume, declared in his *Treatise of Human Nature* (1739–40) that 'reason is, and ought only to be the slave to the passions'.[6] Moral and social philosophers of the age of Sensibility devoted themselves to proving that our emotions could be our guide to what is right; our feelings for others were what softened the differences and strengthened the bonds between the socially fortunate and the socially unfortunate.

Perhaps most influential for writers of Sensibility and Romanticism was the Scottish philosopher Adam Smith. Best known to us now as one of the earliest theorists of laissez-faire economics in his *Wealth of Nations* (1776), he was most famous in his time for his *Theory of Moral Sentiments* (1759). In that book, he argued that *sympathy*—the ability to enter into the situation and feelings of another person—is the mechanism that regulates ethical relations between persons. The powers of sympathy—between the well and the suffering, between rich and poor, even between writers and their readers—is a crucial theme in many of the poems, plays, and novels of the writers of Sensibility and Romanticism, for whom it became an important theory of art as well as of moral and social relations. The influential Romantic prose writer Thomas De Quincey, for example, wrote about the role of sympathy—'the act of reproducing in our minds the feelings of another'—in our responses to works of literature.[7]

The culture of Sensibility popularized not only new philosophies of human thought and feeling, but also new scientific theories of the human body. The Lockean revolution in philosophy, which stressed sensation, was closely linked to a scientific and medical revolution, following the work of Sir Isaac Newton, which stressed the nervous system as the body's receptacle for sensation. Eighteenth-century doctors and scientists theorized that some individuals had more sensitive 'vessels' and more 'vital fluids' than others—and thus transmitted the vibrations of the nervous system more quickly (see *Oxford Companion to the Romantic Age*, pp. 170–7). These new scientific developments played a crucial role in late eighteenth- and early nineteenth-century literature. In Laurence Sterne's novel *A Sentimental Journey* (1768), for example, the sensitive narrator describes the effects of performing an act of benevolence on his body: 'In doing this, I felt every vessel in my frame dilate—the arteries beat chearily together, and every power which sustained life, perform'd it with . . . little friction.'[8] Individuals with sensitive bodies had greater Sensibility, but they were also susceptible to overstimulation, melancholy, and madness. We can see the Romantic poets' fascination both with the sensitive body (as in Coleridge and Percy Bysshe Shelley's conception of the poet as an Eolian harp—see Coleridge, 'The Eolian Harp'; Shelley, 'A Defence of Poetry') and with the proximity of imaginative creativity to madness (as in Byron's *Manfred*) as legacies of Sensibility.

Politics

Sensibility has always been bound up with politics. Because it stressed the importance of humanitarian feelings for others, the culture of Sensibility fostered the development of liberal and republican politics throughout Europe and America. Its vocabulary of tears, impassioned exclamations, and pathetic descriptions of suffering was a powerful resource for reforming politicians of the era, such as the English parliamentarians William Wilberforce and Charles James Fox. It played a crucial role in humanitarian movements on behalf of the poor, on behalf of native peoples around the globe, as well as on behalf of the abolition of slavery. Political poems on these subjects sprouted up all over the place, such as Sensibility poet William Cowper's 'Pity for Poor Africans' (1788). Some of Blake's and Wordsworth's best-known shorter poems, such as 'The Little Black Boy' or 'The Chimney Sweeper' from Blake's *Songs of Innocence and Experience* (1798), come directly out of this tradition (see also chapter on 'Post-colonialism').

The French Revolution had an enormous impact on the ways Sensibility's political legacy was handed on to the Romantics (see *Oxford Companion to the Romantic Age*, pp. 17–26). In France, the revolutionaries were inspired in part by the writings of one of the most eminent writers of the era of Sensibility, Jean-Jacques Rousseau (1712–78). While the Swiss-born writer's extravagant novel of star-crossed lovers, *Julie, ou la Nouvelle Heloïse* (1761) influenced novelists across Europe, his writings on education and society such as the *Discourse on the Origin of Inequality* (1753) and *The Social Contract* (1762)—which stressed the fundamental equality of all people in a state of nature—had a vivid impact on French politics. Sympathetic English observers, such as the poet Helen Maria Williams, praised the revolutionaries for their sensitivity. 'The leaders of the Revolution', she wrote glowingly,

are men well acquainted with the human heart. They have studied to interest in their cause the most powerful passions of human nature, by the appointment of solemnities perfectly calculated to awaken that general sympathy which is caught from heart to heart with irresistible energy, fills every eye with tears, and throbs in every bosom.[9]

But while the revolution seemed to some a natural outgrowth of the culture of Sensibility, it had complex consequences. English opponents of the revolution were quick to accuse its supporters of having *excessive* and misdirected Sensibility (see the chapter on 'The historical context'). The leading anti-revolution magazine of the time, the *Anti-Jacobin Review*, described the radical writer Erasmus Darwin (grandfather of Charles), as 'that high priest of absurdity and impiety . . . who lavishes his sensibility on the sufferings of cabbages and carrots, but had not a tear to bestow on his nearest relatives'.[10]

Indeed the debates surrounding the revolution hastened a growing trend that always, paradoxically, coexisted with the culture of Sensibility, at least since the 1770s: the Anti-Sensibility movement. Anti-Sensibility thinkers warned against Sensibility's effects on several grounds. They sometimes argued that devotees of Sensibility were hopeless slaves of fashion, who did not genuinely feel the extravagant emotions they expressed. They warned that, by putting individual feeling first, the devotees of Sensibility were engaging in irrational and anti-social practices. And the conservative critics of Sensibility feared for the nation, as they saw the cult of feelings destroying law and order. A cartoon in the *Anti-Jacobin Review* called 'New Morality' showed a figure representing Sensibility weeping over a dead bird. The figure holds the works of Rousseau, and steps on the head of the deposed French King Louis XVI. By 1793 when the French Revolution turned into the Terror (see *Oxford Companion to the Romantic Age*, pp. 513–14), it had definitively turned the tide of European culture against Sensibility, leaving a mixed legacy for Romanticism. Ambivalence about emotion still ran high, for example, even in 1807—some years after the worst of the revolution's violence—when Anna Seward (herself an old Sensibility poet) greeted Wordsworth's new *Poems in Two Volumes* with a mixture of 'admiration' and 'disgust'. She thought his description of his heart dancing with the daffodils in his now-famous poem 'I Wandered Lonely As A Cloud' was a parody: 'Surely if his worst foe had chosen to caricature this egotistical manufacturer of metaphysic importance upon trivial themes, he could not have done it more effectually!'[11]

An international movement

As the example of Anglo-French relations might suggest, Sensibility was truly an international literary movement. It spread across Europe and America, and was crucial to the ways in which Europeans and Euro-Americans learned to understand other parts of the world as well. Certain authors of the era gained truly international reputations. In addition to Rousseau, who was as famous, both as loved and reviled, as a rock star today, other international stars of the movement included the German writer Johann Wolfgang von Goethe—in particular his novel *The Sorrows of Young Werther* (1774). Translated immediately into many languages, this book—which purports to be a posthumous collection of letters by a young man who commits suicide for the sake of a young lady named Charlotte—was a sensation. It allegedly contributed to an actual rise in the suicide rate across the Continent, as young people emulated the tragic Werther. Its effects appear in the pages of numerous other texts across Europe and Euro-America; the poet Charlotte Smith wrote five sonnets 'Supposed to be Written by Werther' (*Elegiac Sonnets*, 1782). In America, the protagonist of William Hill Brown's *The Power of Sympathy* (1789)—the first novel written and published in the new nation—leaves a copy of *Werther* next to his own suicide note (see also chapter on 'Americas').

Indeed, Sensibility played an especially important role in the imagination of the New World. Not only did the novels of the early American republic look to the language of Sensibility to bring home to readers the ideals of the Founding Fathers; the European imagination also made 'contact' with the New World (as well as with the new Old Worlds of the Indies, the Orient) *through* the language of Sensibility. Helen Maria Williams wrote a long epic poem about the conquest of Peru, sympathetically imagining the Inca's plight (*Peru: A Poem; in Six Cantos*, 1784). There was one transatlantic sentimental tale—the story of the British trader Thomas Inkle and his love for the Caribbean Indian maiden Yarico—which captured the imagination of scores of poets, essayists, and dramatists from around the world. Versions of the melodramatic tale of Yarico and Inkle (in most versions, the perfidious Inkle cruelly sells Yarico into slavery) were published in England, North America, the Caribbean island of Barbados, France, Germany, and even Russia.[12] In the language of Sensibility, images of the far west (the Americas) and of the Far East converged: both the title figure of Wordsworth's 'Complaint of the Forsaken Indian Woman' (*Lyrical Ballads*, 1798) and the countless exotic females of Byron's oriental tales (such as Leila from *The Giaour*, 1812), all derive from Sensibility's trade in exotic, tragic females from around the globe.

The tears, intimate scenes, and sad stories of Sensibility truly seemed to onlookers to travel the world, uniting persons through the universal language of the heart. Sensibility was able to be a globalizing movement that spread well across distances and differences *precisely because*, paradoxically, its currency was intimate exchanges: between characters, and between writers and readers. Its rhetorical mode was the direct address or apostrophe to a reader, imagined as a friend—a technique that influenced the Romantics enormously, as in, for example, Wordsworth's

> Surprised by joy—impatient as the Wind
> I turned to share the transport—Oh! With whom
> But thee . . .

The culture of Sensibility, with its optimism about the expression of feeling in print as something that could bridge vastly different groups of people, irrevocably transformed the culture of writing, printing, publishing, and reading in which the major Romantics found themselves.

Gender

Sensibility is important to the study of Romanticism because for readers and writers of this era it had a powerful impact on ideas and beliefs about literature and gender. As stressed earlier in this essay, Sensibility was often seen as a social phenomenon associated with femininity, and as a literary mode associated with women writers. This was a mixed blessing. The eminent late eighteenth-century literary critic Lord Kames declared 'women have more imagination and more sensibility than men; and yet none of them have made an eminent figure in any of the fine arts.' But women writers could certainly take advantage of this association. Speaking of the new style of emotional poetry, the writer Hester Thrale remarked, 'This fashion makes well for us Women however, as Learning no longer forms any part of the Entertainment expected from Poetry—Ladies have therefore as good a Chance as People regularly bred to Science in Times when *fire-eyed fancy* is said to be the only requisite of a Popular Poet.'[13]

Women writers throughout the late eighteenth and early nineteenth centuries were able to use the vocabulary of Sensibility to give voice to their concerns. Beginning in 1759, with the publication in the *Edinburgh Chronicle* of a poem called 'A Prayer for Indifference' by Frances Greville, women poets debated back and forth about whether it was better for women to be subject to powerful feelings, or to have no feelings at all. The speaker of Greville's poem prays to 'Oberon, the Fairy' to release her from the curse of feminine feeling:

> Take then this treacherous sense of mine,
>   Which dooms me still to smart:
> Which pleasure can to pain refine,
>   To pain new pangs impart.

While Greville complained that Sensibility was simply too painful, other women poets, such as Helen Maria Williams, responded by suggesting that to renounce 'the sacred power to weep' was to renounce what small power women could have.[14] In seizing upon the issue of feeling as a way of talking about gender, the many poets who participated in this debate anticipated a crucial theme in Mary Wollstonecraft's analysis of women's position in *A Vindication of the Rights of Woman* (1792). Sensibility represents for Wollstonecraft a key factor in the degradation of women. By being linked to feeling, women had 'acquired . . . all the follies of civilization':

Their senses are inflamed, and their understandings neglected, consequently they become the prey of their senses, delicately termed Sensibility, and are blown about by every momentary gust of feeling.[15]

However, we should be wary of overgeneralizing, and seeing Sensibility as always linked with women and with femininity. Women have, throughout Western history, been strongly linked to the emotions; the great revolution of the era of Sensibility was that it permitted *men* to get credit for crying; and in doing so it opened up whole new arenas for masculine power and prestige. Sensibility, that is, may have accorded women *some* new powers, but it vastly expanded men's sphere of cultural influence. The invention of the 'Man of Feeling', in novels such as Henry MacKenzie's *The Man of Feeling* (1771) and Laurence Sterne's *A Sentimental Journey* (1768), and the self-dramatizing, trembling feeling in the works of Sensibility poets such as William Collins and William Cowper, glamorized and dignified masculine emotion, ultimately creating the conditions in which Romantic male poets such as Wordsworth, Coleridge, Keats, Shelley, and Byron could write of their own feelings.

Poetry

Understanding the culture of Sensibility can help us read Romantic-era literature. Even famous passages from the best loved of Romantic poems that can seem melodramatic and embarrassing to us—such as, for example, Shelley's exclamation 'I fall upon the thorns of life! I bleed!' from the 'Ode To The West Wind'—can seem less so when put into the context of Sensibility. Take the exclamation point, for example. The ubiquitous use, in the poetry of Sensibility and Romanticism, of the exclamation point—which has been banished from *serious* poetry for at least the last hundred years!!!—was not, in this era, considered a crutch for lame poets, but was rather a highly innovative device! Though it had been around since the 1400s, the exclamation point became cool and modern in the late eighteenth century, in part through debates among grammarians and elocutionists who sought to define how best to put feelings on to the printed page.[16] Thus, the expostulations of Sensibility poet William Collins—'Ah *Fear*! Ah frantic *Fear*! | I see, I see Thee near!'—were not as ridiculous as they might seem to us.

Thinking about Sensibility as a poetic category may also give us a way to make sense of the many poets who wrote poetry during the Romantic era but who have not, until recently, been counted as Romantic poets along with Wordsworth, Coleridge, Keats, Byron, and Shelley. It might help us place women poets such as Felicia Hemans and Letitia Landon, who rivalled and sometimes eclipsed their male contemporaries in popularity. While the writings of Hemans, Landon, and others manifest definite similarities with the work of the male poets, their work is also undeniably different in style, mood, and theme. One possibility is to assert that there are two 'Romanticisms', a masculine and a feminine one. But another possibility is to see some poets, both male and female, as following a 'poetics of Sensibility' that persisted right through the first decades of the nineteenth century and beyond. An understanding of Sensibility as a poetic style might help us place, for example, a passage from Landon's poem 'Disenchantment' (1838):

Life's dark waves have lost the glitter
  Which at morning-tide they wore,
And the well within is bitter,
  Nought its sweetness may restore:
For I know how vainly given
  Life's most precious things may be,
Love that might have looked on heaven,
  Even as it looked on thee.

Ah, farewell!—with that word dying,
  Hope and love must perish too.
For thy sake themselves denying,
  What is truth with thee untrue?
Farewell!—'tis a dreary sentence,
  Like the death-doom of the grave,
May it wake in thee repentance,
  Stinging when too late to save!

The peculiar emotional tone of this passage—a settled, compounded, everything-is-too-late dreariness in which emotions have their own self-cancelling feelings (hope and love deny *themselves?*)—along with the particular syntax and rhythm of the imagery ('Life's dark waves') are all characteristic of the poetry of Sensibility, from Thomas Gray and Charlotte Smith onwards. Passages from the poetry of Sensibility such as this one often seem both sincere and insincere (clichéd, perhaps?) at the same time, and this is one of their great cultural achievements: they make us aware of the ways in which our emotions come embedded in culture, rather than straight from the heart. Seeing Landon as a 'late' Sensibility poet makes her a crucial link between the poetry of the eighteenth century and the poetry of the Victorian era to come—think of Alfred, Lord Tennyson's 'Tears, Idle Tears', for example. From this perspective, the well-known Romantic poets may be seen as a minority, an anomaly in the broader currents of literary history.

The novel

The Romantic-era development of the novel gained much energy from the culture of Sensibility, not only by drawing on Sensibility's interest in individual feeling, but also through parodying its excesses. Fiction in the age of Sensibility also brought about some surprising innovations in narrative form. When subjected to plot summary, most of the novels of Sensibility either sound predictably melodramatic (variations on the damsel-in-distress-pursued-by-dastardly-villain story: Charlotte Smith's *Emmeline* (1788) is a good example), or dissolve into nothingness. For example: in Henry Mackenzie's *The Man of Feeling* (1771), a young man from the country named Harley goes on an errand to London (he never gets there), meets with various pathetic people along the way, returns home, and dies. In Laurence Sterne's *A Sentimental Journey* (1768), an elderly man named Yorick crosses the English Channel, and gets as far as Paris, where the book abruptly ends. Yorick has many touching encounters (with a young lady who has lost her mind, with a dead donkey), but nothing happens: six whole chapters take place in an unmoving vehicle. But this state of narrative non-incident allowed the authors of the novels of Sensibility to experiment with other aspects of fiction. Both Mackenzie and Sterne, for example, used the forms of fiction to represent the fragmentary, fleeting nature of human experience: Harley's story appears in the novel as pieces of a ripped up manuscript a country curate was using as wadding. Thus, the Sensibility novelists anticipated and participated in the interest in fragments so important to the Romantic poets (see chapter on 'The fragments'). The innovations in form and the emphasis on emotional effects in novels of Sensibility opened up the experimentation of the novels of the Romantic era, for example Mary Shelley's *Frankenstein* (1818) or James Hogg's *Private Memoirs and Confessions of a Justified Sinner* (1824).

Indeed, the development of modern, novelistic realism—famously born in the Romantic era in the works of Jane Austen and Sir Walter Scott—could not have happened without Sensibility. Austen's first published novel was *Sense and Sensibility* (1811) which was significantly *after* the heyday of the most heated controversies between the pro-Sensibility and anti-Sensibility forces during the 1780s and 1790s. How did reviving such a seemingly dead issue help Austen get a start? Probably in at least two ways. First, by writing a novel that parodies Sensibility and dismantles the beliefs of her oversensitive, emotional, and impractical heroine Marianne Dashwood, Austen announced that she was finally killing off Sensibility in order to draw attention to what was *new* in her fiction: a commitment to representing a sensible (in the modern sense), probable world. At the same time, however, Austen draws upon the literary energy of Sensibility, its powers to move us in spite of our will. She honours the residue of Sensibility that remains even at the end of her story, for example when Marianne's more sober sister Elinor (the novel's representative of 'Sense') finds herself highly susceptible to the charms of her sister's perfidious lover, even when she knows he is wrong. 'She felt that it was so, long, long before she could feel his influence less', says the narrator, in a nice allegory for the 'long, long' influence of Sensibility.[17]

Though we can think of Sensibility as having a continuous presence throughout the Romantic era and beyond, its most comprehensive beliefs and forms did eventually die out in the nineteenth century. The word itself ceased to denote a whole set of beliefs about emotion, morality, and art. Under the growing influence of more modern psychological and materialist understandings of the emotions, 'sensibility' came to be defined, for example, in *Chambers Encyclopaedia* of 1862, merely as the physiological capacity to feel.[18] However, the study of Sensibility continues to pose fascinating questions of relevance to modern philosophers, psychologists, and students of literature.

FURTHER READING

Barker-Benfield, G. J., *The Culture of Sensibility: Sex and Society in Eighteenth-Century Britain* (Chicago: University of Chicago Press, 1992). A rich, detailed account of Sensibility as a social phenomenon, placing emphasis on the growth of consumerism in eighteenth-century England, and stressing changing gender roles.

Chandler, James, 'Moving Accidents: The Emergence of Sentimental Probability', in Colin Jones and Dror Wahrman (eds) *The Age of Cultural Revolutions: Britain and France, 1750–1820* (Berkeley: University of California Press, 2002), pp. 137–70. Makes a compelling case for why Romanticism and Sentimentalism (the term the author prefers over the nearly synonymous 'Sensibility') should be seen as part of the same 'cultural revolution', rather than as opposed to each other, and emphasizes the significance of *sympathy* for the entire period.

Ellis, Markman, *The Politics of Sensibility: Race, Gender, and Commerce in the Sentimental Novel* (Cambridge: Cambridge University Press, 1996). Discusses the novel of Sensibility as a new literary form that was specifically capable of addressing political issues such as slavery, capitalism, and prostitution.

Ellison, Julie, *Cato's Tears and the Making of Anglo-American Emotion* (Chicago: University of Chicago Press, 1999). Argues that the Age of Sensibility actually lasted from the late sixteenth century to our own day, and has always been fundamentally concerned with refashioning men as attractive public actors and speakers in an increasingly liberal political culture in both England and America.

Frye, Northrop, 'Towards Defining an Age of Sensibility', *English Literary History*, 23 (1956), 144–52. Provides a clear, useful description of the features of the literature of Sensibility.

Jones, Chris, *Radical Sensibility: Literature and Ideas in the 1790s* (London and New York: Routledge, 1993). Stresses the importance of Sensibility to radical, egalitarian thinkers in England during the French Revolution; it contains chapters on William Godwin and Mary Wollstonecraft, Helen Maria Williams, Charlotte Smith, and Wordsworth.

McGann, Jerome, *The Poetics of Sensibility: A Revolution in Literary Style* (Oxford: Clarendon Press, 1996). Champions the poetry of Sensibility—in particular, by women—as a neglected but highly sophisticated literary tradition that challenges the Romantic tradition.

Mullan, John, *Sentiment and Sociability: The Language of Feeling in the Eighteenth Century* (Oxford: Clarendon Press, 1988). Contains chapters on the philosophical and medical backgrounds to Sensibility.

Pinch, Adela, *Strange Fits of Passion: Epistemologies of Emotion, Hume to Austen* (Stanford, Calif: Stanford University Press, 1996). This book also stresses the continuities between Sensibility and Romanticism, seeing both movements as concerned with identifying the origins of emotion.

Reddy, William, *The Navigation of Feeling: A Framework for the History of Emotions* (Cambridge: Cambridge University Press, 2001). Explores different approaches to studying emotions in culture, and presents a study of Sensibility in France, 1700–1850.

Todd, Janet, *Sensibility: An Introduction* (London: Methuen, 1986). Concise, clearly written book that offers an excellent starting-place for further study of Sensibility as a literary movement in England.

WEB LINK

A Dictionary of Sensibility.

http://www.engl.virginia.edu/~enec981/dictionary/index.html

A helpful site with links to a range of full texts from the era online, organized by key terms ranging from 'benevolence' to 'taste'; contains useful bibliographies of primary and secondary texts.

NOTES

1. *Encyclopaedia Britannica*, 3rd edn. (Edinburgh, 1797).
2. Thomas Bridges, *Adventures of a Bank-Note*, 4 vols. (London: 1770–1), iii. 85–6.
3. Some scholars distinguish between 'Sensibility' and 'Sentimentalism' as distinct literary movements with distinct meanings, but it makes more sense to treat these terms as roughly synonymous. Although late eighteenth-century writers sought to create firm definitions for 'feeling', 'sentiment', 'passion', etc., these words' clusters of meaning often overlapped.
4. Samuel Taylor Coleridge, from *The Friend* (1809), quoted in Susie I. Tucker, *Enthusiasm: A Study in Semantic Change* (Cambridge: Cambridge University Press, 1972), p. 19.
5. John Keats, letter to Benjamin Bailey, 22 Nov. 1817, in *Selected Letters of John Keats*, ed. Lionel Trilling (New York: Farrar, Straus, and Young, 1951), p. 88.

6. David Hume, *A Treatise of Human Nature*, ed. P. H. Nidditch, 2nd edn. (Oxford: Clarendon Press, 1978), p. 415.

7. Thomas De Quincey, 'On the Knocking at the Gate in Macbeth', in *Confessions of an English Opium-Eater and Other Writings*, ed. Grevel Lindop (Oxford: Oxford University Press, 1985), p. 83.

8. Laurence Sterne, *A Sentimental Journey Through France and Italy* (Oxford: Oxford University Press, 1968), p. 4.

9. Helen Maria Williams, *Letters from France* (London, 1790), pp. 61–2.

10. *Anti-Jacobin Review* (Dec. 1806), 346.

11. Anna Seward, *The Letters of Anna Seward*, 6 vols. (Edinburgh, 1811), vi. 367.

12. See Frank Felsenstein (ed.) *English Trader, Indian Maid: Representing Gender, Race, and Slavery in the New World: An Inkle and Yarico Reader* (Baltimore: Johns Hopkins University Press, 1999).

13. Henry Home, Lord Kames, *Elements of Criticism*, 2 vols. (Edinburgh, 1774), ii. 3. Hester Lynch Thrale Piozzi, *Thraliana: The Diary of Mrs Hester Lynch Thrale, 1776–1809* (Oxford: Clarendon Press, 1942), ii. 730; quoted in Mary Poovey, *The Proper Lady and the Woman Writer* (Chicago: University of Chicago Press, 1984), p. 37.

14. See Frances Greville, 'A Prayer for Indifference', ll. 29–32, in D. Nicol Smith (ed.) *The Oxford Book of Eighteenth-Century Verse* (Oxford: Oxford University Press, 1926), pp. 426–38. Helen Maria Williams, 'To Sensibility', l. 64, in *Poems in Two Volumes* (1786).

15. Mary Wollstonecraft, *A Vindication of the Rights of Woman*, ed. Carol H. Poston (1792; New York: W. W. Norton, 1975), p. 61.

16. M. B. Parkes, *Pause and Effect: An Introduction to the History of Punctuation in the West* (Berkeley: University of California Press, 1993), pp. 49, 92.

17. Jane Austen, *Sense and Sensibility* (Oxford: Oxford University Press, 1990), p. 292.

18. Gesa Stedman, *Stemming the Torrent: Expression and Control in the Victorian Discourses on Emotions, 1830–1872* (Aldershot: Ashgate, 2002), p. 34 n. 21.

5 | The visual arts and music

Stephen C. Behrendt

We usually associate Romantic visual art and music with a period extending from the mid- to later eighteenth century until the middle and (for music) later nineteenth century—some would say even beyond that. One of Romantic art's distinctive features is the artist's desire to express the ideal in terms of the real. Like some of William Wordsworth's and Charlotte Smith's poems, it is firmly grounded in actuality and dependent for its force upon precise details about real things. Fundamental truths and principles are revealed through their appearances within 'everyday life'. Like the poet, the Romantic artist renders the familiar unique by presenting it in an unaccustomed way to help the viewer to 'see' what has been there all along, hidden in plain sight within the ordinary external universe.

This is especially true when it comes to nature. Romanticism transformed the natural universe from a mere generic backdrop to human activity to a central character. Romantic art largely rejected the neoclassical preference for generalization when depicting human activity and the natural world. William Blake, for example, wrote that 'To Generalize is to be an Idiot. To Particularize is the Alone Distinction of Merit.'[1] For Blake, what is most individual and idiosyncratic is what is most valuable to the artist; it is the physical kernel that holds within it the universal value or truth that is accessible only via the particular detail, accurately and minutely rendered. Romantic paintings are therefore often filled with carefully executed details, whether their subject-matter is nature, human activity, or both. Like Romantic literature, Romantic art often suggests that nature is both consoling and restorative: seen (and enjoyed) correctly, nature provides the catalyst for altering the individual consciousness, most often for the better. Thus Romantic visual art often depicts people—especially *ordinary* people—enjoying pleasant, salutary activities within natural settings, which suggests to viewers how they might improve their own situations at minimal expense (financial or psychological) through the medium of nature. At the same time, however, visual art comes increasingly to recognize that nature is both 'Destroyer and Preserver', as Percy Shelley called the West Wind: the stormy scenes of Constable and Turner, the cataclysmic visions of John Martin, and the starkness of some of Caspar David Friedrich's works anticipate Tennyson's nature, 'red in tooth and claw'. At other times, artists simply call attention to the sheer immensity of nature, often by having their human figures wholly dwarfed by the natural setting, as in Friedrich's *Landscape with Oaks and Hunter* (1811).

Romantic art is also concerned with *heroism*, which European art and culture were entirely redefining during this period. The revolutions in America and France had begun to reduce the daunting distance between the ordinary citizen's situation and that of the traditional hero or heroine. Like those revolutions, which sought to define the sovereignty of 'the people'—and thereby of the individual—in defiance of inherited social, political, and economic hierarchies, a revolution in Romantic art dignified the sort of individual whom the fine arts had historically either treated as a butt of humour or overlooked altogether. Now George Crabbe wrote about common villagers like Peter Grimes, William Wordsworth wrote poems featuring beggars and retarded children, and Mary Robinson wrote about London street people and military camp followers. To choose such subjects, and then to treat them seriously and with dignity, as Romantic artists began to do, was to declare art far more truly 'open' and representative of the universality of human experience than had previously been the case. Romantic art began to demand that attention be paid not just to the glittering, privileged few but also to the vast majority of humankind, in each of whom resided material appropriate for tragedy or comedy of the highest sort. This is not to say that depictions of prominent public figures and events faded from view (or prominence) during the Romantic period; it *is* to say, however, that by the end of that era it was no longer remarkable to find treated with complete seriousness subjects like Goya's victims of war, Géricault's wounded soldiers and asylum inmates, and Constable's rustic farmers.

Above all, Romanticism emphasized individuality. Every individual is unique, Romanticism argues, and possesses by nature an infinite capacity for experience. Romantic art and literature created a cult of individualism by linking the individual with historical, mythological, and symbolic precursors and prototypes while cultivating personal independence of mind. Hence Romantic writers remind their contemporaries again and again to think for themselves, to bypass or ignore the 'middle-men' (professional reviewers and cultural critics), and in the process to *know themselves.* The Romantic artist relishes those characteristics that distinguish the individual from the mob, even if it results in our accepting, like Lord Byron (and like his immensely popular protagonists who frequently appear in Romantic visual art), that none of us is perfect or ideal, that each of us is compounded of mixed and frequently contradictory elements, desires, and idiosyncrasies that leave us torn between what we aspire to and what we can actually achieve. Romantic art is therefore more than usually preoccupied with subjects dealing with trial, with testing, with triumph, and of course with failure.

This emphasis upon the personal reflects Romantic art's firm grounding in the emotions and in subjectivity. Jean-Jacques Rousseau's ideas concerning human subjectivity influenced the rise, during the later eighteenth century, of *sentimentalism*, which emphasizes feeling and intuition rather than reason and empirical knowledge: what happens is less important than what one *feels* about what happens. Romantic visual art and music engage their audiences first through the senses and the emotions and only secondarily through the analytical intellect. In music, the crisp intellectuality of Bach's fugues or Handel's sonatas gives way to the sheer energy of Beethoven's Fifth

Symphony or the emotional extremes of Berlioz's Requiem. Likewise, Romantic paintings typically demand active emotional *engagement*, rather than passive spectatorship, as happens with John Martin's massive apocalyptic canvasses or J. M. W. Turner's swirling, misty scenes.

British art and Romanticism

British Romantic art reflects most of these characteristics (see *Oxford Companion to the Romantic Age*, pp. 250–60). It is, however, less immediately concerned than French art with the events of the revolution and the Napoleonic era, although later in the period artists like Sir David Wilkie, the most important genre painter in the first part of the century, painted many historical subjects, including scenes from contemporary history. Landscapes and seascapes are, on the other hand, comparatively more prominent. John Constable and J. M. W. Turner (see below) were only the most prominent of many landscape artists. William Delamott and James Ward painted landscapes influenced by precursors like Rubens, while the paintings of Clarkson Stanfield and Francis Danby evoke the many moods inspired by nature and the sea. The sea was also a favourite subject of Richard Parkes Bonington, whose delicate and brilliantly coloured works were influenced by French Romanticism, and of John Sell Cotman, who worked primarily in watercolours.

The work of William Blake (see below) and followers like Samuel Palmer is visionary and spiritual. Palmer's early work reflects his acquaintance with the Bible, Milton, Bunyan, Christian mysticism, and the visual style of Blake and John Linnell, both of whom he knew. His early works are intense and highly spiritualized pastoral landscapes. Like the Germans Caspar David Friedrich and Otto Runge, Palmer sought in his art to explore the sacred symbolism of natural phenomena. Paintings like *Coming from Evening Church* (1830) seem to merge human figures and rustic architecture with the landscape itself in a timeless vision of a rural paradise.

The Swiss immigrant Henry Fuseli gained fame for his dark, wild, and sensuous treatments of mythic and literary subjects, especially from Shakespeare and Milton. Best known now for his several versions of *The Nightmare* (1781–1820), Fuseli was expert at portraying psychological intensity and extreme behaviours, including cruelty and masochism. John Martin was famous for large paintings of cataclysmic events involving broad panoramas, extraordinary architecture, and great numbers of tiny figures dwarfed by the immensity of the other details. Best known in his life for paintings like *Belshazzar's Feast* (1821) and *The Plains of Heaven* (1851–3), Martin also created book illustrations for literary works like Milton's *Paradise Lost*. Less successful was William Etty, whose mythological and historical subjects, though technically correct (especially with the nude human body), lacked vitality and authenticity of experience. The most prominent portrait painter was the brilliant Sir Thomas Lawrence. Lawrence was a favourite of the royal family, whose portraits he painted and whose patronage he enjoyed. The Prince Regent (later George IV) commissioned him in 1815 to execute portraits of the rulers and statesmen involved in the struggle against Napoleon. Richard Cosway was a highly regarded miniaturist. His wife, Maria Cosway, was an accomplished painter (she exhibited more than thirty pictures at the Royal Academy) and musician. Louisa Stuart Costello also gained an early reputation as a miniaturist, although she subsequently directed her energies into literature. Among history painters, the well-known Angelica Kauffman (1741–1807) was influential also on the Continent, while the visionary but eccentric James Barry (1741–1806) defied the Royal Academy's protocols of patronage and died penniless. The best-remembered history painter is Benjamin Robert Haydon (1786–1846), the great rival to the elder American-born Benjamin West (1738–1820, second president of the Royal Academy). Haydon never achieved the broad public success he sought; his debts and disappointments led him finally to commit suicide. His most famous painting, *Christ's Entry into Jerusalem* (1820), included among the spectators portraits of Keats, Wordsworth, and even Voltaire. Haydon's greatest memorial is not a visual work, though, but rather his *Autobiography*, which appeared posthumously in 1853 and which provides important information about artists and their publics during Haydon's lifetime.

Romantic nationalism produced great interest in illustrating the works of native British authors. Fuseli, for instance, prepared a one-man exhibition, the Milton Gallery (1799–1800), devoted entirely to scenes based upon that author's works. Earlier, John and Josiah Boydell had sponsored a successful large exhibition, the Shakespeare Gallery, which opened in 1786 and featured paintings by all the major—and many minor—British artists. Intended to promote the British school of history painting, this exhibition also fuelled the popularity of reduced-scale engraved prints based on the original paintings. Like caricature prints, discussed below, these engraved prints disseminated British art (and increased British visual literacy) by making available to the general public relatively inexpensive versions of paintings otherwise unaffordable.

Many of the engravers involved in these projects were also commercial book illustrators. The growing popularity of illustrated books, made possible by new mass printing techniques and a consequent decrease in book prices, also contributed to the visual education of the general public. Illustrated editions of Shakespeare and Milton, the Bible, and classical and contemporary literature abounded, and books of travels and discovery, history, science, and morality were often illustrated as well, anticipating the later popular illustrated annuals and periodicals. Illustration became an increasingly important venue for artists. William Blake largely supported himself through commercial engraving, preparing prints based both on his own originals and on other artists' pictures; George Cruikshank did the same, concentrating though upon his own designs. One final graphic artist of great importance was Thomas Bewick, whose wood engravings of birds and animals set new standards for accuracy of observation and reproduction and are thus analogous to the strict fidelity to the details of natural history found in the works of poets like Charlotte Smith and John Clare. Illustrations, whether to literary, scientific, travel, or religious texts, contributed to both an increasingly sophisticated public 'eye' (or visual literacy) and a growing public awareness of (and susceptibility to) the particular appeal of visual art.

John Constable and the characterization of nature

John Constable (see *Oxford Companion to the Romantic Age*, pp. 464–5) is often considered the premier English landscape artist. He joined the Royal Academy of Art as a student in 1799 and became a full academician in 1829. Throughout his career, Constable drew upon the scenery of his native Suffolk for the works on which his reputation now rests. Large paintings like *The White Horse* (1819) and *The Hay Wain* (1821) gave Constable the physical space to demonstrate his remarkable skill with highly particularized detail; not only are vegetation and cloud formations rendered with great care, so too are even the most minor details of objects like the hay wagon or the brick and stucco work on the house. And yet, paradoxically, these paintings do not replicate actual places so much as they attempt to capture the immediacy of experience associated with particular times, places, and moods, much in the manner of William Wordsworth's poems, to which they are sometimes regarded as visual analogues. These are the sort of paintings for which Constable is most remembered, along with his images of Salisbury Cathedral, which he painted from many perspectives. But neither these nor the more conventional portraits and religious subjects he was commissioned to paint secured him either wealth or popularity during his lifetime; it was not until the first biography (by C. R. Leslie, published in 1843) that his work began to gain widespread and serious attention.

Constable seems to have coined the expression 'natural painture', by which he meant an approach to landscape painting that rejected academic conventions and sought instead an entirely pure representation of nature. Such representation was, for Constable, grounded in careful and minute observation; convinced that all natural phenomena are unique and individual, he made innumerable sketches (including especially oil sketches) 'on location', in the open air, in order to capture phenomena like changing cloud formations with absolute fidelity. The range of subject-matter in Constable's major landscape paintings is surprisingly narrow; they depict rural settings (with mills and other features of the Stour valley), changeable summer weather, daytime hours, and an emphasis upon the variety and vitality of the natural world. Indeed, in Constable's paintings nature becomes a principal character in what action there is; we are expected to study and reflect upon the carefully delineated details of the natural world at least as much as we are the activities of the few humans present in those settings. Nature's 'stage presence' is heightened by Constable's remarkable skill at rendering the effects of light upon colours. The immediacy and particularity Constable brought to his depictions of nature form an important break with academic convention

Fig. 2 John Constable, 'The Hay Wain', 1821.

and, although Constable's art took a very different direction from that of his contemporary, J. M. W. Turner, it served no less an important function in laying the groundwork for Impressionism and modernism.

William Blake's interdisciplinary art

The work of William Blake (see *Oxford Companion to the Romantic Age*, pp. 427–8) is extraordinary in its variety and intensity, its technical range and its intellectual and psychological penetration. Known in his time principally as a somewhat old-fashioned but technically excellent engraver and an eccentric painter, Blake was an enormously prolific visual artist and poet. A champion of historical and spiritual art, Blake broke from the Royal Academy in protest of both the Academy's exclusion of engravers and its betrayal of artists like James Barry in what he perceived to be its deferral to the retrogressive tastes and preferences of its wealthy patrons. Blake's own style involves an abstract Gothic linearity that typically produced elongated human figures deployed upon a relatively flat plane. The bulk of his work is done in watercolour, which he handles with great skill to produce delicate, luminous figures. Unfortunately, watercolours are notoriously susceptible to the effects of light, and many of Blake's pictures are now sadly faded, though they remain compelling nevertheless.

Although Blake championed exactitude and the individual, he regarded what he called 'Minute Particulars' as visionary gateways to Eternity. Spiritual vision was more important to him than material observation, which bound the senses to the analytically recorded natural world rather than freeing them to unlock the eternal world. Blake regarded the artist as a prophet whose duty it was to open the eyes of a recalcitrant and error-bound people to Truth and to a redemption that was at once spiritual, intellectual, and socio-political. Blake's principal subjects are drawn from the Bible and Milton, both of which he interpreted with great insight, often 'correcting' what he perceived to be errors in the originals or in the public's understanding of them. Indeed, Blake conceived of many of his projects as illustrations, even when they did not always result in conventional engravings. In addition to Milton and the Bible, he created large series of illustrations for Shakespeare, Dante, Edward Young, Thomas Gray, and others.

Blake also illustrated his own poems using a technique of relief etching which he devised. He composed and printed his poems on his own press, then detailed the pages by hand to produce elaborate images that combine verbal and visual art in a composite art form, or 'metatext', that is significantly more than the mere sum of the component parts. Blake called his technique 'illuminated printing', which we should understand in the sense of the medieval illuminated manuscript whose highly detailed pages are intended as objects for reflection and meditation. Among the illuminated poems, *Songs of Innocence and of Experience* (1789–94) is best known.

Fig. 3 William Blake. *Europe: A Prophecy*, plate 9: 'Enitharmon slept', 1794.

Longer illuminated narrative poems (which Blake called prophecies) run from the brief *Book of Thel* (1789) to the hundred-page *Jerusalem* (1804–19). In these Blake formulated a highly personal cosmology or mythological history of the universe. Because each copy was individually coloured over the course of Blake's career, works like the *Songs* reveal Blake's evolution as a stylist, colourist, and printmaker in their increasingly finely detailed pages.

J. M. W. Turner and the directions of Romantic art

Joseph Mallord William Turner (see *Oxford Companion to the Romantic Age*, pp. 739–40) was one of the most prolific of all English artists (he created no fewer than 370 oil paintings and nearly 96,000 watercolours, sketches, and engravings) and one of the most enigmatic. A largely self-taught painter who rose to prominence in the Royal Academy of Art and whose personal life uneasily combined confidence and misanthropy, humour and tragedy, classical aesthetic values and idiosyncratic independence of vision, Turner enjoyed considerable patronage, especially when he chose subjects from classical antiquity or Scripture that reflected the idea that 'high art' required 'serious' subjects. He is best known for his innumerable studies of both urban and rural scenes—including powerful seascapes—depicting the subject-matter under varying conditions of daylight or moonlight. Such pictures place him in the vanguard of what would become Impressionism, even though Turner's art was always grounded more in expressiveness than in naturalism.

Unlike Constable, Turner tended not to sketch in oil, choosing instead to prepare many watercolour sketches before beginning a version in oils: among the vast archives of Turner's art, therefore, we find a great many 'unfinished' sketches. While Turner's earlier paintings are representational images of natural phenomena, his work became increasingly non-naturalistic, featuring especially his characteristic fascination with swirling lines and masses of colour. These are most apparent in scenes set at sea, like *Snow Storm: Steam-Boat off a Harbour's Mouth* (1842), where the rough seas and tempestuous clouds are often indistinguishable from one another. Turner's engaging humour is also visible in pictures like *Rain, Steam, and Speed—The Great Western Railway* (1844), in which a hare outruns the chugging engine, and *Sunrise with Sea Monsters* (*c.*1845), while *The Slave Ship* (1840), an eloquent and moving protest against the inhumanity of the slave trade, reflects Turner's involvement with key social and political issues of his time. Unlike Constable, Turner was less and less interested in fine detail, so that his pictures often have the hazy, dreamlike quality of private interpretations of their subject-matter rather than any sharp, documentary quality.

The caricature print

The Romantic artistic establishment was dominated by wealthy patrons and collectors whose strong influence upon both the content and the style of formal art ensured that much of that art would reflect the tastes and preferences of the aristocracy. This meant large-scale pictures and sculptures, elevated or otherwise learned subject-matter (as in history painting), formal portraiture, and an élite, aristocratic connoisseurship. But other important artists flourished outside this exclusive coterie, creating 'popular' works whose intended audiences were not exclusively members of the privileged classes. Caricaturists like Thomas Rowlandson, James Gillray, and George Cruikshank, for instance, designed satirical prints that occupied the windows of print shops all over London where they could be seen, studied, and purchased by anyone with the relatively modest sum they cost. Unlike highly finished paintings that were accessible during a public exhibition and then sequestered within their purchasers' private spaces (e.g. residences), the caricature print was a determinedly *public* art form whose artists counted upon their works receiving wide viewing. Caricature prints assured their creators considerable intellectual and ideological independence, since the artists' financial success depended upon their skill in assessing the market for such prints: *the public*—not some individual purchaser—was this artist's patron.

This artistic independence was, nevertheless, relative rather than complete. For just as the élite artist needed to satisfy the patron in order to ensure a purchase, so did the caricaturist have to engage the public viewer in order to entice him or her to purchase a print (see *Oxford Companion to the Romantic Age*, pp. 207–13). 'Mass appeal' was often more important than esoteric appeal, which meant that the subject-matter of caricature prints was as a rule both topical and political in nature, while the dominant idiom was that of satire. Subjects ranged widely, but particular favourites involved political corruption, military and civil incompetence, and *ad hominem* attacks, especially upon the royal family and other prominent celebrities. Despite the anti-establishment posture of much caricature art, artists like Gillray were often ideologically conservative, even when they did not align themselves with one political party or another. Like classical Greek comedy, caricature art ridiculed excess of all sorts, whether it be the portly Prince of Wales's gluttony (Gillray, *A Voluptuary under the horrors of Digestion*, 1792) or the king and queen's penny-pinching (Gillray, *Temperance enjoying a Frugal Meal*, 1792). Set against such embodiments of privilege was the stout, homely, blunt, and long-suffering figure of John Bull, the emblematic 'Englishman' forced to bear the social and economic burdens imposed upon the nation by the excesses of the royal and aristocratic lifestyle (Gillray, *John Bull and his dog Faithful*, 1796).

Much of British Romantic caricature is unabashedly nationalistic and therefore also soundly anti-republican and anti-Gallican, attacking all things French (Gillray,

Sans-Culottes feeding Europe with the Bread of Liberty, 1793)—and Napoleon in particular, whether through ridicule or direct attack (Cruikshank, *Snuffing Out Boney!*, 1814). Moreover, much Romantic caricature is also highly sexual in nature and surprisingly explicit, a perhaps inevitable feature of an art form designed to capture the broadest public audience, whether through this sort of (often witty) graphic allusion or through the prints' frequently garish hand-colouring. Like his beautifully executed water-colours, Rowlandson's prints are, for the most part, good-humoured rather than dark deflations of human foibles, although they too are frequently highly sexual—even pornographic—in nature. By 1830 the tradition of the single print was disappearing as a consequence of the rise of illustrated periodicals and annuals. Rowlandson, for example, created a series of prints illustrating William Combe's 1813 poem, *The Tour of Doctor Syntax in Search of the Picturesque*, while Cruikshank left off producing individual prints to create illustrations for political works like the radical publisher William Hone's *Political House that Jack Built* (1819) and for later collections of fiction like *Roscoe's Novelist's Library*.

Some notes on sculpture

In the decade between 1802 and 1812 alone Parliament voted more than £40,000 for national monuments to military and political figures, in addition to the large sums raised by cities and private corporations. In the two decades that followed these vast sums actually increased. Founded in 1802 to eliminate the bickering that had always attended the creation of public monuments, the government Committee of National Monuments oversaw allocation of funds, selection of designs, and placement of sculp-tures. As happened with caricature prints, which addressed and educated a much more broadly based and 'democratic' public than traditional academic paintings produced for private patrons, this explosion of public monumental sculpture inevitably affected the everyday English consciousness. No longer were churches and graveyards the prin-cipal repositories of public sculpture (they were becoming crowded anyway); all public spaces became exhibition spaces. Two major sculptors who benefited from public and private commissions were the popular and long-lived Joseph Nollekens, who prepared neoclassical busts of many celebrities, and Sir Richard Westmacott, whose monuments to General Sir Ralph Abercromby (1802–5) and the 1st Baron Collingwood (1813–17) are in St Paul's Cathedral. Marianne Hunt, wife of the liberal journalist Leigh Hunt, was a proficient sculptor whose bust of Percy Bysshe Shelley is perhaps her best remembered work.

The two greatest British Romantic sculptors are Sir Francis Chantrey and John Flaxman. The largely self-taught Chantrey, who spent his early years in Sheffield before settling in London by 1808, produced more than a hundred elegant busts, like those of John Horne Tooke (1811) and Sir Walter Scott (1820). His public monument of William

Pitt (1831) stands in Hanover Square, London, and the much-photographed mounted George IV (1828) in Trafalgar Square is also his. He was equally skilled with sentimental subjects like *The Sleeping Children* (1817), in Lichfield Cathedral, Staffordshire, which evocatively combines naturalistic touches (like the snowdrops one child holds) with serenity in rendering these dead children. Chantery died a rich man who had done much to liberate British sculpture from the bloodless formality of academic neoclassicism. Like so many Romantic artists, Chantery was unhesitatingly committed to the human particularity of his subjects, once telling a contemporary: 'all our feelings are with men like ourselves. To produce any real effect, we must copy man, we must represent his action and display his emotions.'[2]

John Flaxman, the best-known pre-modern British sculptor, was widely influential in sculpture and in the other arts, both in England and abroad. The Royal Academy created its Chair of Sculpture for him in 1810. Best remembered for his remarkable linear designs, Flaxman early on showed great interest in classical antiquity. Entering study at the Royal Academy in 1770, he became friends with William Blake and Thomas Stothard, the latter soon to become a fashionable designer of book illustrations. A deeply moral man dedicated to serving Protestantism through his art, Flaxman in his maturity created powerful large sculptures on classical themes, like *The Fury of Athamas* (1790–4), and on contemporary subjects, like his monument to Lord Nelson (1808–18) in St Paul's Cathedral. But he also worked on a more modest—and no less public—scale as a book illustrator whose elegant line drawings (like those for an edition of Homer) were widely copied, and as a designer for the famous Wedgwood porcelain factory.

British music

After Thomas Arne, who wrote principally for the theatre, English music declined, partly because music came to be considered less an 'art' than an 'accomplishment' chiefly involving upper-class women. The best-known 'popular' English composers included James Hook, William Shield, and theatre songwriters like Stephen Storace and John O'Keeffe. While nationalism in all other areas of British culture was on the rise, in music the public focused for 'serious' music instead on the foreign virtuoso, and on Italian opera and the work of composers like Giovanni Paesiello and Domenico Cimarosa. This was, after all, the age of Mozart (who died in 1791), Beethoven, Mendelssohn, Paganini, and Berlioz (see *Oxford Companion to the Romantic Age*, pp. 242–50). When Franz Josef Haydn visited London in 1791–5, for instance, the energetic and sociable composer became a great public favourite while his music was adored in the concert hall and the press alike. His time in England was also productive: he composed nearly 800 pages of vocal and instrumental scores encompassing everything from 150 Scottish songs to twelve symphonies.

Perhaps the most important British Romantic composer was the Irishman, John Field, whose popular success Haydn had predicted. A virtuoso pianist and composer of popular concertos that influenced Robert Schumann, Field largely invented the piano Nocturne form that Chopin would later take to a new level of brilliance. Field's Nocturnes are simple and unaffected in form, delicate and evocative. Less well remembered are two other Irish composers, Michael William Balfe and William Vincent Wallace. Balfe began as a violinist at Drury Lane before becoming manager of the Lyceum Theatre in London, where he specialized in producing operas, including his own *The Bohemian Girl* (1843), which achieved some considerable popular success. Wallace, an organist and violinist, lived an adventurous early life in Australia and New Zealand, India, Mexico, and the United States before settling in London in his early thirties to devote himself to producing light piano music and his enormously popular operas *Maritana* (1845) and *Lurline* (1860).

'Popular' music

The popularity of composers like Balfe and Wallace, whose operas played both in major theatres in London and in travelling opera companies, usefully reminds us that, like visual art, music had a much wider audience than just the privileged patrons. Because only the licensed theatres in London—Drury Lane, Covent Garden, and later the Haymarket—were permitted to present 'legitimate' dramas (i. e. works like Shakespeare or Sheridan consisting of standard dialogue), other theatres had to attract audiences with other forms of entertainment, including pantomime, equestrian shows, 'spectacles', and musical entertainments. The number of establishments offering this fare in fact outnumbered the licensed theatres, and the licensed theatres closed down during the summer months, to be replaced by institutions like the English Opera House. Indeed, it is worth recalling that the first dramatic version of Mary Shelley's *Frankenstein*, Richard Brinsley Peake's *Presumption; or, The Fate of Frankenstein*, which ran for thirty-seven performances at the English Opera House in 1823 (where Mary Shelley attended a performance), included a musical score and a variety of songs sung by virtually every character except the Creature. Musical theatres of this sort, together with the more strictly formal opera, propelled singers like Elizabeth Billington, Angelica Catalani, and Giuditta Pasta to great popular fame.

Nor were the theatres the only venue for music. Other settings included large and popular public 'pleasure gardens' like Vauxhall Gardens, which was flourishing already in the eighteenth century and where visitors might enjoy a variety of musical and theatrical entertainments. The popular song itself was enjoying a rapid rise in British Romantic society, in part because periodicals like *La Belle Assemblée*—and gift books and annuals after them—often included in their pages both lyrics and scores for songs. Taken together with the growing popularity of the piano (pianoforte), which more and more people were beginning to be able to afford for their homes, and the formation of popular singing societies (or 'glees'), the publication of musical scores in periodicals and in 'stand-alone' forms spread both music and the ability to produce it to an ever-increasing segment of the population. Already familiar from their religious practices with musical forms like hymns (Charles Wesley and his son Samuel were prodigious hymn composers), and from their populist roots with folk and street music, British citizens provided a hungry audience for the productions of composers in the popular idiom, as is evident for instance from the popularity of the sea songs of Charles Dibdin. Just as Romantic literature, visual art, and politics worked to democratize society and its attitudes, so did music contribute to the phenomenon.

FURTHER READING

Clay, Jean, *Romanticism* (Oxford: Phaidon, 1981). This is a large and lavishly illustrated survey of European Romantic art, arranged thematically.

Haydon, Benjamin Robert, *Autobiography and Journals*, ed. Malcolm Elwin (London: Macdonald, 1950). This useful record of the artistic scene in Romantic-era England provides the entire text of Haydon's *Autobiography* as published in 1853 by Tom Taylor, with additional selections from Haydon's journals of 1821 to 1846.

Honour, Hugh, *Romanticism* (New York: Harper and Row, 1979). This volume surveys the art and ideas of Romanticism from the late 1790s until the middle of the nineteenth century.

Hunt, Leigh, *The Autobiography of Leigh Hunt*, ed. J. E. Morpurgo (London: Cresset Press, 1949). This is a lively and readable survey of the political and artistic culture and leading luminaries of the Romantic age in England, written by a liberal journalist whose friends included Shelley and Keats, among others.

McCalman, Iain (ed.) *An Oxford Companion to the Romantic Age: British Culture 1776–1832* (Oxford: Oxford University Press, 1999). For good brief summaries of the principal issues, see the chapters on 'Viewing' (ch. 19), 'Prints' (ch. 22), 'Popular Culture' (ch. 23), 'Theatre' (ch. 24), 'Music' (ch. 26), and 'Painting' (ch. 27).

Paulson, Ronald, *Representations of Revolution (1789–1820)* (New Haven: Yale University Press, 1983). An illustrated, interdisciplinary study of some of the ways in which the French Revolution furnished subjects for the visual arts and literature, especially in England.

Temperley, Nicholas (ed.) *Music in Britain: The Romantic Age 1800–1914* (London: Athlone Press, 1981). The best and most extensive study of the subject.

Vaughan, William, *Romanticism and Art* (London: Thames and Hudson, 1994). This is a comprehensive, readable introduction to Romantic art, with many small but good illustrations.

Whinney, Margaret, *Sculpture in Britain, 1530 to 1830*, rev. John Physick (London: Penguin, 1988). This is an excellent, thorough, and well-illustrated survey of British sculpture that traces the evolution of the main themes and styles of pre-modern sculpture.

Wolf, Norbert, *Painting of the Romantic Era* (Cologne: Taschen, 1999). This is a sumptuously illustrated survey of Romantic art, arranged by country.

NOTES

1. *The Complete Poetry and Prose of William Blake*, ed. David V. Erdman (New York: Doubleday, 1988), p. 641.

2. George Jones, *Sir Francis Chantrey, Recollections of His Life, Practice and Opinions* (London, 1849), p. 301.

6 | Print culture and the book trade

John Barnard

The increasing availability of printed texts of all kinds between 1770 and 1830 at once reflected, and was instrumental in, creating new readerships of imaginative literature. This expansion of the reading public (a term invented at this time), together with technological innovations in printing and papermaking after 1800, laid the basis for the mass audience of the Victorian period.

The eighteenth-century book trade had established an homogeneous class-based readership by 1770. However, the storming of the Bastille, the Declaration of the Rights of Man in 1789, the Terror of 1793, and the consequent political crisis in Britain, dislocated readerships. Contemporary observers agreed that the 1790s marked a watershed. In 1824 an anonymous writer in *Blackwood's Magazine* said, 'Since the interesting era of the French Revolution the people of these Kingdoms have been an inquisitive, doubting and reading people. ... Their feelings received then an extraordinary impetus.'[1] By 1830 a newly self-conscious middle-class audience had emerged, encouraged by an expanded periodical press, alongside of the beginnings of a mass audience, and a growing radical readership. The period also saw a shift from publishing methods, which in 1770 were conservative and restrictive, to innovatory ways—partly enabled by technological developments—of reaching newly identified audiences on an unprecedented scale.

The widening reading publics and the power of the press created anxieties encapsulated in Wordsworth's Preface to the second edition of *Lyrical Ballads* (1800). Like many, Wordsworth believed that he was living in a period of exceptionally rapid change. If *Lyrical Ballads* is a revolutionary poetic document, the Preface of 1800 takes up a reactionary stance towards recent developments in the reading public: 'a multitude of causes, unknown to former times, are now acting with a combined force to blunt the discriminating powers of the mind . . . [reducing them] to a state of almost savage torpor.' Wordsworth identifies the roots of this cultural crisis:

The most effective of these causes are the great national events which are daily taking place [the war with France and political repression at home], and the encreasing accumulation of men in cities, where the uniformity of their occupations produces a craving for extraordinary incident which the rapid communication of intelligence [through national and provincial newspapers] hourly gratifies . . .

The danger was that a mass of undiscriminating readers, fed only with what was fashionable and popular and accustomed to sensational daily news, would drive out serious literature.

Throughout the period the widening access to print was seen as a threat by many different constituencies, whether it took the form of paternalistic fears about the debilitating effects of novels on women readers, or the government's efforts to restrict readership to the middle and upper classes by imposing stamp duties and taxes on paper, on periodicals, and, later, pamphlets, or Coleridge's belief in the 1820s that the evils of a 'multitudinous PUBLIC' could only be controlled through the intellectual efforts of an educated Christian minority, the 'clerisy'.

Others perceived the phenomenon quite differently. In 1809 Thomas Holcroft, the self-educated dramatist and radical, recalled the scarcity of books during his years as a stable-boy in the early 1760s: 'Books were not then, as they fortunately are now, great or small . . . to be found in almost every house.' It was a widely shared perception. James Lackington, a shoemaker, became a highly successful bookseller at his 'Temple of the Muses' in Finsbury Square (1780–98) by selling remaindered titles and new books substantially below their normal retail price, relying on high turnover for profit. He famously claimed in 1792, 'all ranks and degrees now READ'.

Wordsworth, Holcroft, and Lackington echo a common perception, but their accounts are in some respects exaggerated. First, although literacy between 1775 and 1830 in the 'middling classes', including shopkeepers and skilled tradesmen, both urban groupings, rose from 75 to 95 per cent, among the labouring classes less than a half were literate by 1800, though that proportion increased to some 60 per cent in the early nineteenth century. Second, throughout this period the price of new books was kept artificially high by the dominant London trade, and grew proportionately more expensive over the years. The highest paid workmen in the country, London artisans, earned only between a pound and two pounds weekly, while farm labourers were paid 9s. (£0.45) or less a week. Scott's *Rokeby* (1813), handsomely published in quarto with large type and wide margins at two guineas, represented nearly five weeks' work for a farm labourer, and even a sixpenny pamphlet amounted to a substantial part of his daily wage. What all three men, Wordsworth, Holcroft, and Lackington, testify to in the years between 1792 and 1809 is the increasing numbers of readers and books in their time, an increase that was to continue. 'The reading public, it is estimated, quintupled in the whole period 1780 to 1830, from 1 to 7 millions.'[2] Books exported to North America, the Caribbean, India, and other colonies further boosted an already buoyant market.

Radical publishing

From the early 1790s radicals and reformists saw the printed word as an agent of change. In William Hone's satirical *The House that Jack Built* (1819), Cruikshank's technically detailed wood engraving depicts the new Stanhope iron press as 'THE THING' which will overcome government repression (see Fig. 4). Hone's satire is a response to the second major government campaign against the press, the first of which followed the publication of Thomas Paine's *Rights of Man* (1791–2), a vindication of the principles of the American and French Revolutions in answer to Edmund Burke's *Reflections on the Revolution in France* (1790). Burke's prophesy of social disintegration and the destruction of traditional hierarchies sold 30,000 copies in its first two years. The first part of Paine's reply, helped by the distribution of free copies to workers by the middle-class London Constitutional Society, sold 50,000 copies at 3*s*. in a few weeks, far outstripping Burke's sales. The second part of the *Rights of Man*, advocating radical social reform, sold at 6*d*. It was published in February 1792 and banned in May, but even so sold some 200,000 in the first year. In the ensuing pamphlet war, Thomas Spence's weekly miscellany, ironically entitled, *Pig's Meat; or, Lessons for the Swinish Multitude* (1793), circulated radical ideas in reply to Burke's fear that the French Revolution would 'cast down [learning] in the mire' to be 'trodden down under the hoofs of the swinish multitude'.

In the counter-revolutionary backlash which followed the beginnings of war with France, the dangers posed by a radical press seemed overwhelming. Pitt's government took repressive action, suspending Habeas Corpus (which prevented arbitrary imprisonment) and tightening the laws on libel and treason. James Gillray's savagely satirical print, *The New Morality* (1798), depicts well-known radical writers clutching opposition newspapers like the *Morning Chronicle*, with incendiary pamphlets spilling out of their pockets (reproduced in *Oxford Companion to the Romantic Age*, pp. 112–13). The cartoon forcefully acknowledges print culture's power in an age of revolution, and it is worth noting that 1770–1830 was the heyday of satirical prints by George Cruikshank, Thomas Rowlandson, James Gillray, and others. (This was also a time when fine prints brought high art to the middle class.)

The revelation that there was a large audience for Paine's revolutionary ideas sparked off attempts to reply in kind, most notably through Hannah More's *Cheap Repository Tracts* (1795–8), of which two million were sold or distributed. More, a conservative Christian feminist, opposed the ideas of the French Revolution and those of Mary Wollstonecraft on women's rights. Her cheap pamphlet tales embodied traditional family, Christian, and social values, and were aimed at a working-class readership feared to be on the edge of revolution. The same impulse lay behind the foundation of the British and Foreign Bible Society in 1804, which had, by 1819, circulated more than two and a half million Bibles and Testaments, mostly in Britain, and the Religious Tract Society, which printed 314,000 tracts in 1804.

Government oppression and patriotic support of the war against France quietened radical publishing until Napoleon was finally defeated in 1815. Thereafter there was a second major phase of radical and reformist publishing. When the tax on paper was increased in 1816 to a punitive 4*d*., William Cobbett reduced the price of his weekly *Political Register* (1802–35) to a mere 2*d*. ('Two-Penny Trash; or Politics for the Poor'),

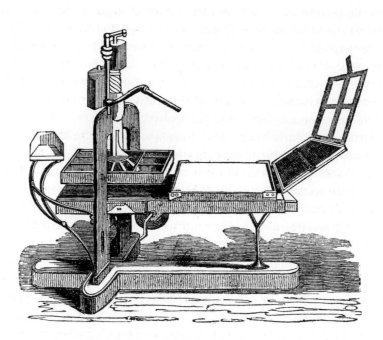

" Once enslaved, farewell !

*　　　*　　　*　　　*

Do I forebode impossible events,
And tremble at vain dreams ? Heav'n grant I may !"

THIS IS

THE THING,

that, in spite of new Acts,

And attempts to restrain it,

by Soldiers or Tax,

Will *poison* the Vermin,

That plunder the Wealth,

That lay in the House,

That Jack built.

Fig. 4 Engraving of Stanhope's new iron printing press by George Cruikshank, reproduced in William Hone, *The Political House that Jack Built* (1819).

and continued to attack the government. This attempt to suppress popular protest was followed in 1817 by the suspension of Habeas Corpus and the renewal of the 1795 Treason Acts. William Hone typifies the radical publishers who stood out against political persecution. He founded the *Reformist's Register* and *Black Dwarf*, and was put on trial three times for publishing satirical blasphemous parodies. In order to cover the ruinous expense of the trials he published his *Three Trials of William Hone* (1818), each costing a shilling, which swiftly ran into many editions. Hone went on to publish satires on the government and establishment, marrying his words with the woodcuts of George Cruikshank, and selling them at sixpence or less.

Alongside Hone, other 'underground' publishers, like Richard Carlile, William Benbow, William Sherwin, and J. Ohnwyn, all published cheap editions in defiance of the government's attempt to shut down their businesses. When the first two cantos of Byron's *Don Juan* appeared in 1819, John Murray, to save himself from the danger of prosecution, had it published anonymously and in an expensive quarto (£1. 11s. 6d.) to limit readership to the wealthy. Anonymity meant, however, that Murray had no copyright. The radical press immediately reprinted *Don Juan*, Cantos I–II, in cheap, small-format pirated editions. These rival publications, about which Murray could do nothing, recruited Byron's satire to the radical cause. This association, which revealed the poem's true colours, undermined the public's, and in particular women readers', popular 'romantic' image of Byron, author of the oriental tales and *Childe Harold*. By 1823 Murray was sufficiently concerned with his own social and political reputation to hand on the increasingly outspoken *Don Juan*, Cantos VI–VII, to John Hunt, brother of Leigh Hunt, who did not fear prosecution.

Even more extraordinary is the case of Shelley's *Queen Mab* (1813), privately published in an edition of probably only 250 copies for a minority audience of like-minded readers. However, from 1821 cheap pirated editions began to appear. By 1845 at least fourteen of these editions were in circulation, including those published by Richard Carlile. Its popularity was due not to Shelley's allegory, but to his extensive notes. These provided translations of key radical texts, continental and classical, advocating anti-monarchical views and arguing for atheism, vegetarianism, democracy, and free love. *Queen Mab* became the 'Bible' of the Chartists in the 1840s.

New books

Although religious books of one kind or another made up the largest part of the market for books between 1770 and 1830, literature had a very substantial readership. Of all books, including reprints, published between 1701 and 1800 now in the major British research libraries, religion accounts for some 54,000 titles, the social sciences (including politics) some 48,000, and literature about 38,000. The novel, the first major literary genre created by the printing press, became a major genre in these years, the number of new novels published increasing steadily from 1770 to 1799 (over 1,400 titles in all), levelling out between 1800 and 1829 (over 2,000 titles); from the 1780s women outnumbered men among identifiable authors. These figures reflect the growing leisure market for reading in these years, but also demonstrate that women readers made women writers. Further, by selling their copyright, women, as much as men, could receive a worthwhile fee from their publisher. Although there are no comparable figures for poetry, the same general pattern seems to apply to that market—women were the majority of readers. Other important new genres emerged or become more important after 1770, like conduct books written for or by women (see *Oxford Companion to the Romantic Age*, pp. 463–4), and children's books. John Newbery began to specialize in publishing the latter in 1744, and they became a particular preserve of women writers, including Anna Laetitia Barbauld, though William Godwin and Charles and Mary Lamb also wrote for children (see *Oxford Companion to the Romantic Age*, pp. 551–3). Educational reforms and population growth made the publishing of schoolbooks a new growth area for the trade.

The apparent paradox of a widening readership and the development of new publishing genres at a time when the prices of new books increased is due to the increasing commodification of literature in these years. During the eighteenth century the book trade established a stable national market for the sale and circulation of new books. Until challenged by Edinburgh in the early years of the next century, London booksellers had a virtual monopoly, and were therefore able to keep prices high, though their ability to do so depended upon their customers' belief that expensiveness was an assurance of a book's enhanced cultural value—and therefore worth paying more for.

Where the normal pattern in the eighteenth century was for groups of booksellers to finance new books jointly, and so spread the risk, this period sees the emergence of publishing houses run by individuals (some of which, like Murray and Longman, became family dynasties lasting into the twentieth century), and the beginnings of the modern separation of retail bookselling from publishing. Publishers of this kind acted as middlemen between the public and authors. The radical publisher, Joseph Johnson, held literary dinners over his bookshop in St Paul's Churchyard. His ownership of the *Analytical Review* enabled him to give employment to his own stable of authors, which included Joseph Priestley, Thomas Paine, Henry Fuseli, Blake, Mary Wollstonecraft, William Cowper, and Erasmus Darwin. He also encouraged the growth of Romantic literature, publishing early work by Wordsworth (*Descriptive Sketches* in 1793), Bowles, and Lamb. John Murray, who took over his father's business in 1799, gave up retailing books altogether, becoming a publisher in the modern sense—'The business, he said, of a publishing bookseller is not in his shop, or even in his connections, but in his brains'. He too cultivated his authors, who included Byron. In Edinburgh, Archibald Constable, Scott's publisher, set out to challenge the dominance of London, and was regarded by his authors as a 'generous patron and payer of all promising publications'. Individuals like Murray and Constable set the pattern for nineteenth-century publishing houses, but the trade in general still depended on selling new books at a premium price in small editions of less than a thousand. This limited the financial risk, and tested the market: if successful, the work could be reprinted.

The extraordinary success of Scott's poems, and even more so of his novels, proved that high prices were no deterrent to buyers. *The Lay of the Last Minstrel* (1805), a lavish quarto costing 25*s.*, sold over fifteen thousand copies in five years. *The Lady of the Lake* (1810), priced at 42*s.*, sold 20,300 copies in the first year. Sales of this order were exceeded by Murray's success with Byron: in 1814 his *Corsair* sold 10,000 copies on the first day of publication. When Constable published Scott's *Waverley* (1814) the first edition of 1,000 copies sold out in a matter of weeks, and a further 2,000 copies were sold within three months. By 1829 Constable had sold some 40,000 copies. With the publication of *Kenilworth* (1821), Constable and Scott established the form of the 'three-decker' novel (three volumes priced at one and a half guineas or 10*s. 6d.* a volume), which became the standard form and price for the Victorian novel, and meant that an individual buying a copy of a first edition paid a premium to do so.

In the context of this highly commercial publishing world, William Blake's decision to publish his poems himself represents a total rejection of the period's commercialization of literature (and, indeed, its industrialization—the 'Waverley' edition of Scott's collected novels was printed on the new steam press). Refusing to use letterpress type, Blake, beginning with *Thel* and *Songs of Innocence* in 1789, invented his own technique for creating plates, which allowed his own handwriting to be integrated into the illustrated pages. These were later hand-coloured, so that each print-image is unique, creating tiny limited editions of his visionary poems for circulation to a few admirers. His marginal income was derived from the print trade and from help given by patrons. The decision of Wordsworth and Coleridge to publish the first edition of *Lyrical Ballads* (1798) with Joseph Cottle in Bristol should also be seen as a gesture against the hegemony of the London trade—a futile one since the unsold stock was remaindered by a London bookseller

Libraries

New books were semi-luxury possessions, bound to their new owner's specification. By the late eighteenth century private libraries were an expected part of any well-to-do household. High prices did not deter this dependable clientele, and worked to the publishers' benefit, but the prohibitive cost for any but the well-off led to the development of various kinds of lending libraries. Because libraries circulated a single copy of a new book to multiple readers, the potential for retail sales was further diminished, forcing prices even higher. Lending libraries began as offshoots of individual retail booksellers, aimed at local readers. These circulating libraries, like those in Bath catering for the leisured readers of a seasonal spa town, included women readers among their clientele. They formed a growing and increasingly important audience both for poetry and novels, particularly the novels of Sensibility and Gothic fiction.

'Book clubs' or 'book societies' were local informal associations of middle-class families who bought and exchanged books. The *Monthly Magazine* reported that in 1821 there were 6,500 of 'these useful institutions' meeting the needs of 'above 30,000' families. William Lane's Minerva Press and Library notorious for its sensationalist Gothic novels was by 1791 offering ready-made libraries of between one hundred to 10,000 books to tradesmen, like grocers and tobacconists, who wanted to cash in on the demand for the borrowing of novels in particular. However, Lane's annual subscription fee of one guinea put his books beyond the reach of any but the middling classes. On the Continent there was a sufficiently large body of English readers for Giovanni Galignani to set up a Paris bookshop and circulating library from *c*.1799. Its success led to the founding of a widely circulated and long-lived newspaper, *Galignani's Messenger* (1814–94), a reading room, and, from 1828, the publication of cheap editions of poets, like Wordsworth and Byron, and of novels.

In large conurbations and, particularly, the emergent manufacturing cities like Birmingham, Newcastle, Manchester, and Leeds, the wealthier professionals and businessmen founded proprietary libraries, intended for both recreation and serious reading. These had their own buildings and librarian, made regular purchases, and were controlled by their members, who each held a share and paid an annual subscription. Leeds in 1817 was typical of other cities in terms of libraries and other forms of access to printed matter. Members of the social, professional, and commercial élite, mostly from the city but some from the neighbouring countryside, held shares in the Leeds Library, founded in 1768 by, among others, Joseph Priestley. The number of owners, who paid ten guineas for their share and a guinea a year subscription, was limited to 500 members. Book purchases were made by a committee, whose choices relied heavily on the reviews in the metropolitan periodicals. In 1817 its owners included no fewer than seventy four women, and its holdings comprised novels (11%), poetry (14%), history (16%), theology (9%), and law, politics, and commerce (16%). Until 1814 the Library also included a separate foreign section, begun in 1779, which bought books in French, Spanish, German, and Dutch. The later New Subscription Library, founded in 1795, and known locally as the 'Jacobin' library, had an initial charge of five guineas and a yearly fee of 25*s*. The Methodist Library (one guinea and 5*s*. a year) extended readership further, though it was still limited to the relatively affluent middle classes. There were, in addition, a medical library in the Infirmary, booksellers' circulating libraries, a mid-town Coffee Room, which took newspapers, the Commercial News Room for tradesmen, thirteen booksellers or stationers, and two weekly newspapers, the Tory *Leeds Intelligencer* (established in 1754) and the Whig *Leeds Intelligencer*. The new Leeds Philosophical and Literary Society, set up in 1819 quickly created a library for its members. Leeds had, like the rest of the country, a stratified but substantial reading public, very largely middle class but including tradesmen, and divided along political and religious grounds.

Although libraries of this kind widened the reading public, they could not reach far beyond the well to do, unless servants read the books borrowed by their masters or mistresses. It was not until the mid-1820s that Henry Brougham, inspired by Dr George Birkbeck's work in Glasgow, encouraged the setting up of Mechanics' Institutes in the industrial cities. Through lectures and libraries, these establishments sought to make books more widely available to artisans and craftsmen. Although idealistic, this initiative was an essentially utilitarian scheme, intended as a form of educative social control to negate the risks of unrestricted, and therefore dangerous, reading by the lower classes.

Cheap print

The most common forms of print for the poor were the almanacs, ballads, and chap-books sold on the streets and through pedlars in the countryside for a penny or two-pence. This was a conservative trade going back to the sixteenth century and still circulated many of the same texts: *Guy of Warwick*, for instance, had been on sale in the sixteenth century and the texts crossed class boundaries. Wordsworth records their importance for his imaginative development during childhood. After 1800 publishers of street literature (see *Oxford Companion to the Romantic Age*, pp. 621–2, 720–1), most notably James Catnach, sold sensationalist illustrated broadsheets, execution sheets, and twopenny chapbooks which gave condensed (and plagiarized) versions of books like Pierce Egan's *Life in London* (1821), otherwise too expensive for this class of readers.

Newspapers and periodicals

Newspapers were the most widely available form of newly written printed texts. They were the main driving force in developments in print technology, and their advertise-ments of books, which reached every corner of the kingdom, provided a vital resource for the London book trade. Like periodicals, they mediated cultural and literary matters to their readers and created reading communities. Any adequate explanation of the development of the literary market and of the new reading publics in this period is dependent upon an understanding of the dynamic role played by newspapers and periodicals, both of which had undergone substantial transformation by the 1830s. They were the economic platform which made the phenomenon of the Victorian 'man of letters' possible. (See further the chapter on 'Essays, newspapers, and magazines' below.)

The reprint trade

Although the cost of new books or a library subscription put them beyond the reach of most of the population throughout this period, cheap reprinted books reached a wider audience. The reprint trade changed significantly after 1774, when perpetual copyright (whereby publishers had indefinite control over the titles they owned) was abolished. This had unforeseen consequences. An Edinburgh publisher, John Bell, decided to challenge the historic monopoly of the London trade by publishing cheap editions of writers whose works were now out of copyright. His pocket edition of *The Poets of Great Britain Complete from Chaucer to Churchill* (1776–83) in 109 volumes, was published in Edinburgh at 1*s*. 6*d*. a volume, each with an engraved title or portrait and set in a new French-influenced typeface. Bell also published an edition of Shakespeare (1774) at 1*s*. 6*d*. a volume (6*d*. on coarse paper), and Bell's *British Theatre* (21 volumes in 1776–81, 36 volumes 1791–1802). In the closing years of the century Charles Cooke issued his editions of pocket editions of British poets (48 volumes, 1794–1805) even more cheaply, selling them in weekly sixpenny numbers. Hazlitt, Leigh Hunt, William Hone, and John Clare all recorded buying Cooke's edition when young. Hazlitt later reported, 'the world I had found out in Cooke's edition of the British Novelists was to me a dance through life, a perpetual gala day'. Cheap reprints of this kind were reinforced by the circulation of second-hand books, so increasing the number of books available, and creating a trickle-down effect. It is that effect which lies behind Holcroft's comments on the increasing availability of books during his lifetime and was the basis of James Lackington's commercial success.

Reading and writing: a case history

The career of the working-class poet Robert Bloomfield demonstrates the intersections between print, reading, and the business of publishing. At 15 years old Bloomfield was sent from the country to London in 1781 to become a shoemaker. His first task was to read out yesterday's newspaper sixpenny part books to the older men working in their garret. He borrowed others, and was encouraged to publish in the 'Poet's Corner' of the *London Magazine* in 1782. After years struggling to write while making ladies' shoes, he sent the manuscript of a long poem to Capel Lofft, a lawyer and *litterateur*, who found Bloomfield patrons and a publisher. *The Farmer's Boy* (1800) was an immediate success. It was published by Vernor and Hood in a pocket-sized octavo, with delicate wood-engravings by Thomas Bewick. There were three London editions in 1800, and New York, Philadelphia, and Leipzig editions the following year. In 1804 Keats's future publisher, John Taylor, reported that Bloomfield had already earned more than £4,000 from his first two books of poems.

Bloomfield's example is telling in several ways. His picture of an idyllic rural England offered the public an antidote to the anxieties caused by the French wars and the threat of revolution from within, fitting safely into the role of the eighteenth-century worker-poet typified by the 'Thresher poet', Stephen Duck. The part played by cheap print and initial newspaper publication in Bloomfield's self-discovery as a poet shows how literary culture could reach beyond the middle class (the very different careers of Chatterton and Henry Kirke White demonstrate the same point). Bewick's illustrations, which used wood engraving with a new freedom, and the use of stereotype to print later editions, show Vernor and Hoods's alertness to the latest technological developments, and also the critical role played by publishers throughout this period. Finally, this publishing sensation was part of the poetry boom evident from at least 1792, when Thomas Cadell's edition of Samuel Rogers's nostalgic *Pleasures of Memory* went into four editions in its first year and had sold 23,000 by 1816.

Readers

The most resistant subject of enquiry for the study of print culture is how books and printed matter actually affected individual readers. Coleridge's lifelong habit of annotating his own and other's books offers a remarkable insight into his reading habits and intellectual development, as do his early borrowings from the Bristol subscription library. Mary Shelley's journal records her reading and that of Shelley, and writers' letters, for instance those of Byron, Leigh Hunt, and Clare, include frequent comments on their own reading, those of their contemporaries, and their attitudes to publishers and literary politics. Keats's attitude to books is instructive. He owned relatively few books when he died in Rome, and his first major poem, 'On First Looking into Chapman's Homer', was written after being shown a borrowed copy of the George Chapman's translation. Keats's schoolteacher, Charles Cowden Clarke, also kept a manuscript commonplace book for copying out interesting poems and passages, which in turn influenced Keats's taste. Keats annotated his copies of Shakespeare and Milton. He copied out his 'Bright star!' sonnet for Joseph Severn on a blank page of his 1806 Shakespeare, and gave a copy of Cary's *Dante* (1814) to Fanny Brawne, in which she too copied out 'Bright star!' on the flyleaf of Volume I, and as he lay dying Keats wanted books about him. This fetishization of books went along with a remarkable verbal memory—Keats's letters and poems are full of allusions to and quotations from other writers, most notably Shakespeare and Milton. Keats's ability to remember, to possess poems in his mind, seems to have been common at the time—Hazlitt's *Liber Amoris* (1823), much of it written while travelling, is replete with quotations and echoes from English and other literatures.

Individual reading patterns of people other than writers have been relatively little explored. Diaries, journals, or commonplace books, which record the traces of an individual's reading, can also be used to reconstruct reading communities, and there is some evidence of reading habits among women and servants. Other evidence is given by catalogues of private or lending libraries (and, where extant, their borrowing records). However, a good deal can be inferred about the intended readership from the physical and commercial characteristics of books themselves—size and price (large poetry quarto at two guineas, sixpenny pocket-sized political satire), title-page layout, type size, paper quality, the sophistication or crudity of illustrations, style of binding, or the number and nature of subsequent editions. The textual strategies employed by the author to define the readers of his/her text are indicators of the intended readership, while contemporary reviews reveal a work's immediate reception and impact.

The changing roles played by the printed text in these years are demonstrated by the increasing availability of print from 1770 to 1830; an ever larger body of readers; the invention of new publishing genres like children's books, the seasonal gift or album books of the 1820s, or the 'three-decker' novel; and the emergence, by the end of the period, of a self-conscious—if politically and religiously fragmented—middle-class readership, and the beginnings of the mass audience of the Victorian era.

FURTHER READING

Altick, Richard D., *The English Common Reader: A Social History of the Mass Reading Public 1800–1900* (Chicago: University of Chicago Press, 1957). A pioneering study which remains relevant.

Brewer, John, *The Pleasures of the Imagination: English Culture in the Eighteenth Century* (London: HarperCollins, 1997), chs. 2–3. A very good account of publishers and readers to 1800.

Chilcott, Tim, *A Publisher and his Circle: The Life and Work of John Taylor, Keats's Publisher* (London and Boston: Routledge and Kegan Paul, 1972). Readable and very informed account, detailing most features of literary publishing from 1803 to 1836.

Feather, John, *The Provincial Book Trade in Eighteenth-Century England* (Cambridge: Cambridge University Press, 1985). Introductory account of an important topic.

—— 'British Publishing in the Eighteenth Century: A Preliminary Subject Analysis', *Library*, 6: 8 (1986), 32–46. Covers 1701–1800.

Forster, Geoffrey, Hamilton, Alice, and Robinson, Elaine, *'A Very Good Public Library': Early Years of the Leeds Library* (Newcastle upon Tyne: Allenholme Press, 2001). The fullest available account of a provincial proprietary library in these years.

Garside, Peter, Raven, James, and Schöwerling, Rainer (eds.), *The English Novel 1770–1829: A Bibliographical Survey of Prose Fiction Published in the British Isles*, 2 vols. (Oxford: Oxford University Press, 2000). See James Raven's important introduction on the numbers and kinds of novels published in these years.

Jackson, H. J., *Marginalia: Readers Writing in Books* (London and New Haven: Yale University Press, 2001).

Klancher, Jon P., *The Making of English Reading Audiences 1790–1832* (Madison: University of Wisconsin Press, 1987). A compact but sophisticated analysis of how periodicals created new reading publics in this period.

Millgate, Jane, *Scott's Last Edition: A Study in Publishing History* (Edinburgh: Edinburgh University Press, 1987). A detailed account of the writing, printing, and publication of a publishing phenomenon.

Raven, James, Tadmor, Naomi, and Small, Helen (eds.), *The Practice and Representation of Reading* (Cambridge: Cambridge University Press, 1996). The opening chapter provides a good introduction to the subject, and is followed by a series of case studies.

Siskin, Clifford, *The Work of Writing: Literature and Social Change in Britain 1700–1830* (Baltimore and London: Johns Hopkins University Press, 1998). A demanding book which raises interesting issues.

Sutherland, Kathryn, ' "Events . . . have made us a world of readers": Reader Relations 1780–1830', in David Pirie (ed.), *The Penguin History of Literature*, v., *The Romantic Period* (Harmondsworth: Penguin, 1994), pp. 1–48. An extremely informed, thought-provoking, and taut essay of broad interest, which brings together material production, the book trade, and readership.

Woods, Marcus, *Radical Satire and Print Culture 1790–1832* (Oxford: Clarendon Press, 1994). A good account of the radical press, centring on the careers of Daniel Eaton, Thomas Spence, and William Hone.

NOTES

1. Quoted in Jon P. Klancher, *The Making of English Reading Audiences 1790–1832* (Madison: University of Wisconsin Press, 1987), p. 27.
2. Kathryn Sutherland, ' "Events . . . have made us a world of readers": Reader Relations 1780–1830', in David Pirie (ed.), *The Penguin History of Literature*, v., *The Romantic Period* (Harmondsworth: Penguin, 1994), p. 6.

7 | Science

Tim Fulford

'The one Life within us and abroad | Which meets all motion and becomes its soul.' When Coleridge wrote these words from his poem 'The Aeolian Harp' in 1816/17, he expressed an ideal that he and a number of literary innovators we now call Romantics had shared since the 1790s. They shared it with a new generation of men whom we now call scientists: all wanted to discover the vital powers that animated mind, matter, man, nature—everything. In the 1790s, though, the word 'scientist' did not exist: there were natural philosophers and 'men of science' but almost no professional full-time researchers working in institutions or universities. It was not until the end of the Romantic era that such researchers became common and only then, in 1833, that Coleridge proposed that a new name was needed for them. He made his proposal in disappointment: the new researchers, he felt, had abandoned the quest to find the vital powers, settling for more pragmatic aims like inventing processes to aid industry. Such men did not deserve the name 'philosopher'. And so 'scientist' was coined, marking the end of Coleridge's Romantic science and the beginning of an era we still live in, an era in which science operates very differently from literature and in which scientists and poets are poles apart.

They were not poles apart in the 1790s: in those years of political revolution a revolution in knowledge also seemed possible. Poets and natural philosophers thought they were lifting the veil that covered the workings of nature. They made common cause: poets would give new insight into human nature; men of science would reveal the processes of physical nature. Their methods were different, their goal the same: they would discover the forces that animated the 'one life' within us and without us, revealing the dynamic interplay of creative powers that made humankind and the world. This was the project of Romantic science as conceived by poets including Shelley and Erasmus Darwin and by experimentalists including Joseph Priestley and Humphry Davy. It was a project that changed both literature and science, one that spawned new disciplines and genres, one that created symbols that haunt us still. But it was also a project that fell foul of opposition from conservatives who saw its ambitions as a threat to the established order.

Geology

The one life ideal seemed possible because of the transformations in perception simultaneously occurring in different areas—none more so than the study of the earth. In the early 1790s, most Britons believed that the earth had been created in six days, approximately 6,000 years ago. Only extreme radicals such as Thomas Paine publicly cast doubt on the Bible's reliability. In Scotland, however, James Hutton was staring obsessively at rocks. What he saw, line after line of different strata, folded and squashed one on another, confirmed his theory that the earth was immensely old (see also *Oxford Companion to the Romantic Age*, pp. 519–21).

Hutton's vision was itself Romantic in the way it looked to nature rather than to Scripture or God. It may have influenced Wordsworth's vision of man alone in a cyclical landscape, 'rolled round . . . | With rocks and stones and trees' for it was certainly akin to it.[1] Nature is not decorative in Wordsworth but a place that, as in Hutton, opens under one's feet into visions of vast, slow ineluctable power. So too in Shelley, who admired both men and saw Mont Blanc more as a process than a place, since the mountain is being built and destroyed by nature's huge forces as the poet, fascinated, watches.[2]

Hutton had opened up a vast abyss of time. Other researchers began to fill that abyss with even more unsettling finds. The pioneer anatomist John Hunter was bringing his surgical expertise to bear on fossil bones.[3] He could not discover their age, but he was able to extrapolate from them the size of the whole skeleton. He realized it was larger than any animal still living.

Hunter's conclusions helped begin a great wave of fossil research. Collectors pored over sea cliffs and quarry faces. Mary Anning, the greatest of these, was a labouring-class girl from Lyme Regis, a figure who might have stepped from the pages of *Lyrical Ballads*, when she began to pull old bones from the crumbling cliffs. By the time of her death she was a professional fossil hunter who had sold specimens for hundreds of pounds. Her most sensational finds included the crushed bones of plesiosaur and pterodactyl, which were reassembled and displayed in the museums of the scientific gentlemen who, from 1807, had taken for themselves the name geologist.

What to make of these strange skeletons? To the Oxford professor William Buckland, the bones were awe inspiring because they came from a time far older than the biblical record suggested, a time when what was now dry land was under the seabed. Moreover, they came from creatures now extinct. Clearly the creation of the world had not occurred as Genesis stipulated. Christians now faced a profound challenge: if Hutton's cyclical nature threatened belief in a providential God, mass extinction undermined it utterly. How could a just God allow whole species to die out?

Buckland and other Anglican geologists had an answer of sorts. Following the great French anatomist Georges Cuvier, they noticed that it was everywhere the case that certain kinds of fossil were specific to particular rock strata. Human bones were altogether absent and, as one went deeper and deeper into the earth, the lowest-lying strata had fewer large bones until, in the lowest of all, none was present. On the one hand this discovery provided a useful scientific tool: by their fossils (or lack of them) the strata could be identified and their relative age established. By applying this tool as he walked up and down the kingdom, the surveyor William Smith constructed the first geological map of Britain, a feat as imaginative and laborious as the writing of an epic poem. On the other hand, the discovery offered Christians a way of reconciling what they saw in the rocks with what they read in the Bible. In his *Reliquiae Diluvianae* (1823), Buckland argued (after Cuvier) that the fossil layers showed that earth had suffered a series of catastrophes, which had brought epochs and their life-forms to an end, followed in each case by the creation of new ones. The most recent of these, an overwhelming deluge, perhaps corresponded to Noah's flood.

While Buckland's catastrophism allowed orthodox Christians to retrieve faith from the abyss revealed in the rocks, it increased others' doubts. Some, at least, of the anxiety that Byron made his name articulating came from the latest geological theories. In 'Heaven and Earth' (1823) he viewed Noah's flood in catastrophist terms. Mountain caves recently excavated by Buckland revealed a God who had allowed whole worlds to die before man ever appeared. Byron's God is cruel and selfish; man, by contrast, is noble, full of ideals even though he knows himself doomed in a world of death. Byron's humanism, that is to say, grows in scale and glamour in proportion to his doubt in the Christian God. Both the humanism and the doubt, however, are related to the dramatic changes in world-view produced by geology.

Botany

No one was better informed about new science and its impact than the botanist, amateur experimentalist, and country doctor Erasmus Darwin. He versified science in his poem *The Botanic Garden* (1789–91), a work of rhyming couplets and eccentric speculations, which became a storehouse of images and ideas raided by later poets. Darwin, essentially, brought two important advances to the attention of general readers. The first was the 'sexual system', the method developed by the botanist Carl Linnaeus of classifying plants by their sexual characteristics. Darwin personified this system in his poem, treating flowers as if they were people and chronicling their fertilization as if they were love affairs.

Darwin's second achievement was to develop arguments about evolution that, in some respects, anticipated those that his grandson Charles would later make. Studying plants' responses to stimuli led Erasmus to believe that they possessed a degree of consciousness and animation and that this was inheritable. Thus a plant might inherit a propensity towards a certain kind of behaviour that its ancestors had begun to adopt as a result of their environmental situation (see *Oxford Companion to the Romantic Age*, pp. 429–30, 477).

Erasmus did not make the crucial conceptual advance of Charles—natural selection. Nor could he prove his ideas about consciousness in plants. Nevertheless his work helped initiate the idea of 'one life within us and abroad' because it suggested that all nature—even the vegetable world—was imbued with the creative consciousness that reached its apogee in humans. Shelley was to explore this idea (and the mimosa, one of Darwin's symbols of it) in his poem 'The Sensitive Plant'. It also stands behind the opinion of another of Darwin's readers, Wordsworth, that people discover in nature 'A motion and a spirit that impels | All thinking things, all objects of all thought, | And rolls through all things' ('Lines Written a Few Miles above Tintern Abbey', ll. 101–3). Here Romantic nature bore the traces of the latest scientific thought.

Joseph Priestley and Humphry Davy

Darwin was part of a network that gave young intellectuals career impetus and political direction. This network aided Southey and Coleridge. Middle class in rank, it was provincial, anti-government, anti-church but above all scientific. Its centre was the Lunar Society, an informal group of natural philosopher friends who met monthly when the moon was full. Darwin was a member, so were Josiah Wedgwood, Matthew Boulton, and James Watt—three of the most innovative industrialists of the age. It was, however, another member who did most to inspire Romantic science—Joseph Priestley, a Unitarian, political radical, theologian, and experimental researcher. In 1772–4 Priestley performed a series of seminal experiments in which he showed that plants renew air's breathability and that it was composed of different gases. Vegetables were indeed vital parts of the one life, since they acted to maintain the stuff that all life depended on. Priestley knew that the gas that they renewed was essential to the combustion process: he called it 'dephlogisticated air'.

Priestley had, in effect, discovered oxygen (though he refused to adopt the concept) and his work led others to revolutionize chemistry: Antoine Lavoisier broke through to a new understanding of the principle of chemical combination while Jan Ingen-housz made advances in plant biology. Priestley himself, however, combined his experimental researches with campaigning for political liberty and with theorizing the relationship of matter to the divine. To Coleridge, he seemed a scientific prophet, who predicted that advances in knowledge (of which his own air pump was a symbol) would destroy tyranny and bring about enlightenment and equality. Priestley was resented by conservatives who feared that free-thinking intellectuals would foment a revolution in Britain such as the bloody one then occurring in France. These conservatives whipped up a mob into burning Priestley's house and laboratory in Birmingham. Priestley escaped but emigrated to America in 1794 (*Oxford Companion to the Romantic Age*, pp. 660–1). It was, however, as an exiled lost leader, unjustly driven out, that he inspired a younger generation. For Coleridge, Priestley promised to reveal the very principles by which elements combined and substances cohered. He sanctioned the visionary hope of a society led to harmony and peace by scientific sages who understood the relationship between man, world, and God:

> From Avarice thus, from Luxury and War
> Sprang heavenly Science; and from Science Freedom.
> O'er waken'd realms Philosophers and Bards
> Spread in concentric circles; they whose souls,
> Conscious of their high dignities from God,
> Brook not Wealth's rivalry!
>
> ('Religious Musings,' ll. 225–30)

Priestley's friends accepted Coleridge as a disciple of great promise. The Wedgwoods gave him an allowance while Thomas Beddoes involved him in further experiments on gases at his Pneumatic Institution in Bristol. Beddoes wrote anti-government pamphlets and practised anti-establishment medicine. He aimed to bring free health to the people by having them inhale newly isolated gases rather than by treating them with doctors' traditional cures. To this end, he hired a young assistant called Humphry Davy who rapidly proved a brilliant experimental chemist. Davy had Southey and Coleridge breathe his latest discovery, nitrous oxide (laughing gas) and Beddoes published their reactions. Davy embraced the role of Romantic scientist that Coleridge and Southey set out for him, writing verse in which he rhapsodized about the idea of the discoverer as genius.

In 1800 Davy read an article by the Italian scientist Alessandro Volta discussing the theories of his compatriot Luigi Galvani. According to Volta, the electrical or galvanic fluid that Galvani thought he was conducting from the bodies of dead beasts was in fact generated accidentally by Galvani himself. It was, Volta, showed, the contact of two dissimilar moist metals that produced the flow of electricity. From this he deduced that placing many pieces of different wet metal together would allow him to generate electricity, and built his own battery: the 'Voltaic pile'.

Volta had made a breakthrough; in April 1800 the natural philosopher Anthony Carlisle, seizing on the potential of the pile, proceeded to decompose water into its elements. Davy began experiments with a battery of his own make. In November 1800 he told Coleridge that he had made 'some important galvanic discoveries which seem to lead to the door of the temple of the mysterious god of Life'.[4]

By 1801 Davy was on his way to London. The instrument that would give chemists power had come via the metropolis, not via Beddoes's provincial network. Under pressure from satirical attacks, tarred by association with the French Revolution, that network was under pressure. Davy left for the scientific mainstream, knowing he needed more support and more funding if he was to build a pile big enough to achieve the spectacular interventions in nature that he aimed at. Going to London meant going, directly or indirectly, to Sir Joseph Banks, the well-connected President of the Royal Society whose patronage opened doors. It meant remodelling one's self and one's practice to suit the social and political context in which science was now pursued under Banks's aegis. Davy turned electrochemistry away from the radical context that its association with Priestley had given it. He caused a change in its symbolism in the process. After his Royal Institution years, electricity was no longer a figure for representing republican liberty or nature's revolutionary agency. Instead it stood for a depoliticized metropolitan hero—a remodelled Romantic experimentalist who now worked in isolation before revealing his work to the world. Davy, in short, made electrical research the hallmark of the experimentalist as sublime egotist.

Davy succeeded because he showed great flair in staging his research. He wooed an audience of socially powerful people with stunning sounds and sights: the fizz of escaping gas, the crack of a blue spark, and, rarest of all, the pure light of a new metal that burnt under water. He first decomposed the fixed alkalis, liberating sodium and potassium, then the alkaline earths. He showed that chemical affinities were related to electrical powers and that elements could be identified in electrochemical terms, sodium being the most electropositive, oxygen the most negative.

To Coleridge, Davy's work seemed a vindication of the Romantic project they had developed together in the 1790s, stripped of the political implications which had made both men distrusted in the Tory centres of metropolitan and national authority. Davy was still a sublime genius who promised to reveal the one law that powered both mind and matter. Electricity was one manifestation of this law, chemical attraction another, gravitation a third. When Davy had demonstrated the unity of these forces 'it will then', Coleridge concluded, 'only remain to resolve this into some law of vital Intellect—and all human knowledge will be Science and Metaphysics the only Science'.[5]

There were no literary responses to Davy more glowing than Coleridge's but there was one more profound, one, moreover, that perfectly illustrates the different symbolic value that experimentalists had acquired in the wake of Davy's London achievements. Mary Shelley had grown up on Davy's brilliance: her father was an early supporter and her husband had constructed his own Voltaic pile at university. Mary herself read Davy's electrochemical papers in late 1816; shortly afterwards she began working on *Frankenstein*. Critics Anne K. Mellor and Maurice Hindle, among others, have demonstrated that Victor Frankenstein is a hero made, in part, in the electrochemist's image.[6] It is power that fascinates Victor, the power that electricity gives the lone experimentalist. He is a would-be Davyan master, inspired by the exalted conception of the experimentalist that Davy had formulated in his writing and embodied in his public demonstrations. He is a new figure, a Romantic experimentalist armed with electricity but cut off from the social networks that would preserve his humanity and discipline his research. In this latter respect he is a critique of the remodelled Romantic genius, the master of nature operating alone, rather than in a society of equals. Victor represents, in other words, not only the power and the glory that modern chemists garnered after Davy, but also the dreadful dangers involved in separating science from the critical and emotional relationships provided by kinship with others (especially women). Shelley spelt out in Frankenstein the failings of egotistical Romantic masculinity, failings inherent in the Wordsworthian poet and in the Davyan experimentalist. It is because many scientists in the nineteenth and twentieth centuries lived out the scientific role as Davy defined it (but ignoring Davy's warnings about hubris and isolation) that her story became talismanic. But it was because the politics of electricity in the 1790s became so suspect that Davy defined the role in those terms. The scientist as master-manipulator of nature working alone in his laboratory was a potent fiction born of the Romantics' forced retreat from the radical electricity of provincial dissent to the conservative electrochemistry of the Royal—and loyal—Institution and Society (for more on Davy see *Oxford Companion to the Romantic Age*, pp. 479–80).

Medicine

Political battles affected the course of another of the sciences in which Romantics placed their hopes—medicine. Surgeon John Hunter trained pupil after pupil in the rigorous methodology of dissection. One of them, Edward Jenner, turned this empiricist training to revolutionary use. In 1798 he established the truth of the country tradition that getting cowpox stopped you getting smallpox. Jenner then turned this into a preventative medicine—vaccination—and by the 1830s had saved tens of thousands of lives all over the world (see *Oxford Companion to the Romantic Age*, p. 743). But Jenner did not succeed without having first to allay the suspicions of metropolitan conservatives. Like Davy, Jenner had to live down his association with radicalism and with the lower classes to achieve acceptance in London and then across Europe. Coleridge and Southey had a similar path to tread and trod it by acting as Jenner's publicity campaigners. To them, vaccination was a triumph of the provincial science which had nurtured them. Coleridge and Southey extolled Jenner in the press, helping him (and themselves) to live down the reputation of being a rural crank and dangerous revolutionary. Here, literary Romantics were not simply responding to a scientific discovery but helping to shape its public profile and to create the image of the experimentalist as not only a genius but a disinterested benefactor of humanity, a national hero above mere political disputes and free of financial motives.

While Jenner was giving new life to the world, other followers of Hunter were arguing over its meaning. At the Royal College of Surgeons, John Abernethy claimed that he was promulgating the doctrine that Hunter himself had failed to publish before he died—that life was a principle independent of bodily organization, since it was present in blood as well as more complex organisms. Abernethy thought that because electricity, as Davy had shown, effected chemical changes, the life principle must be analogous to it (or even *be* the electric fluid). His former assistant, William Lawrence, publicly challenged this view, denying that life existed independently of bodily organization and claiming Abernethy's life principle illogically 'explained' the ultimate cause of one material substance by inventing another.

The dispute went to the heart of Romantic science and for this reason intrigued

Coleridge, Keats (who trained as a surgeon), and Shelley. Coleridge was prompted to write his own *Theory of Life* in 1817–24. In this work he rejected Lawrence's position, linking it with French materialism and atheism. Mind could not be explained as the result of structure. Coleridge supported Abernethy, but recognized that Abernethy's analogy of the life principle with a naturally occurring substance was philosophically incoherent. The life force, for Coleridge, was in origin ideal and divine and could not be equated with a purely material object, though it evolved in and as nature. Coleridge's Christian idealism continued to be inflected by his effort to reconcile the discoveries of experimentalists with the latest theological and philosophical perspectives and so to formulate the relationship between mind, matter, and the creative forces by which God animated all. Shelley too, interested himself in the debate, as a friend of Lawrence, and an intellectual who styled himself an atheist. In fact, Shelley's frequent invocation of 'Power' or 'Necessity' can be likened to contemporary definitions of a vital principle—in his case, as in Lawrence's, identified not with the divine but with the material (see *Oxford Companion to the Romantic Age*, pp. 399, 579–80).

Race

Hunter's legacy persisted not just through his pupils' dispute but also through his collection. Hunter had helped introduce a new methodology. Comparative anatomy placed specimens of different organs and structures next to each other, allowing comparison of human anatomy with the anatomy of different animals. Armed with their collections, natural historians were soon extending their survey to the differences within the human family, classifying people into different races on physical evidence. Hunter and Cuvier invented criteria to distinguish between races, but the central figure in the field was the German, J. F. Blumenbach, with whom Coleridge studied in 1799. Blumenbach coined the term 'Caucasian' and distinguished five different races on the basis (principally) of the shape of their skulls.

Though Blumenbach himself refrained from turning his classification into a hierarchy, others did not. The Dutch anatomical draughtsman Pieter Camper placed black people's skulls at the bottom of a racial scale, just above those of apes. More extreme surgeons, including Hunter's pupil Charles White, argued that black people were a different, lesser, species, justifying their enslavement. White's position was relatively unusual, but even relatively orthodox followers of Blumenbach like Lawrence took blacks' mental inferiority to Caucasians to be anatomically demonstrable. Coleridge, accepting the validity of these methods and measurements (having inspected Blumenbach's skull collection in 1799), concluded that providence had chosen whites to colonize blacks, so as to educate them out of their degenerate state. Blake's reception of current racial theory can be seen in the line 'O African! black African! Go, wingèd thought, widen his forehead!', referring to the emphasis, after Blumenbach, on the width of the occipital bone as a key sign of racial superiority.[7]

Romanticism was not, then, untainted by the development of racist science on the back of a crude empiricism. It was also coloured by a further development that made racial classification possible—the dispatch of scientific expeditions by sea and land to observe and collect natural phenomena (including native people's skulls). These expeditions were also to claim territory for Britain; exploration and empire went hand in hand and literature responded and contributed to both. The items and impressions explorers brought back prepared Britons for empire and gave them a taste for the exotic. Poems such as Southey's *The Curse of Kehama* (1810) and Moore's *Lalla Rookh* (1817) cashed in on this taste: they were full of references to the flora that British botanists had collected, to the customs that British ethnographers had studied, and to the temples British engineers had surveyed in the Orient. Science fed the poetic fashion for the exotic, inspiring in turn a new generation to become scientific explorers.

Astronomy

No explorers were more glamorous than the astronomers. Advances in technology now made it possible to view previously invisible planets and stars. William Herschel (see *Oxford Companion to the Romantic Age*, p. 541) discovered the planet Uranus through his home-made telescope in 1781. Later, he made observations of star-clusters and speculated that life might exist on some, opening to public consciousness the huge depth of space and the immensity of worlds. Keats, in tribute, made Herschel embody the romance of exploration, writing of 'some watcher of the skies | When a new planet swims into his ken' ('On First Looking into Chapman's Homer', ll. 9–10). Byron, likewise, followed Herschel's gaze, to find wonder but also terror in the sight of distant worlds:

> shapes
> Unequal, of deep valleys and vast mountains;
> And some emitting sparks, and some displaying
> Enormous liquid plains'
>
> ('Cain', II. i. 184–7).

Byron's excitement at the possibilities revealed by science became an embarrassment to many of the new researchers, because it led to religious scepticism and moral unorthodoxy. It was precisely to avoid an association with these ideas that, from the 1830s, the newly named 'scientists' adopted a pragmatic, non-controversial agenda. The new men, with their new professional organizations, assured the public of their work's compatibility with Christian belief, solidifying the social authority that their discoveries brought them.

Technology

Nothing gave more authority than the visible effect of science on technology. Not just James Watt's and George Stephenson's steam engines and railways, not just James Brindley's and Thomas Telford's canals, but William Murdock's gaslight, Isambard Kingdom Brunel's bridges, and John McAdam's roads, transformed mobility. Simultaneously, Joseph Bramah's hydraulic pumps and Samuel Crompton's mule revolutionized work: the new machines necessitated the factory system, creating new classes of people, new towns, and a new society. Romantic writers did not ignore these changes but neither did they adequately comprehend them: such comprehension would only be possible for later generations. Instead, they greeted them with a mixture of delight, admiration, and horror. Charles Lamb revelled in the display of new manufactures on offer in London's brightly lit shops; Southey revered Telford, the engineer who tamed nature; Wordsworth recoiled from the new railway bringing hordes of tourists to his rural sanctuary; Blake reviled the 'dark Satanic mills' spreading over England's 'green and pleasant land';[8] Coleridge campaigned against the employment of children in cotton factories. In the face of industrial exploitation, the Romantics called for a renewal of the human values and social relations of former times, of the revolutionary era of liberty, fraternity, and equality, or of the rural community of paternalist duty. They acted as the conscience of an age that increasingly moved to the clockwork pace first announced, ironically enough, by one of their mentors, Josiah Wedgwood, who declared prophetically of his new factory that it 'would make machines of men as cannot err'.[9]

'Scientist'

By 1833, as the new name 'scientist' was born, the project of Romantic science died. In the face of industrial capitalism and political conservatism, few any longer nursed hopes of discovering the powers that made all one life. Yet that project was never the whole story. Also happening in the period was Black's work on latent heat and Dalton's atomic theory of matter. Thomas Young refined the wave theory of light; Michael Faraday, building on Oersted's work, made breakthrough experiments in electromagnetism. The discoveries were numerous, too numerous for this chapter to describe or for literature to respond to them all. All the discoverers, however, owed something to Romantic literature: they owed the image of the researcher as a sublime, lonely genius and they owed the image of the new pragmatic, institutionalized 'scientist'.

FURTHER READING

Bewell, Alan, *Romanticism and Colonial Disease* (Baltimore and London: Johns Hopkins University Press, 1999). Superb discussion of Romantic writing in the light of the medical debates that were precipitated by the spread of imperial diseases.

Cadbury, Deborah, *The Dinosaur Hunters: A True Story of Scientific Rivalry and the Discovery of the Prehistoric World* (London: Fourth Estate, 2000). Entertaining and enlightening portrait of the early fossil-hunters and their theories.

Gascoigne, John, *Science in the Service of Empire: Joseph Banks, the British State and the Uses of Science in the Age of Revolution* (Cambridge: Cambridge University Press, 1998). An important discussion of one of the most central figures in science and exploration, and of his influence on all aspects of its study.

Golinski, Jan, *Science as Public Culture: Chemistry and Enlightenment in Britain, 1760–1820* (Cambridge: Cambridge University Press, 1992). Unparalleled study of Priestley, Davy, and radical electrochemistry.

Grabo, Carl, *A Newton among Poets: Shelley's Use of Science in Prometheus Unbound* (Chapel Hill, NC: University of North Carolina Press, 1930). An old but not outdated study of Shelley's response to science.

Heilbron, John, *Electricity in the Seventeenth and Eighteenth Centuries: A Study of Early Modern Physics* (Berkeley and Los Angeles: University of California Press, 1979). The classic discussion of the development of research into electricity.

Hoskin, M., *William Herschel and the Construction of the Heavens* (London: Oldbourne, 1963). Informative reading of Herschel's astronomical work.

Levere, Trevor H., *Poetry Realized in Nature: Samuel Taylor Coleridge and Early Nineteenth-Century Science* (Cambridge: Cambridge University Press, 1981). The best study of the scientific involvement of the most scientifically knowledgeable of all the Romantics.

McIntyre, Donald B., and McKirdy, Alan, *James Hutton: The Founder of Modern Geology* (Edinburgh: The Stationery Office, 1997). Pithy and pellucid guide to Hutton's life and achievements.

Ritterbush, Philip C., *Overtures to Biology: The Speculations of Eighteenth-Century Naturalists* (New Haven and London: Yale University Press, 1964). The best one-volume survey of changing theories of life in the period.

Uglow, Jenny, *The Lunar Men: The Friends Who Made the Future* (London: Faber and Faber, 2002). Lively and perceptive study of radical science and industry, illuminating the whole period.

Wolf, Abraham, *A History of Science, Technology and Philosophy in the Eighteenth Century*, 2nd edn., 2 vols., ed. D. McKie (New York: Harper, 1961). Authoritative and comprehensive survey: the place to start.

NOTES

1. Lines 7–8 of Wordsworth's 'A slumber did my spirit seal', *Lyrical Ballads* (1800).
2. 'Mont Blanc. Lines written in the Vale of Chamouni' (1816).
3. Hunter set out his conclusions in 'Observations on the Fossil Bones Presented to the Royal Society by his Most Serene Highness the Margrave of Anspach', *Philosophical Transactions of the Royal Society*, 84 (1794), 407–17.
4. Trevor H. Levere, *Poetry Realized in Nature: Samuel Taylor Coleridge and Early Nineteenth-Century Science* (Cambridge: Cambridge University Press, 1981), p. 32.

5. Ibid. 34.
6. See the introduction to *Frankenstein; or, the Modern Prometheus*, ed. Maurice Hindle (Harmondsworth: Penguin, 1992) and ch. 5 of Anne K. Mellor, *Mary Shelley: Her Life, Her Fiction, Her Monsters* (New York and London: Routledge, 1988).
7. William Blake, 'A Song of Liberty', *The Marriage of Heaven and Hell*, plate 26.
8. William Blake, 'Preface', *Milton* (*c*.1804–18).
9. Quoted in Michael Ignatieff, *A Just Measure of Pain: The Penitentiary in the Industrial Revolution 1750–1850* (London and New York, 1989), p. 68.

8 | Philosophy and religion

Alan Gregory

Romanticism has often been described as a 'revolt' against the eighteenth-century 'Enlightenment'. Enlightenment thinkers emphasized the role and authority of 'Reason' in religious matters and in assessing traditional Christian ideas such as miracles, original sin, and the atoning death of Christ. 'Have courage to use your own reason', wrote the German philosopher, Immanuel Kant, 'that is the motto of the enlightenment.' By contrast, Romantic writing and art frequently affirmed the value of feeling, the importance of unconscious forces, the mysterious depths of religious experience, and the limits of human rationality.

Put so baldly, though, the idea of a Romantic revolt obscures vital continuities between Romanticism and Enlightenment (*Oxford Companion to the Romantic Age*, pp. 299–311). Romantic religion involves not so much a seismic break with eighteenth-century thought as a new range of responses to questions concerning the nature and grounds of religious belief. The relationship between religion and philosophy became critical. Does philosophy liberate humanity from religion? Or does it come to the aid of faith? Following the seventeenth-century philosopher Descartes, questions about religious experience had been answered with particular reference to human subjectivity, a strategy that Romantic writers also adopted while being critical of its earlier deployments. Below, I examine the religious thought of a German theologian, Friedrich Schleiermacher, and two English poets, Coleridge and Shelley. The relationship between Romanticism and 'enthusiasm', a theme throughout this chapter, is addressed specifically in the final section.

By and large, 'enthusiasm' was a term even enthusiasts would not own. The philosopher John Locke, whose *Essay Concerning Human Understanding* (1690) was foundational for the British Enlightenment, condemned enthusiasm as abandoning reason 'for the ungrounded fancies of a man's own brain'. Enthusiasts, wrote Edmund Gibson, Bishop of London, 'have a strong persuasion on the mind, that they are guided in an *extraordinary* manner, by immediate impulses and impressions of the Spirit of God'. John Wesley, the founder of Methodism, thought that enthusiasm was a form of 'religious madness', although for many orthodox Anglican clergy Wesley was himself a prominent enthusiast. Enthusiasm involved breaching limits, stirring fears of lawlessness, madness, insurrection, and revolution: 'how can I tell what that person may be prompted to do?' asked the critic and lexicographer Samuel Johnson. For many, enthusiasts were literally beyond the pale. From the mid-eighteenth century, though, positive references to 'enthusiasm' started to appear. In his poem *Night Thoughts* Edward Young associated enthusiasm with a 'godlike height' to which 'Some souls have soared'. This chapter discusses how Romantic writers negotiated and breached the limits that Enlightenment writers placed upon religious discourse. In this, and other respects, the trajectories of Romanticism and enthusiasm cross, overlap, and influence one another.

Immanuel Kant

Through the discovery of gravity and other mathematical researches, the scientist Isaac Newton was able to argue that nature and the created universe was a gigantic machine that could be rationally explained and understood. Reflecting on Newton's achievement, the poet James Thomson wrote:

> Nature herself
> Stood all subdu'd by him, and open laid
> Her every latent glory to his view.

Another admirer of Newton's, John Freke, set about researching electricity by supposing 'that the world is a machine', adding that this was a supposition so obvious that 'no reasonable man can doubt it'. The mechanical model of the universe, however, posed a range of thorny problems for theology. What was the relationship between God and a mechanistic, mathematically predictable world? Did Newton's discoveries mean that belief in God was intellectually redundant? Was religious belief possible?

The readiest answer to such questions was that God was necessary to sustain the workings of nature and to account for its complexity. Both of those claims, though, fell under philosophical challenge. The Scottish philosopher, David Hume (see *Oxford Companion to the Romantic Age*, p. 550) argued that to consider the universe as 'designed' was a religious prejudice, unjustified by any evidence we possess and convincing only to those who were already believers. The French *philosophe*, Denis Diderot, added that a transcendent Creator was in any case unnecessary to explain the complexity and orderliness of the world. Besides raising awkward questions about God and the possibility of belief, Newtonian science had awkward implications for morality. If the universe worked in mechanical ways that were entirely predictable, how could human beings exist as free individuals enjoying free will? Was humanity just another part of the mechanical complex?

Inheriting these problems, the German philosopher Immanuel Kant sought a solution that would preserve moral freedom and the integrity of Newton's ideas. Kant accepted Hume's scepticism regarding the proofs for God's existence, but he was alarmed that such scepticism also undercut the grounds of scientific knowledge. After all, Hume had argued that we accept the principle of cause and effect not because it is a necessary law but out of prejudice, a habit of connection arising from the regularities of our experience. In a bid to outflank such radical doubt, Kant proposed that the structures of the Newtonian universe were the products of the mind's ordering activity which, day by day, gives us the experience we have of ourselves and the world around us. The mind makes our experience by imposing structure upon sensory data, and this 'phenomenal' world—that is, the world as it appears to us—is the only one we know. We have no knowledge of any 'noumenal' world, of 'things-in-themselves' beyond the terms of our experience. The phenomenal world, however, is a seamless web of cause and effect with no room for moral freedom. To secure both morality and faith in God, Kant distinguished between reason as the basis of our knowing the phenomenal world and reason as it guides our wills, or 'practical' reason. That we are capable of willing according to reason makes us free, moral agents. Moral experience is the experience of duty, of actions that must be willed or not willed simply because they are right or wrong. For instance, telling the truth is right, Kant argued, and stealing wrong, not by virtue of culture or experience, but because to claim the opposite is irrational. Therefore, though the world we know is entirely bound by the law of cause and effect, we nevertheless find our wills under the moral law that we must obey irrespective of all the empirical forces that bear down on us. This situation threatens the tragic absurdity of moral beings in a mechanistic world that has no place for them. Taking morality seriously, then, requires faith in the God who harmonizes our moral obedience with a world we know only as mechanism, to bring about, ultimately, a world shaped by a righteousness that leads, as it rarely does now, to happiness. Faith in God is faith in our freedom and in the immortality necessary to the ultimate goal of an endless rule of righteousness. We cannot know that God exists but our moral experience requires us to 'postulate' that he does. Kant's solution is dualistic: he sets the world of our experience against the world as it really is; mechanical nature against morality, freedom, and reason, and the sway of feeling against moral willing. The ultimate unity is hidden from us, an object of faith.

Schleiermacher and the experience of religion

This brings us to Berlin, Romanticism, and the young Friedrich Schleiermacher finding in religion an experience that takes humanity beyond Kant's dualism. In 1799, Schleiermacher published *On Religion: Speeches to Its Cultured Despisers*. The 'cultured despisers' were, in the first place, his own friends, members of the Berlin Romantic circle, who had challenged Schleiermacher to defend his Christian faith. This group of young intellectuals included Friedrich Schlegel, responsible for some of the manifestos of German Romanticism. Schlegel announced Romantic 'poetry' as a progressive art of infinitely expanding inclusivity, the expression of a freedom for which the leadings of emotion were not inimical or alien. This poetry is to spill into life's moral business, seeking to make 'poetry lively and sociable and life and society poetical'. In this spirit, *On Religion* violates most of what contemporaries would have expected of a religious work. There is no systematic discussion of Christian doctrines, barely any mention of God, and no treatment of Christ until the very end. The work is urgent and passionate and deploys an arsenal of literary devices: complex metaphors, startling images, shifts of tone, suspense, direct address, satire, and irony. The detached enquiry 'what is religion?' is less important to Schleiermacher than 'what is the *experience* of religion?' He wants to stir up this inner life in an audience already more inwardly religious than it knows, 'despisers' though they are.

Religion, for Schleiermacher, is an intuition and feeling of the universe, 'the immediate consciousness of the universal existence of all finite things, in and through the Infinite, and of all temporal things in and through the Eternal'. In themselves, even the ecstasies of art and the duties of morality leave us unsatisfied: religion alone is able to fulfill the restless energies within us. The religious person receives life 'in the infinite nature of the Whole ... having and possessing all things in God, and God in all'. Again, this relationship is known to us, not through intellectual construction or moral agency, but at a level of experience that is prior to them both—the level of pre-reflective 'awareness'. The key terms, 'intuition' and 'feeling', name the two-sidedness of religious experience. Intuition indicates the experience of the universe *upon* us, feeling identifies religion as an experience *within* us. What is felt inwardly arises from what acts upon us. Thus, Schleiermacher attempts to avoid both subjectivism—'religion is just a way of feeling about the world'—and 'objectivism' whereby religion is reduced to specified ways of acting or doctrinal creed. The taproot of religion is a most powerful yet fugitive experience in which the duality of subject and object is transcended: a formative awareness of ourselves and all things as *in* the Infinite.[1]

As an intuition of the divine life, religion binds together the universal and the particular. Morality deals with laws that transcend individual situations and philosophy deals in general concepts. Religion, though, delights in the infinite as diversely manifested through the particular. Schleiermacher's religion like Schlegel's 'poetry' is infinitely expanding and inclusive. The truly religious person does not impose her religious life on others. Rather, she delights in the birthing of that religious life, that cast and tone of experience, peculiar to each person. True religion is communicated by inspiration, a subtle gentleness of influence, not by commands or precepts.

This interpretation of religion allows Schleiermacher to reappropriate some traditional religious concepts in the face of Enlightenment prejudice. For the religious person miracles are not singular wonders: rather, all things are miraculous or potentially miraculous in so far as anything finite may be received as a glorious sign of an infinite life. Similarly, traditional ideas receive a new placing. For contemporaries, a startling aspect of *On Religion* was the paucity of references to God. Schleiermacher's most common terms in connection with the 'object' of religion are 'universe', and 'infinite'. Religion, as such, is not identical with acceptance of a particular idea of

God. There are many such ideas, varied and incompatible with one another, and religion may even exist without any idea of God, just as it may be absent where an impeccably traditional account of God is upheld. Proceeding from the intuition of the infinite, particular ideas of God are shaped by the imagination. Schleiermacher warns us not to take offence at this: 'you will know that imagination is the highest and most original element in us . . . that it is our imagination that creates the world for you, and that you can have no God without the world.'[2] This statement reflects Kantian philosophy but involves a religious application that goes well beyond Kant, for whom imagination had little place in his discussion of 'moral faith'. Schleiermacher thus invests imagination with a creativity and centrality that we will find also in the work of the Romantic poet and philosopher S. T. Coleridge.

Beyond understanding: Coleridge on the imagination

Samuel Taylor Coleridge is best known as a poet. He spent much of his life, however, writing prose designed to educate the 'higher and middle classes' in religious, moral, and political responsibility. He claims frequently that whenever we act out of principle, we are in a position to understand both the necessity of Christianity and the distinctive capacities of the human mind. Among these capacities or 'powers', the imagination has a crucial role with respect to religion. Using his theory of the imagination, Coleridge extends Kant's account of knowledge, though in a way Kant would have deemed unacceptably enthusiastic.

Coleridge rejects Kant's attempt to drive a wedge between reason and faith and he insists that reason does yield true *knowledge* of God. At the same time, he rejects the concept of reason that he believes characteristic of Newtonianism and the Enlightenment. Those movements, Coleridge argues, confused 'reason' with 'understanding'. The understanding, Coleridge wrote, is 'the faculty by which we generalize and arrange the phenomena of perception'. It is the mind's power to organize sensory data and the world of experience. Understanding is also deployed in the conscious operations by which we negotiate the world of objects, analysing, abstracting, plotting cause and effect, and discovering means for ends. The world of the understanding is also the Newtonian world of our science. So, if we conform religion to its limits then, Coleridge concludes, God becomes 'an hypothetical watchmaker', and we lose any proper basis for affirming moral freedom or artistic creativity. The understanding, however, must be carefully distinguished from 'reason'. Reason is the power by which the mind recognizes and knows 'Truths above Sense'; it is the 'power of [acquaintance] with invisible realities or spiritual objects'.[3] Reason knows intuitively the embracing mystery of God, and the moral law, together with the freedom that our responsibility presupposes. Furthermore, Coleridge argues, reason enables our recognition of God's revelation, as represented in the Scriptures. For Coleridge, the truths of revelation—Trinity,

Incarnation, Atonement—prove themselves in the rigours of a moral life, acquainted as it must be, with sin and the need for redemption.

Our experience is formed by the activity of the 'understanding'. The intuitions of reason, however, are of realities that transcend the understanding, of 'truths above sense'. The mystery of God is not a reality we know through our senses and, since the job of the understanding is to organize sensory data, its categories are not applicable to God. Here is a grave problem. If human experience is constituted by the understanding, how can we recognize within that experience truths that transcend the understanding, those 'invisible realities or spiritual objects'? Also, our language is similarly earthbound, it articulates a finite world. How then can the transcendent world be expressed? Coleridge's theory of the imagination is his answer to these questions.

In *The Statesman's Manual* (1816) Coleridge identified the imagination as the mental power through which the world of the understanding is opened up to participate in the spiritual intuitions of reason. Imagination mediates between the 'ideas' of reason and the categories of the understanding, enabling the understanding to recognize and express the truths that transcend it. The scientist is thus able to recognize laws that, because they are *universal*, transcend the understanding which may generalize but cannot of itself make the leap to the universal. Through the imagination, too, morality finds its ideal in what is good as such, irrespective of particular circumstances; and we come to distinguish between manipulable 'things' and the sacredness of all 'persons' that prohibits their mere 'use'. While the poet finds in the power of imagination the idealizing and vital image, the religious person recognizes divine mystery in material and linguistic symbols. The imagination thus renders particular, temporal objects, events, persons, images, stories, and words 'translucent' to the universal and eternal. As '*Educts* of the Imagination', symbols incorporate 'the Reason in Images of the Sense'. The pre-eminent examples are found in Scripture where divine truth and its representative symbols move in complete harmony as imagination infuses with reason what the understanding has made of the senses. Symbols are intersections of time and eternity, points at which the whole becomes visible through the particular. They manifest reality as a system of relations in which 'each has a life of its own yet all are one life', expressing that intuition of things 'which arises when we possess ourselves, as one with the whole'. Again, this theory of imagination and symbol must be understood as a response to the Newtonian world, 'a lifeless Machine whirled about by the dust of its own Grinding'. Coleridge identifies the imagination as the means by which human beings are freed from the confines of a merely mechanical account of the world in order to participate in a sacramental universe. In this way, they discover their home in the *creation* of God, for whose work of making the poet provides a better metaphor than the watchmaker.

Imagination is one of Romanticism's defining concepts and Coleridge's a particularly influential account. Whilst more explicitly theological than some, his theory informed significantly the process whereby imagination became a vehicle of liberating and humanizing truths otherwise too deep for words. Although Coleridge later dropped the imagination from his discussions of the mind's powers, its activity of mediating and symbolizing remained a crucial one. This dynamic in which human experience is irradiated by the intuitions of reason becomes, increasingly in his later work, the task of 'true religion', 'the Poetry and Philosophy of all Mankind' that mediates the 'noblest materials' of reason to the objects of understanding.

Shelley: after Jupiter

On 25 March 1811, Shelley's pamphlet 'The Necessity of Atheism' occasioned his expulsion from Oxford, not just for the argument but because Shelley sent it to all the bishops and heads of colleges. His argument follows Locke: 'the senses', Shelley writes, 'are the sources of all knowledge to the mind'. The atheistic conclusion, however, depends on the philosopher David Hume. The proposition 'God exists', Shelley argues, fails demonstration by sensible experience, by reason reflecting on experience, and, even by that weakest of all demonstrations, third-party testimony to experience. Strictly speaking, therefore, 'the mind *cannot* believe the existence of a God'.[4] Both Schleiermacher and Coleridge insisted that knowing God was a distinctive form of knowing, appropriate to the transcendent and unique character of its object. Shelley, though, following the Lockean tradition, assumes that one asks after God as after the Loch Ness monster or any other elusive reality.

Shelley recycled his atheism pamphlet as a long footnote to his poem *Queen Mab*, noting that the argument applied only to a theistic creator, not to 'the hypothesis of a pervading Spirit co-eternal with the universe'.[5] Shelley's humanism demands this hypothesis. A formative, inexhaustible, and unifying power makes reality fecund, unlike the Newtonian mechanistic universe. Though unknowable and 'imageless', this power justifies hope in an ultimate bias toward good, a favouring of 'Love', persistent through 'Fate, Time, Occasion, Chance, and Change'. This persistence is celebrated in Shelley's dramatic poem *Prometheus Unbound*. The drama suggests that, for Shelley, atheism demanded that we redirect rather than suppress religious motivation: awe, sacrifice, hope, and love must invest in immanent not transcendent reality. The drama's decisive event occurs in the first scene in which Prometheus, crying out his agonies, turns from relentless defiance to compassion even for Jupiter who, though he now persecutes and punishes, is ultimately doomed (compare the discussion in the chapter entitled 'Romantic Forms: An Introduction'). This turn to pity begins the process by which Jupiter, the force of tyranny, is overthrown and Asia, the power of love, is recalled from exile as the estrangements of humanity and cosmos are healed. Shelley's powers of reconciliation are a reworking of the Christian virtues 'faith, hope, and love'. Of the three, 'faith' is the most ambiguous term: all tyrannous religion demanded sacrifice of thought under this name. Shelley almost abandons it, subsuming 'faith' into 'hope'. 'Love', the insatiable desire for good, and 'hope', constant before

'Destruction's strength', are the energies of renewal and the only means by which oppressive violence is to be overcome. Represented mythically in *Prometheus Unbound*, Shelley's ideals find political expression in the appeal for non-violent protest in his poem 'The Masque of Anarchy', occasioned by the violent Peterloo massacre of 1818:

> With folded arms and steady eyes,
> And little fear, and less surprise
> Look upon them as they slay
> Till their rage has died away.

Prometheus Unbound is a mythological rendering of human history that also demands reading on psychological and political levels, dramatizing the overcoming of psychic and social alienations. Whilst the drama is inspired by Aeschylus, Shelley ransacks the imagery of biblical hope and Christian salvation to create his humane, atheist vision. He opposes Jesus of 'gentle worth' to the Christian religion that transformed his words into 'swift poison'. Shelley both identifies Prometheus with Jesus and distinguishes him. Prometheus, like the crucified Jesus, is in torment, sweating 'drops of bloody agony' (cf. Luke 22: 44). However, unlike the single, historical figure of Jesus, Prometheus, the power of human thought and creativity, is inexhaustible and transcends the most woeful of evils. Shelley rewrites the apocalyptic hope of John's Revelation, so that judgement falls on heaven not earth: 'earth can console', Shelley writes, 'Heaven can torment no more.' The plagues and judgements of Revelation evaporate in a this-worldly resurrection of humanity, and a millennial peace in which 'thrones were kingless and men walked | One with the other even as spirits do'.

Reworking biblical and theological language, Shelley liberates human thought from oppressive religion. He treats Scripture somewhat in the spirit of Schlegel's aphorism, 'an admirable everyday book whose only fault is that it should have become the Bible'. Despite Shelley's aversion to didactic poetry, *Prometheus Unbound* is decidedly instructive. Much of it is proclamation, and it ends in the mode of sermonic exhortation. It appears that humanity cannot do without Scripture and Shelley has set about writing a new one, the authority of which, because it is in harmony with human hope, good, and destiny, requires no threatenings.

Enthusiasm: the witness of the spirit

Both Schleiermacher and Coleridge pressed beyond received restrictions upon religious discourse in order to expose the subjective foundations of faith and knowledge of God: Schleiermacher in intuition and feeling; Coleridge in imagination and reason. Shelley, too, moves beyond the negative scepticism of Hume to a reorientation of religious motivation and a new 'scriptural' proclamation. It is at these points, arguably, that Romanticism becomes 'enthusiastic'.

To the annoyance of John Wesley Methodism (see *Oxford Companion to the Romantic Age*, pp. 756, 601), a popular, lay movement for religious renewal, was constantly denounced as enthusiasm. Despite his cautious clarifications, Wesley himself fuelled the charge. The subjective certainty of salvation, he argued, is prior to the witness of a good conscience, resting on a 'feeling possession of God in the soul' or 'an inward impression of the soul, whereby the Spirit of God immediately and directly witnesses to my spirit that I am a child of God'. Methodism, Evangelicalism (*Oxford Companion to the Romantic Age*, p. 500), and Revivalism in Britain and North America, Pietism and Moravianism (*Oxford Companion to the Romantic Age*, p. 610) in Protestant Europe share, despite some important doctrinal differences, in a common remapping of religious subjectivity. For these 'religions of the heart', 'feeling' is central. The language of affections thus predominates in many of Charles Wesley's (*Oxford Companion to the Romantic Age*, p. 756) hymns, the emotional appeal pushing towards ecstasy in an infinitely expanding and joyous horizon:

> True pleasures abound
> In the rapturous sound;
> And whoever hath found it hath paradise found.

How and why feeling possessed moral and spiritual power was answered in various ways but the conviction that it did was common to enthusiasts, to the writers of 'sentimental' and Gothic literature, and to the Romantics (see chapter entitled 'Sensibility' and 'Gothic', and *Oxford Companion to the Romantic Age*, pp. 102–14, 528). Schleiermacher's theology has roots in his 'enthusiastic' Moravian upbringing. The authority accorded to intensities of feeling also offered a way for self-proclaimed prophets to legitimate their claims and oracles, and there was considerable interest in contemporary prophets and prophetic fulfilments. Though it invited more charges of enthusiasm, Wesley visited a number of such prophets and met with some within the Methodist movement itself. Wary of scandal, he was cautious but did not reject their claims on principle. By the 1790s, stimulated by revolutionary events that only biblical language seemed powerful enough to articulate, prophecy was in keeping with the apocalyptic temper of the times. We are watching, proclaimed Joseph Priestley, 'great calamities, such as the world has never yet experienced',[6] our guide to which is biblical prophecy. In Scripture the book of Revelation illuminated the times—though only through divinely inspired interpreters according to the anonymous author of *Dissertation on the Prophetic Powers of the Human Mind*.

Among the candidates for divine inspiration, Richard Brothers and Joanna Southcott (see *Oxford Companion to the Romantic Age*, pp. 433, 713) achieved a national following. Brothers, a former naval officer, began his prophetic career in 1792. He claimed that God, albeit a little reluctantly, had accepted his intercession for London, the 'Babylon the Great' of Revelation 18: 'All, All! I pardon London and all the people in it, for your sake; there is no other man on earth that could stand before me to ask for so great a thing.'[7] Brothers discovered himself to be descended from King David, by way of

James, the brother of Jesus. As the 'nephew of the Almighty', he was to lead those Britons who were descended from Israel back to Jerusalem. In 1795, alarmed by his popularity and his warnings against armed conflict with France, the government had Brothers investigated by a Privy Council committee. It declared him insane and locked him away.

Though Brothers continued to write, interest in him declined and many of his supporters turned to Joanna Southcott, a farmer's daughter from Devon, who also began her prophetic ministry in 1792. Southcott predicted national events and claimed to be the 'woman clothed with the sun' of Revelation 12 and, later, to be miraculously pregnant with 'Shiloh' who was the one 'to rule all the nations with a rod of iron' (Revelation 12: 5). Her teachings accorded a counter-cultural role to women, who, through her calling, were vindicated from the ancient charge of a peculiar culpability in the Fall:

> And more than Adam men will stand amazed,
> And more than Adam every one will gaze,
> To see the knowledge from the woman's hand,
> That by their wisdom, they cannot command.

Southcott died in 1814 shortly after the signs of her pregnancy disappeared and she herself concluded 'it all appears delusion'. However, she has followers to this day.

Brothers and Southcott illustrate the fluidity of the relationship between 'inspired interpreter' and 'prophet'. As interpreters of Scripture, which they claimed to be, they serve the traditional authority although neither remained within that role. Both claimed apocalyptic status for themselves and both interpreted Scripture to the point of rewriting it. 'The alterations', Brothers declares, 'I have made in copying some of the prophecies, is by the direction and command of the Lord God.' This enthusiastic bursting of Scriptural authority in a new writing and proclamation constitutes a common religious strategy for Brothers and Southcott, Shelley, and also the poet and painter, William Blake.

Support for these millenarian movements (*Oxford Companion to the Romantic Age*, p. 603) largely parallels that of Methodism and many followers had been or were involved with Methodist meetings, as had Joanna Southcott herself. Artisans and tradesmen, therefore, form the largest group among supporters. The term 'popular' for these movements also needs qualification, though. Brothers and Southcott gained national attention through the support of a small number of wealthy and influential adherents, including Anglican clergy, professionals, businessmen, and, in Brothers's case, an MP, Nathaniel Halhed. Their writings, though crude in themselves, appealed to a tradition according to which natural phenomena and contemporary events, from the national to the intimate and individual, possess spiritual significance for those who have eyes to see. Halhed declared the necessity of reading 'the modern history of Europe in the prophetic records of the Old and New Testament'. Coleridge announces his agenda in similar terms, today the statesman must read events 'in the spirit of prophecy'. Certainly, Coleridge's theory of the symbolic is a sophisticated one designed to exclude the uncontrolled applications, and the potentially radical politics, of the enthusiast. Nevertheless, the romantic theory of the symbol sustained the conviction that Scripture, nature, and history were the living speech of God. Enthusiasm and Romanticism converge in resisting the reductions of Enlightenment rationality.

FURTHER READING

Abrams, M. H., *Natural Supernaturalism: Tradition and Revolution in Romantic Literature* (New York: W. W. Norton, 1973). In this very wide-ranging study of Romanticism in relation to philosophical and religious tradition, Abrams includes a helpful guide to the unusual dramatic structure of *Prometheus Unbound*.

Ferber, Michael, *The Poetry of Shelley* (London: Penguin, 1993). Devotes a lengthy chapter to an act by act commentary on *Prometheus Unbound*.

Gerrish, Brian, 'Friedrich Schleiermacher', in Ninian Smart *et al.* (eds.), *Nineteenth Century Religious Thought in the West* (Cambridge: Cambridge University Press, 1985). A very clear survey of Schleiermacher's work that places *On Religion* within the context of his later theology.

Gregory, Alan P. R., *Coleridge and the Conservative Imagination* (Macon, Ga.: Mercer University Press, 2003). With special reference to the imagination, Gregory traces the relationships between Coleridge's politics, theology, and philosophical psychology.

Harrison, J. F. C., *The Second Coming: Popular Millenarianism, 1780–1850* (New Brunswick, NJ: Rutgers University Press, 1979). Harrison presents a detailed study of Brothers, Southcott, and other millenarians, taking care to treat seriously their aspirations and popularity.

Knox, Ronald Arbuthnott, *Enthusiasm: A Chapter in the History of Religion with Special Reference to the XVII and XVIII Centuries* (New York: Oxford University Press, 1961). This is a classic study of enthusiasm, covering a wide variety of its manifestations; Knox has little sympathy for what he regards as a diseased form of religion.

Livingston, James C., *Modern Christian Thought: From the Enlightenment to Vatican II*, 2nd edn., vol. i (Upper Saddle River, NJ: Prentice Hall, 1988). In addition to treating Romanticism within the Protestant sphere, Livingston discusses the influence of Romanticism upon Catholic theology.

McFarland, Thomas, *Coleridge and the Pantheist Tradition* (Oxford: Clarendon Press, 1969). Brilliant discussion of Coleridge's attempts to escape from Spinoza by way of Christian Trinitarianism.

Mee, Jon, *Romanticism, Enthusiasm, and Regulation: Poetics and the Policing of Culture in the Romantic Period* (Oxford: Oxford University Press, 2003). Mee examines the persistence of anti-enthusiastic discourse into the nineteenth century, and the ambiguities of the relationship between Romanticism and enthusiasm.

NOTES

1. Friedrich Schleiermacher, *On Religion: Speeches to Its Cultured Despisers*, ed. and trans. Richard Crouter (Cambridge: Cambridge University Press, 1988), p. 47.

2. Ibid. 53.

3. Samuel Taylor Coleridge, *The Friend*, in *Collected Works of Samuel Taylor Coleridge* IV,, ed. Barbara E. Rooke, 2 vols. (Princeton: Princeton University Press, 1969), i. 156.

4. Percy Bysshe Shelley, 'The Necessity of Atheism', in *Selected Essays on Atheism* (New York: Arno Press, 1972), pp. 6, 9.

5. Percy Bysshe Shelley, *The Poems of Shelley*, i. *1804–1817*, ed. Geoffrey Matthews and Kelvin Everest (London and New York: Longman, 1989), p. 381.

6. Joseph Priestley, 'The Present State of Europe compared with Antient Prophecies; preached on the fast-day in 1794', in *Two Sermons* (Philadelphia: Thomas Dobson, 1794), p. 23.

7. Richard Brothers, *Wonderful prophecies. Being a dissertation on the existence, nature, and extent of the prophetic powers in the human mind: with unquestionable examples of several eminent prophecies, of what is now acting and soon to be fulfilled, upon the great theatre of Europe*, 6th edn. (London, 1795), p. 18.

9 | England, Ireland, Scotland, Wales

Fiona Stafford

When William Wordsworth landed in Dover in September 1802, after a month in Calais, he was moved to write a sonnet on the scene that met his eye:

> Dear fellow Traveller! here we are once more.
> The cock that crows, the smoke that curls, that sound
> Of Bells, those Boys that in yon meadow-ground
> In white sleeved shirts are playing by the score
> And even this little River's gentle roar,
> All, all are English.[1]

Foreign travel often heightens the homecomer's feeling for his own country, but this powerful celebration reflects an acute awareness that across the Channel, all, all were certainly not English. Wordsworth's personal reasons for the trip gave his return to England a particular emotional charge. He had been meeting his former lover, Annette Vallon, and their daughter, Caroline, before his own marriage to Mary Hutchinson, which would take place in October. For readers of the poem, published five years later in a series of political sonnets, however, the sentiments expressed seemed an eloquent articulation of the national feeling that welled up during the prolonged war with France.

Wordsworth's visit to France had been possible only because the Peace of Amiens, signed in March 1802, afforded a few months' respite from the international conflict. War, which did so much to intensify national feelings during the Romantic period, had been declared in February 1793, rendering travel to Europe hazardous, and France virtually inaccessible to British citizens. Although some writers, including Byron, were in a position to take alternative routes to the Mediterranean during the long war, most were confined to Britain. The difficulty of going abroad stimulated domestic touring, which in turn contributed to the new sense of the nation, and its essential differences from continental Europe. As Wordsworth's sonnet continues, the speaker draws a clear contrast between Europe 'yet in bonds' and his own country, which remains 'free'. With the apparently unstoppable rise of Napoleon and the expansion of French power, English liberty seemed more valuable than ever before.

Wordsworth's affirmation of English liberty draws on a long tradition of political writing. But it also reflects a more recent development: the consciousness of different national identities within the newly created United Kingdom. In January 1801, the Act of Union between Britain and Ireland had come into effect. As England, Scotland, Wales, and Ireland were united, each experienced a renewed sense of its own individual identity, within the larger whole. If the four nations were constructing a collective sense of British identity in the Romantic period, the moment of Union also brought a clear recognition of regional differences. While the continuing threat from France made a strong, unified, political power attractive, the literature of the period also registers the importance of local attachments, as writers everywhere celebrated, chastised, mocked, or mourned for 'England', 'Ireland', 'Scotland', or 'Wales'.

The forms that appealed to Romantic writers reveal the new value being invested in native culture. In place of the neoclassical genres preferred by Pope and Dryden, poets were excited by the traditional songs and ballads that had been passed down through rural communities for many years, and were now available to readers in collections such as Percy's *Reliques of Ancient English Poetry* or Herd's *Ancient and Modern Scottish Songs*. Burns's *Poems, Chiefly in the Scottish Dialect*, Blake's *Songs of Innocence and Experience*, Wordsworth and Coleridge's *Lyrical Ballads*, Moore's *Irish Melodies*, and Felicia Hemans's *Welsh Melodies*, all demonstrate the interest in home-grown oral culture and in lyrics that seemed to have flourished naturally in British soil. The revival of the sonnet, too, reflects the general elevation of English literary culture, through which Elizabethan England came to be seen as a Golden Age and vital source of inspiration for contemporary poets (see also chapters on 'The Sonnet' and 'Narrative Poetry').

Unlike poetry, the late eighteenth-century novel was largely free from inherited traditions and was in the process of developing new subgenres. The Romantic period saw the birth of the 'regional novel', the 'national tale', and the 'historical novel', as Maria Edgeworth, Lady Morgan, Sir Walter Scott, and John Galt turned the new enthusiasm for places and their pasts into popular fiction. Flexible enough to accommodate a host of different accents, tones, and locations, the novel was particularly well suited to articulating new senses of the nation (see chapter on 'The novel').

The impact of these publications was underlined by the simultaneous development of a vigorous reviewing culture. The *Edinburgh Review* was founded in 1802, the *Quarterly Review* in 1809, and *Blackwood's Edinburgh Magazine* in 1817. Many of the critics, like Francis Jeffrey or John Lockhart, were Scots, whose own national perspectives, as Byron pointed out in *English Bards and Scotch Reviewers*, frequently seemed to colour their critical assessments. Since Byron was provoked by the attack on poems inspired by his own Scottish childhood, however, it is clear that the identification of 'English' and 'Scotch' was by no means straightforward. As he observed in *Don Juan*, 'I am half a Scot by birth, and bred | A whole one'.[2]

The internal dynamics of British Romantic culture are complicated, but crucial. Although consciousness of old differences often produced anxiety and sometimes hostility, it also acted again and again as a creative stimulus. Whether the idea of 'England', 'Ireland', 'Scotland', or 'Wales' provoked affection or dismay, the related desire to praise or compete contributed enormously to the rich literature of the Romantic period.

Crossing borders

Awareness of national identity was heightened, but not created, by the Union between Britain and Ireland. Almost a century earlier, the 1707 Union between England and Scotland had stirred up energetic debate over the traditional differences and common interests of the sister countries. Eighteenth-century Scots displayed a strong sense of their Northern character, not only through the revival of older Scots poetry and the recovery of Gaelic culture, but also through their determination to master a correct English style and prove their equality with Southerners. Many writers, including James Thomson, Tobias Smollett, and James Boswell, moved to London to take advantage of the wider opportunities of the capital city. While some subsequently returned, others retained imaginative links, revisiting Scotland in their writings. By the end of the eighteenth century, numerous Scottish writers had crossed the Border, but the pull of the North continued to emerge in their work, inviting readers to take a journey, mental or physical, to the further reaches of the islands.

One of the first novels to capture the growing interest in the varied character of 'Britain' was *The Expedition of Humphry Clinker* (1771). Smollett takes the hypochondriac Matthew Bramble and his family from their home in Wales, through the spas and cities of England to his native Scotland. The epistolary narrative allows for contrasting perspectives on the places and manners encountered on the journey. Bath might strike Bramble as 'the very centre of racket and dissipation', but to his niece Lydia, it seems 'an earthly paradise', while the Welsh maid writes home in astonishment: 'O Molly! you that live in the country have no deception of our doings at Bath!'[3] With Wales as the psychological touchstone, the Highlands as the goal, and a number of memorable Irish characters appearing en route, Smollett creates a comic anatomy of the nation. The variousness of *Humphry Clinker* matches that of contemporary Britain, and opened the way for Romantic novelists to develop the enormous potential of the fictional tour.

The 1770s also saw the publication of *A Journey to the Western Islands of Scotland*, by Samuel Johnson, whose penetrating observations provided an alternative model for the tour of Northern Britain. When Boswell published his own version of the same trip, he included more conversational detail about the people whose hospitality they had enjoyed, together with vivid descriptions of the great English lexicographer in often surprising surroundings. Taken together, the two accounts unite old and young, humour and melancholy, Highland and Lowland, Scotland and England, through the shared experience of a single journey. In both accounts, too, the border between fact and fiction seems even less certain than the physical boundaries being described.

The literary journey established by Smollett, Boswell, and Johnson could be adapted for a variety of imaginative purposes, but was especially suited to novels. Crossing borders was a realistic device for moving along the plot or the characters, but it could also become a metaphor for transformations of various kinds, offering the threshold to an unknown world, a new life, or a self not yet understood or recognized. Like *Humphry Clinker*, novels of the Romantic period frequently began with a border-crossing from one country to its neighbour: a symbolic change that would permit the action to begin. In Scott's *Redgauntlet*, the story begins when Darsie Latimer, a young Englishman who has been brought up in Scotland, follows his deep-seated 'impulse towards the South'.[4] The desire to see his 'native country' sends Darsie into the rugged lawless terrain of the Borders—a suitable setting not only for romantic adventure but also for explorations of personal and national identity. *Redgauntlet* follows the pattern already established by Scott in *Waverley*, and *Rob Roy*, where a young Englishman visits Scotland and, in addition to being struck by the strangeness of the people, becomes embroiled in major historical events of eighteenth-century Highland history. Border-crossings allowed Scott to explore recent Scottish history sympathetically, while at the same time maintaining the viewpoint of a modern British citizen. By dramatizing historic events from a particular angle, and focusing on the lives of individual Highlanders, Lowlanders, and Englishmen caught up in the national upheavals, Scott could draw on his country's past without endangering its present stability. Edward Waverley's marriage to the Scottish Rose Bradwardine is both a traditional ending to a romantic narrative and an allegory of political Union.

Scott was not the first novelist of the period to exploit the motif of the English traveller in love. *The Wild Irish* Girl, Lady Morgan's hugely popular post-Union romance, takes a young Englishman across the Irish Sea to visit the estate owned by his father in remote Connaught. The device of the English visitor allows for admiration of the Irish countryside and sympathy for the dispossessed Catholics, whose ruins and poverty only seem 'picturesque' on an initial, superficial view. Although the romantic plot appears to endorse political Union by marrying the beautiful Irish Glorvina to the young Protestant landowner, the implacable anger of her father is only overcome through his convenient death in the last few pages of the novel. Maria Edgeworth's sympathetic portrayal of Ireland in *The Absentee* took a slightly different form, as she made her fictional traveller a young Irish lord, returning him to the neglected family estates. Like Morgan, Edgeworth encourages sympathy for Ireland through creating a novel which entertains as it makes its social comment. Her success helped to inspire Scott, who recognized the diplomatic power of fiction to introduce the natives of one country to another and to strengthen the Union through imagination rather than legislation. As Smollett had demonstrated, national differences could be the stuff of romance, allegory, satire, or comedy, and although some readers might be more interested in the story than the politics, Romantic novels did much to foster greater understanding between the different regions of Britain and Ireland.

Physical differences in the landscape also excited contemporary readers, as the popularity of travel books by William Gilpin and Thomas Pennant shows. Scotland, Ireland, Wales, and the North of England possessed lakes, rocky seascapes, and mountains, and thus the possibility of Alpine sublimity closer to home. Literary works that could transport their readers to such destinations had powerful appeal. The ruined castles of

Scotland, Wales, and Ireland seemed perfect sites for Gothic mystery: Ann Radcliffe's first novel, *The Castles of Athlin and Dunbayne*, drew not on the mountainous strongholds of Italy, but rather on the romantic scenery of the Highlands. Charles Maturin's *Melmoth the Wanderer* exploits the imaginative possibilities of a ruined mansion that seems uncomfortably close to contemporary readers, as he adapts the Romantic travel motif for Gothic horror. John Melmoth's short trip from Dublin to Wicklow unleashes pages of extraordinary narrative, in which the conventional limits of experience are removed, and yet perpetually desired, by a wanderer who cannot die. Such crossing of spatial and temporal borders is part of the vast creative impact of political union, which had apparently rendered old borders obsolete, while actually heightening their symbolic significance.

The presentation of the local as strange also reflects the self-consciousness of the regional novelist who recognizes a more distant audience beyond the immediate circle. James Hogg, who grew up in the Scottish Borders, was acutely aware that what seemed normal to him could appear uncouth and even weird to readers further afield. Hogg's use of supernatural elements in his fiction is particularly unsettling because it is presented as a natural part of the rural community that is conjured up so vividly. Ghosts appear frequently in his fiction, while the living perpetually cross into the world of the fairies, or visit the dead, or experience prophetic dreams. In Hogg's tales, the borders between natural and supernatural, fiction and non-fiction, life and death, are permeable; in his best-known work, *The Private Memoirs and Confessions of a Justified Sinner*, uncertainty is the key narrative principle. The doubleness of Hogg's novel, with its two narratives, two brothers, and the strange alter ego, Gilmartin, creates a powerful psychological thriller, in which the mystery is never resolved. It is also a profound personal expression by a regional novelist, perpetually torn between his home and the reading public, in a country deeply divided by religious, political, and cultural differences, and yet bound together by the printed word.

The influence of England

Hogg's self-consciousness about his native community, which was accentuated by his comic persona of the clumsy 'Ettrick Shepherd', typifies the difficulties faced by writers who had not been brought up in the higher social strata of English society. The development of British identity in the eighteenth century went hand in hand with a new emphasis on the standardization of language, reinforced by battalions of dictionaries, grammars, and elocution manuals. Edgeworth may have made fun of Lady Clonbrony's aspirations to pass for '*Henglish*, born in *Hoxfordhire*'[5] in *The Absentee*, but for many writers the question of correct pronunciation was no laughing matter. Even a brilliant man such as David Hume was troubled by his ability to write pure English because he spoke in Scots (the traditional language of Lowland Scotland, as distinct from Gaelic, the old Celtic language of the Highlands and Islands). In response to such anxieties, the Irish elocutionist, Thomas Sheridan, filled theatres up and down the land with his lectures on English diction.

In his preface to *A Dictionary of the English Language*, Johnson wrote movingly of the linguistic disorder that had greeted him when he began his great work: 'wherever I turned my view, there was perplexity to be disentangled, and confusion to be regulated'.[6] For Johnson, lexicography was a heroic task: bringing order from chaos, in an attempt to preserve 'the spirit of English liberty' from both creeping Gallicism and from enemies within. What Johnson regarded as a patriotic endeavour, however, had far-reaching and not always beneficial consequences for those furthest from the English centre. Writers in Scotland, Ireland, and Wales were faced with conforming to the new linguistic standard, or with continuing in familiar modes of speech that might provoke critical contempt or worse—complete neglect. The doubleness manifest in the work of Scottish writers has been read by twentieth-century scholars as a response to the kind of internal bilingualism imposed by the need to write in English. As influential Scottish professors such as Hugh Blair in Edinburgh began to promote the English prose writing of Addison as the ideal model for his students, the scope for serious writing in non-standard English dwindled away.

In the context of the widespread obsession with perfect English, the success of Burns's *Poems, Chiefly in the Scottish Dialect* is all the more remarkable. But it is perhaps the very refusal to conform that constitutes the real excitement of the volume. For despite the apparent humility of the preface, Burns's collection of poems challenges pretty much every kind of contemporary authority—linguistic, clerical, aristocratic, even monarchical. As Burns admitted, he was 'determined to flatter no created being, either in prose or verse' and 'set as little by kings, lords, clergy, critics, &c as all these respectable Gentry do by my Bardship'.[7] With such an outlook, Burns was unlikely to feel over-intimidated by pressures to conform to elegant Englishness. His poetry is a celebration of the Scots language and its traditions, but it is also infused with his reading of English literature—Pope, Swift, Milton, Shakespeare, Shenstone, Gray. While the Scots dialect initially startled readers outside Kilmarnock, Burns's blend of Scots and English contributed to the creation of a distinctive and very versatile poetic language. 'To a Louse, On Seeing one on a Lady's Bonnet at Church' concludes with a wish:

> O wad some Pow'r the giftie gie us
> *To see oursels as others see us!*
> It wad frae monie a blunder free us
>   An foolish notion[8]

Burns was only too aware of how others saw himself, and so his work plays on the expectations of an audience conditioned to condescend to an Ayrshire ploughman. His own reputation may have suffered from the skilful manipulation of prevailing critical attitudes, but his poetry made an immense contribution to Romanticism nevertheless, by breaking through constricting linguistic assumptions and revealing the power of native poetry.

While Burns negotiated the tricky linguistic challenges of his situation by glossing words and blending poetic languages, the expansion of English proved much more devastating to the ancient Celtic languages of these islands. Scots might mix imaginatively with literary English, but Gaelic, Irish, and Welsh could not. Anxiety about the fate of Celtic languages sounds loudly in the first published collection of Gaelic poems, Alexander MacDonald's *Ais-Eiridh ne Sean-Chanoin Albannaich* ('The Resurrection of the Ancient Scottish Language', 1751). The destruction of Gaelic culture accelerated after the Jacobite defeat at Culloden in 1746, although, by the end of the century, the modern nation had begun to recognize the value, rather than the threat, of the Highlands. The international success of Macpherson's versions of the ancient, heroic poetry of Celtic Scotland, which appeared in the 1760s as *The Poems of Ossian*, helped transform the perception of Gaelic from barbarous tongue to national treasure, linking British culture to the ancient world. The controversy surrounding his 'discovery' of native epic poetry also stimulated general interest in Celtic languages: in both Wales and Ireland, scholars rallied to dispute Macpherson's version of Celtic culture and to produce more authentic translations. Evan Evans's *Some Specimens of Ancient Welsh Poetry* and Charlotte Brooke's *Reliques of Irish Poetry* were both landmarks in the histories of Welsh and Irish literature, and made the early poetry of the different nations accessible to modern, English-speaking readers. Celtic mythology fed Romantic writers with an exciting alternative to the familiar, authoritative legends of Greece and Rome and provided inspiration for Blake, Southey, Wordsworth, Coleridge, Byron, Hemans, and Keats.

The spread of standard English, promoted by Scottish and Irish intellectuals, helped to cement the Union by driving the distinct languages of the different nations into obscurity. While the old languages receded before the rising tide of English, however, the symbols of Celtic Britain remained very visible. In 1757, Thomas Gray had created the iconic figure of 'The Bard' in a stirring Pindaric on the massacre of the Welsh bards under Edward I. The appeal of the native poet was boosted by Macpherson's depiction of the ancient Bard among the mountains, singing mournfully beneath an oak tree to the strains of a harp. Although in Ireland, the Celtic harp became a symbol of non-English nationalism, evident in the 1798 uprising of the United Irishmen, the note struck by the ancient Bard of Scotland was strongly elegiac. After 1801, even the Irish harp tended to play laments in English-language collections such as Moore's *Irish Melodies*. The Romantic Celtic revival tended to direct attention to the past, not the present. As readers throughout the islands went into raptures over Macpherson's Anglicized *Ossian*, accomplished poets in Ireland, Wales, and Gaelic Scotland continued to compose verse for very limited audiences. The names of Duncan Bán Macintyre, Rob Donn, Evan Evans, Goronwy Owen, and even Brian Merriman are rarely mentioned by students of Romanticism, even though they were living in Britain and Ireland during the late eighteenth and nineteenth centuries, and composing fine poetry in the indigenous languages of the islands.

The power of Scotland, Ireland, and Wales

If Gray's Bard is an early sign of Romantic Celticism, Collins's 'Ode on the Popular Superstitions of the Scottish Highlands' (written *c*.1750, published 1788) demonstrates more explicitly the modern English poet's awareness of the imaginative resources that lay hidden in the North and West. Collins's 'Ode' urges the Scottish playwright, John Home, to draw inspiration from the legends of his country, just as Shakespeare had turned to Scotland for *Macbeth*. Remote, mountainous regions were rich in legend and superstition, and even seemed to have preserved a capacity for prophetic experience that was lost to modern urban life. Poets of the Romantic period were drawn to Scotland, Wales, and Ireland, seeking inspiration from worlds that seemed fascinatingly different, and yet close enough to represent a link to their own origins.

In *The Prelude* (written, but not published, in 1805), the chaos of revolutionary France is followed by the climactic ascent of Snowdon: it is as if the ancient Celtic landscape can somehow refresh the troubled modern poet, infusing energy and clarifying essential truths. Much earlier in the poem, Wordsworth pauses to consider William Wallace, who, like the Welsh bards in Gray's poem, suffered defeat under Edward I, but yet remains a symbol of the heroic commitment to the 'independence and stern liberty' of his 'dear Country'.[9] Although he never wrote an epic poem on Wallace, the inclusion of these lines near the beginning of his great poem indicates the importance of Scotland, as well as Wales, to Wordsworth's poetry.

For readers of the period, unable to enjoy the unpublished *Prelude*, Wordsworth's attraction to Scotland was most apparent in the *Poems, in Two Volumes*, which contained several poems inspired by the tour he had made in the summer of 1803 together with Dorothy Wordsworth and Coleridge. In a series of beautiful lyrics, Wordsworth demonstrated the imaginative stimulation of Scottish history, scenery, poetry, and, perhaps most of all, the people. From the orphaned sons of Burns to the unnamed women at Loch Ketterine, Wordsworth's Scottish poems are filled with human presence. Yet it is the elusiveness, rather than the permanence of what he encounters that gives the lyrics their haunting quality. 'The Solitary Reaper' is the most eloquent embodiment of the fascination of the North, its mystery conveyed in the simplest language:

> 'Will no one tell me what she sings?'[10]

The girl remains distant and strange like the Hebrides, her songs in Gaelic—a language inaccessible to the English traveller. When Dorothy Wordsworth recorded her *Recollections of a Tour Made in Scotland in 1803*, she recalled a moving moment, when the scene, 'solitary and huge', was filled with 'a half-articulate Gaelic hooting'.[11] The appearance of a boy herding his cattle at twilight seemed to encapsulate for the Wordsworths the compelling strangeness of the Highlands: 'it was a text', she observed, 'containing in itself the whole history of the Highlander's life—his melancholy, his simplicity, his poverty, his superstition, and above all, that visionariness which results from a communion with the unworldliness of nature.'

The Wordsworths and Coleridge were encouraged to visit Scotland by the poetry of Burns, Macpherson, and Scott. Later visitors had the additional incitement of Wordsworth's Scottish poems. When Keats travelled north in 1818, he went via the Lake District to Dumfries and Ayrshire before going on to the Highlands and Islands. The trip was a literary pilgrimage to the places that inspired Wordsworth, to the home of Burns, and eventually to Fingal's Cave, named after the legendary father of Ossian. A few months earlier, Keats had heard Hazlitt lecture on Burns, praising the Scottish poet's immediate response to the world around him and the physicality of his poetry. The walking tour was a determined effort by the young English poet to experience dramatic natural scenery first hand, and furnish his mind with grand images to equal his epic ambitions. The letters Keats wrote during his trip reveal the overwhelming sensations he felt on seeing mountains for the first time: 'I shall learn poetry here'.[12] Although he composed few poems during the tour, its effects can be seen in 'Hyperion', which he began in the months following his return to Hampstead. Keats's fallen Titans lie on 'hard flint', in a dark cavern, deafened by 'the solid roar | Of thunderous waterfalls and torrents hoarse'.[13] The images harvested in Staffa and the unyielding mountains of North Britain resurface in *Hyperion*, itself presented as a fragment of some unmanageable giant.

Apart from the desire to be overwhelmed by mountains, Keats hoped the tour would toughen him up. The physical hardship of the journey and the unfamiliar sights were meant to strengthen his poetry, an anxiety that may reflect his sensitivity about the perceived effeminacy of his poetry. It was not only the landscape or the language that startled Keats on his travels; the greatest shock was the poverty he witnessed on his trip across the Irish Sea: 'worse than nakedness, the rags, the dirt and misery of the poor common Irish—A Scotch cottage, though in that some times the Smoke has no exit but at the door, is a pallace to an Irish one'.[14] Such wretched conditions were deeply distressing and cast an ironic shadow over contemporary pride in English liberty and the natural independence of the native Briton.

Keats's disgust at the existence suffered by the Irish poor is an important element in the complicated perception of Britain in the Romantic period. For while numerous English writers admired the history and poetry of the neighbouring countries, the problem of contemporary poverty was very considerable. Dorothy Wordsworth's epitome of the Highlander's life yokes 'melancholy', 'simplicity', superstition', 'visionariness' with 'poverty', while in the figure of Burns, the idea of genius was inseparable from that of suffering. Nor was the problem confined to rural areas. When Shelley visited Dublin in 1811, he was appalled by the scenes he encountered—'I had no conception of the depth of human misery until now.—The poor of Dublin are assuredly the meanest and most miserable of all'.[15] Shelley's *Address to the Irish People* advocates Catholic Emancipation and the Repeal of the Union, while his radical poem, *Queen Mab*, envisaged more wholesale reforms. British radicals might feel some sense of progress following the abolition of the slave trade, but those aware of conditions in parts of their own country knew that there was still a long way to go.

The imaginative and intellectual interaction between England, Scotland, Wales, and Ireland during the Romantic period was extraordinary. While Scottish and Irish novelists represented their home communities through the eyes of imaginary English travellers, English writers walked energetically through the neighbouring countries, pouring out lyric poetry, startled letters, rapturous descriptions, indignant political pamphlets, and Celtically tinged epics. Scottish, Irish, and Welsh writers tried hard to reconcile their desire to adopt standard English literary models with attachments to local forms and speech patterns. English writers in turn found their works being severely judged by Edinburgh critics who not only drew on the influential aesthetic ideas of the Scottish Enlightenment, but also sharpened their rhetorical skills with legal training. The poverty of rural Scotland or the Dublin slums upset the humanitarian idealism of writers throughout the islands; at the same time the literary works that made the most money were the poems of Scott. What emerges is a picture of dynamic interchange, as writers and readers of the four nations viewed each other with fascination, delight, surprise, or suspicion. While the threat from France may have encouraged the adoption of a larger British identity, it is clear from the writings of the Romantic period that the distinctions between England, Ireland, Scotland, and Wales were as much part of the heightened sense of national identity as the new idea of Great Britain.

FURTHER READING

Carruthers, Gerard, and Rawes, Alan, *English Romanticism and the Celtic World* (Cambridge: Cambridge University Press, 2003). A collection of essays by different scholars exploring the importance of the Celtic inheritance to writers of the Romantic period; especially useful for its inclusion of Welsh material as well as Scottish and Irish.

Colley, Linda, *Britons: Forging the Nation, 1707–1837* (London and New Haven: Yale University Press, 1992). An influential, controversial history of the development of British identity in the long eighteenth century, emphasizing the importance of both frequent warfare and Protestantism to the construction of the nation.

Crawford, Robert, *Devolving English Literature*, 2nd edn. (Edinburgh: Edinburgh University Press, 2000). A ground-breaking discussion of Scottish literature from the eighteenth century to the twentieth, arguing for the importance of recognizing the national and cultural contexts of literary texts.

Davis, Leith, *Acts of Union: Scotland and the Literary Negotiation of the British Nation, 1707–1830* (Stanford, Calif.: Stanford University Press, 1998). A discussion of the literary implications of the 1707 Union between England and Scotland, emphasizing the importance of writing to the construction of new ideas of the nation.

Demata, Massimiliano, and Wu, Duncan (eds.), *British Romanticism and the Edinburgh Review* (London: Palgrave, 2002). A collection of essays by different scholars examining the role of the journal in British culture, including discussion of the Scottish philosophical context and the representation of Ireland and Scotland in the *Review*.

Ferris, Ina, *The Romantic National Tale and the Question of Ireland* (Cambridge: Cambridge University Press, 2002). A concise, perceptive analysis of Irish novels in the Romantic period, following the Act of Union in 1800.

Fulford, Timothy, *Land, Liberty, and Authority: Poetry, Criticism and Politics from Thomson to Wordsworth* (Cambridge: Cambridge University Press, 1996). A well-informed critical analysis of poetic representations of the landscape, exploring the significance of picturesque theory and Gilpin's tours.

Kiberd, Declan, *Irish Classics* (Cambridge: Granta, 2000). A lively discussion of Irish writing from the seventeenth to twentieth centuries, remarkable for its critical expertise in both Irish language and English literary texts.

Leerssen, Joep, *Remembrance and Imagination: Patterns in the Historical and Literary Representations of Ireland in the Nineteenth Century* (Cork: Cork University Press, 1996). The early chapters provide well-informed analysis of literary texts written in the wake of the 1798 Rebellion and the Union.

Thomson, Derick, *An Introduction to Gaelic Poetry* (London: Gollancz, 1977). A critical history of Scottish Gaelic literature, including extensive translation of eighteenth- and nineteenth-century Scottish Gaelic poetry.

Trumpener, Katie, *Bardic Nationalism: The Romantic Novel and the British Empire* (Princeton: Princeton University Press, 1997). A substantial, wide-ranging study of the influence of eighteenth-century antiquarianism on Romantic ideas of national identity.

NOTES

1. 'Composed in the Valley, near Dover On the Day of Landing', in *William Wordsworth: The Major Works, including The Prelude*, ed. Stephen Gill (Oxford: Oxford University Press, 2000), p. 284.

2. *Don Juan*, Canto X. 17, in *Lord Byron.: The Complete Poetical Works*, ed. Jerome J. McGann, 7 vols. (Oxford: Clarendon Press, 1980–93), vol. v.

3. Tobias Smollett, *The Expedition of Humphry Clinker*, ed. Lewis M. Knapp and Paul-Gabriel Boucé (Oxford: Oxford University Press, 1984), pp. 34, 39, 42.

4. Walter Scott, *Redgauntlet*, ed. Kathryn Sutherland (Oxford: Oxford University Press, 1985), p. 29.

5. Maria Edgeworth, *The Absentee*, ed. W. J. McCormack and Kim Walker (Oxford: Oxford University Press, 1988), p. 2.

6. *Samuel Johnson: The Major Works*, ed. Donald Greene (Oxford: Oxford University Press, 2000), p. 307.

7. 'To Mrs Dunlop', 30 Apr. 1787, in *The Letters of Robert Burns*, ed. J. De Lancey Ferguson, rev. edn. G. Ross Roy, 2 vols. (Oxford: Clarendon Press, 1985), i. 108.

8. *The Poems and Songs of Robert Burns*, ed. James Kinsley, 3 vols. (Oxford: Clarendon Press, 1968), i. 94.

9. *The Prelude*, I. 219.

10. 'The Solitary Reaper', 17. The inspiration for the poem came from Thomas Wilkinson's *Tours to the British Mountains* (1824), which Wordsworth saw in manuscript—see *William Wordsworth: The Major Works*, p. 717.

11. *Journals of Dorothy Wordsworth*, ed. E. de Selincourt, 2 vols. (London: Macmillan, 1941), i. 286.

12. To Tom Keats, 25–7 June 1818, in John Keats, *Selected Letters*, ed. Robert Gittings, rev. edn. Jon Mee (Oxford: Oxford University Press, 2002), p. 97.

13. See 'Hyperion. A Fragment', II, 5–17, in *John Keats: The Major Works*, ed. Elizabeth Cook (Oxford: Oxford University Press, 2000).

14. To Tom Keats, 3, 5, 7, 9 July 1818, in Keats, *Letters*, p. 112.

15. To William Godwin, 8 Mar. 1812, in *The Letters of Percy Bysshe Shelley*, ed. Frederick L. Jones, 2 vols. (Oxford: Clarendon Press, 1964), i. 268.

10 | Europe

Christoph Bode

As early as 1924, the critic Arthur O. Lovejoy argued that there was no such thing as a European Romanticism: 'The word "romantic" has come to mean so many different things that, by itself, it means nothing. It has ceased to perform the function of a verbal sign.'[1] One should either stop talking about 'Romanticism' altogether or at least 'learn to use the word "Romanticism" in the plural', since 'the "Romanticism" of one country may have little in common with that of another, and at all events ought to be defined in distinctive terms'.[2] Sceptically comparing the British, German, and French varieties of 'Romanticism', Lovejoy concluded: 'There may be some common denominator of them all; but if so, it has never yet been clearly exhibited, and its presence is not to be assumed *a priori* [from the beginning].'[3]

It is true that Romanticism varies in its literary aspects from country to country, and that, as a word, it does not have the same meaning everywhere. It is also true that Romanticism as a movement does not occur simultaneously in different European literatures. Moreover, in some European cultures its predominance stretches over decades, in some it is a matter of a few years only, and in others its existence has been flatly denied. And yet even the use of 'Romanticisms', in the plural, suggests that all these literary phenomena do have something in common, however tenuous the similarity may be. Why else refer to them by a common name? As long as such usage persists, somebody will continue to look for common denominators. Therefore, it could not come as a total surprise when, twenty-five years after Lovejoy, another critic, René Wellek, pleaded impressively for the 'unity of European Romanticism', arguing that 'we find throughout Europe the same conceptions of poetry and of the workings and nature of poetic imagination, the same conception of nature and its relation to man, and basically the same poetic style, with a use of imagery, symbolism, and myth which is clearly distinct from that of eighteenth-century neoclassicism'.[4] Whom are we to believe, Lovejoy or Wellek?

It is a good thing that one does not have to choose between Lovejoy's no-nonsense scepticism and Wellek's careful optimism. For it is, of course, perfectly permissible to speak of a singular European Romanticism provided one keeps in mind that we are then speaking of a *construct* (a concept we have developed because we have reason to believe it is useful as a *tool*) that focuses our discussion and helps us detect both similarities and discrepancies that may have escaped our notice before. 'Unlike dates, periods are not facts', declared the British historian G. M. Trevelyan.[5] Periods and concepts like 'Romanticism' are conceptions that we form retrospectively, in our own interests, and for specific purposes.

Once we are aware of Romanticism as a construct, a number of problems become easier to deal with:

Terminology. Self-designation is neither a sufficient nor a necessary condition for inclusion. Some European Romantics designated themselves Romantics, or were called so in their time; others did not (or were not). Some may have called themselves Romantics, but may fail to qualify when we have formed a sufficiently clear idea of what the theory and practice of Romanticism actually was. The 'thing' and the word do not necessarily have to coincide.

Chronology. In some European countries Romanticism begins early, in others later. That need not be a reason for concern—quite the contrary, in fact: it will stimulate fascinating questions about trailblazers and latecomers, about which conditions may be conducive and which ones obstructive to new intellectual and literary movements.

Heterogeneity. Some Romantics, self-professed or not, were politically progressive and others reactionary; some were internationalist and cosmopolitan, others fiercely nationalistic; some of them believed in the Enlightenment project of rational perfectibility, while others opposed it. Some Romantics were religious sceptics, while others converted to Catholicism; some vested their hopes in absolute Truth, while others acknowledged the inevitability of relative, subjective truths. Some subscribed to a poetics of subjectivity, others to a literary ideal of non-subjectivity; some wanted literature and the arts to be organic, others highly self-conscious, self-reflexive, auto-referential, and ironic. Some regarded poetry, some the novel, and others the drama as the supreme genre. All this variety need not worry us, if we reconceptualize European Romanticism as a *set of responses*, highly differentiated and at times downright contradictory, to a historically specific *challenge*: the challenge of the ever-accelerating modernization of European society.

The European cultural scene profited immensely from such intellectual and literary intermediaries as Mme de Staël, August Wilhelm Schlegel, or Samuel Taylor Coleridge. More important was the direct influence—transcending national, cultural, and linguistic borders—of writers such as Jean-Jacques Rousseau, Johann Wolfgang von Goethe, or Lord Byron, who created a truly international European literature, fed by many sources, spreading in different directions. Still more intriguing, however, is the idea that even where there were no direct contacts whatsoever and no relationships to speak of, individual European writers came up with surprisingly similar solutions to the political, poetical, and philosophical problems that defined the era. If we see European Romanticism as a transpersonal, cultural shift of paradigms, in which pressing social and cultural concerns were creatively negotiated according to new, revolutionary rules, then the diversity of European Romanticism can no longer be held as proof against its unity or even against its existence. On the contrary, overwhelming diversity would then be the form in which European Romanticism unfolded, as a vast range of possible responses within a new framework.

The continental scene—Germany

Curiously enough, the writers and works which for many outside Germany are the clearest manifestations of German Romanticism are not called Romantic in Germany itself. Goethe's epistolary novel, *The Sorrows of Young Werther* (1774) and his drama *Götz von Berlichingen* (1774); Friedrich Schiller's wildly anti-authoritarian play *The Robbers* (1781); and Gottfried August Bürger's spooky ballad *Lenore* (1773/4) are traditionally placed in the eighteenth-century movement known as *Sturm und Drang* (Storm and Stress) rather than under Romanticism.

The misconception has an identifiable source. When Madame de Staël held up German culture and literature as models to be emulated in her three-volume manifesto *De l'Allemagne* (1810; first English edition, 1813), she presented Goethe, Schiller, and Bürger as Romantic poets of the North, whose enthusiasm, feeling, inspiration, and depth of thinking, she believed, were superior to the cold classicism of the South. Confusingly, in her attempt to sell German Romanticism to the rest of Europe, de Staël paradoxically bypassed large sections of German Romanticism in silence: she made no mention of Friedrich Schlegel's scandalous novel *Lucinde* (1799), Heinrich Wackenroder's *Herzensergiessungen eines kunstliebenden Klosterbruders* (1797), or Novalis's only novel *Heinrich von Ofterdingen* (1802). Instead, de Staël praises writers such as Goethe and Schiller who, after their *Sturm und Drang* phase, had become *Klassiker* (both 'classical authors' and 'classicists'), and against whom these Romantics had begun to define themselves.[6]

It is of course true that *Sturm und Drang* displays many elements which qualify as, at least, pre-Romantic: a revolt against literary conventions; a belief in the importance of original, rule-breaking genius, with Shakespeare as the new hero; a revolt against orthodoxy in politics; a strong interest in the past, in ancient epics, in mythology, fairy tales, and folksongs. Much of this was directed against what was felt to be an oppressive predominance of French taste and ideas, though one major aspect of the *Sturm und Drang* movement was certainly of French origin. The cult of feeling and of nature was propagated by the philosopher Jean-Jacques Rousseau.

The first generation of German Romantics—Wackenroder, Ludwig Tieck, Friedrich von Hardenberg (who called himself Novalis), Friedrich Schlegel, and his elder brother August Wilhelm Schlegel—are called *Frühromantik* (early Romanticism) or the Berlin-Jena group. Their most active period was 1790 to 1804, and their prime achievement was a radically new and philosophically well-founded literary practice. Taking their cue from the idealist philosophies of Immanuel Kant, Johann Gottlieb Fichte, and Friedrich Schelling, the Schlegel brothers and Novalis set a dialectic of *becoming* against the classicist ideal of perfection of *being*, and devised a Romantic 'transcendental poetry' that was forever reaching out, forever trying to encompass ever greater realms of reality and human experience.

When Friedrich Schlegel defines Romantic poetry as 'progressive universal poesy' (in the *Athenaeum*, 1798–1800), what he has in mind is a total mixture of all genres and all styles, an ongoing integration of all knowledges. The German word *Poesie* should not mislead us. Here it means not poetry alone, but literature in general; and, of course, the genre that lends itself most easily to the kind of radical mingling the Romantics aim at is the relatively new and characteristically variable genre of the novel (*Roman*, in German). By definition, a novel can contain practically anything.

But why should literature, above all other forms of culture, be able to achieve that kind of overall integration and synthesis? The answer is that in literature alone language can display an awareness of its own inevitable limitations: in the finite medium of language, literature points self-reflexively to its *form* as the finite representation of the infinite. Romantic literature is therefore not only a highly self-conscious and self-reflexive art, it is also invariably *ironic* in that it can never really say what it wants to say—but *that*, it can say. Very often, therefore, German Romantic texts have fragmentary forms signalling that they are symbolically gesturing to a something beyond, signalling that the text itself is not the 'real' thing. Small wonder, then, that the prototypical German Romantic novels—from Schlegel's *Lucinde* through Jean Paul's *Siebenkäs* (1796–7) up to E. T. A. Hoffmann's *Lebens-Ansichten des Katers Murr* (1819–21)—have stronger affinities with Cervantes and Sterne or with paradoxical postmodern novels of today than with the contemporary Gothic novel, or with Jane Austen, or Sir Walter Scott.

In their heyday, the Jena Romantics hoped to romanticize the world, to make the world poetic (Novalis's 'magic idealism'). But if one reads Novalis's *Hymns to Night* (1800) alongside the darker *Die Nachtwachen des Bonaventura* (by E. A. F. Klingemann, 1804), it is easy to see how quickly a universal optimism, based on a belief in the transforming powers of the subjective imagination, can collapse into scepticism, pessimism, and downright despair.

The second generation of German Romantics—Achim von Arnim, Clemens Brentano, the Brothers Grimm—are called *Hochromantik* (high Romanticism), or the Heidelberg group, because it was there that they gathered around 1805. Their interests were less philosophical than philological, less universal than national. Marked by the fight for German independence against Napoleon, they not only collected old poetry and songs (von Arnim and Brentano, *Des Knaben Wunderhorn*, 1806–8), fairy tales, folk tales, and legends (Brothers Grimm, *Kinder- und Hausmärchen*, 1812–15; *Deutsche Heldensagen*, 1816–18), hoping to salvage a folk culture they saw on the verge of extinction, but, faced with the turbulences of the present, they also looked for security in the supposed stability of a medieval corporate state or the organized creed of established Christian religion. As *Hochromantik* turned into *Spätromantik* (late Romanticism, c.1815 to 1830, primarily in Vienna, Munich, and Berlin), conversions to Catholicism were not uncommon, and a reactionary chauvinism, sometimes including misogyny and anti-Semitism, could gain ground. The nation, not humanity, the past, not the future, define German *Hoch-* and *Spätromantik*.

Quite apart from these ideological differences, there is, in terms of literature, an enormous range between the extreme lyricism of Novalis or of Friedrich Hölderlin on the one hand, and the forced experimentalism of Tieck (*Der gestiefelte Kater*, 1797), of the self-reflexive novels of the 1790s, or the tales of the uncanny and the fantastic by E. T. A. Hoffmann (*Fantasiestücke*, 1814/15; *Die Elixiere des Teufels*, 1815–18; *Nachtstücke,* 1816) on the other. But behind all these diverging manifestations of German Romanticism, even behind the dream to re-create the German nation out of a glorified and mystified past, there lies a shared assumption about the relation between language and thought—and, deriving from that, the common belief that literature is not merely a handmaiden to reality, that it is not its task to mirror and imitate reality, but rather to add something to it, to enrich it, ultimately to *transform* it. Disunited, oppressed, and unable to stage a revolution, the German people invested its creative energies in literature and philosophy and placed its hopes in the powers of the imagination and the spirit. In France, they ordered this matter differently: a starker contrast, in this respect, could hardly be imagined.

France

The revolutionary years in France are marked by a conspicuous dearth of innovative, original works of literature. Rousseau's influence is still pervasive in Jacques Henri Bernardin de Sainte-Pierre's exotic novel *Paul et Virginie* (1788), in which the tragic story of the innocent young couple in their island paradise serves, like so many other exotic, 'oriental' tales of the eighteenth century, as a fundamental criticism and indictment of pre-revolutionary France. The same can be said of his prose fable *La Chaumière indienne* (1791). A similar exoticism exists in François-René de Chateaubriand's 'American' novels *Atala* (1801) and *René* (1802), though here the themes of moral conflict and *ennui*, world-weariness and melancholy are introduced to give support to Chateaubriand's extensive, anti-Enlightenment apology of Christianity.

Both during the Republic and the Napoleonic years the doctrines of neoclassicism had quasi-official status. It was only through Madame de Staël's *De l'Allemagne* (helped by the translation of A. W. Schlegel's lectures, which established the dichotomies of classic versus romantic, mechanical versus organic) that an anti-classicist, romantic aesthetics infiltrated the French scene. In contrast to Chateaubriand, Madame de Staël and her circle had strong liberal, progressive, and republican ideals and that would define 'le mouvement romantique' when it finally emerged as late as in the 1820s: French Romanticism is indeed basically a phenomenon of the 1820s and of the following decade.

It was Victor Hugo who, in the programmatic prefaces to his dramas *Cromwell* (1827) and *Hernani* (1830), made the explicit link between literature and politics when he proclaimed that the liberty of art had to go hand in hand with political liberty and that liberty of art was by definition directed against any despotism of systems, of codes, and of rules. This progressive, revolutionary art Hugo called Romanticism. With Hugo's victory in the so-called battle of *Hernani*, French Romanticism found its culmination—at long last the hegemony of neoclassicism on the French stage had been broken.

In poetry, as a less public art, it was easier to make inroads into unchartered territories. The poems of Alphonse Prât de Lamartine, though classical in form, introduced a new meditative tone to French poetry (*Méditations poétiques*, 1820; *Nouvelles méditations poétiques*, 1823); the isolated, misunderstood genius becomes a central theme in Alfred de Vigny's *Poèmes* (1822) as well as in his *Poèmes antiques et modernes* (1826); and Alfred de Musset's outstanding cycle *Les Nuits* (1835–7) develops, in dialogic form, a poetics of submission and, eventually, epicurean composure. But probably the most fascinating of all French Romantic poets is Gérard de Nerval (who, in his tales, follows the dark Romanticism of Hoffmann), who celebrates in his sonnet collection *Les Chimères* (1854) a fusion of a variety of dark ideas which paves the way for Charles Baudelaire, Stéphane Mallarmé, and Arthur Rimbaud, for symbolism and modernism. More than in other European literatures, perhaps, the connection between Romantic and modernist poetry is a strong and secure one in France.

The novel, too, took a different turn in France because, following Hugo's liberal programme, writers aimed at literary realism, at the exact reproduction of social and psychological reality—a development diametrically opposed to the self-reflexive German Romantic novel. For lack of candidates, Stendhal (*Le Rouge et le noir*, 1830; *La Chartreuse de Parme*, 1839), Prosper Mérimée (*Carmen*, 1845), the early Gustave Flaubert, and the early Honoré de Balzac are sometimes called Romantics—but that only draws attention to the fact that in France Romanticism began comparatively late and then did not last long. Wedged between a neoclassicism that would not die and the early stirrings of realism, naturalism, and modernism, French Romanticism functions as an important bridge between two totally different periods of literary history—but it is a remarkably short bridge.

Spain and Italy

Spanish Romanticism began even later: it is essentially a phenomenon of the 1830s and 1840s. It is true that through the mediation first of J. N. Böhl von Faber and then of the Barcelona periodical *El Europeo* (1823–4) the ideas of Schiller, Kant, and A. W. Schlegel found entry into absolutist Spain. Schlegel's enthusiastic endorsement of the Spanish drama of the *Siglo de oro* (the Golden Age of Spanish literature, which encompasses a great part of the sixteenth and most of the seventeenth centuries, up until the death of Calderón in 1681) as 'Romantic' found at first little favour with more liberal circles since they regarded the non-classical, organic forms of this kind of drama as too closely associated with the oppressive institutions of the crown and the Catholic Church.

Only after the death of King Ferdinand VII in 1833 can one register the advent of a 'liberal' Spanish Romanticism, much influenced by Hugo, but also inspired by the historical novels of Scott: 1834 was a particularly fertile year for historical dramas in the new 'Romantic' vein because it saw the productions of the Duque de Rivas's *Don Alvaro o La fuerza del sino*, Mariano José de Larra's *Macías*, and A. García Gutiérrez's *El trovador*. These plays tried to forge a genuine Spanish literature out of an imaginative re-creation of the national past, along lines that Alcalá Galiono had demanded in his famous preface to Rivas's long narrative poem *El moro expósito* (1834, *the* manifesto of Spanish Romanticism). But because the dramas were formally relatively open, in the older Spanish tradition, they did not constitute the decisive break with conventions achieved by French Romantic drama.

After only a few years a conservative reaction set in against the supposed excesses of Romanticism (the Catalan *La Religión* group, 1837–41) and a return to binding rules, both in matters of literature and religion, was called for (Juan E. Hartzenbusch, *Los amantes de Teruel*, 1837; Mesonero Romanos, *Escenas matritenses*, 1842; José Zorilla y Moral, *Don Juan Tenorio*, 1844). But in contrast to that reaction Spanish Romantic poetry found its uncontested climax in José de Espronceda, the 'Spanish Byron' (*El estudiante de Salamanca*, 1839/40; *El diablo mundo*, 1840), and in Gustavo Adolfo Bécquer (his most famous collection, *Rimas*, appeared posthumously in 1871). The radical and unconditional search for intensity in life in Espronceda and the wistful longing for a purer world in Bécquer describe two poles in the brief history of Spanish Romanticism that seem to mirror, on a subjective plane, the collective attempt to conjure up a better future, because evidently the present had not kept the promises of a glorious, golden past. Much more than in France Romanticism in Spain is primarily a negotiation of national identity, an imaginative reconstruction of historical continuities, of which some are rejected, others incorporated, so as to arrive at an idea of the nation that would be at once 'rooted', forward-looking, and viable.

In this aspect, the situation in Spain resembles that of Italy between the Napoleonic occupation and the *Risorgimento*. But in Italy the situation was further complicated by the fact that so much of Italy's cultural heritage was justifiably seen in (neo)classical terms. So it was all right for the Milan Romantics, who gathered around the progressive periodical *Il Conciliatore* (1818/19) and who regarded Giovanni Berchet's essay on Bürger's *Lenore* (1816) as their manifesto, to speak out against all rules and norms which were not in accordance with the 'spirit of the people', to look for truth in simple language and in the lessons of the past, and to style themselves as educators of their people. But the 'spirit of the nation' in a civilization as deeply steeped in classical antiquity as Italy was, of course, an aspect of neoclassicism; which is why the three leading Italian writers of the age—Ugo Foscolo, Giacomo Leopardi, and Alessandro

Manzoni—are often called, though this may seem a contradiction in terms, 'neoclassical Romantics'. And it certainly adds to the confusion that both Foscolo and Leopardi (*Discorso di un italiano intorno alla poesia romantica*, 1818) distanced themselves from Romanticism but are believed to display Romantic traits in their works (see Foscolo's *Werther*-like novel *Ultime lettere di Jacopo Ortis*, 1799, and his poem *Dei sepolcri*, 1807, as well as Leopardi's *Canti*, 1831), whereas Manzoni's Romanticism, deeply Catholic and patriotic, would probably count in other countries as religiously based restorative conservatism (cf. his monumental historical novel *I promessi sposi* (1825–7)).

In Italy even more than in Spain, the Romantics tried to revivify the legacy of an overpowering past for future use, although the best minds, like Leopardi, recognized that something was irretrievably lost, that one could not simply return, and that it was perhaps the obligation and burden of literature to acknowledge that loss and to mediate between the ideal of a naïve, unspoilt, harmonious state of things and the bleak reality of the here and now.

Poland and Russia

Polish Romanticism is said to begin in 1822, with the publication of Adam Mickiewicz's *Ballady i romanse*, and to end in 1849, with the deaths of Juliusz Słowacki, the poet and dramatist, and Frédéric Chopin, the famous composer. It is traditionally divided into two phases, the crucial dividing line being the year 1831, when the defeat of the Polish freedom fighters forced many Polish intellectuals and writers into exile.

Polish Romanticism is defined almost exclusively in terms of the fight for national independence. Following Kazimierz Brodzinski's treatise *O klasycznosci i romantycznosci* (1818), who had taken his cue from Herder, the Schlegels, and Madame de Staël, the Polish Romantics believed in a literature that should reflect the 'spirit of the nation' (see also Julian Ursyn Niemcewicz, *Spiewy historyczne*, 1816). Often in historical guise (Mickiewicz, *Konrad Wallenrod*, 1818, and—Poland's great national epic—*Pan Tadeusz*, 1834), they interpreted Poland's suppression and long history of suffering as analogous to the passion of Jesus Christ (Mickiewicz, *Dziady*, 1823–32). This idea—that oppression made the Polish people a chosen kind, whose world-historic and spiritual mission was to save mankind—was the core of what is called 'Polish messianism' (Zygmunt Krasinski, *Irydion*, 1836).

Nowhere in Europe did Romanticism, patriotism, and Catholic religiosity (with a strong dose of mysticism) form a stronger alliance than in Poland. Characteristically, Słowacki—whose rivalry with the towering figure of Mickiewicz is obvious both in his play *Kordian* (1833) and in his digressive long poem *Beniowski* (1841)—depicts Polish history in his unfinished magnum opus *Król Duch* (first part published in 1847) idealistically as a dialectical unfolding of a spiritual reality (Król Duch = King Spirit). Not hampered by the legacy of a classicist past, like Italy, nor dwarfed, like Spain, by the splendours of a *Siglo de oro*, Poland displays what is possibly the most unified, coherent of European Romanticisms.

Russian Romanticism begins with the restless activities of Wassili Shukovskij, who not only translated Schiller, Byron, and Scott, but whose ballad *Ludmilla* (1808) is the first Romantic poem of Russian literature, although it reminds one very strongly of Bürger's *Lenore*. In the early 1820s, especially after the quelling of the Decabrist revolt (1825), Russian literature becomes noticeably politicized ('Decabrist *Sturm und Drang*': Count Wjasemski, Konstantin Batjushkew, Konrat Rylejew, Wilhelm Küchlbecker). The poet is expected to interfere, Byron-like, in political struggles. But soon a rift occcurs between Westernizers and Slavophiles—an opposition that was to dominate a large part of the nineteenth century, and by no means in literature alone.

If one accepts that the meditative verse of Fjodor Tjuttchew was published relatively late (*Stichotvorenija*, 1854) and fully recognized only by the Russian symbolists at the turn of the century; if one admits further that poets like Delwig, Jasykow, and Jewgeni Baratynski (*Piry*, 1821; *E da*, 1824), who formed part of the Pushkin pleiade in the 1820s and 1830s, had little public response, then one is left with the question of whether, at least, the two most impressive and successful Russian poets of the nineteenth century—Alexander Pushkin and Michail Lermontov—can in some way be addressed as acknowledged, popular Romantics. The happy news is that indeed they can, because there is good reason to regard major works of these outstanding writers as Romantic: both Pushkin's novel in verse, *Evgenij Onegin* (1825–33), and Lermontov's *Geroj nasego vremeni* (*A Hero of Our Time*, 1840) are Byronesque epics, modelled on *Childe Harold's Pilgrimage* and *Don Juan*, ironic dissections of *Weltschmerz* and ennui attitudes, which are diagnosed as the *mal de siècle*. While both works point forward to the psychological and social novels of a later period, they also look back upon literary forerunners such as *Werther* or *René*. In ironically distancing themselves from their protagonists (a move not unknown in Byron), these works also mark the twilight of Romanticism: a frame of mind that knows it is an attitude can only take itself, at best, half-seriously.

By comparison, Russian Romanticism seems a fleeting phenomenon and unusually dependent upon foreign, especially German and English influences. But, as in France, it looks as if this young and vital literature can hardly wait to storm forward to the heights of a new, indigenous kind of prose fiction, as it is before long exemplified in the canonical works of Gogol, Goncharov, Turgenev, Tolstoi, and Dostojevskij, to say nothing of Chechov and Gorki.

Family likenesses and the unity of opposites

As our brief survey shows, the continental literary scene in the Romantic age is highly diversified. If we look at it in conjunction with the British scene, it is apparent that some characteristics are shared by some 'national' Romanticisms and other traits by others, while it would be very difficult to name a number of features shared by all. The picture that emerges is maybe best summed up by the concept of 'family likenesses', as developed by the Austrian philosopher Ludwig Wittgenstein in his *Philosophical Investigations* (1953). Some members of a family may have similar noses, others similar eyes, yet others similar ears and so on, but because of their family likenesses they are all recognizably members of a family although no member of that family need display *all* 'characteristic traits' in order to be identified as a member of said family. Neither is it necessary that every member of the family is directly linked by some particular likeness or other to all other members of the family—they are all interconnected by a 'net' of likenesses. It seems European Romanticism can be regarded as such a family.

Upon that basis, one could abstract and conceptualize further and argue, as indicated above, that even the apparent contradictions and seeming incompatibilities within European Romanticism have common roots in that they form diverging responses to the same set of cultural challenges: the fascination of the past (the Middle Ages in particular) as well as dreams of a utopia to come, the lure of the exotic as well as the cult of domesticity and the familiar, revolutionary cosmopolitanism as well as rampant nationalism, active political partisanship as well as cautious withdrawal from the political sphere—they all form possible answers to a unique historical situation in which, it seems, nothing can be taken for granted any more and in which a reaching out for new (or old) securities is the order of the day. The ideology of childhood innocence as well as the attractions of sin and satanism; the belief in common sense and reason as well as the contrary belief in the superior reasonableness of the emotions and the heart; the acknowledgement of the sublime in nature or human consciousness as well as the thrills and threats of the irrational, the supernatural, the Gothic, and the grotesque; and, lastly, the reversion to traditional established religion (the older the better) as well as the descent into existentialist despair—all of these categories bespeak a juncture at which the individual becomes (falteringly or enthusiastically) aware of his or her own range of possibilities. Finally, note the interest in folk tales and songs, fairy tales, legends, and myths coexisting with the propagation of a highly artificial and self-conscious 'language art', celebrating wit, satire, irony, the optimistic belief that it should be possible to revolutionize the world poetically alongside the pessimistic conviction that, since language can never express the absolute and the ideal, poetry can only draw attention to its inherent, unalterable insuffcencies: all these can be regarded as first manifestations of the insight that the relationships between language and mind, between sign and meaning, between literature and life, are by no means secure and stable but rather precarious, dynamic, and evolving—and therefore quintessential to man's changing place in the world, as an absolute opposition between subject and object can no longer be upheld.

In that sense, Romanticism is an ongoing, undeniably European project, whose very diversity is, paradoxical as it may sound, the hallmark of its unity: between them, the various European Romanticisms play out both the potential and the vicissitudes of modernity.

FURTHER READING

Bone, Drummond, 'The Question of a European Romanticism', in J. Beer (ed.), *Questioning Romanticism* (Baltimore and London: Johns Hopkins University Press, 1995), pp. 123–32. An original discussion of terminological problems.

Esterhammer, Angela (ed.), *Romantic Poetry* (Amsterdam and Philadelphia: Benjamins, 2002). Arguably the most intriguing and ambitious collection in the field, it contains first-class essays by international experts, comparing motives, genres, and poetics both in European and non-European literatures.

Furst, Lilian R., *Romanticism in Perspective: A Comparative Study of Aspects of the Romantic Movements in England, France and Germany* (London, Melbourne, and Toronto: Macmillan; New York: St Martin's Press, 1969). A classic monograph, rightly praised for its expertise and readability as well as for the depth of its readings; introduces 'family likeness' idea, but inconsistently falls back upon common denominators 'individualism', 'imagination', and 'feeling'.

——(ed.), *European Romanticism: Self-Definition* (London and New York: Methuen, 1980). An excellent small anthology of carefully selected passages from essays, letters, manifestos, and so on, which gives deep insight into the complexity of Romantic self-description; texts from outside Britain are given in the original and in English translation.

Porter, Roy, and Teich, Mikuláš (eds.), *Romanticism in National Context* (Cambridge: Cambridge University Press, 1988). In addition to essays on Wales, England, and Ireland (but not Scotland), this collection offers helpful essays on France, Germany, Spain, and Greece, and recommendable ones on Poland and Russia; there are also good introductions to the lesser known Romanticisms of Scandinavia, Switzerland, Hungary, and the Netherlands.

NOTES

1. Arthur O. Lovejoy, 'On The Discrimination of Romanticisms', *PMLA* 29 (1924), 229–53, repr. in M. H. Abrams (ed.), *English Romantic Poets: Modern Essays in Criticism*, 2nd edn. (Oxford: Oxford University Press, 1975), pp. 3–24, here p. 6.
2. Ibid. 8.
3. Ibid. 9.
4. René Wellek, 'The Concept of Romanticism in Literary History', *Comparative Literature*, 1 (1949), 1–23 and 147–72, repr. in René Wellek, *Concepts of Criticism* (New Haven: Yale University Press, 1963), pp. 128–98, here pp. 160–1.
5. Quoted in Malcolm Bradbury and James McFarlane (eds.), *Modernism 1890–1930* (Harmondsworth: Penguin, 1976), p. 19.
6. See Lilian R. Furst, *The Contours of European Romanticism* (London and Basingstoke: Macmillan, 1979), esp. pp. 56–73.

11 | Easts

Nigel Leask

'Stick to the East;—the oracle [Madame de Staël] told me it was the only poetical policy. The North, South, and West, have all been exhausted . . . the public are orientalizing, and pave the path for you.'[1] Thus Lord Byron to the Irish poet Tom Moore in May 1813, a year after he had achieved fame with the first two cantos of *Childe Harold's Pilgrimage*, based on his own Levantine Grand Tour of 1809–11. Byron's remarks give us insight into the workshop of Romantic orientalism, spiriting us behind the splendid façade to the nitty-gritty of poetic production. His canny exhortation 'stick to the East' suggests both the importance of oriental settings and materials for Romantic poets, as well as the sheer popular demand which stimulated them. Byron was the most accomplished orientalist poet of his generation: by 1813 he had completed *The Giaour*, the first of a series of *Turkish Tales* (*The Bride of Abydos, The Corsair, and The Siege of Corinth*). Stealing the laurels from Walter Scott, who achieved fame with a brilliant sequence of patriotic medieval romance poems, Byron's tales of exotic love and adventure quickly won him fame in the eyes of a readership growing weary of jingoism and Tory medievalism.

Byron's advice was not lost on Moore, whose Indo-Muslim poem *Lalla Rookh* was published in 1817. Moore received an enormous advance of 3,000 guineas from his publishers Longman, who later dubbed his poem 'the cream of the copyrights' because it had gone through twenty editions by 1841. (Byron's *Corsair* allegedly sold 10,000 copies on the first day of publication.) Byron and Moore's financial success provides a striking contrast with Robert Southey's *Thalaba the Destroyer* (1801) and *Curse of Kehama* (1810; see also the chapter on 'Epic'). Meticulously researched and (in formal terms) experimental poetic romances, these lacked popular appeal, but nevertheless exerted a powerful influence on Romantic long poems like Shelley's *Alastor* and *Prometheus Unbound* and Keats's *Endymion*. The cluster of poems to which I am referring here might be said to constitute a core canon of Romantic orientalism, although as we will see the orientalist *topos* also pervaded drama and prose fiction as well as poetry.

The great map of mankind

In 1777 Edmund Burke remarked that 'now the Great Map of Mankind is unrolld at once; and there is no state or gradation of barbarism, and no mode of refinement which we have not at the same instant under our View.'[2] Burke emphasizes the importance of (what today we would call) anthropology in constructing the moral science of the Enlightenment, in the older sense of 'mores', pertaining to human manners in general, and based largely upon the enormous body of travel literature generated from the second age of exploration. The 'great map' metaphor is also evident in the famous opening couplet of Dr Johnson's 'Vanity of Human Wishes': 'Let Observation with extensive View, | Survey Mankind, from China to Peru.'

Such tropes are premissed upon the notion of an all-seeing, imperial European eye with the power to command the rest of the world. In the eighteenth century, this was still largely a fantasy, but would become a reality by 1820, when imperial Britain alone ruled over 26 per cent of the world's population. But the eighteenth-century rise of what Mary Louise Pratt has termed European 'planetary consciousness', with its impulse to survey and 'civilize' the rest of the world, could also result in deep anxiety, a fear of being swamped by a plethora of alien cultures. Raymond Schwab links this to the 'dark sublime', suggesting that 'it was logically inevitable that a civilization believing itself unique would find itself drowned in the sum total of civilizations, just as personal boundaries would be swamped by over-flowing mobs and dislocations of the rational'.[3]

Orientalism: theory and history

Although literary orientalism was for long an obscure byway of eighteenth-century and Romantic studies, the publication in 1978 of Edward Said's *Orientalism* gave a new importance to the genre by connecting it with the rise of empire. Said argued that orientalism was a form of 'imaginative geography' conceived initially in the form of fantasy, and only subsequently as an academic 'science of the Orient' (however spurious its claims to scientific objectivity). Far from being merely an exotic literary *topos*, orientalism was 'a Western style for dominating, restructuring, and having authority over the Orient'. For Said, European poetic imaginings about the Orient (a deliberately vague, essentialized term, given its status as an ideological rather than geopolitical reality) tells us more about European than Asian culture, as the former 'set itself off against the Orient as a sort of surrogate and even underground self'. Most problematically, though, Said went further in arguing that 'every European, in what he could say about the Orient, was consequently a racist, an imperialist, and almost totally ethnocentric'.[4]

Critics have pointed out that Said falls into the trap of constructing 'the West' in exactly the same ahistorical, essentialist terms as Europe's 'Orient', the object of his critique. It would be truer to say that the 'Easts' of literary orientalism are as manifold, various, and historically contingent as the 'Wests' which produced them. Moreover, whilst Said is correct in mapping orientalism on to the historical rise of empire, he seriously overestimates the confidence and unity of purpose of European imperialists and writers, failing to register adequately the anxiety, not to mention the critical scruples, which often underwrite orientalist texts.[5] Nevertheless, at a time when literary critics were showing a new interest in historical contexts, Said's post-colonial revision of European cultural history permitted a reconsideration of those elements of the literary tradition (such as orientalism) which had been excluded precisely because they were linked to empire. The strengths as well as weaknesses of Said's book reveal the importance of a more nuanced understanding of the relationship between literature and history in our retrospective interpretation of Britain's imperial heritage.

For eighteenth-century Europeans, 'the Orient' comprised those non-Christian civilizations east of the Mediterranean which had progressed beyond the primitive stage of social development to the point of 'barbarism'. Fixed by tyrannical rulers and superstitious priests, such 'barbarous' societies seemed to be condemned to lag behind progressive, enlightened Europe. The enormous Asian landmass—of which Europe really comprises an outlying western promontory—was in the seventeenth and early eighteenth centuries largely controlled by three powerful land-based Islamic empires, still sufficiently strong to contain Europe's growing military and commercial power; the Ottoman, based in Turkey, the Savafid in Persia, and the Mughal in India. In contrast to Tokugawa Japan and the powerful late Ching Chinese empire (mainly closed to Western trade and influence), the Muslim empires formed part of the proto-capitalist world system, and by the eighteenth century had been frequently visited and described by European travellers, diplomats, and merchants. The eighteenth-century rise of European colonialism in Asia was largely a result of the internal crises in the Muslim empires rather than external pressure, although it permitted the swift maritime ascendancy of France, Britain, and Holland in the eastern Mediterranean and Indian Ocean.

By 1765 Britain controlled the Mughhal province of Bengal, and would thereafter rapidly annex territory around its commercial factories in Madras and Bombay, to the point (by Byron's death in 1824) when it exercised paramount power in India. The impeachment of Warren Hastings, Governor-General of Bengal, in 1786–94 drew public attention to British India, as did a succession of Indian travel books by the likes of William Hodges, Lord Valentia, and James Forbes. Given their numerical weakness and inexperience in ruling large non-European, non-Christian populations, the British East India Company depended upon the administrative and commercial infrastructures of its Mughal precursors. The Persian language spoken by the Mughals remained the official idiom of British India until 1835, encouraging an enthusiasm for Persian poetry which was a marked feature of British Romantic literature.

In other parts of Asia, the war against Napoleon saw British intervention in Egypt in 1799–1804 as well as the acquisition of an eastern Mediterranean empire, which explains the topicality of Byron's *Childe Harold* and *Turkish Tales*. Fears of French incursions in India led to intensive diplomatic negotiations with the Persian emperor, and the publication of a spate of travel books concerned with central Asia. Lord Macartney's embassy to the Chinese emperor Chien Lung in 1793–4 in a bid to win trading concessions from China was a spectacular failure, but travel books by Sir George Staunton and John Barrow (both members of the British delegation) created a new vogue for the largely unknown Chinese empire, stimulating amongst other works Coleridge's poetic evocation of the Tartar despot Kubla Khan, 'ancestor' of the current Manchu emperor.

Eighteenth-century orientalism and Sir William Jones

Since the publication of Galland's *Arabian Nights Entertainment* in 1704–12, Chinese, Arabian, Persian, Indian, and Abyssinian 'costume'[6] had been popular with European writers, who played on the demand for exotic and transgressive settings. Often such writing burlesqued oriental cultures themselves, but could also serve as vehicles for satire or moral critique of European manners. The diverse 'Easts' of my title are matched by widely divergent settings for eighteenth-century 'oriental tales', from Dr Johnson's 'Abyssinian' *Rasselas* (1759) and Frances Sheridan's 'Arabian' *History of Nourjahad* (1767) to Goldsmith's 'Chinese' *Citizen of the World* (1762) and William Beckford's 'Arabian' quest romance *Caliph Vathek* (1786). Henry Weber collected many of these works in his *Tales of the East* (1812), giving them new currency for the Romantic age. In general an earlier eighteenth-century fascination for China was replaced by Indian or Arabian settings in Romantic orientalism, symptomized by William Hazlitt's criticism of the millionaire Beckford's collection of tacky chinoiserie seen at Fonthill Abbey (see *Oxford Companion to the Romantic Age*, pp. 418–19).

None the less, orientalism was never able to lose the stigma of commercialism and cheap glamour. In his poem *Beppo*, Byron sardonically offered to 'sell you, mix'd with western sentimentalism, | Some samples of the finest Orientalism'. Desire and moral scruples merged in the fascination with oriental luxury and its commodification, both in Europe's mercantilist trade with the East, and in exotic literature consumed by metropolitan readers. Despite (or because of) their low generic standing, oriental tales played a major role in contesting the dominant neoclassicism and spearheading a Romance revival (alongside Gothic novels such as Horace Walpole's *Castle of Otranto*) against the fictional realism of Defoe, Richardson, and Fielding. Eighteenth-century literary historians such as Thomas Warton, Clara Reeve, and John and Laetitia Aikin went as far as to claim an oriental provenance for Romance prose narrative itself. Oriental tales might variously represent Asian culture as dominated by voluptuousness, cruelty, and the sexual tyranny of the harem (*Nourjahad*), or else as the sites of forbidden magic and wonders (*Vathek*), or stoic wisdom (*Rasselas*). Montesquieu's influential *Spirit of the Laws* (1748) attributed oriental despotism to torrid climate, but it is often forgotten that the same author's *Persian Letters* (1721) represented tyranny in the heart of modern Europe and revolution in the Persian harem, collapsing any stable 'climatic' distinction between torrid Persia and temperate Paris.

The 'Arabian Nights'—style eighteenth-century oriental tale was transformed by the scholarship of Sir William Jones and the Asiatic Society of Bengal which Jones co-founded at Calcutta in 1784, symptomatic of Britain's changing agency in India from trading company to colonial state. The publications of Jones, Charles Wilkins, H. T. Colebrooke, and other scholars, in *Asiatic Researches* and elsewhere, inaugurated an 'oriental renaissance' which had a profound influence on Romantic literature as well as philosophy, painting, and music. Jones's belief that 'Reason and Taste are the grand prerogatives of the European mind, while the Asiatics have soared to loftier heights in the sphere of Imagination'[7] inspired him to embark on a series of translations of Hindu, Persian, and Arabic works of literature, most famously Kalidasa's drama *Sakuntala*, published in 1790, which profoundly influenced European poetry from Shelley's *Alastor* to Goethe's *Faust*.

In his seminal *Essay on the Poetry of the Eastern Nations* of 1772, Jones praised the rhapsodic and expressive poetry of the Hindus and Persians, and recommended that study of oriental models might rejuvenate the tired neoclassicism of European literature: 'If the languages of the Eastern nations were studied in our great seminaries of learning . . . a new and ample field would be opened for speculation: . . . we should be furnished with a new set of images and similitudes; and a number of excellent compositions would be brought to light, which future scholars might explain, and future poets might imitate.'[8] Jones's remarks are a manifesto for Romantic orientalism, and scholars and poets were not slow to take up the challenge. In his influential essay *On the Gods of Greece, Italy and India* (1784) Jones built on his discovery of the common linguistic roots of Sanskrit and European languages by comparing the Hindu with the Graeco-Roman classical pantheon, concluding that the gods worshipped under different names were in fact identical. Ganesa of the Hindus was none other than Janus of the Romans; Ceres, Lakshmi, and Jupiter, none other than the Hindu triad, and so on. This work of mythographical syncretism had a powerful influence on poets of the next generation; Shelley for example exploited the mythographical analogy between Greek and Hindu deities in his orientalized lyrical drama *Prometheus Unbound*, and represented Prometheus' rebellion against the tyrannical Jupiter as a geopolitical reunification of the 'European' hero with his lover 'Asia'.

A more palpable attempt to combine Hindu and neoclassical sources is evident in Jones's *Hindu Hymns* published through the 1780s, which reworked the Pindaric ode popular in late eighteenth-century England with a Hindu rather than a Greek setting and mythological apparatus. The *Hymns* celebrated the rejuvenation of Hindu culture as a British initiative. Jones argued that, grotesque as they might seem, the fables and images of the Hindus constitute 'at this moment the prevailing religion of a most extensive and celebrated EMPIRE, and are devoutly believed by many millions, whose industry adds to the revenue of *Britain*'. Jones's message of benign imperialism, typical of the so-called 'orientalist' phase of British rule in India, is manifest in the closing lines of the Hymn to Lacshmi:

> Oh! bid the patient *Hindu* rise and live . . .
> Now, stretch'd o'er ocean's vast from happier isles,
> He sees the wand of empire, not the rod:
> Ah, may those beams, that western skies illume,
> Disperse th' unholy gloom!

Footnotes

The Indo-orientalism which Jones unleashed upon the late Enlightenment profoundly influenced the emerging nationalisms of Europe, particularly Germany. The German Romantic scholar Friedrich Schlegel, unconnected to Asia by any colonial ties, exclaimed, after intense study of Jones's work: 'Everything, absolutely everything, is of Indian origin!' The Indo-European 'Aryan' tradition provided German intellectuals with a more ancient, spiritual, and venerable heritage than the 'Frenchified' civilizations of the Mediterranean with their materialist and republican legacy. By the early years of the nineteenth century, the scholarly orientalism of Jones, Anquetil Du Perron, and Schlegel had helped transform European literature. An earlier vogue for decorative arabesques or chinoiserie had diversified and proliferated into a demand for specifically Egyptian, Ottoman, Mughal, and Hindu mythologies, narratives, and styles.

A new realism of orientalist description was called for, inaugurated by Reverend Samuel Henley's notes added to Beckford's novel *Vathek* (1786). Henley drew on the writings of Jones and other orientalist sources in order to add a sense of cultural *typicality* to a genre which had often (as in Johnson's *Rasselas*) preferred neoclassical *generality*. 'Surely for instance Vathek mistaking the tattered awnings and chintzes for large flowers—would be better expressed by *palampores* instead of *chintzes*', wrote Henley to Beckford in 1785. Palampores it would be, as a generalized and dated chinoiserie gave way to a more ethnographically informed, Middle Eastern 'costume'. Henley's notes to *Vathek* set the standard for subsequent oriental narrative poems by Southey, Byron, and Moore, contributing to the sense of 'authenticity' singled out by Byron: '[*Vathek*] bears such marks of originality, that those who have visited the East will find some difficulty in believing it to be more than a translation.' Writing of Moore's *Lalla Rookh* (unlike Byron, Moore had never visited the East) the Indian expert Colonel Wilks joked that it proved 'reading D'Herbelot is as good as riding on the back of a camel'. D'Herbelot's *Bibliotheque orientale*, 1697, was an encyclopaedic compendium of the Orient (itself translated from Ottoman sources), upon which Moore drew heavily in the poem's footnotes, one of the eighty or so orientalist works cited.

In similar vein, the new importance of footnotes is revealed in Elizabeth Hamilton's epistolary novel *Letters of a Hindoo Rajah* (1797), allegedly the work of a pious Hindu travelling in corrupt Georgian Britain. Hamilton's novel drew heavily upon the orientalist learning of the Asiatic Society (her late brother Charles had been a distinguished member) and was dedicated to its founder, Jones's patron Warren Hastings. Beyond its learned footnotes, the *Hindoo Rajah* was prefaced by a 'Dissertation on the History, Religion, and Manners of the Hindoos', one of the most notable contributions to oriental scholarship by a women writer of the period. In contrast to such works where orientalist research buttressed the claims of imperial power, the notes to Byron's *Childe Harold* punctured the gloomy *weltschmerz* of the verse, in order to cast British designs on Greece and the Ottoman world in a highly critical light.

By 1800, then, orientalism had been transformed from the status of an exotic mercantilist commodity—a token of oriental 'luxury'—into a form of knowledge which incorporated the iconography and mythology of Britain's Asiatic subjects into the nation's image repertoire, in precisely the manner demanded by William Jones. Take for example Robert Southey's *Curse of Kehama*, published in 1810 after a decade of laborious research in the orientalist archive. In Southey's elaborate romance Ladurlad, an Indian peasant yeoman, and his faithful daughter, Kailyal, struggle against the evil Rajah Kehama and the ghost of his murdered son Arvalan. Southey represented the triumph of the solid Indian peasant (buttressed by the values of 'British' moral virtue) against wicked Brahmin priests and 'asiatic despotism', at a time when British colonial rule sought to consolidate the landholding of the Indian peasants, or *ryots*, to safeguard the company's rent revenue.

In the poem's preface Southey apologized for the extravagance of Hindu mythology, later adding 'the spirit of the poem was Indian, but there was nothing Oriental in the style'. His invocation of Miltonic sublimity was, however, hardly sufficient to excuse the strangeness of the verse in the eyes of its readership. At one point, Southey added as a footnote a fifteen-page extract from the recently translated Sanskrit epic *Ramayana*, on the grounds that readers would be less disposed to condemn the fictions of Kehama as 'extravagant' when compared with this genuine article. The evangelical reviewer John Foster supported Southey's 'colonial' appropriation of Indian mythology, yet balked at the gross paganism which he read into the poem, comparing it with a fleet of East India Company ships returning triumphantly to Britain, their holds laden with 'gods of crockery, or some portion of that material with which the Lama of Thibet is reported to enrich the craving hands of his devotees [human excrement]'.[9] In contrast to Jones's *Hindoo Hymns*, the critics complained that *Kehama* glorified pagan religion and was simply inaccessible to the European imagination. Even the notes, which aimed to translate oriental sublimity into ethnographic knowledge, failed to provide a *cordon sanitaire* for Southey's mythological monsters.

Desire and quest romance

In *Practical Education*, Maria Edgeworth described how literary orientalism stimulated the colonial aspirations of young male readers, greedy to 'discover in the east the secret of Aladdin's wonderful lamp . . . [and] the treasures of Aboulcasem'. Negative eighteenth-century stereotypes of the 'nabob' (the British adventurer who returned from India laden with riches) gave way in the Romantic period to a more positive image, exemplified in Walter Scott's novel *Guy Mannering* (1815). Scott's eponymous hero employs his loot in restoring the ousted Bertram family to their feudal estate of Ellangowan. The orientalism of Scott's novel (including the 'internal orientalism' of the exotic gypsy soothsayer Meg Merrilies) upheld the values of Tory neo-feudalism at home whilst it supported the expansion of empire in the East. But such novels joined established orientalist fictions of the sort described by Edgeworth to create a *desire* for the East, fundamental to the education of young British empire builders.

Hence the frequent Romantic representation of the East as a sexually enticing, although sometimes dangerous, female, in the venerable tradition of Shakespeare's *Cleopatra*. While Eros was sidelined in Southey's more politically orientated quest romances *Thalaba* and *Kehama*, the oriental poems of Byron, Shelley, and Moore focused on the romance plot, which could produce several different narrative resolutions. In Byron's 'serial' *Turkish Tales*, erotic fascination for oriental women on the part of the 'Western' heroes, like the Giaour, the half-Greek Selim (in the *Bride of Abydos*) or Conrad the Corsair, bears tragic fruit, as the hero fails to liberate his love object or else 'turns Turk', while the idealized female dies or disappears. In these complex fables of empire, desire for the Orient is both all-consuming and fatal to classical civic humanist values. So Byron's 'anxieties of empire' paradoxically fed the orientalist vogue at the same moment as he condemned British imperial conquest.

Tom Moore's 'Veiled Prophet of Khorassan' (the first poem of *Lalla Rookh*) exposed the Thalaba-style oriental revolutionary as the false prophet Mokanna, whose doctrines proved fatal to the lovers Azim and Zelika. Hinda, heroine of 'The Fire-Worshippers', is daughter of the commander of the Arab invaders who have driven the Fire-Worshippers out of their native Persia, and her lover Hafed is the leader of the 'anti-colonial' resistance. Predictably, this tale of transgressive love (partly based on the plot of Byron's *Bride of Abydos*) ends tragically, although Moore was able to imply an allegorical reference to the suppressed condition of his native Ireland, revealing the complex interplay between ethnic identities within Britain, and in her empire at large. The tragic weight of these two Byronic poems is balanced by the light-hearted arabesque quality of the other two tales, 'Paradise and the Peri' and 'The Light of the Haram', and the happy resolution of the love between the Princess and Feramorz, Prince of Bucharia, in the prose frame narrative. Although critics censured *Lalla Rookh's* 'excessive finery' and 'the extravagance of excessive wealth', Moore was praised for having avoided the manner of Southey's 'unsaleables', by mixing oriental matter with

'Western sentimentalism'. Jeffrey believed that it was 'the poetry of rational, honourable, considerate, and humane Europe' filtered off from 'the childishness, cruelty, and profligacy of Asia'.

Shelley's version of the orientalist quest romance is distinct on account of his avoidance of footnotes and cultural typicality. In accordance with his belief that every expression in a poem ought to be 'an intelligible picture', Shelley transferred the 'typical' oriental settings of Southey or Byron or Moore into dream landscapes where the drama of cultural encounter was troped as a psychological quest for the (feminized) 'epispsychidion' or 'soul within a soul'. In *Alastor* (1815), the *Revolt of Islam* (1817), and *Prometheus Unbound* (1820) Shelley drew inspiration from his scholarly reading of Sir William Jones as well as works of popular orientalist fiction like Lady Morgan's novel *The Missionary* (1811), on which he wrote, in the same year, 'since I have read this book I have read no other—but I have thought strangely'. Morgan's tale of the love between Hilarion, a Portuguese missionary in India, and the Brahamachira priestess 'Luxima' (Lakshmi) allegorizes the mutual desire of cultural encounter: 'silently gazing, in wonder, upon each other, they stood finely opposed, the noblest specimens of the human species, as it appears in the most opposite regions of the earth; she, like the East, lovely and luxurious, he, like the West, lofty and commanding'.[10] Anticipating the Byron/Moore plot resolution, Luxima is killed by Catholic bigots and the grieving missionary retires to a cave in Kashmir to venerate her memory, true to Morgan's liberal opposition to evangelical activity in British India.

In *Alastor*, Shelley deploys quest narrative in describing his protagonist's journey East in search of enlightenment, or the 'thrilling secrets of the birth of time'. His version of the erotic encounter in the Vale of Kashmir builds upon the encounter between Hilarion and Luxima, although it is clearly a dream vision. Moreover, Shelley's description of the visionary maid at lines 153–4 decontextualizes its source by representing the maid as a prophetess of secular republican, rather than orientalist, enlightenment. Keats's 1818 narrative poem *Endymion*, written in response to Shelley's *Alastor*, reworks the quest romance structure and bows to the orientalist fashion by affording a crucial role to the 'Indian Maid' in the poem's final book. In Shelley's *Revolt of Islam*, a similarly narcissistic relationship between the visionary seeker and the 'veiled maid' is worked out in the revolutionary partnership of Laon and Cythna, heroes of Hellenic enlightenment who overthrow the oriental despotism of the 'Golden City' before they themselves fall victim to the inevitable counter-revolution. In the complex, syncretic fabric of *Prometheus Unbound*, Shelley returns to the quest romance in orientalizing the setting of Aeschylus' tragedy, now located in the Hindu Kush, and naming the Caucasian Prometheus' lover 'Asia'. This time the lovers triumph, and Prometheus and Asia are reunited in the cave after the fall of Jupiter, the tyrannical deity of imperialism and dogmatic religion. (Jupiter's drinking of the 'Daedal cup' [III. 1. 26–32] and subsequent dethroning are based on *Kehama*'s draining of the 'Amreeta Cup' at the end of Southey's Hindu epic.)

Oriental infections

The gradual decline of Jones-style imaginative sympathy for Asian cultures can be gauged by a new, ethnocentric 'anglicism' in the governance of British India: a 'Pious Clause' inserted into the 1813 India Act, which legitimized the activities of missionaries and challenged indigenous religious practices; the publication in 1817 of James Mill's utilitarian *History of British India* with its denunciation of Sir William Jones and the whole orientalist programme; and Thomas Macaulay's 1835 *Minute on Indian Education*, with its notorious declaration 'a single shelf of a good European library was worth the whole native literature of India and Arabia'. Increasingly the exotic lure of the Orient was converted into the duty of the 'white man's burden', as in the evangelical Charles Grant's insistence in 1792 'we cannot now renounce them [the Indians] without guilt, though we may also contract great guilt in the government of them'.

Guilt and terror had long coexisted with erotic and burlesque accounts of the East in earlier orientalist literature and discourse, as in Burke's figures of 'dark sublimity' during the impeachment of Warren Hastings, or the Gothic cruelty of Charlotte Dacre's oriental villain in her 1806 novel *Zofloya, or the Moor*, but by 1820 they struck the dominant note. In a best-selling travel book published that year, Giovanni Belzoni describing the grisly immolation which revenged his plundering of the tombs and pyramids of Egypt: 'I sunk . . . among the broken mummies, with a crash of bones, rags, and wooden cases . . . I could not pass without putting my face in contact with that of some decayed Egyptian.'[11] Belzoni's Egyptian Exhibition, held in Piccadilly in 1821, presented a Gothic simulacrum of the terrors of the tombs of Thebes and Karnac. It created a sensation among the metropolitan public, who increasingly viewed the Orient as an exhibition of Gothic sublimity. But the 1820s and 1830s also saw the publication of James Morier's comic picaresque novel *Hajji Bhabah of Ispahan* (1824), in which the Oriental was presented as a wily buffoon, as well as melancholy, picturesque images of harem life and female abjection in the popular verse of Felicia Hemans, Letitia Landon, and Emily Roberts.

Orientalism's most symptomatic expression in late Romanticism was, however, that of Thomas De Quincey, 'the English Opium-Eater'. John Barrell has described how De Quincey's 'life was terrorised by the fear of an unending and interlinking chain of infections from the East, which threatened to enter his system and to overthrow it, leaving him visibly and permanently compromised and orientalised'.[12] In his popular *Confessions of an English Opium-Eater* (1821), De Quincey expressed his horror of a composite 'East' which inverted the desire and fascination of Jones and earlier orientalists. He quite literally ingested the Orient so that the European self became a stranger to itself, transformed by the *pharmakon* of opium, at once cure and poison. (Opium was also the staple commodity of British colonial commerce in East Asia.) In one episode, De Quincey attempts to poison a Malay who has called at his cottage in Grasmere (and whom he fears is a sexual threat to his young servant Barbara) with 'the gift' of an enormous lump of raw opium 'enough to kill three dragoons and their horses'. Yet the Malay will not die, and returns to haunt his dreams, betokening a nightmarish condensation of the Orient as a 'dark sublime': 'in China, over and above what it has in common with the rest of southern Asia, I am terrified by the modes of life, by the manners, and the barrier of utter abhorrence, and want of sympathy . . . I could sooner live with lunatics, or brute animals.' De Quincey's racialist paranoia elaborates Belzoni's fantasy of immolation in the mummy-pits of Qurna: 'I was buried, for a thousand years, in stone coffins, with mummies and sphynxes, in narrow chambers at the heart of eternal pyramids. I was kissed, with cancerous kisses, by crocodiles; and laid, confounded with all unutterable slimy things, amongst reeds and Nilotic mud.'[13] Like the opium-eater, Europe had become dependent upon—literally *addicted* to—the oriental other, just as its economy was dependent upon the material expansion of its huge empire: to De Quincey, Europe seemed to have forfeited both cultural and ethical autonomy.

The legacy of Romantic orientalism to the Victorian age (also the age of high imperialism) was an image of the East split between racial mockery and guilt-ridden anxiety. Elements of both persist in the novels of Philip Meadows Taylor (*Confessions of a Thug*, 1839) and Rudyard Kipling (*Kim*, 1901) as well as in much of the neo-Romantic orientalist poetry produced throughout the nineteenth century. De Quinceyan fear of infection is also evident in the fables of 'internalized orientalism' produced by popular writers like Conan Doyle and Wilkie Collins, racialist anxieties about the pollution and degeneration of 'advanced' Europe by its Asian and African colonies. The moral imperative of the white man's burden is turned upon its head and figured as a dreadful infection from which Europe would never recover.

FURTHER READING

Barrell, John, *The Infection of Thomas De Quincey: A Psychopathology of Imperialism* (New Haven and London: Yale University Press, 1991). Gripping psychoanalytically inflected study of De Quincey's psychoses and British imperialism in the East.

Bayly, C. A., *Imperial Meridian: The British Empire and the World, 1780–1830* (London and New York: Longman, 1989). A revisionist 'global history' of Britain's second empire in relation to the extra-European empires.

Fulford, Tim, and Kitson, Peter (eds.), *Romanticism and Colonialism: Writing and Empire, 1780–1830* (Cambridge: Cambridge University Press, 1998). Wide-ranging collection of essays covering many aspects of Romantic orientalism.

Leask, Nigel, *British Romantic Writers and the East: Anxieties of Empire* (Cambridge: Cambridge University Press, 1992). A historically contextualized reading of orientalism in Byron, Shelley, and De Quincey, drawing on post-colonial theory.

—— *Curiosity and the Aesthetics of Travel Writing 1770–1840: From an Antique Land* (Oxford: Oxford University Press, 2002). A study of Romantic-period travel writing in Egypt, India, and Mexico in relation to the aesthetics of 'curiosity'.

Majeed, Javed, *Ungoverned Imaginings: James Mill's History of British India and Orientalism* (Oxford: Oxford University Press, 1992). A brilliant historical reading of the intellectual contexts of Mill's critique of orientalism, with chapters on Sir William Jones, Tom Moore, and Robert Southey.

Makdisi, Saree, *Romantic Imperialism: Universal Empire and the Culture of Modernity* (Cambridge: Cambridge University Press, 1998). A sophisticated theoretical reading of orientalism and empire in Blake, Scott, Wordsworth, Shelley, Byron, and others.

Marshall, P. J., and Williams, Glyndwr, *The Great Map of Mankind: British Perceptions of the World in the Age of Enlightenment* (London: J. M. Dent, 1982). Still the most exhaustive account of British attitudes to the wider world in the long eighteenth century.

Richardson, Alan, and Hofkosh, Sonia, *Romanticism, Race, and Imperial Culture, 1780–1834* (Bloomington, Ind.: Indiana University Press, 1996). A stimulating collection of essays on Romantic orientalism and related topics.

Said, Edward, *Orientalism* (1998; Harmondsworth: Penguin, 1985). Seminal critique of the relationship of European discourse on the Orient in relation to imperial power.

Schwab, Raymond, *The Oriental Renaissance: Europe's Rediscovery of India and the East, 1680–1880* (New York: Columbia University Press, 1984). Encyclopaedic study of European orientalism in the Romantic period as the fulfilment of a 'global humanism'.

NOTES

1. *Byron's Letters and Journals*, ed. Leslie Marchand, 12 vols. (London: John Murray, 1973–82), iii. 101.
2. *Correspondence of Edmund Burke*, ed. Thomas W. Copeland *et al.* 10 vols. (Cambridge and Chicago: Cambridge University Press and University of Chicago Press, 1958–78), iii. 350–1.
3. Raymond Schwab, *The Oriental Renaissance: Europe's Rediscovery of it India and the East, 1680–1880* (New York: Columbia University Press, 1984), p. 18
4. Edward Said, *Orientalism* (1978; Harmondsworth: Penguin, 1985), pp. 3, 206.
5. See my *British Romantic Writers and the East: Anxieties of Empire* (Cambridge: Cambridge University Press, 1992).
6. On 'costume' see my 'Wandering through Eblis: Absorption and Containment in Romantic Exoticism', in Tim Fulford and Peter Kitson (eds.), *Romanticism and Colonialism: Writing and Empire, 1780–1830* (Cambridge: Cambridge University Press, 1998), pp. 175–82.
7. *Works of Sir William Jones*, ed. Lady Jones, 6 vols. (London, 1799), i. 11.
8. *Sir William Jones: Selected Poetical and Prose Works*, ed. Michael Franklin (Cardiff: University of Wales Press, 1995), p. 336.
9. Lionel Madden (ed.), *Southey: The Critical Heritage* (London and Boston: Routledge, 1972), p. 144.
10. *The Missionary, an Indian Tale*, 2nd edn., 3 vols. (London, 1811), i. 156.
11. *Narrative of the Operations . . . within the Pyramids, Temples, Tombs*, 2nd edn. (London: John Murray, 1821), p. 157.
12. *The Infection of Thomas De Quincey* (New Haven and London: Yale University Press, 1991), p. 15.
13. *Confessions of an English Opium-Eater, and Other Writings*, ed. Grevel Lindop (Oxford: Oxford University Press, 1985), p. 73.

12 | Americas

Susan Manning

By the mid-eighteenth century, all of the 'settled' Americas were subject to one of the great European imperial powers: England, Spain, Portugal, and France. Transplanted religion and language, legal, political, and education systems, were the base on which their colonial cultures developed. 'Romanticism' in the Americas is usually associated with emancipation from colonial status; but dates alone demonstrate that British and American Romanticism will not simply equate: for Britain we tend to think of the period 1789 to 1832; Romanticism in the United States followed the Anglo-American War of 1812–14 which crystallized national feeling and gave a strong impetus to the development of an indigenous literature between 1835 and 1865; Canadians distinguish between francophone and anglophone dominions, and, prior to Confederation in 1867, neither literature was markedly radical or reflective. Latin America underwent a series of national revolutionary struggles marking a transition from European colonies to independent republics between about 1820 and 1870 (only anglophone works from, and about, South America are considered here). So in this international, transatlantic context what emerges is less a Romantic period than a sprawling century of Romanticisms.

Romanticism was in every sense a transatlantic cultural movement. Romantic writing *in* the Americas cannot be separated from America as Europe's imaginary space for thinking 'Romantically'. In historical reality and in imagination, the Americas have been associated with transformations: new beginnings, egalitarian ideas about humanity, struggles for freedom, engagements with nature, the realization and the defeat of empire, exploration, travel, and self-discovery. 'American Literature' as a self-consciously conceived subject has been inseparable from the aesthetics of Romanticism and the ideology of nationalism: speaking instead of 'Americas' and 'Romanticisms', we can begin to think more fluidly, not of essential features and peculiar characteristics, but of transformations and processes, of shared preoccupations given local inflection. Experience from new perspectives required new forms, new voices; imported genres and conventions underwent metamorphosis. The satirist Oscar Wilde was not far wrong in declaring the newness of America to be its oldest tradition.

The promise of the new

Some forms presented themselves as immediately appropriate. In the early eighteenth century, Alexander Pope considered writing American eclogues—short pastoral poems often in dialogue, modelled on Virgil, these were believed to represent human society in a golden age in harmony with nature. The Americas abounded in the topographical 'prospects' of a progressive Whig vision; the landscape promised plenty, both literal and figurative. It became an article of national faith for American writers in the post-revolutionary period that Europe's tired poetic forms might be refreshed by a trans-atlantic voyage, and the classical relation between form and content renewed. Late eighteenth-century questions about the authenticity of literary 'voice' became the American issue of how to write 'Americanly', when the linguistic tools available came freighted with centuries of British experience. In *Canada: A Descriptive Poem* (1806), for example, Cornwall Bayley's diction followed British poetic convention: an Indian wears '*snow-sandals*' and a '*crown* of Feathers'. In the nationalistic years following the war of 1812–14, the United States showed markedly less tolerance for its inherited linguistic medium. Noah Webster and others experimented with orthographic ways of distinguishing 'American' from 'English'; as Margaret Fuller put it, 'Books which imitate or represent the thoughts and life of Europe do not constitute an American literature . . . an original idea must animate this nation and fresh currents of life must call into life fresh thoughts along its shores.'[1] Writers of the 'new-found land' aligned themselves ideologically with Wordsworth's and Coleridge's celebration of the tran-scendent poetic value of originality. The difficulty was to enact rather than declaring literary difference.

British Romanticism in America

In the absence of international copyright protection, American reading publics consumed the same literature as Europe, often more cheaply. The work of Burns, Coleridge, Wordsworth, Byron, and Scott was enthusiastically received, adapted, and absorbed throughout the Americas. Moments of transcendence are, as one might expect, frequent in a new landscape characterized by sublimity; the scenic grandeur encountered by travellers in the Americas readily answered to eighteenth-century aesthetic categories: the romantic hero of the first Canadian epistolary novel, Frances Brooke's *History of Emily Montague* (1769), exclaims 'you see here not only the *beautiful* which it has in common with Europe, but the *great sublime* to an amazing degree'.[2] The only transformation insisted on here was of scale; it was hardly surprising that Niagara Falls was a favoured location for spiritual experience:

Voluminous and ceaseless still, forever swift descend
Thy waters, in their headlong course—then, turning, heaven-ward wend;
Now, disenthralled, their essence hath its spirit shape resumed,
Bright, bodiless, and pure, its flight to yon empyrean plumed![3]

The stiff couplets of the Canadian John Breakenridge (1820–54) express an orthodox view of the Falls (and by extension North America) as a gateway to transcendence on the grandest scale imaginable. Combining a Burkean sublime with a Wordsworthian epiphany, Margaret Fuller would write of losing separate consciousness as she contemplated Niagara. From the 'blest calm' of Charles Sangster's *Sonnets in the Orillia Woods* (1859) to Charles Roberts's 'The Skater' (1901), a Wordsworthian therapeutics of sublimity also emerges through personal voices encountering North American landscapes.

The poetry of William Cullen Bryant (1794–1878) was also infused with Wordsworthian vocabulary, forms, and sentiments; the opening of 'Thanatopsis' invokes 'Tintern Abbey' with an insistence that seems perilously close to pastiche: 'To him who in the love of Nature holds | Communion with her visible forms, she speaks . . .'[4] But the poem that a few lines later invokes the 'still voice' of Nature as balm to a mind in tumult, goes on to represent human life as overwhelmed, absorbed, and mastered by its depersonalizing, irrevocable power. Nature was simply *too large*; it overwhelmed, and its benignity could never be assured; transcendence would occur rather differently in America.

Romantic exploration

Before the land could be settled, it had to be surveyed; a notable number of American writers, including Henry David Thoreau, were surveyors by profession. Before it could be surveyed, it had to be imagined. Keats, at home in Hampstead, perched 'stout Cortez' his surrogate surveyor, 'Silent, upon a peak, in Darien' ('On First Looking into Chapman's Homer'). Travel accounts mythologized space and distance in the Americas, attempting to find correlatives for the new hemisphere. South America was of particular picturesque, exotic, and antiquarian interest: the fabled Aztec and Inca lands of Mexico were Eldorado, a land that combined the exoticism of the tropics with the natural riches (ripe for exploitation) of the American dream. 'In the new world,' wrote Alexander von Humboldt—perhaps the greatest travel writer of the Romantic age, and a man of revolutionary sympathies—'man and his productions . . . disappear in the midst of a wild and outsize nature.'[5] South America offered a unique combination of majestic ruined civilizations and the infinite potential of spectacular scenery and enormous empty spaces, peopled only by Byronic noble outcasts and Romantic free spirits. Byron himself, in libertarian mood, called his yacht *Bolívar*, after the great Spanish-American revolutionary whom Humboldt had met in Paris in 1804. Frances Inglis, born in Scotland that same year, became the wife of the Spanish ambassador to

Mexico; as Madame Calderón de la Barca, her observations of the New World showed the impress of Romantic racial theories popularized in works like Germaine de Staël's *De la littérature* (1800) that differentiated the 'peoples of the North' (industrious, orderly, melancholy, and creative) from those of 'the South' (indolent, passionate, and imitative), but managed to complicate national stereotypes through the imposition of a composite, hybrid narrative perspective that combined elements of 'Scots', 'American', and 'Spanish' sensibilities. Her *Life in Mexico* (1843) drew on Walter Scott's use of picturesque narrative conventions (like his narrators, she was fond of invoking scenic parallels with the paintings of Salvator Rosa), and on the descriptive techniques of Robert Southey's epic poem *Madoc* (1805), from which she quotes directly.

The Americas remained a source of fascination and mystery to Europe right into the nineteenth century, requiring of their interpreters new ways to describe the encounter. Generic boundaries between travel narratives (often cast in epistolary form), emigrants' guides, and radical political tracts became mutually permeable, entangling documentary and hortatory impulses. If the Americas did not have the familiar-strange allure for travellers of the exotic Orient, or the ancient classical destinations of Greece and Rome, their attraction for Romantic writers lay instead in their imagined combination of unformed possibility and radical purity. Conveniently eliding its travelling native inhabitants, who did not build palaces or erect monuments, they emerged as resource-rich but culturally barren, a topographical blank slate on which European Enlightenment ideas could be put into practice.

American utopias

Before France, America was the location for revolutions and new beginnings; the English radical Tom Paine sailed to Philadelphia in 1776, to announce the impending transformation: 'We have it in our power to begin the world over again.'[6] After the revolution, many more dreamed of a future in free America than travelled to accomplish it. 'On the Prospect of Establishing a Pantisocracy in America' written (probably by Coleridge) in 1794, expresses both the disillusion of the anti-Jacobin years and the transferred idealism of young radicals, in a vision of 'kindred minds' hastening to enjoy 'Content and Bliss on Transatlantic shore'. Southey and Coleridge's scheme for settling on the Susquehanna in Pennsylvania remained a fantasy; others attempted to realize utopian possibilities in the American landscape. Their vision was informed by a series of French travellers including the Marquis de Chastellux and Chateaubriand, who conveyed information and opinion about conditions in countries so materially involved with French imperial interests.

Amongst British radical sympathizers was Frances Wright who, fired by enthusiasm for liberty, travelled to New York where her play *Altorf* about Switzerland's battle for independence from Austria (previously rejected for the London stage) was performed and praised by Jefferson; she became a close friend of the Marquis de Lafayette, French hero of the American Revolutionary war. Her *Views of Society and Manners in America* (1821) was full of enthusiasm for her adopted country, but Wright was deeply troubled by slavery's blot on American egalitarian ideals. Having met the socialist reformer and mill owner Robert Owen (who later established the New Lanark industrial village on the model of his utopian community New Harmony in Indiana), she started the first of a projected series of enlightened communities in the American South where slaves would work to pay for their own freedom. It collapsed within four years; Wright, convinced of the economic hopelessness of the case, transferred her energies to other libertarian causes.

Anglophone Canadian writing, by contrast, was strongly anti-revolutionary and generically unadventurous: British North America was largely populated by colonists who had successfully resisted French domination, reinforced by loyalist refugees from the American Revolutionary war (at this time the adjective 'Canadian' referred to the indigenous population). Oliver Goldsmith (1794–1861), great-nephew of the English poet, offered an optimistic counterpart to his more famous namesake's *Deserted Village* (1770): *The Rising Village* is pervaded by echoes of Pope's 'Windsor Forest', Thomson's 'Summer', and other Augustan poems that tell of peace, plenty, and a contented workforce in a pastoral landscape untouched by revolution, as the poetry is unaffected by the momentous formal and attitudinal upheavals which had transformed British and European writing between 1770 and 1825. *The Rising Village* is a utopian vision, an emigration tract, and an accomplished poetic idyll. It is also a fable of historical progress: this peaceful scene was once a gloomy, forested landscape inhabited by 'wandering savages and beast of prey'. But these 'rising' views are darkened by a cautionary fable which may be a political allegory of Britain's 'abandonment' of Nova Scotia following the Napoleonic wars, an interpretation that gives an altogether sharper slant to the mercantile idyll.

In the 1830s Louisiana sheltered republican dissidents fleeing counter-revolutionary turmoil in post-Napoleonic France; their settlement consolidated New Orleans's community of intellectuals whose radicalism opposed anti-democratic legislation in the southern state. The French émigré Milo Mower established *Le Libéral*, a newspaper dedicated to defending the rights of the slave population and disenfranchised free people of colour. Immigrants from the French-speaking Caribbean island of San Domingue, notably Victor Séjour, settled in Paris and published stories and plays on the abuses of slavery. Victor Hugo's *Bug Jurgal* (1818) had already drawn French attention to the slave revolution in San Domingue (in which Séjour's father had been involved), while Alphonse de Lamartine commemorated a Haitian uprising in his play *Toussaint Louverture* (1842). Toussaint, the son of a slave who became governor of Haiti, resisted Napoleon's edict to reinstate slavery on the island, and was imprisoned in Paris. In 1802, Wordsworth addressed a sonnet to him as a source of inspiration to lovers of freedom.

In New England, the issue of female emancipation became inextricable from discussions of slavery. Sarah Willis Parton (1811–72), who had her own newspaper column and (as 'Fanny Fern') was one of the best-paid American authors of the first half of the century, wrote powerfully about the position of women in a society notionally dedicated to equality. The association was also made in London by William Blake, who engraved plates for J. G. Jacobs's description of slavery in South America, and created the allegorical *Visions of the Daughters of Albion* (1793), where the rape and subjection of the 'soft American plains' of Oothoon by the imperial ambitions of Bromion unites the oppression of women and slaves. *Albion* is, however, a deeply ambiguous vision of utopia, as was Nathaniel Hawthorne's fiction about the Brook Farm community in which he briefly participated in 1841. *The Blithedale Romance* (1852) casts a sceptical look at the idyll of pastoral simplicity which has haunted American imagination as an alternative to progress and profit. An ironic parallel between the 'Transcendental' community and the original Puritan enterprise runs through the book. The narrator Coverdale (whose very name suggests his inability to give a straightforward account of events) is passive by nature, and rendered more so by illness; he becomes a detached observer like Washington Irving's Rip Van Winkle with no real 'business' in life. In fact, the whole affair seems only a masquerade, repeatedly described in theatrical metaphors, and involving a melodramatic subplot of sham mesmerism. The uncertainty that suffuses the community is the consequence of the metamorphosis of the clear, if harsh, Puritanism that impelled early New England, into the subjective vision of Transcendentalism.

Transcendentalism and its antagonists

De Staël's *De L'Allemagne* had an enormous impact in New England intellectual circles: both Fuller and Longfellow were prompted by their reading to learn German in order to discover more about the new 'transcendent' philosophy for themselves. Transcendentalism was the name given to the German-inflected manifestation of Romanticism in the writing of a small group around Emerson in Concord, Massachusetts, with whom Hawthorne associated loosely in the 1840s and 1850s. In 1829 Coleridge's *Aids to Reflection* was republished in America with a lengthy philosophical essay by James Marsh; four years later, F. H. Hedge wrote on Coleridge and new German thought for the *Christian Examiner*. These, with Thomas Carlyle's early essays, catalysed Emerson's rethinking of the foundations of spiritual experience, the relationship of self and world, and the nature of consciousness. The result was the essay *Nature*, published in 1836, the great foundational text not only of Romanticism in America, but of the ideology of American *exceptionalism*—its special destiny—expressed in literary terms, and America's riposte to the long histories and social complexities of European states: here was a spiritualized landscape which had power to redeem centuries of sinful civilization.

Nature's defiant presentism demands 'an original relation to the universe'.[7] The thought is immediately re-expressed in personal terms; questions about the world become matters of self-enquiry: 'Every man's condition is a solution in hieroglyphic to those inquiries he would put' (36). In transcendentalist writing, natural sight is over-written by inner vision; this is a Romantic insight, reimagined through the strong religious structures of American Calvinism. But in the new landscape there is no burden of Original Sin. Emerson democratizes this election to universal availability. Sceptical of the claims of revealed religion, he had in 1832 resigned his position in the Unitarian ministry, and spent the remainder of his life as a lecturer and essayist, apostle of the new.

Nature was the outcome of a personal epiphany that occurred as he scrutinized the marvellous intricacy of natural specimens whose structures seemed to hint at the unity of all life. Look hard enough at, into, matter, Emerson writes, and the experience is visionary, the distinction between 'Nature' and 'the Soul' dissolves with a thought—as long (and this is the vital, Wordsworthian, condition), as perception enjoys the simplicity and clarity of the child 'whose inward and outward senses are still truly adjusted to each other; who has retained the spirit of infancy even into the era of manhood'. At this point in his writing, it appears that Emerson's solution to the dualism between mind and nature that haunted Western thought was to deny the reality of nature. British Romanticism, even in its most 'German' exponent, Coleridge, never took this step (which is arguably based on a misreading of Kant and Schelling). Emerson's dissolution of the material is an act of American aggression, in which language and expression, no longer defined by their labelling relationship to external things, become symbols of spirit. His essays replace American linguistic and verbal dependency on Europe by a fantasy of self-sufficiency able to make the constitution of matter reflect the structure of the mind. It takes the form of an imagined ideal language in which words and things (as in a prelapsarian world) equate directly, a newly spiritualized imperial vision. He—it is, with Emerson, definitely 'he'—who controls language controls the world. The most indicative Shakespeare play for the American Romantics was not (as it was for Coleridge, or Lamb) *Hamlet*, but the scene-shifting, world-dissolving vision of *The Tempest*, with its artist-magician Prospero who conjures a world into being and, like the Emersonian poet, dispels it again to the realms of vision.

Fuller (who married an Italian count and sent letters from Italy for the *New York Tribune*, and whose first book translated *Conversations with Goethe*) was unusual in her active engagement with European culture: transcendentalists tended to stay at home, finding ample new worlds within. Scholars have become alert to the symbiosis between walking, radicalism, and poetry for British Romantic writers; in American writing this Romantic activity was ideologically always westwards, away from Europe and towards the frontier; it covered spiritual rather than land-bound miles. Thoreau's posthumously published essay 'Walking' offers a geography of spiritual freedom; the symbolic movement westwards, pedantically enacted. Though a great walker, Thoreau did not travel far or gladly: 'What I got by going to Canada was a cold,' he observed sourly of his only venture outside the United States.[8] The antecedents of both Thoreau's insistence on seeing for himself and Emerson's revolutionary manifesto lay with Coleridge and Kant and, behind them, with Plato and schools of Idealist thought. This New World was the location where not only politics, history, and language might be begun again, but the very conditions of being renewed, through the acts of seeing and thinking for oneself. Pragmatism, which half a century later took shape as the most important indigenously American philosophy, extended the implications of Emerson's moments of vision to deny any truth or origin outside experience itself. In seeing and encountering, the perceiver makes himself and the world separate identities. From the essentially religious insight of transcendental vision emerged a philosophy firmly grounded in the circumstantial. 'Transformation' is again at the heart of the issue: the particular and the universal are modalities of one another.

This was the (not altogether independent) insight of Whitman, the greatest Romantic poet of the American republic. His *Song of Myself* (1855), a work of *Prelude*-like ambition, projects the egotistical sublime across a canvas as large and confident as the United States of which the self is a synecdoche:

> I celebrate myself, and sing myself,
> And what I assume you shall assume,
> For every atom belonging to me as good as belongs to you.[9]

Whitman's transcendent self of 1855 is earthier, sexier, and more demanding than Emerson's or Wordsworth's; less concerned with 'Universal Being,' more with particular than absolute affirmations. It is urban and rural, rowdy rather than contemplative. This 'Turbulent, fleshy, sensual, eating, drinking and breeding' self is 'No sentimentalist, no stander above men and women or apart from them'. Evil, and sin, have only hazy, bewildered, negative places in the cosmic visions of both Emerson and Whitman; for those one has to look to their reclusive contemporary Emily Dickinson, whose poetry meditates obsessively and self-reflexively on the conditions of vision. Her fractured lyrics of the terrorized imagination fantasize concealment and revelation: 'Creation' itself is a conspiracy, 'a mighty Crack— | To make me visible—' | and personal alienation threatens at every turn.[10]

New World Gothic

The brave New World contained some very dark corners. 'One need not be a Chamber—to be haunted' one of Dickinson's poems (670) begins, typically locating terror in the soul rather than the world. Praising the 'blackness, ten times black' of Nathaniel Hawthorne's short stories in 1850, Herman Melville more aptly characterized his own work.[11] This 'blackness' was figuratively and literally embodied in two great blots on the libertarian conscience of democratic America. In one form or another slavery and Indian genocide haunt the most enlightened narratives of the post-revolutionary United States. They mark some of the earliest fiction of the new nation, which borrows European Gothic modes that conceal and reveal these dark secrets at the heart of Enlightenment. Charles Brockden Brown (1771–1810) was a philosophic and political radical, a follower of William Godwin. He was also a patriot, who intended a series of moral and improving narratives illustrating the social progress of Enlightenment in America. But his novels are highly ambiguous psychological thrillers that throw the whole notion of Enlightenment, and indeed of 'truth', into question in an American setting. *Wieland; or, The Transformation* (1798), *Edgar Huntly*, and *Ormond* are nightmares of immigration; they dramatize what may happen to 'Enlightenment' when it is translated to an American setting. Brown shows it to be quite literally 'transformed'—and not for the better. The Wieland family are of German extraction; their self-created environment in Pennsylvania is a microcosm of European Enlightenment: sociable sentiments, classical principles, the arts as elegant but strictly rational adornments to industrious activity. Their idyll is shattered by unexplained, disembodied impersonations of the protagonists' voices; nothing in their system can account for this: if the evidence of vision is contradicted by the evidence of hearing, which should be believed? How may a true American voice be distinguished from a counterfeit?

In *The Declaration of Independence*, Thomas Jefferson had brought America, textually speaking, into being with the confident announcement that 'We hold these truths to be self-evident . . .' By 1798 Brockden Brown was asking what a self-evident truth might be, and how we should know it from a false one. Just as how should we tell a 'true' or authentic person from an imposter. As a fictional exploration of the propositions of the *Declaration, Wieland* brings sharply into question just how many of its 'self-evident' axioms are workable or even plausible when put inside people's heads and played out in social practice rather than laid down as theoretical principles. The 'transformation' involved in reproducing a voice or an idea in a new context potentially undermines the whole notion of authenticity—and the authority by which this may be judged. *Wieland* anticipates a whole strain of subsequent American writing that concerns itself with forgery, counterfeiting, and the problematics of authoritative evidence in works such as Melville's 'Bartleby,' 'Benito Cereno', and *The Confidence-Man: His Masquerade*.

Similar ideals of unity and singleness inform Edgar Allan Poe's writing, with equally catastrophic disturbances; but—deeply antagonistic to transcendental vagueness and tutored by careful study of Germanic stories of doubling and self-division in *Blackwood's Magazine*—he drew attention to the perfectly conscious and mechanical construction of these as literary 'effect'. Tales like 'William Wilson', 'The Fall of the House of Usher', and 'Ligeia' focus around the struggle between division and unity: two beings seek blindly to join, which can only be achieved in death. The cannibalistic ego, seeking autonomy, invades the self of the other. Destroying it, consciousness finds its own annihilation; idealism and scepticism cancel out. Poe's narrators operate from restricted locations which emphasize their dissociation from 'normal' experience: dungeons, tombs, locked rooms curtained to exclude natural light. History and the reality of external things are rejected, as narrative unfolds into self-negation. In Poe's quasi-metaphysical *Eureka*, 'Life' itself is characterized as unnatural division: unity is a state of non-being, both pre- and post-Creation, before and after the extension of the created work. It is perfection, but it is also annihilation.

As narrative contexts are dismantled and reconstructed in disorientating ways, so the Romantic ego quavers. When all the layers are stripped off and rearranged, does a heart or soul remain undisturbed at the centre, or are the layers themselves identity, constantly liable to dissociate? Repeatedly—and again the influence of the *Blackwood's* tales is apparent—Poe's writing charts fragmented, disordered states of perception. Because the narrator tries to account rationally for strange effects, a reader is led, temporarily, to assume the narrator's perspective on the horrors of the scene. The language ceases to articulate content and the standing of its speaker and becomes an infinitely manipulable, self-reinventing mask of surfaces: American, and modern. The dystopian vision of American Romanticism is as intransigent as its utopian counterpart; a hoaxing strain in Poe's writing expresses the gullibility of the reading public with a spurious display of reasoning power.

Encountering others

Beyond the realms of Gothic fantasy, documentary travel accounts supplied material for imaginative and sentimental engagement with native Americans. Felicia Hemans, for example, based her poem 'Indian Woman's Death Song' (1828) on an *Expedition to the Sources of St Peter's River*. Her epigraph from James Fenimore Cooper's *The Prairie* (published the previous year) indicated her close engagement with American writing and gives this Wordsworthian lyrical ballad of desertion a complex transatlantic voice in the Indian's elevated diction borrowed from the fabricated Scottish epic *Poems of Ossian*. Native Americans appear in writing of and from the Americas either in elegaic mode, as noble, often solitary, representatives of a race destined to extinction by the march of civilization; or as symbolic projections of fear and savagery. Susannah Moodie, a British emigrant to Canada, declared 'the Indian is one of Nature's gentlemen—he never says or does a rude or vulgar thing. The vicious, uneducated barbarians who form the surplus of over-populous European countries, are far behind the wild man in delicacy of feeling or natural courtesy.'[12] This kind of native embodies the melancholy implicit in the 'Manifest Destiny' of America. Cooper's Indians supplied cultural density and nostalgia for a disappearing way of life in novels of national evolution and consolidation of cultures modelled on Scott's romances—with three significant differences. Firstly, Cooper was an anti-monarchical democrat committed to the American republican experiment; he despised Scott's Tory sympathies and sentimental Jacobitism. Secondly, unlike Scott's attempts to capture 'real' Scottish manners and original characters (albeit in a picturesque and sentimental mode), Cooper's Indians are not 'originals'; their function is entirely mythic and symbolic. Uncas in *The Last of the Mohicans* (1826) speaks like an Ossianic warrior; 'good' Indians are pitted against 'bad', in figurative—though highly dramatic—wars on which the future of the American continent will depend. Bad Indians are demonic, crazed beings who appear first in the novels of Brockden Brown, as one amongst several types of dangerous 'others' who invade national, rational, and emotional territories with their disordering tendencies, transforming enlightened novels of ideas into melodramas of outraged sensibilities.

The relationship between plot resolution and historical progress is the third significant difference between Cooper's tales of nation formation and those of Scott. In Scott's novels both are achieved by racial intermarriage, while Cooper's protagonist Leatherstocking is tangential to a progressively residual romance plot, and never marries; racial mixing is viewed with horror. Only once, in *Mohicans*, does it appear a possibility, in the attraction between the 'dark' heroine Cora and the good Indian Uncas; both die, leaving her 'fair' half-sister to marry the novel's young white soldier-hero. Racial guilt was often personified in Indians or Black savages who lurk at the margins of stories. Some believed Indians to be one of the lost tribes of Israel: in *The Prairie*, their doom is duplicated by Cooper's plains-wandering family of pariahs led by Ichabod Bush, a figure of the Old Testament patriarch who recurs as a specifically American version of the Gothic, Byronic Wandering Jew more fully developed in the paired protagonists Ishmael and Ahab in Herman Melville's *Moby-Dick* (1852).

History and romance

The Sketch-Book of Geoffrey Crayon, Gent. (1819–20) contained 'The Legend of Sleepy Hollow', discovered among the papers of 'Diedrich Knickerbocker', fictitious Dutch historian of Washington Irving's earlier successful *A History of New York, from the Beginning of the Dutch Dynasty to the Present Day* (1809). A 'Postscript' that offers an oral genealogy for the tale's transmission complicates its authenticity, and Burns's *Tam O'Shanter* and Bürger's 'The Wild Huntsman' are clear literary sources. Ichabod Crane supplied the qualities for the caricature Yankee; the tale celebrates a wishful triumph of peace, plenty, and indolence over the acquisitive ethos of the new American republic. 'Sleepy Hollow', like its companion piece 'Rip Van Winkle', was an exercise in national myth-making; it naturalized European folk tale in a rural American setting to produce a story of identity in transformation. Rip, wandering in the Appalachian mountains, sleeps through the American Revolution and awakens twenty years later to find a new regime in place. The Revolutionary war has been won against England as he slept, and he returns not to a Dutch colonial village, but the bustling world of the new American republic. Amazed to find himself an old man with a flowing beard, Rip is further alarmed to see his double, the vision of his earlier self, in a son grown to adulthood during his absence. It causes him to doubt his identity: 'I'm not myself—I'm somebody else—I'm changed, and I can't tell what's my name, or who I am!'[13] For a moment, it seems as though he will be cast out as a fraud or a spy, but on recounting his strange experience, Rip is welcomed back into the community as a harmless teller of tales.

In 1833 Rufus Choate delivered an address entitled 'The Importance of Illustrating New England History by a Series of Romances like the Waverley Novels'; imitations of Scott's novels appropriated the romance model as a theoretical and ideological distinction for a new 'kind' of literature. The idea that 'romance', loftier and more like epic than the novel, was the distinct and appropriate form for American fiction remains powerful in critical orthodoxy. The most famous French Canadian example was Philippe Aubert de Gaspé's *Les Anciens Canadiens* (1863), a romantic adventure liberally sprinkled with descriptions of *Québecois* customs and folklore, that openly challenges Scotland's 'monopoly of witches and wizards'.[14] It includes an inset 'supernatural' tale after the manner of Scott's *Redgauntlet*; like Burns's Tam or Irving's Rip, its protagonist undergoes a metamorphic experience which calls his identity into question. Gaspé's novel was associated with the patriotic Quebec Literary Movement which during the 1860s celebrated the local peculiarities of French-Canadian tradition, in self-consciously mannerist prose. A more typical example was Henri-Raymond Casgrain's *Légendes canadiennes* (1861), which drew on Scott's model equally clearly but with less irony.

The great nineteenth-century histories of the Americas created a cast of heroic pioneers and idealists involved in epic enterprises. If figures like the doomed French leader La Salle were Byronic, the methodology and structure of these dramatized confrontations of 'old' cultures with the 'new' forces that will inevitably supplant them derived directly from Scott. Coleridge had described the 'great theme' of the Waverley novels as 'the contest between the two great moving Principles of social Humanity—religious adherence to the Past and the Ancient, the Desire and the admiration of Permanence, on the one hand; and the Passion for increase of Knowledge, . . . the mighty Instincts of *Progression* and *Free-agency*, on the other.'[15] This was the story, too, told (with a changing cast of characters and backdrops that spanned the Americas) by George Bancroft's *History of the United States*, William Hickling Prescott's *Conquest of Mexico*, and Francis Parkman's *Montcalm and Wolfe*. These historians were in no doubt that their destiny was protestant, Teutonic, and Anglo-Saxon, and that the freedom of America lay in defeating forces of reaction and superstition, personified equally (though differently) by native Americans and Roman Catholic Spaniards or Frenchmen. Their Romanticism was thoroughly Germanic: admirers of Goethe and Schiller, they were also—particularly Bancroft—attached to Kantian philosophy and German academicism.

American Romanticism, then, looked eastwards and faced west in equal measure. Melville's Redburn retraced his father's pilgrimage to Liverpool, guidebook in hand, but found everything changed; he must make his own way in this transformed world. A decade later, Hawthorne's *The Marble Faun* of 1860 (subtitled, like *Wieland*, 'Transformation') marked American Romanticism's re-encounter with Europe to inaugurate a new subgenre, the 'International Novel'; in another seven years Canadian Confederation would precipitate a further wave of North American Romantic transformations of genre and language in the New World.

FURTHER READING

American Poetry: The Nineteenth Century, 2 vols. (New York: The Library of America, 1993). An essential collection of nineteenth-century poetry in the United States.

Bercovitch, Sacvan (ed) *The Cambridge History of American Literature, ii. Prose Writing 1820–1865* (Cambridge: Cambridge University Press, 1995). A detailed and broad history of American literature in the period from many perspectives; extensive suggestions for further reading.

Buell, Lawrence, *Literary Transcendentalism: Style and Vision in the American Renaissance* (Ithaca, NY: Cornell University Press, 1973). An excellent survey of the formation and criticism of American transcendentalism.

Daymond, Douglas, and Monkman, Leslie (eds.), *Literature in Canada*, 2 vols. (Toronto: Gage Publishing, 1978). A wide-ranging anthology of Canadian literature from first contact through to early post-colonial writing.

Emerson, Ralph Waldo, 'Nature', in *Emerson's Prose and Poetry*, ed. Joel Porte and Saundra Morris (New York: W. W. Norton, 2001), pp. 27–55. A foundational text in American Romanticism and the transcendental literary movement.

Fernandez-Armesto, Felipe, *The Americas: The History of a Hemisphere* (London: Weidenfeld and Nicholson, 2003). A modern history of the Americas as a whole; an important starting place for understanding the interrelated cultural development of the continents.

Glickman, Susan, *The Picturesque and the Sublime: A Poetics of the Canadian Landscape* (Montreal and Kingston: McGill-Queens University Press, 1998). Challenges traditional theories about Canadian literature and asserts the importance of Romanticism in the formation of a national literary style.

Jozef, Bella, trans. Carol Tully, 'Romanticism', in *Encyclopedia of Latin American Literature*, ed. Verity Smith (London and Chicago: Fitzroy Dearborn Publishers, 1997), pp. 726–8. Useful survey of Romanticism in Latin American literature as an aesthetic inspiration and response to political and social independence from Europe; a good starting-point with further reading.

Levin, David, *History as Romantic Art: Bancroft, Prescott, Motley, and Parkman* (Stanford, Calif.: Stanford University Press, 1959). An influential argument for the importance of travel writing and historical scholarship on the development of Romanticism in North America.

Tanner, Tony, *Scenes of Nature, Signs of Men* (Cambridge: Cambridge University Press, 1987). Classic collection of essays including 'Notes for a comparison between American and European Romanticism'.

NOTES

1. Margaret Fuller, 'American Literature', in *Papers on Literature and Art* (New York: Wiley and Putnam, 1846), ii. 298.

2. Frances Brooke, *The History of Emily Montague* (1769), ed. Mary Jane Edwards (Ottawa: Carleton University Press, 1985), pp. 5–6.

3. Quoted in Douglas Daymond and Leslie Monkman (eds.), *Literature in Canada*, 2 vols. (Toronto: Gage Publishing Ltd., 1978).

4. William Cullen Bryant, 'Thanatopsis', in *American Poetry: The Nineteenth Century*, 2 vols. (New York: Library of America, 1993), i. 122.

5. Alexander von Humboldt, *Personal Narrative*, trans. Jason Wilson (Harmondsworth: Penguin, 1995), p. 12.

6. *Common Sense* (1776), ed. Isaac Kramnick (Harmondsworth: Penguin, 1976), p. 120.

7. Ralph Waldo Emerson, 'Nature', in *Emerson's Prose and Poetry*, ed. Joel Porte and Saundra Morris (New York: W. W. Norton, 2001), p. 27.

8. Henry David Thoreau, 'A Yankee in Canada', *The Writings of David Henry Thoreau*, (New York: AMS Press, 1968), v. 3.

9. Walt Whitman, 'Song of Myself', in *Leaves of Grass* (1855), ed. Malcolm Cowley (Harmondsworth: Penguin, 1976), p. 25.

10. Poem 891, in *Emily Dickinson: The Complete Poems* (London: Faber and Faber, 1975), p. 422.

11. Herman Melville, 'Hawthorne and His Mosses' (1850), in *The Norton Anthology of American Literature*, 6th edn., vol. B. *1820–1865* (New York: W. W. Norton, 2003), p. 2295.

12. Susanna Moodie, *Roughing it in the Bush* (1852), ed. Carl Ballstadt (Ottawa: Carleton University Press, 1990), pp. 20–1.

13. Washington Irving, *The Sketch-Book of Geoffrey Crayon, Gent.*, ed. Susan Manning (Oxford: Oxford University Press, 1996), p. 45.

14. Philippe Aubert de Gaspé, *The Canadians of Old*, trans. Charles Roberts (1890), in Douglas Daymond and Leslie Monkman (eds.), *Literature in Canada* (Toronto: Gage Publishing, 1978), i. 90.

15. Samuel Taylor Coleridge, 'Letter to Thomas Allsop 8th April 1820', in *Samuel Taylor Coleridge: Selected Letters*, ed. H. J. Jackson (Oxford: Oxford University Press, 1988), p. 219.

Part II

Reading Romanticism

13 | New Historicism

Kenneth R. Johnston

A method of literary interpretation called 'New Historicism' is, at the present moment, the dominant procedure for studying British Romantic literature in the Anglo-American academy. Indeed, its practice is so pervasive that its *hegemony* is being protested by scholars who feel they might be penalized if they write in any other way. The present volume itself is a product of the impetus given to Romantic studies by the New Historicism, especially in its representation of authors who would not have appeared in such a volume a generation ago, most of whom have been rediscovered by New Historicist imperatives.

This is not to say that no other kinds of criticism are being written. Yet even Romantic criticism that is not in the New Historicist vein often proceeds today by referring to it, either antagonistically or apologetically, as what historicist philosophers like Michel Foucault or Louis Althusser would call the 'dominant ideological formation' among current literary critical methods. Of course, there have always been intellectual trends in the methods of literary study, just as there are fashionably favoured subjects and experimental methods in the natural sciences. But the current default predominance of New Historicist assumptions and procedures in the academic field of British Romantic literature and culture is noteworthy for additional reasons.

First, the recency of its appearance and rapidity of its spread: essentially, the last twenty years. Second, the fact that its methods and goals have been relatively little theorized by its practitioners (though more so by its opponents), whose procedures are so diverse that it is hard to deduce a coherent theory from them. And thirdly, the fact that this hegemony is so pronounced within the field of British Romantic studies. There are New Historicists in all fields of literary study nowadays, but in none has it assumed the dominant position it holds in the field of Romanticism—which suggests that there may be a special affinity between historicism and Romanticism.

All this being the case, we cannot explain 'how to do New Historicist criticism' without first trying to understand what *historicism* is (old and new), what problems it tries to solve (and what other problems it creates in doing so), and, of course, whence it arose historically, in both the long run and the short term. It is abundantly clear that New Historicism means studying literature in relation to its historical contexts, but a wealth of possibilities and problems lie buried in the innocuous phrase, 'in relation to'.

Definitions, origins, and problems

A first definition of historicism is a theory that 'all social and cultural phenomena, all categories, truth, and values [are] relative and historically determined, and . . . [can] be understood only by examining their historical context, in complete detachment from present-day attitudes', and that historians must therefore 'study each period without imposing any personal or absolute value system' (*Oxford English Dictionary*, 1989). But another definition is 'the belief that historical change occurs in accordance with laws, so that the course of history may be predicted but cannot be altered by human will', and that 'history is determined by immutable laws and not by human agency' (*Webster's Unabridged Dictionary*, 1987). Already we can feel a tension between immutable laws and human agency: all phenomena are culturally determined, but by immutable laws or by contingent human beings? And the stress on the behaviour required of historians suggests that human agency and attitudes do have a tendency to interfere with strictly law-governed behaviour. Could anyone do research and writing completely insulated from the time in which he or she is working? By extension, this problem seems to give rise to a third definition: 'a profound *or excessive* respect for historical institutions, as laws or traditions' (italics added). This suggests that the project of historicism has been dogged by its own pretensions from the outset.

To anticipate: we can say that most current Romantic New Historicists do presume that all texts, literary or otherwise, are culturally determined, and that these determinations most often come from the actions of other texts upon the primary texts in question. Immutable 'laws' do not enter very actively into current criticism, except in the very broadest way (for example, the increase in commercial activity in eighteenth-century England) which of course is far from being an insignificant way.

The words 'histori*cism*' and 'romanti*cism*' were both first widely used in the early years of the nineteenth century in Germany and in England. After the decimation of Germanic territories in the post-revolutionary Napoleonic wars (see chapter on 'The historical context'), many German historians set about trying to establish their land's historical integrity, 'Germany' being then only a loose confederation of thirty-nine states, not unified in its modern form until 1871 (see chapter on 'Europe'). Hence these historians began their researches with a *purpose*, although their idealized goal was a history without prior interpretations, only 'what really happened', as Leopold von Ranke repeatedly stated his aim. Rigorous scientific rules of evidence and interpretation were marshalled to produce 'results' of a definite ideological tendency.

In this foundational episode of historicism, we see an eighteenth-century philosophical ideal—a belief in the rational progress of all mankind (though usually limited to European civilization in practice)—giving way to a new nineteenth-century national or political 'law' of *origins*, technically applicable to any people anywhere, but implicitly intended to justify the existence of this or that European nation.

Marxism was the strongest version of historicism to emerge out of this post-revolutionary Germanic milieu. Karl Marx, rejecting the nationalistic pretensions of his compatriots—which he witheringly dismissed as 'The German Ideology'—elaborated a vision of an economic, class-defined (not national/political) progress of world history: the rise of the proletarian industrial working class and its eventual triumph over the bourgeois class of capitalists (who had already supplanted the aristocrats of feudalism), leading to a final withering away of the state and the advent of a classless society.

Not all currently practising Romantic New Historicists are Marxists, but many of them are explicitly critical of illiberal phenomena in the Romantic past—slavery, or the condition of women, for example. In addition, many also see themselves as activists in larger progressive movements for the liberalization of contemporary society—in post-colonial studies, for example, or in raising the level of social consciousness in what they see as a class-biased aestheticism—mere 'art appreciation'—in much teaching of literature in modern universities.

Some critics of historicism see such intellectual activism as a kind of 'presentism' in which scholars import their own values anachronistically into arguments about the past. This can be true, when contemporary political possibilities are applied unreflectively into past disputes. But on the methodological level, the sophisticated historicist recognizes and indeed welcomes such involvements with the past as being, in any case, unavoidable. Acknowledging the presence of the investigating observer is as important to a well-informed historicism as it is to contemporary anthropology or nuclear physics: as the critic Marjorie Levinson puts it, in one of her typically pithy statements, 'We are the ones who, by putting the past to a certain use, put it into a certain order.'[1]

It has even been argued (most extensively by James Chandler in *England in 1819: The Politics of Literary Culture and the Case of Romantic Historicism*), that the major Romantic writers were *essentially* historicist—a hypothesis that is given weight by the closely contemporaneous first appearances of the two terms. Wordsworth said that every great writer must help to create the *taste* by which he could be understood; in much contemporary New Historicist Romantic scholarship, Romantic writers are regarded as creating the *history* by which they must be understood.

The characteristics of current New Historicism

Probably the most useful way to understand the difference that New Historicist criticism has tried to make in the past twenty years is to appreciate its methodological suspicion of older assumptions about 'background' and 'foreground' in literary history. Until very recently, any Romantic poem, like Wordsworth's 'Lines written . . . above Tintern Abbey', for example, has stood, front and centre, in the foreground of Romantic literary history. In the background is almost everything else you could know about it:

where Wordsworth was in 1798 when he wrote it, where he had been in 1793 ('Five years have passed . . .'), who was with him on his trips up the Wye valley, what was going on there at the time(s), and so on.

The New Historicist reaction to this comfortable distinction between background and foreground is twofold. First, it points out that the distinction *privileges* the poem, giving it a special status that will distort what we think about it, even before we have begun studying it in earnest. Second, it asserts that privileging the poem effectively cuts it off from the very 'backgrounds' that are being evoked to help explain it, or that it establishes a tacit (i.e. silently assumed) cause/effect relation between background and foreground that needs to be examined.

Thus most contemporary New Historicist criticism jettisons the old background/ foreground distinction in favour of the widest possible field of textual objects, denominated 'culture'. In this field, Wordsworth's poem, Wordsworth himself (who cannot be assumed to be a psychological unity), the political history of the 1790s, the economic history of the Wye valley (the charcoal industry there, glanced at in the poem's 'wreaths of smoke'), and anything else that appears in whatever picture the historian is drawing acts and reacts with everything else in it. Of course, the frame of this picture also keeps expanding, and we soon run into one of the commonest complaints about New Historicist methods: where do they stop? How do we know when to stop? What is our warrant for stopping anywhere?

These complaints are real, both in experience ('I've got to finish my paper in two days!') and in theory (on what basis would we rule anything out of the picture?). But let's acknowledge two advantages of the method first.

One, it makes the poem a living actor in its times. For example, 'Tintern Abbey' is apparently not a political poem, but by opting so strenuously for 'Nature' over society it does raise questions about human social life: is it really as bad as the speaker suggests? And we know that fundamental questions about human life-in-society were being raised almost everywhere in Europe during the revolutionary era in which the poem was composed. Secondly, the rejection of conventional notions about background and foreground illustrates how the two extremes of historicism with which we began tend to collapse into each other. The 'conservative' view says it wants to regard only the facts, without interpretation, so even its historicism could be called 'new' in the research scenario just described: the smoke is there in the poem, and we know from other records that it was also there in the valley, so we have to take it into account, somehow.

Another characteristic of New Historicist criticism is its reliance on the telling anecdote or coincidence to open up larger tracts of history, though this strategy has been used more in early modern studies. For example, Wordsworth landed at Calais on 13 July 1790, at the beginning of his summer walking tour of France and Switzerland. On the same day Helen Maria Williams, the best-selling poet of Sensibility, landed in Dieppe on her way to Paris, where she gained her greatest fame as the author of *Letters from France*. This appeared in six volumes in the mid-1790s, and became England's most popular source of information about the progress of the revolution. The next year, in the autumn of 1791, Wordsworth himself headed for Paris, carrying a letter of introduction to Williams written by Charlotte Smith, the popular liberal novelist and Sensibility poet. Then, on 13 July 1793, the revolutionary Jean-Paul Marat was murdered in his bathtub by Charlotte Corday. And 13 July 1798 is the date Wordsworth put as the last words in the title of his 'Lines written . . . a few miles above Tintern Abbey'. Can we make anything of this collection of coincidences and near-misses, fleshed out by other textual, biographical, and historical parallels? Several New Historicist critics have tried to do so, with interesting results.

But to what historical arguments are such anecdotes attached? What is the ground or warrant for connecting them? The telling anecdote is not really telling until it is attached to some larger explanation, or system of explanations. Similarly, collapsing a text's foreground and background may be interesting, but it is not really significant until we understand on what plausible terms the two grounds can be made to negotiate with each other.

The question of whether the ruined Cistercian abbey at Tintern is present or absent in Wordsworth's poem is a good example of this historicizing problem. Some New Historicists, notably Marjorie Levinson, have made much of the abbey, its history, its organization, and its communal ethos, as contrasted to the Protestant, individualist assumptions which Wordsworth brought to it. Opponents of this line of argument have pointed out that the abbey is not in the poem, which Wordsworth's title clearly sets 'a few miles above' it. But textual formalists cannot have it both ways: clearly 'Tintern Abbey' is there in the title—unless we want to take the dubious position that words in a poem's title are not a legitimate part of its text. Hence the abbey is there textually but not descriptively, and much of the argument here depends on how one negotiates the difference. For example, how might the presence/absence of the abbey affect our interpretation of the devotional rhetoric of the poem's closing lines?

This challenge, of negotiating plausibly between published text and historical evidence, is pertinent to almost all New Historicist writing. An even stronger challenge is presented by its frequent recourse to deconstructive arguments. Deconstruction is a philosophical concept that posits the priority of the written or textual word to spoken or so-called 'natural' language, giving rise to its slogan that there is 'nothing outside the text', that all our knowledge is textual. Setting aside the large philosophic arguments engendered by this claim, the most specific use of deconstruction in literary criticism lies in its observation that the objective *reference* of all words (especially the figurative language common to literature) tends to break down under close formal analysis. The terms of any metaphor, not just of bad ones, will inevitably become 'mixed', and therefore ultimately undecidable.

Language in 'Tintern Abbey' can be made permeable to different meanings under the pressure of such analysis: not only its religious and philosophical discourse, but also its landscape descriptions, its physiological language, and, perhaps most surprisingly, its romantic and erotic phrases. For example: 'one who sought the thing he loved', 'coarser pleasures', 'haunted me like a passion', 'an appetite: a feeling and a love', 'aching joys', 'dizzy raptures', 'the language of my former heart', 'my former pleasures', 'the shooting lights of thy wild eyes', 'never did betray the heart that loved her', 'these wild ecstasies', 'warmer love', and others. The traditional critic will say that these are all 'just' metaphors or similes, and that we 'know' they simply *refer* to Wordsworth's picturesque appreciation of landscape and to his brotherly affection for his sister Dorothy. But the deconstructionist critic asks, 'how can you be so sure?' And the historicist critic adds, 'could this pervasive pattern of language have something to do with the fact that Wordsworth, when he "first came among these hills" in 1793, had just left his lover Annette Vallon and their baby Caroline in France and was seeking ways to help them?' And so the interpretive argument is engaged.

The two most important frameworks for historicist explanations of all such kinds of evidence in Romantic studies today are those of Marx and Foucault, and, of the two, Foucault's is now the most common. Marx's historicism has a linear tendency, in its desire to gauge a text's contribution to the larger economic progression Marx envisioned. All cultural texts are by definition (for Marx) part of society's super-structure of consciousness, which rests on, and is formed by, its base of economic production and reproduction. So a text's or author's intention is interpreted according to which class interests it seems to assume or defend, the struggle between social classes being, for Marx, the real matter of history.

Wordsworth's 'oversight' (to use Levinson's term) of the busy charcoal industry around Tintern thus could be, through its very oblique presence in the poem ('wreaths of smoke'), a kind of hint that he wishes to ignore the economic industrial realities of his time and place. Such a suggestion becomes more pointed if we interpret his speculation about the smoke's likely source ('some uncertain notice, as might seem, | Of vagrant dwellers in the houseless woods', ll. 20–1) as his way of *not* acknowledging what every visitor to the abbey knew, that it was inhabited by vagrants and beggars of the meanest sort, whose number had been notably increased by the economic disloca-tions of the unpopular 'Ministers' war' against republican France. Thus class warfare raises its head in a prospect poem that might seem determined to avoid economic evidence that would complicate its personally reassuring message.

Foucault's historicism is less linear and more diffuse, charting the circulating move-ments of power in many spheres of society outside the strictly political. Besides the power of class and money, there is, for example, the power of professions or discip-lines, the complex powers of gender, the power of language—which is the source and form of the discourses in which we inevitably chart past contests of power. The New Historicist working in the Foucauldian vein most commonly attaches her findings to one discourse or another existing at the time (the anti-slavery discourse, for example), for which she can readily find contemporary parallels.

A final word about procedure. Historicism is not inconsistent with formalism, cer-tainly not at the level of practice: the historicist critic can also be a good formalist critic. Some egregious historicist errors are committed when a reader fails to understand the conventions of a text's genre, for example, or has a tin ear in responding to a poem's tone. Historicism typically values poems more for their historical influence or socio-political impact, but the literary historicist need not give up her ability to distinguish a good poem from a worse one, even if she feels that that is not necessarily the most important decision to make about the text in question.

The importance of sensitive close reading of texts continues even when we venture outside a text into its *archive*, meaning not just the library but all the kinds of evidence that can be brought to bear upon it. All facts are not equal, and some may be false, or even falsified. Some understanding of the rules governing historical evidence will save the novice historicist the embarrassment of treating different orders of information as if history outside the text were all the same thing, an undifferentiated mass. The original authority and subsequent provenance of all evidence should be known, so far as possible. Corroboration of source evidence is at least as important in scholarly writing as it is in journalism. The anecdotes and memoirs surrounding famous texts and artists can be distorted by petty or significant interests as often as those attaching to famous political figures and events, if not more so.

Almost by definition, the historicist critic seeking to do original work should not rest content with what the authorities say. Historicist research can be pushed as far into the text as formalist readings, with analogous risks and rewards for breaking through into deconstructive insights. Finally, what the literary critic can bring, at best, to historicist research is the ability to respond to the nuances of texts (for example, correspondence and memoirs) in a way that a traditionally objective historian may lack. But at this point we would leave the historicist controversies among literary critics and enter those of historians themselves, about the presence, absence, danger, or inevitability of rhetorical interpretation in historical writing and research, questions raised by Hayden White (among others) in books like *Tropics of Discourse* (1978), *The Content of Form: Narrative Discourse and Historical Representation* (1987), and *Figural Realism* (1999).

A short backwards history of Romantic New Historicism

Rather than trace the present history of Romantic historicism from its beginnings, it may be more illuminating for our present purpose (a guide to current research methods) to trace this history backwards, to see how present methods and contro-versies link up with some of the same controversies in the object of our study itself: the literature of the Romantic period.

The advent of present-day Romantic New Historicism can be dated with useful accuracy to Jerome McGann's publication in 1983 of *The Romantic Ideology*. McGann's book was not the sole cause of the new movement; David Erdman, Carl Woodring, E. P. Thompson, and other scholars of the 1950–80 generation are regularly cited as examples of the continuing vitality of traditional literary history. But McGann's was a polemical book that hit its target: the professional practice of Romantic scholarship in the Anglo-American literary academy. The book had an effect far greater than McGann imagined.

His polemical edge glints sharply on the book's first page: 'The poetry of Romanticism is everywhere marked by extreme forms of displacement and poetic conceptualization whereby the actual human issues with which the poetry is concerned are resituated in a variety of idealized localities.' But McGann's real target was less Romantic literature itself than the academic ideology of its present interpreters, which glossed over and explained away such extremes of evasion. He historicized the methods of Romantic criticism and scholarship as he found them, *c*.1980, and he found them to be, in a word, thoroughly 'Romanticized'. McGann charged that academic Romanticists had come to understand Romanticism so well that they were writing as practising Romanticists themselves, losing their scholarly objectivity by overidentifying with their object of study. They might be very good propagandists for Romantic art, but they were, in McGann's view, insufficiently critical.

What led McGann to level such charges? It is important to see that his attack came from *within*, and at a time when the scholarly fortunes of Romanticism had never been higher. It had weathered the storms of New Critical Modernism and, canonized for the classroom by textbooks like Cleanth Brooks and Robert Penn Warren's *Understanding Poetry* (1938), had been taken up by a new generation of intellectual historians, of whom M. H. Abrams was the most important, especially in two of his books, *The Mirror and the Lamp* (1953) and *Natural Supernaturalism: Tradition and Revolution in Romantic Literature* (1971). The latter broadly synthesized differences between several varieties of Romantic art as versions of secularized Judaeo-Christian traditions. It was the success of this homogenizing intellectual history, wedded to a chastened New Critical canon of Romantic writers, that formed the context, in intellectual historical terms, of McGann's attack on 'The Romantic Ideology'.

Brooks and Warren were relatively generous towards Romantic poets when they included them in their landmark textbook. They and their intellectual cohort (John Crowe Ransom, Allen Tate, Donald Davidson, and others, including William Empson and I. A. Richards in England) were academic modernists. They institutionalized a practice of reading poetry that followed the literary tenets of the modernist revolution in the arts which began just before the First World War, and which is represented in literature above all by the critical example of T. S. Eliot.

Like its sister arts, literary modernism favoured abstraction over representation, discontinuity over narrative sequence, and irony over sincerity. It was militantly anti-Romantic, anti-emotional/personal, and anti-historical/political. For Eliot, poetry was, famously, 'poetry, and not an other thing'. That is, it had to be studied in the first instance without reference to anything but itself: no 'inner life' of the poet, no editorializing political allegiances. 'A poem should not mean | but be', in the words of Archibald MacLeish. Romanticism was caricatured as 'spilt religion' by T. E. Hulme, one of modernism's propagandizing critics. Irving Babbitt (1865–1933) was another: a leader of the so-called 'New Humanism', author of *Rousseau and Romanticism* (1919) and other works decrying the influence of Romantic emotional spontaneity on modern arts and education, and, as a Harvard professor, an important early influence on Eliot. Romantic literature had come to represent, for these writers, immature adolescent emotion and pathetic sincerity. An appreciation for Shelley was for Eliot something that one would hopefully grow out of, like puberty.

In the face of such a determined cultural opposition, Brooks and Warren's inclusion of Romantic poetry in their influential textbook was something of a concession. But it came at a high price. The standard for inclusion was relatively short poems in which the modernist—now 'New Critical'—requirements of ironic and structural tension were most clearly present. In a word, those Romantic poems which most closely resembled the poetry of John Donne (1572–1631) and the other Metaphysical poets of the early seventeenth century, which exemplified for Eliot the ideal of poetry. In the end, the New Critical canon of Romantic literature included the shorter major lyrics of Wordsworth and Keats (the only two Romantics represented in Brooks's 1947 book, *The Well Wrought Urn: Studies in the Structure of Poetry*), plus so many of Coleridge's that he appeared to have been as poetically productive as his contemporaries, which was hardly the case. But Coleridge enjoyed a privileged position because much of his literary criticism could be read as an 'anticipation' of certain New Critical tenets, like the concept of *organic form* (see also the chapter entitled 'Formalism').

Why did modernism react so violently against Romanticism? The modernists were not only reacting against a certain kind of poetry, but, as they saw it, virtually all poetry in English, *c.*1890–1910. Poetry had *become* Romanticism, or rather, that kind of vague, melodious rhyming of sweetly melancholy emotional states that characterizes some of late Tennyson and hosts of his imitators. Arthur Symons's survey, *The Romantic Movement in English Poetry* (1909), is an especially useful example in the present context. It included far more authors (89—plus 56 'Minors'!) than are mentioned even in *Romanticism: An Oxford Guide*. But Symons's book is a clear instance of historical distortion caused by an insufficiently historicized (that is, critically *un*self-aware) view of its object. For Symons, writing at the end of the nineteenth century—and after nearly a century of determined *de*historicizing of Romantic literature—'Romantic literature' had become a category that contained all literature written in England between 1750 and 1850.

How had poetry come to this pass? Of course, I have been oversimplifying matters to a great extent, and the further back we go, the greater the degree of oversimplification. But in Matthew Arnold we find an important link between this late, limp Romanticism and the *idea* of Romanticism cast out by Eliot and Hulme and other modernists. In Arnold, we see how emotionalism came to be associated with Romanticism precisely at the cost of its historical dimension: '. . . the English poetry of the first quarter of this century, with plenty of energy, plenty of creative force, did not know enough. This makes Byron so empty of matter, Shelley so incoherent, Wordsworth even, profound as he is, yet so wanting in completeness and variety.'[2] Arnold connects the Romantic poets to the French Revolution, but only to their detriment: 'Nay, and the true key to how much in our Byron, even in our Wordsworth, is this!—that they had their source in a great movement of feeling, not in a great movement of mind.' For Arnold, as for most of his Victorian contemporaries, it was an article of faith that the French Revolution had failed.

But Arnold's critique of Romanticism was also an act of recuperation. Though he is regarded as a godfather of the New Criticism because of his critical insistence on seeing the object 'as in itself it really is', his essay on 'the *function* of criticism *at the present time*' is a profoundly historicizing effort, trying to recover 'the best that is known and thought in the world'—by the Romantic poets, in this case—by excusing their unreflective emotionalism in terms of the 'times' in which they lived. In Arnold's cultural scheme, those were times of feeling, not times of thought; the revolutionary period was an epoch of zealous spiritual expansion, not the '*epoch of concentration*' which the revolution created in opposition to itself, and 'the great force of that concentration was England; and the great voice of that epoch of concentration was Burke'.

In preserving Romantic poetry for posterity, the cost, according to Arnold, would have to be its naïve, emotional politics: in short, its allegiance to the ideals of the French Revolution. If the claims Shelley and Wordsworth and others made for poetry could be understood as applying only to poetry, or to the expression of a purely personal emotion, fine. But to the extent that they were connected to revolution, they were taboo in mid-nineteenth-century Victorian England, whose domestic political ideology had as its first article the imperative to avoid anything like the French Revolution occurring in England. In literary historical terms, this conservatism meant the rejection of the poetry of the first quarter of the century which took favourable views of the French Revolution—and that in practice meant very large tracts of Romantic poetry. For it included not simply those works which took a positive view of overtly revolutionary acts, but all the many texts which engaged themselves seriously with revolutionary thought, pro *or* con.

To summarize then, in a purposely algebraic shorthand: Romantic poetry was made culturally acceptable in mid-nineteenth-century England by severely playing down its allegiances to, or interest in, the French Revolution. This produced a canon of poetry and of concomitant reading practices that contained much emotional excitement but little historical reference. When this conception of poetry ran up against Modernism, which held personal emotion in contempt, the result was a further reduction of Romanticism's cultural valence. The New Criticism reinvestigated the Romantic canon and found some examples worth saving. Then came the huge rise in prominence and prestige of the Anglo-American literary academy after the Second World War, leading to *The Romantic Ideology* of 1983 and, subsequently, to restive complaints against the very success of the New Historicist programme today.

Thus the issue of history in Romantic poetry concerns not only the abstract philosophical and methodological issues with which we began. It also concerns the presence or absence of a very specific history—England's response to the French Revolution—

which for a variety of cultural reasons and by a rich variety of critical and editorial means has been edited out of its subsequent reception in the English-speaking world. To uncover the buried presence of this particular history in Romantic texts is, therefore, to be an actor in that same history oneself, most especially if one happens to be a citizen of Great Britain today.

READING: William Wordsworth, 'Tintern Abbey'

At first glance, Wordsworth's 'LINES (Written a few miles above TINTERN ABBEY, on revisiting the banks of the WYE during a tour. July 13, 1798)' does not seem to be an obvious candidate for historicist interpretation. Of course, any text's historical context can be studied, presumably with some profit, however small. But unless features of the text itself offer some reason for pursuing historical research, the result is likely to seem adventitious: it may be curious or interesting, but so what? But if we can, as a critical rhetorical exercise, construct a warrant for historicizing this, by now the most historicized text in the Romantic pantheon, we will have a better understanding of both New Historicism's procedures and of its goals.

For most of the more than two hundred years since its first publication in the first edition of *Lyrical Ballads and a few other poems* (1798), 'Tintern Abbey' (to use its traditional, but now hotly contested, short title) has enjoyed a high reputation in both critical and popular estimation. But almost no one bothered to read it in historical frames of reference, apart from textual scholars trying to establish the circumstances of its composition and publication. As one of the 'other poems' in *Lyrical Ballads*, it was spared the wrath some reviewers vented on that landmark volume of English Romanticism, because it did not manifest the radical 'ordinary language' poetics of most of Wordsworth's contributions. Indeed, it looked reassuringly familiar: a good example of the loco-descriptive or landscape prospect poem which had been appearing in English literature for over 150 years, from John Denham's *Coopers Hill* (1640) and John Dyer's *Grongar Hill* (1726) to Thomas Gray's 'Ode on a Distant Prospect of Eton College' (1747) and William Crowe's *Lewesdon Hill* of 1788.

Indeed, viewed in this tradition, one of the notable things about 'Tintern Abbey' is that it is so *un*historical. Earlier English prospect poems offered some description of the natural scene spread out in front of the narrator/speaker, but typically ended with reflections about the scene's economic, political, or national 'prospects'. As the eighteenth century wore on, prospect poems became less chauvinistic and more philosophical—if we want to call the weary resignation in Gray's poem philosophical ('Where Ignorance is bliss, 'tis folly to be wise'). Compared with these instances of the tradition, Wordsworth's 'Lines' are less descriptive, more metaphysical, *and* more personal—all hallmarks, as literary criticism would ultimately decide, of the emergent 'Romantic' movement.

And this is pretty much what was said about it until late in the twentieth century; it was a largely uncontested masterpiece. According to N. S. Bauer's *Reference Guide to British Literature* (1978), there were no references at all to 'Tintern Abbey' in British periodical literature between 1816 and 1868. True, in 1930 William Empson accused it of failing to achieve successfully the fourth of his *Seven Types of Ambiguity*, where 'alternative meanings combine to make clear a complicated state of mind in the author'.[3] He challenged the transcendental rhetoric of its fourth paragraph from the perspective of logical positivism and found it to be, if not exactly meaningless, then very bad grammar, resulting in very vague

reference. (If the 'presence' of line 95 was the same as the 'something far more deeply interfused' of line 97, it was then more deeply interfused *than what*?)

In the 1960s, David Ferry, Richard Havens, Harold Bloom, Geoffrey Hartman, and others, starting from formalistic New Critical premises, found the poem's affirmations to be less philosophically suspect than personally strained and ambivalent. Its speaker, a self-proclaimed 'worshipper of Nature' (l. 153) seemed to express his quasi-religious faith in very doubtful terms: 'If this be but a vain belief', 'somewhat of a sad perplexity', 'Nor, perchance, if I were not thus taught', and similar locutions. For some of these New Critics, these doubts qualified or undercut the substance of Wordsworth's religion of nature; for others, they strengthened the poem by making its speaker seem more sincere, admitting to the kind of doubts we all experience; still others read such expressions as examples of the characteristic tension so valued by the New Criticism, not to be resolved by philosophical or biographical explanation, but held in suspension as a hallmark of the architectonics of a great work of art.

But no one offered a *historical* explanation of these tensions. The last twenty years have changed all that. Long recognized as Wordsworth's 'signature' poem, 'Tintern Abbey' is now the textual site on which some of the most ferocious battles for and against Romantic New Historicism have been fought. The only other Romantic text around which the New Historicist hurricane has swirled so furiously is Keats's 'To Autumn'—like 'Tintern Abbey', a poem of apparently calm and peaceful affirmations about human life in nature, that is now sharply contested for neglecting troubling contemporary historical phenomena that are argued to fall within its purview (particularly the Peterloo massacre of 16 August 1819, shortly before Keats composed 'To Autumn'; see also *Oxford Companion to the Romantic Age*, p. 643).[4]

How could we begin to look at Wordsworth's text historically? His title mentions a well-known touristic location in Wales, Tintern Abbey, and stations itself along the Wye river 'a few miles above' it. A date is given, but it is not noteworthy to modern readers, nor was it, I think, to most contemporary ones. If 'July 13, 1798' reminds us of 'July 14, 1789' we would have to admit, in fairness, that the association is a random sleight-of-eye—though it does remind us that the poem is still well within the time-frame of the French Revolution.

But, as far as references to time and space outside the text go, that is about it. However, the poem asserts three times in its first two lines that 'five years have passed', so that, with the subtitle still in our line of sight as we begin reading, we can hardly avoid making a quick calculation to 'July 13, 1793'. Whether this date means anything to a fresh modern reader is doubtful. But some of Wordsworth's contemporary readers would have registered that it refers to the year England and republican France declared war on each other (a war still very much in progress in 1798), a year which saw the beginning of the French Reign of Terror (1793–4), with which the entire revolution had come to be identified, especially in England. Perhaps only readers who kept themselves up on current events would remember that July 13, 1793, was the day on which Jean-Paul Marat, the incendiary Jacobin journalist, was assassinated in his bathtub by Charlotte Corday, a famous political assassination which marked the point at which the tide began to turn against Marat's enemies (and Wordsworth's friends), the moderate Girondin party, leading to their mass execution in October of that year. But the poem following after this hint seems to have nothing to do with Marat or the revolution, and so most readers would probably drop the association.

Other references in the text that go somewhat beyond the speaker's private experience are the 'wreaths of smoke' sent up by 'vagrant dwellers in the houseless woods' (l. 21) and 'the sneers of selfish men' (l. 130). But though the former seem poor and the latter mean, they do not seem to have much of a historical dimension, especially as the social problem of vagrancy is muted by the slightly oxymoronic phrase, 'vagrant *dwellers*'. However, as we follow closely the speaker's progress toward his closing affirmation that 'this green pastoral landscape' is still very dear to him, we note two things about his worship of 'Nature': it is firstly defined at every point by its sharp contrast and positive difference from Society, and secondly represented as a faith hard won from doubts and anxieties that are, like the poem's social references, expressed in every one of its five verse paragraphs (compare the discussion in the chapter on 'Ecology').

To this point, then, we can say that the speaker's reaffirmation of his faith in nature, stimulated by his return to the beautiful landscape of the Wye valley above Tintern after a five-year absence, is set off against his experience in society, apparently during the same intervening five years. More colloquially, we can say that this poem is put in the mouth of a speaker who loves the country and hates the city: a common enough preference, though by no means a universal one, and a preference, furthermore, that is very conventional in prospect poems like this.

Our intra-textual historicizing has not taken us very far, to this point, and it may be far enough for many readers. Yet it leaves us with an understanding of the poem that may make it, for other readers, unsatisfactory: so he has had bad experiences in the city and wants to escape to 'Nature'—so what? Of course, few readers nowadays would be able to read the poem without some prior knowledge of Wordsworth, but even if all they know is that 'Wordsworth loves nature', that still does not rescue the poem from a perception that it presents a rather one-sided view of human existence. In short, is human social life really so bad, that the best thing to do is escape from it into 'Nature'?[5] Conversely, other readers may have had experiences of 'Nature' in its less pacific forms, and be less disposed to give it such an unqualifiedly high valuation.[6]

Where can we turn for further relevant information, if we want to find better answers to these questions? Before heading off to the library, we should look at the other poems in the volume to which 'Tintern Abbey' is the conclusion, a procedure that even the strictest formalist cannot disallow, since an immediately relevant context for any text is the context of which it forms a part: its volume. Looking at the twenty-two other poems in *Lyrical Ballads*, we find only a few poems by Wordsworth that are like 'Tintern Abbey': four shortish poems of natural description/appreciation with the same head-title ('Lines') and variously explanatory subtitles, some even longer than 'Tintern Abbey's': for example, 'Left upon a Seat in a YEW-TREE, which stands near the Lake of Esthwaite, on a desolate part of the shore, yet commanding a beautiful prospect'. Almost all the rest of the poems are ballads about suffering poor people in the countryside, for which *Lyrical Ballads* is chiefly known: e.g. 'The Mad

Mother', 'The Idiot Boy', 'The Female Vagrant', and the like. So we can say that the volume as a whole manifests the same split (or whatever we choose to call it: tension, or contrast), between praise of natural beauty and expressions of sympathy or concern for the poor, that we find in 'Tintern Abbey's' references to 'vagrant dwellers' and 'the still, sad music of humanity'. Furthermore, though the ballads of suffering say little in praise of nature's beauty, most of the 'Lines' express their praise with overtones of ambivalence that are similar to those in 'Tintern Abbey', most notably the 'Lines Written in Early Spring':

> To her fair works did Nature link
> The human soul that through me ran;
> And much it grieved my heart to think
> What man has made of man.
>
> (ll. 5–8)

Hence we can conclude that the nature/society tensions in 'Tintern Abbey' are not accidental or random, but a central part of this author's comprehensive *vision* for his poems. Coincidentally with this conclusion, we can see that it is going to be hard to maintain the distinction between 'speaker' and 'author' of some formalist and generic readings of lyric expressions: if nearly twenty poems by the same author express the same tension, this is more than mere convention can account for. Hence this thematic tension in 'Tintern Abbey', like the running sense of ambivalence in its grandly affirmative statements, must be included as an important part of its overall meaning. The speaker 'worships' nature, but he has a hard time affirming this faith. And the reason seems to be not simply that he dislikes cities, but that, on the contrary, the human suffering represented in the poem by phrases like 'the din of towns and cities' is something towards which he feels a sense of responsibility, however unhappily. Far from being escapist, the poem's self-created difficulties are, if not *what* it is about, then clearly *how* it goes about expressing itself.

Indeed, the poem tells us so directly. Any reader, then or now, might well ask, 'why is the speaker so amazed and grateful that this scene in the Wye valley reappears to him as beautiful in 1798 as it did in 1793?' Five years is not a huge amount of time; it is not as though a middle-aged speaker is returning to scenes of his childhood (though Wordsworth wrote a lot of poems doing just that). Rather, the speaker seems to be a fairly young man. He says he has 'changed, no doubt, from what I was, when first | I came among these hills' (ll. 67–8), but he specifies that even then 'The coarser pleasures of my boyish days, | And their glad animal movements [were] all gone by' (ll. 74–5). We might guess he was a late teenager in 1793 and is now in his early twenties, a calculation not too far off from Wordsworth's actual chronological ages in 1793 and 1798.

The main difference between the two dates that the poem expresses, however, is not in years but in maturity. He tells us that in the interim he has *grown up*, and he phrases that growing up precisely in the terms of his changed attitude towards the human suffering that he struggles to overcome in order to affirm his worship of nature. Indeed, he formulates this as the *raison d'etre* for his entire poem, the reason for its amazed gratitude that the natural scene can still speak to him so powerfully:

> For I have learned
> To look on nature, not as in the hour
> Of thoughtless youth [1793 and earlier], but hearing oftentimes
> The still, sad music of humanity,
> Nor harsh nor grating, though of ample power
> To chasten and subdue.
>
> (ll. 89–94)

In case we miss the force of this explanatory statement ('*For . . .*'), he makes it even stronger, using the language of conclusive logical argument: '*Therefore* am I still | A lover of the meadows and the woods' (ll. 103–4; italics added). He can still love nature, *not* because he has been able to escape into remembered images of its beauty during the past five years, but because he has learned to look upon its beauties while still hearing 'the still, sad music of humanity'. And this is certainly a historical statement, broadly speaking, whatever its personal lyrical dimensions. Hence 'the poem in itself' (to use a favourite New Critical formulation) raises questions about human life that have a clear historical dimension, especially when put in context with the other poems in this volume by this author.

Here, then, we have established *intrinsic* grounds for further *extrinsic* or contextual study of the 'Lines written . . . above Tintern Abbey'. But where we go from here will depend on the kind of questions we want to answer, and the kind of research that seems to offer the best possibilities for answering them. We could say that our further research will be *historical*; but our question-setting, and the provisional or hypothetical answers we propose, is *historicized*. Our questions will require us to go outside the poem, if we are not content to rest with the tension and ambivalence between nature and society that our solely textual reading has produced.

If we want to know more about the life of this speaker-author who feels the nature/society tension so powerfully, that question leads us towards biography. Do we want to know more about why this tension might have been expressed so strongly yet so ambivalently in England in 1798? That question will take us towards political history. Do we want to know why the upper- and middle-class leisure activity of landscape appreciation is brought into tension with social responsibility? That takes us towards sociology or cultural studies. Do we want to know why this volume pays so much attention to the suffering poor, an attention that is less strongly expressed in 'Tintern Abbey' but crucially present at its turning-points? That leads towards economic history, including both private or religious charity and government parish relief systems. Or do we want to know about human responsibility for human suffering? That leads towards philosophy and perhaps towards religion—directions that are surely signposted in the poem's philosophical and religious rhetoric, both generally and in its minute particulars.

FURTHER READING

Abrams, M. H., 'On Political Readings of *Lyrical Ballads*', in Kenneth R. Johnston *et al.* (eds.), *Romantic Revolutions* (Bloomington, Ind.: Indiana University Press, 1990), pp. 320–49. One of the most even-handed critiques of New Historicist methodological assumptions.

Barrell, John, *Poetry, Language and Politics* (Manchester: Manchester University Press, 1988). An excellent combination of theory and practice, especially in the chapter 'The uses of Dorothy: "The Language of Sense" in "Tintern Abbey"', pp. 137–67; for a countering view, compare Alan Grob, 'William and Dorothy: A Case Study in the Hermeneutics of Disparagement', *ELH* (Spring 1998), 187–221.

Chandler, James, *England in 1819: The Politics of Literary Culture and the Case of Romantic Historicism* (Chicago: University of Chicago Press, 1998). The most ambitious effort to date to derive historicist assumptions and methods from the practice of Romantic writers themselves.

Hamilton, Paul, *Historicism* (London: Routledge, 1996). Probably the most useful explanation of historicism's philosophical dimensions. Contrast Karl Popper, *The Poverty of Historicism* (1961).

Johnston, Kenneth, *The Hidden Wordsworth* (New York and London: W. W. Norton, 1998). Historicist method combined with formalist readings in a biographical framework; see for example 'Wye Wandering', pp. 588–608.

Levinson, Marjorie, *Wordsworth's Great Period Poems* (Cambridge: Cambridge University Press, 1986). A path-breaking polemical work that did for New Historicist practice what McGann's *Romantic Ideology* did for its theory; considers 'Tintern Abbey', the Intimations Ode, 'Michael', and 'Peele Castle'.

Liu, Alan, *Wordsworth: The Sense of History* (Stanford, Calif: Stanford University Press, 1989). The most complete and unified critical study of a major Romantic author using historicist methods.

McGann, Jerome, *The Romantic Ideology: A Critical Investigation* (Chicago: University of Chicago Press, 1983). The brilliant polemic which launched a thousand replies, rebuttals, extensions, applications, and qualifications.

Roe, Nicholas, *The Politics of Nature: William Wordsworth and Some Contemporaries* (Basingstoke: Palgrave, 2002). A reconsideration of Wordsworth's supposed 'escapism', in a more contextually informed view of what 'nature worship' might mean, then and now; see for example 'The Politics of the Wye Valley: Re-Placing "Tintern Abbey"', pp. 117–36.

Siskin, Clifford, *The Historicity of Romantic Discourse* (Oxford and New York: Oxford University Press, 1988). A generalizing study that considers Romantic writing practices on a period-wide grid, extending it to include contemporary Anglo-American academic work.

NOTES

1. Marjorie Levinson, 'The New Historicism: Back to the Future', in *Rethinking Historicism: Critical Readings in Romantic History* (Oxford: Blackwell, 1989), p. 20.
2. 'The Function of Criticism at the Present Time', in *Essays in Criticism* (1865).
3. William Empson, *Seven Types of Ambiguity* (London: Chatto and Windus, 1930; 1947), 151–4.
4. See 'Keats and Politics: A Forum', *Studies in Romanticism* (Summer 1986), and compare Nicholas Roe (ed.), *Keats and History* (Cambridge: Cambridge University Press, 1995).
5. A counter-attack to Romantic New Historicism's politicizing of Wordsworth, and of Romanticism's supposed 'escape' to nature, has been mounted by Jonathan Bate, Karl Kroeber, and others under the banner of 'Green Romanticism', which argues that Romantic nature is not escapist at all, but rather posits a new relationship between man and nature that anticipates the ecological and environmental politics of our own time.
6. Cf. Aldous Huxley's classic essay, 'Wordsworth in the Tropics', in *Do What You Will: Essays* (London: Chatto and Windus, 1929), pp. 123–39.

14 | Feminism

Anne K. Mellor

What difference does the social construction of gender make to our understanding of the literature produced in Britain in the Romantic period? As I have argued at length in my *Romanticism and Gender* (1993), paying attention both to the sex of the author and to the ways in which gender is represented in individual literary texts can reveal a very different Romanticism from the one often portrayed in earlier histories of British literature. In order to unpack some of these differences, I will here approach this subject first historically and then thematically.

History

The canon of British Romantic writing has traditionally been centred on the writings of first five, then, after the 1960s, six male poets: Wordsworth, Coleridge, Byron, Shelley, Keats, and then Blake. Conventional descriptions of the nature of literary Romanticism have been founded on the works of these Big Six. Such an exclusive focus has seriously distorted our understanding of the literary culture of the Romantic era, first by occluding the work of many other male writers who have been relegated to the category of minor authors, but, far more important, by virtually erasing the work of women writers from our institutional memory.

In the last decade, feminist literary historians have drawn our attention to the enormous output in England between 1780 and 1830 of women writers, poets, playwrights, and novelists as well as historians, political theorists, and scientists. Their work radically transformed the British literary landscape. To understand why and how it did so, we must turn back to the 1790s and look for a moment at how books were produced and distributed in Great Britain in this period.

Beginning in the 1780s, British booksellers discovered that they could make more money from lending books at a fee to multiple readers than they could make from selling books, which were prohibitively expensive (see also chapter on 'Print culture and the book trade'). Several publishers established circulating libraries, from which annual subscribers could borrow their books. This phenomenon spread rapidly throughout Great Britain, making books widely available for the first time to the literate middle classes. The Sunday School movement furthered this extension of literacy by teaching members of the working classes to read, workers who then clubbed together either to purchase books themselves or to subscribe to lending libraries. Even more important, the demand for the improved education of women, most powerfully articulated in Mary Wollstonecraft's *A Vindication of the Rights of Woman* in 1792, but widely endorsed even by such conservative writers as Hannah More and Beilby Porteus, the Bishop of London, had been effective in extending literacy to women of all classes. Since women of the middle and upper classes typically had more leisure time to read, they had become by 1800 the primary market for works of literature.

This then is the historical moment when female readers for the first time entered British print culture in numbers large enough to form a critical mass. The successful development of over a dozen magazines, gift-books, and annuals specifically aimed at a female audience demonstrated the presence of a literate female public. The phenomenal publishing achievements of such presses as Lane's Minerva Press and John Bell's poetry series rested on a predominantly female taste for romances, Gothic novels, and ballads. The presence of this new female literary market was so strongly felt by the beginning of the nineteenth century that it had even become the subject of satirical prints. James Gillray, for instance, mocked the female taste for Gothic fiction and accounts of the supernatural in his 'Tales of Wonder' published on 1 February 1802, in which he portrays three overdressed, upwardly mobile bourgeois women gathering together to read Matthew Lewis's lurid Gothic novel, *The Monk*, by candlelight (see chapter entitled 'Satire' and *Oxford Companion to the Romantic Age*, pp. 522–3, 689–91).

This development of a new reading audience composed in significant part of women was seen by many male critics and writers as a cultural threat. First, female readers might trivialize literature, substituting their vulgar, low-brow taste for the aesthetic judgements of the better-educated gentlemen who had hitherto controlled the formation of the literary canon. Second, reading exposed women to new ideas, more information, and hitherto unknown desires. As Jacqueline Pearson has documented in her book, *Women's Reading in Britain 1750–1835* (1999), female reading in the Romantic period was increasingly seen as a 'dangerous recreation'. It might increase female rationality, but at the same time it distracted women from their domestic duties. Worse, female reading could arouse transgressive, especially sexual, desires, a fear powerfully captured in Charles Williams's satirical print published on 26 February 1801, titled 'Luxury, or the Comforts of a Rumpford'. Here the lady clearly invites unnatural sexual advances as she warms her naked rump in front of a Rumpford stove while avidly reading Lewis's *The Monk*, having previously been aroused by the other two books discarded on her chamber floor, *The Kiss* and *Oeconomy of Love*.

Third, and perhaps most important, women readers provided a new and increasingly large market for women *writers*, since women preferred to read novels, poems, plays, and books of general information written by other women. The literary market-place was thus increasingly inhabited by a host of female novelists, poets, and playwrights, as well as female historians, critics, and political essayists. As Edward Jacobs has documented in his *Accidental Migrations: An Archaeology of Gothic Discourse* (2000), the circulating libraries not only encouraged a growing taste for fiction but themselves published a disproportionate number of female authors. Statistics compiled by Ann H. Jones in *Ideas and Innovations—Best Sellers of Jane Austen's Age* (1986) show that ten of the dozen best-selling novelists in the 1790s were women. Such poets as Charlotte Smith, Anna Barbauld, Anna Seward, Hannah More, Mary Tighe, Mary Robinson, and, later, Felicia Hemans and Letitia Landon commanded an ever-growing share of the poetry market—as high as 30 per cent in some years between 1790 and 1830; and Hannah More, Elizabeth Inchbald, Hannah Cowley, and Joanna Baillie were among the most successful dramatists of the day.

The emergence of these literate women readers and writers into the print culture of the Romantic era aroused in the male writers of the day a powerful new anxiety. If the male writer could no longer count on a 'band of brothers', a club of gentlemen educated to appreciate his literary efforts, how could he survive economically? The increasing hostility on the part of the male Romantic writers and artists to learned women, called 'bluestockings' in a reference to the coterie surrounding Elizabeth Montagu, is in itself a telling index to the commercial success and cultural impact of these women writers and readers. Beginning in the 1790s, the leading male writers of the Romantic period went out of their way to mock privately or openly condemn learned women.

To take just two examples from many, in his comic opera, *M.P. or The Blue-Stocking*, performed in London in 1811, the Irish dramatist and popular song-writer Thomas Moore openly derided Lady Bab Blue. She is a scientist 'employed in writing a chemical Poem upon *Sal Ammoniac*', whose learned father has 'stuffed her head with all that is legible and illegible, without once considering that the female intellect may possibly be too weak for such an experiment'.[1] Moore's close friend Byron explicitly acknowledged what produced this male hostility to learned women in 1821 in his satirical eclogue, *The Blues*. Here his protagonist, the poet Inkle, first condemns Byron's male competitors, Wordsworth, Southey, Coleridge, and Sotheby. He then warns his best friend against marrying a wealthy Blue: 't'would be your perdition; | She's a poet, a chymist, a mathematician' (I. 65–6). Sir Richard Bluebottle, who has done just that, laments his wife's literary salons, where he must 'hear a vile jargon which addles my brains; | A smatter and chatter, gleaned out of reviews, | By the rag, tag, and bobtail, of those they call "Blues"' (II. 21–3). But Byron's deepest anxiety emerges earlier in the poem, when Inkle's friend Tracy tells him he has just come from a publisher's shop that conveniently lies next door to a pastry-cook's:

> so that when I
> Cannot find the new volume I wanted to buy
> On the bibliophile's shelves, it is only two paces,
> As one finds every author in one of those places
> (I. 18–21).

If the Blues won't buy Byron's poems, his pages can always serve to wrap a loaf of bread!

By taking this large body of female-authored and widely read literary writing into account, students of British Romanticism will develop a far more complex and accurate interpretation of this literary period. Luckily, several recent anthologies make this task far easier. The first teaching anthology to include as much work by women writers as by male authors in the Romantic period, *British Literature 1780–1830*, edited by Anne K. Mellor and Richard Matlak, appeared in 1996, followed in short order by a companion volume to Duncan Wu's *Romanticism: An Anthology*, a second volume devoted entirely to women's poetry, *Romantic Women Poets: An Anthology* (1997). More recently, the Longman's *Anthology of British Literature* (2000) in the section devoted to the Romantic period edited by Susan Wolfson and Peter Manning, derives its format from the Mellor and Matlak anthology, albeit with more limited coverage. In addition, Paula Feldman and Andrew Ashfield have each edited volumes of selected poems by Romantic women writers, and individual modern editions of the works of Charlotte Smith, Felicia Hemans, Anna Letitia Barbauld, Letitia Landon, and Joanna Baillie have appeared.

Themes

How does a consideration of the major work of the most widely read and historically influential women writers change our understanding of the literary culture of Romanticism? Let us assume, for the purposes of comparison, that the canonical male writers of the Romantic period were profoundly concerned with the capacities of the creative imagination; with the possibilities and limitations of metaphorical language, most intensely explored through the genre of poetry, which they assumed to be the highest form of literary art; with the development of an autonomous, even a transcendent self or ego; with revolution either as a process of personal transfiguration or as a political practice; and with the role of the poet as a political leader or religious saviour. This is but a crude summary of the issues that engaged the canonical male Romantic writers, and other essays in this volume will put forth far more complex analyses of their work. But even this inadequate overview is enough to point up the remarkable differences both in content and in style between the male Romantic writers and their female peers. Let us now look at how the women writers of the period dealt with these same issues.

The development of the self

The goal of the masculine Romantic self, as numerous commentators from Meyer Abrams (in *Natural Supernaturalism*, 1971) to Marlon Ross (in *The Contours of Masculine Desire*, 1989) have documented, is to develop an autonomous, transcendental ego grounded in the mental capacity to half-create the world around him that he half-perceives, what Keats in describing Wordsworth called the 'egotistical sublime'. As Wordsworth himself put it in *The Prelude* (1805), his epic quest, his 'heroic argument and genuine prowess' (III. 183–4), is nothing less than the construction of the individual who owns his own body, his own mind, his own labour, and who is free to use that body and labour as he chooses, the achievement of 'Man free, man working for himself, with choice | Of time and place, and object' (VIII. 152–3). This masculine Romantic ego is the Lockean self who possesses property in his own person, Rousseau's maker of the social contract, the modern self who possesses natural rights to life and liberty, and hence the grounding individual ('Every man') of the American and French republican constitutions.

The women writers of the Romantic era conceptualized the self in a very different way. Dorothy Wordsworth imaged the female self as a 'floating island', one that responds to the currents of water and air, one that has no firm moorings, that appears and disappears, that offers 'food, safety, shelter' to birds and plants even as it may itself be absorbed into the lake, 'to fertilize some other ground' ('Floating Island at Hawkeshead, An incident in the schemes of Nature'). This is an extremely suggestive metaphor, enabling us to see that the Romantic-era women writers often embraced what such modern feminist psychologists as Nancy Chodorow in *The Reproduction of Mothering* have taught us to call a *relational self*. This self has no firm ego boundaries, and experiences its place in the world as an entanglement in shifting relationships, with family members, friends, lovers, co-workers. As Keats, who shared this feminine sense of the self as relational, described it: 'the poetical Character itself . . . is not itself—it has no self—it is every thing and nothing—' (letter to Richard Woodhouse, 27 October 1818). To develop the political implications of this relational self, one might invoke the French feminist Luce Irigaray's concept of a 'placental economy', grounded on the image of the pregnant woman who experiences herself always as two-in-one. A relational self does not make economic or political decisions based on the assessment of self-interest (what contemporary economists call 'rational choice'), but rather on what Irigaray calls a practice of 'gift-giving', of submerging one's personal desires into a desire for the good of one's family or the whole community.

Experiencing their selves as relational rather than autonomous encouraged the women writers of the Romantic period to focus on the ways that self interacts with other people, how it functions in relation to the wider community. Jane Austen, for instance, devoted her novels to an exploration of the ways in which people perceive and misperceive each other, how they come to know each other more accurately and profoundly, and how a heroine can overcome her own mental misjudgements and find the partner most suited to her. As Austen insisted, following Wollstonecraft in this regard, the best marriages are those grounded in a rational love, a correct assessment of the genuine compatibility between two people who mutually respect, esteem, and love each other.

When such mutual respect is absent, when the feminine self finds no other into which she can merge, then she feels—not the confidence of the transcendental ego holding its own against the imperatives of nature—but rather desolation. More than any other writer in the Romantic era, the poet Felicia Hemans explores the causes and the effects of female loneliness, despair, even suicidal depression. In her poems and plays, such loneliness is almost always produced by men—men who abandon their female lovers, men who leave home to fight wars, to make money, to explore and conquer new lands. Even as she idealizes the domestic affections and the intense pleasures of the home in a poem such as 'The Homes of England', Hemans is acutely aware that such domestic bliss, such communal sharing among family and friends, never endures—the homes of England quickly become, in her companion poem, the 'Graves of a Household'. Hemans's finest verse-play, *The Siege of Valencia* (1826), poignantly details the willingness of her male protagonists to sacrifice their countrymen and even their children in the pursuit of religious and military conquest (here over the Muslim Moors). Her heroine Elmina alone remains alive at the end of the play to pronounce the funeral oration over her now dead family, an oration that invokes that masculine God 'Whose hand around her hath unpeopled earth' (l. 530).

The relation of human beings to nature

The male Romantic poet often positions himself, as did Wordsworth at the end of *The Prelude*, on top of a mountain, looking down on the natural world, a nature that he claims to understand and therefore speak for. Such a moment is an instance of what Burke and Kant both called the 'sublime', the encounter of the finite human mind with the infinite power of God or the universe. This encounter first overwhelms the mortal poet but then leads to an experience of mental empowerment, one in which the poet feels he can either join with or hold his own against this divine creative power, as does Coleridge in 'This Lime-Tree Bower My Prison' or Percy Shelley in 'Mont Blanc'.

Women writers both condemned this concept of the sublime and offered an alternative model for the appropriate relationship of the human mind to nature. Mary Shelley in her novel *Frankenstein; or, the Modern Prometheus* (1818) offered the most powerful and enduring critique of the male scientific and poetic attempt to appropriate and speak for Mother Nature. Victor Frankenstein's hubristic effort to have a baby without a woman, to pursue nature to 'her hiding places' and steal her reproductive powers, produces not the superior new species of which he dreamed but rather a monster who destroys him and his family. Shelley leaves open the possibility that if Frankenstein had possessed a maternal instinct, if he had been able to love and care for the child he created, then that creature might indeed have benefited mankind. But Frankenstein's failure to mother his child eventually drives that battered and abused child into a violent revenge on his maker and his family.

Instead, Romantic women writers suggested, human beings should see Mother Nature as a friend and co-worker, one with needs of her own, a potentially powerful ally with whom we must cooperate and who will reward our devotion to her. Significantly, the only member of the Frankenstein family left alive at the end of Shelley's novel is Earnest, the son who wished to become a farmer and to live in productive exchange with nature. Charlotte Smith, in her poem 'Beachy Head' (1807), brilliantly images this alternative interaction with nature. She begins by detailing the myriad species of flora and fauna that thrive along the coast of Sussex, using both vernacular and scientific terms, in order to emphasize the variety and abundance of nature, as well as the failure of any one system of terminology or classification to adequately represent her productions. She ends by invoking her hero, Parson Darby, a retired clergyman who devotes his life to rescuing shipwrecked sailors. Rather than celebrating his regular encounters with the sublime (the sea in a storm), Darby does what he can to mediate the elemental powers of nature. He does not attempt to speak *for* nature; rather, he writes his poetry *inside* nature, on the walls of the sea-cave in which he lives. Charlotte Smith's point is clear: the infinite variety and elemental power of nature is far too great for any one mind or linguistic system to encompass. The most we can do is to respect nature, to describe her with reverence, to be grateful for her bounty, and to try to remain in harmonious balance within her.

When female writers do invoke the landscape of the sublime, of alpine mountains and avalanches and devastating storms, as does Ann Radcliffe in her Gothic novels, they do so for very different reasons. Radcliffe locates the terror of the sublime, not in nature, but rather indoors, in the evil that violent, predatory men do to vulnerable women. By domesticating the sublime (often figured as a man raping a woman inside her home, a ruined castle), Radcliffe leaves open the possibility that her persecuted heroines can find solace in nature—and so they do. Ellena di Rosalba in *The Italian* (1796), imprisoned in a convent, regularly gains comfort from climbing to the top of her tower to contemplate the beauty of the setting sun over the Apennine mountains of northern Italy. These traditionally sublime scenes serve, not to remind Ellena of her own mortal limits, but rather to teach her how insignificant her tormentors are.

Politics

Caught up in the revolutionary politics of Jacobin France in the 1790s, many of the first generation of male Romantic writers eagerly embraced the call for the overthrow of the British monarchy and the creation of a democratic republic, founded on the natural rights of man. Women also embraced this demand for a more just society, but they disagreed as to how it could best be achieved. They rejected the belief that a sudden, violent political revolution was the best way to achieve their goal, recognizing—as Charlotte Smith details in her superb poem, 'The Emigrants' (1793)—that too many innocent bystanders, especially women and children, get hurt or killed during such military uprisings; the example of the bloodthirsty Terror which followed the revolution in France vividly proved this.

Instead, they argued that social reform is a process, not of revolution but of gradual evolution, a process that is furthered by educating the populace. Most important, in their view, was the improved education of females, who in the 1790s were denied access to universities. Instead, the girls of the day were educated either at home or at schools where they were taught only the 'female accomplishments'—reading, writing, counting, sewing, dancing, and a smattering of French and Italian (enough to sing songs in those languages). In *A Vindication of the Rights of Woman*, Mary Wollstonecraft railed against the negative consequences of such an inadequate female educational system, one that in her view produced women who were vain, silly, irresponsible, amoral, and selfish.

Instead, Wollstonecraft argued, women should be educated in the same schools in which men were educated, and for the same purposes—to become intelligent, responsible, and moral citizens of the nation (see *Oxford Companion to the Romantic Age*, pp. 161–70). Her call was seconded by the evangelical Christian Hannah More, who in her *Strictures on the Modern System of Female Education* (1799) insisted that women must receive a superior education in order to become good Christians and successful mothers and wives. Although Wollstonecraft focuses on the production of rational, virtuous human beings while More emphasized the production of Christian women, both concurred that an improved, state-supported, co-educational system was essential to the development of a more civilized Britain.

And both Wollstonecraft and More joined their voices to the growing condemnation of what they saw as the greatest social evil in the England of their day, Britain's participation in the African slave trade (see also chapter entitled 'Post-Colonialism'). Numerous women writers joined the abolitionist movement (see *Oxford Companion to the Romantic Age*, p. 399) and they did so far more publicly and consistently than did the canonical male poets, who focused instead on the evils of the monarchy. Perhaps the women writers felt, as Wollstonecraft did, a frightening identification with the enslaved African. As Wollstonecraft argued in her *Vindication of the Rights of Woman*, British females who existed under the legal system of *couverture*, in which their possessions, earnings, children, and even bodies were the legal property of their husbands, fathers, or sons, were no different in law from slaves; hence she proclaimed 'When, therefore, I call women slaves, I mean in a political and civil sense' (ch. 12).

By taking outspoken stands demanding the improved education and employment of women, the abolition of the slave trade and the emancipation of the West Indian slaves, and the right of women to possess property, to control the custody of children, and to elect representatives to Parliament, the women writers of the Romantic era for the first time claimed the right to participate fully in the political culture of the nation. Some, most notably Wollstonecraft, Hannah More, Joanna Baillie, and others discussed at length in my book *Mothers of the Nation* (2000), even insisted that women were better suited to rule the nation than men, because they were more virtuous and more committed to a governmental policy that served the needs of all the members of the body politic. They advocated what the psychologist Carol Gilligan has taught us to call 'an ethic of care', as opposed to an 'ethic of justice'. Under an ethic of justice, everyone is treated the same, regardless of differing needs and abilities; under the more socialist ethic of care, the special needs of individuals (including pregnant women) are acknowledged and met.

Aesthetic theory and genre

Eighteenth-century writers on the whole endorsed a neoclassical aesthetic theory which claimed that the purpose of art was to imitate nature, not ordinary, irregular nature, but an idealized and perfected nature. By depicting both human nature and the physical world in its most virtuous and beautiful forms, they believed, following Horace, that their art would both delight and instruct its consumers. The male Romantic poets vigorously contested this neoclassical mimetic theory, arguing instead that the human imagination is potentially divine, capable of creating a unique world. As Coleridge asserted in his *Biographia Literaria* (1817), the poem is a heterocosm or universe in itself, a world that reconciles the random multiety of experience into a new harmonious unity. Byron, in his poem *Don Juan*, responded more sceptically to this notion, suggesting instead that the poem can only reflect the constant shifting of the universe and must therefore engage in a self-conscious process of creation and de-creation, a process that I have defined as 'romantic irony' in my book *English Romantic Irony* (1980). In both cases, however, these Romantic poets were endorsing an 'expressive' or 'subjective' theory of poetry, arguing that the poem reflected the poet's unique emotional as well as intellectual engagement with the universe. As Wordsworth famously put it in his 1800 Preface to the *Lyrical Ballads*, 'all good poetry is the spontaneous overflow of powerful feelings . . . by a man who, being possessed of more than usual organic sensibility, had also thought long and deeply'. Moreover, these poets assumed that poetry was the highest of the literary genres, because it relied especially profoundly on metaphoric language, those metaphors which, Percy Shelley argued in his *Defence of Poetry*, constituted the governing structures of all human thought. Since metaphors become institutionalized as the laws of the land (e.g. 'the king has two bodies', 'all men are created equal'), poets, Shelley concluded, are 'the unacknowledged legislators of the world'.

The women writers of the Romantic era responded to this dialogue between a mimetic/objective (neoclassical) and an expressive/subjective (Romantic) aesthetics by staking out a middle ground. They argued that the function of art is to teach morality or right feeling by arousing their readers' sympathies through the representation of probable or believable examples of virtuous and evil human behaviour in realistic situations. Rather than giving priority to poetry or drama, they argued that the most realistic and hence the most moral genre was the novel. As Anna Barbauld insisted in her magisterial essay 'On the Origin and Progress of Novel-Writing' (1810), the novel is capable of depicting a social world that is more credible and more psychologically complex than that found in poetry or drama. Further, the novel is a more democratic genre, because it can be read, understood, and enjoyed by any literate person and does not require a prior education in the Greek and Latin languages and literatures. Jane Austen clearly endorsed Barbauld's view, asserting in *Northanger Abbey* (1817) that novels such as Frances Burney's *Cecilia* and *Camilla* and Maria Edgeworth's *Belinda* are works 'in which the greatest powers of the mind are displayed, in which the most through knowledge of human nature, the happiest delineation of its varieties, the liveliest effusions of wit and humour are conveyed to the world in the best chosen language' (ch. 3).

Not only did women writers elevate the genre of the novel to the highest status, they preferred certain kinds of novels to others. Rather than novels which attempted to be 'a comic epic in prose' (Henry Fielding's definition of his novel in his preface to *Joseph Andrews* in 1742), detailing the adventures of a single protagonist as he seeks fame and fortune, they preferred to write novels which focused either on the preservation of an extended human community (as did Maria Edgeworth and Sydney Morgan in their Irish novels) or on the education of a young woman who overcomes her character flaws and intellectual errors and thus finds the right mate. By stressing a companionate and mutually satisfying marriage or the preservation of an extended human community as the goal of a human life, these writers implicitly endorse an ethic of care and the value of a relational self.

When they turn to the genre of poetry, as many women did, they tended to eschew the epic (albeit not entirely) for other forms: the sonnet, the ballad, the lyric, commemorative verse, poetic epistles. These forms enabled them, first, to express their own feelings in an easily comprehensible form and thus to arouse the sympathy and understanding of their readers. Second, they served as records of a dialogue between writer and reader, often memorializing times they had spent together, or serving as 'gifts' to sustain an ongoing relationship. Or they defined the desolation and melancholy experienced by a woman who lacked such sustaining relationships, as did Charlotte Smith's frequently republished sequence of *Elegiac Sonnets*.

Such poems also had a profoundly political dimension. As Lucy Aikin's brilliant revisionary response to Pope, Milton, and the Bible, *Epistles on Women* (1810), suggested, female poetry could correct the traditional but inaccurate representation of woman's character and social function. In this historical poem which rewrites Genesis to suggest that male 'pride of power' (Cain's envy) is the cause of the Fall and of all human misery since, Aikin claims that only the maternal instinct has prevented both the animal and the human species from destroying themselves. Addressed to her best friend, Anna Wakefield Aikin, she calls on all her women readers to rise up against the evils of patriarchal oppression and create a more civilized, benevolent, and egalitarian Britain. The success of such a call requires a response, and numerous female poets of the Romantic era wrote poems to each other, offering support, understanding, and even—by praising each other's work in the literary reviews—economic advancement.

So different were the ideological investments and modes of literary performance of women writers that I have argued for a distinctively different romanticism, one we might call 'feminine Romanticism' so long as we recognize that male writers as well as female writers could produce works of feminine Romanticism—as John Keats notably did in his love poems, in his celebration of female suffering and wisdom in the figure of Moneta in his *Hyperion* poems, and in his letters. To recapitulate, the ideology of feminine Romanticism was based on a subjectivity constructed in relation to other subjectivities, hence a self that is fluid, absorptive, responsive, with permeable ego boundaries. This self typically located its identity within a larger human nexus, a family or social community. Taking the family as the grounding trope of social organization, feminine Romanticism opposed violent military revolutions, especially the French Revolution, in favour of gradual or evolutionary reform under the guidance of benevolent maternal as well as paternal guidance. This involved a commitment to an ethic of care. In this context, nature becomes not a source of divine creative power so much as a female friend or sister with needs and capacities, one who both provides support and requires cultivation, with whose life-giving powers one willingly cooperates. Moral reform both of the individual and of the family politic is achieved, not by utopian imaginative vision, but by the communal exercise of reason, moderation, tolerance, and the domestic affections, an exercise that can embrace the racial or alien other (even Frankenstein's Creature). Above all, feminine Romanticism insisted on the equal value and rational capacities of the female. And finally, this ideology found its appropriate linguistic expression in specific genres: in the novel which enables the author to represent in the vernacular a human community whose multiple relationships extend over time, and in those poetic genres which celebrate the value of the quotidian, of daily domestic and social involvements.

At the same time, I would insist that such a binary division of Romantic-era writing is only an introductory tool that enables us to see differences between male and female writers in the Romantic period that have hitherto been invisible. Recent academic work suggests that women writers varied significantly across the political and generic spectra. Some women writers delighted in portraying female protagonists who were driven by lust, who hated their families, and who enjoyed murdering their rivals, as did Victoria de Loredani in Charlotte Dacre's Gothic novel, *Zofloya, or The Moor* (1806). Others endorsed the status quo, aligning their writings with the patriarchal prescriptions of the dutiful daughter and submissive wife promoted in the conduct books of James Fordyce and John Gregory, as did Laetitia Matilda Hawkins. Others such as Mrs Esme Steuart Erskine (born Eliza Bland Norton), Margaret Holford, and Felicia Hemans turned to the neoclassical epic or the tragic drama to promote their visions of empowered or disempowered women in the very genres hitherto inhabited exclusively by male writers. Such meaningful variations across the wide range of women's writing in the Romantic period will need to be mapped in greater detail by future generations of feminist students and scholars.

READING: Jane Austen, *Pride and Prejudice*

A feminist approach to any literary text begins with these questions: What difference does gender make to this text? How does the sex of the author influence his or her work? How does the text represent the social construction of gender in its historical period? Does it challenge or endorse that construction? Here I raise these questions in relation to what is arguably the finest novel written in the Romantic period, in order to determine the ways in which a feminist approach increases our understanding of Austen's fiction.

Jane Austen begins *Pride and Prejudice* by drawing attention to the severe limitations placed even on relatively well-off women: the Bennets are members of the landed gentry, the upper middle classes. But the Bennet girls receive no useful education—Elizabeth is confined to what she can read in her father's library or glean from conversations with him. She and her sisters learn only the 'accomplishments', on which Austen scathingly comments in Volume I, chapter 8. Miss Bingley first defines the accomplished woman as having 'a thorough knowledge of music, singing, drawing, dancing, and the modern languages . . .; and besides all this, she must possess a certain something in her air and manner of walking, the tone of her voice, her address and expressions'. But when Darcy responds, 'All this she must possess, and to all this she must yet add something more substantial, in the improvement of her mind by extensive reading', Elizabeth Bennet caustically rejoins, 'I am no longer surprised at your knowing *only* six accomplished women. I rather wonder now at your knowing *any*. . . . I never saw such a woman. I never saw such capacity, and taste, and application, and elegance, as you describe, united.'

Because they have no useful education, the Bennet girls are unfit for work—and indeed, the only employment opportunities open to girls of their class, governess or paid companion, are represented in the novel as little short of enslavement or prostitution. Ann de Bourgh's governess Mrs Jenkinson is a cipher who never speaks; Georgianna Darcy's governess Mrs Younge connives at her charge's seduction by Wickham. Since women of this class cannot work to support themselves, they have no financial alternative but to marry, for as Jane Austen commented in a letter to her sister Cassandra, 'Single women have a dreadful propensity for being Poor'. And the Bennet girls in particular must marry, because their father's estate is entailed on the nearest living male heir, their cousin Mr Collins.

In contrast to the Bennet girls, the men in Austen's novel have incomes, either from inheritance (Darcy, Bingley) or from their own labour (Mr Gardiner is in business, Mr Philips is a lawyer, Collins is an Anglican minister, Wickham is an army officer). Because they have money, these men are represented as having autonomous selves that can make choices: they are free to enter a neighbourhood or leave it as they will. Women in contrast are confined to the home where they are put on display to potential suitors. Thus Austen's famous opening sentence—'It is a truth universally acknowledged, that a single man in possession of a fortune, must be in want of a wife'—is deeply ironic. It is women *not* in possession of a fortune who are desperately in need of a husband. Austen's irony continues through her second sentence: 'this truth is so well fixed in the minds of the surrounding families, that he is considered as the rightful property of some one or other of their daughters.' But it is the daughters who under the laws of *couverture* are 'property', to be sold with their dowries to the highest bidder.

Austen's argument, that economic necessity forces women into marriage, is driven home by the example of Charlotte Lucas. At the age of 27 (she is already considered 'an old maid') and not especially handsome, the clear-thinking Charlotte marries a man for whom she has no respect, Mr Collins, because this is her 'pleasantest preservative from want'. She knows that Mr Collins is a sycophant and a fool, yet she willingly accepts his proposal and the limits it brings—she will see less, sitting in the back room, and hear less, ignoring his conversation, yet she will at least have her own household. As Austen finally comments, in an example of her free indirect discourse (in which she enters the minds of her characters), 'Her home and her housekeeping, her parish and her poultry, and all their dependent concerns, had not yet lost their charms' (ii. 15). Austen's brilliant irony emerges here in the word 'yet'—Charlotte Lucas *will* grow bored and unhappy with her life, but as we and she know, she had no choice.

What then is the best that a woman can hope for, in Austen's novel? A happy marriage—and the basic concern of *Pride and Prejudice* is to define what such a marriage is, and how one might achieve it. The novel begins with several negative examples. The Bennet marriage, based on sexual desire, has deteriorated into mutual alienation—the 'invariably silly' Mrs Bennet gossips and manoeuvres, while her contemptuous husband comments ironically on her antics, while at the same time failing to exercise any moral control over her or her daughters. Lydia and Wickham repeat her parents' mistake—their alliance is based entirely on lust, and will cause equal misery to both, which is why Mr Bennet finally says that Wickham is his 'favourite' son-in-law, the one with whom he most identifies. Clearly Austen shares Wollstonecraft's view that sexual desire is not a solid foundation for a good marriage.

The ideal marriage, in Austen's view, is based instead on rational love, one which unites affection, self-esteem, mutual respect, and shared values, what Elizabeth calls a 'reasonable' love. A loving marriage is achieved first by Jane and Bingley, but their union is one in which both partners are equally modest, equally lacking in self-esteem, and hence too easily imposed upon by their friends and relatives. Note that Wickham, at the end of the novel, visits the Bingleys but *not* the Darcys.

The ideal marriage represented in the novel is obviously that of Elizabeth and Darcy. I wish to look first at how they achieve this ideal—and then to ask whether this marriage is as 'ideal' as one might wish. Elizabeth is clearly Jane Austen's favourite heroine; as she wrote to her sister, 'I must confess I think her as delightful a creature as ever appeared in print, and how I shall be able to tolerate those who do not like *her* at least I do not know'. Elizabeth is pert, pretty, intelligent, with the ability to discriminate between simple and complex characters, to use and to appreciate irony, and hence her father's favourite. Although she has had no formal education that we know of, she has read a great deal, she can play the piano with a natural grace, and she has acquired aesthetic good taste, one capable of appreciating the architecture, furniture, paintings, and gardens of Pemberly. She behaves with propriety and good breeding, despite her mother's bad example. And she is capable of deep and lasting affection, as demonstrated by her willingness to risk censure to walk alone to take care of Jane when she falls sick at the Bingleys' house. But above all, and the reason why feminist readers have always liked Elizabeth, she is a rebel, one who refuses to be intimidated by rank or wealth. She defies Lady Catherine de Bourgh, she rejects Collins's proposal, and, most telling, she rejects Darcy's first proposal, believing him—despite his wealth, good looks, and superior education—to be proud, selfish, and unloving. Elizabeth embodies Austen's fantasy of female power, the possibility that a young woman might be able to achieve autonomy and independence based on her intelligence and critical perception. She represents the impact of the French Revolution on Jane Austen's consciousness, the possibility that the natural rights of man might be extended to women as well. But to what extent is this vision of female self-empowerment endorsed by the novel?

Of course Elizabeth has flaws. She is guilty of both pride and prejudice. Her proud insistence on the value of individual moral worth leads her in Austen's view to discount to too great a degree the value of education and good breeding, the good manners which Hannah More had defined as the basis of civilization. She does not always see the evils caused by her mother's vulgar gossip (as when Mrs Bennet provokes Darcy into misreading Jane's feelings for Bingley). More critically, she is too quick to judge others; she has an excessive confidence, even vanity, in the accuracy of her own perceptions of others' characters. As a result, she trusts Wickham when she shouldn't, and rejects Darcy in part on false grounds. None the less, despite her pride and prejudice, Elizabeth is able to learn, to understand both 'intricate' characters and their 'essentials' better. Thus this novel is a novel of education, one in which Elizabeth matures in judgement.

Darcy too is guilty of pride and prejudice, and he too must mature in the course of the novel. His good qualities are numerous—he is handsome, intelligent, superbly well educated, a man of aesthetic taste and good breeding. He is capable of enduring devotion to his sister and his housekeeper, as well as of great generosity (to Wickham, repeatedly). And he is exceptionally wealthy, and hence extremely powerful—as Elizabeth recognizes, 'As a brother, a landlord, a master, . . . how many people's happiness were in his guardianship! How much of pleasure or pain it was in his power to bestow!—how much of good or evil must be done by him!' But Darcy is too proud of his class status, too quick to condemn others (as he says initially of Elizabeth, 'She is tolerable; but not handsome enough to tempt *me*'). And as he himself admits, he lacks the capacity to forgive—'My good opinion once lost is lost for ever.'

For these two proud and prejudiced characters to unite, a reconciliation must take place. In Austen's fiction, as Stuart Tave pointed out, words are always carefully chosen. Here two frequently repeated words define what happens to Darcy and Elizabeth: 'mortification' and 'gratitude'. First the pride of both Darcy and Elizabeth must be mortified, a word that means both a process of humiliation and of ascetic purification, of sacrificing one's former self in order to be born again into a better self. Darcy's pride is mortified, first when he looks again at Elizabeth and finds her extremely attractive; second when his aunt demonstrates as much 'ill breeding' as Mrs Bennet; third when Elizabeth rejects his proposal, delivered, as she points out, in a most 'ungentlemanlike manner'. Finally, in atonement and love, he chooses to mortify himself even further, by bribing his arch-enemy Wickham to marry Lydia. Elizabeth's pride is of course equally mortified, first when Darcy refuses to dance with her; second when she reads his letter and learns how badly she has misjudged Wickham; repeatedly by her mother's bad manners; most intensely by Lydia's elopement and the shame that having a 'prostitute' for a sister would entail; and finally by her father's refusal to believe that Darcy could wish to marry her.

When both Elizabeth and Darcy have been humbled, after Lydia has married Wickham, they meet again. By then Elizabeth knows she would welcome a renewal of Darcy's proposal. What has brought about her desire to marry him? The word Jane Austen chooses to describe Elizabeth's feelings for Darcy is not perhaps what we would expect, not 'love' or 'desire'—it is 'gratitude'. As Elizabeth mulls over her response to meeting Darcy at Pemberly, where he has graciously welcomed her and her aunt and uncle:

above all, above respect and esteem, there was a motive within her of good will which could not be overlooked. It was gratitude.—Gratitude, not merely for having once loved her, but for loving her still well enough, to forgive all the petulance and acrimony of her manner of rejecting him, and all the unjust accusations accompanying her rejection. . . . She respected, she esteemed, she was grateful to him, she felt a real interest in his welfare; and she only wanted to know how far she wished that welfare to depend upon herself, and how far it would be for the happiness of both that she should employ the power, which her fancy told she still possessed, of bringing on the renewal of his addresses.

(iii. 2)

Think about the word gratitude. In what circumstances does one typically feel gratitude? When one has received something one did not expect or deserve, such as a favour or an unexpected gift? When one has been spared a punishment one felt one did deserve? And to whom do we usually owe such gratitude? To parents, perhaps friends. Austen expects us to recognize that gratitude is an emotion produced when there is an unequal relationship, when one person has greater power than another (the power to withhold punishment, to give gifts). It is an emotion most often felt, perhaps, by children or, in the popular literature of the Romantic era, by slaves, as in Maria Edgeworth's novella, *The Grateful Negro*. In *Pride and Prejudice*, gratitude is overwhelmingly felt by Elizabeth rather than Darcy. She 'fancies' that she has 'power' over him, but in fact—once Lydia elopes—Elizabeth is forced to rush home, humiliated and impotent.

Only Darcy's 'ardent love' brings on the renewal of his proposal, a proposal which Elizabeth now accepts 'with gratitude and pleasure'. For she has come

to comprehend that he was exactly the man, who, in disposition and talents, would most suit her. His understanding and temper, though unlike her own, would have answered to all her wishes. It was a union that must have been to the advantage of both; by her ease and liveliness, his mind might have been softened, his manners improved, and from his judgment, information, and knowledge of the world, she must have received benefit of greater importance.

(iii. 8)

As Austen alerts us, Elizabeth recognizes that Darcy has greater power than she does, a power accrued by his wealth, age, education, experience, and sex. From Elizabeth, Darcy 'might' learn better manners; from him, she 'must' learn things of 'greater importance'. Austen wants us to understand that in her day, a time of gender inequality, Elizabeth's fantasy of autonomy and free will is just that, a fantasy—an extraordinarily potent fantasy for her female readers, but none the less a chimera.

For even after Darcy and Elizabeth marry, he maintains his power over her. She finds that it is 'too early' to laugh at him, and even though she 'may take' liberties with him that he does not allow his much younger sister to take, those liberties can be revoked at any moment he chooses. Since, for Austen, money is the basis of all real social power, it is particularly significant that Elizabeth does not share equally in Darcy's wealth. She is 'mistress of Pemberly' but she has only an 'allowance' of her own, a limited amount of funds for her 'private expenses' from which she can, with 'economy', send help to the impoverished Lydia and Wickham.

A feminist approach to *Pride and Prejudice* thus enables us to see beneath the surface fantasy of the novel—its apparent retelling of the fairy tale of Cinderella—to the darker realities of the condition of even the well-off middle-class women of Austen's society. Not only Austen's opening sentences but her entire novel thus operate ironically, telling two opposed stories to two different groups of readers, one to those charmed by her fantasy and another to those who recognize its falsity. Such use of irony may be necessary to feminist writers—certainly Virginia Woolf thought so, when she used it to articulate her fierce condemnation of all military action during the Second World War in *Three Guineas*. If one wishes to express one's anger towards one's rulers without being punished, one must use irony. And so Elizabeth does when she 'politely' refuses Darcy's offer to dance with her after insulting her, 'Mr Darcy is all [here meaning only] politeness'.

FURTHER READING

Butler, Marilyn, *Jane Austen and the War of Ideas* (Oxford: Clarendon Press, 1975). This book situates Austen in the context of the conservative politics of her day.

Copeland, Edward, and McMaster, Juliet (eds.), *The Cambridge Companion to Jane Austen* (Cambridge: Cambridge University Press, 1997). These essays provide a superb introduction to the entire range of Austen's work.

Craciun, Adriana, *Fatal Women of Romanticism* (Cambridge: Cambridge University Press, 2003). Provocatively discusses those Romantic women writers who contested the ethic of care (Charlotte Dacre, Mary Lamb, Mary Robinson, Ann Bannerman, and Letitia Landon).

Fay, Elizabeth A., *A Feminist Introduction to Romanticism* (Oxford: Blackwell, 1998). Offers a useful overview of feminist approaches to Romantic writing for the beginning student.

Feldman, Paula R., and Kelley, Theresa M. (eds.), *Romantic Women Writers: Voices and Countervoices* (Hanover, NH, and London: University Press of New England). An exceptionally fine collection of feminist readings of Romantic women poets, novelists, and dramatists.

Johnson, Claudia, *Jane Austen: Women, Politics, and the Novel* (Chicago: University of Chicago Press, 1988). Analyses Austen as a 'moderate feminist': the best book on Austen's fiction currently available.

Kaplan, Deborah, *Jane Austen among Women* (Baltimore: Johns Hopkins University Press, 1992). Analyses Austen's fiction within the context of a woman's culture of her day.

Keane, Angela, *Women Writers and the English Nation in the 1790s* (Cambridge: Cambridge University Press, 2000). Usefully contests the concept of a division between the public and the private sphere in women's writing in this period.

Kelly, Gary, *Women, Writing, and Revolution 1790–1827* (Oxford: Clarendon Press, 1993). Analyses the political responses of women writers to the French Revolution, from both the radical and the conservative camps.

Kirkham, Margaret, *Jane Austen: Feminism and Fiction* (Sussex: Harvester Press, 1983). The first book to discuss Austen's fiction from a feminist perspective.

Mellor, Anne K., (ed.), *Romanticism and Feminism* (Bloomington, Ind.: Indiana University Press, 1988). The first collection of essays devoted to a feminist approach to British Romantic texts; the essays by Alan Richardson and Stuart Curran have been particularly influential.

—— *Romanticism and Gender* (London and New York: Routledge, 1993). Discusses the issues surveyed in this essay in far greater detail.

—— *Mothers of the Nation: Women's Political Writing in England, 1780–1830* (Bloomington, Ind: Indiana University Press, 2000). Surveys the political views espoused by female Romantic poets, playwrights, novelists, and literary critics.

Poovey, Mary, *The Proper Lady and the Woman Writer* (Chicago: University of Chicago Press, 1984). Usefully surveys the conduct book literature of the Romantic period, but overestimates its influence on Wollstonecraft, Shelley, and Austen.

Roberts, Warren, *Jane Austen and the French Revolution* (New York: St Martin's Press, 1979). Places Austen in the context of the revolutionary politics of her day.

Ross, Marlon B., *The Contours of Masculine Desire: Romanticism and the Rise of Woman's Poetry* (New York: Oxford Univesity Press, 1989). The first book to approach the canonical Romantic poets from a feminist perspective. It gives an excellent overview of 'masculine Romanticism'.

Sulloway, Alison, *Jane Austen and the Province of Womanhood* (Philadelphia: University of Pennsylvania Press, 1989). Analyses Austen's fiction in the context both of the conservative conduct-book literature of her day and of the more progressive novels by Frances Burney and Maria Edgeworth.

Tave, Stuart, *Some Words of Jane Austen* (Chicago: University of Chicago Press, 1973). This book insightfully analyses the function played by key words in Austen's novels.

NOTE

1. Thomas Moore, *M.P. or the Blue-Stocking. A Comic Opera* (London, 1811), p. 64.

15 | Ecology

James C. McKusick

In recent years a new approach to the study of British Romantic literature has fundamentally altered the kinds of questions posed by literary criticism. This new approach,
known as ecological literary criticism, or simply ecocriticism, first came to prominence
during the 1990s, a period of increasing environmental concern throughout the industrialized world. Ecological critics have pondered fundamental questions about the
purpose of literary criticism, and of imaginative literature itself, in a time of ever-
increasing environmental crisis. Literary critic Jonathan Bate, for example, in an
essential book entitled *The Song of the Earth*, enquires: 'What are poets for?'[1] More
specifically, we may ask: Is poetry the authentic representation of reality, or merely the
decoration of life? Should poetry be engaged with social and political issues, or should
it offer merely a pleasant diversion?

These questions are squarely within the domain of poetics, as that discipline was first
conceived by Aristotle. In an era of impending threats to the global environment, the
emerging discipline of ecocriticism is engaged in a vital revision of the fundamental
task of poetry. At present ecocriticism has become more than just a marginal mode of
literary analysis, because nature is more than just a passive backdrop or setting for the
human drama of literature. British Romantic poetry, because it often seeks to address
perennial questions concerning the relationship between humankind and the natural
world, has become one of the most important terrains for the development of
ecological literary criticism.

As Jonathan Bate points out, 'the litany of present and impending catastrophes is all
too familiar'.[2] Any literate person is (or should be) aware of the impending doom of our
planetary ecosystem, due to an array of human-caused environmental hazards that
have no precedent in the entire history of the Earth. Bate presents these grim environmental threats in summary fashion: 'Carbon dioxide produced by the burning of fossil
fuels is trapping the heat of the sun, causing the planet to become warmer. Glaciers and
permafrost are melting, sea levels rising, rainfall patterns changing, winds growing
stronger. Meanwhile, the oceans are overfished, deserts are spreading, forests shrinking, fresh water becoming scarcer. The diversity of species upon the planet is diminishing.'[3] All literate citizens of the developed world know (or should know) these things,
but for some reason the widespread awareness of these horrendous environmental
problems has not resulted in effective remedial action. Why not? Perhaps there is

something amiss in the deep matrix of Western culture. Maybe what is needed is not a quick technological fix, but a fundamental change in human consciousness. If so, then the study of poetry can contribute to the solution of these global problems, because (as Bate argues) 'The business of literature is to work upon consciousness.'[4] In other words, the study of poetry can lead to the interrogation of fundamental ethical values. Ecological literary criticism sets out to explore how literature represents, and may potentially transform, the persistently pragmatic and instrumental awareness of the terrestrial environment that has pervaded Western culture for the last several centuries.

Ecological approaches to British Romantic literature

The emerging discipline of ecocriticism has not (as yet) established a single dominant paradigm for the interpretation of literature. Indeed, several distinct ecological approaches have offered fruitful and suggestive readings of British Romantic literature. One such approach involves looking at the habitat of literary production, and thereby exploring the rootedness of poems in the topography of particular places. This approach was pioneered by David McCracken in *Wordsworth and the Lake District* (1985), which offers a comprehensive study of William Wordsworth's poetry in its concrete geographical context, complete with maps and walking guides, while examining the crucial ways that this poetry is informed by specific images of mountains, lakes, and rivers. Such an approach is especially informative in the case of poets who were decisively influenced by particular places, and much basic research still remains to be done on the environmental contexts of such regional poets as Robert Bloomfield and John Clare. The essential theoretical basis for such an ecological approach was established by Lawrence Buell in *The Environmental Imagination* (1995), which lists four separate conditions that a poem or story must meet to be considered an 'environmental text'. Buell stipulates that in an environmental text, 'the nonhuman environment is present not merely as a framing device but as a presence that begins to suggest that human history is implicated in natural history'. Such environmental texts are especially prevalent in the British Romantic period (see *Oxford Companion to the Romantic Age*, p. 155).

Another important ecological approach to British Romantic literature involves the study of the history of ideas; recent ecocriticism has examined the historical foundations of the Romantic idea of nature, and has sought to elucidate precisely what contributions the Romantic-era writers made to a holistic understanding of the natural world. One of the best available histories of ecological thought is Donald Worster's *Nature's Economy* (1977); this book traces the origins of the modern scientific concept of ecology back to the eighteenth-century conception of the world as a harmonious, self-regulating system, known as the 'economy of nature'. In another wide-ranging historical study, *The Idea of Wilderness: From Prehistory to the Age of Ecology* (1991), Max

Oelschlaeger examines the development of the concept of 'wild nature' with particular reference to William Wordsworth and Samuel Taylor Coleridge. A more sustained and comprehensive analysis of the ecological ideas of Romantic-era writers is offered by Karl Kroeber in *Ecological Literary Criticism: Romantic Imagining and the Biology of Mind* (1994). Kroeber argues that British Romantic poetry was 'the first literature to anticipate contemporary biological conceptions', and that poets such as Wordsworth, Coleridge, and Percy Bysshe Shelley were 'proto-ecological' in their intellectual orientation.[5]

A third ecological approach to British Romantic literature might be termed 'existential', since it seeks to elucidate the history of environmental consciousness from within the imaginative experience of poetry. Perhaps the most influential example of this approach is *The Song of the Earth* by Jonathan Bate (discussed above). Another recent example of this approach is *Romanticism and the Materiality of Nature* (2002), in which Onno Oerlemans endeavours to situate British Romantic poetry in the hard, physical reality of the material world. In this study, Oerlemans seeks to place several of the Romantic poets, especially Wordsworth and Shelley, within the intellectual contexts of their period, while attending closely to the concrete physical substrate of poetic production: the very 'rocks, and stones, and trees' that form the irreducible subject-matter of poetry. Such an 'existential' approach bears an evident affinity with the geographical approach previously described, but it nevertheless remains quite distinct, because it does not endeavour to produce maps or walking guides; rather, it examines the way that natural phenomena are transformed by poetic consciousness into linguistic artefacts.

All three of the approaches outlined above have made important contributions to an ecological understanding of British Romantic literature, and they should be regarded as complementary rather than mutually exclusive. Indeed, the development of ecological literary criticism has been in large measure inspired and sustained by the literature of the British Romantic period, and by the same token, the canon of Romantic literature has been reshaped by the consideration of what constitutes an environmental text. A 'green' reading of Romanticism brings new works and new writers into prominence, and offers new perspectives upon the more canonical writers of the period. The remainder of this chapter will investigate both canonical and non-canonical writers of the Romantic period from an ecological perspective.

The Lake Poets: William Wordsworth and Samuel Taylor Coleridge

The poets William Wordsworth and Samuel Taylor Coleridge collaboratively pioneered new ways of seeing and responding to the natural world. Throughout the nineteenth century, Wordsworth was known to readers on both sides of the Atlantic as the most prominent of the 'Lake Poets', and the deep-rooted affiliation of his writing with a particular scenic locale in the north of England was further confirmed by the publication of his *Guide to the Lakes*, a guidebook to the English Lake District that was the best known and most frequently republished of Wordsworth's writings during his lifetime. More than just itinerant observers of picturesque beauty, Wordsworth and Coleridge were long-time inhabitants of the Lake District, and the poetry that they composed in that region often adopts the persona of a speaker whose voice is inflected by the local and personal history of the place he inhabits. Such a perspective may legitimately be termed an ecological view of the natural world, since their poetry consistently expresses a deep and abiding interest in the Earth as a dwelling-place for all living things. The word 'ecology' (first recorded in the English language in 1873) is derived from the Greek word *oikos* meaning house or dwelling-place, and the poetry of Wordsworth and Coleridge clearly foreshadows the modern science of ecology in its holistic conception of the Earth as a household, a dwelling-place for an interdependent biological community.

William Wordsworth's name is thus ineluctably associated with the Lake District, where he spent his childhood and adolescence, and to which he returned on a permanent basis in December 1799. Settling in Dove Cottage with his sister Dorothy, Wordsworth determined to make his home and his poetic career among the lakes and mountains that had first awakened and nourished his childhood imagination. His is a poetry of place, rooted not only in a concrete awareness of geographic location, but also in the significance that attaches to particular places as a result of childhood memory. In his great autobiographical poem *The Prelude*, Wordsworth states that his earliest memory of childhood was the sound of the river Derwent, whose murmurs 'from his alder shades and rocky falls . . . sent a voice | That flowed along my dreams' (I. 272–4). Wordsworth claims that his first memories were of sounds, a speaking-forth of the river directly into the 'dreams' of the infant, making him an engaged participant in the world that surrounds him, not merely a detached observer.

Beginning in July 1797, Coleridge spent much of his time in the company of William and Dorothy Wordsworth, often walking out in stormy weather to discuss their literary projects. Among these was a collaborative volume of poems, *Lyrical Ballads*, first published in September 1798. *Lyrical Ballads* marks a bold new departure in English verse, heralding the advent of Romanticism as a literary movement. Some of its most innovative features are the revival of ballad stanzas, reliance upon the language of everyday life, and extensive use of natural imagery drawn from direct personal observation (see *Oxford Companion to the Romantic Age*, p. 272). In their composition of *Lyrical Ballads*, Wordsworth and Coleridge shared a perception of the natural world as a dynamic ecosystem and a passionate commitment to the preservation of wild creatures and scenic areas.

Many of the poems in *Lyrical Ballads* are shaped by an underlying narrative of departure and return. This narrative pattern is decisively established by the first poem in the collection, Coleridge's 'The Rime of the Ancyent Marinere', whose protagonist sets forth from his native land on a voyage of exploration, returning home after many adventures, a changed man. This narrative pattern, whose literary analogues go at least as far back as the *Odyssey*, is repeated in Wordsworth's 'Tintern Abbey', the final poem in *Lyrical Ballads*. In this poem, Wordsworth describes his return to a place on the banks of the river Wye that he first visited five years previously. His initial response is one of sheer delight in the evidently unchanged appearance of the landscape; he celebrates the endurance of wild natural beauty, even in the midst of intensive human occupation.

From an ecocritical point of view, 'Tintern Abbey' poses several important questions about the right relationship between humankind and the natural world. The opening lines of the poem depict a human community dwelling in harmonious coexistence with nature; the local farmsteads are 'green to the very door', and the local farmers have acted to preserve a remnant of the primordial ecosystem of that region by allowing their hedgerows to run wild. Considering the increasingly destructive activities of the nearby charcoal-burners, however, it remains an open question whether such an environmentally benign mode of agriculture can be sustained in the long run (compare the analysis of 'Tintern Abbey' in the chapter on 'New Historicism'). The question of whether wildness can be preserved is also crucial to the central meditative development of the poem, in which Wordsworth depicts his younger self as if he were a wild beast, bounding over the mountains, and he later exhorts his sister Dorothy to preserve her own inner wildness. But this poem raises the question of whether such wildness can be sustained in any human relationship with nature. Will Dorothy eventually succumb, as her brother already has done, to the process by which 'these wild ecstacies shall be matured | Into a sober pleasure' (ll. 139–40)? Looking at *Lyrical Ballads* as a whole, it does appear unlikely that such a state of 'wild' awareness can be sustained for long by any individual. The prevailing tone of the collection is tragic; many of the characters in *Lyrical Ballads* are eventually broken, or at least tamed, by their circumstances.

Green language: Robert Bloomfield and John Clare

The democratic ethos of the Romantic era contributed to a flourishing literary marketplace that facilitated the emergence of new voices, including the marginal voices of labouring-class writers and women who had previously been excluded from many forms of literary publication. By writing out of their personal experience as agricultural labourers, Robert Bloomfield and John Clare penned a new kind of poetry, imbued with the concrete imagery of rural life, and (in Clare's case) steeped in the colourful vernacular of his native Northamptonshire.

Robert Bloomfield published his first book, *The Farmer's Boy*, in 1800, and it soon became a phenomenal success, selling more copies than any book of poetry in English had done before it. The key to its popularity was Bloomfield's self-presentation as an uneducated poet, a natural 'genius' whose literary talent allegedly owed nothing to the artifices of literary tradition. In fact, Bloomfield was deeply indebted to the loco-descriptive poets of the eighteenth century, especially James Thomson and Oliver Goldsmith, and his poetry is actually quite conventional in its diction and versification (locodescriptive poetry evokes a specific geographical place, often mentioned in the title of the poem). Bloomfield's originality, and his importance from an ecocritical point of view, lies in his striking attention to the details of agricultural life and natural history, particularly in his description of birds, animals, and insects. Bloomfield attends with great patience and evident affection to the smallest of nature's creatures; he is undoubtedly the first poet in English to describe a beetle from the beetle's own point of view:

> The small dust-coloured beetle climbs with pain
> O'er the smooth plantain leaf, a spacious plain!
> Thence higher still, by countless steps conveyed,
> He gains the summit of a shivering blade,
> And flirts his filmy wings, and looks around,
> Exulting in his distance from the ground.
> ('Summer', ll. 433–8)

Rather than offering a static or 'objective' description of the beetle, Bloomfield evokes the dynamic lived experience of its journey as it clambers across a leaf and clings exultantly to a 'shivering blade'. Who would dare to harm such an intrepid little creature? Such vividly evocative passages seek to bring the reader to a sympathetic appreciation of the essential role played by all living things, even by small insects, in the economy of nature.

John Clare published four volumes of poetry during his lifetime: *Poems Descriptive of Rural Life and Scenery* (1820), *The Village Minstrel* (1821), *The Shepherd's Calendar; with Village Stories and Other Poems* (1827); and *The Rural Muse* (1835). Clare described himself on the title-page of his first collection of poems as a 'Northamptonshire Peasant', a bold assertion of regional identity that situated his voice in an East Midlands county that was becoming increasingly a zone of environmental conflict. Although he had little formal schooling, Clare was an avid reader of English poetry, and he possessed a remarkably detailed and accurate knowledge of natural history. His poetry conveys a detailed knowledge of the local flora and fauna, an acute awareness of the interrelatedness of all life-forms, and a sense of outrage at the destruction of the natural environment. Clare forthrightly denounced the 'improvement' of his local environment through the process of parliamentary enclosure (see *Oxford Companion to the Romantic Age*, p. 155), while evoking with elegiac melancholy the gradual disappearance of the common fields, marshes, and 'waste' lands, and the extinction of an entire way of life in harmony with the natural cycles of the day, season, and year.

Clare's poems typically represent the landscape through the point of view of a local resident, often a peasant, shepherd, or woodman, or even within the imagined consciousness of a native animal, plant, or waterway. In one of his best-known poems, 'The Badger', he depicts with keen sympathy the cruel treatment of a badger captured and tormented by a crowd of villagers:

> He falls as dead and kicked by boys and men
> Then starts and grins and drives the crowd agen
> Till kicked and torn and beaten out he lies
> And leaves his hold and cackles groans and dies
>
> (ll. 65–8)

Clare narrates this episode largely from the point of view of the badger, identifying at a deep emotional level with its role as the helpless victim of human brutality. Like Bloomfield, Clare is fascinated by the inward emotional life of animals, and by evoking the badger's terrible fate, Clare indicates his profound respect for its courage, strength, and determination.

Clare's regional dialect is an intentional feature of his poetry that contributes to his sense of rootedness in a particular landscape. He steadfastly resisted all of his editors' efforts to 'improve' his verse. Clare's fidelity to what he calls the 'Language of Nature' and his resistance to substantive editorial emendations frequently recur in his correspondence, indicating his enduring allegiance to a defiantly 'vulgar' conception of language. Indeed, in 'Pastoral Poesy' Clare refers to his own writing as 'a language that is ever green', suggesting a poetic praxis that emerges from his deep appreciation for the harmony of an indigenous vernacular with its local environment.

The return of the nightingale: Charlotte Smith and John Keats

Charlotte Smith played an influential role in the formation of English Romanticism as a literary movement (see *Oxford Companion to the Romantic Age*, p. 709), and her poetry is essential to an ecological understanding of the period. In her affection for all of nature's creatures, even the lowly green-chafer and the humble hedgehog, Smith evokes the possibility of a new kind of nature writing, intimate in tone and deeply personal in its mode of expression (compare the chapter on 'Sensibility'). Her extensive knowledge of botany, taxonomy, and ornithology exemplifies the convergence between science and poetry in the Romantic era. Smith's first book of poetry, *Elegiac Sonnets* (1784), was remarkable both for its revival of the Petrarchan sonnet form (virtually extinct in English poetry since the time of John Milton) and for the precision and intensity of its nature imagery. In a series of sonnets addressed to the nightingale, Smith evokes the actual presence of the bird: she describes the plaintive sound of its voice at nightfall as it seeks its missing mate. The nightingale is represented not merely as a traditional emblem for poetic inspiration, but more specifically as an analogue for

Smith's own forlorn circumstances of poverty, misery, and heartache. (Deserted by her dissolute, violent, and unfaithful husband, Smith became a professional writer as a means of supporting her twelve children.) The pervasive theme of yearning for lost love, and the intensely personal, introspective quality of her lyric poetry, mark a significant departure from the prevailing norms of late eighteenth-century verse.

Smith's sonnet 'The Return of the Nightingale' (1791) was to prove particularly influential upon later Romantic poetry. Since this poem is rarely anthologized, it is cited here in full:

> Borne on the warm wing of the western gale,
>   How tremulously low is heard to float
> Thro' the green budding thorns that fringe the vale,
>   The early Nightingale's prelusive note.
>
> 'Tis Hope's instinctive power that thro' the grove
>   Tells how benignant Heaven revives the earth;
> 'Tis the soft voice of young and timid Love
>   That calls these melting sounds of sweetness forth.
>
> With transport, once, sweet bird! I hail'd thy lay,
>   And bade thee welcome to our shades again,
> To charm the wandering poet's pensive way
>   And soothe the solitary lover's pain;
> But now!—such evils in my lot combine,
> As shut my languid sense—to Hope's dear voice and thine!

Traditionally regarded as a figure for poetic inspiration, and presented in Milton's poem 'Il Penseroso' (1645) as an emblem of melancholy, the nightingale is here identified with an 'instinctive power' that renews the Earth in springtime, and addressed as a singer whose 'melting sounds of sweetness' charm the wandering poet. Rescued from its melancholy Miltonic associations, the nightingale returns to English poetry as a redemptive female figure that embodies the seasonal cycles of nature and the healing powers of the Earth. To a female poet like Smith, the bird serves as a professional role model in the craft of poetry, offering hope and companionship in a time of pain and solitude.

Smith's revival of the sonnet form, and her dramatic reshaping of the nightingale in the sonnet just cited, directly influenced the work of later poets in the Romantic tradition, particularly Coleridge, whose poem 'The Nightingale' (1798) likewise offers a dramatic reshaping of the Miltonic nightingale. Explicitly citing 'Il Penseroso', where Milton had addressed the nightingale as a 'most musical, most melancholy' bird, Coleridge retorts: 'In Nature there is nothing melancholy' (l. 15). Like Smith, Coleridge invites the return of the nightingale to English poetry, rescued from its mythic associations of mindless melancholy, and presented instead as a real bird that inhabits a real grove in the early springtime; yet Coleridge's nightingale is also a singer or fellow poet (evidently male) whose voice embodies the powerful, transformative emotions of joy and love. Coleridge follows Smith in regarding the nightingale as an embodiment of nature, possessed of mysterious powers.

The nightingale makes its most crucial reappearance in the poetry of John Keats, whose 'Ode to a Nightingale' (1819), while responding most directly to Milton and Coleridge, further elaborates upon Smith's evocation of that bird in 'The Return of the Nightingale'. Like Smith, Keats personifies the nightingale as a female singer—specifically as a dryad, or wood nymph—and he invests the bird with an inscrutable sort of happiness that is immune to mortal woe. The 'Ode to a Nightingale' is rightly regarded as one of the most elusive and ambiguous poems in the entire canon of British Romanticism, and in light of its convoluted literary heritage—from Greek mythology and the poetry of John Milton down through the nightingale poems of Coleridge and Smith—it may be regarded as an embodiment of all the complexity that had come to inhabit the idea of nature during the Romantic period. Keats's nightingale embodies a host of contradictions: it is immortal, yet it is also associated with 'easeful Death' (l. 52); it pours forth its soul in ecstasy, yet it inspires thoughts of 'faery lands forlorn' (l. 70). Every reader of the Ode must wrestle with these contradictions, and an ecocritical reader is unlikely to seek resolution in any version of the taut, sceptical irony that was formerly advocated by the New Criticism. Ecocritical readers are much more likely to linger in that dark, odorous, enchanted forest where 'soft incense hangs upon the boughs' (l. 42; compare the reading of this poem in 'Romantic Forms: An Introduction').

The end of nature: William Blake, Percy Shelley, and Lord Byron

The idyllic Romantic conception of the natural world as a place of vital sustenance and peaceful coexistence is complemented by a nightmare vision of the Earth threatened by imminent environmental catastrophe. Global apocalypse is a theme with a long history in Western literature, going back at least as far as the catastrophic flood depicted in Genesis and the fiery doom foretold in the Book of Revelation. But the dawn of the industrial revolution (see *Oxford Companion to the Romantic Age*, pp. 133–41) marked the first time that such apocalyptic events were imaginable as the result of normal human activity, rather than an inscrutable act of God. In the early years of the nineteenth century, as the manufacturing cities of England disappeared into a thick haze of photochemical smog, it became possible to imagine that new technologies of mass production might alter the climate and eventually destroy the Earth's ability to sustain life.

William Blake, Percy Bysshe Shelley, and Lord Byron each wrote narrative poems of apocalyptic destruction. Blake's critique of industrial capitalism, and his depiction of its ultimate environmental consequences, is apparent in such poems as 'London', and most fully and coherently expressed in his two major prophetic books, *Milton* (composed *c.*1800–4) and *Jerusalem* (composed *c.*1804–7). Both of these narrative poems use the prophetic past tense to describe England's present predicament, with particular emphasis on the grim industrial landscape that was inexorably forming around Lambeth, on the South Bank of the Thames, where Blake lived from 1791 to 1800. Blake is not only concerned with the misery and abasement of the human spirit that inevitably results from the deployment of heavy industry in urban areas; he is also aware that these coal-fired industries entail a serious potential for environmental damage.

In *Jerusalem*, plates 18–19, Blake offers a comprehensive catalogue of environmental damage: the skies over England are darkened with smoke, birds have fallen silent, flocks have died, harvests have failed, apples are poisoned, and the Earth's climate is marked by scorching heat and devastating storms. Albion, the giant personification of England, is 'self-exiled' by the devastation of his homeland; his children cry helplessly, and his Eon (or female companion) weeps as she beholds such terrible destruction. England has been destroyed by its own industrial activity, the 'Starry Wheels' of complex machines, and infernal iron-forges and coal-mines 'that belch forth storms & fire'. Only too late does Albion realize that his relentless drive to industrialize, along with his incessant wars of imperial conquest, have resulted in the desolation of the entire Earth.

Percy Bysshe Shelley's sonnet 'Ozymandias' (1818) is most often read as an ironic commentary on the vanity of political ambition and the inevitable downfall of tyranny (see chapter on 'Formalism'), but from an ecocritical point of view it may also be regarded as an object lesson in unsustainable environmental practices. Well versed in history, Shelley was certainly aware that the ancient Mediterranean world was formerly a place of great agricultural fertility and abundance. Over many centuries, the dense forests described by Homer were felled; the cedars of Lebanon were destroyed; the irrigation of arid areas resulted in the toxic accumulation of salt in the soil; and eventually these paradisal landscapes were converted into barren deserts.[6] The statue of Ozymandias lies shattered in the midst of a desert, and the surrounding landscape offers a grim commentary on the relatively brief duration of the civilization that he commanded: 'Round the decay | Of that colossal wreck, boundless and bare | The lone and level sands stretch far away' (ll. 12–14). The poem implies a critique of any society that believes it can ultimately dominate the natural world: 'Look on my works, ye Mighty, and despair!' (l. 11). Nature will win in the end.

Even more sombre in tone, Byron's poem 'Darkness' (1816) offers an apocalyptic dream-vision of a world that is utterly destroyed. In this bleak narrative, the speaker describes a strange dream: 'The bright sun was extinguish'd, and the stars | Did wander darkling in the eternal space' (ll. 2–3). As the last light fades, and starving people battle over the earth's few remaining resources, the worst aspects of human nature are revealed. Finally, in this dismal scenario, all life is extinguished; the entire earth is frozen into a solid mass; and darkness rules over the entire universe. What does this dream signify? Clearly it offers evidence of Byron's dim view of human nature; and it may also reflect prevailing scientific speculation over the ultimate fate of the universe.

From an environmental point of view, however, this poem may be read as a parable that reminds the reader of the dependence of all living things on the light of the sun, and that points out the inevitable consequence of unsustainable human activity in a global ecosystem. As darkness falls, desperate humans burn everything that will burn:

> Forests were set on fire – but hour by hour
> They fell and faded – and the crackling trunks
> Extinguish'd with a crash – and all was black.
> (ll. 19–21)

To Byron's contemporaries at the dawn of the industrial revolution, such images served as an admonition. To modern readers, faced with the imminent possibility of global climate change, they may offer a prophetic warning.

The Romantic origins of environmentalism

The idea of nature, and indeed the very meaning of the word 'nature', underwent a significant transformation over the course of the Romantic period. The British Romantic writers formulated an innovative and in many respects original way of understanding the natural world. Such an understanding may authentically be termed 'ecological' (and not merely 'proto-ecological'), since for the first time in the Western intellectual tradition their poetry evinces the essential elements of a modern ecological world-view. Especially in such poets as Wordsworth, Coleridge, and John Clare, the Romantic era found itself on the threshold of an ecological perception, a sensibility that understands all of nature to be constituted as an assemblage of biotic communities characterized by diversity, complexity, and symbiosis.

Such traditional literary symbols as the nightingale take on renewed significance in the wake of such ecological understanding; no longer a mythic embodiment of melancholy, the nightingale for Charlotte Smith, Coleridge, and Keats becomes once again a real bird in a real forest, singing its own glad song of springtime, love, and joyfulness. Simply by being itself, however, the nightingale takes on the mysterious complexity of nature, which has the power to give life, and to destroy it, without regard to human desire.

Such ecological understanding also made possible the apocalyptic narratives of Blake, Shelley, and Byron. Blake's poetry, from the *Songs of Experience* to *Jerusalem*, engages in a sustained and bitter critique of the material conditions of production—the 'dark Satanic mills' (*Milton*, plate 1) that constituted the coal-fired industrial base of Britain's mercantile empire (compare the reading of 'Tintern Abbey' in the chapter on 'New Historicism'). Byron's 'Darkness' likewise offers a prophetic vision of the extinction of all life forms and of the earth itself. Such global annihilation, regarded throughout most of human history as a mere poetic fiction, bears a more urgent burden of possibility in the present era of global climate change and impending environmental catastrophe. Blake's visionary protest against the industrial revolution offers informative parallels to our modern ecological concerns.

READING: Samuel Taylor Coleridge, 'The Rime of the Ancyent Marinere'[7]

Samuel Taylor Coleridge's engagement with the integrity of the natural world, and his concern for its preservation, is apparent throughout his contributions to *Lyrical Ballads*, a volume that is constructed with thoughtful attention to the situation of poems in a larger context. 'The Rime of the Ancyent Marinere', a deliberately archaic narrative poem in ballad stanza, appears as the first poem in the 1798 edition of *Lyrical Ballads*. When Coleridge revised the poem for publication in 1817, he normalized the spelling, removed archaic words, and added a marginal gloss. Although many critics, following in the footsteps of a famous essay by Robert Penn Warren,[8] have regarded this poem as a symbolic narrative that is primarily concerned with the sublime transformative powers of the poetic imagination, there is in fact little warrant for such a reading in the original 1798 version of the poem. Indeed, the 1798 version, with its quaint *Argument* and its quirky archaic spelling and diction, may offer modern readers the possibility of seeing the poem afresh, without preconceived notions of its supposed symbolic significance. An ecological reading of this poem could emerge from a stubbornly literal approach to the poem, one that takes seriously its narrative of exploration and discovery in strange seas, and its tale of encounter with wild creatures that live far from human dwelling-places.

Regarded in this way, 'The Rime of the Ancyent Marinere' may be read as a fictional narrative of ecological transgression. The Mariner is portrayed with historical accuracy as a sixteenth-century sailor on a voyage of exploration to 'the cold Country towards the South Pole'. Here he encounters a frigid realm that is apparently devoid of life: 'Ne shapes of men ne beasts we ken | The Ice was all between'.[9] The word 'ken' suggests that the Mariner's plight is fundamentally a crisis in Western ways of *knowing*: an epistemic gap that separates him from the hidden creatures of the Antarctic. The Mariner embarks on this voyage as a philosophical dualist, a detached observer who is cut off from any feeling of empathy or participation in the vast world of life that surrounds him.

The albatross as emissary

The Albatross appears out of the 'fog' as an emissary from the Antarctic wilderness. In a spontaneous act of identification, the mariners hail it as 'a Christian soul', as if it were a human being like themselves:

> At length did cross an Albatross,
>   Thorough the Fog it came,
> And an it were a Christian Soul,
>   We hail'd it in God's name.
>   (ll. 61–4)

The Albatross crosses from the wild ice to the world of men, and its act of 'crossing' the boundary between nature and civilization indicates a possible resolution of the Mariner's epistemic solitude. The Albatross brings companionship to the lonely mariners, it guides them through the pathless ice, and returns 'every day for food or play' (l. 71). The 1798 version of the poem specifies that 'The Marineres gave it biscuit-worms' (l. 65), a homely detail that concretely renders the symbiotic exchange between man and beast: the mariners provide nourishment for the Albatross, while the bird provides them with more intangible benefits of companionship, guidance, and play. These biscuit-worms are more than mere vermin; they play an essential role in the web of life, and they intimate that what we regard as ugly or obnoxious may nonetheless be appealing when considered from another (inhuman) perspective.

The Mariner kills the Albatross with his 'cross bow' (l. 79), a weapon that embodies the relentlessly destructive tendency of European technology at the same time that it invokes, with some irony, the traditional Christian imagery of sacrifice and atonement. If the Albatross is regarded as an innocent emissary from the unspoiled natural realm of the Antarctic, then the Mariner's deed represents an unmotivated act of aggression against all the creatures of that realm. But the Antarctic, through the agency of the Polar Spirit, wreaks a terrible vengeance upon the Mariner, who must witness the death of his shipmates and the decay of the entire living world around him, as if the destruction of a single creature had disrupted the whole economy of nature:

> The very deeps did rot: O Christ!
>   That ever this should be!
> Yea, slimy things did crawl with legs
>   Upon the slimy Sea.
>   (ll. 119–22)

These slimy creatures with legs, unknown to any textbook of natural history, represent with apocalyptic intensity the death of nature as a result of destructive human acts. On a concrete historical level, the voyage of the Mariner may be compared to Captain James Cook's second voyage of discovery in 1772–5, which mapped the Antarctic region, described the incredible abundance of its fauna, and thereby ushered in an era of wholesale destruction of seals, whales, birds, and other marine life.[10]

Creatures of the great calm

As the Mariner's vessel 'made her course to the tropical Latitude of the Great Pacific Ocean' ('Rime of the Ancyent Marinere', *Argument*) a community of living things is gathered around her. Any wooden sailing ship in tropical waters will gradually accumulate a host of fellow travellers, ranging from barnacles and seaweed to schools of fish that shelter within her shadow. The ship comes to resemble a floating reef, and the teeming flora and fauna offer both perils and opportunities to those aboard her. As Coleridge could have learned from several narrative accounts of maritime exploration in tropical latitudes, the fouling of a ship's hull and the rapid rotting of her timbers can lead to her destruction, but the abundance and variety of marine life surrounding the ship was cause of wonder and amazement for many British explorers. In his influential study *The Road to Xanadu*, John Livingston Lowes cites a typical passage from Captain Cook's third voyage of 1776–80:

During a calm, on the morning of the 2d, some parts of the sea seemed covered with a kind of slime; and some small sea animals were swimming about. . . . When they began to swim about, which they did, with equal ease, upon their back, sides, or belly, they emitted the brightest colours of the most precious gems. . . . They proved to be . . . probably, an animal which has a share in producing some sorts of that lucid appearance, often observed near ships at sea, in the night.[11]

The slimy creatures found in the vicinity of Cook's ship display unexpected flashes of beauty to the scientific observer, just as the water-snakes in Coleridge's poem are revealed to be vital participants in the ship's local ecosystem. Their repulsive aspect is eventually shown to have been the result of the Mariner's flawed perception, not their intrinsic nature. The Mariner's act of blessing the water-snakes enables him to see them, with a striking intensity of vision, as creatures that inhabit 'the shadow of the ship', an ecotone (or boundary region) that provides rich habitat for an abundance of marine life:

> Within the shadow of the ship
>   I watch'd their rich attire:
> Blue, glossy green, and velvet black
> They coil'd and swam; and every track
>   Was a flash of golden fire.
> (ll. 269–73)

The luminescent trails of these sea-snakes strongly resemble the tracks of light described by the scientist Erasmus Darwin in his poem 'The Economy of Vegetation' (1791), where he attributes their eerie glow to the 'incipient putrefaction' of 'fish-slime'.[12] Finding the hidden beauty in such slimy substances, the Mariner discovers that all life forms, even microscopic ones, play a vital role in the natural world.

By blessing the water-snakes, the Mariner is released from his state of alienation from nature, and the Albatross sinks 'like lead into the sea' (l. 283), crossing back from civilization into the untamed ocean. The Mariner has learned what the Albatross came to teach him: that he must cross the boundaries that divide him from the natural world, through unmotivated acts of compassion between 'man and bird and beast' (l. 646). In its concern for boundary regions, 'The Rime of the Ancyent Marinere' foreshadows some of the most seminal thoughts of contemporary environmental writers. The American environmental writer Romand Coles, in an essay entitled 'Ecotones and Environmental Ethics', describes the ethical and imaginative significance of such boundary regions:

Natural ecologists know that ecotones (with their intermingling borders) are especially fertile, 'special meeting grounds' charged with 'evolutionary potential'. When we combine this knowledge with the etymology of *ecotone*, *oikos* (dwelling), and *tonus* (tension), we evoke an image of the fertility and pregnancy of dwelling at the edge of the tension between different people, beings, landscapes.[13]

'The Rime of the Ancyent Marinere' likewise ponders the ethical significance of dwelling on boundaries between different realms. In the poem's initial episode, an Albatross crosses from the inhuman world of ice 'as green as Emerauld' (l. 52) into the human community of the mariners. At the poem's climax, the 'shadow of the ship' (ll. 264, 269) delineates a rich tropical ecotone inhabited by sea-snakes that the Mariner must 'bless' in order to survive. At the end of the poem, the Mariner returns from sea to land, drifting across the 'Harbour-bar' (l. 473) and rowing ashore with the help of a Hermit who inhabits yet another ecotone, 'that wood | Which slopes down to the Sea' (ll. 547–8). All of these boundary regions serve as points of departure and arrival for the poem's profound meditation upon the green world of nature and the destructive tendencies of human civilization. Written explicitly in defence of 'all things both great and small' (l. 648), this poem exemplifies the environmental advocacy that is integral to Coleridge's ecological vision.

Archaic words and the conservation of language

Coleridge's use of language in 'The Rime of the Ancyent Marinere' provides crucial evidence of his endeavour to construct a new ecolect.[14] As Lowes points out in *The Road to Xanadu* (pp. 296–310), the 1798 version of the poem is more than just a fake antique ballad on the model of Thomas Percy's *Reliques* (1765) and Thomas Chatterton's 'Rowley' poems (1777). Lowes demonstrates that Coleridge combines three fairly distinct types of archaic usage: first, the traditional ballad lexicon (words like *pheere, eldritch, beforne, I ween, sterte, een, countrée, withouten, cauld*); second, the diction of Geoffrey Chaucer and Edmund Spenser (*ne, uprist, I wist, yspread, yeven, n'old, eftsones, lavrock, jargoning, minstralsy*); and third, seafaring terminology (*swound, weft, clifts, biscuit-worms, fire-flags*). All three types of archaic usage are severely curtailed in the 1800 edition of the poem, perhaps in response to a reviewer in the *British Critic* (October 1799) who denounced the poem's 'antiquated words', citing *swound* (l. 397) and *weft* (l. 83) as flagrant examples of nonsensical diction. Coleridge omitted the vivid seafaring term *weft* in 1800, along with many of the other words listed here. The merits and demerits of Coleridge's 1800 modernization and his later addition of a marginal gloss in *Sibylline Leaves* (1817) have been widely debated; Lowes regards Coleridge's revisions of this poem as a definite improvement, and more recent critics tend to accept this established opinion. Yet the accessibility and stylistic coherence of the 1817 version is accomplished at the expense of the multifaceted syncretic quality of the original version, which bespeaks the author's desire to reassemble the surviving fragments of archaic language into a richly textured and deeply expressive mode of poetic discourse.

From an ecological point of view, the 1798 version of 'The Rime of the Ancyent Marinere' enhances the poem's environmental themes through its conservation of lexical diversity. Coleridge's use of archaic diction and spelling goes well beyond the mere intention to appear quaint, or to follow a literary fashion. Rather than seeking to epitomize the English language at a single time and place, the poem draws eclectically upon many strands of diction from discrete historical periods and social strata. The essential purpose of this lexical variety is to construct an idiolect for the Mariner that embodies a wide assortment of historical features; the adjacence of modern and archaic words enables the poem to characterize the Mariner as a wanderer through geographic space and historical time, and to situate his discourse at the conjunction of modernity and Romantic nostalgia for the remote historical past. Moreover, the use of archaic diction provides a linguistic analogue to the poem's main environmental theme, since the extinction of an archaic word can have unforeseen repercussions upon the integrity of a language. If the English lexicon is regarded as a close-knit organic system, then the loss of a single word may result in consequences as dire as the Mariner suffers upon killing an albatross. Coleridge elsewhere describes 'words as living growths, offlets, and organs of the human soul', and he urges writers to employ the entire 'reversionary wealth in our mother-tongue'.[15] From the perspective of this organic conception of language, it seems apparent that 'The Rime of the Ancyent Marinere' aspires to enrich and revitalize contemporary poetic diction through the recovery and preservation of archaic words.

A particular example may help to elucidate this thesis. Coleridge's term 'Lavrock' (l. 348) derives from Middle English *laveroc*, a precursor of the Modern English *lark*. The Lavrock (like the Nightingale encountered later in the *Lyrical Ballads*) is a 'most musical' bird, and Coleridge's impression of this bird evidently derives from his recollection of Chaucer's version of *The Romaunt of the Rose*:

> There mightin men se many flockes
> Of Turtels and of *Laverockes*
>
> . . . .
> Thei song ther song, as faire and wel
> As angels doen espirituell
>
> . . . .
> Layis of love full wel souning
> Thei songin in ther *jargoning*.[16]

Coleridge likewise uses the word 'jargoning' to describe the Lavrock's song:

> Sometimes a dropping from the sky
> I heard the *Lavrock* sing;
> Sometimes all little birds that are
> How they seem'd to fill the sea and air
> With their sweet *jargoning*.
> (ll. 347–51; emphasis added)

The Lavrock enters the poem at an ecotonal boundary of 'sea and air', lending its mellifluous voice to the Mariner's growing sense of ethical redemption. The 'sweet jargoning' of the Lavrock is metaphorically related in subsequent stanzas to the sound of human instruments, the song of angels, and the 'singing' of a quiet brook. All created beings, and even inanimate objects, are accorded some form of linguistic expression. The voice of the Lavrock exemplifies a radical environmental usage, suggesting that the animate creation has its own language, and its own way of responding to the aeolian influences of the one life. The word *Lavrock* contains a hidden lexemic trace of the word *rock*, possibly foreshadowing the Mariner's return to solid ground and the 'kirk . . . that stands above the *rock*' (ll. 503–4; emphasis added). When Coleridge substituted 'skylark' for 'Lavrock' in the 1800 edition, this subliminal trace of the word *rock* was lost, along with the word's Chaucerian echo and its distinctive contribution to the poem's lexical diversity. The 1800 edition of this poem, bowing to the critical demand for stylistic decorum, was severely impoverished by the loss of such words as *weft* and *Lavrock*. Indeed, the deletion of *Lavrock* obscures the main thematic point of the word 'jargoning', which (according to the *American Heritage Dictionary*) is 'probably of imitative origin', and thus refers to the inscrutable sounds one might hear in a language contact zone (or linguistic ecotone). The archaic word *Lavrock* represents the admixture of diverse linguistic elements that constitutes a *jargon*, in the same way that the Lavrock's song traverses the boundary between human and inhuman language. Just as the Lavrock's song is perceived as a 'sweet jargoning' by the Mariner, so too the word *Lavrock* contributes to the poem's distinctive 'jargon', which might properly be termed an ecolect that emerges from the encounter between humankind and the natural world.

In their collaborative composition of *Lyrical Ballads*, Wordsworth and Coleridge shared a perception of the natural world as a dynamic ecosystem and a passionate commitment to the preservation of wild creatures and scenic areas. Their 1798 volume was designed as a habitat that would provide a nurturing environment for the diversity of poems contained within it. Coleridge's unique contribution to this collaborative endeavour was his conception of language as a living thing, an integral organic system that can be cultivated by the poet for maximum diversity, either through the coinage of new words or the recovery of archaic ones. This holistic conception of language was clearly indebted to the new understanding of the organism that had emerged from eighteenth-century biology, and it represents a metaphorical extension of the cyclical view of natural process that was expressed in the notion of the economy of nature. For Coleridge, the historical development of language is deeply conditioned by its relation to the natural environment, and his aesthetic principle of organicism likewise entails reference to the linguistic habitat of a poem as an essential determinant of its meaning. 'The Rime of the Ancyent Marinere' most fully embodies the poetic praxis envisioned by this organic conception of poetic language; its eclectic use of archaic diction serves to enhance and preserve the lexical diversity of the English language throughout the broad range of its social, geographic, and historical variation. Coleridge's poetic energies were devoted to the development of a distinctive ecolect that might express the proper role of humankind in the economy of nature.

FURTHER READING

Bate, Jonathan, *Romantic Ecology: Wordsworth and the Environmental Tradition* (London: Routledge, 1991). The first major study of British Romantic poetry from an ecocritical point of view, with emphasis on the poetry of William Wordsworth.

—— *The Song of the Earth* (Cambridge, Mass: Harvard University Press, 2000). This important study advocates a new kind of poetics with an ecological inflection—an *ecopoetics*—and argues that the English Romantic poets sought to reimagine the relationship between human communities and the natural world.

Buell, Lawrence, *The Environmental Imagination: Thoreau, Nature Writing, and the Formation of American Culture* (Cambridge, Mass: Belknap Press, 1995). Focusing mainly on American nature writers, this study argues that literary criticism should be centrally concerned with 'environmental texts'.

Harrison, Robert Pogue, *Forests: The Shadow of Civilization* (Chicago: University of Chicago Press, 1993). An insightful and wide-ranging study of the role of forests in Western thought from ancient through to modern times.

Kroeber, Karl, *Ecological Literary Criticism: Romantic Imagining and the Biology of Mind* (New York: Columbia University Press, 1994). Advocates an ecological approach to the study of literature, taking into account recent advances in environmental science.

Lowes, John Livingston, *The Road to Xanadu: A Study in the Ways of the Imagination*, 2 edn. (Boston: Houghton Mifflin, 1930). A fascinating and influential study of Coleridge's intellectual development, with comprehensive analysis of historical and narrative sources for 'The Rime of the Ancient Mariner' and 'Kubla Khan'.

McCracken, David, *Wordsworth and the Lake District: A Guide to the Poems and their Places* (Oxford: Oxford University Press, 1985). A comprehensive study of William Wordsworth's poetry in its geographical context, complete with maps and walking guides.

McKusick, James, *Green Writing: Romanticism and Ecology* (New York: St Martin's Press, 2000). Describes the emergence of ecological understanding among the English Romantic poets, arguing that their approach offered a foundation for American environmentalism in Ralph Waldo Emerson, Henry David Thoreau, John Muir, and Mary Austin.

Oelschlaeger, Max, *The Idea of Wilderness: From Prehistory to the Age of Ecology* (New Haven: Yale University Press, 1991). Traces the history of ideas of wilderness from Paleolithic times through the Renaissance and Romantic periods, up to the 'postmodern idea of wilderness' in our own time.

Oerlemans, Onno, *Romanticism and the Materiality of Nature* (Toronto: University of Toronto Press, 2002). Examines the representation of the natural world in several British Romantic writers, with particular attention to William and Dorothy Wordsworth, Percy Shelley, and John Clare.

Roe, Nicholas, *The Politics of Nature: Wordsworth and Some Contemporaries*, 2nd edn. (London: Palgrave, 2002). An important study of the 'return to nature' by several British Romantic writers in the aftermath of revolutionary defeat: this second edition takes into account recent developments in historical and ecological criticism.

Smith, Bernard, 'Coleridge's *Ancient Mariner* and Cook's Second Voyage', *Journal of the Warburg and Courtauld Institutes*, 19 (1956), 117–54. Coleridge's mathematics teacher was William Wales, a professional astronomer on Captain James Cook's second voyage, who told his students fascinating tales of his exploits in the Antarctic Ocean: Smith argues that these tales first sparked Coleridge's interest in the history of British maritime exploration.

Thomas, Keith, *Man and the Natural World: A History of the Modern Sensibility* (New York: Pantheon Books, 1983). A classic study of the history of environmental ideas in England, with special attention to literary tradition.

Warren, Robert Penn, 'A Poem of Pure Imagination: An Experiment in Reading' (1946), in *New and Selected Essays* (New York: Random House, 1989), pp. 335–423. Warren argues that in 'The

Rime of the Ancient Mariner', the sun represents 'the light of practical convenience' while the moon represents 'the modifying colors of the imagination'.

Worster, Donald, *Nature's Economy: A History of Ecological Ideas*, 2nd edn. (Cambridge: Cambridge University Press, 1994). Investigates the origins of the concept of ecology in Britain and America from the eighteenth to the twentieth centuries.

Wylie, Ian, *Young Coleridge and the Philosophers of Nature* (Oxford: Clarendon Press, 1989). Examines the influence of contemporary scientific discoveries upon the poetry of Samuel Taylor Coleridge, with special attention to 'The Rime of the Ancient Mariner'.

NOTES

1. Jonathan Bate, *The Song of the Earth* (Cambridge Mass.: Harvard University Press, 2000), p. 243.
2. Ibid. 24.
3. Ibid. 24.
4. Ibid. 23.
5. Karl Kroeber, *Ecological Literary Criticism: Romantic Imagining and the Biology of Mind* (New York: Columbia University Press, 1994), p. 2.
6. On ancient Mediterranean deforestation, see Clive Pointing, *A Green History of the World: The Environment and the Collapse of Great Civilizations* (New York: St Martin's Press, 1991), pp. 68–78.
7. This reading is excerpted (with revisions) from James C. McKusick, 'Coleridge and the Economy of Nature', *Studies in Romanticism*, 35 (1996), 385–92. Reprinted by permission of the publisher.
8. See Robert Penn Warren, 'A Poem of Pure Imagination: An Experiment in Reading' (1946), in *New and Selected Essays* (New York: Random House, 1989), pp. 335–423.
9. 'The Rime of the Ancyent Marinere', *Argument* and ll. 55–6. Subsequent citations of this poem refer to the 1798 version by line number. From *The Complete Poetical Works of Samuel Taylor Coleridge*, ed. Ernest Hartley Coleridge (Oxford: Clarendon Press, 1912).
10. For fuller discussion of this historical analogue, see Bernard Smith, 'Coleridge's *Ancient Mariner* and Cook's Second Voyage', *Journal of the Warburg and Courtauld Institutes*, 19 (1956), 117–54.
11. James Cook, *Voyage to the Pacific Ocean*, cited by John Livingston Lowes, *The Road to Xanadu: A Study in the Ways of the Imagination*, 2nd edn. (Boston: Houghton Mifflin, 1930), p. 42.
12. Erasmus Darwin, 'The Economy of Vegetation', in *The Botanic Garden: A Poem, in Two Parts*, 2 vols. (London: Joseph Johnson, 1791), vol. i, additional n. 9. Cited by Ian Wylie, *Young Coleridge and the Philosophers of Nature* (Oxford: Clarendon Press, 1989). p. 154.
13. Romand Coles, 'Ecotones and Environmental Ethics: Adorno and Lopez', in Jane Bennett and William Chaloupka (eds.), *In the Nature of Things: Language, Politics, and the Environment* (Minneapolis: University of Minnesota Press, 1993), p. 243.
14. The term 'ecolect' was invented by Hugh Sykes Davies, *Wordsworth and the Worth of Words* (Cambridge: Cambridge University Press, 1986), pp. 274–5. Davies derives '*ecolect*, from the [Greek word for household], to describe a variation peculiar to a particular household, or kin group' (p. 319 n. 8). In the present chapter the term 'ecolect' is used in a more comprehensive sense, to denote a language that arises from extended human habitation in a particular place.
15. S. T. Coleridge, *Logic*, ed. J. R. de J. Jackson (Princeton: Princeton University Press, 1981), p. 126, and *Biographia Literaria*, ed. James Engell and W. Jackson Bate, 2 vols. (Princeton: Princeton University Press, 1983), i. 86 n.
16. Lowes, *Road to Xanadu*, p. 306, citing *The Romaunt of the Rose*, ll. 661–2, 671–2, and 715–16, as published in Anderson's *Poets of Great Britain* (1795). Emphasis added.

16 | Psychoanalysis

Andrew Michael Roberts

Psychoanalysis and Romanticism seem made for each other. They share many of the same preoccupations: dreaming and waking; terror and desire; childhood; the complexity and multiplicity of the self; the power of the past over the present. These links are a matter of cultural history as well as resemblance. Sigmund Freud, the founder of psychoanalysis, wrote in *Civilization and Its Discontents* that 'I took as my starting-point a saying of the [German Romantic] poet-philosopher Schiller, that "hunger and love are what moves the world"'.[1] The critic Lionel Trilling saw psychoanalysis as 'one of the culminations' of Romantic literature, a literature which Trilling claimed was 'passionately devoted to a research into the self'.[2] Furthermore, it was a Romantic poet, Coleridge, who coined the term 'psycho-analytical' in 1805, long before Freud developed a theory and practice under that name. There are risks as well as opportunities in such a seeming congruence between a critical method and a body of literary texts. Jerome McGann's book *The Romantic Ideology: A Critical Investigation* (1983), which had a major impact on Romantic studies, criticized what he termed the 'romantic ideology': a tendency for critics to echo the ways in which Romantic writers saw their own work. Psychoanalytical interpretation, in a clinical context, involves a certain element of mirroring, in the form of a reflecting back to the analysand (the patient or person being analysed) of his or her projected feelings. It is therefore not surprising that psychoanalytical interpretation of Romantic literature can seem highly implicated with that literature's own theories and procedures.

The key concept of psychoanalytical criticism is the unconscious. The application of this concept to literature can involve the study of the unconscious of the author, of the character, or of the text. Freud's own writings on literature tend to focus on character or author and the same is true of early psychoanalytical criticism. Since the 1960s, however, and under the influence of post-structuralism, psychoanalytical criticism has focused increasingly on the unconscious of the text. The idea that a text has an unconscious may seem odd, but the unconscious is a mode of thought as much as a region of the mind. Freud characterized unconscious mental activity as 'primary process thinking'. This is a mode of thought dominated by fantasy, desire, and 'the pleasure principle' (the quest for instinctual satisfaction). In contrast, 'secondary process thinking' is identified with the conscious mind and with 'the reality principle' (which involves adaptation to the external world). Primary process thinking ignores the normal constraints of space and time. Furthermore it allows images and ideas to combine together or replace each other, processes which Freud called 'condensation' and 'displacement'. So the unconscious of a text might include the way in which images combine outside the formal sequence of time, narrative, or grammar, to suggest feelings and thoughts which are not explicitly stated. The concept of a textual unconscious usually goes further, however. Freud saw the unconscious as the home of wishes and ideas that have been repressed, denied access to consciousness because they are unacceptable. So the idea that a text has an unconscious would also imply that it contains meanings which run counter to its explicit meaning and which are in some sense denied or repressed by the overt structure, images, and statements. For example, Wordsworth's famous 'Lucy' poems (a series of lyrics addressed to a now-dead beloved woman) overtly express devotion, premonitions of her death, bereavement, and a sort of calm acceptance. But the poems are full of ambiguous phrasing, such as the understated: 'But she is in her grave, and, oh, | The difference to me!' ('She dwelt among the untrodden ways'). They also contain many enigmas and paradoxes. These features might suggest a textual unconscious expressing a fantasy desire for the death of 'Lucy'. Such a reading might be biographically based, as in F. W. Bateson's reading of the poems in terms of Wordsworth's suppression of his incestuous love for his sister Dorothy, a love being 'slowly and gently buried alive'.[3] More recent and sophisticated versions of psychoanalytical criticism tend to be wary of the biographical, although the importance of textual self-representations in Romantic literature means that biography is rarely too distant.

So far I have referred to Freud, who tends to remain a point of reference in psychoanalytical theory. However, psychoanalytical ideas have developed in many ways since Freud. These include feminist rereadings and revisions (see the chapter on 'Feminism'), and major schools of psychoanalytical thought such as the object-relations school associated with Melanie Klein and D. W. Winnicott, and the post-structuralist theories of the French analyst Jacques Lacan. The sections which follow in this chapter will refer to these thinkers in discussing how psychoanalytical criticism of Romantic writing engages with certain basic categories, beginning with that of knowledge.

Knowledge

Romanticism was both influenced by, and reacted against, the movement of thought in the eighteenth century known as the Enlightenment, which advocated the use of reason to improve society and the human condition (see *Oxford Companion to the Romantic Age*, p. 299). The Romantic reaction against Enlightenment thought tended to regard it as dry, narrow, over-rationalistic, and deadening to the imagination (*Oxford Companion to the Romantic Age*, p. 310), and instead emphasized imagination, the hidden, irrational, and mysterious aspects of the human mind, the supernatural, and the subjective. Nevertheless, elements of Enlightenment thought persist in the ideas of many Romantic writers, including aesthetic and psychological theories and certain political values such as tolerance. Wordsworth's account of the development of the child in *The Prelude* or Blake's prophetic and visionary strain in one sense react against Enlightenment rationality, but in another sense continue the Enlightenment project of analysing the human self and seeking to improve human society through such knowledge.

Freud's relationship to the Enlightenment was similarly complex. He was overtly committed to a scientific and rational investigation of the human mind by empirical means. Yet as his theories and methods developed, they tended to reveal the subjective nature of psychoanalytical investigation, and to undermine their own rationalistic assumptions. Freudian analysis seeks to cast light into the dark region of the unconscious. But, by definition, the unconscious remains central to the psyche, and psychoanalysis can, at most, shift its boundaries a little. Furthermore, as Freudian analytical techniques developed, the importance emerged of what Freud termed 'the transference'. This is the tendency of the analysand to project on to the analyst repressed feelings about important people in his or her life. Freud came to realize that the transference could be used to re-enact, interpret, and resolve conflicts from the past that trouble or inhibit the analysand. The analyst is no longer a detached, objective observer of the human mind but a participant in a subjective human relationship. This shift was reinforced by the need to confront the 'counter-transference' (the analyst's emotional responses to the analysand's behaviour). Psychoanalysis is a highly imaginative and intuitive process, which involves grappling with a complex and hidden self. Freud emerges as an Enlightenment thinker whose work undermines many assumptions typical of Enlightenment thought.

Romanticism and psychoanalysis are, then, both impelled by a quest for knowledge—of the self, of society, even of human history and destiny—which is to some degree an inheritance of the Enlightenment. But Romantic and psychoanalytical texts are intensely aware that the self is multiple, elusive, perhaps finally unknowable, and that knowledge itself is implicated with the subjectivity of the knower. What does this mean for psychoanalytical reading of Romantic literature? Psychoanalysis can be used to interpret Romantic texts in a way which seems to draw out their meanings and integrate them into a congenial theory of human behaviour. For example, Wordsworth's account of childhood development in *The Prelude* is powerful, effective, and convincing but elusive in its concepts. It fits so well with psychoanalytical ways of thinking and talking, that it can readily be reinterpreted as a proto-analytical account. As a critical procedure this is satisfying but vulnerable to two contrary objections. One is McGann's charge of echoing Romanticism's sense of its self, since such a procedure tends to endorse rather than critique Wordsworth's view of the self. The other is the converse objection, that of projecting on to Wordsworth's poem a twenty-first-century interpretation that distorts its historical meaning.

A key way in which knowledge is implicated with the subjectivity of the knower is through the erotic and gendered aspects of the desire for knowledge. A widespread criticism of Freud is that he represents femininity in negative terms, as an inferior version of masculinity, marked by the absence of the phallus. It has been argued by many feminists that Freud's accounts of fetishism, voyeurism, and 'scopophilia' (the drive or desire to look) associate masculinity with the phallus (the symbolic form of the penis), with active looking, and with power and knowledge, while associating femininity with (symbolic) castration and a passive role as the object of looking and the object of knowledge. Freud's account of the origins of (male) fetishism involves a little boy, who has not yet rejected femininity, discovering that his mother has no penis. He assumes that she has been castrated, and 'fetishizes' some object. This means that the object comes to serve as an unconscious symbol of a contradictory knowledge (the knowledge that his mother lacks a penis combined with the disavowal of that knowledge; a contradiction acceptable to primary process thinking). As a result the object acquires sexual significance. Freud's account of scopophilia (the desire to look) divides this infantile drive into an active form (voyeurism) and a passive form (exhibitionism), and associates voyeurism with the desire for knowledge and mastery. Keats's poem 'The Eve of St Agnes', which describes in rich and sensuous language a lover watching in secret as his beloved undresses and as she sleeps, is readily interpretable in terms of voyeuristic pleasure. Christopher Ricks, in his book *Keats and Embarrassment*, notes the prevalence of voyeuristic images in Keats's art, but ingeniously defends this as morally and aesthetically valuable, in part because it confronts the possibility of guilt and embarrassment without succumbing to them.[4] A psychoanalytical reading of the poem would feel less need to defend or attack it on moral grounds, though a feminist psychoanalytical reading might carry a moral charge, as in those interpretations which take the poem as 'a fantasy of eroticized destructiveness'.[5] What else might a psychoanalytical interpreter make of this poem? 'The Eve of St Agnes' could hardly be interpreted in terms of an unconscious voyeurism or fetishism, since these are explicitly thematized in the text. The element of voyeurism is multiplied, as the reader watches Porphyro watching Madeline, who is also intensely self-aware. There is a fetishistic focus on the objects adjacent to Madeline's body. The way in which the description swerves away from her body and towards surrounding objects as she undresses fits neatly—perhaps too neatly—with Freud's suggestion that fetishism often attaches itself to an object (like a shoe or underclothing) which can 'crystallize the moment of undressing, the last moment in which the woman could still be regarded as phallic'.[6]

A straight Freudian reading of the poem might seem to add little to what the poem itself already knows. However, psychoanalytical interpretation is often most productive when integrated with elements of other theoretical approaches. So Marjorie Levinson reads the poem by combining psychoanalytical concepts such as the pleasure and reality principles, and narcissism, with New Historicist, Marxist, deconstructive, and biographical methods. Levinson divides earlier interpretations of the poem into those focusing on its sensuous, surface richness and those which treat it as an 'allegory of identity'. She associates the first group of interpretations with the pleasure principle, and the second group with the reality principle. However, she goes on to deconstruct this opposition, arguing that both types of interpretation share an underlying view of the poem as enacting an imaginative progress from desire and the sensual to identity and authenticity. She also suggests that the poem represents an imaginative reconciliation of conflicts in Keats's own life.[7] Levinson's argument illustrates the way in which psychoanalytical criticism often becomes meta-criticism: a reflection on critical procedures. This is in keeping with the intense self-consciousness of both Romanticism and psychoanalysis. One might compare the way in which clinical analysis explores the patient's unconscious by focusing on what surfaces in the analytical situation itself: that is, on the transference. The transference involves re-enactment, and, similarly, psychoanalytical criticism of Romanticism often involves a critical, self-conscious re-enactment of Romantic procedures and tropes.

Desire

Freud understood desire in terms of a basic drive: the libido, or sexual energy. He believed this energy could be 'sublimated', that is, displaced from instinctual objects and activities, on to other, more socially acceptable ones. Hence work, creativity, friendship, and art can all be the result of sublimation. This theory tended to give him a reductive view of artistic creation, often emphasizing a form of escapism. Other aspects of his theories of desire have proved more productive for literary criticism. The concept of hysteria has a historical association with female desire. Before Freud hysteria meant physical symptoms without apparent physical causes, and was commonly attributed to unsatisfied sexual and maternal drives, so that it was strongly linked to normative ideas about women's sexuality. Freud saw such symptoms as symbolic conversions of repressed ideas. He rejected implications that hysterical women were self-indulgent, or ruled by their heredity, though he did not escape the tendency of the male doctor to impose patriarchal assumptions on to female hysterics. Hysteria has become a crucial term in the complex set of relations between psychoanalysis and feminism, and its ambivalent and contested status is symptomatic of that troubled relationship. Initially, feminists tended to see hysteria as a form of victimhood, a stereotypical and misogynist construction of femininity as unstable, sick, and in need of patriarchal control. Later feminists, however, have argued that hysteria is a form of resistance to such control, even that it is, in Elaine Showalter's words, 'the "protofeminism" of hysterical protest'.[8] Central to such revision is the idea of the meaningful body, the body which speaks through hysteria that which gender ideology may have suppressed. So Karen Swann interprets Coleridge's 'Christabel' in terms of a hysteria that, she argues, the poem 'both dramatizes and provokes'. The concept of hysteria allows her to link analysis of characters, of genres (which she defines as 'bodies of literary convention'), and implied female readers. She sees the poem as expressing contradictory positions. On the one hand it endorses a gendered ideology by linking its representations of female bodies to 'the "feminine" malady of hysteria and the "feminine" genres of the circulating library'. On the other hand, through 'the logic of dream' it 'exposes "manliness" as a gendered convention', implying, through the operation of desire in the text, that hysteria is 'the condition of all subjects in discourse'.[9]

One of the most influential reinterpreters of Freud has been the French psychoanalyst and theorist, Jacques Lacan. Lacan claims that each individual, by learning to speak, enters the social order, which he calls 'the Symbolic'. By this entry into the Symbolic, the unconscious is created. This entry is simultaneous with the Oedipus complex, which Lacan reinterprets as the intervention of the Father, the Law, and social taboo into the primary relationship with the mother. The result is a divided self, for which desire is always a function of lack: the lack of the imaginary fullness which preceded that intervention. Something of the complexity of Lacan's position will be apparent even from this (highly simplified) account, and Lacanian interpretations tend to be highly complex and opaque. Nevertheless, Lacan's stress on the link between language and desire has been productive for critics interested in the 'unconscious of the text'. Lacan draws on the structuralist concepts of the signifier (in language, this means a written or spoken word) and the signified (the concept conventionally attached to that word). Lacan sees desire in terms of an endless chain of signifiers. Just as language, in a post-structuralist view, never reaches a final point of presence where signifier and signified are unified and stable, so desire is based on lack and absence: it never finds its object. Laura Claridge, in her book *Romantic Potency*, explores the way in which, for Romantic poets, textuality or language 'sustains desire' yet also 'frustrates its consummation'.[10] Lacanian-influenced criticism often emphasizes the way in which textual structures evoke and interact with the desire of the reader and the critic. The critic Peter Brooks compares the structure of literature and the structure of the mind, and sees the creation of narrative truth as analogous to the struggle for meaning and coherence acted out in the psychoanalytical transference. This makes the desire of the reader integral to the process of interpretation, and also allows for the 'resistance' of the text (just as the analysand may resist the interpretations of the analyst). As in the transference, such resistance is incorporated into the process of interpretation.[11]

Such an approach would be helpful in the project of reintegrating into our understanding of Romanticism a figure such as Jane Austen, who until recently was generally read in a different context from her poetic contemporaries. Austen's novels may seem to evoke desire primarily in socially regulated forms, or to punish those figures, such as Marianne in *Sense and Sensibility*, who challenge those forms of regulation. But an awareness of the ways in which the plots and narrative structures of her novels engage the desires of the reader might open up other possibilities of reading. The plots generate a desire for narrative closure, which the endings do indeed offer the reader, normally in the form of 'successful' marriage outcomes. For some readers, then, the fulfilment of narrative desire by socially approved outcomes reinforces the novels' endorsement of the Symbolic order. Other readers, however, may feel that the very formality of the endings, their inability to resolve the desires of the characters other than in formulaic terms, highlights lack and the insufficiency of the supposed objects of desire. Desire in Austen's novels is indeed condemned to inhabit a series of signifiers, beneath which the elusive signified slips away. Her heroines are rewarded for their moral qualities or their ability to learn from experience by the signifiers of satisfaction (money, position, a good marriage), but the disruptive force of desire itself is confined to the unconscious of the text.

Fantasy

Psychoanalysis makes fantasy central to the self, because it sees human behaviour as driven to a large extent by unconscious fantasies. Freud rescued fantasy, dreams, jokes, and mistakes from a marginal status in human psychology, regarding them as ways in which the unconscious communicates itself. This importance is developed by later psychoanalytical thinkers, notably Melanie Klein, whose work shows 'that fantasy is a precondition of any engagement with reality'.[12] According to Klein's object-relations theory, the self is formed through early fantasy relationships with 'objects' (things, people, and parts of people). Fantasy is the primary means by which we establish some relation to the world; it is not an escape from reality but that which mediates between the inner world and external reality. The prevalence of fantasy in Romantic literature is readily apparent: from the fantastical journeys of Coleridge's 'The Rime of the Ancient Mariner' and 'Kubla Khan' to the sensuous fantasies of Keats's Odes or the rich symbolism of the fantasy worlds of Blake's prophetic books. The point is, not that these works share some common meaning or cause, but that the understanding of fantasy as a mode of relation to reality validates and illuminates the diverse impulses and aesthetic strategies that underlie such works. Furthermore, fantasies are intimately connected with the past, since their material is generally drawn from infantile experience; from early desires which have been repressed into the unconscious by the demands of development and socialization. The classic instance of this would be Oedipal conflict: fantasies of desire for the parent of the opposite sex and of jealous destructiveness towards that of the same sex. Although an association between fantasy and infantile experience can lead to reductive interpretations of literary fantasy (as merely symptomatic of general complexes), it can also illuminate critical readings of the relationship between fantasy and the past in Romantic literature. For example, Wordsworth's 'Solitary Reaper', beginning with the sight and sound of a 'Highland Lass' singing in the fields, traces a parabola through exotic locations ('Arabian sands') and an unspecified but emotionally resonant past. The poet wonders whether she sings of 'old, unhappy, far-off things' or 'Familiar matter of to-day? | Some natural sorrow, loss or pain, | That has been, and may be again?'. A psychoanalytic reading might suggest that these are less alternatives than complementary aspects: that the recurrent sorrows of human experience are often repetitions of 'old, unhappy, far-off things', which continue to live in the unconscious, where they repeat themselves and 'may be again'. It is clear from the ending of the poem ('The music in my heart I bore, | Long after it was heard no more') that the song represents a projection of the poet's own feelings, which remain obscure to himself.

The darker fantasies of Romanticism are pervaded by what Freud called 'the uncanny', which he defined as that class of the frightening which 'arouses dread and horror' in the 'familiar and old-established'.[13] This definition draws on etymology: the German term *heimlich*, from which its opposite, *unhemilich* is derived, carries two sets of seemingly opposite meanings: the homely and familiar or the strange and unknown. Freud associates the uncanny with doubles, and with dolls and other things which seem to exist on the border between life and death, with 'uncertainty whether an object is living or inanimate' and with the fear of losing one's eyes (which he takes as representing the fear of castration). Freud suggests that the double expresses the need to insure against death by imagining an other, more permanent self, such as the soul, or an image or representation. But at a later stage in psychic development the double reverses its role and becomes 'the uncanny harbinger of death',[14] a fantasy double associated with self-criticism, self-observation, and conscience, as well as 'the unfulfilled but possible futures to which we still like to cling in phantasy'.[15] Freud's account of the uncanny is rich in ideas rather than precise or definitive.

The life/death border is the crucial site of the Gothic, and the intrusion of the alien into the familiar one of its key tropes. Robert Miles describes the female Gothic (epitomized by the novels of Ann Radcliffe) as centring on the orphaned heroine in search of an absent mother, while the male Gothic (epitomized by the novels of Matthew Lewis) represents the son's Oedipal conflict with authority.[16] These descriptions indicate how central the family (and hence the familiar) is to the Gothic exploration of the unfamiliar and uncanny. James Hogg's *Confessions of a Justified Sinner* is one of the classic treatments of the double, exploring the concept of alternative lives and the idea that one person can be two people. Freudian psychology in a sense rationalizes both these possibilities though its emphasis on fantasy life and its models of the psyche as divided. The uncanny is not limited to the Gothic novel. Keats's fragment of poetry, 'This Living Hand', uncannily speaks to its enigmatic addressee (and hence to the reader) from the standpoint of both life and death:

> This living hand, now warm and capable
> Of earnest grasping, would, if it were cold
> And in the icy silence of the tomb,
> So haunt thy days and chill thy dreaming nights
> That thou wouldst wish thine own heart dry of blood

So in my veins red life might stream again,
And thou be conscience-calmed. See here it is—
I hold it towards you.

The poem traverses the uncanny borders between life and death, between presence and absence. In doing so it foregrounds the uncanniness of writing itself, as the simulated presence of a voice which is absent, and as the visible trace of an absent hand.

Self

The Freudian model of the self stresses the developmental process, exploring the shaping of the self from earliest childhood onwards. In this respect it echoes the Romantic interest in childhood, and the sense that 'The Child is father of the Man' (Wordsworth, 'My heart leaps up when I behold'). Freudian accounts also stress interiority and the flow of energy. Freud's models of mind are topographical, based on interaction between different areas of the mind. But they are also dynamic, representing psychic events in terms of conflicting forces, and economic, describing psychic processes in terms of a flow of energy.[17] The sense of the mind as a complex inner region is congenial to Romantic interiority; Wordsworth describes 'the Mind of Man' as 'My haunt, and the main region of my song' (The Excursion, Preface to the Edition of 1814, ll. 40–1), and writes that, in the human mind, 'there is a dark | Invisible workmanship that reconciles | Discordant elements' (The Prelude, 1805, Book I, ll. 352–4): lines that would seem an apt description of Freud's accounts of the interaction of forces within the mind. Metaphors of flow (streams, rivers) are common in Romantic poetry, as representations of psychic, natural, and spiritual processes, as when Shelley writes that 'The everlasting universe of things | Flows through the mind' ('Mont Blanc').

Object-relations theory focuses less on the internal structure of the self, and more on its relations with the object, or other. The concept of the other, and of the self–other duality, has become crucial to much post-1960s literary theory, notably post-colonial and feminist theory. The distinctive contribution of object-relations psychoanalysis to this field of ideas perhaps lies in its stress on the developmental and dynamic nature of the self's relation to its many objects. M. H. Abrams argues, in Natural Supernaturalism, that Romantic writers reformulated the traditional relation of God to his creation in terms of 'the prevailing two-term system of subject and object, ego and non-ego, the human mind or consciousness and its transactions with nature'.[18] Object-relations theory offers a further reformulation, in which the body of the mother, and especially the breast, is the primary or first object. In the theory of Melanie Klein, the breast (as fantasy object) is split into a threatening 'bad breast' and an idealized 'good breast'. This also involves a split in the ego, and a profound ambivalence. In the first year of life, the 'paranoid-schizoid' position, in which the 'bad breast' threatens the self with punishment, is followed by the 'depressive' position, which involves guilt and desire for reparation, and movement between these positions (as forms of relationship to the object or other) remains a possibility in adult life. The depressive position involves more possibility of integration and the acceptance of ambivalence, and so is linked by some Kleinian critics to the creative process itself, seen as a form of reparation, an attempt to re-create the whole mother. Literary texts may be seen as exploring the two Kleinian 'positions', as well as exploring ambivalence itself. A possible application of such ideas to Romantic texts would focus on the importance of symbolic and mythological figures that represent projections of aspects of the human, in works such as Blake's prophetic books or Keats's *Endymion* and *Hyperion*. Processes of projection and internalization are figured in many of Blake's engravings and poems, while the splitting into good and bad objects, fragmentation and attempts at unification or reparation are key elements of his systems of ideas. In much of Keats's work images of the ideal and of a merging of the poet's consciousness with such an ideal, are crucial, but are haunted by the threat of fragmentation and destruction. Such effects might be seen in terms of what Otto Kernberg describes as a form of psychic defence against the lack of a secure good object within the psyche: 'by means of purified exalted states reflecting fantasies of merging of the self with good, unrealistically idealized objects.'[19]

Geoffrey Hartman has argued that Romantic art seeks to go beyond or overcome self-consciousness, which is 'the product of a division in the self' and achieve a 'Unity of Being', associated with childhood, imagination, and 'recovering deeply buried experience'.[20] An alternative trajectory for the Romantic self is one in which self-consciousness is escaped only by fragmentation or self-extinction. This is a desire which Frances Wilson attributes to Thomas Lovell Beddoes, and which is evoked (in rather different form) in Keats's 'Ode to a Nightingale'.[21] A third trajectory involves the exacerbation of self-consciousness in the service of Romantic irony, an effect associated especially with German Romanticism. The greatest theorist of Romantic irony, the German Romantic philosopher and critic Friedrich Schlegel, saw the role of the artist as one of hovering 'between self-creation and self-destruction', which involves the ego hovering 'between naïve experiences and critical reflections' and 'viewing its own passions with disillusioned detachment'.[22] This process is best exemplified in British Romanticism by the naïve protagonist and the sophisticated, self-reflexive narrator of Byron's *Don Juan*. The impulse to create the self and to escape the self are both strong in Byron and both are elements of the proliferating ironies of *Don Juan*. It is easy to see how psycho-analysis might interpret the first two of these trajectories. The quest for Unity of Being, it could be claimed, expresses the unconscious fantasy of a return to the pre-Oedipal, pre-Symbolic, imaginary bliss of non-separateness. The fantasy is the critic's as much as the author's and, while the link to childhood is explicit, the language of being and soul serves to conceal its unconscious roots by the use of religious and philosophical language. The tendency to fragmentation or extinction of the self might be read by a Kleinian critic as revealing the dominance of the paranoid-schizoid position, a splitting of the ego and its objects, and the projection of destructive impulses on to the bad object.[23] Whether psychoanalysis could interpret the third trajectory, that of Romantic irony, is more doubtful, because Romantic irony has pre-empted it. Romantic irony interprets itself (relentlessly), so that arguably psychoanalysis can only repeat Romantic irony. Psychoanalysis too seeks to view 'its own passions with disillusioned detachment'. Psychoanalysis has its mode of self-creation: the strengthening of the ego, the joint creation by analyst and analysand of a new narrative of the analysand's life. It also has its mode of self-destruction: the intense self-scrutiny of the analytical process leaves intact the unconscious, that permanent dislocation of the self from itself.

READING: Mary Shelley, *Frankenstein; or, The Modern Prometheus*

Frankenstein is one of the richest of Romantic prose texts, and is open to interpretation in terms of many of the psychoanalytical theories that have been outlined. The present reading will concentrate on an interpretation of *Frankenstein* as a study of desire and repression in the family, and as an instance of the role of the fantasy of omnipotence in the Romantic understanding of the creative process (compare the reading of *Frankenstein* in the chapter entitled 'Gothic').

Repression in the family

Frankenstein, when he starts on his project of creating a being, takes it for granted that it will be grateful for being created: 'A new species would bless me as its creator and source; many happy and excellent natures would owe their being to me. No father could claim the gratitude of his child so completely as I should deserve theirs' (54).[24] To make such an assumption is to make gratitude the very grounds of someone's being, to deny them autonomy, by claiming that they belong to you as creator, so that their very being is a debt that must be repaid. Parents sometimes make such an assumption, implicitly or explicitly, and children often respond as Adam does in the lines from *Paradise Lost* which stand as the epigraph to Frankenstein:

> Did I request thee, Maker, from my clay
> To mould Me man? Did I solicit thee
> From darkness to promote me?—

In other words, 'I didn't ask to be born', which of course no one does. To make parental love and care into a debt which must be repaid is to transform love into a contract. One reason for Frankenstein's failure to love the monster may be his expectation that gratitude will stand in the place of love. Why is Frankenstein's creation of the monster so disastrous? Why does he behave in such an irresponsible way, rushing away from his creation, then trying to forget it? Why does he hate and fear this creature which he has anticipated will show gratitude to him? On a literal level he is tired and overwrought, and the fragments of bodies which he was able to face when they were inert are too frightening when they move. By crossing from object to living being the monster evokes the uncanny, with the effect of making birth itself (of which the monster's creation is a form of parody) seem uncanny. On a symbolic level Frankenstein's terror is a form of punishment which the novel stages for the human who tries to emulate God. But we might also explain Frankenstein's failure to love his creation in terms of his own family. Frankenstein presents his family in idealized terms.

His account of them is sentimental in the extreme, and his account of the relationships within his family shows them as dominated by sentimentality. Sentimentality is a way of denying aggression, of pretending that human relationships are different from how they actually are, pretending that they can be wholly pure, wholly loving, wholly altruistic, untouched by irritation, hate, resentment, jealousy, or desire. Frankenstein's account is one in which one sort of feeling or relationship is perpetually standing in for another, in complex mechanisms of denial and repression. His account of his parents' relationship presents his father as 'a protecting spirit' to a much younger wife whom he has rescued from poverty, and characterizes his father's feelings in terms of 'a show of gratitude and worship' in which 'everything was made to yield to her wishes and her convenience. He strove to shelter her, as a fair exotic is sheltered by the gardener' (pp. 32–3). What is being denied here is obviously sexuality. This is a description of a marriage which omits any hint of sexual desire or conflict. Is it a coincidence that the son of this marriage finds a way of creating a being without sex? In the description of Frankenstein's parents, the relationship of guardian stands in for that of husband, while justice, moral approval, gratitude, worship, reverence, and compassion replace love and sex. When Frankenstein comes to describe his own place in this family, there is a similar denial of any aggression, conflict, or desire: 'I was their plaything and their idol, and something better—their child . . . whose future lot it was in their hands to direct to happiness or misery, according as they fulfilled their duties towards me' (pp. 33–4). Notice here the idea of omnipotence, that parents can determine the happiness or misery of their child, as if the child's life was their property, and wholly in their control. It is such control that Frankenstein imagines he will have over his own creation. He also claims that 'while during every hour of my infant life I received a lesson of patience, of charity, and of self-control, I was so guided by a silken cord, that all seemed but one train of enjoyment to me' (p. 34). No such family as the one Frankenstein describes ever existed: a family without sex, without aggression, without conflict. A similar pattern continues in the account of Frankenstein's relationship with his adopted sister and wife to be. Just as his father made guardianship stand in for marriage, by marrying someone to whom he was in the relation of a protector, so Frankenstein makes brotherhood stand in for marriage, by marrying someone who has been brought up as his sister. He claims that they 'were strangers to any species of disunion or dispute. Harmony was the soul of our companionship' (p. 36). We learn that Elizabeth was first introduced to Frankenstein, not as an autonomous person, but as his possession:

On the evening previous to her being brought home, my mother had said playfully,—'I have a pretty present for my Victor—tomorrow he shall have it.' And when, on the morrow, she presented Elizabeth to me as her promised gift, I, with childish seriousness, interpreted her words literally, and looked upon Elizabeth as mine—mine to protect, love, and cherish. All praises bestowed on her, I received as made to a possession of my own.

(pp. 35–6)

He is, to some degree, repeating his father's relationship with his mother, in taking Elizabeth as something fragile to be protected. Prominent in his description, however, are two related fantasies: non-separateness and omnipotence.

The fantasy of omnipotence

'Omnipotence' means unlimited power, and 'power' is a crucial term in much Romantic literature. The psychoanalyst D. W. Winnicott described both infantile development and adult creative processes in terms of the fantasy of omnipotence. Winnicott's work belongs to the object-relations school of psychoanalytical theory, which also included Melanie Klein. Whereas classical Freudian theory describes human behaviour in terms of 'drives' or 'instincts,' this later development describes it in terms of the relationships of the individual to 'objects' (usually people or aspects of people), including 'internal objects' (fantasy images within the self; internal representations of people or attributes), and 'external objects' (people seen as separate from the self). Object-relations theory echoes aspects of Romantic thoughts because both focus on the relationship between inner and outer reality, and both see a process of exchange between self and world, inner and outer, involving a range of emotions such as desire, fear, and loss. In this process forms enter the self ('introjection' in psychoanalytical terminology) and are projected out from the self on to nature, or other people ('projection'). Winnicott argued that a baby, in an 'unintegrated state' (prior to developing a sense of a separate self), is given a brief experience of omnipotence if its basic needs (primarily for food and physical contact) are met. If satisfaction follows on the experience of a need, the subjective experience for the baby is that the need produced the satisfaction: that it controls the world, in the form of the mother (not yet perceived as separate). For Winnicott, while the experience of such omnipotence ends at around age 6 months, this early experience provides a crucial basis for later creativity, for 'a belief that the world can contain what is wanted and needed . . . [the] hope that there is a live relationship between inner reality and external reality, between innate primary creativity and the world at large which is shared by all.'[25] Omnipotence, the belief in a world created by and for ourselves, persists as an unconscious fantasy.

The key elements in Winnicott's account are all found in Mary Shelley's story. In an obvious way, Frankenstein's project of creating a living being is a fantasy of omnipotence, of rivalling God. Frankenstein has a habit of attributing reality to his own desires and fantasies. This, in a sense, is what a creative writer does. But it is also in itself the manifestation of the fantasy of omnipotence, that we can make the world how we want it, that we only have to imagine something, and it is so. Frankenstein expresses this fantasy when he tells us that 'my imagination was too much exalted by my first success to permit me to doubt of my ability to give life to an animal as complex and wonderful as man' (p. 53). The parallels between the creation of the monster and the writing of a fiction are apparent here: to take one's own exalted state of imagination as evidence that one can create is reasonable enough if one is a writer. Frankenstein, however, imagines that he can create life with his imagination: that 'reality'—the real, bodily existence of the monster—depends on his own exalted imaginings. That he succeeds should not perhaps surprise us, since the text in which he appears is evidence that Mary Shelley succeeded in transforming her childhood fantasies into the reality of a novel—the reality of fiction. Frankenstein has a similarly cavalier attitude to facts: he notes that when the idea that the monster may have murdered his little brother occurs to him 'No sooner did that idea cross my imagination, than I became convinced of its truth . . . The mere presence of the idea was an irresistible proof of the fact' (p. 76). Taking the presence of an idea in one's own mind as proof of a fact in the external world is not wise, and it is certainly not a scientific procedure, for all Frankenstein's claims to be a scientist. Again, however, he is right: it was the monster who killed William. Frankenstein seems to be living in a world in which the fantasy of omnipotence works.

Furthermore, his expectations as to the result of his work emphasize only its connection to himself: 'A new species would bless me as its creator and source.' What he is not ready for, is the monster's separate existence as a being with needs of its own. Faced with this, Frankenstein rushes off and leaves it, as if he imagines it will simply disappear—as if it were still part of himself, merely an idea in his mind which he can turn away from. The fantasy of omnipotence as it operates in Frankenstein's view of the monster is presaged, as I have suggested, in his relationships with his family. Encouraged by his mother's introduction of her as a gift, he regards Elizabeth as his possession, as part of himself. He half-recognizes the strangeness of their relationship: 'No words, no expression, could body forth the kind of relation in which she stood to me—my more than sister, since till death she was to be mine only' (p. 36). Though his relationship with the monster appears superficially to be the opposite of this relation with Elizabeth, in fact both are founded on fantasies of non-separateness and omnipotence.

Creativity and the return of the repressed

Winnicott's account of infant development stresses the way in which the sense of self is formed during a coming together of the fragments of the body until a sense of wholeness is created, just as the monster literally comes together from fragments. Winnicott also argues that the experience of omnipotence is a primary factor in the development of creativity. *Frankenstein* is a novel about creativity in various forms: the creativity of a scientist, of a mother, of a writer. The ability to live creatively draws on the early experience of omnipotence, and the persisting unconscious fantasy of omnipotence: the belief that we can, through our own perception, bring into being a meaningful and fulfilling world. Frankenstein's exuberance at the prospect of creating a being shows the pleasure of creativity allied to the traces of omnipotent fantasy. But the traces of this early experience, in the form of the fantasy of omnipotence, can also be a source of despair. Part of the process of development is the discovery that the world continues to exist independently of our needs and desires (which can be frustrating), but also independently of our envy, aggression, hate, and rage (which is reassuring). If, however, we continue to believe at an unconscious level that it is our own creativity alone that gives the world meaning, then at times when that creativity is blocked, when inspiration is lacking, or when spirits fail, the world threatens to become meaningless. This is the experience described by Coleridge in 'Dejection: An Ode', a poem about the loss of inspiration, in which Coleridge presents the risks attendant on the Romantic reliance on the imagination to create a meaningful world. The moment when the omnipotent fantasy collapses, when the poet loses creative power and the self-created world is drained of meaning, is a recurrent moment in Romantic literature and not limited to male poets. The concluding two stanzas of Mary Tighe's poem 'Psyche' represent infantile non-separation in pure form, and move from a vision of eternal loving bliss to a desolate loss of vision.

The monster becomes an externalization of Frankenstein's own aggression and desire. Freud's most famous phrase is 'the return of the repressed', which refers to the way in which unaccepted feeling and desires, which are repressed into the unconscious, return in other forms: as symptoms, as mistakes, as neuroses. The monster can be seen as representing this process. Frankenstein goes to great lengths to emphasize the horrid contrast between its ugliness and destructiveness (as he sees it) and the beauty, purity, innocence, and harmony of his own family. Yet symbolically, the monster springs from within the heart of that family: the monster is the repressed of that family. As already noted, the relationship between Frankenstein's parents, and Frankenstein's own relationship with Elizabeth, both repress any mention of the physical and of sexuality by presenting themselves in terms of protection not desire. What the monster demands from Frankenstein is a mate, and precisely a physical mate, a body which Frankenstein must create. When Frankenstein, in a fit of revulsion, destroys the beginnings of this mate, the monster threatens him with the words 'I will be with you on your wedding night' (p. 168). When his wedding night arrives, Frankenstein says to his bride: 'this night, and all will be safe: but this night is dreadful, very dreadful' (p. 194). And indeed, the monster appears and kills Elizabeth, who is found 'lifeless and inanimate, thrown across the bed, her head hanging down and her pale and distorted features half covered by her hair' (p. 195). Given Frankenstein's relentless sentimentalization of his family and Elizabeth, his denial of aggression and sex, it is not too hard to see why his wedding night should be dreadful to him nor why it should end in disaster.

FURTHER READING

Brooks, Peter, *Psychoanalysis and Storytelling* (Oxford and Cambridge, Mass.: Blackwell, 1994). A fascinating and very readable discussion of psychoanalysis and its relationship to narrative.

Chase, Cynthia, *Romanticism* (Harlow and New York: Longman, 1993). Reprints excerpts from a selection of Romantic criticism, with psychoanalytical approaches especially strongly represented.

Claridge, Laura, *Romantic Potency: The Paradox of Desire* (Ithaca, NY, and London: Cornell University Press, 1992). A psychoanalytical (primarily Lacanian) interpretation of desire in the work of Wordsworth, Shelley, and Byron.

Hertz, Neil, *The End of the Line: Essays on Psychoanalysis and the Sublime* (New York: Columbia University Press, 1985). Examines the crucial Romantic theme of the sublime by reading Romantic and psychoanalytical texts together.

Kirschner, Suzanne, *The Religious and Romantic Origins of Psychoanalysis: Individuation and Integration in Post-Freudian Theory* (Cambridge: Cambridge University Press, 1996). Argues that the roots of psychoanalysis lie in theology, mysticism, and Romantic thought.

Laplanche, J., and Pontalis, J. B., *The Language of Psychoanalysis*, trans. Donald Nicholson-Smith (London: Karnac Books, 1988). A detailed dictionary of psychoanalytical terms, covering Freudian but also Lacanian theory.

Layton, Lynne, and Schapiro, Barbara Ann (eds.), *Narcissism and the Text: Studies in Literature and the Psychology of Self* (New York and London: New York University Press, 1986). Collection of essays applying object-relations psychoanalytical theory to literature, including chapters on Rousseau, Blake, and Wordsworth.

McDayter, Ghislaine (ed.), *Untrodden Regions of the Mind: Romanticism and Psychoanalysis* (Lewisburg, Pa.: Bucknell University Press, 2002). A collection of essays applying psychoanalytical ideas to Romantic literature.

Mellor, Anne K., *Mary Shelley: Her Life, Her Fiction, Her Monsters* (London and New York: Routledge, 1989). A critical and biographical work which includes a detailed discussion of *Frankenstein*, very relevant to the issues raised here.

Phillips, Adam, *Promises, Promises: Essays on Literature and Psychoanalysis* (London: Faber and Faber, 2000). Highly readable and imaginative essays by a contemporary psychoanalyst with wide literary and cultural interests. The first chapter, 'Poetry and Psychoanalysis', pays particular attention to Romantic writers.

Punter, David, *Gothic Pathologies: The Text, The Body and the Law* (Basingstoke: Macmillan, 1998). A study of the Gothic from the eighteenth century to the present, richly informed by psychoanalytical as well as other theories.

Rycroft, Charles, *A Critical Dictionary of Psychoanalysis* (Harmondsworth: Penguin, 1972). A reference work giving clear, succinct definitions of psychoanalytical terms according to Freudian and object-relations theory.

Wright, Elizabeth, *Psychoanalytical Criticism: A Reappraisal*, 2nd edn. (Cambridge: Polity Press, 1998). This book gives a clear account of the range of psychoanalytical theories from Freud to Lacan and their application to literature.

NOTES

1. All references to Freud's work are to *The Standard Edition of the Complete Psychological Works of Sigmund Freud*, translated under the general editorship of James Strachey in collaboration with Anna Freud, assisted by Alix Strachey and Alan Tyson, 24 vols. (London: Hogarth Press, 1953–74); here, xxi. 117.
2. Lionel Trilling, 'Freud and Literature', in *The Liberal Imagination* (London: Secker and Warburg, 1951), pp. 34–57 (p. 35).
3. F. W. Bateson, *Wordsworth: A Reinterpretation*, 2nd edn. (London: Longman, 1956), p. 157.
4. Christopher Ricks, *Keats and Embarrassment* (Oxford: Clarendon Press, 1974), p. 89.
5. Beverly Fields, 'Keats and the Tongueless Nightingale; Some Unheard Melodies in "The Eve of St Agnes"', in *The Wordsworth Circle*, 14 (1983), 246–50 (249).
6. Freud 'Fetishism', *SE* xxi. 155.
7. Marjorie Levinson, *Keats's Life of Allegory: The Origins of a Style* (Oxford and Cambridge, Mass.: Blackwell, 1988), pp. 96–190 (p. 98).
8. Elaine Showalter, *The Female Malady: Women, Madness and Female Culture, 1830–1980* (London: Virago, 1987), p. 161.

9. Karen Swann, ' "Christabel": The Wandering Mother and the Enigma of Form', *Studies in Romanticism*, 23 (1984), 533–53 (pp. 161, 167, 153).

10. Laura Claridge, *Romantic Potency: The Paradox of Desire* (Ithaca, NY, and London: Cornell University Press, 1992), p. 1.

11. Peter Brooks, *Psychoanalysis and Storytelling* (Oxford and Cambridge, Mass.: Blackwell, 1994), pp. 24–5, 51, 61.

12. Elizabeth Wright, *Psychoanalytical Criticism: A Reappraisal*, 2nd edn. (Cambridge: Polity Press, 1998), p. 75.

13. Freud, 'The Uncanny', *SE* xvii. 219, 241.

14. Ibid. xvii. 357.

15. Ibid. xvii. 358.

16. Robert Miles, 'Ann Radcliffe and Matthew Lewis', in David Punter (ed.), *A Companion to the Gothic* (Oxford and Malden, Mass.: Blackwell, 2000), pp. 41–57 (pp. 43–4).

17. See J. Laplanche and J. B. Pontalis, *The Language of Psychoanalysis*, trans. Donald Nicholson-Smith (London: Karnac Books, 1988), pp. 126–30, 449–53.

18. M. H. Abrams, *Natural Supernaturalism: Tradition and Revolution in Romantic Literature* (New York and London: W. W. Norton, 1973), p. 13.

19. Otto Kernberg, *Internal World and External Reality: Object Relations Theory Applied* (New York and London: Jason Aronson, 1980), pp. 32–3.

20. Geoffrey Hartman, 'Romanticism and Anti-Self-Consciousness', in *Beyond Formalism: Literary Essays 1958–1970* (New Haven and London: Yale University Press, 1970), pp. 298–310 (p. 303).

21. Frances Wilson, ' "Strange Sun": Melancholia in the Writing of Thomas Lovell Beddoes', in *Untrodden Regions of the Mind: Romanticism and Psychoanalysis*, ed. Ghislaine McDayter, *Bucknell Review*, 45: 2 (2001), pp. 127–42.

22. Anne K. Mellor, *English Romantic Irony* (Cambridge, Mass., and London: Harvard University Press, 1980), p. 14; Ernst Behler, 'The Theory of Irony in German Romanticism', in Frederick Garber (ed.), *Romantic Irony* (Budapest: Akadémiai Kiadó, 1988), p. 43.

23. Charles Rycroft, *A Critical Dictionary of Psychoanalysis* (Harmondsworth: Penguin, 1972), p. 111.

24. Mary Shelley, *Frankenstein; or, The Modern Prometheus*, ed. M. K. Joseph (Oxford and New York: Oxford University Press, 1969). All references to the novel are to this Oxford World's Classics edition.

25. D. W. Winnicott, *The Child, The Family and the Outside World* (Harmondsworth: Penguin, 1964), p. 90.

17 | Post-colonialism

Deirdre Coleman

In his book *Tropicopolitans* (1999), the post-colonial critic Srinivas Aravamudan captures the drift of current scholarship on 'the new eighteenth-century' by pointing to xenophobia, colonialism, orientalism, and racism as significant omissions from Linda Colley's influential account of the constitution of national identity in her book, *Britons: Forging the Nation, 1707–1832* (1992).[1] Generally speaking, post-colonial critics such as Aravamudan and Saree Makdisi, author of *Romantic Imperialism: Universal Empire and the Culture of Modernity* (1998), concern themselves with those areas identified as absent from Colley's work, areas which reflect a new interest in the cultural effects of colonization and imperialism in the late eighteenth century, as well as their various legacies today.

Since the 1980s a large and diverse group of literary critics and historians of romanticism, increasingly conscious of the intersection of their period of study with Britain's rapidly expanding empire, have begun to explore much more intensively the role of commerce, slavery, racial ideology, and overseas colonization in late eighteenth-century literature and culture. So massive was the expansion of British dominion in the Romantic period—by 1820 Britain ruled 200 million people, over a quarter of the world's population—it was difficult for anyone in the late eighteenth century not to be involved in the imperial system, however remotely. For instance, many of the Romantic authors we study today were connected through family, friends, trade, or the professions to West Indian slavery. Jane Austen's father was trustee of an Antiguan sugar plantation belonging to a close friend from Oxford days. Matthew Lewis, author of the sensational Gothic novel *The Monk* (1796) was a slave holder, inheriting two large Jamaican sugar plantations. William Beckford, who wrote the oriental tale, *Vathek* (1786), inherited enormous sugar wealth, while Thomas De Quincey's father grew rich as an importer of West Indian linen. Even William and Dorothy Wordsworth benefited indirectly from slavery's proceeds, enjoying a rent-free existence in the mid-1790s at Racedown, a house owned by the wealthy John Pinney, Bristol merchant and sugar plantation owner. Later, in 1801, suffering almost continuous poor health, Samuel Taylor Coleridge suggested to Robert Southey that they emigrate to Pinney's large mansion on St Nevis ('A heavenly climate, a heavenly country', he enthused) and get themselves appointed as 'sinecure negro-drivers' at £100 each a year. He seems to have been only half-joking.

The expansion of Britain's overseas empire engendered a vision of imperial greatness and the reality of vast colonial wealth. Positioning itself in the vanguard of the commercial and enlightened world, the British nation saw itself as the exporter of 'civilization' and systems of governance to countries deemed 'backward' or undeveloped. The most visible expression of this burgeoning overseas empire was everywhere evident in the metropolis in the importation and widespread availability of pleasurable, arousing, and in some cases addictive tropical goods, such as coffee, tea, sugar, chocolate, and tobacco. These exotic commodities, which had once been luxury items for the rich alone, embedded themselves into British daily experience, recasting the face of eighteenth-century life. But while the consumption of such exotics brought widespread pleasure, the public's increasing awareness of the evils underpinning the production of colonial goods (like sugar) led to deep anxieties about the morality of Britain's empire (see *Oxford Companion to the Romantic Age*, pp. 181–7).

The American Revolution and the eventual loss of the Thirteen Colonies was a humiliating blow to Britain, reshaping colonial policy in the other areas of the world under British influence or dominion—India, Canada, the West Indies, Australia, West Africa (see chapter on 'Americas', and *Oxford Companion to the Romantic Age*, pp. 51–8). The political hot spot of the late eighteenth century, which left its mark on the great outburst of literary and artistic production of that period, was Britain's leading role in the slave trade, a system involving the kidnapping and export of Africans to the West Indian sugar islands (see *Oxford Companion to the Romantic Age*, pp. 58–65). This burgeoning trade in human flesh, began to attract increasing criticism from the 1780s onwards, which snowballed into a massive popular movement for abolition by the early 1790s (see *Oxford Companion to the Romantic Age*, p. 399). Millions of people petitioned Parliament, demanding an end to atrocities which were graphically, even gruesomely, detailed in tracts, pamphlets, and cartoons. This widespread movement for the abolition of the slave trade, at a time of rapidly increasing literacy and the proliferation of print culture (see chapter on 'Print culture and the book trade'), generated a richly ambivalent and at times deeply troubled discourse in many of the most well-known texts of the period.

But while the interconnection of Romantic literature and British imperial activity at the end of the eighteenth century is now widely accepted, we need to query what kind of connection this is, and what kind of dialogue we might set up between Romanticism and post-colonial studies. Some argue that Romantic literature articulates resistance to, and/or anxiety about cultural imperialism, even as it remains complicit with it. Others, such as Alan Richardson and Sonia Hofkosh, take a more compelling line, arguing that many of 'the rhetorical strategies, literary motifs, and cultural myths of modern colonialism and racism took characteristic form during the years 1780–1834'. Their volume also makes the important point that the inclusion of nationalist, racist, and colonialist discourses is crucial for opening up the boundaries of what we have traditionally called 'Romanticism'.[2]

What does 'post-colonial' mean?

How do we define the term 'post-colonial'? Much ink has been spilt on this issue, but despite the plethora of texts and anthologies devoted to defining what is meant by 'post-colonial', the term remains an elusive and controversial one. The simplest meaning of the word is the chronological one, with 'post-colonial' referring to the post-independence period of former British (and other European) colonies. Post-colonial literature is, therefore, the literature of Africa, Australia, Bangladesh, Canada, the Caribbean, India, Malaysia, Malta, New Zealand, Pakistan, Singapore, South Pacific Island countries, and Sri Lanka. Many writers and critics are, however, automatically troubled by the chronological implications of that prefix, 'post'. Quite reasonably they want to query the extent to which the political, economic, and discursive inequalities associated with colonialism have disappeared into the past, leaving us in a world blissfully free of some of colonialism's most pernicious features, such as xenophobia or racism. As Aravamudan puts it, 'To consider that we are beyond colonialism in any way is to misrecognize—dangerously—the world's current realities.'[3] But the literature of the Romantic period does not of course fit the dictionary definition of post-colonial, meaning 'after the end of colonial rule', so we need to ask: what does it mean to speak of post-colonial approaches to a body of writing emerging from a powerful nation busy *consolidating* its imperial ambitions rather than a former dependency *emancipating itself* from colonial rule?

Leela Gandhi has dealt constructively with the 'post' of post-colonial by defining post-colonialism as a 'disciplinary project devoted to the academic task of revisiting, remembering and, crucially, interrogating the colonial past'.[4] As such post-colonial criticism is very much an engaged scholarship, concerned with unequal relations of power, keen to shift attention away from, in our period, a 'little England' context to the wider non-European world, and alert to textual representations of non-Western peoples and environments. Furthermore, in listening out for voices from the margins and for the voices of resistance and dissent, post-colonial critics are frequently involved in the work of constructing an empire which 'writes back' to the metropolitan centre. But post-colonial analysis often goes beyond overt representation or the voice of the other to explore the ways in which texts themselves can be seen to participate in a colonial logic, involving textual relations of domination, subordination, and othering.

For the purposes of this essay, my particular answer to the question—what does it mean to apply post-colonial approaches' to the Romantic period?—is that the widespread and popular movement for the abolition of slavery, gaining momentum from the 1770s onwards, does itself constitute an important moment of post-colonial critique—a moment in which the political and cultural experience of the marginalized periphery comes vividly to the fore. The texts which embody the voices and the perspectives of the colonized, such as those published by self-liberated slaves Phillis

Wheatley, Ignatius Sancho (see *Oxford Companion to the Romantic Age*, p. 688), Olaudah Equiano (see *Oxford Companion to the Romantic Age*, p. 499), Ottobah Cugoano, and Mary Prince, provide a particularly rich resource for post-colonial analysis. These African writers voice a pungent and moving critique of colonialism, slavery, and racism, dismantling in the process key Eurocentric assumptions, such as the belief in the superiority of Christianity to all other world religions. The challenge these writers posed to British political and cultural hegemony, and to the assumption that whiteness was the colour of spiritual life, forms the subject of the second section of this chapter.

Given the politically activist nature of post-colonial studies, and the pernicious and enduring afterlife of colonialism, post-colonial critics are understandably concerned with the politics of literary interpretation in the present. In important ways, the methodology of post-colonial studies links it to other new humanities, especially feminism, cultural studies, and gay/lesbian studies (see chapter on 'Feminism'). These new humanities seek to recover marginalized voices and knowledges whilst exploring the mechanisms by which these have been obscured and silenced. In the pedagogical realm feminism shares with post-colonial studies the ambition of challenging the privilege and authority of canonical knowledge and the humanist curriculum, especially when (as Gandhi points out) these appear to be based on the belief that 'some human beings are more human than others'.[5] While recently there have been pungent post-colonial critiques of First World feminism, the fit between feminist and post-colonial approaches is nevertheless well established, with the anthology *Feminist Post-Colonial Theory* (2003), making a convincing case for feminism's dynamic role in the early development of post-colonial studies. In exploring the meaning of post-colonial approaches, this essay will itself demonstrate the relevance of feminist methodologies by exploring issues to do with women and empire in the eighteenth century, particularly as these emerge in debates about luxury and the consumption of colonial produce.

More recently, the emancipatory agenda of post-colonialism has come under suspicion, with critics such as Graham Huggan alleging that the rhetoric of resistance has itself been made over into a consumer product in the current highly commercial and neocolonial context of global commodity culture.[6] Complaints about the co-option of Third World post-colonial intellectuals within the very Western institutions they allegedly critique is summed up by the hostile dictum that post-colonialism happens when Third World intellectuals arrive in the First World. Associated with these negative appraisals are some stringent critiques of the more abstruse forms of post-colonial theory, denounced as a form of self-indulgent recreation far divorced from the problems of social, political, and cultural domination. Finally, there has been a growing uneasiness with the centrality to post-colonial theory of the fractured self popularized by post-structuralism. This fissured and cosmopolitan identity, the product of the increasingly global movement of people, leads to a privileging of exile and migrancy, putting at risk some of the specificities of identity as defined by place, time, history, and culture.

Slavery and the Romantic imagination

The historiography of the abolition movement, particularly the relations of slavery and anti-slavery to capitalism, is large and complex. Many scholars still puzzle over the way in which eighteenth-century Britain moved from being a society comfortable with slavery to one which vehemently spurned it. Where did the new humanitarianism of the 1770s onwards come from? What is the crucial explanatory link between capitalism and humanitarianism? In terms of changes in cognitive style and moral sensibility in the period, some might argue that the anti-slavery movement provides a key instance of capitalism's subliminal curriculum of a 'widening of causal horizons'. For the self-interested, Britain's expanding colonial horizons might mean increased wealth and empowerment, but for the scrupulous and for those with powerful imaginations, the newly extended chains of moral responsibility generated by commerce and colonialism sometimes brought about an intolerable burden of guilt.

From the late 1780s onwards, the British public was exposed to an array of detailed evidence about the slave trade, from the storing and shipping of human cargo to the gruesome display of the trade's implements, such as whips, fetters, and iron masks for forced feeding. Coleridge provides just one instance of an imagination haunted by this new knowledge. The diseased bodies that rot the planks of slave ships during the middle passage—a detail mentioned twice in a lecture he delivered against the slave trade in 1795—pass into 'The Rime of the Ancient Mariner':

> I looked upon the rotting sea,
> And drew my eyes away;
> I looked upon the rotting deck,
> And there the dead men lay.

Initially a ballad about discovery and exploration ('We were the first that ever burst | Into that silent sea'), the narrative moves swiftly to the performance of an act of evil ('And I had done a hellish thing, | And it would work 'em woe'), which is then followed by intense physical and mental suffering ('Alone, alone, all, all alone, | Alone on a wide wide sea! | And never a saint took pity on | My soul in agony'). Three years earlier, as a young radical lecturer in Bristol, Coleridge had urged his audience to undermine the trade by boycotting slave-grown sugar and other West Indian products:

A part of that food among most of you, is sweetened with Brother's Blood . . . Surely if the inspired Philanthropist of Galilee were to revisit Earth, and be among the Feasters as at Cana, he would not now change water into wine, but convert the produce into the things producing . . . Then with our fleshly eye should we behold what even now Imagination ought to paint to us; instead of conserves, tears and blood, and for music, groanings and the loud peals of the lash![7]

The highly popular boycott campaign constituted a significant intervention in Britain's global trading system, illustrating the extent of the market, an enhanced understanding of the workings of supply and demand, and the new political power of consumers.

Coleridge's lecture uses lurid rhetoric to harness that power, while his Gothic eucharist reveals the disorienting effects of consumers' growing awareness of moral and personal responsibility. Many boycott tracts took explicit advantage of consumer guilt, imaging sugar as a 'loathsome poison', an (unholy) host 'steeped in the blood of our fellow creatures'. Campaigners even indulged minute calculations: 'In every pound of sugar used . . . we may be considered as consuming two ounces of human flesh.' Since one of the problems with slavery was that it tended to be, for many British people, 'out of sight, out of mind', the metaphor of consumption was a shorthand method of linking the two worlds of black and white, the colony (site of production) and the metropolis.

By means of the Gothic eucharist, Coleridge's lecture sets out to destabilize the binaries of white and black, the 'civilized' and the 'primitive', so that, satirically, the European consumer becomes the 'true' cannibal savage. But instead of collapsing the false dichotomies between Europe and Africa, Coleridge's play with cannibalism and eucharistic rites has the unintended effect of reinforcing the boundaries. For while he inverts the structure of the binary distinction, the validity of the dualism remains intact. The very introduction of the topic of cannibalism—that ultimate boundary marker between self and other—was a sure way of putting his listeners in mind of the chief arguments for justifying slavery—the alleged savagery of Africa and African people. Thus, the mobilization of 'Imagination' in the service of abolitionism inaugurates profound textual disturbance rather than his promised 'truth-painting'.

In his newspaper *The Watchman* (1796), Coleridge characterized his nation as blackened through its many evil connections with empire. Nor could this black complexion be disguised by the rhetorical 'cosmetics' employed by parliamentarians 'to conceal the deformities of a commerce, which is blotched all over with one leprosy of evil'.[8] The allusion to 'cosmetics' invokes a long tradition of misogynistic writing, whilst the 'leprosy of evil' looks forward to that Gothic female figure, the 'Night-mare Life-in-Death' of 'The Ancient Mariner' whose skin is 'as white as leprosy'. The identification of women and domesticity with the conspicuous consumption of exotic products— 'the pestilent inventions of Luxury' as Coleridge called them—is a prominent theme in late eighteenth-century discourse (see chapter on 'Sensibility'). The leisurely etiquettes of tea-drinking, involving West Indian sugar and East Indian tea, were, for instance, so identified with women consumers and the home that teatime was nicknamed the 'shrine of female devotion' (see *Oxford Companion to the Romantic Age*, pp. 60, 102–14). The causal link so often posited in the period between women's desiring bodies and colonialism's worst excesses can be seen in Coleridge's claim that trade with the East Indies had cost eight million lives, 'in return for which most foul and heart-inslaving Guilt we receive gold, diamonds, silks, muslins & callicoes for fine Ladies and Prostitutes. Tea to make a pernicious Beverage, Porcelain to drink it from, and salt-petre for the making of gunpowder with which we may murder the poor Inhabitants who supply all these things.'[9]

Bringing slavery home

Lord Mansfield's ruling in 1772, that a slave owner could not forcibly deport his slave to the colonies, was popularly believed to have banished slavery from British soil, thus increasing the temptation to regard the horrors of the slave system as exclusive to geographically remote colonies. But the abolitionists and boycotters of the 1780s and 1790s were determined to keep the atrocities of slavery firmly at home and in the public eye. So successful were they in infiltrating the consciousness of the nation that sometimes the atrocities they highlighted erupted unexpectedly into scenes of everyday English life. Instances of this can be seen in the dialogue between two images, one illustrating an atrocity of the middle passage, the other a London street scene. The first engraving (by Isaac Cruikshank, April 1792) is of the notorious Captain Kimber case, where a pregnant slave girl was allegedly tied upside down by one leg and flogged to death for refusing to 'dance' on deck. The case received extensive coverage in the periodical and newspaper press, including court transcripts complete with eyewitness accounts. The second illustration, published six months later, is an anonymous engraving entitled 'The Rabbits', apparently referring to Cruikshank's print. It depicts a black rabbit-seller and a well-dressed young white woman. The woman holds one of the dead rabbits by a hind-leg, and complains of its strong smell, a complaint which prompts the rabbit-seller to protest, lewdly: 'Be gar Misse dat no fair. If Blacke Man take you by Leg so—you smell too'.

The kneeling figure of the rabbit-seller alludes to the key emblem of the abolitionist movement, the widely circulated Wedgwood medallion of 1787. This popular medallion depicts a kneeling and fettered slave who, with chained wrists raised in supplication, asks 'Am I not a man and a brother?' The anonymous engraver of 'The Rabbits' mocks this appeal to universal brotherhood by presenting us with a street hawker begging to be rid of his rabbits rather than his chains. But the true butt of the joke is not the rabbit-seller but the young Miss whose sensibilities are so offended. Provocatively the rabbit-seller challenges her to put herself into the position of the dead rabbit, held upside down by him. 'If Blacke Man take you by Leg so—you smell too', he taunts, a proposition which uncannily reverses the Kimber atrocity in racial terms. His words also recall the Wedgwood medallion's motto, substituting for universal brotherhood an appeal to universal sisterhood. For in stating that the young Miss would smell just the same if held in the same position, he effectively asks 'are you not a woman and a sister' to that black female slave tortured and murdered on the middle passage?

Both engravings are unstable in their attempts to imagine or encompass the horrors of the slave trade. They are also notably confused in their stance on the abolitionist question, in particular the endless debates about legitimate versus illegitimate commerce with Africa. Cruikshank introduces a blatantly sexual theme into his imagining of the middle passage, charging that Kimber murdered the woman for her 'Virgin modesty', an allegation altogether absent from surviving court transcripts. 'The

Fig. 5 Isaac Cruikshank, 'The Abolition of the Slave Trade. Or the Inhumanity of Dealers in human flesh exemplified in the Cruel treatment of a young Negro Girl of 15 for her Virgin modesty', London, 10 April 1792. British Museum, Department of Prints and Drawings.

Fig. 6 Anon., 'The Rabbits', London, 8 October 1792. British Museum, Department of Prints and Drawings.

Rabbits' picks up salaciously on the brutality and violence of interracial sex, but reverses the usual abolitionist typecasting of white tormenter and black victim. This racially inverted spectre—black tormenter and white victim—operates on a number of conflicting levels. While on the one hand the rabbit-seller invites the Miss to perform an act of sympathetic identification with the dead rabbit/dead black woman, he is also pointedly misogynistic. Taunting her as smelly dead meat, he not only obliquely threatens her with the same fate as the slave woman, but also implicates her in the guilt of the rabbit's/woman's miserable and degrading fate. That the Miss should, as a consumer, be figured as complicit in the crimes of the slave trade merely restates the theme which we have mentioned already—the pervasive scapegoating of refined (decadent) white women as the principal (savage) consumers of black bodies. But the Miss's disgust—her refusal to enter into the proposed transaction—cuts both ways. It might signal her boycott-inspired (and thus proper) revulsion from slave-grown products, or betray her self-imposed ignorance of the moral precipice on which female consumers stand. The title 'The Rabbits' is curious too, involving a displacement from the lively rabbit-seller himself on to his inert merchandise (a later imitation of this print is entitled 'The Rabbit Merchant'). Even 'The Rabbit' would have been a more apt title, capturing more centrally the comic energy of the cartoon, but instead our attention is directed to the ominous pile of dead rabbits, emerging in seemingly endless, sickening succession from the wicker basket.

Given the widespread belief in some quarters that Africans were no more than animals, 'The Rabbits' aims to trouble our understanding of what it means to be human. As Montesquieu famously stated, with cutting irony: 'It is impossible for us to suppose these creatures to be men, because, allowing them to be men, a suspicion would follow, that we ourselves are not Christians.'[10] The callous view that black people were simply so much dead meat emerged in grotesque form in the case of another notorius and widely publicized middle passage atrocity, involving the slave ship *Zong*. In 1781, the *Zong*'s captain pushed 131 sick slaves overboard in order to deflect their financial loss from the shipowners on to the insurers. When the case came to trial in London, it was heard simply as a matter about property (the slaves were 'things') and the niceties of maritime insurance.

The eruption of the middle passage and its inhuman violence on to the streets of London—the world's imperial centre—reveals the sexual, racial, and moral anxieties generated by Britain's leading role in the enslavement and murder of countless innocent Africans. Furthermore, the city's increasingly visible black population, many of whom had been slaves in America and the West Indies, were a daily (and often uncomfortable) reminder of the trade. The reading below focuses on the autobiography of one of those displaced black Londoners, a former slave whose life and writings reveal a hidden history and identity.

Domesticity and empire

One of the most exciting developments of recent years has been the application of post-colonial approaches to some of the most English, provincial, and domestic of Romantic period authors. Take Jane Austen, for instance, the premiere novelist of England's rural life and of the nation's landed gentry. For a long time critics tended to view Austen as hermetically sealed off from the tumultuous and revolutionary period in which she lived and wrote. The publication of Marilyn Butler's *Jane Austen and the War of Ideas* (1975) set the ball rolling for a revaluation of this received view. Putting Austen back into the context of her times, Butler demonstrated the extent to which her writings were deeply and ideologically engaged with the debates and issues of her day, such as revolutionary Jacobinism, sensibility, the corrosion of the Church's authority, and the weakening of the moral order of society. Since Butler's work, the politicization of Austen's oeuvre has been taken even further by the added dimension of empire. To this end, Edward Said, author of *Orientalism* (1978) and a pioneer of post-colonial criticism, focused on 'the Antigua connection' of *Mansfield Park* (1816)—the fact that Sir Thomas Bertram is an absentee owner of West Indian slave plantations, and that the issue of his slave-holding is explicitly thematized in the novel. Concentrating on slavery as both metaphor and reality in the novel, Said's aim is to 'draw out, extend, give emphasis and voice to what is silent or marginally presented'.[11]

Said's insistence on the 'worldliness' of Austen's novels—that they are always enmeshed in circumstance, time, place, and society—is further explored in a recent volume *The Postcolonial Jane Austen* (2000). Austen's famously miniaturizing reference to her novels as artworks painted with a fine brush on a 'little bit (two Inches wide) of Ivory' is the starting-point for an essay by Jon Mee on the intersection of the exotic and the familiar in *Mansfield Park*, and the privileged place of domestic virtue in relation to nation and empire. Clara Tuite, examining the same novel, plots the coincidence of the Bertram family's domestic contraction and retrenchment with British colonial expansion. Such new work on Austen means that important issues of gender and domesticity, so central to feminist approaches to writing in this period, are now mobilized within the larger context of national and imperial structures of ideas, events, and ideologies, such as racism, the slave trade, military conquest, and travel (see chapter on 'Travel writing').

The new awareness of other cultures engendered by the colonial enterprise can be seen in the major fad for orientalism in the Romantic period, extending from cultural texts (art, literature, philology, ethnography) to interior decoration, where Chinese, Egyptian, and Indian models were highly fashionable (see *Oxford Companion to the Romantic Age*, pp. 232–42). According to Edward Said, orientalism was the discourse 'by which European culture was able to manage—and even produce—the Orient politically, sociologically, militarily, ideologically, scientifically, and imaginatively during the post-Enlightenment period'.[12] Even so-called 'pure' or disinterested knowledge, such as the learned and scholarly eighteenth-century antiquarianism of Sir William Jones, laid the groundwork for two centuries of European imperialist thinking about the East, Said argued. In the twenty-five years since the publication of Said's book there have been numerous critiques and qualifications. The principal complaints are that Said's conception of orientalism is too monolithic, and his methodology too rigidly dichotomized between East and West. These limitations result not only in an Occidental stereotype of the racist Westerner but leave little scope for the multiplicity of orients imagined by hosts of writers, artists, and scholars. Nor did Said's argument take account of what was so palpable in so many orientalist texts—the anxiety of empire and its accompanying sense of European vulnerability (see chapter on 'Easts').

The popular early eighteenth-century collection, *Arabian Nights Entertainments*, was formative of the imaginative development of writers such as Coleridge and Thomas De Quincey. Many of these stories, together with their numerous imitations, feature those negative stereotypes of the Orient which, according to Said, make up a purely 'imaginative geography' of all those values which the West seeks to expel or disavow, such as irrationality, superstition, cruelty, sexual perversion, and effeminacy. Recent readings of the oriental tale *Vathek* (1786), for instance, focus on Beckford's disturbing fantasy of colonial (Eastern) otherness, a fantasy verging on the grotesque in its racist deployment of negative stereotypes. But if orientalism was a distorting medium, it also provided a critical vantage point from which to criticize Western social and sexual arrangements. Many Eastern tales, such as Frances Sheridan's *History of Nourjahad* (1767) are explicitly didactic, mobilizing exotic settings and motifs for the purposes of satire and critique. Others, such as the Eastern poetic utopias of Percy Bysshe Shelley and Thomas Moore offer more complex projections of European fantasies onto orientalism. In other words, eighteenth-century orientalism mirrors the *Arabian Nights* themselves, tales which paradoxically deliver surprisingly feisty heroines alongside predictable stereotypes of cruel, irrational, and oversexed Sultans.[13]

If post-colonial approaches are important for understanding eighteenth-century orientalism they are also germane to Gothic literature, a genre preoccupied with the topics of domination, oppression, and rebellion. The intersection in the Romantic imagination of colonialism with a Gothic language of otherness can be seen in a host of works, from Charlotte Dacre's *Zofloya; or, The Moor* (1806) to Byron's *The Giaour* (1813), Mary Shelley's *Frankenstein* (1818), and Maturin's *Melmoth the Wanderer* (1820). Furthermore, by focusing on monsters, vampires, and the socially and culturally dispossessed, the Gothic challenges Enlightenment rationality and in the process interrogates what it means to be human (see chapter on 'Gothic'). Recently David Punter has given a post-colonial spin to the Gothic by focusing on the genre's view of history, namely, that the past can never be left behind, that there is no escaping from the legacies of imperial rule. Like the ghosts and revenants who haunt Gothic literature, the past will always reappear and exact its necessary price.[14] Gothic's preoccupation with the past and its recurrence in the present usefully disrupts and problematizes any temporal drift post-colonialism might have into becoming yet another grand narrative—a narrative which plots progress from a pre-colonial, to colonial then on to a post-colonial stage.

READING: *The Interesting Narrative of the Life of Olaudah Equiano*

Prominent in the agitation against the slave trade was a free African based in London in the 1780s and 1790s called Gustavus Vassa, or Olaudah Equiano (c.1745–97). A self-styled member of the 'Sons of Africa' (the byline he and other black compaigners used when writing to the newspapers), Equiano wrote an autobiography which doubled as an anti-slavery tract entitled *The Interesting Narrative of the Life of Olaudah Equiano, or Gustavus Vassa, the African, Written by Himself.*[15] The book's argument against slavery carried a particular authority in the public domain, since its author described how he had been kidnapped as a child in Africa and transported as a slave to the West Indies. Equiano's book, the reading for this section, was a best-seller in its day. Published in 1789, the year of revolution, it was quickly and widely reviewed, passing into a second edition in its first year, and into a ninth edition by 1794. It was also translated into several European languages. After a long eclipse in the nineteenth and a good part of the twentieth centuries, Equiano's book is now widely taught and discussed by students of abolitionism and the tradition of early black-British writing.

Generically Equiano's text draws upon a number of narrative traditions—spiritual autobiography, slave narrative, anti-slavery petition, the sentimental novel, travel narrative, and adventure story (see *Oxford Companion to the Romantic Age*, pp. 707–8). The locations of Equiano's story are also varied, from Africa across the middle passage to the West Indies, then on to Britain, North America, the West Indies, Turkey, Central America, and even up into the Arctic Circle. In the course of these far-flung adventures and ordeals, Equiano appears to us in many different roles—the terrified African child, kidnapped with his sister and brutally separated from her, the young slave who buys himself into freedom, the servant, the seaman, the ship's captain, the slave overseer, the committed and outspoken abolitionist. There is another role, too, and that is the role of the independent author. Disdaining the conventional apparatus of white people's letters testifying to the authenticity of author and book, Equiano's narrative is proudly certified on the title-page as 'Written by Himself'. Self-authored and self-authorized, Equiano includes as his frontispiece an engraving of himself dressed in the clothes of an English gentleman. His gaze meets ours confidently, even boldly, his hand holding out an open Bible towards us, as though he were about to speak to the text. The doubleness built into the image of an African man in European clothes reappears on the opening page of his narrative, where his admission of (African) difference is intimately allied to knowledge of (European) sameness. Reviewing his life's experiences he comments, 'did I consider myself an European, I might say my sufferings were great' (p. 31). Later in the narrative he again uses his insider (English) persona to bring his experience of slavery home to his white readers. Whilst acknowledging that (comparatively speaking) his English owner fed his slaves well, he adds that he 'often went hungry, and an Englishman might think my fare very indifferent' (p. 104).

The frontispiece stance of author as a lay preacher or teacher with his Bible is a crucial one. It reverses the usual pedagogic and imperialist hierarchy of European educator and childish, colonized African. It also underscores the interconnection in Equiano's life of literacy and identity. By means of his book and his Anglophone identity, the author writes himself into being, achieving through literacy the crucial transition from slavery to freedom. The importance of English literacy and acculturation in Equiano's self-fashioning must always, however, share space with his African self. This dual identity is prominently inscribed on the book's title-page: *Olaudah Equiano, or Gustavus Vassa, the African*. Gustavus Vassa, a sixteenth-century Swedish nobleman and patriot, was the name given to Equiano by his first owner, and it was this slave name which he invariably used throughout his life. We must conclude, then, that by adding to the title-page the extra name Olaudah Equiano, the author was reclaiming his African identity, an identity which had been erased by slavery and baptism. In terms of marketing and promoting his self-published book, it was also an astute move to add his native name, thus maximizing the impact of the story's authenticity.

Identity politics is an important issue in post-colonial studies. The complexity of Equiano's dual identity, shifting between English and African, is a persistent and at times richly contradictory theme in his life-story, one which neatly illustrates Homi Bhabha's important concept of cultural hybridity, or the condition of in-between-ness. Hybrid identities open up a 'third-space' for oppositional critique, challenging the monolithic opposites which structure so much of our thinking, such as black and white, good and bad, male and female. In Bhabha's words, hybridity allows for 'the construction of a political object that is new, *neither the one nor the other*'.[16] There are dozens of instances of hybridity in Equiano's narrative, where he appears neither African nor English. Some of these moments occur shortly after Equiano's arrival in England as, orphaned and lonely, the young child seeks acceptance into his new environment. For instance, on Guernsey, seeing the face of his little white playmate grow 'very rosy' when her mother washed it, he begins to feel acutely self-conscious about his blackness: 'I therefore tried oftentimes myself if I could not by washing make my face of the same colour as my little play-mate (Mary), but it was all in vain; and I now began to be mortified at the difference in our complexions' (p. 69).

The child's social embarrassment, ironically handled here by the mature author, challenges the reader to think about the process of acculturation, and the extent to which a mind can be colonized by the dominant culture. After several years as a seaman in the British navy, Equiano jokingly boasts of himself as 'almost an Englishman' in his fearlessness at sea. His desire to resemble these 'superior' white men issues in his determination to learn to read and write (pp. 77–8). So intense is this longing to identify with whiteness through mastery of his owner's language that there are moments when he appears to forget or even disown his African identity. When a little black boy on the Isle of Wight rushes to embrace him as a brother, Equiano is confused, turning 'a little out of his way' (p. 85). Equiano handles the issue of his double consciousness, his hybridity, with great skill and complexity, ensuring that the ongoing connectedness and fluidity of that transitional 'third-space' is never lost to view. The issue of his literacy in English and his conversion to Christianity is a case in point. Instead of these acquisitions taking him in a one-way direction away from his native beliefs and language, they actually move him in a circle, returning him to his African origins. The Bible's laws and rules, surprisingly similar to those of his own native country (Equiano tells us), do not obliterate his African self but help him remember his native Ibo 'manners and customs' more acutely and accurately (p. 92). Moreover, despite his conversion to Christianity, Equiano keeps up a steady stream of barbs against the 'Christians' responsible for the slave trade's inhumanity. The savagery and barbarism typically attributed to black people, including the slur of cannibalism, is neatly overturned at the very outset of his tale, when the young Equiano is carried aboard the slave ship loading its human cargo off the coast of West Africa. Terrified at the white complexions and long straight hair of the English seamen, he immediately assumes the worst when his eye falls on a large copper furnace boiling, near which languish many miserable Africans, chained together. Fainting from 'horror and anguish' the child asks his captors 'if we were not to be eaten by those white men with horrible looks, red faces, and long hair?' Although reassured, Equiano records of the 'savage' white people that he had 'never seen among any people such instances of brutal cruelty' (pp. 55–6).

The original moment of enslavement inaugurates Equiano's steady commitment to destabilizing and even reversing eurocentric, racially charged notions of the civilized and the uncivilized. Drawing on Rousseau's primitivism and critique of the decadence of white civilization, Equiano writes feelingly of the simplicity and superior gentility of the African way of life—'we were totally unacquainted with swearing, and all those terms of abuse and reproach which find the way so readily and copiously into the languages of more civilized people' (p. 41). Nor did Africans, in their simplicity, participate in that 'new refinement in cruelty' which led Europeans to aggravate the distress of enslavement by brutally separating family members from one another (p. 61). Drawing upon the horror of being 'torn away from all the tender connexions that were dear to my heart', Equiano's loving re-creation of 'the first scenes' of his African childhood participates in a widespread shift in English sensibility which was lending new meanings to these formative years. The defining moment for celebrating that earlier African self occurs when he purchases his freedom, a moment when he is restored to his 'original free African state'. It is symptomatic of his fluid, dual identity, however, that he has prepared for his new state of freedom by laying out £8 for a blue suit of 'superfine cloathes to dance in', and that his freedom should lead straight to a longing to return to 'Old England', where (he tells us) 'my heart had always been' (pp. 136–8).

But the true motive for returning to England at this time is revenge rather than sentiment, for he wishes to confront and shame his former English owner who had sold him back into slavery after he had purchased his freedom. As many readers have noted, Equiano's trading and mercantile transactions take centre ground in the *Interesting Narrative*, the most important piece of business being, of course, the purchase of his freedom. As a slave, Equiano realizes that it is only through property that he can become his own master. Or to put it slightly differently, a commercial transaction is the only way he can transform himself from an anonymous piece of property into a unique personality. In buying himself—in dealing in the economics of slavery in order to be free—Equiano demonstrates an essential feature of emergent capitalism in this period, namely 'that the economic structure of property and power underwrites the very possibility of individual freedom even as that structure is itself girded by an individualist paradigm, the rights of man'.[17]

The paradox of Equiano's situation, enmeshed as he is in the converging discourses of capitalism, abolition, and individualism, goes some way towards explaining why he is such an enthusiastic advocate of commerce and economic free trade. Pitting himself against the 'illicit Traffic' of slavery, he advocates a legitimate 'commercial Intercourse with Africa', one which would open 'an Inexhaustible Source of Wealth to the manufacturing Interest of Great Britain' (p. 333). Equiano's championing of global commerce and a potentially lucrative African free market goes hand in hand with his daring advocacy of interracial marriage. Instead of prohibition and restraint, which only breed 'secret amours, adultery, fornication and all other evils of lasciviousness', the 'mutual commerce of the sexes of both Blacks and Whites' should (he argued) be liberally permitted. Such couplings would lead the way in encouraging 'open, free, and generous love upon Nature's own wide and extensive plan' without distinction of skin colour (pp. 329–30). In conformity with this romantic ideal of love he married an Englishwoman, Susanna Cullen, from Soham, Cambridgeshire.

Literary influences

Given the popularity of Equiano's *Interesting Narrative*, it is not surprising to find allusions to some if its key episodes in the writings of his contemporaries. It is possible, for instance, that Equiano's description of being a castaway made a deep impression on the young Coleridge. Sailing to Georgia, Equiano's ship succumbs to a storm and he and the crew are washed up on one of the many Bahama islands, a desolate archipelago bereft of fresh water. Lapping 'with much eagerness' a few drops of moisture on some leaves, the men grow increasingly desperate until 'in the midst of our murmuring, the captain, all at once cried out, "A sail! a sail! a sail!" This gladdening sound was like a reprieve to a convict, and we all instantly turned to look at it; but in a little time some of us began to be afraid it was not a sail' (p. 154). The horror of drought, the desperate longing for respite and the combined joy and terror at what appears to be salvation, are replayed in that climactic scene of 'The Rime of the Ancient Mariner':

> With throats unslaked, with black lips baked,
> We could nor laugh nor wail;
> Through utter drought all dumb we stood!
> I bit my arm, I sucked the blood,
> And cried, A sail! a sail!

The *Interesting Narrative* may also have played a role in Blake's well-known poem, 'The Little Black Boy', published in the same year, 1789. The politics of this poem have always puzzled critics: is it a racist and imperialist poem, in which Blake endorses the superiority of whiteness, or is he using lyric irony to expose (as Alan Richardson has argued) Christian anti-slavery literature itself, with its sentimental and neocolonial ethos?[18] While this debate continues, what can be argued with some certainty is that Blake's analysis of the little black boy's psychology, especially his longing for whiteness, owes something to the pathos with which Equiano depicts his younger self's awkward and troubled relation to English culture. In Blake's poem the little black boy sees his complexion (his African identity) in contradictory ways. At first his blackness signifies bereavement, or the social death of slavery, while the white skin of his companion resembles that of an angel:

> My mother bore me in the southern wild,
> And I am black, but O! my soul is white;
> White as an angel is the English child:
> But I am black as if bereav'd of light.

But this hierarchical perspective is reversed when we learn that the little African's blackness is actually the mark of his superiority, enabling him to stand closer to God than the little white boy, to whom he teaches the ways of spiritual love:

> And thus I say to little English boy.
> When I from black and he from white cloud free,
> And round the tent of God like lambs we joy
>
> I'll shade him from the heat till he can bear,
> To lean in joy upon our fathers knee.
> And then I'll stand and stroke his silver hair,
> And be like him and he will then love me.

The poem's ironies continue to the end, for while the little black boy stands on a higher plane he nevertheless struggles with his infatuation with whiteness and whitening—an infatuation with a stinging rationalization for Blake's white readers: 'And then I'll stand and stroke his silver hair, | And be like him and he will then love me.'

In his own time, Equiano's narrative carried special authority because the author himself had been a victim and an eyewitness of slavery in Africa and in the West Indies. Today, too, the cachet of his African identity can be seen in the titles of recent editions of his work, such as *The Kidnapped Prince* and *Olaudah Equiano: The African*. But new evidence (in the shape of a baptism record and a ship muster list) has recently emerged to cast doubt on Equiano's nativity. Emotions run high on this subject, with some scholars arguing that the new documents, suggesting a birthplace of South Carolina, should have been suppressed or destroyed because of their fatal damage to Equiano as the authentic voice of the African diaspora. Others, influenced by post-structuralism, reject such a nativist and essentializing response, arguing that identity and meaning are always unstable, and that modern understandings of subjectivity need to take account of the performative aspect of literary texts (see chapter on 'The idea of the author'). If 'Equiano' was an invented authorial persona, then we need to pay more attention, they argue, to the text's complex rhetorical strategies. John Mandeville's famous travel book is a case in point. Now generally regarded as a complete fabrication, its literary and artistic stocks have never been higher. Others again find a midway point between essentialist and performative notions of identity, arguing that even if

Equiano had not directly experienced the middle passage himself, then surely his parents and/or grandparents had. In this way, his autobiography can be championed as a tremendous source of imaginary coherence to set against the experience of dispersal and fragmentation.

FURTHER READING

Carey, Brycchan, Ellis, Markman, and Salih, Sara (eds.), *Discourses of Slavery and Abolition: Britain and its Colonies, 1760–1838* (Basingstoke: Palgrave Macmillan, 2004). A new volume of critical essays exploring current thinking on the relationship between slavery and the categories of writing, oratory, and visual culture in the 'long' eighteenth century.

Carretta, Vincent, *Unchained Voices: An Anthology of Black Authors in the English-Speaking World of the 18th Century* (Lexington, Ky.: University Press of Kentucky, 1996). This well-annotated and useful anthology brings together sixteen African American and Anglo-African writers from the eighteenth century.

—— 'Olaudah Equiano or Gustavus Vassa?: New Light on an Eighteenth-Century Question of Identity', *Slavery and Abolition*, 20 (1999), 96–105. Reveals two new pieces of archival evidence concerning the 'true identity' of the author of *The Interesting Narrative*; the debate is likely to remain inconclusive, however, since the evidence itself can be read in two ways—as fabrication of an African persona, or simply as Equiano's expedient denial of African nativity at two particular points in his life.

—— and Gould, P. (eds.), *'Genius in Bondage': Literature of the Early Black Atlantic* (Lexington, Ky.: University Press of Kentucky, 2001). A collection of recent critical essays, covering such issues as race, gender, market culture, racial authority, language, and the issue of difference.

Coleman, Deirdre, 'Conspicuous Consumption: White Abolitionism and English Women's Protest Writing in the 1790s', *English Literary History*, 61 (1994), 341–62. This article examines the intersection of Romantic feminist writing with abolitionist rhetoric, focusing in particular on the gendering of consumption.

Davis, Charles T., and Gates, Jr., Henry Louis (eds.), *The Slave's Narrative* (Oxford: Oxford University Press, 1985). A seminal collection for the study of slave narrative and its conventions, which includes Paul Edwards's important essay, 'Three West African Writers of the 1780s' (pp. 175–98).

Ferguson, Moira, *Subject to Others: British Women Writers and Colonial Slavery, 1670–1834* (New York and London: Routledge, 1992). A useful survey, from *Oroonoko* (1688) onwards, of almost two centuries of British women's writing on the topic of slavery.

Gandhi, Leela, *Postcolonial Theory: A Critical Introduction* (St Leonards, NSW: Allen and Unwin, 1998). An excellent, readable critical introduction to the field of post-colonial studies and its wider philosophical and intellectual contexts.

Henry, Lauren, ' "Sunshine and Shady Groves": What Blake's "Little Black Boy" Learned from African Writers', in T. Fulford and P. Kitson (eds.), *Romanticism and Colonialism: Writing and Empire, 1780–1830* (Cambridge: Cambridge University Press, 1998). Henry skilfully draws out the impact on Blake's poem of Equiano's African contemporaries, principally Phillis Wheatley, the Boston slave, and James Albert Ukawsaw Gronniosaw, the African prince.

Hughes, William, and Smith, Andrew (eds.), *Empire and the Gothic: The Politics of Genre* (Basingstoke: Palgrave, 2003). This volume addresses the link between the Gothic and the post-colonial from the eighteenth century (Beckford, Maturin, Dacre, and Mary Shelley) through to contemporary post-colonial literature (Rushdie, Atwood, Roy, and Coetzee).

Kitson, P., and Lee, Debbie (eds.), *Slavery, Abolition and Emancipation: Writings in the British Romantic Period*, 8 vols. (London: Pickering and Chatto, 1999). These volumes contain 3,000 facsimile pages of original texts bearing on topics ranging from parliamentary debates to contemporary drama, fiction, and verse.

Leask, Nigel, *British Romantic Writers and the East: Anxieties of Empire* (Cambridge: Cambridge University Press, 1992). This important book explores the anxieties and instabilities of Romantic representations of the Ottoman empire, India, China, and the Far East.

Lee, Debbie, *Slavery and the Romantic Imagination* (Philadelphia: University of Pennsylvania Press, 2002). This study deploys Romantic theories of empathy and the creative process to analyse the workings of empire in canonical literary texts.

Rajan, R. S., and Park, Y. (eds.), *The Postcolonial Jane Austen* (London and New York: Routledge, 2000). The essays in this volume connect ideologies of gender and of the 'domestic' to an exploration of Austen's novels in the wider culture of imperialism.

Wood, Marcus, *Blind Memory: Visual Representations of Slavery in England and America, 1780–1865* (Manchester: Manchester University Press, 2000). A fascinating study of the visual archive generated by the Atlantic slave trade. Wood analyses the two engravings discussed in this chapter but does not appear to notice the dialogue between them (see *Blind Memory*, pp. 160–2).

NOTES

1. Srinivas Aravamudan, *Tropicopolitans: Colonialism and Agency, 1688–1804* (Durham, NC, and London: Duke University Press, 1999), p. 10. Linda Colley's book is *Britons: Forging the Nation, 1707–1832* (New Haven: Yale University Press, 1992).
2. Alan Richardson and Sonia Hofkosh (eds.), *Romanticism, Race, and Imperial Culture, 1780–1834* (Bloomington, Ind.: Indiana University Press, 1996), p. 4.
3. Aravamudan, *Tropicopolitans*, p. 16.
4. See Leela Gandhi's excellent *Postcolonial Theory: A Critical Introduction* (London: Allen and Unwin, 1998), p. 4.
5. Ibid. 29.
6. See Graham Huggan, *The Postcolonial Exotic: Marketing the Margins* (London: Routledge, 2001).
7. S. T. Coleridge, 'Lecture on the Slave-Trade', in *Lectures 1795: On Politics and Religion*, ed. Lewis Patton and Peter Mann (London: Routledge and Kegan Paul; Princeton University Press, 1971), p. 248.
8. S. T. Coleridge, *The Watchman* (1796), ed. Lewis Patton (London: Routledge and Kegan Paul, 1970), p. 136.
9. Coleridge, 'Lecture on the Slave-Trade', p. 226.
10. Charles de Secondat, Baron de Montesquieu, 'Of the Slavery of the Negroes', *The Spirit of Laws*, 5th edn., 2 vols. (Edinburgh, 1793), i., 263.
11. Edward Said, *Culture and Imperialism* (New York: Alfred Knopf, 1993), p. 66.
12. Edward Said, *Orientalism* (London: Routledge and Kegan Paul, 1978), p. 3.
13. See Alan Richardson, 'Introduction', *Three Oriental Tales* (Boston and New York: Houghton Mifflin Company, New Riverside Editions, 2002), p. 7.
14. David Punter, 'Arundhati Roy and the House of History', in Andrew Smith and William Hughes (eds.), *Empire and the Gothic: The Politics of Genre* (Basingstoke: Palgrave, 2003).

15. The definitive modern edition is Vincent Carretta's *Olaudah Equiano: The Interesting Narrative and other Writings* (Harmondsworth: Penguin, 1995). This edition has explanatory and textual notes, plus six appendices, one of which contains a fascinating collection of hitherto unpublished letters by Equiano. All page references are to this edition.

16. Homi Bhabha, *The Location of Culture* (London: Routledge, 1994), p. 25.

17. Sonia Hofkosh, 'Tradition and *The Interesting Narrative*: Capitalism, Abolition, and the Romantic Individual', in Richardson and Hofkosh (eds.), *Romanticism, Race, and Imperial Culture, 1780–1834*, p. 335.

18. See Alan Richardson's incisive 'Colonialism, Race, and Lyric Irony in Blake's "The Little Black Boy"', *Papers on Language and Literature*, 26: 2 (Spring 1990), 233–48.

18 | Formalism

Richard Cronin

Formalism is more often a tendency in literary criticism than a theory. It is character-ized by a refusal to explain a work of literature by reference to the historical circum-stances, whether biographical, political, economic, or social, out of which it was produced. Rather, the literary work is to be understood as it is 'in itself', which may mean that it is to be understood as a unique object, or, more often, that it is to be understood only in its relation to other literary works. Formalist critics deny that works of literature are either referential or practical; that is, literature does not repre-sent the world, and it does not act upon the world, by, for example, prompting the reader to give to the poor or foment a political revolution. In fact, formalists are happiest when they can represent the literary work as investigating its own status as literature, which is why the easiest way to identify formalist critics is by their predi-lection for reflexive constructions. In this, the title of a recent distinguished work of formalist criticism is exemplary, Michael O'Neill's *Romanticism and the Self-Conscious Poem*. Given this, it is strange that formalism was developed from a stance into a theory in the years 1915–30 by a number of Russian critics who thought of themselves as revolutionaries.

For the Russian Formalists the critical task was to define the 'literariness' of a literary work; that is, to offer an objective description of all the devices employed in a literary work that distinguish its language from ordinary language. The primary effect achieved by such devices is estrangement or defamiliarization, or, in Russian, *ostranenie*. The world is rendered strange so that it is seen as if for the first time. There is no purpose to this. It is an experience to be valued in and for itself. From the mid-1920s the Russian Formalists came under attack in the Soviet Union from more orthodox Marxist critics who valued literature in so far as it offered an accurate reflection of the world and incited its reader to engage in the class struggle. Formalist criticism was represented as bourgeois and escapist, and by 1930 its practitioners had either fallen silent or emigrated from the Soviet Union.

This narrative is of interest because the attack on the Russian Formalists was gently echoed in Romantic studies in the 1980s when charges rather similar to those brought against the Formalists were brought against traditional accounts of Romanticism in the name of a new historicism. In his *The Romantic Ideology* (1983), for example, Jerome McGann argued that students of Romanticism had been complicit with the ideology that informs the work of the Romantic poets, who had themselves espoused the formalist notion that literature might transcend the historical circumstance out of which it was produced. This was curious, because influential critics of the 1940s and 1950s had deprecated much Romantic poetry precisely because of its failure to be formalist enough. Shelley, for example, was often cited as a poet too frequently distracted from the poet's proper task by the appeal of uncontrolled emotionalism—'I fall upon the thorns of life! I bleed!' ('Ode to the West Wind')—or by the temptation to favour the reader with his personal views, such as his opposition to tyranny, disapproval of marriage, and hatred of Christianity.

Were the Romantics formalists?

Lyrical Ballads, for many the founding text of British Romanticism, was, as Coleridge describes it, a project with which the Russian Formalists themselves might have sympathized. The Formalists held that the unique function of literature was to defamiliarize the forms through which we habitually perceive the world. Similarly, Wordsworth's task in *Lyrical Ballads*, Coleridge tells us, was to awaken 'the mind's attention from the lethargy of custom' and disclose to his readers a world which 'in consequence of the film of familiarity and selfish solicitude we have eyes, yet see not, ears that hear not, and hearts that neither feel not understand'.[1] In 'The Defence of Poetry', Shelley seems entirely in accord. Poetry 'makes familiar objects be as if they were not familiar', it 'purges from our inward sight the film of familiarity which obscures from us the wonder of our being', it 'strips the veil of familiarity from the world'. The Russian Formalists focused their attention on the means by which the effect of defamiliarization was achieved, for example the manner in which literary texts disrupt ordinary linguistic usage. Similarly, for Shelley, the principal means by which poets accomplish their end is by the coining of new and hence unfamiliar metaphors. Literary language 'is vitally metaphorical; that is it marks the before unapprehended relations of things, and perpetuates their apprehension', but it is inevitable that such metaphors should in the course of time lose their power to defamiliarize, and as they do so, Shelley argues, again anticipating the Russian Formalists, they lose their literary value, becoming 'signs for portions and classes of thoughts, instead of pictures of integral thoughts; and then, if no new poets should arise to create afresh the associations which have been thus disorganized, language will be dead to all the nobler purposes of human intercourse'.[2] Wordsworth—and here too the Russians were to follow him—went further, intimating in his 'Advertisement' to *Lyrical Ballads* that it was necessary to render not just the language of poetry, but poetry itself unfamiliar. Readers encountering his poems for the first time will 'frequently have to struggle with feelings of strangeness and awkwardness, and will be induced to enquire by what species of courtesy these attempts' may be denominated poems.[3]

So, the Romantics may sometimes seem like precursors of the Formalists, but they are just as likely to assume postures more easily understood as anticipating their opponents. When, for example, Wordsworth expresses his contempt for 'Poets, who think that they are conferring honour upon themselves and their art, in proportion as they separate themselves from the sympathies of men, and indulge in arbitrary and capricious habits of expression, in order to furnish food for fickle tastes, and fickle appetites, of their own creation', he repudiates the linguistic features that distinguish literary from non-literary writing and it is precisely those features that the Russian Formalists particularly valued.[4] For Wordsworth, 'some of the most interesting parts of the best poems will be found to be strictly the language of prose', which could scarcely be more different from the Formalists' concentration on all those elements that distinguish poetry from prose. The Romantics seem to repudiate still more emphatically the Formalist notion that a literary work should not be considered in its relation to the historical circumstances out of which it was produced, but instead should be considered solely in terms of the formal properties of the text. In 'The Defence of Poetry', for example, Shelley offers a summary history of literature in which literary history is construed wholly as a function of political history, and he goes on to insist that the title 'poet' properly belongs not just to those who write literary texts but to all 'Authors of revolutions in opinion'. Plato and Bacon are properly thought of as poets, and so, presumably, is Jesus Christ, even though none of his writing has survived.[5] Clearly within perspectives so vast the proposition that poetry might usefully be defined in terms of its formal properties dwindles into insignificance.

It has long been recognized that Romanticism accommodates this contradiction, and a political explanation has been offered. The contradiction is said to betoken a difference between radical and conservative Romanticism, which may be a difference between writers and may equally well be a difference evident in the work of single writers at different stages of their career. For example, in *Biographia Literaria* (1817), Coleridge dismisses the most striking arguments propounded by Wordsworth in his Prefaces to *Lyrical Ballads* (1800 and 1802). Wordsworth's claims that the language of poetry should be identical with the language 'really used by men' and that it should not differ materially from the language of prose are elaborately refuted. Poetry is distinguished from prose by its use not simply of words in the best order but of 'the best words in the best order' and the best words are not, as Wordsworth had it, those really used by men in 'low and rustic' life, but are words known only to educated people with a philosophical cast of mind.[6] Coleridge, it might seem, is introducing a lexical qualification that will serve in literature much the same purpose that property qualifications served in parliamentary elections, the exclusion of the uneducated. He may claim that he had always recognized these Wordsworthian doctrines as 'erroneous in principle', but, critics have suggested, it was an error apparent to the Coleridge who wrote *Biographia Literaria*, a conservative polemicist in his forties, rather than the young man who had contributed to *Lyrical Ballads*. But this may not be a sufficient explanation. It does not explain, for example, how a single text like 'A Defence of Poetry' might strike at different times extravagantly formalist postures and postures that seem just as extravagantly anti-formalist. It might be best to start not with political divisions, but with a division in the meaning attached to the word, 'form'.

The word, as it was bequeathed to the Romantics, was already a deeply divided term, which might refer either to the superficial characteristics of a thing or to the inward principle that makes that thing what it is. Almost everybody in the period used the word in both those senses. When Shelley denies that Dante and Milton are poets simply because they 'employed traditional forms of rhythm', the word refers to an external characteristic of poetry, its metre, as distinct from its essence. But when he tells us that poems are not essentially damaged by their participation in the moral errors that marked the societies within which they were produced, 'form' becomes a synonym rather than an antithesis of spirit: a poem such as the *Iliad* is not limited by the warrior ethic that it appears to endorse, because 'The beauty of the internal nature cannot be so far concealed by its accidental vesture, but that the spirit of its form shall communicate itself to the very disguise; and indicate the shape it hides from the manner in which it is worn.'[7] For the moment, I will only suggest that, for literary theorists such as Coleridge and Shelley, the fact that a single word, form, might bring together two antithetical concepts was extremely useful. It allowed them at once to assert and to deny the importance of the external characteristics of poetry, and to conceal the self-contradiction. The question that needs to be addressed is why they felt the need to adopt contradictory positions.

It is best to begin by pointing out that Shelley—and in this he is like Coleridge—very rarely uses the word, form, in the sense in which it is most commonly used in more recent literary criticism, in antithesis to content. He cannot do so because he distributes the content of a poem between his two senses of the word form. In so far as meaning is historically contingent it is located in the external form of a poem, in so far as meaning is eternal it is located in the form that is its indwelling principle. One sense of form ties the poem to history, the other releases it. Both positions are necessary for writers who wish to believe that literature transcends history and partakes of the nature of eternity, but also that literary and political history are inseparable. The business of the poet, Shelley tells us, is with 'the eternal truths', but he also insists that the health of a nation's poetry is inseparably connected with the health of the nation's politics.[8] Most writers in all periods have been happy to alternate between these positions, but the impulse to do so becomes especially strong within periods, such as the period of Romanticism, marked by extreme ideological conflict, in which the need to escape into a disinterested, ahistorical aesthetic realm and the need to take sides, to choose between fiercely contested political positions, might both be felt with unusual intensity.

When the word referred to an external characteristic of poetry such as metre, attention to form stressed the difference between poetry and other kinds of writing. When it referred to an indwelling principle it erased the difference between a poet and a prose writer, or even between a poet and other 'authors of revolutions in opinion', who might not be writers at all. When Wordsworth denies that the language of poetry should differ from that of prose he leans towards the second possibility. When Coleridge reasserts the difference he leans towards the first. But, in fact, both are divided on the matter, and so were most of their contemporaries. A significant exception is William Hazlitt.

Form and power: the case of the sonnet

According to Hazlitt, poetry is defined formally, by its difference from other kinds of writing. But to maintain this is not to escape from ideology, rather it is to commit oneself to a particular ideology. Poetry evades rational understanding by making its appeal directly to the imagination. Poetry has an 'exaggerating and exclusive' character which always works to elevate the individual over the species. Hazlitt would have agreed with Tom Paine that Burke's *Reflections on the Revolution in France* is written in a poetic style, and this is what enables Burke to present the misfortunes of Marie Antoinette as outweighing the sufferings of millions of ordinary French people. For Hazlitt, 'the language of poetry naturally falls in with the language of power'.[9]

Hazlitt allows an exception to his general rule. Wordsworth's poetry he thought free from the 'exclusive character' that generally characterized poetry. 'His Muse', he wrote, 'is a levelling one',[10] and results in a poetry that undoes rather than underwrites the distinctions between men. But for the most part poetry, because it is defined by its form, is complicit with a polity which accords more importance to the few than to the many. This seems, on the face of it, an unlikely objection, but it anticipates a hostility to formalism that continues to be felt by the historicist critics who emerged in the 1980s. I will rehearse Hazlitt's case by taking, as an example, the revival by the Romantic poets of a particular verse form, the sonnet (see also chapter on 'The sonnet').

The Romantic sonnet revival was initiated by Charlotte Smith, whose *Elegiac Sonnets* followed Gray's sonnet on Richard West in teasing the boundary between the public and the private. In the hands of William Lisle Bowles and the sonnets Coleridge wrote under his influence the sonnet was adapted to a more general poetry of sensibility in which a hazy melancholy melted the boundary between the mind of the poet and the natural world. It was also Coleridge who in his 'Sonnets on Eminent Characters' first retrieved for the form the possibility of a public, political subject-matter that it had not exercised since Milton. But it was Wordsworth who most fully exploited that potential.[11] In the 'Sonnets Dedicated to Liberty' first published in his *Poems in Two Volumes* of 1807, the sonnet emerges as the most complete formal expression of the political ideal that Wordsworth was developing under the pressure of the Napoleonic threat. One sonnet memorializes Toussaint l'Ouverture for his heroic opposition to Napoleon's reimposition of slavery in his island of Haiti. Toussaint may have been imprisoned, but his mind remains free. It may seem tactless to suggest that Wordsworth imitates his plight by enclosing his celebration of Toussaint within the tight confines of a sonnet, but in 'Nuns fret not at their convent's narrow room', Wordsworth insists on that very analogy. He begins by insisting once again that 'the prison, unto which we doom | Ourselves, no prison is', but by the end of the poem he asserts that confinement is the discipline required by those who have 'felt the weight of too much liberty', and he offers his own commitment to the sonnet as the guarantee that it is a discipline that he has himself willingly undergone:

> and hence for me,
> In sundry moods, 'twas pastime to be bound
> Within the sonnet's scanty plot of ground.

Wordsworth offers the sonnet as figuring a truth that is at once ethical and political, that proper freedom, as opposed to improper liberty, has as its condition the voluntary acceptance of restraint.

It is not a maxim that one would suppose had much appeal for Shelley, who would most often have denied the possibility of 'too much liberty'. But this is to ignore those other moods in which Shelley conceded the need for an overmastering authority. Forms, he notes in the 'Defence', in this case 'forms of opinion and action', once 'copied into the imaginations of men' become 'as generals to the bewildered armies of their thoughts'.[12] Forms, that is, impose a necessary discipline on thoughts that would otherwise constitute only a disorganized rabble. In 'Ozymandias' Shelley confronts the paradoxical position that, according to Hazlitt, the poet who attempts to offer support to 'the cause of the people' inevitably finds himself in. Ozymandias, the Greek name for the Pharaoh Ramses II, had decreed as a monument to his own glory a colossal statue on the pedestal of which is written, 'Look on my Works, ye Mighty, and despair!' But the long course of time, which has reduced the statue to 'two vast and trunkless legs of stone' beside which lies a shattered face, have lent the inscription an unintended irony, mocking the ambition of absolute rulers to an eternity of fame. Poetic power here seems, *pace* Hazlitt, emphatically opposed to kingly power, deriding its pretensions. But appearances, the poem tells us, may not be easy to decipher.

> On the sand,
> Half sunk a shattered visage lies, whose frown,
> And wrinkled lip, and sneer of cold command,
> Tell that the sculptor well those passions read
> Which yet survive, stamped on these lifeless things,
> The hand that mocked them, and the heart that fed.

The syntax of that final line is difficult—presumably the hand of the sculptor mocked the passions that, during his life, the pharaoh's heart had nourished—and so is the sense. It is uncertain whether the word 'mocked' suggests that the sculptor dared to deride the ruler he was appointed to celebrate, or whether the word means only imitated, as when in *Laon and Cythna* spirited steeds 'mock' the thunder peal with their 'neighings' (l. 2737). For this reason, it remains unclear whether the satirical cast of the statue was designed by a foolhardy sculptor or whether it is supplied by a disenchanted observer, and the uncertainty is useful, because it calls attention to a similar difficulty in establishing the relationship between the poet and the poem.

The poems ends in lines that track solemnly over a wide and monotonous landscape:

> Round the decay
> Of that colossal Wreck, boundless and bare
> The lone and level sands stretch far away.

'His Muse is a levelling one', says Hazlitt of Wordsworth, and the same might be said rather literally of a poem that ends by contemplating a vast sweep of level sand. But, for Hazlitt, Wordsworth's achievement required him to work against the inherent bias of his medium, for the 'principle of poetry is a very anti-levelling principle',[13] and the same could surely not be said of Shelley's sonnet. Ozymandias' boast is, like his statue, dwarfed by being placed in so long and wide a perspective of time and space, which is to say that the king's vision is dwarfed in comparison with the vision articulated by the poet, to whom all of time and all of space are laid bare.

Shelley's sonnet derides the monument that Ramses II built to his own magnificence, but, as Shelley knew from Shakespeare, a sonnet is itself a monument, and a peculiarly powerful one:

> Not marble, nor the gilded monuments
> Of princes, shall outlive this powerful rhyme.
> (Sonnet 55)

The achievement of the poem, far from being a levelling one, is to constitute itself a monument beside which the colossal statue of Ozymandias seems shrunken.

It seems likely that Shelley's poem had its origin in a sonnet-writing competition of the kind that Leigh Hunt liked to organize amongst his friends. Shelley's poem was published in Hunt's *Examiner* on 11 January 1818, and three weeks later Hunt published a sonnet by Horace Smith on the same topic and under the same title.[14] Such competitions were friendly no doubt, but they inevitably encouraged a spirit of rivalry. It is hard not to think that Horace Smith would have been chastened when he compared Shelley's poem with his own even if we acquit Shelley of sharing Ozymandias' ambition to compel his rivals to 'despair'. The sonnet is, to use Shelley's metaphor, a particularly powerful general, and though such generals may be necessary to marshal the 'bewildered armies' of our thoughts, reliance on them does little to enforce the contrast between a poet and a warlord such as Ozymandias.

Shelley's sonnet is, we may say, divided against itself, which is what makes it representative. The Romantic poets seem oddly divided in their response to verse form. On the one hand, there is an impulse to develop genres for which there is no established precedent such as the lyrical ballad, the Coleridgean conversation poem, or the English eclogue which, according to Southey, bore 'no resemblance to any poems in our language'.[15] On the other, there was an impulse to revive traditional verse forms, and often forms such as terza rima, ottava rima, Spenserian stanzas, the ode, and the sonnet that make severe formal demands of the poets who employ them. It is the division that seems to me characteristic and it is evident enough even in a poem such as Shelley's 'Ozymandias', which rebels against the formal requirements of the sonnet even as it accepts them. I know of no parallel for Shelley's rhyme scheme, *ababacdcedefef*, and the scheme even strains against its own eccentric order by admitting half-rhymes such as 'frown' and 'stone' or 'appear' and 'despair'. It is the strange conjunction of formal propriety and impropriety within the same poem that makes it characteristic, and the anxiously divided attitude evident in the poem towards established verse forms 'mocks', perhaps, a similar fracture in the poem's ideological stance, which seems simultaneously intent on deriding kingly authority and on ascribing to the poet an authority in comparison with which a king's seems puny.

The Coleridgean solution

Questions of poetic form engaged some of the more troubling questions that confronted writers of the period. Are poems products of their historical moment, or do they transcend it? Are poems better described in terms of their external characteristics or of their internal principles? Ought art to be defined in terms of its product or its producer, the poem or the poet? The key elements of Coleridge's aesthetics are clearly designed to resolve these dilemmas. Coleridge's idea of organic form, for example, unifies the matter and the manner of the poem, its letter and its spirit. His notion of the poetic symbol unifies the temporal and the timeless, the real and the ideal, the particular and the universal. The imagination, for Coleridge, is of supreme importance precisely because the imaginative capacity is ushered into being only by the dilemmas that it works to resolve: it

reveals itself in the balance or reconciliation of opposite or discordant qualities: of sameness with difference; of the general, with the universal; the idea, with the image; the individual, with the representative; the sense of novelty and freshness, with old and familiar objects; a more than usual state of emotion, with more than usual order; judgement ever awake and steady self-possession, with enthusiasm and feeling profound or vehement; and while it blends and harmonizes the natural and the artificial, still subordinates art to nature; the manner to the matter; and our admiration of the poet to our sympathy with the poetry.

But the poems that address these same dilemmas arrive at more tentative conclusions.

Samuel Taylor Coleridge, 'Kubla Khan'

Coleridge's 'Kubla Khan' draws attention to issues to do with poetic form in several ways, all of which, surely not by accident, are hinted at in the short prose explanation with which Coleridge prefaces the poem. Coleridge's claim to have composed the poem while asleep raises the question of how far poetry is the product of the conscious will. It raises, too, the question of the relationship between a dream world and the world of waking experience, for the two though separate are not enclosed from one another: when he awakes Coleridge half-remembers his dream, and the dream itself is instigated by the passage in Purchas's *Pilgrimage* that Coleridge was reading as he fell asleep. 'In Xanadu did Cublai Can build a stately palace', Coleridge read, and drifted into a sleep in which he dreamed a poem beginning,

> In Xanadu did Kublai Khan
> A stately pleasure dome decree.

In his sleep he 'could not', he claims, 'have composed less than from two to three hundred lines', but when he awoke and set about transcribing the poem he was interrupted by 'a person on business from Porlock' and found, when he returned to his manuscript, that he was quite unable to remember the rest of the poem 'with the exception of some eight or ten scattered lines and images'. So the poem of fifty four lines is presented to its readers as a fragment.

A large majority of the poem's critics have seen it as their task to assess the truth of Coleridge's claim and determine whether the poem is best considered a fragment, or, as most of them decide, a complete poem. But it seems more important to point out that the poem itself puts in question its own status. The dome and the carefully measured garden that surrounds it are the products of the emperor's decree, ushered into existence by an imperially autonomous act of will of which the dome in its enclosed, finished perfection of shape is the appropriate emblem. But in its second paragraph the poem entertains a quite different emblem of creative power:

> And from this chasm, with ceaseless turmoil breathing,
> As if this earth in fast thick pants were breathing,
> A mighty fountain momently was forced:
> Amid whose swift half-intermitted burst
> Huge fragments vaulted like rebounding hail.
> Or chaffy grain beneath the thresher's flail:
> And 'mid these dancing rocks at once and ever
> It flung up momently the sacred river.
>
> (ll. 17–24)

In this scene creative power is figured by the uncontrollable gush of water that forces its way up through the earth, a power that signals itself not by the creation of enclosed wholes like the dome, but precisely by its production of 'fragments', the huge slabs of rock that it throws into the air as though they were ping-pong balls. The poem asks, then, whether imaginative power is better expressed by the creation of finished, enclosed forms, or by an energy so great that it shatters into fragments any attempt to embody it.

The poem's first paragraph with its dome and its 'twice five miles of fertile ground' enclosed by walls and towers generates in the second paragraph its own antithesis as the cultivated landscape is supplanted by a 'savage place', a landscape that mocks any ambition to recuperate it within an ordered civility. The genius of the first landscape is the Khan, whose creation, like a God's, is by fiat, but the genius of the second, the 'woman wailing for her demon-lover', embodies a quite different energy, the raw energy of unsatisfied desire.

In the third paragraph the poem returns from the 'deep romantic chasm' in which the river has its origin to the dome, but in this paragraph the dome seems very different. Positioned as it is, its shadow falling exactly 'midway on the waves', at the point at which the noise of the fountain in which the river is born and of the caves in which it falls into the sea mingle, the 'sunny pleasure-dome with caves of ice' seems less a building, a pavilion at the centre of a pleasure garden, than an emblem rather elaborately designed to figure an abstract truth, that the imagination 'reveals itself in the balance or reconciliation of opposite or discordant qualities'. So the civilized space of the first paragraph is countered by the 'savage place' of the second, and the opposition between them generates as its synthesis the somewhat willed and abstract dome of the third paragraph.

It is as if the poem has asked whether measure or measurelessness is the proper gauge of the power of the imagination, and hence whether it is better figured by the 'twice five miles of fertile ground' that Kubla enclosed, and the 'Five miles' that the river meanders, or by the twice mentioned 'caverns measureless to man'. The question is raised most forcefully by the poem's metre, the incantatory power of which seems the product at once of regularity and of irregularity. The four-stress line of the first paragraph, lopped to three stresses in a single line, 'Down to a sunless sea', expands into the iambic pentameters of the second paragraph, several of them hypermetric, before, in the short third paragraph, reverting to the four-stress line until the paragraph closes with a pentameter couplet. But there are other puzzles too. Is the mind in creation possessed of an absolute will, ushering its creations into existence by imperial decree, or is it more like the chasm within which a fountain gushes with a force that cannot be withstood? And what is the relationship between the enclosed world of the work of art and the mortal world of lived experience? Is the artwork so suspended between life and death, between the gush of the fountain and the final fall into the sea, that their opposition is converted into harmony, a 'mingled measure', or is art an enclosed space in which one skulks fearfully. Kubla Khan decrees his dome to celebrate the peace that he has achieved by uniting all of China under his rule, but the peace he has secured is the product of conquest, and Coleridge's Khan dimly foresees that it will not survive him. He hears the fall of the waters,

And 'mid this tumult Kubla heard from far
Ancestral voices prophesying war!
(ll. 29–30)

In the third paragraph the dome is celebrated as the site where contraries are held together: it is a 'sunny pleasure-dome with caves of ice', but the dilemmas that the poem has invoked are too massive to be resolved so patly, which is why the third paragraph is only a mock conclusion to the poem.

In the fourth paragraph the poem seems abruptly to change course; from third to first person, from description to narrative:

A damsel with a dulcimer
In a vision once I saw.
(ll. 37–8)

In a poem that, Coleridge tells us, he wrote in a dream, he recounts a meeting that takes place in a vision. It is an encounter with an exotic Muse, whose song, if Coleridge could only revive it, would give him the power to 'build that dome in air, | That sunny dome! those caves of ice!' The dome appears again, but no longer as decreed by an emperor, nor as reflected on the surface of the river, but as imagined by the poet, and, as if to stress that it is the poem imagined that is the greatest miracle, the dome is not only, like Troy and Camelot, built 'with music', but also built in the air. The notion celebrates the autonomy of art, its freedom from all natural law, even the force of gravitation, and yet at the same time it mocks the business of the artist, dismissing it as the creation of idle fancies, castles in the air. The poet who has this power is the divinely inspired bard:

And all should cry, Beware! Beware!
His flashing eyes, his floating hair!
Weave a circle round him thrice,
And close your eyes with holy dread,
For he on honey-dew hath fed,
And drunk the milk of Paradise.
(ll. 49–54)

The poet here is an inhabitant of an enclosed space: like the dome he is 'girdled round', defined by his separation from the ordinary world. But the walls and towers that surround the dome exclude the world, whereas the bard seems excluded by it. Those who weave the circles around him are impelled by a reverence close to terror. The poet, to borrow Virginia Woolf's description of Shelley, is emphatically 'not one of us'.

But this bard with his flashing eyes and floating hair is the poet in the poem, not the poet of the poem. He is the poet that the poet of the poem aspires to be, but his is, he seems well aware, a hopeless aspiration. He has heard the damsel with the dulcimer, and knows,

Could I revive within me
Her symphony and song,
To such delight 'twould win me,

> That with music loud and long
> I would build that dome in air . . .
>
> (ll. 42–6)

The poem ends by directing us back to its preface, and its account of how the poet 'found, to his no small surprise and mortification, that though he still retained some vague and dim recollection of the general purport of the vision, yet, with the exception of some eight or ten scattered lines and images, all the rest had passed away'. The ambition to revive the visionary song seems unlikely to be attended with any better success.

The dilemmas that the question of poetic form prompted in the poets of the Romantic period can almost all of them be traced in 'Kubla Khan'. The questions as to whether art should be willed or spontaneous, active within history or independent of it, enclosed from or continuous with lived experience are all shown to engage with the issue of poetic form. But in the poem, unlike the critical theory, Coleridge does not arrive at any neat resolution of his dilemmas. He is content rather to present himself as the failed poet, as the poet who sees but cannot realize the possibility of an art so formally perfect that it severs connection with the ordinary world as completely as a dome built in air. He offers his failure, like his inability to remember the bulk of the poem that he had dreamed, as a cause of 'mortification', but it is in the end a mortification that he embraces rather than suffers, because it preserves him from the visionary isolation in which the divinely inspired bard is enclosed. Art, this poem tells us, must aspire to formal perfection, and it must fail, but it is a happy failure because it ensures that the work of art does not lose all connection with the imperfect, time-bound, contingent world that poets and their readers share. (For a contrasting reading, see the chapter on 'The fragment'.)

John Keats, 'Ode on a Grecian Urn'

In 'Ode on a Grecian Urn' Keats, too, cannot disengage from the possibility that the aesthetic realm might not be independent of the world of power. To gaze at a Grecian urn, as Keats had been viciously and recently reminded, was to confront a dead civilization familiarity with which was a crucial test for the exercise of cultural power. J. G. Lockhart had mocked Keats who 'knows Homer only from Chapman', and has acquired from Leigh Hunt only 'a sort of vague idea, that the Greeks were a most tasteful people'.[16] The issue of the relationship between culture and power was sharpened by the bitter dispute over Lord Elgin's attempts to sell to the nation the marbles of which he had despoiled the Acropolis, the British apparently agreeing with their great enemy, Napoleon, at least on this, that the number and quality of art works plundered for the nation was a crucial index of military power.[17] But in this poem Keats does not focus directly on the question of the problematic relationship between art and power. He seems more directly concerned with the problematic nature of reading. The poem repeatedly asks questions of the urn—'What leaf-fring'd legend . . .', 'What men or gods . . .', 'Who are these coming . . .', 'What little town . . .'—and such questions force the reader to confront the problem of what questions it is appropriate to ask of a pot or a poem. The solution hinges on the question of whether the reader ought to attend to what separates the urn from, or what connects the urn to, the world around it. In other words the poem puzzles its readers as to whether they should focus on its form or on its content (compare the reading of this poem in the chapter 'Lyric').

The very first of the poem's questions, 'What leaf-fring'd legend haunts about thy shape', establishes the theme as it directs the eye from the decorative border of acanthus, the leaf fringe, to the scenes with which the urn is illustrated, and then back to the form of the urn, its 'shape', only to leave suspended in the mysterious word 'haunts' the relationship between the urn in its two aspects, as something to be looked at, as 'shape', and as 'legend', literally something to be read. When the urn is seen as shape it charms by its remoteness from the observer, by embodying a beauty that is defined by its perfect enclosure from the world that the observer inhabits, but to 'read' the urn is inevitably to endow it with a life that is lent to it by the observer. The first stanza describes the first of the urn's three scenes, a scene of group rape, and the observer's response seems at first distant enough—'What men or gods are these?'—but as question is added to question the questions lose their interrogative character, and become exclamatory:

> What men or gods are these? What maidens loth?
> What mad pursuit? What struggle to escape?
> What pipes and timbrels? What wild ecstasy?

By the end of this sequence the observer seems to feel an excitement that can only derive from his imaginative participation in the rape that he sees depicted.

Two conclusions follow, their relationship one with another seems paradoxical, but it is the paradox that the whole poem explores. First, it seems impossible to attend simultaneously to the form and to the content of the scene. An observer can see the figures on the urn as shapes, not different in kind from the leaf shapes of the decorative border, and as a depiction of rape only in alternate perceptions. Second, the observer (presumably a male) is freed to relish the scene of rape by his knowledge that he is witnessing a representation rather than a reality. The 'excellence of every Art is its intensity, capable of making all disagreeables evaporate, from their being in close relationship with Beauty & Truth', Keats wrote to his brothers, and directed them for examples to *King Lear*, presumably because it is a play that can accommodate scenes of vile cruelty without disgusting the reader. But the remark also has an erotic context: it immediately follows Keats's report of his disappointment with Benjamin West's 'Death on the Pale Horse', which, according to Keats, offers nothing in which its 'unpleasantness' might be buried: 'there is nothing to be intense upon; no women one feels mad to kiss; no face swelling into reality.'[18] The demand that in art content should be subordinated to form and the rival demand that form should be subordinated to content are revealed as at once antithetical and complementary. One can be mad to kiss a painted woman only by ignoring painting's two-dimensionality, only by imagining the face 'swelling into reality', but the ability to enjoy that madness rather than to be ashamed or frustrated by it depends just as surely on a knowledge that the face is not really a face at all, but a painted piece of canvas.

The rape that Keats imagines in the poem is an intensification of the kiss that he imagines in the letter, but it scarcely functions to make 'all disagreeables evaporate'. To find that enjoyment at watching a rape is a product at once of a knowledge that the rape is unreal and the ability to imagine it 'swelling into reality' is disconcerting. It prompts the observer to turn the pot in his hands, cancelling the rape for a scene in which the erotic is represented with a pastoral delicacy. The wild music of pipes and timbrels is muted to the melody of a single piper, and the fierce sexual struggle is replaced by a youth leaning over a maiden, the two lovers forever poised, always about to kiss. The scene reconfigures the relationship between the world of the pot and the world of the observer, so that the former is revealed as the product of the latter's deficiencies. The lovers on the urn are prevented from kissing so that they, unlike us, can live forever in the moment of erotic anticipation, and they are spared too any sad discovery that intensity lessens with repetition: the piper on the urn, because his melodies are silent, may be imagined 'For ever piping songs for ever new'. Happiness is conferred on the figures on the urn by their exemption from what Shelley calls 'chance and death and mutability', and in the fourth stanza their happiness is insistently asserted—the word 'happy' appears six times—as if, by sheer force of repetition, Keats could erase the etymology that binds the idea of happiness so tightly to the contingent, mutable world that the observer, not the figures on the urn, inhabits. The central stanzas of Keats's poem attempt to separate the two worlds, but their success is precarious. They celebrate a love that is 'All breathing human passion far above', because, of course, the lovers on the urn do not breathe, and yet their happiness can be complete only if they are granted that ability, if they can be imagined 'For ever panting' as well as 'for ever young'.

In the first stanza Keats tries to imagine that the world of the observer and the world of the urn are continuous one with another, and in the second and third he tries to imagine that the two worlds are quite separate. But both attempts fail, and in the fourth stanza Keats accepts that failure: he recognizes that to look at an urn, and, by implication, to read a poem, is at once to recognize that art has value and meaning only in relation to life and that art is art precisely by virtue of its not being life. The fourth stanza accepts that paradox with a calm that seems possible because of the change of subject. The first two scenes on the urn address the erotic material that in the summer of 1819 provided Keats with his most intense and most perplexing subject-matter, but the third, which seems closely based on one of the marble fragments appropriated by Lord Elgin,[19] describes an ancient form of worship that Keats could contemplate with calm disinterest, a garlanded heifer is led to sacrifice. But this, the scene depicted on the urn, summons other scenes that are not represented; the 'green altar' to which the procession must be winding, and finally the 'little town' that is 'emptied of this folk, this pious morn'. The thought with which the stanza ends, that the town must remain silent and desolate for ever, is beautifully poised, because the town has been summoned into existence only by an imagination unable to accept that the world represented on the urn is autonomous and enclosed, and invested with pathos only by an imagination that recognizes that on the urn time, as it never can be in life, is frozen.

In the ode's final stanza the urn continues to generate paradox: the urn inhabits its own timeless world which makes it a 'Cold Pastoral!', chillingly indifferent to all the dying generations that it has outlived, and yet it is on this account, too, 'a friend to man', its marble repose consoling him for his own mortality. Although the matter has been much discussed, it seems clear that the urn should be understood as speaking the whole of the poem's last two lines and not simply the aphorism about truth and beauty:

> 'Beauty is truth, truth beauty',—that is all
> Ye know on earth, and all ye need to know.

The urn, the perfect solipsist, can imagine nothing other than the coincidence of beauty and truth that it embodies. It is a notion to which all of living experience gives the lie, and yet a notion that cannot be rejected, and it is the peculiar function of art, the poem suggests, to express such notions. So the poem ends with the urn exposed as a work of art, its men and maidens carved from marble, its timelessness dissevered from the time-bound world in which we live. All encounters with works of art, whether urns or poems, end similarly, with the urn revealed as an urn, the poem as a poem. But, as we read it, the poem invites its reader to live through such an encounter, and to recognize that it is marked by an oscillation, a repeated shift of focus, in which the 'men and maidens' on the urn are imagined as flesh and blood creatures and then recognized as figures carved from marble, and that it is this oscillation that defines all referential arts such as sculpture and poetry.

'Ode on a Grecian Urn' offers itself as a lesson on how to read poetry, and in particular a lesson in how to read poems like 'Kubla Khan', 'Ozymandias', and 'Ode on a Grecian Urn', that is, Romantic poems. To approach such poems simply as a formalist, the poems themselves suggest, is quite inadequate, but it is also, those same poems suggest, indispensable. From one point of view, given the current critical climate, it is the second of these injunctions that needs stressing. But, from the other point of view, the same perception, that Romantic poems alternately demand and refuse a formalist reading, itself demands explanation in terms of the historical moment within which the poems were produced.

FURTHER READING

Armstrong, Isobel, *The Radical Aesthetic* (Oxford: Blackwell, 2000). The most powerful recent defence of formalist criticism; Armstrong argues that the category of the aesthetic must be reinstated if art is to perform its proper function of playfully positing alternative realities.

Bennet, Tony, *Formalism and Marxism* (London: Methuen, 1979). A lucid account of the Russian Formalists and their opponents, and an ingenious argument that formalist and historicist criticism are not incompatible.

Curran, Stuart, *Poetic Form and British Romanticism* (New York and Oxford: Oxford University Press, 1986). A lively and scholarly account of the importance of poetic genres in the Romantic period.

Eagleton, Terry, *The Ideology of the Aesthetic* (Oxford: Blackwell, 1990). Traces the idea of the aesthetic to the Romantic period, and proposes that from the first it was an idea that served malign ideological purposes.

McGann, Jerome, *The Romantic Ideology* (Chicago and London: University of Chicago Press, 1983). Convicts the Romantics of an ahistorical formalism which it is the modern critical task to unmask.

O'Neill, Michael, *Romanticism and the Self-Conscious Poem* (Oxford: Clarendon Press, 1997). Impressive, formalist readings of a selection of major Romantic poems.

Vendler, Helen, *The Odes of John Keats* (Cambridge, Mass.: Harvard University Press, 1983). A reading of Keats's odes that robustly refuses all historicist attempts to locate in the poems tensions that have to do with politics or class.

Wolfson, Susan, *Formal Charges: The Shaping of Poetry in British Romanticism* (Stanford, Calif.: Stanford University Press, 1997). Argues that it is possible to redirect attention to the formal characteristics of Romantic poems while avoiding formalism.

NOTES

1. *Samuel Taylor Coleridge*, ed. H. J. Jackson (Oxford: Oxford University Press, 1985), p. 314.
2. Percy Bysshe Shelley, *The Major Works*, ed. Zachary Leader and Michael O'Neill (Oxford: Oxford University Press, 2003), p. 676.
3. *Wordsworth's Literary Criticism*, ed. W. J. B. Owen (London and Boston: Routledge, 1974), p. 65.
4. Ibid. 71.
5. Shelley, *The Major Works*, p. 679.
6. *Biographia Literaria*, chs. 17 and 18.
7. Shelley, *The Major Works*, pp. 677, 679, 681.
8. Ibid. 690, 700.
9. *The Selected Writings of William Hazlitt*, ed. Duncan Wu, 9 vols. (London: Pickering and Chatto, 1998), i. 125–6.
10. Ibid. vii. 161.
11. On the Romantic sonnet and its development, see Stuart Curran, *Poetic Form and British Romanticism* (New York and Oxford: Oxford University Press, 1986), pp. 29–55.
12. Shelley, *The Major Works*, p. 688.
13. *The Selected Writings of William Hazlitt*, i. 126.
14. Smith's sonnet is reprinted in Percy Bysshe Shelley, *Poems and Prose*, ed. Timothy Webb (London: J. M. Dent, 1995), p. 463.
15. Southey's preface to *Poems* (1799).
16. G. M. Matthews (ed.), *Keats: The Critical Heritage* (London: Routledge and Kegan Paul, 1971), p. 103.
17. On the debate see William St Clair, *Lord Elgin and the Marbles* (London: Oxford University Press, 1967).
18. *The Letters of John Keats*, ed. Hyder Edward Rollins, 2 vols. (Cambridge: Cambridge University Press, 1958), i. 192.
19. See Ian Jack, *Keats and the Mirror of Art* (Oxford: Clarendon Press, 1967), p. 219.

Part III

Romantic forms

19 | Romantic forms: an introduction

Michael O'Neill

Romantic poetry reveals a creative concern with form, taking that word to mean both a poem's genre (or kind) and all that is involved in its design as a verbal artefact. 'Creative' is a key word here. In Romantic writing, traditional forms undergo transformation. Part of a movement that is often 'tameless, and swift, and proud', to adapt a phrase from Shelley's 'Ode to the West Wind' (1820; such parenthetical dates refer to the year of first publication, unless stated otherwise), Romantic poets are rarely content merely to imitate a pre-existent model. At the same time, as Shelley's poem reveals, the wild or transgressive energies of Romanticism frequently house themselves within literary forms of some sophistication.

This sophistication extends to the minute particulars of formal invention. In its use of metre, rhythm, rhyme, and verse form, Romantic poetry challenges the reader and shows much technical cunning. So, Leigh Hunt in *The Story of Rimini* (1816) and Keats, after him, in *Endymion* (1818) flaunt their liberal loosening of the closed couplet of Augustan poetry: a formal freedom that, arguably, corresponds to a political hope. Shelley brings to a head the perplexing, fluid interplay between mind and world central to 'Mont Blanc' (1817) by rhyming 'things' and 'imaginings' in the closing lines. Wordsworth persuades the line-endings of his blank verse to mimic the endless-ness of mental activity as he describes his brain working with 'a dim and undetermined sense | Of unknown modes of being' in *The Prelude* (quoted from the 1805 version). And in *Lara* (1814) Byron marshals secretive psychological processes within disciplined couplets. He recalls Pope and Dryden in his phrasing's antithetical precision, but he departs from them in his refusal to supply a stable moral vantage point,

Romantic poets were accomplished in their use and reworking of form. They were at ease, for instance, with the ode (Wordsworth's 'Ode: Intimations of Immortality', 1807), the sonnet (Shelley's 'England in 1819', composed in 1819), the ballad (Keats's 'La Belle Dame sans Merci', composed in 1819), the epistle (Hunt's 'To Thomas Moore', 1816), the romance (Keats's *The Eve of St Agnes*, 1820), and the epic (Blake's *Jerusalem*, title-page dated 1804). The period abounds, too, in hybrid genres, the demands of one entwining with or redefining the imperatives of the other: Wordsworth's and Coleridge's *Lyrical Ballads* (1798) or Shelley's *Prometheus Unbound: A Lyrical Drama* (1820) are examples. Different poets use the same form differently. Shelley uses the ballad form in *The Masque of Anarchy* (composed in 1819) to voice satirical anger and visionary hope; Coleridge explores a series of personal and metaphysical obsessions in his ballad, 'The Rime of the Ancyent Marinere' (1798).

Romantic poets frequently build into their use of a form awareness of the associations evoked by that form: associations which they go on to modify. So, in *Songs of Innocence and of Experience* (1794), Blake adapts a sing-song hymn form associated with religiously improving verses for children, and makes it a vehicle for psychological diagnosis and social critique. His lyric art is one of exposure. The speakers in his poems assert, and often betray, their vision of life through rhythmic, metaphorical, and tonal emphases. When the speaker of 'The Chimney Sweeper' in *Songs of Innocence* concludes with the admonition, 'So if all do their duty they need not fear harm', there is a suggestion that he is passing on oppressive advice to which he has been subjected. Again, Shelley's 'Hymn to Intellectual Beauty' (1817) calls up and departs from the religious orthodoxy associated with the hymn as a form. Shelley addresses the humanist notion of intellectual beauty the way that a Christian believer would petition his God.

Romantic epic (and a note on Romantic fragments)

English Romantic literature shows a resurgence of interest in epic poetry (see chapter on 'Epic'). Shelley defines 'epic' in his *A Defence of Poetry* (written in 1821) as a poetry which bears 'a defined and intelligible relation to the knowledge, and sentiment, and religion, and political condition of the age in which [the poet] lived, and of the ages which followed it'. Often the relation between Romantic epic and 'the age' is oppositional. In his *Jerusalem*, William Blake sets the poetic principle, embodied in Los, against the materialism and warmongering of contemporary England, personified by Albion. By the poem's close, after much creative toil on Los's part, toil which includes subduing his Spectre (that side of Los which fears and denies), Albion is united with Jerusalem, his Emanation, or female counterpart. The poem concludes with a majestic vision of the humanizing of all things, 'All human forms identified, even tree, metal, earth and stone' (see also discussion of *Jerusalem* in chapter entitled 'Ecology').

The form of *Jerusalem* is unique to Blake in three ways. First, it is organized into four chapters and one hundred plates or sections, as though Blake were willing his materials into some final order. Second, as with much of his poetry, words coexist with illustrations; there is a constant effect of interplay and interaction between words and pictures. Third, Blake uses a strikingly unusual verse line, one that recalls the prose of the King James Bible and anticipates the long lines employed by the nineteenth-century American poet, Walt Whitman. He breaks not only with rhyme, but also with the use of what he calls 'a monotonous cadence' (by which he appears to mean the iambic pentameter, the staple line of Milton's *Paradise Lost* and Shakespeare's plays). In his preface to the poem's first chapter, he asserts: 'I . . . have produced a variety in every line, both of cadences and number of syllables'. *Jerusalem* shares many preoccupations with traditional epic, but it gives them individual treatment. If Virgil sings of arms and the man in the *Aeneid*, Blake makes his hero not a warrior but an artist; the warfare approved by the poem involves 'mental fight', not military bloodshed. Traditional epic involves at some stage a descent into the underworld, the world of the past with which the hero must come to terms before he can fulfil his destiny. Blake finds the here and now of early nineteenth-century London to be such an underworld; at the same time he is always on the look-out for moments of affirmative vision.

Blake's emphasis on vision illustrates the inwardness that marks Romantic epic, and is apparent in Wordsworth's *The Prelude*, with its emphasis on consciousness. This is not to see Romantic epic as ignoring or evading the claims of history. *Jerusalem* is recognizably the product of an artist made indignant by, yet seeking adequately to respond to, the pressures of living through a time when the nations of Europe were involved in a long military struggle following the French Revolution and the coming to power of Napoleon. *The Prelude* recalls the young Wordsworth's rapturous response to the onset of the French Revolution and his subsequent if tangled disenchantment with the course taken by the revolution. But, for all the force of these accounts, it is Wordsworth's subjective response to history which takes centre stage (see below under 'Readings' for a fuller account).

Romantic epic also incorporates the digressive antics of Byron's capacious *Don Juan* (1819–24), simultaneously epic in its sweep and anti- or mock-epic in its debunking of pretensions. Byron's tones are pervasively duplicitous, allowing him to eat his cake and have it, too: his poem is both epic and mock-epic. His pleasure in throwing the epic rule-book out of the window is evident. 'Most epic poets plunge *in medias res* [in the middle of things]', he tells us in Book 1, before he goes on with poker-faced solemnity to assert, 'That is the usual method, but not mine; | My way is to begin with the beginning.' And yet the poem has an ambitiousness of scope that makes it more than merely mock-epic. Full of self-description, it is, as the opening of canto 7 phrases it, 'A versified Aurora Borealis, | Which flashes o'er a waste and icy clime': a brilliant and mobile poetic display that illuminates a difficult historical period. 'I want a hero', the poem begins, but Byron's true epic hero is less the young man who gives his name to the poem than the narrative consciousness of the work. Digressive, open to the multi-fariousness of experience, contemptuous of bourgeois hypocrisy, and alert to the ebb and flow of recent history, this consciousness is to the fore throughout, and finds a perfect medium in the *ottava rima* stanza which Byron uses (a stanza rhyming *abababcc*, and full of comic possibilities).

John Keats also entertained epic ambitions in his fragment, *Hyperion* (1820), as is acknowledged in the back-handed compliment which Byron pays the poet and poem in *Don Juan*, Canto XI, stanza 60. There, after a snobbish reminder that Keats was 'without Greek', Byron says that Keats 'Contrived to talk about the Gods of late, | Much as they might have been supposed to speak.' Whereas Byron's seriousness in *Don Juan* is inseparable from irony, Keats's seriousness in *Hyperion* is more straightforward. In the poem Keats contrives to talk in a style that is at once Miltonic and his own. Keats finally abandoned the *Hyperion* project, the second instalment of which was *The Fall of Hyperion* (composed in 1819), because he felt it was flawed by the overpowering presence of Milton, a presence which was silencing, so Keats felt, what he called in a letter of September 1819 'the true voice of feeling'. Certainly Milton's *Paradise Lost* influences the language and plot of Keats's *Hyperion*. Keats admired *Paradise Lost*, impressed by Milton's evocative compression and grandeur. The opening portrait of the fallen 'grey-haired Saturn' reaps the fruits of Keats's study of Milton. Saturn dominates a landscape that is in sympathy with his utter dejection. The poetry's life derives from its capacity to conjure up an atmosphere of lifelessness. In the second book of the fragment, the debate between the fallen Titans recalls the debate between the fallen angels in the second book of *Paradise Lost*.

Hyperion is far from being a study in a worn-out poetical form, however. Keats departs from Milton in intriguing ways. His story does not involve a cosmic clash between good and evil; rather, it centres on the fact of evolution, of progressive movement from one order of things to another that is more developed, from the rule of the Titans to that of the Olympians. In Book II Oceanus, the fallen god of the seas, counsels his fellow Titans to accept defeat on the grounds that ' 'tis the eternal law | That first in beauty should be first in might'. This counsel seems to be the poem's 'message'. But the poem will not be restricted to a single viewpoint. It counts the cost of pain, defeat, and overthrow, encouraging the reader to sympathize with the overthrown Titans. Moreover, it emphasizes the pain of being 'The first in beauty'. Apollo's development into an all-knowing god is the subject of the truncated third book, and what Keats stresses is the suffering endured when, under the watchful eye of Mnemosyne, symbol of cultural memory and muse-figure, the young deity experiences the onset of 'Knowledge enormous'. The process is akin to the development involved in being a poet, the subject of many of Keats's poems. When he reworked *Hyperion* in *The Fall of Hyperion*, he took as his epic model Dante rather than Milton, placed his own subjective concerns with poetry at the forefront of the poem, and wrote one of the most compelling accounts of poetic anxiety in the language. Epic matter in this reworked version centres on the question, 'Am I a poet?' and involves Keats in arduous self-questioning, as he imagines a visionary encounter between a poet-dreamer and the goddess Moneta.

Both versions of *Hyperion* are fragmentary, and the Romantic fragment is a sufficiently new phenomenon to deserve a separate if brief notice in this survey (see also the chapter on 'The fragment'). Sometimes intended (Coleridge's 'Kubla Khan', 1816), sometimes the result of accident (*The Triumph of Life* (1822), left unfinished as a result of Shelley's untimely death, or *Don Juan*, similarly unfinished as a result of Byron's death in Greece), the fragment emerges as a central form in the period, given legitimacy by dawning theories of the Romantic as bound up with the indefinable. Traditionally, epic strives for completeness. The fragment confesses and at times celebrates incompleteness, which can be seen as a sign of infinite possibility. *Hyperion* and *Don*

Juan refuse epic completion: Keats abandons the former, leaving it unfinished like the torso of some ruined statue; in the case of Byron's epic, the accident of his death conspired to confirm the resistance to finality that is everywhere evident in his poem. As 'Kubla Khan' and *The Triumph of Life* show, the fragment can take different generic forms: lyric in Coleridge's poem, dream-vision in Shelley's poem. But it has, when associated with epic, a vivid capacity to suggest either an affecting failure to achieve poetic wholeness or, more positively, a recognition of what Wordsworth calls 'something evermore about to be'.

Drama

Drama is a form central to the Romantic imagination. It is no accident that the Romantic period is a great age of Shakespearean criticism. Though acting styles could be bombastic, especially when actors had to speak into vast theatres, the period also saw the emergence of charismatic actors and actresses: Edmund Kean, for example, whose acting was compared by Coleridge to reading Shakespeare by flashes of lightning; or Eliza O'Neill, whom Shelley had in mind in writing the part of the heroine of *The Cenci* (1819). William Hazlitt, Charles Lamb, and Coleridge all write with energy and insight about the experience of responding to Shakespeare's plays. Even though Lamb felt that no production could equal the imaginative experience of reading Shakespeare, he was an avid and acute critic of contemporary drama. All the major Romantic poets tried their hand at drama, often writing for the stage, but sometimes writing plays that were meant primarily to be read (see also chapter on 'Romantic drama').

Such mental theatre, the forerunner of Victorian fascination with the dramatic monologue, is to be found in Byron's *Manfred* (1817) and Shelley's *Prometheus Unbound*. Byron's work is subtitled 'A Dramatic Poem', Shelley's 'A Lyrical Drama': subtitles that show a characteristic Romantic interest in mixed or hybrid genres. *Manfred*, modelled on various treatments of the Faust legend, including Goethe's as translated orally to Byron by his friend M. G. ('Monk') Lewis in 1816, deals with remorse, guilt, and the courage required to surmount these emotions, and asserts the mind's power. Byron's mixture of incantatory lyrics and melodious blank verse wins from his hero's predicament a seductive, melancholy beauty. *Prometheus Unbound* locates its principal dramatic action in Prometheus' coming to terms with the impulse to exact revenge. His turning away during his first speech from hatred for the tyrannical Jupiter is the key moment in the play, a play fascinated by what in the preface Shelley refers to as 'operations of the human mind'. These 'operations' affect vitally, in Shelley's view, the world which human beings inhabit, and the poem is an extended celebration, using many different poetic forms (including epic struggle, pastoral, lyric, and masque), of the need 'to hope, till Hope creates | From its own wreck the thing it contemplates'.

Romantic drama tends to focus on the psychological, on inner experience, often of guilt and experience. So, Joanna Baillie published 1798–1812 her three-volume *Series of Plays; In Which It Is Attempted to Delineate the Stronger Passions of the Mind*. It is clear that the major poets saw drama as a means of registering the repercussions of revolutionary ideas and events in the world of the mind and of feelings. 'Action', remarks Rivers in the third act of Wordsworth's *The Borderers* (composed in 1797; published in revised form, including changed names for the two main characters, in 1842), 'is transitory', but 'suffering' is 'permanent, obscure and dark, | And shares the nature of infinity'. The play focuses on the mind, but it calls into question Rivers's exaltation of experience unmoored from morality. In *The Borderers* Wordsworth replays the scenario of temptation in *Othello*. However, whereas Iago tempts Othello into sexual jealousy, Rivers lures Mortimer into helping to kill an old man almost purely as a demonstration of intellectual power. The play speaks of Wordsworth's fascinated revulsion from the rationalism he associates with an extremist, revolutionary cast of mind, a rationalism memorably defined by Rivers's lines in Act 3 praising 'the only law that sense | Submits to recognise, the immediate law, | From the clear light of circumstances, flashed | Upon an independent Intellect'. By the close of Act 5 and the play, the folly of this confidence in 'Intellect' is exposed, as Mortimer condemns himself for his complicity in evil, and sentences himself to be (in the revised version of 1842) 'A Man by pain and thought compelled to live, | Yet loathing life'.

Shakespeare is both an influence on, and a lion in the path of, Romantic drama. Shelley's *The Cenci* alludes to Shakespearean and Jacobean drama, but usually in order to point up difference. Awaiting execution for arranging the death of her father (in revenge for his incestuous rape of her), Beatrice echoes a speech in *Measure for Measure* where Claudio expresses terror of death, yet her terror is not of the unknown, but of the all too well known, the fear that the afterlife might consist of one permanent paternal rape. The play explores the question how to respond to tyrannical oppression, a theme with strong political implications for an age seeking to learn lessons from the French Revolution and its apparent descent into bloody revenge. Shelley also suggests that Beatrice does not, so to speak, belong to the world of her play. She belongs with other unhoused consciousnesses in Romantic literature. The play strikes a balance between revealing that Beatrice has assumed the moral outlook of Renaissance Italian Catholicism and indicating, through imagery of veils and masks, that her true being awaits a different culture and value-system; much emphasis, accordingly, is placed on the inadequacy of speech, a topic brought into the play by her refusal to speak of her rape, but widening in implication. *The Cenci* is shaped formally to bring not only tragic but also utopian discourse to mind; a world in which Beatrice might not experience oppression has yet to be invented.

Byron, too, in plays such as *Marino Faliero* (1821) explores political dilemmas and contradictions that involve a clash between the individual and a dominant political culture. Marino Faliero, Doge of Venice, engages in a conspiracy against the state of which he is the head, after slander against his wife has resulted in a punishment for the slanderer that he regards as too lenient. Byron's own political ambivalence about the militant tendencies of middle- and working-class reform movements (apparent in the Cato Street conspiracy of 1820, when a plot to assassinate the Cabinet was thwarted) is at work in scenes involving the Doge and other conspirators. So, in response to the use of 'we' by one of the conspirators (Israel Bertuccio), the Doge replies, '*We—We!*—no matter—you have earn'd the right, | To talk of *us*' (3.1.65, 66–7). The play's themes and situations are often Shakespearean (with its scenes of conspiracy and concern with honour, *Julius Caesar* is unsurprisingly echoed on a number of occasions). But its verse—austere, relying on run-ons from line to line that create a sense of actual speech—shows Byron's wish to escape the Shakespearean shadow and strive for a drama of reflection, harangue, and debate.

Lyric

Lyric poetry, where that term means shorter poems which devote heightened if often unostentatious poetic music to expressing the feelings of a real or imagined speaker, is among the major formal achievements of Romantic poetry (see also the chapter on 'Lyric'). Romantic poets use much art to convey the sense of 'the spontaneous overflow of powerful feelings' of which Wordsworth speaks in his Preface to *Lyrical Ballads*. Wordsworth himself innovates continually in his shorter poems. In his 'Lucy' poems, he blends balladic impersonality with seemingly confessional intimacy, the bareness of limpid song with heart-piercing directness, as is typified by the close of one poem: 'But she is in her grave, and oh! | The difference to me!' Grief, if that is what the speaker's unfathomable emotion amounts to here, is incommunicable, and yet the sense of loss communicates with great power. Elegy, in which grief for the dead is expressed and consolation sought, becomes a form of extended lyric in the Spenserian stanzas of Shelley's *Adonais* (1821), which concludes with a depiction of poetic inspiration. The Spenserian stanza rhymes *ababbcdcd*, and tends towards a slow-moving richness which is accentuated by the closing alexandrine (twelve-syllable line); it suits a poem that, in a letter of June 1821, Shelley calls a 'highly wrought *piece of art*'. Formal artifice helps him to express his deepest feelings about the value of poetry. Elegy serves in Letitia Landon's briefer 'Felicia Hemans' (1838) as a way of disclosing veiled personal anxieties about the predicament of being a female poet. In a moment of heightened self-awareness, in which the 'song'-like quality of the writing is pointed up, Landon asserts: 'We say, the song is sorrowful, but know not | What may have left that sorrow on the song.' Later, Thomas Lovell Beddoes intersperses the scenes of his unfinished play, *Death's Jest-Book* (first version finished in 1829) with shorter poems such as 'The swallow leaves her nest', where, as in lyrics by his master Shelley, images and rhythms coalesce to create mood-pieces about loss and recovery that can be read—partly because of their very unspecificity—politically as well as personally.

The variousness of lyric forms in the Romantic period is remarkable. Coleridge's conversational poems consist of subjective meditations in blank verse, shaped with artistic skill and apparent naturalness into a poetic vision that accommodates shifts of mood and accidents of experience. 'Frost at Midnight' (1798) starts with a state of stillness and a mood of 'Abstruser musings' as the poet looks at his baby sleeping beside him. It moves through a series of carefully managed transitions into Coleridge's own childhood and an imagining of his child's growing up under the eye of nature, before it comes full circle, rounding out the poem's imaginative experience with an image of icicles 'Quietly shining to the quiet Moon': an image that embodies a natural harmony with which the poet wishes to bring his own life and that of his child into relationship.

No form benefited more from Romantic fascination with reworkings of the traditional than the sonnet. Charlotte Smith's *Elegiac Sonnets* (first edition 1784) reminded poets of the form's suitability as a vehicle for the control and release of feeling (compare the discussions of Smith in 'Sensibility' and 'Feminism'). The first sonnet reflects self-consciously on the hurt that lies behind art through an allusion in its last line to Pope's *Eloisa and Abelard*. Smith writes: 'how dear the muse's favours cost | If those paint sorrow best who feel it most!' Wordsworth and Keats are just two of the canonical poets of the period who experiment with the sonnet. Wordsworth uses the form for public purposes in 'Milton! thou shouldst be living at this hour' (1807), a poem that shifts in its last six lines (the sestet) from criticism of contemporary England as 'a fen | Of stagnant waters' to celebration of Milton's power and humility. He also employs the form for personal ends in 'Surprised by joy' (1815), a moving poem addressed to his dead daughter that draws on the sonnet's ability to capture a 'surprised' moment of feeling. Keats complains of the form's limitations in the innovatively interlacing rhymes of his sonnet 'If by dull rhymes our English must be chain'd' (composed in 1819), and remodels it as the basis for the ten-line stanzaic form adopted in most of his odes (a fuller account of one of these poems, 'Ode to a Nightingale' (1819), is provided under 'Readings').

Keats's odes are only the most marked example of how the form of the ode is given new life by the major Romantic poets. The eighteenth century witnessed a revival of interest in the ode, whether Pindaric, used for wilder flights, or Horatian, the vehicle of calmer meditation. Poets such as Thomas Gray recognize the capacity of the ode to convey turns and counter-turns of feeling. The set-piece, declamatory nature of the eighteenth-century ode is still apparent in the highly wrought stanzas of Shelley's 'Ode to Liberty' (1820), itself a republican alternative to Coleridge's 'France: An Ode' (1798), in which Coleridge expresses his rejection of allegiance to revolutionary France. Both odes dramatize their poets' subjective responses to major public themes.

Often formal boundaries blur. Wordsworth blends ode and blank-verse meditation in 'Lines Written a Few Miles above Tintern Abbey' (1798). The poem reflects on change and continuity: change pointed up by Wordsworth's admission that he 'cannot paint | What then I was'; continuity forged by memory and projection into the future as the poet imagines his 'dear, dear Sister' as a second self. The poem balances between 'loss' and 'Abundant recompence'; it moves between hope and anxiety, and includes within the meditative flow created by the gravely haunting blank verse the inner debate associated with the ode (compare the reading of 'Tintern Abbey' in the chapter entitled 'New Historicism'). In a note to the 1800 edition of the *Lyrical Ballads* Wordsworth wrote of the poem: 'I have not ventured to call this Poem an Ode; but it is written with a hope that in the transitions, and in the impassioned music of the versification would be found the principal requisites of that species of versification.' Such 'transitions' and 'impassioned music' are evident, too, in Wordsworth's 'Ode: Intimations of Immortality', as in the change from lament to residual hope at the start of stanza 9: 'O joy! that in our embers | Is something that doth live'.

Shelley's 'Ode to the West Wind' illustrates how Romantic writers negotiate with past forms, but make them new. Few changes of mood in the English lyric have the affective power of the speaker's descent into desolate confession in the fourth section ('I fall upon the thorns of life! I bleed!') and subsequent recovery and assertion of poetic authority in the fifth section. Shelley reshapes a rhyming scheme rarely used in English poetry, *terza rima*, a mode of rhyme found in Dante's *Divine Comedy*. In each tercet (three-line stanza) the first and third line rhyme; the second does not, but rhymes with the first and third lines of the next tercet. Shelley adapts this form into a series of five sonnets, closing all the poem's sections with a couplet. The resulting form suits the poet's concern with rebirth and regeneration, constantly reaching out through its rhymes towards new poetic life. In section 5, Shelley asks the wind to 'Drive my dead thoughts over the universe', but he goes on to assert the importance of 'the incantation of this verse', the significance, that is, of the poem he is composing. The rhyme between 'universe' and 'verse' is expressive. It implies a close relationship between poetry and the world in which we live, and shows how details of poetic form tell us a great deal about the larger ambitions of Romantic poetry.

Poetic narrative, including romance

Much Romantic poetry delights in story, even as it complicates our understanding of what story is. The forms of narrative poetry are many, and include the reworking of pastoral which Wordsworth offers in *Michael* (1800). The poem focuses on an old but vigorous shepherd, his fears for the loss of his land, his love of his son, Luke, and his heartbreak when Luke goes to the bad. The throat-catching, understated climax in which Michael is described returning day after day, after Luke's desertion, to a scene of former labour and never lifting up a single stone illustrates poignantly how for Wordsworth 'the feeling . . . gives importance to the action and situation, and not the action and situation to the feeling', as he puts it in the Preface to *Lyrical Ballads*. Wordsworth is probably the most original narrative poet of the period, because of a trust in 'feeling' that makes for daringly internalized poetry. Operating at a less demanding level, tales by Walter Scott (such as *Marmion; A Tale of Flodden Field*, 1808) and Robert Southey (*Thalaba the Destroyer*, 1801, see also chapter on 'Epic') express and shape a vogue for narrative that treats the past or the culturally other (the exotic or oriental), a vogue expressive of the desire to explore the present by reference to alternative perspectives. Byron's eastern tales cash in on, and take in new directions, the taste for such stories. His tales express a glamorous, troubled mood of aristocratic and individualist discontent. There is, in *The Giaour* (1813), a complex effect of suspense and fragmentation created by the narrative mode, which often involves lyric meditation on events that are obscurely veiled but always dark.

Romance, a form involving strange, supernatural, or marvellous experience, compels the Romantic imagination. Coleridge's unfinished *Christabel* (1816) is oblique in manner, its narrator's voice puzzling over events that are not fully understood. The poem feels like episodes from, and in search of, a larger, enigmatic plot. Is Geraldine, the mysterious lady who exerts power over Geraldine, an embodiment of evil? Or is she herself possessed by a force beyond her control? The questions multiply as the narrative travels into a mist of unknowability. The two Conclusions that follow each of the poem's two parts virtually mock the idea of narrative closure; they do not bring anything to a finish so much as offer digressive bafflement. The effect is to undo the morally straightforward as well as to blur narrative clarity.

Particularly in *The Eve of St Agnes, Isabella*, and *Lamia* (all 1820), Keats offers narrative variations on his obsessive theme of dream and imagining. In various ways and with shifts of emphasis, the poems move between the real and the imaginary, the ironic and the enchanted, disappointment and desire. Keats's verse forms suit his different approaches to this complex of concerns: the busy, changeable *ottava rima* of *Isabella* adapted to frequent narratorial interventions gives way to the slow-moving, sumptuously descriptive Spenserian stanzas of *The Eve of St Agnes*; in turn, the often sardonic, Drydenesque couplets of *Lamia* handle their form with a knowingness and force wholly different from Keats's earlier practice in *Endymion*. Byron had already put Spenserian stanzas to unusual use in the four cantos of his romance (or 'Romaunt') *Childe Harold's Pilgrimage* (1812–18), imbuing the stanza with a restless agitation at odds with its tendency towards a musically calming union of sound and sense. The poem is, among other things, an account of Byron's travels to Turkey, Greece, and Italy; it broods on contemporary history, and on the process of self-fashioning which occurs in poetry. Always it is conscious of the way that 'we endow | With form our fancy' and create a life in art that fends off the fear of nothingness, mortality, and incoherence. It is, in this respect, a mere step away from the comic works of Byron's maturity such as *Beppo* (1818), a miracle of playful art that contrives to be in its own way 'doubly serious', partly through its self-awareness about its own formal procedures (see 'Readings' for a fuller account).

Gender and genre in Romantic poetry

One of the major developments in criticism of Romantic poetry in recent years has been the rediscovery of the work of Romantic women poets, such as Mary Tighe, Charlotte Smith, Felicia Hemans, and Letitia Landon (see chapter on 'Feminism'). There have been attempts to argue that women poets treat poetic forms with a gendered awareness, that they subvert the values associated with the way these forms are handled by male Romantic poets. Certainly there are thematic differences: on many occasions, Romantic women poets lay more emphasis on female experience than is found in works by Romantic male poets. Hemans's *Records of Woman* (1828) is only a step away from the Victorian dramatic monologue in some of its poems, such as 'Properzia Rossi', a poem spoken by 'a celebrated female sculptor of Bologna', who 'died', according to Hemans's authorial headnote, 'in consequence of an unrequited attachment'.

Yet it is evident from Hemans's work that she sees herself, not as working in a separate female tradition, but in a poetic culture full of diverse voices. Her lyrics pay tribute and artfully allude to Wordsworth and Byron. At the same time, they establish, as do the lyrics of Landon, a space of their own, through a fusion of formal skill and the suggestion of stoical, often withheld melancholy. The result is less one of female separation from male Romanticism than a reworking of its larger affirmations and a further contribution to its impassioned questionings, as when Hemans ends 'The Graves of a Household' (1828) with an exclamation that holds within it a far-reaching metaphysical question, or when Landon conveys through the terse stanzas of her self-reflexively entitled 'Lines of Life' (1828) her own, trauma-ridden version of the concern with, or indifference to, fame found in poets such as Byron and Shelley.

William Wordsworth, *The Prelude*

It is characteristic of the paradoxes that beset Romanticism that a poem which seems at the movement's very heart was not published until 1850, the year of the poet's death. Wordsworth himself appeared to feel that he ought to write a more philosophical poem, the never-completed *Recluse*. But his failure to write this poem connects intimately with his success in writing *The Prelude*. In its 1805 and 1850 versions, the poem begins with a nod towards the end of *Paradise Lost*, only to underline the fact that, for the Romantic poet, the exploration of the self is matter equal in epic significance to Milton's attempt to 'justify the ways of God to men'. At the end of *Paradise Lost* Milton describes the departure of Adam and Eve from Eden in this way: 'The world was all before them, where to choose | Their place of rest, and Providence their guide.' History, about to begin, offers Adam and Eve (and their descendants) an array of possibilities. The shape taken by the future will depend in large part on human choice, even as it will also rely on the guidance of 'Providence'. Wordsworth starts his epic of consciousness by exclaiming, 'The earth is all before me!' Here he echoes Milton's 'The world is all before them', concerned, like the seventeenth-century poet, with the possible, the yet to be called into being. However, Wordsworth relies, not on Providence, but on inspiration: 'should the guide I choose | Be nothing better than a wandering cloud, | I cannot miss my way.' He cannot miss his way because of his trust in his imaginative powers, a trust that assures him he will be guided to his goal by 'nothing better than a wandering cloud'. That goal differs from Milton's. Wordsworth's epic will not attempt to justify the ways of God to men; instead, it will reveal the godlike power of the human imagination.

The epic's master-theme is the growth of a poet's mind; fundamental to that growth is the poet's belief in his imagination. The poem's form shares common ground with traditional epic. As in Blake's *Jerusalem*, contemporary London serves as a vision of the underworld, 'a hell | For eyes and ears!' There is an Odyssean quality, too, in the emphasis on the poet's literal and metaphorical wanderings and homecoming. But at the poem's heart is a radically new self-consciousness. The poem's theme is the poet's discovery that he is a true poet; the evidence for that discovery is the poem we are reading—and, indeed, the poem Wordsworth is himself writing. Few poems give so strong a sense of the difficulty of finding an appropriate theme as *The Prelude* does in its opening book. Here a feeling of wasted talent and frustrated creativity shadows the initial state of delighted creative freedom. The poem gives the impression of stumbling, despite itself, on its real subject: the sources of the poet's creative power in remembered experience.

Memory and imagination are the poem's major characters. Nature plays a strongly supporting role, while history, given a walk-on part, threatens to steal the scene in the account of the poet's engagement with the French Revolution. In one sense, the poem sees this engagement as well-nigh traumatic, a dangerous distraction; it is only when the poet returns to nature and realizes the value of the human love offered by his sister, Dorothy, that he recovers his 'true self' and is guided 'through the weary labyrinth' to 'open day'. In another sense, the power of the poet's imagination informs his accounts of the feelings induced in him by the revolution, as when he returns to Paris a short time after the September massacres of 1792, when many prisoners were slaughtered, and 'seemed to hear a voice that cried | To the whole City, "Sleep no more" '. Shakespearean tragedy sweeps through Romantic epic in that allusion to Macbeth and his terrifying sense of being condemned to eternal insomnia because of his murder of Duncan. Wordsworth's echo hints at his sense of guilt by proxy (because of his revolutionary sympathies) over the bloodbath of the September massacres.

The epic simile, beloved by Homer, Virgil, and Milton, becomes in Wordsworth's hands a means of describing his poem's river-like course when in Book IX he compares his 'motions retrograde' to 'a River . . . | Yielding in part to old remembrances'. Wordsworth's blank verse is a capacious instrument, capable of such river-like yieldings. It also mimes on many occasions the process of walking that permits the encounters between mind and other at the poem's centre. *The Prelude* is a conversational poem (addressed to Coleridge) as well as an epic of consciousness. Wordsworth delights in juxtaposing the ordinary with the sublime, taking risks whose warrant is the fineness of the resulting poetry. In Book VI, seeking to cross the Alps, he describes a conversation with a peasant which elicits the fact that he has already crossed the mountain range. The response is not deflated disappointment, but an elated address to the Imagination and its capacity to drive us onward with its permanent sense of 'possible sublimity' (to quote a phrase from an earlier part of the poem). A major carrier of significance in the poem are the 'spots of time', which Wordsworth delineates in strikingly original ways. Such spots involve earlier experiences that are frequently fearful, even terrifying, though they are remembered by the mature poet with gratitude as proof of his capacity to imagine and, therefore, to be a poet. Wordsworth deploys two main formal devices to bring these spots to our attention. The first, and most original, is his use of concrete images and rhythms that re-create the original experience in all its fascinating and often incomprehensible strangeness. Thus, in the eleventh book (1805) he records an experience of 'visionary dreariness' that invests elemental (and repeated) images—a beacon on a hill, a girl with a pitcher on her head, and a naked pool—with uncanny power. The second is the addition of commentary after the event. The fact that such commentary, for all its intelligence and insight, at times fails to exhaust the meaning of the original experience, and that this mismatch is allowed for in the poem's form, gives one reason for the greatness of the poem: even as Wordsworth seeks to explain the self's development, he preserves a sense of its mystery.

John Keats, 'Ode to a Nightingale'

In 'Ode to a Nightingale', as in his other odes, Keats imitates the associative flow of consciousness, as one emotion and feeling lead into another. Transition is all in this ode, and the key that unlocks its workings is the question 'how did we get to this point after starting from that one?' The verse form, a quatrain using pentameters followed by a sestet with varying lengths of line, captures switches of direction with great sureness. These switches of direction are one reason why the poem cannot be labelled as 'merely escapist' (compare the account of this poem in the chapter on 'Ecology'). Often the poem appears to wish to leave behind 'The weariness, the fever and the fret' of life in this world, yet the wish is complicated by two forces, each of which is caught in the poetry's formal web. One is that the desire to escape consciousness paradoxically triggers a heightening of consciousness. So, the second stanza calls for 'a draught of vintage' that would allow the poet refuge through drunken intoxication from the cares of living. But the poetry delays, caught by the sensuous beauty of the 'Dance, and Provencal song, and sunburnt mirth' linked with the wine. The other is that Keats's imagination is fundamentally dialectical: he cannot conceive of one state without summoning up its opposite.

The poem begins with the words 'My heart aches', with, that is, the poet's 'heart', traditional seat of emotional experience, and with a marked stress shift; the second foot is reversed so that instead of the expected fourth syllable taking the emphasis of the voice the word that takes this emphasis is 'aches'. The effect is, apparently, one of suffering. And yet, in keeping with the swerves of feeling that pervade the poem, this apparent suffering passes into the altogether stranger 'drowsy numbness' which 'pains | My sense'; near opposites come together in the wording, there. A few lines later, the poet protests that his 'drowsy numbness' does not proceed from 'envy' of the bird's happiness, but from a state of over-intense fellow feeling, of being 'too happy in thine happiness'. The relations established between poet and bird here are developed and complicated in what follows.

Lyric thrives on a significant other: a 'thou' to be addressed with longing or desire, and conceived of as 'signifying', or making meaning, in a way denied to the word- and form-bound poem. Towards the end of the first stanza of Keats's poem, a pun flickers in the description of the bird dwelling among 'shadows numberless', 'numbers' being the old-fashioned word for a poet's words put into metre. It is as though the bird's song comes from a dimension beyond poetic speech. 'Ode to a Nightingale' is about longing and desire for a state it cannot know, the bird's pure, unreflective flow of sound. And yet if there is a chasm between the bird's song and the poet's self-divided poetry (self-divided because he is unable not 'to think', and 'to think', as the third stanza tells us, 'is to be full of sorrow'), there are also brief moments of connection. Keats is self-aware about his role of poet in the poem, expressing his desire, in the fourth stanza, to join the bird 'on the viewless wings of Poesy', and wooing 'easeful Death', in the sixth stanza, 'in many a mused rhyme', where 'mused' suggests both the poet's musings and the presence in them of the muse's inspiration. In both cases, there is a momentary if illusory sense of closeness to the bird's song. In stanza 4, the poet exclaims, 'Already with thee!' In stanza 6, the lyric flow of the poem imitates the way that 'thou [the nightingale] art pouring forth thy soul abroad | In such an ecstasy!' There, an original meaning of 'ecstasy', namely, leaving the self behind, emerges, and there is a fugitive mingling of lyric voice and nightingale soul.

In stanza 7 Keats views the bird's song in a changed light, allowing it, a symbol with many facets, to stand for art when removed from its origins in the artist's experience. Unsurprisingly, the attempted farewell to the nightingale in the final stanza is very much a provisional 'Adieu! adieu!' Keats is unabashed about his use of the nightingale as a symbol, and it is instructive to contrast his practice with that of John Clare in 'The Nightingales Nest' (1832). For Clare, the nightingale is fascinating in and for itself. In his poem, he wishes, above all, not to 'plunder music of its dower', to 'be hush' as he draws close to the bird's 'secret' habitat. As a result, his formal choices move away from the dramatic transitions permitted by Keats's use of the ode form; Clare prefers loose-knit, irregularly rhymed, and low-key pentameters.

As has been indicated, Keats exploits to the limit the transitional possibilities of the ode in 'Ode to the Nightingale'. The failure in stanza 4 to be united with the nightingale and its condition of carefree joy leaves the poet in his bower in stanza 5, unable to 'see what flowers are at my feet'. But from this state of apparent deprivation Keats wins an imaginative vision of natural process as he thinks of 'Fast fading violets' and 'The coming musk-rose'. The effect is close to acceptance of transience, but the poem finds itself, one turn in the poetic road later, rehearsing the desire for death, before it pulls back from that desire, with a palpable shudder. In a similar way, the 'faery lands forlorn', which conclude stanza 7, seem the essence of delightful enchantment, but at the start of stanza 8, the last stanza, the 'forlorn' or desolate nature of such enchantment impresses itself on the speaker. Keats repeats a word he has just used, hearing another, darker meaning in its syllables. In so doing, he holds up a formal mirror to associationism (the explanation of ideas as coming into being through apparently chance connections). At the same time, he implies a trust in the directions taken by his 'shaping spirit of Imagination', to borrow a phrase from Coleridge's 'Dejection: An Ode'. As the final stanza unfurls, Keats turns on 'fancy' as a 'deceiving elf', a phrase whose rhyme-induced nature (Keats needs a rhyme for 'sole self') itself supports the mood of disillusion with imagination and poetry. Not that this is the poem's last word, though, and Keats will conclude, as Shelley ends his 'Ode to the West Wind', with a question that makes us reconsider the poetic experience we have just undergone: 'Do I wake or sleep?'

Lord Byron, *Beppo*

Byron's *Beppo*, much more than a dry run for *Don Juan*, illustrates how the Romantics rework genres in an individual fashion. Byron excels at turning the expectations of a form inside out. If *Don Juan* is at once epic and mock-epic, *Beppo* is both story and anti-story. It contains a story: the departure of the merchant Beppo from his wife Laura, his prolonged absence during which she takes a Count as 'a vice-husband, *chiefly to protect her*', and his return to Venice. There is, too, a running counterpoint between the moral rigidities and shortcomings of Regency England and the civilized freedoms of a Venice at a time when 'That sea-born city was in all her glory'. So, Beppo, Laura, and the Count come to an unconventional, amicable arrangement; of Beppo we are told in the last stanza that 'Though Laura sometimes put him in a rage | I've heard the Count and he were always friends'.

And yet Byron does not so much tell a story as play with the conventions of narrative. Indeed, the true plot of *Beppo* is Byron's relish of the sheer variety to be found in Venetian manners (and, by implication, in life itself), and of the capacity of language to convey this variety. In the first twenty stanzas, Byron's flexible *ottava rima* accommodates, by turns, an account of the Venetian Carnival, the evocation of paintings by Giorgione, and a description of a gondola, doing so in ways that draw attention to the poet's linguistic brilliance and worldly knowledge. Setting himself to describe a gondola 'exactly', he finds 'exact', amusing rhymes for the adverb: he depicts the boat as 'built lightly, but compactly' and as gliding 'along the water, looking blackly'. Byron is able to sustain our interest in reality, and to underscore his and our awareness of his poetic activity.

This underscoring communicates through impudently daring rhymes (as when, during her parting from Beppo, Laura 'on her sad knee' is compared to an 'Adriatic Ariadne'), and through Byron's self-dramatization as 'A broken Dandy lately on my travels', nonchalantly spinning out rhymes and digressing from the story as he chooses. Yet this self-awareness never grows complacent or merely indulgent. Rather, it is inseparable from Byron's appetite for the particulars of human experience that crowd in at the edge of his narrative. In one way, Byron points up the fact all narrative is arbitrary; in another way, he takes exuberant pleasure in the fact that narrative is a means of entrance into fuller recognitions. The poem's concluding lines are quintessentially Romantic as well as Byronic. If they mock the conventions of 'story', suggesting that the poem only ends because the poet's 'pen is at the bottom of a page', they affirm the ability of poetic form to indicate modes of escape from limitation. It is Byron's rhythms and rhymes, after all, that make us realize how 'stories somehow lengthen when begun'.

FURTHER READING

Cronin, Richard, *In Search of the Pure Commonwealth: The Politics of Romantic Poetry* (London: Macmillan, 2000). Pioneering work that attempts to fuse formal and historical considerations.

Curran, Stuart, *Poetic Form and British Romanticism* (New York: Oxford University Press, 1986). Curran discusses the treatment of different forms in the period with great learning and insight—this is a book that students of form in the Romantic period must read.

Hartman, Geoffrey H., *Wordsworth's Poetry 1787–1814* (New Haven: Yale University Press, 1964). Still among the very finest accounts of the connection between poetic structure and feeling in Wordsworth.

Keach, William, 'Cockney Couplets: Keats and the Politics of Style', *Studies in Romanticism*, 25 (1986), 182–96. Influentially argues for a connection between style and politics.

McGann, Jerome, *Fiery Dust: Byron's Poetic Development* (Chicago: University of Chicago Press, 1968). Remains an indispensable critical guide.

—— *The Poetics of Sensibility: A Revolution in Literary Style* (Oxford: Clarendon Press, 1996). Argues that much Romantic poetry must be read in relation to Sensibility; provides many brilliant, suggestive insights into the implications of style, and contains ground-breaking pages on poets such as Hemans and Landon.

Mellor, Anne, *Romanticism and Gender* (New York: Routledge, 1992). Links the two nouns in its title with clarity and flair; full of implications for a gender-inflected reading of poetic form in the period.

O'Neill, Michael, *Romanticism and the Self-Conscious Poem* (Oxford: Clarendon Press, 1997). Contains detailed readings of many poems from the period; focuses on the poetry's formal self-awareness.

Stabler, Jane, *Burke to Byron, Barbauld to Baillie: 1790–1830* (Basingstoke: Palgrave, 2001). Excellent survey of the use of the major literary genres made by male and female writers of the period.

—— *Byron, Poetics and History* (Cambridge: Cambridge University Press, 2002). Examines Byron's uses of poetic form in relation to contextual and historical issues.

Vendler, Helen, *The Odes of John Keats* (Cambridge, Mass.: Harvard University Press, 1983). An attentive and elegantly written study of the structures and workings of Keats's poems.

Wolfson, Susan J., *Formal Charges: The Shaping of Poetry in British Romanticism* (Stanford, Calif.: Stanford University Press, 1997). Highly recommended for the sophistication of its theoretical discussions and the sensitivity of its close readings.

Wolfson, Susan J. (ed.), *The Cambridge Companion to Keats* (Cambridge: Cambridge University Press, 2001). Contains stimulating essays on the poetry, including a good piece by Paul D. Sheats on 'Keats and the Ode', pp. 86–101.

Wordsworth, Jonathan, *William Wordsworth: The Borders of Vision* (Oxford: Clarendon Press, 1982). Attuned to the movement and feeling of Wordsworth's poetry, including *The Prelude*.

20 | The sonnet

David Fairer

Why did Romantic poets find the confined space of the sonnet so congenial? The extraordinary popularity of the form during the 1776–1832 period seems something of a paradox—like the sonnet itself. In an age that breathed the spirit of liberty, explored the visionary sublime, and cultivated the incompleteness of the fragment, its poets (with two notable exceptions: Blake and Byron) enthusiastically embraced the fourteen-line sonnet with its emphasis on discipline, tightness, and wholeness. Wordsworth, who wrote more than five hundred of them, suggests in his 'Prefatory Sonnet' (discussed in the 'Reading' section below) that working within its 'narrow room' could actually bring a sense of creative release. His phrase, 'the weight of too much liberty' (l. 13), catches the irony at the heart of the form: that its constraints of length and rhyme scheme might free poets from wider distractions and allow them to focus their energies. The sonnet's compression could release the essence of a thought, feeling, or situation; and the formal variations possible within its structure gave opportunities for shaping an idea in new ways. Indeed, many Romantic sonneteers eagerly tested themselves against the formal demands, conscious that the great European poets of the past (Dante, Petrarch, Ronsard, Spenser, Tasso, Shakespeare, and Milton) had all excelled in the sonnet.

It would be wrong to think of 'Romantic' poetry as shedding earlier formal constraints. 'The mind of Man naturally hates every thing that looks like a Restraint upon it', wrote the critic Joseph Addison in 1712, 'a spacious Horizon is an Image of Liberty', and his words remind us that it was the eighteenth century that discovered the sublime, celebrated original genius, theorized about the imagination, and chafed at critical 'rules'. In fact, the revival of the sonnet during the 1770s and 1780s occurred at a time when there was a new curiosity about the verse forms used by English writers of previous centuries. A rapidly increasing knowledge of the pre-1660 tradition brought a desire to extend poetry's structural and expressive possibilities. By the second half of the eighteenth century the sonnet, which had been defunct for a hundred years, attracted a new generation of admirers who were familiar with its history and appreciated the range of choices it offered. It is useful, therefore, to begin with a brief sketch of the earlier sonnet tradition because it underlies much of the work that the Romantic poets did with the form.

The sonnet form and its development

The sonnet was a pan-European phenomenon. The earliest known sonnets were composed in the 1230s by Giacomo da Lentino, a poet at the Sicilian court of the Emperor Frederick II, who from the beginning established the Italian model of a fourteen-line poem written in pentameters (lines of five stresses) and consisting of two unequal parts of eight and six lines respectively: the *octave* and the *sestet*. In the next century through Dante and especially Petrarch (who wrote 317 sonnets about his love for the beautiful Laura) this form spread across Europe. Thanks also to them it became associated with idealized and often frustrated love. The earliest English examples are by Sir Thomas Wyatt and the Earl of Surrey, courtiers of Henry VIII, both of whom translated Petrarch originals. What is still known as the Petrarchan or Italian form, uses the octave–sestet model. The sestet brings a fresh set of rhymes, and the 'turn' from one section to the next is an important structural feature. It means that the sonnet can move dramatically from statement to counter-statement, or more organically from a situation to its implications, or from a simple idea to its complex or ironic reassessment. The possibilities are many. The opening move may be extended, qualified, complicated, blocked, or even withdrawn. As the Romantics saw, this could be used to bring a dramatic element to a lyric mode. The Petrarchan form has a basic pattern of five different rhymes: *abba abba/cde cde*, with the sestet capable of being varied, perhaps alternating two rhymes (*cdcdcd*), or creating a more interlinked structure such as *cdeced*. Petrarch used all three versions. Given these shapes it is clear that the octave tends to fall naturally into two *quatrains* (four-line units), and the sestet into two *tercets* (three-line units). This offers further structural possibilities to the poet.

By the mid-sixteenth century in England, however, another sonnet type appeared, partly owing to the difficulty of finding four rhyming words for the Petrarchan octave. The English or Shakespearean sonnet, named after its most celebrated practitioner, uses seven rhymes rather than four or five, and features three quatrains of alternate rhymes followed by a concluding couplet: *abab cdcd efef gg*. This opens up fresh structural possibilities, while closing down others; in particular it has a tendency towards a final dramatic turn, depending on how emphatic the couplet is. One sonnet that delivers an appeal to 'Devouring Time' closes defiantly: 'Yet do thy worst, old Time, despite thy wrong, | My love shall in my verse ever live young' (Shakespeare, Sonnet 19). The English form can build up through three equal stages until it finds a kind of resolution at the end. The Petrarchan sonnet lends itself to a more inconclusive structure.

In the hands of the Elizabethan poets of the 1590s variations on the English sonnet were the norm, and in long 'sonnet sequences' they worshipped an idealized mistress or wooed an unwilling one. But this craze was over by 1609 when Shakespeare's *Sonnets* were finally published (most of them had been written during the 1590s). The sonnet nevertheless remained a poem that lent itself to speaking from the 'heart', compressing a plea or meditation into a shape presentable not only to a mistress but also to God. In the hands of John Donne and George Herbert the religious sonnet achieved strong effects, whether in Donne's dramatic appeals ('Batter my heart, three-person'd God') or in Herbert's distilling of 'The spirit and good extract of my heart' ('The Sinner'). In a spiritual context the final couplet of the English type could work well by leaving a powerful image imprinted on the reader's mind.

A further dimension was added by John Milton (1608–74), who, although he wrote only twenty-three sonnets (five in lush Italian), had a remarkable influence on the development of the form, especially during the Romantic period. Influenced by sixteenth-century Italian models he avoided a complacent smoothness by introducing an ungraceful, sinewy word order that overran line divisions and broke across the old formal structures of octave, sestet, quatrain, tercet. This introduced new resonances, and the sonnet began to sound different. The Romantics therefore inherited not only the sonnet of soul-searching ('With this key | Shakespeare unlock'd his heart', said Wordsworth) but also the sonnet of public declaration (Wordsworth's contemporary Walter Savage Landor wrote that Milton 'caught the Sonnet from the dainty hand | Of love, who cried to lose it; and he gave | The notes to Glory'. In Milton's hands the sonnet became a means of arguing or wrestling with political ideas. Like Tasso before him, he tackled heroic and controversial subjects ('On the Late Massacre in Piedmont') and his addressees included General Fairfax and Oliver Cromwell. With the Restoration of Charles II in 1660, however, the Elizabethan lover, the struggling soul, and the republican controversialist were all out of favour. The sonnet virtually disappeared as a literary form for a hundred years. What is known as the 'sonnet revival' in the later eighteenth century was exactly that—a historically informed reanimation of the earlier forms. Poets of the Romantic period who returned to the sonnet were aware of the range of opportunities and choices that faced them.

The sonnet revival

The years 1775–7 were crucial for the development of the Romantic sonnet. They saw the publication of the two most influential sonnets of the century, and also a volume of Petrarch in English. In Thomas Gray's 'Sonnet on the Death of Richard West' (first printed in 1775 but written in 1742) the joyous springtime renewal of life is set against the poet's lonely grief. The natural cycle is ironically reflected in the Petrarchan structure, which begins and ends with the words 'in vain', suggesting his very different, endlessly repeatable round of pain. There is no decisive final couplet, just a return to the beginning: 'I fruitless mourn to him, that cannot hear, | And weep the more, because I weep in vain.' Extra irony comes from the fact that Gray's West sonnet is modelled on Petrarch's sonnet 'Zephiro torna' (*Rime* 310), where the West wind (Zephyr) brings warmth and love to the earth ('Zephyr returns and leads back the fine weather and the flowers and the grass . . . the waters and the earth are full of love'), until the sonnet's turn into the sestet ('But to me, alas, come back heavier sighs . . .'). It was this combination of natural description and lyric emotion that encouraged Romantic sonneteers to return to Petrarch, and this taste is evident in John Nott's collection, *Sonnets, and Odes Translated from the Italian of Petrarch* (1777), where his versions of what he considered the thirty 'most beautiful' *sonetti* are printed alongside their Italian originals (he included 'Zephiro torna'). The volume's significance is noted in his preface: 'The English reader cannot have any idea of Petrarch, no material portion of his poetry having yet been attempted in English verse.' Nott evidently reflected the taste of the time, since out of the four sonnets translated by Charlotte Smith, three are in his selection. He thoroughly revised his translations and added a further fifty for an edition in 1808, for the next generation.

The historical recovery of the sonnet took a different path in Thomas Warton's *Poems* (1777), which included an influential group of nine sonnets. Samuel Johnson, the literary dictator of the day, mocked the volume for its

> Phrase that Time has flung away,
> Uncouth words in disarray:
> Trickt in antique ruff and bonnet,
> Ode and Elegy and Sonnet.

Johnson thought that the sonnet should be left alone as a historical curiosity; but Warton (who disliked what he called 'the capricious and over-strained invention of the Italian poets') deliberately set out to accommodate the sonnet to an earlier British manner, in the way that he considered Lord Surrey had done by 'setting it into a track of tenderness, simplicity, and nature'.[1] Warton therefore uses the sonnet to explore various acts of historical recovery, whether through old books ('Written in a blank leaf of Dugdale's Monasticon') or ancient artefacts ('Written at Stonehenge', 'On King Arthur's Round Table at Winchester'), or through the record of personal memory, which functions as another receding text that he wants to make readable in the present. This is the subject of his last sonnet, 'To the River Lodon', which revisits the river of his childhood:

> Ah! what a weary race my feet have run,
> Since first I trod thy banks with alders crown'd,
> And thought my way was all through fairy ground.

Warton structures the sonnet in temporal terms by staging an emotional 'turn' back to the river at the opening of the sestet: 'Sweet native stream! those skies and suns so pure | No more return, to chear my evening road!' But at this point there is a second 'turn' to what becomes in effect a concluding quatrain:

> Yet still one joy remains, that not obscure,
> Nor useless, all my vacant days have flow'd,
> From youth's gay dawn to manhood's prime mature;
> Nor with the Muse's laurel unbestow'd.

After this, many Romantic sonneteers revisited a favourite riverbank to weigh their past and present selves, trace loss and gain, and locate an organic continuity in their lives—and in Wordsworth's 'Tintern Abbey' we have Warton's structure extended well beyond the bounds of the sonnet.

The sonnet, sensibility, and the self

The sonnet-writers of the 1780s and 1790s followed the lead of Gray and Warton by developing the form's potential for linking natural landscape to subjective experience. One of the most influential figures in this was Charlotte Smith, whose volume of *Elegiac Sonnets* (1784) continued to be expanded and reprinted, reaching an eighth edition by 1797. In the preface she cautiously offered the public her 'little Poems which are here called Sonnets', each being the 'vehicle for a single Sentiment'. They grew, she said, out of specific situations: 'Some very melancholy moments have been beguiled, by expressing in verse the sensations those moments brought.' These confessional words hint at the hope underlying many an early Romantic sonnet: that its localized 'moment' of exquisite feeling will be shared by a sympathetic reader. This assumed intimacy is a characteristic of eighteenth-century Sensibility (see *Oxford Companion to the Romantic Age*, pp. 102–14). Smith directs her sonnets at those sensitive enough to empathize with the 'I' of the sonnet and project themselves into the scene: 'I can hope for readers', the preface concludes, 'only among the few, who to sensibility of heart, join simplicity of taste.' For Smith and many other sonneteers of the 1780s and 1790s it is the reader's sensibility that completes the poem.

Given its compressed structuring of a lyrical impulse, the sonnet seemed to Smith and others the perfect *vehicle* for crystallizing a fleeting experience. Many of her sonnet titles locate themselves in time and place: 'Written on the Sea Shore—October, 1784', 'To Melancholy. Written on the Banks of the Arun, October, 1785', or 'Composed during a walk on the Downs, in November 1787'. This gives them a mixture of spontaneity and thoughtfulness. The sonnet form exploits the immediacy of a 'fragment' while redeeming it from fragmentariness. In 'Written on the Sea Shore', for example, Smith immediately places herself amongst nature's fragments and fractures ('On some rude fragment of the rocky shore, | Where on the fractur'd cliff, the billows break, | Musing, my solitary seat I take, | And listen to the deep and solemn roar'). From this precarious position she evokes the howling winds and the storm's 'dark waves'. By the end of the second quatrain, however, this potential drama has been brought into harmony with her self ('the wild gloomy scene has charms for me, | And suits the mournful temper of my soul'). After this moment of poise, in the third quatrain she imagines herself as a shipwrecked mariner who waits to be overwhelmed by the tide, and in the closing couplet his terrible fate and her own have fused into a single image: 'Faint and more faint are heard his feeble cries, | 'Till in the rising tide, th'exhausted sufferer dies.' The art of the sonnet has brought an element of composure to the fragments. Smith has combined an effective octave–sestet 'turn' with a final couplet in which faintness and exhaustion, far from being artistically embarrassing, and for all their uncompromising bleakness, manage to achieve a formally satisfying close.

Recognizing the sonnet's ability to capture moments of strong feeling, poets cast around for situations from fiction and drama that could give them subjects for sonnet treatment. In several of Charlotte Smith's novels her characters, especially in melancholy mood, find relief in structuring their emotions in sonnet form, and fourteen of these were later collected into her expanded *Elegiac Sonnets*. Like other poets of the period she also wrote some sonnets in the character of Werther, the suicidal hero of Goethe's *The Sorrows of Young Werther* (1774). In 1793 Alexander Thomson even floated the idea of putting virtually the whole of Goethe's novel into sonnet form: 'Such a series', he considered, 'would exhibit a more natural and pathetic picture of the various fluctuations in the mind of a lover than any publication of amorous poetry, even than the effusions of PETRARCH himself', and he added: 'The number of sonnets, which could be thus collected, might probably amount to a hundred' (*Essay on Novels*, p. 16). It seemed as though any intense experience or situation could find its artistic consummation in fourteen lines. In his *Sonnets from Shakespeare* (1791) John Armstrong offered forty-two sonnets in the voice of various characters, with an appendix of the relevant passages from the plays. There are twenty-one sonnets exchanged between Romeo and Juliet, four between Troilus and Cressida, and others spoken by Viola, Florizel, Lorenzo, and others. Reading these it is fascinating to watch drama turning into lyric, and a quite musical effect is achieved at many points, recalling the world of opera where a lyric 'aria' would halt the action and allow a character briefly to explore a particular emotion or situation.

An ambitious series of sonnets of this lyric kind is Mary Robinson's *Sappho and Phaon* (1796). The speaker is the Ancient Greek lyric poet Sappho, and we follow the course of her doomed love for Phaon through forty-four Petrarchan sonnets, each strictly rhymed *abba abba cdcdcd*. There is no variation in this structure, and the reader has the experience of repeatedly revisiting the same mental space while her passions mount to their inevitable self-destructive climax at the cliff edge. The effect is a subtle one: the unvarying rhyme scheme begins to have a fatalistic tread; but it also provides a silent supporting framework for her emotions; and in a poem where there is little sense of Sappho's immediate physical presence, the sonnet form acts as a series of embodiments for what might otherwise become drifting abstractions. The sequence, after all, is not only about expressing passion, but about finding some order and direction through it. In the penultimate sonnet, spoken before she plunges from the 'dizzy precipice', she waits for the 'transcendent blaze' of the sun to give way gratefully to the 'cool concave' of the moon, declaring: 'So shall this glowing, palpitating soul, | Welcome returning Reason's placid beam.' Her scrupulous care in handling the form plays its part in a powerful drama of frenzy and coolness.

Friendship and the heart

In the work of Smith and Robinson, the voice of the sonnet seems an essentially lonely one, and the poet has to reach out to the natural world for sympathy: 'Oft do I seek thy shade dear with'ring tree, | Sad emblem of my own disast'rous state' (Robinson, 'To Evening'). Nature tends to be a projection of the self. In the sonnets of William Lisle Bowles, however, nature's effects are subtly different, and the self is responsive and more outgoing. In 'Written at Tinemouth, Northumberland, after a Tempestuous Voyage' the speaker, while climbing a cliff, pauses and turns round ('Pleas'd I look back, and view the tranquil tide'). Down below his eye notices a bright detail: 'The lifted oar far off with silver gleam | Is touch'd, and the hush'd billows seem to sleep!' But rather than read the scene in terms of himself, at this moment his thoughts move outward: 'Sooth'd by the scene, ev'n thus on sorrow's breast | A kindred stillness steals, and bids her rest.' We expect 'Sooth'd by the scene, *I* . . .', or 'bids *me* rest', but instead, in his moment of pleasure he is reminded of a sorrowing figure. This is a small point, perhaps, but on it hinges the difference between egoism and sociability. Where some poets might be thinking of themselves, Bowles is prompted to a *kindred* impulse.

Bowles's *Sonnets, Written Chiefly on Picturesque Spots, During a Tour* (1789) were hugely admired by Coleridge, Wordsworth, Charles Lamb, and Robert Southey. The teenage Coleridge transcribed forty copies of them for his friends, and in 1796 he published privately *Sonnets from Various Authors*, in which he printed a selection of Bowles sonnets intermingled with those of himself and his friends. He sensed a kindred spirit in the older poet, 'a style of poetry, so tender, and yet so manly, so natural and real'. For Coleridge, sonnets were meant to be memorized: 'Easily remembered from their briefness . . . they domesticate with the heart, and become, as it were, a part of our identity.' Sonnets, in other words, could be an organic part of yourself, and link others' intimate experiences with your own in a kind of friendly converse, or sharing of correspondent feelings. In his sonnet, 'To the River Otter', for example, Coleridge revisits his childhood river, while echoing Bowles's riverbank sonnet to the Itchin, and its source in the river Lodon sonnet of Thomas Warton (Bowles's Oxford friend and mentor). In this way a personal memory becomes a shared revisiting of the landscape of youth: 'Dear native Brook! wild Streamlet of the West!', Coleridge's sonnet opens,

> How many various-fated Years have past,
> What blissful and what anguish'd hours, since last
> I skimm'd the smooth thin stone along thy breast,
> Numbering its light leaps!

And with that last phrase the enclosed *abba* quatrain is joyfully transgressed with the lightest of touches. Coleridge's friend Southey, in his sonnet 'To a Brook near the Village of Corston', makes his own contribution to this poetry of echoes:

As thus I bend me o'er thy babbling stream
And watch thy current, Memory's hand pourtrays
The faint form'd scenes of the departed days.

The brook becomes the current of memory itself, and at the close of the sonnet Southey leaves the scene echoing in the reader's mind: 'Dim are the long past days, yet still they please | As thy soft sounds half heard, borne on the inconstant breeze.' The quiet phrase 'half heard' is redundant to both the meaning and the metre (it turns the pentameter into a six-stress 'alexandrine'), but its effect of prolonging the close is perfectly judged.

Amongst Coleridge and his friends the sonnet played an important role in cultivating friendship itself. They addressed intimate sonnets to each other, completed or revised one another's efforts, and used the form to explore how poetry and friendship shared a potential for organic growth. Their images are often of unfoldings, ripenings, fosterings, and nurturings—words that convey a sense of growing into one's full powers under a guiding amicable spirit. In their sonnets Charles Lamb and Charles Lloyd are sensitive to how precarious and vulnerable this trusting to benign impulse can be. Lloyd introduced his earliest volume of *Poems* (1795) with a 'Dedicatory Sonnet *Ad Amicos*' ('to my friends'), where the idea is stated in the second of its elegiac quatrains:

How would the soul unsatisfied, and cold,
Pine all unconscious of its secret powers,
Those powers did fostering Friendship ne'er unfold,
Nor ward with fond attempt each storm that lowers.

(*Fond* can mean both 'loving' and 'foolish'.) As 'a small poem, in which some lonely feeling is developed' (Coleridge's definition), the sonnet often longs for company, and can be painfully sensitive to fleeting hopes or sudden betrayals. The betrayal came when Coleridge in 1796, under the assumed name of 'Nehemiah Higginbottom', satirized his two friends in a set of sonnets that parodied their sensitive intimacies:

And then with sonnets and with sympathy
My dreamy bosom's mystic woes I pall;
Now of my false friend plaining plaintively,
Now raving at mankind in general.

These mocking sonnets mark not only a personal disillusionment, but a more significant crisis in the form's development. The sonnet's potential to engage with wider national issues was in danger of being forgotten.

The public voice of liberty

The sonnet, as Milton had shown, could also speak with a public voice; and in mid-1790s Britain amidst repressive legislation, treason trials, and threatened liberties, it was inevitable that poets should recall his rousing tones. In 1794–5 Coleridge pub-lished eleven sonnets in the *Morning Chronicle* addressed to contemporary public fig-ures who embodied the spirit of freedom. These poems return repeatedly to images of the human voice speaking out. Those to Thomas Erskine the advocate, Sarah Siddons the actress, and Richard Sheridan and Edmund Burke the great parliamentary speakers, celebrate their respective powers of eloquence. Perhaps with a thought to his own future, Coleridge finds in Sheridan a genius who can move with ease from private lyricism to public oratory; in the octave of the sonnet he is like Petrarch in retreat at Vaucluse: 'sweet thy voice, as when o'er Laura's bier | Sad music trembled thro' Vauclusa's glade'; but the sestet opens with Sheridan in full rhetorical flow:

> Now patriot Rage and Indignation high
> Swell the full tones! And now thine eye-beams dance
> Meanings of Scorn and Wit's quaint revelry!

The effect is startling. Coleridge gives his sonnet its full tones, which incorporate both Petrarch and Milton; and he concludes with Sheridan as St Michael defeating Satan:

> Writhes inly from the bosom-probing glance
> Th'Apostate by the brainless rout ador'd,
> As erst that elder Fiend beneath great Michael's sword.

It is a knotty, muscular sentence that could have come from *Paradise Lost*.

But the private/public distinction need not mark a difference in kind: behind the sonnet's louder public voice is still that core principle of personal integrity, a thought growing authentically from heartfelt experience. This idea particularly fascinated Wordsworth. In 1802 it was hearing Milton's sonnets read aloud that converted him to the form, and in his *Poems in Two Volumes* (1807) he grouped together twenty-six 'Sonnets Dedicated to Liberty', in which he consciously turned up the volume. Addressing Liberty in the opening quatrain of 'Thought of a Briton on the Subjugation of Switzerland', he reaches for sounds to express the unstoppable organic forces of nature:

> Two Voices are there; one is of the Sea,
> One of the Mountains; each a mighty Voice:
> In both from age to age Thou didst rejoice,
> They were thy chosen Music, Liberty!

We have seen how the sonnet is appropriate for quiet intimacies; but its contained energies are also effective for a brief, urgent declaration. It can have the power of a trumpet fanfare, or 'sennet' (in Marlowe's *Dr Faustus* the Pope enters to the stage direction 'Sound a Sonnet'). With especial daring Shelley in 1819 took hold of this idea, and his remarkable 'Ode to the West Wind' consists of five sonnets with the interlocking rhyme scheme of *aba bcb cdc ded ee*. Shelley allows the sound to build to its brass-note climax in the final couplet:

> Be through my lips to unawakened Earth
> The trumpet of a prophecy! O Wind,
> If Winter comes, can Spring be far behind?

Another feature of the sonnet, its formal constraints, could be turned to advantage by a freedom-loving poet. Like any authority, its rules were there to be tested or overthrown. In the preface to his *Poems* (1797) Southey virtually apologizes for his sonnets. Had he been writing them now, he says, 'I would have adopted a different title, and avoided the shackle of rhyme, and the confinement to fourteen lines'. He was recalling Coleridge, who the previous year had recategorized all his sonnets as 'effusions' ('pourings out') and printed them under that title with some of his longer poems. Coleridge's friend, the radical activist, John Thelwall, attacked the concept of the 'legitimate' sonnet (i.e. the strict Petrarchan form) as a mere 'arbitrary' regulation: 'The time is coming, I hope, when we shall estimate things, not by their titles, but their merits' (*Universal Magazine*, 1792). For him, the rhyme scheme of a sonnet, even its number of lines, 'ought surely to be left to the genius of the writer'. Two years later, imprisoned and awaiting trial for his life, Thelwall passed the time writing twelve sonnets (*Poems Written in Close Confinement*, 1795). In his preface he describes them as 'transcripts of the heart' written in a situation of 'rigorous confinement'—itself not a bad definition of the sonnet. And no two of them have the same shape: each is a fresh attempt to find freedom within constraint: in 'The Cell' he deliberately makes the 'narrow room' even narrower by writing in four-stress octosyllabics; and 'The Phoenix' invokes Freedom in its final line—the fifteenth.

Strength and stillness

In one of the finest sonnets of the Romantic period, Wordsworth's 'Composed upon Westminster Bridge, Sept. 3, 1803', London is transformed into an image of strength and beauty:

> Earth has not anything to show more fair:
> Dull would he be of soul who could pass by
> A sight so touching in its majesty:
> This City now doth like a garment wear
> The beauty of the morning . . .

The delicacy of 'touching' and 'garment' is cast momentarily over the substantial and symbolic strength, the 'majesty', of the metropolis. It is a convergence the sonnet is well equipped to make. Wordsworth appreciates how London can be held for an instant as a symbol of calm, contained power, summed up in his last line: 'And all that mighty heart is lying still!' It was this ability of the sonnet form to let beauty, strength, and stillness coalesce that John Keats particularly explored.

It is characteristic of the sonnet to compress the lyric impulse, and in Keats this can be used to build up pressure, as it does in the sonnet to his painter friend, Benjamin Robert Haydon, 'Great spirits now on earth are sojourning' (1816). Keats can hardly contain his excitement at the creative geniuses all around him, and in a final quatrain the tension almost snaps:

> These, these will give the world another heart,
> And other pulses. Hear ye not the hum
> Of mighty workings?—
> Listen awhile ye nations, and be dumb.

The ellipsis suddenly commands quiet, and perhaps only in a sonnet could that continuing silent pulse and the unheard rhyme be felt so strongly. Repeatedly in Keats's sonnets there are moments of stillness when beauty asserts its power and becomes something sublime, whether it is a distant bright star 'watching, with eternal lids apart, | . . . The moving waters at their priestlike task | Of pure ablution round earth's human shores', or the Elgin marbles torn from the Parthenon, which momentarily form themselves into an insurmountable edifice he can never climb: 'each imagined pinnacle and steep | Of godlike hardship tells me I must die | Like a sick eagle looking at the sky' (see also the chapter on 'The Fragment').

Keats feels the pressure of the sonnet, not as a 'narrow room', but as an elemental power contained within art and within his mind. It is like the river Nile in a sonnet by his friend Leigh Hunt, which 'flows through old hush'd Ægypt and its sands, | Like some grave mighty thought threading a dream'. This internalized silent strength forms the climax of Hunt's sonnet before sound and movement reassuringly return:

> Then comes a mightier silence, stern and strong,
> As of a world left empty of its throng,
> And the void weighs on us, and then we wake,
> And hear the fruitful stream lapsing along.

Hunt and Keats enjoyed challenging each other in sonnet competitions (see Keats's 'On the Grasshopper and Cricket' in the 'Readings' section), and 'The Nile' was written on such an occasion. In his posthumously published 'Essay on the Cultivation, History, and Varieties of the Species of Poem Called the Sonnet', Hunt gives as his final requirement for the 'perfect sonnet' that its close should be 'simple, conclusive, and satisfactory; strength being paramount, where such elevation is natural, otherwise on a level with serenity; flowing in calmness, or grand in manifestation of power withheld.' In that last phrase we are close to paradox, but in Keats this simultaneous strength and calmness, the sense of *power withheld*, is often evident. Hunt may have been thinking of his favourite sonnet, Keats's 'On first looking into Chapman's Homer', which ends on a moment of discovery when the old boundaries fall away and potential seems limitless. Keats felt, he says, 'like stout Cortez when with eagle eyes | He star'd at the Pacific—and all his men | Look'd at each other with a wild surmise—| Silent, upon a peak in Darien.' The poem ends with this rapt, visionary stillness, suggesting that the limits of the sonnet can turn out not to be walls, but horizons.

READINGS

Charlotte Smith, 'To the Moon'

Queen of the silver bow!—by thy pale beam,
  Alone and pensive, I delight to stray,
And watch thy shadow trembling in the stream,
  Or mark the floating clouds that cross thy way.

And while I gaze, thy mild and placid light
  Sheds a soft calm upon my troubled breast;
And oft I think,—fair planet of the night,
  That in thy orb, the wretched may have rest:

The sufferers of the earth perhaps may go,
  Releas'd by death—to thy benignant sphere,
And the sad children of despair and woe
  Forget in thee, their cup of sorrow here.

Oh! that I soon may reach thy world serene,
Poor wearied pilgrim—in this toiling scene!

Charlotte Smith's poem from her *Elegiac Sonnets* (1784) is a good example of the links between the Romantic sonnet and eighteenth-century elegy. I have emphasized this by supplying spaces to expose the poem's structure of three elegiac stanzas (*abab cdcd efef*) followed by a couplet (*gg*).

Smith exploits these units to plot the stages of her meditation on earthly sorrow and human mortality. Over it presides the 'silver bow' of the moon; but this is also the bow of Diana the huntress, the classical moon goddess and emblem of female chastity. This image of aggressive purity is turned by Smith into one of maternal love; just as she emphasizes the moon's calmness, not its traditional changeableness. In her poem the moon looks down on the earthly state of change, decay, toil, and passion from which the poet longs to be rescued. According to the old cosmology everything beneath the moon (the 'sublunary world') was subject to time and mortality, and Smith draws on this idea to contrast the 'despair and woe' on earth with the eternal higher 'sphere'.

The first quatrain registers the visual effects of the scene (ll. 3–4), and at this stage the 'I' is also the 'eye' of the poem. The second quatrain brings the speaker's response as the 'calm' mood is internalized, and nature and human nature meet to create what we can think of as a self, or focus of individual experience. In the third quatrain this self opens out to include 'the sufferers of the earth', and a personal sorrow is subsumed into the human condition. The successive quatrains mark the stages by which the experience is widened and deepened.

But with its final word 'here' (l.12) the third quatrain returns us to the speaker, and the concluding couplet opens with her sigh ('Oh! . . .). Fitted into its space of fourteen lines,

Smith's imagination has been necessarily circumscribed: it has not opened out into a sustained transcendent vision, but has had to remain, as the poem concedes, within its own 'sphere'. The sonnet form has given Smith an appropriate limit to her 'reach'—at least for now. It has been her allotted span.

William Wordsworth, 'Prefatory Sonnet'

Nuns fret not at their Convent's narrow room;
And Hermits are contented with their Cells;
And Students with their pensive Citadels:
Maids at the Wheel, the Weaver at his Loom,
Sit blithe and happy; Bees that soar for bloom,
High as the highest Peak of Furness Fells,
Will murmur by the hour in Foxglove bells:
In truth, the prison, unto which we doom
Ourselves, no prison is: and hence to me,
In sundry moods, 'twas pastime to be bound
Within the Sonnet's scanty plot of ground:
Pleas'd if some Souls (for such there needs must be)
Who have felt the weight of too much liberty,
Should find short solace there, as I have found.

In his *Poems in Two Volumes* (1807) Wordsworth used this poem to introduce two sets of sonnets, forty-six in all, divided into 'Miscellaneous Sonnets' and 'Sonnets Dedicated to Liberty'. He was conscious of the range of the form, using it to explore both childhood memories and big public themes of war and peace in Napoleonic Europe. In this 'Prefatory Sonnet', 'liberty' is made to acknowledge a personal need for familiar routine and peaceful retreat; yet at the same time these seeming retreats are productive—there is spinning and weaving, gathering of honey, and the potential for releasing the human spirit.

To read Wordsworth's sonnet for the first time is something of an adventure, because only at line 11 do we learn that its subject is the sonnet form itself. Up to that point its progress is mysterious and rather disconcerting. We move through a series of constricting spaces that open themselves out into happy activity: imprisoning 'Cells' become 'Citadels' of thought; the body may be confined but the spirit is free. Work spontaneously turns into play. Wordsworth clinches his paradox with the twin images of the bees: we glimpse them soaring up to the mountain-tops of 'Furness Fells', then contentedly enclosed in the 'Foxglove bells'. In those four rhyming words ('Cells', 'Citadels', 'Fells', 'bells') the sonnet catches the double movement: there is delight in expansiveness and flight but also in intimacy and concentration; the poet relishes both nature's sublimity and its minute detail. All these ideas come into focus once the word 'Sonnet' appears, and we learn that its 'scanty plot of ground' is a special place for the poet, not one of limitation, but one where things will potentially grow. By the close of his sonnet the poet's pleasure is increased by being offered to the sympathetic reader.

Appropriately for a poem about the resources to be found in self-limitation, Wordsworth confines himself to just four rhymes: *abba abba cddccd*. The Petrarchan structure of octave–sestet, however, is deliberately overridden. The octave climaxes in the portentous word 'doom', only to run on benignly into the next line. It is not fate being imposed on us, but a willing restriction, and the crucial word 'ourselves' transforms a negative imposition into a free choice. The move from octave to sestet marks a decisive turn in the poem, but its drama is in this way reassuringly underplayed. In later editions Wordsworth altered 'short' (l. 14) to 'brief', and in the process sacrificed a witty reminder that the sonnet is a small poem.

William Wordsworth, 'London, 1802'

Milton! Thou should'st be living at this hour:
England hath need of thee: she is a fen
Of stagnant waters: altar, sword and pen,
Fireside, the heroic wealth of hall and bower,
Have forfeited their ancient English dower
Of inward happiness. We are selfish men;
Oh! raise us up, return to us again;
And give us manners, virtue, freedom, power.
Thy soul was like a Star and dwelt apart:
Thou hadst a voice whose sound was like the sea:
Pure as the naked heavens, majestic, free,
So didst thou travel on life's common way,
In cheerful godliness; and yet thy heart
The lowliest duties on itself did lay.

Printed among the 'Sonnets Dedicated to Liberty', Wordsworth's poem was written on his return from the Continent during the precarious Peace of Amiens, which had temporarily halted the war with France. This is Wordsworth recovering the public tones of Milton, who exactly 150 years earlier had addressed a sonnet to the nation's protector, Cromwell, in which he remarked that 'peace hath her victories | No less renowned than war'. Wordsworth 'at this hour' echoes Milton's concern about what needs to be fought for in peace, and how the country must reconstitute itself by rediscovering its inner values.

Wordsworth uses the disciplined dynamics of the sonnet form to curb the kind of expansiveness that neglects personal principle. He redefines heroism in terms of the domestic fireside ('the heroic wealth of hall and bower'). Those who represent the nation through 'altar, sword and pen' (i.e. the clergyman, the soldier, and the writer) need to assert 'freedom' and 'power', but under the guidance of 'manners' and 'virtue'. Ambition must be combined with duty, and the nation rebuilt from within.

The sonnet therefore simultaneously arouses and restrains. Energetic movement is wanted to stir the 'stagnant waters' and give England a sense of direction, and this is what Milton the visionary poet seems to offer. Coming at the end of the octave, the rhyming word 'power' has a strong effect, and the sestet builds on this as it surges to a climax with what appears to be an emphatic couplet: 'Thou hadst a voice whose sound was like the sea; | Pure as the naked heavens, majestic, free'. But at this point the recoil comes. Rather than continuing with a predictable line such as 'So didst thou soar beyond the realms of day', we meet a disconcerting contradiction: 'So didst thou travel on life's common way'. With a sudden shift from sublime flight to the daily journey, the reader is reminded of Milton's humanity. The last line allows Wordsworth to end dutifully himself. A poem that begins like a public ode finishes as a sonnet completing its appointed task. At the end the reader is conscious of the poem closing down around what is essential and achievable. After the declamatory opening this may seem an anticlimax, but its modesty and manageability are crucial to Wordsworth's point. At the end he wants dignity and restraint—a certain measure in things, such as the sonnet has placed on him, and which he hopes will mark a new national discipline.

Leigh Hunt, 'On a Lock of Milton's Hair'

It lies before me there, and my own breath
Stirs its thin outer threads, as though beside
The living head I stood in honoured pride,
Talking of lovely things that conquer death.
Perhaps he pressed it once, or underneath
Ran his fine fingers, when he leant, blank-eyed,
And saw in fancy, Adam and his bride
With their heaped locks, or his own Delphic wreath.
There seems a love in hair, though it be dead.
It is the gentlest, yet the strongest thread
Of our frail plant,—a blossom from the tree
Surviving the proud trunk;—as if it said,
Patience and Gentleness is Power. In me
Behold affectionate eternity.

In contrast with the rousing opening of the previous sonnet, Leigh Hunt evokes Milton's spirit with a quiet confidence that is content to play with an idea much as his own breath plays with the lock of hair. Hunt lets his imagination indulge itself and he spins a poem from its 'threads' (l. 2), picking up the word metaphorically in line 10 to suggest organic continuities—threads linking death to life, past to present, the real to the imagined. To enter his world of the poetic 'fancy' is to sanction fictions and conjectures, and these become the subject of the poem. The repeated conditional 'as though' (l. 2) and 'as if' (l. 12) establishes this realm of possibility which the reader is invited to share. We are asked not only to see Hunt musing over the lock, but to superimpose an image of the blind Milton writing *Paradise Lost* and toying with his hair while he pictures Adam and Eve in the Garden of Eden and dreams of the 'Delphic wreath' (Apollo's laurel crown) that will encircle his head. Here Milton is not a public figure, but an intimate and palpable presence. In a surprisingly sensuous way the threads of hair intertwine Hunt, the old poet, and the reader. Indeed the sestet begins with a suggestion of a secret affinity: the phrase 'There seems a love in hair' (l. 9) reproduces exactly the rhythm and rhyme of the sonnet's opening phrase ('It lies before me there'). With the subtlest of effects, therefore, Hunt creates an aural sympathy between octave and sestet, and it is typical of this sonnet that the idea of 'a love in hair' is not asserted but offered to us ('There seems'). The links are tenuous, but vital ones, and Hunt is taking risks (especially from a critical audience). He spins out his sentiments in this way, trusting to the reader's sympathies as he guides us back to Milton's Paradise and towards what is the sonnet's version of the Tree of Life. Characteristic of this benign leading of the reader is the use throughout of run-on lines, especially towards the poem's close. It culminates in a final pair of lines that do all they can to avoid becoming a couplet. This sonnet does not work by clinching anything, and it is appropriate that the word 'Power', which brought Wordsworth's octave to a climax, here loses its prominence and is subsumed into 'Patience and Gentleness'. Similarly the awesome final concept of 'eternity' is woven into the idea of 'affectionate' humanity. For Romantic writers Milton was not just the great visionary, but also a human poet, and here Hunt exploits the sonnet's potential for what Coleridge called 'domesticating with the heart' in order to claim Milton as a friend rather than a figure of sublime authority who overshadowed his successors. In doing so, Hunt makes an important point about literary history by showing how a poetic influence can transfuse itself benignly from one generation to the next.

John Keats, 'On the Grasshopper and Cricket'

The poetry of earth is never dead:
   When all the birds are faint with the hot sun,
   And hide in cooling trees, a voice will run
From hedge to hedge about the new-mown mead;
That is the Grasshopper's—he takes the lead
   In summer luxury,—he has never done
   With his delights; for when tired out with fun
He rests at ease beneath some pleasant weed.
The poetry of earth is ceasing never:
   On a lone winter evening, when the frost
     Has wrought a silence, from the stove there shrills
The Cricket's song, in warmth increasing ever,
   And seems to one in drowsiness half lost,
     The Grasshopper's among some grassy hills.

On 30 December 1816 Keats and Hunt challenged one another to write a sonnet with this title in only fifteen minutes. Both completed on time, and this is Keats's version.

Here Keats unlocks the narrow room of the sonnet to explore two landscapes and two poetic worlds. He chooses a clear structure of octave (*abba abba*) and sestet (*cdecde*), and marks the division boldly by repeating his opening phrase in line 9, but with a nice variation that introduces fresh rhymes. The symmetry of the sestet is in turn reinforced by a further echo ('ceasing never'/'increasing ever'). The doubling emphasizes the contrast between summer day and winter night and the distinct characterization of the two tiny, noisy crea-tures. Keats's grasshopper and cricket represent an age-old contrast (his equivalent of Milton's L'Allegro and Il Penseroso): first the convivial spirit who joins in and celebrates the life going on around him, and then the solitary spirit who creates an alternative world in the imagination. 'The poetry of earth' is forever divided between them. In the world of the grasshopper the language tends appropriately towards comedy: it is a tad vulgar ('tired out with fun') and slightly ludicrous ('at ease beneath some pleasant weed'). The cricket's more refined creativity magically emerges out of the darkness, 'when the frost Has wrought a silence' (as Hunt read this he exclaimed 'Ah! That's perfect! Bravo Keats!'). The grasshop-per's simple happiness in his own situation is countered by the cricket's meditative ability to transform experience and change winter to summer. In doing so he represents the power of the fancy. Within the imagination of 'one in drowsiness half lost' the sonnet finally brings the two voices together. Not a bad achievement at a line a minute.

Percy Bysshe Shelley, 'England in 1819'

An old, mad, blind, despised, and dying King;
Princes, the dregs of their dull race, who flow
Through public scorn,—mud from a muddy spring;
Rulers who neither see nor feel nor know,
But leechlike to their fainting country cling
Till they drop, blind in blood, without a blow.
A people starved and stabbed in th'untilled field;
An army, whom liberticide and prey
Makes as a two-edged sword to all who wield;
Golden and sanguine laws which tempt and slay;
Religion Christless, Godless—a book sealed;
A senate, Time's worst statute, unrepealed—
Are graves from which a glorious Phantom may
Burst, to illumine our tempestuous day.

In Shelley's angry poem the compactness of the sonnet form works to powerful satiric effect. The time is out of joint, and as if to mimic this the sonnet inverts octave and sestet: *ababab cdcdccdd*. The insistent alternate rhymes work up to a climax with the final emphatic doub-ling of *ccdd*. The poem does not unfold as an argument, but is set out as an indictment, a mounting list of grievances. The time for explaining, arguing, and justifying has passed, and Shelley's indignation cuts through such niceties. The alliteration adds to this stacking effect: 'country cling . . . blind . . . blood . . . blow . . . starved . . . stabbed'. As the poet surveys the nation, the accumulated wrongs pile up and Shelley creates a list from the abuses of the system. All is concentrated into an essence of corruption. Like the vivid image of the bloated leech that finally drops off the body through its own weight (ll. 5–6), the sonnet lets every-thing compound together until the moment when it can be swept away for good. The impetus builds relentlessly to the closing couplet, which supplies a double shock. With the simple word 'Are', the main verb of the poem finally arrives like a withheld breath, and the last line bounces off the word 'Burst', as if a boil on the body politic has been lanced. But this climax is additionally disconcerting, as we notice that the image of apocalyptic resurrection is only a hope—the promised 'day' remains dependent on the verb 'may'.

FURTHER READING

Cruttwell, Patrick, *The English Sonnet* (London: Longman, 1966). A concise introductory summary of the sonnet's history and development in English literature; personal and quirky judgements are balanced by some good detailed analysis of individual sonnets.

Curran, Stuart, *Poetic Form and British Romanticism* (New York: Oxford University Press, 1986), pp. 29–55 ('The Sonnet'). An authoritative and scholarly discussion of the sonnet from the 'rebirth' of the form in the 1770s, in which issues of style and structure are related to larger matters of poetic form during the Romantic period; the critical analysis is acute, and the continuing influence of the Petrarchan sonnet is convincingly shown.

Fairer, David, 'Coleridge's *Sonnets from Various Authors* (1796): A Lost Conversation Poem?', *Studies in Romanticism*, 41 (Winter 2002), 585–604. A critical analysis of the structure of Coleridge's collection of his contemporaries' sonnets which emphasizes the role played by the sonnet in the poet's friendships during the 1790s.

Fuller, John, *The Sonnet* (London: Methuen, 1972). This 'Critical Idiom' volume is a useful technical handbook to the sonnet written by a practising poet; the form's rigorous structural requirements are stressed, and the analyses are thorough and detailed.

Kerrigan, John, 'Wordsworth and the Sonnet: Building, Dwelling, Thinking', *Essays in Criticism*, 35 (1985), 45–75. This article sees Wordsworth's continual return to the sonnet form as a feature of the poet's need for rootedness and repose; Kerrigan argues that the fourteen-line sonnet became for him 'a uniquely comforting abode in which to dwell'.

Robinson, Daniel, ' "Work Without Hope": Anxiety and Embarrassment in Coleridge's Sonnets', *Studies in Romanticism*, 39 (Spring 2000), 81–110. Robinson regards Coleridge's sonnets as 'the most intimate poems in his oeuvre'; his article sees the poet's use of the form as characterized by a combination of defensiveness and anxiety, and a nagging self-consciousness in relation to his poetic models.

Zillman, Lawrence John, *John Keats and the Sonnet Tradition: A Critical and Comparative Study* (Los Angeles: Lymanhouse, 1939). Zillman stresses Keats's 'versecraft' and the specific influences of Milton, Shakespeare, and Leigh Hunt. Keats's sonnets are printed in an appendix.

WEB LINK

There is a useful online anthology of Romantic-period sonnets at <http://www.sonnets.org/romantic.htm>

NOTE

1. Thomas Warton, *History of English Poetry* (London, 1774–81), iii. 32, 12.

21 | Lyric

Paul D. Sheats

To see where the word 'lyric' comes from, look up on a clear summer's night at Lyra, the lovely constellation that seemed to the ancient Greeks to resemble a lyre, or harp. For them a lyric was a poem sung to the lyre or another instrument. It might be a choral ode, danced and sung to honour Olympic victors, a hymn to the gods, a drinking song, an elegy, or a love poem. The philosopher Aristotle distinguished such musical kinds, or genres, from the other grand divisions of poetry, the narrative that tells a story and the drama that enacts it.

This sense that lyric implied music was still intact thousands of years later in the Romantic period, although, because poetry was now usually read in silence, a lyric came to be thought of as a poem suitable for musical accompaniment. Wordsworth so defined it in 1815, when introducing his collected poems, but his better-known phrase describing poetry as a 'spontaneous overflow of powerful feelings' pointed to the split between lyric and music that took place in the nineteenth century.[1] Although that century produced great narrative poems and some verse drama, the lyric soon became its dominant poetic form, and Edmund Gosse could write in 1911 that 'lyrical poetry is, really, nothing more than another name for poetry itself'.[2]

Today, of course, songs are sung to instruments, although the guitar has replaced Sappho's lyre, and we speak of the 'lyrics' of a song. As a way of classifying poetry, however, lyric inherits the ambiguities of its ancestry. It may provide an umbrella term for a host of particular kinds, like the sonnet and the elegy, or refer loosely to poems that are obviously neither narratives nor dramas. In practice, however, the word usually calls attention not to a poem's music but to its size and psychology, suggesting that it is relatively brief, passionate, and personal.

This truncated sense of the word hardly describes the great lyric achievements of the various poets we group together as Romantics. Each in his or her way took advantage of the genre's broadening possibilities, its musical and dramatic heritage, or its ancient visionary authority, often articulating a distinctly modern sense of the individual self and its various communities, social, political, and natural.

Broadening possibilities

For commercial as well as literary reasons, the Romantic period was especially propitious for writers of lyric poetry. Between 1780 and 1820 the reading public grew in numbers, income, and sophistication, and lyric poems appeared in a host of books, anthologies, magazines, and newspapers, where their brevity recommended them to impecunious editors. Men and women of widely different classes and opinions invoked the lyric muse, from aristocrats to farm workers, from radical democrats to staunch supporters of Church and King. A new generation of popular women poets found certain varieties of lyric particularly congenial, in part because they did not boast the classical education that with few exceptions was still reserved for men.

The forms of poetry were also evolving. Traditional generic divisions eroded, often with the blessing of political radicals who equated formal constraint with political repression. Inspired not only by the Greek and Roman classics but the Hebrew Bible, native folk song, and even nursery rhymes, lyric kinds proliferated, cross-fertilizing each other and transforming other genres. The increasingly popular sonnet took new forms and addressed new subjects, and in *Lyrical Ballads*, the landmark volume published by Wordsworth and Coleridge in 1798, the humble ballad aspires to the heights of the ode. The final act of *Prometheus Unbound*, Shelley's 'lyrical drama', consists of little else but passionate lyrics. Perhaps the most impressive long poem of the age, Wordsworth's *Prelude*, begins with a spontaneous lyric 'preamble', and mingles lyric with epic elements throughout its narrative. Hence the frequent necessity of distinguishing a lyric *poem* from lyric *effects*, and the difficulty of assigning Romantic poems to clear-cut generic categories. Is Coleridge's 'Rime of the Ancient Mariner' a lyric or narrative poem, or both?

The resonant lyre

The Romantic lyric was nourished by a literary and popular culture rich in song. All the major poets wrote songs suitable for accompaniment by the harp or piano, like Thomas Moore's *Irish Melodies* and Lord Byron's *Hebrew Melodies*, and many inserted songs in plays or narrative poems. During the last decade of his short life Robert Burns wrote or rewrote lyrics for over 350 Scottish songs, including many, like 'O my luve's like a red, red rose', and 'Green grow the rashes, O', that have long since transcended national boundaries. Working men who gathered in Manchester in 1792 sang their hearty support of the young French Revolution, and when navy tars mutinied for better treatment and higher wages in 1797, at the risk of their necks, they presented their case not only by petition but in song:

> Good Providence long looked with pity at last
> For to see Honest Jack so shamefully thrashed,
> But still held his arm for to let Jack subdue
> The pride of those masters whose hearts were not true.

The melody of this earnest chorus has been lost, but in a well-made Romantic lyric we continue to sense its presence.

Here are the first lines of an *ariette*, or 'little song', which Shelley wrote for his friend Jane Williams not long before he drowned off the Italian coast:

> The keen stars were twinkling,
>   And the fair moon was rising among them,
>   Dear Jane!
> The guitar was tinkling,
>   But the notes were not sweet till you sung them
>   Again.
>   ('The keen stars were twinkling', ll. 1–6)

All poetry involves ordered sounds and rhythms, but here they are concentrated and intensified. 'An animated or impassioned recitation', Wordsworth observed, can replace 'the classical lyre or the romantic harp'; the language of poetry, that is, can furnish its own musical accompaniment.[3] The 'animated' voice of his 'Mad Mother' suggests why he called his ballads 'lyrical':

> Suck, little babe, oh suck again!
> It cools my blood; it cools my brain;
> Thy lips I feel them, baby! they
> Draw from my heart the pain away.
>   (ll. 1–4)

These simple, unpoetic words are as democratic in their social origin as the song of the mutineers, and like that song they are given form by a stanza (Italian for 'room'), and by the modulations of a four-beat iambic rhythm, which partly controls the emphasis we place on each word. (Unlike the three-stress anapests of the mutineer's song, the iamb is a metrical unit of two stresses, the second of which is stronger than the first; we hear it clearly in lines 2 and 3.) Certain words are weighted further by repetition ('suck', 'cools'), and by a rich network of echoing sounds, including rhyme ('again'/'brain'), alliterating consonants ('blood'/'brain'), and assonance of vowels ('baby'/'pain'). Such effects are 'musical' because, like a piano sonata, they depend on the arrangement of sounds and rhythms. But at the same time they function as semantic signifiers, inseparable from the words they order and qualify, and the sensations, feelings, and thoughts those words in turn represent. If we ask *why* a given word receives more emphasis than another, one answer (and there are many) will point into the 'animated' consciousness of the woman speaking.

As Mother Goose reminds us, the pleasure of this word-music is in part autonomous and physical:

Wee Willie Winkie
Runs through the town,
Upstairs and downstairs
In his nightgown.

Like nursery rhymes, chants, and incantations, the lyric offered Romantic poets an opportunity to recover what much earlier eighteenth-century poetry had lost, language's organic power to awaken responses rooted deep within the living, unthinking body.

As the glancing rhythms of Shelley's song suggest, the Romantic poets experimented freely with different lyrical forms, borrowing stanza patterns from Renaissance and Baroque predecessors or inventing their own. William Blake may have recalled Wee Willie when he used nursery-rhyme effects to mock his neoclassic arch-enemy, the critic Samuel Johnson:

Lo! the Bat with leathern wing,
Winking and blinking,
Winking and blinking,
Winking and blinking,
Like Dr Johnson [.]
('An Island in the Moon', ch. 9, ll. 3–7)

Thomas Lovell Beddoes exploits the dissonance between a macabre Gothic imagery and a lilting anapestic rhythm:

Is that the wind dying? O no;
    It's only two devils, that blow
Through a murderer's bones, to and fro,
    In the ghosts' moonshine.
('Old Adam, The Carrion Crow', ll. 9–12)

The musical effects of John Keats's 'Ode on Melancholy' are characteristically intense:

Or if thy mistress some rich anger shows,
Emprison her soft hand, and let her rave,
    And feed deep, deep upon her peerless eyes.
                    (ll. 18–20)

Long vowels join with weighted stresses and pauses, and with consonants focused on the lips (m, f, v, p), to retard the movement of attention, as if to savour the perverse pleasure of this sexual confrontation.

Language in action: lyric as drama

Like their classical and Renaissance predecessors, Romantic poets freely exploited the dramatic potential of the lyric voice. Usually single and passionate, often bent on some purpose, this voice naturally invites dramatic elaboration. Who is speaking, and to whom? Where and why? Such questions may be suspended, of course, and in many lyrics we hear a voice that tells a story or describes a landscape but takes no part in the action, as in Felicia Heman's vivid and much-recited 'Casabianca' ('The boy stood on the burning deck'). In a delightful lyric by Burns, on the other hand, a farmer commiserates with a mouse—a 'wee sleeket cowran tim'rous beastie'—whose nest he has upturned with the plough, and the dramatic situation expands to include an invented speaker, a listener, and a landscape; only the reader is left out. Any or all of these dramatis personae may appear in a given Romantic poem. Invented or not, the lyric voice may address practically anything, from a Greek Titan, in Byron's 'Prometheus', to an abstract idea, in Helen Maria William's admired ode 'To Sensibility' (see also the chapter on 'Sensibility'). In 'The Nightingale's Nest', John Clare hospitably invites his reader along on a country walk: 'Up this green woodland ride lets softly rove' (l. 1), and the narrator of Wordsworth's 'Simon Lee' interrupts a meandering tale to stage an ironic confrontation with his 'gentle Reader' (l. 61).

Especially popular from the later eighteenth century on was the reflexive situation we find in Charlotte Smith's *Elegiac Sonnets* (1784), where a speaker, apparently solitary, reflects on a landscape, relating it in some fashion to her life and feelings. 'To Spring' begins, for example, by describing an English countryside:

> Again the wood, and long with-drawing vale,
>   In many a tint of tender green are drest,
> Where the young leaves unfolding, scarce conceal
>   Beneath their early shade, the half-form'd nest
> Of finch or wood-lark . . .
>
> (ll. 1–5)

Smith describes this landscape as if it were actually present—she uses the present tense, and implies through her choice of images the approach of the observing eye to its object. At the sonnet's close, however, attention turns inward, as she reflects that these springtime charms 'have power to cure all sadness—but despair' (l. 14). We seem to overhear her private thoughts and feelings, their sincerity guaranteed, as it were, by her solitude. This appeal to the reader's sensibility (see chapter on 'Sensibility' and *Oxford Companion to the Romantic Age*, p. 102) is thus grounded in the poem's dramatic mode. Judging from its popularity—*Elegiac Sonnets* went through six editions by 1792— readers relished this illusion of uncompromised intimacy, of artlessness within a finished work of art. So did other poets, judging from the many Romantic lyrics that adopt and elaborate this reflexive model, which was itself celebrated in Shelley's evocative portrait of the poet as a 'nightingale, who sits in darkness and sings to cheer its own solitude with sweet sounds'.[4]

Such dramatic effects can become more sophisticated. We are expected, for example, to infer a 'plot' from overheard speech in Wordsworth's 'Mad Mother' (quoted above), where the speaker has been betrayed by her lover, her baby's father. What her monologue dramatizes, however, is not only her misery, but the empowering strength she draws from her child. This lyric drama steers us away from a stereotyped response shaped by the ideals of sensibility, and asks us to explore its meaning imaginatively for ourselves. The period's major lyrics often do the same. In Coleridge's great 'conversation' poems, for instance, a speaker meditates within changing, vividly realized landscapes, natural and domestic. In the odes of Keats and Shelley it is a speaker's relationship to an object, a nightingale or the west wind, that evolves as the poem proceeds. Such poems were first classed as 'greater' romantic lyrics by the critic M. H. Abrams, who pointed out that they often dramatize a particular plot, in which a personal crisis is confronted and resolved, and the speaker's psychic integrity regained.

In Wordsworth's 'Lines Written a Few Miles above Tintern Abbey', to take a definitive example, a speaker who has returned to a remembered landscape reflects on his own destiny and his changing relationship to nature. We assume he is alone until, more than halfway through the poem, he unexpectedly addresses his sister, who has been there from the beginning, a surprise entrance that enlarges the poem's theme and allows it to contemplate (and demonstrate) human love as well as love of the natural world. But the drama of this remarkable poem takes place on a smaller scale as well. As its third paragraph begins, for example, we witness a struggle in the speaker's mind between doubt and belief:

> If this
> Be but a vain belief, yet, oh! how oft . . .
> (ll. 49–50)

The conditional sentence that expresses rational scepticism ('If . . . belief') is never completed. Instead, a second train of thought passionately intervenes ('yet, oh!'), and a new sentence forms before our eyes ('how oft'), bringing with it in succeeding lines a train of powerful memories that testify to the truth of this 'belief'. Syntax and lyric music work together to dramatize a living consciousness in the act of discovering who and what it is (compare the reading of 'Tintern Abbey' in the chapter on 'New Historicism').

Vision quests

What we loosely call 'visionary' poetry can range from momentary insight to apocalypse, an unveiling of ultimate reality. When the speaker of 'Tintern Abbey' claims the power to see 'into the life of things' (l. 49), he invokes an ancient and influential tradition that links lyric with exalted and unusual states of mind. The Delphic oracle was something of a lyric poet, chanting riddling messages from the gods, and the philosopher Plato, who mistrusted poetry's civic effects, joined his classical contemporaries in acknowledging it as a kind of divine madness, one exemplified for later ages by the 'wild' odes of the Theban poet Pindar (see *Oxford Companion to the*

Romantic Age, p. 625). In the later eighteenth century this tradition revived, aided by growing interest in the poet-bards of medieval Scotland and Wales, by British psychological philosophy, which tended to elevate the authority of the creative imagination, and by a growing impatience among younger poets with Enlightenment rationalism and the paradigms of neoclassical correctness (see *Oxford Companion to the Romantic Age*, p. 299). In the looser lyric forms, like the irregular Pindaric ode, a neoclassic poet could bend the rules with relative impunity, in the name of original genius. As the poet and critic John Aikin wrote in 1772, the 'modern ode' invites 'the boldest flights of poetical enthusiasm, and the wildest creations of the imagination'.[5]

For the Romantic poets, notably those young men who exalted the figure of the poet, the higher forms of lyric offered a natural vehicle for lofty imaginative and philosophic vision. Unfortunately, however, it was these very forms, and especially the ode, that risked becoming fashionable clichés; in 1797, according to a scornful critic, even a hackney coachman could publish Pindaric odes. A serious poet might respond to this difficulty by democratizing the parameters of visionary poetry, in poems that reveal the extraordinary in the ordinary, 'the world', as Blake put it, 'in a grain of sand'. Another solution was offered by unconventional forms like the ballad, the children's song, or the biblical 'prophecies' of Blake. Or a poet could accept traditional forms but forcefully reassert their ancient height and difficulty. In his ambitious 'Ode to the Departing Year', Coleridge adopted the strict Pindaric form, with its intricate rhyme scheme and stanza structure, to indict a world gone morally and politically awry. In a difficult but masterful irregular ode that became one of the nineteenth century's most influential poems, Wordsworth lamented the loss of vision brought by age, and celebrated the 'Intimations of Immortality' that sustain human hope through life. In *Adonais*, his great elegy for Keats, Shelley skilfully adapted the classical pastoral to his own visionary purposes, using it not only to mourn the dead poet but to strive after him towards another realm of being.

The sense of struggle and difficulty is virtually absent from the visionary lyrics of William Blake. In his *Songs of Innocence and Experience* (1789, 1794) we hear an assured voice that speaks across centuries:

> In futurity
> I prophetic see,
> That the earth from sleep,
> (Grave the sentence deep)
>
> Shall arise and seek
> For her maker meek.
> And the desart wild
> Become a garden wild.
> ('The Little Girl Lost', ll. 1–8)

In 'The Tyger' the humble nursery rhyme, with its incantatory word-music, becomes a workshop where the human mind creates its myths:

Tyger, Tyger, burning bright,
In the forests of the night;
What immortal hand or eye,
Could frame thy fearful symmetry?

.   .   .   .   .   .

What the hammer? What the chain,
In what furnace was thy brain?
What the anvil? What dread grasp
Dare its deadly terrors clasp?
(ll. 1–4, 13–16)

As we read, the imagination of the frightened but fascinated speaker begins to shape the titanic blacksmith god that framed the tyger as well as the lamb.

More enigmatic still is Coleridge's 'Kubla Khan', a lyric vision that has inspired its own mythology, providing generations of readers with an epitome of the Romantic imagination (compare the reading in the chapter on 'Formalism'). After circulating in manuscript for nearly nineteen years, it was published in 1816 with an apologetic preface, in which Coleridge presented it as a fragmentary dream-vision, induced by an 'anodyne' (that is, opium), and interrupted by the now-famous 'person on business from Porlock'. Through the power of its verbal music and its concentrated, suggestive imagery, which encompasses the sacred and demonic, autocratic power and aesthetic beauty, this dream-vision has from the beginning fascinated and provoked its readers. It ends with not the vision but the visionary poet, seen as an object of wonder and fear:

And all should cry, Beware! Beware!
His flashing eyes, his floating hair!
Weave a circle round him thrice,
And close your eyes with holy dread,
For he on honey-dew hath fed,
And drunk the milk of Paradise.
(ll. 49–54)

This famous portrait may enchant us into assuming that it speaks for other poets or for Romanticism itself. When Mary Robinson read 'Kubla Khan', it is true, she replied by composing her own visionary lyric, which enthusiastically extended and praised Coleridge's: 'I'll raptured trace the circling bounds | Of thy rich Paradise extended' ('To the Poet Coleridge', ll. 55–6). Only a few months before he composed the poem, however, Anna Barbauld had warned him to resist the seductions of 'mystic visions' that 'swim | Before the cheated sense', and to exert himself instead 'for friends, for country' ('To Mr C[olerid]ge', ll. 8–9, 41). Years earlier the poet and future playwright Joanna Baillie made her own modest comment on visionary aspiration, informing the 'mighty spirits of the song', the Muses, that their 'wild obscuring heights' were 'too great' for her:

it will avail
With simple words to tell my tale;

And still contented will I be,
    Though greater inspiration never fall to me.
            ('Address to the Muses', ll. 141–4)

Representing the self

It was during the Romantic period that the lyric assumed its modern cultural role as the poetic voice of the individual self. Long accustomed to the use of the first-person singular, the 'I', and shaped by the historical assumption that, as the oldest poetic form, it represented a pristine freedom and integrity, the later eighteenth-century lyric had welcomed the construction of exemplary poetic selves, which embodied the virtues of sensibility or original genius. In later poems, however, these lyric constructions of self take on a distinctly modern form: the individual consciousness becomes a unique subject-matter in itself, potentially infinite in depth and complexity, and a component of all perception and knowledge, perhaps inescapably so. The word 'subjectivity' first appears in English in 1812, in a sentence written by Coleridge's friend and fellow poet, Robert Southey, to suggest the bias of the perceiving mind.

These developments may be dramatized by placing a Romantic lyric alongside its neoclassical antitype, a didactic poem. Here is how Alexander Pope, in his *Essay on Criticism* (1711), celebrated 'Nature':

First follow Nature, and your judgment frame
By her just standard, which is still the same;
Unerring Nature, still divinely bright,
One clear, unchanged, and universal light,
Life, force, and beauty must to all impart,
At once the source, and end, and test of art.
                (ll. 68–73)

The speaker of this brilliant display of neoclassic artistry might be described as articulate and forceful, even passionate, but to ask after a self seems somewhat beside the point. That is not the business of the poem, which seeks to guide a reader in the arts of judging and writing well. As befits a didactic poem, attention centres not on the speaker's personality or motives but on 'Nature', which Pope celebrates as an idea in the human mind, a universal norm.

As he walked back to Bristol in 1798, after a tour of the river Wye, William Wordsworth composed his own celebration of nature, which ends the first part of 'Tintern Abbey':

                Therefore am I still
A lover of the meadows and the woods,
And mountains, and of all that we behold
From this green earth; of all the mighty world
Of eye, and ear,—both what they half create,

And what perceive; well pleased to recognise
In nature and the language of the sense,
The anchor of my purest thoughts, the nurse,
The guide, the guardian of my heart, and soul
Of all my moral being.

(ll. 102–11)

These climactic lines remind us that nature is as mutable an idea as self, and that successive ages give such primary concepts distinctive poetic forms. Unlike Pope, Wordsworth finds nature roughly where we do today, in the physical world, 'the meadows and the woods', which he perceives as living, holy, and redemptive. Although the word 'ecology' did not exist in 1798, its invention seems only a matter of time (see chapter entitled 'Ecology').

But the more striking change lies in the representation of self, which gives Wordsworth's poem not only its subject but its guiding formal principle. As he tells us in a later note, he thought of it as an ode, a form he evidently regards as fit for serious meditation, which here touches (in 'half create') on a philosophical problem that had haunted British empiricism for nearly a century. Describing such lyrics merely as the 'overflow of powerful feelings', as we are often taught to do, thus profoundly misunderstands their point. Like the Metaphysical poets of the seventeenth century, Wordsworth rejects generic distinctions between deep feeling and deep thinking, and uses the lyric's musical powers to dramatize a consciousness, a self, that exemplifies both. One might profitably ask of the above lines, for example, why a momentary disturbance of the iambic rhythm imbues the word 'green' with such feeling, or why the briefest of all sentences, 'I am', simply refuses to end, taking advantage of the freedom of blank verse to prolong itself from line to line (as it never could in Pope's couplets), adding, qualifying, rising finally to religious solemnity, as the speaker probes his own identity and asserts what he now is.

This foregrounding of individual consciousness takes many different lyric forms, from Wordsworthian introspection to the poignant self-analysis of John Clare's 'I am' and the brilliant self-display of Byron's or Mary Robinson's verses to their estranged partners. Its apparent preoccupation with self did not escape criticism. In a moment of impatience Keats protested against 'the Wordsworthian or egotistical sublime', and the conservative critic Francis Jeffrey could agree with his liberal counterpart, William Hazlitt, that much of the new poetry was self-centred and erratically idiosyncratic. Related charges have been made ever since, mostly on the basis of lyric poetry. Before taking sides in this perennial dispute, however, we should remember that idiosyncrasy often lies in the eye of the beholder, and that a Romantic speaker may function as a representative model or type of human consciousness. In dramatic lyrics, furthermore, even the most profound introversion enters into dialogue with the mind's more outward-looking impulses.

Lyric communities

In 1772, in front of a distinguished audience that included Lord North, the Prime Minister of England, and Benjamin Franklin, the former Agent of the colony of Pennsylvania, the Orator of Oxford University read an 'Ode to the Lyric Muse'. In intricate and lofty strains, it asserted the lyric poet's civic responsibility, and urged the poets of England to embrace the cause of Liberty, the 'Patriot Virtues', and 'Public Zeal'.

Had we been present on this solemn occasion we might have wondered at Shelley's portrait of the poet as a solitary nightingale, singing to itself. For much of its history the lyric had performed public and social functions, and during the Romantic period it continued to reach outward towards various communities from the family to the nation, binding together 'by passion and knowledge the vast empire of human society', as Wordsworth wrote in the Preface to *Lyrical Ballads* in 1802.[6] As schoolboys, future poets imitated Greek songs that celebrated the fall of tyrants, and sang ballads about heroic deeds in the British past. When they grew up, depending on their politics, they hailed such events as the fall of the Bastille, or Wellington's victory over Napoleon at Waterloo, or both, in songs and odes. Nearly all the major male poets addressed formal, occasional lyrics to a national audience. and so, less frequently, did women (see chapter on 'Feminism').

Lyrics served less heroic social purposes as well. Domestic communities provide the subject of a substantial class of poems, many but not all composed by women. As she sets out to describe 'Washing Day', Anna Barbauld imagines a 'domestic muse' suitable to her subject, and in a variety of lyrics she approaches family and household with affection and humour. Joanna Baillie's dramatic lyrics movingly connect family members across generations. In other senses, too, lyrics furnished a kind of social currency, circulating among local communities. An ode by Ann Yearsley, a gifted country milk-woman, helped fund a local hospital. Keats left a famous sonnet on a friend's doorstep as a token of gratitude. Under the exotic pen names of Della Crusca and Anna Matilda, Robert Merry and Hannah Cowley engaged in a public exchange of florid lyrics (see *Oxford Companion to the Romantic Age*, pp. 481–2). If what these occasions display is not exactly 'Public Zeal', they show the lyric working to consolidate communities of affection and concern.

Nor is it always easy to see the civic relevance of certain lyrics written by radical poets, who with some reason feared suppression or reprisal. Such poems often work by indirection; they may seem private but are designed to have far-reaching public effects, working through individual readers to reform England and its institutions. In several *Lyrical Ballads*, for example, Wordsworth uses sly strategies of drama, sound, and rhythm to raise his reader's political and moral consciousness, as well as to challenge the reigning conception of poetry. Blake's imagery often reveals but does not name the causal links that bind the perpetrators of social misery, in his view the Church

Fig. 7 The 'Lyric Muse,' as depicted by the Frontispiece to the *Universal Magazine* of January, 1791. Clasping a lyre and companioned by the winged god Eros, she represents Erato, the classical muse of the love lyric. The dancing ladies in the background may be her sister muses, in a setting that recalls the landscaped grounds of an English country house.

and State, to their human victims. To walk with him through the streets of London is to see

> How the Chimney-sweepers cry
> Every blackning Church appalls,
> And the hapless Soldiers sigh
> Runs in blood down Palace walls.
>   ('London', ll. 9–12)

Such outraged compression of cause and effect may bewilder a reader used to more conventional imagery, because it cannot be read and understood passively; it requires the cooperation of the reader's imagination. 'I give you the end of a golden string', Blake wrote in *Jerusalem*,

> Only wind it into a ball;
> It will lead you in at Heaven's gate,
> Built in Jerusalem's wall.
>   (plate 77)

'Only' help me, he offers, making it sound easy, and my poetry will bring about your salvation. And, he might add, the salvation of England.

As we see here, the line between public and private is not always easy to draw. It is better, perhaps, to recognize that both coexist in the encounter, implicit in all lyrics, between a speaker and the other always postulated by the human voice. It is the rich diversity of such encounters, as well as a newly sensed freedom to explore their implications, formal musical, and thematic, that distinguishes the Romantic lyric. At this point in its history, the lyric form provided a melodious theatre in which the competing claims of self and community, of nature and the supernatural, could be dramatized in their power and complexity.

READINGS

James Fordyce, 'To Spring'

Relenting Spring, who to my earnest prayer
    Hast hearken'd, and thy footsteps hither turn'd,
With those sweet smiles, and that delightful air,
    To chase the wint'ry glooms I lately mourn'd;

Haply to end the elemental strife,
    And brighten universal Nature's face,
To call her various kingdoms into life,
    And lend her all thy loveliness and grace!

With thee, alluring Spring, I'll daily walk,
    Attentive listen to thy tuneful voice,
And while with thee, and God himself, I talk,
    In thy benignity and his rejoice.

In a tradition as old as the medieval *reverdie*, this lyric welcomes the return of spring. It does so, moreover, in a distinctive way, by imagining the season as a person, who listens, moves, and feels. In many poems of the period an opening apostrophe to an abstraction would signal an author's lofty visionary ambitions, but here it provides a graceful way of celebrating the season and the benign cosmic order it exemplifies. The actual sights, sounds, and smells of the spring landscape are only partly concealed by the poet's fiction; if we choose we can read Spring's 'delightful air' as a breeze, and her 'tuneful voice' as birdsong. We are invited to enjoy this fictional encounter, in other words, not to believe in it. What *is* taken seriously in the poem are the moral and philosophical ideas in stanza 2: the goodness of the natural order and the comprehensibility of its benign creator, who appears in the final stanza to join nature and man in earnest conversation. Postponed to the very end is the joyful response of the human heart. The poem presents the arrival of spring as an Enlightenment rationalist might conceive it, an occasion neither for mystery, suspense, nor displays of uncontrolled passion, but for calm gratitude.

The form of the poem reflects this sense of harmonious order. The three stanzas move logically from past to future time, in one long suspended sentence that postpones action and encourages reflection. The regular alternation of weak and strong beats (iambic meter) is seldom disturbed, and the speaker's thought-patterns fit comfortably into their formal compartments, the ten-syllable line and the stanza. The language of the poem makes no attempt to imitate Spring's 'tuneful voice', nor would we expect a poem that prizes 'talk' to take much pleasure in verbal music for its own sake.

The poem was published in 1786, not long before the outbreak of the French Revolution, at a time of deepening cultural and political division in England. Some of those divisions can be detected in the poem. Its author assumes, for example, that we understand Latinate abstractions like 'benignity', know the scientific context of life's 'kingdoms' and 'elemental strife', and enjoy 'poetical' words like 'hearken' and 'hast' and 'thee'—all assumptions that place us within a relatively small and privileged minority. Fordyce himself was an eminent Presbyterian minister, known for his eloquent sermons and a popular book, *Sermons to Young Women*, which Mary Wollstonecraft vigorously attacked, and the Reverend Collins reads to the Bennet girls in Jane Austen's *Pride and Prejudice* (much to their displeasure, as they prefer novels). Fordyce's decorous lyric shows us what a respectable, educated reader might expect and enjoy at the outset of the Romantic period.

William Blake, 'To Spring'

Blake's lyric addresses a 'thou' whose hair is wet with morning dew—an image that invites us not to name it but to imagine seeing and touching its body, as it looks down, like the rising sun, from the heights of the morning sky. As the speaker implores it to 'turn' and look, we realize that Spring has yet to come, and that the poem is both a celebration and a cry of urgent desire, sung not by one speaker but many, from 'our western isle', England. Each stanza restates this desire, and the last reveals Spring as a virile bridegroom about to consummate his marriage to his bride, the 'love-sick land' of England.

We see in this early poem a central theme of Blake's later work, the holiness of the body and its desires. He conceives the coming of Spring as a sexual union, modelled, in part, on the Old Testament Song of Solomon, where frank desire mingles with reverence and oriental ceremony. But desire shapes the poem's form and language as well. Its repetitive structure expresses urgent and unfilled need, not logic. It strictly avoids the abstract language of the reason, in favour of an imagery rich with concrete objects of feeling and sensation. It encourages us to apprehend 'Spring' not as a personification, an artful construction of the poet's imagination, but as an independent existence: this being who walks on 'holy feet' compels the attention and belief we might give to a god. In each respect this little lyric forcefully challenges the central philosophical and moral values of the Enlightenment.

Other formal effects implicate the body by enhancing the poem's verbal music. We may not even notice the absence of traditional rhyme, because the rest of its language is so sonorous. Its first line interweaves vowel and consonant sounds in patterns Blake may have imitated from his lyric predecessor, William Collins; the sequence of 'dewy locks' / 'lookest down' moves the lips and tongue in especially delightful ways. The next line ends with a forceful imperative verb, the first of several in the poem:

> Through the clear windows of the morning: turn
> Thy angel eyes . . .

The transitive power of 'turn' overwhelms the normal pause at the line-end, contributing its syntactical energy to the poem's dynamic representation of the season.

Far from being solitary and introspective, this lyric asserts the vital stake of the English people in the fertilization of their land and the abundance of its future produce. On the satisfaction of desire, it implies, depends the welfare of the state. Written in 1783, it is a radical poem in multiple senses, in that its politics, morality, and poetic form grow out of a single passionate vision. It comes as no surprise that an older Blake would become a dedicated supporter of the French Revolution, which he would interpret in terms of the energy of desire. In this, as in other respects, Blake's poem rewards comparison to Fordyce's complementary vision of spring.

John Keats, 'Ode on a Grecian Urn'

This ode has left readers intrigued and delighted for nearly two centuries. Keats composed it at a time when many British artists were turning to ancient Greece for inspiration and subject-matter. He had seen various vases and funerary urns, among them, perhaps, the delicate bas-reliefs on the Portland Vase, and had composed a sonnet on the sculptures recently brought back from Athens, the Elgin marbles. Keats wrote a number of famous odes, but here the ancient Hellenic form seems especially appropriate to its marble subject-matter, and to a celebration of the mystery and power that gathers about an artwork that persists through time (compare the reading of this poem in the chapter on 'Formalism').

As a poem written about another work of art, a popular lyric type at the time, the ode depicts an act of interpretation (the 'on' of its title means that it is 'prompted by', or 'about', the urn). Reading it for the first time, then, we might do worse than to follow the example of its speaker, who approaches the urn with intelligence and sympathy, questioning its meaning and at the same time exploring it in imagination. Like the urn, the ode is not slow to provoke our questions: the 'unravished bride' of its opening apostrophe, for example, gestures, riddle-like, at a darker meaning that remains obscure, even as the richness of Keats's slow verbal music, with its patterned repetition of sounds, especially long *i* and *s*, encourages us to linger in contemplation.

> Thou still unravish'd bride of quietness,
> Thou foster-child of silence and slow time . . .
>
> (ll. 1–2)

The urn is a 'foster-child' and a 'sylvan historian' (l. 3), each name pointing towards unexplored possibilities. Is this foster-child's original parent the mortal artist who made it, who never enters the ode? What histories, or legends, does it tell? In the fifth line, a critical point in each stanza where the rhyme scheme shifts from a four-line quatrain to a six-line sestet, the speaker begins to ask questions directed at particular scenes depicted on the urn, seeking identities, place-names, and explanations of various human activities—a rejected sexual advance, a mad pursuit, musical instruments, a 'wild ecstasy' (l. 10).

Fig. 8 In the 'Portland Vase,' with its carved figures arranged in discrete scenes, we see the kind of funerary urn Keats may have had in mind. Made around the time of Augustus Caesar, perhaps in Rome or Alexandria, it was lent in 1810 by the Duke of Portland to the British Museum, where Keats probably saw it and where it remains today.

These increasingly excited questions are never answered in the poem, which leaves the urn's mysteries intact. But they do suggest a change in the speaker, whose attitude towards the urn alters throughout the poem. In this sense the ode is a dramatic lyric; its five stanzas trace an arc of imaginative approach and withdrawal, as the speaker is attracted and then distanced by the urn's teasing, exquisite beauty. Keats balances the competing claims of art and life with great subtlety, as in the image of the young lover who can 'never, never' kiss his immortal mistress (l. 17), a lover whom the speaker envies yet consoles, as if he were not marble but warm and breathing flesh. Keats's contemporaries would have appreciated the way such images imply the superiority of poetry to its sister art, sculpture (whose marble pipers do not make music). At the ode's very centre, in the daring repetitions of 'happy' (ll. 21–5), the speaker's feelings reach an aching climax; but as he turns the urn and explores a new scene we sense a cooling of tone. This mountain landscape, with its priestly sacrifice and distant citadel, prompts renewed questioning, and gradually the urn recedes into an aesthetic form, an 'Attic shape' (l. 41), a 'Cold Pastoral' (l. 45). And yet it remains a 'friend to man' (l. 48), which will move on through time, away from the mortal speaker, to future generations of readers, carrying the enigmatic message that ends the poem. That message has provoked spirited debate, in part because of teasing textual inconsistencies, in part because it crystallizes an aestheticism that has itself become highly polarized. All of which seems quite appropriate to this enigmatic lyric and the mysterious object it addresses, as they journey on through time.

Samuel Taylor Coleridge, 'This Lime-Tree Bower My Prison'[7]

This poem exemplifies a new and distinctively Romantic genre, the 'greater' Romantic lyric, which evolved out of the meditative and descriptive poetry of the eighteenth century. One of a series of 'conversation poems', Coleridge wrote it in the summer of 1797, at his cottage in the little village of Nether Stowey, in Somerset. As we learn from the introductory note, it was inspired by a household accident that kept the lamed author from accompanying a group of friends on a walk through the local countryside.

As the poem begins his friends have set out, and the speaker sits alone in his garden beneath a lime tree—a majestic shade tree with broad, heart-shaped leaves. 'Well, they are gone' he begins, musing to himself in an easy, informal blank verse, the metrical form that least advertises its differences from everyday conversation. He speaks in the present tense, referring to a present time, a 'now', that gradually changes, as we read the poem, from late afternoon to night, and at times flashes by within a single line: a flying bird is 'now a dim speck, now vanishing in light' (l. 72). In the foreground of this monologue are the speaker's changing thoughts, sensations, and feelings, or what would be called a century later a 'stream of consciousness', inflected and modulated by the lyrical powers of sound and rhythm.

The plot of the poem springs from the metaphor in its title: to the unhappy speaker this garden bower is a 'prison'. His solitary confinement not only separates him from his friends, whom he 'never more may meet again' (l. 6), but denies him precious and irreplaceable memories,

> Beauties and Feelings, such as would have been
> Most sweet to my remembrance, even when age
> Had dimmed mine eyes to blindness!
>
> (ll. 3–5)

In the reverie that follows he nevertheless escapes this 'prison' and shares the 'beauties' and 'feelings' of this well-known walk. He first follows them down into a 'roaring dell' (l. 10), a strange, uncanny place, not unlike the underworld of classical epic, where, shut out from the light of day, ordinary things assume preternatural aspects. A fixed, horizontal ash tree 'flings' itself across the narrow gorge (l. 13), its sickly leaves moving in the stillness, framing the waterfall beyond, and, 'a most fantastic sight', the row of ferns that

> Still nod and drip beneath the dripping edge
> Of the blue clay-stone.
>
> (ll. 18–20)

Here the first of the poem's three paragraphs comes to an end, and we might pause to observe the changes silently taking place before us. The speaker has forgotten his self-pitying complaints of a moment before, his attention captured by these powerful, specular images. His consciousness has become transparent, unconscious of itself, and the reader seems to see through his eyes, just as he sees through the imagined eyes of his friends. What we may forget is that this 'blue clay-stone', seemingly so substantial, is part of a daydream, a figment of the speaker's imagination. An observant reader may thus look more deeply into the speaker's mind than the speaker himself, to appreciate the healing strategies of a wish-fulfilling imagination, as well as this poet's power to suspend our disbelief.

The ascent to the hilltop in the second section presents sharp and symmetrical contrasts. It lies open to 'the wide wide Heaven' (l. 21), revealing a magnificent prospect of land and sea. The speaker no longer muses to himself, but speaks directly to one of his friends, Charles Lamb, as if he were physically present:

> but thou, methinks, most glad,
> My gentle-hearted Charles!
>
> (ll. 27–8)

At the beginning of a formal ode we would recognize this apostrophe as a literary convention, but here, well into this lengthy poem, its extravagance is justified psychologically as an expression of the speaker's love for his friend. The next lines deepen the connection to Lamb with a private allusion to Milton's *Paradise Lost* (see IX. 444), a poem both friends had shared and admired, and by revealing that Lamb too has struggled and suffered:

> for thou hast pined
> And hunger'd after Nature, many a year,

In the great City pent, winning thy way
   With sad but patient soul, through evil and pain
And strange calamity!

                    (ll. 28–32)

The reader is not told that this 'calamity' was a tragic version of the domestic accident that occasions this poem: in a temporary fit of insanity Lamb's sister had murdered their mother. As if in response to that unspoken horror, however, the speaker's enthusiasm intensifies, and he commands nature itself, from the lowly heath-flowers to the ocean and the 'glorious Sun', to bestow 'deep joy' upon his friend (ll. 32–8). This second part ends with a grand metaphysical surmise, that in this sublime landscape Lamb sees not the 'bodily' material world but a vision of God himself (ll. 40–4). 'You remember, I am a Berkleian?', Coleridge commented in a letter, referring to the English philosopher who famously denied the existence of matter (and after whom he named his first son).

A lesser poem might have ended here, at a climax of intimate affection and cosmic speculation, where the imaginative reconstruction of the speaker's loving community seems complete. But this reconstruction itself now becomes the object of the speaker's conscious attention, as he reflects upon the significance of the experience dramatized in the poem—an intimate history that the reader shares. The lyric genre here becomes truly philosophical, as it dramatizes a mind examining itself, reasoning about its own feelings and faculties, and arriving at rational and general truth. A sudden perception of his own happiness rouses the speaker from his reverie:

            A delight
Comes sudden on my heart, and I am glad
As I myself were there!

                 (ll. 44–6)

He looks about him, realizing that this humble bower, no longer a 'prison', offers the beauty and delight of the scenes he had imagined. Sitting in near darkness, he recalls how the sun touched the leaves of the lime tree:

          Pale beneath the blaze
Hung the transparent foliage; and I watch'd
Some broad and sunny leaf, and lov'd to see
The shadow of the leaf and stem above
Dappling its sunshine!

                (ll. 48–52)

Here, in the poem's third descriptive passage, it becomes apparent that the speaker's vision of the natural world has been transfigured. These images, now the product of immediate sense-perception, confirm his emergence from subjective reverie, and demonstrate a new capacity to cherish the ordinary world before him. His 'community' now includes the natural world as well as his absent friends; he shares the darkening garden with a solitary 'humble' bee, whose name now describes him as well. At this point the experience the poem has dramatized is distilled by the generalizing reason into a principle that will guide future action:

> Henceforth I shall know
> That Nature ne'er deserts the wise and pure . . .
> (ll. 60–1)

The achievement of this poem is measured by the difference between this abstract moral and the drama of its emergence from a living consciousness. It comes close to realizing the theoretical ideal Coleridge would propose twenty years later, of a poetry that 'brings the whole soul of man into activity'.

In the final lines the speaker reaches out to Lamb once more, using a common bird, a rook, as a visual talisman of the affection that links them and nature: both watch as it flies into the disc of the setting sun, their sightlines forming a vast isosceles triangle of love. The image binds the poem's two complementary actions, the recentring of the self and the restoration of a loving community, into one.

FURTHER READING

Abrams, M. H., 'Structure and Style in the Greater Romantic Lyric', in *The Correspondent Breeze: Essays on English Romanticism* (New York: W. W. Norton, 1984), pp. 76–108. This classic article defined the terms of modern critical discussion.

Curran, Stuart, *Poetic Form and British Romanticism* (Oxford: Oxford University Press, 1986). A detailed and incisive history of Romantic genres, including various kinds of lyric and the particular poems that comprise them.

Hollander, John, *Vision and Resonance*, 2nd edn. (New Haven: Yale University Press, 1975). A modern poet's eloquent discussion of the music of verse; see especially 'The Poem in the Ear', pp. 1–43, and 'Romantic Verse Form and the Metrical Contract', pp. 187–211.

—— *Rhyme's Reason*, 2nd edn. (New Haven: Yale University Press, 1989). A delightful introduction to the forms of English verse.

Hosek, Chaviva, and Parker, Patricia (eds.) *Lyric Poetry: Beyond New Criticism* (Ithaca, NY: Cornell University Press, 1985). The articles in Part III exemplify the diversity of modern critical approaches, and offer stimulating discussions of particular poems.

Maclean, Norman, 'From Action to Image: Theories of the Lyric in the 18th Century', in R. S. Crane (ed.), *Critics and Criticism* (Chicago: University of Chicago Press, 1952), pp. 408–60. Another scholarly classic, this article places the Romantic lyric, and especially the ode, in historical context.

Magnuson, Paul, *Coleridge and Wordsworth: A Lyrical Dialogue* (Princeton: Princeton University Press, 1988). This book examines the exchange of lyrics between two great poets, with sensitive readings of particular poems, including the 'conversation poems'.

Stillinger, Jack, 'Imagination and Reality in the Odes', and 'Who Says What to Whom at the End of *Ode on a Grecian Urn*', in *'The Hoodwinking of Madeline' and Other Essays on Keats's Poems* (Urbana, Ill.: University of Illinois Press, 1971), pp. 99–119, 167–73. The first of these articles illuminates a central theme in Keats's odes, and the second provides the best analysis yet of the hermeneutic problems raised by the Grecian Urn's famous motto.

Vendler, Helen, *The Odes of John Keats* (Cambridge, Mass.: Harvard University Press, 1983). Students interested in the structure and style of Keats's odes will be rewarded by these sensitive, probing, intertextual readings.

Wolfson, Susan J., *Formal Charges: The Shaping of Poetry in British Romanticism* (Stanford, Calif.: Stanford University Press, 1997). This book explores the power and craft of formal devices in lyrics by Blake, Coleridge, Keats, and Shelley.

—— 'Blake's Language in Poetic Form', in Morris Eaves (ed.), *The Cambridge Companion to Blake* (Cambridge: Cambridge University Press, 2003), pp. 63–84. This informative essay examines Blake's use of English verse forms, especially in the poetry of the 1790s.

NOTES

1. *Prose Works of William Wordsworth*, ed. W. J. B. Owen (Oxford: Clarendon Press, 1974), iii. 27, i. 126.
2. *Encyclopaedia Britannica*, 11th edn. (Cambridge: Cambridge University Press, 1911), xvii. 181.
3. *Prose Works*, iii. 29.
4. *Shelley's Poetry and Prose*, ed. Donald H. Reiman and Sharon B. Powers (New York: W. W. Norton, 1977), p. 486.
5. John Aikin, *Essays on Song-Writing*, 2nd edn. (London: Joseph Johnson, 1774), p. 20.
6. *Prose Works*, i. 141.
7. Published in *Sibylline Leaves: A Collection of Poems* (London: Rest Fenner, 1817), pp. 189–93.

22 | Epic

Lynda Pratt

The Romanticism with which we are now most familiar is that represented in numerous excellent, easily available anthologies. It is inevitably a selective Romanticism, one still shaped (if no longer entirely owned) by the six canonical male poets and dominated by shorter poetic forms, for example, the ode, the lyric, and the sonnet. With a mere handful of notable exceptions, such as William Wordsworth's *Prelude*, Romantic long poems—or at least long poems in their entirety—do not sit easily in this format. It is therefore not surprising that it is easy to overlook the contributions made by longer poetic forms, in particular the epic, to Romantic-period culture. The following quotations give some indication of what we might be missing:

I should not think of devoting less than 20 years to an Epic Poem. Ten to collect materials and warm my mind with universal science . . . the next five to the composition of the poem—and the five last to the correction of it. (S. T. Coleridge, letter to Joseph Cottle, early April 1797)

> The morning dawned, Urizen rose, and in his hand the flail
> Sounds on the floor heard terrible by all beneath the heavens;
> Dismal loud redounding, the nether floor shakes with the sound,
> And all the nations were threshed out, and the stars threshed from their husks.
> (William Blake, *The Four Zoas*, Night the Ninth, ll. 650–3)

> Most epic poets plunge *in media res* . . .
> That is the usual method, but not mine . . .
> (Byron, *Don Juan*, Canto I, ll. 41–2)

Coleridge, Blake, and Byron all draw attention to the interest of Romantic-period writers and readers in the epic. The very different ways in which they approach the genre—Coleridge's emphasis on the long, serious preparation needed to write one, Blake's use of elliptical personal mythology, and Byron's playful dismissal of epic convention—remind us of how diverse and various their engagement with it was. This diversity, which is mirrored in the works of numerous other writers, suggests that it might be more accurate to speak of 'Romantic epics' rather than 'Romantic epic'. They even open up the possibility that it might be best to approach the term 'epic' with caution or avoid it completely.

What is an epic?

In our own culture the word 'epic' is frequently used in a non-literary context, as shorthand for anything that is perceived as being extremely long. A long journey through hostile or unfamiliar terrain may be referred to as an 'epic journey' or a film lasting over two or so hours as an 'epic film'. A good recent example of the latter is Peter Jackson's *Lord of the Rings* film trilogy, which lasts for some nine hours in total and has consistently been described as 'epic'. The appropriation of 'epic' for non-literary forms indicates the word's flexibility. It also gestures towards our own culture's ambivalence: 'epic' is something we are both familiar and unfamiliar with. In a culture of sound-bites, anything 'long' is distinctive and perhaps unsettling enough to attract comment.

According to the *OED* an 'epic' is 'a long poem narrating the adventures or deeds of one or more heroic or legendary figures'. Literary epics are frequently divided into three types. Primary epic: poems derived from an ancient oral tradition, for example, *Beowulf*, Homer's *Iliad* and *Odyssey*. Secondary epic: an epic written down and a conscious imitation of the primary epic, for example, Virgil's *Aeneid*. Tertiary epic: epics which exist in a culture where the genre has achieved a high status and become part of literary tradition and which often have a complex relationship to the primary and secondary models, for example, John Milton's *Paradise Lost* (1667).

What might we look for in a traditional epic? In his study of *Romantic and Victorian Long Poems*, Adam Roberts has provided a helpful summary of the features of what he calls the standard or paradigmatic epic. It should be divided into either 'twelve or twenty-four books' and 'written in the same metre and style throughout', preferably in a 'high' style. It should start '*in media res*' ('in the middle of things'). It should tell a continuous narrative of the 'adventures of a heroic figure', these should include 'war . . . or lengthy travels . . . or both'. It should have 'supernatural machinery'; it should contain lists; it should include a visit to the underworld; and it should begin with an address to the muse. Other features such as epic similes, recognition scenes, and an emphasis upon 'home' and a return 'home' are optional. These are features that writers and readers of the Romantic period would have recognized. Yet they would also have argued over them, perhaps insisting that optional features such as epic machinery (the use of supernatural beings to intervene in the actions) were actually not so optional after all; or claiming that only certain subjects (for example, episodes from the Bible) were suitable. They were, of course, features that Romantic writers were able to ignore or subvert at will.

Whilst labelling and placing poems in generic categories can have its uses, it is important to remember that it can raise further problems. Many of the longer poems written and published during the Romantic period resist categorization, not least because their authors tended to adopt a complex, ambivalent attitude to the genres they engaged with (see the chapter 'Romantic Forms: An Introduction' for more on hybrid genres). Romantic long poems are marked by generic indeterminacy and tend to slip between categories, but perhaps this is what makes them Romantic poems rather than merely Romantic epics.

A short history of epic

Critics have pointed out that the early eighteenth century produced very few epics, or at least few epics that survived the years following their immediate publication. For example, Richard Blackmore's *Alfred: an Epick Poem in Twelve Books* (1723) and Richard Glover's *Leonidas* (1737) and *The Atheniad* (1788). This does not mean that other writers showed no interest in the genre, rather that they thought about writing, planned, and even began epics, but did not complete them. For example, from the 1670s to the 1690s John Dryden talked about publishing a poem on the Black Prince and King Arthur but never did so. The youthful Alexander Pope wrote 4,000 lines of an epic on Alcander, Prince of Rhodes, which he then mostly destroyed on the instructions of a friend. In later life he returned to the genre, planning and writing the opening lines of a poem on Brutus, the mythological founder of Britain. His principal effort at epic was his translation of Homer.

Various reasons have been cited as causes of this decline of epic in the eighteenth century. It has been argued that *Paradise Lost* had a debilitating impact on the next couple of generations of poets, making them feel that there was nothing left to be achieved with the genre and that any poem they produced would inevitably compare poorly with Milton's. Some have argued that Enlightenment thought and technological progress made the epic an outmoded form. It was not, as the writer Horace Walpole observed, 'suited to an improved and polished state of things' and was therefore out of place in a more advanced society such as existed in eighteenth-century Britain. Another line of argument finds significance in the rise of mock or burlesque epics such as Dryden's *MacFlecknoe* (1682) and Pope's *The Rape of the Lock* (1712) and *Dunciad* (1726, 1743). The only way for writers of the period to engage with epic was through parody.

Although relatively few epics were published in the eighteenth century, it is important to remember that it did not lose its status as one of the pre-eminent genres and that any decline in its popularity and prevalence was temporary. Moreover, as the mock-epic indicates, poets could and did assume that their readers were familiar with the tropes and conventions of the epic and could respond accordingly to them. With James Macpherson's publication of the Ossianic epics *Fingal, an Ancient Epic Poem, in Six Books* (1762) and *Temora* (1763), and the resulting controversy over their authenticity, the epic was on the rise again.

Epic revival

The latter half of the eighteenth century saw a massive revival of interest in the epic. William Hayley in his *An Essay on Epic Poetry* (1782) marked a change in the critical climate, condemning the rules which he felt actively discouraged young poets from trying their hand at epic and hoping that his poem would act as a catalyst:

> Haply, inspiriting poetic youth,
> Our verse may prove this animating truth,
> That Poesy's sublime, neglected field
> May still new laurels to Ambition yield;
> Her Epic trumpet, in a modern hand,
> Still make the spirit glow, the heart expand.
> Be such our doctrine! Our enlivening aim
> The Muse's honor, and our Country's fame![1]

The *Essay* provides an encapsulated history of the epic, ranging from Homer to more recent efforts. It also offered ambitious young British writers not just encouragement but potential materials to work with. With its blank verse complemented by extensive notes, the *Essay* is in fact an early example of what would become an important genre in the Romantic period—the annotated poem. Hayley's notes are packed with biographies of epic poets and samples of epic poems, most notably drawn from non-British contexts. For instance, he devotes several pages to a detailed analysis of *La Araucana*, an epic poem on the Spanish conquest of the Arauco region of Chile by Alonzo de Ercilla. In addition, the notes suggested possible themes for future epics:

The Indian mythology . . . is finely calculated to answer the purpose of any poetical genius who may wish to introduce new machinery into the serious Epic Poem . . . Our great Historian of the Roman empire has intimated, in a note to the first volume of his immortal work, that 'the wonderful expedition of Odin, which deduces the enmity of the Goths and Romans from so memorable a cause, might supply the noble ground-work of an Epic poem.' The idea is certainly both just and splendid.[2]

In a period which celebrated Camoens's *The Lusiad* as the epic poem of commerce and which saw the growth of Britain's imperial ambitions and possessions, Hayley opens up both extra-British epic achievements and indeed extra-European areas of epic potential. His *Essay* seems to have struck a nerve.

The revival of interest in the epic gathered pace in the 1790s and continued through the 1800s, 1810s, and 1820s. This took several forms. For example, the publication of William Cowper's translations of Homer's *Iliad* and *Odyssey* (1791) and of Hayley's *Life of Milton* (1796) was evidence of a new preoccupation with epics and their authors. The period also saw the recovery of earlier epics such as *Beowulf* and the translation of works from other languages, such as the Spanish *Poema del Cid*.[3] Taking Hayley's advice, poets were now producing epics on an almost unprecedented scale—and interest was not restricted to literary circles. Napoleon Bonaparte confessed that his well-thumbed copy of Ossian accompanied him on campaign.

The epic's renewed popularity attracted widespread comment. For example, the anonymous author of an appraisal of John Ogilvie's *Britannia: a National Epic Poem. In Twenty Books* (1801) observed that:

Posterity will consider it a singular phaenomenon, that at so late a period as the beginning of the nineteenth century, the number of candidates for epic fame should exceed, as is the case at present, those of the early and middle ages of the world.[4]

The reviewer of Hannah Cowley's *The Siege of Acre* (1801) assured readers that 'no one surely will venture to say, that the present period is not sufficiently productive in Epic Poetry', while the bemused reviewer of Henry James Pye's *Alfred, an Epic Poem in Six Books* (1801) noted that 'the Public have lately been presented with a sort of Series of Epic poems'.[5] By the turn of the century the outpouring of epics was sufficient for the *Poetical Register* to set aside a separate section for reviews of 'Epic and Historical Poems' and for one poet, himself the author of more than one epic, to suggest the period was suffering from 'epomania'.[6]

Why was the epic revived? Was it merely the case of ambitious poets taking Hayley's advice and seeking to capitalize on a high-status but recently neglected genre? Or did other factors contribute? The 1790s was, after all, a decade of political and social revolution and not just a period marked by a change in literary fashion. It was a decade when conflict abroad (Britain was at war with revolutionary France from February 1793) was accompanied by trouble at home (for example, the government's suppression of British radical movements in 1792–3 and the naval mutinies at the Nore and Spithead in 1797). Could these events have impacted on the epic? Was the revival of interest in the genre galvanized by a need to define both self and nation at a time of crisis—and did this identity crisis continue throughout what is traditionally thought of as the Romantic period, shaping the works of writers as diverse as Blake, Wordsworth, Shelley, Byron, and Keats?

There is no doubt that Britain in the late eighteenth and early nineteenth centuries was a country increasingly aware of what the contemporary essayist and genre theorist Nathan Drake defined as the 'national advantages . . . to be derived from perpetuating the memory of any remarkable event, or deed'.[7] However, 'national advantages' took different and frequently contradictory forms. These ranged from the alternative versions of the political nation proffered by writers such as Burke and Paine, to opposing official and radical celebrations of victories such as that at Cape St Vincent in 1797. The government established a committee to oversee the erection of monuments to recent national heroes, and there was a plan to convert St Paul's Cathedral into a kind of national shrine—a British version of the French Pantheon. Whilst it was believed that the national character could be restated through the process of seeing, particularly through viewing state monuments to the heroic dead, it was also realized that *reading* was an effective way of affirming national identity. Acknowledged by most writers as the highest of literary forms, the epic—in particular the epic about the nation—offered contemporary poets a highly attractive and suitable means of achieving a desirable and also much-needed national end.

The epic, moreover, was suited to the demands of the period in another and perhaps less obvious way. As the reactions of writers, reviewers, and readers of the numerous epics produced in the Romantic period illustrate, in spite, or possibly as a result of, its high status and considerable lineage, the epic was also an essentially unstable form. Reiterating earlier debates, Romantic producers and consumers of the genre were unable to agree on what an epic was, on what subject-matter was most suitable for it, or on the appropriateness or inappropriateness of epic machinery. Such lack of unanimity is indicative of the complex state and allegiances of literary and political cultures in the Romantic period. Both national identity and the epic were beset by a fundamental instability. In the case of the national epics produced in this period, generic/formal instability echoes the frequently inchoate, contested nature of what the national poem was being asked to inscribe. As Hugh Cunningham has suggested in relation to late eighteenth- and early nineteenth-century writings on patriotism, the 'outpourings [of epics] from the presses are not so much a celebration of national unity as an exercise in persuasion'.[8] The epic therefore is the ideal form to encapsulate the divided nation. Moreover, in terms of writing epics about the nation, this double instability is both the poet's greatest asset and his or her greatest challenge.

The profusion of new epics which confronted readers in the period therefore implied neither certainty about how the nation should be defined nor agreement about the kind of poetry best suited to inscribe so-called national values. What they did indicate was that literary culture in late eighteenth- and early nineteenth-century Britain was a battlefield and that nowhere was the conflict fiercer, or potentially of greater significance, than in the field of epic.

Diversity

Given the inability of writers to agree on what constituted an epic and the sheer numbers of poems produced in the period, it is not surprising that these covered a wide variety of subjects. As Stuart Curran has shown, booksellers' shelves groaned under the weight of epics on stories from the Old and New Testaments (e.g. James Ogden's *Emmanuel; or, Paradise Regained* (1797) and James Montgomery's *The World Before the Flood* (1812)); the founding of Britain (e.g. John Ogilvie's *Britannia* (1801)); the Anglo-Saxons (e.g. Henry Hart Milman's *Samor, Lord of the Bright City* (1818) and John Fitzgerald Pennie's *Rogvald* (1823)); and events from recent history (e.g. James Ogden's *The Revolution* (1790) and Thomas Northmore's *Washington, or Liberty Restored* (1809)). There were epics which supported the established order of things (e.g. Henry James Pye's *Alfred* (1801)) and those which criticized the status quo (e.g. Percy Shelley's

Queen Mab (1813) and William Blake's *Jerusalem* (1804–20)). This tremendous diversity of subject was mirrored by variety in style. Not all Romantic epics were written in the same way. Some, for example, employed epic tropes and the Latinate diction and syntax thought by many critics to be suitably elevated; others favoured simpler modes of expression. For example, Joseph Cottle's *Alfred* (1800) avoided classical allusions and 'adopted a studious simplicity of phrase' that verged on the prosaic. As he explained to his readers: 'In the following Poem, the Reader will find neither classical or scientific embellishments, neither learned references, nor metaphysical illustrations of abstract sentiments'.[9]

Contemporary disagreements are central to any understanding of epic during the Romantic period. Moreover, the fact that the epic attracted the attention of so many writers of different persuasions offers an important link between the familiar and the less well known. Epic ambitions connect the high Romanticism of writers such as Blake, Shelley, and Wordsworth with hitherto marginal figures such as Ann Yearsley, John Thelwall, and Robert Southey.

Gender

Contemporary reviewers expressed concern about the 'female pen', particularly when it was set loose on the epic.[10] Yet women writers were not deterred, and notable examples of epic poems published by them in the period include Ann Yearsley's 'Brutus, A Fragment' (1796), Mary Linwood's *The Anglo-Cambrian* (1818), Eleanor Ann Porden's *Coeur de Lion; or the Third Crusade* (1822), and Helen Maria Williams' 'brief' epic *Peru* (1784).[11]

Yearsley's poem provides an interesting illustration of how a controversial female writer took on the challenges posed by the epic. An example of the period's interest in labouring-class genius, Yearsley's first publication, *Poems on Several Occasions*, had appeared in 1785. Her career was not halted by a spectacularly public quarrel with her patron, the formidable Hannah More. Indeed, she went on to publish further volumes of poetry, a novel *The Royal Captives* (1795), and a play entitled *Earl Goodwin* (1791). Her final collection of miscellaneous poems, *The Rural Lyre*, appeared in 1796. It opened with 'Brutus, a Fragment', a work which she explained in a brief prefatory 'Argument':

The Author offers this humble specimen as a spark, from whence she wishes a body of fire may arise in the imagination of some more able Poet. The Aeneid is not so eventful, nor so interesting, but that an Epic Poem from the History of England might vie with it. If the Author may presume to offer an opinion, her opinion will be, that some of the greatest geniuses of this island neglect the choice of subjects best suited to their learning and their natural powers.[12]

The 'Argument' is testimony to Yearsley's ambition and to her confidence in theorizing and pronouncing on contemporary culture. Building on the foundations of Hayley's

Essay, she sets herself up as a national poet, muse, and cultural critic. The fragment of epic Yearsley published in *The Rural Lyre* reveals her interest in what makes up national identity, the constituents of 'Britishness'. In legend Brutus is a great-grandson of the Trojan prince Aeneas (hero of Virgil's epic *The Aeneid*). He comes to England, bringing with him a band of Trojan followers, founds the city of Troynovant (London), and is the first in a line of British kings that includes Cymbeline, Vortigern, and Arthur. Yearsley's short epic manages to squeeze in all these elements of the Brutus myth, suggesting that it is not really a fragment at all. It pictures the orderly and successful nation Brutus achieved through following the advice of 'Liberty', responding to the genius loci of Britain, and establishing a compact with the native inhabitants of his new country. Brutus does not conquer or enslave the Britons—he works with them. In so doing, he establishes a relationship between monarch and subject which is integral to the nation's character and to its commercial and political success. Brutus (Trojan prince married to a Trojan wife, Hermia) is the ancestor of George III (member of the German house of Hanover, despite his pride in being 'Briton born', and married to the German princess, Charlotte of Mecklenberg Strelitz). Yearsley's epic therefore offers a picture of a nation united and flourishing under the auspices of a benevolent constitutional monarchy.

Politics

Yearsley's poem reveals how the epic provided poets with a means of commentating on contemporary politics, although not all writers of the period were as reassuring about the condition of Britain. For example, in 1801 the radical lecturer John Thelwall published a fragmentary epic poem based on an incident from David Hume's *History of Great Britain* (1754–62). 'The Hope of Albion, or Edwin of Northumbria' is about the Anglo-Saxon prince who 'distinguished himself, both by his influence over the other kingdoms, and by the strict execution of justice in his own dominions'. Thelwall claimed that his poem would celebrate Edwin's 'establishment of English liberty' and would portray how:

> [Edwin] from the strife
> Of feuds and deadly factions, haply wrought
> A nation's bliss: whence union, wisdom, power,
> Spread thro' the Seven-fold isle [Britain]; and cheering lights
> Of Holy Truth—and Liberty, and Laws.[13]

Yet the fragment of the poem Thelwall published in his volume *Poems chiefly written in Retirement* presents a much less comforting vision of the nation. Instead it concentrates on Edwin as the victim of a degenerate society which persecutes him. Exiled since infancy from his rightful position as king of Northumbria, Edwin is pursued by the devilish agents of his hostile sister and brother-in-law, who have usurped his throne and wish to have him murdered. Like the hero of William Godwin's novel *Caleb Williams* (1794), Edwin flees in order to save his life. The portrayal of Edwin gains greater resonance from the literary context in which it appeared. *Poems* opened with a 'Memoir' detailing Thelwall's experience as a radical in the 1790s: his hounding by the government and its agents, and the hostility he encountered when he retired from public life and tried to set up as a farmer in Wales. Read in tandem, the 'Memoir' and the epic connect Edwin, the original prototype for the movement for freedom, with his modern double, John Thelwall. Edwin the patriot and national hero had opposed the illicit rulers of Northumbria; now John Thelwall offers an alternative to the bogus, warmongering patriotism promoted by the British government and its supporters. Similarly, the poem's use of Miltonic allusion constructs a line of literary descent in which the mantle of national poet is transferred from the republican author of *Paradise Lost* to his modern heir, Thelwall.

Thelwall never completed 'The Hope of Albion'. Personal pressures as well as the outpouring of other epics may have discouraged him. As he noted in *Poems* (1801), his cherished plan to write an epic for the good of his country had been pre-empted by others and the press was 'teeming, and, perhaps, the public already satiated with NATIONAL HEROICS'. However, he did not abandon his belief that 'The Hope of Albion' was a work 'in which ... the glory of his Country is not altogether unconcerned'.[14] Unable to continue as a political lecturer, Thelwall became instead a teacher of elocution, travelling the country giving public talks on the importance of correct speaking and accurate use of language. His published works on elocution linked language with national identity. Political opponents such as the *Edinburgh Review* were attacked for their 'deplorable want of acquaintance with the meaning of English words' and a 'lie' was renamed a 'Jeff' as testimony to the truthfulness of the periodical's editor, Francis Jeffrey. He often used his own writings to provide illustrations of key points and 'The Hope of Albion' was put to good use. It became a kind of elocutionary epic, and sections from it were published alongside extracts from *Paradise Lost* as examples of different types of rhetoric and of language used to good patriotic effect.

The fact that the republican and atheistic Thelwall chose as his subject a princely hero responsible for converting his people to Christianity, indicates some of the problems facing would-be Romantic writers of epic. Their choice of subject-matter was not always wholly compatible with their political commitments. For example, how was a pacifist writer such as the poet-publisher Joseph Cottle going to tackle the link between epics and warfare? His first epic, *Alfred*, dealt with the Anglo-Saxon king's defeat of the Danish invaders at the battle of Edington in AD 878. However, Cottle was keen not to endorse militarism and made it clear that anyone who claimed that battles in epic had a good moral tendency was wrong. The fights traditionally found in epic literature were clichéd, and they had a pernicious effect on their readers. Indeed, Cottle went further, pointing out that too many epics had glorified men who were unworthy of the name of hero:

The generality of persons almost imperceptibly admire strength and heroism, without nicely examining the justice of that cause which calls them into action, and which alone renders such qualities estimable . . . many *wars* have been undertaken, and much blood may have flown, from the glowing and unqualified commendation, which writers have sometimes heaped on men, who possessed prowess and intrepidity, but who were strangers to the virtues, which, alone, could rightly direct those powerful engines.[15]

Cottle's revisionism was shared by many of his contemporaries.

Ambivalence

As we have already seen, the Romantic epic was characterized by its instability—by the refusal of Romantic-period writers to agree what an epic was or what it should be about. This instability affected even those writers who had definite, and frequently revisionist, ideas about what an epic should or should not be. This is very evident in the case of one of the most prolific writers of Romantic-period epic, Robert Southey. Between 1796 and 1813 Southey published five long poems. Three of these, *Joan of Arc* (1796), *Madoc* (1805), and *Roderick, the Last of the Goths* (1813) could loosely be described as epics. The remaining two, *Thalaba, the Destroyer* (1801) and *The Curse of Kehama* (1810), are of epic length but could be described as oriental romances. A lover of public controversy, Southey was more than willing to stake a claim for his poems. *Madoc* rejected the 'degraded title of epic', whilst *Joan* openly violated the decorum of the national poem by celebrating a labouring-class, French heroine at a time when England was at war with revolutionary France. He also claimed that they were highly influential, noting that *Joan* had single-handedly revived 'the epomania that Boileau cured the French of 120 years ago'. In general, Southey was critical of other practitioners of the genre, and so keen to point out the follies of bad epics that he devoted some fifty-seven pages of the second edition of *Joan*, published in 1798, to a satirical analysis of *La Pucelle*, an epic on the Maid of Orleans by the French writer Jean Chapelain. At one point he considered publishing a volume devoted to the 'Analysis of Obscure Epic Poems' in which he would display his own talents: 'perhaps sometimes when I see a fine subject massacred [by another writer]', Southey mused, 'I may throw off a passage of my own to show what could have been made of it.'[16]

Southey was often more successful at articulating what his own epics were not doing—what they were reacting against—than he was at explaining what their philosophy was. This emerges most clearly in *Madoc*, published in 1805, though begun as early as *c*.1789. The Welsh prince Madoc is a figure from legend, younger son of Owen Gwynedd, a real-life ruler of North Wales in the twelfth century. He was reputed to have left his homeland and sailed to the Americas, where he founded a colony. The legend was potent enough for some of Southey's contemporaries to finance searches for Madoc's descendants, the so-called 'Welsh-Indians' of popular mythology. For

Southey it provided the perfect subject for a revisionist poem that rejected the 'degraded title of epic'. Southey's hero leaves his war-torn homeland and eventually lands in North America. Although he establishes good relations with a tribe of native Indians, his attempts to establish a permanent settlement are thwarted by the rulers of the country, the ferocious Aztecas, whom Madoc is forced to fight and defeat. The remnants of Aztecan civilization are destroyed by a volcanic eruption and the Azteca king, Yuhidthiton, decides to move elsewhere, leaving Madoc behind as sole ruler of the country. In the version of 1805, *Madoc* is an epic of colonization and conversion, the Aztecas who remain behind are converted to Christianity.

Yet although *Madoc* is an interesting and important example of Romantic-period narratives of imperial expansion, it is also a poem which left contemporary readers bemused. Here, for example, is John Ferriar, reviewing *Madoc* in the *Monthly Review*:

It has fallen to the lot of this writer to puzzle our critical discernment more than once. In the *Annual Anthology*, we had reason to complain that it was difficult to distinguish his jocular from his serious poetry; and sometimes indeed to know his poetry from prose. He has now contrived to manufacture a large quarto, which he has styled a poem, but of what description it is no easy matter to decide . . . The poem of *Madoc* is not didactic, nor elegiac, nor classical, in any respect. Neither is it *Macphersonic*, nor *Klopstockian*, nor *Darwinian*,—we beg pardon, we mean *Brookian*. To conclude, according to a phrase of the last century, which was applied to ladies of ambiguous character, *it is what it is*.[17]

According to Ferriar, Southey's poem invites comparison with others, be they classical or near contemporary, but it also almost defies description. It is an epic, which rejects the 'degraded' title of the genre, a literary prostitute that is prepared to be promiscuous in its generic affiliations but that in the end can be defined only against itself. This ambiguity emerges very clearly in its handling of the tropes of the foundation epic.

Madoc has clear links with the foundation epic. Like Virgil's *Aeneid*, it is a poem about the founding of a new society. Yet there is a crucial difference. Virgil's poem connects Aeneas' society with that of Augustan Rome. Southey's revisionist epic is about a society with no direct lineal descendants, as all the expeditions to find the 'Welsh-Indians' had failed. Moreover, *Madoc* is a poem with a distinct reluctance to think about sex. Its hero displays no 'amorous propensities either towards the ruddy damsels of Wales, or the olive princesses of America' and the one example of the interracial marriages (between Madoc's sister Goervyl and the Azteca warrior Malinal) necessary to produce 'Welsh-Indians' is deferred. Indeed, the strongest relationships in the poem are those between men. It is, therefore, a strangely revisionist foundation epic in which nothing lasting is founded and in which male friendship takes the place of the breeding of future citizens. It is a poem in which 'So did not Madoc' takes on a great significance and in which Southey is more successful in describing what he is both repelled and fascinated by (be it in European or Aztecan society) than he is in inscribing the values he supports.

The counter-factual literary history of the great, unwritten Romantic-period epics is a substantial and significant one: inability to write an epic was as important a feature of

Romantic-period culture as the numerous epics that in fact rolled off the presses. In some cases the epics planned by Romantic-period writers went no further than entries in commonplace books or references in letters, for example Coleridge's suggested epic on the destruction of Jerusalem, and his projected collaboration with Wordsworth on 'The Brook'. In the opening book of his verse autobiography *The Prelude* Wordsworth listed the historical/mythological themes he had considered but rejected for his great poem, indicating that he shared Southey's ability to cast the new epic in terms of what it was not.

Wordsworth's epic-writing ambitions, his determination to be a new Milton, manifested themselves in public and private forms. To his Romantic readers he was, from 1814, known as the author of *The Excursion*. Consisting of nine books, some 8,916 lines of blank verse, the poem offers a series of meditations on man and society, human suffering and endurance. Its importance was recognized by contemporary critics such as Francis Jeffrey, and by contemporary poets such as Shelley, Byron, and Keats, who all felt the need to engage with it. The poem opened with a lengthy preface in prose and verse which offered a dramatic recasting of Wordsworth's own oeuvre and of his relationship to literary history. It announced that not only was the poem the middle section of a far larger work, 'The Recluse', but also that all of his previous publications were subordinate to his epic-scale meditation on 'man, nature and human life'. In addition, Wordsworth's determination to reclaim and reformulate the epic for a new age was made apparent in his appropriation of Milton. Whereas in his fragmentary epic *Milton*, William Blake subsumed the author of *Paradise Lost* into his own person, Wordsworth took the more conventional path of invoking Milton's muse, Urania, or an even greater one if she proved to be available.

Wordsworth's contribution to the Romantic epic revival also emerged in a poem not available to the majority of his Romantic-period readers, and only named and published after his death in 1850. *The Prelude* initially started life as a series of autobiographical blank verse meditations, written ostensibly because of Wordsworth's inability to work on 'The Recluse', the great poem planned by himself and Coleridge. It provides an extended analysis of Wordsworth's development as a poet and explores his suitability to write the great poem of the age. As Stuart Curran has argued, *The Prelude* is an example of the hybrid nature of many Romantic-period engagements with genre. Whilst it contains some of the features of conventional epic, it also offers a dramatic recasting of the genre. It replaces the heroic warriors and nation builders found in Homer and Virgil with the figure of the poet himself, and substitutes the growth of the poet's mind for the history of a nation. In *The Prelude* epic is transformed into autobiography, and autobiography—that most characteristic of Romantic forms—acquires the scale and status of epic.

The adaptability of epic—its ability to be different things to different poets—is also demonstrated in the work of one of Wordsworth's greatest critics, Byron. From his early satire *English Bards and Scotch Reviewers* (1809) to *Don Juan* (1819–24) Byron's attitude to epic was equivocal and ironic. *Don Juan* runs to some 16,064 lines but is incomplete and breaks off in Canto XVII. Digressive and comic in the manner of Sterne's novel *Tristram Shandy, Don Juan* also demonstrates the vigour of Byron's engagement with contemporary culture. He originally planned to open the poem with a Dedication attacking the poetry and politics of the Lake School, ridiculing Coleridgean metaphysics and the pretensions of Southey and Wordsworth. In a sub-version of Southey's delight in generic revisionism, the Poet Laureate is dismissed by Byron as an 'epic renegade'. The phrase is appropriate and deeply ambiguous. Southey, author of three epics at least two of which were self-consciously revisionist, is a 'renegade' to the tradition of epic writing. However, as Poet Laureate, reviewer for the Tory *Quarterly*, and a member of the Lake School, his apostasy from his early radical principles has also made him a 'renegade' on a truly epic scale. Byron moreover had nothing good to say about the epic-writing pretensions of another Lake poet, Wordsworth. He dismissed the *Excursion* as overlong and incomprehensible, a contemporary addition to the linguistic confusion and nonsense found in the biblical Tower of Babel. His fascination with the epic mistakes of his contemporaries continues in Canto I of *Don Juan*. Byron uses the opening section of his poem to compare his own work with the generic expectations raised by the epic, and the poem that follows demonstrates the complexity of his engagement with the genre. It contains self-consciously epic features (such as the set-piece Siege of Ismael), and consistently questions the nature of epic and the subject-matter suitable for a heroic poem (see for example Byron's rejection of contemporary heroes in Canto I and his choice of Don Juan, a figure from popular culture, as his 'hero'). It replaces the consciously high style of many Romantic-period epics with a style which mixes high and low culture, epic set-pieces with the burlesque, and which substitutes *ottava rima* for Miltonic (or sub-Miltonic) blank verse. In addition to its reconfiguration of the epic, *Don Juan* is inclusive—or promiscuous—in its use of other genres. For example, it incorporates features from romance, mock-epic, and elegy alongside its more self-consciously epic moments. The end result is a poem whose digressive, hybridized style and content reflects and responds to the generic complexity and diversity of the period within which it was written. A Romantic epic which is simultaneously not epic, the poem offers a commentary on a culture in which the epic was both elevated and deflated, in which it was simultaneously everything and nothing.

READING: John Keats, *Hyperion*

Hyperion was central to Keats's ambitions and achievements as a poet. He began work on it in autumn 1818 but abandoned it, unfinished, in April 1819. The fragmentary poem, consisting of 884 lines of blank verse, was published in 1820 in his third volume *Lamia, Isabella, The Eve of St Agnes and Other Poems*. In late July 1819 Keats returned to the poem, recasting it as a new work *The Fall of Hyperion. A Dream*. This contained an adapted version of the narrative of *Hyperion* but introduced a framing narrative in the form of a dream-vision. Keats abandoned work on this second poem in late 1819 on the grounds that its Miltonic style was too prevalent and too artful, and hence not truly poetic. This 529 line fragment was not published until 1848, more than twenty years after his death.

Whereas many of the epics discussed in the first part of this chapter deal with subjects from British history or from the Bible, the characters in *Hyperion* are taken from Greek mythology, indicating that the classical world was still a potent resource for writers in the early nineteenth century. *Hyperion* tells the story of the replacement of the old gods with new ones, the overthrow of the Titans by the Olympians. It is divided into three books (the third breaks off in mid-sentence). In the first we meet the fallen Saturn, leader of the Titans. He is in despair, but his sister-wife Thea advises him to meet with his fellow fallen gods. In the meantime Saturn's brother, the sun-god Hyperion, who lives in a glorious palace in the sky, is still unfallen. He is, however, increasingly concerned about his own future and is advised by his father, Coelus, to travel to the Earth and find Saturn. Book II returns to the fallen Titans. Saturn addresses them, asking for advice on how they can make war on the Olympians and their leader, his own son Jove. The sea-god Oceanus counsels against war, arguing that their fall was inevitable, part of an unchangeable, natural cycle. Other gods, however, suggest that their hopes rest on the as-yet unfallen Hyperion. At this point, Hyperion appears. Book III shifts the focus of the poem away from the Titans and to Apollo. One of the Olympians, he is destined to overthrow Hyperion and become the god of the sun, music, and healing. Apollo encounters the goddess Mnemosyne and the fragment ends with his transfiguration, breaking off mid-sentence with the word 'Celestial'.

Placed in the context of Keats's previous attempt at a long poem, the controversial romance *Endymion* (published in 1818), *Hyperion* marks a radical departure in style, though both poems share the same classical subject-matter. In a letter to the painter Benjamin Haydon, 23 January 1818, Keats noted the differences between the two, claiming that *Hyperion* replaced the 'sentimental cast' of *Endymion* with 'a more naked and Grecian manner'. His desire to separate *Hyperion* from *Endymion* could indicate a reformulation of his literary and stylistic allegiances. Whereas the earlier poem was greatly influenced by his friend and mentor Leigh Hunt, the later one is evidence of a move from Hunt to Milton. It was a timely move, especially given that its connections with Hunt had led to *Endymion* being savaged on literary and political grounds by the Tory reviewers of the *Quarterly* and

Blackwood's Magazine. Certainly, some of Keats's contemporaries appreciated the dissimilarity between the two poems, preferring what Thomas De Quincey described as 'the majesty, the austere beauty' of *Hyperion* to the more decorative *Endymion*.

Yet *Hyperion* is not just an indicator of Keats's development as a writer. It is also an example of the Romantic revival of interest in the epic and John Milton. Like other Romantic-period epics, *Hyperion* adopts some of the features of the genre but rejects others. Indeed, in some respects, it is more 'epic' than other more experimental poems of the period. For example, it begins in *media res* and is concerned with war between mythological beings. It contains an epic list (the roll-call of fallen Titans in Book II) and an addresss to the Muse (Book III). However, it does not make use of supernatural machinery as this is a poem concerned with gods who are preoccupied with their own affairs, not with humans whose affairs are shaped by acts of divine intervention. It also contains evidence of Keats's characteristically Romantic displacement of epic conventions. For example, the invocation of the Muse occurs at the beginning of the third book and not at the commencement of the poem, as any reader familiar with epic conventions would have expected.

Hyperion shares another feature found in epics of the Romantic period: a preoccupation with Milton, whose *Paradise Lost* Keats had been reading and annotating since 1817. The poem can be interpreted as a reconfiguring and rewriting of *Paradise Lost*, replacing Satan and his fallen angels with Saturn and his displaced Titans, Adam with Apollo. For example, the council of fallen Titans (Book II) offers parallels with the council between Satan and his followers in *Paradise Lost* (Book II). Yet it is important to remember that, as Lucy Newlyn has argued, its relationship to Milton's poem is a revisionary one, championing experience and suffering over Christian redemption. Moreover, its engagement with *Paradise Lost* is more coded than that found in other works of the period. It can be contrasted with Wordsworth's conscious verbal engagement with Milton, signalled by the use of quotation marks, in the Prospectus to *The Recluse*, first published in *The Excursion* in 1814.

The product of a culture deeply engaged with *Paradise Lost, Hyperion* also reads Milton through Keats's own contemporaries. It engages directly with Romantic-period interpretations of Miltonic epic and offers, as Vincent Newey has argued, a counterpoint to the generic and cultural ambitions of *The Excursion* and its author. In addition it attacks the Romantic epic on another front. It rebuts the anti-classicist tendencies of Keats's epic-writing contemporaries, who had preferred subjects from the modern world. An important example of how Romantic epic could deploy classical subject-matter, it replaces the Wordsworthian hills and lakes of Cumberland with the shady vales and olive groves of ancient Greece, and Wordsworthian characters such as the Solitary and the Wanderer with the Greek gods.

Yet *Hyperion* also has important extra-literary dimensions. Its engagement with the theme of suffering may reflect Keats's own biographical circumstances and his experiences whilst a medical student at Guy's Hospital. In addition, the poem offers a salutory reminder of Keats's contemporary reputation as a political poet. This is an epic about changes in a hierarchy, the conflict between an old set of rulers and those who are in the process of replacing them. There are a number of possible historical comparisons. The relationship between Saturn and his son and conqueror, Jove, could be paralleled with that between

George III and his son the Prince Regent. The exiled, melancholy Saturn compares with the figure of Napoleon Bonaparte, finally defeated at Waterloo in 1815 and exiled to the remote island of St Helena where he would die in 1821. In addition, the theme of regime change echoes the reshaping of post-Napoleonic Europe that was taking place in the late 1810s, a process being thrashed out by the victorious powers, including Britain, at the Congress of Vienna. The reactionary nature of the post-Napoleonic settlement raises possible questions about the nature of Jove and his new regime. One of the unseen figures in the epic, the new king of the Olympians remains a mystery, as does the nature of the rule he will impose. Will it be better than what has gone before, the same, or worse?

The fragmentary state of *Hyperion* means that it is notoriously tricky to make judgements about what the poem might have been like if it had been completed. We are given only brief glimpses of central characters such as Hyperion and Apollo and none at all of the other Olympians. The shift in style detected by some critics in Book III may even indicate that it would have adopted more than one stylistic register. We can only speculate. The fragmentary nature of *Hyperion* shapes our reading of it in other ways, and we need to be aware of the possibility that we as readers bring different expectations to a poem labelled 'A Fragment' than we do to one either unlabelled or complete. Compare, for example, the experience of reading *Hyperion* with reading Coleridge's 'Kubla Khan'.

Hyperion is an ambitious poem that demonstrates the renewed possibilities Romantic-period writers found in the epic. It might be tempting to read its incompleteness as evidence that Keats found the problems of engaging with and rethinking the highest of literary forms to be insurmountable. Yet *Hyperion* also reveals the cultural possibilities of revision and the inevitability of transformation. In terms of Keats's own career, the fragment marks the change in style and direction evident in the turn away from *Endymion*. Politically, it is a poem about the replacement of an old regime, written at a time when Europe was trying to resolve a post-Napoleonic political settlement and when England was beset by internal conflict. Generically, *Hyperion* engages with the need to revitalize and transform the epic and to take on poets such as Milton and Wordsworth. As the concluding sections of Book III reveal, *Hyperion* is also a poem about the process of becoming. It figures forth the painful coming into being of both a poet (Apollo/Keats) and a poem (*Hyperion* itself). By implication, then, Keats's epic is about the replacement of an old poetry by a new poetic. This new regime is bodied forth in Apollo, destined to defeat Hyperion and become the new god of the sun and of poetry. It is also embodied in Keats's fragmentary epic, a poem whose ending—suspended halfway across the page—enacts something that is ongoing, inevitable, and 'Celestial'.

FURTHER READING

Curran, Stuart, *Poetic Form and British Romanticism* (Oxford: Oxford University Press, 1986). Two chapters, 'Epic' and 'Composite Forms', contain detailed accounts of Romantic engagements with the epic.

Griffin, Dustin, *Regaining Paradise: Milton and the Eighteenth Century* (Cambridge: Cambridge University Press, 1986). Includes material on the decline of epic in the eighteenth century.

McWilliams, J. P., *The American Epic: Transforming a Genre, 1770–1860* (Cambridge: Cambridge University Press, 1990). Very detailed account of the ways in which American writers engaged with the epic, which offers comparisons with British Romanticism and a reminder of the international dimensions of generic revisionism.

Newey, Vincent, '*Hyperion, The Fall of Hyperion*, and Keats' Epic Ambitions', in Susan Wolfson (ed.), *The Cambridge Companion to Keats* (Cambridge: Cambridge University Press, 2001), pp. 69–85. Lots of detail about Keats and the epic.

Newlyn, Lucy, *'Paradise Lost' and the Romantic Reader* (Oxford: Clarendon Press, 1993). Detailed study of the responses of Romantic-period writers to Milton. Includes section on *Hyperion*.

O'Neill, Michael, ' "When this warm scribe my hand": Writing and History in *Hyperion* and *The Fall of Hyperion*', in Nicholas Roe (ed.), *Keats and History* (Cambridge: Cambridge University Press, 1995), pp. 143–64.

Quint, David, *Epic and Empire: Politics and Generic Form from Virgil to Milton* (Princeton: Princeton University Press, 1993). Deals mainly with earlier epics, and has important and useful material on traditions of counter-epic.

Richardson, Alan, 'Epic Ambivalence: Imperial Politics and Romantic Deflection in Williams's *Peru* and Landor's *Gebir*', in Alan Richardson and Sofia Hofkosh (eds.), *Romanticism, Race, and Imperial Culture, 1780–1834* (Bloomington, Ind.: Indiana University Press, 1996), pp. 265–82. Material on the connections between Romantic revisionary epics and the politics and poetics of empire.

Roberts, Adam, *Romantic and Victorian Long Poems: A Guide* (Aldershot: Ashgate, 1999). Introduction to and summaries of a number of important Romantic-period long poems.

Roe, Nicholas, *John Keats and the Culture of Dissent* (Oxford: Clarendon Press, 1997). Keats and politics; includes discussion of *Hyperion*.

Strachan, John, *The Poems of John Keats: A Routledge Literary Sourcebook* (London: Routledge, 2003). Introduction to texts and criticism.

Wilkie, Brian, *Romantic Poets and Epic Tradition* (Madison: University of Wisconsin Press, 1965). Detailed study of Romantic writers and the epic; contains a useful chapter on Landor and Southey, as well as chapters on Byron, Keats, Shelley, and Wordsworth.

NOTES

1. W. Hayley, *An Essay on Epic Poetry* (London, 1782), p. 5.
2. Ibid. 297–8.
3. For *Beowulf*, see Stuart Curran, *Poetic Form and British Romanticism* (Oxford: Oxford University Press, 1986), p. 245 n. 10. The *Poema del Cid* was translated by Robert Southey as *The Chronicle of the Cid* (London: Longman, Hurst, Rees, and Orme, 1808).
4. *Anti-Jacobin Review*, 11 (1802), 272.
5. For the review of Cowley, *The British Critic*, 18 (1802), 517. Henry James Pye, *Alfred, an Epic Poem in Six Books* (London: J. Wright, 1801), reviewed in *Monthly Review*, NS 37 (1802), 179 n*.
6. Curran, *Poetic Form*, p. 158; R. Southey, *Life and Correspondence*, ed. C. C. Southey, 6 vols. (London: Longman, Brown, Green and Longmans, 1849–50), ii. 121.
7. Nathan Drake, *Literary Hours, or Essays Literary and Critical*, 2nd edn., 2 vols. (Sudbury: J. Burkitt, 1800), i. 130.

8. Hugh Cunningham, 'The Languages of Patriotism', *History Workshop Journal*, 12 (1981), 63.

9. Joseph Cottle, *Alfred; an Epic Poem in Twenty-Four Books*, 2nd edn., 2 vols. (London: Longman and Rees, 1804), i, p. xlix.

10. Review of Cowley, *The British Critic*, 18 (1802), 518.

11. For Williams's 'oblique' relationship to the epic, see Alan Richardson, 'Epic Ambivalence: Imperial Politics and Romantic Deflection in Williams's *Peru* and Landor's *Gebir*', in Alan Richardson and Sofia Hofkosh (eds.), *Romanticism, Race, and Imperial Culture, 1780–1834* (Bloomington, Ind.: Indiana University Press, 1996), pp. 266–73.

12. Ann Yearsley, *The Rural Lyre* (London, 1796), 'Brutus', 'Argument' (unpaginated).

13. J. Thelwall, *Poems chiefly written in Retirement* (Hereford: W. H. Parker, 1801), pp. 177–202.

14. Ibid., pp. xliii, xliv.

15. Cottle, *Alfred*, p. xxxxvii.

16. Southey to Thomas Southey, 1 Mar. 1799, quoted in Lynda Pratt, 'Patriot Poetics and the Romantic National Epic', in Peter J. Kitson (ed.), *Placing and Displacing Romanticism* (Aldershot: Ashgate, 2001), p. 103.

17. R. Southey, *Madoc* (London, 1805); for all versions of the poem see R. Southey, *Poetical Works, 1793–1810*, 5 vols. (London: Pickering and Chatto, 2004), ii. *Madoc*, ed. Lynda Pratt. Ferriar's article is in the *Monthly Review*, NS 48 (1805), quoted in L. Madden, *Robert Southey: The Critical Heritage* (London: Routledge and Kegan Paul, 1972), pp. 102–3.

23 | Narrative poetry

Peter Vassallo

Narrative poetry in English literature is often associated with the Middle Ages when 'romances' were considered to be stories of adventure told in 'rime' (compare Coleridge's ballad 'The Rime of the Ancyent Marinere'). The revival of interest in the medieval world, in 'golden tongued romance with serene hue' (Keats's phrase), was an important aspect of Romantic verse narrative, particularly in its exploration of the exotic and the fantastic. At times the dynamic was a personal one—an attempt to revive lost worlds in the imagination, as in Coleridge's tantalizingly unfinished 'Kubla Khan' where the landscape of the pleasure dome built by Kubla Khan becomes a symbol for the poet's introspective mind—in effect, a poetic *paysage interieur*, an inner voyage (compare the reading of 'Kubla Khan' in the chapter entitled 'Formalism'). In Wordsworth's autobiographical poem *The Prelude*, the narrative is internalized and becomes a profound exploration of the influence of nature on the poet's mind and soul (see chapter entitled 'Romantic forms: an introduction').

Italy and Italian literature were a comparably fertile source during the Romantic period, influencing the narrative style and versification of Romantic poets. Byron, for example, made powerful use of the Italian narrative mode, the *ottava rima*, in his mature satirical poetry (see chapter on 'Romantic forms: an introduction'). The exotic Orient, with its alien customs and traditions, was also a source of inspiration to poets who tended to indulge their own fantasies and project their dreams of wish fulfilment. The popularity of these oriental poems was such that they came to be regarded as a potential rival to the Gothic novel, in their concern with the mysterious and the supernatural.

Narrative revival

The revival of verse narrative, influenced by Thomas Percy's antiquarian work, *Reliques of Ancient English Poetry* (1765), a collection of ancient ballads from several sources, was one of the main facets of British Romanticism in the first decades of the nineteenth century. The opening lines of 'The Marriage of Gawaine' from the *Reliques* give the flavour of this narrative, with its ballad versification and archaic vocabulary:

King Arthur lives in merry Carleile,
   And seemely is to see;
And there with him queene Guenever,
   That bride soe bright of blee.

And there with him queene Guenever,
   That bride so bright in bowre:
And all his barons about him stoode,
   That were both stiffe and stowre.

The king a royale Christmasse kept,
   With mirth and princelye cheare;
To him repaired many a knighte,
   That came both farre and neare.

Percy's *Reliques* inspired Sir Walter Scott who collected Scottish Border ballads and folk songs in his *Minstrelsy of the Scottish Border* (1802–3, see also the chapter on 'Lyric' and *Oxford Companion to the Romantic Age*, pp. 413–14). Scott's 'The Battle of Otterbourne' has a distinct linguistic identity, and the ballad rhythms set up a firm narrative pace from the outset:

It fell about the Lammas tide,
When the muir-men win their hay
The doughty Douglas found him to ride
Into England, to drive a prey.

He chose the Gordons and the Gaemes,
With them the Lindesays, light and gay;
But the Jardines wald not with him ride,
And they rue it to this day.

Popular interest in Percy's and Scott's ballads gave rise to the composition of longer narrative poems dealing with love, adventure, and the supernatural. This aspect of the Romantic narrative poem is initially represented by the longer poems of Robert Southey and Sir Walter Scott.

In *Thalaba the Destroyer* (1801) and *The Curse of Kehama* (1810) Robert Southey extravagantly transposed the medieval quest romance to exotic lands enlarging the horizons of the readers' expectations and providing historical and mythological interest with copious annotations. In these oriental verse epics Southey exploited the popular taste for the exotic, mingling oriental opulence with interest in strange customs and unbridled sensuality (compare the chapter untitled 'Easts'). Scott for his part combined a lasting interest in the medieval past with a sense of stirring in his readers the virtues of loyalty and patriotism in order to counteract the threat of Napoleon. In his imaginative re-creation of historical episodes, Scott subtly used the minstrel as a framing device to dramatize Anglo-Scottish history and legend. This device is best seen in his popular narrative poems *The Lay of the Last Minstrel* (1805) and *Marmion* (1808); the former sold over 20,000 copies in the first year. Much of the success of *The Lay of the Last Minstrel* depended on the lilting rhythm Scott had borrowed from Coleridge's *Christabel*:

> The feast was over in Branksome tower,
> And the Ladye had gone to her secret bower;
> Her bower that was guarded by word and by spell,
> Deadly to hear, and deadly to tell—
> Jesu Maria, shield us well!
> No living wight, save the Ladye alone,
> Had dared to cross the threshold stone.
>
> (I. 1–7)

Scott's artful welding of past and present proved popular, as did his poem's mingling of fantasy and fiction—the minstrel is unable to vouch for the truth of the song ('I cannot say how the truth may be: | I say the tale as 't was said to me' II. 262–3). The ageing minstrel, fallen on bad times, mediates past and present preserving the old legend for the entertainment of Ann, the widowed Duchess of Buccleuch, and her coterie of aristocratic ladies who have offered him hospitality. This was Scott's way of trying to revive the dignity of the bard while at the same time paying tribute to his ancestors. The nostalgia for the past, including the turbulent border skirmishes, is eventually resolved in a contest of minstrels and a tournament between champions in which chivalric values are restored. In *Marmion* Scott focused on the tensions in the character of his guilty hero, Marmion, Lord of Fontenaye, who callously abandons his mistress Constance (after persuading her to break her vows as a nun) and causes her death. Marmion was to fascinate Byron who judged him in *English Bards and Scotch Reviewers* (1809) 'not quite a felon, yet but half a knight'—the crowning irony being that Scott probably modelled his caddish hero on Byron himself. *Marmion* blends historical fact—the decisive battle of 'Flodden's fatal field', in which Marmion is killed—with picturesque fantasy bolstered by the brio of the verse.

Scott shrewdly used the narrative form to exploit public sentiment and anti-Napoleonic feeling, transposing his theme from the minstrelsy of the Scottish border to the Peninsular campaign being fought in Spain (see *Oxford Companion to the Romantic Age*, p. 642). In *The Vision of Don Roderick* (1811) Scott indulged his Tory patriotic sentiments in leisurely Spenserian stanzas (the stanza form of nine lines devised by Edmund Spenser for the *Faerie Queene*; see also the chapter on 'Romantic Forms: An Introduction') which, he felt, were appropriate to modern war. The third and last of Roderick's visions provides Scott with a timely opportunity to sing the praises of the British forces particularly the gallantry of the Scottish contingent and the heroism of the Highlanders at Fuentes d'Honoro and Barossa. Significantly, Sir John Moore, the commander of the British forces, who died in the retreat to Corunna, does not feature in Roderick's vision probably because Scott, like Moore's Tory critics, felt that Moore's strategic retreat was in fact ill-advised and amounted to a national disgrace. The poem ends with a tribute to Arthur Wellesley, Duke of Wellington, who replaced Moore as commander of the British forces. In *The Vision of Don Roderick* the poetry is overwhelmed by strident patriotic sentiment. Scott himself was aware of this and later dismissed it as a 'Drum and Trumpet performance'.

Byron's poetic 'romaunt'

Byron's *Childe Harold's Pilgrimage. A Romaunt*, has been acclaimed by critics (notably by Stuart Curran) as the romance, par excellence, of the period. The first two cantos of *Childe Harold*, written in Spenserian stanzas, chart the quest of Childe Harold (Byron's aristocratic poetic persona) for experience and adventure. Like a latter-day Ulysses—Homer's epic hero—the Childe wanders around the exotic Mediterranean commenting on customs, mores, and superstitions. The quest, which takes the form of a verse travelogue, subtly transmutes life into art, self-consciously focusing on the aesthetics of self-projection. The autobiography is thinly disguised, for Byron often failed in his endeavour to remove himself from himself, as he put it. Aristocratic world-weariness and cynicism pervade his narrative in ironical observations, gloomy perceptions, and dramatic posturing before his public, creating a number of fictional selves which were to merge into the popular Byronic hero in which Byron's real life, his aspirations, frustrations, and delusions, assume mythical significance. For example, Byron's brief sentimental attachment to the aristocratic adventuress, Constance Spencer Smith, during his 1809 sojourn in Malta, is transmuted into a scene reminiscent of the *Odyssey* in which Harold, on Calypso's isle, resists the blandishments of this new Calypso 'Sweet Florence' and withstands the 'lustre of her gaze'.

The heroes of Byron's verse narratives, Harold, Lara, the Giaour, and the Corsair, are poetic instances of Byron's mythologizing of himself. The quest for self-renewal in Byron's poetry in the years 1812–18 is subtly linked with the renewal of the Mediterranean cultural values that had sustained Europe over the years. In the first canto of *Childe Harold* (1812) Byron, in visiting some of the actual sites of the Peninsular campaign, pays tribute to the Spanish freedom fighters and extols the bravery of the Maid of Zaragoza who was boldly resolute 'to lead in Glory's fearful chase' while at the same time ambivalently expressing his misgivings about the outcome of the campaign lest 'desperate Valour acts in vain'. After cynical observations on the dubious outcome of the Convention of Cintra (1809), *Childe Harold* focuses despairingly on Greece—'Fair Greece, sad relic of departed worth'—which becomes a symbol of an ideal against which the political shortcomings of modern states, including Britain, can be measured. The suppression of liberty and democracy in Greece was, in Byron's view, a constant reminder of the frailty of political institutions in the West, and a glaring example of the indifference of Europe to the plight of the modern Greeks abandoned to the tyranny of their masters.

Nature in *Childe Harold* can be a source of consolation. Shelley had 'dosed' Byron with Wordsworth's poetry when both men were at Geneva in 1816 and, responding to that influence, Byron in *Childe Harold* reflects on the possibility of a reconciliation between man and nature which might enable him to transcend his 'clay-cold bonds':

> I live not in myself, but I become
> Portion of that around me; and to me,

High mountains are a feeling, but the hum
Of human cities torture: I can see
Nothing to loathe in nature, save to be
A link reluctant in a fleshly chain,
Class'd among creatures, when the soul can flee,
And with the sky, the peak, the heaving plain
Of ocean, or the stars, mingle, and not in vain.
(III. lxxii. 680–8)

In the fourth canto of Byron's poem, Childe Harold in his dual role of rebel and oracle responds to Italy emotionally and philosophically. Italy's 'fatal gift of beauty' has been its ruin over the centuries and in recalling Italy's illustrious past Childe Harold mourns the passing of Italy's great artists, poets, and philosophers. The Romantic vision of Italy urges the modern Italians, so divided among themselves, to shake off the yoke of foreign tyranny, and unite and restore that pristine glory which was a beacon for all nations. Significantly, Childe Harold's quest ends in Rome, where most pilgrimages ended, but the experience projected in the final canto is aesthetic rather than religious. The splendid architecture of St Peter's basilica with its massive harmonizing architectonic structure is subtly linked with the splendour of the Colisseum with its 'arches on arches' producing an effect of perfect balance and harmony: 'Vastness which grows—but grows to harmonize | All musical in its immensities' (IV. 1399–1400). The abiding architecture of Rome becomes a metaphor for Romantic transcendence, apart from the religious experience, which subsumes the sensitive traveller into the sea of Eternity, 'Dark-heaving—boundless, endless, and sublime' (IV. 1644). The questing pilgrim's shrine is achieved, not through religious conversion, but through an awareness of an aesthetic experience where the quest is internalized. In the persona of the aristocratic Childe Harold Byron, somewhat histrionically, strives to come to terms with himself, especially after the crisis of his separation from his wife, Annabella Milbanke.

'The Italian strain'

In a series of articles in the *Monthly Magazine* (May 1806 and June 1807), the scholar John Herman Merivale introduced the British public to the 'wonders and eccentricities' of Italian romance. Merivale focused in particular on Luigi Pulci's *Morgante Maggiore* on which he later composed a verse adaptation, *Orlando in Roncesvalles*, published by John Murray in 1814. This was praised by Byron who claimed that the metre (the *ottava rima*) 'was uncommonly well chosen and wielded'. The *ottava rima*, an Italian verse form with stanzas of eight lines each with eleven syllables rhyming *abababcc*, was used by the Italian masters Tasso and Ariosto and by the burlesque poets, and notably by Pulci and Casti, to ridicule the social mores of their times by writing a travesty of the old chivalric romances. Tasso's famous chivalric epic on the liberation of Jerusalem during the first Crusade was entitled *Gerusalemme Liberata* (1581). Ludovico Ariosto had written his *Orlando Furioso* in 1516 dealing mainly with the hero Orlando's insane love for the beautiful Angelica. Pulci's burlesque of the chivalric epic was entitled *Morgante Maggiore* and appeared in 1478. Giambattista Casti's *Novelle Galanti* (first published in 1790) consisted of licentious narrative poems (*novelle*) in the *ottava rima* dealing with the corrupt Venetian social mores and was much admired by Byron who admitted that he had 'almost got them by heart'. These humorous *novelle* considerably influenced Byron's poetic style when he composed *Beppo*, a Venetian narrative making satirical comparisons between English and Italian customs and manners.

John Herman Merivale's English version, focusing on a few select cantos of Pulci's burlesque of the chivalric romances, had in effect toned down the genial and boisterously irreverent spirit of Pulci by making the *Morgante* palatable to his conservative readers. In adapting Pulci to an English audience, Merivale had dressed the comic, burlesque Pulcian mode in the garb of Miltonic 'high seriousness' (the lofty moral tone adopted by John Milton in his epic poem *Paradise Lost*). Merivale's *Orlando* caught the attention of the Cambridge wit John Hookham Frere, a prominent member of the publisher John Murray's coterie of literary advisers. Frere tried his hand at grafting Pulci's Morgante on to native English stock, preserving Pulci's rollicking buffoonery while tactfully steering the narrative away from the dangerous reef of blasphemy and heresy—especially Pulci's digressions on the nature of God's justice and mercy. Frere concentrated instead on the antics of the oafish giant Morgante, who, after a farcical siege of the monastery, is converted and domesticated by the timorous Monks—they are decidedly English monks with a penchant for bell-ringing or 'tintinabulation', as Frere facetiously calls it. Frere's anglicizing of his Italian source is evident in his playful description of one of the monks who was particularly fond of angling and of a hearty English breakfast:

> The Monk with handy jerk, and petty baits,
> Stands twitching out apace the perch and roach;
> His mightier tackle, pitch'd apart, awaits
> The groveling barbel's unobserv'd approach:
> And soon his motley meal of homely Cates
> Is spread, the leather bottle is a-broach;
> Eggs, Bacon, Ale, a Napkin, Cheese and Knife,
> Forming a charming Picture of Still-life.

Frere's *The Monks and the Giants* (or *Whistlecraft,* as it came to be known after Frere's fictitious authors William and Robert Whistlecraft) skilfully adapts most of Pulci's stylistic traits of the Italian burlesque including the use of colloquialisms, doubles—entendres, broken rhymes, bathos, and loose digressions to which he adds an original touch—the flourish of stanzas in Latin to preserve the medieval flavour of his text while providing cultured amusement. In his thumbnail sketch of the knights of Charlemagne, Frere poked fun at some of his friends in the Tory Cabinet (the character of

Sir Tristram is based on his friend George Canning, the Foreign Secretary). But realizing that this might cause embarrassment, he decided it would have been improper to continue adapting the poem, observing that he had no inclination to 'persevere in a nonsensical work for the sake of good judges of nonsense'.

In a fine article on the 'Narrative and Romantic Poems of the Italians' published in the *Quarterly Review* (April 1819) Ugo Foscolo, an Italian exile in London and a member of the Murray circle, authoritatively discussed the salient features of the Italian burlesque poets. He encouraged Frere to continue his 'Specimen' adaptation of Pulci which he felt could 'become completely English, and be truly naturalized by English wit and English feeling'. Byron who admired Frere's *jeu d'esprit* immediately realized the potential of the Pulcian chiaroscuro style with its flippant impiety and abrupt shifts of seriousness and levity ('scorching and drenching' simultaneously). Byron later defended Pulci in the Advertisement to his translation of the first canto of the *Morgante*, pointing out that Pulci's manner was tolerated in the capital of Christianity centuries earlier but considered immoral and irreligious in hypocritical Regency England (see *Oxford Companion to the Romantic Age*, pp. 671–2). The moral and political Tory cant of his day (which had inhibited Frere) had imposed on the poet a concern with propriety which Byron found stultifying. His publisher John Murray, cautious as ever, had tactfully pointed out that, as far as the cultivated reading public was concerned, Pulci was the sort of writer who 'went without clothes'.

Byron was indignant that Murray's advisory coterie of literati failed to see that a dose of irreverence and buffoonery in the manner of the Italian burlesque poets could be salutary, and he was quick to realize the devastating potential of the Pulcian burlesque style if applied to the English political scene. Robert Southey's pompous and sycophantic poem on the death of George III, *A Vision of Judgement* (1821), provided Byron with an opportune purpose to deflate Southey's smug Toryism and to 'put the said George's Apotheosis in a Whig point of view'. The Italian burlesque narrative style with its droll irreverence could, in Byron's version, *The Vision of Judgement* (1823), be harnessed to the contemporary political scene. A convenient parallel could also be drawn between the battle of Roncesvalles at the end of the Morgante and 'the crowning carnage of Waterloo' (compare the discussion in the chapter on 'Satire'). Both battles, poetically imagined, caused a commotion in the infernal regions, since the devils could not cope with the sudden influx of damned souls. Southey's limping, ponderous hexameters ringing with fulsome praise are deflated by the volubility of the *ottava rima* with its irreverent, and somewhat disconcerting, admixture of seriousness and levity.

Pulci's bizarre humour and spirited religious parody gave Byron his cue when it came to writing his scathing rejoinder to Southey's canonizing of George III, unleashing latent energies within him which Byron appropriated as his 'finest, ferocious, Caravaggio style'.

Leigh Hunt's *The Story of Rimini*

The fashionable English interest in Italian literature in Regency England was not limited to the burlesque poets. It focused as well on the classics of Italian literature, in particular Dante, the great Florentine poet and author of *La Divina Commedia*, and Boccaccio whose great collection of stories, entitled the *Decameron*, dated from the middle of the fourteenth century. Byron met the English journalist and poet Leigh Hunt in 1813, when Hunt was in prison for libelling the Prince Regent in his newspaper *The Examiner*. In prison Hunt was making the fifty-six volumes of the *Parnaso Italiano* his 'favourite reading'. Pulci's gay levity and tolerance were, in Hunt's view, more congenial than Dante's occasional 'melancholy absurdities'. However, Dante's poetic rendering of the tragic love of Francesca da Rimini in the *Inferno* absorbed Hunt's interest and in order to alleviate the discomfort of his term in prison ('with which I cheer my long | And caged hours . . .') he set himself the task of composing a narrative poem that would elaborate Dante's terse account of the fate of Paolo and Francesca. As adulterous lovers Paolo and Francesca are, in Dante's moral scheme of things and in accordance with befitting retribution ('la legge del contrappasso'), condemned to be buffeted eternally by the 'bufera infernal'. Hunt departs from the traditional account followed by Dante, which has Giovanni surprise and kill the lovers in a fit of anger. Hunt's version (in the 1816 edition) makes the brothers fight a duel in which Paolo is killed and Francesca dies of a broken heart. Hunt deliberately evokes the epic romances in his account of Francesca's fatal passion for Paolo where she finds solace in a secluded garden or bower in which the lovers eventually meet, protected from the prying eyes of censorious onlookers. His strategy is to narrate the events as they occur thereby pre-empting moral judgement while indulging his love of elaborate decorative detail (he associated such verse textures with the 'luxuries' of Spenser's poetry). In his *The Story of Rimini*, scented flowers, luscious trees, and babbling fountains assail the senses in Francesca's secluded garden, conspiring to make the lovers' attraction to each other irresistible and eliciting the reader's sympathy for their fatal intimacy. This is Hunt's actual description of the bower in Canto III:

> It was a beauteous piece of ancient skill,
> Spared from the rage of war, and perfect still;
> By most supposed the work of fairy hands,
> Famed for luxurious taste, and choice of lands,—
> Alcina or Morgana,—who from fights
> And errant fame inveigled amorous knights . . .
>
> (III. 456–61)

Hunt's sympathetic rendering of the adulterous love of Paolo and Francesca ensconced in the artifice of nature ('the fairy hands of an Alcina or Morgana') and protected from the prying eyes of the stern moralist forestalls moral censure. In Dante's *Inferno* the sympathy aroused by Francesca's account of her tragedy is tempered by the poem's overriding concern with a sense of divine justice—Dante the pilgrim does swoon with pity for the plight of the lovers, but Dante the poet's concern with moral righteousness compels him to consign the lovers to the second circle of Hell. In Dante's poem Francesca and Paolo are made to endure eternal punishment by being relentlessly tossed by the strong winds of their illicit passion. In Hunt's *Rimini* Paolo and Francesca are placed in a setting which is strongly reminiscent of Dante's earthly paradise as described in the final cantos of the *Purgatorio* and the emphasis is subtly shifted from adultery to empathy with the lovers' plight. Hunt's version presents Francesca as the victim of the 'secret snare' of Giovanni's calculating collusion with her father Guido, Duke of Ravenna, in that they use the more attractive Paolo to woo her by proxy. Hunt's Tory reviewers (notably 'Z' in Blackwood's *Edinburgh Magazine* (July 1818, p. 453)) predictably censured his rendering of the story of Rimini for its 'extreme moral depravity' which they chose to see as an insidious violation of the marriage code (Tory orthodoxy) in accordance with the radical programme of Hunt's *Examiner* and the subversive sexual politics of the Cockney School of poetry.

The Orient

Southey's *Thalaba* had catered to the vogue for oriental tales at the end of the eighteenth century by offering oriental adventure in poetic form. In this long narrative poem, complete with learned footnotes and lengthy annotations, the youthful hero (an illiterate boy, brought up by Bedouin Arabs) is taken to Baghdad and the ruins of Nineveh, and then into a paradisiacal and somewhat sinister underworld garden, where he is reunited for a short while with his childhood sweetheart, evading the snares of wily sorcerers and magicians. In *Thalaba* Southey projected his contemporaries' prejudices and fantasies about the East, in a narrative that combined grotesque Gothic horrors with insights into the archetypal nature of myths and exotic religious practices and beliefs. Although little studied now, the poem was popular and widely read and influenced Scott's Romantic historical poems.

Byron, too, exploited the public's craving for the oriental narrative poem. In 1813 he advised his friend the poet Tom Moore to 'stick to the East' as the cultured 'oracle' Madame de Staël had suggested. From Scott's *Marmion* Byron developed the notion of narrative poems that focus on a mysterious guilty hero. Lara, the Giaour, and the Corsair are all developments of the Byronic hero who had captured the public imagination in the early cantos of *Childe Harold*. They are moody, brooding, and domineering outlaws haunted by a secret guilt, characters who are larger than life, forever defying malignant fate. The description of Lara is typical of the Byronic hero:

> There was in him a vital scorn of all
> As if the worst had fall'n which could befall,
> He stood a stranger in this breathing world,
> An erring spirit from another hurl'd;

A thing of dark imaginings, that shaped
By choice the perils he by chance escaped;
But 'scaped in vain, for in their memory yet
His mind would half exult and half regret:
With more capacity for love than earth
Bestows on most of mortal mould and birth,
His early dreams of good outstripp'd the truth,
And troubled manhood follow'd baffled youth . . .

(Lara, XVIII. 313–24)

This could be seen as Byron's attempt to mythologize himself in an oriental setting—in March 1814 he sat for his portrait (by Thomas Philips), in Albanian costume.

The heroes of Byron's Eastern tales have something in common: their love for a woman which endures beyond the grave. Leila in *The Giaour* possesses the Giaour's soul and he craves to spend eternity with her, beyond his mortal confines. This quality of the transcendence of love was the main reason behind the sensational commercial success of Byron's Turkish tales. The tales could also be read as allegories of the fascination of the East upon the European mind, Islamic culture and religion being regarded as an alternative culture to the West and possessing its own moral code and peculiar traditions.

The Bride of Abydos, Lara, and *The Giaour* show Byron's understanding of, and sympathetic engagement with, the East, to which he had travelled earlier in 1809–11. These poems invite comparisons with Eastern religions and mores. *The Giaour* has a suggestive political resonance, its central theme being the subjugation of modern Greece, and, by implication, the inability of the Western powers to understand Levantine politics. The underlying message of *The Giaour* is that the intervention of the European powers, one is led to assume, would be the replacement of one form of despotism by another, in this case by European monarchical government in the guise of liberalism. The Turkish Tales go beyond the exotic adventure narrative. Byron adds an element of unprecedented sophistication to the Romantic narrative poem. The narrative technique of *The Giaour*, for instance, is complex. The story is told from different perspectives: sometimes the narrator is Byron himself, sometimes the old Turkish fisherman who narrates the story from an unsympathetic point of view, and, towards the end of the poem, it is the Giaour himself and the monk to whom he is speaking who take over. Byron constantly revised the poem inserting additional passages and later referred to it as 'a snake of a poem'.

The romantic narrative poem is given a new dimension in Shelley's longest poem, *The Revolt of Islam*, written in Spenserian stanzas and published in 1818. Shelley's original uncensored version had been entitled *Laon and Cythna; or the Revolution of the Golden City: A Vision of the Nineteenth Century*. In that poem Shelley uses myth to interpret history and to come to terms with the failure of the French Revolution, exploring its unfulfilled potential and advocating perseverance in questing for an attainable earthly paradise. The original *Laon and Cythna* is in effect a mythologized version of the French Revolution, a vision in which the possibility of change and progress is idealistically projected. Cythna's eventual revelation of the paradise of the heart nostalgically takes the reader back to the poet's vision of the world in which 'mankind was free Equal and pure and wise in wisdom's prophecy' (VII. xxxiii. 8–9). The narrative shifts on to the sphere of allegory, and this contains one of the major themes of the poem. The narrator witnesses an aerial battle between an eagle and a serpent, an emblem of the cosmic struggle between Good and Evil, in which evil is the apparent victor. The poet's prophetic vision extends beyond the immediate present into the future where the battle will be renewed and the serpent eventually overcome:

> The victor Fiend
> Omnipotent of yore, now quails, and fears
> His triumph dearly won, which soon will lend
> An impulse swift and sure to his approaching end.
> (I. xxxiv. 429–32)

Laon and Cythna are in fact brother and sister, and they embody the refining spirit of the revolution as well as the virtues of love and forbearance, which ennoble man in defeat. Shelley provocatively introduced the taboo theme of incest by way of advocating a liberal, uncensorious attitude to unconventional relationships but when his publisher Charles Ollier threatened to withdraw the poem Shelley agreed to tone down its radicalism and *Laon and Cythna* was issued as *The Revolt of Islam*. In both poems, however, the revolutions against Eastern despots have a bearing on the corrupt old regimes of Europe; the Golden City—Constantinople—becomes the *beau ideal* of the French Revolution, purged of its excesses. The narrative ends with an affirmation of historical evolution and progress which, the poet believes, is destined to overcome the tyranny of cynical monarchs, and projects a vision of America the mighty land where 'freedom and truth | are worshipped'.

So Shelley's orientalism in *The Revolt of Islam* was a means of alluding to analogues between events in the narrative and the process of the French Revolution and the Napoleonic wars. In his narrative poems his imagined East could thus interact significantly with Western political and religious concerns. At the same time, Shelley avoided cultural specificity.

In the 'Witch of Atlas' (1820) Shelley playfully restates his notion of political and social reform, in jocose *ottava rima* stanzas in the manner of the Italian burlesque poets. The Witch, actually a beautiful enchantress born in the North African Atlas Mountains, is a typically Shelleyan creation. Travelling over North Africa into Egypt on her magic carriage, she bestows her enchanted antidote to the evil propensities of mankind and 'gave | strange panacea in a crystal bowl' (lxix. 594). Shelley here seems to be poking fun at those visionaries, like himself, who naïvely believe that the world might be redeemed by lofty idealisms.

In the dedication of *The Corsair* (1814) Byron had advised Tom Moore to pursue the oriental mode in order to proclaim 'the wrongs of your own country'. Moore followed Byron's suggestion and published *Lalla Rookh: An Oriental Romance* in 1817, shrewdly attuning his harp, as Irish minstrel, to the popularity of the fashionable oriental romances with their interplay of voluptuousness and terror in an exotic setting. Moore's poem consists in effect of four long narrative poems with a connecting tale in prose. *Lalla Rookh* focuses on the journey of Lalla Rookh, the daughter of the Emperor Aurungzebe, from Delhi to Kashmir where she is to be married to the King of Bokhara. On the journey she is entertained by stories told by the Feramorz, the young poet from Kashmir who joins her retinue (with whom Moore identifies). Feramorz is ridiculed by the pompous vizier Fadladeen (mainly a caricature of Francis Jeffrey, the editor of the Whig *Edinburgh Review*, who had criticized Moore's poems). Moore sentimentalizes his romance by supplying a harmonious, improbable ending in which Lalla Rookh discovers that the poet Feramorz, with whom she has fallen in love, is none other than her prospective husband the King of Bokhara. The longer poems which follow, 'The Veiled Prophet of Khorassan' and 'The Fire-Worshippers', while exploiting the public craving for sensational themes of cruelty and revenge, are also fables of contemporary imperialism which would have appealed to the liberal-minded British readers. 'The Fire-Worshippers' celebrates the heroic resistance of the Gherbers (the fire-worshippers of the ancient Persian religion) against the invading Islamic army. In the persona of Feramorz, the wise poet, Moore displays his own suitably camouflaged political bias in favour of religious tolerance (the question of Catholic emancipation) and political independence (emerging Irish nationalism). Literary encounters with the East, as mediated in the longer narrative poems, often enabled the Romantic poets to engage with another culture and civilization in a manner which obliquely reflected their own particular social, political, and religious concerns.

READING: John Keats *Isabella; or, the Pot of Basil*

In *The Rime of the Ancyent Marinere*, first published in *Lyrical Ballads* (1798), S. T. Coleridge revitalized the archaisms of traditional ballad narrative, and transformed it into a haunting tale of guilt and retribution. As the mariner sets sail, an albatross crosses the ship and then follows it like a guardian spirit: 'And every day for food or play | Came to the Marinere's hollo!' Coleridge's mastery of eerie effects enabled him to play up this traditional feature of the ballad, as when he describes how

> In mist or cloud on mast or shroud
> It perch'd for vespers nine,
> Whiles all the night thro' fog smoke-white
> Glimmer'd the white moon-shine.
>
> (ll. 73–6)

In the verse that immediately follows this ghostly scene, we learn that the mariner inexplicably 'shot the Albatross' with his cross bow. By killing the albatross, he severed the harmonious bond between nature and humankind, and the sense of spiritual violation is enhanced by the poem's Christian imagery (especially references to the 'cross'). In this psychologically sophisticated 'ballad', Coleridge's treatment of the old mariner's story concerns a voyage of discovery that eventually becomes a nightmarish journey into the unknown in which the supernatural and the spectral are 'naturalized'. After a voyage that brings the mariner intense suffering and, eventually, an ambiguous atonement, he eventually returns to his homeland with 'strange power of speech' to tell of his 'ghastly aventure'. *The Ancyent Marinere*'s startling juxtapositions of traditional ballad features (verse form and rhyme structure, metre, supernatural visitation, and Gothic retribution) with the real world of 'Old men, and babes, and loving friends, | And Youths, and Maidens gay' (ll. 641–2) was also attempted by John Keats in his own modernization of Italian romance narrative.

The fashionable English interest in the Italian Renaissance poets and in the narrative poetry of the Italians was fostered by Merivale and Frere, and influenced Hunt and Byron. John Keats's poem *Isabella; or, the Pot of Basil* was composed between February and April 1818, and eventually published in Keats's third and final book of poetry in 1820. It was originally intended as part of a collaborative project with Keats's fellow poet John Hamilton Reynolds. They planned to produce verse tales based on Giovanni Boccaccio's collection of tales from many sources, assembled between 1349 and 1351 and entitled *The Decameron*. By this time the possibilities of an Italian theme had already been suggested to Keats by Hunt's *The Story of Rimini*. He had also enjoyed the Italianate pleasures of Hunt's library at his home in the Vale of Health, Hampstead, which included a portrait of the Italian poet Petrarch and a fifty-two-volume edition of the Italian poets. The idea of using Boccaccio as a source, and the tale of Isabella in particular, was suggested by the journalist and critic William

Hazlitt in his lecture on the poets Dryden and Pope of 3 February 1818, which Keats attended. In the course of this lecture, Hazlitt had urged poets to emulate Dryden by versifying some of the serious tales in Boccaccio: 'I should think that a translation of some of the . . . serious tales in Boccaccio . . . as that of Isabella . . . if executed with taste and spirit, could not fail to succeed in the present day.' Keats was listening, and took the hint.

Keats read Boccaccio's *Decameron* in the fifth edition of the first English translation dating from 1620. He saw immediately that Boccaccio's short tale of Isabella offered the potential Hazlitt had remarked upon, and as he set to work on his own modern version the narrative grew to four times the length of the briskly paced Italian original. Keats adopted the eight line Italian *ottava rima* verse form, and embroidered the narrative with sentimental and macabre scenes that go beyond anything in Boccaccio's tale. In the lines that follow here, Keats is describing the two lovers, Isabella and Lorenzo:

> Parting they seem'd to tread upon the air, A
>   Twin roses by the zephyr blown apart B
> Only to meet again more close, and share A
>   The inward fragrance of each other's heart. B
> She, to her chamber gone, a ditty fair A
>   Sang, of delicious love and honey'd dart: B
> He, with light steps went up a western hill, A
> And bade the sun farewell, and joy'd his fill. B
>
> All close they met again, before the dusk C
>   Had taken from the stars its pleasant veil, D
> All close they met all eves, before the dusk C
>   Had taken from the stars its pleasant veil, D
> Close in a bower of hyacinth and musk, C
>   Unknown of any, free from whispering tale. D
> Ah! better had it been for ever so, E
> Than idle ears should pleasure in their woe. E
>   (x–xi. 73–88)

The imagery of 'roses' parted by 'the zephyr' (the west wind), and references to Isabella's 'chamber', a 'ditty fair', 'delicious love', and the perfumed 'bower' all combine to create a richly romantic ambience, while the allusion to the 'honey'd dart' of love has an overtly erotic thrust. All of this is exactly what one needs in a poem of romantic interest, one might suppose, but Keats was dissatisfied with the effects he had created. Why was this?

When the poem was finished Keats had misgivings about publishing it, and was especially aware of shortcomings which he confided to his friend Richard Woodhouse (who had insisted on the poem's worthiness). *Isabella*, in Keats's view, was 'too smokeable'—by which he meant too easily ridiculed and 'laugh'd at'. There was much 'inexperience of life' and 'simplicity of knowledge' in it, Keats thought. Projecting himself into the role of a hostile reviewer, he surmised that *Isabella; or, the Pot of Basil* was 'a weak-sided Poem' with 'an amusing, sober-sadness about it'. Keats often belittled his own achievements, and was only too ready to find fault with what he had written (he dismissed his 'poetic romance' *Endymion* as another weak perfomance that should 'die away'). Yet in spite of *Isabella*'s weaknesses, the sickly mawkishness of parts of the narrative (for example 'delicious love') and the lapses into bathos (like 'joy'd his fill'), there are moments where the narrative is restrained and gains considerable dramatic power when it departs from its source in the pathetic story as told by Boccaccio.

Keats's vigorous, modern narrative style is most obvious when he writes about Isabella's brothers. They are merchants of Florence whose wealth derives from the exploitation of workers in 'torched mines and noisy factories' and from slave labour driven by the 'stinging whip'. The brothers also profit from the suffering of men who dive for pearls, and from the brutal trade in animal furs:

> For them the Ceylon diver held his breath,
>   And went all naked to the hungry shark;
> For them his ears gush'd blood; for them in death
>   The seal on the cold ice with piteous bark
> Lay full of darts . . .
>
> (xv. 113–17)

Notice the different physical qualities of Keats's vocabulary here: 'naked', 'hungry', gush'd blood', 'cold ice'. The cruel 'darts' that kill the seal deliberately recall the 'honey'd dart' of Isabella's love song, and emphasize the violently predatory world beyond the veiled bower. In Keats's poem the malign creatures who populate Spenser's romance landscape in the *Faerie Queene* have been reshaped as capitalist businessmen, and all of the issues Keats touches upon are contentious in today's world of relentless globalization. By attending to Keats's updating of Boccaccio and earlier romances, we can see how he aimed to remake narrative poetry for his own times and ours. Isabella's brothers are as terrifying as the evil magicians in the older romance mode, because they appear unassailable and all-powerful:

> How was it these same ledger-men could spy
>   Fair Isabella in her downy nest?
> How could they find out in Lorenzo's eye
>   A straying from his toil? Hot Egypt's pest
> Into their vision covetous and sly!
>   How could these money-bags see east and west?
> Yet so they did—and every dealer fair
> Must see behind, as doth the hunted hare
>
> O eloquent and famed Boccaccio!
>   Of thee we now should ask forgiving boon
> And of thy spicy myrtles as they blow
>   And of thy roses amorous of the moon
> And of thy lilies that do paler grow
>   Now they can no more hear thy ghittern's tune
> For venturing syllables that ill beseem
> The quiet glooms of such a piteous theme.
>
> (xviii–xix, 137–52)

The furtive passion of Isabella and Lorenzo is crudely interrupted by the cold, calculating schemes of the brothers who have, inexplicably, become aware of the faintest signs of their love. The narrative focuses on the darker side of human nature by suggesting that the rapaciousness of the merchant brothers should have blinded them to the secret love of their innocent sister. And yet, somehow, these 'money-bags' managed to see both 'east and west'. The brothers are ruthless and calculating in their financial dealings as merchants, and their predatory instinct, these stanzas suggest, has sharpened their awareness. This sudden imposition of a temporal frame enables the narrative to impose a modern sensibility on to an ancient theme. This is apparent in Keats's self-conscious address to the 'eloquent and famed Boccaccio!' at the precise moment when he is about to elaborate on his source in the process of modernizing an old tale—'to make old prose in modern rhyme more sweet' (xx. 156) and applying his 'dramatic capacity by entering fully into the feeling'.

Keats's sense of the dramatic made him reject an earlier stanza, inappropriately satirical in tone, which makes use of facile reference to the callous world of commerce in rationalizing the brothers' greed, by attributing this to the fact that their mother had dreamed of money when she was pregnant. Calculating that they can marry their sister profitably to some rich nobleman, the two brothers get rid of her lover Lorenzo by murdering him and burying him in a wood. The poem's focus hereafter is on the macabre details of Lorenzo's ghost, Isabella's determination to find and exhume his corpse (first 'a soiled glove', and then 'the horrid thing' itself), the gruesome detail of how she cut off the head, and the narrator's empathy with her feelings as she reburies the head in a 'garden-pot'. These unsparing horrors all suggest that Keats was attempting to introduce a note of 'manliness' to forestall the criticism that he wrote especially for fashionable drawing-room female readers. Certainly Keats's gruesome embellishments are in excess of Boccaccio's crisp account of how Isabella 'brought a keen Razor [and] . . . divided the Head from the Body'. In Keats's version, she labours three long hours to dig up Lorenzo's body with her bare hands, and then 'cut away' his head with a knife of 'duller steel'. As Jack Stillinger pointed out in his essay on 'The "Reality" of Isabella', the lengthening of time and the emphasis on the 'dullness' of the knife adds realism to 'the unemotional bare bones of the story Keats was recasting'.

The 'modernization' of Boccaccio's medieval tale necessarily entailed the highlighting of physical horror, and the insistent dwelling on what Keats called 'wormy circumstance' which accounts for Isabella's eventual insanity. She plants 'Sweet Basil' in the pot containing Lorenzo's head, and tends the plant obsessively until she dies of a broken heart. Her anguish, 'weeping through her hair', is obvious. But at the same time Keats's attempts to enlist the readers sympathy for the forlorn heroine's plight leads him into the serious difficulty of maintaining an appropriate tone and stance. In stanza 16, for example, there are several feeble rhetorical exclamations concerning her brothers—'Why were they proud?' and 'Why in the name of glory were they proud?'—all of which have a hollow ring, and exposed this part of the poem to the reviewers' ridicule. Towards the end of the poem Keats's exclamation—'O Music, Music, breathe despondingly!' | . . . For Isabel, sweet Isabel, will die'—might be felt to direct the reader's response too overtly. Keats himself always had reservations about poems with a 'palpable design' on the reader.

Irony, in Keats's mature style, was a way of introducing modern sensibility to the narrative voice and of inserting an anti-romantic note into the romance mode. The gruesome appearance of Lorenzo's head 'with green and livid spot' strikes this note in *Isabella*, and helps turn the poem to its conclusion when the brothers discover the rotting head in the pot and flee into exile. Likewise, Keats's narrative poems *Lamia* and *The Eve of St Agnes*, as Tilottama Rajan has observed, both affirm and reject the values of romance they seem to project. Within the artifice of traditional romance, which binds hero and heroine to their conventionalized roles, Keats's characters Porphyro and Madeline in *The Eve of St Agnes* undergo a deep erotic experience while acting out their respective roles in a romantic narrative. *The Eve of St Agnes*, as Jack Stillinger provocatively suggested in his essay on the 'Hoodwinking of Madeline', is ironic at the expense of Madeline who is naïvely credulous and therefore 'amort' to the real world and easily 'hoodwinked with faery fancy' (the word 'amort' means 'dead', and Keats wants this darker tone to colour his poem). Porphyro, in Stillinger's account, steps beyond the limits of fantasy sanctioned by romance into the world of reality, taking on the role of a 'villainous seducer' rather than a lover. Indeed, it is Porphyro's role that enables Keats to mingle the ideal with the physical, and wish-fulfilment with sensual consummation of the lover's passion.

> Beyond a mortal man impassioned far
> At these voluptuous accents, he arose,
> Ethereal flushed, and like a throbbing star
> Seen mid the sapphire heaven's deep repose;
> Into her dream he melted, as the rose
> Blendeth its colour with the violet,
> Solution sweet—meantime the frost wind blows
> Like love's alarum pattering the sharp sleet
> Against the window panes; St Agnes' moon hath set.
> (xxxvi. 316–24)

The sexually explicit aspect of the poem dismayed Woodhouse, who felt that Porphyro initiates Madeline into the pleasures of physical passion ('this is no dream my bride, my Madeline!'). In Woodhouse's view, Porphyro 'acts all the acts of a bona fide husband, while she fancies she is only playing the part of a Wife in a dream'. The passage also alarmed Keats's publisher John Taylor, who thought that Keats was taking too much of a risk with his readers and was recklessly 'flying in the face of all Decency & discretion'. Keats's narrative in effect enacts the uneasy merger of the dream world of fantasy which sustained his early poems, into the real world of physical consummation and decay. In the *Eve of St Agnes* Richard Woodhouse was also disturbed by the death of the nurse Angela who dies 'palsy-twitch'd, with meagre face deform'. This was one of Keats's deliberate alterations to his poem: 'He says he likes that the poem should leave off with this Change of sentiment', Woodhouse reported, 'it is what he aimed at, & was glad to find from my objections to it that he had succeeded.' Keats was deliberately importing discomforting material details into the 'faery' world of St Agnes Eve, but at the same time he was reluctant to abandon that fanciful world altogether. While Keats embraces the sharpness of human desire, pain, and suffering his narrative also lingers in the shadows of the old medieval tradition revived by Percy and Scott and seems to regret its demise: 'And they are gone: ay, ages long ago.'

FURTHER READING

Barnard, John, *John Keats* (Cambridge: Cambridge University Press, 1987). An interesting revaluation of Keats's major poems which contains an illuminating chapter on 'Four "medieval" love stories'.

Butler, Marilyn, *Romantics, Rebels and Reactionaries: English Literature and its Background 1760–1830* (Oxford : Oxford University Press, 1981). A comprehensive account of the Romantic movement in its political and historical setting.

—— 'Orientalism', in David Pirie (ed.), *The Penguin History of Literature: The Romantic Period* (Harmondsworth: Penguin, 1994), pp. 395–447. A first-rate essay dealing comprehensively with some of the significant ways in which the Romantic poets portrayed and 'constructed' the Orient.

Cox, Jeffrey N., '*Lamia, Isabella and the Eve of St Agnes*: Eros and "Romance"', in Susan Wolfson (ed.), *The Cambridge Companion to Keats* (Cambridge: Cambridge University Press, 2001). A stimulating study of Keats's narrative poems and their relation to the culture of dissent.

Curran, Stuart, *Poetic Form and British Romanticism* (Oxford: Oxford University Press, 1986). An indispensable reference work on the ways in which the Romantic poets adopted traditional literary forms. Contains a superb chapter on 'The Romance'.

Everest, Kelvin, 'Isabella in the Market Place: Keats and Feminism', in Nicholas Roe (ed.), *Keats and History* (Cambridge: Cambridge University Press, 1995). A stimulating essay containing a perceptive close reading of *Isabella*.

McGann, Jerome, 'The Book of Byron and the Book of a World', in the *The Beauty of Inflections* (Oxford: Clarendon Press, 1988). An excellent study of Byron's skill at manipulating his publications and of the political aspects of Byron's oriental romances.

Rajan, Tilottama, *Dark Interpreter: The Discourse of Romanticism* (Ithaca, NY: Cornell University Press, 1980). Complex but rewarding study of the ironic mode of Keats's narrative poems.

Stillinger, Jack, *The Hoodwinking of Madeline and Other Essays* (Urbana, Ill.: University of Illinois Press, 1971). Contains seminal essays 'The "Reality" of *Isabella*' and 'The Hoodwinking of Madeline'.

Sutherland, John, *The Life of Walter Scott: A Critical Biography* (Oxford: Blackwell, 1995). Sir Walter Scott's life and achievement as poet and novelist, with particularly illuminating remarks on Scott's chivalric romances.

24 | The novel

Corinna Russell

'I hate to read new books', announced William Hazlitt in 1826. With this, the opening line of his essay 'On Reading Old Books', the foremost commentator on his age begins an exercise in subjective canon-formation. Looking back, four years before his death, over a reading career spanning most of the Romantic period, the essayist makes a wry boast of his 'scanty library', comprising 'twenty or thirty volumes that I have read over and over again, . . . the only ones that I have any desire ever to read at all'.[1] Where 'old books', as the repository of associations formed during first readings in youth, are 'links in the chain of our conscious being', new books seem to him, like the reading of the Prince Hamlet, merely ' "Words, words, words" ' without ' "matter" '.[2]

Hazlitt's rejection of recent publications refers simply to 'new books' of all kinds, but the terms with which he fleshes out his repudiation are borrowed from contemporary debate concerning a genre eponymously linked with the idea of newness: the novel. In distinguishing his reading habits from those of women, who 'judge of books as they do of fashions or complexions', or from 'those who trouble the circulating libraries', the critic also signals his ambivalence with regard to a form of publication popularly associated in this period with both these readerships: 'the wet sheets of the last new novel from the Ballantyne press [Edinburgh publisher of Scott's *Waverley* novels], to say nothing of the Minerva press in Leadenhall-street [a popular publisher of "horrid" novels]'.[3] It is clear, however, that all novels are not anathema to Hazlitt, since he learned his love for 'old books' from 'Cooke's edition of the British Novelists', and is still inclined to 'solac[e] himself' with 'a volume of Peregrine Pickle or of Tom Jones'.[4]

The paradox implicit in Hazlitt's essay is one that informs much contemporary assessment of the Romantic-period novel. In the decades surrounding the turn of the eighteenth century, novels are associated both with the 'new'—in the sense of the ephemeral, the fashionable, and the culturally belated—and with the familiar—in a spectrum of senses ranging from 'contemptibly ubiquitous' to 'historically established'. They are imagined as involved with the ethics of novelty, and with the promiscuous, extensive reading eschewed by Hazlitt in favour of faithful, intensive *re*reading, yet, following the abolition of perpetual copyright in 1774, a proliferation of 'standard' editions and multi-volume 'Novelist's Libraries' locates some novels, at least, in a tradition worth future investment.

The contradictions governing the reception of the novel between 1770 and 1830 do not prevent readers, critics, and, in particular, novelists of this period from writing about the genre with increasing confidence in their subject. The ambiguous status of the novel in relation to other 'Romantic forms', combined with the generic experimentation of the age itself and the formal heterogeneity already associated with this mode of prose fiction, might suggest that Romantic period novels are peculiarly resistant to the kind of literary historicizing that seeks to draw out a set of distinctive characteristics. And yet this is a period in which practitioners of the genre continually comment, within and outside of the boundaries of narrative, on the distinguishing features of their chosen form, and in which to write a novel is to participate in a national conversation about the 'progress' of the craft.

In examining what can be said to be distinctive about the Romantic-period novel, this chapter will take its cue from the analysis and commentary offered by Romantic-period writers, but will also place its findings in the context of present-day critical discourses, concerning the history of the novel and the definition of Romanticism in literature. To this end, what follows will be framed by one section, called 'Origins and Directions', detailing some of the predecessors and descendants of the Romantic-period novel, and one on the various manifestations of narrative voice in novels of this time, which also asks to what extent the Romantic-period novel confirms or challenges existing definitions of the Romantic movement. Book-ended by these two sections will be a brief survey of the diverse subgenres that come under the heading of the Romantic-period novel.

The ideas of reading and rereading foregrounded by Hazlitt's 'On Reading Old Books' are strongly deterministic in the self-definition of the Romantic-period novel. Readers are considered at this time, not only as growing in number (see *Oxford Companion to the Romantic Age*, p. 287), but as congregating, amassing, becoming that amorphous, shadowy community known as a 'reading public'. Romantic-period writing is characteristically preoccupied with this collective unknown, but it is the novel, perhaps more frankly than other genres, that acknowledges the almost co-creative influence of its readers on its development as a form. It does so explicitly, by means of prefaces, direct addresses by a narrator to a fictional 'Reader', and through the recurrent inclusion of reader-figures or substitutes in its stories; and implicitly, by its involvement in increasingly sophisticated marketing strategies (see *Oxford Companion to the Romantic Age*, pp. 664–5), and by creating formal analogies between the experiences depicted in its fictions and the experience of reading them. This last technique is fundamental to the transformation of the generic identity of the novel in the Romantic period, and requires further explanation.

One way in which the late eighteenth- and early nineteenth-century novel seeks recognition as a genre in its own right is by asserting its difference from the romance. This is at no stage a stable opposition: the novel arguably furthers its own progress by appropriating some conventions of romance, and the application of the terms 'novel' and 'romance' can in some cases appear arbitrary and inconsistent. But the defining line is in all cases drawn with reference to the likely experience of the reader, and according to the degree of continuity or rupture between that experience and the world of the fiction. The greater the likelihood of such a continuity, the fitter the work to be placed in the category of 'novel'. Clara Reeve, the author of the self-proclaimed Gothic novel, *The Old English Baron* (1778; see *Oxford Companion to the Romantic Age*, p. 670), appealed to this test in her history of narrative fiction, *The Progress of Romance* (1785). Seeking 'to mark the distinguishing characters of the Romance and the Novel, to point out the boundaries of both',[5] she offers the following definition of the 'modern Novel':

The Novel gives a familiar relation of such things, as pass every day before our eyes, such as may happen to our friend, or to ourselves; and the perfection of it, is to represent every scene, in so easy and natural a manner, and to make them appear so probable, as to deceive us into a persua-sion (at least while we are reading) that all is real, until we are affected by the joys or distresses, of the persons in the story, as if they were our own.[6]

In dispensing with or mitigating the 'marvellous' and supernatural improbabilities of romance, novelists flattered their readers, implying that they had grown too discerning to be played upon like their credulous ancestors. Reeve, however, draws attention to a new kind of 'deception' practised on the reader, '(at least while we are reading)', in which the 'easy and natural' style of the writing distracts attention from the act of reading itself, thereby creating a new layer of experience, temporarily indistinguishable from the fiction.

The absorption of the reader by his, or more usually her, reading material is a para-digmatic concern in Romantic-period novel-writing and criticism, but it is a concern which runs parallel to a frequently articulated awareness of the role played by form in encouraging or disrupting such absorption. This heightened formal self-consciousness is wielded initially as a moral tool, to prevent the errors that might proceed from inadvertent reproduction in real life of attitudes or actions encountered in fiction. Increasingly in this period, however, it is incorporated into narratives as part of the repertoire of pleasures available to a sophisticated novel reader.

The poet, essayist, and educationalist, Anna Laetitia Barbauld, acknowledged the power of a novel's formal organization to shape the reading of reality, in an essay 'On the Origin and Progress of Novel-Writing', prefixed to her fifty-volume collection, *The British Novelists* (1810). Here she reminds readers that, unlike real life, novels can be understood as 'a *whole*, in which the fates and fortunes of the personages are brought to a conclusion, agreeably to the author's own preconceived idea'. Sir Walter Scott com-plained, in the *Quarterly Review* of January 1821, that some authors' preconceived designs were too apparent, and that, far from allowing readers' own conclusions to coincide with the end of their reading, these didactic novelists 'first thought of a moral, and then framed a fable to illustrate it'. A self-defeating pattern is identified, too, in novels whose design has the opposite tendency; namely, to keep from the reader for as long as possible, through continual mystification and prolongation of narrative, the conclusion of its fiction. In such works, noted Coleridge's review of Ann Radcliffe's

Mysteries of Udolpho (*Critical Review*, August 1794), the 'interest is completely dissolved when once the adventure is finished, and the reader, when he is got to the end of the work, looks about in vain for the spell which had bound him so strongly to it'. Where this is the case, implies the reviewer, there is little incentive to reread a novel, and a novel that cannot be reread is perpetually fixed in the *arriviste*, subliterary category of the 'new book'.

Origins and directions

Other Romantic-period readers did not concur with Coleridge's assessment of Radcliffe's most famous work. *The Mysteries of Udolpho* is in one way the subject of more rereadings than most novels between its publication in 1794 and the early years of Victoria's reign: for decades, novelists writing after *Udolpho* revise and reinterpret its mysteries and their effects, with more or less conscious intent. Best known of these rereadings is of course Jane Austen's early fable of readerly education, *Northanger Abbey* (1818), in which the formative, if subsequently qualified, influence of the Gothic romance on the young heroine is a covert allegory for its important, if subsequently superseded, contribution to the history and progress of the novel (see also the chapter on 'Gothic'). *The Mysteries of Udolpho* is just one such 'horrid novel' mentioned by Austen in what has come to be known as the 'Northanger canon', a collection of titles unusual in novels of this period for attempting to create neither a role call of ignominy, from which the book in hand is by implication exempt, nor a canon of exception, in which select novels are plucked from infamy to provide a genealogy for the current work. The wider function of these lists of titles, sometimes located, as in Frances Burney's *Evelina* (1778) or Maria Edgeworth's *Belinda* (1801), in the preface, is to locate the novel, as a genre, in an historical narrative of its own.

Perhaps the most significant date in this narrative was 1774, the year that saw the abolition of 'perpetual copyright', or the author's permanent right of ownership in his literary 'property' (see *Oxford Companion to the Romantic Age*, pp. 466–7). This defeat brought about a historical disjuncture, between texts by living authors still able to exert their rights, and the legitimately reproducible works of dead writers. In the case of the novel, this sense of the availability of the past finds its most tangible expression in large edited collections such as John Cooke's series (1794–5), from which Hazlitt learned to love the 'British Novelists'.

The selections made by the editors of such collections point to the origins and directions being chosen for the novel in the Romantic period. The ten-volume Ballantyne's Novelist's Library (1821–4) is often considered as doubly representative of this selection process, since its editions are prefaced with biographical and critical essays by Scott, also an innovative practitioner of the novel form. In close association with Scott's Janus-faced role as guardian of the history, and architect of the future of the novel, the Standard works in the Ballantyne volumes suggest an influential tradition for the kind of novelistic practice he wishes to endorse. Perhaps unsurprisingly, the spirit of adventure is identified as the original impulse behind the form. The picaresque plot, enabling the greatest number and variety of encounters between hero and world, is conspicuously represented by the works of Cervantes, Le Sage, Swift (*Gulliver's Travels*), Fielding, and Smollett, as well as more obliquely in Samuel Johnson's philosophical fable, *Rasselas*, and by the non-human protagonist of Charles Johnstone's *Adventures of a Guinea*. The novel of sensibility or sentiment takes up a number of the volumes, not least because of the disproportionate length of the epistolary contributions of Richardson (*Pamela*, *Clarissa*, and *Sir Charles Grandison* published in full), followed by the comparatively slight works of Goldsmith, Mackenzie, and Sterne. The third dominant school of novel-writing in this collection is the Gothic, the history of which is traced from Walpole's *Castle of Otranto*, through Clara Reeve's *Old English Baron*, into the early Romantic period, where five romances by Radcliffe conclude the collection.

One possible interpretation of the progress traced out here is that it does not unambivalently represent 'Progress' in the newer, Whiggish sense of steady improvement or inevitable civilization. Scott's prefaces notice a frustrating reluctance to move forward in the fictions presented by the Library: the leisured prolixity of Richardson's epistolary art, in particular, is presented as rather provoking to the expectations of the modern reader. Even the mysteries of the Radcliffean plot, designed, as it seemed to Coleridge in 1794, to whet the 'vulgar appetite' of curiosity, appear to Scott in 1824 more like a soothing confection for the palate of an invalid. A common explanation for the growing impatience with slow-moving or 'redundant' fictions, perceived in the reading public during the Romantic period, was the pace at which events in public life were communicated by the print media. Wordsworth's Preface to the *Lyrical Ballads* in 1800 diagnoses in the reading public a 'craving for extraordinary incident which the rapid communication of intelligence hourly gratifies', which he attributes to 'the great national events which are daily taking place'.[7] In an essay on 'Standard Novels and Romances' in the *Edinburgh Review* (1815), Hazlitt regrets a falling off, in modern novels, from the Shakespearean study of character in the tradition bequeathed by Cervantes to the likes of Fielding, Sterne, and Smollett. He attributes this dying art to the changes in public life and its representation since the middle of the eighteenth century: whereas '[t]he reign of George II was, in a word, in an eminent degree, *the age of hobby-horses* [personal eccentricities or obsessions]', the warmongering of the Regency government has driven out all interest in 'our own affairs, or laughing at each other', and replaced it with a national fascination with 'the returns of killed and wounded', and 'the manufacture of newspapers and parliamentary speeches'.[8]

The rapid transition from a period in which the 'whole surface of society appeared cut out into square enclosures and sharp angles' and 'each individual had a certain ground-plot of his own to cultivate his particular humours in', to one where the nation was united in breathlessly following 'the tumult of events crowded into this period',[9] is one way of accounting for the decline in popularity of the epistolary novel at the beginning of the nineteenth century. Audiences schooled in reading by the 'manufacture of newspapers' and reviews that increasingly praised novels written in a higher journalistic style, discouraged the production of fictions where the narrative was passed from hand to hand, and where the plot was dependent on the 'particular humours' of each letter-writer. Another possible reason for the discrediting of the epistolary mode is, as Nicola Watson has argued (see 'Further reading', below), its association with the dangerously excessive sensibility of novels imported from the Continent. One novel in particular was both celebrated and vilified for its depiction of the exquisite and amoral sensations of romantic love: *Julie, ou La Nouvelle Héloïse* (1761), by the Genevan-born philosopher, Jean-Jacques Rousseau. Swiftly translated into English, the novel was a great popular success in the decades leading up to the revolution in France, but, throughout the 1790s, criticism from both sides of the political divide held it up as a model of everything that was most harmful to the morals of English readers.

The connection between acute feeling and virtue proposed by the British novel of sentiment or sensibility was already subject to critical scrutiny. By 1785 even Henry Mackenzie, the author of the influential *Man of Feeling*, was voicing his concern, in his periodical journal, *The Lounger* (20), that the sentiment in such novels remained isolated in the aesthetic sphere, rather than giving rise to virtuous actions. The events of 1789 made such a breach between art and life seem relatively harmless. When the egalitarian sentiment of Rousseau's social philosophy spilled over into revolutionary action in Paris, the possibility of similar transgressions resulting from reading his novels seemed very real. The seduction plot of *La Nouvelle Héloïse* (in many ways a response to the ruination by letters of Richardson's heroine, Clarissa) was accused of recommending in domestic life the same subversion and government by the passions that Rousseau's theoretical writings had brought about in the arena of European politics.

In 1792, Charlotte Smith published her epistolary novel, *Desmond*, set in revolution-era France. Here the letter form is exploited both as a fitting convention for her Rousseauvian account of a young man's love for a married woman and as a kind of fictional 'foreign correspondence', in which the letter written 'to the moment' fulfils a reportorial function as well as providing a moral guarantee by its unpremeditated appearance (see also the chapter on 'Letters, Journals, and Diaries'). The novel was initially well received, but, in the more conservative climate that developed in England after the French regicide of 1793, critical response to Smith's work grew more hostile and mistrustful. The epistolary mode could no longer suggest the same degree of artlessness as it could for Frances Burney's *Evelina* in 1778, and novels of the post-revolutionary period that make use of letter-writing in their narratives (e.g. Mary Shelley's *Frankenstein*, 1818) do so in such a way as to demonstrate their awareness of the partial or relative truth contained in a letter.

La Nouvelle Héloïse was not the only European novel to provoke anxiety about the dangers of unmediated subjectivity and sentiment in the epistolary form. The sensational reception on the Continent of *Die Leiden des Jungen Werther* (*The Sorrows of Young Werther*, 1774), by the German writer, Johann Wolfgang von Goethe also caused a frisson of concern to be felt in British periodical reviews. 'Wertherism' became short-hand for an over-literal translation of literature into action, after the epidemic of sui-cides that was understood to sweep through late eighteenth-century continental Europe, by sentimental young men seduced into shooting themselves in imitation of Goethe's lovelorn hero. Whilst it is difficult to obtain empirical data concerning the real number of such deaths, it is clear that the idea of a novel as the cause of such desperate action was taken very seriously indeed, and contributed to a transformation in the form and function of the novel after the end of the eighteenth century.

This transformation is signalled not only by the disappearance of the epistolary novel, but also by the systematic undermining in prose fiction of the Romantic period of the principle of self-representation. It is as if isolated and unmediated subjectivity has become too volatile a force to be entrusted to a popular prose medium such as the novel, and uninterrupted first-person narrative is increasingly confined to poetry. Indeed, it is difficult to think—with the significant exception of Godwin's *Caleb Williams* (1794), discussed below in the section on narrative voice—of a novel pub-lished between Sterne's *Tristram Shandy* (1759–67) and Charlotte Brontë's *Jane Eyre* (1847), in which a first-person narrative is presented as the entirety of a novel, without being embedded in an ironizing or relativizing editorial framework (as in Edgeworth's *Castle Rackrent* or Hogg's *Confessions of a Justified Sinner*).

This is not to suggest that the eighteenth century and the Victorian period were golden ages of unproblematic, unambiguous first-person narratives: of the two examples given above, Sterne's novel can be read as an exercise in reducing to the point of absurdity the notion that a man can be his own historian, whereas Brontë's journal-izing governess continually, and troublingly, hints that a first-person narrator can withhold as much as she discloses. But the Romantic period does represent a hiatus in the production of novels narrated entirely in the first person. It is interesting to note that Scott's tradition-creating choices for Ballantyne's Novelist's Library omit not only the European epistolary novel in the works of Rousseau and Goethe, but also the early, English, first-person narratives of Daniel Defoe. Scott remarked in a *Quarterly Review* article of 1821 that Defoe's novels 'have been oftener mistaken for true narratives, than any fictions that ever were composed'.

When, in the mid-nineteenth century, the first-person narrative became once more an essential part of the novelist's craft, it was in large part owing to the histories that had been created in the Romantic period. The narrative history of the novel prepared by British fiction-writers of the preceding generation had given the form its own story, and it was now used to record the growth of novelists themselves. Goethe's later work, *Wilhelm Meister's Lehrjahre* (*Wilhelm Meister's Apprenticeship*, 1795–6), translated by Thomas Carlyle in 1824, provided at this stage a more measured and detached model for a novel charting the development of selfhood, later to be termed the *Bildungsroman* or novel of 'education'. Typical, and in many ways prototypical of such endeavours in

English, is Charles Dickens's *David Copperfield* (1849–50). This quasi-autobiographical work follows the experience of the hero from birth to maturity as a novelist and the supposed author of his own Life. In this way, and through its representation of David's childhood reading as a collection of eighteenth-century Standard Novels, *David Copperfield* maps the history of an individual on to the progress of the novel form.

Genre and subgenres

In the late 1790s, a series of conversations between Wordsworth and Coleridge resulted in a collection of poems that adapted existing genre categories. The *Lyrical Ballads* of 1798, Coleridge recalled, was conceived with 'the two cardinal points of poetry' in mind, namely 'the power of exciting the sympathy of the reader by a faithful adherence to the truth of nature, and the power of giving the interest of novelty by the modifying colours of the imagination'. But, as the hybrid nature of the collection's title suggests, the poems were also designed to demonstrate the interfusion of the naturalistic and the imaginative, so that the 'supernatural, or at least romantic' could be presented with a 'semblance of truth', and 'the charm of novelty' could be given to 'things of every day'.[10]

A similar dialogue can be seen at work in the Romantic-period novel, between verisimilitude and fantasy, truth and transcendence, rationality and romance. This inherent hybridity is less likely to be presented by novelists and critics of the period as epoch-making and experimental, perhaps because, unlike poetry, the novel had for some time been considered as existing outside the neoclassical hierarchy of genres, or as a kind of magpie genre that picked up and assimilated the characteristics of other categories. But a continual negotiation between more or less naturalistic and romantic principles of creation is what makes many of the texts under consideration in this chapter distinctively Romantic novels.

The terms of this negotiation are to a considerable degree set by the Gothic novel, a subgenre which has recently come to be considered as a Romantic form in itself (see the chapter on the 'Gothic'). The publication of *The Mysteries of Udolpho* in 1794 with the subtitle, 'A Romance; Interspersed with Some Pieces of Poetry', announced a new age of novel-writing that placed the Mystery at the centre of its thematic, rhetorical, and moral projects. The notorious episode of the 'veiled picture' is emblematic of this paradigm shift: Radcliffe's incarcerated heroine, Emily, wandering through 'obscure and desolated' chambers of the castle of Udolpho, peers behind the black silk veil that covers a particular picture frame.[11] What she sees causes her to lose consciousness from sheer terror, but is not fully described to the reader for another 400 pages; the true nature of the horrendous sight is never revealed to Emily.

Subsequent novelistic essays in the Gothic—notably, Matthew Lewis's *The Monk* (1796) and Charlotte Dacre's *Zofloya* (1806)—associated the idea of Mystery more strongly with the deliberate obfuscations of religion or the dark machinations of satanic forces, but in Radcliffe's influential version the trope is more broadly representative of that which transcends, eludes, or prevents knowledge. As such, Radcliffean Mystery comes to stand for everything militating against the education or moral growth of the individual, thereby defining the fundamental conflict dramatized by at least two important subgenres of the novel around the end of the eighteenth century. The Jacobin novel (so-called because of a real or perceived sympathy with French revolutionary radicalism) and the Moral Tale both project an ideal of fiction as in the service of a more rationally oriented society, in which unjust and arbitrary social restraints are replaced by the voluntary and virtuous self-restraint of the individual. Where the Moral Tale, as epitomized by Maria Edgeworth's *Belinda* (1801), sets out to present a new form of fiction committed to the reform of the glamorous Mysteries of aristocratic vice, Jacobin novels such as Godwin's *Caleb Williams* (1794) and Mary Wollstonecraft's *The Wrongs of Woman* (1797) often borrow Gothic motifs of incarceration and persecution, the better to expose the Mysteries with which the institutions of oppression cloak their misrule.

The Wrongs of Woman begins by invoking the 'ABODES OF HORROR' and 'castles, filled with spectres and chimeras' of the Gothic novel, only to depreciate their imaginary terrors by comparison with the de facto legal status of women such as her heroine, wrongly committed to a mental asylum on the instruction of her tyrannical and unworthy husband.[12] As the novel progresses, however, it becomes apparent that the imaginary incarcerations of romance are the more hopelessly imprisoning, since they rob the mind of women readers of their rightful liberty and immure them in vanity and false sentiment. Wollstonecraft's demystifying strategy is fraught with danger, as her tale so closely shadows the fictions of sensibility and romance as to risk readerly engagement with the forms she warns against.

Edgeworth's *Belinda*, whilst ostensibly charting the development 'by circumstances' of the already unimpeachable character of her heroine, invests considerable narrative energy in the more rewarding story of the reform of the Lady Delacour, whose dissolute lifestyle is a self-created Mystery thrown up to mask the real pain of secret ill-health. Belinda, who declares, 'I hate all mysteries',[13] undertakes the spiritual and physical medication of her aristocratic patroness, not least through a course of exemplary reading, until Lady Delacour, freed from the canker of secrecy, is herself able to provide the moral of the tale and end the novel. *Belinda* abounds with indications that reading can be character forming only when teleological; that is, aimed at the end or moral of the story rather than at tantalizing, mysterious fragments.

Another strand in the generic definition of the Romantic-period novel is the study of manners, a concern connecting the society novels of Frances Burney, Maria Edgeworth, and Jane Austen with the historical and national tales that became increasingly popular with the second wave of Romanticism in Britain. When he warns his readers to expect, from *Waverley* (1814), 'more a description of men than manners', Scott is signalling his novel's deviation from the ephemera of the tale of fashionable life as much as from the 'romance of chivalry'. The study of 'manners' here is relegated to the level of the trivial, contingent, and merely external, where the study of 'men', it is suggested, is more likely to identify enduring, inward, and fundamental qualities that transcend time and place. And yet the historical novel as pioneered by Scott is no more nor less than a minute investigation into the influence of accidents of birth, education, and ethnicity, as well as of larger currents of philosophical and political thought, on the external habits of speech and behaviour that culture teaches us to read as an index of inner being. What redeems this investigation from mere relativity or triviality is a whole apparatus of literary devices, including a framework of popular antiquarianism and a deflating, distancing narrative commentary. The study of 'manners' is raised into a study of 'men' by the universalizing action of the literary.

The same principle applies to the vignettes of provincial manners presented in the novels of Austen, represented as in themselves contingent, local, and even petty, but worthy of sympathy and deeper scrutiny because related through the allusive and ironic voice of a judge of literary taste as well as human nature. Both Scott and Austen learnt from the national tales of Maria Edgeworth, whose *Castle Rackrent* (1800) is both, as its preface suggests, a record of 'the manners of a certain class of the gentry of Ireland some years ago', and a study in the various literary methods of recording manners so as to suggest resonances beyond the merely historical or regional.[14]

The narrator in the Romantic-period novel

One of the devices by which Edgeworth broadens the field of reference of *Castle Rackrent* beyond late eighteenth-century rural Ireland is ambiguity. The particular form of the ambiguity she employs is highly historically and geographically specific, since it consists in splitting the narration of her tale on the page between the voice of Thady, the Irish Catholic steward of the landowning Anglo-Irish Rackrent family, and that of the drily academic 'editor' figure who provides frequent footnotes to Thady's account. In a typographical enactment of the diglossia or dual register that enters a language under colonialization, the body-text and footnotes undercut and relativize each other through linguistic divergences, even where the factual basis of their shared history is consistent. The reader is obliged to read not simply between the lines but also between the two voices, with the result that neither seems entirely trustworthy.

Closer analysis of other novels of this age suggests that this is a typical narrative device, and that in fact the Romantic-period novel not only foregrounds the heteroglossia or multivocal quality that the Russian critic Mikhail Bakhtin identified with novelistic discourse as a whole (see Further reading, below), but often locates the divergence in voices within the mode of narration itself. This tendency destabilizes the common association of Romantic literature with the representation of privileged, primary, and unified subjectivity: narrative heteroglossia in the Romantic-period novel results not so much in subjective realism—the idea that there are several ways of telling every story—as in the suggestion that every way of telling is itself divided or inhabited by several voices.

The apparent mistrust of self-representation in Romantic prose fiction was touched on above. An important, though qualified exception to the general absence of first-person narratives in this period is *Caleb Williams* (1794) by William Godwin. Presented in the form of a memoir or testimony, part self-vindication and part self-accusation, the novel is really the story of two men locked together in a psychological fight to the death. The narrator, Williams, in his position as secretary to the benevolent Mr Falkland obtains access to documents that prove the squire guilty of murder. Though his devotion to his employer determines him to remain silent, his relentless persecution at the hands of Falkland eventually forces Williams, in despair, to make a public accusation, and the narrative ends with a full confession by Falkland, who subsequently dies, leaving Williams to recriminate with himself: 'I began these memoirs with the idea of vindicating my character. I have now no character that I wish to vindicate.'[15]

Godwin claimed in a preface written for the 1832 edition of *Caleb Williams* that he began the narrative 'as is the more usual way, in the third person', but soon realized that the first-person narrative would better enable him to employ his 'metaphysical dissecting knife in tracing and laying bare the involutions of motive'.[16] Self-representation is here demonstrated as the last resort of a subject divided against itself by the unnatural and inhumane mechanisms of power, and narrative unity lays itself open to the 'dissecting' methods of forensic psychological study. Motive, too, is revealed as involuted or turned in upon itself, in an anatomical metaphor that suggests a painful retrogression of the will into incarcerating self-consciousness: concluding his memoirs, Williams laments, 'Why should my reflections perpetually centre upon myself?'[17]

Recent critical fashion has meant that the paradigm of Romantic consciousness privileged in academic discourse has moved closer to the self-contradictory mock-epic of Byron's *Don Juan* (1819–24) than to the 'egotistical sublime' of Wordsworth's narrative poetry or to the intense, luxuriant inwardness of Keatsian lyric. Critical consensus over what constitutes the Romantic in literature has increasingly centred around the ideas of Romantic irony introduced by German writers of the period such as Friedrich Schlegel. Schlegel suggested that the novel was the most suitable literary form for the Romantic ironist, since it allowed a perpetual oscillation between illusion and disillusion, or between engagement and withdrawal on the part of the narrator. It is likely that when Schlegel made this suggestion, he had in mind English novels such as Sterne's *Tristram Shandy*, in which the narrator takes such exaggerated pains to re-create the minutiae of real events that the reader becomes exasperatedly aware of the impossibility of a literal mimesis. This kind of ironic awareness is occasionally fostered by the narrator in Austen's novels, as towards the end of *Northanger Abbey*, where readers are credited with a consciousness of literary convention that will allow them to deduce from 'the tell-tale compression of the pages before them, that we are all hastening together to perfect felicity'.[18] More often, however, Austen's narrative irony functions on a smaller scale, drawing attention to literary form at the level of the sentence rather than the whole book.

This is pre-eminently the case in her last work, *Persuasion* (1817), where the repetition of the same phrase mediated by different modes of narration can convey multiple and divergent interpretive possibilities. So, when Anne Elliot hears from her insensitive and vain sister that her former lover, Captain Wentworth, has remarked upon her changed appearance, there is a difference between the reported speech within her sister's dialogue, and the repetition of the phrase, 'So altered that he should not have known her again!' in a subsequent paragraph.[19] On the latter occasion the phrase is received as an echo in Anne's mind of Wentworth's judgement, coloured by her consciousness that he has had cause to find her culpably, morally changeable in the past. The next paragraph in this sequence modulates into a presentation of Wentworth's interior monologue, and when the phrase is repeated once more as a summary of the captain's sentiments, it is with the intention that, like his speech a few lines later, it should eventually 'be contradicted' by the reader's awareness of the gradual reawakening of his esteem for Anne.[20]

Repetition for ironic effect is a feature of the many parodic novels of the Romantic period, ranging from conservative mockeries of the excesses of sensibility and credulity in formula romances, such as Eaton Stannard Barrett's *The Heroine* (1813), to the dialogic novels of Thomas Peacock, with their exaggerated representations of the conversation of poets and philosophers. An increasingly apparent phenomenon in the Romantic-period novel is that of parody as a first means of entering into the realm of authorship. Whilst parody in this period is frequently used as a means of deterring the socially disenfranchised from literary creation, it also seems to serve as a rite of passage for aspirant but marginalized writers such as women (Austen, Charlotte Brontë) or working-class men. This is one way of reading the extraordinary *Private Memoirs and Confessions of a Justified Sinner* (1824), by James Hogg, the 'Ettrick Shepherd'.

The reiteration of the same tale of apparently demonic doubling, firstly by an Editor's Narrative and secondly in the form of the confessions of the Sinner, generates uncertainty as to which is the pre-text and which the repetition. Furthermore, the final pages of the Editor's Narrative introduce an extract from an 'authentic letter, published in *Blackwood's Magazine* for August 1823', 'signed JAMES HOGG' and offering a third version of the Sinner's story from the perspective of a local historian.[21] The Editor betrays a nervous desire to fix the nature of the work in some more recognizable and stable literary form, such as 'allegory' or 'religious PARABLE', but the embedding of the Confessions in two other narratives implies that any analogue for the story will not be found outside of the text but within the novel as a whole. Just as the Sinner of the story is encouraged by his sinister double to devise increasingly elaborate means of justifying his own atrocities, so the Editor and letter-writer resort to ever more tortuous devices for 'justifying' or squaring up the various competing and divergent narratives. In this way, the *Confessions* parody the narrative heteroglossia of many Romantic-period novels, without providing the satisfaction for the reader of a master-narrative in which to resolve the conflicting voices.

Fanny Burney, *Evelina; or the History of a Young Lady's Entrance into the World*[22]

Evelina makes an Entrance

On the first night of her first ever visit to London, the inexperienced young heroine, Evelina, is taken to Drury Lane theatre, where she has the good fortune to see 'the celebrated Mr Garrick' (p. 27). She writes the same night to her guardian, Mr Villars, in 'raptures' at the 'ease' of the great actor's performance: 'I could hardly believe he had studied a written part, for every word seemed spoke from the impulse of the moment . . . And when he danced—O how I envied Clarinda. I almost wished to have jumped on the stage and joined them' (pp. 27–8).

Burney's first novel abounds with reported scenes of performance and audience, literal and metaphorical; part of the lesson Evelina must learn on her entrance into the world concerns the appropriate degree of participation or passive response to what she observes. This early episode in the theatre immediately positions her response in terms both of the world she has entered and of the novel as an art form at this point in its history.

Evelina's astonishment at Garrick's naturalistic acting would have recalled for many late eighteenth-century readers the reaction of another naïve, country-educated playgoer. Partridge, the schoolmaster in Fielding's great comic novel, *Tom Jones* (1749), famously finds Garrick's Hamlet so realistic that he refuses to believe that he has witnessed a theatrical performance at all, insisting that the actor's response to the 'ghost' was one of real, not dissembled, fear. *Tom Jones* was itself seen as pioneering a new, naturalistic style of novel which made it harder for readers to differentiate between fact and fiction. The critic Samuel Johnson suggested that this confusion increased the novel's potential for imperceptible moral influence on its readers, for good or ill. In the second half of the century, the type of reader most likely to suffer from such confusion and to succumb to the influence of a novel was increasingly identified as female.

Evelina's comments in this letter therefore situate her in terms of contemporary beliefs about the novel and its readers, and signal that the history unfolding will be to some extent narrated by a 'typical' female reader-figure. Crucially, however, she stops short of acting on her desire to become part of the fiction she responds to: she only '*almost* wished to have jumped on the stage and joined them' (my emphasis). Here as throughout *Evelina*, the spatial organization of the theatre demarcates boundaries which cannot be overstepped without socially mortifying consequences.

The trope of the theatre as an 'epitome of the world' (cf. p. 413 n. 27) is common to many forms of eighteenth-century literature, and one employed in various forms by Burney in

Evelina. Social rank is nicely indicated by seating arrangements in the auditorium, as in the episode in Volume I where Evelina is obliged to accompany the trading-class branch of her family to the opera; the dangerous error of judgement she makes in agreeing to leave, unchaperoned, with Sir Clement Willoughby is in part occasioned by her terror of being seen in the one-shilling gallery by her socially superior connections in the pit (p. 95). In another visit to a play earlier in the volume, the preposterous coxcomb Mr Lovel asserts that the theatre is a place one comes to, not to watch the proceedings on stage, but merely 'to shew that one's alive' (p. 82), and Evelina quickly learns that it is her own visibility or otherwise that is at stake as she makes the rounds of the fashionable 'entertainments' of the capital. This ritualized emergence into public view is signified by the novel's subtitle, but there is another sense in which *Evelina* is a history of its eponymous heroine's 'entrance into the world'. Evelina must appear before polite society in order to cast light on her obscure birth; literally, to show that she is alive.

In her second novel, *Cecilia* (1782), Frances Burney made the first recorded use of the phrase 'to come out' to describe a young woman's formal emergence into society, especially by means of presentation at court. The expression was also current during the Romantic period to describe someone making their debut on stage, and in use, then as now, for the publication of books. The ambivalence displayed by the author of *Evelina* about the publication of her first book is well documented in Burney's journal and letters, and forms the basis of much modern criticism of the novel (see 'Further reading', below). The constellation of ideas surrounding Evelina/*Evelina*'s emergence as public figure, 'actress', and published work of fiction also gives rise to a kind of ambivalence in the reader who tries to read the novel as a Romantic form.

Evelina as a Romantic-period novel

As its subtitle suggests, *Evelina* can be read as a narrative of socialization, charting the experiences of a young woman learning how to conduct herself in public life. Part of the pleasure of this immensely entertaining narrative comes from playful hints that, in following Evelina's progress, the reader may be undergoing the same process of education and socialization. At one stage, Evelina remarks in exasperation that 'there ought to be a book, of the laws and customs *à-la-mode*, presented to all young people, upon their first introduction into public company' (p. 84). There is a sense in which the heroine's own reports of her errors and new experiences act as just such a guide; as in the first lesson she has to learn about politely refusing a partner at a ball (Volume I, letter xi), or in the numerous new phrases for fashionable activities, such as 'shopping' (p. 28) or 'seeing sights' (p. 39), which the novel introduces. Some critics have suggested analogies between the kind of advice explicitly or indirectly communicated by *Evelina*, and the influential 'conduct books' aimed at young women in the later eighteenth century (see *Oxford Companion to the Romantic Age*, p. 464). Burney chose to present her narrative in the form of a novel, however, rather than a conduct manual, and this means that *Evelina*'s commitment to sociality is altogether more ambiguous.

In her preface to the novel, Burney lists what she calls 'our predecessors, to whom this species of writing is indebted for being saved from contempt, and rescued from depravity' (p. 9). Amongst the six names to whom she gives this credit are two who made especially famous the epistolary form of novel used for *Evelina*: Samuel Richardson, author of *Clarissa* (1747–8), and Jean-Jacques Rousseau, the French political philosopher whose novel *Julie, ou la Nouvelle Héloïse* (1761) was to some extent a revised version of *Clarissa*. Richardson, in particular, had insisted throughout his career on the virtues of his novels as socializing forms, teaching the values of polite culture and religion. This insistence was maintained in the face of growing fears that the private reading experience encouraged by novels rendered consumers of the novel peculiarly unfit for social intercourse or public virtue.

Both Richardson and Rousseau use the epistolary form to tell the stories of innocent young women whose entrance into the world is beset with the same kinds of dangers which threaten the reputation of Evelina. Unlike Evelina, however, there is no triumphant emergence from the trials faced by the heroines of these cautionary tales: Clarissa's history culminates in her abduction, rape, and eventual death; Julie's consists of seduction, illegitimate pregnancy, and enforced marriage to a respectable man she cannot love. The fate of both these women is traced back to their initial, culpable engagement in a private exchange of letters with their undoers, whereas Evelina never replies to what she believes to be Lord Orville's attempts to instigate an improper private correspondence with her (p. 257). It is as if what Evelina instinctively knows, but her epistolary predecessors do not, is that any aspects of a young woman's behaviour, even letter-writing, which are not public or at least communally oriented risk endangering her life and, worse, her reputation. She assures the Revd Villars that she has 'an aversion the most sincere to all mysteries, all private actions' (p. 260).

Rousseau's *Nouvelle Héloïse* was interpreted by many Romantic-period readers as promoting the kind of private experience it ostensibly cautions against, through the attractive, passionate sincerity expressed in the lovers' letters. The epistolary form in this case stands as a guarantee of the kind of immediate, unsocialized interiority often considered to be a special property of Romantic literature. It is much harder to decide whether Burney's use of this form in *Evelina* offers a similar guarantee.

Some critics of *Evelina* have questioned whether the apparent 'artlessness' of Evelina's letters masks a more knowing, manipulative character, who is in turn manoeuvred into such disingenuousness by the restrictions imposed on her by a patriarchal society (cf. 'Further Reading', below). This approach, whilst it encourages a useful attention to Evelina's epistolary style, is perhaps asking the wrong kind of question, proceeding as it does from an assumption that there is a 'real' self behind the character presented to us as 'Evelina'. The absence of such a core, hidden interiority seems perpetually dramatized by the novel; in its employment of theatrical metaphors for its heroine's situation: in its identification of her 'entrance into the world' with her social rebirth as the true daughter of her biological father (the emotional scene of her reunion with Sir John Belmont itself resembling a set-piece of sentimental theatre); in Evelina's instinctive avoidance of the pitfalls of 'private actions'. The absence of a typically Romantic self at the centre of *Evelina* is above all signalled by the novel's insistence on social embarrassment, or shame, rather than, say, the promptings of private conscience, as the ultimate moral sanction for its heroine. On this scheme of things, more distress is occasioned by the misuse of one's name by socially inferior relations (p. 246) than by the sight of two poor, dependent old women forced to engage in a footrace (pp. 311–12).

There is, however, implicit in *Evelina* a belief in a form of consciousness distinct from the society depicted through the letters: that of a new breed of novel-reader, with a sensibility educated and refined by her choice of literary entertainment, accustomed to cultivate in private a sense of moral judgement or sympathy which is not an explicit part of the narrative's public voice, and capable of an engagement which nevertheless differentiates between fiction and reality.

Sir Walter Scott, *Waverley; or, 'Tis Sixty Years Since*[23]

'The romance of his life' and 'real history'

Towards the end of the third and final volume of *Waverley*, the young man referred to as 'our hero' by the novel's occasionally sardonic narrative voice finds the leisure to review his recent experiences. From his position of hiding in the Lake District he hears of the failure of the cause with which he has, quasi-accidentally, aligned himself and fought 'in civil conflict'. Whilst Charles Stuart, figurehead of the Jacobite insurgency, makes his retreat from the deadly efficiency of the Duke of Cumberland, Waverley comes to a rare, pragmatic conclusion:

[H]e felt himself entitled to say firmly, though perhaps with a sigh, that the romance of his life was ended, and that its real history had now commenced. He was soon called upon to justify his pretensions to reason and philosophy. (p. 283)

Such a clean distinction, between 'romance' and 'real history' is not one which the novel *Waverley* facilitates. In the case of Edward Waverley, the 'real history' of his life will entail a withdrawal from political conflict into domestic tranquillity; it is the details prior to this withdrawal with which the novel is concerned and which therefore constitute the 'history' of Waverley in the sense that *Evelina* is 'the History of a Young Lady's Entrance into the World'. These prior details, designated 'romance' by our hero, happen to occupy the same terrain as what is often considered to be 'real history': the actual events surrounding the attempt by supporters of the house of Stuart, in 1745, to reclaim the British throne from the Hanoverian dynasty.

The sentence following Waverley's evaluation of his life story hints at further ambiguity, referring as it does to the young man's 'pretensions to reason and philosophy'. The verb *to pretend* is heavily loaded in this context, since 'the Pretender' was a term used of both Charles Stuart and his father, James III, by those who did not believe they had a just claim to the throne. Thus even as Waverley seems to be leaving behind the romance of a lost cause in favour of 'reason and philosophy'—the watchwords of the Scottish Enlightenment which, we are later informed, ensued from 'the total eradication of the Jacobite party' (p. 340)—the use of this word 'pretensions' pulls him, and the reader, backwards, in the direction of older claims.

Scott is frequently given credit for making respectable the denigrated, feminized genre of romance by infusing it with the masculine, empirical essence of real history. It is certainly true that history was widely considered at this period to represent a superior form of reading matter to novels and romances: Catherine Morland acknowledges this genre hierarchy in Austen's *Northanger Abbey* (pub. 1818), when she admits that she feels obliged to read 'real solemn history' occasionally, 'as a duty'. This does not prevent her from making unfavourable comparisons between such virtuous reading and novels, in terms which shed an interesting light on to Scott's hybrid 'historical romance':

'I often think it odd that it should be so dull, for a great deal of it must be invention. The speeches that are put into the heroes' mouths, their thoughts and designs—the chief of all this must be invention, and invention is what delights me in other books.'[24]

Austen is not merely poking fun at her heroine's limited reading. Catherine's ingenuous identification of 'invention' in the work of empiricist historians like 'Mr Hume' hints at the existence of common ground between the genres of history and romance, even before it was mapped out by the historical novel.

Since, as we have seen above, the narrative tone of *Waverley* itself teaches us to be cautious about any easy distinctions between 'romance' and 'real history', can the 'historical' part of the subgenre 'historical romance' or 'historical novel' have any real meaning when applied to Scott's prose fiction? One level on which we might expect the novel to be driven by the 'historical' is that of plot: the details of what happens, when, and in what order. This is true of *Waverley* in so far as the outcome of certain events in the novel is already determined; the reasonably well-informed reader knows from the start that Bonny Prince Charlie will not be restored to the throne. But the actual experience of reading *Waverley* is such as partially to suppress the knowledge of this outcome, since the novel frequently sidelines or postpones the narration of historical events as they occurred.

At one stage, indeed, the narrator assures us that it is 'not our purpose to intrude upon the province of history', but that he wishes merely to 'remind our reader, that about the beginning of November the young Chevalier, at the head of about six thousand men at the utmost, resolved to peril his cause upon an attempt to penetrate into the centre of England, although aware of the mighty preparations which were made for his reception' (pp. 263–4). In a similar vein is the '*Postscript, which should have been a Preface*' (pp. 339–41), in which an overview of the economic and cultural consequences of the Hanoverian victory is compressed into a brief chapter, appended like an afterthought to the story.

The plot of *Waverley* takes liberties with historical chronology in other respects, too, choosing not to divulge until the end details of the arrangements made for the hero's kidnap and delivery to the Jacobite forces. The narrator belatedly alludes to 'such points of our narrative, as, according to the custom of story-tellers, we deemed it fit to leave unexplained, for the purpose of exciting the reader's curiosity' (pp. 308–9), appealing to the conventions of romance as justification for the collusion of the plot of the novel with the plotting of the Stuart sympathizers.

The pleasures of the past

Enlightenment is delayed for the hero as well as for the reader: Waverley spends much of the novel in a state of polite ignorance, whether as guest or as prisoner of an unfamiliar society. At one stage he is to be found contemplating 'the strangeness of his fortune, which seemed to delight in placing him at the disposal of others, without the power of directing his own motions' (p. 186). The lack of heroic agency frequently displayed by Waverley aligns him with the benighted and perpetually incarcerated heroines of Radcliffean Gothic, a species of fiction ostensibly disavowed by Scott's narrator in the introductory sequence to the novel (p. 3). The opening chapters also take pains to attribute this passivity to the desultory romance reading that has formed our hero's mind from childhood, awakening his imagination at the expense of his understanding (p. 18).

Throughout his travels in Scotland, Waverley is recognized by those he encounters as a kind of historical tourist; a connoisseur with a taste for the pleasures of the past. As a result, he is repeatedly practised upon by more knowing characters, who procure for him romantic experiences in exchange for the cultural capital he possesses as a Hanoverian soldier and landed English gentleman with political connections. Thus we see Edward Waverley passing through a series of impeccably managed romance tableaux: the torch-lit interior of the cave of Highland bandits (p. 80); the dazzling court of Charles Stuart at Holy-Rood (p. 193); the appointment by a waterfall with Flora, who 'gave the romance of the scene, and other accidental circumstances, full weight in appreciating the feelings with which Waverley seemed obviously to be impressed' (p. 106). Even the warrior-like Fergus avails himself of the 'remnants' of Cervantes in order to 'frame his language to befit romantic ears' (p. 121).

It is not only Waverley's taste that is gratified by these manipulations of the romance paradigm. Each episode in our hero's progress represents a vicarious pleasure offered for the enjoyment of the reader. Unlike Waverley, however, the reader is also made party to the novel's detached, often bathetic narrative commentary, with the reassuring effect that these scenes of romance are revealed, and so can be savoured, as pure commodities, purveyed by the author through the worldly, commercial mechanisms of publishing and bookselling. One could argue that this intermittent, ironic prompt to readerly consciousness constitutes the most distinctively Romantic feature of Scott's novel, but it is not necessarily the defining principle of *Waverley*.

The mystery with which Scott and his publishers deliberately surrounded the authorship of *Waverley* certainly did nothing to diminish the commercial appeal of the book, and in one respect emphasizes the novel's canny repackaging of the mysteries of romance to flatter a new readership's sense of its own perspicacity. The cultivation of this notorious anonymity was for many readers a polite fiction, or just one of the range of romantic pleasures available from the publication of *Waverley*, since the knowledgeable presentation of Scottish folk culture—in particular, the inclusion of Border ballads—was powerfully associated in the popular imagination with the collections of songs and metrical romances published by Scott in previous decades (see *Oxford Companion to the Romantic Age*, p. 692). The absence of an author's name on the title-page of *Waverley* was in a sense consistent with Scott's previous identity as a prominent mediator of 'lost' forms for a modern audience, and still facilitates a reading of these miscellaneous forms as contained, not so much in the design of one man's mind, but by the larger form of the novel itself.

Waverley is above all a collection of curiosities, presented in the heterogeneous shapes of the contents of Aunt Rachael's commonplace book (p. 22), of David Gelattly's old songs (p. 55 and *passim*), of Flora's poetry (pp. 107–9), or the pedantic phraseology of feudal law and classical scholarship with which the Baron Bradwardine seams his speech. Its very narrative is a ragbag: interspersing the minute realism of descriptions of rural poverty (p. 34) or despoiled, war-torn countryside (p. 295) amidst accomplished essays in the sublime and picturesque, breathless battle exercises and passages of direct address to the reader; always celebrating the 'mutability' of the novel's style (p. 91).

In one especially unsettling episode, during which the captive Waverley is interrogated by Major Melville, it becomes apparent that the narrative is able to assume, not merely different voices and styles, but different perspectives altogether: the 'equivocal circumstances' (p. 154) of Waverley's history, by virtue of being collected by a strange hand, are arranged to form a very different, far less sympathetic story from the one presented up to that point (pp. 156–9). Unusually for this novel, reader and protagonist are confronted here with the convincing possibility of a stark difference between the 'romance of [a] life' and 'real history', where the latter is presented as a configuration of evidence, dispassionately considered. A few pages later, the narrator states, only half-jokingly, that 'It is the object of this history to do justice to all men' (p. 171). With the memory of the interrogation scene still fresh in the reader's mind, it is apparent that such justice is not to be found in the narrative organization of the law or of 'real history', but rather in the heterogeneous and curious record of mixed motives which Scott makes of the Romantic-period novel.

FURTHER READING

Bakhtin, M. M., *The Dialogic Imagination*, trans. C. Emerson and M. Holquist (Austin, Tex.: University of Texas Press, 1981). Includes the essay on 'Discourse in the Novel', outlining Bakhtin's theory that a novel is the site of interaction for multiple voices or modes of discourse.

Burney, Fanny, *The Journals and Letters of Fanny Burney (Madame D'Arblay)*, ed. Joyce Hemlow *et al.*, 12 vols. (Oxford: Clarendon Press, 1972–84). The best place to look for first-hand accounts of the publication and reception of *Evelina*, as well as a lively record of the literary and social circles in which Burney moved.

Duncan, Ian, *Modern Romance and Transformations of the Novel: The Gothic, Scott, Dickens* (Cambridge: Cambridge University Press, 1992). Usefully positions Scott between Radcliffe and Dickens in an eloquent and insightful account of Scott's fictional nation-building.

Epstein, Julia, *The Iron Pen: Frances Burney and the Politics of Women's Writing* (Bristol: Bristol Classical Press, 1989). Raises interesting questions about the sincerity of the epistolary form in *Evelina*, and places these questions in the context of the politics of women's writing.

Kelly, Gary, *English Fiction of the Romantic Period, 1789–1830* (London and New York: Longman, 1989). Full and lucid survey of the relation of novelistic forms to historical context, with extended readings of key texts.

Klancher, Jon, *The Making of English Reading Audiences, 1790–1832* (Madison: University of Wisconsin Press, 1987). Useful history of the changing circumstances of publication and reception in the Romantic period.

Lukács, Georg, *The Historical Novel*, trans. Hannah and Stanley Mitchell (Harmondsworth: Penguin, 1962; 1981). Influential Marxist reading that places Scott at the head of a genealogy of the historical novel in Europe.

Price, Leah, *The Anthology and the Rise of the Novel from Richardson to George Eliot* (Cambridge: Cambridge University Press, 2000; 2003). A brilliant and original account of how one facet of publication history defined the practice of, and attitudes to, the eighteenth- and nineteenth-century novel.

Tandon, Bharat, *Jane Austen and the Morality of Conversation* (London: Anthem, 2003). Close study of the novel of manners and the representation of conversation in prose fiction; relevant to other novels of the period as well as Austen.

Watson, Nicola, *Revolution and the Form of the British Novel 1790–1825: Intercepted Letters, Interrupted Seduction* (Oxford: Clarendon Press, 1994). Influential account of the demise of the epistolary novel.

NOTES

1. William Hazlitt, 'On Reading Old Books', *The Plain Speaker* (London: Henry Colburn, 1826), ii. 63.
2. Ibid. 66, 75.
3. Ibid. 63, 68.
4. Ibid. 69, 66.
5. Clara Reeve, *The Progress of Romance, Through Times, Countries, and Manners; with Remarks on the Good and Bad Effects of it, on them Respectively; in a Course of Evening Conversations* (Colchester: W. Keymer, 1785), i, vi.
6. Ibid. i. iii.
7. William Wordsworth, Preface to *Lyrical Ballads* (1800), ed. R. L. Brett and A. R. Jones (London: Routledge, 1991), p. 249.
8. 'Standard Novels and Romances', *Edinburgh Review*, 24 (1815), 335.
9. Ibid.
10. Samuel Taylor Coleridge, *Biographia Literaria*, ed. James Engell and W. Jackson Bate, 2 vols. (Princeton: Princeton University Press, 1983), ii. 5–6.
11. Ann Radcliffe, *The Mysteries of Udolpho*, ed. Bonamy Dobrée (Oxford: Oxford University Press, 1998), pp. 248–9.
12. Mary Wollstonecraft, *The Wrongs of Woman; or, Maria*, ed. Gary Kelly (Oxford: Oxford University Press, 1998), p. 1.
13. Maria Edgeworth, *Belinda*, ed. Kathryn Kirkpatrick (Oxford: Oxford University Press, 1999), p. 131.
14. Maria Edgeworth, *Castle Rackrent*, ed. George Watson (Oxford: Oxford University Press, 1995), p. 4.
15. William Godwin, *Caleb Williams*, ed. David McCracken (Oxford: Oxford University Press, 1982), p. 326.

16. Ibid. 339.

17. Ibid. 325.

18. Jane Austen, *Northanger Abbey, Lady Susan, The Watsons, and Sanditon*, ed. John Davie with an introduction by Terry Castle (Oxford: Oxford University Press, 1998), p. 203.

19. Jane Austen, *Persuasion*, ed. John Davie (Oxford: Oxford University Press, 1998), p. 61.

20. Ibid. 62.

21. James Hogg, *The Private Memoirs and Confessions of a Justified Sinner*, ed. John Carey (Oxford: Oxford University Press, 1999), p. 240.

22. All page references for *Evelina* are to the edition by Edward A. Bloom with an introduction and notes by Vivien Jones (Oxford: Oxford University Press, 2002).

23. All page references for *Waverley* are to the edition by Claire Lamont (1986; Oxford: Oxford University Press, 1998).

24. Austen, *Northanger Abbey*, p. 84.

25 | Satire

Steven E. Jones

According to conventional literary histories, Romantic literature is predominantly sincere, spontaneous, subjective, otherworldly, and transcendent. Satire, on the other hand, is usually understood as rhetorical, strategic, worldly, and topical. The construction of the Romantic canon, therefore, along with the establishment of Romanticism as the dominant movement of early nineteenth-century British literature, was accompanied by the relative devaluation of Romantic-period satire by literary historians. It used to be common to say that satire 'died' with the 'Augustan' writers of the eighteenth century and was displaced by the emergence of sentimental and sincere Romanticism. In many twentieth-century critical studies satire was treated as everything that Romanticism was not—as in effect Romanticism's generic other.

In recent years this reductive opposition of satire and Romanticism has begun to be dismantled, in part through comprehensive scholarly surveys of the wealth of satires actually written during the Romantic period (see works by Dyer, Stones, and Strachan in 'Further reading'), and in part through critiques of the opposition itself,[1] but also through the accumulation of evidence for the critical importance of specific satiric poems, novels, graphical prints, and dramatic works.[2] Satire was in fact extremely important in early nineteenth-century culture, not only as a strain running through what later came to be called Romanticism, but also a force helping to shape the boundaries of 'the Romantic' from the outside, as it were. The study of satire offers a valuable critical perspective on Romanticism, as a movement and critical construct, and on the assumptions that shaped the Romantic canon and continue to influence studies of Romantic-period literature. But even considered in its own right, satire was an extremely important feature of the era's cultural landscape. Romantic-period satires flourished in a wide range of venues: novels, drama, reviews and pamphlets, graphical prints, and poetry.

Novels and prose satires

According to literary theorist, Mikhail Bakhtin, the novel has its roots in satire. Early satiric forms—the prose satires of Menippus and Petronius, for example, or the later work of Rabelais—can be seen as ancestors of the novel. This genealogy makes intuitive sense in the case of obviously satirical novels such as *Don Quixote, Gulliver's Travels*, and *Tristram Shandy*, but the Bakhtinian argument actually runs much deeper. It implies that the polyvocal, heteroglossic quality of *all* novels, along with their tendency, like the epic, to take the form of stylistic medleys or generic mixtures (one traditional etymology for satire ties it to *satura*, or 'mixed feast'), and the carnivalesque inversions and subversions of hierarchy their discourse makes possible, means that *any* novel possesses at least a latent family relation to satire, which is to say to early prose-medleys that undermined the pretensions and exposed the follies of their targets. This connection is valid to some extent even in novels we think of as self-contained and generically unified, or as more gently comic in tone, like those of Jane Austen.

In fact, no one better exploited the satiric potential of the novel than Austen. Not a Romantic in the usual sense of the term, she is one of the most celebrated Romantic-period authors in part because of the satiric qualities of her work: her wit, moral judgement, analysis of subtle social interactions and the dangers thereof (especially for young women), her illustrative or exemplary characters, and carefully crafted narratives involving the 'chastening' or correction of those characters. She undoubtedly saw herself as working in the tradition of the novelists Henry Fielding and Tobias Smollett and the poet Alexander Pope. One of her earliest juvenile works, written at 16, was a satirical parody of historical writing, a *History of England* (composed around 1791). Though all of her six major novels contain satiric passages and are governed by a broadly satirical point of view, her *Northanger Abbey* (1818) is predominantly a parodic satire, an exposé of contemporary Gothic fiction and its many fans, focused especially on the extremely popular novels of Ann Radcliffe. Austen's young heroine, Catherine Morland, looks as though she might become a victim of her enthusiastic reading, until she is in the end educated in the important difference between novelistic conventions and social conventions.

The popular Gothic (see *Oxford Companion to the Romantic Age*, p. 291), so often satirized during the Romantic period, already contained within itself the seeds of its own satire. Gothic literary works were so over the top, so non-naturalistic, that they often winked at their own artificial conventions. The Gothic seemed modern in part because it was so knowing, so self-referential a mode. Many of the most famous and influential examples can be read as at least partly self-satirizing, beginning with Horace Walpole's *Castle of Otranto* (1765), which at points verges on camp self-parody. In many ways, Austen's *Northanger Abbey* simply follows the lead of Gothic novels like Walpole's and Anne Radcliffe's but seizes upon and emphasizes the latent satiric potential of Gothic excess.

Traditionally, satire has been a highly topical mode: it names names and refers to contemporary events and institutions. Thomas Love Peacock's seven novels (see *Oxford Companion to the Romantic Age*, pp. 294–5), sometimes labelled Menippean satires, have often been read as keys to his friends and contemporaries, the stories and ideas merely an excuse for caricatures of Lord Byron and Percy Shelley and Leigh Hunt, for example—much in the way that Max Beerbohm has often been looked at (and read) as a caricaturist of eminent Victorians such as Oscar Wilde and William Morris. But Peacock's satire extends beyond his cartoons of famous writers to include telling representations of contemporary trends in art and science as well as social and political controversies. The chatty, often absurd universe of Peacock's *Headlong Hall* (1816), *Nightmare Abbey* (1818), and *Crotchet Castle* (1831) is compelling for the texture of its dialogue, as well as for its topical references. Those references are clearly central to the effect of Peacock's novels, however, which represent some of the key ideological debates, party and class conflicts, fashions, and intellectual ferment of the era.

Outside the novel, prose satires of various kinds were among the most popular of the period. One prominent example is the satirical correspondence of the anonymous 'Junius', coming just before or at the beginning of the conventional Romantic period. Junius wrote mocking letters to newspapers in support of John Wilkes and against George III and his ministers, publishing most actively in the early 1770s, with powerful effect. Robert Southey argued that he was in fact the most perniciously influential writer of his age, an instigator and example of the general 'disaffection' with the government. Byron was still paying tribute to Junius in his own 1822 satire on the Georges, *The Vision of Judgement* (1822), a parody of Poet Laureate Robert Southey's elegy for the king, *A Vision of Judgement* (Byron's mocking title declares that *his* version offers the definitive vision). Byron's poem, published in *The Liberal*, a periodical he produced with Leigh Hunt in Italy, owes a great deal to the iconography and methods of pamphlet satires and satiric prints, including for example George Cruikshank's 'Doctor Southey's New Vision', one plate from the pamphlet, *A Slap At Slop* (1821). The print shows Southey playing a poetic barrel-organ (which is also the butt of sack, or barrel of wine, he earned as Poet Laureate). The wine draining out of it is labelled 'A Vision of Judgement'. George IV ascends to his role as Apollo and king—or anyway, he ascends a few feet off the ground, fat and dressed in a classical toga but still wearing his boots and spurs.[3] Here we glimpse the influence of Junius as well as the concentrated satiric nexus out of which Byron wrote: the Cruikshank plate was accompanied by the text of William Hone's own parody of the same Southey poem that Byron satirizes in his *Vision*. Byron joins and betters his precursors, Southey and Hone (and the newspaper correspondent, Junius, too), in part by making some of them appear in his satire. Even in Heaven, Byron imagines, everyone is still trying to guess the identity of the anonymous gadfly, Junius. When Junius appears, he speaks with calm, yet sublime, indignation, matching his newspaper satires against the royal reputation itself: 'My charges upon record will outlast | The brass of both his epitaph and tomb,' he declares to the Archangel Michael. The satirist, for Byron, easily trumps the monarch: 'I loved my country, and I hated him,' Junius declares, offering at once a patriotic and a personal justification for his satire (compare the discussion in the chapter on 'Narrative poetry').

The theatre

At a famous juncture in Jane Austen's novel, *Mansfield Park*, the characters engage in an amateur (and socially inappropriate) production of the extremely fashionable play, *Lovers' Vows*. The play within the novel (like a play within the play in Shakespeare) mirrors the complicated relationships among the characters in the main plot. But of course Austen is at the same time satirizing this very interpretive tendency: the narcissistic, 'romantic' desire to see all the world as a stage and life merely as an opportunity for a sublime or sentimental performance. In this sense, at least, the importance of the 'theatrical' in the Romantic period has long been appreciated. Only relatively recently, however, has the vital importance of the drama, the actual theatre, in the Romantic period begun to be established (see *Oxford Companion to the Romantic Age*, pp. 223–31). The vitality of the theatre survived even in the face of intense censorship by John Larpent, the Lord Chamberlain's Deputy Examiner or Examiner of Plays from 1778 to 1824 (a tenure which included the increased censorship during the war with France), and in the delimited market-place created by the Licensing Acts of 1737, which had restricted the production of legitimate drama with spoken parts to two licensed or 'patent' theatres, Drury Lane and Covent Garden (and Haymarket, as well, during the summer season). By default, this led other, illegitimate theatres to stage lower forms of drama, spectacles without spoken parts, often set to music or involving dance and tending to sensational special effects. Thereby, among other results, the English pantomime (*Oxford Companion to the Romantic Age*, pp. 635–6) reached its full development as a popular theatrical form during the Romantic period (compare the chapter on 'Romantic drama' and, in Part IV, 'The theatre').

In a January 1817 review, Leigh Hunt referred to the pantomime as 'the best medium of dramatic satire' in the Romantic period.[4] Surely he said this in part because the pantomime was so popular, so successful with audiences. In fact, it came close to what we would now call a mass entertainment, in the sense that at holiday times around the calendar it drew a mixed audience from almost every level of English society, often putting middling types and royalty together in the same theatre. As the London *Times* commented on 27 December 1823, 'Every body "pooh-poohs" the pantomime, but every body goes to see it.'

The form derived from the traditional Italian *commedia dell'arte*, with its recognizable type characters, Harlequin, Pantaloon, Columbine, Clown, *et al.*, and its basic plot of eloping young lovers being pursued by an authoritarian father. Songs and staging, including extravagant special effects, along with extended improvisation, filled in the rest. The pantomime (especially as it was first established by John Rich and was later popularized in productions by Charles Dibdin) tended to have a two-part structure.[5] An opening story, often based on romance, fairy tale, novel, or other traditional or well-known narrative, is followed by a 'transformation scene', in which a benevolent agent—a Mother Goose or fairy godmother figure, for example—magically (using trapdoors, lights, and the removal of 'big heads' or masks) changes everyone into their *commedia* types. The final movement is the Harlequinade, driven by the elopement and pursuit, often degenerating into a slapstick chase scene. People dive through windows and fall through traps as props metamorphose into characters or, for example, the scenery rolls by in a panoramic mechanical backdrop.

Within all this spectacle there were opportunities to evade censorship restrictions through mimed or sung topical reference, visual caricature, or structural parody, but mostly the pantomime tended towards a universal form of moral satire: the general type of the authoritarian father-figure is mocked rather than any specific prince, for example, or the traditional carnivalesque inversions of the Harlequinade gesture towards the vulnerabilities and limits of all forms of power and oppression. This may be another reason Leigh Hunt considered it 'the best form of dramatic satire' in his day—its universal language and populist comic appeal. But it also seems likely that he recognized pantomime's affinities with then-emergent Romantic modes that he was helping to construct and promote. The pantomime was all about rapid succession, startling transformations, metamorphoses, and chameleonic identities. In this sense, by way of a kind of popular Romantic irony, it satirized the rage for order, stability, and hierarchy. Though on occasion the famous Clown, Joseph ('Joey') Grimaldi, mocked specific public figures or institutions, and though pantomime plots or settings did indeed refer to the French Revolution or to London fashion, topicality was not the only (or even the major) form taken by its satire. By implication, the pantomime's structure allowed it to satirize its own romantic (derived from romance) narratives, as well. Thus it indulged in a kind of doubleness that insincerely celebrated change and passion and youthful sexuality, and implicitly celebrated fluid forms of self-directed irony as a way of transcending fixed social roles, stable identities, and the controls of authority and convention. In this sense, pantomime was indeed the most Romantic form of dramatic satire in the period.

Reviews and pamphlets

The Romantic period coincided with the great age of the reviews, which dominated the periodical press at the time. Much of the writing in the reviews—especially in the two great rivals affiliated with political parties, the Whig *Edinburgh* and the Tory *Quarterly*, but also in other reviews, such as the ubiquitous *Anti-Jacobin*—was satirical. Seeing themselves as the makers and upholders of public standards of taste, as well as the defenders of their parties, the usually anonymous reviewers frequently turned to acerbic, even violent rhetoric. Party conflict and wartime paranoia often overrode literary and aesthetic judgements. Outright polemic involved satire of literary targets and vice versa: reviews of novels or poems sometimes became merely occasions for polemic. Wordsworth, Coleridge, and Southey (as leaders of the 'Jacobinical' Lake

School or 'new school' of poetry) were widely attacked in the reviews, often for their 'vulgar' simplicity and usually in satirical tones mixing derision with moral condemnation. In fact, Southey (from time to time himself a writer of satirical reviews) counter-attacked in the *Quarterly Review* (December 1811) quoting from the *Edinburgh Review* in order to expose the rival's viciously satirical methods:

A burlesque description of the contents of the volume follows, together with a few passages, most easily susceptible of ridicule, as specimens of the poetry; and the critique is thus wound up. 'We cannot laugh at this any longer. . . . When every day is bringing forth some new work from the pen of Scott, Campbell, Rogers, Baillie, Sotheby, Wordsworth, or Southey, it is natural to feel some disgust at the undistinguishing voracity which can swallow down three editions of songs to convivial societies, and verse to a pillow.'[6]

When *Blackwood's Edinburgh Magazine* and other reviews later attacked a second generation of poets in the 1820s—the new 'new school' associated with the Leigh Hunt circle, including Keats, Shelley, and sometimes Byron—it compared them to the earlier satiric targets, the Della Cruscans and memorably dubbed them the 'Cockney School'. Satiric parody was again deployed, in one case in a mocking imitation by William Maginn of Shelley's long elegy for John Keats, *Adonais*: 'O weep for *Wontner*, for his leg is broke, | O weep for Wontner, though our pearly tear | Can never cure him.'

Powerful satirical reviewers or editors of reviews included John Wilson Croker, John Gibson Lockhart (who often signed himself 'Z'), William Maginn, and Francis Jeffrey. But one of the strongest voices belonged the editor of the *Quarterly* from 1809 to 1824, William Gifford, who had made a name for himself as translator of the Roman satirist Juvenal and, even more notoriously, as the satirist of the contemporary liberal school of sentimental poets, the Della Cruscans (*Oxford Companion to the Romantic Age*, pp. 481–2). Gifford's verse satires, *The Baviad* (1791) and *The Mæviad* (1795), when collected in one volume, were introduced by a scathing critical essay which compared Della Cruscan poetry to the spread of a disease: 'a thousand nameless names caught the infection; and from one end of the kingdom to the other, all was nonsense and Della Crusca . . . the evil grew every day more alarming (for now bedridden old women, and girls at their samplers, began to rave).' The rhetorical tone, here, adapted from the tradition of Juvenal, Addison, Swift, and Pope but reflecting new anxieties about women and plebeian authors, characterized not only Gifford's but many others' reviews from the 1790s to the 1820s, as well as other verse satires (and their sometimes essay-length prose footnotes) by Richard Polwhele and T. J. Mathias.

Gifford also edited the weekly *Anti-Jacobin* (1797–8), which became famous as a venue for clever and scathing parodies of contemporary poetry, first embedded in review articles and later republished in book form as *The Poetry of the Anti-Jacobin* (1799). These parodies, by authors such as George Canning, as well as Gifford himself, mocked in order to defuse fashionable trends in poetry and political and intellectual liberalism. 'The Friend of Humanity and the Knife-Grinder', for example, satirizes through the device of parody the Lake School's fascination with 'rustics':

> 'Needy Knife-grinder! whither are you going?
> Rough is the road, your wheel is out of order—
> Bleak blows the blast;—your hat has got a hole in't,
>   So have your breeches!

'La Sainte Guillotine' denounces those who supported the French Revolution: 'From the blood bedew'd vallies and mountains of France, | See the Genius of Gallic invasion advance!' And 'The Loves of the Triangles' mocks Erasmus Darwin and the fashion for science and mathematics, tellingly linking it to a new dominance of the middling classes (and women) in London life:

> Presses round Grosvenor Gate the' impatient throng;
> White-muslin'd misses and mammas are seen,
> Link'd with gay Cockneys, glittering o'er the green:
> The rising breeze unnumber'd charms displays,
> And the tight ancle strikes the'stonish'd gaze.

> But chief, thou Nurse of the Didactic Muse,
> Divine NONSENSIA, all thy soul infuse;
> The charms of *Secants* and of *Tangents* tell,
> How Loves and Graces in an *Angle* dwell.

Since all parody contains at least a germ of homage or tribute (and sometimes a great deal more than a germ), some of the *Anti-Jacobin* parodies read today as (negative) close studies of Romantic and sentimental verse forms and themes. Twenty-first-century critics who deal with the Romantic ideology and its formal expressions can learn a great deal from these first, sometimes critically astute, poetic critiques of emergent Romanticism.

If the Romantic ideology values art that is transcendent, timeless, and universal, then topical, ephemeral satire on particular targets is bound to be construed as un-Romantic. No form of publication better exemplifies the ephemeral nature of much of Romantic-period satire than the pamphlet, a cheap and quick form of publishing descended from seventeenth-century tracts and chapbooks but, in the era of the French Revolution, newly associated with Tom Paine's and William Cobbett's populist radicalism (compare the chapter on 'Print culture and the book trade'). Pamphlets in the late eighteenth and early nineteenth centuries included sincere political, social, and religious publications, but also an overwhelming flood of satiric texts and images. By far the best-known pamphlet satirist of the era was William Hone (1780–1842) (*Oxford Companion to the Romantic Age*, pp. 547–8), a radical publisher and bookseller as well as a writer who successfully faced a government prosecution in 1817 for blasphemous and seditious libel. Hone was particularly adept at satires in the form of religious parody, such as *The Late John Wilkes's Catechism* (1817), one of the works that prompted the government prosecution, and *The Clerical Magistrate* (1819). The latter included the text of the Form of Ordination for priests, ironically cited under an image, by the artist George Cruikshank, of a literally two-faced authority—one side a priest in the pulpit and the other side a punitive 'hanging' judge on the bench.

Hone had begun a very productive artistic and business collaboration with Cruikshank in 1815 and their satirical pamphlets against the Prince Regent, especially, were notorious. These culminated in works about the Queen Caroline affair of 1818–21 (when the Prince, now George IV, sought to bring divorce proceedings against his wife), such as *The Queen's Matrimonial Ladder* (1819). But perhaps the best-known Hone–Cruikshank satire was *The Political House that Jack Built* (1819), a pamphlet written as a parody of the children's rhyme but with scathing political content, including especially a pointed reaction to the Peterloo massacre in Manchester, on 16 August 1819, when local yeomanry and militia rode into a demonstrating crowd, killing at least eleven and wounding hundreds. The pamphlet is interesting in part for its successful mixture of high and low satirical modes, its grafts of bantering parody and sublime anger. As Kyle Grimes has argued of the *Political House*, by 'combining his parodic doggerel verse with George Cruikshank's brilliant woodcuts and the epigraph quotations from Cowper's *The Task*, Hone was able to generate an ironic complexity that far exceeds the mere sum of the assembled parts'.[7] In fact, this is an apt description of the work's rhetorical structure as a whole, which takes its cue from the original jingle and accumulates layered significations plate by plate: 'This is the house that Jack built', is depicted as a temple symbolizing the kingdom itself, built by Jack (John Bull or the people), and topped with a figure of Liberty; 'THE WEALTH | That lay in the house' is the Magna Carta, Habeas Corpus, etc.; 'THE VERMIN | That plunder the wealth' are (in the image) depicted as government officials of varying types; and so on. It is difficult to estimate the 'readership' (including those who heard it read aloud or only looked at its images) and potential influence of such a work, but it was surely considerable. We do know that *The Political House* went through fifty-four editions and spawned numerous imitations as well as conservative, counter-satiric rejoinders.

Graphic prints

The powerful example of Hone and Cruikshank serves as a reminder that, in early nineteenth-century London, the most common form of satire was not literary in the strict sense at all—it was graphic. This was the great age of satiric prints (*Oxford Companion to the Romantic Age*, pp. 207–13), cartoons on a wide range of political and social topics. Prints by Rowlandson, Gillray, or Cruikshank, as well as lesser-known artists, were widely available both in crude pamphlet form (like those of Hone and Cruikshank, with simple woodcut illustrations) and in more expensive engravings or etchings, hand-coloured on individual sheets. The latest ones were sometimes posted in shop windows, illuminated from behind, so that even those who did not purchase copies could see them. A whole subgenre of images grew up: representations of people looking at prints in the printshop window (*Oxford Companion to the Romantic Age*, pp. 195–6). One well-known self-referential satire by Gillray, *Very Slippy Weather*

(1808), depicts just such a scene before a shop window covered in colourful prints—all miniature images of actual published prints and in the window of an actual shop where Gillray sold his work. An audience of respectable persons with one iconic clownish member of the 'lower orders' stands on the walk viewing the prints with such rapt attention that they entirely ignore an elderly gentleman in the foreground who has fallen on the slippery paving stones. Prints such as these were arguably much more widely known than most novels or books of poetry. Anyone interested in satire during the Romantic period must attend to this and other extra-literary forms of satire, and would be well advised to make good use of M. D. George's volumes of the British Museum's *Catalogue of Political and Personal Satires* as a research tool.

Graphic satirical prints were mixed-media works. They included text as well as images and possessed a distinctive verbal and visual language, part of a popular semiotic discourse going back to seventeenth-century chapbooks and broadsides, mixing caricature, parody, and multilayered allusion (invoking contemporary works as well as Shakespeare or the Bible) with a conventional visual iconography. Etched or engraved images were often accompanied by labels, captions, even word balloons like those in modern comics. It was thus possible to read such satires on more than one level, employing very different kinds of literacies. Because of their multilayered but highly conventional verbal and visual language, and because they were widely reproduced and found in lending libraries and shop windows as well as made available for purchase, satiric prints reached a wide and diverse, mixed-class audience. Many literary authors deliberately cultivated or borrowed from the satiric modes of the prints, clearly aspiring to the rhetorical effectiveness (and audience) of this extremely popular extra-literary form. This downwardly mobile borrowing is evident in any number of Romantic works, from Coleridge's early political newspaper satires, such as 'Fire, famine and Slaughter'; to Shelley's political satires (*The Mask of Anarchy, Peter Bell the Third*, and *Swellfoot the Tyrant*); to Keats's fragmentary satire on the Prince Regent and Lord Byron, *The Jealousies*; to Byron's own better-known satires, for example, *The Vision of Judgement*, 'The Curse of Minerva', and *Don Juan*.

Poetry

The righteous indignation conventionally associated with (an idealized) Juvenal was accepted by many as the proper, 'high' tone of great poetic satire in the age that also celebrated displays of refined sensibility and intense passion in poetry. Percy Bysshe Shelley once began but never finished or published a 'Satire upon Satire', which was fuelled by his own hatred of Robert Southey, whom Shelley and Byron believed had spread rumours about them from across the political party divide. 'If Satire's scourge could awake the slumbering hounds of conscience,' Shelley began at one point (but then cancelled most of the line), then who would not 'exclaim . . . Lash on & be the keen verse dipped in flame | follow his flight on winged words, & urge | The strokes of the inexorable scourge.' Shelley's draft implodes in a series of cancellations and false starts, but seems to be attempting a structural turn, a kind of dialectic in which the invective against Southey gives way to a quieter, sincere renunciation of satire. On second thought, Shelley proposes, someone should just talk to Southey: 'Far better than to make innocent ink | With the stagnant truisms of trite Satire stink.' A complex and ambivalent document of rhetorical 'small knives' or hidden daggers (as Shelley admitted), this 'Satire upon Satire' none the less reminds us of the ways in which Romantic poets and their critics—from the very early stages of the formation of the Romantic canon—opposed satiric rhetoric to an ostensibly more Romantic rhetoric of sincerity and authenticity, expressive rather than corrective poetry.

Of course this does not mean that even Shelley ever really renounced satire altogether, as some critics used to assume. The fragment is probably best read as a canny dramatic monologue; at least in this draft form, it does not entirely erase its own aggression. And the rest of Shelley's late poems, *The Mask of Anarchy* (1819) and especially *Oedipus Tyrannus; or Swellfoot the Tyrant* (1820), argue for his continued interest in writing satire. Satiric rhetoric, ridicule, violence, topical caricature, run throughout canonical Romanticism. But taking a historical census of satires published in the Romantic period is one way to step outside the relatively narrow, posthumous boundaries of canonical Romanticism, to correct the proportions, as it were, of our understanding of Romantic-period poetry. Much of the poetry, including much of the satire, written during the period was demonstrably un-Romantic, though popular and influential at the time.

'Peter Pindar' (John Wolcot, 1738–1819; *Oxford Companion to the Romantic Age*, pp. 765–6) was by any objective measure one of the better-known poets of the era. His verses, usually in couplets, rather than displaying Juvenalian loftiness or righteous indignation, were colloquial and mocking in their sometimes direct attacks on contemporaries including the painters of the Royal Academy and, most famously, King George III. None the less, Wordsworth acknowledged 'the redoubted Peter' as a representative satirist of his day, placing him in a tradition that ran from Horace and Juvenal to Pope.[8] Wolcot's satires were conversational in style and vivid in their imagery, boldly topical, usually Whiggish or generally populist in politics. All this the burgeoning audience for satirical prints and pamphlets would have found familiar and seem to have found congenial. *The Lousiad* (1785–95), for example, is a relatively light comic work, a five-canto mock-heroic tale of a louse found in a dish served to the king. The *Ode upon Ode* (1787) mocked the Romantic-period's predilection for public declamation—and mocked George III as well. *Bozzy and Piozzi; or, the British biographers, a Town Eclogue* (1786) made wicked fun of Dr Johnson's disciples, Boswell and Hester (Thrale) Piozzi, in a style of gossipy personal satire that matched their own chatty texts.

A similar political-cartoon style informs the epistolary satires of Thomas Moore, from *Intercepted Letters: or, the Twopenny Post-Bag* (1813) to the extremely popular *Fudge Family in Paris* (1818). The former pretends to be a collection of found letters written by the royal family and other public figures and intercepted by the notorious Society for the Suppression of Vice. The satire works by revealing the contents of the letters while simultaneously exposing the Society's reactionary moralism and the bad behaviour among the Regency aristocracy and royalty. The *Fudge Family* letters pretend to have been written by an Irish family touring Europe after Waterloo. Topical references to English and French culture and politics (and of course the Irish) come naturally with the premise. As Gary Dyer has argued, Moore's *Intercepted Letters* by their very form satirize the climate of surveillance that dominated England during the war with France and its aftermath.[9] Moore's letter-conceit builds on the kind of satire his friend Lord Byron was busy creating during exactly the same period, in which a personal, even confidential form is used to expose the inevitable link between private and public matters.

Byron began his career in earnest as a young curmudgeon, a poet who admired Pope and Dryden and not Wordsworth and Southey and proved it with a heroic-couplet satire on the contemporary scene, *English Bards and Scotch Reviewers* (1809). We should resist the anachronistic Whiggish tendency (under the influence of the Romantic ideology) to read Byron's career as a march of inevitable progress away from this Augustan satire and towards the mature Romantic forms based on the Italian *ottava rima* stanza of his later career. The later-named Romantics did not know that the heroic-couplet satire was to be seen as a moribund, pre-Romantic form (though some did grumble about the oppressive dominance of Pope in the schools and critical reviews). *English Bards* made a splash with Byron's contemporaries, after all, and Byron went on to write other couplet satires, starting with *Hints from Horace* (1811), which he called a sequel to *English Bards*, and *The Curse of Minerva* (1812) on Lord Elgin's Parthenon marbles, but including as well the late poem, *The Age of Bronze* (1823). Nevertheless, few readers in the past century would disagree that the *ottava rima* satires, from *Beppo* (1818) to *The Vision of Judgement* (1822) and, especially, *Don Juan* (1819–24), are among the brilliant poetic achievements of the era.

READING: Lord Byron, *Don Juan*

Near the end of *Don Juan*, Canto XIV, Byron comments self-consciously and teasingly on the narrative we are reading at that very moment, as well as the narrative we are no doubt anticipating:

> Whether Don Juan and chaste Adeline
>   Grew friends in this or any other sense,
> Will be discuss'd hereafter, I opine:
>   At present I am glad of a pretence
> To leave them hovering, as the effect is fine,
>   And keeps the atrocious reader in *suspense*;
> The surest way for ladies and for books
> To bait their tender or their tenter hooks.
>
> Whether they rode, or walk'd, or studied Spanish
>   To read Don Quixote in the original,
> A pleasure before which all others vanish;
>   Whether their talk was of the kind call'd 'small,'
> Or serious, are the topics I must banish
>   To the next Canto; where perhaps I shall
> Say something to the purpose, and display
> Considerable talent in my way.
>
> Above all, I beg all men to forbear
>   Anticipating aught about the matter:
> They'll only make mistakes about the fair,
>   And Juan too, especially the latter.
> And I shall take a much more serious air
>   Than I have yet done, in this Epic Satire.
> It is not clear that Adeline and Juan
> Will fall; but if they do, 'twill be their ruin.
>   (XIV. xcvii–xcix. 769–92)

That last stanza contains one of the most often quoted self-definitions of the poem as an 'Epic Satire' (comically rhymed with 'latter'). In one sense this is a joke that simply means a *massive* satire—a reference to *Don Juan*'s length. But in another sense, Byron seems quite serious about trying to write a new kind of epic, and he repeatedly refers to it elsewhere as a satire. *Don Juan* is the Romantic poem that best illustrates what epic and satire have in common: the generic licence to contain mixed modes and to represent a little of everything. In fact, every kind of Romantic-period satire that I have discussed in this essay can be found in *Don Juan*'s sprawling *satura*, its extravagant Regency banquet of mixed modes and multiple forms.

Don Juan as satiric novel in verse

The passage just quoted toys with the audience's narrative expectations (regarding suspense and serial instalments) that were in Byron's day already most commonly associated with the novel. In its multiple plots, analysis of social relations, cast of thousands, and self-conscious narrative structure (including its deconstruction of narrative structure), *Don Juan* is a kind of serial novel in verse, the historical link between comic-epic poets such as Ariosto and Laurence Sterne's *Tristram Shandy*, as well as, from our later vantage, Pushkin's *Eugene Onegin*. As these examples indicate, the specific tradition within the history of the novel to which *Don Juan* belongs is satiric. As if to underscore this, in the highly novelistic 'Epic Satire' passage quoted above, Byron tellingly names Cervantes's *Don Quixote*, the great precursor to almost all satiric novels in the Western tradition.

In a long catalogue in Canto VII, Byron includes Cervantes among those who have undercut humanity's moral pretensions. Later, in Canto XIII (ll. 58–64), he cites *Don Quixote* in support of his own misanthropic tendency to 'sneer' at human nature:

> If I sneer sometimes,
> It is because I cannot well do less,
> And now and then it also suits my rhymes.
> I should be very willing to redress
> Men's wrongs, and rather check than punish crimes,
> Had Cervantes in that too true tale
> Of Quixote, shown how all such efforts fail.

Don Quixote he calls 'that real Epic unto all who have thought' (l. 72) and in a famous stanza sums up the profoundly destructive—and (literally) un-Romantic—power of its satire:

> Cervantes smiled Spain's Chivalry away;
> A single laugh demolished the right arm
> Of his own country;—seldom since that day
> Has Spain had heroes. While Romance could charm,
> The world gave ground before her bright array;
> And therefore have his volumes done such harm,
> That all their glory, as a composition,
> Was dearly purchased by his land's perdition.
>
> (stanza xi)

An elegy for Spain's lost chivalric culture, this passage also declares Byron's serious, satanic bargain with satire. When he says elsewhere that his epic, unlike classical models, is actually *true* (l. 202), he means it in the sense that Cervantes's 'real Epic', his invention of the satirical novel, reveals a deeper truth about the self-divided human condition, a truth to which Byron's poem is also dedicated. This satiric insight is profoundly un-Romantic, contrary to the impulses and wishes of Romance and of the Romantic ideology. But pursuing that truth and confessing ironically to its allure in a novelistic narrative poem with self-conscious lyric passages is a profoundly Romantic gesture.

Don Juan as pantomimic satire

The doubleness of this Romantic confession of un-Romantic beliefs falls under the conventional category of Romantic irony (*Oxford Companion to the Romantic Age*, pp. 682–3). The term was coined by Friedrich Schlegel, who based his theories on the works of the eighteenth-century Venetian satirist, Carlo Gozzi, whose works updated and revised the *commedia dell'arte* forms—from which the English pantomime was also derived. Byron has traditionally been treated as the best English exemplar of Romantic irony; it seems likely that he absorbed this mode from going to the pantomime as much as from reading Schlegel (or his translators and popularizers).

Don Juan opens with a kind of casting call that ends in a declaration of provenance:

> I want a hero: an uncommon want,
>   When every year and month send forth a new one,
> Till, after cloying the gazettes with cant,
>   The age discovers he is not the true one;
> Of such as these I should not care to vaunt,
>   I'll therefore take our ancient friend Don Juan,
> We all have seen him in the pantomime
> Sent to the devil, somewhat ere his time.

I take the famous penultimate line literally, as revealing that Byron's satiric anti-hero is of the same family as the Don Juan of London stage pantomimes, theatrical sources with which Byron was extremely familiar, not only as a theatregoer but as chairman of the Drury Lane Theatre Committee. Byron even knew and reportedly admired Joey Grimaldi, the famous pantomime Clown (the poet is said to have visited him backstage and given him a snuff box), as well as the writer and producer, Thomas Dibdin.[10]

From the pantomime—and the milieu of popular theatricals in general—Byron got more than his titular hero. He also got a Romantic-ironic mode of satire that he then brilliantly versified in *Don Juan*. Contemporary readers would have recognized this quality of the epic satire. One 1819 review classified *Don Juan* as a 'serio-comic melo-dramatic harlequinade' and referred to Juan's 'prototype in the pantomime'.[11] Like the pantomime, Byron's poem mixes contrasting modes—comedy, melodrama, slapstick, lyrical meditation, and theatrics—and often combines Romantic with ironic perspectives. Like the pantomime, *Don Juan* presents itself as a series of outrageous improvisations on a well-known, legendary narrative. And like pantomime, Byron's poem often plays to (and with) the audience (including those in the cheap seats) and makes use of a poetic version of stagecraft and spectacle, the verbal equivalent of tricks and props, such as trapdoors and Harlequin's magic slapstick bat.

Don Juan everywhere echoes the pantomime and its popular milieu, from the rescue of the shipwrecked Juan by Haidée in Canto II to the cross-dressing seraglio episode in Canto V, and the bed-tricks and chase scenes throughout. The entire Haidée episode—the story of two star-crossed lovers thwarted by an authoritarian father in an exotic, 'Oriental', setting—is broadly pantomimic. When Haidée's father, the pirate Lambro, comes home unexpectedly, the highly theatrical party going on includes this telling figure, straight out of the pantomime:

> Afar, a dwarf buffoon stood telling tales
>   To a sedate grey circle of old smokers
> Of secret treasures found in hidden vales,
>   Of wonderful replies from Arab jokers,
> Of charms to make good gold and cure bad ails,
>   Of rocks bewitch'd that open to the knockers,
> Of magic ladies who, by one sole act,
> Transform'd their lords to beast, (but that's a fact).
>   (III. 34)

This last joke even calls to mind the female benevolent agent who effects the transformation scene in pantomimes, and suggests how the overdetermined materials of popular theatricals could be turned to Byron's personal satiric purposes. In this case, however, the usual transformation goes in reverse, from man to beast, and, instead of producing a magical reconciliation, Byron kills off Haidée and sends Juan into slavery. On the slave ship (IV. 81) Juan meets an Italian *opera buffa* troupe (like the English pantomime, another theatrical form descended from the *commedia dell'arte*). *Don Juan* seems to take the transformations so characteristic of pantomime as both its subject and its primary structuring device ('*What after all*, are *all* things—but a *Show*?' VII. 2). In *Don Juan*, Byron himself serves as both the transforming agent *and* satirist-clown.

What Leigh Hunt called the 'best means of dramatic satire' of the Romantic age even gives Byron a theatrical model for a kind of dialectic we have come to recognize as one of his characteristic poetic moves, the deeply Romantic gesture of satirizing his own Romantic tendencies: 'And the sad truth which hovers o'er my desk | Turns what was once romantic to burlesque' (IV. 3). Like the shift in countless pantomimes from enchanted fairy tale or tale of romance to knockabout slapstick, Byron's movement here and throughout the poem is downward, towards the burlesque. But the act of incorporating in his epic satire his self-consciousness of this movement Romanticizes again, on another level, the experience of Romantic imagination confronting satiric truth. *Don Juan*, like the pantomime, works by paradoxical combinations of Romantic and *buffo* modes and perspectives.

Don Juan, pamphlet satires, and graphical prints

Don Juan was at first published expensively by John Murray, then, in part to compete with the flood of piracies, Byron switched to the radical publisher, John Hunt, beginning in 1823, who brought out later cantos in less-expensive editions. The relationship of Byron's very literary satire to the sub-literary realm, in which not only the pirates of *Don Juan* but even more ribald and violent satirists operated, was competitive in more than one sense. Byron's work was in fierce competition with the culture of pamphlets and prints, for sales, for an

Haslett, Moyra, *Byron, 'Don Juan', and the Don Juan Legend* (Oxford: Clarendon Press, 1997). Persuasively situates Byron's figure of Don Juan in relation to an anthropological theory of myth and the historical contexts of contemporary drama, pantomime, opera, and popular culture. In the process, this study shows how Byron's epic was designed to appeal to audiences from different social classes and political persuasions.

Jones, Steven E., *Satire and Romanticism* (New York: St Martin's/Macmillan, 2000). Argues that Romanticism was constructed and canonized in part by opposition to its 'generic other'—satire. Offers readings of this differential and oppositional construction as found in the work of canonical and extra-canonical authors.

——(ed.) *The Satiric Eye: Forms of Satire in the Romantic Period* (New York: Palgrave Macmillan, 2003). A collection of essays by twelve prominent scholars which argues by its very existence and table of contents for the range and diversity of satiric forms during the Romantic period, in terms of genre, venue, audience, medium, high as well as low cultural productions.

Mayer, David, *Harlequin in His Element: The English Pantomime, 1806–1836* (Cambridge, Mass.: Harvard University Press, 1969). Definitive critical treatment of the popular British pantomime in its heyday, this book provides historical context and generic analysis of individual scripts, explains the stagecraft of pantomimic productions, and describes the conventional structures and themes of pantomimes.

Stones, Graeme, and Strachan, John (eds.), *Satires of the Romantic Period*, 5 vols. (London: Pickering and Chatto, 2003). A convenient scholarly collection of satires from the Romantic period, some otherwise quite difficult to find; the edition is capacious enough to allow for complete longer works as well as numerous shorter satires, a mix of satires by anonymous and canonical authors.

WEB LINK

Grimes, Kyle (ed.) 'Hone and Cruikshank', *The Political House that Jack Built*, Romantic Circles Website, <http://www.rc.umd.edu/editions/contemps/hone/coverp.htm>. Online scholarly hypertext published by the peer-reviewed Romantic Circles Website, this edition includes photofacsimiles of the 1819 pamphlet (including, as in the original pamphlet, 'The Clerical Magistrate'), textual transcriptions, notes, and a link to Grimes's useful Hone Web pages and bibliography.

NOTES

1. Steven E. Jones, *Satire and Romanticism* (New York: St Martin's Press/Macmillan, 2000).
2. Steven E. Jones (ed.), *The Satiric Eye: Forms of Satire in the Romantic Period* (New York: Palgrave Macmillan, 2003).
3. Mary Dorothy George, *Catalogue of Political and Personal Satires in the British Museum* (London: Trustees of the British Museum, 1870–1954), x. 238–9.
4. Quoted in Jones, *Satire and Romanticism*, p. 178.
5. David Mayer, *Harlequin in His Element: The English Pantomime, 1806–1836* (Cambridge, Mass.: Harvard University Press, 1969).
6. Quoted by Trott, in Jones (ed.), *The Satiric Eye*, p. 83.
7. Kyle Grimes, 'The Political House that Jack Built: Introduction and Contents', at Romantic Circles Website: http://www.rc.umd.edu/editions/contemps/hone/intro.htm.

8. *The Letters of William and Dorothy Wordsworth*, ed. E. de Salincourt, 2nd edn., i. *The Early Years, 1787–1805*, rev. C. Shaver (Oxford: Clarendon Press, 1967), p. 169.

9. Gary Dyer, 'Intercepted Letters, Men of Information: Moore's Twopenny Post-Bag and Fudge Family in Paris', in Jones (ed.), *The Satiric Edge*, pp. 151–71.

10. Moyra Haslett, *Byron, 'Don Juan', and the Don Juan Legend* (Oxford: Clarendon Press, 1997), p. 59.

11. Quoted ibid. 60.

| **Romantic drama**

Judith Pascoe

In May of 1780, the notorious Lady Craven arrived at the Drury Lane theatre in London to see her comedy *The Miniature Picture* being performed as an afterpiece to Shakespeare's *The Winter's Tale*. The arrival of Elizabeth Craven probably caused as large a rustle in the audience as the moment of curtain rising; she was enveloped in scandal and dressed to catch the eye. According to another member of the audience, the letter-writer Horace Walpole, Lady Craven wore 'a profusion of white bugles and plumes, to receive the public homage due to her sex and loveliness', and she seated herself in the middle of the front row of the stage box, so that homage could be easily received.

It was not a great night for theatre, at least not by conventional dramatic standards. William Parsons 'murdered' the role of the Scottish Lord Macgrinnon, and the ingenue Mary Robinson, cast as Eliza Camply, 'thought on nothing but her own charms'. According to Walpole, Robinson was rumoured to be the favourite of the Prince of Wales. The romance of Florizel and Perdita (as the lovestruck Prince and Robinson would come to be designated in printed satires) won the actress a prominent position in the annals of public scandal. There, also, was recorded Lady Craven's fling with a French ambassador. If one takes into account the larger social stage of the audience and the networks of gossip to which they subscribed, the joint performance of *The Winter's Tale* and *The Miniature Picture* resulted in a brilliant night of theatre.

Walpole lovingly chronicles this broader drama and its attendant pleasures. The prologue to Lady Craven's play, penned by the renowned playwright Richard Brinsley Sheridan, gestured chivalrously towards the female author seated prominently in the stage box. 'It is a lady writes—and hark—a noble Muse', Sheridan wrote. Walpole depicted this line as a frank solicitation of applause on behalf of Lady Craven, and interpreted the audience's reticent response as a failure of gallantry. He took malicious delight in the moment, noting that Lady Harcourt would have suffered several deaths rather than encounter such an 'exhibition'. Lady Craven's tranquillity, he continued, 'was the ascendant of Millamant and Lady Betty Modish and Indamora', that is, of famous theatrical heroines, and so she met the audience's snub with equanimity.[1]

Lady Craven's night at the theatre hints at some of the reasons why 'Romantic drama' is such a curiously fraught phrase. The several spectacles the evening provided stand in contrast to the unstageable productions of the writers most famously associated with the period. The 'lyrical drama' of Percy Shelley's *Prometheus Unbound* and the 'mental theatre' of Byron's *Manfred* represent efforts to borrow on the emotional power of dramatic characterization while keeping a safe distance from the staged frivolity of socialite playwrights and royal mistresses.[1] Poets like Shelley and Byron innovated verse drama forms in order to attempt serious explorations of human feeling and consciousness,[ ] a project whose most ambitious practitioner was Joanne Baillie, author of a series of plays each devoted to a single human passion (see *Oxford Companion to the Romantic Age*, p. 413). Baillie's plays were actually performed on stage. William Wordsworth, who claimed he had written his verse drama *The Borderers* without 'any view to its exhibition upon the stage', but who relished the thought of a successful production none the less, denied feeling any disappointment when the piece was rejected by the manager of the Covent Garden theatre.[2]

Students of late eighteenth- and early nineteenth-century poetry have grappled with the question of whether the term 'Romantic poetry' should be used as a temporal or an aesthetic marker (see also the 'Introduction'). That is, should we use this phrase to indicate all works written by poets who share a view that poetry is endowed with a special insight and transcendent power. Or should we simply use 'Romantic poetry' to designate poems written between 1789 and 1832? A similar dilemma is raised by the phrase 'Romantic drama' which I use here to encompass both the introspective verse drama of the Romantic poets *and* the plays they attended, a mixed bill of fare dominated by Renaissance and Restoration theatrical favourites (compare the discussion of Victorian theatre in the chapter on 'The theatre' in Part IV). Shakespeare was arguably the most popular playwright of the Romantic period, with revivals of his plays in constant rotation, but Romantic theatre managers felt no obligation to adhere faithfully to Shakespeare's scripts. *The Winter's Tale* was most commonly performed in David Garrick's version, which cut Shakespeare's five-act play down to three acts, and foregrounded the pastoral high jinks. Romantic-era Shakespeare productions were adaptations rather than revivals, selective cullings from the original plays to suit the theatrical and political exigencies of the day.

Romantic drama also encompassed more modest productions, 'private theatricals' staged in domestic settings or provincial venues. *The Miniature Picture* was first performed in the town hall at Newbury, and its author became known for the performances she staged in domestic settings. A year after the Drury Lane production of *The Miniature Picture*, Lady Craven directed her own children and those of other persons of fashion in a pastoral opera performed at Queensberry House, Burlington Gardens. Her home became the site of the Brandenburgh House Theatre beginning around 1800, and the Brandenburgh theatricals blurred the line between public and private performances. A staging of Craven's *The Statue's Feast*, in 1802, featured the professional assistance of Joseph Madocks and the dancer Miss Darville, and was attended by 250 persons of distinction. In order to characterize Romantic drama, one must take into consideration a diverse bill of fare, but also the stage conditions, star turns, and audience proclivities that shaped particular productions.

The repertoire

The evening Lady Craven ventured to the theatre in order to see her own play performed was typical in its offering a main production (in this case, *The Winter's Tale*) and a shorter afterpiece (*The Miniature Picture*). If there had been a musical interlude during one of the intervals of the main piece or during a break between the two productions, that, too, would have met the expectations of an audience for whom an evening at the theatre often lasted as long as five hours, and was embellished with separate musical and dance productions. Lady Craven was fortunate in having her play introduced to the audience with a prologue written by Sheridan, but the prologue feature was standard; each of the night's main offerings was preceded by one of these poetic preludes pronounced, in the traditional fashion, by an actor standing before the curtain. Prologues were judged on their own merits; Sheridan's prologue to *The Miniature Picture* was so admired that, at the request of the Duchess of Devonshire and other members of the nobility, it was respoken by an actor hastily enlisted for the duty because the actor originally featured had already left the building.

Richard Brinsley Sheridan's comic masterpiece *The School for Scandal* stands as representative of one strain of theatregoing experience in the era, the social comedy's clever skewering of bourgeois values in a gentler variation of Restoration comedy. First performed in the year after Sheridan took over the management of the Drury Lane theatre in 1776, *The School for Scandal* contrasts the two nephews of the wealthy Oliver Surface, who unexpectedly returns from India and puts their characters to the test. The sincere affections of Charles (who auctions off his family's paintings but insists on preserving a portrait of his uncle, described as 'the ill-looking little fellow over the settee', much to the chagrin of eavesdropping Oliver Surface) win out over the opportunistic machinations of Joseph. The play reproduces the witty repartee of urbane London social gatherings, while, at the same time, revealing and rebuking the shallowness of fashionable alliances.

Sheridan's prologue to *The Miniature Picture* exhibited the wit that made *The School for Scandal* so celebrated, but it was ultimately enlisted for a very different kind of production, one that anticipated the theatrical counterpart of popular social comedies. Sheridan resurrected the first thirty lines and the concluding couplet to serve as prologue to the only play he wrote after being elected to Parliament in 1780, an adaptation of the German dramatist August von Kotzebue's *Die Spanier in Peru*, produced in 1799 at Drury Lane as *Pizarro*. Sheridan's story of Rolla, a brave commander who is pitted against the brutal title character, foreshadows the popularity of melodrama, a dramatic genre invented by Romantic playwrights. Officially inaugurated with the performance of Thomas Holcroft's *The Tale of Mystery* in 1802, Romantic melodrama is difficult to distinguish from other emotionally fraught plays which predated Holcroft's play. The term 'melodrama' referred to the use of music to enhance the emotional expressiveness of key dramatic moments in a play, but it came to designate, more generally, a highly sensational mode of drama which often pitted a victimized hero against a series of inequities (see *Oxford Companion to the Romantic Age*, pp. 599–600). Sheridan's *Pizarro* featured 'Musick, Airs and Chorusses', and a symphony composed for the occasion was performed before the play began and between the acts. In keeping with the new genre's emphasis on sensational experience, *Pizarro* was acclaimed for its spectacular theatricality; the theatre in which it was to be performed went dark for one evening to allow time for *Pizarro*'s elaborate staging. Stretching to five hours in length, *Pizarro* was performed thirty-one times before the end of the season, and 27,000 printed copies of the play were sold within a few weeks of its first performance (see *Oxford Companion to the Romantic Age*, p. 230).

Joanna Baillie's *Plays on the Passions*

If Sheridan's two most successful plays, *The School for Scandal* and *Pizarro*, stand as opposite extremes of a spectrum of Romantic drama that ranged from barbed comedy to lachrymose tragedy, the ambitious project of Joanna Baillie—to write two plays, one comedy and one tragedy, on each human emotion—represents another attempt to encompass that range of entertainment experience. The first volume of Baillie's *A Series of Plays: in which it is attempted to delineate the stronger passions of the mind* was published anonymously in 1798, the year before the spectacle of Sheridan's *Pizarro* dazzled theatregoers. Baillie believed that the drama could serve as a school for moral instruction, that audience members could learn from the dramatic tracing of passions 'in their rise and progress in the heart'. Possibly drawing on Adam Smith's notion of sympathetic identification as espoused in his 1759 *Theory of Moral Sentiments*, Baillie used the phrase 'sympathetick curiosity' to describe what she saw as a constitutive aspect of the human mind: a universal desire 'to behold man in every situation, putting forth his strength against the current of adversity, scorning all bodily anguish, or struggling with those feelings of nature, which, like a beating stream, will oft'times burst through the artificial barriers of pride'.[3] In her 'Introductory Discourse' to the first volume of her series of plays, Baillie portrayed human beings as obsessively fascinated with the tiniest nuances of others' feelings. '[E]ven the smallest indications of an unquiet mind, the restless eye, the muttering lip, the half-checked exclamation, and the hasty start, will set our attention as anxiously upon the watch, as the first distant flashes of a gathering storm', she wrote.[4] Baillie sought to exploit this human proclivity by presenting theatrical studies of particular emotions which could allow audience members to understand the workings of their own minds by watching these passions unspool in performances on stage. Her plan to explore the trajectory of an emotion in both tragedy *and* comedy stemmed from the different kinds of situations portrayed in these opposing genres. As her object was to trace passion through all its varieties, she did not want to limit herself to the heroic figures of tragic drama, but sought additionally to trace the workings of a passion in more humble settings. '[M]any a miserable being', she wrote, is halted from the commissioning of crimes that we might expect from a tragic hero because of 'timidity of character' or 'fear of shame'. The comparatively mousy protagonists of comedy, however, with their less grandiose infatuations and grievances, could educate viewers, especially those of a similarly mild disposition. The grand seducers or bold spoilers in the audience might not benefit from the more quotidian portrayal of human passions—'exposing them in an absurd and ridiculous light, may be shooting a finely-pointed arrow against the hardened rock'—but for less hardened theatregoers, Baillie posited, comic enactments of the passions might afford the most effective moral lessons.[5]

Baillie's plays, until recently, have not been treated kindly by theatre historians, one of whom listed the purported weaknesses of her work: 'a tendency toward abstraction, diffuse construction, "romantic" characters too often unbelievable, and unreal dialogue and language.'[6] The high moral seriousness of a Baillie, and also of her literary compatriots Wordsworth, Coleridge, Byron, and Keats, can be off-putting to modern readers (that all these writers' plays are available to us as texts rather than as stage realizations further complicates critical assessment). The experimental quality of these writers' plays and their grandiose ambitions to raise drama to new heights contribute to the difficulty of reception. Percy Shelley described drama in his 'Defence of Poetry' as 'a prismatic and many-sided mirror, which collects the brightest rays of human nature and divides and reproduces them'. As Stuart Curran reminds us, Shelley's mirror reflects not actions but passions, that is, the same subject around which Baillie organized a catalogue of plays. Curran goes on to locate the power and potential significance of English Romantic drama in moments of inaction, in the emotional impasses that resonate in both Baillie's staged dramas and in Shelley's unstageable one.[7]

The pursuit of novelty

Baillie's stripped-down theatrical enactments of single passions stand in contrast to the hyperkinetic stage business that was coming to dominate the theatrical world, a world which encompassed not just the patent theatres of Covent Garden and Drury Lane, but illegitimate theatres as well. The two patent theatres were granted exclusive rights to stage tragedies and comedies by the 1737 Licensing Act, but along with this monopoly on the standard dramatic repertoire came the constraints of censorship. All the plays were inspected and often edited by the Lord Chamberlain. However, no government official censored the slack-rope dancing, the pantomimes, the Italian operas, the burlettas, and the extravaganzas staged at venues like the Sadler's Wells theatre or Astley's Amphitheatre, and these venues' comparative freedom from surveillance allowed for more overt engagement with political events. As Jane Moody puts it, the illegitimate theatre became the 'dramatic newsreel of the modern metropolis'.[8] Allusions to the royal family were routinely censored in plays submitted for performance at Drury Lane or Covent Garden. Because the pantomimes and burlesque performances that were staged at the minor theatres did not have to undergo review by the Examiner of Plays, they could mock royal peccadilloes with comparative impunity. For example, the Coburg theatre on the other side of the Thames was able to stage *George III, the Father of his People* (1824), in which the members of the royal family were given stage counterparts. Although the play was mild in its treatment of George III—it ended with the king ascending to heaven in a balloon—there was still something unseemly about having a second-tier actor play the reigning king. The performance threatened to tarnish the lustre of kingship, and to underscore the theatrical underpinnings of the ruler's reign (compare the chapter on 'Satire').[9]

The minor theatres were factories of innovation that lured audiences with the wondrousness and novelty of their offerings. Philip Astley became famous for the equestrian acts he managed; working within the confines of this stable genre, his performers outdid themselves in startling derring-do. Astley exhibited the 'Little Learned Military Horse' which amazed audiences with its ability to mind-read, feign death, and fire a pistol. Astley's wife became renowned for 'circling the arena on horseback with swarms of bees covering her hands and arms like a muff'. And Astley's 5-year-old son vaulted, danced, and played the violin while riding a horse at full gallop.

Joanna Baillie's earnest ambition to educate theatregoers through the enactment of human passion, and the Romantic poets' ambition to be the Shakespeares of their day, might seem to be operating in an entirely different world from Astley's bee-wearing and violin-playing horseback riders, but all these theatrical endeavours can be situated within a consumer culture that placed a high premium on novelty. Shelley wrote of *Prometheus Unbound*, 'It is a drama, with characters & mechanism of a kind yet unattempted'.[10] And in Baillie's 'Introductory Discourse', according to one recent critic, 'passions function as discrete items available for inventory, display, and sale'.[11] In William Wordsworth's Preface to the *Lyrical Ballads*, a poetic manifesto published two years after Baillie's explanation of her play writing scheme, he decries 'the degrading thirst after outrageous stimulation', a desire that, in his disapproving view, fuelled the market for 'frantic novels, sickly and stupid German Tragedies, and deluges of idle and extravagant stories in verse'. But Wordsworth also emphasized the novelty of his own project, his plan to present ordinary things in an unusual aspect, and he identified the task of poetry as being 'to produce excitement in co-existence with an over-balance of pleasure'. Even Romantic literary figures who distanced themselves from the tawdrier aspects of the stage participated in the quest for new modes of sensational experience.

The theatres

They were always burning down. The Covent Garden theatre went up in flames in 1808, and the Drury Lane theatre was destroyed by a devastating conflagration the following year. Astley's Amphitheatre burned down in 1794, and was rebuilt by the following year, only to have the second building gutted by fire in 1803. The periodic levelling of theatres by fire only served to reinforce a general trend towards their enlargement. A 1794 redesign of the Drury Lane theatre enabled it to house 3,600 spectators, an increase of a thousand bodies from its prior manifestation.

The visitors to the theatre on the night Lady Craven's play was performed were, as usual, segregated by seating arrangement. The most affluent theatregoers, the upper classes and gentry, sat in tiers of boxes that circled the perimeter of the interior and extended beyond the proscenium so as to frame the stage itself; each could seat a small party of spectators. The vast area directly in front of the stage, known as the pit, seated mostly middle-class or professional visitors who paid a more modest price (3s. as opposed to the box holders' ticket price of 5s.) to pack themselves on to benches and watch the play. Frugal theatregoers—artisans, servants, soldiers, sailors—paid a shilling or two to watch the play from the gallery behind the pit. Even more economical theatregoing was made possible by the half-price custom; audience members were admitted to the gallery for 6d. after the end of the third act of the main play. This tradition created a sense of entitlement among theatregoers that caused them to protest when this pricing scheme was revoked at Covent Garden in 1792. More violent and sustained rioting took place in 1809 when ticket prices rose after the post-fire reconstruction of that theatre.

Audience members exerted an influence over the proceedings in other ways as well. When David Garrick, in his adaptation of *The Winter's Tale*, addressed the gallery spectators affectionately as 'my hearts of oak', he did so out of a need to court their favour. Gallery members were not averse to manifesting their displeasure with a play or performance by showering the stage with rotting fruit or dried peas. Outside the theatre, these audience members may have submitted to their lowly status in society; stationed in theatre galleries, they spoke in a collective and raucous voice.

The separately priced seating areas might give us the false impression that theatre-goers mingled only with their social equals. But box, pit, and gallery all abutted each other, especially in the intersection of the three sections at the rear of the theatre where an aristocratic denizen of a facing box (one of those that faced the stage) might have tossed her handkerchief and hit either a pit or gallery spectator. Audience members within the same section were on especially cosy terms; the main seating area of the theatre was packed tightly enough to make the leg room on a contemporary airliner seem generous. Only one foot nine inches was allowed between the back of one seat and the back of another, despite the fact that a moderately sized person could not be comfortably limited to a space of less than two feet.[12]

The increasingly cavernous theatre buildings accommodated extraordinary special effects aimed at dazzling both the lucky members of the royal family occupying a box just left of the stage, and the stable boy craning his neck in the outer reaches of the gallery. The period's master of scenic innovation, the Swiss artist Philippe Jacques De Loutherbourg, made Drury Lane a laboratory for scenic experimentation. He used painted transparencies, skilful perspective painting, and coloured side lights to achieve startling new effects, to create sets that were both shockingly realistic and fancifully wondrous. The year after Lady Craven's *The Miniature Picture* was staged, De Loutherbourg set out on his own. His 1781 *Eidophusikon*, an exhibition of moving pictures designed to imitate the 'Phoenomena of Nature', featured scenic enactments of a sun setting after a rainy day and a moon rising with a water spout. In moving from Drury Lane to the house near Leicester Square where the *Eidophusikon* was staged, De Loutherbourg dispensed with actors and streamlined theatrical experience to pure spectacle. His bracing grand finale depicted Satan arraying his troops on the banks of the fiery lake.

Star turns

Actors may have shrunk in proportion to the steadily enlarging theatres, but the performances of the best of them loomed larger than life. Romantic-era theatregoers did not come to the theatre in order to see particular plays, but rather to see beloved actors perform in striking scenes. This was partly because regular theatregoers were so familiar with the standard repertoire that popular plays could have been staged by audience members calling out lines from memory. But it was also because theatre stars inspired fierce devotion in their fans.

Coleridge's comparison of Edmund Kean's acting to reading Shakespeare by flashes of lightning characterizes the way Romantic theatrical experience has survived in glimpses of memorable moments or points that audiences eagerly anticipated. When Sarah Siddons controversially chose to enact Lady Macbeth's sleepwalking scene without carrying a candle, audience members were so familiar with the traditional bit of stage business that they registered this omission as a significant departure (see further, *Oxford Companion to the Romantic Age*, pp. 569–705). Siddons went on to invent a point of her own. After setting down the light, she rubbed her hands, 'making the action of lifting up water in one hand at intervals'.[13] In its enactment of a woman whose movements were being dictated by the urgings of guilt-ridden fancy, her performance was celebrated for psychological truth. All her actions had a 'wakeful vigour', wrote one commentator: 'she laded the water from the imaginary ewer over her hands—bent her body to listen to the sounds presented by fancy, and hurried to resume the taper where she had left it, that she might with all speed drag her pallid husband to their chamber.'[14]

Siddons also performed memorably in *The Winter's Tale*. The statue scene, featuring a supposed dead Hermione brought back to life, was so popular in the eighteenth century that it was sometimes played on its own as a prelude or coda to other dramas; by the nineteenth century, it was a reliable crowd pleaser, 'a miniature sentimental warhorse', in the words of Stephen Orgel.[15] Siddons made the scene her own by giving a sudden action of her head as the first gesture of Hermione's reanimation, startling audience members. Siddons's Hermione was rendered even more memorable on one occasion when the white muslin robe she was wearing was set on fire by lamps positioned behind the pedestal on which she stood, another reminder of the combustible nature of Romantic-era stage properties.

Besotted theatre fans paid loving tribute to their favourite stars by minutely recording the smallest alterations in a particular performance. After detailing his first impressions of Edmund Kean's performance as Shylock, William Hazlitt took in a second performance and noted, 'He assumed a greater appearance of age and feebleness than on the first night.' Hazlitt was not alone in his obsessive attention to variations in a particular actor's performance. When Kean played Richard in a weak voice, the audience cried 'No, no', upon the announcement of the next night's performance. According to Hazlitt, they were in one accord regarding 'the impropriety of requiring the repetition of this extraordinary effort, till every physical disadvantage had been completely removed'.[16]

Star turns like those of Siddons and John Philip Kemble became so iconographic that a subgenre of thespian mimicry evolved: 'to see Mrs Wells not acting one of the parts made famous by Mrs Siddons or Mrs Abington, but imitating them in those same parts, gave their admirers great delight', writes the theatre historian Charles Beecher Hogan.[17]

If the more famous Romantic writers were not entirely successful as dramatic writers, they were eloquent recorders of their favourite actors' roles and nostalgic memoirists of their visits to the theatre. 'O, when shall I be such an expectant again!' Charles Lamb wrote of his first trip to the theatre as a small child, going on to describe the disenchantment he felt when he returned to the theatre as a jaded teenager. 'The green curtain was no longer a veil drawn between two worlds', Lamb wrote, 'The actors were men and women painted.' Nevertheless, after Lamb's first visit to Drury Lane during the 1781–2 season (the year following Lady Craven's eventful descent upon that theatre), he returned again and again; despite adolescent disillusionment, the theatre was still, for Lamb and his contemporaries, 'the most delightful of recreations'.[18]

READING: Elizabeth Craven, *The Miniature Picture*

Dangling affections

The miniature picture of Elizabeth Craven's play is a portrait of Eliza Camply which she has given to Mr Belvil, whose affections for her are in doubt. When the play opens, Eliza Camply enters her brother's Oxford study in masculine disguise. She pretends to be Sir Harry Revel, a cousin of the Camplys just arrived from France. Sir Harry claims he is going to marry Miss Flirtilla Loveless, much to the dismay of Mr Camply, who is smitten with that aptly named young woman and uncertain of her devotion. Eliza Camply reveals herself to her brother, and outlines her plan to court Miss Loveless in the guise of Harry Revel so as to test the affections of Mr Belvil and also to steer Miss Loveless into the arms of Mr Camply. As Eliza unfolds her plan, she regretfully recalls her last meeting with Mr Belvil, when he laughed at her jealous criticism of Miss Loveless's flirtatiousness, and left the house with Eliza's picture 'hung about his neck' (1.1.138).

Miss Camply's miniature picture is not the only thing left hanging in this play. When Miss Loveless's aunt chides her for playing with men's affections, she says, 'do not you know that Mr Belvil has even been attached to Miss Camply, and yet you have suffered him to dangle after you for a whole week' (2.1.120–4). In a later scene, Miss Loveless refers to her suitors as 'danglers', criticizing her aunt for fancying that 'every dangler one has is to offer', in other words, that every one of Miss Loveless's hovering beaux will propose marriage (2.1.269–70). All the lovers in this play dangle as they wait for confirmation of reciprocal affections.

The miniature picture becomes the focal point of the series of comic misadventures that follow, passing from Mr Belvil to Miss Loveless, and then getting co-opted, much to Mr Belvil's chagrin, by Miss Loveless's pretend suitor, Sir Harry Revel. The picture becomes a mark of good faith and faithful representation in a play in which lovers conceal their true identities and their true affections. 'I will put it in my pocket | till I have an opportunity of comparing it with the | original', Miss Loveless says of the miniature picture (2.1.84–6). As the play proceeds, Eliza Camply, once again pretending to be Sir Harry Revel, spars with the risible Lord Macgrinnon, another aspirant for Miss Loveless's affections, but one motivated solely by mercenary concerns. Toward the end of the play, Lord Macgrinnon is hoodwinked by a second woman in disguise: Miss Loveless's servant Susan impersonates her mistress and literally leads Macgrinnon down a garden path to his final humiliation at the hands of her faithful suitor John.

The play contrasts the steadfastness of true affection with the fleeting vagaries of social fashion. When we first meet Miss Loveless's aunt, Mrs Arabella Loveless, she is visiting the Camply household in order to see Mr Camply's new plants. 'Pray, Mr Camply', she announces in her first speech, 'have you not built a new | hot-house lately?' (1.1.184–5) Mr Camply's hot house is one marker of a social world in which exotic imports are prized more highly than native plants, a concern that is taken up as well by the play's prologue, which notes a decline in native stock. Sheridan writes: 'Thus while with Chinese firs, and Indian pines, | Our nurs'ries swarm, the British Oak declines' (p. viii).

When Eliza adopts the role of Sir Harry Revel, she portrays him as an enthusiast for all things French; in Revel's guise, she greets her brother 'à la Françoise', and when Sir Harry later enters Miss Loveless's drawing-room, he uses this same phrase to register his admiration. 'Heavens and earth, ma'am', exclaims Sir Harry/Eliza, 'I did not expect to find a salon so truly à la francoise in this horrid country' (2.1.172–4). The frivolous fashion for things French is underscored in the prologue, in which Sheridan invents a critic who rises from his bench to fault Lady Craven's play for not being French. Sheridan goes on to conjure up a hilarious scenario in which celebrated English actors become French actors through the intervention of an opportunistic language coach, who vows to have them speaking 'pure flippant French' within a week, but provides, instead, more indiscriminate language training.

> *Dodd* spoke good Flemish, *Bannister* bad Dutch;
> Then the rogue told us, with insulting ease,
> So it was Foreign it was sure to please:
> Beaux, Wits applaud, as Fashion should commend,
> And Misses laugh—to seem to understand—
>
> (p. vii)

Sheridan's fake French actors—the perfectly adept English actors James Dodd and John Bannister, forced to declaim incomprehensible foreign phrases—provide a suitable prelude to a play which explores the truthfulness of artistic representation.

The traffic in pictures

The actress Mary Robinson, in the role of Eliza Camply, first enters the stage in the disguise of Sir Harry Revel, which seems a risky theatrical move. In Shakespeare's cross-dressing scenes, an actor is usually well established in a particular role before being called on to adopt a false persona. Elizabeth Craven assumed that her audience would be able to figure out that the young gentleman in breeches introduced by a servant as Revel was really another female character playing a trick. This complicated sorting out of roles was made easier for audience members by the recognizability of Robinson, whom they had just watched perform the role of Perdita in *The Winter's Tale*, and who was increasingly visible in London social circles. In her 1801 *Memoirs*, Robinson recalled the attention she elicited an an ingenue: 'I was consulted as the very oracle of fashions; I was gazed at and examined with the most inquisitive curiosity' (ii. 18). Robinson was the subject of dozens of portraits (many of which depicted her playing the role of Perdita, and often in miniature format), as was Elizabeth Craven, a celebrated beauty who, like Robinson, was painted by Thomas Gainsborough, Joshua Reynolds, and other renowned portrait painters of the period. Horace Walpole was inspired by the performance of *The Miniature Picture* to rehang a George Romney portrait of Lady Craven that he owned, writing to his friend William Mason, 'I have brought hither her portrait and placed it in the favourite blue room.'[19]

The Miniature Picture was performed at a moment when portraiture was enjoying an extraordinary vogue in England. George Romney booked 593 portrait sittings in 1783, and in the early years of the 1780s portrait paintings made up the largest percentage of works submitted to the Royal Academy, the official arbiter of English painting (see *Oxford Companion to the Romantic Age*, pp. 656–9). The fad for collecting engraved 'heads', inspired by works like James Granger's 1769 *Biographical History of England*, pushed up the price of books with engraved portraits. It also meant that collectors sliced out engravings to interleave the pages of Granger's volume with suitable illustrations.

The art of portraiture was strongly associated with the theatre, thanks in part to works like John Bell's *British Theatre* series, which, from 1775 on, reprinted British plays with engraved full-length portraits of performers in costume and gesturing as they would in particular roles. A portrait of Mary Robinson playing the role of Amanda served as illustration for Bell's 1777 publication of Colley Cibber's *Love's Last Shift*. Sarah Siddons's exalted stage career was immortalized in Bell illustrations which presented her in a variety of roles, including her celebrated turn as Lady Macbeth. But even portrait subjects who were not actresses enjoyed posing as historical and theatrical figures or mimicking admired poses struck by previous portrait sitters; Joshua Reynolds's clients could flip through a portfolio of prints taken from his portraits in search of pleasing attitudes.

Elizabeth Craven's play highlights the personal vanity that helped to fuel the market in portraits. Her stage directions signal the characters' preoccupation with their own appearances. Belvil exits the stage during the second act in order to tend to his coiffure: 'With your leave, ladies, I shall | go and put a little powder in my hair' (2.1.106–7). Flirtilla Loveless spends a good portion of the same act 'arranging her hair in a pocket-glass' (2.1.148). Her pocket mirror provides a visual echo of the miniature picture that is the characters' central concern. The picture's miniature size and circulating status make it comparable to pocket change, and remind us that Eliza Camply's beauty, circumscribed by the portrait, serves as a commodity in the marriage market.

Craven uses Eliza to draw attention to the staginess of portraiture. In the guise of Sir Harry Revel, Eliza claims to detest 'modern daubs' and faults English artists' propensity for over-saturated colour: 'your English artist here gives you ladies a yellow | purple complexion, and then to set it off | dresses you in a bright rose colour or blue drapery' (2.1.209–11). In the comic centrepiece of the play, Sir Harry adopts a connoisseur's stance, and orders Miss Loveless into a series of silly poses so as to make her match his memory of a Madonna by Guido that he once saw in Florence. 'Be so good to turn your head a little this way; no, no, I | mistake, recline it on the other side, lean it upon the right shoulder: no, no, I mean the left | —aye, there—now half shut your eyes', he directs the vain Miss Loveless who is happy to oblige. Craven allows Eliza Camply to demonstrate the limitations of the portrait genre, to realize the stark contrast between the confining pose depicted by a static portrait and the 'variety of expressions' conveyed by an actual woman (2.1.259).

A late winter's tale

'This Comedy of Three Acts was originally written as a Farce in Two Acts, and never intended for the Public theatres, nor the Public Eye', states the Advertisement to the printed version of *The Miniature Picture*. Elizabeth Craven claimed that Sheridan had staged the play at Drury Lane against her will. 'I was very angry with him for it', she wrote, 'and kept up my resentment, till he made me laugh, one night in a crowd coming out of the Opera House. We were squeezed near one another by chance, and he said, "For God's sake, Lady Craven, don't tell any body I am a thief, for you know very well, if you do, every body will believe it." '[20] The thieving Sheridan did Craven a service by coupling her play with *The Winter's Tale* because Shakespeare's play, particularly in the versions most familiar to Romantic viewers, perfectly complemented her own.

In any production, *The Winter's Tale* is a play about artistic representation, most famously in its staging of a statue coming to life, the scene in which a statue of Hermione, who had been long assumed dead by Leontes, is discovered to be the ageing Hermione herself. The scene contrasts the static perfection of art with the mutability of breathing human beings. 'Hermione was not so much wrinkled, nothing | so aged as this seems', Leontes exclaims when he first sees the statue.[21] As Christopher Rovee notes, Hermione is transformed into an aesthetic representation and likened to a portrait miniature long before the statue scene; Leontes complains that he 'wears her like her medal, hanging | about his neck', a line that is echoed by Camillo, at the end of the play, when he says of the restored queen: 'She hangs about his neck.'[22]

In *The Miniature Picture*, even though Eliza Camply's picture gets passed from hand to hand, a neat reversal occurs in the central confrontation scene between Eliza and Belvil. Eliza, in the guise of Sir Harry, has regained her portrait from Miss Loveless and flaunts it before Belvil, telling him that she/he plans to use it 'as a passport | to the good graces of the lady who sat for it' (2.1.288–9). As Belvil grows more and more distraught, Eliza learns, to her satisfaction, the depth of his affection when he reveals his desire to marry her. Still playing Sir Harry, she exclaims, 'What then you really are ready to hang yourself about Eliza, hey!' (2.1.374–5). Where Belvil once wore Eliza's portrait dangling from his bosom, here he becomes a bauble that can be hung around her neck. In a further complication of the association of the female with aesthetic objects, Eliza's brother Mr Camply interrupts Miss Loveless's sardonic description of her aunt dancing to demand that he be the subject of her portraiture. 'Now draw | my picture', Mr Camply abruptly demands (3.1.19–20).

Mary Robinson's career as an actress ended soon after *The Miniature Picture* was staged at Drury Lane, but she became associated with another miniature picture, a portrait of the Prince of Wales which caught the eye of Marie Antoinette when Robinson visited the French court. According to Robinson's 1801 *Memoirs*, the French queen 'appeared to survey, with peculiar attention' the miniature of the Prince of Wales that Robinson wore on her bosom, and on the following day she requested the loan of this object. When Robinson obliged, the queen reciprocated with the gift of a netted purse. In a neat inversion of conventional gender roles, the Prince of Wales, like Belvil in Elizabeth Craven's play, becomes a dangler, an object of miniaturization and exchange.

Sheridan's prologue to *The Miniature Picture* encourages us to draw connections between the Shakespeare offering and its afterpiece. He presents Craven's play as 'a Winter's Drama', the last gasp of a cold season that refuses to make way for spring.

> Chill'd by rude gales while yet reluctant May
> With-holds the beauties of the vernal day
>
> .   .   .   .
>
> The season's pleasures too delay their hour,
> And Winter revels with protracted pow'r:
> Then blame not, Critics, if, thus late, we bring
> A Winter's Drama—but reproach—the Spring.
>
> (p. v)

Shakespeare's *The Winter's Tale*, in its Romantic-era adaptations, foregrounded the highly wrought spring of the pastoral, the love affair of Florizel and Perdita played out against a backdrop of cavorting rural folk in flowery Bohemia. When Hazlitt excerpted a few passages from the play for his *Characters of Shakespeare's Plays*, he focused on Perdita's speeches, her conjuring up of the flowers of spring:

> Daffodils,
> That come before the swallow dares, and take
> The winds of March with beauty; violets dim,
> But sweeter than the lids of Juno's eyes
> Or Cytherea's breath; pale primroses,
> That die unmarried, ere they can behold
> Bright Phoebus in his strength.
>
> (4.4.118–24)

The pastoral presents an idealized version of nature, and inspires nostalgia for its lost utopia. Recalling passages from the play and the actors who performed them, Hazlitt succumbs to this longing for a more perfect theatrical past. 'We shall never see these parts so acted again; or if we did, it would be in vain. Actors grow old, or no longer surprise us by their novelty.'[23]

Elizabeth Craven, too, understood the appeal of pastoral fantasy. She designed a cottage so that it was surrounded entirely by willows, and she orchestrated the planting of grape vines. Her friend William Beckford wrote in the late 1780s to enquire what she was up to: 'What are you about?—gathering roses perhaps or composing pastorals full of grace and sprightliness.'[24] But the winter's drama she depicted in *The Miniature Picture* provided no pastoral reprieve; it is situated squarely in the midst of town life and of uncertain social alliances. Still, Hazlitt's sad musing on the loss of the theatrical past rings especially true for *The Miniature Picture* which exists only as a printed text that deviates from its Drury Lane staging. The Advertisement to its printed form notes that the author published it only so she could correct its misrepresentation on the stage at Drury Lane: 'she chuses to submit Faults which are really her own, to the Judgment of the World, rather than be accused of those which she never committed', the Advertisement concludes. The printed version of the play is an odd entity; it cannot be a faithful rendition of Elizabeth Craven's original farce in two acts, which was privately staged, because it has three acts like Sheridan's Drury Lane version. It must be a composite text which corrects perceived mistakes in Sheridan's version without entirely reverting back to the original form. That is, *The Miniature Picture* stands as a perfect representative of Romantic drama, a genre whose virtues no one could or can agree on, and whose plays seem most vivid in the snapshot recollections of the audience members who first saw them staged.

FURTHER READING

Baillie, Joanna, *Plays on the Passions*, ed. Peter Duthie (Peterborough, Ont.: Broadview Press, 2001). The introduction provides an excellent overview of the philosophical context of Baillie's plan to write a comedy and a tragedy on each human emotion, and also of the theatrical milieu in which her plays were performed.

Bartholomeusz, Dennis, *'The Winter's Tale' in Performance in England and America 1611–1976* (Cambridge: Cambridge University Press, 1982). A history of *The Winter's Tale* performances which provides a survey of its Romantic-period permutations.

Bolton, Betsy, *Women, Nationalism, and the Romantic Stage: Theatre and Politics in Britain, 1780–1800* (Cambridge: Cambridge University Press, 2001). Bolton explores the ways in which Romantic women performers and playwrights—most notably Emma Hamilton, Mary Robinson, Hannah Cowley, and Elizabeth Inchbald—used theatrical conventions to intervene in the political debates of the 1780s and 1790s.

Burroughs, Catherine, *Joanna Baillie and the Theatre Theory of British Romantic Women Writers* (Philadelphia: University of Pennsylvania Press, 1997). Burroughs focuses on Baillie as a theorist of theatre, provides an analysis of several of the *Plays on the Passions*, and describes closet drama as a form of experimental theatre.

——*Women in British Romantic Theatre: Drama, Performance, and Society, 1790–1840* (Cambridge: Cambridge University Press, 2000). An anthology of essays focusing on Elizabeth Craven's female contemporaries, with particular emphasis on Elizabeth Inchbald and Joanna Baillie.

Carlson, Julie A., 'Trying Sheridan's *Pizarro*', *Texas Studies in Literature and Language*, 38 (1996), 359–75. Carlson explores the interplay between Sheridan's political oratory and the theatrical rhetoric of his most famous play. Her essay is part of a special issue of *TSLL* devoted to 'Romantic Performances'.

Cave, Richard Allen (ed.), *The Romantic Theatre: An International Symposium* (Totowa, NJ: Barnes and Noble Books, 1986). See especially Timothy Webb's essay on Romantic poets' ambivalent relationship to the stage in this series of essays on Romantic drama.

Cox, Jeffrey N., 'Spots of Time: The Structure of the Dramatic Evening in the Theatre of Romanticism', *Texas Studies in Literature and Language*, 41 (1999), 403–25. Cox explores how the scheduling of plays affected the reception of particular works; his essay is part of a special issue of *TSLL* that focuses on 'Romantic Drama in Place'.

Donahue, Joseph W., *Dramatic Character in the English Romantic Age* (Princeton: Princeton University Press, 1970). Donahue focuses on the Romantic concept of dramatic character and in so doing provides fascinating analyses of the performances of Siddons, Garrick, and Kean.

Hume, Robert D. (ed.), *The London Theatre World, 1660–1800* (Carbondale, Ill.: Southern Illinois University Press, 1980). An anthology of essays providing excellent historical accounts of theatre architecture, audiences, repertory, management, and scenery, among other topics.

Moody, Jane, *Illegitimate Theatre in London, 1770–1840* (Cambridge: Cambridge University Press, 2000). An exploration of the range and significance of performances staged in the minor playhouses.

Pointon, Marcia, *Hanging the Head: Portraiture and Social Formation in Eighteenth-Century England* (New Haven: Yale University Press, 1993). A comprehensive history and analysis of the centrality of portraiture in the eighteenth century.

Richardson, Alan, *A Mental Theater: Poetic Drama and Consciousness in the Romantic Age* (University Park, Pa.: Pennsylvania State University Press, 1988). Richardson explores Romantic poets' verse drama innovations.

Russell, Gillian, *The Theatres of War: Performance, Politics, and Society, 1793–1815* (Oxford: Clarendon Press, 1995). Russell details the significance of the theatre as a political arena in the Romantic period, and also the use of theatricality in the conduct of war.

NOTE ABOUT THE TEXTS USED

Elizabeth Craven's *The Miniature Picture; A comedy in three acts: performed at the Theatre-Royal Drury Lane* (London: G. Riley, 1781) was consulted at Literature Online, August 2003 <http:lion.chadwyck.com>. For accounts of the play's performance, I used *The London Stage 1600–1800*, Part 5. 1776–1800, ed. Charles Beecher Hogan (Carbondale, Ill.: Southern Illinois University Press, 1968), i. 344–5, and also John Genest's *Some Account of the English Stage from the Restoration in 1660 to 1830*, 10 vols. (Bath: H. E. Carrington, 1832), vi. 134–5. A. M. Broadley and Lewis Melville's two-volume *The Beautiful Lady Craven* (London: John Lane, 1914) provided details of Craven's life and career. Marc Baer's *Theatre and Disorder in Late Georgian London* (Oxford: Clarendon Press, 1992) and James J. Lynch's *Box, Pit and Gallery* (Berkeley: University of California Press, 1953) were sources of information on audience activism. Jerome McGann's *The Romantic Ideology* (Chicago: University of Chicago Press, 1983) informed my account of the debate over the definition of Romantic poetry. My descriptions of the Astley family performances, and of Philippe Jacques De Loutherbourg's productions are indebted to Philip Highfill, Jr., Kalman A. Burnim, and Edward A. Lanhans's *A Biographical Dictionary of Actors, Actresses, Musicians, Dancers, Managers & Other Stage Personnel in London, 1660–1800*, 16 vols. (Carbondale, Ill.: Southern Illinois University Press, 1973–93). Marcia Pointon's *Hanging the Head: Portraiture and Social Formation in Eighteenth-Century England* (New Haven: Yale University Press, 1993) surveys the rise of portraiture in the eighteenth century, and Kalman A. Burnim and Philip H. Highfill Jr.'s *John Bell, Patron of British Theatrical Portraiture: A Catalog of the Theatrical Portraits in His Editions of 'Bell's Shakespeare' and 'Bell's British Theatre'* (Carbondale, Ill.: Southern Illinois University Press, 1998) reproduces Bell's portraits of *The Winter's Tale*. Mary Robinson's four-volume *Memoirs of the Late Mrs Robinson* (London: R. Phillips, 1801) provides accounts of her celebrity, and my *Romantic Theatricality: Gender, Poetry, and Spectatorship* (Ithaca, NY: Cornell University Press, 1997) analyses her portrait exchange with Marie Antoinette.

NOTES

1. Horace Walpole to William Mason, 28 May 1780, *Horace Walpole's Correspondence with William Mason*, ed. W. S. Lewis, Grover Cronin Jr., and Charles H. Bennett, *The Yale Edition of Horace Walpole's Correspondence*, 48 vols. (New Haven: Yale University Press, 1939–83), xxix. 43–5.

2. William Wordsworth, *The Poetical Works of William Wordsworth*, ed. Ernest de Selincourt and Helen Darbishire, 5 vols. (Oxford: Clarendon Press, 1952–9), i. 342.

3. Joanna Baillie, 'Introductory Discourse', *Plays on the Passions*, ed. Peter Duthie (1798; repr. Peterborough, Ont.: Broadview Press, 2001), pp. 91, 69, 70–1.

4. Ibid. 73.

5. Ibid. 103.

6. Michael Tait, 'England: Nineteenth Century and Edwardian', in John Gassner and Edward Quinn (eds.), *The Reader's Encyclopedia of World Drama* (New York: Thomas Y. Crowell Company, 1969), p. 232.

7. Stuart Curran, 'Shelleyan Drama', in Richard Allen Cave (ed.), *The Romantic Theatre* (Totowa, NJ: Barnes and Noble Books, 1986), p. 71.

8. Jane Moody, *Illegitimate Theatre in London, 1770–1840* (Cambridge: Cambridge University Press, 2000), p. 7.

9. Ibid. 106–17.

10. Percy Shelley to Thomas Love Peacock, 6 Apr. 1819, *Letters of Percy Bysshe Shelley*, ed. F. L. Jones, 2 vols. (Oxford: Clarendon Press, 1964), ii. 94.

11. Andrea Henderson, 'Passion and Fashion in Joanna Baillie's "Introductory Discourse"', *PMLA* 112 (1997), 199.

12. Edward A. Langhans, 'The Theatres', in Robert D. Hume (ed.), *The London Theatre World 1660–1800* (Carbondale, Ill.: Southern Illinois University Press, 1980), pp. 48–9.

13. G. J. Bell's notes on Sarah Siddons's acting included in H. C. Fleeming Jenkin, *Mrs Siddons as Lady Macbeth and as Queen Katharine*, Papers on Acting, III (New York: Dramatic Museum of Columbia University, 1915), p. 67.

14. James Boaden, *Mrs Sarah Siddons*, 2 vols. (London: Grolier Society, 1900), ii. 99.

15. Stephen Orgel, 'Introduction' to William Shakespeare's *The Winter's Tale*, ed. Stephen Orgel (Oxford: Clarendon Press, 1996), p. 63.

16. William Hazlitt, *A View of the English Stage*, in *The Complete Works of William Hazlitt*, ed. P. P. Howe, 21 vols. (London: J. M. Dent, 1930), v. 180, 183.

17. Charles Beecher Hogan, 'Introduction', Part 5. 1776–1800, *The London Stage 1660–1800* (Carbondale, Ill.: Southern Illinois University Press, 1968), p. lxxxvi. *The London Stage*, which gathers performance information gleaned from playbills, newspapers, and theatrical diaries of the period, stands as the definitive reference manual for students of eighteenth-century theatre.

18. Charles Lamb, 'My First Play', *The Works of Charles and Mary Lamb*, ed. E. V. Lucas, 5 vols. (1903; repr. New York: AMS Press, 1968), ii. 98, 100.

19. Horace Walpole to William Mason, 28 May 1780, *Horace Walpole's Correspondence*, xxix. 45.

20. A. M. Broadley and Lewis Melville (eds.), *The Beautiful Lady Craven* (London: John Lane, 1914), ii. 146.

21. William Shakespeare, *The Winter's Tale*, ed. Steven Orgel (Oxford: Clarendon Press, 1996) 5.3.28–9.

22. Christopher Rovee, '"Everybody's Shakespeare": Representative Genres and John Boydell's *Winter's Tale*', *Studies in Romanticism*, 41 (2002), 524–5.

23. William Hazlitt, 'The Winter's Tale', *Characters of Shakespeare's Plays*, *The Complete Works of William Hazlitt*, iv. 326.

24. William Beckford to Lady Craven, 30 May 1788, *The Life and Letters of William Beckford of Fonthill*, ed. Lewis Melville (New York: Duffield and Company, 1910), p. 176.

27 | Essays, newspapers, and magazines

William Christie

Periodicals—printed forms that recur *periodically*—had been around in Britain since the beginning of printing in the fifteenth century in the form of almanacs, annals, and annuals. It took a number of legal, cultural, and political changes, however, as well as changes in what we would call communications and technology, to allow that network of newspapers, magazines, journals, and Reviews that the Romantics were the first to identify as 'the periodical press' to develop and flourish. Some of the changes necessary for the development of a periodical press had themselves been accelerated by it. One obvious example would be the adoption of the vernacular rather than Latin as the language of prose around the turn of the eighteenth century. A sound English prose style then became one of the objects of polite education and a prerequisite for participation in the communal literary culture that, after Jürgen Habermas, we call 'the public sphere'. Another concomitant cultural change was the new pride taken by a progressively better educated public in having informed opinions. Throughout the eighteenth century, newspapers, magazines, and Reviews joined a steady stream of pamphlets and encyclopaedias in offering, in a condensed form, information and argument otherwise available only in protracted and expensive works of philosophical and political speculation.

Other changes conducive to the rise of the periodical press were more immediately and directly effective, not the least of these being the suspension of the Licensing Act in 1695, when what has since been identified as a publishing revolution took place. The number of books available for purchasing or for borrowing from the new libraries starting up everywhere climbed steadily throughout the eighteenth century (quadrupling between 1750 and 1800). But the surest sign that a publishing revolution had taken place and a print culture had become established—or the surest symptom, depending on your point of view—was the proliferation of periodicals (see also the chapter on 'Print culture and the book trade').

Sweeping politico-legal changes like the lapse of the Licensing Act (which was, in fact, more accidental than I make it sound) would have come to nothing without the technology to produce and distribute the periodicals themselves. It was not until 1814 that *The Times* newspaper finally installed a steam press capable of meeting any demand the reading public might make of it, but this came at the end of developments in the printing press that had halved production time and of concomitant improvements in the speed and extent of transportation. The eighteenth century had been a period of systematic road building and improvement so that, by the Romantic period, navigable roads existed from London to all major cities and, with that, a system of coaches, hostelries, and horse-exchange. In 1740, one coach had run from London to Birmingham daily; by 1763, passengers could choose from thirty. And the coaches themselves were covering the distance more and more quickly as each year went by. Cross-country mail services and the introduction of scheduled mail coaches later in the eighteenth century allowed a national postal system begun a century earlier to develop into a reliable and swift service.

Physical (technological) developments like these have always played an important role in enabling and to some extent directing the way we communicate with each other. No account of the periodical press can ignore them, any more than it can ignore the cultural and ideological questions raised by that press's accelerated development. Why (for example) *did* the British public become a reading public? Why was so much importance placed by this consolidating print culture on being informed and on having opinions? In the meantime, however, it is enough for our purposes to know that in the eighteenth century a periodical press had evolved to meet a new demand for information ('intelligence') and for a critical position on most aspects of communal life. In a complicated symbiosis, periodicals (to quote Francis Jeffrey, see below) saw themselves as 'among the legitimate means by which the English public both instructs and expresses itself'—and, one hastens to add, amuses itself.

Newspapers

Ephemeral publications (pamphlets) discussing contemporary events had been common enough during the Elizabethan period to have become the butt of satire, and newspapers or newsbooks (called 'corantos') had begun to appear in numbered sequences during the 1620s. It was not until 1702, however, that the first successful London daily paper commenced publication. Thereafter the number of newspapers that started up became so alarming that in 1712 the government had introduced a tax (known as 'stamp duty') to keep up their price and restrict their readership. In spite of stamp duty, however, which had been regularly increased throughout the century, the number of newspapers—defining 'newspaper' as a daily through to weekly periodical (some came out every two or three days) carrying the most recent political, commercial, and social information relevant to the life of the community it serviced—had grown steadily throughout the eighteenth century. By 1800, there were well over 250, more and more of them featuring the foreign and domestic news that was once the exclusive province of the élite, while at the same time offering some interpretative commentary. By 1800, moreover, the press had become the ubiquitous presence we recognize it as today. With the political and cultural consciousness of the nation having quickened in the 1790s under the impetus of the war with France and its effect on trade and prices, the newspaper had made itself indispensable.

There is disagreement amongst scholars as to the extent of subsidization enjoyed by different newspapers at different times, though ample evidence that senior government ministers and members of the opposition invested heavily in newspapers as an effective form of party propaganda. Even when subsidized, however, the press seems to have relied on sales and advertisements to survive. Like so many other aspects of British culture in the Romantic period, the world of newspapers—and to these we should add the rest of the periodical press—was a world of supply and demand, driven more by commercial than by political interests. This is not to say that individual newspapers were politically disinterested. Far from it. In most cases, however, commercial interests encouraged a kind of diplomacy in which a variety of interests and opinions could be represented within the pages of one newspaper.

Newspapers do not usually feature prominently in literary histories of this or any other period—not as prominently, certainly, as the Reviews and literary magazines. However, it is worth remarking on the cultural continuity between the world of daily and weekly journalism and the so-called 'republic of letters', if only because there has been until recently a Romantic tendency to keep the two apart. Many writers and thinkers involved themselves in daily and weekly journalism, especially in the form political commentary. The poet, critic, and cultural theorist Samuel Taylor Coleridge used to brag that the political essays he contributed over a twenty-five year period to Daniel Stuart's *Morning Post* and *Courier*—the first a morning daily for which he began writing in 1797 and the second an evening newspaper started up in 1804—had been responsible for raising the profile of newspaper journalism. There is an element of truth in this. Coleridge's confirmed and conjectural contributions to newspapers are certainly extensive enough to have filled three volumes of his *Collected Works*—five if we include the short-lived periodicals *The Watchman* (1795) and *The Friend* (1809–10), started up and written by himself. But the newspaper only achieved a secure social status and authority when in 1817 Thomas Barnes took over the editorship of *The Times* (established in 1788), when it became at once more independent and more effectual, almost doubling its sales to around 14,000 in 1820 at the time of the Queen Caroline affair (see *Oxford Companion to the Romantic Age*, pp. 668–9). Besides relying on the network of foreign correspondents that *The Times* had established—including Henry Crabb Robinson, friend of the poet William Wordsworth—Barnes used copy from prominent insiders like Henry Brougham (1778–1868), the lawyer and Whig politician (later Lord Chancellor) who was also the mainstay of the *Edinburgh Review*.

Better known amongst the political journalists were Leigh Hunt and William Cobbett. After three years as a theatre critic, Hunt became editor and leading political writer for his independent weekly *The Examiner*, founded in 1808 with his brother John. Though hardly a radical democrat or even a republican, Hunt infused political writing with what he called 'a philosophical spirit', which amounted to an at times quite trenchant reformism, severely critical of government policies and practices and of corruption in the establishment generally. The Hunt brothers soon learned the limits of official tolerance. After successfully diverting and defending themselves against a number of charges, they were eventually fined and sentenced to two years in prison in 1812 for libelling the Prince Regent ('a violater of his word, a libertine over head and ears in debt and disgrace, a despiser of domestic ties, the companion of gamblers and demireps, a man who has just closed half a century without one single claim on the gratitude of his country or the respect of posterity!'). *The Examiner* later became less politically aggressive and Hunt himself turned to poetry and criticism and from political journalism to the familiar essay.

The Hunt brothers certainly caused a stir, but William Cobbett was the leading journalist of the day, and far and away the most widely read. Establishing his weekly *Political Register* in 1804 with support from members of the government, he soon became disillusioned with what he called the 'Old Corruption' and turned to vigorous advocacy of parliamentary and other reforms. He, too, was convicted of libel and sentenced to prison. What stands out most clearly from Cobbett's curious mixture of reactionary and progressive politics is his conviction and contentiousness, and the unpatronizing directness of his address to working people.

From the beginning, newspapers had circulated opinions to a wider audience than that enjoyed by the political pamphlets which were such a pronounced feature of political life throughout the seventeenth and eighteenth centuries. A genuinely popular press, however, was another matter. It would be wrong to imagine that by the early nineteenth century newspapers had anything like the habitual and universal appeal they have today. Like the books and magazines with which they shared the market, they remained the preserve largely of the middle and upper classes. It was not until after William Cobbett began issuing his *Political Register* for 2*d*. in 1816 that a radical, unstamped ('pauper') press began to develop, opening up the possibility of mass circulation.

Magazines

The discussion of *The Examiner*, one of the 'Sunday newspapers' according to Hunt himself, is a reminder of how difficult it is to classify the products of the periodical press. What *The Examiner* promised was 'Politics, Domestic Economy and Theatricals', what it delivered was anything that suited its editor, including original poetry and literary criticism along with the political intelligence and polemic that amounted to at least half of each issue. In its heterogeneity, it more nearly resembled the monthly magazine than some of the daily and weekly newspapers—though newspapers, too, especially the weekly newspapers, published poetry and songs and anecdotes and book extracts and reviews of books, as they still do. (Already by 1769, the *Worcester Journal* can be found commenting that newspapers, once 'dry registers of common intelligence', had become 'annals of history, politics and literature'; that the newspaper was, indeed, 'now a magazine'.)

Though not confined to the magazine, then, this formal heterogeneity was the magazine's distinguishing feature. The magazine had become increasingly popular throughout the eighteenth century, and had been around some time before Edward Cave's *Gentleman's Magazine* (1731–1914) first used the word in its title and described itself as 'a monthly collection, to treasure up as in a magazine' ('magazine', from the original Arab word meaning 'a storehouse'). The very number, variety, and brevity of the magazine's various components or contributions—and in the eighteenth century readers were more often than not invited to contribute, so that a genuine confusion of writer and reader resulted—were central to its appeal. The essence of the magazine (to quote the author Oliver Goldsmith) was 'never to be long dull upon one subject'. Like so many eighteenth-century pamphlets and periodicals, for example, the *Gentlemen's Magazine* offered the stimulant of the true-life crime story with its commentary on all aspects of social life and of language. But information was usually as important in magazines as diversion, so that any one of the many that were aimed exclusively at women—like the *Ladies' Diary* (1704–1840)—might contain articles on history or geography or even mathematics along with the more predictable Society gossip.

A magazine market already amply supplied by the late eighteenth century was glutted by the 1820s. Only some of these stand out for the quality of their critical and creative work, however—like *Blackwood's Edinburgh Magazine* (1817–1980), or *Maga* as it was known, the *London Magazine* (1820–9), and the *New Monthly Magazine* from 1821, when it was under the editorship of the poet Thomas Campbell. Of the first two of these, the Tory *Maga* not only had priority but was the more innovative, ushering in two decades in which the literary magazine dominated British literary history. It was also the more controversial. If the poet Alexander Pope can be said to have made hatred into an art form, the contributors to *Maga* made malice and manic irreverence into an art form, one that had its proprietor William Blackwood regularly paying out compensation for libels committed. The two prime movers involved were John Gibson Lockhart (self-titled 'the Scorpion which delighteth to sting men's faces') and John Wilson (writing as 'Christopher North'), the two of whom developed a clever, verbally energetic, and sneering form of satire that might take any form from a mock-scholarly treatise to a stinging literary criticism. The butt of their attacks was anything they took to be liberal or radical (and a lot else besides), though the immediate provocation was the cultural domination of the Edinburgh Whigs around Francis Jeffrey of the *Edinburgh Review*. A number of snobbish attacks by Lockhart on 'the Cockney School' of Hunt, Hazlitt, and the poet John Keats have gone down as his and *Maga's* most ignoble campaign.

There was more to *Maga* than malice, however, and much of it talented: some excellent poetry and tales by James Hogg, serialized novels by John Galt and Susan Ferrier, and Wilson's own serialized dialogues, *Noctes Ambrosianæ* ('Nights at Ambrose's

[Tavern]'). In these last, a caricatured Wilson, Lockhart, Hogg, William Maginn, and sometimes others (including the Romantic essayist Thomas De Quincey), all thinly veiled by pseudonyms, debate any and every topic from poultry farming to poetry with gusto and occasional point.

As editor of the *London Magazine* when it started in 1820, John Scott was generous in his recognition of the precedent set by the older *Maga*—which only makes it that much more tragic that he should have lost his life a year later to Lockhart's 'second' or stand-in, John Christie, in a duel over *Maga*'s insults. But the *London* itself, if it does not have the same sense of collective, performative endeavour as *Maga*, was and is renowned for having published an extraordinary number of individual works of distinction. Keats and John Clare and Thomas Hood published poetry in the *London* and Charles Lamb's *Essays of Elia* first appeared in its pages, as did De Quincey's *Confessions of an English Opium-Eater* and much of Hazlitt's *Table Talk*.

For our purposes it is with the literary magazine in the age introduced by *Maga* that we identify the occasional or familiar essay so characteristic of the later Romantic period. The persistence with which new magazines were launched throughout the period, in spite of the short life most of them would enjoy, suggests how potentially lucrative they must have been for publishers. The essayist had certainly never had such opportunities, though payments varied dramatically and were never as generous as those offered by the big Reviews, to which we must now turn.

Reviews

It was the cultural authority assumed and enforced by the two big Reviews of the early nineteenth century—the *Edinburgh Review* and the *Quarterly Review*—that confirmed the power of the periodical press in the culture of Romantic Britain. This is not surprising if we think of the publishing revolution that took place during the eighteenth century, when the London booksellers had been obliged for various commercial and copyright reasons to advertise and promote their books more actively, especially in the provinces. The widely distributed and successful *Gentleman's Magazine* mentioned earlier had included from the start accurate and comprehensive lists of recent books, but 'intelligence' had not been enough. To make more informed choices, readers overwhelmed by the expanding numbers of titles published each year looked to the recommendations or warnings of book reviews.

The first Review—a periodical devoted exclusively to publishing reviews of books—was the *Monthly Review* established by Ralph Griffiths in 1749. It had been followed not long after in 1756 by the *Critical Review*, edited and managed by the novelist Tobias Smollett. Many more were to follow, and when changes to the law of copyright in 1774 made the living author and recent books a more lucrative commercial proposition, publishers had become even more reliant upon reviewing, and reviewing itself even more central to the network of ancilliary institutions servicing the publishing revolution.

But however exigent the commercial pressures on the establishment and development of Reviews, their centrality and influence had never been limited to the promotion of reading generally or to promoting specific books as commercial objects. From the beginning they were also engaged in the culture of ideas and ideologies. Reviews mapped and modified the various emerging knowledges—commenting on natural philosophy (our 'science'), for example, on moral philosophy, historiography, political economy, aesthetics, linguistics, and so on. And they did this in ways that participated in and fuelled political and cultural wars that would become more open and divisive after the French Revolution. The Tory *Critical Review*, for example, had been established in political reaction to the success of the Whig *Monthly Review*, setting a pattern for the early nineteenth century when the Whig *Edinburgh Review* (1802) would be followed by the Tory *Quarterly Review* (1809) and reviewing would become even more heavily politicized.

These two big Reviews, as I said, dominate our period—not just its reviewing but also its thinking. Changes to reviewing practice introduced by the *Edinburgh* enabled Reviews to become a discursive force throughout the whole of the nineteenth century. For one thing, in their twelve issues per year, the *Monthly* and the *Critical* had tried to discuss or at least to register as many publications as possible, with the result that they were bound to remain closely affiliated with the book trade. The *Edinburgh*, on the other hand, published only quarterly, with a determination 'to be distinguished, rather for the selection, than for the number of its articles'. And it paid well—three to five times the rate offered in the eighteenth century, and this increased even more dramatically over the first three decades of the nineteenth century. Under the *Edinburgh* editorship of Francis Jeffrey from 1803 to 1829, moreover, the book review gradually expanded. What in 1800 might have occupied two or three, at most ten pages, say, was soon running to twenty or thirty or even as much as fifty and sixty pages.

More to the point, however, the priorities of book reviewing changed. In many cases the reviewer and his ideas on the topic in question end up taking priority over the publication under review. Indeed, while there usually *is* a book being reviewed (not always), that book not infrequently becomes the mere occasion or excuse for a reflective (and self-reflective) political and cultural *essay*. The Scottish lawyers and other professionals who formed the 'distinct and marked set' that launched the *Edinburgh* (Jeffrey, Brougham, the philosopher Thomas Brown, the political economist Francis Horner, and the English wit Sydney Smith) drew on an intellectual heritage in the Scottish Enlightenment—they drew on its empirical, inductive approach to an encyclopaedic range of ideas and disciplines; they drew on its 'conjectural' or philosophical historicism; they drew on its political economic priorities. Little wonder that by 1831, in the pages of the *Edinburgh* itself, Thomas Carlyle was looking apprehensively towards the day when 'all Literature has become one boundless self-devouring Review'.

All of this, incidentally, was conducive to a cultural authority that had an enormous effect on writers no longer enjoying formal patronage and dependent for their livelihood on the sale of their works—and thus an enormous effect on Romantic writing itself. An uneasy relationship already subsisted between the reviewer and the professional author, one which dated back to the eighteenth century when they had been born and raised together by the needs of a radically revised and rapidly enlarging book trade. By the Romantic period, however, Review criticism could make or break a reputation, with the reviewer often identifying with consumers and conspiring with them against the pretensions of an author. Francis Jeffrey hounded William Wordsworth throughout the early years of the nineteenth century, for example, retarding Wordsworth's reputation as a poet even while he enhanced Lord Byron's and made George Crabbe's. For another thing, while in the *Edinburgh* what we call 'literature' (poems, plays, novels) is given the respect of being one of society's significant endeavours, it is only one. And no less than other social institutions, literature is occasionally subjected to historical scrutiny and thus to a degree of demystification. Not surprisingly, then, the often antagonistic attitude taken by nineteenth-century reviewing played a crucial role in reinforcing the self-consciousness of authorship in our period.

The periodical essay

The miscellaneous nature of individual periodicals, not to mention the variety and unevenness of the periodical press as a whole, makes it difficult to generalize about the periodical essay as a Romantic form. A few traits and certain anxieties are shared across the different media, however. One characteristic and controversial aspect of periodical literature, for example, has always been its marriage to time and to the transient—a temporality and transience that are inherent in the epithet 'periodical' itself, which suggests not just its recurrent, sequential production but also its remaining at least to some extent irrecoverably *of its period*. The latest turnpike or the digging of a canal, a slip in grain prices or the Prince of Wales's latest affair, Edmund Kean's impersonation of Shylock or Lord Byron's latest Turkish tale—whatever their pragmatic relevance at the time of their becoming news, they are hardly likely to be of comparable interest beyond the day of their original notice and discussion. This is especially obvious in the case of contributions to a newspaper, but it was not difficult then, as it is not difficult now, to derive the same uneasy sense of a society's ever-shifting priorities from reading the more intellectually ambitious essays of the big Reviews. It is not the least of the legacies of the Romantic period that talent and economic necessity brought a qualified respectability to all departments of journalism, but none of the writers I have mentioned who involved himself in the different forms of periodical did so without at least occasional misgivings about being in some way contaminated by it as a *trade*, of little social and historical consequence.

We should never forget that periodical publication was driven by commercial interests—not exclusively, perhaps, but without some measure of popularity survival was impossible. Indeed, it was the manifestly rapid development of competitive, commercial publishing and the proliferation of commercially viable publications like the periodical that precipitated a Romantic redefinition of 'literature' as a uniquely gifted cultural form transcending the fashions of taste and whims of contemporary history. Literature—imaginative literature, creative literature—was to be identified and valued precisely in contrast to the ephemerality of periodical writing, with its investment in the momentary, the fleeting both in subject-matter and in sentiment and value. Literature, in short, was everything periodical writing was not.

Not surprisingly, then, the periodical essay, like the periodical itself, is often haunted by an awareness of the transient nature of its material—as it is by an awareness of the contingent nature of its own authority. Born to meet the new demand for opinions it is also aware of being limited to just that: opinions. It was a crisis of confidence that ironically derived from the very developments in eighteenth-century empirical philosophy that had helped to foster the growth of journalism in the first place. Preoccupied with the way the mind experienced the world as phenomena (appearances, perceptions, mental images) and with what we mean when we say we 'know' something, eighteenth-century philosophy ended by giving to the individual experiencing mind an exclusive, if severely limited authority. In the absence of certainty, truth becomes more and more a matter of consensus. This encouraged and informed the development of journalism and, ultimately, of its political counterpart in democracy. (The periodical essay, in other words, as the root meaning of 'essay' as an 'attempt' suggests, claimed only a limited or tentative authority, but it was starting to look like all authority could only ever be tentative.)

Different periodical writers deal with the ephemerality and contingent nature of their form in different ways. Those unembarrassed by periodicals as a trade, of course, were not concerned in the least. Others, however, claim the privilege of the imaginative writer in being able to transform passing events and personal opinions into something of more permanent interest. Some, arguably the best writers, will turn the ephemerality and contingency of the periodical essay to account. Hazlitt, for instance, will make them at once the condition and the topic or issue of an essay, or offer an unapologetically 'impressionistic' or even prejudiced reading of ideas or events.

But we have to beware of running together the different kinds of periodical essay. A familiar essayist like Hazlitt—or Lamb or Hunt or Wilson or De Quincey—is far more likely than is a political journalist or a reviewer to use personality and personal experience as interpretative. For the sake of clarity, then, we can discriminate between these three significant kinds of Romantic essay (loosely associated with the three different kinds of periodical):

1. The political essay: a short, rhetorical and argumentative piece concerned to record and influence immediate events or conditions or personalities (Coleridge on the

character of William Pitt; Hunt on the Prince Regent or Queen Caroline; Cobbett on popular rural culture);

2. The occasional or familiar essay: licensed musing on miscellaneous aspects of social or individual behaviour (Lamb on his schooldays or the 'Behaviour of Married People'; Hazlitt on boxing, Indian jugglers, or on hating and its satisfactions; De Quincey 'On Murder, Considered as One of the Fine Arts');

3. The historico-cultural review: a sustained, historical interpretation of contemporary culture, like the political essay (only less directly) designed to intervene and change its direction (Hazlitt on 'The Periodical Press' itself; Jeffrey on the influence of the *philosophes* on the French Revolution or on changes in literary culture since the Elizabethan period; Thomas Carlyle on 'The Signs of the Times'; Thomas Babington Macaulay on the seventeenth century and its legacy).

Of these it is the familiar essay, especially after Waterloo (1815), that is seen as the characteristic contribution of the Romantic period, if only because the familiar essay shares so many of its assumptions and techniques with Romantic poetry. The Romantic essay inherited its peculiar blend of the familiar, the topical, and the reflective from the *Spectator* (1711–12) of Joseph Addison and Richard Steele, an innovative periodical which sought self-consciously to bring literature and philosophy to the educated middle- and upper-class reader of the early eighteenth-century London coffee-houses and clubs. But its exploitation of personality and its self-conscious, confessional mode the Romantic essay inherited from the philosopher Jean-Jacques Rousseau, the novelist Laurence Sterne, and the Romantic poets. Lamb writes his 'Confessions of a Drunkard', De Quincey his *Confessions of an English Opium-Eater*; Hazlitt launches into his meditation 'On Living to One's-Self' with a characteristically disarming intimacy that recalls nothing so much as the conversation poems of Coleridge:

I never was in a better place or humour than I am at present for writing on this subject. I have a partridge getting ready for my supper, my fire is blazing on the hearth, the air is mild for this season of the year. . . . I have three hours good before me, and therefore I will attempt it. It is as well to do it at once as it is to have it to do for a week to come.

If the writing on this subject is no easy task, the thing itself is a harder one. It asks a troublesome effort to ensure the admiration of others: it is a still greater one to be satisfied with one's own thoughts. As I look from the window at the wide bare heath before me, and through the misty moon-light air through the woods that wave over the top of Winterslow . . . my mind takes its flight through too long a series of years, supported only by the patience of thought and secret yearnings after truth and good, for me to be at a loss to understand the feeling I intend to write about; but I do not know that this will enable me to convey it more agreeably to the reader.

How self-revealing the confessions of the Romantic essayist either are or were intended to be remains a moot point, but each in his own idiosyncratic way exploits confessional techniques that take the familiarity of the essay to new extremes: extremes of subject-matter (focusing, often perversely, on trivial or bizarre details of everyday life);

extremes of personality (indulging nostalgias, anxieties, or obsessions); extremes of stylistic exhibitionism (in the case of Lamb and De Quincey, certainly). In the Romantic essay, a rambling, associative, musical, often mannered prose is being pushed to its expressive limits.

READING: William Hazlitt, 'My First Acquaintance with Poets'

The germ of William Hazlitt's 1823 essay 'My First Acquaintance with Poets'[1] can be found in a letter he wrote to *The Examiner* on 12 January 1817 professing his surprise at the attacks upon 'Jacobinism' made by the poet and cultural commentator Samuel Taylor Coleridge. Hazlitt's letter recalls Coleridge in his younger, radical days expressing sentiments quite the reverse of those with which the now conservative polemicist is identified. By way of example, he quotes the substance of the sermon delivered in the Unitarian church at Shrewsbury which appears early on in 'My First Acquaintance with Poets'. Hazlitt signed the letter with the pseudonym SEMPER EGO AUDITOR, an elaborate pun that in itself antici-pates the later essay. 'I am still (*or* always) the listener' is what it says, but what it suggests is that (1) Hazlitt is *still* waiting to hear (from Coleridge) and that (2) when Coleridge talks he turns everybody into a listener (because he is so entrancing and/or because it is simply not possible to get a word in!). But (3) the Latin word *auditor* was also often used to refer to 'a disciple' and Hazlitt is nothing if not genuinely grateful for the part the charismatic Coleridge has played in his own intellectual development.

Coleridge, then, was the occasion and remains the central figure of the essay, both in his person and as a symbol of his generation. The difference between the letter and the essay, however—and the difference is a crucial one—is that in the essay the autobiographical mode takes over from the portrait of the older poet. For Hazlitt, it was no less true of our ideas and opinions than it was of our affections that they simply could not be disjoined 'from the impressions of time, place, and circumstance, without destroying their vital principle' ('The New School of Reform', *Works*, xii. 189). Indeed, so intimately bound up with each other are our ideas, our experience, and our feelings that for Hazlitt the only way of discussing a topic *was* autobiographically. The most faithful way for him to represent Coleridge was to express to the reader the 'involuntary movement of the imagination and passion' that Coleridge inspired *in himself*, as the poet's *auditor* or disciple (*SW* 308–9). This expression does not pretend to keep faith with Coleridge in any objective sense, rather with the essayist's own *experience* of Coleridge.

It is this complex expressiveness that makes Hazlitt a supreme essayist. In an intense, direct, plain-spoken, apparently effortless yet various and always musical prose, Hazlitt sets about making what was vital to himself seem vital to the personal and political life of every thinking, feeling individual. In 'My First Acquaintance with Poets' he uses his own youthful and middle-aged selves to mediate in a recollection that turns out to be a meditation on genius and on a whole generation of thinkers, on intellectual and emotional development, time and memory, loss and disappointment.

First acquaintance with Coleridge

The autobiographical mode is apparent in the title, highlighting as it does the personal involvement of the essayist: *'my* first acquaintance'. And in an opening sentence in which Hazlitt endeavours to establish a matter-of-fact context for Coleridge's appearance in his life, the impulsive essayist cannot resist betraying the quasi-apocalyptic significance of the event in a pre-emptive aside: 'My father was a Dissenting Minister at W—m in Shropshire; and in the year 1798 (*the figures that compose that date are to me the "dreaded name of Demogorgon"*) Mr Coleridge came to Shrewsbury, to succeed Mr Rowe in the spiritual charge of a Unitarian Congregation there' (*SW* 211 (italics added)). The quotation is from that great paradigm of Romantic poetry, John Milton's *Paradise Lost* (II. 964–5), and the allusion is to a primal Chaos, arguably neutral in itself but foreboding in so far as it is out of Chaos that all the dark gods are spawned.

The full force of this disturbing and ambivalent quotation from a poem about the loss of paradise will not become apparent until later in the essay, however. At this stage, we are aware only of the significance of the arrival of the poet, who brings with him all the magic of language:

the Welch mountains that skirt the horizon with their tempestuous confusion, agree to have heard no such mystic sounds since the days of

> 'High-born Hoel's harp or soft Llewellyn's lay!'

(*SW* 211)

Characteristically, the true power of those 'mystic sounds' is best revealed by the revolution they effect in Hazlitt's own life, a revolution captured by his comparing his younger self, prior to his meeting with Coleridge—'dumb, inarticulate, helpless'—with his present, mature self, in the act of composition and at last sharing in Coleridge's command of language: 'my ideas float on winged words, and as they expand their plumes, catch the golden light of other years' (*SW* 211, 212).

Then, as so often in his essays, Hazlitt cannot resist a sudden access of self-pity. He is, however, quick to counter: 'But this is not to my purpose'—that purpose being, he implies, to tell Coleridge's story, which he goes on to do in a justly famous passage in which he recalls going to hear Coleridge preach:

When I got there, the organ was playing the 100th psalm, and, when it was done, Mr Coleridge rose and gave out his text, 'And he went up into the mountain to pray, HIMSELF, ALONE'. As he gave out this text, his voice 'rose like a steam of rich distilled perfumes', and when he came to the two last words, which he pronounced loud, deep, and distinct, it seemed to me, who was then young, as if the sounds had echoed from the bottom of the human heart, and as if that prayer might have floated in solemn silence through the universe. The idea of St John came into mind, 'of one crying in the wilderness, who had his loins girt about, and whose food was locusts and wild honey'. The preacher then launched into his subject, like an eagle dallying with the wind . . .

'And for myself', he concludes, 'I could not have been more delighted if I had heard the music of the spheres' (*SW* 212–13). Again, note, the true measure of the sublimity of the poet's rhetoric is Hazlitt's own response.

'An archangel a little damaged'

At this moment and throughout the opening pages of the essay, Coleridge's genius is allowed to reign unchallenged, a matter of public record, so to speak, underwritten by its power over the essayist as an enchanted youth. It is not until Hazlitt's description of the Tuesday after the sermon, when he meets Coleridge face to face for the first time, that he allows his adult consciousness and his knowledge of what Coleridge has become—and has failed to become—abruptly to intervene: 'His mouth was gross, voluptuous, open, eloquent; his chin good-humoured and round; but his nose, the rudder of the face, the index of the will, was small, feeble, nothing—like what he has done' (*SW* 214). Coming on the heels of the soaring passage inspired by and reproducing Coleridge's sublime sermon, this is a deliberate rhetorical anticlimax, a sudden sinking (*bathos*) or collapse of grand pretensions to reveal the shabby reality behind. Anticlimax, it turns out, is for Hazlitt the prevailing trope of human life.

When the revelation of Coleridge's inconsequence finally does come, prior signs suddenly take on extra meaning. The incessant talking that is the subject of Hazlitt's gently comic characterization in the opening paragraph ('He did not cease while he staid; nor has he since, that I know of' (*SW* 211)) is suddenly revealed as a substitute for action and resolution, what we would call *sublimation*. This is entirely appropriate when we think of Coleridge's extraordinary verbal skills. Suddenly the very sublimity of the sermon—the height to which it rises, like the expectations of the essayist, the congregation, and the reader—now appears to flirt with disaster, like Icarus flying in the face of the sun.

Suddenly, too, we are reminded that it was the *young* Hazlitt's perspective—'it seemed to me, who was then young'—and that Coleridge's oratorical achievement is hedged around by conditionals: '*as if* the sounds had echoed from the bottom of the human heart, and *as if* that prayer might have floated in solemn silence through the universe.' For the self-conscious young radical Hazlitt the struggle of the sun to liberate itself from the thick mists 'seemed an emblem of the *good cause*' (*SW* 213). *Seemed*, not *was*. The inspired Coleridge, we note, is really only 'half-inspired' (*SW* 214).

The passage of time mocks young Hazlitt's enthusiasms and hopes: 'So at least I comment on it after the event' (*SW* 214). When Coleridge's nose is said to reveal his fatal flaw, both essayist and reader are suddenly made aware of a tension between the younger Hazlitt's original experience and the older Hazlitt's disillusioned understanding. Two visions of Coleridge compete for attention, as it were, and the essay characteristically inhabits the tension between them. The anticlimax, however, is, like time itself, irreversible. The essay is about loss and about the darkly ironic gap opened up between the past and the present by memory.

A history of the growth of Hazlitt's mind

What alters with the shift from Hazlitt's younger to his older consciousness at the point of anticlimax is not just the reader's image of Coleridge—from archangel to 'an Arch angel a little damaged' (to quote Charles Lamb)—but also the emphasis of the essay itself, which is no longer on Coleridge but is now firmly back on the history of the growth of Hazlitt's own mind. We have already noted a continuous oscillation in the opening of the essay between Coleridge as the object of Hazlitt's admiration on the one hand and Hazlitt the admirer on the other—between the impressive orator and the impressionable *auditor*. The two are inseparable. Now, however, Hazlitt's priority is confirmed.

When I refer to the essay as a history of the growth of Hazlitt's mind, I am adapting a description Wordsworth once gave of his epic poem of the self that we know as *The Prelude* (the poem 'on my earlier life or the growth of my own mind'). The autobiographical tech-nique of 'My First Acquaintance with Poets' is very similar to that of *The Prelude*: the same imaginative re-creation of special events from the past—what Wordsworth called 'spots of time', Hazlitt called 'standing resource[s]' (*Works*, xvii. 320); the same interplay of two consciousnesses; the same vital geography ('How was the map of my life spread out before me, as the map of the country lay at my feet!', *SW* 222). Wordsworth also and more habitually referred to *The Prelude* as 'the poem to Coleridge', which only serves to highlight the similarity.

As the narrative of the subsequent days and months unfolds in 'My First Acquaintance with Poets', we witness a diffident young Hazlitt growing in confidence and beginning to risk the ideas that he has arrived at independently. John Chester is introduced into the Somersetshire idyll precisely to distinguish Hazlitt's relationship with Coleridge from that of the poet's less critical disciples. Chester was 'one of those who were attracted to Coleridge's discourse as flies are to honey, or bees in swarming-time to the sound of a brass pan' (*SW* 226)—a characterization that flatters neither the disciple nor the teacher—and is 'aston-ished that I should be able to suggest any thing to Coleridge that he did not already know' (*SW* 229). By the end of the narrative, in other words, Hazlitt's two consciousnesses start to fuse, as the youthful acolyte is well on the way to becoming the mature thinker who can look with a critical eye upon most of the recollected utterances of the '*half*-inspired' sage.

The anticlimax of history

Coleridge's is not the only anticlimax in the essay, and indeed is seen to reflect the anticlimax of a whole generation. 'I set out in life with the French Revolution, and that event had considerable influence on my early feelings', Hazlitt writes in his essay 'On the Feeling of Immortality in Youth'; 'Little did I dream, while my first hopes and wishes went hand in hand with those of the human race, that long before my eyes should close, that dream would be overcast, and once more set in the night of despotism' (*Works*, xvii. 197). Throughout 'My First Acquaintance with Poets', Hazlitt bears historical witness to the promise held out by the French Revolution and the social and intellectual debate of the 1790s, no less than by the new poetry of Wordsworth and Coleridge:

Somehow that period (the time just after the French Revolution) was not a time when *nothing was given for nothing*. The mind opened, and a softness might be perceived coming over the heart of individuals, beneath 'the scales that fence' our self-interest. (*SW* 222)

Besides being a veritable anthology of the contentious philosophical and political issues of the decade, the essay is a 'Who's Who' of its influential thinkers: Edmund Burke, James Mackintosh, Mary Wollstonecraft, William Godwin, Thomas Paine, and Thomas Holcroft. But his writing on the other side of the defeat of Napoleon in 1815 means that Hazlitt also bears historical witness to the return of monarchy and legitimacy ('the night of despotism'), and thus to what he sees as the failure of the ideals of the French Revolution. (Hazlitt was a staunch supporter of Napoleon against the monarchies of Europe and wrote a long biography of the man Coleridge had characterized as an 'upstart Corsican'.)

In re-creating the past in this way, 'My First Acquaintance with Poets' can also be seen as mapping the twin intensities of the Romantic period, with its two generations: the 1790s and the radical years of Wordsworth and Coleridge on the one hand, and on the other the darker, more pessimistic radicalism of the post-Napoleonic period—of Byron and Shelley, for example. Hazlitt straddled the generations. He was 20 in 1798 when the story is set, only six years younger than Coleridge himself. (Byron and Shelley had been 10 and 6 respectively.) Because he had been personally familiar with Wordsworth and Coleridge and had shared in the euphoria of the revolutionary decade, Hazlitt saw himself as uniquely able to mediate, explaining the 1790s to a younger generation that he felt consistently underrated its achievement even while he attempted to shame a misguided older generation by offering it a dramatic re-enactment of its own hopes and dreams.

The vanity of human wishes

Finally, however, there is another, self-consciously ahistorical or apolitical dimension to Hazlitt's allegory of failed promise, one that works against a sense of the uniqueness of the revolutionary and post-revolutionary years of Hazlitt's own life. In this dimension, the personal history of William Hazlitt senior, the essayist's father, proves exemplary. Genial, pious, loving, Hazlitt senior is also politically idealistic ('a veteran in the cause') and stubbornly independent, so he is 'tossed about from congregation to congregation in the heats of the Unitarian controversy' and ends by living out an anticlimactic life in relative obscurity (*SW* 215). The lives of all men confirm that failure is inevitable:

So if we look back to past generations (as far as eye can reach) we see the same hopes, fears, wishes, followed by the same disappointments, throbbing in the human heart; and so we may see them (if we look forward) rising up for ever, and disappearing, like vapourish bubbles, in the human breast! (*SW* 215)

In his own life, certainly, the essayist can see only a frustrated idealism: 'My soul has indeed remained in its original bondage, dark, obscure, with longings infinite and unsatisfied' (*SW* 212). A prose poem on the vanity of human aspiration and idealism, 'My First Acquaintance with Poets' is Hazlitt's equivalent to Wordsworth's *Ode* ('Intimations of Immortality') in which loss and anticlimax are seen as fundamental to human life and the

Coleridge preaches his sermon, Hazlitt his. Hazlitt's sermon is an exemplary tale about blighted hope and the vanity of human wishes, without any of the consolation we might expect from this kind of sermon—either in this world or in the next. Hazlitt refuses his father's recourse to the consolation of theology, in other words, just as he refuses Wordsworth's and Coleridge's consolation of a divinely sanctioned establishment. We are left with Hazlitt, having climbed the mountain with Coleridge and glimpsed a brighter future in an experience that had shown all the signs of being an apocalyptic moment, now alienated from his mentor and without consolation: 'HIMSELF, ALONE'.

Though not quite alone. Hazlitt discourses through people and personalities, moving them around like chess pieces. Even seemingly casual appearances in his life leave their mark and in his essays are charged with significance. 'My First Acquaintance with Poets' begins with Coleridge and discovers (briefly and less sympathetically) Wordsworth. Even when Coleridge and Wordsworth are making the compromises Hazlitt finds so contemptible, there is still a sense in which he will turn to them for understanding and vision:

Wordsworth, looking out of the low, latticed window, said, 'How beautifully the sun sets on that yellow bank!' I thought within myself, 'With what eyes these poets see nature!' and ever after, when I saw the sun-set stream upon the objects facing it, conceived I had made a discovery, or thanked Mr Wordsworth for having made one for me! (*SW* 225)

Coleridge has given Hazlitt words, Wordsworth has given him eyes, and they have become part of the history of his personal development, testifying to the power of ideas and literature to give insight and open up vistas, mapping our landscapes and our lives.

The essay concludes with another 'first acquaintance', moreover—with Charles Lamb. Like Hazlitt, Lamb was a friend and contemporary of Coleridge and Wordsworth. Like Hazlitt, Lamb would come into his own as a periodical essayist late in life and, again like Hazlitt, would retain his liberal sympathies while resisting the utilitarianism and commercialism often associated with rational reform. 'Lamb', he says, 'always appeared to me . . . with a *bon mot* in his mouth':

It was at Godwin's that I met him with Holcroft and Coleridge, where they were disputing fiercely which was the best—*Man as he was, or man as he is to be.* 'Give me,' says Lamb, 'man as he is *not* to be.' This saying was the beginning of a friendship between us, which I believe still continues. (*SW* 229)

The apostasy of Coleridge and Wordsworth could never be a source of humour for Hazlitt— as it could, say, for Byron. Hazlitt found few things laughable in that way. But it is not quite fair to suggest with Virginia Woolf that he had no sense of humour. Certainly if there is any consolation at the end of 'My First Acquaintance with Poets' it comes in the form of Charles Lamb and his wry joke about human imperfectability.

FURTHER READING

Altick, Richard D., *The English Common Reader: A Social History of the Mass Reading Public 1800–1900* (Chicago and London: University of Chicago Press, 1957). A classic study of the reading habits of the nineteenth century.

Black, Jeremy, *The English Press 1621–1861* (Stroud: Sutton Publishing, 2001). Traces the growth and establishment of the newspaper in British culture with frequent reference to interesting details of form and content in different periods.

Bloom, Harold (ed.), *William Hazlitt: Modern Critical Views* (New York, New Haven, and Philadelphia: Chelsea House, 1986). A collection of representative essays, all of them interesting and some—like Christopher Salvesen's 'A Master of Regret' (pp. 29–46)—wide-ranging and excellent.

Bromwich, David, *Hazlitt: The Mind of a Critic* (New Haven and London: Yale University Press, 1983). A thorough, revisionary study that concentrates throughout on the literary criticism and on Hazlitt as philosopher and theorist of imagination, rather than on the essays as essays.

Butler, Marilyn, 'Culture's Medium: The Role of the Review', in Stuart Curran (ed.), *The Cambridge Companion to British Romanticism* (Cambridge: Cambridge University Press, 1993), pp. 120–47. An excellent short critical introduction to the Reviews as cultural and ideological enterprises that concentrates on early issues of the *Edinburgh*.

Feather, John, *A History of British Publishing* (London and New York: Routledge, 1988). A necessarily general but informative and readable account of the development of the British publishing industry which mentions vital changes in relevant laws (including copyright) and in publishing business practices.

Gilmartin, Kevin, *Print Politics: The Press and Radical Opposition in Early Nineteenth-Century England* (Cambridge: Cambridge University Press, 1996). A detailed account of 'the radical press' of the early nineteenth century focusing on politics and including a chapter each on Hunt and Cobbett along with an afterword on Hazlitt.

Grayling, A. C., *The Quarrel of the Age: The Life and Times of William Hazlitt* (London: Weidenfield and Nicholson, 2000). This biography offers an excellent introduction to the family, cultural, and intellectual background by a popular academic philosopher.

Jack, Ian, *English Literature 1815–1832*, Oxford History of English Literature, Vol. X (Oxford: Clarendon Press, 1963). Though the new Oxford histories of English literature are now coming out, Ian Jack's opening chapter contains an accurate and readable account of the major Reviews and magazines of the period.

Klancher, Jon P., *The Making of English Reading Audiences, 1790–1832* (Madison: University of Wisconsin Press, 1987). A brilliant discussion of the social and political assumptions and interpretative strategies of the major Romantic periodicals.

McFarland, Thomas, *Romantic Cruxes: The English Essayists and the Spirit of the Age* (Oxford: Clarendon Press, 1987). A set of general lectures on Lamb, Hazlitt, and De Quincey, though with more on 'the spirit of the age'—'the convulsive disruptions and accumulating stresses that defined Romanticism'—than on what was actually going on in the age itself.

Natarajan, Uttara, *Hazlitt and the Reach of Sense: Criticism, Morals, and the Metaphysics of Power* (Oxford: Clarendon Press, 1998). A study focusing on 'metaphysics' in an effort to establish Hazlitt's stature as a 'philosophical critic', with a long chapter on 'The Self as Focus in Hazlitt's Theory' that is of interest.

Park, Roy, *Hazlitt and the Spirit of the Age: Abstraction and Critical Theory* (Oxford: Clarendon Press, 1971). A general discussion of the resistance to abstraction in Hazlitt's criticism and theories of poetry and painting, though again (as with Bromwich, Natarajan, and Paulin below) little discussion of Hazlitt as a *periodical* essayist or of the essay form.

Parker, Mark, *Literary Magazines and British Romanticism* (Cambridge: Cambridge University Press, 2000). Good discussion of a selection of major writers (not all essayists) in the major magazines, arguing the importance of the periodical context.

Paulin, Tom, *The Day-Star of Liberty: William Hazlitt's Radical Style* (London: Faber, 1998). An engaged and appreciative study of Hazlitt as a man and as a feeling, thinking *stylist*.

NOTE

1. See William Hazlitt, *Selected Writings*, ed. Jon Cook (Oxford: Oxford University Press, 1991), pp. 211–30, hereafter *SW*, references to be given in the text. References for quotations from essays not included in the Oxford World's Classics edition will be to *The Complete Works of William Hazlitt*, ed. P. P. Howe, 21 vols. (London and Toronto: J. M. Dent, 1930–4), hereafter *Works*, references to be given in the text.

28 | Biography and autobiography

Anthony Harding

The half-century from 1776 to 1832 marked the arrival of biography and autobiography as major literary genres. Their rise to prominence is one of the most significant features of the literary culture that defines the Romantic movement. Reading biography and autobiography of this period is rewarding, not only for what the texts themselves tell us about the lives of prominent women and men of the period, but more especially because the rapid emergence of the genres at this time marks a crucial stage in the development of the modern idea of 'the author', as a figure of cultural significance.

The author as a legal entity was a creation of copyright law as it developed in the eighteenth century. The 1710 Copyright Act and subsequent interpretations (especially a 1769 case which gave legal recognition to the author's interest in the work) created a basis in law for the modern assumption that the author is the chief originator of a literary work. The belief that by learning about an author's life-experiences we can understand that author's work is so deeply ingrained in modern culture as to seem almost a common-sense proposition, but it is actually part of a set of cultural assumptions inherited from the Romantic period. It was not until the late eighteenth century that interest in the lives, personalities, and experiences of authors grew to be a major preoccupation of the book-buying public. The first major author whose personal life became as culturally significant as his published writing was Samuel Johnson, thanks to James Boswell's massive *Life of Johnson* (1791). Johnson himself had a great interest in biography, and his own *Lives of the English Poets* (1779–81), written at the behest of more than forty London booksellers who invited him to contribute biographical prefaces for a series of elegantly produced editions of the poets' works, constituted a major part of his literary legacy. After Johnson, the creation of the modern idea of the 'great writer' became a dominant feature of literary culture. Between 1780 and 1850, a number of literary figures owed their fame or notoriety as much to their lives—or what was communicated about their lives through various biographical accounts—as to their own writings: Robert Burns, Mary Wollstonecraft, Sir Walter Scott, Lord Byron, and Percy Shelley, to name a few. If we include those known in part from their autobiographical or semi-autobiographical writings, we can add Helen Maria Williams, Mary Robinson, Mary Hays, S. T. Coleridge, William Hazlitt, Leigh Hunt, and Thomas De Quincey to the list. William Wordsworth's *The Prelude*, usually read as an autobiographical poem, was withheld from publication until after the author's death in 1850, but was well known, in its successive versions, to Wordsworth's family and close friends.

The emergence of autobiography is particularly significant in the development of this focus on the character and life of the author. The word 'autobiography' does not appear in book titles until later: it was not until the mid-nineteenth century that the term came into common use as the title for a personal narrative, or story of the author's own life. The term did not even appear in Henry J. Todd's revised edition of Johnson's *Dictionary* (1818). Leigh Hunt, whose *Autobiography* appeared in 1850, was one of the first writers to use it as a title. However, writings that were autobiographical in all but name achieved unprecedented prominence in the Romantic period.

The phenomenon did not go unnoticed by the critics. As John Gibson Lockhart commented dourly in the *Quarterly Review*, 'England expects every driveller to do his Memorabilia'.[1] Certainly, the rage for writing memoirs, recollections, and reminiscences was responsible for a vast amount of trivia finding its way into print; but what conservative critics like Lockhart were resisting was in one sense a revolt, on the part of those who had very limited access to the public sphere, against the domination of public discourse by a predominantly male and upper-class clique. Life-writing, particularly autobiography, lent itself to the reformist and revolutionary agendas. Helen Maria Williams, Mary Wollstonecraft, William Godwin, and Mary Hays all saw the potential of personal narrative to document injustice, and initiate social or political change. Life-narratives were also a powerful weapon in the hands of the movement to abolish the slave trade: accounts of their own experiences of slavery and the slave trade by James Albert Gronniosaw and Olaudah Equiano appeared in 1772 and 1789 respectively, and helped to arouse public outrage against the cruel, murderous, but highly lucrative trade in African slaves.

Social, economic, and cultural context

The massive increase in the number of life-narratives published, particularly in the British Isles, can be traced to a number of social, economic, and cultural factors, some of them purely commercial. At the end of the eighteenth century, a much higher proportion of the population could read and write than was the case in 1700. After 1800, technological advances in printing and papermaking, such as the advent of mechanical, steam-driven presses, and the development of machine-made paper, made it possible to print large quantities of books at low cost. Printers and booksellers saw an irresistible opportunity to market biographies of famous people. These appealed to the leisured middle class, a new reading public fostered by the magazine culture of the time and eager for useful knowledge (see *Oxford Companion to the Romantic Age*, pp. 203–6). Johnson and other respected authorities recommended the reading of biographies as a ready way to learn history, since lives of notable individuals offered historical information in an easily digestible form. Still more important was the fact that many children of poorer families were taught to read in Sunday schools, run by churches and philanthropic foundations. These children were urged first of all to read the Bible, but teachers often recommended reading biographies as well, since they could offer examples of virtue for the young to follow. In 1791, when John Wesley (popular preacher and founder of the Methodist movement) died, enterprising book-sellers saw an opportunity and hastened to produce several rival 'Lives' to be offered for sale to the thousands who visited the chapel in City Road, London, where Wesley was buried. Lord Nelson, British admiral and hero of Trafalgar, was an even more popular biographical subject: between 1805 (the year of his death) and 1830, no fewer than twenty-three biographies of him were published. One did not have to be a national hero like Nelson to merit a biography, however. The Evangelical movement encour-aged promulgation of biographies of almost anyone whose life could be held up as an example of Christian virtue, and this notion of biography as a vehicle of moral instruction—a holdover from the eighteenth-century view of the genre as furnishing useful examples of how to lead a good life, but given a more overtly religious slant—was a powerful incentive both to publishers and to many amateur biographers.

These social and commercial developments converged with a new valuation of the personal and subjective in both imaginative literature and political debate. The idea that a life-narrative might be a good vehicle for recording a thinker's opinions, captur-ing the essence of a person's engagement in the culture of the time, and even propagat-ing a particular political stance, was in some sense validated by Boswell's *Life of Johnson*. This was a landmark achievement in that it showed how an intimate record of a man's life and conversation could weigh almost equally with his own writings in extending his reputation. Johnson's skill in argument and his ability to deliver emi-nently quotable epigrams and apophthegms made him an ideal biographical subject; but the influence of Boswell's *Life* was broader than even Johnson's admirers could have imagined. In confirming the reputation, and extending the influence, of a literary figure, it virtually created the modern concept of the great writer as a figure of national importance whose life would be interesting to the public in its own right.

The same economic conditions that encouraged the proliferation of biographies applied also to the writing and publishing of autobiographies, but with some differ-ences. Writing a memoir of oneself, or 'self-biography', could easily appear prompted more by sheer vanity than by a genuine desire to serve the public good. The critical press was merciless against any 'self-biography' that looked like mere self-promotion. Jean-Jacques Rousseau's *Confessions*, most English critics felt, should be taken as a warning against the danger of exposing one's own faults and follies to public view. The very term 'autobiography' did not exist until the last few years of the eighteenth century: its first recorded use was in 1797, by William Taylor, in the *Monthly Review* (see *Oxford Companion to the Romantic Age*, p. 411). Robert Southey used the term in the *Quarterly* in 1809; he was also one of the first to give currency to the term 'autobiographer', when he complained in the *Annual Register* that 'booksellers, public lecturers, pickpockets, and poets become autobiographers' (quoted in *Oxford Companion to the Romantic Age*, p. 411). Southey is clearly suggesting that there is something indecorous about publishing a narrative of one's own life. Carlyle's description of the era as 'These Autobiographical times of ours' has a similarly satirical edge.[2] Nevertheless, many compelling autobiographies were written and published in this period, usually with a preface stating that the author came forward reluctantly, writing these recollections not from any desire for self-aggrandizement but only because they contained some knowledge useful to the reader. De Quincey's *Confessions of an English Opium-Eater* purports to be written to correct public ignorance about opium, its likely effects, and how the opium user can avoid its dangers; but for most modern readers the book is fascinating not for the medical data about narcotics, but because of De Quincey's exploration of the subconscious mind through his dreams and memories.

Individualism, natural rights, and life-writing

Johnson's approach to biography was conservative in several respects, particularly in the suggestion that biography could teach virtue, and the neoclassical belief that the human condition was essentially the same everywhere. Even though Johnson advised the biographer to examine the 'domestick privacies' of the subject, since such details revealed more of a person's true character than what he or she did in public, he argued that these details had value for readers only because human beings all shared one common nature. Reading biography thus had a high moral purpose: we can learn from the example of others—from their errors, as well as from their achievements. Romantic life-writing is generally marked by a more individualistic outlook, stressing the *uniqueness* of a person's experience and situation. Gender, race, social class, and geography (being born far from centres of wealth such as London and Edinburgh, for instance) all made obvious differences to one's life-experiences. Those who were committed to social reform, whether liberals or radicals, could use these disparities in exposing social injustices.

Radicalism and liberalism both challenged the last remnants of the older social system, with its relatively fixed and stable social classes. The liberal individualist believed that a person's own talents and industry, rather than parentage or inherited fortune, should determine his or her place in society. Radicals wanted the abolition of all inherited privileges and a democratic political system (see *Oxford Companion to the Romantic Age*, pp. 37–41). In practice, the liberal and radical agendas sometimes overlapped, and both could claim a philosophical basis in the Lockean concept of 'natural rights' (see *Oxford Companion to the Romantic Age*, p. 586).

Towards the end of the eighteenth century many life-narratives, especially autobiographical writings, were designed to be read either as accounts of how a talented young man could make his way in the world, if the emphasis was on successful achievement (Benjamin Franklin's autobiography is a classic example),[3] or as protests against social injustice. Wollstonecraft's *A Short Residence in Sweden, Norway, and Denmark* (1796) blends descriptive travel narrative with observations on the damaging effects of poverty, illiteracy, and class distinction, but the most persistent theme in the work is the emotional and physical suffering the narrator has to undergo simply because she is a woman, in a world controlled by men. Other reformist thinkers of the period, such as Mary Hays and William Godwin, cast their accounts of social injustice in the form of fictionalized life-narratives (Hays's *Memoirs of Emma Courtney*, Godwin's *Caleb Williams*).

Even narratives by conservative writers could reflect a concern with the struggles of impoverished and marginalized individuals. J. G. Lockhart (a Tory in politics and associated with the conservative *Quarterly Review*), in his *Life of Robert Burns* (1828) does censure Burns for his womanizing, and takes exception to some of his criticisms of the clergy, but near the end of the biography he also praises Burns for his 'boldness' in choosing to write in his own Scots dialect, and remarks that the poverty in which Burns was forced to spend the last years of his life, after being denied a state pension, was a disgrace to Scotland.

Biography: lives in contention

In the *Rambler* for 13 October 1750, Johnson set out what was to remain for the next century one of the most influential claims for the value of biography. Johnson stresses the pleasure to be derived from reading biographies, as well as their usefulness and wide appeal: 'no species of writing . . . can be more delightful or more useful, none can more certainly enchain the heart by irresistible interest, or more widely diffuse instruction to every diversity of condition.'[4] Moreover, Johnson argues, biographers should not conceal the errors and faults of their subjects, even out of friendship or respect for the dead. In the eighteenth century it was far from being generally accepted that biographers should tell the whole truth. Boswell, for example, was criticized for revealing too much of Johnson's melancholia and self-doubt. The debate reflects the fact that social changes were redrawing the boundaries between the public sphere and private life.

The most dramatic demonstration of how fiercely this boundary was contested is the unprecedented frankness of Godwin's *Memoirs* of Wollstonecraft, and the hostile reaction which it provoked in the conservative press. Godwin was clearly taken aback by the outrage which greeted the first edition of the *Memoirs*. The decorum which was still supposed to govern what could be publicly revealed about a person's private life, particularly a woman's life, had been, according to conservative critics, grossly violated. They ridiculed Godwin's account of Wollstonecraft's hard struggle to establish an independent career, and of her love affairs, as a revealing example of 'Jacobin morality'.

To conclude that the whole genre of biography changed after the appearance of these *Memoirs* would be quite wrong, however. Godwin's contemporaries (even the more progressive ones) were generally agreed that biographers had a duty to be selective about what they revealed, a principle sometimes known as the 'dignity of biography'. Just as eighteenth-century historians espoused the principle of the 'dignity of history', meaning that the historian should focus on events and personages of wide significance, not on circumstantial details and minor players, so critics, and many biographers of the more conservative kind, held that it was indecent for a biographer to dwell on the subject's private life, particularly on anything discreditable. Biography should highlight the subject's public life and great achievements. (The standards of what was discreditable were different for men and for women, of course, a point that Godwin chose to ignore.) On this issue—whether the biographer should 'tell all' or select only the materials that would enhance the reputation of the subject—Johnson was actually more in tune with modern judgement than most nineteenth-century critics.

Robert Southey, in the reviews he wrote for the *Quarterly*, was at the forefront of those who argued that it was a biographer's duty to avoid delving into the subject's private life, and overwhelming the reader with a mass of material from letters or diaries. Rather, the biographer should present a boldly drawn portrait and a readable narrative. He followed these principles when he agreed to write a life of Lord Nelson for the publisher Murray. In commercial terms, this was one of Southey's most successful works, going through many reprintings in Southey's lifetime and up to the twentieth century. In the foreword, Southey proclaimed his purpose: he wished it to be 'a manual for the young sailor, which he may carry about with him, till he has treasured up the example in his memory'.[5] Nelson's reputation for heroism was unassailable, but this is still a rather extraordinary statement, since the book portrays Nelson as flagrantly disobedient towards his commanders. One wonders what the young men who did take Southey's *Life* to sea with them made of the promotion of such a figure as an exemplary naval officer. Southey did make *selective* use of Nelson's private letters. He felt that quoting from these letters was justifiable, since they showed how Nelson himself felt about the situations he was placed in, and the strategic blunders of his superiors. Yet Southey scrupulously avoided revealing details of Nelson's private life.

On this issue of the biographer's use of personal material, it is instructive to see what James Field Stanfield says in an essay published at about the same time. *An Essay on the Study and Composition of Biography* (1813), often pedantic in style, is still a good indicator of how the middle-class reader would have viewed life-narratives (see *Oxford Companion to the Romantic Age*, p. 425). Stanfield's argument is contradictory, but the very contradiction reveals the conflict that lay behind all life-writing in this period, and that every biographer had to resolve in his or her own way. For Stanfield, the object of a biography is truth, and its purpose instruction. The need for truth dictates that biographers must not glamorize their subjects, but rather describe any failings honestly. However, Stanfield clearly believes that the 'truth' of a person's life is to be found less in the record of that person's career than in his motives, hopes, and values, interpreted according to a distinctly heroic model.[6] The use of private documents can thus be justified because, as Stanfield puts it, 'letters convey, not merely acts, but thoughts and purposes'.[7] Stanfield agrees that private life reveals more of a person's true nature than public life, but he gives the idea a new emphasis on subjectivity. He does not seem aware of the problem here. If the biographer quotes letters, diaries, and other private documents, but does so selectively, then the biography is open to the charge that it is presenting a falsified version of the subject's animating 'spirit', or that this 'spirit' is a pure invention of the biographer. Stanfield is caught between the two dominant expectations of biography in the early 1800s: that it should be truthful, and that it should be inspirational. With the Evangelicals, he believes that biography should respect the dignity of its subject and inspire readers to do good works; but with Johnson, he also holds that biography should show the truth of the inner man or woman, though he goes further than Johnson in emphasizing the 'sentiments' and 'designs' of the biographical subject. Carlyle's *Life of Friedrich Schiller* (1825) is a good example of literary biography written according to this heroic model. Schiller emerges as a man dedicated to the literary calling, despite the obstacles that pettiness of circumstance throws in his way.[8]

The controversy which erupted in 1814 about the republication of a memoir of Robert Burns, first written as a preface to his poems by Dr James Currie, is a perfect illustration of how many conflicting interests came to bear on biography, especially when the subject was a figure of such importance to a nation's self-image as Burns was for Scotland. Currie's *Life*, originally published in 1800, scandalized readers not only by printing many of the poet's private letters, but also by claiming that it was overconsumption of alcohol that killed him. In 1814, attempting to repair Burns's public image, Alexander Peterkin (a friend of the Burns family) published a corrective account, with letters from the poet's brother, Gilbert, and from James Gray, a friend of the poet. Unfortunately for Burns's reputation, this more positive account was overshadowed by the republication of Currie's biography. William Wordsworth was drawn into the controversy when James Gray wrote to him with a copy of Peterkin's book, asking for advice about the best way to defend Burns's 'injured reputation'. Wordsworth responded with *A Letter to a Friend of Burns*, which he published as a pamphlet in 1816.

In this pamphlet, Wordsworth defends an author's right to privacy—even after death—criticizing the 'coarse intrusions . . . the gross breaches upon the sanctities, of domestic life' which had become all too characteristic of biographies in the early 1800s. He attacks Currie's *Life* as 'a revolting account of a man of exquisite genius, and confessedly of many high moral qualities, sunk into the lowest depths of vice and misery!'[9] He points out, probably with good reason, that when Currie's account first appeared many people were quick to judge Burns by their own high moral standards.

They seized on the shocking revelations, and rushed to condemn Burns as an improvident drunkard without taking the time to weigh all the evidence or consider how fair it was to judge a great poet in this way. Moreover, the picture Currie gave was incomplete, since he did not publish all of Burns's letters, only a selection of the more damaging ones. Thus the reader was invited to react to a partial representation of the poet's personal life that highlighted his flaws and overlooked his generosity and his genius.

The concept of the 'dignity of biography', then, continued to influence the way biography was written well into the nineteenth century. It was as if Boswell had set a standard for revealing literary portraiture that later biographers could not hope to emulate. It is instructive to compare Boswell as biographer with Lockhart. In Sir Walter Scott, Lockhart, who was Scott's son-in-law, had a subject that rivalled Johnson in literary stature. He had access to Scott's private papers, including an autobiographical memoir that Scott had written in 1808 and later annotated (the 'Ashestiel Fragment'). Most modern critics, however, agree that in *Memoirs of the Life of Sir Walter Scott* (1837–8) Lockhart chose to be an editor—a highly selective editor—more than a biographer, relying heavily on extracts from Scott's letters and journals, but suppressing much of the material according to his own notion of what the public image of Scott should be. Lockhart had not solved the problem of how to write a biography that would balance the revealing personal details of the private life with what he felt was the respect owed to a public figure.

Autobiography: confession, self-exploration, self-making

One of the paradoxes of the Romantic period is that even while writers such as Wordsworth and Coleridge were attacking the intrusion of biographers into the private lives of poets, they were making free use of personal and domestic experience in their own writings. Domestic life had become simultaneously sacrosanct and a source of publishable material. In an era when 'sensibility' was valued, it no longer seemed inadmissible to appeal to emotion, even in order to support a political viewpoint. Edmund Burke had done exactly this in protesting against the revolutionists' treatment of the French royal family; and Helen Maria Williams, a passionate supporter of the revolution, freely blended narration of public events in France with accounts of her own emotional reactions. Predictably, Williams was castigated for daring, as a woman, to comment on political affairs. It may have been Williams that the novelist Jane West had in mind when she complained, at the end of *A Tale of the Times* (1799), that 'Female letter-writers teach us the arcana of government', and that 'books of travels are converted into vehicles of politics'.[10]

In fact, just as the genre of biography merged into and incorporated elements of the personal reminiscence, the memoir, and the critical essay, so autobiography during this period refused to be contained within neat boundaries. Coleridge's *Biographia Literaria*, though containing some autobiographical elements, consists of (to quote its subtitle) 'sketches' of the author's 'Literary Life and Opinions', and like most such works it had a definite cultural and political agenda (see *Oxford Companion to the Romantic Age*, p. 411). Travel narratives, such as Wollstonecraft's *Short Residence* (1796), contained autobiographical elements. Olaudah Equiano's *Interesting Narrative* (1789), originally written to vindicate the author from charges of financial dishonesty, conveyed a vivid picture of the horrors of life on the slave ships, and became a key document in the campaign to abolish the slave trade (see *Oxford Companion to the Romantic Age*, pp. 63–4, 499). It is not only a slave narrative, however, but a narrative of the author's conversion to Christianity, and (since he travelled with his successive masters to the Caribbean and various parts of the Americas) also a travel narrative.

An older tradition that contributed to Romantic autobiography was the Christian practice of assessing one's own spiritual state by writing a personal narrative. This practice was widely adopted by Protestant sects in the seventeenth century: converts would tell their story either orally or in writing. Of course, the object was not to vaunt the gifts or achievements of the writer, but the very opposite: to demonstrate his or her need for God's grace, and readiness for salvation. The oldest Christian precedent for such writings was the *Confessions* of St Augustine. The narrative pattern established by these spiritual narratives could easily be adopted to non-religious purposes, however. In a conversion narrative, the author writes from a position of (supposedly) greater knowledge and self-understanding about the errors and struggles of her or his past life. In a similar way, a self-biographer like Benjamin Franklin tells us how he overcame obstacles and used his talents to achieve social success and material gain. In their more elaborate, introspective, and philosophizing autobiographical works, Johann Wolfgang Goethe and William Wordsworth trace their development as poets, demonstrating their ability to make art out of personal experience while in some sense mythologizing their own pasts.

The most influential confessional work of the period was that of Jean-Jacques Rousseau. His *Confessions* (published 1782–9) set an example of candour in self-disclosure that most British critics saw as simply immoral, exposing the author as not only vain but lustful, deceitful, and hypocritical (see *Oxford Companion to the Romantic Age*, pp. 684–5). In one sense its influence was not that of a model to be imitated, but a bad example, a precedent to be avoided at all costs. Nevertheless the *Confessions* showed how compelling self-biography could be. When Byron wrote of his own travels and adventures in *Childe Harold*, adopting the most transparent of disguises, and even more in *Don Juan* where he adopts the tone of the experienced tale-teller, well acquainted with worldly pleasures, he is knowingly trading on the public's prurient taste for the exploits and passions of the ostracized, alienated writer, a taste originally cultivated by Rousseau. William Hazlitt's essay 'On the Character of Rousseau' exemplifies the ambivalent reaction to Rousseau in the English-speaking world. On the one hand, Hazlitt characterizes the Rousseau of

Confessions as a great egotist, concerned with the rest of the world only as it affects himself. Hazlitt implies such egotism is a fault in a writer and threatens his credibility. On the other hand, Hazlitt clearly admires the way Rousseau makes us share the states of his soul, his *états d'âme*, as if they were our own. Here Hazlitt puts his finger on one of the main attractions of a well-written autobiography: it gives us the sense that we can understand the world from an entirely different perspective. The unbeliever can feel what it is like to be religious, the lonely can feel what it is like to be popular and successful, and so on.

There is always a price to pay for self-disclosure, however. Hazlitt's own auto-biographical memoir, *Liber Amoris*, telling the story of his passion for the daughter of his landlady, was attacked as immoral, and even more tolerant critics in the twentieth century have described it as self-indulgent and unreadable. Thomas De Quincey's *Confessions of an English Opium-Eater*, now considered a classic, was attacked for encouraging people to take up opium use, and De Quincey wrote extensive revisions in which he tried to justify the work and clarify its original purpose.

The centrality of life-writing in the Romantic period

The fact that biography and autobiography were so often a focus of contention between 1776 and 1832 demonstrates how all parties to the debate recognized the new importance of these genres. The public appetite for biographies of notable personages, and the eagerness of publishers to feed this appetite, meant that successful novelists like Scott and poets like Wordsworth, Byron, and Shelley could not help but be aware that the image of them that would be transmitted to posterity would depend in part on the biographies that were written. Mary Shelley, knowing that her husband's reputation had suffered as a result of his sexual infidelities, wrote biographical notes to be appended to her edition of the poems. There were disputes among Keats's friends as to which of them would be best qualified to write the biography; the first full-length biography of Keats, by Richard Monckton Milnes, did not appear until 1848. After Byron's death at Missolonghi in 1824, several of his friends and acquaintances brought out volumes of 'recollections' or 'reminiscences'—none of them an 'authorized' life, in the sense in which Lockhart's *Scott* was authorized. The most authoritative account to appear in the decade after Byron's death was Thomas Moore's *Letters and Journals of Lord Byron, with Notices of his Life* (2 vols., 1830).

In a sense, however, Byron had already fashioned a persona that towered over any possible biographical account, through his partly fictionalized autobiographical poems. With the posthumous appearance of *The Prelude* in 1850, Wordsworth too gave the public a version of himself that was at least an alternative to any future biographer's. Elizabeth Barrett Browning's *Aurora Leigh* (1857), through its fictional heroine, tells the story of the coming-to-self-consciousness of an aspiring young woman poet. Like the many prose autobiographies that appeared in the later nineteenth century, it testifies to the endurance of Romantic ideas of self-formation, and the role that narratives of the author's life, more or less fictionalized, continue to play in literary culture.

READING: William Godwin, *Memoirs of the Author of A Vindication of the Rights of Woman*

Reshaping Mary Wollstonecraft's public image

When William Godwin wrote his *Memoirs* of Mary Wollstonecraft, he judged that her reputation as a serious writer would be enhanced, not damaged, by a candid account of the material difficulties and emotional crises she faced, and the conflicts into which her strong passions and commitment to social change led her. This biography is of particular interest today, not only because Wollstonecraft's reputation stands higher than it did in her own lifetime, but also because Godwin's narrative was unprecedentedly frank in what it revealed of her personal life. It anticipates what the modern reader has come to expect of serious biography: that it should show the faults and misjudgements of the biographical subject, as well as her strengths and achievements.

Godwin presents Wollstonecraft first and foremost as a writer, however, giving his interpretation of her career and her 'genius', or particular character, as a thinker. He thus combines several roles in the *Memoirs*: that of the conscientious biographer of a famous person, but also that of a moral philosopher who assesses her conduct and critiques her ideas, and that of the lover and husband, speaking to the world about those virtues which were revealed only in her private life.[11]

A salient feature of Godwin's practice as a biographer is that he believes the rules of decorum and social delicacy to be 'factitious' (p. 103),[12] and therefore something the enlightened and liberal writer should simply ignore. His decision to put these radical principles ahead of social custom and decorum may have been (from a worldly point of view) imprudent, but it is characteristic of his commitment to the moral and philosophical value of candour and the avoidance of hypocrisy.

Becoming an author

The opening paragraph of the *Memoirs* is worth careful study, first, because it avows the biographer's commitment to the same cause which he identifies as the goal of Mary Wollstonecraft's life: 'public welfare and improvement' (p. 43). The term 'memoirs' already suggests a political dimension to the story, and here Godwin shows that this will be a biography with a *social purpose*, not just a pious tribute. He invokes the Johnsonian argument that reading biography is educative, since it shows us the 'excellencies' of the biographical subject: only when we are shown the private as well as public conduct of eminent people do we fully understand the ideals by which they lived. He goes further, however, in grounding his narrative on a reformist interpretation of the usefulness of biography.

Biographies of people like Wollstonecraft offer encouragement to those who would follow them in working for the improvement of society.

The first six chapters of the book, dealing with Wollstonecraft's upbringing, her passionate friendship with Fanny Blood, and her writings up to 1795, chart the formation of her character and abilities. It is possible for a biographer to narrate the events of a writer's youth without interpreting them as prophetic of a future career, but most Romantic-era biographers happily seized on any evidence of nascent talent in the subject's childhood. Godwin is no exception. Indeed, he introduces a quotation from Wollstonecraft's novel *The Wrongs of Woman*, describing the heroine's sufferings as a young girl, and comments that it is 'the outline of the first period of her own existence' (p. 45). It is a signal that this is to be a *writer's* life. He describes her father's violence towards her and her mother, but does not dwell on these sufferings at great length, though he does say that Mary's 'superiority' to the rest of the family both in intelligence and in firmness of character rapidly became evident.

Wollstonecraft's close relationship with Fanny Blood dominates the account of her youth, largely because Godwin saw it as the most formative of her early relationships. When the two women first met, Fanny (then aged 18) had acquired the accomplishments considered suitable for young middle-class women. She became mentor to the younger girl: 'Mary found Fanny's letters better spelt and better indited than her own, and felt herself abashed . . . Fanny undertook to be her instructor; and, so far as related to accuracy and method, her lessons were given with considerable skill' (p. 51). The phrase 'so far as related to accuracy and method' is significant. Godwin portrays the friendship as useful to Mary, but later says that she had more originality and soon overtook her older friend.

He also takes a critical view of Wollstonecraft's eagerness, once she reached adulthood, to help not only Fanny herself, but Fanny's entire family. He cannot resist a moralizing comment on the danger of supplying other people's needs, to the detriment of one's own, noting that she was 'the victim of a desire to promote the benefit of others' (p. 55). This is one instance where Godwin appoints himself critic not only of Wollstonecraft's writing, but of her conduct. He seems both to praise her for her selflessness, and criticize her naïvety in expecting those she helped to change in character. The end of chapter 3, however, gives Mary herself the last word on this relationship: when Fanny dies, with Mary at her bedside, Godwin quotes a passage from *A Short Residence in Sweden, Norway, and Denmark* in which Wollstonecraft recalls the ineffaceable memory of their friendship.

The winter following the death of Fanny Blood marks the beginning of Wollstonecraft's career as a writer for the literary market-place, and her connection with the radical publisher Joseph Johnson. Godwin emphasizes that Wollstonecraft harboured no ambition to be 'regarded . . . in the character of an author' (p. 68). The initial motive was financial. But Godwin also shows that much of the work Wollstonecraft did between 1782 and 1787 was motivated by her desire to contribute to society through education: the girls' school which she set up, with her sisters and Fanny Blood, and her first two published works, *Thoughts on the Education of Daughters* (1787) and *Original Stories from Real Life* (1788).

The champion of women

Godwin's positive assessment of *Mary: A Fiction* (Wollstonecraft's first novel), at the end of chapter 4, is in marked contrast with the critical view he takes of her 'miscellaneous literary employment' as translator and reviewer for Joseph Johnson (p. 69). His narrative has turned into a study of a literary career. Work that hampers her career is seen as problematic; work that advances it is beneficial. In keeping with this theme, Godwin offers forthright opinions on the faults and merits of each of her writings, and this applies in particular to her most famous work, *A Vindication of the Rights of Woman*.

Chapter 6 locates this work in the context of the period of intellectual ferment that followed the fall of the Bastille. Up to 1789, she was learning her trade, and she had earned money but not fame. From 1790 on, however, 'she was destined to attract the notice of the public, and perhaps no female writer ever obtained so great a degree of celebrity throughout Europe' (p. 72). Her best-known writings, then, were a joint result of her own maturity as a writer and contemporary events: 'The French revolution, while it gave a fundamental shock to the human intellect through every region of the globe, did not fail to produce a conspicuous effect in the progress of Mary's reflections' (p. 72). The sudden shrinking of scope in this sentence, from global impact to the 'reflections' of one mind, is revealing. Godwin clearly wants to portray Wollstonecraft's mature work as part of a necessary revolution in ideas, sparked by the conjunction of one individual's genius with the reality of political change.

Godwin says little about *Vindication of the Rights of Men* (1790) beyond the fact that it was written in a 'burst of indignation' in answer to Edmund Burke's *Reflections*, and that it succeeded because it rode the wave of strong anti-Burke feeling among the 'liberal and enlightened' (p. 73). The treatment of the second *Vindication*, too, emphasizes less its overt agenda of questioning received ideas about gender and starting a 'REVOLUTION in female manners' than what Godwin considers its strengths and shortcomings as polemic.[13] Godwin moves quickly from Wollstonecraft's indignation at women's low social status—'standing forth in defence of one half of the human species' (p. 74)—to considering the reaction of hostile critics. To us, the rapidity with which Godwin moves from his very brief characterization of her actual arguments to a somewhat defensive series of concessions about the 'rigid' and 'amazonian temper' of parts of the book seems inexplicable, if not inexcusable, as if he were more concerned with the critical reactions of contemporaries than with Wollstonecraft's actual arguments. It seems, in short, an unnecessarily negative assessment: 'Many of the sentiments are undoubtedly of a rather masculine description. . . . There are . . . occasional passages of a stern and rugged feature . . .' (p. 75).

Modern readers will have a variety of explanations for Godwin's reluctance to argue in defence of Wollstonecraft's style in *A Vindication*. Perhaps he was repelled by the 'unfeminine' rhetoric—by Wollstonecraft's skill in taking up and using against male writers their own rationalistic style of argument. He tries to correct what he sees as the false image of herself that she inadvertently created. From her writing, he says, people expected 'a sturdy, muscular, raw-boned virago', not a 'lovely' and 'feminine' woman (p. 76). The terms of praise seem oddly inappropriate, if not sexist. However, it is also true that by 1798 *A Vindication* was well enough known to need no defence: it had marked out for itself a dominant space in the arena of public debate. Godwin leaves it to future readers to carry on the work Wollstonecraft began.[14] Much as he may have been in thrall to the gender conventions of his time, he is asking the reader of the *Memoirs* to remember that *A Vindication* was written not by a 'virago' but by a real woman who was herself enmeshed in a social context.

Love, marriage, and death

Godwin now has to introduce a new and sensitive aspect of his subject: the sexual relationships in which Wollstonecraft had the deepest emotional investment. In describing her relationship with the painter Henry Fuseli, which she broke off once she realized it could not be fulfilled, he includes a summary of her principles regarding sexual relations between men and women, stressing that, contrary to the public perception, 'She set a great value on a mutual affection between persons of an opposite sex' (p. 79). Anti-Jacobin commentators certainly did attack Wollstonecraft's sexual conduct, so Godwin tries to give a fair summary of her considered views on sexual relationships, and her reasons for being opposed to marriage.

Godwin's picture of the period Wollstonecraft spent in Paris is one of happiness and literary productivity. There is no attempt to conceal the nature of her relationship with the American businessman Gilbert Imlay, a fact that shocked his first readers but testifies to Godwin's consistency of purpose. (He made several changes in the text for the second edition, trying to make the account more circumspect, but by then the damage had been done.) Despite Imlay's abandonment of Mary after she had borne him a daughter, and her subsequent suicide attempt, Godwin refrains from overtly condemning him, in part because of his understanding of Wollstonecraft's own feelings, and what he has already explained was her commitment to the sincerity of affections. 'It is of the very essence of affection', he comments in moral-philosopher mode, 'to seek to perpetuate itself' (p. 91).

The chapters narrating Wollstonecraft's relationship to Godwin, their subsequent marriage, and her death from an infection contracted after the birth of her daughter, show the overlap of public and private at its most intense—or, as some eighteenth-century readers felt, at its most intolerable. It was a crucial part of Godwin's philosophy, however, that lies and concealment were a social evil. He viewed marriage as an institution that compelled men and women to live in a dishonest manner. Given that this biography was written not just to honour Wollstonecraft's private self and virtues, but to encourage the better understanding of her ideas and values, including those she shared with him, Godwin judged that this purpose would be served only by being as truthful as possible. He emphasizes, then, the unusual degree of mutuality which marked the progress of their love, with neither of them pursuing or courting the other, and he carefully explains why they decided—in apparent contradiction to their well-known views—to marry when she became pregnant.

The narrative of Wollstonecraft's death may shock the modern reader, as it did many in 1798. For Godwin's readers, the medical details of the labour and its aftermath were repellent in themselves, and entirely inappropriate for inclusion in a biography. Modern readers are perhaps more likely to be disturbed by Godwin's tone in describing his own feelings, as his wife suffered through several days of pain and fever. Godwin's desire to hold to a firm state of mental clarity and avoid being deceived by false hopes seems to have transgressed almost into a refusal of emotional response.

It is evident elsewhere in this chapter, however, that Godwin *did* feel the loss of his wife deeply: not simply as a loving husband, but as a thinker. Consistently with his intention to describe a relationship of two enquiring minds, he emphasizes, in his closing tribute to Mary, not love and affection but 'the improvement that I have forever lost' (p. 121). Again, the phrase takes us by surprise, and may seem too much the response of a thinker, not a lover. What Godwin clearly intends here, however, is to close the *Memoirs* not with the grieving husband's tribute to his love ('this is a subject', he says tactfully, 'for meditation, not for words' (pp. 120–1)), but with testimony to her qualities of mind, especially the quickness of her intuition. Godwin reminds the reader that with Wollstonecraft's sudden death the world lost a woman of great powers. Whether he succeeded in conveying the meaning of her life and literary career is something for each reader to judge, but Godwin's book certainly marks a watershed in the development of literary biography, not just for its remarkable candour, but also for its serious engagement with the career and reputation of an exceptional woman and feminist.

FURTHER READING

Bradley, Arthur, and Rawes, Alan (eds.), *Romantic Biography* (Aldershot and Brookfield, Vt.: Ashgate, 2003). The editors' introduction examines the part played by biography in the creation of Romanticism; particularly relevant to the study of biography in the Romantic period are the essays by Mark Storey on Southey as biographer, by Gerard Carruthers on Lockhart's biographies of Burns and of Scott, by Jennifer Wallace on biographies of Keats, and by Michael O'Neill on poetry and biography.

Buss, Helen M., 'Memoirs Discourse and William Godwin's *Memoirs of the Author of A Vindication of the Rights of Woman'*, in Helen M. Buss, D. L. MacDonald, and Anne McWhir (eds.), *Mary Wollstonecraft and Mary Shelley: Writing Lives* (Waterloo, Ont.: Wilfrid Laurier University Press, 2001), pp. 113–25. This essay explores the mixture of roles Godwin adopts in the *Memoirs*, arguing that, in making public the more intimate aspects of Wollstonecraft's life, Godwin pushed the 'memoir' genre beyond what was acceptable in the ethos of the period.

Egan, Susanna, *Patterns of Experience in Autobiography* (Chapel Hill, NC: University of North Carolina Press, 1984). Describes such 'patterns' as the progression from 'innocence' to 'experience,' the 'heroic journey', and the formation of the artist, with analyses of works by Rousseau, Wordsworth, De Quincey, Carlyle, and others; the main focus is on the nineteenth century.

Myers, Mitzi, 'Godwin's Memoirs of Wollstonecraft: The Shaping of Self and Subject', *Studies in Romanticism*, 20 (1981), 299–316. This article views Godwin as an 'innovator' in the genre of biography, stressing the transgressive quality of the *Memoirs*.

Newey, Vincent, and Shaw, Philip (eds.), *Mortal Pages, Literary Lives: Studies in Nineteenth Century Autobiography* (Aldershot and Brookfield, Vt.: Ashgate, 1996). Includes essays by Peter Swaab on Wollstonecraft; by Keith Hanley on Wordsworth; by Julian North on De Quincey; and by Nicholas Roe on Leigh Hunt.

Rajan, Tilottama, 'Framing the Corpus: Godwin's "Editing" of Wollstonecraft in 1798', *Studies in Romanticism*, 39 (2000), 511–31. In a subtle analysis of the collaboration that characterized their relationship in 1797–8, Rajan explores the way Godwin's writing of the *Memoirs* is related to his editing of Wollstonecraft's Posthumous Works; she suggests that Godwin found the meaning of Wollstonecraft's life to reside in 'utopian possibility' (p. 531).

Reed, Joseph W., Jr., *English Biography in the Early Nineteenth Century: 1801–1838* (New Haven: Yale University Press, 1966). Though old-fashioned in its focus on a 'men of letters' tradition, this has informative treatments of Johnson's continued influence, of the Evangelical movement's contribution to the genre, and of biographers such as Southey and Lockhart.

Smith, Sidonie, and Watson, Julia (eds.), *Women, Autobiography, Theory: A Reader*, Wisconsin Studies in American Autobiography (Madison: University of Wisconsin Press, 1998). A compilation of short readings on theory and practice of autobiography (including diaries) by women; it includes two essays that focus on eighteenth-century writing, Felicity Nussbaum's 'The Politics of Subjectivity' (pp. 160–5) and Patricia Meyer Spacks's 'Female Rhetorics' (pp. 232–8).

Stelzig, Eugene, 'Introduction', in *The Romantic Subject in Autobiography: Rousseau and Goethe* (Charlottesville, Va.: University Press of Virginia, 2000), pp. 1–23. This 'Introduction' places the emergence of autobiography in the broad context of developments in European philosophy, religion, and psychological theory, emphasizing the 'confession' as the basis of the genre.

Todd, Janet, *Mary Wollstonecraft: A Revolutionary Life* (New York: Columbia University Press, 2000). A thorough, richly detailed, and readable modern biography of Wollstonecraft.

NOTES

1. Quoted from *Quarterly Review* (1827), in Joseph W. Reed Jr., *English Biography in the Early Nineteenth Century: 1801–1838* (New Haven: Yale University Press, 1966), p. 3.
2. Thomas Carlyle, *Sartor Resartus*, ed. Kerry McSweeney and Peter Sabor (Oxford: Oxford World's Classics, 1999), p. 73.
3. Modern editors point out that the title 'Autobiography' as used for Franklin's narrative is anachronistic. In his letters, he refers to the work as 'memoirs'. Selections from it appeared in various magazines in 1790, a French version of Part I was published in Paris the following year, and another version (translated from the French) in London, in 1793. The version edited by William Temple Franklin finally appeared in 1818. See *The Autobiography of Benjamin Franklin: A Genetic Text*, ed. J. A. Leo Lemay and P. M. Zall (Knoxville, Tenn.: University of Tennessee Press, 1981), pp. xvii, xlviii–liii.
4. Samuel Johnson, *Works*, iii. *The Rambler*, ed. W. J. Bate and Albrecht B. Strauss (New Haven: Yale University Press, 1969), p. 319.
5. Robert Southey, *Life of Lord Nelson*, quoted in Reed, *English Biography*, p. 86.
6. 'Man, pursuing his objects, encountering dangers, overcoming difficulties, employed in acts of magnanimity and benevolence, glowing with elevated sentiments, or actuated by designs of splendour and importance—man, thus highly engaged, cannot be contemplated, without communicating to the observer, a portion of that spirit which guides and animates him in the conflict.' James Field Stanfield, *An Essay on the Study and Composition of Biography* (Sunderland: Printed by George Carbutt, 1813), p. 109.

7. Ibid. 77.

8. 'Literature was his creed, the dictate of his conscience; he was an Apostle of the Sublime and Beautiful, and this calling made a hero of him.' *Life of Friedrich Schiller, Works*, 30 vols. (London: Chapman and Hall, 1895), xxv, 200.

9. William Wordsworth, *A Letter to a Friend of Robert Burns*, in *Prose Works*, ed. W. J. B. Owen and Jane Worthington Smyser, 3 vols. (Oxford: Clarendon Press, 1974), iii. 122, 119.

10. Jane West, *A Tale of the Times*, 3 vols. (London: Longman and Rees, 1799), iii. 387.

11. On this matter of Godwin's multiple roles as biographer see Helen M. Buss, 'Memoirs Discourse and William Godwin's *Memoirs of the Author of A Vindication of the Rights of Woman*', in Helen M. Buss, D. L. MacDonald, and Anne McWhir (eds.), *Mary Wollstonecraft and Mary Shelley: Writing Lives* (Waterloo, Ont.: Wilfrid Laurier University Press, 2001), pp. 118–21.

12. Page references are to William Godwin, *Memoirs of the Author of A Vindication of the Rights of Woman*, ed. Pamela Clemit and Gina Luria Walker (Peterborough: Broadview, 2001).

13. The phrase 'a REVOLUTION in female manners' is Wollstonecraft's. See Anne K. Mellor, *Mothers of the Nation*, (Bloomington, Ind.: Indiana University Press, 2002), pp. 44–5, 73, 87, 100, 122.

14. On this aspect of Godwin's presentation of Wollstonecraft see Tilottama Rajan, 'Framing the Corpus: Godwin's "Editing" of Wollstonecraft in 1798', *Studies in Romanticism*, 39 (2000), 511–31, and Gary Kelly, *Revolutionary Feminism: The Mind and Career of Mary Wollstonecraft* (London: Macmillan, 1992).

29 | Romance

Greg Kucich

When Keats pronounced the need to write 'a tale of chivalry' near the outset of his poetic career, he was responding to a recent surge in the historical development of the literary genre of romance (see Keats's 'Specimen of an Induction to a Poem'). In heavy demand from its medieval point of origin and throughout its many post-Romantic formulations—such as science fiction; the Western; potboiler supermarket novels of love and lust—during the Romantic age romance soared to an unprecedented high point and outstripped all other literary genres in popularity. It grew so fundamental to the culture of Romanticism, in fact, that the term 'romance', particularly in its nine-teenth-century meanings of exotic and otherworldly, became associated with the imaginative proclivities of Romantic literature and thus supplied the etymological root for what came to be know as 'Romanticism'. (In a different sense, the term 'romantic' was first applied to the literature of the age by August William Schlegel, in his *Courses of Lectures on Dramatic Art and Literature* as a way of defining the era's ironic sensibility).

The prevalence of literary romance during the Romantic age emerged in a staggering range of popular manifestations, which often but not always took the form of medieval quests driven by a central love plot. As Clara Reeve pointed out in *The Progress of Romance* (1785), the form extended to any type of narrative in prose or verse that ventured into strange or exotic terrain. Such examples of the widespread Romantic engagement with this literary type include: Ann Radcliffe's sensational Gothic novels; the related proliferation of Gothic dramas like Charles Maturin's *Bertram* (1816); Sir Walter Scott's wildly popular metrical romances and his equally famous works of historical romance in fiction, which branched out from the era's prolific inundation of sentimental romance novels; Byron's trend-setting Turkish tales in verse; Robert Southey's ground-breaking oriental epic *Thalaba the Destroyer* (1801); Coleridge's *Christabel* (1816); epic-length poems by Keats, *Endymion: A Poetic Romance* (1818), Byron, *Childe Harold's Pilgrimage: A Romaunt* (1812–18), and Shelley, *The Revolt of Islam* (1818); shorter poems like Keats's *The Eve of St Agnes* (1819) and 'La Belle Dame Sans Merci' (1819) that have struck many readers as the quintessence of Romanticism; the prodigious amount of scholarly writings by Scott, Southey, William Godwin, Joseph Ritson, and many others on the history and aesthetics of romance. That all this approached something like a mania for literary romance, became a commonplace of the Romantic age. Byron titled one of his earliest poems 'To Romance'. Keats saturated his early verse with chivalric motifs. Shelley proudly imagined himself when completing his epic labour on *The Revolt Islam* as 'some victor Knight of Faëry' (Preface, l. 3).

Literary romance has always provoked detractors, however, and there was no shortage of examples during the Romantic period, from Jane Austen's parodic *Northanger Abbey* (1818) to the broad circulation of dire warnings against the debauching influence of romance literature on the minds of impressionable young, particularly female, readers. Even those who cherished 'old Romance', like Keats (*Isabella*, l. 387), could feel compelled to reject its pleasures as the misleading allurements of 'Golden-tongued Romance' ('On Sitting Down to Read *King Lear* Once Again', l. 1). Such resistance and equivocation has led many critics to associate literary romance of the Romantic period merely with the superficially exotic. Conflicts over the form during the Romantic era, however, point to a profound duality at the heart of the Romantic experience of romance, which can provide a useful reference point for comprehending the breadth of such a multifaceted genre as well as its aesthetic complexity and cultural significance. Not just a literary form, romance also functioned as a dualistic mode of cultural vision that powerfully addressed the most urgent aesthetic, social, and political tensions of the volatile Romantic era.

The origins of romance

The *Oxford English Dictionary* dates the word 'romance' to the thirteenth century, as a term designating the new European vernacular languages—primarily French, Spanish, and Italian—emerging from Latin. That linguistic term became associated simultaneously with the vernacular literature of the time, particularly with popular tales in verse detailing aristocratic court life and chivalric adventures often linked to France's King Charlemagne and England's legendary King Arthur and his Knights of the Round Table. These narratives derived from earlier oral traditions, but their first and most influential appearance in textual/manuscript form occurred with the writings of the French poet Chrétien de Troyes in the later part of the twelfth century (*Érec et Énide; Lancelot, le chevalier de la charette; Perceval; Le conte del Graal*). Chrétien's foundation in literary romance would be expanded by many poets over the next two centuries throughout France, Spain, Italy, and England, particularly by Chaucer, Langland, Malory, and the anonymous author of *Sir Gawain and the Green Knight*. The popularity of literary romance had swelled to such a degree by the late fourteenth century that Chaucer not only experimented at length with its possibilities but also parodied its excesses in *The Tale of Sir Thopas*, as would Cervantes even more famously two centuries later in *Don Quixote* (1605–15).

One functional though somewhat limited method of grouping this wide body of works as a distinctive literary genre has been to catalogue its recurrent narrative plots.

Medieval romances typically combine, for instance, narratives of military heroism and love relations set within exotic or supernatural landscapes. They focus on aristocratic court life but also feature the chivalric exploits of young knights questing into strange landscapes where they succour the downtrodden and wage battle against evil, often supernatural forces in order to rescue distressed maidens and win their hands in marriage. The strong emphasis on the love plot in these narratives actually provides the basis for our modern association of the term 'romance' with love interests. Much as this formalist type of genre definition helps outline the central narrative patterns of medieval romance, it does not adequately explain the complexity of the form, its persisting grip on later generations, and its elastic openness to various types of adaptations (see also 'Romantic forms: an introduction').

Modern theorists of medieval romance have tracked its abiding cultural influence to specific structural levels on which its most complex systems of meaning operate: the mythopoetic, the psychological, and the socio-political. Northrop Frye, one of the great twentieth-century scholars of literature and myth, finds the exotic quest motif of medieval romance—such as the Arthurian search for the Holy Grail—acting out deep cultural desires for spiritual ideals that are profoundly difficult to attain: salvation, redemption, eternal union with God. This mythic structure produces a fundamental dialectic in the romance plot, manifested in perpetual struggles against enormous foes—giants, dragons, sorcerers—that rarely find complete resolution. Frye also notes how this mythic structure frequently merges with a related psychological form of action in the medieval quest romance, which functions on both thematic and narrative levels. Chrétien's *Lancelot*, for instance, features Lancelot's anguished vacillation between his devotion to chivalric honour and his illicit love for King Arthur's wife, Guinevere. Such deep mental divisions in medieval romance often assume the form of sustained interior monologues, as in Chaucer's *Troilus and Criseyde*, whose poignant turns of mind receive intensification from a framing split between the narrator's overarching voice and the inner thoughts of his characters.

These divisions of mind, which would figure prominently in Romantic adaptations, sprang in many cases from historically specific social pressures. Fredric Jameson expands Frye's notion of the political agency of medieval romance—an élite court genre propping up aristocratic ideals and power structures—by stressing the acute tensions in medieval romance between anxious nostalgia for a fading feudalistic society and the pressing realities of a new social order moving towards secular, economic modernity. The celebrated idolization of women in chivalric romance can be understood, moreover, as part of a troubled effort to reassert masculine social hierarchies—with women contained as beautiful, passive objects—in the face of shifting gender dynamics and the beginnings of modern female empowerment. Even the basic aristocratic character of medieval romance as a court genre written about and for the political élite clashed with the form's more popular appeal, particularly in its oral dissemination, to low-brow audiences. Romance, Frye contends, always sustained a disruptive proletarian underpinning.

It was the interplay of these deep structural tensions, usually linked together by a central quest narrative, that enabled medieval romance to flourish as a mode of cultural outlook incorporating major elements of earlier literatures—classical as well as biblical—and undergoing so many significant adaptations in literary forms of succeeding eras, such as: the romance epics of Spenser, *The Faerie Queene* (1590–6), and the Italian poet Ariosto, *Orlando Furioso* (1532); Renaissance prose romances like Sir Philip Sidney's *Arcadia* (1590); Shakespeare's late romance plays; the outpouring of romance fiction, Gothic novels and drama, and Spenserian poetic imitations in the eighteenth century. In addition to the original medieval works, these various continuations exerted considerable influence over the shape of Romantic romance, with Spenser's mammoth chivalric allegory, *The Faerie Queene*, standing out as the single greatest transmitter of the narrative motifs and the deep structures of medieval romance to the Romantic imagination.

Virtually every significant and scores of little-known poets of the Romantic period essayed Spenserian adaptations, usually situated like Keats's *The Eve of St Agnes* in some form of medieval or quasi-medieval context. The sheer musical wizardry of Spenser's verse fascinated many Romantic poets, but Spenser's greatest appeal stemmed from his magnificently imaginative deployment of the deep structural tensions of medieval romance. The poignant drama of unresolved pursuits of heavenly ideals, for instance, permeates all levels of *The Faerie Queene*. Each book features the recurring plot line of a virtuous knight questing through exotic landscapes towards a specific goal that is allegorically linked to a form of spiritual redemption often figured in the union of two lovers. Yet each quest remains problematically incomplete. Redcrosse defeats the evil dragon in Book I and redeems the Edenic land of Una, but his marriage to her remains deferred. Such divisions also inform some of the most poignant individual scenes of yearning in *The Faerie Queene*, such as Redcrosse's grief-stricken realization that he cannot enter the golden New Jerusalem he glimpses from afar but must return to sojourning along the dreary paths of mortal suffering. Blake and other poets of his time would take notice when they set forth in creative labour to build Jerusalem in 'England's green & pleasant Land' (Blake, Prefatory Poem to *Milton*).

This endless dialectic in the quest plots of *The Faerie Queene* merges with a similarly recurring drama of mental divisions on the allegory's psychological level. Although Romantic writers on Spenser frequently dismissed the allegory's moral function, they shared a keen interest in its function as psychodrama. Coleridge, for instance, found the action of *The Faerie Queene* taking place in mental space. The Redcrosse Knight's spiritual pilgrimage thus functions as a complex interior drama of shifting mental states as he grapples with moral hopelessness in the Cave of Despair (an episode Keats identified with during his own bouts of depression), undergoes psychic renewal under the tutelage of the hermit Holy Contemplation, and eventually approaches a type of visionary insight with his apprehension of God's heavenly city and his final defeat of the Satanic dragon. The recurrent centring of Spenser's allegorical quests in such evocations of the divided mind would provide a compelling model for Romantic writers seeking literary methods to explore related kinds of mental dualities. Spenser's own expressions of mental torment in his swerves between glorifying the Elizabethan court of his day and lamenting its ruthless hostility to the arts (see particularly *The Teares of the Muses* (1590)) would also alert his Romantic descendants to the vexed politics of romance writing.

The progress of romance

Literary romance underwent certain, though sometimes overestimated, drops in cultural prestige from the mid-seventeenth century through to the first half of the eighteenth century. Increasing historical distance from the functioning of chivalry as a meaningful social institution, coupled with religious resistance to exotic art during the Puritan Commonwealth of the middle seventeenth century, made the romances of the medieval past seem obsolescent and morally suspect. With some regret, Milton would reject the 'tedious' tales of 'fabled knights' when assuming the 'more heroic' tone of Protestant epic for his masterwork, *Paradise Lost* (Book IX, ll. 14, 30). The priorities of rational thought and classical balance in early eighteenth-century aesthetic theory and practice, while far from universal in their application, tended nevertheless to marginalize medieval and Spenserian romance as excessively exotic and obsolete literary forms. Romance never disappeared utterly, however, from the eighteenth-century literary scene. Swift's *Gulliver's Travels* (1726) and Defoe's *Robinson Crusoe* (1719) incorporate elements of the romance tradition in their travel motifs and unusual settings, while the rise of the eighteenth-century novel entails significant transformations of the romance plot into modern commercial society. It would be somewhat inaccurate, then, to claim that literary romance undergoes a startling 'revival' in the later part of the century. However, after a century or more of diminished cultural significance, it does generate such a new upsurge of interest and adaptation that John Foster, digging in his heels, associates the word 'romantic' in his essay 'On the Application of the Epithet Romantic' (1805) with an utter 'violation' of sound reason.

The rapid progress of romance in the second half of the eighteenth century involved a myriad number of interrelated types of literary productions, all of which significantly influenced the course of Romanticism. These developments included: a prodigious amount of original scholarship that recovered medieval literary texts and analysed the social institutions and aesthetic theories informing them, such as Thomas Percy's three-volume *Reliques of Ancient English Poetry* (1765; see also the chapters on 'Lyric' and 'Narrative poetry'), Richard Hurd's ground-breaking *Letters on Chivalry and Romance* (1762), Reeve's equally significant two-volume work, *The Progress of Romance*, Thomas Warton's monumental *Observations of the Fairy Queen* (1754; revised 1762), and Warton's massive *History of English Poetry* (1774–81), which concentrates two of its three volumes on pre-Renaissance material; a captivating new vogue for alleged discoveries of ancient manuscripts from the medieval period and earlier, realized most spectacularly in the forgeries of Thomas Chatterton and James Macpherson; four new editions of *The Faerie Queene* in the 1750s, and a large outpouring of poems imitating Spenser's chivalric medievalism in *The Faerie Queene*; the emergence of a sensational new genre of medieval adaptation, the Gothic novel or Gothic romance, in works like Horace Walpole's *The Castle of Otranto* (1764), William Beckford's *Vathek* (1787), and Ann Radcliffe's *The Mysteries of Udolpho* (1794); and the new flourishing of sentimental romance fiction in such forms as *The Castle of Mowbray, an English Romance* (1788) and *The Solitary Castle. A Romance of the Eighteenth Century* (1789).

Such a dazzling expansion of literary romance derived from multiple cultural and political factors, many of which would continue to influence the shape of Romantic adaptations. The emergence of Enlightenment historiography as a major discipline altered previous stereotypes about the barbarous quality of medieval life by situating the period within progressive cycles of historical development. This progressive approach to history also entailed a fresh consideration of the roles of literature and the arts in historical development, which gave the literary romances of the Middle Ages a new cultural significance. That revaluation gathered momentum from important shifts in eighteenth-century aesthetic theory about imagination and original genius—as propounded by such critics and poets as Joseph Addison and Edward Young—which celebrated the type of exotic landscapes and extraordinary adventures featured in medieval and Spenserian romance. A sharp nationalistic interest further energized this overall scholarly and creative fascination with early forms of imaginative genius in Britain. Recovering, celebrating, and adapting them took part in a larger national process of canon-formation that helped fuel the rapidly developing emergence in the national imaginary of a consolidated 'Great Britain'—including England, Scotland, Wales, and Ireland—opposed to France in particular and pre-eminent among the nations.

The interplay of these various cultural forces not only transformed literary romance into a prominent and malleable genre for Romantic writers to inherit, but it also shaped the particular contours of their further experiments in adapting its deep structures to their own cultural conditions. Those scholarly efforts to comprehend the aesthetic integrity and social functions of medieval romance highlighted, for instance, the form's mythic and spiritual components. Reeve called Homer the Father of Romance and drew analogies between medieval romancing and the myths of classical Greece. In their efforts to comprehend how England's romance traditions function on this deeper level, later eighteenth-century scholars of the form emphasized its intrinsic structural dualities. This focus on doubleness was particularly strong in the revisionary evaluations of Spenser's achievement. Hurd, Warton, and John Upton all contended, for instance, that Spenser adapted the structural patterns of French, Italian, and English medieval romance in order to produce an irregular Gothic form of allegorical narrative for *The Faerie Queene*, which conflicts with patterns of classical unity woven throughout the poem, such as the device of radiating various knightly quests outward from the central pivot of Glorianna's fairy court. This basic kind of structural division, Upton elaborated, actually revealed Spenser's own mental conflicts between the aesthetic delights of poetic ornamentation and the moral demands of virtuous instruction. Such a concern with the psychological dualities of Spenserian romance became a hallmark of eighteenth-century scholarship on the traditions of romance, which provided a crucial model for creative adaptations of the form in both the later eighteenth century and throughout the Romantic era.

While the eighteenth-century transmission of romance to Romantic writers took a wide variety of pathways, the most compelling line of influence came through the flood of Spenserian poetic imitations, many of which adapted Spenser's medieval motifs and his psychological dualities to a modern, commercial age. Thomas Denton's *The House of Superstition* (1762) and William Jones's *The Palace of Fortune* (1769), for instance, feature a dream-vision motif (adapted from *The Faerie Queene* and later deployed by Shelley in *Queen Mab* (1813)) in which a human protagonist becomes magically transported to a celestial fairy world where he observes the persisting war of mind in human history between the attractions of sensual pleasure and the rigorous pull of duty. James Thomson's *The Castle of Indolence* (1733–4), a favourite of Wordsworth, Coleridge, and Keats among many other Romantic writers, centres this kind of division precisely in the mind of the poet. Such an interior drama receives substantial elaboration in James Beattie's *The Minstrel* (1771–4), arguably the single most influential form of eighteenth-century poetic romance on the shape of Romanticism. Its protagonist, Edwin, appears as a young medieval poet-pilgrim questing not exactly for religious enlightenment but rather to solve a modern aesthetic division between the poet's attraction to imaginative ideals and his commitment to social reality and intellectual truth. In characterizing such a quest as 'The Progress of Genius', Beattie supplied an invaluable blueprint for adapting medieval and Spenserian romance to one of the primary concerns of Romantic poets, what Wordsworth (who strongly identified with Beattie's Edwin) would famously term as the subtitle to *The Prelude*: 'The Growth of a Poet's Mind'.

Beattie also showed how the 'Progress of Romance' towards such a conflicted narrative of the poet's mental growth could engage with the social and political tensions of his own time. And here again, we find the deep structures of medieval and Spenserian romance transported into a modern age. For Beattie, this historical adaptation entailed a final, somewhat mournful repudiation of aesthetic pleasure in favour of the poet's responsibility to promote modern science, industry, and, particularly, the British nation's 'various' military and commercial 'powers' for achieving global hegemony (ii. 488). This lesson in the political applicability of literary romance would not be lost upon Romantic writers, though they would put it to very different uses.

One of the most intriguing signs of the political tension emerging in eighteenth-century romance lies in the narrative framework of Reeve's history of the progress of the form. Cast as a debate among three conversationalists—one man and two women—about the origins, development, and functions of romance, Reeve's *Progress* concludes with a spirited evocation of the gender politics involved in the later eighteenth-century enthusiasm for literary romance. Already by this time identified as a female genre, particularly in its novelistic modes, romance had begun in all its popularity to generate a groundswell of critical complaints about the corrupting influence of its exotic and sensual extremes on female readers. Reeve clearly recognized that such protests signalled the rise of a major social battle over female liberties in both the literary and political spheres. She thus presents what was rapidly becoming a characteristic masculine response to the vogue of romance when her male conversationalist, Hortensius, rails against the vices of romance and argues for preventing women's access to it. The quick reaction of Reeve's female speaker, Euphrasia—that women should be free to legislate their own reading and writing habits—throws down the gauntlet of a burgeoning women's rights movement in the lists of romance. That arena would soon become one of the main cultural battlegrounds for the gender politics of the Romantic era.

The Romanticism in romance

To comprehend the great boom in scholarly and creative responses to romance traditions during the later eighteenth century is to recognize how the explosive force of Romantic romance came not so much as a revolutionary event but rather as an intensification of movements well underway throughout the previous half-century. We can also now see how many of the principal patterns of eighteenth-century romance conditioned not only the aesthetic and political contours of Romantic romance but also contributed significantly to the overall shaping of the culture of Romanticism. Although Romantic adaptations of romance assumed a myriad variety of forms, the most numerous and culturally powerful examples tended to extend the fundamental patterns of duality in eighteenth-century romance, particularly regarding the deep structural levels incorporated from medieval traditions. Nevertheless, shifting aesthetic and political developments during the Romantic era produced a new kind of intensity in the adaptations of these structures, giving such experiments an unprecedented cultural centrality as well as a modified range of formulations distinctively aligned with the historical pressures of the age. These developments included a considerably expanded project of recovering the original texts of medieval romance, a new and powerful myth-making enterprise grounded in the creative psyche's divisions between visionary idealism and material reality, and the earth-shattering historical phenomenon of the French Revolution

One of the features that so heightened the relevance of romance was, paradoxically, its very difference as a medieval genre from the modern world. This stronger alertness to cultural difference was created by the exponentially increased editorial and scholarly labour of recovering textual examples of medieval romance and explicating their origins, structures, and cultural functions. Though an outgrowth of eighteenth-century scholarship on romance, this enterprise far exceeded what had come before in textual production and depth of analysis. The following sample only gestures towards its vast extent: Joseph Ritson's three-volume *Ancient English Metrical Romances* (1802); Walter Scott's popular three-volume *Minstrelsy of the Scottish Border* (1801–3) followed by a fourth volume one year later; George Ellis's three-volume printing of *Specimens of Early English Metrical Romances* (1805); Henry Weber's three-volume set of *Metrical Romances* (1805); modern English translations of medieval romances originally written in other languages, such as separate versions of *Amadis of Gaul* by Robert Southey and William Stewart Rose in 1803, as well as Southey's editions of *Palmerin of England* (1807) and *The Chronicle of The Cid* (1808); Southey's reprinting, with Joseph Cottle, of Chatterton's medieval imitations and his own edition of Malory's *Morte d'Arthur* in 1817; Henry Weber's three-volume edition of the *Arabian Nights* in 1812, under the title of *Tales of the East: comprising the most popular Romances of oriental Origin*. Most of these works featured lengthy introductions and annotations on medieval history and romance, which were elaborated on in numerous periodical reviews.

Adding more than a little to this voluminous body of works were Scott's lengthy introductions and high number of detailed notes on medieval history and literature for his own metrical romances. *The Lay of the Last Minstrel* (1805), for example, contains a prose introduction nearly one-third as long as the six-canto poem and ninety notes, most of them several paragraphs long. Scott also published long, minutely detailed essays on chivalry and medieval romance for the *Encyclopaedia Britannica*, 'An Essay on Chivalry' in 1818 and 'An Essay on Romance' in 1824. William Godwin composed a theoretically complex essay 'Of History and Romance' in 1797, though it did not appear in print until 1988. Romanticism's massive reinvestment in the literary and social traditions of romance was further augmented by an unprecedented burst of Spenserian materials pouring from the presses throughout the era: the first variorum edition of Spenser's works (an eight-volume set published in 1805 by John Henry Todd, who included a formidable amount of biographical, historical, and critical essays and notes); hundreds of poems written in explicit imitation of *The Faerie Queene*, which frequently included extensive prefaces and notes on Spenser's incorporation of medieval romance backgrounds; an equally prolific industry of periodical reviews of these works and critical essays devoted to Spenser.

This staggering body of collective editions, adaptations, and critical works on Spenser and his precursors in romance had the overall effect of making 'old Romance' both extremely familiar and intriguingly distant as the product of ancient, exotic cultures. Such a paradox of closeness and estrangement created much of the special allure of romance throughout the Romantic era, partly because it appealed to an ongoing nostalgia for antiquity carried over from the eighteenth century but even more so because it keenly addressed an elemental split in the creative consciousness of the age. Ever since the monumental studies of the Romantic imagination by M. H. Abrams, scholars of the period have located a core feature of Romantic literary experience in the pressing, yet endlessly forestalled, desire to recast the great spiritual systems of Western religion into secularized, visionary myths appropriate to a modern, revolutionary age. This powerful imaginative drama of indeterminate yearning for new visionary ideals drives many of the high achievements of Romantic poetry—such as Blake's prophetic works, Wordsworth's *Prelude* (1805; 1850), Shelley's *Prometheus Unbound* (1819), Keats's *Hyperion* fragments and his great odes of 1819. Such an intensive pursuit of visionary ideals evermore about to be realized found a compelling literary outlet in the divided status of 'old Romance'.

It was a mode of writing also grounded in forms of myth-making and spiritual quests that—as Southey's myth-making experiments in *Thalaba* and the essays by Godwin and Scott on romance illustrate—had now become deeply familiar to Romantic writers. Those earlier visionary enterprises were also shown, in their irresolute character, to be apt models for Romantic forms of divided imaginative questing. However, an abiding confidence in the legitimacy of the spiritual ideals pursued in 'old Romance'—Spenser rarely doubts the promise of the New Jerusalem, only the struggle to attain it—made these ancient quests pointedly different from the erratic, self-doubting sojourns of the Romantic imagination. To adopt the quest form of romance was thus to highlight and vividly explore the tension between older belief and modern indeterminacy at the centre of Romantic poetics. Such a paradoxical correspondence explains not only why so many Romantic writers turned to the form of literary romance for their own major works but also why so many examples of Romantic romance foreground, sometimes in seemingly incongruous ways, the obsolescence of romance for modern poetics: Scott opens his series of medieval romances with a work about the end of minstrelsy, *The Lay of the Last Minstrel*; Byron subtitles *Childe Harold's Pilgrimage* 'A Romaunt' but prefaces the poem with a cynical rejection of 'the monstrous mummeries of the middle ages' and deliberately inserts archaic verbiage and the 'anachronism' of chivalric motifs as well as the 'old structure of versification' (the Spenserian stanza) for a poem about Napoleonic-era European conflict.

In his influential article 'The Internalization of Quest Romance', Harold Bloom has emphasized a new kind of mental drama in these transformations of romance—the perpetual struggle of poetic consciousness to realize visionary ideals—which he also presents as a primary innovation of Romanticism. Rather than justifying the ways of God to man, as Milton had done in *Paradise Lost*, Romantic poets found their 'high argument' (as Wordsworth announced in his 'Prospectus') in the creative mind's divided pursuit of its own imaginative ideals. Such a psychodrama certainly powers the major poetic achievements of the Romantic period. Its emergence, however, was not so much a striking innovation on the background of medieval quest romance but rather an intensification of the deep psychological fissures we have already observed running throughout literary romance from the Middle Ages through Spenser and up to the eighteenth century.

Although earlier romance writers may have trusted more confidently in what Spenser calls God's 'pillours of Eternity' (*The Faerie Queene*, VII. 8.2) shoring up this mortal sphere of mutability, they repeatedly questioned their ability to reach that glorious resting place. Such interior dramas of the mind in medieval romance drew concentrated notice from Romantic writers. Godwin's essay 'Of History and Romance', for instance, elevates romance as the higher form of writing because it delves intensely into human passions and unveils the psyche's deepest truths. Much of the Romantic enthusiasm for Spenser, moreover, centred on his astonishingly varied modes of rendering mental division, particularly regarding that profound split between visions of God's New Jerusalem and the constant prickings of frail mortal flesh. It was a modernized version of this conflict in eighteenth-century Spenserian imitations—the conflict between imaginative enchantment and material responsibility—that inspired many of the Spenserian poems of the Romantic era. When Beattie modified this psychodrama into the minstrel story of the poet's creative maturation, the deep psychological structures of medieval romance had evolved into a form that captivated the imaginations of Romantic writers and helped them to articulate their own elemental divisions between visionary ideals and the interference of modern experience.

While the myth-making and psychological dualities of romance made it such a fertile mode for Romantic adaptation, its political applicability to French revolutionary events gave it an irresistible appeal utterly unique among the genres of Romanticism. The eighteenth-century Spenserian writers had established the political significance of romance traditions for a commercial age, but their model of romance politics underwent acute changes by the end of the century with the development of a charged new association between romance and revolution. Among the many different types of British response to the French Revolution, the strongest and most comprehensive was sheer amazement at the unimaginable transformations of conventional reality transpiring on a daily basis in France. There was nothing like such an astonishing phenomenon, Burke proclaimed at the outset, in all of human history. To many British observers the ongoing sequence of these marvellous events gave France the appearance for good or bad of an enchanted world, reminiscent of the exotic, often dangerous landscapes of medieval romance.

Not surprisingly, then, the rhetoric surrounding the revolution from all sides of the political spectrum frequently invoked the language of romance. Burke, initiating a strategic ploy to revive interest in chivalry as a conservative way of supporting long-established political institutions, famously lamented that hateful revolutionary innovations had put an end to the age of chivalry. Byron, representing those on the radical side, answered in the Preface to *Childe Harold's Pilgrimage* that its death was long overdue. Wordsworth, caught between extremes, described revolutionary France as a country in chivalric romance (*The Prelude*, XI. 112) whose oscillations between delightful enchantment and sinister threat embodied a powerful new political application of the characteristic dualities of medieval romance. Scott's metrical romances typically feature bitter rivalries from Britain's medieval and Renaissance past—English and Scots; warring Scottish clans; royalists and parliamentarians—whose resolutions posit models, albeit shaky ones, for healing entrenched internecine conflicts in the face of

Napoleon's looming threat. Hunt, when released from prison in 1815 for his liberal critiques of a conservative British government, quickly moved his political fight into the lists of romance by seeking to wrest away Burke's conservative purchase on the form through his own creation of a liberal group of writers, including Hazlitt, to be christened as politically progressive Arthurian Knights who would contribute to a series in Hunt's *Examiner* newspaper called 'The Round Table'.

This potent relevance to the age's major upheavals would also extend to pressing social issues, particularly the movement for women's rights and gender equality. Here, again, striking paradoxes and competing appropriations of romance traditions would abound. The eighteenth-century masculine resistance to women's indulgence in literary romance continued with a vengeance during the Romantic period, as exemplified by Joseph Robinson's warnings in *An Essay on the Education of Young Ladies* (1798) about the licentious influence of romance fiction on the minds of young women. In a very different use of chivalric tradition to limit women's entry into the literary marketplace, male writers like Richard Polwhele (author of the notoriously bigoted *The Unsex'd Females* (1798)) deployed hyperbolic postures of gallantry towards women to represent them as frail damsels in need of male protection and guidance. These gender-biased forms of romance, reinforced by educational treatises like Robinson's that linked women's reading habits with only the lightest, most superficial types of romance, provoked an innovative counter approach to literary romance by early feminists like Mary Wollstonecraft. Instead of arguing with Reeve for women's freedom to choose in the circulating library, Wollstonecraft (in *Thoughts on the Education of Daughters* (1787) and *Vindication of the Rights of Woman* (1792)) recommended against women's engagement with conventional forms of romance fiction because they stunted intellectual development and promulgated the same stereotype of female weakness advanced by the pseudo-chivalry of male detractors like Polwhele. Wollstonecraft responded with ironic types of anti-romance, but she did not do away with romance entirely. Instead, along with other early advocates of gender equality, like Mary Tighe in her Spenserian poem, *Psyche* (1795), Wollstonecraft followed the liberal strategy of putting romance to subversive political functions and developed, as we shall see in the next section, a transformative mode of feminist romance that advanced her age's more radical claims for women's empowerment.

Lord Byron, *Childe Harold's Pilgrimage*

Byron's *Childe Harold's Pilgrimage* was the single most popular and arguably the age's most complex form of literary romance, functioning with ingenious sophistication on the myth-making, psychological, and political levels of Romantic adaptations of the form. We have seen how Byron's fundamental mixture of archaism and modernity in his incongruous 'Romaunt' advanced these levels of action in a general way. His management of these intersecting dualities on the micro levels of narrative mode, poetic form, and allegory fully exemplifies the aesthetic richness and cultural significance of the deep structural functions of Romantic romance.

On the narrative level, for instance, Byron calls attention to the visionary trajectory of modern poetics by recurrently associating his protagonist's journey with the spiritual quest motifs of medieval and Spenserian romance. Harold is a young knight-errant of medieval tradition, technically known as a 'Childe', embarked on what appears from the poem's title to be a holy 'pilgrimage' directed, like the Crusades of the Middle Ages, toward 'Paynim shores' (I. 99). Yet Byron flags, from the outset, the stark differences between those earlier quests and Harold's alienated modern pursuit of indeterminate ideals. The Preface fore-grounds this dislocation in its cynical modern perspective on those 'mummeries of the middle ages', and the opening narrative sequence further widens the distance between medieval and modern questing. Harold's quest originates not from a venerable institution like King Arthur's Round Table or Glorianna's court in *The Faerie Queene* but rather from his own satiety of indulgence in 'Sin's long labyrinth', which he has experienced amid the polluted confines of the ancient family pile, a ruined 'Monastic dome' (I. 59) transparently associated with Byron's own estate at Newstead Abbey. Harold morbidly departs from this seat of vice without the specific direction provided to traditional knights of romance, and his quest aims towards no particular objective. It is thus a 'weary pilgrimage', unlike the difficult but ever forward moving journeys of Spenser's moral knights, with no 'fix'd . . . goal' (I. 85, 328). Although the narrative of this weird pilgrimage follows no specific course in its random peregrination through Napoleonic Europe (a virtual map of Byron's own travels), it is not completely aimless. For it persistently brings Harold and the poem's narrator into confronta-tion with false or unrealizable ideals—Portuguese religious icons in Canto I; mountain sub-limity in Canto III; Rome's Apollonian statuary in Canto IV—thus forwarding the poem's central theme of thwarted visionary questing. The one 'shrine' to which the narrative finally leads, a quintessential symbol of such Romantic pilgrimages, consists of the eternally restless 'deep and dark blue ocean' (IV. 1603).

To illuminate the inward turn of this type of pilgrimage into mental space, Byron deploys numerous adaptations of the psychodynamics of Spenserian allegory. His reformulation of

Spenser's Mutabilitie sequence in Canto IV of *Childe Harold's Pilgrimage* reveals how much Romantic experiments in romance both draw from and modernize the form's traditional structures. Mutabilitie's procession of change in the two cantos of Mutabilitie appended to *The Faerie Queene* poignantly illustrates the impermanent condition of all 'living wights', who are 'Still tost, and turned, with continuall change' (VII. VII. 21). Yet Spenser juxtaposes this state of ongoing flux, whose imaginative representation anticipates Byron's own ever rolling ocean, with the qualified solace of belief in God's eternal, unchanging paradise. Spenser's Nature thus silences Mutabilitie's claims to dominance over human affairs by appealing eschatologically to God's steadfast 'pillours of Eternity . . . contrayr to Mutabilitie' upon which 'all shall rest eternally' (VII. VIII. 2). Byron's revisionary form of Mutabilitie's pageant reverses the Spenserian movement from sublunary change to divine permanence, figuring instead symbols of Roman aspirations to permanence that crumble under the irresistible forces of time, change, and human corruption. The Colosseum's astonishing architecture, for example, appears as so many 'loops of time' whose eternal glory, worshipped from 'Saxon' days to the present, defies temporal change. So gleams Apollonian statuary with the 'ray of immortality'. Yet all these Roman pillars of eternity, the narrator finally concedes, loom as monuments of 'Ruin' and human inability to redeem experience from the ravages of time (IV. 1290–1466). This allegory, like Spenser's, contrasts symbols of change and permanence as pictures of the poet's mind torn between hope for the eternal and despair over the frailty of all that is human. Byron's picture tips Spenser's upside down, but in doing so it also demonstrates how Romantic romance achieved a vision of modernity through its creative tension with the form's deepest traditions.

This contrapuntal use of romance for modern psychodrama extends to Byron's formal experimentation with the Spenserian stanza. Spenser's mellifluousness of sound entranced his followers throughout the centuries. However, Romantic poets and critics became particularly intrigued by his rhythmic swerves between enchanting harmony and cacophonous discord, which struck them as the musical complement to his allegorical dualities. The melodious sound of Nature's first appearance in the Mutabilitie cantos,

> And all the earth far vnderneath her feete
> Was dight with flowers, that voluntary grew
> Out of the ground, and sent forth odours sweet;
> Tenne thousand mores of sundry sent and hew,
> That might delight the smell, or please the view:
>
> (VII. VII. 10)

thus contrasts with the tortured rhythms of the lines describing Mutabilitie's rule of 'changes infinite',

> Now, boyling hot: straight, friezing deadly cold:
> Now, faire, sun-shine, that makes all skip and daunce:
> Streight, bitter storms and baleful countenance,
> That makes them all to shiuer and to shake:
> Rayne, hayle, and snowe do pay them sad penance.
>
> (VII. VII. 23)

Byron mobilizes similar tonal divisions in his reactions to the Colosseum, contrasting the soothing rhythms of his description of those eternal 'loops of time',

> the rising moon begins to climb
> Its topmost arch, and gently pauses there;
> When the stars twinkle through the loops of time,
> And the low night-breeze waves along the air . . .
> (IV. 1288–91)

with the grating sounds of his portrait of the dying gladiator who dreams of his native homeland as he falls amidst the barbaric shouts of spectators in the Colosseum,

> Butcher'd to make a Roman holiday—
> All this [his dreams] rush'd with his blood—Shall he expire
> And unavenged?—Arise! ye Goths, and glut your ire!
> (IV. 1267–9)

Discords of this sort intensify Spenserian dissonance, and they expectedly recur with much greater frequency in Byron's poem. Nevertheless, their collision with aural enchantment draws from Spenser's world of romance the very patterns of sound that, adjusted to a new setting, give articulate voice to modern consciousness. Keats and Shelley would hear it all when shaping the Spenserian stanzas of their modern versions of romance psychodrama, *The Revolt of Islam* and *The Eve of St Agnes*.

We have seen how these interior structures of Romantic romance also functioned on the political level, and here, too, *Childe Harold's Pilgrimage* provided an exemplary model for other poets. Byron's invocation of 'Chivalry' when narrating the Napoleonic war in Spain reinforces the type of incongruities between past and present that advance the poem's main psychodrama. However, just as his repudiation of Burke's chivalric nostalgia in the Preface argues against political retrenchment, so his dexterous use of chivalric tropes in the Spanish passage extends radical appropriations of medieval chivalry for strategic political critiques of state power. In championing Spanish patriotism against the tyranny of Napoleon's French invaders, Byron associates 'Chivalry', the 'ancient goddess' of Spain, with radical republican virtue and opposition to despotism. 'Chivalry', therefore, does not wield her 'thirsty lance' of old but flies on the 'blazing bolts' of artillery and proclaims a thunderous shout for the progress of liberty in modern Europe. Byron further complicates his politics of chivalry by combining this subversive appropriation of the form with the radical strategy of denouncing conservative celebrations of chivalry like Burke's. Thus the physical forms of chivalry displayed by the warring hosts—'rival scarfs of mix'd embroidery'—appear as garish, obsolescent symbols of state tyranny. The military troops on all sides act but as 'The broken tools . . . that tyrants cast away | By myriads' for their own bloodthirsty, power hungry aims (I. 405–58). That chivalry could thus assume so many ideological shapes on the battlefields of nineteenth-century Europe illustrates the complex potency of the politics of romance in Byron's time.

Leigh Hunt, *The Story of Rimini*

Hunt's creative experiment with chivalric politics in *The Story of Rimini* (1816) also deserves notice as an influential landmark in the progress of radical romance during the Romantic era. For the most part written while Hunt was still serving his jail sentence, *The Story of Rimini* provides an elaborate setting of medieval chivalric pageantry for its narration of Dante's story of the tragic, incestuous love of Paulo and Francesca. Hunt calls attention to the politics of this chivalric experiment with overt references to his 'caged hours' while composing *Rimini* behind the 'dull bars' of a state prison (III. 4, 6). The poem's most subversive effect stemmed, however, from a more systematic and highly distinctive adaptation of radical chivalry on the level of narrative emphasis. In his lengthy descriptions of chivalric pageantry, for instance, Hunt prioritizes its aesthetic and sensual delights—colourful plumes, canopies, and costumes; dashing courtiers and blushing ladies—over its military purposes. This overwhelming preference for 'shapes of gallantry' (I. 170) serves as a prelude to the poem's main emphasis on the frankly erotic love between Paulo and Francesca, whose incestuous nature defies all social and legal codes but receives Hunt's clear endorsement. Although official violence and a broken spirit lead to the deaths of Paulo and Francesca, they are interred in a shared grave that becomes a noble monument to future lovers. By thus celebrating his lovers' transgressions against the established institutions of their medieval time, Hunt also presents a thinly veiled attack, noted by all of his conservative enemies in the reviewing press, against the restricting moral and political ideologies of his own day.

Hunt's critique acquired another layer of subversive energy from the jocular, Cockney rhymes and witticisms he deliberately infiltrated into the narrative—Francesca 'had stout notions on the marrying score' (II. 28). Instead of simply acting as a parody of high romance, this kind of Cockney performance insinuates an arrogant voice of the lower orders into the centre of élite cultural production. Such a strategic manœuvre blurs the distinctions between high and low art, and, by extension, subverts the hierarchical divisions between the political élite and the democratic masses. Such controversial innovations in *The Story of Rimini* would exert a strong influence on the major liberal writers of second-generation Romanticism. Byron worked with Hunt on manuscript revisions of the poem. Keats wrote imitations of *Rimini* and a sonnet in honour of it. Shelley began adopting his knightly postures around this time. And the radical Knights of Hunt's *Examiner* Round Table would begin to gather just as *Rimini* moved forward in composition. The political force of all this Huntian chivalry registers in the outcry it provoked among conservative guardians of culture and politics. By the time that *Blackwood's Edinburgh Magazine* began its notorious series of hostile reviews entitled 'On the Cockney School of Poetry' (1817), which assailed *Rimini*, the *Examiner* Round Table, and Hunt's knightly pretensions, the poetry and politics of Romantic chivalry stood at the forefront of national dispute about the fate of culture and country.

Mary Wollstonecraft, *Maria; or, The Wrongs of Woman*

The controversial eroticism of *Rimini* also shares elements of a subversive Wollstonecraftian pattern of linking radical romance and sexual liberty with nascent women's rights movements. Where Wollstonecraft had previously resisted the sexual excess of romance fiction, she puts a new kind of emphasis on sexual freedom in the romance plot for her final, incomplete novel, *Maria; or, The Wrongs of Woman* (1798). The heroine of *Wrongs*, Maria, first appears as a typically distressed female protagonist of Gothic romance, though she is imprisoned in a horrifyingly real rather than a fictitious dungeon: 'Abodes of horror have frequently been described and castles, filled with spectres and chimeras, conjured up by the magic spell of genius to harrow the soul, and absorb the wondering mind' (p. 7). Maria advances through a series of sensational adventures fitting for the heroine of a Gothic romance. She falls into prison under the insidious pressure of her scoundrel husband, yearns for her mysteriously stolen daughter, and plots to escape with her fellow prisoner, Darnford, who possesses all the characteristics of a hero of romance in his dashing good looks, his virtuous republican politics, and his deep literary sensibility. Wollstonecraft pointedly alters the conventional romance plot, however, which might have featured Darnford's heroic rescue of the distressed Maria. Instead, Wollstonecraft lends a radical form of agency to Maria, who defies her legal bonds of marriage to a despicable husband and chooses of her own accord to take Darnford as a lover. Maria's actions do not exactly undermine the typical romance plot; rather they transform it into one of female agency and sexual freedom, a more radical version of the kind of liberty for women espoused by Reeve in *The Progress of Romance*.

Yet Wollstonecraft remains uncomfortable with conventional romance fiction, and she further combines a keen critique of its masculine biases with an even more advanced type of feminist transformation of its basic plot. Darnford, the quintessential chivalric hero of romance in appearance, turns out to be a fake who heartlessly abandons Maria after impregnating her. In tracing the course of Maria's infatuation and bitter disappointment with this attractive cad, Wollstonecraft repudiates the tendency of romance fiction to give women readers false expectations about fulfilment through a quest to marry a knightly figure conjured out of the traditions of romance. Rejecting this type of romance and its intrinsic devaluation of women, Wollstonecraft invents a new romance plot even more radical in its feminist politics than the story of Maria's sexual liberation. In the novel's final plot twist, left in a fragmentary state when Wollstonecraft suddenly died from childbirth complications, Maria escapes from prison without Darnford's assistance and finds a special haven with her own infant daughter and the trustworthy Jemima. This female haven, curiously anticipating a similar union in Shelley's *Rosalind and Helen* (1818), transforms the marriage plots, utopian idealism, and gender subordinations of romance tradition into one of the period's most extreme forms of radical romance: the romance of female community, with Maria and Jemima acting as paired 'mothers' to the baby girl. Thus stretching the form so far from Burke's chivalric nostalgia or Scott's chivalric model of national unity while also pushing to a different political edge than Byron or Hunt sought in their subversive chivalry, Wollstonecraft demonstrates the astonishing adaptability of Romantic romance to the full spectrum of the period's most pressing social and political tensions. So it was that all those writers of the Romantic era felt, with Keats, that they 'must tell a tale of chivalry'.

FURTHER READING

Abrams, M. H., *Natural Supernaturalism: Tradition and Revolution in Romantic Literature* (New York: W. W. Norton, 1973). Presents a magisterial overview of the visionary poetics of Romanticism.

Bloom, Harold, 'The Internalization of Quest Romance', in *The Ringers in the Tower: Studies in Romantic Tradition* (Chicago: University of Chicago Press, 1971), pp. 13–35. Explores the interior drama of Romantic poetry and its roots in earlier forms of quest romance.

Chandler, Alice, *A Dream of Order: The Medieval Ideal in Nineteenth-Century English Literature* (Lincoln, Neb.: University of Nebraska Press, 1970). Provides a comprehensive survey of uses of medieval traditions in nineteenth-century English literature.

Chandler, James, *England in 1819: The Politics of Literary Culture and the Case of Romantic Historicism* (Chicago: University of Chicago Press, 1998). A complex account of the intersections between literature, historical thought, and liberal politics during the Romantic period, particularly in the year of the Peterloo massacre, 1819.

Curran, Stuart, *Poetic Form and British Romanticism* (Oxford: Oxford University Press, 1986). An excellent study of Romantic poetic genres, including a chapter on romance.

Duff, David, *Romance and Revolution: Shelley and the Politics of a Genre* (Cambridge: Cambridge University Press, 1994). Offers a comprehensive analysis of the political functions of chivalric tropes throughout the Romantic period and, particularly, in the writings of Percy Bysshe Shelley.

Frye, Northrop, *Anatomy of Criticism* (Princeton: Princeton University Press, 1957). A major study of literary archetypes, this book provides sustained analysis of the mythical and political functions of romance in world literature.

Jameson, Fredric, 'Magical Narratives: Romance as Genre', *New Literary History: A Journal of Theory and Interpretation*, 7 (Autumn 1975), 136–63. A stimulating theoretical interpretation of the politics of romance.

Kucich, Greg, *Keats, Shelley, and Romantic Spenserianism* (University Park, Pa.: Pennsylvania State University Press, 1991). Traces the influence of Spenser on eighteenth-century and Romantic literature, and includes a detailed section on *Childe Harold's Pilgrimage*.

Labbe, Jacqueline M., *The Romantic Paradox: Love, Violence and the Uses of Romance, 1760–1830* (London: Macmillan, 2000). Studies the unstable gender politics of literary romance in the eighteenth and nineteenth centuries.

Parker, Patricia A., *Inescapable Romance: Studies in the Poetics of a Mode* (Princeton: Princeton University Press, 1979). Presents a comprehensive history of the development of literary romance from the Renaissance until the nineteenth century.

Roe, Nicholas (ed.), *Leigh Hunt: Life, Poetics, Politics* (London: Routledge, 2003). A collection of critical essays on Leigh Hunt, many of which address his politics as well as his literary writings, including Greg Kucich's study of Hunt's 'Cockney Chivalry'.

Ross, Marlon B., 'Scott's Chivalric Pose: The Function of Metrical Romance in the Romantic Period', *Genre*, 19 (1986), 267–97. Analyses the political acts of nation-building in Scott's metrical romances.

Vicario, Michael, 'The Implications of Form in *Childe Harold's Pilgrimage*', *Keats-Shelley Journal*, 33 (1985), 103–29. Provides a detailed analysis of the formal poetic structures of Byron's poem.

Vinaver, Eugène, *The Rise of Romance* (Oxford: Clarendon Press, 1971). A comprehensive introduction to the development of medieval romance.

30 | Gothic

Nicola Trott

The Gothic existed long before it became a genre-word. In origin, it is a race-term, referring to the Goths who, from their tribal homelands in Germany or Scandinavia, invaded central and southern Europe and helped to bring down the Roman Empire (Goths under Alaric sacked Rome in AD 410). For the Renaissance scholars who recovered Roman culture, the Gothic meant whatever was pre-Roman. For the Italian art historian Vasari, it meant non-classical architecture, built in the perpendicular or pointed-arch style, and dating from the twelfth to sixteenth centuries. By extension, then, the Gothic came to signify whatever was medieval (Horace Walpole relied on this sense when in 1765 he subtitled the second edition of *The Castle of Otranto* 'A Gothic Story', and founded what we now think of as the Gothic novel). Throughout the eighteenth century and beyond, such counter-classical and medieval associations made 'Gothic' operate as a sort of swear-word. On the one hand, it suggested all things primitive, barbarous, and savage; on the other, it designated a historical period, known evocatively as the 'dark ages'. This darkness was post-classical, clearly, but also pre-Enlightenment or (in a British context) pre-Reformation. In the light of modern advances in civilization, the Gothic past represented an era of ignorance, irrationality, and superstition. At the same time, however, it also testified to an era of belief; and this access to modes of faith no longer strictly credible became central to Gothic writing.

Gothic nationalism

References to the Catholic dark ages have a Protestant history—and, all too plainly, Protestant prejudices—at their beck and call. And yet the meaning of Gothic is also tied up with the origins of Englishness. Goths invaded Britain as well as Rome; and these northern tribes (Angles, Saxons, and Jutes, who settled in 447–450) were collectively known as the English. Since they put an end to Roman domination, they also came to be thought of as free, and the source of England's democratic laws and institutions. As a result, the word 'Gothic' came to have favourable, nationalist connotations of patriotism, liberty, and constitutional monarchy. Such connotations were taken up in literary or cultural terms: Joseph Addison, for instance, characterized the English as an especially fanciful people, and hence especially gifted in what Dryden called '*the Fairie way of Writing*', which demands 'an Imagination naturally fruitful and superstitious'.[1] Such claims came often to be made in association with Shakespeare, as a national poet. What, from a pejorative point of view, was regarded as alien irrationality, could also be admired as native creativity.

That the Gothic was available as a term of either abuse or endearment is fundamental to the writing gathered under its name. Equally fundamental is the spirit of opposition in which the semantics of 'Gothic' developed: the *Oxford English Dictionary* suggests that '"romantic", as opposed to classical', was a meaning acquired by 1762. Just three years later, Walpole managed to turn the negative implications of Gothic to a similarly positive advantage, in English literature's first example of 'A Gothic Story'. By identifying appeals to the marvellous with the free play of the writer's 'fancy', *The Castle of Otranto* laid claim to a freedom from aesthetic restriction—specifically, from the restrictions of both matter-of-fact realism and neoclassical rules, the one being described as a feature of English fiction, the other of French drama (see Walpole's preface to his second edition). This dual nationality was further complicated by the fact that *Otranto* had originally posed as a translation from the Italian (see the first-edition title-page and preface), and set itself, in a fashion that became typical, in the Catholic Mediterranean: like British tourists, British novelists had to go abroad in order to effect their escape. Victor Sage also points out that Walpole's style was at odds with his theory, being 'suffused with the rational virtues of eighteenth-century prose';[2] but in staging a Shakespeare-justified overthrow of 'French'-instituted unity, probability, and decorum, his story introduced the possibility, taken up by later generations of writers, of a fiction that was energized by the excessive, the improbable, and the monstrous.

Gothic aesthetic

Crucially, a Gothic sensibility or aesthetic was established in the fifty years prior to *Otranto*. Foundations were laid by John Dennis's inclusion of the principle of fear, in his *Grounds of Criticism in Poetry* (1704); by Daniel Defoe's ghost story, *A True Relation of the Apparition of One Mrs Veal* (1706); by Addison's *Spectator* papers on the pleasures of imaginary terror and horror;[3] and in works of criticism which rescued a British romance tradition, from Thomas Warton's *Observations on the Faerie Queene of Spenser* (1754) to Richard Hurd's *Letters on Chivalry and Romance* (1762). In architecture the Gothic Revival got underway in the 1740s by converting ecclesiastical and medieval Gothic to domestic and gentlemanly uses, as in Walpole's Strawberry Hill, Beckford's Fonthill Abbey, and Scott's Abbotsford (see *Oxford Companion to the Romantic Age*, pp. 417–18, 747). Most important, perhaps, were the hints given by the poets, from the 'graveyard school' (Robert Blair, *The Grave*, 1743; Edward Young, *Night Thoughts*,

1742–5) to the 'primitives' (Thomas Gray's 'Odin', 1768, and James Macpherson's Ossian, the supposedly fourth-century Gaelic bard of *Fingal*, 1762, and *Temora*, 1763). An early, and influential, example, Pope's *Eloisa to Abelard* (1717), placed melancholia and forbidden passion in a conventual setting so as to use these Gothic surroundings to passionate psychic effect: Eloisa speaks as the haunting figure of a 'rebel nature', lost in 'a convent's solitary gloom', with only her 'phantom' lover and her own 'illusions' for company. This tradition of indulged instability was later cultivated by Thomas Warton, in *The Pleasures of Melancholy* (1747):

> when the world
> Is clad in Midnight's raven-colour'd robe,
> 'Mid hollow chancel let me watch the flame
> Of taper dim, shedding a livid glare
> O'er the wan heaps; while airy voices talk
> Along the glimmering walls; or ghostly shape
> At distance seen, invites with beckoning hand
> My lonesome steps, through the far-winding vaults.
>   (ll. 42–9)

Gothic writing, as Warton's vaults and chancel indicate, was much indebted to Gothic building. This was largely because medieval architecture provided a clear opposition to the classical: as Walpole put it, in his *Anecdotes of Painting* (1762), though 'taste' was necessary to appreciate 'Grecian architecture', 'one wants only passions to feel the Gothic'. The antithesis of Grecian and Gothic building became a standard way of describing the dichotomy between 'classic' and 'Romantic' art—the one dedicated to principles of order, proportion, and completeness, the other to irregularity, vastness, and indeterminacy. Gothic architecture seemed to speak to unenlightened states of mind (despite being 'stripped of its altars and shrines' at the Reformation, Westminster Abbey, Walpole dared to suggest, 'is nearer to converting one to popery than all the regular pageantry of Roman domes'; *Anecdotes of Painting*)—and so also to correspond to obscure or unexplored recesses of consciousness.[4]

Gothic (anti-)modernity

In many respects, then, the Gothic passes for a product of counter-Enlightenment or a move against the modern. The superstitiousness it values is of the kind which, in enlightened thinking, is attacked as a feature of primitive culture perpetuated only by the childish, uneducated, or defective:

It was shrewdly remarked by Voltaire, that the early stages of society are the times for prodigies—Scotland was not civilized when Macbeth met the Witches; nor was Rome, when Curtius leaped into the gulph. People of weak intellects, have, at all times, believed in apparitions.[5]

That the Gothic started life in a spirit of opposition has been one of the main routes to its interpretation. The proponents, on the one hand, of a rational philosophy of mind, and, on the other, of an experience which 'anticipates our reasonings', are, respectively, John Locke and Edmund Burke. An exemplary encounter between the two occurs when Burke's *Philosophical Enquiry into the Origin of our Ideas of the Sublime and Beautiful* (1757) contradicts Locke's lucid explanation of the commonly held, and in Locke's view irrational, association of darkness with ghosts and goblins.[6] Burke's facing down of Locke implies the kind of historical shift which has been often associated with the rise of Romanticism: Eino Railo has commented that 'the whole terror-romantic movement resolves itself, as it were, into an experiment with Edmund Burke's theory', which 'attempts to awaken by suggestion the emotions of suspense, fear and terror'.[7] This confrontation—the spectacle of rational empiricism being answered by an aesthetics of terror—is a defining moment: the novelists Ann Radcliffe and M. G. Lewis expressly allude to it; and it is endlessly replayed in the structure of the Gothic novel. But the line of thought which presents the Gothic as a reaction-formation cannot account for the way in which, for instance, the author of 'The Ghost' (quoted above) feels constrained to add: 'It is unnecessary now to say, that stories of Ghosts are mistakes or impositions, and that they might always be detected, if people had ingenuity to discover the trick, or courage enough to search out the cause of their fright.' To say that it 'is unnecessary . . . to say' testifies to the very persistence of such 'prodigies'; and saying that it is unnecessary to say it 'now' implies that, for all the attempt to cast them definitively in the past, 'stories of Ghosts' are precisely expressions, or 'apparitions', of modernity. Despite an official hostility and disbelief, the possibility of the paranormal attracted even the most sophisticated: Dr Johnson paid a visit to the Cock Lane Ghost, and Sir Walter Scott spent at least two nights in the haunted chambers of Scottish castles (Glamis in 1793 and Dunvegan in 1814).[8] Emma Clery has recently argued that the rise of the supernatural is a function not of metaphysics—'the old opposition of belief and scepticism, truth and error'— but of the 'spectacle' of urban consumer culture; and that 'the literature of terror arose in the late eighteenth century as a symptom of and reflection on the modern'.[9]

Gothic (anti-)rationality

Instead of being the work simply of reaction, Gothic writing took part, even if it also took sides, in an *unresolved* argument between rationality and more suggestive and mysterious states of mind. The terms of this argument are greatly complicated by the historical identification of superstition as 'Romish'. The heyday of the British Gothic novel is framed by the anti-Catholic Gordon riots of 1780 and the Catholic Emancipation Bill of 1829, with a French Revolution dedicated to secular Reason in between; and many texts offset Catholic superstition against Protestant rationality.[10] Like the classic–Romantic antithesis that is contained in the word Gothic, this religious divide can be seen as another version of the polarizations in Enlightenment thinking. Sometimes, as with Radcliffe's Adeline (in *The Romance of the Forest*) or Maturin's Spaniard (in *Melmoth the Wanderer*), the protagonist's outlook is manifestly at odds with his or her Catholic background, and takes on the Lutheran or Calvinist cast of the author's mind. Alternatively, as with M. G. Lewis's citation of German sources and Mary Shelley's Swiss locations, the Gothic is partly returned to its northern tribal origins. Elsewhere again, as in Scott's assessment of Walpole, Gothic writing is understood as an 'attempt to reconcile the superstitious credulity of feudal ages with the philosophic scepticism of our own' (from *Lives of the Novelists*). These encounters indicate that the Gothic novel had a special role in the culture of the day, as the popular—and fantastic—version of its various antagonisms and contradictions.

Gothic novels are remarkable for their entertainment of the irrational rather than their subservience to it. Far from simply endorsing the supernatural, the novels often register ambivalence about its phenomena, and about the mental and emotional conditions under which these appear. At the same time, they seek to engineer situations in which superstitious fears take charge, and to offer potent symbolizations of these provocations and responses (the subterranean vaults of abbeys and castles in early Gothic, or the simultaneous appearances of moon and monster in *Frankenstein* (see the creation scene, vol. I, ch. 4)). The subrational is typically housed within a rational superstructure. This housing is historically specific. In Horace Walpole, reason figures as the cultural authority against which his own story is written ('I wrote it in spite of rules'; letter to Mme du Deffand, 13 March 1767): more playful than defiant, his fiction invokes, and breaks, the 'rules' in order surreptitiously to evade its assumed reader's training in polite or sceptical habits of mind. In Ann Radcliffe, the rational is incorporated into the fabric of the novel, and, officially at least, acts as the default position, which is periodically and deliberately overcome by the sequence of events: while the author's 'explained supernaturalism' to some extent pursues the Enlightenment project of 'search[ing] out the cause of . . . fright', the heroine's sensibility provides the reader with a pleasurable succession of Gothic terrors and uncertainties. In M. G. Lewis and C. R. Maturin, reason drives a partisan satire of Catholicism: Lewis combines a sarcastic anticlericalism and an Anglo-Saxon attitude to miracles with a full-blooded commitment to the most luridly outlandish Germanic legends; Maturin, an eccentric Irish clergyman, invents a fantastic elaboration of the Faust story while at the same time conducting a withering exposure of Jesuit impostures, in 'The Spaniard's Tale', as the instruments of a system of power which exploits credulity for its own institutional ends. Mary Shelley's is the most complex case, due to her inheritance from her father, William Godwin, of an ultra-rationalist political philosophy, to which elements of *Frankenstein* imperfectly or ironically subscribe: Shelley's anti-hero, Victor, has an enlightened vision of human society transformed by the creation of a new and perfect race; but the creature he brings to life in fulfilment of that vision he can see only as an inhuman 'monster'.

Gothic novels seek to undermine, manipulate, or critique the logic of Enlightenment rationalism even as they appeal to it for clarification. Where the result seems too nearly superstitious, or is stigmatized as credulous, the fiction tends to adopt a sceptical or forensic stance towards the possibilities it opens up. And yet the form depends for its effects on the continual renewal of those same possibilities. Gothic narrative thrives on the suspense surrounding the unknown. Having said that, even its most irrational promptings are animated as much by curiosity and conjecture as by ignorance. Gothic itself, then, is characterized by a pursuit of knowledge; it is just that the pursuit is invariably tangled up in the imaginary—in terror or mystery, alchemy, diabolism, or the occult.

Gothic taboos

The Gothic novel built on many existing Gothic structures. But it seems fair to say that Gothic writing was not organized until it emerged in novel form (a transition from 'mode' to 'genre' that can be traced to an episode in Smollett's *Adventures of Ferdinand Count Fathom*, 1752). Here, an extended interplay of rational and irrational forces could take place; and the loose tendencies of a Gothic aesthetic could be given shape, through their connection with the prose romance and its expectation of fanciful or improbable adventures. But the Gothic novel from the first established specialized excitements of its own. And it was these that made it the first fully popular literature for a newly enlarged reading public (see chapter on 'Print culture and the book trade'). The infringement of physical laws by supernatural events seems to have encouraged other kinds of outrage: persecution and abduction, incarceration and rape (whether actual or threatened), incest and infanticide (or some equally familial crime). These violations of moral and social order have been labelled, by G. R. Thompson, as 'dark Romanticism'. In marketing terms, they gave the Gothic novel brand recognition. The genre's added value, and a key to its popular success, lay in combining the fear and suspense which already had a home in the Gothic aesthetic, with sex and violence—which had a more remote ancestry, in oral ballads and Shakespearean or Jacobean tragedy.

Across the genre as a whole, transgressiveness varies considerably, both in kind and degree. Interestingly, ethical shocks are often proportional to physical ones: the more morally circumspect the writer, the more sparing, as a rule, his or her recourse to the supernatural (Reeve and Radcliffe are comparatively restrained; Walpole and Lewis much less so). Censurable elements often enter by way of dream, or by appeal to the other—those conventional lovers, Spanish friars, and Mediterranean machiavels, whose illicit passions, forbidden lusts, or Italian revenge, exhibit the emotional and psychical excess which Austen's *Northanger Abbey* rejects as inherently un-English. For all its taboo acts, however, the Gothic plot frequently revolves around the same set of aristocratic or bourgeois interests, to do with lineage and primogeniture, marriage and inheritance, as are found elsewhere in eighteenth-century fiction. (In its concern with reproduction both in and outside the family, even *Frankenstein* can be seen as taking up this thread, though with radical twists of its own making.)

Gothic genres

So far I have referred confidently to the Gothic novel as a genre. But in many ways the form defies the concept of kind. One area of difficulty arises from the fact that *Frankenstein* has in recent years become the core text (see also the discussion of stage versions of *Frankenstein* in the chapter on the 'Theatre' in Part IV). This canon change presents complexities that are especially challenging to genre criticism, in that the Gothic novel—or the writing which is habitually grouped together in that name—is now associated primarily not with its relatively coherent early phase, but with its later sophistication and diversification. Another area of difficulty has already been mentioned: the sheer diversity of materials out of which the novels are constructed means that generic boundaries are repeatedly crossed. The Gothic method of production, which ostentatiously draws attention to this eclecticism, has been often compared to the making of the monster in *Frankenstein* (following a lead in Shelley herself: see her 1831 Introduction). More than this, the Gothic novel is deliberately announced as a work of generic fusion: Walpole's stated aim, in the preface to the second edition of *Otranto*, the edition that named itself 'A Gothic Story', was to reconcile what he called 'ancient' and 'modern' romance. From the first, then, the Gothic novel was defined as a mixed creation. Or, to put it another way, the narrative form was marked by the same kind of opposition and doubleness that featured in the semantic development of the word 'Gothic': on the one hand, it registered a simple antagonism to prevailing cultural standards; on the other, it was itself intrinsically divided. And it is the interaction—or contestation—of these different positions that seems to be constitutive.

So is the Gothic novel definable only by reference to its diversity and plurality? In effect, the history of Gothic is a history of subgenres. Contemporary taxonomies of supernatural fiction readily identified a number of subdivisions, among them 'terrorist', 'German', 'Jacobin', and 'Inquisitional'. Two of the most important early distinctions are between 'terror' and 'horror' (corresponding, roughly, to Radcliffe and Lewis), and between 'explained' and 'assumed' or 'asserted' supernaturalism (corresponding to Radcliffe and Walpole). Over the nineteenth century, Gothic narrative split into several distinct genres: sensation novels, horror fiction, detective stories, and so on. By the same token, however, the Gothic novel would not be categorizable at all but for its conventions. These were established almost at once, largely by Walpole, and there is plenty of evidence to suggest that they were quickly recognized as a set of standard ingredients. In setting (medieval and southern European castles and convents), scenery (bat-haunted ruins, banditti-infested mountains), characterization (persecuted heroines and murderous villains, garrulous servants and wicked guardians), props (trapdoors, expiring tapers, concealed chambers), and narrative techniques (found manuscripts, multiple narrators, inset tales and poems), the Gothic novel was briefly standardized enough to be exploited in parody, most famously by Peacock and Austen, and satirized in 'recipes', by Beckford, Coleridge, and others. That the form is formulaic may indicate that it is little other than a series of framed conventions (testifying, in Elizabeth Napier's view, to its limitation and failure). And yet, to see it as no more than the sum of its devices would be too simply reductive. Besides, the devices alone are by no means definitive: as they grew tired, so they were reinvented—the castle beloved of early Gothic does not feature in *Frankenstein*—and the rubrics were no sooner announced than they were self-consciously worked, in a spirit of imitation, homage, or pastiche: Scott's *Redgauntlet*, for instance, marvellously does the Scottish Gothic after the manner of James Hogg (author of *Confessions of a Justified Sinner*), in 'Wild Willie's Tale', an inset story which encodes in lurid Gothic script the familial-political mystery of the novel as a whole.

Gothic criticism

The mix out of which the Gothic novel arises has shaped the history not only of its writing, but also of its interpretation. The questions that criticism has asked of the Gothic novel correspond to the antitheses and ambiguities of the form itself, revealing, by turns, sharp divisions of opinion and of methodology. Critics have disputed whether the Gothic novel is light- or serious-minded? deep or superficial? coherent or incohate? escapist or engaged? reactionary or revolutionary? permissive or repressive? In putting such questions, a basic fault-line has developed. To some, the Gothic novel is best analysed as a set of formal codes or textual practices. To others, on the contrary, it is best analysed as an expression of psychological drives or ideological regimes. These two methods could be restated as 'discursive' and 'symbolic' approaches to the form. The first is implicit in *The Castle of Otranto*, which Virginia Woolf describes as 'a parasite, an artificial commodity, produced half in joke in reaction against the current style, or in relief from it';[11] and which, in modern criticism, produces 'a guardedness against reading the Gothic as if it were governed by a model of surface/depth, of there being a deep structure that would explain Gothic's irrationalisms'.[12] The second has found powerful allies in psychoanalysis, cultural materialism, and feminism, and can cite as contemporary evidence the dream origins of Gothic texts (*Otranto* and *Frankenstein*), and their uncanny appeal to what Addison calls 'those secret Terrours and Apprehensions to which the Mind of Man is naturally subject'.[13]

Much recent criticism of the Gothic novel has seen those terrors in socio-political terms, following David Punter's suggestion that there is a 'very intense, if displaced, engagement with political and social problems'[14]—whether these are conceived in terms of class struggle and alienation; the rise of 'economic man'; anxieties surrounding sexuality and childbirth; or the limitations of domestic life and the values inculcated by the novel of social manners. Another important strand of historical criticism seeks to contextualize Gothic novels by reference to the conditions of their making or reception, an approach which has found a starting-point in the French Revolution. This revolutionary link is romantic but wrong in the founding case of Walpole, whose *Otranto* predates the events of 1789 by twenty-five years; yet it has considerable relevance for the outpouring of Gothic fiction that began in the 1790s, at a time when a fondness for Burkean and physiological terror coincided with the Terror in France. Ideological and radical applications of Gothic to the unmasking of a state apparatus or the disclosure of 'things as they are' are apparent in William Godwin's *Adventures of Caleb Williams* and Mary Wollstonecraft's *Maria; or, the Wrongs of Woman*.

The Gothic is especially remarkable for two things: for proliferation and for persistence. It has become a multimedia idiom, migrating effortlessly from text to drama to image, and has capitalized (above all via *Frankenstein*) on the modern technologies of film and video. The Gothic novel really took off with—and is indeed a symptom of—the surge in the volume of printed matter that occurred towards the end of the eighteenth century. This Gothic dimension of the new print culture can in turn be linked to various other factors: the rise or development of commodification; of the female reader and writer; and of the periodical press. In its various prose forms, the Gothic is defined by an almost sinister capacity to 'go forth and prosper' (Mary Shelley's 1831 Introduction to *Frankenstein*). The novelists, and certainly their critics, were highly alert to this productive and reproductive power, an awareness which culminated in Mary Shelley's 'monster', which turned what was a routine term of critical abuse for the Gothic novel in the 1790s into a literal creature of the novelist's own making and an archetypal symbol of the social reject run amok. Increasing numbers of leisured and literate women, meanwhile, made their mark in what Ellen Moers has named 'female Gothic', a distinctively feminized romance which hijacked the existing novel of sensibility for the mutual satisfaction of the woman writer and reader through the suggestive and sensitive medium of the Gothic heroine. Finally, the numerous magazines, reviews, and periodicals meant that the Gothic novel was one of the first genres to develop entirely within a culture of public criticism. As a result, the Gothic has a long and fascinating reception history. It has found a generous host in the modern academy, and itself given ample scope to the pursuit of every major theoretical development. But the genealogy of Gothic criticism stems from the earliest analyses of Gothic writing—in prefaces, essays, lectures, and reviews, by Walpole, Hurd, Reeve, Aikin (later, Mrs Barbauld), Coleridge, Hazlitt, Lamb, Maturin, Scott, Radcliffe, and innumerable anonymous or lesser-known figures. First-phase Gothic (roughly, 1764–1820) is often seen as the occasion or victim of vociferous and often hostile criticism from the outside; but it may be more accurate to say that Gothic fiction had always itself included—or at the very least been framed by—the scrutiny to which it came to be subjected. The critical limits that were applied in order to condemn Gothic novels in particular (rationality, probability, propriety—especially in relation to female conduct—and norms social, formal, and sexual) corresponded to elements that were displayed within or tested by the novels themselves, even if the overall effect of Gothic writing was to allow for the overcoming of those limits. The category of Gothic ought, then, to include the whole critical apparatus out of which the fiction arose and into which it has since expanded, in ways as monstrously productive and unstoppable as its early critics often feared. As Woolf puts it, 'Mrs Radcliffe may vanish, but the craving for the supernatural survives', even if 'It is at the ghosts within us that we shudder, and not at the decaying bodies of barons or the subterranean activities of ghouls.'[15]

READINGS

Horace Walpole, *The Castle of Otranto*

Horace Walpole wrote *The Castle of Otranto* under a mixture of impulses, which together illustrate the movement of the Gothic away from antiquarianism into as yet uncharted psychological territories (see his letters of 5 January 1766 and 9 March 1765). Walpole's assertion of the counter-classical is embodied in the very form his principal supernatural agent takes—grotesque, gigantic, and fragmentary. In *Otranto*'s opening paragraphs, a vast helmet falls from the sky, killing the sickly heir of the Castle on what was to have been his wedding day. His father, Manfred, responds, first, by unjustly imprisoning a youth who is arbitrarily (and absurdly) accused of the crime, and then by himself pursuing his son's widowed bride in defiance of Church law and a sequence of ghostly portents. For this he is punished by mistakenly killing his own daughter and by the eventual loss of Otranto itself, through the revelation of an ancestral crime of usurpation perpetrated by Manfred's family upon Alfonso, the man whose supernatural armoury started the chain of events, and whose true heir is none other than the youth Manfred condemned.

Not only is the Gothic removed to the 'dark ages' (preface to first edition), it also has a 'dark' or prohibited content. In this respect, the work's dream origin, confessed in the letter of 9 March 1765, is entirely characteristic: Walpole's Gothic story is full of taboo acts, which cohere around the figure of the usurper and tyrant, a key convention of the new genre. George E. Haggerty identifies Manfred's pursuit of Isabella through subterranean passages as the archetypal scene of Gothic fiction, which 'in a single image . . . combines the sexual anxiety of a victimized female, the incestuous desire of a libidinous male, the use of the physical features of the castle itself to represent political and sexual entrapment, and an atmosphere deftly rendered to produce terror and gloom'.[16] Manfred's attempts to cling to power impel a reversal of the Oedipal plot, resulting in the slaying or seduction of his children and dependants. However, infanticide conceals or gives way to a fantasy of parricide, as a domestic tyrant is overcome by a masculinity even more gigantic, and Manfred the Bad is toppled by Alfonso the Good, in the shape of the conventional romance hero (and, by the etymology of his name, God's gift), Theodore. At the same time, Manfred emerges as a scapegoat who is being punished for ancestral wrongdoing: the first preface observes that 'the sins of fathers are visited on their children', while Manfred himself histrionically declares, 'I pay the price of usurpation for all!' (ch. 5). And, for all his tyrannical bluster, his desires are constantly (and often comically) frustrated: just as Manfred's biological line dies out, so Walpole initiates the Gothic method of an interrupted and disorderly narrative line.

All this suggests a complex and ambivalent awareness of patriarchal authority. Manfred is by turns a principle of 'terror' (and as such the 'engine' of Gothic fear (first preface)), an (occasional) object of sympathy, and a figure of fun. A transgressive overreacher uttering satanic impieties—'Heaven nor hell shall impede my designs' (ch. 1)—he is also an irascible parent in a mid-life crisis, who is constantly 'relapsing into rage' and sexual indiscretion (ch. 4). It may not be irrelevant that Walpole was much the youngest son of an extremely powerful father, Robert Walpole, Whig Prime Minister and latterly first Earl of Orford, who had fallen from office in 1742, and in 1737, the year in which Horace's much-loved mother died, had married his mistress of long standing. Certainly, power, and the loss of influence, together with an 'incestuous design' (ch. 2), are much on display in *The Castle of Otranto*'s tale of (dis)inheritance and contested ownership.

Walpole establishes the Gothic novel as a product of opposite tendencies, at once primal and artful, primitive and bookishly self-conscious. The first edition of *Otranto* disguised its true author twice over, by posing as a translation, by an English gentleman, from an Italian original of uncertain date, written by a Canon of the Catholic Church. (Surprisingly, some readers were taken in.) The second edition lost the sobriquets of scholarly translator and monastic novelist, and gained the crucial subtitle, 'A Gothic Story', together with a new preface, which classified the work as 'an attempt to blend the two kinds of romance, the ancient and the modern', and claimed for it a precedent in the 'mixed' drama of Shakespeare—to whose five-act form, comic subplot, credulous and insubordinate domestics, prince-in-peasant's clothing, and paternal ghost (after *Hamlet*) the novel is clearly indebted, and whose example licenses the frequently unnerving tonal shifts and the theatrical props of trapdoor, expiring lamp, and 'subterraneous regions', all three of which appear in the first chapter and rapidly became stock devices of the genre.

Modern readers are likely to find Walpole's narrative tonally unstable. His contemporaries tended to miss the comedy, and instead pick up on the fear and sentiment—as Thomas Gray reported of his Cambridge set, *Otranto* 'makes some of us cry a little, and all in general afraid to go to bed o' nights' (letter, 30 December 1764). Those twin strands of Gothic fiction were to be more deftly interwoven by Radcliffe.

Ann Radcliffe, *The Romance of the Forest*

With Radcliffe, Gothic fiction became a craze. Her enormous popularity was associated with a number of innovations. Not the least of these was money. Radcliffe ushered in a new era of publishers' advances, made on the back of circulating-library subscriptions: she was offered £500 for *The Mysteries of Udolpho* (1794), a sum then unprecedented, and £800 for *The Italian*. This market-value ensured that her style was widely imitated, and indeed one can speak, with Scott, of a Radcliffe 'school'.

The Romance of the Forest, which reached a fourth edition by 1795, and was translated into French and Italian, made Radcliffe's reputation. Her third Gothic novel, it testifies to several developments in the genre. For one thing, it incorporates the Gothic Revival: taking refuge in a partly ruined abbey, Radcliffe's Parisian exiles are aware of an extension that 'appeared to have been built in modern times upon a Gothic plan' (vol. I, ch. 2).

Neo-gothic—the retro-chic of which Walpole's *Castle of Otranto* claims, tongue in cheek, to be unaware—is now recognized as part of a layered historical setting, in which the 'Gothic' is as much contemporary as medieval, and the imagining of history becomes one of the motives to Gothic response: 'fancy bore him back to past ages' (vol. I, ch. 2).

Radcliffe's *Romance* is set in mid-seventeenth-century France, but written and published in the immediate aftermath of the French Revolution (1789). In this volatile context, the Marquis de Montalt may readily be seen as a stereotypical corrupt aristocrat of the *ancien régime*. But Radcliffe's Marquis is also a new style of Gothic villain, whose intellectual 'sophistry' shows the bad uses to which 'philosophy' may be put. His rational justification of murder (vol. II, ch. 14), with its conflation of rhetorical and physical violence, makes him the prototype of other 1790s studies in unscrupulous force. In so far as they are allowed to be persuasive, the Marquis's arguments register a growing cultural anxiety about the influence of ideology; while his 'love of pleasure' adds a touch of hedonism to the Gothic villain's customary sex-and-power drives (vol. III, ch. 23). Adeline, for her part, is comparable to Burke's Marie Antoinette, an ideal of womanhood, for whom (male) chivalry is either 'dead' or alive, to whom either the 'sentiment' of respect, or lecherous disrespect, is shown.

In ways that strikingly both resemble and depart from Walpole's experiment, Radcliffe combines two kinds of romance: the sentimental novel and the Gothic adventure, a 'mixed' form linked to the development of what has been called 'female Gothic'. *The Romance of the Forest* presents an especially clear example of the patriarchal trap in which the Gothic heroine—in this case Adeline—finds herself: 'On one side was her father, whose cruelty had already been too plainly manifested; and on the other, the Marquis pursuing her with insult and vicious passion' (vol. II, ch. 8). Yet the heroine's flight from one peril to another gives her a surprisingly active role. Remarkably, too, the *Romance* identifies the Gothic itself with female forms of writing. Adeline's own life-story is included as a first-person narrative. The title-page advertises a novel 'interspersed with pieces of poetry', and their 'author' is for the most part none other than the heroine herself (ahistorically, she writes in a knowledge of eighteenth-century English verse). Female Gothic is associated with a kind of poetic prose. (Radcliffe was christened, by Scott, in response to her second novel, *A Sicilian Romance*, as 'the first poetess of romantic fiction'.) Contemporaries tended to find poetry in her descriptions of landscape. Her models here lay partly in visual art—the rugged scenery of Salvator Rosa, and the idyllic views of Richard Wilson—but her settings also reveal an application to fiction of Edmund Burke's *Philosophical Enquiry into the Origin of our Ideas of the Sublime and Beautiful* (1757). By introducing Burkean aesthetics to the novel (and so to a mass audience), Radcliffe vitally redefined the 'Gothic'. Her landscapes are frequently designed to recognize, for instance, that objects are especially terrible, and imaginings especially vivid, where obscurity, or darkness, denies any clarity of vision or understanding: Gothic fear is partly equated with the pleasurable 'terror' which the *Enquiry* identified as the source of 'sublime' experience, and which overwhelms the mind's powers of reason. In Burke, the 'sublime' and 'beautiful' represent opposed gender ('male' and 'female') as well as aesthetic categories; but in Radcliffe, the sublime is seen in relation to specifically female experience. At times, this experience suggests a displacement of sexuality—Adeline 'thrilled' (or pierced) with a 'pleasing dread' which 'filled all her soul' (vol. I, ch. 2). Elsewhere, by contrast, the 'beauties of nature', to which Adeline is virtuously sensitive, imply a parallel between her beauty and that of the landscape (vol. I, ch. 1): both conform to contemporary taste by being artfully displayed to best advantage—that is, by a partial exposure to the male gaze.

Radcliffean Gothic works by relying on the suggestibility which is assumed to operate in the mind of character and reader alike. As Robert Bisset perceptively observed, in 1800, 'Mrs Radcliffe has not introduced ghosts, but the effects of the belief of ghosts on the human imagination'.[17] This absence of bona fide spectres sharply divides Radcliffe's Gothic from Walpole's (though she did make an exception in her last, posthumously published, novel). It is also linked to her most significant narrative innovation, known as 'explained supernatural-ism': as the *Critical Review* put it, in 1794, 'mysterious terrors are continually exciting in the mind the idea of a supernatural appearance . . . and yet are ingeniously explained by familiar causes'. In solving the vexed issue of the status of the supernatural in fiction, Radcliffe was seen as having been led into another kind of 'improbability', and her tricksy endings become a byword for narrative bathos and deflation: by 1824, a reviewer in the *Edinburgh Magazine* was referring to 'the awkward windings up and lame explanations of Mrs Radcliff's romances'. But a more complex, and more sympathetic, reading than the teleological[18] emerges when attention is focused instead on the ongoing fictional processes, of a continu-ous alternation between rational explanation and irrational suggestion. In characters such as Adeline and La Motte, this divided allegiance is expressed in terms of psychological conflict, as they repeatedly check the impulses they repeatedly fail to control. It is on just such contradictions that Austen capitalized when parodying the Gothic novel and its heroine in *Northanger Abbey*. Austen's irony makes a distinction between heroine and reader; Radcliffe's lack of irony identifies them. The effectiveness of the female Gothic depends upon the reader being able to share in the heroine's superstitious promptings. This identifica-tory process is recognized most fully when Radcliffe uses the trope of discovering an old document. Her manuscript is not (as in Walpole) a discovery made by a fictitious author in a preface which serves to mystify the novel's origins. Rather, it is incorporated into the novel as the discovery of the heroine herself (vol. II, chs. 8–9), and serves ultimately to unravel the mystery of her own origins. It also turns the heroine into a fellow reader, suggesting that Adeline's responses are a mirror for those of Radcliffe's ideal audience, the text a model of Gothic transference and identification.

Matthew Gregory Lewis, *The Monk*

Lewis is a pivotal figure in the history of the Gothic novel. He may have been inspired by Radcliffe (whose influence is felt in the use of epigraphs, verses, dreams, and a usurpation plot impelled by fratricide), but he also rewrites the book. If Radcliffe is the epitome of 'female Gothic', Lewis is the pattern of the 'masculine' form, which, as Alison Milbank observes, features 'plots of transgression of social taboos by an excessive male will, and explorations of the imagination's battle against religion, law, limitation and contingency'.[19] As such, *The Monk* is a precursor of the Romantic satanism of Byron's *Manfred*, and, more obliquely, Shelley's *Frankenstein*. It also heralds an eclectic and continental style of fiction. To 'terror' is added the perverse fascination of 'horror', which Radcliffe rejected, but which had a model in German *Schauerromantik* (literally, 'shudder-romanticism'), and strove to induce disgust as well as fear, repugnance as well as dread, aversion as well as alarm.

The first edition was on the whole well received, but the second, in 1796, created a huge furore, because it was subscribed with the author's name and new status, 'M. G. Lewis, Esq. M.P.'. At the age of 20, 'Monk' Lewis was famous. He was however cautious enough to remove offending passages, on sex and religion, in the revised fourth edition of 1798. (Predictably, the result was that unexpurgated copies were selling at a guinea apiece by 1801.) The main plot, which seems to originate with the Persian poet Sáadi, but which Lewis knew from Steele's *Guardian*, tells of an austere hermit who is tempted into transgression and damnation. In *The Monk*, this plot is much expanded. To some extent, the expansion moves in the direction of the psychological portraiture of Angelo, Shakespeare's priest-turned-statesman, in *Measure for Measure* (whose name Lewis adopts for his Madrid-based Abbot). Mostly, though, it leads to an escalating series of sex crimes, involving everything from incestuous rape and murder to insinuations of necrophilia. Small wonder that in its day *The Monk* was synonymous with 'hyperbolical atrocity'.[20] Beyond the headlines, though, Lewis's interest seems to lie in the spectacular nature of Gothic fiction, in the sense that his novel presents scenes of prurience or voyeurism which in turn implicitly comment upon the reader's own involvement. At the same time, attraction repeatedly turns to repulsion, and excessive lust to excessive disgust (vol. III, ch. 11: 'He felt himself at once repulsed from and attracted towards her, yet could account for neither sentiment'). To twentieth-century eyes, these sensationalist extremes look like the sex-and-death drives of Freudian theory. But they also work, in literary terms, to reinvigorate the Gothic trope of continuously deferred gratification. Lewis reinvents the Gothic method of suspended narration as a sort of sexual odyssey. That carnal appetites are shown to be dulled or blunted by excess could be seen as poetic justice of a kind appropriate to a morality tale. In effect, it is as though Lewis has chosen to base his fiction on the law of diminishing returns which critics pervasively recognized as the (false) economy of the Gothic itself; but which, in his hands, becomes the justification for ever more extreme and taboo situations.

The anti-monastic strain in *The Monk* raises the question of how Lewis approaches the perennial issue of the Gothic novel's attitude to its supernatural appearances. Byron records Lewis's 'mania' for 'the marvellous'. And yet his novel would seem an interesting case of the Gothic being constructed from the extremes of *both* sceptical *and* credulous viewpoints. Disconcertingly, this involves interweaving ludicrous sham-supernaturalisms with lurid appeals to the real thing. That there is a kind of conscious method at work is suggested by Lewis's use of the German Bleeding Nun legend: her history is recounted 'in a tone of burlesqued gravity' by Agnes (vol. II, ch. 4); but Agnes's personation of that history leads to Raymond's actual haunting. That is, a supernatural being is introduced as a tall tale, but then turns up for real, to the terror of all concerned. The sequence crucially disrupts and reverses

Radcliffean Gothic, in which the apparently supernatural yields to natural explanation. Sometimes, Lewis elects to pre-empt the rational response mechanism by making it the preamble to a genuinely supernatural mode. Elsewhere, he plays 'imaginary' off authentic horrors: sounds in the nunnery vaults are thought to be ghosts, or one of the 'miracles' of the St Clare, but turn out to come from Agnes, a real victim, and object, of terror (vol. III, ch. 10). At times, the antitheses of superstition and scepticism are presented as a contradiction in character: Ambrosio scoffs at the maid Jacintha's story of a ghost (vol. III, ch. 9), while at the same time freely accepting the black magic art of raising devils. Meanwhile, at Castle Lindenberg (which is both a mock- and truly haunted house), Lewis breaks with the class-bound convention of Walpole and Radcliffe, whereby the upper crust are relatively immune from the credulity that afflicts their inferiors: Raymond and Agnes are sceptics, but 'the baron, his lady, and Don Gaston . . . agreed in believing the existence of spectres'. A good deal of fun is had at the expense of the credulous (viz. the nuns who listen to Theodore's Gothic stories in vol. III, ch. 8), while the more sophisticated display a consciously Radcliffean attitude—at once 'susceptible of terrors' and made to blush at such weakness when 'their natural and insignificant cause' is discovered (vol. III, ch. 9).

Mary Shelley, *Frankenstein; or, The Modern Prometheus*

Shelley's novel was generated out of the convergence of three powerful influences: her mother, Mary Wollstonecraft, who died shortly after her birth, the author of *A Vindication of the Rights of Woman*; her father, William Godwin, whose rational-anarchist philosophy had a controversial role in the debate surrounding the French Revolution, and whose Jacobin novel-of-ideas, *Things as They Are; or, the Adventures of Caleb Williams*, was a conscious narrative model; and her lover, the poet Percy Bysshe Shelley, whom she came to know, as an unhappily married man, in May 1814.

In *Frankenstein*, superstition and science (electricity, galvanism, vitalism, somnambulism), Gothic magic and rational enquiry (such questions as 'whether man was to be thought merely an instrument' and the possibility of discovering the 'principle of life'), undergo a spectacular fusion. In her Introduction to the third, Standard Novels, edition (1831), Shelley attributed her impulse to write, beginning with the creation-scene itself (first edition, vol. I, ch. 4), to her waking vision of an 'artist' bringing a creature to life, and the horrific implications of his achievement. This daydream may in turn be linked to the death of her own first child, and to the ghost-story competition that was held by the runaway Shelleys and their circle, including Lord Byron, while they were staying on the shores of Lake Geneva in 1816 ('Monk' Lewis later joined the party). As the novel's 1818 title-page indicates, this 'modern' myth of creation has two ancient ones behind it: the Greek god Prometheus, fire-giver and man-maker; and, more potent still, perhaps, the first man—and woman—from Milton's epic retelling of the Christian story of Genesis, in *Paradise Lost*. Genesis and anatomy, alchemy and chemistry, John Milton and Humphry Davy, God and man, the archetypal and the individual, all intersect; and the revolutionary search for perfection through knowledge is told in terms of the age-old code of its forbidden and dangerous pursuit.

As the tale of a human maker, *Frankenstein* subjects Milton's interpretation of Genesis to a number of crucial reversals. The creator has to share the same world as his creature; yet acts as though he were free to abandon his work. For his part, the creature is more mighty than his creator; but is also a hideous distortion of his creator's image, and, as such, a 'one-off', without hope of a companion. In all of this, Shelley may be seen as taking up an antagonistic stance towards Milton's theology, and especially to the power relations it embodies; while at the same time adopting a sympathetic relation to Milton's creatures—Adam and Satan, in particular. Surprisingly, then, Frankenstein's 'monster' becomes as much a creature of sympathy as of horror (compare the reading of *Frankenstein* in the chapter on 'Psychoanalysis').

The monster's narrative, in the central confrontation of the novel (beginning at vol. II, ch. 2), provides clear evidence of the influence of Godwin's thinking. Despite his origins in irrational obsession, the monster explicitly uses the Godwinian method of rational persuasion to claim 'justice' from his creator. He also reveals how, in Godwinian terms, he was not born, but became, evil. Endowed with a capacity for benevolence, he was systematically brutalized by the humans with whom he came in contact; and his treatment is an indictment of society, or 'things as they are'. In this sense, the monster may be seen as a type of the oppressed—a category which includes the rebellious outcast (as Milton's devil is reconceived, in the radical tradition of Godwin and Percy Bysshe Shelley), and the history of female subjection (in Wollstonecraft's understanding of the misogynist tradition, which conceives Eve or 'woman' as the—potentially monstrous—inferior of the male).

Unlike Milton's Adam, Frankenstein's creature is an innocent born into a fallen world—in Godwinian terms, a world of institutionalized injustice. But there are other forces at work, too. The 'monstrosity' of Frankenstein's creature is inherent as well as imposed. Owing to his appearance, Godwin's hopeful rationality is of no avail. His ugliness makes his goodness unrecognizable, even unbearable; and he is contaminated with the anti-social (and anti-heterosexual) instincts of his creator. He is also driven to a diabolic revenge, and to a cycle of retribution of the kind which Percy Bysshe Shelley consistently opposed.

What, then, of the creator, the ambiguous hero of the story? Frankenstein is often, and rightly, seen in relation to Percy Bysshe Shelley—the ardent humanitarian idealist, who, as letters to Godwin record, spent much of his youth in fiery alchemical experimentation. Yet the character may also include traits of Mary herself: in her father's observation, 'Her desire of knowledge is great, and her perseverence in everything she undertakes almost invincible.' Frankenstein registers this kind of daring. His phases of frenzy and lassitude, intoxication and disgust, reflect Romantic ideas about the moods of creative genius. Yet, as a creator of life, he assumes a divine power within human limitations. In so far as Frankenstein stands for an idea of God, the novel implies the scepticism about Christianity that was the common currency of the Shelley circle. But the work also casts grim reflections on the perfectibility theses with which Shelley's atheist father and lover sought to replace the Christian God. And in these twin criticisms it is possible to detect the ambivalence with which she regards not only traditional religion, but also theories of man-made redemption—and, indeed, the secular Enlightenment values of the whole French Revolutionary era.

Frankenstein and his creation repeatedly echo or mirror one another. In their relationship lies the core, antagonistic double or dualism around which the novel is structured. In crucial ways the narrative also doubles back on itself. That is, the resemblances or mirrorings often involve reversals or inversions. The 'pursuit' theme, which Shelley skilfully adapts from *Caleb Williams*, is a case in point. Frankenstein's pursuit of knowledge transforms into his pursuit by 'remorse and guilt'. The monster, meanwhile, turns from innocent victim to serial murderer. Most of all, in their dealings with one another, the roles of master and slave, pursuer and pursued, are transposed.

In Shelley's reinvigoration of the genre, the Gothic is made to 'speak to the mysterious fears of our nature'—and it has gone on doing so ever since, latterly in the forms of mass entertainment and mass anxiety. The myth has played host to every cultural shift, from race theory to genetic engineering (Frankenstein foods). The 1831 Introduction finds in the creation-scene an analogy for the making of the novel itself; and so allows it to reflect upon the reception of the literary 'monster', Gothic itself. Shelley's monster, who is created out of human and animal parts, may bear a relation to her own complex assimilation of influences. Part of the novel's enduring power, however, lies in the way it seems to resist this amalgamation, by conducting an experiment in synthesis which goes horribly wrong, and which instead results in radical disharmony and dismemberment: the novel speaks indirectly but powerfully of the stresses and incompatibilities in the rational and Romantic traditions of which she was the inheritor.

FURTHER READING

Birkhead, Edith, *The Tale of Terror: A Study of the Gothic Romance* (London: Constable, 1921). Informative history which finds the roots of modern Gothic in antiquity, and makes room, alongside Walpole and Radcliffe, Lewis and Maturin, for Barbauld and Drake, for Beckford's oriental tales, Godwin's Rosicrucian novels, for satires of Gothic, and for Scott.

Clery, E. J., *The Rise of Supernatural Fiction, 1762–1800* (Cambridge: Cambridge University Press, 1995). Cultural history of the later eighteenth century, which relates the rise of supernatural fiction to the growth of consumerism.

——and Miles, Robert (eds.) *Gothic Documents: A Sourcebook 1700–1820* (Manchester and New York: Manchester University Press, 2000). Wide-ranging selection of secondary texts and excerpts arranged in six handy thematic sections with further subsections.

Ellis, Kate Ferguson, *The Contested Castle: Gothic Novels and the Subversion of Domestic Ideology* (Urbana, Ill., and Chicago: University of Illinois Press, 1989). Feminist study which shows Gothic novels to be alarmingly, or empoweringly, true to the domestic life of their time.

Ellis, Markman, *The History of Gothic Fiction* (Edinburgh: Edinburgh University Press, 2000). Up-to-date historical survey which takes in Walpole, Radcliffe, Lewis, Brockden Brown, Shelley, Byron, Stoker; vampires, zombies, and slaves.

Gamer, Michael, *Romanticism and the Gothic: Genre, Reception, and Canon Formation* (Cambridge: Cambridge University Press, 2000). Historicist account of the Gothic, as a genre that was defined by its producers, consumers, and critics; and as the unacknowledged low underside to high Romanticism.

Howells, Ann, *Love, Mystery, and Misery: Feeling in Gothic Fiction* (London: Athlone Press, 1978). Intelligent history, ranging from Radcliffe to Bronte, via Lewis, Austen, Maturin, and Minerva Press Fiction, 1796–1819.

Kilgour, Maggie, *The Rise of the Gothic Novel* (London and New York: Routledge, 1995). A thematic and authorial history, which usefully summarizes different models of reading the Gothic while itself grappling with the difficulty of providing a definition. Does for Gothic what Ian Watt has done for the 'rise' of the novel in general.

Miles, Robert, *Gothic Writing 1750–1820: A Genealogy* (1993; 2nd edn., Manchester and New York: Manchester University Press, 2002). Lucid Foucault-influenced study ('discourse-centred' as opposed to 'author-centred', 'genealogical' rather than 'historical'), which defines Gothic as both an 'aesthetic' which 'pre-existed, and then coincided with, Gothic writing', and 'a carnivalesque mode for representations of the fragmented subject'.

Moers, Ellen, *Literary Women* (1976; London: Women's Press, 1986). The originator of 'Female Gothic' (Part I, ch. 5) and Gothic 'Heroinism' (Part II, ch. 7): *Frankenstein* is a monstrous 'birth myth'; Radcliffe's fiction 'a device to send maidens on distant and exciting journeys'.

Norton, Rictor (ed.) *Gothic Readings: The First Wave 1764–1840* (London and New York: Leicester University Press, 2000). Extracts and samples, designed to introduce students to both long classics and lesser known works.

Punter, David (ed.) *The Literature of Terror: A History of Gothic Fictions from 1795 to the present day*, 2 vols., 2nd edn. (London and New York: Longman, 1996). An important and comprehensive study which (drawing on Marx and Freud) analyses Gothic as an expression of a collective psyche, shaped by social and historical forces; and, in a final chapter, works 'Towards a Theory of the Gothic'.

——*The Blackwell Companion to the Gothic* (Oxford: Blackwell, 2000). A good starting-point, treating Gothic in history and in Europe, in its 'original' phase (including drama), in its nineteenth- and twentieth-century transmutations, and in theory, genre, and modern culture.

Richter, David H., *The Progress of Romance: Literary Historiography and the Gothic Novel* (Columbus, Oh.: Ohio State University Press, 1996). Argues for a reading of Gothic novels based in reception theory, and against the historical-allegorical models of interpretation which link them to, for example, the French Revolution (Ronald Paulson) or the position of women (Kate Ferguson Ellis).

Sedgwick, Eve Kosofky, *The Coherence of Gothic Conventions* (1980; London and New York: Methuen, 1986). A theoretically informed close reading of Gothic conventions, and the first attempt to unpick the relationship between 'surface' and 'depth' in criticism of the Gothic. Extends to De Quincey and the Brontës.

WEB LINKS

http://www.litgothic.com/index_fl.html
A handsome gathering of resources for literary Gothic, including e-texts and web links.
http://www.wlu.ca/~wwwgac/
Website for the International Gothic Association; membership gains subscription to the twice yearly international journal *Gothic Studies* (Manchester University Press).

NOTES

1. *Spectator*, no. 419 (1 July 1712).

2. Victor Sage, 'Gothic Novel', in Marie Mulvey-Roberts (ed.), *The Handbook to Gothic Literature* (Basingstoke: Macmillan, 1998), pp. 81–9: p. 82.

3. *Spectator*, nos. 44, 110, 419 (20 Apr., 6 July 1711, 1 July 1712).

4. Horace Walpole, *Anecdotes of Painting in England*, 4 vols. (Strawberry-Hill, 1762–71); David S. Miall, 'Gothic Fiction', in Duncan Wu (ed.), *A Companion to Romanticism*, (Oxford: Blackwell, 1997), pp. 345–54: p. 346.

5. 'The Ghost', *The Aberdeen Magazine*, 3 (Aug. 1798), 369–70.

6. See *A Philosophical Enquiry into the Origin of our Ideas of the Sublime and Beautiful* (1757), Part IV, sect. xiv.

7. *The Haunted Castle: A Study of the Elements of English Romanticism* (1927; New York: Gordon Press, 1974), pp. 387–8 n. 307.

8. Johnson agreed to serve on a committee set up to investigate the phenomenon in 1762. For 'Scott's Experiences in Haunted Chambers', see *Modern Philology*, 30 (1932), 103 ff.

9. *The Rise of Supernatural Fiction, 1762–1800* (Cambridge: Cambridge University Press, 1995), pp. 17, 10.

10. See Victor Sage, *Horror Fiction in the Protestant Tradition* (London: Macmillan, 1988), pp. 26–39, 140–73.

11. Virginia Woolf, 'Gothic Romance', in *The Essays of Virginia Woolf*, ed. Andrew McNeillie, 4 vols. (London: Hogarth Press, 1986–), iii. 305.

12. Robert Miles, *Gothic Writing 1750–1820: A Genealogy* (1993; Manchester and New York: Manchester University Press, 2002), i. 3.

13. *Spectator*, no. 419 (1 July 1712).

14. *The Literature of Terror: A History of Gothic Fictions from 1795 to the Present Day*, 2 vols., 2nd edn. (London and New York: Longman, 1996), p. 54.

15. Virginia Woolf, 'Across the Border', in *Essays of Virginia Woolf*, ed. McNeillie, ii. 218; 'Gothic Romance', ibid. iii. 307.

16. George E. Haggerty, *Gothic Fiction/Gothic Form* (University Park, Pa.: Pennsylvania State University Press, 1989), p. 223.

17. Robert Bisset, *Douglas; or, The Highlander*, 4 vols. (London: Anti-Jacobin Press, 1800), i. xxi.

18. A reading that is produced by looking to the novels' conclusions.

19. Alison Milbank, 'Female Gothic', in Mulvey-Roberts (ed.), *Handbook to Gothic Literature*, p. 54.

20. Richard Payne Knight, *An Analytical Inquiry into the Principles of Taste* (2nd edn., 1805), Part III, ch. 1, sect. 42.

31 | The fragment

Sophie Thomas

In March of 1818, an impressive collection of architectural fragments arrived on English shores, aboard HMS *Weymouth*, from the Roman ruins of Leptis Magna on the Libyan coast of North Africa. The contents of this shipment were listed as having included an extensive assortment of granite and marble columns, capitals, pedestals, pieces of cornice, inscribed slabs, and various fragments of sculptured figures (for example, 'Statue in halves Head and Feet deficient'). Also part of the shipment, taken on board at Malta, was the bust of Ramses (now in the British Museum) that inspired Shelley's poem 'Ozymandias'. Such large-scale plundering of ruins abroad was not unusual at this time—this is in fact only a few years after Lord Elgin acquired a number of fragmentary marbles from the Parthenon in Athens. For the early nineteenth century, though, the cultural importance of these bits and pieces can be inferred from two things that happened to them next. First of all, nothing: they languished in a disorderly heap in the courtyard of the British Museum for eight years. Then, in 1826, King George IV's architect, Wyatt, came up with a plan to erect them in the king's gardens, on the southern shores of Virginia Water, an artificial lake in Windsor Great Park. Wyatt refashioned them into what he referred to as his 'Temple of Augustus', in which he arranged the fragments to convey the impression of a temple in ruins, suggestively submerged in the landscape, through which the king could pass on his private ride to the lake.

Two aspects of the contemporary attitude to fragments can be deduced from this story: confusion, on the one hand, and pleasure on the other. Confusion not only because the king's men were at a loss as to what to do with that assortment of ruins—what indeed can one do with something that is not complete?—but also because fragments are, by definition, disturbing entities. They play upon the imagination by promising or suggesting more than what they are, while reminding the viewer or reader that what they promise can never be recovered or fully experienced. Fragments simultaneously raise and disavow the possibility of totality and wholeness, thus becoming suitable figures for all manner of disruption and discontinuity. The more evocative aspects of the fragment may even be felt as threatening and haunting, perhaps especially where the fragment in question is a ruin: for ruins bring us an element of the past embedded or locked into the present, suggesting the uncanny suspension of time and history. The solution in the case of the Leptis Magna ruins was finally to make those architectural fragments into a folly, to harness ambivalent fragmentariness and use it playfully.

Fragments, fashion, and fakery

This was certainly in keeping with the more frivolous side of the fashion for fragments that had emerged distinctively in the eighteenth century, when the wealthy regularly erected sham ruins in their gardens for picturesque effect. The very idea, of course, of building a ruin is intriguingly paradoxical. All ruins require a kind of double vision, whereby they are perceived both in their current ruinous state and in their formerly whole one. A sham ruin, however, had to be predicated on a building that had never actually existed, and fooling the viewer was an important measure of success. This vogue had a direct literary equivalent: not only were fragmentary texts increasingly published and read on their own terms, but sometimes, as in Thomas Chatterton's *Rowley* poems of 1777, which claimed to be the recovered work of a fifteenth-century monk, found secreted away in a rural church, they were actually hoaxes or forgeries— modern compositions faked up to look like ancient texts. Another good example of this was James Machperson's *Ossian* poems, which purported to be the rediscovered and translated relics of a blind Scottish poet from the third century (see *Oxford Companion to the Romantic Age*, pp. 448, 630). These were popular texts well before the controversy that followed upon the discovery that they were hoaxes.

The taste for fragmentary forms had become so widespread that in 1813 Francis Jeffrey, editor of the *Edinburgh Review*, was prompted to remark that 'the greater part of polite readers would now no more think of sitting down to a whole Epic than to a whole ox'.[1] Marjorie Levinson, in her study of the Romantic fragment poem, has argued that the phenomenon of the hoax poems contributed to the popularization of the fragment, by bringing out its potential literariness. She suggests that it helped to cultivate a sympathetic readership, one willing to engage creatively in the reading process as an act of imaginative completion. It was no doubt the case that by the end of the eighteenth century fragments had become marketable in a way that made it possible for serious writers to publish their own literary remains while they were still very much alive. We should keep in mind, though, not only the importance of the ruin industry (and its attendant *sentiment des ruines*) for fuelling this fashion, but also the impact of the popular sentimental novels of the eighteenth century, which skilfully made use of the fragment for both comic and emotional effect.

In one of many amusing episodes in Laurence Sterne's *A Sentimental Journey* of 1768 (a text, like Sterne's *Tristram Shandy*, that is thoroughly fragmentary and digressive), Yorick's servant brings him his butter upon a bit of paper, which, once turned over, is found to have upon it a fragment of narrative in faded old French. The novel's hero, thoroughly engrossed by this dramatic tale (which Sterne includes verbatim for the reader), translates it as far as he can—but it is soon revealed that the continuation, contained on a second sheet of paper, has been wrapped around a bouquet of flowers and given by the servant to his lover, who in her faithlessness has already passed it on to another, and so on. Narrative suspense, like erotic impulse, must remain undischarged. In a similar vein, Henry Mackenzie's *The Man of Feeling*, of 1771, is entirely made up of scraps of found manuscript, which the fictive editor must arrange—and indeed rescue, for example, from use as gun wadding. Digressions, strategic ellipses, and the interpolation of apparently unrelated stories are meta-fictional devices of long standing; the explicit use of fragments in sentimental novels, though, emphasized (and often satirized) qualities of spontaneity and immediacy, values much privileged by the eighteenth-century cult of Sensibility (see *Oxford Companion to the Romantic Age*, pp. 102–14). The fragment was thus (artfully) deployed as a consummately artless form.

The ruin and the unfinished

Because it is a spatial object, a ruin is a particularly accessible and familiar form of the fragmentary. It illustrates nicely the primary definition of 'fragment' in the *Oxford English Dictionary*, as 'a broken off, detached, or incomplete part . . . a part remaining when the rest is lost or destroyed'.[2] Like a fragmentary piece of antique sculpture, the ruin generally presents a historical object eroded by the effects of time and chance, by the activity of man and/or nature. The contemplation of ruins is often construed as a melancholy activity—one which (like fragments in general) invites the viewer to reflect on the relation of part to whole, presence to absence, and present to past. Ruins particularly evoke an awareness of past accomplishment and present loss. This is especially the case for classical Greek and Roman architecture and sculpture, which are seen to embody particular aesthetic and cultural ideals that were still potent—indeed whose potency was renewed, even rediscovered—in the period (see *Oxford Companion to the Romantic Age*, pp. 539–40).

A good example is the statue of the Venus de Milo: unearthed in 1820 by a peasant digging in his field, on the island of Melos, the statue was immediately hailed as the finest example of a nude female figure to survive from Greek antiquity. The statue, however, was further damaged during the diplomatic fracas that followed its discovery—and its final arrival in Paris was greeted by competing schemes for its restoration, founded upon varying (but equally passionately held) views of the whole as it *must have been*, and often based upon the ambiguous evidence of a few spare parts unearthed at the same time. While the statue enthralled successive generations of Romantic writers and artists, controversy raged throughout the nineteenth century over questions of its dating, its precise provenance, and the mode, as well as the desirability, of its reconstruction.[3]

Fig. 9 'The Artist Overwhelmed by the Grandeur of Antique ruins', by Henry Fuseli.

Ruins such as the Venus, however, represent only one kind of fragment: a material and spatial one that we tend to associate with the past. Readers of Romantic-period literature encounter a surprising number of canonical literary texts that are fragmentary for many different reasons: Coleridge's 'Kubla Khan' and 'Christabel'—even his *Biographia Literaria* which was undertaken in the first instance as a preface to a volume of poems; Wordsworth's *Prelude*—also intended as a preface, to his incomplete work *The Recluse*; Keats's *Hyperion* and *The Fall of Hyperion*, both incomplete attempts to write on the same subject; Shelley's *The Triumph of Life*—cut short, with terrible irony, by his death. Any full edition of the poetic works of period authors reveals a surprising number simply entitled 'fragment', and the list above is only a partial one, intended to present a range of possibilities for which the second *Oxford English Dictionary* definition of 'fragment' would be apposite: 'an extant portion of a written work which as a whole is lost; a portion of work left uncompleted by its author; a part of anything uncompleted'.

In most cases, rather than being the remnants of past wholes, such fragmentary texts held out the promise of future completion; and although their authors had every intention of finishing them, that completion often became either practically or inherently impossible. Coleridge's 'Christabel' is a case in point. Though compared by a contemporary reviewer to a 'mutilated statue, the beauty of which can only be appreciated by those who have knowledge or imagination sufficient to complete the idea of the whole composition', the poem is in fact not one fragment, but an assemblage or sequence of fragments.[4] To each of its two main parts, written at a three-year interval, Coleridge appended concluding poems that were, in one case at least, composed for an entirely different occasion. As in the case of the Venus de Milo, the problems are thus intensified by the presence of spare parts that the whole cannot readily assimilate. Readers of the poem, moreover, have often remarked upon an apparent gap or void lurking somewhere in the conception as well as the execution of the poem—something not just missing but also concealed. Its Gothic central drama, of the encounter of the virtuous young Christabel with the spell-binding and demonic figure of Geraldine, whom she encounters while praying at midnight in the woods, is not only left unresolved, but also inflected throughout by paralysis, anomaly, and a sense of things disturbingly out of place.

For reasons arising arguably from the poem itself, Coleridge found himself unable to go on. And yet, like the case of the Venus de Milo, projected endings abound and the poem has always invited speculation not only about *if*, but about *how*, it could continue. Although Wordsworth would deny that Coleridge ever had a specific conclusion in mind, a number of phantom endings—by turns appealing and implausible—have been passed down by Coleridge's son Derwent, and his biographer James Gillman. Coleridge, for his part, persistently claimed to have the whole poem in his head, and attached a brief preface to the poem to this effect when he first published it in 1816: 'as, in my very first conception of the tale, I had the whole present to my mind, with the wholeness, no less than the liveliness of a vision; I trust I shall be able to embody in verse the three parts yet to come'.[5] In spite of this optimism, it is clear that Coleridge ultimately felt himself to be thwarted or blocked by the poem's central 'Idea', which he identified as 'the most difficult, I think, that can be attempted to Romantic Poetry—I mean witchery by daylight'.[6]

Aesthetic and antiquarian contexts

We have already seen how the eighteenth century regarded and valued the ruin as a picturesque motif. Fragmentariness comes up often in the work of key theorists of the picturesque (see *Oxford Companion to the Romantic Age*, pp. 646–7). William Gilpin, for example, argued that the ideally picturesque landscape included varied and contrasting terrain and partial concealments of the view, while suggesting intricate (even rough) surfaces, motion, and change. Nothing completed this 'picture' more effectively, however, than a fortuitously located ruin—'the elegant relics of ancient architecture; the ruined tower, the Gothic arch, the remains of castles, and abbeys'—with its evocative antiquarian appeal.[7] But the fragment found a place in other central aesthetic discourses of the eighteenth century, most notably in that of the sublime (see *Oxford Companion to the Romantic Age*, p. 723). The fragment is related to the sublime in so far as it represents what eludes representation, and conveys a limitlessness that cannot be reduced to a concrete, finite, or present object. Edmund Burke, in his influential treatise of 1757, identified obscurity, vastness, infinity, and terror as key producers of sublime effects. The first three of these particularly relate to situations in which the whole is impossible to see or grasp, where boundaries or limits have been effaced or obscured. Burke also argued that a pleasurable experience of the infinite could be aroused by an unfinished object, such as an artist's sketch, because 'the imagination is entertained with the promise of something more, and does not acquiesce in the present object of the sense'.[8]

The pursuit of picturesque scenery and sublime experience fuelled the tourist industry both at home and abroad; antiquarian interests similarly encouraged the commodification and domestication of various fragmentary forms (see *Oxford Companion to the Romantic Age*, pp. 328–38). At home, antiquarianism popularized an interest in the historical features of the English landscape, but it had a literary component too, for example in Percy's *Reliques of Ancient English Poetry*, a compilation inspired largely by Macpherson's purported Ossian poems, or in Walter Scott's ballad collecting. The impulse to collect demonstrates the power of part objects to represent, even recover, lost cultures through their artefacts. The profusion and popularity of sculpture galleries in the eighteenth century attests, in a similar vein, to the broad interest among the wealthy in acquiring and displaying objects, relics, from their experience abroad on the Grand Tour. This demonstration of taste and cultural authority encouraged a flourishing trade in casts and copies, but it underlay serious collecting, such as that of Charles Townley, whose extensive gallery of classical marbles was purchased by the

British Museum in 1805 (see *Oxford Companion to the Romantic Age*, pp. 187–97). Perhaps the most momentous episode from this period, however, was Lord Elgin's acquisition, as controversial then as now, of marbles from the Parthenon. He collected various fragments of figures and friezes from the site, with the permission of the Turks who then controlled Athens, and he subsequently offered them for sale to the English government. It is likely that this expensive venture saved them from destruction, but it was denounced by many at the time—by Byron for example in *The Curse of Minerva*—as an act of vandalism.

Responses

The prominent place of the fragment in the Romantic period is linked to a wide range of cultural and philosophical preoccupations—from changing aesthetic ideals to increasing historical self-consciousness. In many instances, ruin and fragmentation are themes rather than physical features of the work. They may be linked to the aspirations and limitations of the human condition. Their presence may also reflect an acute awareness of one's own historical moment. Here, a sense of melancholy, and conservative nostalgia, may well be implicated; on the other hand, the ruin may be seen more positively as a sign that decline is an inevitable feature of oppressive, authoritarian, institutions (the monastery, the baronial pile), and may reorient the viewer's thoughts towards ideas of progress and change. As Anne Janowitz's has shown in her study, *England's Ruins*, the ruin motif in English poetry has important political and historical dimensions; it has done much to shape British national identity, and to encourage nationalist feeling—feeling of the very kind now, ironically, prompting Greece to argue for the return of the Elgin marbles.

Keats's sonnet, 'On Seeing the Elgin Marbles', charts the poet's reaction to his first sight of the fragmentary sculptures, to which his friend Haydon memorably introduced him in 1817. The marbles epitomize the achievement of classical art, but the poem, while implicitly celebrating their impossible perfection, is not about how they look, but rather about thoughts of death and poetic inadequacy. The broken sculptures are, it seems, experienced by the poet as a source of distress: these 'dim-conceived glories of the brain' (l. 9) are oppressively burdensome. Human mortality 'weighs heavily . . . like unwilling sleep' (l. 2); the poet sees in them heights ('each imagined pinnacle and steep | Of godlike hardship'(ll. 3–4)) that his inevitable death will prevent him from scaling. In his distress, he compares himself to 'a sick eagle', that can only look impotently at the sky, powerless and marginalized in his own domain. The poem's sestet reflects pointedly on the force of such fragments ('these wonders'), by linking the sense of disturbance they evoke—'a most dizzy pain'—to the mingling of beauty and decay, to prized objects and their wasting: 'Grecian grandeur with the rude | Wasting of old Time' (ll. 11–14).

Fig. 10 Fragments of the Elgin marbles.

By contrast, Shelley's sonnet 'Ozymandias' presents not the force but the farce of the fragment: impotence is not the poet's problem, but that of the tyrant, who builds himself up (literally) and believes he is immortal. Inscribed, with terrible irony, on the pedestal upon which his massive statue once stood, is the declaration 'My name is Ozymandias, King of Kings, | Look on my Works, ye Mighty, and despair!' (ll. 10–11). Ozymandias derives from a Greek version of the name for the Egyptian pharaoh, Ramses II, and it is alleged that Shelley's poem was inspired by the sight of the colossal granite head of the pharaoh, which was hauled across the desert from the temple at Thebes, brought to England with the ruins of Leptis Magna, and put on display in the British Museum. In the sonnet, the statue's frowning face, with its 'sneer of cold command' (l. 5) lies shattered and half sunk in sand; his 'vast and trunkless' (l. 2) legs still stand, looking faintly ridiculous, but 'nothing beside remains' (l. 12) in the unfrequented expanse of desert in which he is said to lie. The artist is cannier than the ruler in this vignette, as the work of the sculptor, who 'well those passions read' (l. 6), has outlasted the works of the pharaoh himself. The fragments here function as an ironic warning against the dangers of self-aggrandizement, as well as a reminder of the evitable decline and fall of empires. But perhaps there is also an element of satire in the lightness of the poem's treatment of its subject, directed against the melancholic view of the ruin as the repository of inaccessible truths, one that leads to the veneration of old tyrannies (on Keats and Shelley, see also the chapter on 'The sonnet').

Form or genre?

Shelley and Keats's sonnets enable us to see how a preoccupation with fragments operates in a broader cultural context, one that includes art, architecture, and archaeology. But to what extent can the fragment be considered a distinct form or genre in Romantic writing? From sentimental novels to canonical Romantic poems, we have seen examples of works planned and executed as fragments, which suggests at least a certain generic coherence—one that could extend to literary texts whose fragmentation, though circumstantial or accidental, nevertheless features prominently in the published work. Such is the prevalence of fragments in the Romantic period, that one commentator has claimed that the fragment should be regarded as the 'ultimate' Romantic form—'ultimate in the sense that it matches Romantic ideals and tone as fully and completely as the closed couplet matches the ideals of eighteenth-century neoclassicism' (see also the 'Introduction').[9]

On the surface, the fragment seems the epitome of minor or marginal forms. Maxims, aphorisms, anecdotes, *pensées*, marginalia—all depend, to different degrees, on the relationship of contraction (of expression) to unfolding (of meaning). The long tradition of such writing, from Montaigne's essays, to Pascal's *Pensées*, and the English and French moralists (Shaftesbury, La Rochefoucauld, Chamfort) informs the use of fragments in a deliberate manner that takes positive advantage of what might otherwise be the result of contingency and accident. This tradition stands behind the more radical use of the fragment made by the German writers of the Jena circle (chiefly the Schlegel brothers, and Novalis) who made it a central feature of their literary theory and practice. In their view, the fragment was the Romantic genre par excellence, and, appropriately, their arguments were made in series of remarkable philosophical fragments published in their journal, the *Athenaeum*.

Many of these fragments convey a reflection (often ironically stated) on the fragment itself, and thus on the practice of their authors: 'Many of the works of the ancients have become fragments. Many modern works are fragments as soon as they are written' (*Athenaeum Fragment* 24). Or: 'In poetry too, every whole can be a part and every part really a whole' (*Critical Fragment* 14). Written as a series (not one but many: a collection even) of evidently complete statements, their fragments urge the independence of the fragment from other forms: 'A fragment, like a miniature work of art, has to be entirely isolated from the surrounding world and be complete in itself like a hedgehog' (*Athenaeum Fragment* 206).[10] The *Athenaeum* fragments play explicitly on a dynamic of complete incompletion in so far as each fragment is thought to enfold completion and incompletion within itself. In spite of their individual distinctiveness, these fragments must also be seen to add up (though not in a straightforward or teleological way). They are more than straightforward aphoristic statements, since they intermix the generic conventions of the aphorism with inherently inconclusive reflections—sketches, perhaps, of a systematic philosophy of literature. Even more precisely, the work of the Jena circle puts the very possibility of the whole into question, while celebrating the fragment as the only effective mode of engagement with a subject that exceeds presentation: an ideal form for the Ideal, so to speak, the elusive 'literary absolute'.

The theoretical problems and enticements of the fragment were an important part of German Romantic discourse: less so in England, in spite of the proliferation and popularity of fragmentary works there. Obviously there is a great deal of difference between the fragments of the *Athenaeum* and the fragment of *The Prelude*. Many recent critical works on the fragment, such as Marjorie Levinson's *The Romantic Fragment Poem* and Elizabeth Wanning Harries's *The Unfinished Manner*, work hard to distinguish different kinds of fragments from one another. Levinson's taxonomy includes the true, the deliberate, the completed, and the dependent fragment; Harries asserts that we must distinguish the 'consciously generic' fragments prevalent in the later eighteenth century from, on the one hand, those of Schlegel (dismissed as merely 'pithy, ironic aphorisms'), and, on the other, those high-Romantic fragments that derive from 'some disproportion between idea and execution'—those ambitious poems conceived 'in terms that made conclusion impossible'.[11]

Finally, though, it is important to think about the characteristics that all fragments share, particularly since these bear directly—and disruptively—on the question of genre. All fragments occupy an ambivalent space between parts and wholes: as both more than the part and less than the whole, they belong to neither. By definition, they are what disturbs categorization, even such categorization of the fragment as a form. If the fragment's mode of fulfilment is *other* than through the unified whole, if it functions on the basis of deferral, interruption, or what Maurice Blanchot refers to as 'unworking', then it is precisely what *deforms* form. The fragment is the 'form' of formlessness. As a figure for insufficiency or cessation, it constitutes (if any) the genre of the nearly: nearly a genre. This has implications for the reading of fragments, as they are arguably indexes of the unreadable, but also for literary criticism. Hans-Jost Frey, in his study *Interruptions*, asserts that literary scholarship and the fragment are actually incompatible. The fragment, as that which interrupts meaning, and whose structure is an 'inexplicable interruption', undermines the distinctions that criticism depends on, such as a clear sense of the limits and borders of texts—of what is inside or outside a text, of what marks it off for the purposes of study. Understanding the fragment (which for Frey always means integrating it, making it into a whole) has the effect of suppressing fragmentariness, since it creates 'context' where relations insistently break off.

The afterlife of the Romantic fragment

In spite of the challenge the fragment presents for criticism, over recent decades a number of works, such as those by Thomas McFarland, Marjorie Levinson, and Anne Janowitz, have resituated the fragment as central to Romantic concerns. Where once literary critics emphasized the importance of the organic whole in Romantic aesthetic ideology, we now privilege the fragmentary and the discontinuous. One might suggest here that shifts in critical fashion reconstitute their object of study. Although many of the most decisive theoretical interventions of recent centuries directly engage either the question or the form of the fragment, certainly part of the current taste for fragments can be derived from the impact of post-structuralist theory, where the problems for signification presented by fragments illuminate features and effects (dispersion, unworking, discontinuity) of textuality more broadly. Moreover, many key concepts for deconstruction entail the logic of the fragment.

Does the fact that the fragment is unfinished mean that we will never be finished with it? The Jena Romantics advanced the view of Romantic poetry as perpetually in the process of self-achieving, but never achieved in the sense of being finished, fixed, or finite: 'the romantic kind of poetry is still in the state of becoming; that, in fact, is its real essence: that it should forever be becoming and never perfected' (*Athenaeum Fragment* 116).[12] How, then, does an unfinished Romanticism relate or extend to the concerns of the present? Philippe Lacoue-Labarthe and Jean-Luc Nancy have argued that the Romantic project is still underway: 'Romanticism will always be more than a period ... in fact, it has not yet stopped in-completing the period it began.'[13]

Romantic assumptions, in their view, still govern current literary-critical and theor- etical practices. Or, to put it differently, one could argue that the prominence of the fragment in Romanticism is a response to the dilemmas of representation—a dilemma to which Romantic writers responded, and with which we are still preoccupied.

If the fragment directs us, finally, towards the future, it is only fitting here to con- sider a final example that evokes (but with a difference) Wyatt's 'Temple of Augustus' at Virginia Water, with which we began. In the park at Ermenonville near Paris, where Rousseau is buried, is to be found a 'Temple of Philosophy', modelled on the Temple of Vesta at Tivoli. What first appears a ruin, with some of its fragments strewn around it, is in fact only half-built: those stones on the ground are waiting to be erected. The names of six Enlightenment philosophers are inscribed on the temple's columns (Newton, Descartes, Voltaire, Rousseau, William Penn, Montesquieu), along with a Latin word characterizing each. Several spaces, however, are left blank, awaiting the names of those to come, future philosophers who will accomplish what remains impossible: the 'completion' of all knowledge. The temple as a whole is dedicated, somewhat contra- dictorily, to Montaigne, 'who had said everything'. The keyword there is perhaps 'had': all *had* been said, but now, everything remains to be said (again).

READING: Samuel Taylor Coleridge, 'Kubla Khan'

Part or whole?

Coleridge's best-known fragment poem, 'Kubla Khan', is thought to have been written in 1798, during the productive period of the *Lyrical Ballads* project, a period that included 'The Rime of the Ancient Mariner' and 'Christabel'.[14] There are, indeed, some notable similarities between 'Christabel' and 'Kubla Khan'. Both were first published along with 'The Pains of Sleep' in a slim volume of 1816—itself a fragment, it has been noted, of a proper book. More significantly, both poems share a distinctive (and disjunctive) two-part structure, prefaced by a lengthy prose note describing the history of the poems' composition, that introduces the theme of fragmentation, and alerts the reader to the author's intention, eventually, to complete the work. In the early published version of the preface to 'Christabel', Coleridge confidently claimed, as we have seen, that he had the whole poem in mind and would one day write it. In the more lengthy preface Coleridge added to 'Kubla Khan', he made no such claim: the preface tells the story of the loss of his vision, thanks to the untimely visit of the man from Porlock. Interestingly, though, 'Kubla Khan' explicitly projects, in the very terms of the poem, the existence of a *potentially* comprehendible whole (the possibility of a unifying poetic vision is at least one of its major themes), while 'Christabel' does not.

The fragment's most characteristic feature, as I have argued above, is its ambiguous location between the part and the whole: it is, at the same time, more than the part and yet less than the whole. Readings of 'Kubla Khan' have been thoroughly preoccupied by this problem. The poem has been assailed with competing claims for its wholeness, its partialness, its partial wholeness, and because its status as fragment is so much debated, the poem can be said to display the essential ambivalence of the fragment. In its own time, its fragmentary status was either cause for outright dismissal (as Hazlitt famously complained, 'The fault of Mr Coleridge is that he comes to no conclusion'), or, occasionally, open lament ('Still, if Mr Coleridge's two hundred lines were all of equal merit with the following which he has produced, we are ready to admit that he has reason to be grieved at their loss').[15] In ours, the poem has been appreciated as much for its fragmentariness as for the 'wholeness' of its remains, though each perspective depends upon the other, by contrast, for its explanatory force. In this we see that the two perspectives are closely intertwined: necessary parts, even, of the same view.

Clearly it is not so much the poem itself as its relation to the preface that makes the poem such an exemplary fragment. Generations of critics and readers have found the poem formally satisfying in spite (or perhaps because) of its enticing, but partial, articulation of visionary experience. The poem has been often read as the symbolic part of an unavailable but promising whole. The addition of the preface, however, complicates matters: so much a literary, self-conscious fiction in its own right, it makes an enormous difference to how we understand the poem. In describing the genesis of the poem, the preface establishes the conditions for its reading. By identifying and even re-enacting key themes such as the power of poetic vision and the loss of inspiration, the content of the preface further complicates those themes. Superficially, 'Kubla Khan' becomes a fragment poem because the preface claims that it is. But the close connection between preface and poem makes it apparent that Coleridge is not simply, or only, providing an inventive explanation for the poem's relative incompletion. Rather, he is responding to tensions, or difficulties, present in the poem itself—tensions that, as the preface and particularly the combination of preface and poem demonstrate, resist resolution.

The preface

Coleridge's addition of the preface is not without precedent. Many other poems contain brief prefatory notes, or epigraphs, that inform or guide the reader. Coleridge wrote this preface for the poem's first publication, and it has posed editorial problems ever since. Some editors have suppressed it entirely and anthologized the poem on its own; or, in other cases, printed only part of the preface (usually leaving off the first paragraph and the conclusion); in still other cases, the preface has been reduced to a (rather lengthy) footnote. A number of reasons have been advanced for the writing of this preface, few of them flattering. Some critics find it an expression of Coleridge's embarrassment or lack of confidence about the poem (which is also suggested by the delay in publishing the poem, a delay of nearly twenty years after its initial composition). Others argue that Coleridge anxiously attempts to deflect judgement by claiming that the poem is incomplete—even though it has the ring of termination about its final lines. It has also been suggested that Coleridge creates the prefatory fiction to evade responsibility, a possibility raised by his disclaimer that the poem is a mere 'psychological curiosity', whose publication is justified by Lord Byron's admiration, rather than by its literary merits.

Other, more positive, justifications for the preface are often advanced. David Perkins, for example, argues that Coleridge wished to impose a 'plot' upon the poem to compensate for an internal lapse: without the explanation advanced by the preface, the poem would consist only of two separate, discontinuous (though related) passages. Broadly put, this two-part structure is shared by certain examples of Romantic lyric poem (Keats's 'Ode to Psyche', Shelley's 'Ode to the West Wind') in which the first part postulates a challenge or ideal that the poet aspires to reach or overcome, while the second, following from that, offers a concluding 'credo', a personal statement perhaps of desire or ambition. Because 'Kubla Khan' fails to integrate two such parts, Perkins suggests that Coleridge solves the problem by superimposing a narrative: the introductory note both explains the structure of the poem and converts it into the 'dramatic enactment' of a story. The preface, while suggesting a certain unity, invites us to locate the interruption occasioned by the visitor from Porlock, and identify the scattered fragments. The theme of lost inspiration is, one might say, represented as it occurs.[16]

Similar debates surround the untimely interruption of the person on business from Porlock, whose entry, given the above, could well be a Coleridgean expedience rather than a real historical occurrence. But his potentially fictional status matters little; he makes his mark, both cutting short and defining the structure of the poem. For many readers, he has come to represent the end of poetry, or more specifically, a stone cast on the smooth surface of visionary, poetic inspiration—akin to Sara's reproving glance in 'The Eolian Harp', which serves somehow to curb the poet's imaginative flight. Elizabeth Harries argues for his membership in a 'generic cast of characters'—'a descendant of those many careless and unpoetical figures who destroy or mangle manuscripts in countless novels'.[17] Leslie Brisman goes so far as to suggest that his entry 'might be called a primal scene of interruption', where Porlock is the serpent in the garden of poetic paradise—a place of original and immediate inspiration.[18] By contrast, Kathleen Wheeler proposes that the man from Porlock may be 'a personification of a faculty of the mind', and reads his intervention as having ironical, not anti-aesthetic, force.[19] Regardless of the effects of his intervention, he is as often perceived as a very creative invention indeed.

Towards the end of his preface, Coleridge illustrates the dispersal of the poet's vision with a passage, a fragment, taken from another of his poems, 'The Picture; or, the Lover's Resolution' of 1802. The lines he excerpts (ll. 91–100) describe the fragmenting of a surface of a stream, so that the charm produced by the reflection (in the poem, of a fair maiden) is broken. The downcast youth (beholder of this vision, thus a reflection of the poet) is urged to stay, with the promise that the fragments of the dispersed vision will reunite and again become 'a mirror'. While Coleridge uses these lines to describe the loss of his own vision (he claims that 'with the exception of some eight or ten scattered lines and images, all the rest had passed away like the images on the surface of a stream into which a stone has been cast'), he admits that in his case there was, 'alas! [no] after restoration of the latter' (ll. 31–4). Nor, for that matter, had there been in the case of 'The Picture', where the return of the stream's smooth reflective surface revealed only that the fair maiden had fled. Ironically, 'Kubla Khan' re-enacts the very aspect of 'The Picture' that Coleridge suppresses in the preface.

However one views it, the preface both echoes and repeats important structural and thematic aspects of the poem. In spite of the clash of genres ('plain' prose for the preface and 'sublime' verse for the poem) and disparate locations (a lonely Somerset farmhouse versus the exotic Xanadu), a similar scene is played out: at centre stage is the character and activity of the poet. In the preface, the poet's activity is the result of chance, of a drug-induced slumber overcoming him while reading *Purchas his Pilgrimage*. Once the slumber ends, the poet must hasten 'instantly and eagerly' to record his 'distinct recollection of the whole' (ll. 23–5). The fragility of this operation is, of course, exposed by the untimely entry of the visitor from Porlock.

The poem

The poem itself (like the preface) begins with a description of the contents of the poet's dream. The first stanza details the Khan's paradisal pleasure ground with its dome, its sacred river, and its caverns. The creative activity of the Khan is in considerable contrast with the efforts of the poet in the preface. Where one creates by decree, by simple verbal utterance, the other labours with 'pen, ink, and paper' (l. 24) to arrest his vision before it slips away. The passionate, if hypothetical, terms in which Coleridge dramatizes poetic creation in the third stanza (or second part) of the poem register this disparity by presenting an inspirational ideal—a model of a poet who, like the Khan, is fully possessed by his vision. Not surprisingly, then, Coleridge emphasizes the delirium of the poet in the preface. This serves to ennoble his failure, while indicating a degree of closure by framing both preface and poem as a thematic unit. This effect is especially interesting since it is this final passage, with its celebration of the power of the poet, that is felt to be a satisfying conclusion to the poem *as it stands*, and that thus, for readers who consider the poem whole, renders the preface unnecessary.

Further analogies between preface and poem are remarked upon by Kathleen Wheeler. Looking at the basic structure of the poem, one observes that the first part (ll. 1–36) offers an account of the poet's dream, and the second part (the final stanza), a meditation on its recovery; this two-part structure is also present in the preface. The last portion of the poem, often referred to as an epilogue, is thus (like the preface as a whole) distinct from the main body of the poem. When the poem and preface are structurally examined in this way, its internal fragmentation becomes more obvious. Both preface and epilogue, Wheeler suggests, refer to part one of the poem and maintain a certain aesthetic distance from it. Both attempt to make constructive sense of a prior experience: in the preface, the 'author' is trying to build a poem (to put it bluntly) and in the epilogue, the poem's narrator 'would build that dome in air, | . . ., those caves of ice!' (ll. 46–7). In keeping with a common change in register from a representation of immediate experience to its mediation and reception, the preface and the poem begin in the descriptive third person and then shift into the first person. Finally, I would suggest, in their respective second parts, both express ambivalence about what has been achieved: Coleridge's self-quotation from 'The Picture', while implying the possibility of a restored 'Kubla Khan', rehearses, as we have seen, a moment of loss; and in the second part of 'Kubla Khan', the triumph of the imagination is couched, logically and grammatically, in the conditional ('*Could I* revive within me' (l. 42, emphasis added)).

This sketch of thematic and structural echoes reveals how closely integrated preface and poem are. They thus appear to present a unified front, but we nevertheless perceive profound disjunctions—disjunctions perhaps typified by that infinitely deep romantic chasm, and by the poem's irreconcilable oppositions, by its successive scenes of fragmentation and division, by the dialectic of fragmentation and totalization present in both preface and poem. Perhaps the most rigorous reading of the poem's fragmentariness has been undertaken by Timothy Bahti in his article, 'Coleridge's "Kubla Khan" and the Fragment of Romanticism'. Bahti examines and exposes the endless play of 'self-reflecting notions of part and whole, fragment and totality' in the language and structure of the poem. In the first stanza, several dichotomies and oppositions are established and split apart, and this process is repeated in subsequent stanzas. Particularly noteworthy are the oppositions between finite and infinite, between the outside and the inside ('girdled round' and 'enfolding'), and between 'the hyperbolic and the defined'. As a scene of fragmentation, the second stanza splits apart such oppositions (in the fountain, for example, 'Amid whose swift half-intermitted burst | Huge fragments vaulted like rebounding hail' (ll. 20–1)). Rapid part/whole inversions are expressed through such terms as 'amid' and, of course, 'fragment', and Bahti observes that this fountain of fragments may be understood as the very origin of the poem. Close observation reveals that in this sequence of divisions, whereby 'a part within a whole becomes a whole for yet another part', the categories of parts within wholes, fragments of pre-existent totalities, finally invert themselves.[20]

Coleridge's extended preface is not only a rhetorical tour de force, but also a key factor in the debate about the poem's status as fragment or unified whole; until the preface was taken seriously, the problem of the 'fragment' of 'Kubla Khan' was largely overlooked. Critics have observed that the addition of the preface, in emphasizing a disjunction, disrupts an apparently complete poem—a self-destructive poetic act. On the other hand, the revisionary effect of the preface is seen to turn the poem from an achieved, finite artefact into an open-ended fragment symbolizing an infinite array of meanings beyond itself—which would be a vote for creative possibility. Many readers of the poem tend, not surprisingly, to occupy a compromise position on whether or not the poem is finally fragmentary.

Discussions of the poem often return to the preface and its insistent force, which is an effect of the troublesome person from Porlock, whose arrival, if slightly comic, has serious implications. Coleridgean interventions—such as this mysterious figure, or the putative friend (Coleridge himself) whose letter interrupts the philosophical preparation for Coleridge's exposition of his theory of the imagination in *Biographia Literaria*—do not occur only as external interruptions, fabricated or real. They are more frequently internally generated, arriving in the form of negligence or forgetfulness, as failures of memory or of the will. The intervention, though apparently external, reveals an internal lapse. But problems arise around the question of textual identity as well as integrity. Which poem are we reading: the one on the page before us or the one projected around it? If a fragment of a poem claims to represent (or 'symbolize') a whole poem, can it also claim to *be* that poem? A poetic text is never identical with all the meanings it may signify. Yet if the signified text is never exactly the same as the text before us, how much more true this must be of the fragment, where the 'whole' text is signified in absentia, and where there is an overtly ambiguous relationship between the poem and its extra-poetic surround.

If it is difficult for readers to agree on whether or not 'Kubla Khan' is really a fragment, part of the problem is that the 'fragment' is by definition an unstable concept. The fragment's key feature, as I have suggested, is that it is caught up between partiality and wholeness, identifiable with neither term, but conceptually dependent on both. Clearly, more than just the preface is at stake. 'Kubla Khan' does not necessarily suffer as a poem because it has been 'interrupted', but it is the case that Coleridge's introductory note compounds (rather than simply adds to, or even clarifies) a complex of representational and interpretive difficulties that its fragmentary status makes impossible to ignore. The poem exemplifies the irresolvability of the fragment as either part or whole since the problem of fragmentation is apparent on so many levels: it is at work *in* the work, it guides Coleridge's reading and presentation of his work, and it represents a major preoccupation for literary criticism. For 'Kubla Khan' is experienced not only with both extremes (visionary wholeness and fragmentation) in view, but more precisely in the ambivalent and richly suggestive space between those extremes. (For a contrasting reading, see the chapter on 'Formalism'.)

FURTHER READING

Chambers, G. E., 'The "Ruins" at Virginia Water', *Berkshire Archaeological Journal*, 54 (1953–4), 39–52. An intriguing and thorough account of the Leptis Magna ruins and their transport to London.

Frey, Hans-Jost, *Interruptions*, trans. and introd. Georgia Albert (Albany, NY: State University of New York Press, 1996). An exploration of fragmentation from a critical and theoretical perspective, which performs its observations through the inclusion of short fictional texts and meditations.

Harries, Elizabeth Wanning, *The Unfinished Manner: Essays on the Fragment in the Later Eighteenth Century* (Charlottesville, Va., and London: University Press of Virginia, 1994). This book discusses the eighteenth-century cultural context, and is helpful for understanding the fragment in Romanticism.

Janowitz, Anne, *England's Ruins: Poetic Purpose and the National Landscape* (Oxford: Blackwell, 1990). Examines the poetics of fragments and ruins, using generic analysis to explore the political and historical dimensions of the subject.

Levinson, Marjorie, *The Romantic Fragment Poem: A Critique of a Form* (Chapel Hill, NC: University of North Carolina Press, 1986). Levinson brings a New Historicist approach to readings of a number of canonical Romantic fragment poems, emphasizing their epochal specificity, and their ideological determinants as a form.

McFarland, Thomas, *Romanticism and the Forms of Ruin: Wordsworth, Coleridge, and Modalities of Fragmentation* (Princeton: Princeton University Press, 1981). McFarland's account is largely phenomenological, and views fragmentation, ruin, and the unfinished (his 'diasparactive triad'), as endemic not only in Romanticism, but also in all human endeavour.

Rauber, D. F., 'The Fragment as Romantic Form', *Modern Language Quarterly*, 30 (1969), 212–21. One of the first critical texts to argue that the fragment has a privileged place in the Romantic period, and is implicated in key Romantic concepts such as infinitude, the sublime, and the imagination.

Schlegel, Friedrich, *Philosophical Fragments*, trans. Peter Firchow, foreword by Rodolphe Gasché (Minneapolis and Oxford: University of Minnesota Press, 1991). Brings together, with a helpful introduction, the fragments published in the *Athenaeum* by Schlegel and his circle.

Thomas, Sophie, 'The Return of the Fragment: "Christabel" and the Uncanny', in *Bucknell Review*, 45: 2 (2002), 51–73. Examines the fragmentary status of 'Christabel' from a psychoanalytic perspective, with an emphasis on the problems of reading and interpreting fragmentary works.

Woodward, Christopher, *In Ruins* (London: Chatto & Windus, 2001). A wide-ranging and accessible exploration of the appeal of ruins, across cultures and epochs.

NOTES

1. Jeffrey makes this remark in a review of Byron's *The Giaour, a Fragment of a Turkish Tale, Edinburgh Review*, 21 (July 1813), 299.
2. *The New Shorter Oxford English Dictionary* (Oxford: Oxford University Press, 1973, 1993), p. 1018.
3. For an excellent account of the Venus, and the cultural and psychoanalytic significance of its fragmentary state, see Peter Fuller's *Art and Psychoanalysis* (London: The Hogarth Press, 1980).
4. Josiah Condor, in the *Eclectic Review*, 2nd ser. 5 (June 1816).
5. *Poetical Works*, ed. E. H. Coleridge (1912; London: Oxford University Press, 1969), p. 213.
6. *Table Talk*, ed. Carl Woodring, 2 vols. (Princeton: Princeton University Press, 1990), i. 409–10 (1 July 1833).
7. Essay II, 'On Picturesque Travel', in *Three Essays* (London, 1794), p. 46.
8. Edmund Burke, *A Philosophical Enquiry into the Origin of our Ideas of the Sublime and Beautiful*, ed. Adam Phillips (Oxford: Blackwell, 1987), p. 77.
9. D. F. Rauber, 'The Fragment as Romantic Form', *Modern Language Quarterly*, 30 (1969), 214–15.
10. The *Athenaeum* fragments cited here are from Friedrich Schlegel, *Philosophical Fragments*, trans. Peter Firchow, foreword by Rodolphe Gasché (Minneapolis and Oxford: University of Minnesota Press, 1991), pp. 21, 2, 45.
11. Elizabeth Wanning Harries, *The Unfinished Manner: Essays on the Fragment in the Later Eighteenth Century* (Charlottesville, Va., and London: University Press of Virginia, 1994), p. 2.
12. Schlegel; *Philosophical Fragments*, p. 32
13. Philippe Lacoue-Labarthe and Jean-Luc Nancy, 'Genre', *Glyph*, 7 (1981), 2; see also *The Literary Absolute: The Theory of Literature in German Romanticism*, trans. Philip Barnard and Cheryl Lester (Albany, NY: State University of New York Press, 1988).
14. All line references to the poem and preface are from *Poetical Works*.
15. Hazlitt, *The Examiner* (2 June 1816); reviewer unknown, *Literary Panorama*, 2nd ser. 4 (July 1816).
16. David Perkins, 'The Imaginative Vision of *Kubla Khan*: On Coleridge's Introductory Note', in J. Robert Barth and John L. Mahoney (eds.), *Coleridge, Keats, and the Imagination: Romanticism and Adam's Dream* (Columbia, Mo., and London: University of Missouri Press, 1990).
17. *The Unfinished Manner*, p. 159.
18. Leslie Brisman, *Romantic Origins* (Ithaca, NY: Cornell University Press, 1978), pp. 30–7.
19. Kathleen Wheeler, *The Creative Mind in Coleridge's Poetry* (London: Heinemann, 1981), p. 39.
20. 'Coleridge's "Kubla Khan" and the Fragment of Romanticism', *Modern Language Notes*, 96 (Dec. 1981), 1038–40.

32 | Forgeries

Debbie Lee

'There are upwards of 10,000 practising scoundrels in London, whose manoeuvres are daily directed against its unsuspecting inhabitant', wrote William Kidd in his 1832 book *London and All Its Dangers, Frauds, Iniquities, Deceptions, &tc.* Kidd was not the only one warning Britons to beware of impostors and forgers. On any day, a person in Romantic England could open one of the newspapers to find headlines like: 'Infamous Impostor', 'Singular Case', 'Fabrication', 'Celebrated Hoax!' Impostors and forgers were important figures not only in London street culture, but also in Romantic literature and history.

Impostors and forgers routinely disrupted seemingly stable cultural categories. Cross-dressers like Mary Lacy and Mary Talbot, who put on men's clothes and sailed with the British navy, or Monsieur D'Eon, the French diplomat and spy who at mid-career and mid-life suddenly announced that *he* was *she*, cast serious doubt on the construction of gender in the period. Class-crossers like Beau Brummell, who died a poverty-stricken beggar but who spent much of his life as the court dandy and friend of George IV, or Edward Wortley Montagu, who gave up the life of an aristocrat to live as a chimney sweep, disputed the official view of the social world in which a person's identity was largely determined by inheritance. Travel hoaxes, among the most notorious Christian Frederick Damberger, the Wittenberg printer whose fake travel narratives to Arabia and Africa confounded British journalists, and Mary Baker, a Devonshire servant who styled herself the exotic Javanese royalty 'Princess Caraboo', raised questions about the European desire to describe national characteristics and then categorize people according to a fixed system. Poetic forgeries, those of James Macpherson, Thomas Chatterton, and William Henry Ireland, challenged the myth of original poetic genius. Disrupting fixed Romantic forms became the de facto vocation of impostors and forgers.

Because of their disruptive qualities, these characters also tell us a great deal about the time and place in which they lived. One of the things impostors and forgers make strikingly clear is the period's idolatrous worship of authenticity and truth. It is what underlies Wordsworth's claim that poetic truth could be found in the language of 'real men'; or J. M. W. Turner's sublime images of uncorrupted English landscapes and ancient castles; or the move, in all art and literature, away from the artificiality of neoclassicism. In fact, when we think of this stretch of history, liars and frauds, the deluded and deceived, are emphatically *not* what come to mind. Instead, the period's most enduring message is John Keats's claim that 'Beauty is truth, truth beauty' (*Ode on a Grecian Urn*, l. 49). Claims like this were no less evident in the social and political realm. Many Romantic women writers such as Mary Wollstonecraft were interested in social truth. In science, explorers and naturalists sought truth when they followed the directions of the Royal Society and returned with facts and drawings that would enlighten both the specialist and the general reader. In spite of all the emphasis on authenticity and truth, or maybe because of it, forgery and imposture played a large counter role in the Romantic period.

Most impostors and forgers came from the least privileged classes in Britain, where it was not the transcendent but the trivial things that decided truth: how one dressed, the language one used, the titles attached to one's name. Though poets were sure that truth was an ideal by which they could authenticate the self, and men of science were positive that truth could be gathered from observable data, impostors and forgers proved that the border between truth and lies was permeable. Truth was constructed and identity conjectural. Impostors and forgers impinged on *all* Romantic forms, from poetry, to medical discourse, to ethnography and travelogues. Since by their very nature impostors and forgers are protean and transformable, slipping in and out of known genres and modes, they are also difficult to categorize. Because they resist absolute classification, these figures and their actions can only be studied as individual cases.

Poetic forgeries

Romantic forgery begins with the figure of James Macpherson. In the mid-eighteenth century, Macpherson claimed he had found the lost epics of the third-century Celtic bard Ossian. He said he had translated Ossian's ballads, and he proceeded to publish these in 1760. The reading public went wild over their familiar but strange melodies, and their popularity continued even when it was discovered that Ossian was by and large Macpherson's invention.

Ossian influenced a whole generation of writers, including Blake, Wordsworth, Coleridge, Byron, Burns, Scott, and the Romantic icon Thomas Chatterton. Chatterton's father, who died just before he was born, had worked at St Mary Redcliffe church in Bristol, where he had access to a small garret over the north porch called the muniment room. This room was filled with fifteenth-century manuscripts, and Chatterton's father helped himself to the stash. Many years later, when Chatterton was 15 years old, he found scraps of his father's manuscript collection. He was so enthralled by these documents that he went himself to the muniment room. This room and these manuscripts apparently inspired Chatterton to create the works of a fifteenth-century monk whom he named Thomas Rowley.

Chatterton invented a whole world for Thomas Rowley, including a patron and a group of peers including writers, architects, and medieval literati. He imagined Rowley as a poet and playwright, a translator of Latin, a scribe and businessman. He created account books, maps, business correspondence, and research notes. Although some enthusiasm developed in Bristol over the fictitious Rowley, there were also detractors such as Horace Walpole. Still, this was just the beginning of a writing career for Chatterton, or so he hoped. He moved to London where he wrote popular verse, then suddenly and unexpectedly he died. His death, whether suicide or accident, created an obsessive interest in his life among other Romantic poets like Coleridge and Wordsworth, who wrote in his poem 'Resolution and Independence': 'I thought of Chatterton, that marvellous Boy, | The sleepless Soul that perished in its pride' (ll. 43–4). In an odd twist, it was Chatterton's mysterious death and his enigmatic forgeries that formed part of the Romantic's obsession with the authenticity of poetic inspiration.

The most notorious forger of the period was a young man named William Henry Ireland. Ireland's father was a London engraver and antiquarian book collector who took his son to Stratford in 1792 and 1793 to absorb all things Shakespearean. In Stratford, Ireland entered a literary holy land, complete with shrines (Shakespeare's birthplace), relics (his father purchased the stool on which Shakespeare supposedly kneeled to court Ann Hathaway), and religious followers (most famously, David Garrick). He also noticed his father's obsession with the playwright. Ireland's father wanted to purchase Shakespeare's birthplace house and then his bed. He succeeded in neither. Ireland, probably sensitive to his father's hopes and disappointments over Shakespearean treasures, came to his father a few years later on the evening of 16 December 1794 with an old mortgage deed signed by William Shakespeare. He told his father he had obtained the deed from some papers he was in the process of purchasing. Ireland's father was ecstatic over the document and deeply grateful to his son.

Over the next few days Ireland produced more Shakespearean relics for his father, including an IOU from Shakespeare to John Heminge of the Globe theatre and a letter to Lord Southampton, Shakespeare's patron. Soon, Ireland was bringing verses, theatre receipts, a love letter from Shakespeare to Ann Hathaway, a handwritten manuscript of *King Lear*, and even new plays. One of them, *Vortigern*, Ireland fabricated by reading Holinshed's *Chronicles* just as Shakespeare had. News of the Shakespeare papers spread from the Ireland household to the London newspapers and literati. In 1795, Ireland's father helped him publish *Miscellaneous Papers Under the Hand and Seal of William Shakespeare*. Meanwhile, Drury Lane theatre had bought *Vortigern* from Ireland and was planning its premiere. But at the same time, London critics suspected foul play. Ireland was attacked in the *Telegraph* and the *Monthly Mirror*, among other newspapers. In 1796, Edward Malone published *An Inquiry into the Authenticity of Certain Miscellaneous Papers and Legal Instruments*, exposing Ireland as a forger.

In the Romantic era, then, forgeries inspired original poetry by some of the period's best-known poets, but forgeries also inspired other forgeries. Chatterton's poetry had included imitations of Ossian, itself a forgery, and then Chatterton's entire legacy stirred the imagination of William Henry Ireland. Chatterton, in fact, was the focus of much of Ireland's verse, in poems like 'Elegiac Lines to the Memory of Thomas Chatterton'. While poetic forgeries begat other poetic forgeries, they were also significant for undoing 'authentic' literary forms and for caricaturing the aesthetic values of the Romantic period: original genius and the cult of the 'true bard'.

Medical hoaxes

At the beginning of the eighteenth century, England's health care system was flexible and patient centred. People called on the medical community when they wanted to, and they took medical practice into their own hands when it was convenient. They were not awed by medical authority, and medical men did not have the kinds of social power they do today. Religion was the most powerful factor in patients' ability to self-diagnose and medicate. In fact, a patient's own interpretation of the causes of his or her illness was given the same credence as those of certified medical men. But by the time the Romantic period came to a close, professional medicine was a major discursive form, having gained more authority than vernacular medicine.

Medical hoaxes of the period were successful because they walked the tightrope between religion and medicine, two contrary yet powerful paradigms for diagnosis. If a bodily ailment could not be explained scientifically, it could be justified through religion as a miraculous sign from God. While the public by and large believed in these medical miracles, physicians were motivated to see the inexplicable ailments of the body as hoaxes, which is why medical impostors came under more severe scrutiny than many other types of frauds. The cases of Mary Toft, a poor woman of Surrey who in 1726 claimed she had given birth to eighteen rabbits; Joanna Southcott, the prophetic poet who in 1814 at age 65 said she was pregnant with the New Messiah; and Catherine Mewis, the child of working-class parents who said she was completely blind except on Sundays, all fooled large numbers of ordinary Britons until medical investigators uncovered them as impostors.

One of the most telling cases of medical imposture was that of Ann Moore. Like most impostors in the era, Moore was born to poor parents and, when she married, her life did not improve. She and her husband fought so violently that they separated, and she ended up living in an adulterous relationship with a local farmer by whom she had a son and a daughter, Mary. In 1805 and 1806, Moore took a job as a servant to a boy named Samuel Orange who was sick with the skin disease scrofula, a job she despised because of the offensive smell of his disease. But since she was unable to find work elsewhere, she was forced to continue. Yet wrapping and unwrapping the putrid bandages took its toll on Moore. She lost all desire to eat solid food and soon she was hardly eating or drinking at all. She thought everything she consumed smelled like the dying Samuel Orange and his pus-flowing ulcers. By 1807, she was finding it painful to swallow. Soon she gave up liquids too, except to wash her mouth with water three times a week. Moore claimed to live this way for fourteen months, with no food, no water, and even no sleep.

Soon the story of the 'fasting woman' spread through local villages. People began to come to see this medical miracle, often leaving behind some money out of pity or awe. But with all the attention, Moore quickly came under medical scrutiny. Local physicians debated whether or not it was really possible for someone to live so long without food and water. Moore said it was, and she volunteered to be observed by medical men to prove her veracity. This 'watch', as it was called, took place between 13 and 29 September 1808. A bed was furnished for Moore, with curtains that could be drawn, and her daughter Mary was the only one who had access to her. Mary would come in every morning and evening to kiss her mother. Otherwise, volunteers from the community monitored her around the clock. After the sixteen days, Mr Taylor, the local surgeon, was so convinced that Moore was a fasting woman, he published an account saying she had lived without food or liquid for the entire time. Much later, it was discovered that her daughter had delivered food and water to her in her daily kisses.

Moore's popularity as a fasting woman increased over the years. Although she had been a woman of questionable morals before her self-imposed starvation, she now claimed to be deeply religious. She was linked to the millenarian prophecies of Joanna Southcott, who included a description of Ann Moore in her 1805 *True Explanations of the Bible* calling her a 'living miracle'. But some were suspicious, most notably a Dr Henderson who published a pamphlet in 1813 denouncing Moore as an 'artful impostor'. Both her supporters and detractors decided she must have a second watch, and that this time it should last four weeks. They also stipulated that the watchers had to be people of unquestionable character and judgement. A crowd of peers—doctors, rectors, surgeons, reverends, curates, and solicitors—was assembled.

When Moore learned of the conditions of the second watch, she refused, but then, after some badgering, consented. The committee first weighed her and then brought her to the watching bed they had constructed and thoroughly searched for any speck of food or liquid. The committee also constructed a special booth so that the watchers could not have access to Moore, and her daughter was likewise not allowed to visit. Towards the end of the first week, the watchers were alarmed because although Moore had taken no food or liquid, she was suffering terribly. She had a fever, which she said made her excessively thirsty, and she begged to have a cloth dipped in vinegar water so she could apply it to her tongue. Mr Wright, a surgeon from Derby, wrung the cloths almost dry before giving them back to the starving Ann Moore. But on one occasion, he admitted that he did not wring out the cloth so that he could see if she really could swallow, since she claimed she had not swallowed in years. Her drama of starvation had now passed beyond medical miracle or medical hoax: it exposed the dichotomy between the world of medical help and that of medical violence.

On the ninth day, Moore was dying of starvation as the medical men and the other distinguished gentlemen from the area watched her waste away. Her voice was feeble, and her pulse, almost impossible to detect in one wrist, was racing at 160 beats per minute in the other. When two of the doctors, Dr Fox and Dr Garlike, thought she would not live more than two more hours, they sent for her daughter. The daughter was admitted and gave Moore some water. Having revived a little, Moore then said she wanted to make a solemn oath that 'for six years she had taken no food whatever'. The oath was administered and the watch terminated, but when the doctors took Moore from her bed they discovered 'unequivocal testimony of recent evacuations'. At last, Moore was said to be 'overwhelmed with confusion', and forced to sign a confession begging the public's forgiveness for her imposture.

Moore did starve herself; that much was true. Her hoax was in claiming she had given up food, drink, sleep, and other bodily functions completely. But this was the only way she could draw attention to herself. Moore's self-starvation was a performance for the medical community, forcing them to recognize that they were implicated in the spectacle they saw. Because her imposture took place when religious magic and vernacular medicine were on the wane, and when medical men and new scientific principles were on the rise, it demonstrated that the body was no longer the patient's own but an object to be poked and prodded, observed and catalogued by professionals. It is no coincidence that Ann Moore's medical fraud made use of hunger, which is often associated with protest (hunger strikes) and with spirituality (the fast). To reduce the female body to a shadow of itself through a medical hoax uncovered the sinister nature of a new Romantic form: medical discourse.

Travel lies

Travel literature was one of the most pervasive forms during the Romantic period. Travel books could centre on scenic walks familiar to many educated people, or they could describe foreign territory hardly visited at all by Europeans. Wordsworth's early work included *Descriptive Sketches, in Verse, taken during a pedestrian Tour in the Italian, Grison, Swiss, and Savoyard Alps*, and Mary Wollstonecraft likewise produced *Letters written during a short Residence in Sweden, Norway, and Denmark*. Soldiers, sailors, independent travellers, and employees of the East India Company and various other associations wrote popular volumes, such as Jonathan Carver's 1778 *Travels Through North America* and John Crawfurd's 1828 *Journal of An Embassy from the Governor General of India to the Courts of Siam and Cochin China*.

Because travel literature sold well, it was an obvious choice for forgers who wanted to make money or gain notoriety. Robert Southey's 1807 *Letters from England: by Don Manuel Alvarez Espriella, translated from the Spanish*, a fake travelogue used to protest against English politics, and Mary Talbot's 1809 *The Life and Surprising Adventures of Mary Ann Talbot, in the name of John Taylor*, a fabricated tale of cross-dressing, both gained popularity. But the most successful travel hoax of the period was written by a man whose identity remains a mystery even today: Christian Frederick Damberger's 1801 *Travels through the Interior of Africa from the Cape of Good Hope to the Empire of Morocco*.

Of all the places on the globe, Europeans knew the least about Africa. During the Romantic period, a number of men ventured into Africa in the name of science, commerce, and trade. One of the earliest and most successful was Mungo Park. Park went to Africa in 1794 and returned in 1799. His sponsor, Joseph Banks, told the African Association that Park had 'opened a Gate into the Interior of Africa into which it is easy for every nation to enter and to extend its Commerce and Discovery'.[1] Park's 1799 narrative of his journey was immediately popular throughout Europe (see also the chapter on 'Travel Writing'). Of course, Park had only travelled a short distance into West Africa, so someone who could claim to traverse the entire continent, from its southern tip to its northernmost point, could be guaranteed a readership.

Damberger's *Travels* was published in 1801 to instant acclaim. In fact, news of Damberger's extraordinary journey spread rapidly before it was even published, while both Paris and London booksellers competed for rights to the translation before it was even printed in German. The *St James Chronicle* filled entire pages with excerpts from the book, which showed Damberger audaciously correcting the ethnography and geography of the much-admired Mungo Park. But soon experts began to suspect the traveller was a fake. The *British Critic*, in its January–June issue of 1801, called the narrative 'a most impudent and fraudulent publication'. Likewise, The *Gentleman's Magazine* of 1801 designated it 'a compilation of falsehood and nonsense'.[2] Still, Damberger's book became one of the most clever travel hoaxes ever because of its amazing amount of circumstantial detail and its subtle mixture of fact and fiction.

But who was Damberger? The only biographical source of the time tells how a mechanic from Saxony named Joseph Schrodter presented to the public a fake travel narrative to the East Indies and Egypt, Mount Sinai, and Bethlehem, during the years 1795–9, where he claimed to witness the occupation of Egypt by the French. The book met a fine critical reception. In 1799, another fake travelogue came out by an Egyptian, Zacharias Taurinius, chronicling his journey to Asia, Africa, and America. This book also advertised a promised travel narrative from the Cape of Good Hope, to Caffaria and the Sahara desert. In this same year, a cabinetmaker named Damberger presented himself to the publisher Martini in Leipzig. He said he was resting in Wittenberg from his long travels in Africa and offered copyright of his exceptional narrative to Martini. Interested in such an extensive journey, Martini went to Wittenberg to visit Damberger and interview him. Damberger was so convincing that Martini signed him up on the spot. Back at Leipzig, the geographer Goldbach was hired to design the map for the travel narrative.

Not long after publication, however, Martini became suspicious and began to compare the narratives of Joseph Schrodter, Zacharias Taurinius, and Damberger. He became so convinced they were all one person with three different names that he took Damberger to court. Damberger confessed he was the author of the work by Taurinius but said he only acted as amanuensis for the work by Schrodter. He also claimed he was in fact Christian Frederick Damberger, although he admitted that Damberger was simply an alias he had picked up in Africa for safety reasons. He affirmed that he had undertaken the great voyage outlined in the narrative. Martini determined, after a thorough investigation, that the three narratives had been fabricated through 'compilation' (from previous narratives) by the printer Taurinius in conjunction with a forger by the name of Junge, also from Wittenberg. Still, even this conclusion remains speculative and Damberger's precise identity will probably never be known.

Damberger may not have overturned the travel craze for knowledge of Africa, but he did expose the rapacious desire of Europeans to know all they could about the continent. What is most remarkable about the narrative is its continuing popularity in the period. In 1807, William Mavor printed an edition called *Travels in Africa by Mungo Park, Surgeon; from the Cape of Good Hope to Morocco by Damberger, and in the Interior Districts of Africa, by Ledyard and Lucas,* apparently in an attempt to cash in on the public curiosity about the interior of Africa, even if the information presented was false.

Exotic others

It was not unusual in the Romantic period for the foreign 'other' to gain widespread attention. Wordsworth describes the ethnic diversity of London in Book VII of *The Prelude*:

> The Swede, the Russian; from the genial south,
> The Frenchman and the Spaniard; from remote
> America, the hunger-Indian; Moors,
> Malays, Lascars, the Tartar and Chinese,
> And Negro ladies in white muslin gowns.
>   (VII. 239–43)

Foreigners from exotic and unknown places found themselves at the centre of attention. The Polynesian Omai, who came to London in 1774 on board the *Adventure* as part of Captain James Cook's second voyage, became an instant curiosity: he was introduced to the king only three days after his arrival and painted by Joshua Reynolds, one of the nation's foremost portrait artists.

Because exotic foreigners received such widespread attention, and because they came from cultures that few knew anything about, they were prime objects for imposture. The most celebrated case of the eighteenth century was George Psalmanazar, who, with the help of a Scottish chaplain Alexander Innes, pretended to be an exile from Formosa (now Taiwan). Psalmanazar invented a language based on Japanese, which he could write and speak. He came before the Royal Society and the Bishop of London, and he produced a fake historiography called *An Historical and Geographical*

Description of Formosa in 1704, before he was eventually uncovered. About a hundred years later, another impostor appeared in England named Mary Baker, also known as Princess Caraboo of Javasu, and she would become one of the most intriguing impostors in British history. Like Psalmanazar, her false identity would question the discourse of empire.

Mary Baker first arrived in Bristol at a parish poor house in 1817, as if out of nowhere. According to eyewitnesses she appeared hungry and tired and, since she did not speak a word of English, she was sent by the parish priest to Mr Worrall, the magistrate, and his wife Elizabeth. As Elizabeth showed the young woman to a well-furnished bedroom upstairs, the young woman pointed to some Chinese figurines perched on the mantlé and uttered a few foreign words, then declared 'Caraboo, Caraboo', pointing to herself. Even though no one, including the servants, could decipher her nationality the assumption now was that she must be oriental.

Over the next few weeks articles appeared in the daily papers and the mysterious visitor came to public attention. People flocked to see her, bringing with them foreigners of their acquaintance in the hope of discovering who she was. At last, a Portuguese man from Malay spoke to Caraboo and said he could understand her perfectly. He translated her entire story. She turned out to be a eastern princess, born of a Malay mother and a Chinese father. One day, while walking in her royal gardens, she was kidnapped by pirates, one of whom she killed with her sword, but this was not enough to effect her escape. She was bound, blindfolded, and carried off, then transported around the world until she managed to jump overboard just off the coast of England. Her language, according to this translator, was a mixture of Eastern languages and she was from a small island called 'Javasu', which had all the characteristics of the recently popularized island of Java.

From here on Princess Caraboo became a national sensation. Her presence was requested at the residences of duchesses and earls, who kneeled before her, took her by the hand, or begged kisses. Experts also arrived on the princess's doorstep, linguists and East Indian travellers, hoping to get a chance to decode her language or observe her as a living foreign specimen. A Mr P. of Cathay, for example, came to see her, bringing a Malay dagger. Princess Caraboo instantly took it and placed it on her right side, where the Malays supposedly wore them, confirming to Mr P. that she was a Malay and a genuine princess. This publicity continued until Caraboo's caretakers received a visit from a Mrs Neale, who had rented a room to Caraboo when she was still Mary Baker. Mrs Neale reported that the Javanese princess was actually just a servant girl who spoke perfectly good English and had not a drop of foreign blood.

A thorough investigation commenced, revealing that Princess Caraboo was in fact a Devonshire woman named Mary Baker who had lived most of her twenty-four years as a beggar, gypsy, and thief travelling between Exeter, Taunton, and London, before she arrived in Bristol in 1817. Her life became so desperate that at one point she almost hung herself. Then she discovered the social currency of an exotic identity.

Mary Baker's performance of foreignness—especially orientalism—revealed one of the roles it *actually* played in Britain. Oriental objects—vases, clothing, china—were displayed in upper-class homes, like the Worralls', where Caraboo resided in Bristol. But beyond the ornamental, the Orient was represented rhetorically through travel literature and descriptive accounts of oriental places. Most notably, the former governor-general of Java, Stamford Raffles, had just published his two-volume *History of Java*, which included word lists, maps, and engraved illustrations, which would supposedly allow any reader to identify a Javan. In fact, the central irony of the Princess Caraboo case was that she pulled off her imposture through the imperial fantasy about how national identity was determined. For instance, a letter writer to the *Edinburgh Review* had this to say: 'the first part of the female foreigner's name, Cara, is either a Tartar adjective signifying black, or the second person imperative mood of the Tartar verb to look; the last part, boo, signifying this or that, is a pronoun in the same language.'[3] The paradox of categorizing Caraboo was that the more seriously observers deployed their system, the more ridiculous and false they revealed it to be. But more importantly, Caraboo's true story is significant because it demonstrates how a fairly typical poor girl's life is given legal and social power only in relation to the invented tale of an exotic oriental identity.

Imposters and forgers showed how readily key concepts of cultural value like 'originality' and 'authenticity' could merge with the copy and the counterfeit. They also demonstrated that the period was permeated by social mobility; by considerable instability in the gender system; and by an attitude towards the foreign that was by no means settled or univocally powerful.

READING: John Hatfield and the Lake Poets

John Hatfield, also known as the Reverend Hatfield, Major Hatfield, and Colonel Alexander Augustus Hope, was tried for forgery on 15 August 1803 at Carlisle, a town about twenty miles north of England's Lake District. Although Hatfield claimed innocence, the jury, after hearing testimony, deliberated for just ten minutes before finding him guilty. He was sentenced to death and hanged on the first Saturday in September 1803. At the execution, Hatfield—a stocky, handsome man of 45 with long dark hair brushed back into a pony-tail—mounted the scaffold, the gibbet towering above him. He was dressed in a 'black jacket, black silk waistcoat, fustian pantaloons, white cotton stockings, and ordinary shoes'.[4] He untied his cravat and wrapped it around his head as a blindfold. The crowd watched as the executioner fumbled with the noose and was finally assisted by Hatfield himself, who instructed him on where to tie the rope and the proper method of driving away the cart. Once everything was in place, Hatfield said quietly, 'my spirit is strong, though my body is weak'. According to one eyewitness, the 'noose slipped twice, and he fell down about eighteen inches.—His feet at last were almost touching the ground. But his excessive weight, which occasioned this accident, speedily relieved him from pain. He expired in a moment, and without any struggle.'[5]

Though by all accounts it was a solemn occasion, the execution was in fact a crowded affair. Hatfield's crimes had been so notorious that people came from miles around to witness the spectacle. Three of the most celebrated visitors were William and Dorothy Wordsworth and Samuel Taylor Coleridge, the three Lake Poets who would go on to become the defining writers of the Romantic Movement. Coleridge, in fact, had more at stake in the execution than almost anyone there, for he was solely responsible for bringing Hatfield to the attention of the nation in five newspaper articles he wrote for the *Morning Post* during the autumn of 1802.

Hatfield's identities

Ten years earlier, in 1792, John Hatfield arrived in the resort town of Scarborough without servants, wearing a tattered waistcoat and breeches. At this time Hatfield was a travelling salesman for a linen draper and the attractions of life in fashionable Scarborough were obvious. He immediately took up residence at one of Scarborough's finest hotels, introducing himself to the most respectable people in town. He told his new acquaintances that he was Major Hatfield.

For three weeks, Hatfield's activities at Scarborough included eating, drinking, gambling, and endless talking with local businessmen. He acted with such gentlemanly grace that everyone was put at ease. Not only that, they found themselves rapt with his stories of military service, in America and Ireland. In Ireland, he said, he had been the Duke of Rutland's personal assistant. He also mentioned that he was connected with the Duke of Rutland by marriage, and that as recipient of the duke's patronage, he expected the duke would ask him to represent Scarborough in Parliament. Hatfield's lies won him friends. But none of this would have been much good without Hatfield's extraordinary talent for storytelling.

After two or three weeks in Scarborough, however, things began to break down. The proprietor at the hotel asked Hatfield for £20 on his quickly escalating account, but of course he was unable to pay, and so he was arrested and thrown in jail. The prison term was extended from a minimum sentence to seven years when various people in London discovered his whereabouts and brought further charges of debt against him. Though he sat in the Scarborough prison until 1800, according to the surviving records he none the less entertained the other prisoners, and even the jailer's wife, with stories of intrigue and adventure. In 1797, he even published *A New Scarborough Guide*. The title-page includes the phrase 'by a Gentleman', just in case anyone would doubt his authority. The epigram to the travel guide, an ironic inside joke, reads:

> No Party Lies I herald for the Press,
> But modest Truth, in artless English Dress.

Coleridge's identities

Like Hatfield, Samuel Taylor Coleridge was constantly in debt. He was also a man riddled by questions of identity and matters of truth that often centred on the meaning of his own being. While John Hatfield sat shackled in Scarborough prison denying his true identity, Coleridge roamed around the country in search of his. Between 1792 and 1799 he shuttled between Cambridge, Oxford, Bristol, the English Midlands, Nether Stowey, Germany, and London. The restless motion that sent him around the country was accompanied by confusion over his personal mission. He planned to be, by turns, a pantisocrat, an urban poet and campaigner, an intellectual in rural retreat, a journalist, a Unitarian minister, and then a scholar in a German university. He married a woman he did not love and fell in love with one he could not marry. These years were Coleridge's times of financial troubles, illness, remorse, suspicion, jealousy, and self-pity, as well as of extreme optimism and epic idealism. In 1797, he formed a friendship with Wordsworth and found what he hoped would be a relationship in which he could establish an unwavering sense of self. They moved in 1800 to the Lake District—Wordsworth to Grasmere and Coleridge to Keswick. Here Coleridge wrote poetry while working as a journalist for the *Morning Post*. He also planned to write a travel guide for Longman titled *A Tour of the North of England*.[6]

Although Coleridge and the Wordsworths were newcomers to the Lake District, the area had long been a place for painters and poets who searched for authenticity. One of the most influential of these was William Gilpin whose 1792 *Observations relative chiefly to Picturesque Beauty* became popular for its landscape descriptions. Yet for Coleridge, the Lake District inspired nothing short of a grand personal drama. He embarked on a walking tour of the region in the summer of 1802 and wrote a series of extraordinary letters to Sara Hutchinson, his forbidden love, pouring all his desire for her into describing the Lake District's dramatic colours and complex textures, its 'black crags and green steeps as the woolly Down on the underside of a Willow Leaf, & soft as Floss Silk'.[7]

At the heart of this region lay the vale of Buttermere. The area had a wild, almost savage character, according to Thomas De Quincey. Buttermere's primary establishment was the Fish Inn, a white stone cottage enclosed by a slate fence yet open to a breathtaking view of the water. The Fish Inn was owned by an elderly couple, the Robinsons, and their only daughter, Mary, worked as a barmaid for her parents. Mary appeared to be another poor country girl. But, in fact, she had the singular distinction of being a tourist attraction in her own right, having been made famous by the Lake tourist Captain Budworth, in his 1792 book *A Fortnight's Ramble to the Lakes*. Budworth had termed Mary Robinson the 'The Beauty of Buttermere', as if she herself were a feature of the landscape. Because of this accidental identification with the Lake District, Mary quickly became a symbol for English purity and innocence. Tourists regularly visited the Fish Inn to see her. Coleridge was one such visitor in August of 1802.

Imposture in the Lake District

But just as Coleridge walked out of Buttermere in August 1802, the ex-convict John Hatfield rode into this region of authentic beauty. He arrived first in Keswick, where he met Coleridge, in a well-furnished, cream-coloured carriage, announcing himself as the Honorable Alexander Augustus Hope, Member of Parliament, army official, and the brother of the Earl of Hopetoun. As Hope, Hatfield not only reprised his previous roles, he intensified them. He had, according to Coleridge, 'an astonishing flow of words, and his language to the generality of men, would appear as choice and elegant as it was undoubtedly fluent and copious'.[8] Touched by Hatfield's interest in their lives and impressed with his status, the people of Keswick embraced him. They threw open their doors to him, invited him to dinner, and lent him money when he was unable to cash a bank draft on a Sunday. In turn, he complimented them excessively, declaring to locals that their daughters were more beautiful and worthy than the women of property with whom he had dined in fashionable London.

Hatfield/Hope made good on his compliments too: he took more interest in the local women than any man they had ever met. He listened to them with sensitive attention and frequently put his hand on his heart. Within weeks of his arrival, he even asked two consecutive women, both far beneath him in status, to marry him. They refused his proposals, but only because their families insisted on following the tradition of a long courtship. For his part,

Hatfield was unruffled by the rejection, partly because he had already moved on. This time, he set his sights on the secluded village of Buttermere.

At Buttermere, Hatfield, again posing as Hope, was greeted with a warm reception. He took up permanent residence at the Fish Inn, where Mary Robinson, still unmarried despite all the attention, served him drinks and dinners. It was not long before he proposed to Mary who, unlike the women of Keswick, cast aside the tradition of a long courtship. Some of the locals were wary of this choice, including Coleridge, who took it upon himself to report the marriage in the *Morning Post* on 11 October 1802. Even without the suspicions, the story was newsworthy because it was not often in England that so great a man as Colonel Hope married so poor a woman as Mary Robinson at so secluded a village.[9] Still, in his article Coleridge reported that the people of the Lakes 'await with anxiety the moment when they shall receive decisive proof that the bridegroom is the real person whom he describes himself to be'.[10] Indeed, Mary's friends did demand that the supposed Hope write to various gentlemen to confirm his identity, but he instead convinced them that such useless etiquette would take too long. He insisted on vouching for himself, reminding his new friends that he had signed his name to letters at the post office in Keswick. In 1802 Britain, this was a distinction given only to MPs. The price of forging such a signature was death, a risk few were willing to take. So the couple was speedily married, and no one had proved that Hope was other than what he claimed to be.

They were wrong, of course, for just a few weeks after Hatfield and Robinson wed and set off for his supposed ancestral estate in Scotland, two letters were printed in the *Morning Post* in response to Coleridge's article of 11 October. The letters, written by Colonel Augustus Hope's brother, claimed that the real Colonel Hope had been in Germany the past six months and could not possibly have married Robinson. As the rumours from these letters stirred uncomfortably through the Lake District, the country pastor who had performed the ceremony in England's tiniest chapel wrote urgently to the supposed Hope in Scotland, begging him to return to Keswick and set the record straight. Oddly enough, Hatfield and his bride did return, where he must have believed he still had enough credibility to carry on his identity theft. He was, however, immediately identified as an impostor and arrested.

From here, Mary Robinson's life moved from tragedy, to sensation, to oblivion. Although she and Hatfield were married for just a few weeks before he was arrested, she was pregnant. Even after he was imprisoned, Mary reportedly carried on correspondence with him and went to see him in jail. After their child was delivered stillborn, she married the local farmer Richard Harrison and eventually faded into obscurity, though one can see her tombstone in the Lake District churchyard at Caldbeck to this day.

In the meantime, locals began the unpleasant task of unravelling the story. Just after the execution, they came across a small chest containing Hatfield's letters and papers. Coleridge read them and ended up writing four more sensational articles for the *Morning Post*. But he was not the only one, because within a year of the trial, Hatfield and Robinson became part of Britain's national mythology. In 1803 alone, five different fast-selling pamphlet versions of the story were printed; Dorothy Wordsworth included it in her *Recollections of a Tour Made in Scotland*; and Wordsworth in Book VII of *The Prelude*. Robinson became the object of visual culture too, in play after play on the London stage and in well-known engravings by James Gillray and George Cruikshank. Novel versions have also remained popular, right up until a few years ago with Melvyn Bragg's 1989 *The Beauty of Buttermere*.

The story's staying power shows the grip it had on the national psyche. Hatfield had violated something very basic in those who were already identified with the Lake District. It was not just that ideas of truth were betrayed. The Robinson affair represented a bizarre coupling of deceit and honesty. The consummation of their marriage also symbolized a terrifying clash of two opposed forces: simple poverty and sophisticated wealth. This became apparent in at least one retelling of the story in 1803 by William Mudford, in which Robinson tells Hope she is 'the humble daughter of a villager! Oh, Sir! Forget me; think not of me; Nature seems to have placed a bar, which custom forbids us to o'er leap.'[11]

Coleridge had come to the Lake District to discover his own inner truth, and instead ended up exposing Hafield's outer falseness. So it is no surprise that he took Hatfield's case personally. Hatfield had developed a pattern of changing lives, as if he were merely changing clothes. When one life seemed to end, he would just abandon it and create a new one. Witnessing this easy transformation threw Coleridge off balance. He was especially unsettled by the way in which the humble folks of Keswick and Buttermere so fiercely defended Hatfield's actions, even after they were convinced of his true identity. Coleridge wrote, 'It will hardly be believed, how obstinately almost all classes at Keswick were infatuated in his favour, and how indignantly they spoke of the Gentleman who had taken such prudent and prompt measures to bring the impostor to detection.'[12]

For Coleridge, the fact that individual identity could be so slippery, that outward appearance could so completely mask the desires of the heart, that personal authenticity had so little meaning in the midst of Britain's most authentic landscape, were unbearable problems. Curiously, these realizations also excited him, urging him to introspection at a depth that was as compelling as it was painful. It is no coincidence that the same weeks he spent travelling the fells writing intense descriptions of the landscape to Sara Hutchinson, then investigating and writing up the Hatfield case, Coleridge also wrote his most desolate poem, 'Dejection: An Ode'. In that poem the growth of the poet's mind is revealed as a process of continuous transformations akin to Hatfield's. Yet he was deeply unsettled by the idea that inner truth did not necessarily manifest itself outwardly, as he wrote in 'Dejection': 'Though I should gaze for ever | . . . | I may not hope from outward forms to win | The passion and the life, whose fountains are within' (ll. 44, 46–7).

Coleridge also had very personal reasons to see parallels between Hatfield's situation and his own. As is well known, at this time Coleridge was deeply unsettled by Wordsworth's impending marriage to Mary Hutchinson, Sara's sister. Although Coleridge must have wanted to, he could not bring himself to abandon his wife and children for Sara. Wordsworth, on the other hand, had a mistress, Annette Vallon, and a child Caroline, in France. This did not stop him from courting and marrying Mary Hutchinson, an event that obviously disturbed Coleridge deeply, as his *Morning Post* publications chronicle. He printed his 'Dejection' ode on the day of Wordsworth's marriage, clearly pitting his personal despair against Wordsworth's happiness. Hatfield's marriage to Robinson took place just two days after Wordsworth's, and Coleridge, who had a deep interest in both marriages, did not trust either of them. The following week he published his first article on Hatfield in the *Morning Post* along with a sonnet called 'Spot in the Sun'. In this poem, he makes a reference to Wordsworth's abandonment of Annette Vallon and their child Caroline in 1792, and of his visit to Calais to see them in August 1802. The poem reads, 'And yet how oft I find the pious man | At Annette's door, the lovely courtesan!' (ll. 3–4). Coleridge centres his poem on a hypocrite: a holy father goes to hear a courtesan's sins, but he ends up treating himself to sexual favours. For Coleridge, both Hatfield and Wordsworth become bigamists in the same week.

The week of Wordsworth's and Hatfield's weddings, Coleridge recorded in his notebook a dream of identity transformation. He wrote, 'I dreamt of Dorothy, William & Mary—& that Dorothy was altered in every feature.' A week later, he had sunk even deeper into questions of authenticity. Coleridge wrote 'The Seems—the Seems—what seems to be & is no—'.[13] Hatfield's appearance in the 1802 Lake District was just that: an appearance, or 'seeming', to borrow Coleridge's term. And yet it was more than that. Ironically, Hatfield migrated to the Lake District to lose his identity, whereas Coleridge came to find his. What Hatfield lost was his life, and what Coleridge found was that even in this pastoral and authentic landscape, in the heart of rural England, true identity was as uncertain as it was anywhere else in the world.

FURTHER READING

Adams, Percy G., *Travelers and Travel Liars, 1660–1800* (New York: Dover Publications, 1962, 1980). Examines the relationship between travel narratives and travel hoaxes throughout the eighteenth century.

Anon., *Of the Shoemaker Schroter, the Printer Taurinas, and the Traveler Damberger, three travelers who never traveled at all but invented their stories in one manufactory* (London, 1801). This anonymous book is the only biographical account of Damberger's hoax.

Bragg, Melvyn, *The Maid of Buttermere* (London: Hodder and Stoughton, 1987). A novel based on the lives of Mary Robinson and John Hatfield written by a native of the Lake District.

Burton, Sarah, *Impostors: Six Kinds of Liar* (London: Penguin, 2000). Discusses Princess Caraboo and other impostors.

Collins, Paul, *Banvard's Folly: Thirteen Tales of Renowned Obscurity, Famous Anonymity, and Rotten Luck* (London: Picador, 2001). A study of impostors, including William Henry Ireland and George Psalmanazar.

De Quincey, Thomas, 'Samuel Taylor Coleridge', in *Tait's Edinburgh Magazine* (Sept. 1834), 590–3. De Quincey remembers the Hatfield hoax and Coleridge's part in it.

Groom, Nick, *The Forger's Shadow: How Forgery Changed the Course of Literature* (London: Picador, 2002). The newest and most innovative study of literary forgery in the Romantic period.

Kirby, Robert S., *Kirby's Wonderful and Eccentric Museum; or, Magazine of Remarkable Characters*, 6 vols. (London: R. S. Kirby, 1820), i. 309–30; 333–44. Carries the fullest account of the Hatfield imposture, including some of his original letters and poetry.

Low, Donald A., *Thieves' Kitchen: The Regency Underworld* (London: J. M. Dent, 1982). Includes a discussion of Hatfield among a larger cast of Regency rogues and characters.

Parry, Edward Abbott, *Vagabonds All* (London: Cassell, 1926). Chronicles a number of hoaxes and mischief makers, including the life of John Hatfield.

Rieman, Donald, 'The Beauty of Buttermere as Fact and Romantic Symbol', *Criticism*, 24: 2 (1984), 139–70. Discusses in detail the chronology of the Hatfield hoax and its relationship to Romanticism.

Russett, Margaret, 'The "Caraboo Hoax": Romantic Woman as Mirror and Image', in *Discourse: Journal for Theoretical Studies in Media and Culture*, 17: 2 (Winter 1994–5), 26–47. A critical article on Romanticism and Princess Caraboo.

Stark, Suzanne J., *Female Tars: Women Aboard Ship in the Age of Sail* (Annapolis, Md.: Naval Institute Press, 1996). Discusses many of the women who cross-dressed and sailed on warships in the Romantic period.

Wordsworth, Dorothy, *Recollections of a Tour Made in Scotland* (New Haven and London: Yale University Press, 1997). On p. 40 of this account, Dorothy Wordsworth details the trial of Hatfield and Wordsworth's and Coleridge's reaction to it.

NOTES

1. *Records of the African Association, 1788–1831*, ed. Robin Hallett (London: Thomas Nelson, 1964), pp. 168–9.
2. *British Critic*, 17 (Jan.–June 1801), 349; *Gentleman's Magazine*, 71: 1 (1801), 249–50.
3. John Matthew Gutch, *Caraboo: A Narrative of a Singular Imposition* (Bristol, 1817), p. 22.
4. R. S. Kirby, *Kirby's Wonderful and Eccentric Museum; or, Magazine of Remarkable Characters*, 6 vols. (London: R. S. Kirby, 1820), i. 341.
5. Ibid. i. 341–2.
6. *The Collected Letters of Samuel Taylor Coleridge*, ed. E. L. Griggs, 6 vols. (Oxford: Clarendon Press, 1956–71), i. 580.
7. Ibid. ii. 853.
8. Samuel Taylor Coleridge, *Essays on His Times*, ed. David V. Erdman, 3 vols. (London: Princeton University Press, 1978), i. 406.
9. Ibid. i. 358.
10. Ibid. i. 357.
11. William Mudford, *Augustus and Mary; or, The Maid of Buttermere* (London, 1803), p. 92.
12. Coleridge, *Essays on His Times*, i. 413.
13. *The Notebooks of Samuel Taylor Coleridge*, 3 vols. ed. Kathleen Coburn (London and New York: Routledge, 1957–73), i. 1250 21.214; 1253 21.217.

33 | Non-fictional prose

John Whale

The prose writings of the Romantic period form a rich and varied body of work which is only now beginning to receive the kind of attention it deserves from critics and scholars. The dominance of the idea of the 'Romantic' in the past has meant that only a selection of this variety has received its due. Because of the foregrounding of the self and the dominance of a poetic aesthetic, the kind of prose writings which have figured most prominently in literary histories have been literary reviews, auto-biographies, and essays. There was a time—as recent as the mid-twentieth century—when the male prose writers of this period were defined under the cosy title of 'Romantic essayists'. Women writers, of course, were rarely dealt with at all. Charles Lamb, William Hazlitt, Thomas De Quincey, and Leigh Hunt were the authors whose multifarious writings were categorized under this problematic heading. It valued short 'familiar' prose writings in which the author manifested his taste in an act of rhetorical intimacy with the reader. Literary intimacy, taste, and the force of immediate impressions were the valued qualities of a prose writing fit to match the singular individualism and autobiographical mode of a Romanticism dominated by poetry and led by Wordsworth. The title of 'essay' fitted much of Lamb's writing under his pseudonym Elia, some of Hazlitt's shorter articles, and a number of Hunt's more whimsical pieces, but it failed miserably to describe any of the more discursively complex productions of De Quincey. The valued essays were more often than not manifestations of hero-worship or memoirs of those who had encountered the poets first-hand. If the prose writers were not mimicking the poets by producing essays that behaved like lesser versions of Romantic odes, they were writing in adulation of the poets themselves. Unsurprisingly, as Romantic criticism changed its focus and became more sophisticated, the early twentieth-century critical appreciation of the aesthetics of the familiar essay fell into decline and the essayists into relative obscurity.

In more recent years, the developing sense of the political aspect of Romantic writing generally has enabled figures like Hazlitt to make a welcome return alongside other writers whose work was formerly considered to be outside the purview of literary studies. Now it is possible to read political, literary, or aesthetic texts alongside each other and to find ways of connecting the non-fictional prose writing of, among others, Edmund Burke, Tom Paine, Mary Wollstonecraft, Helen Maria Williams,

Hannah More, William Cobbett, Charles Lamb, William Hazlitt, Leigh Hunt, Thomas De Quincey, and Dorothy Wordsworth.

One of the ironies of the history of Romantic non-fictional prose I have described here is that many of the most significant works were written by poets: Percy Shelley's *Defence of Poetry*; Wordsworth's Prefaces to the *Lyrical Ballads*; Keats's *Letters*; Southey's *Letters Written in Spain and Portugal*: Coleridge's *Biographia Literaria*. And there is a very strong case for arguing that Coleridge is the most various and creative prose writer of the age if one considers not only his ground-breaking critical experiment in *Biographia Literaria*, but also his various lectures, the publishing enterprise of *The Friend*, his notebooks, and his marginalia. The last two particularly, like the journals of Dorothy Wordsworth or Keats's letters, extend the boundaries of what we still too generally (and narrowly) think of as prose.

This narrowness is exposed by the case of William Cobbett, almost certainly the most prolific prose writer of the Romantic period. His extraordinarily voluminous output included agricultural tracts, economic treatises, political satire, historical commentary, advice literature, and autobiography. Cobbett is as much a publisher as an author. He instigated the publication of parliamentary debate now known as Hansard and acted for most of his career as a conduit for radical agricultural opinion. His publishing activities challenge traditional literary evaluations of the quality of prose writing. His work is almost always occasional, suited to a pressing topical purpose, and is always pushing for a political response. The most famous collections of his work are *Rural Rides*, originally published in his *Political Register*, which move easily from the detailed landscape descriptions of a countryman—appreciation of soil texture and depth, the size of trees, availability of common land—into swingeing attacks on the condition of the labouring poor and the rising cost of central government.

Faced with such a rich variety of prose writing in the Romantic period, it is possible to divide it along generic lines: autobiography, biography, memoir; or according to its mode of publication: journals, magazines, newspapers. The problem here is that many writers made their living by working across the dividing lines of genres and published wherever they could in newspaper columns, journal articles, as well as in books. As Jon Klancher suggests (see *Oxford Companion to the Romantic Age*, pp. 279–86), this was also a period in which a new sense of literature emerges through a culture of reviews: in the early 1780s, journals such as the *Quarterly Review* and the *Critical Review* inaugurated a 'notion of "public opinion" as a newly autonomous force'. This rearticulation of 'public opinion' enabled the radical counter-culture of the 1790s to take place as well as its anti-Jacobin backlash later in the same decade. Literary reviews such as the *Edinburgh* and the *Quarterly* were formative for the way in which the reading public thought of the category of the literary, particularly in relation to politics. By the 1820s, the categories were clearly conflicted even in middle-class liberal journals such as the *London Magazine* and Leigh Hunt's aptly named *Liberal*. Writers of the Romantic period such as William Hazlitt, Charles Lamb, Thomas De Quincey, and Leigh Hunt whom literary criticism has conventionally designated as 'essayists' belong to this review culture which is strongly identified with political argument, and which encourages a mixture of different kinds of writing within the pages of a single publication: reviews, opinion columns, letters, biographies, serialized fiction, poetry, political economy, travel literature. To appreciate fully the nature of what has been termed the 'familiar essay' we need to return these writers and their writings to their original context of miscellaneous magazine writing (see also the chapters on 'Print culture and the book trade' and 'Essays, newspapers, and magazines').

The familiar essay might be seen as a response to the increasing proliferation of literature and print with the advent of the steam press in 1814. Klancher has pointed to the strategy adopted by some of the literary journals in their attempt to come to terms with a burgeoning mass audience: to fabricate a specific identity for a magazine which could pose a staged intimacy against a wider sense of the anonymity of the reading audience in a mass market. Similarly, writers and editors could exploit the mixed nature of the new audience by acting as cultural arbiters and mediators, or, in the case of *Blackwood's Edinburgh Magazine*, by comically and aggressively exploiting the situation, by turns attacking and cajoling the anonymous reader while maintaining a strong sense of learned coterie. This is especially true of their 'Noctes Ambrosianae', articles which regularly regaled the readership with the fictionalized goings-on in their Edinburgh headquarters. The 'Noctes' confidently established a specific cultural and geographical identity. They challenged and risked alienating many potential readers with these tactics while successfully attacking the liberal literary mores of distant London.

Even those texts which might be thought of as most definitely within traditionally defined notions of Romantic introspection and self-expression are often cut through with an ironic playfulness which creatively exploits the magazine context of their publication. At the opening of his *Confessions of an English Opium-Eater* (1822) De Quincey plays with the expectations of his readers by dissociating himself from what he perceives to be a radical liberal tradition of autobiographical writing emanating from the French Enlightenment thinker Jean-Jacques Rousseau, author of the sexually explicit *Confessions*. He immediately forms an intimate system of address with the reader which aggressively betrays the Opium-Eater's privileged role in the culture at large and his affiliation to a much more conservative brand of politics. He also plays upon his reader's sense of public scandal. It is a typically playful and ironizing manœuvre by De Quincey, who engages with the genre of confession while removing himself from the expected version of it. The reader gains an impression of the slippery business of reading autobiographical texts from this period like Lamb's *Confessions of a Drunkard* and Hazlitt's *Liber Amoris* in which different degrees of anonymity, irony, and fiction are strategically deployed in a sophisticated magazine culture.

Aesthetics and politics: politics and aesthetics

The French Revolution generated a concerted and widespread response from different levels of British culture (see *Oxford Companion to the Romantic Age*, p. 19). Opinion was mobilized into print in a way hitherto unprecedented. Between 'loyalist' anti-Jacobin pamphleteers on the one side and the revolution's liberal and radical sympathizers on the other, the war of words covered an extremely wide spectrum of public opinion, much of which had not been formed or seen before on this scale in something as visible as printed texts. The pamphlet war between British writers which has come to be known as the 'Revolution Controversy' also included those, like the poet and engraver William Blake and the philosopher William Godwin, who offered a severe critique of the government with its repression of opinion along with an attack upon the very idea of violent revolution which, they argued, would only create a new kind of tyranny (see also chapter on 'The historical context').

Edmund Burke's *Reflections*

Edmund Burke's *Reflections on the Revolution in France* (1790) set the terms for this more general debate, not only by establishing the historical significance of the moment, but also by deploying a complex mixture of styles and tactics (see *Oxford Companion to the Romantic Age*, pp. 18–19). Burke sought to persuade his politically empowered readers to dissociate themselves not only from the new revolutionary republic but from the liberal and radical opinion at home which sought to challenge the established order and constitution of British society. Burke's powerful anti-revolutionary reflections assume the open-ended and organic form of a letter, offering advice to a young Frenchman. Although much of his book is concerned with matters of political economy, with revenue and taxation as well as an account of the French Church, many of his contemporary readers (like many modern ones) were taken with his more uncharacteristic emotional descriptions of Marie Antoinette and the 'storming' of the queen's bedchamber by the revolutionary mob. In such untypical literary 'scenes', Burke's appeal to chivalry and sentiment was seen by his detractors as turning history into romance, and real-life politics into theatre. Even to his supporters, there appeared to be a risk in his sentimentalizing of history—for all of the book's success as propaganda. Burke's *Reflections* thus becomes as controversial for its mode of argument, its daring literary style, and its deployment of sensibility, as it does for its trenchant critique of the recent French example of political experiment and its staunch defence of the English system of government. By championing an aristocratic culture seen through the rather outmoded idea of chivalry, Burke's fertile imagination created a dangerously heterogeneous text whose complications and contradictions even he could only guess at. For example, in attempting to identify France's new revolutionary society as absurd, overly rationalistic, inhuman, and primitive, Burke can be credited with giving the event its identity as the first truly modern revolution. The effect of Burke's play of different styles, some of them highly literary—occasionally novelistic, sentimental, and theatrical—effectively aestheticized the nature of political argument. At one point he writes of the reciprocal exchange of citizen and state in terms of aestheticized emotion: 'To make us love our country, our country ought to be lovely.'[1] As we shall see, this had great consequences for other writers in this period, especially for those working in the medium of non-fictional prose.

Responses to Burke

While mockingly drawing attention to Burke's 'genius', Tom Paine declared of the *Reflections* that: 'Mr Burke's book is *all* Miscellany.'[2] His attack fastened specifically on Burke's literariness, facetiously suggesting at one point that 'it is in his [Burke's] paradoxes that we must look for his arguments'.[3] Unwittingly, Paine's suggestion here anticipates current analysis of Burke's prose: the use of literary modes of criticism to explore its political meaning.

Many of Burke's opponents seized on this feature of his writing in their attacks on the *Reflections* (see *Oxford Companion to the Romantic Age*, pp. 44–7). The first to do so was Mary Wollstonecraft in *A Vindication of the Rights of Men* (1790). Here Wollstonecraft focuses on Burke's subscription to aristocratic culture and his attachment to sentiment in order to expose the libertine nature of the culture to which they belong. With a ruthlessly rationalistic mode of argument, she portrays Burke as a victim of his own masculinity, a version of Jean-Jacques Rousseau: a man of sensibility wasting his talents on an absurdity. One of Wollstonecraft's tactics is thus to use gender as a means of critique, not to personalize the debate, but to see Burke's position as symptomatic of masculinity within aristocratic culture. She portrays him as the victim of sentiment. She uses gender as a means of undermining his place in (and his defence of) the dominant culture epitomized in the form of the aristocratic male.

The style of Burke's prose, particularly in the most famous passages of his *Reflections*, is ornate and hierarchical. Its structure might be said to reflect the thing he is writing about: the constitution of British society. This is not written and visible, but mysterious and organic, lurking by implication in the workings of history: 'we have given to our frame of polity the image of a relation in blood; binding up the constitution of our country with our dearest domestic ties; adopting our fundamental laws into the bosom of our family affections; keeping inseparable, and cherishing with the warmth of all their combined and mutually reflected charities, our state, our hearths, our sepulchres, and our altars.'[4] In its complex, hierarchically ordered syntax Burke's style mirrors the nature of the society he wants to preserve from revolutionary change. Since Burke's argument is about the spirit of liberty residing within the complex mystery of social relations, his style serves as a reminder of the appropriate respect and awe in which such sanctity of power should be held. It is a style which assumes that truth is complex and difficult and certainly not easily accessible to everyone.

In contrast, Thomas Paine's style operates with a belief in simplicity which assumes that the truth of things is visible, legible, and understandable by all people in the guise of common sense (see *Oxford Companion to the Romantic Age*, pp. 19, 22). It assumes that rights can be written down and codified. Writing is definitive, not failing in the face of higher authority as it sometimes is for Burke. Paine's subscription to openness and transparency assumes that language works best when simplest. When language obtrudes on the reader as an object in its own right it is seen by him to be delusive and dangerous. Paine wants language to be as transparent as possible, even to be invisible in the service of truth—unlike Burke whose language parades its own rhetorical splendour and eloquence. (By the same token, it could be said that Paine's writing masks its own brand of rhetoric under the guise of simplicity.) 'The duty of man', according to Paine, 'is not a wilderness of turnpike gates, through which he is to pass by tickets from one to the other. It is plain and simple, and consists but of two points. His duty to God, which every man must feel; and with respect to his neighbour, to do as he would be done by.'[5] Paine's democratic impulse, evident in his reference to 'every man', is supported by a New Testament ethics and an image which reveals his subscription to an empire of free trade.

In this way, the revolution debate self-consciously exposes the connection between style and ideology. The liberal and democratic impulse of an accessible Painite style encounters the complex, organic eloquence of Burke's commitment to an unwritten constitution to form a conflicted basis for a politicized understanding of style for prose writers later in this period. Burke's legacy is a complex one. William Hazlitt, for example, is renowned for his terse, masculine style of writing, the directness and idiomatic accessibility of which might be seen as confirming his position as a liberal or radical in politics. Yet he is also a great admirer of Burke as a prose writer whose style places him closest to the edge of poetry. Hazlitt is drawn to the poetic, imaginative mystery and suggestiveness of Burke's rhetoric while recognizing the danger of its tendency to be diverted from actualities, practicalities, and, more simply, the truth.

In their very different ways, Hazlitt, Charles Lamb, Thomas De Quincey, and Leigh Hunt produce essays and articles in which prose style inevitably negotiates this conflicted paradigm of Paineite simplicity and Burkean eloquence. Even for the more obviously conservative De Quincey and for the more antiquarian aspects of Lamb, a rhetorical directness to the reader supported by the informal ease of a spoken idiom has its attractions, although it is often subverted by playful or aggressive obscurity and a parade of learning. For Hazlitt and Hunt, both liberal radicals, their attachment to the aesthetic is always likely to complicate their commitment to a democratic intimacy with the reader. And on the other side of the equation, their politically connected idiomatic ease could very easily be seized upon by the literary establishment and their enemies as mere 'vulgarity'. This was the tactic of the aggressively Tory *Blackwood's Edinburgh Magazine* when it attacked writers like Hazlitt, Hunt, and, most famously, John Keats, as members of what it saw as the 'Cockney School', a loose literary grouping of London liberals.

For 'polite' or middle-class radicals like Hazlitt and Hunt, their involvement in literary aesthetics inevitably tempers their writing and makes it retain its difference from other artisanal or working-class radicals within the print culture of the time. Even in Hazlitt's case there appears a reluctance to be associated with non-polite forms of political dissent and radicalism. He values his attachment to a cultured, philosophical position. When he comes to assess William Cobbett's contribution to political writing in the period he distances himself from Cobbett's lack of 'the philosophical structure of opinion'.

Burke's choice of the letter form might also be said to have been significant, for the possibilities which it opened up for other prose writers in the period. Epistolary forms already had a rich and well-established history in the century before Burke wrote his *Reflections*, both in prose and verse. It is a particularly flexible form even for mainstream literary productions. As I have already suggested, Burke could dramatize his act of polemical persuasion in the *Reflections* by presenting it in the guise of an advice letter from a paternal British friend to a French citizen. Early on in the book, Burke makes a strategic claim upon his readers: 'I beg leave to throw out my thoughts, and express my feelings, just as they arise in my mind, with very little attention to formal method.'[6] With such a claim to spontaneity, the text maintains a thinly veiled fiction which can exploit its proximate relationship to events at home this side of the Channel. Burke can present himself as an avuncular man of wisdom. The form also provides him with an opportunity to try out his occasionally emotive acts of persuasion, the theatricalized horror, outrage, and passionately concerned sentiment with which he views events in Paris. The letter form uses sentiment and sensibility to support the more extensive rational economic modes of argument.

While Burke was formulating his response to the French Revolution, Helen Maria Williams was also engaged in letter-writing, in her case while witnessing events in the French capital. Her *Letters Written in France* (1790–4) form a considerable body of work in which, once again, there is a mixture of aesthetics and politics. Here, the letter form is deployed to relay a responsive historical commentary. The narrative of history thus unfolds simultaneously with Williams's response as eyewitness. The capacity of an epistolary text to capture or embody change, often in the individual, had long been one of its successful features. It was prominent in the literature of sensibility, the most famous and influential instance being Goethe's *The Sorrows of Young Werther*. In the case of Williams's *Letters Written in France*, then, history and sensibility fuse in a narrative which fascinatingly converges with the novelistic. At times, the key players in the revolution are reminiscent of the heroes and villains of fiction, as Williams charts the narrative of her love affair with the revolution from its optimistic, idealistic, and philanthropic opening to its degeneration into the Terror of 1793. Williams the letter-writer becomes a character within her own historical romance. As she puts it in Letter IX, after explaining the responsiveness of her 'common sensibility': 'My love of the French revolution, is the natural result of this sympathy, and therefore my political creed is entirely an affair of the heart.' At another point she suggests that 'the leaders of the revolution [have] engaged beauty as one of their auxiliaries'.[7] Simultaneously with Burke's *Reflections*, Williams's *Letters* provide a powerful instance of the fusion between aesthetics and politics in the writing of prose, a mixing in which the flexible and dynamic nature of the epistolary text—its dialectical quality—plays a key role.

Reading discursively

Burke's *Reflections*, according to Olivia Smith, was ground-breaking in the way it inaugurated a revolution in attitudes towards vulgarity of style which lasted at least through the two decades following its publication. Burke's deployment of strong emotion and idiomatic prose ushered in a new wave of political writing which questions previous confidence about what exactly constituted decorum, propriety, and vulgarity.

Many of the leading prose writers of the period perceived a significant shift in the nature of their medium and they saw this change in terms of style. If Samuel Johnson was the abiding stylistic influence of the previous age, then Burke was the model for theirs. Coleridge could not understand how anyone could 'set Johnson before Burke' whose style he valued for its 'discursive and continuous' qualities.[8] For De Quincey, too, it was this latter quality for which Burke's prose was deservedly prized; and he dramatically endorses it as a form of prospective energy: 'two contrasted intellects, Burke's and Johnson's: one an intellect essentially going forward, governed by the very necessity of growth—by the law of motion in advance; the latter, essentially an intellect retrogressive, and throwing itself back on its own steps.'[9] Characteristically, De Quincey sees Burke's prose as natural, dynamic, and organic. When, in his article on Charles Lamb, he comes to disparage the style of his near contemporary Hazlitt, the contrast is marked. Hazlitt lacks the required continuous quality, what De Quincey elsewhere calls 'connection' and 'eloquence'. For De Quincey, Hazlitt's thoughts are 'abrupt, insulated, capricious and . . . non-sequacious' and his style is typified by 'separate splinterings of phrase or image which throw upon the eye a vitreous scintillation for a moment, but spread no deep suffusion of colour'.[10] Put more simply, Hazlitt's flashiness, for De Quincey, represents a dangerously attractive superficiality. There is a fear of the popular mass audience here registered in the language of visual trickery. In contrast, he sees truth as something natural, deep, and eternal. De Quincey takes this analogy further in his meditations on 'Style' where he characterizes the age's prose by reference to the English newspapers. (As if to reinforce his Burkean conservatism, De Quincey sees style as a marker of national identity.) Here the wrong kind of continuousness, a dangerous kind of prolixity, has taken hold of the popular consciousness:

Whereas now, amongst us English, not only is the too general tendency of our sentences towards hyperbolical length, but it will be found continually, that instead of one rise and one corresponding fall . . . there are many. Flux and reflux, swell and cadence, that is the movement for a sentence; but our modern sentences agitate us by rolling fires, after the fashion of those internal earthquakes that, not content with one throe, run along spasmodically in a long succession of intermitting convulsions.[11]

Whereas Burke's style was credited with a smooth, organic nature, the spirit of the age for De Quincey manifests itself in a chaotic, disruptive energy described in a language that suggests revolution and social subversion. Here style, for the conservative De Quincey, is a sign of the age's tendency towards social agitation.

For Hazlitt, too, Burke is the prose writer par excellence, but, for him, the admirable quality of his style is that it straddles social realities and fictions. Its mixed quality means that it acts as a bridge between the world of politics and the world of aesthetics. It is in touch with an empirical notion of truth while recognizing the power of idealizations: 'Burke's execution, like that of all good prose, savours of the texture of what he describes, and his pen slides or drags over the ground of his subject, like the painter's pencil. The most rigid fidelity and the most fanciful extravagance meet, and are reconciled in his pages.'[12] For Hazlitt, non-fictional prose occupies this mixed ground: it aspires towards the poetic, but has to keep itself firmly based on realities and in close touch with the truth of things.

Today we are, perhaps, less concerned with the category of style than these Romantic exponents of non-fictional prose. For them, style is never far removed from ideological intervention and political argument. De Quincey's Tory politics are embedded in the organic principles and metaphors of Burke's *Reflections*. In contrast, Hazlitt uses the same text to support his position as a radical. As we can see from these brief examples, style could also be a useful starting-point for an understanding of the specific nature of prose divorced as it often is from the strictures, conventions, and possibilities of well-defined literary genres. At present, we lack a fully developed poetics of non-fictional prose, particularly one informed by a sense of the way in which ideological position, allegiances, and affiliations inhere in the aesthetics of style. More work needs to be done on the nature of prose: its rhetoric, its capacity for connection, and its coherence into a sense of recognizable style.

The discursive nature of prose also demands attention: how to appreciate its capacity to range across different fields of knowledge, often seemingly free from the strictures of genre. Much of the most fruitful recent work on prose in this period has been informed by an awareness of 'discourses' as defined by the French theorist Michel Foucault. This kind of discursive discourse analysis combines an awareness of the various and discrete nature of sets of vocabularies as well as the ideological subject positions with which they are connected. One could see what Paine disparagingly refers to as 'Mr Burke's Miscellany', the plurality of the *Reflections*, as stemming from his deployment of an intersecting complex of different discourses: of sensibility, civic humanism, political economy, and chivalry. Similarly, one could analyse Paine's claims to common sense, his assumptions of transparency and simplicity as well as his use of a discourse of natural observation. This kind of reading is particularly useful for exposing the underlying contradictions within a prose text, the ruptures and conflicts which emerge as one discourse knocks against another. As in Tom Paine's mischievous suggestion that we find Burke's arguments in his paradoxes, this kind of reading appreciates the miscellaneous nature of prose writing.

William Hazlitt, 'The Indian Jugglers'[13]

Coming forward and seating himself on the ground in his white dress and tightened turban, the chief of the Indian jugglers begins with tossing up two brass balls, *which is what any of us could do*, and concludes with keeping up four at the same time, *which is what none of us could do to save our lives, nor if we were to take our whole lives to do it in.* (emphasis added)

In this way, Hazlitt's 'The Indian Jugglers' (1819) opens with a dramatic re-creation of the act of juggling. The immediate effect is, apparently, to start the essay as the act of juggling starts: to invite the reader to take part in an immediate instance of the visual imagination. As Hazlitt's opening sentence unfolds, however, we realize that this conjuring of a physical phenomenon is wrapped up in a question about ordinariness and exceptionality. The two key relative clauses of Hazlitt's balanced sentence (here italicized) might seem to be there just for their idiomatic responsiveness, their striking a demotic bond with the reader. But as we shall see, their apparent innocence turns out to contain an urgency in an essay which is really concerned with the achievement of a life.

At the beginning of the article, then, the writer shares a rhetorical common ground with the reader, one supported by experience. The ostensible topic of the essay, the Indian jugglers, is used as a means of literary sharing and the opening of the article plays on this sense of mutuality, as if author and reader are sharing in the spectacle of popular culture which appears before them.

This illusion of common ground is dramatically shattered when Hazlitt's text suddenly becomes surprisingly self-referential, as if the mode has switched, within the space of a paragraph, from a cultural commentary handling philosophical questions of perception in a popular, accessible manner to an anguished autobiographical confession:

The hearing a speech in Parliament, drawled or stammered out by the Honorable Member or the Noble Lord, the ringing the changes on their common-places, which anyone could repeat after them as well as they, stirs me not a jot, shakes not my good opinion of myself: but the seeing the Indian Jugglers does. It makes me ashamed of myself. I ask what there is that I can do as well as this? Nothing.

The subject of Indian jugglers rendered in an apparently dramatic and objective manner has suddenly mutated into an agonized self-critique about the limits of essay-writing and the worth of being a writer. The hinge on which this sudden transition turns within a single paragraph is the idea of being 'stirred', being jolted out of an ordinary complacent view of things. This runs through the whole article: a sense of being stimulated out of our everyday perceptions by different kinds of fascination and wonder. At this point, having been fascinated (and to some degree disgusted) by the jugglers, Hazlitt switches abruptly to shame and abjection. The psychological move is from an object of external wonder to one of self-criticism. Such complex movements between subject and object are often a key feature of Hazlitt's writings. In this essay, he now moves on to consider the distinction between mechanical arts and acts of genius, between mere ingenuity or cleverness and a higher form of organic power described here as 'greatness'. He now brings in the idea of time: to be truly great one's achievements must outlast the sensation of the moment—as is the case of the Indian jugglers—and be unique. (This idea has already been raised in the form of Hazlitt's tired—if not cynical—response to the speeches of politicians, quoted above.) Here the plural nature of the essay's title is important: this kind of dazzling dexterity is impersonal and definitely reproducible. (One senses that the Indian jugglers are doomed to be anonymous and interchangeable despite Hazlitt singling out the 'Chief' for notice.) At the heart of the essay is an anxiey about the reproducibility of art and literature in an age which proliferates writing. This is forcibly captured in the melodramatic anxiety of: 'The utmost I can pretend to do is to write a description of what this fellow can do. I can write a book: so can many others who have not even learned to spell.'

At the key point of his essay, Hazlitt trumps the merely mechanical by turning to a higher set of categories in which 'fine art' replaces 'mechanical skill'. We move beyond ordinary sight to a higher mode of seeing. Here the essay reaches a crescendo with its celebration of the poetic and, at this point it breaks appropriately into poetic quotation from Thomas Gray and Alexander Pope. Here is the Romantic heart of the essay:

The more ethereal, evanescent, more refined and sublime part of art is the seeing nature through the medium of sentiment and passion, as each object is a symbol of the affections and a link in the chain of our endless being. But the unravelling this mysterious web of thought and feeling is alone in the Muse's gift, namely, in the power of that trembling sensibility which is awake to every change and every modification of its ever-varying impressions, that,

Thrills in each nerve, and lives along the line.

This power is indifferently called genius, imagination, feeling, taste; but the manner in which it acts upon the mind can neither be defined by abstract rules, as is the case in science, nor verified by continual unvarying experiments, as is the case in mechanical performances.

Having shifted his ground and categories so that not only is there a higher kind of seeing involving the soul, but also that nature is a language, Hazlitt proceeds to a clinching definition based on his key word 'power'. Typically, for him, he keeps this power in touch with the body. (Even in the chosen quotation there is the presence of a 'nerve'.) Most importantly, Hazlitt defines feeling as the agent of this power. The presence of an experiencing self is at the centre of this definition of his aesthetics: 'seeing nature through the medium of sentiment and passion.' Paradoxically, the vision or truth of this aesthetic can only be construed through poetry, not through the prosaic communication of the essay form. The very point of this power, it is claimed, is that it resists the usual, rational, formulation of rules. Even the defining quality of language fails to capture it. It spans the words 'imagination', 'genius', 'feeling', and 'taste'. Hazlitt self-consciously draws attention to this as 'the undefined and the imaginary'. After this high point of mystery, the essay returns to the definable, the mechanical. He then moves on to a more easily defined territory: power in the form of greatness that is measurable through its effects. Here Hazlitt is on firmer ground; now it is a question of communication, and the field of enquiry spreads beyond the fine arts across the full range of great men having an impact upon the world.

The essay ends with his already published obituary to the fives-player John Cavanagh. This returns us to a manifestation of popular culture, to the physical and the unlearned, to the democracy of popular sport, and counters what might appear to be the essay's privileging of high art. What becomes an elegy for Cavanagh also draws the essay away from the autobiographical and towards the life of another. The emphasis is no longer on the shame and inadequacy of one's lot as an essayist. His inclusion of the piece on Cavanagh thus acts as a dramatic illustration of how to escape morbid self-pity through a generous act of the sympathetic imagination, while sticking to the subject of a life's achievement. It dramatically reverses the process which started the essay: the projection from juggler to self; now we move from self to other.

An essay which starts out focused on a particular visual subject turns out to be an analysis of taste. For all its apparent casualness and idiomatic common sense, Hazlitt's essay invites the reader into the complex area of aesthetics and a definition of genius. It does so while situating itself in an accessible middle ground in which the first-hand reference to experience, its empiricism, always keeps it in touch with a determined sense of the tangible and the understandable. It very much inhabits Hazlitt's fraught negotiation of the realms of popular and high culture, his wanting prose to approach the poetic without losing touch with its grounding in truth, perception, and a democratically shared humanity. To that end, the essay does not leave the Indian jugglers behind as if they are a lesser kind of achievement; but they are replaced by Cavanagh who stands in for a return to the territory of popular, physical skilfulness, albeit in a safer, less exotic form. It is fitting, too, that the whole essay is suffused with a sense of the elegiac, an aspect present from the beginning in the apparently innocent phrases 'to save our lives' and 'if we were to take our whole lives to do it in'.[14]

Leigh Hunt, 'On the Realities of Imagination'[15]

There is not a more unthinking way of talking than to say such and such pains and pleasures are only imaginary, and therefore to be got rid of or undervalued accordingly. There is nothing imaginary, in the common acceptation of the word.

Leigh Hunt's 1820 essay from his journal *The Indicator* engages confidently, even brusquely, with a commonplace way of looking at the world. It also embarks, as many more famous Romantic texts do, with a redefinition of the word 'imagination'. Although at this point in the essay they can be overlooked, the key terms of Hunt's recategorization are 'pain' and 'pleasure'; and, in particular, the links between them. At this early stage in the essay it might be thought that the essayist is preparing the ground for a learned argument about the nature of perception: swapping a popular fallacy based on a sloppy use of language for the more rigorous ground of philosophical debate. We might expect the essayist now to come forward as our guide to high culture. But as his subscription to 'Whatever is, is', already indicates, he seems determined to keep within the bounds of ordinary language and to cement his relationship with his audience developed through a repeated use of the pronoun 'we'. This is clearly going to be a shared enterprise using a common language. Questions about 'materialists or immaterialists' are raised only for them to give way to the primacy of our perceptions and then, most importantly, to the perception of our neighbours. Truth here consists in being suspicious of an over-reliance on one's own feelings and in an awareness of the necessary corroboration of the evidence of those of one's neighbours: the idea that others might feel something even if you do not. In case we had not realized, Hunt's third paragraph informs us that: 'We do not profess metaphysics.' Persisting in its strategic use of 'we' the essay now takes a more particular, self-revelatory turn in which the nature of the indicator's empirical value system is brought to our attention:

All that we may know on the subject comes to us from some reflection and some experience; and this all may be so little as to make a metaphysician smile; which, if he be a true one, he will do good-naturedly. . . . Our faculty, such as it is, is rather instinctive than reasoning; rather physical than metaphysical; rather wise because it loves much, than because it knows much; rather calculated by a certain retention of boyhood, and by its wanderings in the green places of thought . . .

Characteristically, Hunt negotiates metaphysics by assuming the power of good will. The true metaphysician smiles at his lack of specialist knowledge; the false metaphysician attacks him for it. As he goes on to state, truth here is goodwill or good nature. Love, not reason, is true wisdom. The essayist's identity and his authority may importantly include 'reflection and experience', but instinct also involves a continuation of childhood. There is perhaps an assumption here that adult rationality entails a loss of vitality, of emotional freshness. Hunt's special brand of ethical feeling is presented to his audience in terms of its instinctive physicality.

   This sense of instinctive corporeality also figures strongly in the essay through its repeated awareness of illness, pain, and suffering. Hunt's first enquiry into perception in his opening paragraphs focused on a patient suffering from 'deliriums' and now his essay returns to this quarter as he articulates the strangely limited nature of his knowledge. His democratic wisdom is defined by goodwill, by the power of sentiment and benign sensibility: 'We pretend to see farther than none but the worldly and the malignant.' Given Hunt's professed physicality and his avoidance of metaphysics, the reader might be forgiven for puzzling over the terms of this definition and his rejection of the 'worldly'. Hunt's belief in the power and truth of feeling now begins to take a more transcendent turn as he announces the possibility of a nobility of nature which operates in spite of the painful—or fallen—nature of our humanity. A complex sense of the continuum of pain and pleasure is now expressed in a fascinating paragraph which defines Hunt's self-sacrificing idea of the transformation of pain into pleasure. There is a low-key religious connection here, almost as if Hunt wants to keep the essay free from an expressly religious or metaphysical ethics. He pulls abruptly out of further definition: 'But we shall be getting into other discussions', and returns to a more physical basis for our existence: our health. At this point, he makes another key shift in the trajectory of the essay. Having shied away from theology, he immediately ushers in the poets and the remainder of the article is taken up with the power of poetry and the role of poets as mediators of the realm of imagination.

Within a Romantic literary context this might be thought to be the richest part of the essay, containing as it does Hunt's own particular definition of the role of the poet, the nature of creativity, and the power of imagination. His instruction to his reader to 'take care' of the ground of his health forms an important basis for his aesthetics. To some extent, this is imagination as healthy cure and its mode is a peculiar mixture of pain and pleasure, composed as it is of 'delicious smiles, or tears as delicious'. True riches are of this imaginary kind, Hunt asserts, and he illustrates the point graphically by having the imaginative man see more in the estate of the landed gentry than its owner. Emphatically, Hunt argues, 'He *is* richer.' 'Knowledge, sympathy, imagination, are divining-rods, with which he discovers treasure.' As in Hazlitt's essay, imagination is conceived of as a form of knowledge working in tandem with feeling.

All this prepares the ground for the greater riches and imaginative intensity provided for us by the poets. 'Let a poet go through the grounds, and he will heighten and increase all these sounds and images.' Hunt moves things up a gear. Greater intensity shifts the categories and this is characteristically clinched by a quotation from Shakespeare. Hunt's empiricism—the terms of experience registered on the senses with which he began the essay—now encompasses the idea of purification. Love and imagination, he argues, 'are the two purifiers of our sense which rescue us from the deafening babble of common cares, and enable us to hear all the affectionate voices of earth and heaven'. Hunt's Christian sensibility is once again evident here; and in his idea of benevolence as truth now registered in the word 'affectionate'. This soon leads on to a definition of poets as creators and makers, confirming their role in a more theological system of value: 'the poets are called creators (Ποιηται, Makers) because, with their magical worlds, they bring forth to our eyesight the abundant images and beauties of creation. They put them there, if the reader pleases, and so are literally creators.' At the high point of Hunt's essay, there seems to be some doubt as to whether the poets are creators or mediators: whether they create something absolutely new or simply make apparent what is already a part of the creation. With this question deemed to be unanswerable, Hunt switches to moments of intense pathos in the ultimate work of poetry, Shakespeare's *King Lear*. Now we return to the question posed at the beginning of the essay about the reality of things imaginary. The power of response, of affective or emotional force, is the ultimate mark of poetic imagination which stands in defiance of the glib common subscription to a negative use of the word 'imaginary'.

As if to reinforce his earlier point about the need for purification and for humanity to move beyond common cares through imagination and love to appreciate the beauty of creation, Hunt shifts the perspective for a final time. The essay ends with a prospect of the metropolis of London which registers its immensity and through an imagination such as that possessed by 'the indicator'—our essayist—its capacity for beauty by day or night. The final resting-place of the essay is fittingly the perspective afforded by the suburb, the space of reflection from which Hunt operates. The writer from the suburbs rises above the common cares and pain of the metropolis through the power of affectionate beauty accessed through imagination whose claim to reality is endorsed through feeling, not only in relation to the individual, but as part of a wider community of feeling in which the poets perform a powerful role as mediators of a divine creation.

FURTHER READING

Bate, Jonathan, *Shakespearian Constitutions: Politics, Theatre, Criticism 1730–1830* (Oxford: Clarendon Press, 1989) The last section of this wide-ranging study offers a detailed consideration of Hazlitt's liberal imagination in his Shakespeare criticism.

Boulton, James T., *The Language of Politics in the Age of Wilkes and Burke* (Westport, Conn.: Routledge and Kegan Paul, 1975). A pioneering historiographical study of the links between politics and prose in the period.

Bromwich, David, *Hazlitt: The Mind of a Critic* (New York and Oxford: Oxford University Press, 1983). A powerful overview of Hazlitt's key ideas as a literary critic.

Cox, Jeffrey N., *Poetry and Politics in the Cockney School: Keats, Shelley, Hunt and their Circle* (Cambridge: Cambridge University Press, 1998). An excellent cultural history of the aesthetic and political context of this circle of writers.

Favret, Mary, *Romantic Correspondence: Women, Politics, and the Fiction of Letters* (Cambridge: Cambridge University Press, 1993). A wide-ranging analysis of the dynamic nature of letter-writing in relation to gender and ideology in non-fictional and fictional texts, including those by Burke, De Quincey, and Wollstonecraft.

Gilmartin, Kevin, *Print Politics: The Press and Radical Opposition in Early Nineteenth-Century England* (Cambridge: Cambridge University Press, 1996). An authoritative account of the formation of political opinion in the period through print culture.

Jacobus, Mary, 'The Art of Managing Books: Romantic Prose and the Writing of the Past', in A. Reed (ed.), *Romanticism and Language* (London: Methuen, 1984). A lively illustration of the ways in which prose writers of the period articulate themselves through a complex awareness of past writers.

Keane, Angela, *Women Writers and the English Nation in the 1790s* (Cambridge: Cambridge University Press, 2000). A welcome study of the discourses of nationalism in relation to the revolution controversy of the 1790s, including chapters on Mary Wollstonecraft, Helen Maria Williams, and Hannah More.

Klancher, Jon, *The Making of English Reading Audiences 1790–1832* (Madison: University of Wisconsin Press, 1987). A ground-breaking study of the ways in which audience is constructed and anticipated in various periodical texts of the period.

McFarland, Thomas, *Romantic Cruxes: The English Essayists and the Spirit of the Age* (Oxford: Oxford University Press, 1987). A traditional account from within the poetics of Romanticism, but one which offers illuminating insights into the prose of Hazlitt, Lamb, and De Quincey.

Park, Roy, *Hazlitt and the Spirit of the Age: Abstraction and Critical Theory* (Oxford: Clarendon Press, 1971). A study of Hazlitt as a thinker in relation to philosophical debates of the time.

Paulin, Tom, *The Day-Star of Liberty: William Hazlitt's Radical Style* (London: Faber and Faber, 1998). A passionate reconsideration of Hazlitt as a politically committed and sensuous prose writer.

Roe, Nicholas (ed.), *Leigh Hunt: Life, Poetics, Politics* (Routledge: London and New York, 2003) A timely and welcome collection of essays on Hunt as prose writer as well as poet.

Smith, Olivia, *The Politics of Language 1791–1819* (London and New York: Oxford University Press, 1984). A wide-ranging historical survey of the key arguments about the nature of prose in relation to political argument in the period.

Whale, John, 'Indian Jugglers: Hazlitt, Romantic Orientalism, and the Difference of View', in Tim Fulford and Peter Kitson (eds.), *Romanticism and Colonialism: Writing and Empire, 1780–1830* (Cambridge: Cambridge University Press, 1998), pp. 206–20. An analysis of Hazlitt's famous essay in relation to its cultural context.

——*Imagination Under Pressure: Aesthetics, Politics, and Utility 1789–1832* (Cambridge: Cambridge University Press, 2000). A study of the key Romantic term of 'imagination' as it figures in the prose writings of Burke, Wollstonecraft, Paine, Hazlitt, Cobbett, and Coleridge.

Woodring, Carl, 'Leigh Hunt as Personal Essayist', in Robert A. McCown (ed.), *The Life and Times of Leigh Hunt: Papers Delivered at a Symposium* (Iowa City, Ia: Friends of the University of Iowa Libraries, 1985), pp. 61–72. One of very few accounts of Hunt the essayist.

NOTES

1. Edmund Burke, *Reflections on the Revolution in France*, ed. Conor Cruise O'Brien (Harmondsworth: Penguin, 1968), p. 172.
2. Tom Paine, *The Rights of Man*, ed. Henry Collins (Harmondsworth: Penguin, 1969), p. 138.
3. Ibid. 71.
4. Burke *Reflections*, p. 120.
5. Paine, *Rights of Man*, p. 89.
6. Burke, *Reflections*, p. 92.
7. Helen Maria Williams, *Letters Written in France*, 'Revolution and Romanticism, 1789–1834' series, ed. Jonathan Wordsworth (Oxford: Woodstock Books, 1989), pp. 66, 62.
8. S. T. Coleridge, *Table Talk*, in *Coleridge's Miscellaneous Criticism*, ed. Thomas Middleton Raysor (London: Constable, 1936), p. 423.
9. Thomas De Quincey, 'Conversation', in *Works of Thomas de Quincey*, ed. Grevel Lindop *et al.* 21 vols. (London: Pickering and Chatto, 2001–3), xvi. 218.
10. Thomas De Quincey, 'Final Memorials of Charles Lamb', *Works*, xvi. 378.
11. Thomas De Quincey, 'Style', *Works*, xii. 20, 371.
12. William Hazlitt, *Complete Works*, ed. P. P. Howe, 21 vols. (London and Toronto: J. M. Dent, 1934), xii. 12.
13. William Hazlitt, 'The Indian Jugglers', in *Selected Writings*, ed. Jon Cook (Oxford: Oxford World's Classics, 1991), pp. 128–42.
14. For a further analysis of Hazlitt's essay in relation to its cultural context, see my essay 'Indian Jugglers: Hazlitt, Romantic Orientalism, and the Difference of View', in Tim Fulford and Peter Kitson (eds.), *Romanticism and Colonialism: Writing and Empire, 1780–1830* (Cambridge: Cambridge University Press, 1998), pp. 206–20.
15. Leigh Hunt, 'On the Realities of Imagination', *The Indicator* (Wednesday, 22 Mar. 1820), 185–92.

34 | Travel writing

Carl Thompson

In his autobiographical narrative *Suspiria de Profundis* (1845), Thomas De Quincey tells (or more probably, invents) an amusing story about his childhood appetite for books. Besotted with reading, he signs up at the local bookseller's to receive a multi-volume series of voyage narratives. Matters go awry, however, when the bookseller jokingly tells him that the series will run to some 15,000 volumes. Taking the bookseller at his word, the young De Quincey has nightmares in which books arrive by the wagonload; and as he imagines them piling up in the front garden, he becomes convinced that he has consigned himself to legal proceedings, bankruptcy, and shame.

Whilst shedding light principally on De Quincey's curious psychological hang-ups, this anecdote also says something about travel writing in the Romantic period, and about contemporary perceptions regarding the genre. De Quincey is obviously exaggerating for comic effect, but enormous multi-volume publishing ventures were not uncommon in connection with the genre known at the time as 'Voyages and Travels'. John Pinkerton's *General Collection of the Best and Most Interesting Voyages and Travels* (1808–14), for example, weighed in at an impressive seventeen volumes, whilst William Mavor's *Historical Account of the Most Celebrated Voyages, Travels and Discoveries* (1796–1801) was still more daunting, running to twenty-five volumes. It was soon supplemented, moreover, by a further six-volume series, comprising twenty-two travelogues, entitled *The British Tourists; or Traveller's Pocket Companion through England, Wales, Scotland & Ireland* (1798).

Pinkerton's and Mavor's collections (and the many others like them that appeared around this date) were attempts to marshal, to delimit, or perhaps just to cash in on, a genre that in the Romantic period was hugely popular, staggeringly prolific, and bewilderingly diverse. Today we tend to think of travel writing as a somewhat marginal genre, a form neither fully 'literary' (in the way that the novel, say, is), nor at the cutting-edge in terms of the information it provides: we do not expect the modern travelogue to lead the way in scientific knowledge, political debate, or news reportage. Romantic-era travel writing held a very different place in the mind of the reading public. It was a form in which almost all were immersed, to a greater or lesser degree. Partly this was the case because the generic label 'Voyages and Travels' embraced such a wide variety of texts, and so was read by all sorts of reader, for all sorts of reasons. But partly this was because the most important travel narratives—John Hawkesworth's account of Captain Cook's first voyage (published in 1773), for example, or the Reverend William Gilpin's 'picturesque tours' (appearing from 1782)—were landmark publications, books that would have been known to almost every literate individual. These were texts which worked a profound effect on British culture in the Romantic period. Stimulating (and sometimes provoking) the contemporary imagination, they shaped fundamentally the consciousness of the age.

Larger historical developments, of course, created the travel-writing boom of the late eighteenth and early nineteenth centuries. On the domestic front, the British Isles were being ever more tightly integrated into a single nation-state, its different regions increasingly interconnected by roads, canals, and—by the end of the period—railways. Along these routes travellers rushed to explore previously remote regions, or just to holiday in them. The middle classes, enriched by the industrial and agricultural revolutions, took up a pastime that had previously been the preserve of the aristocracy and gentry: they chose to travel for pleasure, for purposes of recreation, revitalization, and self-education. In response to this new vogue for travel as a leisure activity, a new synonym for traveller was coined in the 1770s: one could now be labelled, initially without any sense of ridicule or condemnation, a 'tourist'.

Overseas, other developments were further stimulating an interest in travel and travel writing. Over the course of the Romantic period, British military forces were engaged on almost every continent and ocean of the world. The overall result of these campaigns (notwithstanding a major setback with the loss of the American colonies in 1781) was that vast areas of the globe came under British control. Britain's influence extended also by peaceable means, by alliances, trading agreements, and the like, until, by the 1820s, there were some 200 million people, 26 per cent of the world's population, living under British rule. A truly global empire and economic network took shape—a situation that ensured on the one hand a keen interest in far-off lands amongst the domestic population, and on the other hand, a steady flow of Britons to all corners of the world.

Given these contexts, Romantic-era travel writing was in some manifestations and for some readers a highly serious business, a crucial forum for political, economic, and moral debate on matters such as imperialism, colonialism, slavery and Abolitionism, modernity, consumerism, and luxury. In other instances, and for other readers, it was a key source of scientific data relating to diverse fields of enquiry: natural history, geography, anthropology, and so forth. Yet it was also simultaneously a source of adventure stories, and of wonders and curiosities. From shipwreck victims or from those who had escaped captivity at the hands of some far-off 'savage' tribe there came sensationalistic accounts of horrifying ordeals. From more devout travellers there came narratives that could be read as a source of religious instruction. Others again, especially at the more touristic end of the travel-writing spectrum, wrote primers in good taste, narratives intended to educate travellers in a 'correct' knowledge of art and landscape. And some were simply eager to see themselves in print, assuming (often wrongly) that the reading public would relish the fine sentiments expressed in their travel letters and journals.

Travel is also an important theme and preoccupation in the imaginative literature of the Romantic period. Writers drew extensively on travel writing, plundering the genre for storylines, settings and exotic details, for personae and imagery, even for narrative conventions and formal structures. Mary Shelley makes Walton, the narrator of *Frankenstein*, an Arctic explorer; Coleridge's two most famous poems depict on the one hand the sufferings of a mariner in the south Pacific ocean, and on the other an exotic pleasure dome erected by an oriental potentate in far-off Xanadu. Much of Wordsworth's poetry, meanwhile, springs from and describes the rambles and tours he made through both Britain and Europe; it is with some justice that he declares in *The Prelude*, 'A Traveller I am | Whose tale is only of himself' (III. 195–6).[1]

The fictional or poetic handling of travel-related material, and more generally the relationship between 'literature' and travel writing, will be discussed in the final two sections of this chapter. Prior to that, however, the chapter will survey the main branches of Romantic-era travel writing, and the key developments in the genre.

A 'tour-writing and tour-publishing age'

When Dorothy Wordsworth wrote in 1823 of 'this writing and publishing (especially *tour*-writing and *tour*-publishing) age', she identified a major factor underpinning the growing interest in travel, and the sheer quantity of travel books, in the Romantic period.[2] Tourism (understanding this term, for the time being, in a neutral, non-pejorative sense, as denoting travel undertaken willingly, for pleasure and recreation) was a startling new phenomenon in late eighteenth-century British society. In the earlier part of the century, almost the only people travelling in a spirit akin to modern tourism were those engaged in the élite practice of the Grand Tour. This involved the sons of the aristocracy and gentry being sent to the Continent, and especially to France and Italy, often for several years, in order to finish their education and perhaps to sow a few wild oats safely out of harm's way. From the 1760s, however, the traditional Grand Tourist increasingly found himself rubbing shoulders with (or trying *not* to rub shoulders with) other sorts of British tourist: with older men, with women, and with family groups, many of them drawn not from the upper but the middle classes.

The growing middle-class taste for tourism was further boosted in the 1770s, when the domestic tour to regions within Britain became fashionable. To make a tour was increasingly a pleasure, and a mark of taste and privilege, available to an ever-widening portion of British society. Both at home and in Europe (where tourists for the most part continued to travel within the traditional circuit established by the Grand Tour) the numbers of British tourists escalated steadily. The closure of the Continent to British travellers during the long war with France was a temporary bar to the European tour, but each time the Continent reopened to Britons a flood of tourists crossed the Channel. Their numbers astonished contemporaries. Tourism, it was increasingly felt, was one of the defining features of modern culture, a product of the new industrialized, commercialized Britain. And tourism was itself fast becoming an industry. From the 1830s, guidebooks in the modern sense—containing no narrative but just information relating to destinations and routes—were available from publishers such as John Murray and the Baedekers, whilst in the 1840s Thomas Cook introduced the concept of the package holiday, in which an agent organized every aspect of the journey for the traveller.

Many Romantic-era tourists ventured into print with accounts of their travels (amongst them Percy and Mary Shelley, who published in 1817 a *History of a Six Weeks' Tour*). These narratives reveal that diverse agendas underpinned the tourist boom of the Romantic period. Some tourists kept alive the precepts and itinerary of the traditional Grand Tour, emphasizing the cultural authority that accrued from visiting Rome and other sites of classical antiquity. Others were interested not in the classical, but in the primitive and the natural. Influenced by the philosopher Rousseau—and more immediately, perhaps, by the hugely popular Ossianic poems of James McPherson—they sought in regions like the Scottish Highlands places and cultures supposedly uncorrupted by modernity. Others again, however, saw tourism as part of a modernizing, Enlightenment project, a means of gathering technical and scientific knowledge, and also (in the domestic context) of unifying the disparate communities of the British Isles. For example, tourists following the lead of Arthur Young (whose 'farmer's tours' began appearing from 1768) preached the gospel of 'improvement': they aimed to identify and disseminate good agricultural practice, so as to boost the British economy.

These different stimuli to Romantic-era tourism may seem at odds with each other, yet many tourists were capable of overlooking any points of contradiction and combining them all quite happily in a single narrative. Also strongly evident in many of these narratives is a growing appreciation of landscape, and especially of wild or what was often termed 'romantic' scenery. Landscapes that had previously been viewed with distaste and horror—mountains, for example—were increasingly associated with the aesthetic category of the 'sublime', and enjoyed as awesome spectacles. William Gilpin's tour narratives, meanwhile, encouraged tourists to evaluate landscape according to 'picturesque' rules of beauty: that is to say, according to the extent to which they approximated the idealized landscapes found in the art of Claude and Poussin. In many ways, this was a watered-down version of the taste for the sublime: the devotee of the picturesque found beauty in the more rugged, irregular elements of a landscape—a gnarled oak or the distant outline of mountains—and in the judicious combination of such elements to create a correctly composed scene.

Traditionally an exercise in studious empirical enquiry, proceeding along guidelines laid down by the Royal Society in the seventeenth century, most eighteenth-century tour narratives are couched in an impersonal style. The writer foregrounds the information acquired, including just enough personal detail to create a readable narrative, and to convince the reader of his (less commonly, her) presence at a given site. From the latter part of the century, however, a more subjective element becomes apparent in many tour narratives. Increasingly, it was how one was moved by a ruin or landscape that mattered, not just a detailed survey of the scene. A major influence here was the sentimentalism one associates with Laurence Sterne. Sterne's novel, *A Sentimental Journey* (1768), produced a host of real-life imitators, sentimental tourists who hoped for emotional adventures that could demonstrate both their own sensibility and the innate goodness of all men and women. More generally, the sentimental impulse encouraged the growing tendency in (some) tour narratives to prioritize the traveller's impressions, and his or her affective responses.

A more emotive, impressionistic style was also characteristic of many female-authored travelogues in the Romantic period. These were a new and burgeoning branch of the genre. Whilst there were only two travel narratives published by women before 1770, some twenty appear between 1770 and 1800 (Ann Radcliffe and Mary Wollstonecraft being among the authors). A still greater number appeared in the first decades of the nineteenth century. In addition, many women—Dorothy Wordsworth, for example—wrote travel journals that were intended not for publication but for circulation amongst family and friends. Published or unpublished, the female-authored travelogue usually adopted a perspective on people and places, and on the whole business of travel, different from that found in male-authored accounts. Most writers avoided 'masculine' topics such as politics and economics, concentrating instead on domestic details, local 'manners and customs', and the like. A few (Wollstonecraft, for example) challenged these restraints on the female travel writer; many more worked within them to critique subtly male viewpoints and assumptions in travel writing.

The upsurge in tourism generated many outbursts of anti-touristic sentiment. The whole phenomenon was denounced by some; others denounced particular modes or tendencies in the rapidly diversifying sphere of recreational travel. The shallowness of the female tourist, the profligacy, debauchery, and effeminacy of the aristocratic Grand Tourist, the vulgarity and intellectual poverty of many middle-class tourists: these were accusations regularly hurled in contemporary debate. The picturesque tourist especially was much ridiculed (for example, in William Combe and Thomas Rowlandson's illustrated poem, *The Tour of Dr Syntax in Search of the Picturesque* (1812)). To commentators of many different persuasions—conservative landowners, middle-class utilitarians concerned with agricultural improvement, radicals distressed with the lot of the rural poor—picturesque tourism was not just a frivolous but a pernicious exercise, making the traveller a 'consumer' of landscapes who gave no consideration to the larger moral, political, or economic issues at stake in each locality. It was accordingly to counter the perceived superficiality of a merely picturesque engagement with the Lake District, and to encourage a deeper understanding of the history, ecology, and economy of the region, that Wordsworth produced (in prose) a highly popular *Guide to the Lakes* (1810).

Significantly, many such attacks on aspects of tourism came from individuals who were themselves engaged in some form of recreational travel. As tourists took to the roads of Britain and Europe in ever greater numbers, so many of them felt the need to differentiate themselves from the mass, and to assert the superiority of their own practices and responses. Perhaps the most powerful articulation of this desire is Byron's hugely popular poetic travelogue *Childe Harold's Pilgrimage* (1812–18). It is in part a critique of contemporary tourism, as it explores Europe and the Middle East with a poet's heightened responsiveness. At the same time, however, it reflects, and shapes, impulses fundamental to modern tourism. *Childe Harold* became a handbook for travellers anxious to feel that they were not merely tourists: following its self-dramatizing script, they were able to pronounce, at even the most hackneyed tourist destination:

> in the crowd
> They could not deem me one of such; I stood
> Among them, but not of them; in a shroud
> Of thoughts which were not their thoughts
> (III. 1053–6)[3]

Increasingly, the term 'tourist' was reserved for those other travellers in the crowd. The word begins to take on the pejorative aspect that it still bears today, and 'tourism' becomes understood as a set of travel practices that are both a dubious consequence of modernity and the means by which modernity contaminates pristine cultures and environments. Yet when thinking of what tourism signified in the Romantic period, we should keep in mind that 'tourism' and 'tourist' were only *beginning* to acquire this derogatory connotation. Both terms could be used without implicit distaste, and could also be applied to travellers whose activities seem, to our eyes, decidedly unfrivolous and 'untouristic' (Arthur Young, for example), and even to professional travellers such as surveyors.

Explorers: the business of scientific discovery

If the boom in tourism and tour narratives was one major factor in the Romantic-era interest in travel and travel writing, the other single greatest stimulus was exploration. The three voyages of James Cook (1768–71, 1772–5, and 1776–9) inaugurated a great age of discovery—and unlike the voyages of discovery conducted in earlier epochs, this was exploration construed principally as an exercise in scientific enquiry. Cook's voyages pursued scientific objectives, and to this end carried teams of professional scientists, and a daunting array of instruments and equipment. The presiding spirit of this exploratory endeavour was the Swedish natural-historian Carl Linné (better known as Linnaeus). Linnaeus's *Systema Naturae* (*The System of Nature*, 1735) had launched European science on a vast project of taxonomy, the orderly classification of every aspect of the natural world (including, increasingly, human beings: by the end of the Romantic period, scientific theories of race and of physical 'types' had found widespread acceptance in Europe). The purpose of voyages such as Cook's, alongside mapping uncharted coasts and oceans, was to provide the raw material for such classificatory systems.

In Cook's wake, British explorers pursued this intellectual agenda by both land and sea: Alexander MacKenzie, Samuel Hearne, and John Franklin in North America and Canada; Matthew Flinders and Charles Sturt in Australia; James Bruce and Mungo Park in Africa; William Parry and John Ross in connection with the North Pole and the North-West Passage. In many regions of the world (including the British Isles themselves), surveyors and explorers worked assiduously to map the world and catalogue its contents. Their activities were sponsored by a variety of institutions and organizations: the Admiralty, the Royal Society, the Botanical Gardens at Kew, the African Association (founded in 1788 to promote the exploration of West Africa), from 1830 the Geographical Society, and others besides. In many of these organizations, one man especially maintained an important, co-ordinating presence: Sir Joseph Banks, who travelled as naturalist on Cook's first voyage and subsequently engineered for himself a pivotal role in Britain's exploration establishment. Banks stood at the heart of a network that guided and systematized the activities of British explorers, and that processed the vast quantities of data they collected. There were explorers who undertook expeditions outside this exploratory infrastructure (James Bruce at the beginning of the period was a notable maverick) but often they might have difficulty getting their findings accepted back in Britain. Bruce, for example, was for a long time widely denounced as a liar.

This exploratory endeavour was an offshoot of Britain's imperial expansion in this period, and often assisted that expansion. Yet it is important to note that an important part of the rationale behind the new exploration—an important part, equally, of the self-image of many explorers—was that it was not an overtly expansionist, imperialist exercise. Contrasting themselves with the European discoverers of earlier eras, Romantic-era explorers emphasized their pursuit of knowledge rather than booty, and they emphasized also the benefits that should flow to all mankind from a better knowledge of the planet. In the global as well as the domestic context, 'improvement' was a buzzword of the age. The natural world, it was widely felt, was not just to be observed and catalogued, it was also ultimately to be harvested. And where necessary, it was to be transformed, until even waste regions like the Arctic were rendered productive by the guiding hand of British stewardship.

From these voyages and expeditions there came a flood of exploration narratives, catering not only to specialists in the various sciences but also to the general reader.

James Cook, Mungo Park, and many others died in the course of exploratory expeditions: as this will suggest, there was scope for these accounts to incorporate elements of adventure, heroism, even horror, alongside the factual, scientific information. The 'Reading' section of this chapter will discuss this ability to appeal to different readerships, and more generally the key formal and stylistic features of the exploration narrative, in connection with one of the most popular travel publications of the period, Park's *Travels in the Interior Districts of Africa* (1799).

Survivors, missionaries, and other travellers

Beyond the tourist and the explorer, the heterogeneous genre of 'Voyages and Travels' embraced other sorts of traveller, and other sorts of travel writing. Accounts of shipwreck, for example, had a powerful grip on the contemporary imagination. As well as many individual accounts, several multi-volume anthologies of these narratives appeared in the early nineteenth century (for example, J. G. Dalyell's three-volume *Shipwrecks and Disasters at Sea* of 1812). The shipwreck narrative often dovetailed into another popular contemporary form, the captivity narrative. This told of the writer's experience when enslaved or entrapped among some foreign tribe or in some foreign culture (a situation that the survivors of shipwreck often found themselves in when washed up on dry land, hence the connection between the two subgenres).

Such accounts might be sensationalistic, but they could just as frequently contain important ethnographic information about an alien culture, so again they often appealed to several different readerships. Furthermore, many shipwreck and captivity narratives were also heavily infused with religious sentiment. John Newton's *Authentic Narrative* (1768), for example, incorporates scenes of shipwreck and captivity into the tradition of Protestant spiritual autobiography; in a narrative that probably influenced Coleridge's *Ancient Mariner*, Newton's travails as traveller lead him back to God. Another sort of religious traveller was also becoming more common by the end of the Romantic period. The London Missionary Society was set up in 1794, and as British society underwent the Evangelical Revival of the first decades of the nineteenth century, accounts of missions to 'heathen' tribes became another popular strand of 'Voyages and Travels'.

Romanticism and Romantic-era travel writing

The literary figures traditionally thought of as the Romantics (that is, the 'big six' poets, Wordsworth, Coleridge, and Blake, Byron, Shelley, and Keats) have an ambiguous relationship with the travel-writing genre. All read the genre avidly, and all borrow from it extensively, in diverse ways, in their own writing. Yet with the exception of the Shelleys' *Six Weeks' Tour* and Wordsworth's *Guide to the Lakes*, none of them wrote travel writing as such. They incorporated elements of travel and travel writing into their *poetry*—but left the supposedly more mundane task of producing prose travelogue to their (often female) travelling companions. Thus William Wordsworth writes *Poems Written During a Tour in Scotland* (1807), and Dorothy the prose narrative *Recollections of a Tour of Scotland* (circulated privately from 1803). And whilst Byron transforms his tour of 1809–11 (to Portugal, Spain, Greece, and Albania), and his European travels of 1816–18, into *Childe Harold's Pilgrimage*, it is his friend John Cam Hobhouse who produces the prose narratives *A Journey through Albania* (1813) and *Historical Illustrations of the Fourth Canto of Childe Harold* (1818).

In these poetic renderings of travel and travel writing—Byron's *Childe Harold*, Wordsworth's *Excursion* and *Prelude*, Coleridge's 'Rime of the Ancient Mariner'—we often find the theme of travel invested with what we might think of as a characteristically Romantic sensibility. Here we can find travel construed as heroic quest, as a process of simultaneous inner and outer discovery that leads perhaps to a moment of transcendence or a sense of the self's sublimity. Rendered thus, as an act of enormous existential significance and a crucial route to wisdom, self-knowledge, and authenticity, travel not surprisingly becomes one of the master-tropes of Romantic writing. And this Romantic valorization of travel in turn taught the larger public to privilege certain modes of being a traveller, and of expressing that experience. 'Proper' or 'real' travel, contemporaries learnt from texts like Byron's *Childe Harold*, maintained a seriousness of purpose, a profundity of response, and possibly even a spiritual aspect, that was lacking in mere tourism.

In time, many prose travelogues adopted these Romantic attitudes and tropes. William Hazlitt's *Notes of a Journey through France and Italy* (1824), for instance, is an early example of the travel book as a more self-consciously literary exercise, and as the expression of a Romantic sensibility that owes much to Byron. The application of the term 'Romantic' to other travel writing in the period, however, is more problematic. Broadly speaking, one can detect across many strands of Romantic-era travel writing a new concern with the traveller's subjective impressions, and a corresponding narratorial endeavour to chart the flux of thoughts and feelings. Also evident is a keener aesthetic appreciation of wild or 'romantic' landscape. These seem Romantic developments, yet closer inspection arguably tells a somewhat different story. In many (possibly most) cases, these preoccupations enter Romantic-era travel writing in connection with tastes and fashions that the canonical (male) Romantics wish to distance themselves from. Most travellers' responses to landscape are shaped by the picturesque rubric—generally denounced by the major Romantics as an inadequate response to nature. The greater inwardness and subjectivity of much travel writing, meanwhile, is often better understood as a consequence not of Romanticism, but of sentimentalism. The sentimental rendering of the self is in many ways antithetical to the Romantic attitude as traditionally conceived. Typically, it resists (or arguably, fails to achieve) the sublime or transcendent self-fashionings sought by the Romantic writer. Its concern is not with the epic (and in the gender categories of the day, masculine) realm of quest and adventure, but with a more feminized realm of mundane details, inconsequential whims, and passing fancies.

Surveying the whole genre of Romantic-era travel writing, one must also acknowledge that in some branches of the genre there is a pronounced movement *away* from those supposedly Romantic characteristics just described. A tendency towards objectivity and impersonality is apparent not just in the guidebooks being produced by the end of the period by Murray and Baedeker, but also in many travel books that evinced a more hard-nosed scientific or economic interest in far-off regions. In some cases, travellers abandoned any personal element, and any narration of the actual journey, to offer instead just statistical gazetteers and compilations of data. As they did so, some publications previously understood to be part of the 'Voyages and Travels' genre ceased to be regarded in this way: instead, they increasingly fell within the province of the new academic disciplines emerging in the early nineteenth century, political economy, anthropology, and the like.

This bifurcation into more polarized subjective and objective modes is perhaps the major development in Romantic-era travel writing. By the end of the period, the combination of literary pleasure and useful knowledge that had put the travel book at the heart of the eighteenth-century canon is becoming unsustainable. Instead, there are works solely concerned to transmit knowledge, couched quite possibly in a technical language that is daunting to the general reader, and there are works chiefly concerned to entertain and amuse their readers. And the latter class of travel book increasingly seems somewhat inconsequential. Deprived of the remarkable inclusiveness that characterizes it in the Romantic period, travel writing becomes regarded as a lesser genre, the province (bar a few exceptions) of dilettante and amateur writers.

Travel writing and Romantic-era literature

Since the Romantic period, then, travel writing has become far less critically esteemed. As a consequence, travelogues were for the most part excluded from the canon of Romantic literature; and where canonical literary texts did borrow from the supposedly lesser genre—as is so often the case in this period—critics did not give such intersections between literature and travel writing too much consideration. Romantic-era travel writing, it was felt, simply provided source material to the Romantic imagination. And the literary work subsequently produced by that imagination was held to stand apart from travel writing, and from the more worldly social and political concerns that are so often addressed in the genre.

Recovering the contemporary sense of the liveliness and importance of travel writing, we expand the canon of Romantic-era (if not Romantic) literature dramatically.

We can also place those literary texts that rightly remain at the heart of the canon in a far more dynamic and interactive relationship with contemporary travelogues. It becomes apparent, for example, that the original meaning and resonance of many Romantic-era literary texts was to some extent the result of their relationship with the vast hinterland of contemporary travel writing. Exploiting, and sometimes subverting, generic expectations that derived from the reading public's great relish for 'Voyages and Travels', many Romantic-era poems, novels, and plays tap deliberately into debates taking place in the form. Indeed, there are several cases where we probably need to understand Romantic-era poems and novels as being themselves a species of travel writing, notwithstanding the strain this puts on our modern sense of the genre: Byron's *Childe Harold*, for example.

This is a perspective that opens up interesting new vistas on familiar texts. In framing the story of Victor Frankenstein with Walton's exploratory voyage into the Arctic, for example, Mary Shelley exploits the contemporary interest aroused by John Ross's Admiralty-sponsored expedition to this region (in preparation as *Frankenstein* was being written) whilst simultaneously offering a critique of the values underpinning that venture. The Banksian project of global improvement, confident that scientific knowledge can order and transform the natural world, is hardly endorsed by Victor's experience, and Walton's own voyage of discovery will ultimately be abandoned.

In *Frankenstein*, then, we find a literary work (not insignificantly, a female-authored text) subtly rebuking the principal agenda pursued by many contemporary travellers and travel writers. Many other literary works of the period, however, endorse and promote the values and attitudes dominant in contemporary travel writing. In his seminal study *Orientalism* (1978), the critic Edward Said argued that European travel writing, notwithstanding its claims to be pure knowledge or harmless entertainment, must be seen as part of the apparatus of empire. It provided not only the information but also the conceptual framework—the images of 'savages', for example—that enabled imperialism and colonialism. When it borrows from contemporary travel writing so as to circulate such images and ideas more widely in British culture—as it does, arguably, in Wordsworth's depiction of the 'squalid, vengeful and impure' Native American in *The Excursion* (III. 953), or in Southey's exotic epic *The Curse of Kehama* (1810)—Romantic-era literature clearly needs to be regarded as part of this orientalizing mechanism. Other texts, meanwhile, manifest confusion or ambivalence in this regard. At one level, Byron's popular Turkish tales seem intended to rebuke smug British notions that Christian Europeans are morally superior to Islamic adversaries in the Middle East. At another level, however, they confirmed orientalist preconceptions about the East as a place of fantasy, passion, and adventure. Consequently, and paradoxically, Byronic imaginings launched many a glittering career in the service of empire.

There is not space here to discuss the many different ways in which Romantic literary texts interact with contemporary travel writing, and the full complexity of their engagement with both the touristic and the exploratory contexts outlined above. Yet every student of the period should be attentive to these contexts, and they should also be aware of the sheer ubiquity and prominence of travel writing in British culture in the Romantic period. Of huge historical importance, and highly enjoyable in its own right, Romantic-era travel writing is a genre that maintains an insistent dialogue with the canonical literature of its age.

READING: Mungo Park, *Travels in the Interior Districts of Africa*

Mungo Park's *Travels in the Interior Districts of Africa* (1799) was one of the great publishing successes of the Romantic era, going through three editions within a year of its appearance. The narrative recounts an eighteen-month exploratory expedition in West Africa, through present-day Gambia, Senegal, and Mali, that commenced in May 1795. Accompanied by two African servants, the author, a young Scot (born 1771), had headed inland from the African coast in an effort to reach the mighty Niger river. His aim was to ascertain the direction in which the river flowed; if possible, to travel as far along the river as the city of Timbuktu, much fabled for its wealth; and more generally, to gather information on the regions and peoples encountered along the way.

Park encountered considerable difficulties as he travelled. Most disastrously, he was imprisoned and ill-treated by Ali, a Fulani or (in Park's usual terminology) Moorish chieftain. Escaping 'the Moors', and bereft now of his servants, Park proceeded alone, surviving chiefly through the charity of the indigenous West African population. Locating Timbuktu was now out of the question. Notwithstanding his misadventures, however, Park did reach the Niger, which he observed to be 'flowing slowly *to the eastward*' (Park's emphasis).[4] Park then made his way back to the coast, travelling with a slave convoy, and from there returned to Britain in December 1797.

Following the acclaim that greeted Park on the publication of his *Travels*, he was invited to lead a second expedition to the region. Heading a company comprised mostly of soldiers, Park returned to West Africa in January 1805. This time, however, the difficulties proved insurmountable. Disease swiftly killed most of the company: the final remnant, including Park himself, died in late 1805. The precise circumstances are uncertain, but seem to have involved a confrontation with local tribespeople.

Exploration, commerce, and colonialism

Although Park travelled to Africa on his own in 1795, the expedition was not an individual or maverick undertaking. It was sponsored by the African Association, an organization dedicated to acquiring knowledge of the continent, and to putting that knowledge to practical, profitable use. The African Association—and in particular, Sir Joseph Banks, here as elsewhere a leading light in exploratory concerns—accordingly dictated the goals of the expedition, and defined the data Park was expected to acquire. It was also instrumental in the production of the published narrative: Banks arranged for Bryan Edwards to act as editor, and for Major James Rennell to provide two new maps and a seven-chapter appendix summarizing the new geographical knowledge arising from Park's endeavours.

Park's published narrative follows closely the notes he took whilst travelling, and we are meant to recognize this fact. For the greater part of the narrative, a journal format is adopted, and great emphasis laid on specificities of time and place ('Dec. 20th. We departed from Soobrudooka, and at two o'clock reached a large village situated on the banks of the Falemé river . . .' (p. 100)). The narration of the journey, however, is occasionally interrupted with passages—some a few paragraphs long, others taking up whole chapters—that bring together in a more consolidated form Park's findings and thoughts about a particular place or culture or issue. Thus chapter 12 consists of 'Reflections on the Moorish Character, and Manners', and 'Observations concerning the Great Desert, its Animals, wild and domestic, &c'.

This stylistic formula was customary in the Romantic-era exploration narrative. It was calculated to convince the reading public, and the critics, that the explorer was a reliable eyewitness to the events and phenomena described. As Sir Joseph Banks well knew, authenticity and credibility were crucial in ensuring the success of an exploration narrative. Banks had witnessed the savage reception given to James Bruce's *Travels to Discover the Source of the Nile* (1790). Bruce had written in overly flamboyant, egotistical style, paying too little regard to the recognized procedures of scientific observation and telling too many astonishing or self-glamorizing stories (although many were subsequently corroborated). In contrast, Park devotes himself conscientiously to the business of first-hand empirical observation, and he relates his observations in a simple, unaffected style, not overly sophisticated or polished. Personal thoughts and feelings, and more subtle stylistic elements, *are* interwoven (as we shall see in the next section) but they are present only in a restrained way, subordinated to the principal agenda of data collection.

Park's narrative, then, is chiefly preoccupied with the external world. On matters of time and place, on the physical appearance of landscapes, the material properties of things, or the method by which, for example, the Bambarran flute is played, it strives for precision. On occasions, it turns to the more specialized discourses of contemporary science for greater precision and authority. Park can tell us, for example, that the 'small farinaceous berries' known to the locals as '*tomberongs*' are 'the fruit of the *rhamnus lotus* of Linnaeus' (p. 131). In some contemporary exploration accounts, this language was beginning to predominate, in an attempt to present the explorer's findings as wholly objective. Park, however, mostly avoids an over-technical, impersonal scientific idiom just as he avoids excessive subjectivity: compass bearings, degrees of longitude and latitude, and so forth, are generally relegated to Rennell's geographical digest at the end of the volume.

In all these ways, the narrative establishes Park as an eminently trustworthy traveller, an assiduous but plain-speaking gatherer of information. Such data collection is presented to us as a morally neutral, or, indeed, positively beneficial act. On occasions, we are invited to smile at the simplicity (or paranoia) of African leaders who cannot believe that someone travels so far, and takes so many risks, simply to satisfy intellectual curiosity. But in truth the Africans are being perceptive, and Park and his contemporary readers disingenuous, in these scenes. The sort of information Park collects implicitly reveals the more pragmatic agenda underpinning the expedition. It is the 'chief productions' (p. 89) of a locality—its agricultural produce, manufactured goods, and so forth—that are catalogued with particular care: the search for knowledge, it seems, is closely bound up with the search for new commercial opportunities.

Park's narrative is also subtly suffused with the logic of 'improvement', that thinks in terms almost of a moral obligation to render West Africa economically productive and profitable. If the local population will not develop the resources bestowed on them by God, that obligation falls to others. In his closing assessment of the region, Park points the way not just to trading links but to a more active British intervention in West Africa:

It was not possible for me to behold the wonderful fertility of the soil, the vast herds of cattle, *proper* both for labour and food, and a variety of other circumstances favourable to colonization and agriculture; and reflect, withal, on the means which presented themselves of a vast inland navigation, without lamenting that a country, so abundantly gifted and favoured by nature, should remain in its present savage and neglected state. (p. 272: emphasis added)

Along with the reference to possible colonization, Park's use of 'proper' here is worth remarking: 'labour and food' are evidently what cattle are intended for, and it is implicitly wasteful, even sinful, not to put them to this use.

Suffering and sentiment

Clearly, then, there is an acquisitive dimension to the interest being taken in West Africa by Park and his audience. At the same time, however, the huge contemporary popularity of Park's narrative derived in no small way from the skill (and sincerity) with which Park coupled a mercantile and colonialist agenda with other, more moralistic concerns. It did not simply inform its readers as to new commercial opportunities; it also flattered and reassured them with a sense that they might be a force for good in the world.

Of crucial importance in this regard are the many hardships endured by Park in his expedition. Whilst Park, characteristically, is always restrained in his depiction of his own sufferings, this is nevertheless an account of exploration that seems less interested in the explorer's triumphs than in his defeats, and in his dogged perseverance in the face of defeat. The sighting of the Niger is arguably the climax of Park's mission, but the narrative presents this scene with little crescendo, and moves swiftly on to other matters. Rhetorically, this serves several functions. The overall effect is to present an explorer who is conspicuously *not* an ambitious seeker of glory, or a larger-than-life adventurer engaged in some epic quest. This in turn helps Park and his audience conceptualize exploration as an innocent, unaggressive activity, in no way threatening to the local population. In the Enlightened eighteenth century, European discovery is not a violent incursion into a foreign region in the manner of, say, the Spanish conquistadors. Park's is a passive, sometimes helpless persona, and for long stretches of the narrative he is entirely reliant on charity—who could accuse this traveller of exploiting or harming anyone?

The many scenes of suffering also enable Park to introduce religious and sentimental dimensions to the narrative. Park's faith is an obvious if unobtrusive presence throughout the text: he frequently quotes the Psalms, for example. But it becomes more prominent during Park's captivity, when he is tormented by the Moslem Moors for being Christian. And it is most powerfully evident in a key scene towards the end of the narrative, in which Park is so weak, and his position so hopeless, that he almost gives up in despair. At his lowest point, however, the traveller catches sight of a small moss 'in fructification' (p. 227). The 'delicate conformation of its roots, leaves and capsula' suggest the care and love with which God has fashioned even the lowliest parts of creation; with this thought, hope revives in Park, and he finds the strength to continue his journey. Especially significant here is the way Park's narrative marries the languages of Linnaean botany ('fructification', 'conformation', 'capsula') and religion. The precise, discriminating gaze of European science, we infer, is divinely sanctioned and sustained. The explorer, it seems, has a part to play in a larger Providential plan for the globe.

Park's rendering of his ordeal is also rooted in attitudes and stylistic conventions deriving from the late eighteenth-century vogue for sentimentalism. In scenes that would have reminded contemporary readers of novels such as Henry MacKenzie's *The Man of Feeling* (1771) and Laurence Sterne's *A Sentimental Journey* (1768), Park records the many occasions on which he was the recipient of charity from strangers. He thus invites readers to be moved both by his abject condition (as the Africans who helped Park were moved), and also by the motiveless generosity of his African benefactors. Such affective responses, whether occurring in an English drawing-room or a Foulah village, are understood as evidence of a natural benevolence that operates (or should operate) in all of us. Or as Park puts it at one point: 'whatever difference there is between the Negro and the European in the conformation of the nose and the colour of the skin, there is none in the genuine sympathies and characteristic feelings of our common nature' (p. 120; see also the chapter on 'Sensibility').

This sentimental ethos prompts Park to depict the people of West Africa with remarkable admiration and affection. This aspect of his narrative should not be understated. Writing in a pre-colonial era, Park gives us a portrayal of Africa far removed from the vitriolic, overtly racist outpourings of later explorers like Henry Stanley and Richard Burton. In Park's account, the local inhabitants are not only kind and generous individually, they also form collectively a society of considerable complexity and accomplishment. West Africa as described by Park is emphatically not the home of cannibalistic savages who understand only force and are fit only to be enslaved. This was the burden of some anti-abolitionist, pro-slavery commentators of the time, and Park's *Travels* accordingly provided the Abolitionist movement with much valuable ammunition against the slavery lobby.

At the same time, we should not overlook the more insidious effects of this sentimental agenda. Naturally charitable and benevolent they may be, but the lives of most West Africans, according to this account, are severely blighted by technological backwardness, lack of education, and superstition. Furthermore, the indigenous population is increasingly in thrall to 'Moorish', Fulani overlords, and to Islam, the religion of the Fulani. On the 'Moors' and Islam, Park is generally scathing. His more characteristic sentimental idiom gives way to angry denunciations, some of which seem calculated to lend support to the scientific theories of racial and physical types just beginning to emerge in this period: the physiognomy of the Moors, for example, is said to reveal 'a disposition towards cruelty, and low cunning' (p. 171). The West Africans bear the brunt of this cruelty—and just as the Africans were spurred by natural benevolence to help Park during his ordeal, so too should British sympathy and British charity go out to Africa, in a reciprocal outflowing of sentiment.

Park's narrative thus works ultimately to suggest a moral as well as an economic imperative to the extension of British influence in the region. Moving its readers with sentimental set-pieces, it reassures them of their fundamentally benevolent impulses, and invites them to direct these impulses towards West Africa. The British, Park suggests, must play a civilizing or emancipating role in the region, and in this way *Travels in the Interior Districts of Africa* helps to shape the paternalistic attitudes that were a prominent feature of nineteenth-century imperialist and colonialist ideology.

The explorer in Romantic-era culture

Deftly interweaving the languages of science and sentiment, religion and improvement, Park's *Travels* captured the imagination of the British public in diverse ways. As we have seen, it persuaded the hard-nosed commercial strategists of the African Association, and subsequently the British government, to underwrite a more substantial (armed) expedition into West Africa. It moved others, such as Georgiana, Duchess of Devonshire, and the poet George Crabbe, to write songs and poems that expanded on the sentimental aspects of Park's experiences. (The former's 'Negro Song', written after the duchess had read an abstract of the narrative, was incorporated into early editions of *Travels*.) And whilst Park himself takes care in his narrative not to cut an overly epic or sublime figure (or alternatively, whilst the generic conventions of the exploration narrative do not allow Park to cut such a figure), many readers were moved to romanticize the explorer in this way. Mary Russell Mitford's 'Lines, Suggested by the Uncertain Fate of Mungo Park', Felicia Hemans's 'The Flower of the Desert', and Wordsworth's draft verses for his five-book *Prelude* ('Even yet thou wilt vouchsafe') all emphasize Park as a lone traveller in the wilderness, engaged in a heroic quest for knowledge that is also an inner journey whereby the resources of the self, and the guiding hand of God, are discovered by the traveller.

Diffusing more widely through the culture in this way, Park's *Travels* contributed to a significant shift in the British public's attitude to the wider world. Characteristic of the Romantic era is a growing conviction as to Britain's global mission, its role as reformer and improver of the planet, and as steward of the natural resources gifted to mankind by God. Not everyone, of course, subscribed to these views. Byron notes sardonically in *Don Juan* that

> Tombuctoo travels, voyages to the Poles,
> Are ways to benefit mankind, as true,
> Perhaps, as shooting them at Waterloo.
> (l. 1054–6)[5]

Byron refers to Park's and to other, subsequent expeditions to West Africa, as well as to the ongoing Arctic voyages of John Ross and William Parry, driven by the same rhetoric of improvement. But even those who were sceptical about the British imperial project could find themselves fascinated by Park's *Travels*, and by the many other exploration narratives of the Romantic period. In a sense, these narratives opened up the whole planet as an imaginative resource. Remote regions and alien peoples became the objects of Romantic fantasy, conjecture, and aspiration. Gleaning not just factual information from Romantic-era exploration narratives, but also more subtly a sense that they were empowered to make a panoramic survey of the globe, contemporary readers and writers of all political persuasions yearned to legislate for the world, and to launch themselves on heroic quests, epic missions of enlightenment and emancipation. And in this way, Romantic-era exploration narratives such as Park's *Travels in the Interior Districts of Africa* encourage an imperious, if not explicitly imperializing, tendency in British Romanticism, and contribute to those transcendent self-fashionings that we often find in the literature of the age.

FURTHER READING

Batten, Charles, *Pleasurable Instruction: Form and Convention in Eighteenth-Century Travel Literature* (Berkeley: University of California Press, 1978). A formalist analysis that is still the best introduction to the generic requirements of eighteenth-century travel writing.

Buzard, James, *The Beaten Track: European Tourism, Literature, and the Ways to 'Culture', 1800–1918* (Oxford: Clarendon Press, 1993). Exploring the 'anti-tourism' of much Romantic and post-Romantic travel writing, this study has illuminating sections on Wordsworth and Byron, and on the role played by these writers in shaping subsequent attitudes to travel.

Drayton, Richard, *Nature's Government: Science, Imperial Britain, and the 'Improvement' of the World* (New Haven and London: Yale University Press, 2000). Describes the intellectual framework informing Romantic-era exploration, and the religious and philosophical beliefs underpinning the British conviction as to Britain's mission in the world.

Fulford, Tim, and Kitson, Peter J. (eds.), *Travels, Explorations and Empires: Writings from the Era of Imperial Expansion, 1770–1835*, 8 vols. (London: Pickering and Chatto, 2001). Offering extracts from almost 100 contemporary travel narratives, this collection conveys powerfully the sheer scale of Britain's engagement with the wider world in the Romantic era, and the diverse forms and attitudes flourishing within the genre of travel writing.

Leask, Nigel, *British Romantic Writers and the East: Anxieties of Empire* (Cambridge: Cambridge University Press, 1992). A highly nuanced study of the ways in which Romantic-era travel writing, and more generally the imperial expansion of Romantic-era Britain, informs the creative imaginations, and literary productions, of Byron, Shelley, De Quincey, and Coleridge.

Lupton, Kenneth, *Mungo Park, the African Traveller* (Oxford: Oxford University Press, 1979). The best biography of Park, making extensive use of the primary sources.

Nichols, Ashton, 'Mumbo Jumbo: Mungo Park and the Rhetoric of Romantic Africa', in Alan Richardson and Sonia Hofkosh (eds.), *Romanticism, Race and Imperial Culture* (Bloomington, Ind.: Indiana University Press, 1996). Understanding Park as an explorer who travels in a pre-colonial, and therefore more open-minded, period, this essay discusses how his narrative contributed to an emerging Romantic ideology.

Park, Mungo, *Travels in the Interior Districts of Africa*, ed. Kate Ferguson Marsters (Durham, NC, and London: Duke University Press, 2000). This is the only edition of Park's *Travels* currently in print, and comes with an excellent introduction and scholarly apparatus.

Pratt, Mary Louise, *Imperial Eyes: Travel Writing and Transculturation* (London: Routledge, 1992). A seminal work on exploration narratives of the Romantic era and the different rhetorical strategies deployed within them, that includes two chapters on Park.

——'Travel Narrative and Imperialist Vision', in Jame Phelan and Peter Rabinowitz (eds.), *Understanding Narrative* (Columbus, Oh.: Ohio State University Press, 1994). Looking at the accounts of Park and Livingstone, this article explores the shift from a more personalized to a more objective mode of narration in the exploration narrative.

Turner, Katherine, *British Travel Writers in Europe, 1750–1800: Authorship, Gender and National Identity* (Aldershot: Ashgate, 2001). A wide-ranging survey of the different types and modes of tour narrative (including a useful chapter on female-authored narratives).

NOTES

1. *Wordsworth: Poetical Works*, ed. Thomas Hutchinson, rev. Ernest de Selincourt (Oxford: Oxford University Press, 1988). Subsequent quotations from Wordsworth are from this edition.

2. *The Letters of William and Dorothy Wordsworth: The Later Years*, ed. Ernest de Selincourt, rev. Alan G. Hill, 4 vols. (Oxford: Clarendon Press, 1972–88). i. 181.

3. *Byron: The Complete Poetical Works*, ed. Jerome J. McGann, 7 vols. (Oxford: Clarendon Press, 1980–93), ii. 118.

4. Mungo Park, *Travels in the Interior Districts of Africa*, ed. Kate Ferguson Marsters (Durham, NC, and London: Duke University Press, 2000), p. 194. All subsequent references are to this edition.

5. *Byron: The Complete Poetical Works*, v. 50–1.

35 | Letters, journals and diaries

Nichola Deane

Letters and journals of the Romantic period have an uneasy status. They may in some respects be regarded as marginal texts. Until quite recently, Romanticism was thought of as a movement of a few (male) poets and philosophers, and the letters and journals of these few writers and those of their circle were used, by biographers and critics, to show just how essentially Romantic these canonical writers were. Letters and journals were seldom studied for their own sake. Whether or not they were 'Literature', with a capital 'L', had scarcely been discussed let alone decided.

Letters, and, to a lesser extent, journals, were essential to family, intellectual, and literary life. Coleridge wrote copious letters from Germany to his wife Sara and close friend Thomas Poole in 1798–9, and later edited them for inclusion in his prose memoir *Biographia Literaria*. Jane Austen honed and shaped her precise and often barbed wit in her long correspondence with her sister Cassandra. Material from Byron's letters found its way into his verse epic *Don Juan*, and indeed the comic style of the poem owes a substantial debt to Byron's verve and skill as a letter-writer. Keats, along with a number of other poets, found his first audience for his works in letters to friends. He wrote letters in verse, and included whole poems in his letters for his correspondents to read. Many other writers also used their journals and notebooks as a basis for works published in their lifetime, often in the travel genre, examples being Mary and Percy Shelley, and Dorothy Wordsworth. Diarists, such as Henry Crabb Robinson, and letter-writers, such as Anna Seward, wrote with the self-conscious knowledge that their records of the sayings and doings of their celebrated literary friends and acquaintances would make eminently publishable posthumous work.

The advent of feminist criticism has encouraged a reconsideration of letters and journals themselves for their content and also as significant literary forms and genres. The letters of Charlotte Smith and Mary Wollstonecraft, the journals of Frances Burney, Dorothy Wordsworth, and Mary Shelley, to name but a few, have either been reassessed (as in the case of Dorothy Wordsworth) or evaluated for the first time (as in the case of severely neglected writers such as Smith). Feminist critics have also asserted the importance of the subject-matter that these women write about. When William Knight edited Dorothy Wordsworth's *Alfoxden Journal* for its first publication in 1897, he decided that what he thought of as the domestic, and, he implied, trivial details of this diary should not be included in the published text. But not only did he omit these details, he also caused the manuscript to be mislaid or destroyed. Fortunately, the same did not occur with Dorothy's *Grasmere Journal*: the manuscript survives, and thus the domestic records it contains remain intact alongside the more obviously poetic details.

Feminist criticism has sought to oppose the kind of prejudices displayed by Knight, prejudices about what constitutes interesting, important, and literary autobiographical material. A feminist critique helps us to appreciate and have a politically conscious reaction to *all* the material included in letters and journals. Feminism helps us to see the skill involved in Dorothy Wordsworth's meticulous descriptions of strawberry flowers, of light on water, of waterfalls. It also helps us to see the sadness and the anger behind the weaving in together of such details with records of Dorothy's daily work of laundry, darning, cooking, and gardening, and to recognize the poetic quality of all her prose.

Other critical movements have also affected the way in which we read Romantic letters and journals. New Historicist criticism, with its interest in political and social contexts, has found letters and journals fruitful areas for research. An ecologically based approach might be used to elucidate the relationship in evidence in letters and notebooks between writers and their environment. After all, notebooks and letters often show an attempt to write to the moment, to capture what is happening now, and can often demonstrate what appears to be an extremely committed, involved relationship between the writer and the natural world. Formalist approaches to letters and journals may also be helpful in attending to the aesthetic shapes that letters and journals take, without proposing a proscriptive aesthetic.

Popular myths and images

Myths and popular images of the letter-writer and diarist abound in the late eighteenth and early nineteenth centuries. In the popular imagination, the letter-writer was often (but not always) a woman. In drawings, etchings, and paintings, she was depicted alone, pouring out her confessions on paper, her privacy disrupted by the voyeurism of the artist, and, of course, the artist's audience. The fascination for the reader or the observer here is essentially erotic.

By this period, novelists tended not to use the letter to structure their narratives: the epistolary novel was out of fashion. Instead, novelists began to use letters as an occasional device. In Jane Austen's *Persuasion* (1818), for example, a single letter is the means by which Anne Elliot finally discovers that Frederick Wentworth loves her. But despite this change in the use of the letter form within prose fiction, earlier epistolary novels still exerted a strong influence on the way letters were actually written (see *Oxford Companion to the Romantic Age*, pp. 286–95). Samuel Richardson's *Pamela* (1740) and *Clarissa* (1747–8); Jean-Jacques Rousseau's *Julie, ou la Nouvelle Heloïse* (1761);

Frances Burney's *Evelina* (1778) were all influential novels containing letter narratives that reveal and explore the romantic dangers or erotic threats their young female protagonists face when they enter the social world.

In these popular narratives and images, letter-writing and journal-keeping are often barely distinguishable. *Evelina*, for example, contains journal letters, or letters which are not finished and posted on one day. Instead individual letters can be carried on over several days. Thus, in the popular imagination, the practices of letter-writing and journal-keeping are very much linked, and equally sensational.

Another popular image of the letter in the Romantic period is of its use as an agent of revolutionary change. When Edmund Burke wrote his conservative polemic *Reflections on the Revolution in France* (1790) he wrote using the letter form, and offered a formal and ornate but also personal response to the events in France. But because he had used the epistolary form in this way, radical critics of his anti-revolutionary stance offered their own use of epistolary forms when they replied angrily to Burke's reactionary work (see also the chapter on 'Non-fictional prose'). Mary Wollstonecraft used the form to offer a blistering response in *A Vindication of the Rights of Men* (1790). She also used a letter-dedication to the French radical Talleyrand in her next work, *A Vindication of the Rights of Woman* (1792), and Thomas Paine used letter-dedications to address each of the two parts of his *Rights of Man* (1791 and 1792) to different revolutionaries, George Washington and General Lafayette. Helen Maria Williams's *Letters from France* (1790–6) used the letter form to champion the cause of the French Revolution in England.

Political uses of the letter were not confined to print culture. In the five or so years following the beginning of the French Revolution, revolutionary dissent also began to increase in Britain. Organizations such as the London Corresponding Society (the LCS) were formed (see *Oxford Companion to the Romantic Age*, pp. 1–26 and pp. 467–8). The LCS used letters as a means of gathering and sustaining mass opposition to the British government's oppressive laws and unjust treatment of the poor, connecting groups in a large number of towns and cities. Thus, the corresponding societies made the letter a potent symbol of popular, articulate, and organized dissent.

There are other important myths associated with letter-writing and journal-keeping. It is important for writers in both genres to make their writings *appear* as spontaneous as possible. Letters and journals, whether by men or women, must seem to be 'written to the moment'—in Samuel Richardson's phrase. They must be, or rather *seem*, the genuine, sincere outpourings of a refined sensibility; not stiff, stilted, or in any way formulaic (see also the chapter on 'Sensibility', and *Oxford Companion to the Romantic Age*, pp. 102–13). Diaries operate under a similar imperative. Part of the appeal of Coleridge's *Notebooks*, for example, is that they seem to adhere to this rule of sincerity and spontaneity. Coleridge owned a portable inkhorn, and often took his notebooks on journeys to record his thoughts and impressions as he went along. He was even known to take his portable writing kit with him on expeditions to the Lakeland Fells. These *Notebooks* also seem to conform to the contemporary taste for emotional sincerity, confessional revelation—they are so candid, in fact, that Coleridge occasionally uses a code to prevent easy discovery. He uses the Greek characters for the word 'Asra', an anagram of Sara, when referring to his unrequited love for Sara Hutchinson.

Spontaneity demands few, if any, fixed rules. In diaries and letters, subject-matter can often be miscellaneous. In Jane Austen's letters, descriptions of dress fabric sit beside brief references to her novels. In Mary Shelley's *Journals* records of Mary and Percy's reading are interspersed with notes about letters written and friends met. It also appears to be the case that the more private the diary, the more disconnected and associative the writing can be. Letters need to make some kind of sense to their recipients. Diaries can be ostensibly confidential writings (although this is by no means always the case) and as such are under no obligation to be fully comprehensible to anyone but the person who wrote them.

Critical problems

If the popular image of the letter-writer is usually of the desiring and desirable female, writing secret letters to a lover or about a lover, the reality was probably less sensational. In fact, by far the largest percentage of letters sent through the official post were business or legal letters, and these would generally be written by men. Only a small percentage of letters posted were written by women, and, of these, most would not be confidential love letters. The majority of letters not concerned with business would be family letters, directed to more than one recipient. The reasons for this were partly financial. Throughout the late eighteenth and the early nineteenth centuries, posting letters became increasingly expensive. William Pitt the younger (see *Oxford Companion to the Romantic Age*, pp. 648–9), Prime Minister from 1783 to 1801 and from 1801 to 1806, made it part of his policy to use postage charges as a tax to help fund his government's wars with Napoleon. As a result, letter-writing became a prohibitively expensive luxury, and so one family member would write on behalf of others, and letters would be passed around or read aloud. Such letters were not usually the place for confidential outpourings about love. Far from being a place where correspondents could express themselves without restraint, letters instead demanded self-censorship. Correspondence helped to keep the family hierarchy in place in a number of ways: writing them, amongst other things, encouraged young women (and, to some extent, young men) to submit to their parents. In letters, marriages were brokered, family business transacted, and kinship groups strengthened. Correspondence, in short, allowed separate branches of a family to retain a shared identity, sometimes across generations, and helped to keep patriarchal hierarchies in place (see *Oxford Companion to the Romantic Age*, pp. 42–51).

The letter became a potent symbol of popular, articulate, and organized dissent in the period. But although the corresponding societies unnerved the government of the time a great deal, that government was also able quickly to pass legislation (such as the Traitorous Correspondence Act of 1793) that made it increasingly difficult for the corresponding societies to use either the official postal service or unofficial carriers with any safety. Spies and informers could open letters to check for seditious pro-French opinions, which made people cautious.

Both radical epistolary tracts and the activities of the corresponding societies fostered the idea that letter-writing was essentially democratic. In a letter the poorest person could address the richest, and protests against injustice could be organized. But it must also be considered that, in practice, many of the poor were illiterate and could not write. Or, if they could write or find someone to write letters for them, the cost of postage was itself a barrier to writing. In many ways, letter-writing reinforced social divisions.

Several myths about Romantic diarists are also misleading. Diarists might appear to be writing very freely and privately, perhaps even more freely than they can in letters. But diarists' talk of writing confidential material needs to be treated with a little scepticism. To begin with, different diaries and notebooks have different functions, and even the same diarist can use her or his notebooks for different purposes at different times. Levels of confidentiality vary widely. Mary Shelley's *Journals* are a good example of this. Mary does not even begin her own *Journal*. Its opening entries, dating from 28 July 1814, are written in her new lover Percy Shelley's hand, and describe the couple's elopement from London to the Continent. Mary does not become a significant writer of the *Journals* until a fortnight later. But these early remarks by Percy are clearly meant to be read over by Mary: the undated inscription in the flyleaf of the first volume reads

↑not↓
Shelley and Mary's journal book

The '↑not↓' is a typographical way of showing a later insertion by Mary made to denote the change of use. Over time the 'journal book' becomes fully Mary's. But despite this, until Percy's death in 1822 the *Journals*, however often they were in fact read by Percy, seem, at all points, designed to be looked over by him. That is to say, there is very little in them that criticizes Percy's behaviour in any direct way. Despite the couple's intimacy in the early stages of their relationship, there is, nevertheless, some restraint in evidence. This restraint grows more pronounced in later volumes of the *Journal*, until 1822, and Shelley's death, when the tone and function change again. The entry of 2 October 1822 makes Mary's difficulty and her anguish clear:

. . . my thoughts are a sealed treasure which I can confide to none. White paper—wilt thou be my confident? I will trust thee fully, for none shall see what I write. But can I express all I feel? Have I the talent to give words to thoughts and feelings that as a tempest hurry me along?

These comments tell us a great deal about how Mary saw her *Journals* and the practice of journal-keeping in general. Firstly, she shows her awareness that her *Journal* has acquired a new intensity and confidentiality because it now has no audience but herself: Mary is here noting a change in readership. Percy is no longer an actual reader, but an imagined one. Secondly, and perhaps most importantly, she worries about her literary talent. This is, on the surface of it, a paradox. Why, if 'none shall see' what she writes, does she worry about good style? It would appear from her comments here that, even in this moment of intensely private grief, this public function of the *Journals* is beginning to take shape. Mary later used the *Journal* for self-justification and as a way of memorializing Percy. This is why I suggest that even at their most private and confidential, journals, like letters, are still being written with the hope or even intention that they will be read by someone other than their author. But, and this is key, that readership is, for the writer of the personal, highly confidential diary, necessarily posthumous.

Letter-writing

By the late eighteenth century, a substantial literary market had evolved for the published letters of authors, in letter manuals, in collections with titles such as the *Letters of*, or in biographies. Letter manuals became a distinct genre before the Renaissance. They were designed to teach those who could not afford a formal education how to write letters. Their method was simple and did not alter much from the medieval period onwards. They offered the student a series of letters dealing with a variety of social situations that were designed to act as models for imitation. Amongst the examples offered were often 'exemplary' letters, and, by the mid-eighteenth century, these exemplars were often letters by poets and novelists.

In addition, many eighteenth-century writers were well aware of the commercial value of their letters. The novelist Laurence Sterne was a case in point. Sterne wrote to a friend that he thought his letters would 'make a couple of Vol^s' and would 'print & sell to good Acc^t'. And even if writers were not as obviously self-conscious as Sterne, and did not attempt to gather together a collection of their own letters and arrange for posthumous publication, they were often aware that biographers might use their letters as source-material after their deaths.

Such was the commercial value of literary letters in the half-century or so prior to the Romantic period. And it would appear that the public appetite for letters of this kind did not diminish as the eighteenth century closed. To begin with, those who were associated with the more famous eighteenth-century authors continued to publish letters and other biographical material associated with them into the early years of the nineteenth century. Anna Laetitia Barbauld's edition of Samuel Richardson's letters (1804) was not a great commercial success, but the very fact of its publication meant that publishers still calculated that collections of literary letters would sell. If any additional evidence of this were required, one need look no further than the title of Thomas Moore's 1830 biography: *Letters and Journals of Lord Byron with Notices of his Life*. Here, Moore cleverly sidelines his role in writing the *Life* and lets his subject's letters and journals do the talking. In doing so he lets the association between letters, journals, and an authentic voice give his biography authority and a sense of intimacy.

This tactic also has the advantage of giving the book a powerful commercial allure. Moore was right in this—the book was a best-seller.

Self-consciousness necessarily shapes any letter, but from the eighteenth century on the culture of fame meant that letter-writers often had an eye on future publication. Whilst they might wish to appear as artless and spontaneous as contemporary taste demanded, their sense of offering an epistolary performance, both to their readers and to posterity, can be intense. Perhaps the most extreme example of this is, once again, Lord Byron. Byron loved to write highly confidential letters. But he also enjoyed sharing confidential letters (often from lovers) with other confidants. This epistolary game was played with some intensity in the period 1812–16, a time when, at the height of his fame following the publication of *Childe Harold's Pilgrimage*, he had affairs with Lady Caroline Lamb and his half-sister Augusta, but also married Annabella Milbanke, and separated from her. During this period, as he conducted correspondences with these women and with other lovers, he also wrote a commentary on his relationships in letters to an older woman friend, Lady Melbourne. He would enclose letters by Annabella, Caroline, and Augusta to her, and ask for her opinions. This voyeuristic system was clearly exciting to both Byron and Melbourne, so much so that Byron wrote to her on 6 November 1812 that

I never laugh at P——(by the bye this is an initial which might puzzle posterity when our correspondence bursts forth in the 20th century)

Byron's confidence that his letters will be read after his death is unwavering. He is not merely imagining them being read in the twenty or so years after his death, but having a vigorous afterlife—bursting forth—well over a century later.

Romantic correspondents, therefore, inherit a certain type of self-consciousness from their eighteenth-century predecessors, a self-consciousness based on the importance of the letter form in the literary market-place. Byron's self-consciousness was exceptionally pronounced, but he was not alone in his awareness of his letters' public future. Charlotte Smith at one time made an attempt to publish her letters, as did Anna Seward. And of course there were other correspondents, such as Charles Lamb, who tried to prevent the preservation of letters by friends such as Coleridge because he feared publication. Similarly, Keats ensured that the love letters Fanny Brawne sent to him were buried with him in Rome, although Fanny kept and later bequeathed to her relatives the letters he sent to her.

Journals, diaries, and notebooks

These related terms are placed together because they help to suggest how Romantic-period diaries come in a number of different, often specialist, forms. 'Diary' and 'journal' are almost interchangeable terms. Their etymology shows a common root, in the Latin word *dies* (day), and both terms describe a daily record. The practice of keeping a daily record of actions, and thoughts, became increasingly common from the Renaissance onwards. The function of a personal diary was, for many practitioners, essentially religious. In the Renaissance and after, both Puritans and Jesuits kept journals as part of their religious practice. The purpose of this daily writing was to examine the state of the conscience or soul; to track spiritual progress; to improve religious self-discipline. But in parallel to this there were substantial numbers of non-religious diarists. In their cases, the diary allowed the writer to chart actions, thoughts, and feelings, and was not necessarily a conversation with God. The term 'notebook', however, avoids the suggestion that the writer makes entries each day (although daily entries may be made). 'Notebook' also sounds a little less sensational than 'journal' or 'diary', a little more informal. But, of course, the associations we have with these terms may be misleading. A notebook may be as confessional as any journal. Or a journal may be enigmatic and utterly devoid of sensational revelation, and so on. William Godwin, for example, adopted private symbols and a personal shorthand in his diary in order to avoid personal revelation.

The market for diaries and journals, as I noted of Moore's *Life* of Byron, was a significant one. There was a plethora of travel journals published in the period: as Dorothy Wordsworth put it, when considering whether to write and publish her own travel journals, it was 'a writing and publishing (and tour-writing and tour-publishing) age'. Selling a publication such as the Shelleys' *History of a Six Weeks Tour* (1817) might be a way of financing a journey.

Diaries and journals, however, were not always written with immediate commercial gain in mind, and were not necessarily just religious or just travel journals. Instead, they were often hybrids, and may have had one or more specialized functions for the person writing. To take the basic function of the diary, the imperative to write in it every day: this was certainly not the central motivation behind Coleridge's journal-writing. Entries in his notebooks were often rather sporadic, and many were undated. Coleridge also used a number of notebooks at the same time, and carried on using them until they were full. There is, therefore, not even a chronological sequence of entries to rely on. Coleridge was not interested in charting his day-to-day 'progress' through life. He was more interested in the intense impressions made on him by life itself. And yet, the religious function of the journal is still in evidence in his *Notebooks*: many entries are full of religious despair or joy, many are confessions of profound religious guilt.

Contrast this with the approach of Mary Shelley, who *was* concerned to give a daily record of her life with Percy. Here is a small sample of her observations for November 1814:

Sunday 6th
Talk to Shelley—he writes a great heap of letters—read a part of St Leon—talk with him all evening—this is a day devoted to Love in idleness—go to sleep early in the evening—S. goes away a little before 10

Monday 7th

Work all the morning—go to Shelley at 3—return at 5—work & read in the evening. go to bed at 10

Teusday 8th

Write to Izy—& work all morning—go to Shelley in the evening it rains—thunders & lightens—stay with him ~~above an hou~~ about two hours.

Two things are of concern to Mary: work and her meetings with Percy. She is not concerned to record what she worked on or what she and Percy talked about, simply that the work or the conversation took place. And pressing on her very much at this point is *time*. She is precise about when she goes to bed, how long she works for, but above all, how much time she spends with her lover. She even goes so far as to cross out what she feels to be a slight inaccuracy: 'stay with him ~~above an hou~~ about two hours'. Also striking is the present tense in the declaration: 'this is a day devoted to Love in idleness', an expression of pleasure and intimacy set against the pressing sense of time passing, of love passing. The brevity of these entries might suggest that she has little time to record 'the actions of a day', as another diarist, the dramatist Ben Jonson, might put it. But she is keen to record events on the day that they happen: 'This *is* a day' (my emphasis).

Such concerns are particular to Mary's *Journal*, and its form evolves out of her new life and her relationship with Percy Shelley. Coleridge's *Notebooks*, on the other hand, arise in a more haphazard fashion. Coleridge only settles gradually into keeping notebooks. Early entries take the form of mathematical puzzles and equations, and at one point he even jots down a favourite recipe. Many of his notes are very brief, exclamatory, ecstatic. It is only later, around 1803, that making such notes becomes a compulsion, a necessity. Coleridge continues the habit of writing in his notebooks until the end of his life. Not so Mary Shelley or Dorothy Wordsworth. Their journals mark particular and often turbulent periods in their lives, but do not document the entire stretch of their adult existence. Dorothy Wordsworth begins her *Grasmere Journal* because, as she writes in its first entry, she wants to record what happens at home, what she observes, what she does, for the benefit of her brother William whilst he is away. The barely disguised subtext of this motive, of course, is a great deal of anguish and loneliness. And this brings me to another important point about journals: they often begin as a way of countering a perceived absence, the absence of a person or persons to whom the diarist cannot write in letters. In effect the journal is usually a 'dead' letter, an act of desperation, a last resort. When love affairs and/or friendships have failed, the journal becomes the confidant who cannot reply and who does not embrace. Or judge.

READINGS

Letters of Jane Austen

Critics have sometimes sneered at Austen's letters. E. M. Forster was one among many in the early twentieth century to voice their (gender-motivated) dislike for the letters' domestic details and, at times, very barbed wit. What these critics typically fail to appreciate is the importance of the interaction between domestic life and writing life. They also disparage the anger in Austen's letters, and the often surreal quality of her prose. That surreal wit can be employed in deconstructing the letter form itself, as in the letter to Cassandra, Austen's sister and chief confidante, dated 3 January 1801.

I have now attained the true art of letter-writing, which we are always told, is to express on paper exactly what one would say to the same person by word of mouth; I have been talking to you almost as fast as I could the whole of this letter.

Austen shows herself fully aware of how she is supposed to write a letter, but her knowledge of epistolary conventions far surpasses mere attainment of conventional skill. She gives that convention an extra twist by comically suggesting that she can do the impossible, and give the written text an unusually vivid *spoken* quality. Thus she shows that she can do far more than reproduce a style of conversation, as letter manuals of the time demanded. But behind all her animation lurks a perennial problem for this incredibly sharp-witted woman: the tedium of her day-to-day life. This problem creates a particular difficulty for the correspondent, as Austen points out to Cassandra on 21 January 1801:

Expect a most agreable Letter; for not being overburdened with subject—(having nothing at all to say)—I shall have no check to my Genius from beginning to end.

This is a problem for all women of this period belonging to Austen's social group, the upper-middle class. Confined to the home, not having the resources to travel, but needing the social stimulus of letters, they are faced with writing what Austen's contemporary, the novelist Susan Ferrier, called 'Parish News' letters (see *Oxford Companion to the Romantic Age*, p. 510). Austen's response is to attack the problem, and inject a strangeness to everything she touches, including that epistolary staple, gossip. In a letter to her sister of 20 November 1800 she describes, in detail, a ball she has attended:

Mrs Blount was the only one much admired. She appeared exactly as she did in September, with the same broad face, diamond bandeau, white shoes, pink husband, and fat neck.

The first sentence of this carefully constructed description is pure conversational cliché. It describes a social ritual: a group of acquaintances and friends deciding which of the women is most attractive. It is done in impersonal terms, in the passive voice. But here is Austen's skill: instead of being satisfied with this rather commonplace piece of news, she completely turns that news inside out, and to biting comic effect. Firstly, she suggests the boredom she feels at the conversation: Mrs Blount might be admired, but in fact there is not even anything new about her appearance to remark on, because she looks 'exactly as she did in September'. Then Austen precedes with a list of descriptors. Some of these sketch, disparagingly, Mrs Blount's physical appearance: 'Broad face' and 'fat neck'. But placed next to these in the same list is the inclusion of the 'pink' Mr Blount, as though he were a mere sartorial accessory. The way she structures this list gives the same status to the shoes, the fat neck, and the pink husband. The human life of these two people seems no more important or comprehensible than a diamond bandeau. If Austen has been praised in her novels for her insight into human nature, here we see almost the opposite of insight. She suggests in her letters that it is not possible to have much of an insight into the people she meets: in those letters, human life can often seem opaque, utterly tedious, grotesque. A human destiny can be dispensed with in a sentence. Or perhaps illuminated. The Argentinian writer, Jorge Luis Borges once wrote of Shakespeare that he could define a character's identity in a single phrase. Austen, it seems, first learnt a similar skill through the sometimes wearisome duty of writing letters.

Letters of John Keats

If Austen's letters have, at least in the past, been unfairly derided by critics, Keats's letters have, with some exceptions, been seen as almost the ideal literary letters. As far as we are aware, Keats kept no journal (though he did write long journal-letters). He published little in the way of essays and prefaces that explore and justify his mode of writing. Instead, almost all of his comments on this subject appear in letters to friends. Often the letters seem like a way of working out and testing ideas. This is perhaps the most famous and most anthologized example of Keats using the letter in this way. He writes to his brothers George and Tom on 21 December 1817:

Brown and Dilke walked with me back from the Christmas pantomime. I had not a dispute but a disquisition with Dilke, on various subjects. Several things dovetailed in my mind, and at once it struck me what quality went to form a man of achievement, especially in literature, and which Shakespeare possessed so enormously. I mean *negative capability*; that is, when a man is capable of being in uncertainties, mysteries, doubts, without any irritable reaching after fact and reason. Coleridge, for instance, would let go by a fine isolated verisimilitude caught from the penetralium of mystery, from being incapable of remaining content with half-knowledge. This pursued through volumes would perhaps take us no further than this: that with a great poet the sense of beauty overcomes every other consideration, or rather obliterates all consideration.

Recent critics have established that Keats derives these ideas about Shakespeare from his contemporaries Leigh Hunt and William Hazlitt. This discovery, however, does not diminish the importance of the letter. What Keats does with Hazlitt's idea is to make that italicized concept a focus-point for himself. *Negative capability* is a way of deriving power and strength from adversity and from failure. And this is the fascination of the letters, that in them we see Keats gathering strength and developing as a poet, over a period of a few years. During this time he builds up a complex epistolary mythology about himself.

Keats has a very specific way of writing this mythology. To take the negative capability letter as an example: he does not just describe the idea he has, but also tells us how that idea arose and grew. He uses the word 'dovetailed' to announce the key idea: a carpentry metaphor, but also one which suggests the incident in the New Testament where the spirit of God descends, in the form of a dove, at the baptism of Jesus by John the Baptist (Mark 3: 21–2). The word 'dovetailed' is at once mundane and magical.

Such letters about writing poetry are not the only means by which Keats creates a mythology about himself. Like a number of his contemporaries, he also chooses to send copies of his poems in letters, and, when he does so, the text of the letter acts as prelude for, and context to, the poem. A letter from the Isle of Wight illustrates the point. On 17 April 1817, Keats writes John Hamilton Reynolds a letter which is full of descriptions of the landscapes and seascapes of the island, and which also has a second life: an underlying and pressing preoccupation with the sea. In the opening paragraph, a description of the chine at Shanklin is suddenly interrupted by the phrase 'But the sea, Jack, the sea'. Keats then, just as abruptly, returns to the more standard epistolary fare of picturesque description, until he comes to what really obsesses him:

From want of regular rest, I have been rather *narvus*—and the passage in Lear—'Do you not hear the Sea?' has haunted me intensely.

Immediately after this, he launches into a new sonnet, 'On the Sea', but in the above preface, as he does in the negative capability letter, he suggests a kind of magic has taken place, a haunting, and implicitly links his sonnet with Shakespeare. Such rhetorical features are used to add to the sonnet's mystique. This is not to suggest that Keats is being in any way grandiose, but that he has an instinctive understanding of how to use the letter form to create a dramatic, yet often self-deprecating, narrative.

Dorothy Wordsworth, *Grasmere Journal*

Keats wrote letters in the way that he did at least in part because of the nature of the recipients of those letters who kept, read, reread and in some cases circulated his letters amongst themselves. The audience of Dorothy Wordsworth's *Grasmere Journal* also profoundly shaped the form the writing took. The journal begins on 14 May 1800, a day when Dorothy's brothers William and John leave the house at Grasmere which we now know as Dove Cottage. They were to be away for some time, and as a way of dealing with the loneliness and anxiety that beset her as soon as the brothers 'set off into Yorkshire after dinner at ½ past 2 o'clock, cold pork in their pockets', she begins to write. In addition to describing the brothers' departure that first entry also gives specific information about the journal's intended audience:

I resolved to write a journal of the time till W. and J. return, and I set about keeping my resolve because I will not quarrel with myself, and because I shall give W[illia]m Pleasure by it when he comes home again.

This is the purpose in writing: not just to give William pleasure, but also because Dorothy does not want to quarrel with herself. Her motivation is not simple. She wants to be self-denying (this journal is *for* William) but she also recognizes that she cannot be entirely successful in this. Her own desires intrude: she *also* needs to write for herself, as a way of dealing with difficult feelings. Sometimes, as in that first entry, there is a specific confession of Dorothy's emotional state. On that day she writes:

My heart was so full that I could hardly speak to W. when I gave him a farewell kiss. I sate a long time upon a stone at the margin of the lake, and after a flood of tears my heart was easier.

This kind of emotional confession does not predominate in the journals. Nevertheless the melancholy and self-conflict that provokes those tears imbues much of what Dorothy describes, as is the case in the next sentence of the 14 May entry: 'The lake looked to me I knew not why dull and melancholy, and the weltering on the shores seemed a heavy sound.' Equally, however, she can turn in a sentence or two from perceiving landscape as a mirror to perceiving it as a kind of consolation. After describing the lake she goes on to write:

The wood rich in flowers. A beautiful yellow, palish yellow flower, that looked thick and round and double, and smelt very sweet—I supposed it was ranunculus—Crowfoot, the grassy-leaved Rabbit white flower, strawberries, geranium—scent-less violet, anemones two kinds, orchises, primroses.

Such consolations are fragile and temporary. Flowers, or other beautiful objects, excite her eye and stimulate her powers of observation. But her daily activities and meetings with local people can, in a moment, plunge her once more into a sense of rage, frustration, and loss or fear of loss. On 7 August 1800, Dorothy writes

Packed up the mattrass, and sent to Keswick. Boiled gooseberries—N.B. 2 lbs of sugar in the first panfull, 3 quarts all good measure—3lbs in the 2nd 4 quarts—2½ lbs in the 3rd. A very fine day. William composing in the wood in the morning. In the evening we walked to Mary Point. A very fine sunset.

This entry, read in isolation, seems innocuous enough. Dorothy is simply detailing what she has done, and what William did, on one day in August. It is part recipe and part record of work done and time spent. The classic use of the journal, in other words. But, read in sequence, Dorothy's journal entries hint that she does not easily accept her lot as William's helpmate. Dorothy makes notes about the tasks she has completed, *alongside* notes about William's use of his time. The contrast is stark. William is usually free to compose while Dorothy does chores: packing up mattresses, drying linen, 'making shifts', cooking. Dorothy does not openly criticize this arrangement, but her habit of recording these bare facts hints that she feels a sense of loss, if not rage, at this imbalance. But it is often difficult to say for certain how she feels, because her style is very spare. Occasionally, as we see in the first entry, direct expressions of feeling erupt. Sorrow is the safest emotion for her to express, and it is this emotion that is experienced when she meets beggars on the road, or attends a poor woman's funeral. But there are moments of piercing joy too, quiet moments, when she talks of 'sweet' sunlight or writes descriptions such as 'the level meadows seemed very large, and some nearer us unequal ground heaving like sand, the Cottages beautiful and quiet' (22 November 1801). Here the land seems dynamic and alive, and the houses are emblems of peace and rest. But although beauty and quiet are in evidence, there is also the 'unequal ground heaving like sand'. Even at their most benign, Dorothy's landscapes are never quite tranquil, and often heave with unspecified emotion.

Samuel Taylor Coleridge, *Notebooks*

Coleridge's *Notebooks* do not come into being with anything like the troubled resolve demonstrated by Dorothy Wordsworth. The full emotional significance of Coleridge's *Notebooks* emerges only gradually as Coleridge's sense of isolation evolves. The entries he makes in the mid-1790s are frequently brief and playful. But although the humour does not disappear after 1800, by 1805 writing in the *Notebooks* has become an altogether more serious matter. As Coleridge's difficulties begin to arise—with the Wordsworths, with his love for Wordsworth's sister-in-law, Sara Hutchinson, and with his opium dependency—so the *Notebooks* become his 'sole confidants' (No. 463).[1] But it would be a mistake to see these jottings merely as sensational confessions of guilty feeling. They are also meditations born out of a far-reaching loneliness, meditations with nowhere else to go.

Coleridge wrote a very large amount of notebook material, covering an astonishing variety of topics, from poetry to philosophy, and from religion to nature. Often his observations consist of just one sentence, or even, in some cases, one word. An entry dated 1795 reads, simply, 'Protoplast', a word he also uses in some poems written around this time and which means 'The first former, fashioner, creator', i.e. God (No. 11). These micro-jottings are set alongside entries that extend over long paragraphs and whole pages, the longer entries often clarifying a philosophical point.

Whether the entries are long or short, and whatever they may be about, they have at least one thing in common: they are all unusually intense interactions with time. I say unusually intense: in fact, all diary entries are interactions with time, and not all diarists deal with time in the same way. Coleridge seems uniquely preoccupied with *instants* of time, with the force of one particular moment, or another, more than he is with the calendar or the clock. His notebooks are full of attempts to capture moments: moments experienced by one or more of the senses, or moments of cognition.

Those moments of cognition can be Coleridge's perception of what it is to be himself: 'Whirled about without a center—as in a nightmair—no gravity—a vortex without a center' (No. 508). Presumably Coleridge is talking about himself here, although he uses no personal pronoun to do so. Instead, he registers a frightening moment of perceiving the self as a terrifying void.

The moments of sensory perception he records are equally acute. He captures vivid moments of visual perception, such as: 'Severity of the Winter—the King'sfisher, its slow short flight permitting you to observe all its colours, almost as if it had been a flower' (No. 84). There is an almost chilling intensity to this way of seeing, and Coleridge himself is well aware of this, as when he writes, presumably, of Sara Hutchinson: 'As I have been falling to sleep, the Thought of you has come upon so strongly, that I have opened my eyes as if to look at you—' (No. 163).

Coleridge also has an acute ear for how phrases sound. 'Leaves already on the walk scattered' (No. 19) is a melancholy image, but it also has a delicate sound to it. It is written in an unusual poetic metre, as if it were an opening or closing line to a poem. Touch, too, is important in Coleridge's private writings, and has the same extraordinary vividness as his sense of sight. Sara Hutchinson's kiss, he notes, entrances him long after it has happened (No. 102). Coleridge also notes sensations of smell and taste: disgust at the after-effects of herrings, delight at the scent of Poplars (Nos. 359, 90).

Coleridge's notebook entries are like prayers, either full of longing for the intensity of the moment just gone, or full of desire for love, for literary works, for God. To give just one example: 'Poem on this night on Hellvellin | William & Dorothy & Mary | Sara & I' (No. 182) is both an expression of a very sharp sense of loss for a passing moment *and* an invocation for a poem to appear. In this way, the *Notebooks* offer Coleridge consolation pierced by desolation—in the same complicated way that he himself describes one particular colour effect: 'Blue *pierced* white' (No. 332).

FURTHER READING

Altman, Janet Gurkin, 'Political Ideology in the Letter Manual (France, England, New England)', in *Studies in Eighteenth Century Culture* XVIII, ed. John W. Yolton and Leslie Allen Brown (East Lansing, Mich.: Colleagues Press, 1988), pp. 105–22. Gives a good, concise history of the letter manual, and has interesting things to say about English manuals, an area not covered by Roger Chartier's book (see below).

Benstock, Shari (ed.), *The Private Self: Theory and Practice of Women's Autobiographical Writings* (Chapel Hill, NC: University of North Carolina Press, 1988). Useful in linking different autobiographical genres (including letters and journals) and in thinking through the ways in which women use them; also includes articles on Austen's *Letters* and Dorothy Wordsworth's *Journals*.

Chartier, Roger, Boureau, Alain, and Dauphin, Cécile, *Correspondance*, trans. Christopher Woodall (Cambridge: Polity Press, 1997). An excellent book, containing some detailed, thought-provoking perspectives on the history and political uses of letter manuals in France; also stresses the way in which correspondences come to be preserved (in archives), and the function of letter-writing within the family.

Coburn, Kathleen, *The Self-Conscious Imagination: A Study of the Coleridge Notebooks* (Oxford: Oxford University Press, 1974). An important study by the distinguished editor of the complete *Notebooks*.

Corbett, Mary Jean, 'Reading Mary Shelley's *Journals*: Romantic Subjectivity and Feminist Criticism', in Audrey A. Fisch, Anne K. Mellor, and Esther M. Schor (eds.), *The Other Mary Shelley* (Oxford: Oxford University Press, 1993), pp. 73–88. Corbett discusses the reasons for the marginalization of Mary Shelley's *Journals*, but also makes important comments on the position of journals by women within Romantic studies.

Favret, Mary, *Romantic Correspondence: Women, Politics and the Fiction of Letters* (Cambridge: Cambridge University Press, 1993). This gives a feminist perspective on some of the uses made of the letter form within print culture.

Flynn, Carol Houlihan, 'The Letters', in Edward Copeland and Juliet McMaster (eds.), *The Cambridge Companion to Jane Austen* (Cambridge: Cambridge University Press, 1998), pp. 100–14. Insightful, and a good introduction to the criticism available on Austen's letters.

Levin, Susan M., *Dorothy Wordsworth and Romanticism* (New Brunswick, NH, and London: Rutgers State University Press, 1987). A key text, and one which shows the extent to which Dorothy Wordsworth's writing is embedded in women's culture.

Modert, Jo, 'Letters/Correspondence', in J. David Grey (ed.), *The Jane Austen Handbook* (London: Athlone, 1986), pp. 271–8. Brief and suggestive, a useful introduction to Austen's letters by the editor of Austen's *Manuscript Letters in Facsimile*.

Perry, Seamus (ed.), *Coleridge's Notebooks: A Selection* (Oxford: Oxford University Press, 2002). Excellent selected edition of Coleridge's notebooks, with helpful introduction and notes.

Robinson, Howard, *The British Post Office: A History* (Princeton: Princeton University Press, 1948). A good, readable introduction to the history of the post in Britain, from medieval times to the mid-twentieth century.

Ruddick, William, '"As Much Diversity as the Heart that Trembles": Coleridge's Notes on the Lakeland Fells', in Richard Gravil, Lucy Newlyn, and Nicholas Roe (eds.), *Coleridge's Imagination: Essays in Memory of Peter Laver* (Cambridge: Cambridge University Press, 1985), pp. 88–101. A sensitive assessment of Coleridge's *Notebook* entries on local landscape.

Trilling, Lionel, 'The Poet as Hero: Keats in His Letters', in *The Opposing Self: Nine Essays in Criticism* (New York: Viking, 1968). A good example of a critic recasting Keats's letters as ideal and Keats's personality as somehow impeccably 'masculine'.

Watson, Nicola J., *Revolution and the Form of the British Novel 1790–1825: Intercepted Letters, Interrupted Seductions* (Oxford: Clarendon Press, 1994). This book deals, usefully, with the use of the letter within the fiction of the period, and stresses the revolutionary potential of the letter.

Wolfson, Susan J., 'Keats the Letter-Writer: Epistolary Poetics', in *Romanticism Past and Present*, 6: 2 (1982), 43–61. Stimulating reading of Keats's letters, one which sees into Keats's epistolary playfulness and 'speculative' imagination.

Woof, Pamela, 'The Alfoxden Journal and its Mysteries', in *The Wordsworth Circle*, 26: 3 (1995), 125–33. Shows clearly what William Knight wrongly found distasteful and uninteresting in the *Grasmere* and *Alfoxden Journals*.

NOTE

1. Samuel Taylor Coleridge, *Coleridge's Notebooks: A Selection*, ed. Seamus Perry (Oxford: Oxford University Press, 2002). I refer to each *Notebook* entry by using the number assigned to it in Perry's edition.

Part IV

Romantic afterlives

36 | Literary criticism and theory

Seamus Perry

For the Romantic poets, F. W. Bateson once said, language was chiefly 'a device for asking questions and not one for recording answers';[1] and even when not exactly posing questions ('Was it a vision, or a waking dream?', Keats, 'Ode to a Nightingale') Romantic poets are often engaged by questionable speculations, the entertaining of possibilities and second thoughts and half-thoughts ('If this | Be but a vain belief, yet . . .', Wordsworth, 'Tintern Abbey') rather than the placing of settled doctrines on record. Bateson's observation is true enough for us usefully to keep it in mind if we are drawn to define a Romantic position on art (or on anything else)—something which coherently persists to influence later thinkers and theorists. For what matters is the provision, not of a theory or a doctrine or an *ism* which later writers adopt or dispute, but, rather, of a set of interrelated, irresolved dilemmas about literature and author- ship, between which later poets and critics must pick their way. Telling the story of Romantic influence on later literary thinking is complicated further by the fact that (in English at least) 'Romantic' was mostly a retrospective classification—one little used by the writers it normally categorizes, that is to say, but often an all-important term for those who belatedly used it to categorize them. For most of the nineteenth century, the word means quite unambitiously 'the sort of quality you might associate with romance', as it does in 'Kubla Khan' ('But oh! that deep romantic chasm'); but gradually it begins to acquire some much more sophisticated meanings, often (as we shall see) at odds one with another.

The fascination of what's natural

Literary historians used to describe Wordsworth's Preface to *Lyrical Ballads* (1800, 1802) as the declaration of a new epoch in literary history; and while the novelty of the essay and the radicalism of the volume which it prefaced have by now been many times disputed, the Preface still remains a good place to begin because it exemplifies so vigorously one popular understanding of the Romantic revolution in letters. You might summarize this general view as 'the return to nature' or 'the revolt against

Alexander Pope', with 'Pope' there to be understood as shorthand for the abstraction and artificiality that Romantic polemic typically characterized as Augustan—'the dark age of English poetry', as Robert Southey once called it. 'He was, in a word, the poet, not of nature, but of art', says Hazlitt of Pope, summarizing a whole climate of opinion. For all such professions of distaste, Pope remained a secretly fruitful presence in much Romantic poetry; but what concerns us is the Romantic embracing of *nature* as a criterion: as Keats told his friend Taylor (27 February 1818), 'if Poetry comes not as naturally as the Leaves to a tree it had better not come at all'. Here, the most important figure is Wordsworth—a poet to whom, as M. H. Abrams puts it in *The Mirror and the Lamp* (1953), 'the cardinal standard of poetic value is "nature"'.[2] The Preface to *Lyrical Ballads* announced the volume's principal subject to be 'the primary laws of our nature'—Wordsworth generalized impressively in the additions made to the 1802 edition, 'Poetry is the image of man and nature'. Such a natural disposition led to the imaginative interest in the unsophisticated and uncultivated tendentiously manifest in Wordsworth's *Lyrical Ballads*, which severally deal with unlettered peasants, children, and the mentally disabled: Wordsworth provocatively justified his choice in the Preface on the grounds that such characters were composed of elements exemplarily 'simple, belonging rather to nature than to manners'. They conformed, that is to say, to the axiom stated in his later 'Essays on Epitaphs' (1810), that poetry should deal with 'those feelings which are the pure emanations of Nature': the problem with modern verse was the way it had been 'thoroughly tainted by the artifices which have over-run our writings in metre since the days of Dryden and Pope'.

Your attitude towards such a sentiment will, of course, depend in large part on how you regard nature untainted. If, with T. E. Hulme, modernist essayist and conservative philosopher, you believe in Original Sin (that the simple and natural is not good at all but in fact innately wicked) then Wordsworth's ascription of natural simplicity to his subjects would be precisely the reason for properly leaving them uncelebrated: the reasons 'why I believe in Original Sin', as Hulme put it in his 'A Tory Philosophy' (1912), were one and the same as those 'why I cannot stand romanticism'. A good deal of twentieth-century anti-Romanticism found the cult of unartificial naturalness as exemplified by Wordsworth's subjects particularly hard to stomach: 'The whole movement is filled with the praise of ignorance and of those who still enjoy its unappreciable advantages', as Irving Babbitt put it in his brilliant and caustic *Rousseau and Romanticism* (1919), going on to specify some distasteful Romantic favourites—'the savage, the peasant and above all the child'. The literary interest in children and childish experience to which an immense literature over the last two centuries bears testimony—and particularly its governing (Wordsworthian) axiom that adults are not different from their childish selves but continuous with them, and indeed the product of their early experience—must be among the most pervasively influential of all Romantic tenets.

Feeling and wonder

Rejecting artifice in the name of what comes naturally can lead to more than a renewed interest in children and the simple-minded as something to write about. If Pope's artificiality was the work of what Coleridge called 'the logic of wit', merely amounting to 'just and acute observations on men and manners' (*Biographia Literaria*, ch. 1), then poetry that came *naturally* was presumably authored by deeper stirrings of the human being: hoping to reject what he felt to be 'the false beauty proceeding from art', Keats looked to 'the true voice of feeling' for his proper inspiration (Letter to Reynolds, 22 September 1819). Again, Wordsworth is the important spokesman here: 'The reader cannot be too often reminded', he wrote splendidly in a note to 'The Thorn' in the second edition of *Lyrical Ballads*, 'that poetry is passion: it is the history or science of feelings'—or, as the famous phrase from the Preface goes, 'all good poetry is the spontaneous overflow of powerful feelings'. It is Wordsworth's usual habit promptly to qualify such statements: he maintains in the 'Essays on Epitaphs', for instance, that 'a conjunction of Reason and Passion' was what the poet really needed; but later anti-Romantics typically identified unchecked emotionalism as a peculiarly pervasive, and mischievous, element of the Romantic legacy. In *Rousseau and Romanticism*, Babbitt identified an 'extreme emancipation of the emotions' lying at the heart of the Romantic movement—'the assumption that feeling is worthy of trust' (which assumption, needless to say, he did not share).

The critic Yvor Winters, writing later in the century, similarly judged the wrongness of the 'Romantic theory' to begin with its assumption 'that literature is mainly or even purely an emotional experience' (in his exemplarily entitled *In Defence of Reason* (1947)). This was a judgement often handed down in twentieth-century criticism—for example, by the poet and critic Donald Davie, an admirer of Winters, who spoke warmly in his memoirs of 'the Romantic conviction that a sufficient head of passion in a man absolves him from practising the cooler virtues' (*These the Companions* (1982)). The un-Romantic virtues were, as Davie maintained in his critical book *Articulate Energy* (1955), those of 'strong sense' (not 'strong feelings')—the virtues of reasonableness and lucidity, and a forceful clarity of thought, rather than the emotive poetic irrationalism which Davie considered the Romantics' bequest. He presumably had in mind such touchstones as Keats's cry in a letter (22 November 1817) 'O for a Life of sensations rather than of Thoughts!', or his lament in 'Lamia', that all charms fly at 'the mere touch of cold philosophy'; or Wordsworth's declared mistrust in 'The Tables Turned' (*Lyrical Ballads*) of the 'meddling intellect'—'We murder to dissect'. Characteristically, I suppose, twentieth-century authors have shared Babbitt's disapproval of 'Emotionalism as a substitute for thought' (*On Being Creative and Other Essays* (1932)); but of course not everyone was so appalled. An artistic distrust of reason presumably reaches its apogee in surrealism, in which art emulates the pseudo-logic of dreams; and Sir Herbert Read, Britain's leading sponsor of surrealist art, was pleased to see the Romantics anticipate it. In his once important book *The True Voice of Feeling* (1953)—the title comes from Keats—Read praises Coleridge's 'Kubla Khan', a poem supposedly written in a dream, as a precursor of the 'surrealist doctrine of automatism in art' (though he conceded, correctly, that Coleridge himself hardly embraced any such doctrine).

Chief among the emotions that Romanticism sought to cultivate, according to Babbitt's sceptical account, was a particular kind of infantilism: Coleridge, said Babbitt, counselled us to 'sink back to the devout state of childlike wonder'. What Coleridge actually said (*Biographia Literaria*, ch. 4) was a good deal grander, namely that 'the character and privilege of genius' was to 'carry on the feelings of childhood into the powers of manhood; to combine the child's sense of wonder and novelty with the appearance, which every day for perhaps forty years had rendered familiar.' (The notion is a striking reimagining of Christ's injunction (Matthew 18) that the faithful should 'become as little children'.) Coleridge was writing with Wordsworth in mind, and the Preface to *Lyrical Ballads* makes much the same point in a different way: the principal object of the poems, Wordsworth says, is 'to choose incidents and situations from common life', but 'to throw over them a certain colouring of imagination, whereby ordinary things should be presented to the mind in an unusual aspect'. (Shelley revoices the doctrine more mystically in 'A Defence of Poetry' (1821): 'Poetry lifts the veil from the hidden beauty of the world, and makes familiar objects be as if they were not familiar.') This quality of genius, as Coleridge put it in his notebook (1811), was not a matter of writing 'What oft was thought but ne'er so well expressed'—Pope's description of true wit—but rather the placing of 'things *in a new light*'. Wordsworth once pointed out to Hazlitt the way the sun cast beautifully upon a bank, and, recalled Hazlitt in *My First Acquaintance with Poets* (1823), 'I thought within myself, "with what eyes these poets see nature!" and ever after, when I saw the sun-set stream upon the objects facing it, conceived I had made a discovery, or thanked Mr Wordsworth for having made one for me.'

The post-Romantic tenacity of this aesthetic, with its art of the ordinary-made-extraordinary and the commonplace renewed as wonderful, can hardly be overstated: it strikes a modern reader as obvious that an artist's business should be, among other things perhaps, to restore by descriptive power the freshness of a world perceptually lost to us through weary adulthood and the laziness of habit. (David Trotter complains that the verse which such a cast of mind encourages has even come to seem 'the entire scope and value of poetry'.[3]) This cast of mind reveres a vivifying realism, often a vividness of image in particular (as in the Wordsworthian example Hazlitt remembered); and it is underwritten by a moral imperative about the dignity and proper interest of the real world: 'the world is not to be learned and thrown aside, but reverted to and relearned', as Browning nobly said in his 'Essay on Shelley'. Perhaps the most heroic Victorian expression of such a conviction concerns not literature at all but painting: John Ruskin's *Modern Painters* (1843–60)—each volume of which bears an epigraph from Wordsworth—celebrates in extraordinary detail the extraordinary detail that Ruskin found celebrated in the paintings of J. M. W. Turner, a man who painted 'more of nature than any man who ever lived', as Ruskin put it in the preface to the second edition. But this revelatory power was not the mark only of painters: the hero of Charles Kingsley's novel *Alton Locke* (1850), for example, finds that he sees the unremarkable world anew after reading Tennyson—'I always knew there was something beautiful, wonderful, sublime, in those flowery dykes of Battersea Fields; in the long gravelly sweeps of that lone tidal shore; and here was a man who had put them into words for me! This is what I call democratic art—the revelation of the poetry which lies in common things' (ch. 9). Tennyson was evidently fulfilling the task of the poet, as Thomas Hardy defined it in his notebook (1878)—'Paradoxically put, it is to see the beauty in ugliness.'

'He was a man who used to notice such things', Hardy imagined the neighbours saying about him after his death, in his poem 'Afterwards', which would serve well enough as a motto for much modern literary practice and appreciation. I suppose Joyce's *Ulysses* (1922) is the grandest and most programmatic of all attempts to render heroic the undignified paraphernalia of common things, an instinct which Joyce (who thought highly of Wordsworth) had earlier theorized, more preciously, in his doctrine of the epiphany. In an epiphany, something wholly banal becomes suddenly remarkable—such as a clock on a government office which is 'only an item in the catalogue of Dublin's street furniture' until (as Joyce's spokesman says in the novel *Stephen Hero*) 'all at once I see it and I know at once what it is: epiphany'. Writers who otherwise resemble one another scarcely at all nevertheless share in this continuing aesthetic: the authors associated with the Movement in 1950s Britain, for example, with whom Donald Davie was often counted, set themselves as squarely against the flamboyant virtuosity of Joycean modernism as they did 'Against Romanticism' (the title of a poem by Kingsley Amis). But the studied recourse to the ordinary which was their chief mode of retaliation—

> I fell asleep, waking at the fumes
> And furnace-glares of Sheffield, where I changed,
> And ate an awful pie—

remains, from another point of view, eminently Romantic, as is clear enough when Philip Larkin, the author of that marvellous and drab pie, tells an interviewer that the purpose of poetry is 'recreating the familiar' (*Required Writing* (1984)). Such would be the hallmark, too, of the Martian school, nicknamed after Craig Raine's poem 'A Martian Sends a Postcard Home' (1970), in which familiar reality is misdescribed by an attentive but alien eye ('Mist is when the sky is tired of flight'). The blurb to Raine's *Collected Poems 1978–1999* is exemplary: 'the poet forces us to see the most commonplace objects as miraculous'—the Raine speaker is a space-age version of the Romantic child, or of the Romantic poet who has again become as a child, with all the wide-eyed innocence of Adam looking about Eden: 'You look round on your mother earth . . . As if you were her first-born birth, | And none had lived before you!' (Wordsworth, 'Expostulation and Reply').

Ordinary language

A decent poem should be full of 'accurate, precise, and definite description', thought T. E. Hulme, as did the Imagist poets who followed him, celebrating what they took to be a non-Romantic excellence; but its true credentials in fact are not hard to spot: 'I have at all times', wrote Wordsworth in the Preface to *Lyrical Ballads*, 'endeavoured to look steadily at my subject, consequently, I hope that there is in these Poems little falsehood of description.' The desire not to falsify implies my last point about this trend in Romantic thinking: the appeal to nature and naturalness can suggest a number of subjects for poetry, and also a source of inspiration; and it might suggest additionally an ideal for poetic language. From the Preface to *Lyrical Ballads* again: 'I have proposed to myself to imitate, and, as far as is possible, to adopt the very language of men'—not, that is to say, among other things, the language of *poetry*. 'There will also be found in these volumes little of what is usually called poetic diction; I have taken as much pains to avoid it as others ordinarily take to produce it; this I have done for the reason already alleged, to bring my language near to the language of men.' The language of poetry should not be *special*: 'Poetry sheds no tears "such as Angels weep," but natural and human tears', the language of 'a man speaking to men'.

For an artist to define himself against the artful looks bound to involve all kinds of paradoxes, and Coleridge picked about them resourcefully in *Biographia Literaria*. But, whatever imponderables in the theoretical position, we should not be surprised to find one who 'vindicate[s] the rights and dignity of Nature' expressing an emotive hostility to 'the adversary of nature, (call that adversary Art or by what name you will)' ('Essays on Epitaphs'). Wordsworth's attempt at a poetry eschewing a 'poetic' idiom for something closer to 'the language of men' stands at the head of a vigorous modern tradition. Byron, implacably opposed to almost everything Wordsworthian, might yet have surreptitiously concurred with him on the point of 'the very language of men': he built a masterpiece on the principle in *Don Juan* ('never straining hard to versify, | I rattle on exactly as I'd talk'); and John Clare's vernacular poetry has been widely celebrated for its fulfilment of much the same ambition, though admittedly by rather different means. (His verse comes straight from 'the living heart of a language', avers Tom Paulin, admiring 'the in-dwellingness of spoken language' in it.[4]) Robert Browning's experiments with artless colloquialism ('Well, I could never write a verse,—could you?') go hand in hand with his conception of the 'objective' poet, whose interest is in the things that lie outwith the poet ('He took such cognizance of men and things'); and much the same might be said of Hardy, for whom seeing beauty in ugliness was clearly cognate with the deployment, within poetry, of showily unpoetical locutions ('Well, on the whole, I like my life.— | I know I swore I'd be no wife, | But what was I to do?'). The modernist revolution was noisily dedicated to the rejection of, as Ezra Pound put it, 'every literaryism, every book word': rather, he counselled, poetry should use 'nothing that you couldn't, in some circumstance, in the stress of some emotion, actually say' (letter to Harriet Monroe, 1915; compare the chapter on 'Modernism and Postmodernity'). T. S. Eliot insisted similarly on a vital connection between the language of poetry and the language spoken outside poetry ('The music of poetry . . . must be a music latent in the common speech of its time'); and he retrospectively made explicit a connection between the literary revolution of which he was a part and its Romantic precursor: 'a refreshment of poetic diction similar to that brought about by Wordsworth had been called for (whether it has been satisfactorily accomplished or not)' ('The Music of Poetry' (1942)). By the time of F. R. Leavis's highly influential *New Bearings in English Poetry* (1932), the principle appears wholly uncontentious, and Eliot might find himself praised in his own terms: the 'staple idiom and movement' of his poetry, Leavis maintained, 'derive immediately from modern speech'. The strength of Gerard Manley Hopkins too, 'Paradoxical as it may sound to say so' (and it did), lay in the way 'that he brought poetry much closer to living speech'. Such sentiments doubt-less accompany in some way that powerful trend in modern thought which looked to 'ordinary language' for a way through the tangles of philosophy—a line of enquiry pursued in the Cambridge of Leavis's day most notably by Ludwig Wittgenstein.

One way that Wordsworth put the all-important kinship between the language of art and living speech was, slightly confusingly, that 'that there neither is, nor can be, any essential difference between the language of prose and metrical composition'; and this association too has had its important post-Romantic afterlife. 'Poetry must be *as well written as prose*' was how Pound put it (letter to Harriet Monro, 1915): Wordsworth was hardly a fashionable predecessor in the early twentieth century, but even Pound could advise, 'Read as much of Wordsworth as does not seem too unutterably dull' ('A Few Don'ts By an Imagiste' (1913)). Donald Davie did not simply like Wordsworth either, but 'prosaic' is a term of high literary praise in his *Purity of Diction in English Verse* (1952), as it had been for Eliot: 'no poet can write a poem of amplitude unless he is a master of the prosaic' ('The Music of Poetry'). That is hardly vindicating nature in Wordsworth's way, but it is part of the same tradition. Likewise, the contemporary American poet Gary Snyder writes in his own voice but still in an impeccably Wordsworthian spirit when he rejects the principle that 'Good writing is "civilized" language' in favour of the ecological counter-principle that 'Good writing is "wild" language' ('Language Goes Two Ways' (1995)).

But if the 'wild', the prosaic, the ordinary, and the natural can all claim good Roman-tic credentials, still, few if any of the writers I have just quoted would have cheerfully recognized the virtues they were celebrating as Romantic, and nor would many mod-ern authorities either. Both Byron and Clare, for example, have been held up in much recent criticism, not as exemplarily Romantic but, on the contrary, as salutory *alterna-tives* in one way or another to bad Romantic habits of mind (habits that, it is said, continue to shape our modern literary thinking). So, what are the alternative trends in late eighteenth- and early nineteenth-century literature which modern criticism has chosen to adopt in this adversarial spirit as definitionally Romantic? And what afterlife have these trends enjoyed in the modern period?

Egotism and imagination

Part of the case for the realist imagination I have been describing so far is moral: the artist is kept in his place, attendant upon, and not master over, the world he is set to evoke; and since his success is never likely to be complete—for he can hardly rival the realness of reality—this builds a kind of humility into his art. 'However exalted a notion we would wish to cherish of the character of a Poet', writes Wordsworth in the Preface, 'it is obvious, that, while he describes and imitates passions, his situation is altogether slavish and mechanical, compared with the freedom and power of real and substantial action and suffering.' The consequence of this sense of limits is predictable but still striking: 'it will be the wish of the Poet', continues Wordsworth, 'to bring his feelings near to those of the persons whose feelings he describes, nay, for short spaces of time, perhaps, to let himself slip into an entire delusion, and even confound and identify his feelings with theirs.' The poet should seek to evade his own personality and selfhood: this doctrine of Romantic self-effacement has its loftiest expression in Keats's account of the 'camelion Poet': 'it is not itself—it has no self—it is every thing and nothing—It has no character . . . A Poet is the most unpoetical of any thing in existence; because he has no identity' (27 October 1818). Critics sometimes label this poetical character 'negative capability', taking a phrase from another Keats letter: the point at stake is not the poet's self-expression, but his power as a negative spirit some-how to identify with whatever he contemplates and to realize its nature from within. The creativity is the work of the selflessness, a kind of imagination, thought Coleridge, best exemplified by Shakespeare, 'the one Proteus of the fire and the flood' (*Biographia, Literaria*, ch. 15): protean, shape-shifting Shakespeare himself is invisible in his works, 'an omnipresent creativeness' whose poetry is 'characterless' (*Table Talk*)—his personal self-presence dissipates itself among the multiple voices he inhabits from moment to moment. When T. S. Eliot writes of the poet's necessary 'impersonality', the way in which he has 'not a "personality" to express, but a particular medium, which is only a medium and not a personality, in which impressions and experiences combine in peculiar and unexpected ways', he does not sound very Romantic—yet it is hard not to agree with J. A. M. Rillie's spry observation, that the tone is 'simply a device for fright-ening the horses of Romanticism' and that Eliot is really offering a modernist version of the self-elusive type of Romantic poet blessed with no identity.[5]

But there is an alternative sort of Romantic creativity to this—not the magnanimous invisibility of a Shakespeare, but a colossal imaginative egotism: if the first is self-oblivious, then the second is all-absorbingly self-aware. Coleridge looked to both with equal and opposite admiration, and considered the best exponent of the second type to be Milton, who, working in quite the contrary direction to Shakespeare, 'attracts all forms and things to himself, into the unity of his own IDEAL' (*Biographia Literaria*, ch. 15): in his *Table Talk* Coleridge praised the 'intense egotism' of Milton's verse—'it is Milton himself whom you see; his Satan, his Adam, his Raphael—they are all John

Milton'. Keats was also regardful, though much more warily, of the Miltonic possibility: he contrasted his own poetical character with the Miltonic sort of imagination which he saw in Wordsworth—the 'wordsworthian or egotistical sublime; which is a thing per se and stands alone' (27 October 1818). If this does not sound much like the mind of Wordsworth as I have been describing it so far, then that is because (like Coleridge) Wordsworth possesses quite diverse casts of mind; and there are, as a consequence, two quite distinct Wordsworths on show in the critical tradition: if one, the author of the Preface, with his eye steadily on the object, exemplifies a 'return to nature', then the other stands for something quite differently Romantic, an art that dwells instead upon subjectivity and the inwardness of experience. Hazlitt put it most vehemently, and not quite unadmiringly, in his review of Wordsworth's *The Excursion*: 'An intense intellectual egotism swallows up everything ... he lives in the busy solitude of his own heart' (*Examiner*, 21 August 1814). In this account of things, Wordsworth's eccentric choice of subject-matter was not testimony to his egalitarian impulses but, on the contrary, evidence of the unanswerable trust he placed in his own highly private perceptions, convinced of its own imaginative rectitude and heedless to external objection or check. The poet Clough put it best: 'instead of looking directly at an object, and considering it as a thing in itself, and allowing it to operate upon him as a fact in itself, he takes the sentiment produced by it in his own mind, as the thing, as the important and really real fact. The real thing ceases to be real; the world no longer exists ...' (*Poetry and Prose Remains* (1869)). Imagination, to this way of thinking, is not an attentive adherence to nature so much as something that gets done to her, or made of her: it is not, say, the actual natural daffodils by Ullswater that move Wordsworth to spontaneous delight, but rather the flashing idea of them which he experiences when he's back home alone—

> And *then* my heart with pleasure fills
> And dances with the daffodils.
> (emphasis added)

Coleridge puts the powerful magic of poetic subjectivity most wonderfully in his notebook (1804): 'Poets ... are the Bridlers by Delight, the Purifiers ... Gods of Love who tame the Chaos.' The implications for nature and ordinary things in their own right are stark enough: not to be revered and rendered anew, but the stuff of mere 'chaos', raw material to be brought to life and remade in the artwork. Without the imagination's transforming attention, nature remains (as Coleridge says in 'Dejection: An Ode') an 'inanimate cold world'.

Of the two kinds of Romantic imagination, as John Bayley observes in *The Romantic Survival* (1957)—to which account I am much indebted here—it is 'the theory of the self-conscious Imagination' that has been 'by far the more influential'.[6] Frank Kermode's *Romantic Image* (1957) concurs, drawing connections between the literary thinking of the modern period and the subjective aspect of its Romantic precursors. When, for example, Oscar Wilde's spokesman announces in 'The Critic as Artist' (1891) that 'All artistic creation is absolutely subjective', or that 'those great figures of

Greek or English drama that seem to us to possess an actual existence of their own . . . are, in their ultimate analysis, simply the poets themselves', or expresses his approval for the 'deliberate rejection of Nature as the ideal of beauty, as well as of the imitative method of the ordinary painter', he is (as Kermode observes) drawing upon a repertoire familiar from the Romantics. And when, for a slightly later example, T. S. Eliot offers his great description of the poet's mind at work, 'constantly amalgamating disparate experience', he too is recognizably writing within a Coleridgean tradition: 'the ordinary man's experience is chaotic, irregular, fragmentary. The latter falls in love, or reads Spinoza, and these two experiences have nothing to do with each other, or with the noise of the typewriter or the smell of cooking; in the mind of the poet these experiences are always forming new wholes' ('The Metaphysical Poets' (1922)). Eliot's admiration for *Ulysses*, then, was not to be for Joyce's rendering marvellous of mundane experience, but rather for the subjective mastery that his mind enjoyed over such experience—'a way of controlling, of ordering, of giving a shape and a significance to the immense panorama of futility and anarchy which is contemporary history' ('*Ulysses*, Order and Myth' (1922)). Eliot's contemporary Wallace Stevens writes of 'The poem of the act of the mind' ('Of Modern Poetry' (1942)); and his own poems display such acts of control with endless resourcefulness, perpetually moved by the thought of what he calls elsewhere 'Blessed rage for order' ('The Idea of Order at Key West' (1936)).

What matters in such cases is the *differentness* of art from the world, and, by implication, the differentness too of the artist, who enjoys a peculiar kind of authority, occupying what Coleridge admired in Wordsworth as 'the dread watch-tower of man's absolute self' ('To William Wordsworth'). The poet's role becomes, in short, Godlike—not an idea new to the Romantics, but one invested with a new vigour by them; and the corollary to it is that the product of poetic artistry is, like the product of God's artistry, a world—a 'second nature', a *heterocosm*, a new and autonomous world. Shelley says in the 'Defence of Poetry': 'Poetry makes us inhabitants of a world to which the familiar world is a chaos', an idea that persists through a vast range of modern literary thinking. A. C. Bradley, for example, in 'Poetry for Poetry's Sake' (1901), his inaugural lecture at Oxford, announced that poetry's purpose is 'to be not a part, nor yet a copy, of the real world . . . but to be a world by itself, independent, complete, autonomous' (*Oxford Lectures on Poetry*). The point is reiterated so often in modern criticism, in one form or another, that it feels as though the least contentious of critical platitudes is being invoked when a work is praised for the way it creates and occupies 'a world of its own'—'Greeneland' (the imaginative territory where Graham Greene's novels happen) or *The World of C. P. Snow*. If, as I said a moment ago, the idea of ordinary language as a goal for poetry coincides with a more general emphasis upon ordinary language in modern thought, then these doctrines of art's heterocosmic separateness go hand in hand with quite different, but equally influential, trends—in particular, with those brands of critical theory, often gathered under the label 'formalism', which seek to describe artworks not in relation to the world without them but as self-contained systems of signs complete within themselves—to understand, say, poetry 'as poetry and not another thing' (in Eliot's resonant phrase from the preface to *The Sacred Wood* (1928)).

Both Bayley and Kermode identify Romantic origins for modernist literary thinking that its exponents did not themselves confess, and would no doubt have been displeased to hear about: if the deep Romanticism of their notions now seems self-evident, it is because, over the second half of the twentieth century, prevailing conceptions of what is Romantic have shifted. When, for example, Harold Bloom describes Wordsworth's 'revolution in poetry' he means, not a return to nature but, on the contrary, 'the evanescence of any subject but subjectivity', and the Romanticism which this exemplifies produces, in Bloom's provocative phrase, 'an antinature poetry' ('The Internalization of Quest Romance' (1971)). The exemplary Romantic, as described (say) in Bloom's *The Visionary Company: A Reading of English Romantic Poetry* (1962), now becomes William Blake: for Blake would have agreed most vigorously with Wilde that nature should be rejected by the artist, though for reasons of his own (and Wordsworth would have agreed only some of the time). 'Natural Objects always did & now do Weaken deaden & obliterate Imagination in Me', Blake wrote in the margins of his copy of the less single-minded Wordsworth, 'Wordsworth must know that what he Writes Valuable is Not to be found in Nature'.

Current questions

But if a conception of the mind as (in Wordsworth's words from *The Prelude*) 'lord and master' and of 'outward sense' as 'but the obedient servant of her will' currently feels most importantly Romantic about the Romantics, then this emphasis upon subjectivity and the transforming power of consciousness is hardly the subject of warm approval in most of its discerners. 'The idea that poetry, or even consciousness, can set one free of the ruins of history and culture is the grand illusion of every Romantic poet', Jerome McGann writes in his widely noticed *The Romantic Ideology* (1983);[7] and his terms, 'history and culture', imply one group unlikely to be impressed by such visionary Romanticism—the politically engaged, for whom the ability to apprehend the world as it is would seem a minimum necessity, and who might be expected additionally to see the ordinary world as something of intrinsic ethical value. No more likely to be impressed are those to whom nature, untouched, is propositionally a good thing: for the ecologist, such as Gary Snyder, rightly protests 'We do not need to organize so-called chaos' ('Language Goes Two Ways'). Jonathan Bate likewise attacks the view that 'the human mind is its own place' as a principle which opens the way to 'a denigration of material nature and an exaltation of human consciousness'—which bad habit of mind the Romantic artist, 'quasi-magical, quasi-divine', exemplifies in a peculiarly potent way.[8] A critic might also read the imposition of the creative mind's designs upon the world in a symbolical sort of way and forge a figurative connection with varieties of political exploitation—imperialism, say, or patriarchy.

Well, against such multiple failings of the Romantic ego there are salutory counter-voices from the Romantic period to be mustered. McGann has often, and with increasing sophistication, put forward Byron as such a voice, a poet whose greatest work 'puts poetry in its place' by insisting on a world without the mind and so challenging 'the primacy of the Imagination';[9] and McGann has also invoked to similar ends the poetry of George Crabbe, a writer in the Romantic age to be sure but (by this definition) not of it, 'human, non-transcendent' and 'non-subjective', whose work 'represents the discovery that no subject lies outside the province of verse'.[10] Jonathan Bate has eloquently argued the case for John Clare, a poet of 'thing-experience' who bucks the expectations of the egotistical sublime.[11] Aidan Day sets Dorothy Wordsworth's self-effacing journal against the example of her imaginatively appropriative brother, explaining that her kind of writing 'genuinely allows nature a life of its own': women's writing of the period has often been held to voice a morally admirable suspicion of 'the masculinized and egocentric sublime' in this kind of way.[12] Now, the merits of these various objections to Romantic selfness could be debated individually, of course; but what is noteworthy for our purposes is simply the way that the kinds of argument put forward in their favour all participate in one current of the Romantic afterlife while criticizing as Romantic the other. Few critics of the Romantic ideology will invoke the term 'nature' (though ecologists do), but all seek to vindicate the rights and dignity of that which lies without the poet, or outside poetry—and in doing so they follow in the wake of the first brand of Romantic theory as I tried to sketch it out in the earlier pages of this essay.

All this is making the Romantic afterlife sound markedly dualistic: I have separated the goats and the sheep here, hoping to set out the traditions clearly; but, in practice, of course, the different elements mingle incongruously all over the place, just as they do, not only in Wordsworth and Coleridge, but in most of the Romantic writers from whom those elements descend. As I have said, to praise an author for creating a world of his own feels to us an uncontentious sort of gesture, though such grounds for appreciation are quite at odds with the equally inoffensive belief that artists restore the ordinary, common world to us afresh: the two, contrary Romantic notions of poetic excellence rub along well enough in contemporary literary thought. Let me close by mentioning a volume of poetry by Seamus Heaney, the title of which might imply, on its small scale, the continuing fruitfulness of the Romantic contraries and their recurrent encounters: the title in question, *Seeing Things* (1991), deftly interweaves the two dispositions, the subjective poet's creation of what he contemplates—as in, 'but you're seeing things!'—with the objective poet's self-effacing attentiveness—'really seeing *things*'—and Heaney draws poetry out of the contradictions and dilemmas that he discovers, just as, often, his Romantic precursors did.

FURTHER READING

Abrams, M. H., *The Mirror and the Lamp: Romantic Theory and the Critical Tradition* (New York: Oxford University Press, 1953). Still the most comprehensive account of Romantic literary thinking, which offers many suggestive connections and analogies with later writers.

——'From Addison to Kant: Modern Aesthetics and the Exemplary Art', in his *Doing Things with Texts: Essays in Criticism and Critical Theory*, ed. Michael Fischer (New York: W. W. Norton, 1989), pp. 159–87. A lucid and wide-ranging account of the development of the idea of artworks as heterocosmic.

Baker, Carlos, *The Echoing Green: Romanticism, Modernisn and the Phenomenon of Transference in Poetry* (Princeton, NJ: Princeton University Press, 1984). Essays on Yeats, Frost, Pound, Stevens, Eliot, and Auden, and their response to the canonical Romantic poets.

Bayley, John, *The Romantic Survival: A Study in Poetic Evolution* (London: Constable, 1957). One of the earliest studies to argue for the persistence of Romantic attitudes in modern poetry, with particular reference to Yeats, Dylan Thomas, and Auden.

Beer, John, *Romantic Influences: Contemporary—Victorian—Modern* (Basingstoke: Macmillan, 1993). A characteristically original and learned study, tracing influence in part by studying the way fluency appears as a concept and a figure in Romantic writing and since.

Bromwich, David, 'Why Authors Do Not Create Their Own Worlds', in his *A Choice of Inheritance: Self and Community from Edmund Burke to Robert Frost* (Cambridge, Mass.: Harvard University Press, 1989), pp. 247–63. An elegant disagreement with the notion of the heterocosmic work of art.

Kermode, Frank, *Romantic Image* (London: Routledge and Kegan Paul, 1957). A landmark in our revisionary understanding of the great modernists—Hulme, Eliot, Yeats—as participants in (not dissenters from) a tradition extending back to Coleridge, Blake, and Wordsworth.

Lovejoy, A. O., 'On the Discrimination of Romanticisms'; in his *Essays in the History of Ideas* (Baltimore: Johns Hopkins University Press, 1948), pp. 228–53. The most influential account of the term's multiple meanings.

Pinsky, Robert, *The Situation of Poetry: Modern Poetry and its Traditions* (Princeton: Princeton University Press, 1976). In chapter 3, 'The Romantic Persistence' (pp. 47–96) the poet Pinsky places several prominent twentieth-century American poets within a tradition descending from the Romantics, exemplified here by Keats.

Ward, John Powell, *The English Line: Poetry of the Unpoetic from Wordsworth to Larkin* (Basingstoke: Macmillan, 1991). A suggestive study, by a poet, of the 'Wordsworthian' line in post-Romantic English poetry, taking in Tennyson, Hardy, and Larkin, among others.

NOTES

1. F. W. Bateson, *A Guide to English Literature* (1965; 2nd edn. London: Longman, 1967), p. 146.
2. M. H. Abrams, *The Mirror and the Lamp: Romantic Theory and the Critical Tradition* (New York: Oxford University Press, 1953), p. 105.
3. David Trotter, *The Making of the Reader: Language and Subjectivity in Modern American, English and Irish Poetry* (London: Macmillan, 1984), p. 249.
4. Tom Paulin, *Writing to the Moment: Selected Critical Essays 1980–1996* (London: Faber, 1996), pp. 168, 169.

5. J. A .M. Rillie, 'T. S. Eliot', in David E. Cooper (ed.), *A Companion to Aesthetics* (Oxford: Clarendon Press, 1992), p. 131.

6. John Bayley, *The Romantic Survival: A Study in Poetic Evolution* (London: Constable, 1957), p. 8.

7. Jerome McGann, *The Romantic Ideology: A Critical Investigation* (Chicago: Chicago University Press, 1983), p. 91.

8. Jonathan Bate, *The Song of the Earth* (London: Picador, 2000), pp. 137, 68.

9. Jerome J. McGann, *Don Juan in Context* (London: John Murray, 1976), pp. 159, 157.

10. Jerome McGann, *The Beauty of Inflexions* (Oxford: Clarendon Press, 1984), p. 306.

11. Bate, *The Song of the Earth*, pp. 153, 166.

12. Aidan Day, *Romanticism* (London: Routledge, 1996), pp. 195, 197.

37 | Poetry

Charles J. Rzepka

British Romantic poets influenced both the poetry and fiction of the century that followed their own. William Butler Yeats's visionary metaphysics was nurtured by William Blake's lyrics and John Keats's odes. Lord Byron's defiant self-performances inspired the early James Joyce and the mature Virginia Woolf. Samuel Taylor Coleridge's concept of 'organic form' helped shape the critical theory of early twentieth-century formalists, and both Percy Shelley and Keats influenced American writers as diverse as Wallace Stevens and F. Scott Fitzgerald. William Wordsworth's impact, if less obvious, has been more profound.

In 'Michael' Wordsworth expressed the hope that 'youthful Poets, who among these Hills | Will be my second self when I am gone' would carry on his legacy. That hope has been realized, directly and indirectly. Like the air we breathe, Wordsworth's presence circulates throughout the poetic space that surrounds us as readers of verse in English. Also like the air, that presence is not always immediately apparent. We notice it mostly when it moves, as in Charles Tomlinson's allusion to the 'natural piety' of 'My Heart Leaps Up' in his description of stone walls and buildings at 'Holwell Farm':

> Rooted in more than earth, to dwell
> 	Is to discern the Eden image, to grasp
> In a given place and guard it well
> 	Shielded in stone. Whether piety
> Be natural, is neither the poet's
> 	Nor the builder's story, but a quality of air

Few of Tomlinson's contemporaries have found a comparable 'blessing' (*Prelude*, I. 1) in the 'gentle breeze' of the poet's words. Many consider his 'quality of air' a 'spirit breathed | From dead men to their kind' ('Expostulation and Reply').[1] And yet, whatever opinion of Wordsworth contemporary poets may hold, they would all probably agree that poetry as we know it would not exist had he not written it the way he did. The colloquial diction and plain syntax, the wresting of singularly revelatory moments from the quotidian events of life, the attention to socially marginalized individuals, and the generally autobiographical orientation common to poetry today are all indebted to the example set 200 years ago by this courageous but self-centred, and often rude, son of Cumberland. It may be difficult today to appreciate how radical a challenge to the principles of decorum and good taste Wordsworth's verses posed at the time he wrote them. However, there is little doubt that his advocacy for what he called in his Preface to *Lyrical Ballads* 'the language really spoken by men' as opposed to the cold formalities of 'poetic diction', for the 'spontaneous overflow of powerful feelings' and 'wise passiveness' instead of the 'meddling intellect' that 'murder[s] to dissect', for the respect due to ordinary folk, including beggars, children, the infirm, and the mentally impaired, as well as to the influences of nature and the unique powers of one's own imagination, helped clear the ground for a recognizably modern Anglophone poetry.

Plain style: Robert Frost

The influence of Wordsworth's plain style is most apparent in the work of the early twentieth-century American poet, Robert Frost, who also incorporated many of his predecessor's themes and subject-matter, making them his own. Frost's poems are set in the rugged, mountainous state of New Hampshire, a region similar in topography and human inhabitants to Wordsworth's Lake District. Like Wordsworth, Frost adhered to the trimeter and tetrameter lines and rhyme schemes of folk ballad in most of his shorter nature poems, and did much, like Wordsworth, to simplify his language while deepening its intellectual and emotional interest. Natural piety is important to both. In 'Rose Pogonias', Frost's speaker and his beloved, resembling Wordsworth and his sister Dorothy on a typical spring ramble like the one described in 'Lines, written at a small distance from my House', encounter a 'saturated meadow' of wild flowers, hidden by trees from the hay mowers. Before leaving, writes Frost, 'We raised a simple prayer',

> That in the general mowing
>   That place might be forgot;
> Or if not all so favoured,
>   Obtain such grace of hours,
> That none should mow the grass there
>   While so confused with flowers.

A Wordsworthian bias towards natural feeling over bookishness informs Frost's 'To the Thawing Wind', which in other respects resembles Percy Shelley's 'Ode to the West Wind'. Frost's poem reads almost like a homily on Wordsworth's 'The Tables Turned', particularly the line, 'Books! 'tis a dull and endless strife'. 'Come with rain, O loud Southwester!' Frost exclaims, 'Bathe my window, make it flow':

> Melt it as the ice will go;
> Melt the glass and leave the sticks
> Like a hermit's crucifix;
> Burst into my narrow stall;
> Swing the picture on the wall;

> Run the rattling pages o'er'
> Scatter poems on the floor;
> Turn the poet out of door.

It is in his attention to the quiet desperation of mountain life, however, to its hidden pain and loss and harsh resignation, that Frost most clearly betrays his affinities with the Wordsworth of 'Simon Lee', 'The Thorn', 'The Ruined Cottage', and 'Michael'. Frost's portraits are generally rendered in a blank verse style that comes perilously close to prose, almost as if to test the limits of Wordsworth's assertion, in his Preface, that 'there neither is nor can be any essential difference' between 'the language of prose and metrical composition' (l. 253). Frost's laconic tone of voice only deepens the power of what is often too painful to be expressed directly. ' "Out, Out—" ' describes the accidental death of a teenaged boy who bleeds to death when his hand is cut off by a buzz-saw. It ends:

> No one believed. They listened at his heart.
> Little—less—nothing!—and that ended it.
> No more to build on there. And they, since they
> Were not the one dead, turned to their affairs.

In 'The Death of the Hired Man' Frost gives us an evening debate between Mary and Warren, husband and wife, over whether to take in the feckless hired hand, Silas. After much wandering he has returned to their farm, old and near death, but promising to mend his ways. Warren is sceptical. ' "What would you have him say?" ' asks Mary. ' "Surely you wouldn't grudge the poor old man | Some humble way to save his self-respect." ' The conversation recalls Wordsworth's defence of impoverished dignity in 'The Old Cumberland Beggar' and his sympathetic encounter with the homeless discharged soldier in Book IV of *The Prelude*. ' "Warren," she said, "he has come home to die: | You needn't be afraid he'll leave you this time." ' Warren is sullen. ' "Home is the place where, when you have to go there, | They have to take you in," ' he says, to which Mary replies, ' "I should have called it | Something you somehow haven't to deserve." ' But the debate turns out to be bluntly pyrrhic by the end of the poem, when Warren goes off to chat with Silas. To Mary's interrogative ' "Warren?" ' upon her husband's return, ' "Dead," was all he answered'.

Wordsworth and Anglo-American modernism

Respect for the working poor and the marginally subsistent is not prominently featured in the work of modernist poets like T. S. Eliot or Ezra Pound, from whom writers like Frost sought to distinguish themselves. Yet Eliot's autobiographical masterpiece, *Four Quartets*, is indebted to Wordsworth's example in *The Prelude*, particularly in its exploration of connections between the poet's sense of place, personal history, and self-understanding. Elsewhere, in Eliot's depiction of London as an 'Unreal City' of the dead in *The Wasteland*, or in as brief a reflection on the alienating effects of city life as Pound's 'In a Station of the Metro'—'The apparition of these faces in the crowd. | Petals on a wet, black bough'—we can glimpse the depressing dislocations that Wordsworth first registered in Book VII of *The Prelude*, where the 'overflowing streets' become 'A second-sight procession, such as . . . appears in dreams', and the poet thinks, 'The face of every one | That passes by me is a mystery!' (VII. 594–602).

Despite their differences, one might expect to find some affinity between Eliot and Pound, born in the American heartland of Missouri and Idaho respectively, and Wordsworth, a child of the English Lakes. Like Frost, the Americans had inherited from Walt Whitman a native tradition committed to democratizing the language of poetry while opening its rhythms to the cadences of prose, although, unlike Frost, they found little use for Whitman's levelling of the traditional subject-matter of serious poetry. Whitman had grafted that levelling tendency, in large part, on to what he inherited from Wordsworth, and, as a result, it might be safe to say that Wordsworth's long-range impact is most noticeable in the work of American rather than British writers.

This is particularly true for Americans like James Merrill, whose work challenged the formalist tenets of modernism by recourse to chance methods of composition and scientific themes and topics. In 'Mirabell', for instance, the second part of a trilogy entitled *The Changing Light at Sandover* that Merrill wrote with the aid of his lover David Jackson and a Ouija board, Jackson's dead mother says from beyond the grave that she expects to be reincarnated because a friend and fellow dead soul 'Reads her the Wordsworth *Ode* . . . A final life on Earth . . . lies ahead' (p. 103).

The reference to Wordsworth's 'Ode: Intimations of Immortality' is not out of character. Merrill was highly sensitive to the Wordsworthian 'shades of the prison house' that gradually darken what he calls the 'sunbeam gaze' of childhood ('The Green Eye'). 'Verse for Urania', addressed to Merrill's 2-year-old god-daughter, bears an obvious resemblance to 'Frost at Midnight', which Wordsworth's fellow poet, Samuel Taylor Coleridge, addressed to his infant son. But Merrill, like Wordsworth in the 'Intimations' ode, is resigned to the passing of childhood innocence, not hopeful, like Coleridge, of the child's gradually achieving fluency in the language of nature's 'Great Universal Teacher', God. Referring to the astronomical origins of Urania's name, Merrill draws analogies between the dimming of the constellations from the increasing ambient light of cities and the dimming of what Wordsworth called 'our life's star':

> From out there notions reach us yet, but few
> And far between as those first names we knew
> Already without having to look up,
> Children that we were, the Chair, the Cup,
> But each night dimmer, children that we are,
> Each night regressing, dumber by a star.

Merrill's incorporation of astronomy reflects his general interest in exploring the poetic possibilities of science as metaphor, in line with Wordsworth's belief, professed in the 1802 Preface to *Lyrical Ballads*, that 'If the labours of men of Science should ever create any material revolution, direct or indirect, in our condition . . . the remotest discoveries of the Chemist, the Botanist, or Mineralogist, will be as proper objects of the Poet's art as any upon which it can be employed' (ll. 259–60). In 'Laboratory Poem', where a young woman vivisects turtles for scientific research—'taking heart | And a steel saw', 'Easy in the presence of her lover'—Merrill seems to be extending and complicating Wordsworth's famous line, 'we murder to dissect' ('The Tables Turned'). Charles, the lover, is put in mind 'of certain human hearts, their climb | Through violence into exquisite disciplines | Of which, as it now appeared, they all expired'.

The Anglophone world

In former British colonies, from India to the Caribbean, Wordsworth's heritage has persisted, reflecting the lingering institutional influences of the British colonial school system. As Anita Patterson has pointed out, among Guyanese writers like A. J. Seymour and Wilson Harris the older poet's impact is especially apparent.

But Wordsworth's influence extends even into post-colonial territories formerly held by non-English European powers. In his long autobiographical poem *Another Life*, for instance, Derek Walcott, who was raised as an English-speaking Methodist in the Francophone culture of St Lucia, links his coming of age as a poet and painter with his heartbreaking decision to leave his native island at the age of 19 to study at the University of the West Indies in Anglophone Jamaica. While the only overt reference to Wordsworth here is ironic—thoughts of seducing the British Counsel's wife gave Walcott his 'First intimations of immortality. | Other men's wives'—this long work is full of events and scenes, objects and portraits, that assume a significance in the young poet's life similar to the 'spots of time' in Wordsworth's *Prelude*, subtitled, 'The Growth of a Poet's Mind'.

Enumerating the objects he remembers from his childhood in his mother's vine-covered house (his father had died soon after he was born), Walcott pauses to ask, 'Why should we weep for dumb things?' Ushering in the 'radiance of sharing [that] extends to the simplest objects, | to a favourite hammer, a paintbrush, a toothless, | gum-sunken old shoe . . .', the question recalls the Pedlar of 'The Ruined Cottage', who interprets the ruins of dead Margaret's dwelling for Wordsworth's young poet-narrator only to conclude,

> enough to sorrow have you given,
> The purposes of wisdom ask no more;
> Be wise and cheerful, and no longer read
> The forms of things with an unworthy eye.
>   (ll. 508–11).

Walcott's portraits of the common people of his neighbourhood, introduced alpha-
betically in the next section of *Another Country*, reveal still deeper, if culturally
transformed, affinities with the rural population of Grasmere depicted in *Lyrical
Ballads*.

On his native shores

In England, Wordsworth's influence can be felt in the return to country scenes and
subjects in Edwardian pastoral at the beginning of the twentieth century and in the
ostensibly anti-Wordsworthian bestiaries of Ted Hughes's poetry near the end of it.
Hughes's skylark is a far song from Wordsworth's 'Drunken Lark!': 'Joyous as morning
. . . Happy, happy Liver! | With a soul as strong as a mountain River, | Pouring out praise
to the almighty Giver' ('To a Skylark'). Hughes's lark is 'leaden | With muscle | for the
struggle | Against | Earth's centre', 'Obedient as to death a dead thing', frantically,
instinctively 'Scrambling | In a nightmare difficulty | Up through the nothing'. Hughes
finds not unmitigated joy, but desperate confusion, even panic, in the lark's song: 'O
song, incomprehensibly both ways— | Joy! Help! Joy! Help!' Indeed, the glad 'madness'
of Wordsworth's bird is darkened and magnified, in Hughes's imagination, into the
collective insanity of an asylum: 'All the dreary Sunday morning | Heaven is a mad-
house | with the voices and frenzies of the larks, . . . the mad earth's missionaries.' Birds
and beasts in Hughes's poetry seem helpless prisoners of instinctual forces driving
them ultimately to lunacy and death, rather than joyful denizens of a nature who
'never did betray | The heart that loved her' ('Tintern Abbey').

And yet Hughes has acknowledged his admiration for Wordsworth as the last great
English poet. Richard Gravil suggests the reason why: like Wordsworth, Hughes 'has
adopted as a matter of faith' Wordsworth's view 'that human nature is something
properly studied on the fells or in the fields, and that the poet is a diviner, a healer'.[2]
Moreover, for Hughes as for Wordsworth, the human nature the poet seeks in inhuman
nature is his own, awaiting discovery in the creatures he encounters. Gravil cites
Hughes's 'Pike' as an example, where the predatory fish, hidden in 'the dark pond',
finally begins to surface, like 'a dream . . . That rose slowly towards me, watching'.

Another professed admirer of Wordsworth, with more obvious ties to his predecessor, is Seamus Heaney. Heaney has made overt reference to Wordsworth in the
'Glanmore Sonnets', humorously comparing himself and his wife, in their retreat from
the turmoil of Northern Irish politics, to William and his sister, Dorothy, living
together in remote Grasmere: 'I had said earlier, "I won't relapse | From this strange
loneliness I've brought us to. | Dorothy and William—" She interrupts: | "You're not
going to compare us two . . . ?"' (Sonnet 3).

But Heaney sees more than a casual resemblance between himself and the poet of
The Prelude. The title of Heaney's autobiographical *Singing School* is taken from Yeats's

Among Schoolchildren, but his first epigraph comes from Wordsworth's autobiographical poem: 'Fair seedtime had my soul, and I grew up | Fostered alike by beauty and by fear . . .' (*The Prelude*, l. 305–6). *Singing School* describes the poet's political coming of age in Northern Ireland, and the relevance of his Wordsworthian epigraph is accordingly filtered by 'The Troubles' of his native land. The childhood 'spots of time' scattered throughout Wordsworth's poetry, however, especially in *The Prelude*, have provided models for similar moments of self-transformation elsewhere in Heaney's poetry, moments shaped by what Wordsworth calls nature's 'Severer interventions' (*The Prelude*, I. 370) and 'discipline of fear' (I. 631).

In 'Death of a Naturalist', for instance, Heaney describes his spring expeditions as a boy in search of frog's eggs in terms that recall Wordsworth's earliest years as a 'plunderer' of bird's eggs 'in the high places' (I. 336–7) near his home in Cockermouth, or of roaming the hills in search of woodcocks, 'my shoulder all with springes hung . . . a fell destroyer' (I. 317–18). Plying his 'anxious visitation, hurrying on', says Wordsworth, he often felt himself to be 'a trouble to the peace' of the natural world, and sometimes even 'heard among the solitary hills | Low breathings coming after me'. Similarly, Heaney's plundering of frog's eggs continued until the day when, returning to his favourite pond, he heard 'the angry frogs' raise the 'bass chorus' and 'slap and plop' of their 'obscene threats': 'The great slime kings | Were gathered there for vengeance and I knew | That if I dipped my hand the spawn would clutch it.'[3]

Two second selves: Charles Tomlinson and Elizabeth Bishop

Modern poets often draw on Wordsworthian sources when reflecting on the relation of the mind to nature, and on the formal relationships between art and nature in general. Charles Tomlinson is not only a poet, but a graphic artist, and his written responses to nature are often informed by his attention to the visible details of a world that loses integrity and innocence when subsumed under word, myth, and metaphor. In 'Adam', the biblical naming of the beasts by Eden's first human inhabitant becomes, for Tomlinson, emblematic of the subjugation to human meaning that 'an openwork world of lights and ledges' undergoes as it is brought to a second birth in the mind by naming:

> Are we the lords or limits
> Of this teeming horde? We bring
> to a kind of birth all we can name
> And, named, it echoes in us our being.

Lines like these indicate something of a bias against the Wordsworthian 'egotistical sublime', a term coined by the poet's younger contemporary, John Keats, to convey the idea that the deeper powers Wordsworth sensed in nature reflected little more than his own concerns writ large. Elsewhere, however, Tomlinson seems to endorse much of Wordsworth's poetic agenda. In 'The Art of Poetry', for instance, he says disapprovingly of poets in general 'that when the truth is not good enough | We exaggerate', and in 'Observation of Facts' he rejects mythical exaggeration by stating that 'A dryad is a sort of chintz curtain | Between myself and a tree'. These lines resonate with Wordsworth's rejection of 'poetic diction' and mythical ornament in his Preface to *Lyrical Ballads*, where he also expresses his resolve 'to look steadily at my subject' (l. 251).

The rarely beheld Edenic face of our fallen natural world is, for Tomlinson, a 'contemporary counterpart to the apprehension of an "active power" in nature of which Wordsworth documents his discovery in *The Prelude*', argues Joel Wilcox.[4] However, it is a counterpart that according to Wilcox has undergone considerable diminution since Adam's Fall. Thus, he says, the last line of Tomlinson's 'Eden', where the wind 'rings with its meaninglessness where it sang its meaning', serves as a 'corrective' to Wordsworth's invocation of 'a blessing in this gentle breeze' at the beginning of *The Prelude*, a blessing that elicits a 'corresponding breeze' of creative energy in the poet.

But this reading does scant justice to the complexity of the older poet's relation to nature. For Wordsworth, creative energy, like Edenic nature, is rarely available when most desired. Not many lines into *The Prelude*, the poet's 'corresponding breeze' has died away and Wordsworth confesses himself

> baffled by a mind that every hour
> Turns recreant to her task, takes heart again,
> Then feels immediately some hollow thought
> Hang like an interdict upon her hopes.
> (I. 259–62).

Tomlinson shares these Wordsworthian doubts:

> Despair
> Of Eden is given too: we earn
> Neither its loss nor having.

And yet, we must keep wishing it. This seems to be the real point of Tomlinson's last line, which does not stand alone, but is preceded by the statement that there can be no Eden unless we resist the ordinary meaninglessness of the world by actively desiring its transformation:

> no way
> But the will to wish back Eden, this leaning
> To stand *against* the persuasions of a wind
> That rings with its meaninglessness where it sang its meaning.
> (emphasis added)

Elizabeth Bishop's affinities with Wordsworth were remarked long before her death in 1979. Bishop herself confessed them in a letter to the American poet Robert Lowell in July 1951: 'On reading over what I've got on hand'—she was referring to the poems that were to appear in 1955, in *A Cold Spring*—'I find I'm really a minor female Wordsworth—at least, I don't know anyone else who seems to be such a Nature Lover.'[5]

Bishop was not always a fan of William Wordsworth. As early as the mid-1930s, Bishop remarked on Wordsworth's irritating habit of appropriating his sister Dorothy's notebook entries for his own poetic use: 'Wordsworth. "By My Sister"—keep all the honor for himself. . . . Impossible to argue with, or to talk to'.[6] At about the same period, Bishop characterized as 'a great perversity' what she called the 'Romantic' practice of 'using the supposedly "spiritual"—the beautiful, the nostalgic, the ideal and *poetic*, to produce the *material*' world.[7] Within another year or two, however, she was reading Wordsworth's *Prelude*, and it was not long, as Bonnie Costello notes, before Wordsworthian practice and theory were influencing Bishop's adoption, and adaptations, of surrealism.[8] In short, Bishop outgrew her personal resentment of the poet (apparently, he reminded her of her despised paternal grandfather) as she matured into the 'minor female Wordsworth' of her own estimation.

A lifelong concern with childhood states of feeling and cognition looms large in Bishop's poetry, and one can often discern in her portraits of childhood the lineaments of her Romantic predecessor's poetic children. The prototype of the traumatized pubescent Elizabeth of 'In the Waiting Room', dreading the onset of her own nascent womanhood, dizzy and fearful at the sound of her aunt's painful cries in the dentist's chair, and feeling herself 'falling, falling', 'falling off | the round, turning world', 'sliding | beneath a big black wave, | another, and another', is to be found in the 'Intimations' ode, where 'Shades of the prison-house begin to close | Upon' the Wordsworthian child with the advent of maturity, inciting 'those obstinate questionings | Of sense and outward things, | *Fallings* from us, vanishings; | Blank misgivings of a Creature | Moving about in worlds not realised' (ll. 67–8, 141–7; emphasis added). Similarly, despite their apparent differences of temperament, the little maid of 'We are Seven' and the sombre child-mourner of Bishop's 'Death in Nova Scotia' are poetic siblings. The one extends her family circle to embrace the graves of her dead brother and sister, the other believes her dead cousin Arthur was invited by the Royal family to be 'the smallest page at court'. Neither comprehends the terrible finality of death.

Bishop shares with Wordsworth a sympathetic eye for the deep humanity of the common, the vulgar, and even the grotesque. In 'At the Fishhouses', an old Nova Scotia fisherman and his increasingly precarious relationship to the frigid waters from which he draws his livelihood recall a similar relationship between the old Leech-gatherer and the ponds from which he takes an 'honest maintenance' in 'Resolution and Independence'. Often, portraits like these arise in Bishop's verse, like those in Wordsworth's poem, from chance encounters that betray what Wordsworth calls a 'leading from above' (l. 51), or from an act of deliberate, even perverse, misconstruction that brings the poet an unexpected revelation or spiritual epiphany.

In November of 1951, four months after Bishop called herself a 'minor female

Wordsworth' and 'Nature Lover', she landed in Rio de Janeiro for what she thought would be a brief stopover with friends. Her stay lasted sixteen years. The poems she wrote during that time include some well-known studies of tropical landscapes, but many more are about marginal figures, the dispossessed, the rural poor. In those sixteen years, Bishop also began to come to terms with the painful traumas of her early Nova Scotian childhood. She began writing short stories about these experiences, including the incomparable 'In the Village', much as Wordsworth revisited the shaping experiences of his early life in *The Prelude*'s 'spots of time'.

Bishop had long taken an interest in lower-class and socially marginal characters, especially during her earlier residence in Key West, Florida. In the poetry she wrote in Brazil, however, such figures seem to proliferate: feeble-minded squatters and their scavenging children, river-people, fugitive burglers, wooden-clogged denizens of greasy filling stations, truckers and village women overheard conversing at a well outside Bishop's house in Ouro Preto. Perhaps, in the end, Bishop came to resemble Wordsworth less in her self-described love of nature than in her chance portraits of these marginal figures and the narrative epiphanies they incited.

Recompenses

These are only a handful of examples of the complexity and range of Wordsworth's influence on the poetic generations that succeeded him, not only in England and America, but around the world. In theme and subject-matter, in style and focus, Anglophone poetry as it is written today would be inconceivable without the breakthroughs he achieved.

Perhaps the last word on this subject should be left to Charles Tomlinson, whose 'The Recompense' alludes, in its very title, to the 'abundant recompense' that Wordsworth found after the loss of the 'aching joys' and 'dizzy raptures' he had once experienced, according to 'Tintern Abbey', in the presence of nature. The structure of Tomlinson's poem follows the model of disappointment followed by unanticipated joy in the two mountain scenes that mark the halfway point and the end, respectively, of Wordsworth's *Prelude*: the Simplon Pass episode in Book VI and the climb up Mount Snowdon in Book XIII.

In the first episode, the young Wordsworth and his school friend, Robert Jones, eagerly anticipate what they believe will be a sublime experience when they cross the watershed line dividing the Alps. But they are subsequently dismayed to discover that they have already passed this point—'crossed the Alps'—without knowing it. In the second, Wordsworth accompanies a party of climbers hoping to reach the top of Snowdon before dawn to behold the sunrise, only to find themselves enveloped by clouds well below the summit. In each case, initial disappointment gives way to a moment of unexpected sublimity and revelation.

Thus, beyond the Simplon Pass, in the deep gloom and crashing falls of Gondo Gorge, Wordsworth encounters a landscape that seems to speak directly to him:

> rocks that muttered
>
> . . . .
> Black drizzling crags that spake
>
> . . . . . .
> As if a voice were in them
>
> . . . . . .
> Were all like the workings of one mind, the features
> Of the same face, blossoms upon one tree,
> Characters of the great Apocalypse,
> The types and symbols of Eternity . . .
>
> (VI. 562–71).

Similarly, just below the top of Snowdon the clouds suddenly break to reveal, not the sunrise, but the moon standing 'naked in the Heavens': 'and on the shore I found myself of a huge sea of mist', writes Wordsworth, while 'beyond, | Far, far beyond, the vapours shot themselves, | In headlands, tongues, and promontory shapes' (XIII. 41–8). Wordsworth finds in this misty moonlit scene 'The perfect image of a mighty Mind | Of one that feeds upon infinity', or upon 'The sense of God, or whatso'er is dim | Or vast in its own being' (XIII. 69–74). In short, he beholds an image of his own poetic imagination.

Tomlinson's 'The Recompense' describes a late night family expedition to a nearby hilltop to behold the appearance of a predicted comet:

> We waited.
> No comet came, and no flame thawed
> The freezing reaches of our glance: loneliness
> Quelled all we saw.

Disappointed and chilled, 'unwillingly | We took the tree-way down', only to confront the 'growing glow' of the 'immense circle of the risen moon | Travelling to meet us.' Moon-rise here compensates for the loss of the comet, as it does for the anticipated sunrise in Wordsworth's Snowdon passage, but the apocalyptic voices of Gondo Gorge also make themselves felt, if only as echoes of the poet's own desire—his 'wish', as 'Eden' might put it—for meaning:

> trees
> Wrote themselves out on sea and continent,
> A cursive script where every loop and knot
> Glimmered in hieroglyph, clear black:
> We—recompense for a comet lost—
> Could read ourselves into those lines.

Wordsworth's influence on the poets who succeeded him is something like the influence of the moon on Tomlinson's disappointed comet-seekers. Recurrent and largely unremarked, it does not flash forth like some heavenly portent, but patiently announces itself as that glowing 'sea and continent' upon which nearly all modern poets write themselves in a 'cursive script' whose 'every loop and knot | Glimmer[s] in hieroglyph'. Like the moon of his own Snowdon vision, illuminating the misty 'head-lands, tongues, and promontory shapes' of poetic tradition, Wordsworth has become a 'mighty Mind' which these 'higher minds bear with them as their own' (*Prelude*, XIII. 90), 'the very spirit in which they deal | With all the objects of the universe' (XIII 91–2).

FURTHER READING

Costello, Bonnie, *Elizabeth Bishop: Questions of Mastery* (Cambridge, Mass: Harvard University Press, 1991). This fine study places Bishop in relation to her poetic mentors and poetic tradition, and contains many helpful readings of Bishop's poems in historical and geographical context. Costello also has an excellent command of Bishop's early notebook material.

Gravil, Richard, 'Wordsworth's Second Selves?', *The Wordsworth Circle*, 14: 4 (1983), 191–201. A sensitive and informed examination of Wordsworth's multifarious influences on mid-to-late twentieth-century poetry, primarily in England. Gravil focuses mainly on the Wordsworthian legacy in Geoffrey Hill, Ted Hughes, and Seamus Heaney.

Hendry, Diana, 'Up With the Lark(s)', *Critical Survey*, 4: 1 (1992), 67–9. A brief but compact analysis of influences on Hughes's 'Skylarks', beginning with Wordsworth's 'To a Skylark' and including poems by Percy Shelley and Isaac Rosenberg.

Lane, M. Travis, 'A Different "Growth of a Poet's Mind": Derek Walcott's Another Life', *Ariel: A Review of International English Literature*, 9 (1978), 65–78. Lane was one of the first to observe Walcott's indebtedness to the model of Wordsworth's *Prelude*, and makes several keen observations on the unpredictable nature of poetic influence.

Merrin, Jeredith, *An Enabling Humility: Marianne Moore, Elizabeth Bishop, and the Uses of Tradition* (New Brunswick, NJ: Rutgers University Press, 1990). A largely feminist reading of Moore's and Bishop's engagements with the male-dominated poetic tradition dating back to the Romantics.

Patterson, Anita, 'Pastoral Poetry and Transculturation in Guyana: The Contexts of Wilson Harris's "Trail"', *The Journal of Commonwealth Literature*, 37: 2 (2002), 107–35. An excellent study of Harris and his Guyanese contemporaries in a post-colonial setting where English culture and poetic tradition, including Wordsworth, at first predominated, for better or worse.

Patterson, Annabel, 'Hard Pastoral: Frost, Wordsworth, and Modernist Poetics', *Criticism: A Quarterly for Literature and the Arts*, 29: 1 (1987), 67–87. Patterson traces Wordsworth's realist revision of pastoral tradition in its effects on Frost's poetry and Frost's engagement with modernism in his own time.

Profitt, Edward, 'The Long Poem in the Twentieth Century', *Research Studies*, 46 (1978), 20–7. This article traces the influence of Wordsworth's *Prelude* on several long, autobiographical poems, focusing on recurrent themes and figures of speech.

Quinney, Laura, *The Poetics of Disappointment: Wordsworth to Ashbery* (Charlottesville, Va.: University Press of Virginia, 1999). A sensitive examination of the impact of a prevailing Wordsworthian theme in modern poetry, principally American, including the poetry of Wallace Stevens and John Ashbery.

Wilcox, Joel F., 'Tomlinson and the British Tradition', in Kathleen O'Gorman (ed.), *Charles Tomlinson: Man and Artist* (St Louis: University of Missouri Press, 1988), 41–56. An excellent study of Tomlinson's relation to his predecessors, especially William Wordsworth and the interconnections between poetry and landscape.

NOTES

1. All references to Wordsworth's poetry and prose come from the edition of his works by Stephen Gill, *William Wordsworth* (Oxford: Oxford University Press, 1984).
2. Richard Gravil, 'Wordsworth's Second Selves?', *The Wordsworth Circle*, 14: 4 (1983), 195.
3. Seamus Heaney, 'Death of a Naturalist', from *Selected Poems, 1965–1975* (London and Boston: Faber and Faber, 1975), pp. 12–13.
4. Joel F. Wilcox, 'Tomlinson and the British Tradition', in Kathleen O'Gorman (ed.), *Charles Tomlinson: Man and Artist* (St Louis: University of Missouri Press, 1988), p. 42.
5. Elizabeth Bishop, *One Art: Letters*, ed. Robert Giroux (London: Pimlico, 1996), p. 222.
6. Quoted in Jeredith Merrin, *An Enabling Humility: Marianne Moore, Elizabeth Bishop, and the Uses of Tradition* (New Brunswick, NJ: Rutgers University Press, 1990), p. 84.
7. Quoted in Bonnie Costello, *Elizabeth Bishop: Questions of Mastery* (Cambridge, Mass.: Harvard University Press, 1991), p. 4.
8. Ibid. 249 n. 12.

The nineteenth- and twentieth-century novel

Michael Herbert

Romantic influences on the novel are very deep as well as widespread, with the novelistic inheritance from the Romantic poets probably even greater than from the novelists. It would be an impossible task, in the space available, to provide even an overview, let alone a discussion of any large selection of the innumerable later novels influenced by Romantic writers of poetry or fiction. Instead, what is offered here is a consideration of examples of major nineteenth- and twentieth-century novelists who stand out for the qualities they have inherited from the Romantics, and have developed in their own ways. These are the writers who from the middle of the nineteenth century gave the novel the pre-eminence which poetry had enjoyed at the time of the Romantics. All these writers subscribe to such familiar Romantic tenets as turning from merely external events to concentrate upon inner experience, the life of the mind as the essence of existence, but each brings to literature in English an individual voice, a personal vision, a unique psychology.

Though their legacy may be lesser, the Romantic novelists bequeathed much to their successors. Even before them, the pre-Romantic phenomena of the Gothic novel (see *Oxford Companion to the Romantic Age*, pp. 291–2, 526–9) and the novel of Sensibility (see *Oxford Companion to the Romantic Age*, pp. 102–14, 290–1), both dating from the mid-eighteenth century, provided a stimulus for novelists who, in the nineteenth century, adopted and adapted the often sensational and sentimental aspects of these forebears to create works in many cases of superior literary merit. Ripples from the Gothic novel spread particularly widely, inspiring not only the satirical response of that classic novelist of the Romantic era, Jane Austen (1775–1817), in *Northanger Abbey* (1818), but also such effective utilizations of Gothic elements as are found in *The Private Memoirs and Confessions of a Justified Sinner* (1824) by the Scottish writer James Hogg (1770–1835) as well as in the novels of the Brontë sisters discussed below. But it was Sir Walter Scott (1771–1832), poet as well as novelist, who was the Romantic father figure to the Victorian novelists. From him more than any other writer they learned how to use history and folklore, landscapes and ruins, dramatic characters and a quick flow of narrative to tell a vivid tale.

Scott's energetic way of writing was taken up and extended by Charles Dickens (1812–70), often considered the greatest Victorian novelist. Like Austen, but unlike almost every other writer mentioned in this chapter, he did not write poetry; but his fictional output is intensely vibrant, to the extent that it can seem so heightened—and deepened—as to be sometimes exaggerated and extreme. This is all part of what makes Dickens easily recognizable as an inheritor of the Romantic tradition: without such intensity of emotion, intensely conveyed, such overwhelming forcefulness of feeling, both personal and moral, such creative ransacking of a packed imagination, Dickens would not be heir to the Romantics, and he would not be Dickens. Among his greatest achievements are his keeping alive of the Romantic belief in the primacy of the imagination, in what Keats called 'the holiness of the heart's affections', and in the value of the child and the child's vision of the world, and his exploiting of symbolism to explore reality in the novel in ways that poetry had done before, while in addition taking on the modern urban world and contrasting it, rather as Wordsworth does, with nature. In this way he went beyond Scott, as did the Brontës, who so much admired Scott, and who were even more influenced by him, and by other Romantic writers, than Dickens was.

The Brontës

The three Brontë sisters, Charlotte (1816–55), Emily (1818–48), and Anne (1820–49), are archetypal children of the Romantic movement, and in all the arts, not merely the literary: music and the visual arts are important to them, for instance, which is not true of the rather philistine Dickens. They share with Dickens, however, the same passions outlined in the introduction above, and one of the most significant of these is their passionate evocation of feeling, especially in relation to the lives of children and of ignored or slighted or otherwise marginalized or even outcast older people. All three sisters are drawn to similar types of alienated misfits as Dickens is, though in some ways theirs are more closely akin to, for example, Blake's innocents and Wordsworth's rustics, Coleridge's Ancient Mariner, and Byron's Childe Harold, while Dickens's famous children—from Oliver Twist to David Copperfield, or Little Nell to Little Dorrit—are matched by the equally famous children of Charlotte and Emily.

Jane Eyre (1847), however, not only marks a revolution in the way the child's viewpoint is presented, though that is one of the most striking features of the book, and what has most endeared it to generations of readers. It also takes on themes of love and passion and religion and madness, and sets all these revolving around the unprepossessing figure of a plain Jane, with the same slighted profession of governess as Anne's *Agnes Grey*, published in the same year. 'Romantic', in the sense of being a beautiful heroine who loves and is loved by a handsome young man, is exactly what Jane is not. 'Romantic' aspirations, we learn, are not limited to the conventionally beautiful, but may blossom from the superficially stonier seeming but ultimately richer soil, more full of natural goodness, of the more thoughtfully and more sympathetically human. Nor is the dark and rough Rochester a conventional hero, though his type—the

Byronic, from the personality of Byron himself as much as from his poetic (anti-)heroes—has become a stereotype in many lesser romances.

This Byronic figure also appears in at least one even greater novel, Emily's *Wuthering Heights* (published in that same year of wonders, 1847), in which the unruly character of Heathcliff, shocking in his violent extremes of love and hatred, is an archetypal demon lover. This is where some readers lose sympathy, as Charlotte did in her critical reaction to what she saw as her sister's barely human fiend or 'Ghoul', in her Preface of 1850. But what is so remarkable about this unique masterpiece, as more recent critics have not failed to recognize, is that it miraculously fuses Romanticism with Realism, using symbols drawn from an actual life in which they are also concrete exactnesses, domesticating the mythic and bringing the Gothic down to solid Yorkshire earth. We see this in the way the superhuman can be also just the human writ large, the cosmic and general can grow out of the local and specific, the possibly supernatural can be interpreted as natural. The love presented in the elder Catherine and Heathcliff may be immense, like a force of nature, but it is also undermined by the down-to-earth narrative of commonsensical Nelly Dean, who has less time for it than the author has. Yet the author also presents another kind of love, more normal and positive, between the younger Catherine and Hareton. It is this balance, this ability to see both sides of an issue, to rise to a sublime impartiality, that makes Emily Brontë heir not only to the great Romantics but also to Shakespeare. She wrote powerful poems, but in her novel there is also much powerful poetry. It is there in the opening description of the Heights by prosaic Mr Lockwood:

Wuthering Heights is the name of Mr Heathcliff's dwelling, 'Wuthering' being a significant provincial adjective, descriptive of the atmospheric tumult to which its station is exposed in stormy weather. Pure, bracing ventilation they must have up there, at all times, indeed: one may guess the power of the north wind, blowing over the edge, by the excessive slant of a few, stunted firs at the end of the house; and by a range of gaunt thorns all stretching their limbs one way, as if craving alms of the sun.

It is there in Heathcliff's tremendous response, in the twenty-ninth chapter, to Nelly's accusation of disturbing Catherine in her grave:

'... Disturbed her? No! she has disturbed me, night and day, through eighteen years—incessantly—remorselessly—till yesternight—and yesternight, I was tranquil. I dreamt I was sleeping the last sleep, by that sleeper, with my heart stopped, and my cheek frozen against hers.'

And it is there in the final paragraph of the novel, when Lockwood visits the graves of Catherine, Edgar, and Heathcliff:

I lingered round them, under that benign sky; watched the moths fluttering among the heath, and hare-bells; listened to the soft wind breathing through the grass; and wondered how any one could ever imagine unquiet slumbers, for the sleepers in that quiet earth.

As throughout, the option is given to believe, as the locals do, that ghosts walk the earth, or to take the sophisticated southerner's less credulous line—or to adopt the author's even-handed attitude, her double vision, as applied to everything in the novel, from the houses to their inhabitants, polarized but given an equal chance, through the multiple perspectives of a many-layered narrative.

Wuthering Heights is like no other novel. But there is a family resemblance in the novels of the other Brontës. Even Anne, described by Charlotte in her Biographical Notice of 1850 as 'milder and more subdued' than Emily, produced in *The Tenant of Wildfell Hall* (1848) a work that even in its title place-name proclaims kinship with Emily's, shares something of the same complex plotting, the same realism in the presentation of life in the English countryside, with splendid natural descriptions, and suffered from the same accusations of being coarse and brutal and immoral. This is where the sisters part company from Jane Austen, with their very different and at times blatantly anti-Austen attitude to passion and propriety. In particular, the sisters could never free themselves from their Romantic legacy, even if they wanted to. On the first page of *Shirley* (1849), Charlotte seeks to disabuse her reader of any ideas of the 'Romantic' in her soberly realistic 'Condition of England' industrial novel:

Do you anticipate sentiment, and poetry, and reverie? Do you expect passion, and stimulus, and melodrama? Calm your expectations; reduce them to a lowly standard. Something real, cool, and solid, lies before you; something unromantic as Monday morning . . .

But the novel does in fact contain, for all its solid realism, plenty of poetry and passion, sentiment and stimulus, even melodrama: like all the Brontë writings, it is much closer in style and subject to the poetry of Byron than the prose of Austen. It could not be otherwise, given the nature of its author.

In some respects, Charlotte's last novel, *Villette* (1853), is the most thoroughgoing culmination of the Romantic tradition in the Victorian novel, challenged in these respects only by Dickens at his finest, or George Eliot (1819–80), with her equal emotional and greater intellectual reach. It is if possible even more intensely autobiographical and personal than *Jane Eyre*, with a confessional quality that, in its innovative concentration on the inner world of the narrator, Lucy Snowe, relates it closely to contemporary works such as Wordsworth's *The Prelude* (1850).

The American tradition: *Moby-Dick*

It is sometimes argued that the true inheritors of the great Romantic poets are not their conservative successors in Victorian England but the more radical American writers of the nineteenth century. Among their novels, *Moby-Dick; or, The Whale* (1851), by Herman Melville (1819–91), is often proposed as the greatest American work of fiction, although it might better be called 'faction', because of the enormous amount of fact woven into the fictional narrative. Certainly this novel shows its author to be a revolutionary descendant of Blake, Wordsworth, Coleridge, Byron, Shelley, and Keats. It is full of the strange and exotic, of horror and melancholy and madness, of rapture and nostalgia and sentimentality, of the irrational, the dreamy, the visionary, of superstition and legend—any list, in short, of those things regarded as intrinsic to most definitions of Romanticism. It is also stuffed with realistic descriptions, but even the lists to do with whales and whaling carry rich symbolic and mythological freight, while it is at its most heavily laden with legacies from the Romantic poets in the related areas of characterization, theme, and style.

The characters are archetypal, which immediately creates analogies with earlier literature, particularly but not only of the Romantic period. 'Call me Ishmael' is the arresting first sentence of the book, in which the all-too-aptly self-named (nick-named?) narrator declares himself to be, like his biblical namesake, an outcast from the start: 'And he will be a wild man; his hand will be against every man, and every man's hand against him' (Genesis 16: 12). However, the name literally means 'God hears', so he is also, like Jonah in the Bible, the only one of the crew to survive the destruction of the whaling ship, the *Pequod* (named after an extinct tribe), by the eponymous white whale, and the book is his obsessively extensive and intensive account of his experiences, told to the reader in a manner reminiscent of Coleridge's Ancient Mariner buttonholing the wedding guest. Ahab, the captain of the *Pequod*, is even more of an Ancient Mariner, literally in his age and experience and metaphorically in his insane obsessiveness, driven by his monomaniac quest for Moby-Dick. The wild speeches of King Lear in the storm have their echoes in Ahab's maddened speechifying, and his name—literally 'father's brother', for he is an avuncular father figure to Ishmael as well as Pip, the demented cabin-boy—is that of a king in the Bible who angers the Almighty by worshipping another god and is killed in battle. Nothing, it seems, is accidental in all this, and in much more of this leviathan of a novel: all the allusions play their part in making the characters and the theme of the quest richly resonant. Moby-Dick himself is surrounded by a sea of suggestive allusions and a mythic aura of both vindictive monster and godlike wonder that leave him a finally more elusive mystery than even Ishmael or Ahab.

The poetical and mythological and intertextual qualities of *Moby-Dick* connect Melville back to Coleridge, whose 'Rime of the Ancient Mariner' (1798) and 'Khubla Khan' (1816) could be described in many of the same terms that apply to the American masterpiece. All three works could—and do—have scholarly treatises devoted to explicating their multiple levels of meaning, tracking down their myriad sources and influences, and assessing their innovativeness, effectiveness, and, in turn, impact on later literature. Shelley has recently been shown to be behind the shaping of the theme and structure of *Moby-Dick*—its 'Romantic architecture' (see 'Further Reading' below)— more influentially than any other writer, but the closest actual literary analogies are mostly Coleridgean.

It is difficult to know how best to illustrate this discussion of a novel that is, although in some parts itself made up of excerpts, resistant to excerpting: the massive and varied wholeness and 'whaleness' of *Moby-Dick* seem necessary to its proper impact, even if the aim is the relatively specific one of indicating particular Romantic qualities. But, as with *Wuthering Heights* above, perhaps something of the magic of its poetic and peculiar flavour can be conveyed by brief quotation, and the first comes from the first chapter, 'Loomings', with its characteristically Romantic emphases on the aspirational search for meaning in the mysteries of life, even if finally 'ungraspable', as here in explaining the attraction of one of the grandest phenomena in the world of nature, while illustrating Melville's learned allusiveness and habit of directing the reader to look for deeper levels of significance, through metaphor and imagery:

Why upon your first voyage as a passenger, did you yourself feel such a mystical vibration, when first told that you and your ship were now out of sight of land? Why did the old Persians hold the sea holy? Why did the Greeks give it a separate deity, and own brother of Jove? Surely all this is not without meaning. And still deeper the meaning of that story of Narcissus, who because he could not grasp the tormenting, mild image he saw in the fountain, plunged into it and was drowned. But that same image, we ourselves see in all rivers and oceans. It is the image of the ungraspable phantom of life; and this is the key to it all.

The second quotation is the last paragraph of chapter 33, 'The Specksynder', linking Melville back to Wordsworth as much as Coleridge, with their democratic recognition that literature can find heroes and tragedy in ordinary lives, and that the interest and even nobility or grandeur of the outwardly insignificant can be revealed by the writer's re-creation of these qualities through imaginative vision and empathy:

But Ahab, my Captain, still moves before me in all his Nantucket grimness and shagginess; and in this episode touching Emperors and Kings, I must not conceal that I have only to do with a poor old whale-hunter like him; and, therefore, all outward majestical trappings and housings are denied me. Oh, Ahab! what shall be grand in thee, it must needs be plucked at from the skies, and dived for in the deep, and featured in the unbodied air!

That the creative vision involves turning to nature links Melville with his Romantic predecessors in an obvious way, and the third and final quotation from *Moby-Dick* shows him working as a poet of nature as much as they, and relating his own human nature to it as clearly as they. In chapter 87, 'The Grand Armada', in the midst of the frightful carnage of a bloody whale-hunt, the narrator movingly turns aside to wonder at the mother whales nursing their infants, suspended in calm deep below the surface of a 'lake' in the ocean, remote from all the horrors:

And thus, though surrounded by circle upon circle of consternations and affrights, did these inscrutable creatures at the centre freely and fearlessly indulge in all peaceful concernments; yea, serenely revelled in dalliance and delight. But even so, amid the tornadoed Atlantic of my being, do I myself still for ever centrally disport in mute calm; and while ponderous planets of unwaning woe revolve round me, deep down and deep inland there I still bathe me in eternal mildness of joy.

D. H. Lawrence

David Herbert Lawrence (1885–1930) wrote interestingly on Melville in *Studies in Classic American Literature* (1923), praising him as the greatest seer and poet of the sea, and responding to that massive emotional directness so typical of all the writers Lawrence admired—and typical of Lawrence himself most of all. As a seer and poet of such passionate feeling in his own prophetic and poetic novels (though he also wrote poetry), Lawrence may be equalled in places by other modern writers but seems unsurpassed by any and unchallenged overall as the principal legatee of the Romantic tradition in twentieth-century English fiction. Furthermore, he did not just inherit the tradition, but developed it in ways more original and truly revolutionary (in turning it upside down, as it were) than any other writer of the nineteenth or twentieth centuries. Though Lawrence's chief rival, James Joyce (1882–1941), has his undoubted Romantic side, or even sides, he is not without reason generally labelled 'classic' when it comes to the traditional literary divide, with all the connotations of order and control and rationality, formal innovation, perfection of style, and so on, that separate the art for art's sake aesthetes from the art for life's sake emotionalists. There is nothing in Joyce's novels akin to Lawrence's belief in the body, blood, and bowels providing a profounder source of wisdom than the mind, in instinct as a better guide than intellect, or his other similar notions startlingly developing Romantic concepts of the teachings of nature: Joyce is an intellectual, to whom this anti-intellectualism is antipathetic. Joyce's exact contemporary, Virginia Woolf (1882–1941), is perhaps a stronger contender as heir to the Romantics: her novels, with their distinctive prose-poetry, are not only brimming with quotations from, and allusions to, the Romantics, but also at times find in them both thematic and structural pivots. In the end, however, Woolf lines up much more readily with Joyce, whose artistic objectives she shares, than with Lawrence, whose art is fundamentally alien to the other two: they are in what might be called a continental or European (mainly French) tradition; Lawrence, though influenced by European (mainly German and Russian) as well as American novelists, primarily harks back, in an individual way, to a native English tradition stemming from the Romantics. As is the case with Dickens, he would not be the novelist he is without that Romantic tradition, and he cannot be understood, or imagined, apart from it.

Lawrence's first novel, *The White Peacock* (1911), is as easy to place in this tradition as his last, *Lady Chatterley's Lover* (1928), which completes the circle by repeating, with variations, many of the same features. These include not only a gamekeeper who acts as a spokesperson for Lawrence's own views, derived from the Romantics, on the decay of society when it abandons true values for life-denying material ones, but also a heroine who has to choose between a passionate man who is close to nature and one who is more her cultured, educated, wealthier class equal but not as attractive and vital. In the first book the more natural man is rejected; in the last book it is the other way round. It is all very reminiscent of *Wuthering Heights*, and Lawrence adopts this method of using contrasted couples and love-triangles in all his novels, as many nineteenth-century writers had done before him, as one way of exploring his favourite—and essentially Romantic—theme of the conflict between the natural and the so-called civilized. Sexual relationships are at the heart of this theme: more than any other writer before him, Lawrence takes on his characters as sexual beings and explores them with exceptional depth and candour, which got him into trouble with the censors, but has earned him a unique place in the liberation of literature from the restraints of what is regarded as 'improper' by prudish guardians of literary morals. In this way he has extended his literary legacy from the Romantics, likewise criticized in their own times for 'impropriety' of various subjects and treatments, though none was punished as severely as he, having his books not only bowdlerized but in some instances even banned.

One extension of the treatment of sex as early as *The White Peacock* is the homosexual idyll in the chapter entitled 'A Poem of Friendship'; this would be taken further in such episodes as the lesbian relationship in *The Rainbow* (1915), which is probably the main reason the police destroyed all copies they could find immediately after publication, and the male bonding between Rupert Birkin and Gerald Crich in *Women in Love* (1920). Another extension as early as the first novel is the recognition of the potential for destructive cruelty of love, depicted not only in the heroine's rejection and taunting of the 'natural' lover, as in *Wuthering Heights* again, but also, and more perversely, in the marriage of the gamekeeper, Annable, to Lady Crystabel, like the heroine of Coleridge's 'Christabel' (1816) an unwitting agent of evil, who humiliates and destroys her husband. This will be taken to its furthest in the sadomasochistic relationship between Gudrun Brangwen and Gerald Crich in *Women in Love*, which culminates in his almost parodistically Romantic death high on a mountain in the snow. Though he has sometimes been credited with it, Lawrence did not invent this notion of cruelty in love, but he took it to new heights—and depths—of psychological insight as well as erotic physicality.

The eroticism of Lawrence's second novel, *The Trespasser* (1912), led to its being toned down before publication, with similar alterations instigated by the publisher's editor in the case of the third, *Sons and Lovers* (1913). This is Lawrence's first masterpiece. While *The White Peacock* is more pastoral, and *The Trespasser*, built on musical and indeed explicitly Wagnerian principles as it charts a doomed love affair, is perhaps Lawrence's most Romantic novel (even he thought it too personally revealing and emotionally overcharged), neither of them has the originality and impact of *Sons and Lovers*. This is a truly archetypal novel, and, in treating the dominating love of mother and son, the most famous example of the Oedipus complex in modern literature. Incest was a topic of interest to the Romantics, especially Byron and Shelley; here the taboo is taken on deliberately but delicately. Above all, the love of the mother and the hatred of the father, though coming directly from Lawrence's own family life, are transmuted by art to something not only of universal application as myth and archetype, but also much more impartially balanced than the biased autobiographical impulses could have instigated on their own.

The typical fusion, in the best writers of the Romantic tradition, of the realistic depiction of ordinary life—here seen in a coalminer's home, a factory, and so on—with the higher significances supplied by symbolism—here especially of flowers—is notable in this book, and this fusion is yet more subtly achieved in the next two novels. They started out as one, but are very different novels in their separated final state, with even some of their Romantic qualities having different flavours and effects. *The Rainbow* is more traditionally positive as it presents individuals, especially women, in three successive generations of the Brangwen family searching for self-fulfilment, as they move from farm to city, as foreshadowed in the first chapter by an even earlier representative Brangwen woman, revising the usual Romantic imperatives as well as traditional gender roles:

She stood to see the far-off world of cities and governments and the active scope of man, the magic land to her, where secrets were made known and desires fulfilled. She faced outwards to where men moved dominant and creative, having turned their back on the pulsing heat of creation, and with this behind them, were set out to discover what was beyond, to enlarge their own scope and range and freedom; whereas the Brangwen men faced inwards to the teeming life of creation, which poured unresolved into their veins.

The affirmative vision of third-generation Ursula Brangwen in the very last paragraph of the book typifies Lawrence's own Romantic attitudes in his favourite symbol, the rainbow itself:

She saw in the rainbow the earth's new architecture, the old, brittle corruption of houses and factories swept away, the world built up in a living fabric of Truth, fitting to the over-arching heaven.

Ursula has not found fulfilment with another person at the end of *The Rainbow*: she 'gets her man' in the decidedly Lawrentian figure of Rupert Birkin in *Women in Love*. Yet the latter novel, less a consummation than an apocalypse, a modernly episodic rather than a traditional narrative, is more negative overall, because Lawrence develops the Romantic tradition's ambivalence towards the 'corruption' swept away at the end of the former novel, in opposed images of decay, dissolution, and disintegration giving it its due weight as equal of life-affirming vitality, seeing the polarized opposites as necessary to each other, as in the religious concept of death being necessary to rebirth. Such dualities characterize the novel, as when the daisies Birkin throws into the water, in the eleventh chapter, 'An Island', are not only less easily interpreted symbols than the flowers in *Sons and Lovers* but expressive of both exalted and oppressive feelings in the watching Ursula:

A strange feeling possessed her, as if something were taking place. But it was all intangible. And some sort of control was being put on her. She could not know. She could only watch the brilliant little discs of the daisies veering slowly in travel on the dark, lustrous water.

It is not possible to consider the rest of Lawrence's novels here, but a brief return to his last novel provides a final consummation of the Romantic movement in his work. *Lady Chatterley's Lover* is remarkable for many things, not least for giving its author a notoriety possibly even more resounding than Lord Byron's, but it is more tender than titillating, more puritanically moral than pornographically exploitative. And one of its most moving aspects is where the progress of Constance Chatterley's love affair with her husband's gamekeeper is matched by events in the natural world, not with any trite use of the pathetic fallacy, but with both originality and truth to individual inner feeling, as in chapter 8, when images from nature parallel the woman's early feelings of being aroused by the man:

Constance sat down with her back to a young pine-tree, that swayed against her with curious life, elastic, and powerful, rising up. The erect, alive thing, with its top in the sun! And she watched the daffodils turn golden, in a burst of sun that was warm on her hands and lap. Even she caught the faint, tarry scent of the flowers. And then, being so still and alone, she seemed to get into a current of her own proper destiny. She had been fastened by a rope, and jagging and snarring like a boat at its moorings; now she was loose and adrift.

This is beautifully done, with the inherited features, such as the echoes of Wordsworth's daffodils and any number of other Romantic writers' boats in the stream of life, easily and seemingly spontaneously fitted into Lawrence's signature phallic symbolism. In such ways Lawrence both reasserts his Romantic heritage and boldly rejuvenates it.

FURTHER READING

Beer, John, *Romantic Influences* (Basingstoke and London: Macmillan, 1993). A thoughtful and detailed tracing of 'some important lines of influence' from the Romantics through the Victorians to the moderns; particularly relevant to Romantic legacies in the novel is the discussion of Romantic poetic images developed by Hardy, Forster, Woolf, and Lawrence.

Clarke, Colin, *River of Dissolution: D. H. Lawrence and English Romanticism* (London: Routledge and Kegan Paul, 1969). Explores Lawrence's 'debt to the English Romantic poets', especially in their shared ambivalence towards decay and regeneration, 'dying into being'.

Coveney, Peter, *The Image of Childhood* (Harmondsworth: Penguin, 1967). Cogently examines notions of the individual and society, chiefly but not only through treatments of childhood, from Blake and Wordsworth, through Dickens, Charlotte Brontë, and others, to Woolf, Joyce, and Lawrence.

Duncan, Ian, *Modern Romance and Transformations of the Novel* (Cambridge: Cambridge University Press, 1992). Useful in placing the Gothic novel, Scott, and Dickens in relation to each other and the development of Romanticism.

Durer, Christopher S., *Herman Melville: Romantic and Prophet* (Toronto: York University Press, 1996). A concise study of Melville's characteristics in relation to European and especially British Romanticism.

Gravil, Richard, *Romantic Dialogues: Anglo-American Continuities, 1776–1862* (New York: Palgrave/ St Martin's Press, 2000). One of the few studies of transatlantic connections between the major Romantic poets and their American legatees, including Fenimore Cooper, Hawthorne, Poe, and Melville.

Higbie, Robert, *Dickens and the Imagination* (Gainesville, Fla.: University Press of Florida, 1998). Traces Dickens's novels back to Romantic ideas of creativity.

McNees, E. (ed.), *The Brontë Sisters*, Critical Assessments of Writers in English Series, 4 vols. (Mountfield: Helm Information, 1996). This comprehensive collection has much relevant to the Romantic inheritance of the Brontës, especially in the fourth volume.

Pinion, F. B., *A Brontë Companion: Literary Assessment, Background, and Reference* (London and Basingstoke: Macmillan, 1975). Usefully includes material on the sisters' literary sources and influences.

Thomson, Shawn, *The Romantic Architecture of Herman Melville's* Moby-Dick (Madison: Fairleigh Dickinson University Press, 2001). Intricately argues that the ideas of Shelley, in particular, shape both the theme and structure of *Moby-Dick*.

39 | **Film**

Jerrold E. Hogle

The transfer of English Romantic writers and writings to film has produced a dazzling variety at best and a troubling portrait gallery at worst. To be sure, the work of British Romanticism filmed most often has been Mary Shelley's *Frankenstein*, which I will not be treating directly. Usually based more on R. B. Peake's play *Presumption* (1823) than on Shelley's novel of 1818,[1] the many screen versions of it have been so thoroughly studied that I need not repeat what is so well known (see further the chapter on 'The theatre'). Some, after all, have found the Romantic period more accessible in the recent film adaptations of several Jane Austen novels, from *Sense and Sensibility* (dir. Ang Lee, 1995) to *Mansfield Park* (dir. Patricia Rezema, 1999). Yet the most revolutionary and conflicted aspects of England from 1790 to the 1830s are either softened or suppressed in these pictures, save momentarily in *Mansfield Park*. More in touch with what most consider Romantic in this period—the poets and verse dramatists who 'elevated creative imagination, individual genius, and the inward self . . . to cope with commercial and professional changes' in the wake of the American, French, and early industrial revolutions (see *Oxford Companion to the Romantic Age*, p. 2)—are those efforts that are my subject here: the primarily dramatic, rather than educational and documentary, films that visualize the lives and/or works of Blake, Wordsworth, Coleridge, Byron, Percy Bysshe Shelley, Keats, and their close associates, thereby showing us how we see them and their legacies long after their departures. Though these films are not legion, they reveal the complex ways in which modern audiences have come to value *and* distance 'the Romantics', somewhat like Frankenstein and his creature: as simultaneously inspiring creators, on the one hand, and eccentric monsters, on the other.

Such films, I find, have taken four general forms over the last hundred years: the visual rendering of a classic Romantic poem; the film biography on the life and loves of a major Romantic author; dramatizations of key events in the lives of the Romantics that have led to certain famous works; and half-fictional eavesdroppings on the private lives of such poets that claim to give us insight into the origins of Romanticism as a movement. Here I propose to exemplify these forms, one at a time, first by noting each category's range of films and then by highlighting a major example, or a tight group of them, that epitomizes the perspectives most crucial to each form. In this process, I try to pinpoint the interpretation that each main example gives us of the Romantics being treated, including the ways in which these renderings both use and distort documented evidence and Romantic writings. But I also want to expose and explain the most overriding tension that these films share. All of them, despite their differences, dramatize a compelling Romantic creativity, to which filmmakers and audiences seem genuinely drawn as to a saving source of energy, but they *counter* that brilliance too by exposures of irrational strangeness in all the authors they treat, from which we viewers of these films are urged to recoil even as we feel a continuing attraction.

The Romantic poem on screen

In those productions that offer to turn the words of a Romantic poem into moving pictures, the makers almost always comment on the lives of the authors as well. Rare and short are those films that render only a poem, as we see in *La Belle Dame Sans Merci* from Keats (dir. Jonathan Glendening, 1996, 6 min.) and *The Albatross*, a mostly animated short based on Coleridge's 'Rime of the Ancient Mariner' (dir. Paul Bush, 1998, 25 min.). More typical is *Keats and his Nightingale: A Blind Date* (dir. Jim Wolpaw, 1986), a documentary short that intersperses the 'Ode to a Nightingale' with Keats's dreamy conception of it in his Hampstead garden. Granted, the balance between life and work visible here sometimes tilts other filmmakers into surveying works as mere gig-lamps in a life. Such is the fate on film of the engraver-poet in *The Vision of William Blake* (dir. Guy Brenton, 1958, 29 min.) and *William Blake* (dir. Giuseppe Cristiano, 2001, 6 min.). These efforts, though reasonably helpful, however, should be classed with the avowedly educational films on the classic Romantic poets available through the Films for the Arts and Humanities web site.

But the most persistent form taken by this type of production is what we see in filmings of 'The Rime of the Ancient Mariner', the Romantic poem adapted most often. Since Coleridge's original is so much a series of images already, the 'Rime' has been attractive to filmmakers from a very early stage, and their interest in exploring Coleridge through it has only increased. *The Ancient Mariner* was a major studio silent film in 1925 (dir. Chester Bennett and Henry Otto), and this version retells the poem's lurid voyage with some added elements, including some filled-out characters (among them Clara Bow as 'Doris'). Even here, though, a prelude points to the dream-like reverie of a poet feeling the stirrings of his unconscious. By the 1970s, this aspect becomes more dominant even when the poem is accurately rendered, as in the 1977 *Rime of the Ancient Mariner* (dir. Larry Jordan) narrated by Orson Welles, in which the partial animation of Gustav Doŕe's famous 1878 illustrations for Coleridge's poem is framed within an account of Coleridge's addictive personality.

The most forceful example of this sort of film, however, is *The Strangest Voyage* (dir. Raul da Silva and Michael Twain, 1976), which is retitled *Rime of the Ancient*

Mariner in its Kultur video release (1984). This version renders every line of Coleridge's poem, with Sir Michael Redgrave voicing the Mariner's narration, following first a historical and then a biographical prelude. The opening segment, written and read by Donald Moffatt, visualizes the tradition of the sea as a 'strange place, unknown and unknowable', establishing the 'Rime' as the climax of a Western tendency to link ocean voyages with humanity's deepest longings and fears. But this film's next segment quickly relocates that theme within the author's life. Now, mostly through etchings and paintings ranging from Constable's to Hogarth's, Coleridge is presented as the epitome of youthful creativity, energized by the supernatural *Arabian Nights* and the new freedoms allowed briefly in the revolutionary 1790s, *and* the most wildly impractical of men, 'crack-brained' and 'penniless', until his gift for poetry supposedly faded into the 'posthumous', if more prosperous, 'existence', of his post-'Rime' period. Since that poem is therefore seen as the product of the author's early contradictions, the Mariner becomes a re-enactment of that strangeness throughout the film's final segment: the picturing of the complete poem via half-animated drawings from Doré and Edward Hicks that are interspersed with live-action seascapes, all underscored by borrowed music and Redgrave's harrowing narration. The Mariner finally seems like Coleridge reincarnated, as well as the focus of everyone's wondrous fear of the sea, in an intensification of both the poet's passionate voice and his early instability, especially when the camera keeps closing in on still pictures of the Mariner's face as though probing his tortured soul. By the final frames the viewer feels let in on a special 'vision' that is inspiring, yet profoundly 'dangerous' (in the prologue's words) in rendering a feverish mental confusion, repeatedly symbolized in this film by the swirling waters in the wake of the voyaging ship.

Romantic film biography

The prompting of this double bind in the viewer is just as pronounced, though it is more sharply focused, in the life-and-loves film biographies of Romantic poets. Not surprisingly, one author has this type of film almost entirely to himself: Lord Byron, whose calculated confusion of his characters with his sexualized public persona—a theatrical construct he also critiqued, particularly in *Don Juan*—has long made readers interpret his works as windows into his life, both at his own time and since. The litany of films involving Byron the man, consequently, is fairly long, especially if one includes the pieces in which he is a secondary character providing hints of romance and scandal. The Byron film archive, following brief silent renderings of *Mazeppa* (dir. Frank Dudley, 1908) and *The Corsair* (dir. Frank Powell, 1914), begins in earnest with *A Prince of Lovers* (dir. Charles Calvert, 1922), in which an ardently posturing but silent Byron (Howard Gage) is blended with a stereotype of the *old* Don Juan romancing his way through a gallery of women, a figure quite different from Byron's ironic version of him. Such an approach is understandable, since the same decade saw a silent *Don Juan* film (dir. Alan Crosland, 1926) that gives writing credit to the dark Lord by name but uses visual echoes of Mozart's *Don Giovanni* more often than moments from Byron's mock-epic. This trend, which mixes a brooding depth in Byron with mildly lurid shadings of sexual promiscuity, has continued all the way through such television films as *Solo: Lord Byron* with Jeremy Brett (BBC, 1970)—a companion piece to *Solo: Keats* with Ian McKellan the same year—to the recent mini-series film *Lord Byron* (BBC, 2003) with Jonny Lee Miller. In between, Byron has been used secondarily to spice up *The Last Rose of Summer*, a 1937 period musical (dir. James Fitzpatrick); *Beau Brummel* (dir. Curtis Bernhardt, 1954), a remake of a 1924 silent film (dir. Harry Beaumont); *I Remember Nelson*, a 1982 mini-series (dir. Simon Langton, BBC); and most famously *Lady Caroline Lamb* (dir. Robert Bolt, 1972). There Richard Chamberlain overacts Byron opposite the Caroline of Sarah Miles more like a performance of Lamb's fictional portrait of him in *Glenarvon* (her novel of 1816) than the Byron we can discover during his or her own accounts of their affair.

In all these versions, as in the wide variations on the Byronic hero in other films (see 'Further Reading'), the depiction of this 'bad' Lord has primarily extended what Dino Felluga calls 'Victorian culture's pathologizing sexualization of Byron'.[2] Each film in this group, like many Victorians, starts to value *up* his old-world sex appeal as a bold, iconoclastic poet-aristocrat—a sop to the bourgeois admiration for individual initiative and higher-class status—only to value that attraction *down* in the end as perverse and repellant, recasting it as a self-involved resistance to middle-class market circulation. In this way most film versions of Byron render the paradox that becomes '*the* Romantic poet' for the modern middle-class viewer: the creative, passionate, even boundary-crossing overreacher of limits longing for a pre-industrial world of emotional self-expression *mixed* with the unsettling, rampantly sexual questioner of middle-class values and presumed stability, a rebel type that can include Blake, Mary Wollstonecraft, Percy Bysshe *and* Mary Shelley, as well as the early Coleridge.

Much of the time, though, we ask a film to resolve this double bind. Byron in a fictive biography, for example, remains much too uncontainable if his contradictions cannot be explained by some ideological scheme that comes down on a 'good' or 'bad' side. The film biography that most clearly pursues this objective is *The Bad Lord Byron* (dir. David Macdonald), very much a British film of 1949. It begins with Byron (Dennis Price) musing over his past in Greece, where he is dying of fever after coming to fight the Turks (see *Oxford Companion to the Romantic Age*, p. 442). This J. Arthur Rank picture— in a conventionalizing of the poet's own *Vision of Judgement* (1822) that makes it more like the work it parodies, Robert Southey's *The Vision of Judgement* (1821)[3]—then has him imagine a stylized English courtroom between earth and heaven in which he is evaluated as he dies by a judge and jury positioned between a prosecutor and a defence barrister, each of whom proceeds to call witnesses (with the flashbacks that accompany each), most of them the primary women in his life. This trial builds towards a final scene where the judge turns to the audience as jury and leaves the question to them/us:

'Is [Lord Byron] to be remembered by posterity as a poet and a liberator or as a seducer and a libertine?' The testimony of Caroline Lamb (here Joan Greenwood) sways these proceedings towards the latter side at first, but a turn towards the former begins when Augusta Leigh (Linden Travers)—here a married friend and *neither* his lover nor his sister (despite evidence to the contrary)—explains 'bad Byron' with 'You've been hurt too badly [when young] so you can't help hurting others'. What completes the shift towards a 'good' Byron, though, is the final emergence of him as 'liberator' in this highly anti-fascist, post-Second World War production. Byron's supposedly final love, Teresa Guicolli in Venice (Mai Zetterling), proudly testifies about his leaving her side for 'noble purposes', first to support her brother in the *carbonari*, the Italian underground fighting the Austrian occupation, and finally to restore the liberty of Greece, much as Britain and its allies had just done for Western Europe against Hitler and Mussolini. The context of any film's own period is the key to the complex of attitudes towards which its audience is ultimately drawn, whatever the baggage of cultural debate that comes with the central character.

Films on the birth of a Romantic classic

Resolutions like the one in *The Bad Lord Byron*, however, have proven difficult to achieve on film since 1949, particularly in the third kind of Romantic picture that became more prominent after the 1960s, the one focused on a period in the lives of important writers that gave rise to a famous work. The most prominent such moment, of course, is the one that produced the original *Frankenstein*: the gathering on the shores of Lake Geneva in the summer of 1816, when Byron, Shelley, Mary Godwin (not yet legally Shelley's spouse), Clare Clairmont (Mary's sister-in-law and Byron's some-time lover), and Dr John Polidori (then Byron's personal physician) agreed on a ghost story-writing contest among themselves, mostly at the Villa Diodati occupied by Byron (see *Oxford Companion to the Romantic Age*, p. 651). This challenge eventuated, not only in Mary's novel *and* elements in Percy Shelley's and Byron's poetry, but in Polidori's *The Vampyre* (1819; see *Oxford Companion to the Romantic Age*, p. 652), a literary ancestor of Bram Stoker's *Dracula* (1897). Consequently, following the 1960s—which included a revival of Romantic liberalism, a renewed endorsement of self-expression (including freer sex and drug use), challenges to imperialism and war, and movements for civil rights and female equality—we find a quickened interest in this liberal-to-radical second generation of Romantics. One result is a novel, *Haunted Summer* (1972) by Anne Edwards, written in Mary Shelley's voice and claiming to uncover what really happened in and around Diodati beyond what is sketched in diaries, journals, and prefaces.[4] Such efforts, though, reveal great uncertainty about how to view these revived Romantics, since these very writers (like much of the 1960s) challenged middle-class norms almost as much as Byron alone. Edwards offers her own sense of

Frankenstein as stemming mainly from conflicts in Mary herself about her birth causing her mother's death and her 'monstrous' role as a well-read *woman* in what was still a male-dominated society *and* literary circle.[5] But the succeeding years have produced many different explanations as this novel and the events it half-invents have been reworked in three major films: *Gothic* (dir. Ken Russell, 1986), the Anglo-Italian-Spanish co-production *Rowing With the Wind* (dir. Gonzalo Suarez, 1988), and *Haunted Summer* (dir. Ivan Passer, also 1988), the only one of the three explicitly based on the Edwards book.

Such a proliferation of differing versions around a single Romantic encounter is a sign that these writers and their works continue to arouse cultural conflict. Ideological tugs-of-war could hardly be more blatant, in fact, than they are in Ken Russell's *Gothic*, the work of a director with an affinity for the Romantic and the Gothic already (as in *The Music Lovers* and *The Devils*, both 1971). Russell begins and ends *Gothic* with middle-class onlookers gawking from afar at the Villa Diodati (as some did) and projecting visions of drug-assisted excess, without real knowledge, upon the supposedly decadent aristocrats inside. In some contrast to these presumptions, after the call for everyone to 'create a ghost' by Byron (Gabriel Byrne), the gathering in the house becomes a collective, and sometimes drug-induced, journey into a dark night of the soul, especially for Mary (Natasha Richardson). Partly in imitation of the Gothicism in Henry Fuseli's 1781 painting *The Nightmare* (see *Oxford Companion to the Romantic Age*, p. 515), seen here on a Diodati wall where it did *not* happen to be in 1816, each character begins to see a vague spectre that symbolizes his or her deepest phobias now 'called to life' from the deathly world of sleep. Mary's idea of Frankenstein's creature emerges from a conflation of all these ghosts as a 'jigsaw of all our worst fears' in what strives to be a tour de force of preconscious creativity. At the same time, however, Russell also seems to follow Byron's early dictum in this film to 'give [the gawkers] what they want'. Often reduced in size by being photographed from a distance, the members of this circle become hyperbolic grotesques, wild-eyed and drugged puppets of their own irrationalities. Shelley (Julian Sands) stands naked and screaming atop the villa hoping lightning will strike him, while self-loathing Polidori (Timothy Spall) keeps trying to kill himself repeatedly as if he were one of his own mechanical figurines. The Romantics of this piece *are* the stereotypes of mad self-indulgence that have too often been attached to them by those who know too little of their writings and lives—all this in a film (scripted by Stephen Volk) with unusually accurate allusions to the literary sources of the Diodati contest. Even Ken Russell, it seems, wants to celebrate and denigrate these geniuses all at once.

Such general conflict, while emphasizing different obsessions, also underwrites *Rowing With the Wind*, much as Gonzalo Suarez strives to make it more pensive and expansive than Russell's gallery of grotesques. More is made here, as in the title, of the Diodati party taking boat trips on the lake, where they are first drawn out of themselves by the 'wind' of peaceful nature but then drawn back into their psychological nightmares (rowing with an *internal* force) by such dark destinations as the now-empty castle that became the setting for Byron's 'The Prisoner of Chillon'. Heeding this call from the preconscious, Mary (Lizzy McInnery) begins to envision a ghostly creature that again composites personal agonies, though not ones found mainly at the Villa: her own guilt for being her mother's killer and a 'breeder of death', especially given the later drowning of her son William; the abject dependence of Polidori (Jose Luis Gomez) on Byron's mercurial love; the fervent idealism of Shelley (Valentine Pelka) that tempts him towards suicide, or other women, when it is disappointed; and the sceptical belief in Byron (Hugh Grant) that decadence is his destiny, since 'horror', he claims, is the 'point to which all things finally return'. Gradually the cadaverous nemesis in Mary's writing of this summer appears half-seen to all the characters as though haunting them visibly with their internal monstrosities. In the end, as this story continues past 1816 into the circle's later re-encounters in Italy culminating in Shelley's 1822 drowning (here *foreseen* by Mary), the creature, now outside even Mary's novel, dogs the steps of every character. Its combination of guilts, we find, has become a vengeful force of death taking the lives of Polidori, William, Shelley, Byron's daughter by Clare (Elizabeth Hurley), and finally Byron himself, whose demise in Greece, with little emphasis on his heroism, is noted in writing as the film ends. The capacity of the creative imagination to bring the unconscious to external life is given demonstrable Romantic power in this rendition, but that power is seen ultimately as a curse on all who exercise it, turning on them to destroy them with their own extreme views of the world.

By contrast, the tone of Ivan Passer's *Haunted Summer* is much less sombre, even though its final stance on its characters is equally conflicted. This time Mary (Alice Krige) struggles for weeks to find an idea for a tale after Byron (Phillip Anglim) jauntily proposes the ghost story contest, even though she finds him as repugnant as he is seductive, much as we know the real Mary Shelley did.[6] She succeeds in the end, of course, but for unexpected reasons, which stem *both* from screenwriter Lewis John Carlino changing Edwards's novel at key points *and* from a decision to leap finally beyond any evidence in the documentary record of this summer. At the outset, Mary seems content to be part of a free-love, 1960-ish *ménage à trois* (including a three-to-a-bed scene not in the book) with a giddy Clare (Laura Dern) and a happily idealistic Shelley (Eric Stolz), who invites both girls to join him in naked bathing and remains naïvely hopeful for a love-filled world even in the face of Byron's brooding self-involvement. The latter's greater complexity in this version, however, begins to interest Mary in spite of herself, partly because Byron's limp and sadness help her see how his cruelty to others comes from the earlier cruelty of others towards him. After Byron urges some opium on Shelley, whereupon the latter starts seeing Mary as luridly monstrous in the caves beneath Chillon, Mary becomes attracted to Byron's active monstrosity, now more intriguing—and, by implication, more masculine—than Shelley's manipulable passivity. Once Byron acknowledges this tendency, the Mary of this film (not of the Edwards novel nor her actual life) goes to bed with the young lord in the picture's climactic moment, embracing the main model for her monster by joining her sexuality and creativity to his. A certain valuing of personal genius and self-realization, particularly through a freed sexuality, is extolled in this production, to be sure. But, promoted as a tale of 'lust, drugs, alcohol, and depravity' in the real lives of famous authors, the film *Haunted Summer* still reduces its characters to creatures of shifting passions they can never fully control, a view hardly fair to their writings nor to Anne Edwards, though they are not the driven zombies of *Gothic* nor the tragic self-destroyers of *Rowing With the Wind*.

Filming the origins of Romanticism

More recent years, it turns out, have not brought more resolution to this paradox in the beliefs of filmmakers and filmgoers. The ongoing conundrum, I find, has only intensified in the fourth type of Romantic film, the one focused on primal encounters that have had many long-lasting consequences. Most recent forms of this type have turned back with still conflicted attitudes to the presumed beginnings of the Romantic movement in England, possibly because of the 200th anniversary of 1798, the year of Wordsworth's and Coleridge's first *Lyrical Ballads* volume alongside the increased government repression throughout Britain in the wake of the French Revolution and the start of the Napoleonic wars (see *Oxford Companion to the Romantic Age*, pp. 23–6). Perhaps not surprisingly, Ken Russell has been a prime mover in this revisitation of Romanticism's English birth. To inaugurate a British television series called *Clouds of Glory*, which did not continue beyond these first two films, Russell has directed *William Wordsworth: William and Dorothy* with David Warner as William (1994) and *Samuel Taylor Coleridge: The Rime of the Ancient Mariner* with David Hemmings as Coleridge (1995). Granted, quite unlike *Gothic*, these films choose more of a docudrama, if slightly flamboyant, realism to visualize the pressures on these figures as being among the prime causes for their writings. There are, however, moments where brief parts of their works are filmed, and these do have a dreamy quality that threatens to tilt into nightmares of mental anguish. The Coleridge film, moreover, reverses the procedure of *The Strangest Voyage*. Instead of placing a refilming of *The Ancient Mariner* within cultural mythology and its author's troubled life, Russell here makes the Mariner's journey a metaphor for Coleridge's personal development, thereby helping the poet seem to emerge from a phase of revolutionary and drugged extremity (the roots of the 'Rime') into an afterlife as reflective and becalmed as the Mariner's by his poem's end.

The most important recent film on the birth-throes of English Romanticism, though, has surely been *Pandaemonium* (dir. Julian Temple, 2000), a joint venture of BBC and October Films mostly photographed 'where it all happened': Somerset, Cornwall, London, and the Lake District itself. In certain ways this picture is very like, and clearly influenced by, the 'haunted summer' films. Though beginning with a framing encounter at Wordsworth's prosperous home years later, it focuses on the intense relationships in a small circle—a fiery Coleridge (John Hannah), his increasingly disenchanted spouse Sara (Samantha Morton), an often introverted Wordsworth (Linus Roache), and his vibrant sister Dorothy (Emily Woof)—from the first Wordsworth–Coleridge meeting (though not the true one) in 1795 through the whole group's heady days together in 1797–9, out of which have come the *Lyrical Ballads* and much more. The first half of this production, too, is unusual in the history of Romanticism films: it draws the viewer eagerly into the young Coleridge's revolutionary dynamism, all in the face of shadowy government spying and repression embodied in the recurring figure of James Walsh, an actual government agent who really conducted surveillance on these figures. This fervour is connected to Coleridge's poetic capacity during the 1796–7 winter at Nether Stowey, when the tracings of ice on his and Sara's cottage window seem to spin out into the words and interconnections of his 'Frost at Midnight' (1797–8). This tone even extends into the second half with Dorothy gaining her due as a direct inspirer and fervent interpreter of both Wordsworth's and Coleridge's ideas and very words. Though not all the historical references at this stage are strictly accurate, it is hard to fault how close they come to ringing true, at least as dramatic composites.

But most of the second half of *Pandaemonium* brings back the long-standing fear and uncertainty about Romantic extremes, often with more blatant inaccuracy. Leaping beyond any conclusive evidence, screenwriter Frank Cottrell Boyce has Dorothy fall visibly in love with Coleridge, and he with her, to the point where her unfulfilled desires and her distress at his and Wordsworth's quarrels lead her into compulsive drug-taking, here presented as the source of her later dementia, which is used (I think) cruelly in the last frame-scene of the picture as she madly recites 'Kubla Khan' to all those assembled. Drugs, meanwhile, become *the* prime catalyst for Coleridge's rapid creativity of 1797–8 (including 'The Rime of the Ancient Mariner'), in contrast to Wordsworth's initial slowness. They soon become the basis, too, for Coleridge's eventual writer's block as Wordsworth comes to see his colleague as holding him back and flees with his sister and snobbish new wife back to the Lake District. Moreover, in an acceptance and exaggeration of the controversial case made by Kenneth Johnston in *The Hidden Wordsworth* (1998),[7] the Wordsworth of *Pandaemonium* is finally revealed as having betrayed Coleridge by being in league with Walsh, possibly all along, as a still-drugged 'Sam' discovers by catching them together at the end. 'Pandaemonium' at the beginning, as defined by Coleridge, is a revolutionary and poetic upheaval, but ultimately it becomes the habitation from Hell in Milton's *Paradise Lost* as the founding English Romantic circle descends into division, back-stabbing, drug dependence, shattered love lives, complicity with repression, and nostalgic insanity. There is a sense, indeed, of a 'paradise lost' as Dorothy wails out the near-forgotten poetic ravings of the younger Coleridge, yet there is equally the suggestion that they 'brought it on themselves' because of the very drives *inside* them that they are famous for articulating. The ultimate basis of Romanticism on film, we still find, is the tragic flaw seemingly inherent in its own liberating vision.

It is indeed phenomenal that, in the face of many divergent elements in these films on Romantic writers, there is a consistent pattern of love-them-*and*-loathe them—not unlike the ones expressed by the middle-class reviews of their own time (see *Oxford Companion to the Romantic Age*, pp. 281–6)—that has only gained strength as it has continued. What is most revealing is how the curse of Romanticism, the fear of what its radical extremes might do to social order, sexual boundaries, and normal sanity, turns out in films to be inseparable from the movement's best-known gifts to the modern world: its insights into human subjectivity; its remembering of the physical nature obscured and polluted by the industrial revolution; its various hopes for greater social justice in a Western world of lingering hierarchies; and its reinvigoration of the art of writing, energized by these other elements, in ways that have become incorporated into our cultural vocabulary, sometimes in the forms, including film, by which we express our aspirations. Consequently, this brief history of the Romantics on film shows us how much remains conflicted about some of the foundations underlying the ways we articulate ourselves and our culture as inheritors of the Romantic legacy.

FURTHER READING

MacDonald, Gina, and MacDonald, Andrew F. (eds.) *Jane Austen on Screen* (Cambridge: Cambridge University Press, 2003). The best scholarly collection of essays on the films adapted from Austen's novels.

Stein, Atara, 'Immortals and Vampires and Ghosts, Oh My: Byronic Heroes in Popular Culture', in Laura Mandell and Michael Eberle-Sinatra (eds.), *Romanticism and Contemporary Culture* (College Park, Md.: University of Maryland, 2001). A helpful account of many versions of the Byronic hero in recent Western culture and especially on film.

Tropp, Martin, *Mary Shelley's Monster: The Story of Frankenstein* (Boston: Houghton Mifflin, 1976). Still the best introductory account of how the novel is both used and changed in the best-known film adaptations up until Mel Brooks's *Young Frankenstein* (1974).

WEB LINKS

Films for the Humanities and Social Sciences @films.com (Princeton, 1997–2003): www.films.com/films_home The best web site for locating and ordering educational and documentary films—and sometimes dramatic ones—on English Romantic writers and writings.

Internet Movie Database, The (Seattle: IMDb, Inc., 1990–2003): www.imdb.com The widest-ranging site for looking up—and even ordering—nearly all of the films discussed in this essay.

Romantic Circles Praxis Series online: www.rc.umd.edu/praxis/contemporary/stein/stein.html A helpful account of the many versions of the Byronic hero in recent Western culture and especially on film.

NOTES

1. See Richard Brinksley Peake, *Presumption; or the Fate of Frankenstein*, in *Seven Gothic Dramas, 1789–1825,* ed. Jeffrey N. Cox (Columbia, Oh.: Ohio State University Press, 1992), pp. 385–425.

2. Dino Franco Felluga, 'The Fetish-Logic of Bourgeois Subjectivity, or, The Truth the Romantic Poet Reveals About the Victorian Novel', *European Romantic Review*, 14 (2003), 251–60.

3. See E. M. Earl and James Hogg, *Byron and Southey: 'Vision of Judgement'* (Salzburg: University of Salzburg, 1998).

4. See *The Diary of Dr John William Polidori (1816)*, ed. William Michael Rosetti (1911; Folcroft, Pa.: Folcroft Library Editions, 1972), pp. 99–153; *The Journals of Mary Shelley*, ed. Paula R. Feldman and Diana Scott-Kilvert (Oxford: Clarendon Press, 1987), i. 114–32; and 'Mary Shelley's Introduction to the Third Edition (1831)' in *Frankenstein or The Modern Prometheus: The 1818 Text*, ed. James Rieger (Chicago: University of Chicago Press, 1982), pp. 222–9.

5. See Anne Edwards, *Haunted Summer* (New York: Coward, McGann, and Geoghegan, 1972), esp. pp. 211–59.

6. See Emily W. Sunstein, *Mary Shelley: Romance and Reality* (Boston: Little, Brown, 1989), pp. 120–5.

7. See Kenneth R. Johnston, *The Hidden Wordsworth: Poet, Lover, Rebel, Spy* (New York: W. W. Norton, 1998), pp. 526–33, 608–21, 654–70, 847–51.

40 | The theatre

Julie A. Carlson

It is odd to place the afterlife of British Romanticism in the theatre since so much writing during the period was trying to move drama and its readers out of the theatre and so much subsequent writing about the period has denied its interest and competence in drama or theatre. The standard view presented both in theatre histories and criticism on Romanticism is that the period produced no playwright of note, no play that was at once poetic and stageworthy, and that the conditions of early nineteenth-century theatres, especially patent or legitimate theatres, were themselves hostile to classical drama, especially verse tragedy (compare the chapter on 'Romantic drama'). With seating capacities of over 3,000, theatres were cavernous, stages were huge, and audiences were noisy, raucous, and irreverent (see *Oxford Companion to the Romantic Age*, pp. 228, 231). The combined effect was a theatre experience that favoured spectacle over spoken discourse because so many in the audience could not hear what was being said on stage, arrived halfway through a play, or attended the theatre primarily to see and be seen. In its day, discourse regarding Romantic theatre instituted a major separation between stage and page, viewing and reading, popular and cultivated, distinctions that are still operative in discussions about art today and that tend to link viewing with the mindless masses and reading with cultivated individuals. One advantage of recovering the theatre of the nineteenth century is the opportunity that it provides to challenge this division.

Over the past fifteen years, scholarship on Romantic drama and theatre has recovered the enormous vibrancy of this cultural arena and even argued for the literary value of several late-Georgian playwrights or plays. Not only did all the canonical poets (Wordsworth, Coleridge, Shelley, Byron, and Keats) write plays but scholars have also showcased the theatrical ambitions and/or successes of acknowledged playwrights such as Joanna Baillie, George Colman the younger, Thomas Morton, and Elizabeth Inchbald. They have also emphasized the forms of social and cultural legislation effected *by* theatre, not just the legislation applied to it through various licensing acts, patent grants, and censorship (see *Oxford Companion to the Romantic Age*, pp. 224–6). For theatre in this period represents one of the most democratized and diversified cultural arenas at the same time that its various stage representations are active in shaping proper British subjects in the metropolis, provinces, and colonies. This means that discussions regarding character, proper action, and means of embodiment are also always discussions regarding which people, mindsets, and social positions are best suited to representing the nation.

Approaching the legacy of Romanticism through one of its own weakest legacies has several advantages that underlie the arguments of this chapter. As a general principle, it highlights the provisional nature of how scholars define a particular literary-historical period and what they come to see as vital to, or significant about, it. Specifically, it pursues one of the most enduring literary–cultural debates of Romanticism concerning the workings and efficacy of imagination. Imagination is the faculty with which Romanticism is chiefly associated and whose powers are envisioned and applauded in relation to the period's changing tastes for revolution, whether political or artistic. For one of the chief ends of theatre—activating a people's powers to envision alternate realities—is increasingly said in the Romantic period to be invalidated by one of the chief means of theatre—realizing, in the sense of ascribing reality, material, and there-fore limitation to, dreams. As support in Britain for the radical projects associated with the French Revolution waned (see *Oxford Companion to the Romantic Age*, pp. 19–23), debates regarding stage representation were often correlated with a growing reaction against radical innovation of any type. They also occasioned anxious discussions regarding the nature of heroism, triggered by evaluations of the 'Corsican upstart', Napoleon Bonaparte, the leader of the slave revolt in San Domingue, Touissant L'Overture, Shakespeare's tragic heroes, or Lord Byron (see *Oxford Companion to the Romantic Age*, pp. 26–9, 63). This chapter explores the legacy of some of these tensions as pursued on the nineteenth-century stage. It takes up two separate issues with two different ends in mind. The first explores how the nineteenth-century British theatre dramatizes Prometheus—the archetype of rebellious heroism—and reacts to the Pro-metheanism associated with revolutionary Romanticism, epitomized in Byron. The second reflects on post-Romantic spectacle by considering the afterlife of Mary Shelley's *Frankenstein*, which constitutes the most extreme enactment of anxieties regarding the fleshing out of dreams.

Upstaging Prometheus

One measure of the distance that separates Romantic from Victorian world-views con-cerns the growing implausibility of heroes and classical notions of heroism after the 1820s. For various economic, political, literary, and military reasons, Romanticism has often been seen as marking the last stand of mythic or heroic individualism. After that, the theory goes, what is deemed representative—that is, what reading and viewing audiences are ostensibly seeking—concerns the common, the middling, the everyday. This and the next section explore this hypothesis by considering the post-Romantic stage history of two famous Romantic supermen, Prometheus and Byron, both of whom are vital to Romanticism and to measuring the distance between it and the

Victorian age. Romantic writers portray Prometheus as the archetypal revolutionary and friend of man in his twin roles as foe to tyranny (the only god to oppose Jove) and bringer of the arts to humanity (by stealing fire from Olympus). This twin legacy—rebel and artist—already announces the kinship of Prometheus to Byron and, more generally, to Romantic reconfigurations of the hero as poet. Byron is not the only Romantic writer who 'can easily conceive' the 'influence' of the 'Prometheus of Aeschylus' 'over all or anything that I have written'.[1]

Post-Romantic treatments of Prometheanism on stage accentuate several of the features normally ascribed to Victorian theatre in terms of its growing emphasis on realism, the common man, domesticity, commodity culture, and spectacle. Even more than in the Romantic period, the topic divides the dramatic from the theatrical, whereby the former presents a hero not envisioned for the stage and the latter makes a spectacle out of the period's scepticism towards heroism. A useful trajectory goes from Percy Bysshe Shelley's 'lyrical' drama, *Prometheus Unbound* (1820), written expressly for some twenty highly imaginative minds, to James Robinson Planché's *Mr Buckstone's Ascent of Mount Parnassus* (1879), a popular hit and anti-heroic sensation. This trajectory also indicates the interaction between genre and history, as plays concerning Prometheus shift from lyric or comedy to burlesque.

On the lyric or unstageable side are several mid-century translations and adaptations of Prometheus, including Elizabeth Barrett Browning's *Prometheus Bound. Translated from the Greek of Aeschylus* (1833), John Stuart Blackie's *Prometheus Bound. A Lyrico-Dramatic Spectacle* (1850), and Richard Henry [or Hengist] Horne's *Prometheus the Fire-Bringer* (1864). By and large faithful translations of Aeschylus, both Browning and Blackie's versions make some interesting 'Victorian' alterations to the Promethean legend. Browning's preface rebuts the view of the 'present age', that 'it has no need of translations from classic authors' on the grounds that 'there is one step from dreaming nobly to sleeping inertly; and one, from frenzy to imbecility'.[2] Indeed, it redefines 'classical' in a way that makes it indistinguishable from Romantic (not 'what is necessarily regular, and polished, and unimpassioned' but passionate and daring) and instances Prometheus of all classical heroes as one of the 'most original, and grand, and attaching characters ever conceived by the mind of man' (compare the chapter on 'Classical inheritances').[3] Blackie's Prometheus resembles Christ, overturning the Romantic alliance of Prometheus with Satan and their unrepentant spirits of rebellion. For example, Might tells Hephaestus to 'pierce his feet through with these nails' and Prometheus describes himself as being 'crucified' for having brought 'arts' and 'comforts' to humanity.[4] Moreover, the signs of Jove's tyranny are sentimentalized; he 'withhold[s] | The fellow-feeling and the tear', and denies 'merc[y]' to 'him whose crime was mercy to mankind'.[5] Plus, chances and mishap take the place of fate.

Horne's *Prometheus the Fire-Bringer* focuses on the earlier part of the legend that explains why Prometheus is bound, as punishment for bringing the arts to humanity. A prefatory note continues the Christianizing of the classics evident in Blackie by regarding Prometheus as 'the grand old Pagan archetype, and providential foreshadowing of the Divine Master who came upon the earth many centuries afterwards'. It also raises an up-to-date theatrical point about contemporary stagings of the classics. In protesting the 'vulgar' notion that 'Prometheus stole fire from Heaven', the preface attributes such views to the 'brutal prostitution of the popular taste' that is occasioned by 'burlesquing, with prodigal costliness, the noblest and the most beautiful subjects'.[6]

This protest voices a reality of Victorian staging, for burlesque *is* the chief form in which Prometheus and his fellow gods and goddesses make their appearance on stage from mid-century on. (In fact, burlesque is the distinguishing feature of Victorian theatre overall and is inseparable from its delight in spectacle.) This tendency, of representing the gods from an irreverent but affectionate perspective, is epitomized in the career of Planché, a hugely prolific playwright (author of some 180 pieces) who is best known for his extravaganzas and burlesques, eight of which concern familiar Greek myths. Initiating his fame in this genre is the punningly named *Olympic Revels*, mounted to celebrate the opening of the newly redecorated Olympic theatre on 3 January 1831, whose subtitle is *Prometheus and Pandora*. Memorable about this deflationary Prometheus is his status as 'an eminent *Man*-ufacturer', who 'pilfered coals' from the 'kitchen range' of Olympus to make men out of clay and whom Jupiter plans to punish by having him 'die of a liver complaint'.[7] Even more in the spirit of Victorian thematics, the men that Prometheus manufactures do not hold up well in battle because he has 'no English stuff to make 'em stronger'.[8] The hearth is stressed in Pandora's demand that Prometheus wed her, even though her sole possession is a (theatre) box.

One of Planché's last burlesques, *Mr Buckstone's Ascent of Mount Parnassus* (1879), makes the further linkage of stage Prometheanism to Byron. Written to celebrate J. B. Buckstone's assumption of the management of the Haymarket theatre in 1853, the play foregrounds the bankruptcy of poetic drama by having Buckstone decide that his best chances for theatrical success lie in producing an 'entertainment' on the model of Mr Smith's wildly popular *Ascent of Mont Blanc*. This decision comes after Buckstone has been visited by the spirits of several theatres who provide a revue of the most recent hits on stage (including *The Spirit of the Corsican Brothers*, *Gold*, and *Six Uncle Toms*) and their chief ingredients: 'Give me fun, splendour, music, dancing, dress | Those are the elements of my success.' Having rejected the 'horrid jargon' of contemporary drama, Buckstone's task is to find an appropriate mountain for his 'Ascent', to which Fortune proposes Parnassus, long unfrequented owing to the lack of aspirants to poetry.[9] Indeed, so foreign is Parnassus to the spirit of Fortune that a scene painter is called in to sketch the way, underscoring the huge divide between poetry and spectacle, especially on the score of turning a profit.

This expressed longing for the spirit of poetry to be revived introduces Byron, described as 'the latest, greatest, English pilgrim' to Parnassus. Twice Byron is cited approvingly as capable of 'improv[ing] the Drama's fortune'—and this in express contradistinction to Shakespeare.[10] Such preference for Byron is an accurate characterization of the state of Romantic poetic drama on the nineteenth-century stage, for Byron's are the only plays of the canonical poets that are staged during this period and his are neoclassical, rather than Shakespearean, in their tone of austerity and allegiance to the unities. The characterization also indicates the intellectual savvy, not mindlessness, of burlesque. For burlesque depends on an audience recognizing its puns and allusions to serious drama and, in its referencing Byron, playing off of Byron's own high spirit of fun. In citing the lines from *Don Juan* regarding the difficulty of making an adequate beginning, Planché's *Ascent* implicitly alludes to the poem's more famous comment on the lack of credible heroes that begins Canto I. It is this Byron, who 'wants a hero' and who mocks epic pretension, which Victorian stage representations of Byron most frequently take up. In this attitude as well he becomes their hero.

Lord, Byron

The fact that only Byron of the canonical Romantic writers survives on the post-Romantic stage speaks volumes about the ironies that attend theatre as a literary–cultural institution. The least Victorian of Romantic poets in terms of his attitudes toward sex, domesticity, morality, money, or England, Byron is the most Victorian in his delight in show. Put another way, whereas the conflicts explored by other Romantic poet-dramatists make them and their dramatic characters introspective, antitheatrical, and prone to monologue, Byron and his characters, even in their moodiness, are highly theatrical—despite, but also in, his declared ambivalence to theatre. For Byron is also the only Romantic poet to go so far as to get a legal injunction against Drury Lane for attempting to stage *Marino Falerio* (on 25 April 1821) while also continuing to write a series of plays thereafter (eight plays in total). Post-Romantic theatre has no such ambivalence about profiting from Byron's popularity, whether as poet, playwright, sexual iconoclast, or cultural icon, even when certain managers and actors, most notably Charles Kean and William Macready, try to honour the classical spirit of his plays. Victorian theatre produces several of his plays, transforms several of his poems into plays, and ascribes Byronic features to conventional or newly composed stage heroes.

Productions of Byron's plays throughout the nineteenth century confirm the anti-heroism and dominance of spectacle ascribed to Victorian theatre. We see this most vividly in his two most successfully staged plays, *Sardanapalus* and *Werner*, but accounts of the production of all of them foreground visual over verbal appeal. This is partly because at least half of the lines of Byron's history plays have to be cut in order for them to be staged—a normal acting play comprising no more than 1,800 lines and Byron's often exceeding 3,000—but it is also because of the spectacular nature of all of Byron's settings. Although Byron classifies *Manfred* 'A Dramatic Poem' and deems it '*quite impossible* for the stage', its Alpine setting and supernatural plot make it a likely stage sensation, especially once the Promethean and Faustian features of Manfred have been downplayed or excised.[11] This is the case with Alfred Bunn's 1834 *Manfred*, which capitalized on the current craze for witch drama and even required the construction of a new stage to accommodate the extensive scenery and amplified cast. With a success-ful run of thirty-three performances, Bunn's version established a stage tradition revived at Drury Lane in 1863 and the Princess theatre in 1873. To the extent the Promethean features of Manfred are recognized, they invite burlesque. Across town at the Strand theatre in 1834 Man-Fred is an unemployed chimney sweep.

Byron's history plays, even in their general sobriety, feature spectacular settings and stagecraft, which is always part, if not most, of the rationale underlying decisions to mount them. Of the three, *Sardanapalus* is the most successful (the other two being *Marino Faliero* and *The Two Foscari*), owing both to the peculiar nature of its protagonist and the exotic nature of its setting. The last of the Assyrian kings, Byron's Sardanapalus is a striking revision of heroism, composed as he is of indolence and courage, effemin-acy and power. Stage versions, instituted by Macready in April 1834, downplay the philosophical dimensions of Byron's rewriting of kingship that would be dwarfed in any case by this production's self-description as a lavish Assyrian panorama. Charles Kean's version (Princess, 1853) upped the spectacular ante by having live horses pull Sardanapalus's coach, accompanied by troops of spearmen, dancing girls, archers, standard- and fan-bearers. Hardly any play can compete with the terrific conflagration that ends the drama as Myrrha ascends Sardanapalus's funeral pyre. This scene was staged so effectively that, in more than one performance, audiences had to be reassured from the stage that the theatre was not on fire. But both productions also highlight the antiquarian and interdisciplinary dimensions of the period's delight in spectacle. Macready models the play's final scene on John Martin's famous painting, *The Fall of Nineveh*, and playbills to Kean's version boast that his is the first to present authentic Assyrian architecture and costume, thanks to the recent archaeological discoveries published in Sir Austen Henry Layard's illustrated *Nineveh and its Remains* (1849).

Virtually no one makes a positive argument for any of the elements that make *Werner* the acknowledged Byron favourite on the Victorian stage. Instead, they suggest that its popularity is partly owing to the weaknesses found in Byron's play—his shabby prot-agonist, repetitious dialogue, derivative and melodramatic plot—that some critics contend are an intentional commentary on the depraved tastes of nineteenth-century audiences. Sell-out or not, *Werner* is Byron's most popular play on stage, the only popular play that the Romantic poets contributed to the English theatre, and one of the most popular plays in the repertoire of the most important actor of the age, Macready (indeed, fifth, after his *Macbeth, Hamlet, The Lady of Lyons*, and *Virginius*). While the dignity that marks Macready's usual stage demeanour is arguably in keeping with Byron's classical tastes, the nature of the actor's fame in *Werner* bespeaks another irony of theatre history. For *Werner's* appeal is domestic, not neoclassical, a sentimental version of an anguished father. In this, it accords with another irony of the staging of *Manfred*, whose music, a major source of its success, is composed by the same man credited with writing 'Home, Sweet Home'. These facts help to identify through contrast the kind of anti-heroism that Byron enacts in and through his various protagonists, who, when all is said and done, finally have more in common with classical heroes than with the anti-heroes offered by domestic tragedy and its corollaries, bourgeois tragedy and she-tragedy. In this regard, it is not simply ironic that the most popular of all Byron's works in the theatre is not a play at all but the poetic frame tale, *Mazeppa*, adapted by H. M. Milner and first performed as an equestrian drama at Astley's Amphitheatre in 1831. Even more than its wild horses and scenery, the popularity of *Mazeppa* rests in a 1864 revival, when the title role was played by Adah Isaacs Menken dressed in exceptionally tight fleshings (in fact, posters depict her strapped to a horse naked). If this *Mazeppa* exceeds Byron's own delight in sexualized gender-bending, at least it does not commit the, to him, greater sin of treating love on stage in a 'melting & maudlin' fashion rather than as '*furious—criminal—*and *hapless*'.[12] For Byron is the least Romantic *and* the least Victorian in his wildly theatrical and self-dramatizing approach toward women and love.

Hideous stage progeny: *Frankenstein; or, The Modern Prometheus*

No fictional creation of any period is better suited to illustrating the discrepancies between page and stage or reading and viewing than Mary Shelley's *Frankenstein; or The Modern Prometheus* (1818). The most famous of modern-day myths, Frankenstein in the popular imagination has virtually nothing to do with Shelley's novel or the original Prometheus—right down to its reputation as spectacle rather than text and its name as referencing the creature (worse, 'monster') rather than its creator. From the start of its transformation into visual media in the 1820s and up to its still-current recurrent status as cult film, *Frankenstein* accentuates the spectacular over the textual, compressing the multi-layered action and soul-searching of the novel into highly melodramatic and/or Gothic scenarios. In virtually every nineteenth-century stage version, the creature not only steals the show but also is reduced to dumbshow—a far cry from the novel's focus on its moving life story that includes an account of its humanization through reading. Film only heightens this spectacle of the creature-as-spectacle, whose most enduring image remains an inarticulate Boris Karloff, stitched and bolted, arms outstretched, seeking its next victim.

On another level, the history of stage and filmic visualizations of *Frankenstein* has everything to do with two key aspects of Shelley's novel, beyond the obvious point that the book explores the dangers of materializing one's dreams. Admittedly to different ends and less-special effects, Shelley's *Frankenstein* itself is preoccupied with differences between viewing and reading. The creature's account emphasizes the leap in knowledge that comes when one learns to read books, not simply observe one's immediate surroundings. More importantly, it explains its eventual transformation into a fiend as the consequence of society's habit of judging others according to how they look rather than what they say or do, a point that underlies the feminist and anti-racist messages of the novel. This critique of a mindset or culture that prefers snap judgements to a careful reading of character is linked to the Prometheanism that the novel explores. But rather than establishing an opposition between heroic, or intellectually ambitious, young men (like Victor and Walton) and hoi polloi who pursue their menial routines, Shelley's *Frankenstein* censures its would-be heroes for not reading another's character—let alone the character of the other—in a sympathetic fashion.

Perhaps for these reasons, Shelley delighted in the first stage version of her novel, *Presumption; or, the Fate of Frankenstein*, adapted by Richard Brinsley Peake and performed at the Lyceum from 28 July to October 1823. While it seriously oversimplified the storyline, she found that *Presumption* also captured much of her novel's spirit, primarily owing to the acting skills of the well-known stage villain, T. P. Cooke, who played the creature. In fact, Cooke (the Boris Karloff of the day) played the role of the creature some 365 times over the next seven years and is credited with the extreme durability of the play. Though initiating the trend to portray the creature as mute and hyper-athletic, Cooke's portrayal does not associate its inarticulacy with dehumanization. One sign of this creature's sensitivity is its captivation by music (underscored in most subsequent versions), rendered even more touching by its efforts to grasp the sounds in its hand.

Meanwhile, Frankensteins were appearing all over the theatrical world, often already in burlesque form such as Frankenstitch (a tailor who stitches together parts of his workers' bodies), and Frank-n-Steam, or the Hobgoblin of Hoxton. Within three years of the first performance of *Presumption*, fourteen other English and French versions appeared, the most influential being Henry M. Milner's *The Man and the Monster; or, The Fate of Frankenstein* (Coburg, July 1826) and Jean Toussaint Merle and Antoine Nicolas Beraud's *Le Monstre et le magicien* (1826), translated by John Kerr and performed at the New Royal West London theatre in October 1826. To date more than 100 dramatizations have been undertaken, with a huge surge of plays in the 1970s, including Richard O'Brien's *The Rocky Horror Show* (1973) and Lemuel E. Harris's *Frankenstein is a Soul Brother* (1974). Even during the nineteenth century, far more people knew Frankenstein through visual media than the book, partly because later adaptations adapted earlier stage versions rather than returning to the novel. Similarly, popular print allusions to Frankenstein relied on the stage tradition, using the name to refer to the creature and to warn against innovation of any kind—whether freeing the slaves, reforming Parliament, or enfranchising the Irish. By the time that Frankenstein assumed its now-primary form as film, in 1931 with James Whale's version for Universal Studios, it had become totally unloosed from its textual origin. Moreover, its already rich stage history of parody, topical commentary, and buffoonery (for example, the 1940 play, *Goon with the Wind*) invited increasingly zany filmic extensions, most notably *I Was a Teenage Frankenstein* (1957), *Dr Frankenstein on Campus* (1970), *Young Frankenstein* (1974), and, in a more serious register, *Gods and Monsters* (1998).

This history of visual adaptations of *Frankenstein* becomes doubly ironic when versions are made to warn against or outright reject technology, since their appeal has always depended upon, and indeed triggered, ever-increasing technical ingenuity. Throughout the nineteenth century, the primary criterion for selecting which features of Shelley's novel to dramatize was the opportunity they provided for stage pyrotechnics. This is why stage versions invariably included Frankenstein's laboratory, the creature's animation, the burning of the De Lacy's cottage, the murders, and Alpine scenery and almost never portrayed the Walton frame narration, Victor's domestic upbringing, scenes of reading, or the creature's self-narration. Moreover, the specific nature of the warning against technology in *Frankenstein* also accurately characterizes the means and end of theatre: the dangers inherent in creating life artificially as well as animating artificial life. This is not to say that stage and film versions do not misconstrue or oversimplify Shelley's novel or that technology, in its interventions in and usurpations of human life, cannot get out of control. But the extraordinary vibrancy, multiplicity, and inventiveness of adaptations of this modern Prometheus underscore two lessons. Myths are never faithful to origins; humans cannot control what the creation of any new life will do to them, it, or the future. In sending forth her hideous progeny, Shelley displays a less phobic reaction to theatre, life, and its modes of reproduction than do poets who, in their alleged stage fright, seek to preserve their creations from the light or dark of day.

Afterlife now: Romanticism unbound; or 'cut'

The afterlife of Romanticism in the last two decades suggests that the drama of the Romantic period is finally coming of age. Signs of this maturity can be found in contemporary theatres and on the screen (both silver and computer). In the case of theatre, two situations converged in the past fifteen to twenty years that make it possible for audiences finally to see even the most allegedly un-actable Romantic drama on stage. One is a return to the more intimate setting and stage conditions of pre-Romantic theatre, available to managers and production companies since the tail end of the nineteenth century. The other is renewed scholarly interest in Romantic plays other than Byron's that makes at least certain persons eager to attend these plays.

Not surprisingly, viewing opportunities usually have been offered by university theatres, often in conjunction with an academic conference on Romanticism. For example, Yale Theatre Studies produced Wordsworth's *The Borderers* in 1987 and *Sardanapalus* in 1990, and the Rude Mechanicals performed Percy Bysshe Shelley's

Prometheus Unbound at the University of Texas, Austin, in 1998, with each act situated in a different venue on campus. Annual conferences of the North American Society for the Study of Romanticism have seized the opportunity to produce or sponsor several plays, including John Fawcett's *Obi; or Three-Fingered Jack*, Thomas Beddoe's *Death's Jest Book*, and Joanna Baillie's *Count Basil*. Arguably great plays, like Percy Bysshe Shelley's *The Cenci*, only had to await the first condition (coupled with a loosening of stage censorship) for various performances of it to occur during the late twentieth century, especially a brilliant production at the Alameida theatre in London in 1997 and a striking rewriting in George Elliott Clarke's *Beatrice Chancy*. A widening of audiences beyond Romanticists is promised by projects such as The First 100 Years: The Professional Female Playwright organized by the Juggernaut Theatre Co. in New York, devoted to reading and staging the works of Hannah Cowley, Elizabeth Inchbald, and Joanna Baillie (among others). But there are also popular plays that dramatize the lives of Romantic writers, including Howard Brenton's *Bloody Poetry* (1985) in which Byron, the Shelleys, and Claire Clairmont irritate each other to the amusement of Harriet Shelley's ghost, Ann Jellicoe's *Shelley; or, The Idealist* (1966), and, most famously, Tom Stoppard's *Arcadia* (1993) that updates the personages and activities of the Byron circle.

Most playnotes and commentary on the revivals (or, often, premieres) of Romantic plays assert that contemporary theatre conditions and sensibilities are more conducive to achieving the playwright's intended reception of these plays. If so, this stage history showcases the length of time that can separate the time of writing from the time of reception, especially when compositions are attempting to create new worlds. At the same time, we should not hurry to preclude entirely the dissonance attained by envisioning these plays on the spectacular stages of the nineteenth century. Surely *somebody* at the time had to be writing with these conditions in mind, possibly even to underscore experientially that any character's actions or soul-searchings always compete with surrounding attractions and, no matter how important, are overwhelmed by the splendours, congestion, and sheer scope of reality. From such a busy and enlarged perspective as is provided by the world of that stage, Victorian spectacular theatre reminds viewers that even supermen with their world-changing ambitions appear pathetic in their heroism and heroic in their pathos. Without this perspective, audiences in more intimate theatre settings become over-invested in feelings.

The second venue suggests Romanticism's renewed popularity to a wider audience. Screen images feature the unconventional lives of several Romantic writers and foreground precisely those elements that were decidedly unpopular in their day. The 'league of incest' known as the Byron–Shelley circle is a box-office draw, as evident in several recent films that foreground their sex lives as writers. Best known is *Gothic*, directed by Ken Russell (1986) and featuring Gabriel Byrne as Byron, Julian Sands as Percy Bysshe Shelley, and Natasha Richardson as Mary Shelley, but there is also *Haunted Summer* (dir. Ivan Passer, 1988), *Don Juan de Marco* (dir. Jeremy Leven, 1995), and *Remando al viento* (dir. Gonzalo Suarez, 1987, rereleased as *Rowing with the Wind* on Miramax video, 1999) with Hugh Grant as Byron and Elizabeth Hurley as Claire

Clairmont. (Truth is as strange as Romantic fiction.) Dozens of web sites attest to the iconic stature of Romantic writers and texts, including the voluminous links to *Frankenstein*, the interactive Villa Diadoti web space that places participants within the villa that Byron rented in 1816 on Lake Geneva, the bibliographies of 'Popular Romanticism' compiled by *Romantic Circles*, and Shelley Jackson's hypertext *Patchwork Girl*, that not only finally animates the female creature but also gives each of its body parts a separate life story.

Taken together, these contemporary acts of recovery show the vibrancy of current reincarnations of Romanticism and accentuate two other aspects of the myth comprising *Frankenstein*. Material is ideal in its powers of reproduction. There is something about the deadness of made objects that keeps both them and their receivers spirited, mutable, alive. Moreover, the longevity of Shelley's Prometheus shows that when women steal and catch fire, they underscore certain redundancies of life. The afterlife of Romanticism in the theatre puts into perspective what was opposed in discourse regarding the theatre of its day: recreation is art and is an art, but also art is dead.

FURTHER READING

Booth, Michael R., *Victorian Spectacular Theatre, 1850–1910* (Boston, London, and Henley: Routledge and Kegan Paul, 1981). Focuses on the spectacular aspect of Victorian theatre production as it was expressed in a variety of forms, especially melodrama and pantomine, and reconstructs two important productions by Henry Irving and Herbert Beerbohm Tree.

——*Theatre in the Victorian Age* (Cambridge and New York: Cambridge University Press, 1991). A comprehensive overview of the theatres, plays, actors, and managers of Victorian theatre that also provides a helpful chronology of dates associated with major theatrical events.

Cave, Richard Allen (ed.) *The Romantic Theatre: An International Symposium* (Totowa, NJ: Barnes and Noble Books). Contains four essays by different authors that discuss the textual and stage histories of plays by the canonical Romantic poets. It gives particular focus to Byron and Shelley.

Fisher, Judith L., and Watt, Stephen (eds.) *When They Weren't Doing Shakespeare: Essays on Nineteenth-Century British and American Theatre* (Athens, Ca: University of Georgia Press, 1989). A collection of essays describing the range of theatrical and dramatic material on the nineteenth-century stage, including melodrama, historical drama, pantomime, and spectacle.

Forry, Steven Earl, *Hideous Progenies: Dramatizations of 'Frankenstein' from Mary Shelley to the Present* (Philadelphia: University of Pennsylvania Press, 1990). Part I of this book focuses on three phases of dramatizations of *Frankenstein*: 1823 to 1832, the years of transformation and proliferation; 1832 to 1900, years of diffusion among the populace and in various media; 1900 to 1930, years when dramatic and cinematic interpretations vied for popularity. Part II provides the text of four plays from the first period.

Gillespie, Gerald, 'The Past is Prologue: The Romantic Heritage in Dramatic Literature', in Gerald Gillespie (ed.), *Romantic Drama* (Amsterdam: John Benjamins Publishing, 1994), pp. 429–51. A helpful overview of the legacy of Romantic drama in Victorian dramatic literature and theatre; it also discusses Romantic images in post-Romantic European and South American theatre with some attention to film and television.

Howell, Margaret J., *Byron Tonight: A Poet's Plays on the Nineteenth Century Stage* (Windlesham, Surrey: Springwood Books, 1982). Explores the productions of Byron's plays throughout the nineteenth century; contains a series of very helpful appendices, concerning twentieth-century productions of Byron, commentary on his alleged stage fright, and details relating to the staging of *Werner*.

Powell, Kerry, *Women and Victorian Theatre* (Cambridge: Cambridge University Press, 1997). An overview of women as actresses, theatregoers, and playwrights in Victorian England; it characterizes Joanna Baillie as mother to various Victorian daughter-playwrights.

Rowell, George, *The Victorian Theatre: A Survey* (Oxford: Clarendon Press, 1956). A good overview of the buildings, audiences, and types of plays associated with the Victorian theatre; also includes a play-list from 1792 to 1914.

St Clair, William, 'The Impact of *Frankenstein*', in Betty T. Bennett and Stuart Curran (eds.), *Mary Shelley in Her Times* (Baltimore and London: Johns Hopkins University Press, 2000), pp. 38–63. Surveys the publishing history of *Frankenstein* and the interaction between stage and filmic representations of *Frankenstein* and reprints or new editions of the novel.

Taylor, George, *Players and Performances in the Victorian Theatre* (Manchester and New York: Manchester University Press, 1989). Reconstructs what Victorian actors thought they were doing on stage; examines how changes in social, economic, and scientific conditions affected theatrical performances and underscores the seriousness of purpose, rather than extravagance, that characterized these performers.

Thorslev, Peter L., *The Byronic Hero* (Minneapolis: University of Minnesota Press, 1962). Explores various incarnations of the Byronic hero in Byron's works, including a chapter on Prometheus.

NOTES

1. *Byron's Letters and Journals*, ed. Leslie A. Marchand, 9 vols (London: John Murray, 1973–9), v. 268.
2. Elizabeth Barrett Browning, *Prometheus Bound* (London: A. J. Valpy, 1833), pp. vii–viii.
3. Ibid. pp. x, xiv.
4. *Prometheus Bound* (pp. 175–212) in *The Lyrical Dramas of Aeschylus*, trans. John Stuart Blackie (London: J. M. Dent; New York: E. P. Dutton, 1906), pp. 185, 186.
5. Ibid. 187, 189.
6. Richard Henry [or Hengist] Horne, *Prometheus the Fire-Bringer* (Edinburgh: Edmonston and Douglas, 1864), p. 7.
7. James Robinson Planché, *The Extravaganzas of J. R. Planché*, ed. T. F. Dillon Croker and Stephen Tucker, 5 vols. (London: Samuel French, 1879), v. 43, 46, 59.
8. Ibid. v. 54.
9. Ibid. v. 279, 282.
10. Ibid. v. 283.
11. *Byron's Letters and Journals*, v. 170.
12. Ibid. viii. 57.

41 | The idea of the author

Andrew Bennett

William Wordsworth's Preface to the second edition of *Lyrical Ballads* (1800) was written as a defence of the poems collected in those two extraordinary, ground-breaking volumes. In order to defend his often rather odd poems from what he felt had already been a hasty and unjust reception, Wordsworth developed an extended analysis of the nature of poetry itself. Revising the Preface in 1802, he elaborated this point by exploring a related but prior question: 'Taking up the subject, then, upon general grounds', he says, 'I ask what is meant by the word poet? What is a poet?'[1] Wordsworth's question marks a turning-point in the history of literature and literary criticism and expresses what we might take to be a central legacy of Romanticism. The question asserts the importance of thinking about the poet or author when we think about poetry or literature. In other words, it places at the centre of the literary work the subject who creates the work, the inspired author as original and originating genius. Wordsworth is asserting that to ask 'what is poetry?' is to ask 'what is a poet?' According to this thinking, poetry in particular *is*, in effect, an effect of the thoughts and especially the feelings of the author. To read a literary text is to read—to gain insight into, to understand, to communicate or commune with—its author.

The idea that the poet or, more generally conceived, the author is at the centre of the literary work is certainly not one that originates with Wordsworth. But it is an idea that was crucial to the reconception or even invention of literature at the end of the eighteenth century, and it is an idea that transforms the way literary texts are understood. If it changed the way texts are read, it changed too the way that, in their different ways, poets, novelists, dramatists, think about themselves as writers—and therefore the way that they write. The twentieth century saw repeated attacks on the Romantic idea of the author, including T. S. Eliot's modernist emphasis on the 'impersonality' of the author in 'Tradition and the Individual Talent' (1919), W. K. Wimsatt and Monroe Beardsley's seminal New Critical essay 'The Intentional Fallacy' (1946), and iconoclastic and equally influential post-structuralist essays by Roland Barthes ('The Death of the Author' (1967)) and Michel Foucault ('What is an Author?' (1969)). But the Romantic idea of the author continued and continues today to haunt literary criticism and the institution of literature itself. Indeed, one of the most important legacies of Romanticism is precisely the reaction *against* its celebration of the author that characterized literary criticism and theory for much of the twentieth century.

Even in the opposition that it has aroused, this privileging, this celebration of the author constitutes one of the enduring legacies of Romanticism. In this chapter we will examine some of the ways in which this uniquely paradoxical of figures, the Romantic author, is theorized, represented, and performed.

Lives of the poets

In many of the most well-known, most canonical works from the Romantic period, the very topic of the work becomes—either explicitly or as an easily decodable representation—the author himself. Thomas De Quincey, for example, became famous in 1821 by revealing intimate details of his life of opium dependency in *Confessions of an English Opium-Eater*. Although he carefully refrains from confessing his addictions, Samuel Taylor Coleridge's most important prose work, *Biographia Literaria* (1817), ranges unpredictably across languages, genres, discourses, and disciplines while still being, at least nominally, based around his own life. Despite his protestations against such readings, Lord Byron originally named the witty, world-weary hero of *Childe Harold's Pilgrimage* (1812–18) Childe Burun (an older version of his own name), and he leaves it open for us to think of Childe Harold as well as the perhaps more cynically ludic narrator of *Don Juan* (1819–24) as a version of himself. John Keats's lyric 'I' and its yearning invocations of nightingales, urns, and classical figures in his odes of 1819 appears to express, directly and sincerely, the sensations, feelings, and thoughts of the poet himself. Percy Bysshe Shelley's poems characteristically present a figure who might only too easily be taken for the poet himself: the visionary Poet embarks on an interminable quest for a 'Being whom he loves' in *Alastor* (1816), the eponymous hero engages in an agonistic struggle to speak, to produce language or poetry in *Prometheus Unbound* (1820), while the speaker laments Keats's death and dreams of joining him in the 'abode where the Eternal are' in *Adonais* (1821) (l. 495). And Wordsworth, undoubtedly the most self-obsessed of the canonical Romantic poets, insists despite his better instincts that he must write a thirteen-book autobiographical account of 'The Growth of a Poet's Mind' in *The Prelude* (1805) before he can embark on his projected epic, *The Recluse*; while in the Preface to the only major part of that epic published in his lifetime, *The Excursion* (1814), Wordsworth explains that although his work concerns 'Man, Nature, and Society' it has for its 'principal' focus the 'sensations and opinions of a poet living in retirement'.[2] There is perhaps nothing surprising, therefore, in the fact that writers such as Mary Shelley, in *Frankenstein* (1818), Thomas Love Peacock, in *Melincourt* (1817) and *Nightmare Abbey* (1818), and Byron himself, in *English Bards and Scotch Reviewers* (1809) and *Don Juan*, satirize, in very different ways, the aspirations of the Romantic author.

Characteristic of the Romantic idea of authorship is the sense that the experiences, the consciousness, the imagination of the author—and especially of the poet—are themselves the proper topic for the literary text. Indeed, as he begins the narrative of his own life in *The Prelude*, Wordsworth spends some time considering the various topics that an epic poem might address before declaring that there is only one suitable theme, the narrative of his own development as a poet. According to this somewhat tautological reasoning, the proper topic of poetry concerns the way that the poet's life has prepared him to write a poem about his own life. But there is a similar insistence on the importance of the author in Wordsworth's shorter, less conventionally autobiographical poem 'Tintern Abbey' (1798). Here he focuses on his own sensations and perceptions, his own thoughts and memories, as he stands in the Wye valley contemplating the scene and contemplating his experiences in the five years since he last visited the spot. Although Wordsworth in particular and the Romantic poets in general are often said to celebrate nature, what is meant by 'nature' in Romantic poetry involves a modification of the natural by the prosthesis of authorial consciousness: what is important in a poem such as 'Tintern Abbey' is not nature as such but the poet's perception of it, and indeed the sense that what the 'eye and ear' perceive they also 'half-create'. As Wordsworth establishes, the significance of the Wye valley, its very meaning, is contained within our understanding of the poet's experience of it. And the meaning of the poem is not so much the poem itself or the natural surroundings that it describes, as a 'presence that disturbs' the poet—the prior experiences, feelings, thoughts, perceptions, to which the poet alludes and by which he is inspired:

> And I have felt
> A presence that disturbs me with the joy
> Of elevated thoughts, a sense sublime
> Of something far more deeply interfused,
> Whose dwelling is the light of setting suns,
> And the round ocean, and the living air,
> And the blue sky, and in the mind of man—
> A motion and a spirit that impels
> All thinking things, all objects of all thought,
> And rolls through all things.
>
> (ll. 94–103)

The role of the reader, as she or he overhears this conversation of the poet with himself (and later with his sister), is to identify with, to experience, this experience, these feelings, this consciousness, and these thoughts. There is an explicit universalism in these lines, a declaration that this is the condition of all 'men'. But this universality is at the same time complicated by the singularity, the specificity, of the experience. The poet, author, or genius, in this high Romantic sense is constituted by his ability to be universal, to be an exemplary man, precisely by being unique. We are invited to respond to the author's sense of himself as at one with nature, to identify with the author's ability to transcend himself, to become nature. And it is this ability that, at the same time, marks the poet out as singular, unique, and uniquely privileged.

Inventing the author

What is it that engenders such a radical rethinking of the function of literature and the role of the author in the late eighteenth and early nineteenth centuries? There have been many attempts by critics and historians to link this literary revolution with wider social, cultural, and economic transformations in the eighteenth century. In particular, critics have pointed to dramatic changes in relationships between individuals, including authors and readers, consequent upon the complex social, political, industrial, and commercial developments analysed elsewhere in this volume (see also *Oxford Companion to the Romantic Age, passim*). These include the repercussions of the American and French revolutions in the last quarter of the eighteenth century; the expansion of the British empire; the move from a primarily agricultural to a primarily industrial economy, mass migration into cities, and a rapid growth in population; the increased availability of books consequent upon developments in print technology, distribution networks, and circulating libraries; the spread of literacy and public education, especially amongst women, and the increasing importance of women in the literary market-place; developing notions and practices of democracy and the popular franchise, the growing influence of corresponding societies on the political consciousness of artisans and working men, and the treason trials of the 1790s; the increasing commercialization of society and social relationships, and the burgeoning extent and influence of the middle classes; and finally the movement for the abolition of slavery and for the legal and political rights of women. These cultural and political changes were reflected in important and influential reconceptualizations of personal identity and the nature of subjectivity in the work of the British philosopher David Hume and the German philosopher Immanuel Kant as well as in a new recognition of the political subject's human rights in Thomas Paine's *The Rights of Man* (1791–2), Mary Wollstonecraft's *A Vindication of the Rights of Woman* (1792), and other works. Indeed, it is not too much to say that *authority* itself is in the process of being reconceived and redescribed in the late eighteenth and early nineteenth centuries. Such developments produced new reading audiences and new markets for books, newspapers, and literary journals, but they also radically altered the position of writers and the expectations of readers. Alongside and partly as a result of these important philosophical, social, political, and commercial developments in eighteenth-century culture, there were critical changes in the book trade and in the law of copyright that placed the author at the centre of the trade. Between 1710 and 1814, new copyright laws instigated a fundamental shift from booksellers' to authors' rights. Some historians of copyright and publishing even argue that what we might call the 'invention' of the modern concept of authorship in the eighteenth century was driven, not least, by developments in copyright law (see *Oxford Companion to the Romantic Age*, pp. 466–7). According to this argument, as the law changed to give authors—as opposed to publishers or booksellers— ownership rights over their works, literary and critical conceptions of the poem, novel, essay, or play shifted to emphasize the autonomy and originality of the individual who composes the work.

The new, Romantic conception of literature as a body of autonomous, imaginative writing was itself part of a paradoxical response to, as well as a reaction against, what amounted to a commodification of authorship. During the eighteenth century the economics of writing gradually began to shift away from the patronage system towards a more distinctly commercial transaction whereby authors are paid royalties and become central to the whole, newly commercialized publishing industry. On the one hand, the author rather than the bookseller or printer comes to be seen as the owner of the work, a work that is properly embedded within the capitalist economic system, within a commercial system of exchange. On the other hand, in direct contradiction to social, legal, and commercial reality, this commodification of authorship itself produces a counter-reaction in the ideal of the author as fundamentally *outside* any commercial system. When Samuel Johnson famously insisted that 'No man but a blockhead ever wrote, except for money', his 'strange opinion' (as his biographer James Boswell puts it) is at least in part a response to a fashionable eighteenth-century sense of the aristocracy of authorship, its rejection of payment for writing.[3] The aristocratic Lord Byron continued this tradition during his early writing career, but the Romantic poets more generally developed it into a declaration of independence from the market, from readers, booksellers, editors, and audiences. Indeed, Romanticism may be said to be defined in important respects in terms of its particular emphasis on the separation of one form of authorship from another—on the separation of the solitary, inspired, autonomous, intellectually or culturally aristocratic and even prophetic figure of the genius on the one hand, from the hack who writes for money or immediate acclaim, the professional writer, the 'useful drudge' (in Wordsworth's phrase), the hourly paid artisan or the professional wordsmith, on the other.

Posterity

Through a high-minded assertion of the poet's independence from the patronage of readers, the Romantic idea of the author is therefore inextricably bound up with the question of audience. As John Stuart Mill suggests in an 1833 essay 'What is Poetry?', and as is repeatedly asserted in the early years of the nineteenth century, the true poet, being 'overheard' rather than 'heard', should reject popular applause and write for posterity, for a timeless and anonymous audience of the future.[4] But this again produces a paradox in relation to the Romantic conception of authorship, since while major figures of the period rejected considerations of popularity, they were also acutely aware of the potential rewards to be gained from tapping into the new audiences for literary works. Poets such as Byron, Sir Walter Scott, Mrs Hemans, and Letitia Landon were able to sell thousands, indeed tens of thousands of volumes of their books. By contrast, the sales figures for poets such as Wordsworth (until he was well into middle age), Coleridge, Blake, Shelley, and Keats were almost always disappointing—and all except the virtually unknown Blake were subject to mixed and often aggressively critical reviews in literary journals. The tempting but out-of-reach prospect of a mass audience provoked a sense of dislocation, alienation, and disillusionment in poets who rarely managed to sell more than a few hundred copies of their volumes of verse, and this uncertain and difficult reception might itself be said to have increased the significance of a proper posthumous appreciation.

A new emphasis emerges in Romantic writing, then, an overriding emphasis on the traditional distinction between two different kinds of poetic reception: immediate and popular applause on the one hand and an initial rejection followed by a more lasting and a more properly appreciative reception on the other. Itself a traditional trope of literary reception, the idea produces a relatively new celebration of the neglected poet and a firming-up of the idea that the genius is, to put it anachronistically, avant-garde, ahead of his time. William Hazlitt declared that true fame is 'the recompense not of the living, but of the dead'; Coleridge insisted on the distinction between eternal 'fame' and contemporary 'reputation'; Keats declared that he would be 'among the English Poets' but only *after* his death; Shelley argued that the poet is the '*unacknowledged legislator*' of the world. And in his 1815 'Essay, Supplementary to the Preface', Wordsworth presents a brief and historically inaccurate history of English poetry designed to demonstrate that contemporary neglect has always been the fate of poets of genius: every original writer, Wordsworth sententiously declares, 'has had the task of *creating* the taste by which he is to be enjoyed'.[5] It is this conception of authorship that becomes established in the later nineteenth century and the early twentieth century as an 'aestheticist' conception of art, of 'art for art's sake', and as a celebration of the author as 'ahead of his time', as avant-garde. Modernist writers like Stéphane Mallarmé, James Joyce, Ezra Pound, and T. S. Eliot developed a taste for what (in a poem of that name) W. B. Yeats calls 'The fascination of what's difficult' (1910), cultivating an aesthetics of obscurity which was specifically designed to resist the bourgeois satisfactions of what Samuel Johnson called the 'common reader'.

Genius, originality, inspiration

The Romantic rethinking of the role of the author, then, places a crucial emphasis on the idea of the author as fundamentally apart from, fundamentally separate from, society. Indeed, the Romantic author is ultimately seen as different from humanity itself, as both an exemplary human and as somehow above or beyond the human, as literally and figuratively *outstanding*. The Romantic author—particularly the poet in the fullest, most ideal sense—is opposed to the writer, the scribbler, the journalist, or literary drudge and is conceived as a subject inspired by forces outside himself, forces that allow him to produce work of originality and genius. The work of the genius is fundamentally new: that is what makes him a genius (see *Oxford Companion to the Romantic Age*, pp. 629–30). One of the most influential proponents of originality in literature was the eighteenth-century poet Edward Young. Young's *Conjectures on Original Composition*, first published in 1759, helped to establish originality as a key component in thinking about literature. In an argument that is itself in fact far from original, Young identifies originality with genius. But this originality is itself profoundly strange. It is, at some level, inexplicable. Genius, Young argues, involves 'the power of accomplishing great things without the means generally reputed necessary to that end'.[6] Such a formulation points to another paradox of Romantic authorship: in the ideal author, in the genius, there is a mysterious disjunction of cause and effect. There is no reason why the genius is able to create the works that he creates. The idea is fundamental to an understanding of the Romantic theory of authorship, a theory that both asserts the importance of the genius himself and, at the same time, asserts that the genius is beyond the self of the genius. Coleridge, for example, declares that genius involves 'unconscious activity' and that this activity is itself 'the genius in the man of genius'. Similar analyses can be found throughout the Romantic period and beyond, particularly in relation to the way that genius is linked to inspiration. In his *Essay on Genius* (1774), for example, Alexander Gerard argued that 'the fire of genius, like a divine impulse, raises the mind above itself, and by the natural influence of imagination actuates it as if it were supernaturally inspired'. More prosaically, in an essay entitled, precisely, 'Whether Genius is Conscious of its Power?', William Hazlitt declared that the very definition of genius is 'that it acts unconsciously' and that 'those who have produced immortal works, have done so without knowing how or why': Shakespeare, he argued, 'owed everything to chance, scarce anything to industry or design'. At its most radical, William Blake asserted, apparently without irony, that he had written *Milton* (1803–8) 'from Immediate Dictation without Premeditation & even against my Will'.[7] While Romantic poetry and poetics celebrate the individuality of the author or genius, then, they also assert that the essence of genius is an ability to transcend the self, to go beyond that which any mortal, fallible individual is capable. The poet, John Keats declares in a letter of 1818, is 'not itself—it has no self—it is everything and nothing—it has no character': the poet is 'the most unpoetical of any thing in existence, because he has no identity'.[8] In addition to instituting the self as at the centre of poetics, Romantic writers in fact also developed a sense of the impersonality of the poet that was to be developed in reaction *against* Romanticism by writers such as Gustave Flaubert, Stéphane Mallarmé, Paul Valéry, T. S. Eliot, Ezra Pound, and James Joyce in the later nineteenth and twentieth centuries.

If a defining element in the Romantic invention of the modern sense of authorship is the notion of genius, then, a defining element in the notion of genius is the genius's own ignorance—what Keats calls his 'negative capability'.[9] Writing in around 1775, the French writer and encyclopaedist Denis Diderot wittily summed up this sense of the poet's own ignorance of his work when he declares that poetry 'supposes an exaltation of the brain that comes, one could almost say, from divine inspiration. The poet', he goes on, 'has profound ideas without knowing their cause or their effects. The philosopher, in whom these same ideas are the fruit of long meditation, is amazed at this, and exclaims: Who inspired so much wisdom in that maniac.'[10] Along with classical notions of inspiration expressed in such texts as Plato's *Ion* (c.390 BC) and Longinus' *On the Sublime* (1st century AD), such ideas had enormous influence on the work of the poet and literary theorist Percy Bysshe Shelley (compare the chapter on 'Classical Inheritances'). In his 'A Defence of Poetry' (written in 1821), Shelley argues that ignorance both is and fundamentally is not intrinsic to poetry, to the work of the poet. Responding to Peacock's declaration in 'The Four Ages of Poetry' (1820) that modern poets are 'wallowing in the rubbish of departed ignorance', Shelley declares both that poetry is the 'centre and circumference of knowledge', and that it is 'not subject to the control of the active powers of the mind' and has 'no necessary connection with consciousness or will'.[11] Poets, Shelley says, are themselves 'the most sincerely astonished' at their own work, 'hierophants' as they are of an '*un*apprehended inspiration', their words expressing 'what they understand *not*'.[12] Shelley's declaration of poetic independence serves to resurrect and radicalize the ancient tradition of the poet as irrational, crazed, or inspired: he is responding, not least, to Socrates' declaration in *Ion* that the poet is a 'light and winged and sacred thing' who is unable to compose 'until he has been inspired and put out of his senses, and his mind is no longer in him'.[13]

Craze

Such was the attention to the sublime capabilities of the man of genius that in certain cases the figure of the author was something of a craze in the early nineteenth century. Lord Byron in particular achieved the kind of popularity to which only pop stars, actors, models, and sportsmen and women can aspire in our own age. But if the author was a craze, authorship was itself in some respects crazed, or seen as crazed. As we have seen, for Diderot the inspired author is a 'maniac', in an intensification of the ancient tradition that the poet's mind is, in Socrates' words, 'no longer in him'. The Romantic craze of authorship, though, had its darker side and, crazed or not, inspired or not, a major dimension of authorship was the representation of the poet or genius as a danger to conventional, respectable society, to the morality and mores of, especially, the burgeoning middle classes. Byron's fame had much to do with his aristocratic affront to such conventions. His fame, indeed, was largely based on a sense—a sense that he wittily and wittingly exploited both in his poems and in his behaviour—that, as Lady Caroline Lamb excitedly declared, he was 'mad, bad, and dangerous to know'.

More generally, the Romantic author was increasingly represented as allied with the mad, the vagrant, the subversive, even the criminal. Coleridge's protagonist in his mock-balladic 'The Rime of the Ancient Mariner' (1798; 1817) is perhaps the most famous example of an isolated, tortured, and self-torturing figure. With his 'glittering eye', his 'skinny hand', and his gloomy, compulsive sense of having committed an obscure, irredeemable crime, the Mariner embodies a peculiarly Romantic conception of the outsider. But he is also a storyteller, a poet of sorts. The Mariner stops the wedding guest in his tracks, turning him away from the matrimonial feast, and insists, despite the guest's protestations, that he will recount his strange, appalling tale—a tale of crime, isolation, starvation, death, haunting, and of supernatural retribution and redemption. As he ends his narrative, the Mariner explains that, like a poet, he is both gifted and cursed with 'strange power of speech'. He is indeed gifted with poetic powers, with the power to enthrall his listener, and cursed at the same time by this very gift and by the impulse to wander the world telling his ghastly tale:

> Since then, at an uncertain hour,
> That agony returns,
> And till my ghastly tale is told,
> This heart within me burns.
>
> I pass, like night, from land to land,
> I have strange power of speech;
> That moment that his face I see,
> I know the man that must hear me—
> To him my tale I teach.

(ll. 582–90)

This strongly compelling figure of the poet is not just socially outcast but is also socially disruptive, subversive, a dissonant voice of sanity and insanity, of sanity *in* insanity. In 'Kubla Khan', a poem written at about the same time as 'The Ancient Mariner', in the winter of 1797–8, Coleridge presents a similar conception of poetic alienation. When it was eventually published (in 1816), 'Kubla Khan' was prefaced by an explanation that it had originated in a dream. Coleridge explains that his dream and therefore his poem was catastrophically interrupted by a man from Porlock coming to call. The poem and the dream are incomplete, fragmentary: that catastrophe is the source of their power. At the end of 'Kubla Khan' the poet declares that if he had been able to remember his dream-vision, if he had been able to 'build that dome in air'—if he had been able to write the vision and become a poet, an author—then society would have had to guard against his power by observing rituals of exorcism and control:

> And all should cry, 'Beware! Beware!
> His flashing eyes, his floating hair!
> Weave a circle round him thrice,
> And close your eyes with holy dread—
> For he on honey-dew hath fed
> And drank the milk of paradise'.

(ll. 49–54)

The Romantic idea of the author is a site of paradox. The author is celebrated for being himself and celebrated for going beyond himself; he is at the same time personal and impersonal; he is neglected in his own time but is destined to be revered by posterity; he is all too human and he is beyond humanity; he is at the centre of culture but proudly marginal; he is neglected but can be the subject of a craze; he is crazed but his insanity is also a deeper form of sanity; he is powerless, disenfranchised, politically subversive, or socially irresponsible but also celebrated as the unacknowledged legislator of the world; he is unique, singular, individual, and he is universal, everyman, an exemplary human being. And while the Romantics made Wordsworth's question 'what is a poet?' as well as the wider question 'what is an author?' central to their radically new poetics and literary theory, the legacy of the Romantic idea of the author is itself paradoxical. Later in the nineteenth and in the early twentieth centuries, writers such as Gustave Flaubert, Stéphane Mallarmé, James Joyce, Katherine Mansfield, Ezra Pound, and T. S. Eliot developed theories of the impersonality of the poet, and in the mid-twentieth century the new critics rejected the 'intentional fallacy' and post-structuralist theorists announced the death of the author. Such poets and critics may be understood to be reacting against, to be resisting, the Romantic concentration on, the Romantic celebration of, the author. But, in a final paradox, it is precisely in this resistance to authorship that modernists, New Critics, post-structuralists, and others may be said to pay homage, may be said to be most in thrall, to an essentially Romantic idea of the author.

FURTHER READING

Abrams, M. H., *The Mirror and the Lamp: Romantic Theory and the Critical Tradition* (New York: Oxford University Press, 1953). The standard account of the move from classicism to Romanticism in literary theory; still a basic starting-point for the study of ideas of authorship in the period and for an understanding of later critiques of the Romantic author.

Bennett, Andrew, *Romantic Poets and the Culture of Posterity* (Cambridge: Cambridge University Press, 1999). Explores Romantic poets' anxieties concerning audience and the importance of the idea of posthumous reception for their poetry and their poetics.

Clark, Timothy, *The Theory of Inspiration: Composition as a Crisis of Subjectivity in Romantic and Post-Romantic Writing* (Manchester: Manchester University Press, 1997). An important post-structuralist analysis of the role of inspiration and its centrality for a certain rethinking of Romantic poetics.

Clery, E. J., Franklin, Caroline, and Garside, Peter (eds.) *Authorship, Commerce and the Public: Scenes of Writing, 1750–1850* (Basingstoke: Palgrave Macmillan, 2002). Essays on the material conditions of authorship, writing, and publication in the period.

Newlyn, Lucy, *Reading, Writing and Romanticism: The Anxiety of Reception* (Oxford: Oxford University Press, 2000). A wide-ranging discussion of Romantic conceptions of readership and audience and their implications for the Romantic rethinking of authorship.

Ross, Marlon, *The Contours of Masculine Desire: Romanticism and the Rise of Women's Poetry* (New York: Oxford University Press, 1989). Ground-breaking discussion of the importance of masculinity in the high Romantic ideal of authorship, arguing that this is itself a response to the threat perceived in the 'rise of women's poetry'.

NOTES

1. William Wordsworth, Preface to *Lyrical Ballads*, in Duncan Wu (ed.), *Romanticism: An Anthology*, 2nd edn. (Oxford: Blackwell, 1998), p. 360: unless otherwise stated, quotations from Romantic poems are taken from this anthology.

2. William Wordsworth, *The Poems*, ed. John O. Hayden, 2 vols. (Harmondsworth: Penguin, 1977), ii. 36.

3. James Boswell, *Life of Johnson* (1791), ed. R. W. Chapman (Oxford: Oxford University Press, 1980), p. 731

4. John Stuart Mill, 'Thoughts on Poetry and its Varieties', in *Autobiography and Literary Essays*, ed. John M. Robson and Jack Stillinger (Toronto: University of Toronto Press, 1981), p. 348.

5. *The Complete Works of William Hazlitt*, ed. P. P. Howe, 21 vols. (London: Dent, 1930–4), v. 143; *Collected Letters of Samuel Taylor Coleridge*, ed. E. L. Griggs, 6 vols. (Oxford: Oxford University Press, 1956–71), iii. 277–8; *The Letters of John Keats*, ed. Hyder E. Rollins, 2 vols. (Cambridge, Mass.: Harvard University Press, 1958), i. 394; Percy Bysshe Shelley, 'A Defence of Poetry', in Wu (ed.), *Romanticism*, p. 956; *The Prose Works of William Wordsworth*, ed. W. J. B. Owen and J. W. Smyser, 3 vols. (Oxford: Clarendon Press, 1974), iii. 80.

6. Edward Young, *Conjectures on Original Composition*, ed. Edith J. Morley (Manchester: Manchester University Press, 1918), p. 13.

7. Samuel Taylor Coleridge, 'On Poesy or Art', in *Biographia Literaria*, ed. J. Shawcross, 2 vols. (Oxford: Oxford University Press, 1907), ii. 258; Alexander Gerard, *Essay on Genius*, in *Eighteenth-Century Critical Essays*, ed. Scott Elledge, 2 vols. (Ithaca, NY: Cornell University Press, 1961), ii. 894; Hazlitt, *Works*, xii. 118; *The Poetry and Prose of William Blake*, ed. David Erdman (New York: Doubleday, 1965), p. 697.

8. Wu (ed.), *Romanticism*, p. 1042.

9. Ibid. 1019.

10. Quoted in Paul Bénichou, *The Consecration of the Writer, 1750–1830*, trans. Mark K. Jensen (Lincoln, Neb.: University of Nebraska Press, 1999), p. 31.

11. Thomas Love Peacock, 'The Four Ages of Poetry', in *Romantic Critical Essays*, ed. David Bromwich (Cambridge: Cambridge University Press, 1987), p. 208; Shelley, 'Defence', in Wu (ed.), *Romanticism*, pp. 953, 955.

12. Ibid. 956; emphasis added.

13. Plato, *Ion*, trans. W. R. M. Lamb (London: William Heinemann, 1952), p. 423 (534B).

| # Modernism and postmodernity

Edward Larrissy

Modernism is a movement which, while it had various different tendencies, often prized a concentration on the essential, the avoidance of extraneous comment, and an analytic approach to form such as one can find in Cubism. Many canonical modernist writers define their work in opposition to Romanticism, or to nineteenth-century writing in general. In the latter case, it is clear that they are opposed to tendencies which they believe originated in the Romantic period, and it is easy to show that late nineteenth-century writers still found models there. Oscar Wilde, for instance, when he visited Rome, went to the Protestant cemetery to pay respects at Keats's grave, which he did by prostrating himself upon it. A more serious way of putting it would be to observe that the late nineteenth-century cult of beauty and intensity, in which Wilde participated, was indeed indebted to Keats—or at least to a certain reading of Keats. Again, W. B. Yeats, whose mature work is often classified as modernist, began his career by taking Blake and Shelley as models. He subsequently turned his back on what he came to see as the vagueness of late Romanticism, but this may not be sufficient to establish that he turned his back on Romanticism. And it must be doubted whether he ever repudiated Blake. Of course, as we shall have to remember, Romanticism is a big word covering many and diverse phenomena. But there is no doubt that the qualities the modernists depreciated can be found in many Romantic writers. Among these are discursiveness, the emphasis on personality, the use of the language of the emotions, and the aesthetic ideal of organic form. Furthermore, modernists may go on to implicate these qualities in a threat to civilization itself. Irving Babbitt, professor of French at Harvard, was an important influence on T. S. Eliot, who attended his lectures as a student there. In his *Rousseau and Romanticism* (1919) he traces the threat back to the eighteenth-century philosopher Rousseau (see *Oxford Companion to the Romantic Age*, pp. 684–5). Babbitt sees a link between Rousseau's Romantic emphasis on individual experience and what he regards as the dangerous simplicity of his political ideas, which are profoundly influential on modern liberal and democratic thought. By contrast, Babbitt espouses tradition and classicism. This connection sheds light on Eliot's prizing of tradition and impersonality in his essay 'Tradition and the Individual Talent', where he also aims a blow at Wordsworth's idea of 'emotion recollected in tranquillity', laying emphasis rather on the impersonality of the artistic process. Furthermore, in line with Babbitt's suspicion of Rousseau's political inheritance, one must see Eliot's later profession of 'conservatism' as intimately related to his own anti-Romantic and supposedly classical critical theories. On the other hand, it should be noted that Eliot's conversion to Christianity would not have been pleasing to Babbitt, who espoused classical humanism. There are parallels between Babbitt's thought and that of T. E. Hulme, who is best known as an Imagist poet and associate of Ezra Pound. In his *Speculations* (1924) Hulme contrasts the vague idealism of Romantic art with the 'dry hardness' of classicism, and he sees the twentieth century as bringing a new classical movement to birth. In particular, he prizes the precise rendering of a physical image; and one can see how this ideal is related to his involvement with Imagism. Pound himself advocates 'direct treatment of the thing' and derides the 'slither' and 'mush' of the nineteenth century. The modernists, then, tended to prize impersonality, direct- ness of presentation, and often, as one finds in Pound, the analogy of mechanical or sculptural form, as opposed to organic form. These ideals correspond to identifiable features of modernist writing, and they were worked out in conscious opposition to Romantic models (compare the chapter 'Literary criticism and theory').

As new modes of writing became established, academic critics, especially in the newly developing subject of English Literature, developed techniques of reading which were consonant with a distrust of vague feeling and unanalysed response. The trad- ition of Practical Criticism initiated by I. A. Richards sought to specify the features of the poem from which affect, and therefore value, was derived, and this way of reading was deeply influential upon F. R. Leavis, William Empson, and ultimately the American New Criticism. Often Romanticism was found to be wanting: Leavis, for instance, analysed the supposed incoherence of the imagery in Shelley's 'Ode to the West Wind' and castigated the poet for his 'weak grasp upon the actual'. By 1936, F. L. Lucas, in his *Decline and Fall of the Romantic Ideal*, though agreeing with many of the criticisms, felt it necessary to defend Romanticism from the worst excesses of the anti-Romantics.

Modernist debts to Romanticism

But the situation is not clear-cut. It is also possible to think of modernism as a continu- ation of Romanticism. Perhaps the most abidingly influential exposition of this idea is to be found in Frank Kermode's *Romantic Image* (1957), which shows how the concen- tration on the image in Yeats, Pound, and Eliot has its roots in the Romantic period: to be more specific, it demonstrates how distrust of discursiveness, and a concomitant reliance on the radiance of the image, had already begun in that period. The images of the dancer and the chestnut tree in Yeats's 'Among School Children' have a lineage which goes back through *symbolisme* to the epoch of Wordsworth: *The Prelude*'s 'spots of time', the depiction of the Leech-Gatherer. On these grounds, Kermode sees even Hulme as indebted to Romanticism. The thesis is persuasive, and it is possible to won- der if Kermode could not have found even broader support for it than he offers: for instance, more could surely have been made of radical developments in dramatic monologue in the Romantic period, such as can be found in Blake's *Songs of Innocence and of Experience* (1794), where part of the point is to offer inwardness with the particularity of a state of mind (innocent or experienced) rather than an abstract account of it.

Other critics have followed in Kermode's path: George Bornstein, for instance, in works such as *The Postromantic Consciousness of Ezra Pound* (1977), has demonstrated the influence of the Romantic tradition on Pound. Carlos Baker, in *The Echoing Green* (1984), has noted the importance of certain Romantic poems for key modernists. And Michael O'Neill, in *Romanticism and the Self-Conscious Poem* (1997), shows how the self-consciousness of the modern poem about its own status as artefact has deep roots in the similar self-consciousness of Romantic poems. Keats's 'Ode on a Grecian Urn' provides a usefully obvious example.

Much of the influence is unacknowledged. And in line with this point, some critics have gone even further, claiming that the rejection of Romanticism often conceals a debt to the very qualities that are decried. Thus Eliot, despite his talk about classicism and his concept of the 'objective correlative', remains a poet of 'feeling', as his theoretical pronouncements confirm. And while 'feeling' may not be 'emotion' (a word less favoured by Eliot), it is hard to see it as a centrally classical or neoclassical critical category. Indeed, Edward Lobb, in *T.S. Eliot and the Romantic Critical Tradition* (1981) sees even Eliot's critical ideas as profoundly indebted to Romanticism, especially to Coleridge and Keats. But it is equally important to recognize that his poetry is evocative and emotive in ways which exhibit a debt to the Romantic tradition.

But the debt may be larger even than that. Geoffrey Thurley, in *The Romantic Predicament* (1983), points out that one of the most significant changes to occur in much Romantic writing is that it concentrates on objects, apparently for their own sake. So far from being vague about the object, Romantic writers (and painters) exhibit an unprecedented tendency to record it accurately. In painting, one might claim that the work of Constable (see *Oxford Companion to the Romantic Age*, pp. 464–5) provides analogies with certain accuracies to be found in, for instance, the landscape poetry of Coleridge and Wordsworth. Thurley does not claim that most Romantics are content, as some modernists might be, with the accurate recording of impressions: they often have an ulterior motive, for instance of a transcendentalist kind, and this also comes across. The point is that by the Romantic period it had become very difficult simply to assume that nature is a book of sacred emblems, the keys to which are handed down by tradition: the world is now a problem to be recorded, explored, and probed for solutions by the individual artist. That sounds close to the predicament of the moderns; and furthermore, it is hard to avoid the conclusion that modernist precision is indebted to the prior experiments of the supposedly vague Romantics and their Victorian successors.

The story so far leads to a rather odd-sounding conclusion: that many modernists are indebted to Romanticism both for a suggestive evocativeness they affect to despise and for a clarity which they admire but claim is anti-Romantic. In my own book on *Reading*

Twentieth Century Poetry (1990) I seek to offer a partial explanation of this strange formation in modernist poetry as the performance of ideologies of gender, and the poet's self-representation in these terms: thus some canonical male modernists represent themselves as possessing a kind of masculine hardness in virtue of the accuracy and precision they profess, and the supposed Romantic qualities to do with feeling, suggestion, and the organic are disavowed as too feminine. Pound's critical pronouncements are fairly explicit on these lines. At the same time, the spell exerted by those supposedly feminine qualities remains strong. However, this can hardly be an exhaustive explanation, and other factors, such as the spread of technological innovation, probably play their part.

Modern Romantics

'Modernism' is a big word, covering a variety of phenomena. Furthermore, we can be misled by it into thinking that all writers in the modern period were 'modernists'. This is a tendency which is increasingly encouraged by university courses which concentrate on the highly significant innovations of modernism. But things did not seem so clear-cut in the age when the modernists themselves were writing. Some writers continued to imitate nineteenth-century models, and some innovators appear to be working with assumptions which are most sensibly described as Romantic. D. H. Lawrence is an example of an important writer who, while he exhibits modernist tendencies, can just as easily be classified as belonging in the Romantic tradition, and not merely, like Pound and Eliot, as indebted to Romanticism at certain points (compare the chapter on 'The Novel'). Relevant facts here would be the strong visionary strain in both his fiction and his poetry, the invoking of analogies from nature (for instance, in *The Rainbow*), and the unabashed use of the language of the emotions. One might attempt to offer his brief association with Imagism, his use of free verse, and his prizing of directness as evidence to the contrary, but, as we have seen, these things are not sufficient in themselves to establish a clear divorce from Romanticism. Slightly more contentiously, a similar claim, though on different grounds, can be made about Yeats. If one accepts Kermode's thesis about the Romantic provenance of modern uses of the Image, then there can be little doubt about the self-contained organicism embodied in the Dancer and the Tree in 'Among School Children': they are late Romantic developments. And this is a late poem, from Yeats's supposedly post-Romantic phase. Furthermore, Yeats's doctrine of the Mask, which is often said to be impersonal and modernist, is itself intimately connected with the Image: the Mask is an image of a person. Yeats's great occult system, expounded in *A Vision* (1926 and 1933) makes the position clear: the great organizing symbol of this work is that of the phases of the moon, with their cycle of changing darkness and light. The light of the moon, or lunar quality, represents subjectivity, dreaming, the ages of romance and heroism; the dark, or solar quality, represents reason and objectivity. Yeats is in no sense impartial: he clearly prefers the subjective, and the terms in which he makes this preference clear seem to align him with Romanticism. Harold Bloom, in his *Yeats* (1970), has done much to ensure that readers acknowledge these facts.

Later Romantics

Furthermore, after the period of high modernism there continue to be writers who think of themselves as working within the Romantic tradition: Dylan Thomas, for example. Or else, like Kathleen Raine, the debt seems clear enough, even if, as in her case, they might claim to be invoking a tradition older still than Romanticism. Thomas's work, for instance in 'Fern Hill', is indebted to Blake, to the Wordsworth of 'Intimations of Immortality', and of course to Yeats, for images of innocence and experience, of a redeemed and miraculous nature, and of the poet as visionary. As a critic, Kathleen Raine reads Blake as a visionary reinterpreter of an ancient mystical tradition incorporating the truths of neo-Platonism, the Kabbalah, and philosophical alchemy. While her own poetry is gentler and less assertive than that of Blake, it is clear that she sees herself as being in the same tradition. Both Thomas and Raine began to publish in the 1930s, and achieved strong recognition in the 1940s, a period when there was a neo-Romantic revival in Britain, for which the explanation is often sought in a sense of spiritual crisis occasioned by the Second World War. This, at any rate, was the decade of the New Apocalypse, a grouping associated with the anthology of that name (1939), which included Henry Treece and Vernon Watkins, and which recognized Thomas as a master. In the 1940s it was still possible for Herbert Read, in a widely read critical book, *The True Voice of Feeling* (1947), to claim that T. E. Hulme, T. S. Eliot, and Ezra Pound were the heirs of Wordsworth and the Romantics. He identified the concept of 'organic form' as the chief element in this tradition, but also referred to imagination, sympathy, and feeling.

The continuation of Romanticism did not go unrecognized in the following decade. In the same year that Kermode's *Romantic Image* was published (1957), John Bayley's *The Romantic Survival* appeared. Its thesis is rather different and states that Yeats, Auden, and Dylan Thomas are indebted to Romanticism for their prizing of qualities of mysteriousness, wonder, and innocence, but have given it new life by engaging with the reality of the modern world. Auden is something of a surprise, and indeed, if these big words mean anything he cannot be described as a Romantic. Nevertheless, there is the troubling fact that the young Auden recognized Blake as his master, along with Marx, Lawrence, and Freud. This influence makes itself felt in the sharp antagonisms of the early work: the encounters between the Enemy and a sick society, the parodies of a degraded Christianity in *The Orators*. Arguably such effects are indebted to Blake's *The Marriage of Heaven and Hell*. Here we have an example of the way in which the moderns (not all of them: Eliot would be an exception) often find Blake more palatable than the other Romantics. This is a significant fact, which provides us with a neat way into our next topic.

Modern constructions of Romanticism

If Modernism is a big misleading word, so is Romanticism. The writers we now describe as Romantic are not always the same as those who were regarded as important in the Romantic period—during which the word 'Romanticism' as we use it did not even exist. In that period, Samuel Rogers and Thomas Moore were highly regarded poets, there was a significant readership for Charlotte Smith (see *Oxford Companion to the Romantic Age*, pp. 680–1, 609–10, 709), and Blake was seen as a minor figure. Rogers wrote *The Pleasures of Memory* (1792), in its day one of the most celebrated poems of the 1790s. It is composed in heroic couplets which are squarely in the neoclassical trad-ition, and owe nothing in respect of form to the innovations or revaluations being promoted by other poets of the period. As with modernism, so with Romanticism, we need to see beyond later constructions in order to gain a more objective impression of the past. Over the nineteenth century the list of Romantic poets who have dominated the anthologies in the twentieth century emerged. And when one looks at the qualities which promoted them, one finds that it is possible to fit them into an account which leads up to modernism. One may start in the early Victorian period by noting the emphasis on the pleasure of poetry in the critical thinking of John Stuart Mill (see *Oxford Companion to the Romantic Age*, pp. 602–3) or Tennyson's friend Arthur Hallam. This pleasure is ensured by the poet's concentration on feeling or states of mind, which the poem must become an instrument for embodying. The mood poems of Tennyson, 'Mariana' for instance, answer to this type of description. But the source of the critical ideas is to be found in the Romantic period, especially in Coleridge's *Biographia Literaria*. Such thinking leads on to the poetry of the Pre-Raphaelites, to the theories of Walter Pater, and to the emphasis on lyric poetry exemplified in the most widely read anthology of the second half of the nineteenth century, *Palgrave's Golden Treasury* (1861), a volume which conveys no notion of the longer poems of Wordsworth or Shelley. It does not seek to do so: it avowedly represents only lyrical poetry, but this choice, and the popularity of the anthology, are both significant of a movement in taste. Of course, it would be a grotesque oversimplification to claim that the Victorians never wrote a more reflective or discursive type of poetry: some of the Pre-Raphaelite poets found that Tennyson and Browning were too long winded. But by the end of the nineteenth century the doctrine of pleasure and the intense realization of feeling and states of mind leads to the impressionism to be found in the lyrics of Wilde or Arthur Symons, the latter a great supporter of *symbolisme* and an influence on both Yeats and Eliot. The impressionistic urban poetry of Symons's *London Nights* (1895), with their gaslights and actresses, constitutes a definite link between the Romantic tradition and poems such as Eliot's 'Preludes'. In sum, one can offer a plausible account of the development of modernism as the acceleration of tendencies towards directness and intensity of presentation which have their roots in the Romantic period.

It often seems that Blake is more favoured than other Romantic artists in the modern period. In this connection, then, it is instructive to note that Symons was also an admirer of Blake, and wrote a book about him (1907). It is not surprising to find that he emphasizes the intensity and suggestive power of Blake's poetry, effectively assimilating him to a tradition that includes Pater and the French *symbolistes*. And this was the way in which Blake started on his progress towards the eminence he enjoys today, even though the political radicalism we nowadays refer to was not much discussed, and the detailed workings of his symbols were relegated in favour of the idea that he was a pure lyric poet. Blake seemed to offer an aesthetic boldness, suggestiveness, and ardour. This is what Wilde meant when he said that in modern times, Blake was one of the greatest exponents of 'the Greek spirit'. That Blake also offered a kind of immoralism in *The Marriage of Heaven and Hell* (1793) did not hurt his case with writers who admired Baudelaire. Thus Blake began to enjoy fame in an environment where what one might call 'pre-modernism' was being gestated. It seems that adventurous writers were looking for models in certain types of Romantic writing, while rejecting other types. All of this indicates that Romanticism as the twentieth century knew it only came into existence at the same time as tendencies towards modernism were developing: indeed, it suggests that the two processes are intimately related.

Postmodernity and postmodernism

As we move into the latter half of the twentieth century we enter the age of postmodernity, an age of increasing doubt, uncertainty, and moral relativism. In Britain, although critics such as Kermode and Bayley might chronicle the Romantic survival, the 1950s writers reacted against Romanticism: Kingsley Amis's poem 'Against Romanticism' castigates dangerous apocalypticism and vagueness, and also reveals a desire for an age completely cleansed of faith or ideology: in post-war Britain one should avoid the fanaticisms which led to totalitarianism and war. And by the same token, one should avoid the neo-Romanticism of Dylan Thomas. Amis is associated with the Movement, a group of poets which also included Philip Larkin, Thom Gunn, and Donald Davie. Their ideals comprised reason, clear structure, unostentatious diction, metrical conservatism, and ironic wit. Even so, rebellions against predecessors are not always clear-cut: the early poetry of John Wain, also associated with the Movement, still bears the imprint of Thomas's influence. A contemporary of these poets, Ted Hughes, was often unconvincingly bracketed with Gunn. But Hughes always seemed to owe more to Lawrence than to the rationality invoked by the Movement, and in the quasi-mythological and decidedly unmelodious songs in *Crow* (first edition 1970), which sometimes parodies Genesis, critics have discerned a similarity with another book that does this, Blake's *The Book of Urizen* (1794). This is not a far-fetched suggestion. Hughes's interest in mythology and philosophical alchemy (alchemy interpreted as spiritual symbolism), although it owed something to the psychologist C. G. Jung, makes Blake a sympathetic forebear. Such a suggestion would be supported by works such as *Cave Birds: An Alchemical Cave Drama* (1978), which presents the reconciliation of the sexual contraries by reference to the idea of an alchemical marriage: that is, to the many symbols of the marriage of opposites which are to be found in the alchemical tradition, a tradition upon which Blake was drawing in *The Marriage of Heaven and Hell*.

In America significant poets are clearly indebted to Romanticism: Allen Ginsberg's long-lined urban prophecies recall Blake, who is an oft-mentioned point of reference in his poems. When Ginsberg asserts in *Howl* (1956) that 'Everything is holy!', he is nearly quoting Blake from *The Marriage of Heaven and Hell*. Nor is this merely a matter of the vague adoption of prophetic uplift, for Ginsberg is also influenced, in his critique of American imperialism, by the political element in Blake's works, specifically by *The French Revolution* (1791). The poets associated with Black Mountain College combine indebtedness to Pound and William Carlos Williams with a conscious Romanticism: Charles Olson's notion of the poet's energy being conveyed to the page in an open form is a contemporary reinterpretation of organicism, and often comes accompanied with a rather inflated idea of the poet, as in the appropriately entitled *Maximus Poems* (1960); Denise Levertov has written an essay on the concept of organic form; and Robert Duncan's work includes 'Variations on two Dicta of William Blake' and 'A Set of Romantic Hymns'.

Another important fact is the increasing popularity, on both sides of the Atlantic, of Gothic fiction (a mode related to Romanticism: see *Oxford Companion to the Romantic Age*, pp. 526–7). This suggests that we are haunted, in an increasingly complicated and technologized world, by dark dreams which cast doubt on the rationality which is supposed to govern our lives. There appears to be an understanding of the close link between the literature of terror and the contemporaneous phenomenon of Romanticism: this, at any rate, is indicated by a popular novel such as Tom Holland's *The Vampyre: The Secret History of Lord Byron* (1995), or by Ken Russell's film *Gothic* (1987), an excited representation of Byron and the Shelleys in Switzerland.

The most obvious concept which relates to the Gothic within high Romanticism is that of the sublime (see *Oxford Companion to the Romantic Age*, p. 723), an aesthetic and experiential category which, like the Gothic, comprises the emotion of terror, especially in the version of it promoted by Edmund Burke (see *Oxford Companion to the Romantic Age*, pp. 435–8) in his *Philosophical Enquiry into the Origin of our Ideas of the Sublime and Beautiful* (first edition 1757). Other ideas Burke relates to the sublime include 'vastness' and 'obscurity'. These last points are subject to a development in the German philosopher Immanuel Kant's *Critique of Judgement* (1790), such that there is an emphasis on the gap between the vastness of the conception and our inability to represent it. This idea is picked up by the contemporary French philosopher Jean-François Lyotard in his much-discussed theories about postmodernism. He claims that the modernist avant-garde, with its problematization of representation, is the inheritor of the Kantian Sublime. Furthermore, he claims that postmodernism is similarly indebted. But there is also a difference: modernism remains nostalgic for a great truth, or a 'grand narrative', as he sometime calls it, whereas postmodernism is liberated from this requirement and happy to engage in the play of forms. This would certainly accord with the common usage, which has more or less gained acceptance, whereby postmodernism (unlike postmodernity) is a term referring to cultural phenomena which exhibit in their very technique (and not just their themes) the uncertainty and relativity of our age. Postmodernist works are often acutely self-conscious, parodic, or they foreground indeterminacy. In these characteristics, they are sometimes indebted to modernism. That is to say, in terms of artistic form there does not seem to be much that Joyce or Eliot or the early Auden could learn from a postmodernist, were they to come back and visit us. But Lyotard's contention is that the postmodernist may learn from modernist techniques but does not share in the nostalgia which, for instance, leads Eliot and Auden back to Christianity. From our point of view, however, the most interesting thing about Lyotard's analysis is that it states that the ancestry of both modernist and postmodernist aesthetics is to be found in the Romantic period, specifically in the concept of the Sublime.

But possibly a distinction between modernist nostalgia and postmodernist irony would be too rigid. Indeed, perhaps the Romantic period itself contains harbingers of postmodernist irony. For instance, could not the pervasive irony, the scepticism, the playfulness, and the ironic use of form in the poetry of Byron provide a case in point? Such, at any rate, is the claim made by Drummond Bone, in my edited volume *Romanticism and Postmodernism* (1999). So we are beginning to accumulate a number of features of postmodernism which may have remote antecedents in the Romantic period: irony, the attempt to represent the unrepresentable with the assistance of formal innovation, a strong interest in Gothic romance. To this we might add a tendency on the part of some writers to lose patience with Anglo-American modernist ideas about accuracy and the fear of abstraction or adjectives. One way of losing patience is to write in a loftily expressionist manner which is indebted to a certain strain in Romanticism. Thus the American poet John Ashbery can start a poem with these lines: 'How much longer will I be able to inhabit the divine sepulcher | Of life, my great love?' Ashbery, an ironic poet addicted to self-conscious parody, whose work often conveys a disquieting sense of the isolation of the contemporary city, is uncontroversially seen as a postmodernist, and he quite often uses language such as this. One has the feeling that he is thumbing his nose in a rather camp fashion at modernist aesthetics.

So there is evidence that Romanticism can be found in the postmodern. A refinement of this idea (and one that is itself typically postmodern) is to realize that we are probably continuing to create Romanticism in our own image, just as the modernists did. So we are confronted with a kind of two-way street: the postmodern is both indebted to Romanticism, and at the same time creating it. In any case, it appears that there can as yet be no end to the usefulness of the words 'Romantic' and 'Romanticism' in describing new art. Possibly this is because, since the period of the bourgeois revolution, of which the French Revolution is the most striking manifestation, innovations in art have tended in a certain direction: have borne the imprint of isolation and alienation, and offered art as a surrogate for religious certainty or as a rebellious means of challenging an intolerable status quo. This would mean that postmodernist art can be understood in relation to a deepening of uncertainty and alienation in the contemporary period. At least one postmodernist poet shows an awareness of this kind of possibility: Paul Muldoon, in his long poem *Madoc* (1990), creates a parallel universe where Coleridge and Southey go to America and carry out their plan to found a primitive communist community, something they never in fact did. In depicting their encounter with the native Americans, the poem raises troubling questions about the implication of Romantic ideology in self-deceiving narratives about the enlightening effects of colonization. But this is only one of the ways in which it suggests that we are still in the post-Romantic universe. The poem is playfully divided into many subsections which are given the names of thinkers, from the pre-Socratic Thales to the contemporary Stephen Hawking. In this respect, the poem looks like a potted history of Western thought. Yet it is set in the Romantic period. One implication is that we can only see the big questions about existence in terms bequeathed to us by Romantic philosopher-poets such as Coleridge. As yet we cannot see beyond the Big Bang with which, the poem suggests, that universe may come to an end.

FURTHER READING

Bloom, Harold, *The Visionary Company: A Reading of English Romantic Poetry*, 2nd edn. (London and Ithaca, NY: Cornell University Press, 1971). The poet glimpses a transcendent vision, but this is threatened by reality; this is the problem for the Romantic tradition, which stretches into the twentieth century.

Kermode, Frank, *Romantic Image* (London: Routledge and Kegan Paul, 1957). Modernist concentration on the image has its roots in Romanticism.

Larrissy, Edward, *Reading Twentieth-Century Poetry: The Language of Gender and Objects* (Oxford: Blackwell, 1990). Modern poets are indebted to the descriptive precision to be found in much Romantic poetry, even as they seek to stigmatize Romanticism as vague in terms which suggest that it is too 'feminine'.

——(ed.), *Romanticism and Postmodernism* (Cambridge: Cambridge University Press, 1999). A collection of essays exploring the theoretical issues and analysing examples of the connection.

O'Neill, Michael, *Romanticism and the Self-Conscious Poem* (Oxford: Clarendon Press, 1997). The unparalleled self-consciousness of the Romantic poem is the corollary of the poet's anxiety about the significance of poetry, and modern poets inherit this situation and are conscious of their Romantic forebears.

What was the political legacy bequeathed to us by the Romantics and how positive is it? At first it might seem odd or even perverse to want to view the Romantic poets and writers as political thinkers rather than as creative artists and visionaries; yet, even in their own day, the leading Romantics were perceived as very political animals and their works were seen as contributing to the current debates of the times. The period coincided with the French Revolution and Napoleonic wars; with the most intense agitation against the transatlantic slave trade and the institution of slavery (formally ended by Britain and its colonies in 1807 and 1833 respectively); with the development of colonial and imperial ambitions around the globe, but especially in India and the Near East; and with the rise and professionalization of new sciences, such as anthropology and ethnology. Most of those whom we regard as the canonical Romantic poets wrote political tracts and treatises, or made their views known in other ways. Not simply important for their own times, the Romantic writers have left us with a series of legacies and problems, not always inspiring and aspirational.

A Romantic ideology?

One of the most influential ways of reading the political and cultural legacy of the Romantics is defined in Jerome McGann's phrase 'A Romantic Ideology'. McGann famously accused the canonical Romantic poets (chiefly Wordsworth and Coleridge) of achieving a separation between politics and art, stressing the transcendent and universal at the expense of the political and local. McGann argued that the scholarship of Romanticism and its works is dominated by this 'Romantic Ideology', that is, by an uncritical absorption in the ways in which the poets represented their own work and art. He argued that Romantic poetry is characterized by its employment of forms of displacement which resituate human issues in idealized localities beyond the realm of the political. The 'Romantic Ideology' thus displaces and idealizes, privileging imagination at the expense of history and hiding social conditions in its quest for transcendence. This idealistic image of an organic society and a progressive history serves the interests of the ruling class and helps to maintain the status quo. Thus Wordsworth's theory of 'natural piety' whereby human beings are nurtured and sustained by the permanent and abiding forms of nature, as developed in, for instance, 'Lines written a few miles above Tintern Abbey' and *The Prelude*, is seen as complicit with a conservative-minded project to turn people away from attempting to change society by political means. Similarly, Coleridge's interest in the transcendentalist philosophies of Immanuel Kant and his idealist successors, Fichte and Schelling, marked an attempt to divert people from material protest to a spiritual politics which is essentially quietist. The notion that the Romantic ideology displaces the historical, social, and political tensions of the time into an ideal realm of imagination, or nature, is one that has encouraged an extensive debate in Romantic studies and has been the catalyst for the production of a substantial number of books and articles. Generally associated with McGann in what became known as the New Historicist school of Romantic studies are the names of David Simpson, Marjorie Levinson, Marilyn Butler, and Alan Liu. These critics have accused the Romantics of a variety of historical displacements, absences, and evasions by which the historical, social, and economic realities are repressed in fabricating an ideology of unity and harmony.

Behind such criticism is the assumption that any movement from the economic, social, and particular, to the pastoral and domestic, is de facto an act of apostasy which all will recognize as such. All turns from economic and social realities are therefore to be characterized as evasions. Wordsworth should be depicting charcoal furnaces in the Wye valley and Keats should be discoursing about the Corn Laws in his ode 'To Autumn' rather than the mysterious cyclical processes of nature. This view, however, excludes from consideration the Romantics' other, political poetry as well as their many letters, essays, and other documents that indicate humanitarian, social, and political concerns in the period; the method is to define by exclusion. So, for such critics, the Romantic political legacy is one of betrayal, in which we are encouraged to avoid the concerns of the material world and seek solace in a transcendental world of art.

A green Romanticism?

Rather than the Romantic concern with the natural environment constituting an evasion of the political, others see this very concern as representing a valuable legacy for the present time. Such critics trace a line from Wordsworth and Coleridge through the nineteenth-century thinker John Ruskin to our present 'green' or ecological consciousness, regarding the interest in the functioning of the natural economy not as an escape from political reality but as an immersion in the debates of the day. One of the consequences of this ecocritical endeavour has been the recovery of the 'peasant poet', John Clare, for the Romantic canon. For critics such as Jonathan Bate and James McKusick, the chief political legacy of Romantic writing lies in its broadly political concern with the environment, a green politics clearly present and not evaded by the poetry. Though others may take Wordsworth to task for reneging on his youthful political activism, Bate argues that Wordsworth's politics were truly green and that he is the first authentic ecological poet in English. His message has a strong relevance to our own contemporary concerns with the depletion of the ozone layer, the damages of acid rain, the disappearance of the tropical rainforests, the development of energy-saving technology and cleaner engines, and the problems of industrial pollution generally.

In Romantic works, such as Coleridge's 'Eolian Harp' and Wordsworth's 'Ruined Cottage', an environmentalist view of the world is developed. Despite the suffering involved in the story of Wordsworth's Margaret, a victim of economic distress, there is a consolation and inner peace to be gained from contemplating her human tragedy in the context of the natural world. Humanity perseveres in the face of suffering but is also somehow transformed by it and reconciled with the natural cycle. For Bate and others, an ideology based on a harmonious relationship with nature goes beyond the narrow parameters of political programmes and reaches out to human sympathy and embraces a holistic conception of our place in the world. It is a plea for human understanding and community against the alienating tendencies of modern, especially urban, life. Crucial to this reading is Wordsworth's ideal of the independent landowner, the statesman, as representative of the free liberty-loving human being. Similarly, in Coleridge's concern with the organic metaphor as a way of describing human society and artistic composition, Romantic ecocritics have discovered an attempt to develop the idea of a holistic conception of poetic form. In a different way, the writings of the poet John Clare have been understood to represent an ecological consciousness. Clare was an impoverished Northamptonshire agricultural labourer who wrote extensively about the local flora, fauna, and village life of Helpston and its environs. He decried the incursions of economic and social progress into the local environment, criticizing the destructions of forests and wetlands, the disappearance of streams, and the enclosure of common lands. He writes about the value of weeds and of wastelands in a poetic language which he describes as 'green'.

Radicals or reactionaries?

The green reading of Romantic writing attempts to evade the left–right political division that originated with the French Revolution and which still describes our political activity today; however, many contemporary political thinkers have directly responded to the Romantic political inheritance. Some critics of the Romantics have argued that their work forms a part of a radical, or at least, a democratic and reformist tradition. Certainly the traditional reading of British Romanticism, prior to the New Historicist critique, was that it was somehow related to the revolutionary tide sweeping the Western world in the late eighteenth and early nineteenth centuries. William Wordsworth, widely regarded as the chief poet of the movement, was a supporter of the revolution and a democratic and republican. He became interested in the revolution while at Cambridge and toured France on foot in 1790 and again in 1791–2, enthusiastically witnessing the Fête de la Federation celebrating the first anniversary of the revolution. His unpublished political pamphlet of 1793, 'A Letter to the Bishop of Llandaff', defended the regicide and attacked the established government of the day. Samuel Taylor Coleridge, along with his fellow West Country poet Robert Southey, were both radicals in their youth; Coleridge was a Unitarian Christian, a dissenter in politics and religion. Southey and he developed a scheme for emigration to the United States where they would found a small communal settlement of twelve couples practising community of property, a scheme referred to by them as 'Pantisocracy' (see *Oxford Companion to the Romantic Age*, p. 635). Coleridge lectured in Bristol in 1795 against the established Church and state, arguing for a more representative government and for civil and religious liberties. William Blake developed a more extreme and visionary form of revolutionary politics which transcended the political framework that contemporary radicals and reformers operated within. His prophetic writings made up an apocalyptic politics which called for the overthrow of all hierarchies, political, religious, and artistic, and a re-evaluation of humanity. Blake remained sympathetic throughout his life to the French Revolution and subsequent revolutionaries have found his ideas tractable to their own projects. Of all the canonical Romantic writers, however, it is Percy Bysshe Shelley whose work is most apparently revolutionary in scope and style. Karl Marx's daughter, Eleanor Marx Aveling, argued that the poet had anticipated the leading tenets of nineteenth-century socialist thought. Shelley combined a visionary politics and poetics in works such as his 'Ode to the West Wind', *Queen Mab, The Revolt of Islam, Prometheus Unbound*, and 'The Masque of Anarchy' with some detailed pragmatic political critiques, such as his 'A Philosophical View of Reform'. He was famously expelled from Oxford in 1811 because of his pamphlet, *The Necessity of Atheism*, and he proselytized against the Act of Union of Ireland and England and in favour of Catholic Emancipation. Intimately related to his political radicalism was his advocacy of vegetarianism. In his 'A Vindication of Natural Diet' and 'On the Vegetable System of Diet' he considered meat eating as a consequence of the Fall and argued that it led to disease and ill health, and involved extensive animal cruelty (see *Oxford Companion to the Romantic Age*, p. 744). Certainly vegetarians and socialists, such as George Bernard Shaw, have often quoted the examples of Percy and Mary Shelley. The legacy of the political and radical writings of the Shelley circle was not simply concerned with domestic politics. Shelley's writings and those of his friend George Gordon, Lord Byron, have been seen as important works in the struggle for national liberation in Europe, especially in the case of Greece. The highly influential cult of the Byronic hero as national liberator began to take shape in this period. Byron espoused the cause of the Greek people and their bid for national independence from the oppressive and faltering Ottoman empire. He intervened in the politics of Greek nationalism taking charge of his own brigade of Greek soldiers, but died from illness at Missolonghi in 1824. Byron became for many an image of disinterested patriotism and a Greek national hero, remaining a powerful icon, certainly to revolutionaries and nationalists such as the Italian liberators Mazzini and Garibaldi.

If one trend of Romantic writing has been seen to lead to a political tradition of radicalism and reformism then another led to a politics of conservatism. The main thrust of this charge results from the accusations of Byron, William Hazlitt, Thomas Love Peacock, and others that Wordsworth, Coleridge, and Southey forsook a radical youth for a conformist and staid maturity. The implication is that, in doing so, they essentially sold out. Wordsworth certainly sought the patronage of Sir William Lowther, the Earl of Lonsdale, the head of the most powerful aristocratic family in Cumbria and was appointed, with his patron's help, to the lucrative sinecure, the post of Distributor of Stamps for Westmorland in 1813; a favour he repaid by assisting the Lowthers in parliamentary elections. Robert Southey became the Poet Laureate in 1817 and published his *Vision of Judgement* in 1820, which depicted the joyful admission to Heaven of George III, and the consequent damnation of his radical critics, in whose ranks Southey was once enlisted. Similarly Coleridge renounced his earlier Unitarianism dissent for a socially conservative platform; yet Coleridge's 'recantation' or, according to Byron and Shelley, his apostasy, was not quite so simple. Even as a dissenter in *The Watchman* (1796) and elsewhere, he had argued for the positive role of government in education and in improving the lives of the lower classes. Always wary of the kind of demagoguery he himself once essayed, he developed a philosophy of government that was paternalist but also progressive. He consistently argued against the harsh materialist utilitarianism that came to dominate the nineteenth century, pleading that human beings should not be treated as things or abstract qualities in the calculations of political economists. In his mature work, *On the Constitution of the Church and State* (1828), he proposed the formation of an educated class, or clerisy, which would mediate between the demands of the growing commercial economy and that of the landed interest. Optimistically, he believed that the Church of England was capable of being reformed and energized to perform this educative task. Nevertheless these views were profoundly influential on the new generation of Christian Socialists, such as F. D. Maurice, and the later idealist political thinker T. H. Green, and they lay behind the foundation of King's College, London. Importantly Coleridge was an influence on the 'one nation' conservatism of Benjamin Disraeli: a strain of thinking that remains influential to the present day. Although 'one nation' thinking has been eclipsed on the right in recent years by the hegemony of Margaret Thatcher's revival of economic liberalism within the British Conservative Party, many might argue that it remains present in the New Labour emphasis on duties as well as rights, a political attitude that derives its pedigree from Christian socialist forebears.

Nationalism, imperialism, and orientalism

Recently, it has been claimed by a number of critics that Romantic writing is complicit with both the growth of nationalism and with theories of biological racism, which, having led to the later twentieth-century excesses of National Socialism, continue to bedevil the relationships within and between communities of peoples today. The issue is an extremely sensitive and complex one, too dangerous to be given up to easy summary, but basically the argument maintains that there is some kind of analogy or congruence between the development of Romantic theories of art and the idea that human beings can be divided into morphologically stable types with fixed physical, moral, and mental characteristics. These trends, one scientific and one cultural, were also concomitant with the rise of a new imperialism in which the Western European powers (and especially Great Britain) came to dominate the globe; a hegemony predominantly justified by ideas of racial superiority.

This charge against the Romantic poets and writers is based on their participation in two different, but related, intellectual currents of the late eighteenth and early nineteenth centuries: the first is cultural and political, the second, scientific. The first relates to the growing nationalist consciousness which the Romantics as a whole did so much to foster. In 1960 the intellectual historian Elie Kedourie argued that German idealist and Romantic writing fostered a belief in the national consciousness, and especially the German psyche, that contributed to the rise of Adolf Hitler's National Socialism. More recently, Martin Bernal has argued that Romantic writing, in particular that of German writers, was complicit with the exclusionary project of eighteenth-century neoclassicism to deny the contributions of black African history and thought to Greek classicism, nurturing an Aryan myth of the origins of Western civilization. For Bernal the influential philosopher J. G. Herder's work was crucial in constructing a linguistic community of people, united by their contribution to their nation's culture; each ethnic group thus possesses a *Volksgeist* (or folk soul) manifested in a language, folklore, poetry, and the arts. Herder was a cultural pluralist, arguing that all nations' cultures were equally authentic; nevertheless he wrote of the importance of each nation preserving its cultural inheritance and remaining separate from foreign or cosmopolitan contamination. Herder's preference for the national state as the authentic political voice of a people was combined with the privileging of the northern European at the expense of the cultures of other nations. Wordsworth's championing of the independent statesman of the Cumbrian Lake District and his insistence on the authenticity of the experience of the rural denizens of this area over and above the refinements of metropolitan civilization could be seen as complicit with this tendency. In *The Excursion* (1814) he writes how such values as these will be exported to the rest of the world in a hegemonic enterprise. These tendencies have led post-colonial critics, such as Gauri Viswanathan, to argue that colonial administrators in nineteenth-century India and elsewhere discovered an ally in English literature to support them in maintaining their hegemonic control of native peoples. Indeed, Thomas Babington Macaulay's famous 'Minute on Education' of 1835 dismissed the entirety of oriental learning as inferior to 'a single shelf of a good European library'. Certainly Romantic-period texts came for many to embody the superiority of Britishness and Christianity. It is not fair to blame Romantic writers for the uses made of their work by others; nevertheless it could be argued that these imperial tendencies were implicit in their writings. Coleridge, for instance, supported colonialism as an important national duty. This imperial dimension is also evident in Anna Letitia Barbauld's apocalyptic satire, *Eighteen Hundred and Eleven* (1812) which links English language and culture to the imperial project. In this work, Barbauld imagines a future in which the intellects of the peoples of the globe are instructed with the philosophies of Locke and Paley and in which the works of Milton, Shakespeare, Pope, and others provide the educational basis of their lives.

It is not just the exporting and universalizing of British culture that have troubled critics of Romanticism in recent years, but also the way its writings represent other cultures and peoples. The Romantic period coincided with the most intense activity in opposition to the transatlantic slave trade and the institution of slavery as well as with colonial activity in the Near East and India. Numerous male and female writers wrote in opposition to the slave trade during the period (and some in its favour), including William Cowper, Hannah More, William Blake, Anna Barbauld, Samuel Taylor Coleridge, Olaudah Equiano, and many more. Though opposing the trade, many of the representations of African people in these writings are deeply suspect. Ultimately most, including Equiano, favour the commercial development of African nations combined with a Christianizing project: the beginnings of the substantial Protestant global missionary endeavour of the nineteenth century.

So too in its representations of the East has Romantic writing left, or at least contributed to, an abiding legacy. Edward Said argued that from around 1798 onwards (the date of Napoleon's invasion of Egypt) British and French imperial ambitions in the East were reflected in the growth of the scholarly discourse known as 'orientalism', which he believes to be a Western mode for allowing the domination of the Orient (see also the chapter 'Easts'). Said has argued more recently that this discourse of orientalism, which pretends to know and classify the East, persists today and informs the ways in which the West interprets its other. For Said the prevalence of such semi-mythical ideas in the Western consciousness has contributed to its misunderstanding of the Gulf War of 1991, the spate of suicide bombings following the outbreak of the second Palestinian Intifada, the events of 11 September 2001, and (at the time of the writing of this chapter) the American and British occupation of Iraq. Said has argued that traditional Western orientalist scholars have helped to justify the Gulf War and the war in Iraq by appealing to ideas about the 'Arab mind' and that they are implicated in the dehumanization of Arab and Muslim peoples who are increasingly regarded as violent irrational terrorists, oppressors of women, and exponents of barbaric punishments and mutilations. Said singles out contemporary scholars as perpetrators of these views but he argues that the origins of their distortions lie in the late eighteenth century. Certainly some of the stereotypes of the oriental East, developed in a series of works by Romantic writers, artists, and architects, have contributed to this process. Substantial numbers of Romantic writers contributed to the fashion for orientalist writing, including Walter Savage Landor, Robert Southey, William Beckford, Sir William Jones, Anna Letitia Barbauld, Sydney Owenson, Elizabeth Hamilton, Thomas Moore, Coleridge, Percy Shelley, Thomas De Quincey, and, most popularly, Byron in his several eastern tales. The East in such writings is usually seen as a homogenized world of despotism, magic, irrationality, luxury, sensuality, and passion. It is usually feminized in a binary opposition to Western masculine, rationalist, and progressive Europe. As scholars such as Nigel Leask and John Barrell have argued, its denizens are possessed of extreme passions whether they be of love, like the women in Byron's tales, or hate, like the sorcerers in Southey's *Thalaba the Destroyer*. It is also the place of effeminacy: Byron's drama *Sardanapalus* (1821), for instance, depicts the tragedy of an effeminate Assyrian king. It is sometimes imaged as the place of plague and infection as in De Quincey's opium dreams, Barbauld's verse *Epistle to William Wilberforce*, and Mary Shelley's apocalyptic novel *The Last Man* (1821). The afterlife of Romantic orientalism, which coincided with the invention of the discipline of scholarly orientalism and the expansion of British and French influence in the Near East, is perhaps the impact that influences our daily lives and expectations most pressingly today.

Romanticism and racism

The most urgent issue that faces humanity today relates to how the various peoples of the world share out its resources. In the eighteenth and nineteenth centuries these peoples were classified into various physical types, varieties, or races, an extremely slippery and ambiguous set of terms. Recently a number of critics have investigated how Romantic writing may reflect, or even propagate, such potentially dangerous dogmas. Historians of race argue that a kind of paradigm shift occurs towards the end of the eighteenth century in ideas about the differences between peoples and cultures, one that signals a move from an interest in cultural to physical or bodily markers. The Enlightenment natural historians Buffon and Linnaeus attempted to describe and categorize humans in terms of their physical appearance: skin colour, hair texture, and anatomical form and other physical features. These classificatory or descriptive systems were fed by a huge increase in ethnological data resulting from a series of British, French, Russian, and other voyages of exploration to the hardly known or completely unknown parts of the globe; of which the voyages of Captain James Cook (1769–75) were only the most famous. Linnaeus classified humanity into first four, then five varieties: ferus (wild man), americanus (American), europaeus (European), asiaticus (Asian), and afer (African). Beginning as varieties such groupings soon became ossified into morphologically stable types with equivalent moral and intellectual capacities. Linnaeus described African people as phlegmatic and indulgent and Asian people as melancholic and inflexible. His categories were combined with neoclassical notions of physical beauty derived from Greek and Roman statuary to create an aesthetic hierarchy of races with Europeans at the top because of their alleged beauty.

It is, however, in the writings of Immanuel Kant that we first encounter what may be described as explicitly biological arguments for the modern notion of race. The general consensus held that physical human differences were created chiefly by climatic effects; however, Kant argued in 1775 that the ancestral human stock was endowed with latent powers which could be activated in response to differing climactic conditions. Once this racial programming was activated it was not possible to reverse its effects. Kant's generative force created four races, White, Negro, Mongolian, and Hindu, each deriving from an ideal stem genus that corresponded to the white European and these were permanent. As one might expect, Kant believed that hot and sunny climates brought out the worst in humanity and that African peoples were lazy, soft, and desultory in temperament and lacking in intelligence compared to the white European.

Kant's hypothesis received support from the most influential anthropological writer of the period. J. F. Blumenbach. He argued for a 'formative force' in nature which ordered and structured the world. Like Kant, he divided humanity into varieties, Caucasian (he coined the term), Mongolian, Ethiopian, American, and Malayan; he believed that Europeans were the originary and historic race from which descended (degenerated in his terms) the other varieties with the Ethiopian and the Mongolian at the foot of this scale. Blumenbach discussed human variety in terms of physical characteristics describing skin colour, hair texture, skull, and anatomical detail. Although he argued against fixed and permanent human types, Blumenbach's fetishization of the human skull and his notorious collection of crania, his 'Golgotha', had a pernicious history as later craniometrists sought to construct tables of measurements confirming the racial inferiority of non-Europeans. Blumenbach's Golgotha, greatly augmented over the years, formed the basis of the collection later used by National Socialist scientists as an evidential basis for their theories of racial inferiority.

By and large Romantic poets and writers avoided narrowly biological expressions of racial thinking. One can indict Wordsworth for his privileging of the northern English in his work and see this as complicit with the general trend of race thinking in the period. One can also draw attention to the numerous and problematic representations of African and Eastern peoples in their works, many of which can be seen as racist in one way or another. Scholars have argued whether or not Romantic writing, such as Blake's 'The Little Black boy' from *Songs of Innocence and of Experience*, is racist and the case has been made that the Romantics challenged the current paradigms of racial thinking. Nevertheless some Romantic writers did take up explicitly racialist stances. The political writer and journalist William Cobbett, for instance, clearly believed in the racial inferiority of African people and supported the slave trade. Thomas De Quincey represented Asian peoples as not entirely human in his *Confessions*; when he meets a Malay traveller in the English Lakes, he can only describe him in terms of the rats and tigers of the animal kingdom and the diseases and infections that he feared.

It is in the later writings of Coleridge that the most troubling signs of Romantic racism are discovered. Coleridge certainly began his literary career as someone who opposed the slave trade and who fully believed in the Christian universalist consensus concerning the origins and unity of humanity; however, in 1798, when he studied at Göttingen, he encountered the anthropology of Blumenbach and saw his collection of skulls. Coleridge seems to have accepted Blumenbach's hypothesis of a formative force, which coincided with his own intuitions of an active and vital force in nature; he also accepted Blumenbach's fivefold typology of mankind. Coleridge, unfortunately, was to go even further than Blumenbach. Integrating this racist anthropology with his own attempts to provide a systematic philosophy, he began to argue that the European race was the original race from which all others have degenerated both physically and morally. Combining Christian eschatology with an idealist version of natural history, Coleridge argued, in a series of notes, unpublished essays, and other pieces, that it would be the historic mission of the European race to reunite and perfect the rest of the peoples of the world thus fulfilling the master narrative of world history. Famously, Coleridge could never accept that Shakespeare intended Othello to be represented as a black African and he also commented that one of the anecdotal proofs of his belief that white was the primary racial colouring consisted in the allegation that African slaves came to admire the whiteness of the scars inflicted by their overseers.

What therefore are the political legacies of Romanticism and in what does its afterlife consist: political quietism and visionary evasion, revolutionary enthusiasm, nationalist liberation, Christian socialism, ecological awareness, nationalism, colonialism and imperialism, or racist thinking? There is no one simple political or cultural legacy from this wide range of writing but there are many possible legacies there to be discovered. Romanticism has its afterlives in its advocacy of the aesthetic realms of imagination, its cultivation of the unity of consciousness in a striven-for harmony with the exterior world, its various political and social concerns, and in its engagement with the global dimension of human experience.

FURTHER READING

Barrell, John, *The Infection of Thomas de Quincey: A Psychopathology of Imperialism* (London: Yale University Press, 1991). Ground-breaking study of the psychopathology of one of Romanticism's foremost commentators on the Far East.

Bate, Jonathan, *Romantic Ecology: Wordsworth and the Environmental Tradition* (London and New York: Routledge, 1991). Key text in establishing the ecological dimensions of Romantic writing.

Bernal, Martin, *Black Athena: The Afroasiatic Roots of Classical Civilization* (London: Vintage, 1987). Argues that Romantic figures are complicit in the scholarly fabrication of an Aryan myth of the origins of Western civilization.

Fulford, Tim, and Kitson, Peter J. (eds.), *Romanticism and Colonialism: Writing and Empire, 1780–1830* (Cambridge: Cambridge University Press, 1998). Ground-breaking collection which discusses the interrelationship of Romantic writing and the material processes of empire.

Kedourie, Elie, *Nationalism* (London: Hutchinson, 1960). Study of the involvement of Romantic and idealist philosophers with ideas of nationalism.

Leask, Nigel, *British Romantic Writers and the East: Anxieties of Empire* (Cambridge: Cambridge University Press, 1992). Important study of Romantic writers and the East.

Levinson, Marjorie, *Wordsworth's Great Period Poems* (Cambridge: Cambridge University Press, 1991). New Historicist reading of canonical Wordsworth poetry.

Liu, Alan, *Wordsworth: The Sense of History* (Stanford, Calif: Stanford University Press, 1989). New Historicist study arguing that Wordsworth's work represents a denial of history.

McGann, Jerome J., *The Romantic Ideology: A Critical Investigation* (Chicago: University of Chicago Press, 1983). Key text in establishing the New Historicist reading of Romantic poetry.

McKusick, James C., *Green Writing: Romanticism and Ecology* (Basingstoke: Macmillan, 2000). Study of Romanticism's green writings in Britain and America.

Makdisi, Saree, *Romantic Imperialism: Universal Empire and the Culture of Modernity* (Cambridge: Cambridge University Press, 1998). Blake as post-colonial critic of empire before his time.

Morton, Timothy, *Shelley and the Revolution in Taste: The Body and the Natural World* (Cambridge: Cambridge University Press, 1994). Study of the political implications of Shelley's vegetarianism and the seriousness of his stance.

Richardson, Alan, and Hofkosh, Sonia (eds.), *Romanticism, Race, and Imperial Culture, 1780–1834* (Bloomington, Ind.: Indiana University Press, 1996). Another key collection of essays concerning Romanticism and empire.

Said, Edward, *Orientalism* (New York: Pantheon, 1978). Seminal work arguing that the West views the Middle East in terms of stereotypes located in late eighteenth-century scholarship on the Orient.

Thomas, Helen, *Romanticism and Slave Narratives: Transatlantic Testimonies* (Cambridge: Cambridge University Press, 2000). Sound overview of the subject, which argues that Romanticism, Evangelism, and African beliefs mutually reinforce each other.

The legacies of Romanticism in science include concepts such as the age and origin of the earth and of life; discoveries such as oxygen and electricity, theories of light, sound, and colour; inventions such as steam engines, tin cans, hot-air balloons, bicycles, umbrellas, sewing machines, cotton underwear, carbon paper; and the organization of the sciences as professions and disciplines, with credentials, languages, societies, and publications. By 1830 individual sciences in the modern sense had emerged, including astronomy, biology, physics, chemistry, anatomy, palaeontology, geology, botany, and zoology.

The natural world, the subject of science, had been represented in eighteenth-century literature, philosophy, and theology as a fallen world, created about 6,000 years before, and marked by signs of God's wrath and power. In twenty years, from 1785 to 1805, this image of the world was reconceived as older, larger, and more diverse than anyone had previously believed. It was packed with an incalculable number of invisible particles, suffused with 'imponderable fluids', driven by mysterious forces, and, according to the astronomer William Herschel, located in a 'boundless' universe (see *Oxford Companion to the Romantic Age*, p. 542). This was a world of process, transformation, conflict, destruction, generation, evolution, with 'no sign of a beginning . . . no prospect of an end', according to James Hutton, the founder of modern geology (see *Oxford Companion to the Romantic Age*, pp. 551–2). Such a universe was not created for human beings (as had been earlier thought); human beings were belated intruders working out their own destiny in a landscape that was indifferent to their comfort or survival. Coleridge, one of the most learned of his generation, condemned the 'subtle fluids, impacts, essences, | Self-working tools, [and] uncaused effects' of this new science because it had 'Untenant[ed] creation of its God' ('*Destiny of Nations*', ll. 32–5).

Art and science shared the subject of 'Man, Nature, and Human Life' (as Wordsworth described it in *The Excursion*). They also shared a colloquial style, aesthetic values, and a unity of knowledge or 'consilience'. Erasmus Darwin's encyclopaedic poems responded to the very latest developments in contemporary science (see *Oxford Companion to the Romantic Age*, p. 477) as did Mary Shelley's novel *Frankenstein* (see *Oxford Companion to the Romantic Age*, pp. 699–701). The chemist Humphry Davy (see *Oxford Companion to the Romantic Age*, pp. 479–80) prepared the second edition of the *Lyrical Ballads* for publication. William Blake engraved the scientific papers published by the

Royal Society; Coleridge found emotional comfort in chemistry; and Wordsworth, in the headnote to 'The Thorn', defined poetry as 'the history or science of feelings'. In 1834, William Whewell (see *Oxford Companion to the Romantic Age*, pp. 758–9) coined the word 'scientist' as an analogy with 'Artist', acknowledging their common imaginative and creative dimension.

Beyond inventions, solutions, and attitude, the Romantic legacy to modern science includes much that is anomalous and mysterious like quantum physics and chaos theory. To function in such a universe, to know it at all, requires the opposite of what conventional science values; requires what Keats called 'negative capability', the capacity to be in 'uncertainties, mysteries, doubts, without any irritable reaching after fact and reason'.

Normal science

'Normal science', according to Thomas Kuhn in *The Structure of Scientific Revolutions*, represents the collective beliefs of the scientific community. It constitutes a paradigm in which young scientists are indoctrinated as part of their entry into the profession. Revolution and progress occur when someone encounters an anomaly, challenges conventions, and eventually forces his colleagues to discard one paradigm in favour of another. Before the Romantic period, the common paradigm accounting for the origin of the earth and of life was theological, derived from literal readings of the Bible such as Thomas Burnet's *Sacred Theory of the Earth* (1681). Burnet believed that God had created the earth 6,000 years ago as a round, smooth, symmetrical sphere under a dome-like heaven across which the stars were evenly distributed. Under the weight of sin, the surface of the earth had collapsed releasing the inner waters in a great flood that produced irregularities of landscape, caves, and shorelines, and left the world 'lying in its own Rubbish' as a monument to human error and God's power. However, given Noah's careful gathering of pairs, every species that God had originally created survived. Since there were no extinct species, fossil bones were believed to be the remains of the monstrous offspring created by angels and the human women they fell in love with—the sin for which the Flood had been a punishment.

As President of the Royal Society from 1778 to 1820, the great botanist Sir Joseph Banks (see *Oxford Companion to the Romantic Age*, p. 415) sponsored voyages of exploration such as Captain Cook's on the *Endeavour* and Captain Bligh's on the *Bounty*, voyages that were as expensive and risky as space exploration in the twentieth century (see also chapters on 'Travel writing' and 'Politics'). From data gathered on these voyages came natural histories, reports, drawings, collections, and engravings that celebrated the empirical world—that is, the visible, observable, tangible, palpable, and diverse world of nature. The study of imponderables (phenomena for which there was no explanation) languished or was relegated to theology. For example, although

Benjamin Franklin had experimented with electricity in 1752 and Joseph Priestley (see *Oxford Companion to the Romantic Age*, pp. 660–1) wrote a history of it in 1767, no one thought of using electricity for light or power for at least fifty more years. Electricity remained a mysterious force, a 'something' that might be described as a fluid. Voyages of exploration inspired other inventions: inflatable boats, portable watches that allowed sailors to keep time at sea, and the chronometer to measure longitude (see Dava Sobel's book *Longitude: The True Story of a Lone Genius who Solved the Greatest Scientific Problem of his Time* (1995)). The Royal Astronomer Nevil Maskelyne made Greenwich, England, the centre of the earth by establishing it as the location for the prime meridian, the place from which all distance was measured and all clocks were set, everywhere in the world.

Counting and measuring, establishing standards and weights, naming and ordering occupied the best minds of the period. They produced methods for statistics, accounting, insurance, instruments for standardizing and regulating products and commerce, the concept of hourly wages, and, in 1802, the first census. In this spirit, Linnaeus (Carl von Linné) classified all of nature according to its sexual identity and means of reproduction. Likewise, Caroline Herschel published the first catalogue of stars in 1798, composed from her patient and scrupulous 'sweeps' or 'reviews of the heavens' that her brother William had started in 1781. She added 3,000 stars and several thousand nebulae, and doubled the radius of the known universe (see *Oxford Companion to the Romantic Age*, pp. 541–2).

Ironically, this preoccupation with measuring and enumerating led to a sharper awareness of incalculables. 'Time', Hutton wrote, 'which measures everything in our idea, and is often deficient to our schemes, is to nature endless and as nothing.'[1] John Dalton's *New System of Chemical Philosophy* (1808) proposed that all matter is made up of a stable but incalculable number of atoms (see *Oxford Companion to the Romantic Age*, pp. 474–5). He was 'confounded with the thought' that these particles, the building blocks of the perceptible world, were infinitesimally small and more numerous than the stars. Perception, which the Romantic writers identified with the subjective, became the assumption behind Einstein's theory of relativity. The inescapable nature of the subjective is also expressed in Werner Heisenberg's uncertainty principle, which Stephen Hawking calls a 'fundamental and inescapable property of the world'.[2] While it is elusive and has many applications, the uncertainty principle acknowledges that the act of measuring alters the size, location, and speed of whatever is being measured, or, as Blake said, 'The eye altering, alters all' ('The Mental Traveller').

Geology

Burnet's theory of creation, which established the Flood as a formative influence on the surface of the earth, took a scientific and secular turn in 1775. Abraham Werner, a German mineralogist, claimed that the earth had originated in water that eventually evaporated and left behind sedimentary layers in the rocks and soil. This neatly explained why seashells are sometimes found on mountain tops. Georges Cuvier also believed that a great flood, caused by a comet, had overwhelmed the world, and that there had been multiple creations and catastrophic deluges which accounted for the fossil remains of extinct species (for more, see the chapter on 'Science').

James Hutton, a learned gentleman-farmer reflecting on the ordinary problems of arable land, conceived a theory of landscape that became a theory of creation (see *Oxford Companion to the Romantic Age*, pp. 551–2). Like Werner, Burnet, and Cuvier, he also believed that water helped form the surface of the earth, but he did not believe that the features of the landscape were symbolic reminders of God's presence and his power to punish or reward human beings. 'The volcano', Hutton wrote, 'was not created to scare superstitious minds . . . into fits of piety'; it is 'the vent of a furnace'. Patiently watching the weather, the seasons, and their effect on the landscape, Hutton concluded that the elemental forces operating around him were the ones that had shaped the landscape over a period of time too long to calculate, far more than the conventional 6,000 years of biblical chronology. Wind and rain eroded the hills, and sediments washed into the sea. Layer on layer of sediment produced pressure, and generated heat, earthquakes, subterranean fires, and volcanic eruptions from which the whole cycle started again. In a paper he first presented to the Royal Society of Edinburgh (1785), and later published as his *Theory of the Earth* (1788), Hutton presented a vision of a self-sustaining earth, an earth that decayed and was renovated, renewed, shaped by wind, water, and heat, by erosion, deposition, combustion, and uplift. With John Playfair, who wrote *Illustrations of the Huttonian Theory* (1802), Hutton transformed the landscape into an ecological system, replacing the 6,000 years of biblical history with a staggering tract of time:

Having in the natural history of the earth seen a succession of worlds, we may from this conclude that there is a system in nature; in like manner as from seeing revolutions of the planets . . . there is a system by which they are intended to continue these revolutions . . . The result, therefore, of our present inquiry is, that we find no vestige of a beginning—no prospect of an end.[3]

With Hutton, 'deep time' was born, a stunning realization that the history of life is in the history of the earth.

Hutton initiated the golden or heroic age of geology (see *Oxford Companion to the Romantic Age*, pp. 519–21) although for some time his work was overshadowed by Cuvier's and Werner's. To accusations that his geology had produced a godless world, Hutton responded:

Why refuse to see in this construction of things, that wisdom of contrivance, that beautiful provision which is so evident, whether we look up into the great expanse of boundless space where luminous bodies without number are placed, and where, in all probability, still more numerous bodies are perpetually moving and illuminated for some great end; or whether we turn our prospect towards ourselves, and see the exquisite mechanism and active powers of things, growing from a state apparently of non-existence . . . decaying from their state of natural perfection and renovating their existence in a succession of similar beings to which we see no end.[4]

Nevertheless, like Darwin's *The Origin of Species* or *The Descent of Man*, Hutton's grand and optimistic reading of natural history became a terrifying negation of individual human history. The earth, in Hutton's thesis, simply occurred; human life was an accident; and human beings merely stages in a great recycling process. Working independently, Dalton and all the atomic theorists who followed him were to propose that human beings are made of indestructible atoms endlessly recycled in the universe, coming together to form individuals before they drift off to become something or someone else. Each of us could have up to a billion atoms from Machiavelli, Shakespeare, or Hutton himself. As Bill Bryson says in *A Short History of Nearly Everything*: 'We are all reincarnations'.[5]

Forty years after publishing his *Theory*, Hutton was vindicated by Charles Lyell's *Principles of Geology, Being an Attempt to Explain the Former Changes of the Earth's Surface by Reference to Causes Now in Operation* (1830–3). As Carlyle wrote the same year in *Sartor Resartus*, 'we know enough: what with the labours of our Werners and Huttons, what with the ardent genius of their disciples, it has come about that now . . . the Creation of a World is little more mysterious than the cooking of a dumpling.'[6] Although Hutton did not know about glaciers, ice ages (described by the Swiss-American geologist, Louis Agassiz, in 1840), plate tectonics, or even about the impact of meteors, his theory, his approach, even his conclusions were confirmed repeatedly, not only by modern uniformitarians such as Richard Dawkins in *Climbing Mount Improbable* (1996), but also by James E. Lovelock, in the *Ages of Gaia: A Biography of our Living Earth* (1987). The Gaia hypothesis turned Hutton's self-regulating machine into a self-sustaining organism with every part, down to the smallest bacteria, functioning for the good of the whole.

When William Smith was excavating new canals in 1793, he observed that rocks appeared in strata; that the fossils in each layer were different; and that the layers ran across England and Wales and probably beyond. In 1815, he created the first geological map of England, reproduced on the cover of Simon Winchester's *The Map that Changed the World: William Smith and the Birth of Modern Geology* (2002). Smith's map helped others make their fortunes from iron, coal, and oil—and provided grist for competing geological theories. Although Smith's geological maps illustrated perfectly Hutton's version of the earth's inner life, catastrophists (who clung to the biblical history of the world) were also able to make use of them. In 1811, the Reverend Joseph Townsend, who had befriended Smith, began publishing theological interpretations of his discoveries with titles such as *The Character of Moses Established for Veracity as an Historian, Recording Events from the Creation to the Deluge* (1815) and *The Stratigraphical System of Organized Fossils* (1817). Like Cuvier, Townsend concluded that God had created each strata or layer separately for the new life forms he had generated after wiping out the previous ones. Consequently, the earth was a many-layered tribute to a powerful, creative, and governing deity who was nevertheless given to violent fits of frustration and rage. The conflict between uniformitarians and catastrophists continues into contemporary science: for example, in opposition to Richard Dawkins who conceives evolution as steady and progressive, Stephen J. Gould proposed a theory of 'punctuated equilibrium', to account for changes, extinctions, earthquakes, volcanoes, floods, and comets that altered the climate and so changed or destroyed the life forms dependent on it.

Astronomy

As early as 1734, Emanuel Swedenborg, a Swedish geologist, had proposed that the universe began in an explosion of concentrated gasses that cooled in great swirls forming the earth and planets. Others followed with various theories of explosion to explain the origin of the universe. In *Theory of the Earth* (1749), for instance, the Comte de Buffon proposed that planets came from fiery comets colliding with, and then ejected by, the sun. In the twentieth century Albert Einstein restated the theory of the explosive origins of the universe, and in 1950 Fred Hoyle called it the 'Big Bang theory' (a derisive name for a concept he was refuting in favour of a solid state universe). Hoyle also proposed that life must come from somewhere else: the planet had been seeded by cosmic dust and from this all life forms have sprung.

Extraterrestrial life has been a persistent idea. William Herschel believed that the planets, and even the sun, would contain life forms suited to the environment. The moon had a population of Lunarians, a landscape with lunar forests, and round lunar cities. In 2001 the North American Space Agency set up an Astrobiological Institute, convinced that if there is one planet with life, there must be more—a claim which updates and restates Herschel's theory. Herschel was born in Germany in 1738 and brought up to be a musician. Having come to Britain as a refugee, he encountered advanced scientific ideas at a Philosophical Society in Bath and determined to pursue his interest in astronomy. With his sister Caroline he devised new telescopes for which he ground and polished the lenses. In 1781, he became the king's astronomer and moved to Windsor where George III could visit him. There Herschel built a telescope so huge that it required a ladder to use, and in the chill and darkness that astronomers accepted as the condition for studying stars, he patiently counted stars and mapped the heavens. Among his many distinguished visitors were Lord Byron, Thomas Malthus, and Maria Edgeworth. John Keats's famous lines, 'Then felt I like some watcher of the skies | When a new planet swims into his ken' ('On First Looking into Chapman's Homer'), refer to Herschel's discovery of the planet Uranus in 1781.

As important as Herschel's developments of the telescope was the 'art of seeing' that he developed, from which he concluded that the earth is a very small part of the Milky Way, and that the Milky Way itself is not a band of clouds obscuring the stars but millions of stars emitting light. He also conjectured that the universe was expanding, evolving, and 'fathomless' (compare Blake's observation in *The Marriage of Heaven and Hell*: 'If the doors of perception were cleansed, everything would appear to man as it is, infinite.') By likening the heavens to a 'luxuriant garden', Herschel drew on a popular image that Erasmus Darwin had used as a microcosm of the natural world in his *Botanic Garden* (1791)—a poem that did much to disseminate the work of advanced scientists and astronomers like Hutton and Herschel.

Herschel had emancipated astronomy from Scripture to reveal a universe that evolved on its own inscrutable schedule, in which human beings were aliens and human history utterly insignificant. The demystification that Herschel began turned the heavens into 'space'—the 'intense inane' of Shelley's *Prometheus Unbound*, the 'blinder vacancy' of Wordsworth's Prospectus to *The Excursion*. This vast, impersonal, and threatening concept inspired the controversial 'anthropic principle' of the late twentieth century, which places human beings once again at the centre of the universe (as they had been in the Bible). First proposed by John Wheeler in the 1960s, the anthropic principle assumes that if the world was other than what it is, human beings would not exist. As Stephen Hawking explains, human beings hypothesize that the Big Bang took place 10,000 million years ago because it took that long for them to evolve the intelligence to understand it (further evidence here of the Romantic assumption that the world is as one sees it, or, as Blake said, 'the eye altering, alters all' (*The Mental Traveller*)). As the titles of some recent books emphasize, the universe can be seen as domestic space: Dennis Overby, *Lonely Hearts of the Cosmos* (1992), John Wheeler, *At Home in the Universe* (1992), Fred Hoyle, *Home is Where the Wind Blows* (1994), and Stuart Kauffman, another book called *At Home in the Universe* (1995).

While Herschel was honoured in his lifetime, his astronomy had little use before space exploration (the visible stars were adequate for navigation at sea). But just as Hutton's geology had to be repeatedly rediscovered, so did Herschel's astronomy. In 1923 Edwin Hubble (after whom the orbiting telescope was named) and Henrietta Swan Leavitt (who did the counting as Caroline had done for Herschel) looked at what others had called clouds and discovered galaxies—billions of them. He called them 'island universes', as Herschel had before him, measured by rays comparable to the infra-red that Herschel had discovered. And Hubble's discoveries raised the same questions about human life as Herschel's: if the universe was not created by God for human life, then, as May Swenson asks in her poem, 'The Universe' (1974), 'What is it about? | And what about *us?*'

Sciences of life

The sciences of life during the Romantic period—chemistry, anatomy, biology, to name the most significant—tied human beings to the natural world in new and interesting ways, mainly as biological expressions of life forces that they did not yet comprehend. By performing dissections for medical students and artists such as Blake, the surgeon James Hunter (see *Oxford Companion to the Romantic Age*, pp. 551–2) noticed likenesses between the body parts of animals and humans, and exhibited specimens to demonstrate the similarities between wings and arms, skulls, fingers, and paws. Wanting the historical awareness of a Herschel or Hutton, and without the sense of process and transformation they had brought to geology and astronomy, Hunter and his contemporaries were unable either to question or to account for physical similarities in creatures that were otherwise different. Biologists and palaeontologists, those most concerned with the study of life, such as Cuvier, could not account for the emergence of different life forms without resorting to a creative god. As we have seen, however, ideas of evolution were current in astronomy, geology, chemistry, and in Erasmus Darwin's poetic readings of natural history. Such was the inheritance from Romantic science that lay behind Charles Darwin's ground-breaking *Origin of Species* (1859).

Other developments in Romantic science met with opposition. Because the process of photosynthesis in plants transferred the basis of life from divinity to nature, it was resisted. It took thirty years from Priestley's discovery of the photosynthesis of oxygen (1772) until it was common knowledge that life was sustained by a process involving rain, sun, plants, oxygen, and carbohydrates, and that plants cleansed the air of the carbon dioxide and other poisonous gasses that human beings exhaled and machinery produced. As Humphry Davy said: 'No more sublime idea can be formed of the motions of matter than to conceive that the different species are continually changing into each other.' Another legacy of Romantic science is the recognition that human beings are physically dependent on the natural world and participants in its processes and transformations. Ironically, since Priestley's time manufacturing and technology have been choking the planet, depleting resources, contaminating the water, and destroying the natural world.

While photosynthesis could explain some processes of life, philosophers and physicians still debated the origin of life itself. John Hunter (see *Oxford Companion to the Romantic Age*, p. 551) claimed that life was a force separate from the physical organization of matter into bodies; John Abernethey (see *Oxford Companion to the Romantic Age*, p. 399) claimed that life was analogous to electricity and added to organization; and William Lawrence (see *Oxford Companion to the Romantic Age*, pp. 579–80) claimed in *Lectures on Physiology* (1819) that life could be explained by chemistry, that its origins are 'forever beyond our reach'. Since the Romantic period, that debate about when and how life begins continues in subjects ranging from DNA and the human genome, to controversial issues such as abortion and euthanasia.

The Romantic legacy is science itself: the assumptions, style, and problems solved and unsolved; time, space, nature, and life as we understand them; the relationship between human life and nature; how human beings know and how 'to imagine that which we know', as Shelley wrote in *The Defence of Poetry*; and how to live with the mystery, as Keats said, in 'half knowledge' through 'negative capability'. In 1943, when quantum physics was new to the Western vocabulary, Herbert Muller, who could have been speaking of Wordsworth or Blake or Keats, wrote: 'Modern science is distinguished by the calm acceptance of empty spaces, the calm awareness of the meaningless question.'[7] With the same assumptions and 'calm acceptance' as Hutton and Herschel, the same strata and fossils as Smith and Cuvier, scientists now speculate that the earth is fifteen billion years old and that recognizable human life appeared between six and seven million years ago—although exactly what this looked like remains a matter of speculation. Romantic scientists identified the geological functions of earthquakes, volcanic eruptions, tornadoes, droughts, and floods, but contemporary scientists are still unable to predict when they will happen or how to defend ourselves against them. A great deal is now known about evolution, although no one can anticipate how things will evolve. Debate continues on when life begins, and when it ends. But because Herschel, Hutton, Priestley, Davy, Dalton, and all the other Romantic scientists looked at nature with what Keats called in the 'Ode to Psyche' 'awakened eyes', contemporary science at the very least has questions worth pursuing.

FURTHER READING

Brockman, John, *The Third Culture* (New York: Simon and Schuster, 1996). Drawing on the most influential contemporary scientific figures, Bockman shows how science is the new intellectual centre in contemporary society.

Eiseley, Loren, *Darwin's Century: Evolution and the Men Who Discovered It* (New York: Anchor Books, 1961). This eloquent study shows the basis of Darwin's theories in the geology of the Romantic period, and the invention of time.

Gaull, Marilyn, *English Romanticism: The Human Context* (New York: W. W. Norton, 1988). This cultural history of British Romanticism includes sections on contemporary science and its relation to literature, art, philosophy, and theatre.

Gould, Stephen Jay, *Time's Arrow; Time's Cycle: Myth and Metaphor in the Discovery of Geological Time* (Cambridge, Mass: Harvard University Press, 1987). This book is the classic introduction to the study of 'deep time', how it was discovered and what it means.

Horgan, John, *The End of Science: Facing the Limits of Knowledge in the Twilight of the Scientific Age* (New York: Broadway Books, 1996). Horgan's lucid and engaging survey of contemporary scientific thought leads to the conclusion that there is no more that can be known.

Lussier, Mark S., *Romantic Dynamics: The Poetics of Physicality* (New York: St Martin's Press, 2000). Wide-ranging study showing the relationship between the conception of nature in Blake, Coleridge, Byron, and Shelley and contemporary science.

Uglow, Jenny, *The Lunar Men: Five Friends Whose Curiosity Changed the World* (New York: Farrar, Strauss and Giroux, 2002). Describes the life and times of Erasmus Darwin, James Keir, Matthew Boulton, Josiah Wedgwood, and Joseph Priestley, among others, the inventors and philosophers whose ideas shaped the industrialization of England in the eighteenth century.

Wilson, Eric G., *The Spiritual History of Ice: Romanticism, Science, and the Imagination* (New York: Palgrave, 2001). This study demonstrates how literature and science collaborated in the re-evaluation of a facet of nature.

NOTES

1. James Hutton, *The Theory of the Earth, from the Transactions of the Royal Society of Edinburgh*, 2 vols. (Edinburgh, 1788), i. 215.
2. Stephen Hawking *A Brief History of Time* (New York: Bantam, 1988; 1996), p. 57.
3. Hutton, *Theory of the Earth*, i. 304.
4. Ibid. ii. 468–9.
5. Bill Bryson, *A Short History of Nearly Everything* (London: Doubleday, 2003), p. 134.
6. Thomas Carlyle, *Sartor Resartus: The Life and Opinions of Herr Teufelsdröckh*, ed. Charles Frederick Harrold (New York: Odyssey Press, 1937), p. 4.
7. Herbert Muller, *Science and Criticism: The Humanistic Tradition in Contemporary Thought* (New Haven: Yale University Press, 1943), p. 78.

45 | Environmentalism

Timothy Morton

Environmentalism is a set of cultural and political responses to a crisis in humans' relationships with their surroundings. Those responses could be scientific, activist, or artistic, or a mixture of all three. Environmentalists try to preserve areas of wilderness or 'outstanding natural beauty'. They struggle against pollution, including the risks of nuclear technologies and weaponry. They fight for animal rights and vegetarianism in campaigns against hunting and scientific or commercial experimentation on animals. They oppose globalization and the patenting of life forms.

The Romantic legacy

Environmentalism is growing broader. You can be a communist environmentalist, or a capitalist one, like the American 'wise use' Republicans. You can be a 'soft' conservationist, sending money to charities such as Britain's Woodland Trust; or a 'hard' one who lives in trees to stop logging and road building. And you could, of course, be both at the same time. You could produce scientific papers on global warming or write ecocritical literary essays. You could create poems, or environmental sculpture, or ambient music. You could do environmental philosophy (ecosophy), establishing ways of thinking, feeling, and acting based on benign relationships with our environment(s).

The scientific, political, ethical, and aesthetic worlds are coming under the sign of the environment. Even postmodernism, held in suspicion by much ecocriticism, may eventually appear as a moment in the process of including the environment in thinking, doing, and making. Two hundred years hence, people may recognize in the Romantic period the beginning of environmental ways of understanding and acting. There are many legacies of Romanticism in current environmental movements. The trouble is not that these legacies are obscure; rather, there are *too many* connections. The relationships are overdetermined—a sure sign that we are in the warped space of ideology.

The period literary historians define as Romantic—1780–1830, roughly—witnessed the birth both of animal rights and anti-racism, and of fascism and eugenics. In 1809 Lord Erskine gave the first speech in Parliament supporting animal rights. Social experiments such as Coleridge's Pantisocracy included animals (see *Oxford Companion to the Romantic Age*, p. 635). Nationalisms emerged, invoking an environing nature as a powerful image of the nation as land. Thinking mapped the ways in which culture was shaped by nature, for instance in Alexander von Humboldt's idea that different places had different forms of cultural-conditioning *Stimmung* ('mood', 'atmosphere'). The new term 'culture', hovering somewhere between nature and nurture, evoked a surrounding world. Moreover, Romanticism has persisted in the growth of industrial capitalism; nationalism; the idea of organic form; colonialism, imperialism and globalization; changing attitudes towards children and animals; and the modern idea of *nature* itself. Let us consider these in turn.

Industrial society and its discontents

In industrial society, with its symptoms of alienation and pollution, the logic of unintended consequences plays out such that, despite class differences, risk becomes increasingly democratic. In 1986 a disaster at the Chernobyl nuclear reactor in the Soviet Union spread radiation across a vast expanse of Asia and Europe. Radiation is ignorant of national boundaries. In a bitter irony, the equality dreamt of in the 1790s has come to pass—we are all (almost) equally at risk from the environment itself. No matter what our nationality or class affiliation is, we share the toxic legacy of Chernobyl.

Romantic writers were aware of the perils of industry and its philosophy of reason. Coleridge and Shelley noticed that, despite the promises of republicanism and democracy, the unequal distribution of wealth generated famine, disease, and crime. Industrialism gave rise to rationalization, the ordering and control of social and natural systems, and utilitarianism. Yet animal rights emerged from utilitarianism: Jeremy Bentham opposed cruelty to animals. Evolution, whose first hints appeared in the later eighteenth century, displaced humans from their position at the top of a great chain of being, compelling them to acknowledge their entanglement with other species. Along with discoveries by geologists such as Charles Lyell of the astonishing age of the earth, the Darwins (Erasmus and grandson Charles) diverted thinking from the supremacist idea that humans were exceptional beings existing outside the world.

Some opposed reason, promoting mystical-participatory forms of holism or anti-rationalist celebrations of life lived on the pulses—in short, political versions of aesthetic experience. Romantic pantheism—believing that the universe and the godhead are one and the same—informs religious and ontological varieties of environmentalism. Some embrace a strong version of James Lovelock's Gaia hypothesis, the idea that the self-regulating systems of the biosphere constitute an entity, if not a personality. Ecofeminism holds that the ecological crisis results from long-term patriarchal social structures and beliefs. Ecofeminists observe that the domination of women is a symptom of a larger oppression: nature has been objectified, turned into an other, a mute object of sexist sadism.

Let us consider a potent example of anti-rationalist environmentalism. Like nature, Englishness seems mysteriously more than the sum of its parts. It exists, apparently, alongside monarchs, checks and balances, strawberries, and bluebells, irreducible to them yet somehow caught up in them. Organicism, that peculiarly English form of nature ideology, paints society as a non-systemic heap of classes, beliefs, and practices, as ramshackle and spontaneous as a pile of compost. This is a rich, compelling, and finally authoritarian fantasy—there is no arguing with it. Many environmentalist values—complexity is good, the world cannot be totalized though it is a whole—are slices of Romantic organicism typified in Edmund Burke's reactionary prose. But environmentalism need not be organicist, not even in the Romantic period. *Franken-stein* shows how organicism fails. Incapable of loving his creature spontaneously, Frankenstein would benefit from a more rational and planned social structure that treated all social actors as equal participants with equal rights.

Nationalism, a quintessentially Romantic ideology, motivated the re-enchantment school of environmental poetics. The nation-state remains a real yet fantastic thing. As the idea of world (*Welt*) became popular in German Romantic idealism, so the nation-state was imagined as a surrounding environment. The idea of the nation as homeland, as in American Homeland Security or the German *Heimat*, demanded a poetic render-ing as an ambient realm of swaying corn, shining seas, or stately forests. Nature appeared sublime, 'there' and yet fundamentally beyond representation, stretching beyond the horizon and back into the distant, even pre-human past. It was a suitable objective correlative for the *je ne sais quoi* of nationalist fantasy. Walter Scott's inven-tion of historical novels, realist fictions generating an entire world in a bubble of past-tense narrative, did as much for environmental nationalism as explicitly Romantic criticisms of modern society and technology.

The Shire in J. R. R. Tolkien's trilogy *The Lord of the Rings* depicts this world-bubble as an organic village. Tolkien narrates the victory of the suburbanite, the 'little person', embedded in a tamed yet natural-seeming environment. Nestled into the horizon as they are in their burrows, the wider world of global politics is blissfully unavailable to them. Tolkien's trilogy embodies a key nationalist fantasy, a sense of *world* as real, tangible yet indeterminate, evoking a metonymic chain of images. *The Lord of the Rings* establishes not only entire languages, histories, and mythologies, but also a surrounding world (*Umwelt*). If ever there was evidence of the persistence of Romanticism, this is it.

Like some 'nature writing' and ecocriticism, Tolkien's *Umwelt* edited out those signifi-cant moments in Romantic literature (even and especially in Wordsworth, the icon of 'nature writing') involving hesitation, irony and ambiguity. Consider Romantic irony: how the narrator becomes the protagonist, unnervingly aware that the world they have constructed is a fiction. Must ecological and ecocritical worlds be absolutely self-contained, utterly sincere—and how Romantic is that? Irony involves distancing and displacement, a moving from place to place, or even from homey place into lonely space. 'Ecology' comes from the Greek *oikos*, 'home', and early ecological science developed terms resonant with the idea of home, such as 'niche'. Science itself can be

Tolkienesque. Where does that leave migrating birds, hominids, pilgrims, gypsies, and Jews? If irony and movement are not part of environmentalism, such beings are in danger of exclusion, ostracism, or worse.

While we are on the subject of self-containment we should clarify the Romantic idea of holism. Holism constitutes the 'feel' of nationalism—'we' are interconnected in a whole greater than the sum of its parts. The struggle between individualism and holism offers an attenuated choice between absolute liberty and absolute authority—in other words, the dilemma called America. Americans are caught between the constitution and a militarized state, between placards and pepper spray, just as models of nature give to organisms with one hand, while taking with another. Organisms are politically all-important, and yet they are easily sacrificed for the sake of the greater whole. The ideological supports of American capitalism have gradually shifted away from individualism and towards corporatism. Holism is not as oppositional as some environmentalists claim. It may be better for environmentalism to think in terms of *collectivism* rather than *holism*. A collective does not imply an organic whole that is greater than the sum of its parts.

In the Romantic period, capitalism moved from its colonialist to its imperialist phase. Intense war, plunder and slavery spread over the earth. Monocultures appeared: unfeasible ecosystems where business produces only one crop. Ireland was the test case, its potatoes transplanted from South America. In the resulting potato famine, countless people died or emigrated to America. Language blanketed places from Kingston, Jamaica, to Calicut, India, as 'spice islands', 'the Indies'. This alone indicates how Europe was thinking. English, Portuguese, and French psychic and political maps of the world included special open, empty places (empty of society and/or Western social norms), soaked with desire, producing goods spontaneously, a fruit machine in permanent jackpot mode. Poetry caught wind of the coordination of imperialism and ecological destruction.

Nevertheless, one did not have to oppose capitalism to have environmental awareness. Indeed, global commerce gave rise to poetry that celebrated the global. We think of globalization as new, but it is just the most recent form of social processes that existed in the Romantic period. Powerfully depicted in Coleridge's 'Rime of the Ancient Mariner', empty wilderness spaces owe something to imperial geography and the 'because it's there' attitude of Everest climbers: imperialism in the abstract, the attempt to grasp the pure space, the abstract spacious*ness* of the environment. We are now witnessing a reverse, internal colonization: the insides of life forms provide new products such as patented genomes. In the language of the exhilarating rush to the new genetic frontier it is not hard to detect the strains of the Romantic voyage.

Private property aided ecological awareness, however strange that may sound. In eighteenth-century Britain the enclosure movement privatized land held in common, obliterating feudal and communal relationships with the earth (see *Oxford Companion to the Romantic Age*, pp. 496–7). Some ecological movements have since been trying to get it back, materially and/or symbolically. In returning to Romanticism, ecocriticism highlights those aspects that celebrated the bygone life of feudal hierarchy. Primitivist environmentalisms yearn for a lost golden age of interconnectedness with the environment. They look to pre-feudal, sometimes prehistoric, pasts to discover forms of primitive communism. Futurist environmentalisms have also appeared. Beginning with the notion that the golden age has not happened yet, they acknowledge that, despite the medievalist glamour, most people never had much of a relationship with their land under a feudal hierarchy. These futurist environmentalisms are also distinctively Romantic, in the tradition of William Blake and the Shelleys.

By the Romantic period the nuclear family had become a dominant form of kinship. On the one hand, this dominance isolated people from one another and from their world. On the other hand, it created, in the negative, a desire for connection. Individualist environmental awareness emphasizes the sublimity of open space, potential value, and, in Wordsworth's phrase, 'something ever more about to be'. The texts of contemporary nature writers are obsessed, in Romantic fashion, with the act of writing alone in the wilderness. Wordsworth, John Clare, and Henry David Thoreau each promoted this idea, inscribing the aloneness deeply into their poems and prose. The legacy continues: a recent scandal revealed that Edward Abbey's wilderness literature was not written alone, as claimed—his wife accompanied him as amanuensis.

Society began to value children differently, as beings possessing basic intrinsic goodness embodied in the imagination. They were little versions of the 'noble savage', more attuned to that gigantic concrete abstraction, nature. From an ecological point of view, social relations include relationships with animals: pets became very popular; vegetarianism was no longer a medical fad or mystical radicalism but a growing movement; animal rights was on the rise.

'Nature' is a key Enlightenment and Romantic term. Nature can be an abstract principle, an intrinsic value including a widening circle of beings: 'man', woman, child, slave, animal . . . plant? mineral? 'Nature' is used and abused. It is no comfort to see the word 'natural' in front of the word 'flavourings', since 'natural' carries no legal weight; the very term 'organic' has been appropriated for describing foods that contain no pesticide residues or genetically modified ingredients. The history of modernity is partly the story of the fortunes of 'nature'. On the one hand, nature continues to have politically progressive significance as natural rights extend towards more and more beings. On the other, postmodern theory and philosophy, for example disability studies and queer theory, have contested the idea of natural and unnatural altogether.

Frankenstein is about the origin and properties of life. It poses the basic mythological question of 'where we came from' (the earth or ourselves?) in a distinctively modern, biological, and sociological way. No wonder then that the story has come to embody contemporary anxieties about technical and scientific forms from nuclear power to genetic engineering. *Frankenstein* serves as a template for the nature debate. The creature is both utterly natural (made of pieces of other life forms) and unnatural—and perhaps the most monstrous thing about him is his plangent Enlightenment eloquence. Students never fail to be touched and disturbed by the eloquent voice of the creature requesting that Frankenstein make a mate for him and that they depart for a peaceful vegetarian exile in South America.[1] The creature is literally a talking piece of butcher's meat, made from pieces from the slaughterhouse as well as bodies from the grave. But his speech transcends his physicality. He may *appear* an unnatural monster, but, at heart, he is more human than humans. In the key Enlightenment diction, he is *humane* (essentially human).

Romantic consumerism, green consumerism

In 1988 Prime Minister Thatcher 'greened' herself, proclaiming something like 'The first thing we have to do is get this country really, really *tidy*'. It was the force—the tidiness—of that 'tidy' which grated. As if ecology were about rearranging the furniture. Thatcher, like Hitler, was thinking in terms of living rooms; Hitler proposed that the destiny of Germany was to increase and purify its *Lebensraum* ('living room'). The 1980s had witnessed one of the least tidy critiques of modernity in the transgressive form of the Greenham Common women, who camped outside a proposed cruise missile base in the UK and practically created an alternative society. Thatcher was not reacting directly to the Greenham women, whom, like the rest of the establishment, she dismissed as dangerously marginal, probably witches (ironically some *did* consider themselves witches). Thatcher was reacting to a growing pile of 'environmentally friendly' products. Green consumerism made it possible to be both pro-capitalist and green, repeating the Romantic struggle between rebelling and selling out.

Thatcherite 'tidiness' included processing the world's nuclear waste at Sellafield, a concern so lucrative that British Nuclear Fuels now has an interest in the clean-up at Rocky Flats nuclear bomb trigger factory near Boulder, Colorado. Rocky Flats was renamed, temporarily, an 'environmental protection site'—which means removing enough plutonium to accord with 'safe' levels for the establishment of an open space wilderness reserve; not safe enough for suburban houses, but safe enough apparently for microbes that will eventually enter the ground water. Against such crass co-opting of green politics, a Romantic scream seems entirely justifiable. Romantic cultural artefacts usually take the form of a rage against the machine of modern life. This is why Alan Ginsberg's 'Plutonium Ode', commemorating an action on the rail tracks towards Rocky Flats, is a gigantic paratactic list deriving from Romantic experiments with expansive lineation by William Blake and Walt Whitman.

And yet—and this is a big 'and yet'—Romanticism *is* consumerism; consumerism is Romanticism. Notice the word 'consumer*ism*', not 'consuming': a particular style of consuming that arose as a result of the growth of consumer society throughout the long eighteenth century.[2] One can take this notion too far. Other forces were in play: the rise in the price of meat, for example, meant that working-class food actually deteriorated. In the seventeenth century the high cost of bread was not vitally important to the lower classes: they lived on other sorts of cheap food and occupied the land. By the Romantic period they could hardly afford meat, while tea and white bread had become necessities. But consumerism is indeed a Romantic development.

Consumption became *reflexive*. This reflexivity generated such roles as that of the bohemian, the consumer who consumes for the sake of experiencing some general essence of consumption itself. As consumer society developed, more and more divergent groups evolved Kantian, self-reflexive bohemian forms of consuming. Now many people behave like Thomas De Quincey or Charles Baudelaire, both in the precise sense that drug use is rising, and in the broader sense that those writers typify Romantic consumerism. For the sake of a clear image we could reduce this to the notion of window shopping—aesthetic consumption without purpose or purchase.

It became possible to *be* a consumer: to highlight one's consuming role through self-reflection. One available role is refusal: that of the abstainer, the boycotter. These are quintessential Romantic, bohemian roles: they reflect upon the idea of what it means to be a consumer altogether. Romantic-period sugar boycotts and vegetarianism exemplify a style we would now recognize as ecological. The same forms confront today's green consumers as confronted the earlier Romantic consumers. Will buying organic food really save the planet? Romantic consumerism at once broadened and narrowed the idea of choice. The sense that we have a choice, while giving rise to utopian desires, indicates social deadlock as well as possibility.

Romantic consumerism influenced the construction and maintenance of the actually existing environment. Consider how Wordsworth's Lake District became the National Trust's Lake District; or the American wilderness. Environments themselves were caught in the logic of Romantic consumerism. Wildernesses embody both soft, shallow Romanticism—a provisional getaway from the mechanical or totally administered hurly-burly—and, in deep terms, a radical alternative. Wilderness therefore expresses various kinds of negative: fingers wagging, strongly or weakly, at modern society. To the extent that wilderness spaces and the laws that created them persist, we are still living, literally, within the Romantic period. It is strange to discover a secret passage between bottles of detergent and mountain ranges. But there is one, and it is called Romantic consumerism.

Ecological criticism

To be a consumerist is not simply to be caught in the stuff-your-face logic of capitalism, but to have the potential to resist and challenge it. One could use one's refusals to consume certain things in certain ways as modes of critiquing modern society. Without doubt, there are those green Romantic consumerists who have gone so far as not to consider themselves consumerists at all. A deep ecologist such as Julia Butterfly Hill will surely protest that she is not a consumerist, and activists in the Earth First! group would be shocked to find that its tactics derive from consumerism. When *Adbusters*, the American fashion magazine for the tortured anti-consumerist, proclaims itself a journal of 'the mental environment', it is promising something beyond consumerism. But this promise typifies the paradox of the Romantic avant-garde. If we could just get the aesthetic *form* right, then we could crack reality, open it up and change it. The *Adbusters* approach is simply greener-than-thou consumerism, 'outconsumerisming' other consumerists. Surely this is why deep ecology names itself in opposition to what it calls 'shallow ecology'. Those shallow ecologists are just day-trippers, from the deep point of view.

There is nothing intrinsically wrong with avant-garde consumerist forms. Like art, they embody what Theodor Adorno—a great Romantic in his engagement with Hegel—calls the negative knowledge of reality. This negativity is negative not in the sense of 'bad', but in terms of a dialectical moment of negation. Romantic consumerism embodies what has been negated, left out, excluded, or elided. It shows just how far one would need to go really to change things. Boycotting and protesting are both ironical, reflexive forms of consumerism. By *refusing* to buy certain products, by *questioning* oppressive social forms such as corporations or globalization, such activities point towards possibilities of changing the current state of affairs, without actually changing it. They are a cry from the heart in a heartless world, a spanner in the works (Dave Foreman's term for green direct action is 'monkeywrenching'). They thus have not only a practical, but also a religious aspect. Many religious practitioners are involved in environmental movements: nuns who hammered on Colorado's nuclear missile silos, the Church of Deep Ecology in Minneapolis. The nuns did not change the missiles into flowers, but did draw attention to these weapons of mass destruction lurking almost literally in people's backyards.

We may usefully understand the process of green consumerism via Hegel's dialectic of the beautiful soul, a moment in his history of different kinds of consciousness.[3] The beautiful soul maintains a split between self and world, an irresolvable chasm created by the call of conscience—or 'consciousness raising', as an activist might put it. This is despite the fact that the beautiful soul also yearns to close the gap. The title of a popular ecological book in the late 1980s, by David Icke, the erstwhile deputy secretary of the British Green Party, says it all: *It Doesn't Have to Be Like This*. (Since then, Icke has embraced a more extreme refusal, to the point of paranoia.) Modern art and green consumerism have this refusal stamped on them: rage against the machine. Just how deep the stamp goes is the issue. Integrity and hypocrisy become the ways to calibrate commitment.

Nature remains a reified object, 'over there'. As Marx maintains about his university experience, 'the kingdom of poetry glittered opposite me like a distant fairy palace and all my creations dissolved into nothingness'.[4] The Romantic environment twinkles and glitters like Bambi's blinking eyes. We could think of a thousand ecological examples of what Marx meant. But the name of many of them, in America, is Thoreau. The choice for engagement appears as a strong tension between, and blending of, quietism and activism. In the mid-nineteenth century, Thoreau practised both—he was prepared to go to prison and advocated non-violent resistance, and wrote about the importance of contemplating the natural world.

At its extreme, beautiful soul syndrome can lead to fascism. The composer Richard Wagner, who had a bad case of it, dramatized his life as a resistance to the inexorably commercial, capitalist aspect of the music business. In part this consisted in anti-Semitism. The core of Wagner's 'beautiful' resistance was a fantasy object of hate around which he generated all kinds of biological essentialist (racist) thoughts. But beautiful soul syndrome can also lead to hippiedom: if we think hard enough, the rain will stop, as the MC said at the Woodstock festival in 1969. Likewise, there are fascist and New Age versions of environmentalism.

The beautiful soul distinguishes between theory and practice so sharply that reflection and hesitation is seen as inane cloud-castle building, and pure action becomes solidly material and absolutely, guilt-inducingly vital. Or it comes to the same conclusion in reverse: reflection becomes ethereal transcendence, action a rather grimy thing that other, less enlightened, people do. The notion of *praxis*, however, is that reflection can be a form of action; and that action—such as a non-violent protest—can be theoretical, reflexive. Ecocritical *praxis* could strangely invert beautiful soul syndrome. If ideology relies upon enjoyment as well as disguised truth claims, one could adopt a paradoxical strategy towards ideology's fantasy spaces, images, and objects. Instead of spitting them out, or refusing to inhabit them, one could instead identify, over-identify, or paradoxically inhabit them, like the Latinos who have recently begun to transform cities such as Los Angeles.

Current environmentalist literary criticism (ecocriticism) is thus drastically limited. Ecocriticism is another version of Romanticism's rage against the machine, a refusal to engage the present moment. Like imperialism, ecocriticism produces a vision of the text as a pristine wilderness of pure meaning. Some are beginning to theorize ways in which pure celebration of the pristine wilderness is only one facet of an ecological-political spectrum of responses. Although among ecocritics themselves there has persisted the survival mentality of the small group, turning ecocriticism into ecoideology, ecocriticism now has greater potential to become a contested field: a healthy symptom of arrival or legitimation.

Ecocriticism wavers between the apolitical or quasi-political spilt religion of a call to care for the world, and the New Left inclusion of race, gender, and environment in socialist thinking. Both have significant ties to Romanticism. While capitalist ideology had been formulated by Adam Smith in 1776, out of Romanticism there emerged, eventually, figures such as Karl Marx and William Morris. Some right-tending ecocriticism, in its return to Romanticism, regresses to a historical state in which precisely these socialist and communist developments had *not yet happened*. Moreover, the regression is redoubled in championing an anti-modern, medievalist form of Romanticism. Regression can assume the form of rousing environmental rhetorics seeking to convey a *sense* of the empirical in an aesthetic of the touchy-feely, combined with a motivational sense that ecocriticism is good for us. Both empiricism and its experiential equivalent, specialized components of capitalist ideology itself, act as correctives to 'tarrying with the negative' and seeing the shadow side of things. If ecological criticism is to progress, it must engage negativity fully rather than formulate suppressants against perceiving it.

Ecological criticism must face up to the radically different senses of Romantic *nature*. All in all, 'nature' has two distinct meanings: *essence* and *substance*. As *essence*, nature is the inalienable rights of a sentient being, akin to private property: a kind of ghost that haunts the world like a possibility or a promise. This essence is ethical, political, and scientific. In the Romantic period, 'natural history' became 'biology' (a term coined simultaneously in Germany and England). There was a fundamental change in what counts as an object of knowledge. Natural-historical facts consist in classifications along a pre-established grid, such as Linneaus' system of genus and species. Biology, on the other hand, seeks to discover the essence of life itself.

As *substance*, nature is a thing, indeed a fantasy 'thingy', palpable, squishy, and self-generating—it *is* life, one might say. Substantialism usually underpins reactionary, nostalgic, or conservative forms of Romanticism. And yet essentialism has often proved lacking, an empty set, an oppressive blankness. This blankness is reproduced in the very postmodern criticism that pretends to deconstruct Enlightenment thinking. The trouble with this sort of criticism is not that it ignores the substantial realities of nature, as if what postmodernists need is a night out in a thunderstorm in Kansas. Some contend that Mother Nature herself should punish postmodernists with the tornado from *The Wizard of Oz*.

The real problem is not the debate between postmodernism and ecocriticism, which sounds like two sides of the same warped record. The trouble is that as intoxicants go, clichéd post-structuralist relativism, even chic nihilism, is no match for something more religious: it is indeed religion's inverted form. Believing in nothing, while strictly untenable, is still a form of belief. Both sides miss seeing that it is not so much technology and language that are the issue, as oppression and suffering. Both bypass earthly conditions: one by cancelling it, the other by preserving the mere idea of it, in however compelling and squidgy a shape.

Instead of serving up lashings of guilt and redemption, might ecological criticism not engage the ideological forms of the environment, from capitalist imagery to the very ecocriticism that partly opposes capitalism? Such 'ecocritique' would serve the establishment of collective kinds of identity that included other species and their worlds, real *and* possible. It would subvert those fixating images of 'world' that inhibit humans from grasping their place in an already historical nature. Subverting fixation is the radical goal of the Romantic wish to explore the shadow lands. The hesitations of a Wordsworth, the unreliable narrators of a Mary Shelley—the whole panoply of irony and linguistic play is not marginal, but central to Romanticism.

The environment was born at exactly the moment at which it became a problem. The word 'environment' still haunts us, because in a society that took care of its surroundings in a more comprehensive sense, our idea of environment would have withered away—hence 'environmentalism'. Society would be so involved in taking care of 'it' that it would no longer be a case of some 'thing' that surrounds us, that environs us, and differs from us. Indeed, humans may return the idea of the 'thing' to its older sense of 'meeting place'. In a society that fully acknowledged that we were always and already involved in our world, there would be no need to point it out.

FURTHER READING

Adams, Carol J., *The Sexual Politics of Meat: A Feminist-Vegetarian Critical Theory* (Cambridge: Polity Press, 1990). Adams links together feminism and vegetarianism in a ground-breaking study of Romantic-period writers such as Mary Shelley and Joseph Ritson.

Beck, Ulrich, *Risk Society: Towards a New Modernity*, trans. Mark Ritter (London: Sage, 1992). Beck shows how the modern age democratizes risk by spreading unintended consequences, such as ecological risk, wider and wider.

Callicott, J. Baird, and Nelson, Michael P., *The Great New Wilderness Debate* (Athens Ga., and London: University of Georgia Press, 1998). This collection of essays is a wide-ranging rethink of the idea of wilderness so crucial to Romantic cults of nature.

Davis, Mike, *Late Victorian Holocausts: El Niño Famines and the Making of the Third World* (London and New York: Verso, 2001). Davis analyses the ways in which British imperialism shaped the earth's ecosystems in the nineteenth century, resulting in tremendous suffering.

Ferry, Luc, *The New Ecological Order*, trans. Carol Volk (Chicago: University of Chicago Press, 1995). While his book does not acknowledge all the strengths of environmentalism, it does explore very significant strands of Romanticism in contemporary ecology, and especially their political implications.

Levinson, Marjorie, 'Pre- and Post-Dialectical Materialisms: Modeling Praxis without Subjects and Objects', *Cultural Critique* (Fall 1995), 111–20. Levinson's essay is hard reading, but it is an excellent polemical introduction to ideas in radical ecological philosophy.

Lovelock, James E., *Gaia: A New Look at Life on Earth* (Oxford and New York: Oxford University Press, 1979; repr. 1987). This classic text suggests that we consider the function of the earth's ecosystems holistically.

Plumwood, Val, *Environmental Culture: The Ecological Crisis of Reason* (London and New York: Routledge, 2002). Plumwood investigates new ways of doing philosophy influenced by ecological thought.

Shiva, Vandana, *Biopiracy: The Plunder of Nature and Knowledge* (Boston: South End Press, 1997). Shiva critiques the recent ways in which corporations have engaged in a colonization of living beings in the search for new medicines, potentially profitable genomes, and so on.

Thomas, Keith, *Man and the Natural World: Changing Attitudes in England 1500–1800* (London: Allen Lane, 1983; repr. Penguin, 1984). In this seminal text, Thomas explores how ecological ways of looking at plants and animals arose over a span of 300 years; there is a significant chapter on vegetarianism and animal rights.

NOTES

1. Mary Wollstonecraft Shelley, *Frankenstein; or, the Modern Prometheus: The 1818 Text*, ed. James Rieger (Chicago and London: University of Chicago Press, 1974, 1982), p. 142.

2. Neil McKendrick, John Brewer, and J. H. Plumb, *The Birth of a Consumer Society: The Commercialization of Eighteenth-Century England* (Bloomington, Ind.: Indiana University Press, 1982).

3. Georg Wilhelm Friedrich Hegel, *Hegel's Phenomenology of Spirit*, trans. A. V Miller, analysis and foreword by J. N. Findlay (Oxford: Oxford University Press, 1977), pp. 383–409.

4. Karl Marx, *Selected Writings*, ed. David McLellan (Oxford and New York: Oxford University Press, 1977), p. 8.

46 | Romanticism in the electronic age

David S. Miall

The computer has a place in the Romantic period. Byron's daughter Ada was born in December 1815, a few months before Byron left England following the breakdown of his marriage. She grew up to become a competent mathematician, and worked with Charles Babbage on programmes for his Calculating Engines, generally considered the prototype of the modern computer (although they were not built in Ada's lifetime—she died in 1852).

In the wider perspective we can also see that the Romantic ethos has permeated the electronic realm. Concepts of unity, community, fragmentation, and dispersal that structure discourse about computing, what it has or will make possible, come down to us from the Romantic period. As Richard Coyne showed in his book *Technoromanticism* (1999), the power of the computer has made it seem the agent of a new sensibility, one in which 'the physical is transcended by information, providing opportunities for participation in a unity beyond the multiplicity and individuation of the material realm'.[1] Perhaps the experience of Romantic transcendence, whether through hypertext, virtual reality, or artificial intelligence, will one day be represented in cyberspace.

These two visions, that of Ada the programmer and the promise of cyberspace, mark the two ends of a continuum along which we can locate the achievements of electronic Romanticism. At the technical end we can find studies in text analysis, based on mathematical models of textual meaning. At the other end lie experiments in hypertext, imaginative responses to the themes of a Romantic writer: so far Shelley Jackson's hypertext novel *Patchwork Girl* (1995) has been the most striking example, developing the abortive female monster of Mary Shelley's *Frankenstein* into a fully realized, if bizarre, creature who lives for 175 years. In between lie several other significant applications, in particular the creation of electronic editions of Romantic writers that exploit the expressive or representational power of the computer.

The two ends of the continuum are thus very different, suggesting that the first challenge faced by those employing the computer is to assess what kinds of thinking it makes possible. This has been a source of contention. Theorists such as George Landow assert that in its hypertext mode the computer models the functioning of language and thought, being associationist and decentring; on the other hand critics of this approach argue that hypertext trivializes or reifies thought. In text analysis we count the patterns and distribution of words, usually aiming for a better understanding of the formal characteristics of a text. But in separating words to count them do we not eliminate the power of the text as a literary work? This is one way of pointing to the limitations of the computer as a tool for literary study, a tool that is not yet ready to replace the printed book, although it can supplement it in a number of important ways. Because the computer has computational powers, has vast storage capacity, is interactive, and can be adapted to the personal needs of its user, we have expected much from it, perhaps prematurely. But the development of more adequate resources and more powerful programs for Romantic study undoubtedly lie in the future.

In the following sections I offer a critical review of the main computer-related work in Romanticism. This will necessarily be highly selective. A more comprehensive listing of resources and references will be found on the websites listed at the end of this chapter.

Text analysis

The study of words and their distributions is the oldest literary application of the computer, dating back to the 1940s. It has been employed to study distinctive features of an author's style, to decide the authorship of disputed texts, and to examine the formal structures of a text. It has made little headway with scholars in the mainstream of the literary discipline, being confined to the specialist prepared to invest time in preparing electronic texts and learning how to use (or write) the required programs. This remains true in the example studies I will mention in a moment, but the advent of new programs for text analysis, including one Internet-based program, and the availability of numerous Romantic texts in electronic form, may begin to open text analysis to wider use.

The first three studies I will mention focus on Jane Austen's novels. The questions raised by text analysis methods can be illustrated by this short passage from *Emma*. About a third of the way through the novel, during a visit to her house by Emma and Harriet Smith, Miss Bates says:

Mrs Cole was so kind as to sit some time with us, talking of Jane; for as soon as she came in, she began inquiring after her, Jane is so very great a favourite there. Whenever she is with us, Mrs Cole does not know how to shew her kindness enough; and I must say that Jane deserves it as much as any body can.[2]

Miss Bates, we have been told earlier, 'loved every body, was interested in every body's happiness'.[3] Her vocabulary here is typical: her generosity to Mrs Cole and to her niece Jane Fairfax is shown by such words as 'favourite', 'kindness', and 'deserves'. But Miss Bates's words of goodwill are heard with an ironic ambience. This is due not only to the situation (Emma's dislike at having to listen to Jane's letters) but to the connotations of a word such as 'deserves'. For example, in the first chapter Emma remarks of Mr Elton: 'I must look about for a wife for him. There is nobody in High-bury who deserves him.'[4] A little later we hear Emma deciding that Harriet Smith 'must . . . deserve encouragement'.[5] The subtle moral conceptions (and misconceptions) of what is deserved resound through Austen's novel, making Miss Bates's evaluation of Jane Fairfax when we meet it very questionable. Text analysis shows us that the word and its variants (deserves, deserved, deserving) occurs 43 times (0.027 per cent of the 160,498 words in *Emma*). It appears to be one of Austen's more distinctive words, as we can see by comparing its frequency with some other novels: in Dickens's *Dombey and Son* (359,031 words in length) it occurs only 27 times (0.008 per cent); and in Emily Bronte's *Wuthering Heights* (117,276 words) it occurs 15 times (0.013 per cent).

One of the first comparative studies of this kind with Jane Austen's texts was that by Karl Kroeber, published in 1969. He studied small groups of key words in the novels and compared their frequencies with several other nineteenth-century novels. For instance, he showed that in comparison with George Eliot, Austen used a smaller pool of abstract nouns (such as 'love', 'manners', 'sensibility'), but used them more often, and in connection with social events and interactions; in contrast, Eliot's abstract nouns pointed more often to the examination of states of consciousness.[6]

The occurrences of a word or group of words can be studied with the help of a concordance programme (for readily obtainable programmes see *Concordance* or *WordSmith*; for an Internet program, see *HyperPo*). A concordance will list each occurrence of a given word in a text, usually with a few words of context on each side. It is thus useful for analysing the manner in which the word is used. It also enables the reader to see where a given word is distributed across a text. In *Emma* it is worth noting the uneven distribution of the 'deserve' group of words: half occur in the last quarter of the novel where the moral conflicts of the plot are finally worked out; every main character, so to speak, gets what they deserve. A concordance can also help analyse the environment within which a word occurs, that is, the co-occurring words, or all those words occurring within a span of up to (say) five words before the key word and five after. It will sometimes be found that an author's style is distinctive in this respect, that particular words will be associated more frequently than in the work of comparable authors.

Many other kinds of analysis and comparison are possible on the basis of word frequencies. One of the most detailed and elaborate studies, also based on Austen's work, is that of J. F. Burrows (1987). He examines the most common, frequently occurring words—prepositions, pronouns, modal verbs (would, must, may)—and their roles in developing the characters in Austen's novels. We behave as critics, says Burrows, as though these words, making up from two-fifths to a half of the text of a novel, were not really there. In fact they make up the thirty or so commonest words not only in Austen's but in any fiction text. Burrows is able to show that in Austen's work the frequency of a word such as 'the' or 'we' varies considerably from one character to another: such common words can thus be used to identify differences in the idiolects of characters (i.e. their particular speech patterns), and to trace shifts in idiolect over the course of a novel.

For example, he shows that in *Emma*, use of the first-person singular and plural markedly distinguishes Miss Bates's dialogue. She uses the plural forms far more than other characters (especially 'us'), and the singular forms far less (as the short passage cited earlier shows). Burrows explains that 'The difference appears to arise from idioms that tend to objectify the family group for which she customarily speaks and tend to acknowledge a certain passivity or submissiveness as part of its inevitable role'.[7] Burrows develops his thesis primarily by describing the different statistical methods that were used in examining the Austen novels and comparing these novels with several others. The reader thus needs a rather strong interest in Burrow's statistical method to appreciate how the findings were reached, but there are numerous felicitous discussions of Austen as a result.

A third study involving Austen by Mary DeForest and Eric Johnson (2001) is based on identifying words originating in Latin or German sources. The use of Latinate vocabulary tends to typify characters of higher class, education, and intellect. In contrast, Germanic words tend to typify a popular dialect, those who work closer to the soil. Their study enabled them to show the proportions of Latinate words in the dialogue of individual characters. In the quotation from Miss Bates above, for example, three Latinate words occur: 'inquiring', 'favourite', and 'deserve'.

The proportion of Latinate words indicates the status of a given character. Darcy, in the opening scenes of *Pride and Prejudice*, 'barricades himself behind a wall of Latinate diction'; however, by the end of the novel the proportion has dropped by over 9 per cent, corresponding with the amendment of his behaviour towards Elizabeth.[8] Latinate words also tend to characterize the insincere characters: Frank Churchill in *Emma*, Mary Crawford in *Mansfield Park*, Mr Elliot in *Persuasion*.[9] The overall score for Latinate diction in Miss Bates's speeches is about ten percentage points below the average for Austen's novels overall. Alongside Burrow's work, this approach makes clear how individually distinctive Austen's characters are, and how firmly located in their contemporary social and class contexts. Other text analysis studies with Romantic authors include those of Nancy Ide with Blake (1989) and Thomas Rommel with Byron (1994).[10]

Digital editions

Electronic versions of Romantic texts are now widely available over the Internet. Texts can be downloaded freely from several repositories, and guides to which texts are currently available can be found on *The Voice of the Shuttle*, or the *Internet Public Library*. The copy of *Emma* I have, for example, was provided by Project Gutenberg. This is a plain copy of the text, the only coding being the underscore mark to indicate words in italics. Texts from other sources may be encoded: that is, special marks are placed within the text to indicate such structural and formal details as poem titles, chapters, stanzas, the use of italics, and the like. I briefly describe encoding practices and their implications later in this chapter.

Many Romantic texts have been 'repurposed' to be read on the computer, but in this respect we find an interesting reconfiguration of the traditional Romantic canon. The area that has developed most actively has been the recovery and electronic publication of lesser-known or forgotten texts, especially by women writers. Such texts have long been available outside copyright. In contrast, texts by authors such as Wordsworth or Byron have been republished in book form in edited, copyrighted editions, which excludes them from the electronic domain. Where electronic copies of the canonical writers exist they are usually based on out of copyright editions—a collected Wordsworth on the Internet, for example, is based on an edition of 1888. There are a few exceptions: Graver and Tetreault's multiple-version edition of *Lyrical Ballads* that I describe below is one. This situation thus, ironically, privileges the lesser-known writers and has undoubtedly been a catalyst in restoring them to the attention of readers and scholars. The Women Writers Project at Brown University, for example, now offers electronic copies of a wide range of women writers from the Romantic period.

The hypertext environment of the Internet provides a much less constrained context for presenting a text than does a printed book. Several editors have taken advantage of this in significant ways, providing ancillary texts, variant versions, or graphical materials. In the remainder of this section I describe three such editions: Vargo and Muri's *Barbauld*, Graver and Tetreault's *Lyrical Ballads*, and *The Blake Archive*.

In writing about her work Lisa Vargo points to the virtues of the web in recovering the work of Anna Laetitia Barbauld. Although one of the most widely read poets of her period, she was displaced later in the nineteenth century as the canon of male Romantic poets came into place and virtually disappeared; thus there has been no continuous tradition of reading Barbauld as there has been for writers such as Wordsworth or Keats. The web can help to create a sense of Barbauld's original context: 'The hypertext links we have assembled invite readers to navigate through a series of documents so as to work from a sense of reading the poems when they were [first] produced.' This includes not only high quality facsimile images of each page from Barbauld's first editions, but much other contemporary material and commentary. For example, the short poem 'On a Lady's Writing' in the Romantic Circles edition of *Poems* (1793), brings together images and texts in a hypertext environment: this, says Vargo, 'is meant not only as a teaching tool, but as a model for hypertextual editing'.[11]

Another notable electronic edition is the *Lyrical Ballads* of Bruce Graver and Ronald Tetreault, published (again) on Romantic Circles, but also bearing the imprint of Cambridge University Press. First published in 1798 jointly by Wordsworth and Coleridge, *Lyrical Ballads* went through three further editions with significant changes in 1800, 1802, and 1805, before the poems were repossessed for later publications by each poet separately. The electronic edition is designed to provide access to all four editions and to enable the revisions to the poems to be examined. Unlike a print edition, where the variants would be relegated to footnotes, the complete text of each edition is available, with the text of all four versions of a poem each visible in its own window. A key to the variants is provided in another window at the left of the screen. This 'variant map', as Tetreault calls it, 'is an abstraction of the poem which does not privilege one version of the text over another and that piques the reader's curiosity by means of gaps in the text to pursue the significance of revisions made in successive versions'.[12] Unlike the use of footnotes, this design facilitates reading rather than interrupting it. More important, it does not privilege one version of *Lyrical Ballads* over another, as a print edition is obliged to do.

The third notable digital edition I will mention here is oriented towards presenting graphics. *The Blake Archive* is a remarkable, ground-breaking endeavour designed to present copies of Blake's illuminated works, as well as a number of other non-illuminated texts. It also makes Blake's texts available (based on a transcript of the text on each page). Examination of a particular text, such as *The Book of Thel*, is focused on a facsimile of the original page of the book. The reader first selects an edition to examine—in the case of *Thel*, four copies are available. Each page can be examined in turn. Images are shown on the computer screen at a resolution matching the original by invoking the Calibration Applet. At the same time as viewing a page, the reader can request a textual transcription (this is one of the Text & Image Options available from a drop down menu on the lower left of the screen); since Blake's own script is small and sometimes difficult to read directly, this is a useful supplement. As there are four different copies of *Thel*, the reader can also call up two or more images of the same page side by side by clicking on Compare, then choosing which editions to examine. The images are often surprisingly different, calling into question any single-edition copy of Blake's work available in print. For students who are developing their understanding of Blake's graphics, the Image Descriptions are often very valuable, and in themselves an important work of scholarship: these explain what appears to be happening in an image, and relates it to the text of the poem. For studying Blake's graphical achievements, this Internet-based edition supersedes any paper-based edition. A helpful recent account of the archive and its principles is provided by Morris Eaves and his colleagues.

Among non-Internet editions of Romantic writing, the most comprehensive is *Romanticism: The CD-ROM*, edited by David Miall and Duncan Wu (1997), distributed with the second edition of Wu's *Romanticism: An Anthology*. This includes numerous non-canonical texts relating to history, science, travel, Gothic fiction, etc., and an extensive archive of prints and paintings from the period. At the time of writing, it seems possible that this will be replaced by an edition reformatted for web browsing.

Text encoding

Each of the digital editions I discussed in the previous section is based on text encoded in SGML (Standardized General Markup Language) or its derivatives (TEI and XML). Unlike the HTML code that supports hypertext on the Internet, which is designed primarily for presentation and formatting, SGML allows a text's structure to be captured and represented. Moreover, the great advantage of SGML is its independence of any particular program or computing system. As its proponents have argued, a text coded in SGML should in principle be extremely long lasting, accessible to all future programs that recognize SGML.

SGML and its derivatives are based on an hierarchical model of a text: thus, within a book we find chapters, within which we find paragraphs, within which we find sentences. While this model of text has been taken as exemplary by some scholars (e.g. Allen Renear), others (e.g. Jerome McGann) have pointed out that the meaning of literary texts is more diverse and ambivalent than current text encoding standards can accommodate. While it is so far the best technology we have for presenting texts on the computer (especially as it is machine and programme independent), it cannot yet be made to serve the interpretive functions that we depend on as readers. McGann suggests that non-hierarchial mark-up models will eventually come to dominate, since literary texts so often present features that overlap, cutting across hierarchical structures.[13] In addition, while SGML can indicate links to other media, such as images or sound files, it provides as yet no tools for encoding them as it does for text.

In practical terms, while students of Romanticism will encounter SGML-encoded texts on the Internet, at the moment software for exploiting the power of the coding is hard to obtain, unless built into an application such as *The Blake Archive*. But this is likely to change in the near future: *The Orlando Project*, for example, will soon make available over the web its richly encoded text and database of information on British women writers, including many from the Romantic period. Other SGML-based applications are also in prospect.

Romanticism on the Internet

A wide array of Romantic texts and secondary materials is now available over the Internet. As with all Internet sources, students must know how to evaluate them: before using a web site for study it should be examined for reliability (whether it originates from an authoritative scholarly source, such as a library or university), and whether it is current (up to date, not superseded by other, later research). These decisions may not always be easy to make: even when a university hosts the site, material posted may reflect enthusiasm rather than accurate research. Where possible, quotations or factual materials should be cross-referenced against other sources. In the following paragraphs I mention several notable sources; even these, however, as I will mention, are not without error.

Romantic Circles is currently the most elaborate set of resources on the web. It provides editions of several primary texts edited to a high standard, collections of scholarly essays on specific topics, information on Romantic publications (monographs, anthologies), and materials for high school students. The resources are invariably well designed and highly reliable. Apart from *The Blake Archive*, it is perhaps the best place to see the expressive powers of the web in presenting Romantic materials. In the High School project participating schools make use of the resources in the design of English courses on early nineteenth-century literature, and students participate in online discussions with Romantic scholars through a live discussion facility.

The Romanticism Chronology, hosted by the University of California at Santa Barbara, provides a detailed, year-by-year outline of events, publications, and people. Well-designed and easy to use, it draws on a database of information that is formatted for the screen whenever the user makes a request. It can be searched like a database, with word combinations in different fields. A simple search can often provide a wealth of helpful information: for example, searching on 'Coleridge' brings up 53 entries. Read in sequence these provide a helpful overview of Coleridge's life and main publications, although (oddly) omitting to provide his date of birth.

For each entry, a Details link on the left does not, as one might expect, provide further detail of the event, but more general information; for writers, a list of references to primary and secondary texts is shown, with links to Internet resources for the writer, thus the Chronology can often provide a useful departure point for further research. Not all Details provide further information, and there are occasional errors: Maturin's *Bertram* (1816) is a play, not a novel. The Chronology can also be organized by Topic, although this is somewhat uneven in scope and requires further development. For example, while 'Abolition' is richly furnished with 75 entries, 'Gothic' is limited to 11, all entries being titles of Gothic novels from Walpole (1765) to Peacock (1831). Some of the key novels in the genre are missing, such as Radcliffe's *The Mysteries of Udolpho* (1794). Entries can occasionally be misleading: against June 1816 Byron's movements are described: 'after touring the Alps and visiting the Chateau de Chillon with Percy Shelley, Byron leaves for Italy at the end of the year.' The visit to Chillon occurred during a tour of Lake Geneva with Shelley, 22–30 June; the tour of the Alps occurred after Shelley had left for England, 17–29 September. Users of the Chronology should thus treat it with caution, but as the major searchable database for Romanticism it is often very helpful; and nothing similar to it is available elsewhere.

Women of the Romantic Period is based on *The Unsex'd Females* by Richard Polwhele. A poem of 206 lines published in 1798, it consists mainly of hostile references to contemporary women writers. But the editors have designed the website in order to foreground the women writers derided by Polwhele and provide some information about them: this includes short biographical entries and online references to their writing, where this is available. The reader can thus consider Polwhele's criticism in the light of each woman's actual achievement. The site is, of course, limited to considering only those writers mentioned by Polwhele.

A major source for critical work on the Romantic period is the online journal *Romanticism on the Net*. Since its inception in 1996 it has become a vehicle for publication by many leading Romantic scholars; it also includes valuable full-length book reviews in each issue.

Students will find many other Romantic resources on the Internet. *The Voice of the Shuttle* provides a generally reliable and up-to-date index of what is available (the *Shuttle* is itself the brainchild of a well-known Romantic scholar, Alan Liu). The web has played a major role in opening up the traditional canon of Romantic writing to work by other writers. At a conference session on the issue in 1996 entitled *The Canon and the Web*, the organizers noted that the web is

a medium that at least in principle does away with space limitations, rethinks the logic of the 'page' (the result of a centuries old negotiation between textual, visual, and oral media with their affiliated population groups), diminishes the role of capitalized middlemen (editors and publishers), has no permanence, and resists hierarchical structure.

Romantic scholars have been at the forefront in envisioning how the Internet can serve our discipline and in providing innovative resources. The present moment is thus a particularly interesting time, with new materials appearing online, and new configurations of Romantic topics and historical contexts that can only be realized in the electronic medium. The Internet with its hypertextual links is particularly suitable for representing the richly intertextual environment in which Romantic writers worked, as the *Romanticism Chronology*, for example, demonstrates. Whatever it becomes, it is clear that the advent of the Internet has already had a major impact in changing understandings of Romanticism.

Learning how

Many resources are now available over the Internet for students wishing to do more than use the Internet to read. For work in text analysis, *HyperPo* can be used freely over the Internet with a text on either the user's own computer or the Internet (noting that the programme is still under development, and is not yet entirely reliable). The *Concordance* programme can be downloaded and used free for a trial period. By using the Help facility a student can quickly learn how to prepare a text and create a concordance. For an overview of research on text analysis Susan Hockey's book *Electronic Texts in the Humanities* (2000) provides a rich source of examples and ideas.

An increasing number of teachers and students of Romanticism are now making use of the Internet to reshape the classroom. While it has become common for the syllabus and some reading materials to be placed on an Internet course site, students can also be asked to post their essays or other written work on the web, making it available not only to their fellow students but to anyone else who cares to read it. For web authoring many products are now available; at the time of writing *Dreamweaver* offers a powerful and readily learned tool (it can also be downloaded and used free for a limited period). Assessed work may take more varied forms than the conventional essay: students might provide an annotated edition of a Romantic text, or a hypertext collection of texts and images around a historical topic, perhaps working in a small group rather than individually. A suggestive account is provided by Joel Haefner, who lists a number of possible approaches to a hypertext edition of Charlotte Smith's poem 'Beachy Head'. Students' work can also, of course, be maintained on the web after a particular course is over, and even added to by later students. Miall and Wu's *Romanticism: The CD-ROM* contains a separate section with advice and suggestions for carrying out projects on Romantic topics.

On the horizon lie better tools and environments for the study of literary and other texts. The organizing concept on the Internet will be the portal, a gateway offering a range of texts, programmable procedures, and outputs that users will be able to personalize to facilitate their specific interests (for an example description see *TAPoR*). While there seems no immediate likelihood that the medium of the book will soon disappear, or that we will be able to work without library collections, the Internet portal will in time provide a conducive environment for much basic study of Romantic texts and the production of multimedia essays or resources. Students interested in monitoring these possibilities and studying current applications will find a list of links on the webpage accompanying this chapter.

FURTHER READING

Burrows, J. F., *Computation into Criticism: A Study of Jane Austen's Novels and an Experiment in Method* (Oxford: Clarendon Press, 1987). A landmark study in computer-based analysis of a Romantic author; with its heavy focus on statistical method this is not an introductory text, but it still offers many accessible insights for readers of Austen.

DeForest, Mary, and Johnson, Eric, 'The Density of Latinate Words in the Speeches of Jane Austen's Characters', *Literary and Linguistic Computing*, 16 (2001), 389–401. Some interesting discriminations between Austen's characters emerge from considering the different rates at which they use words of Latin origin.

Haefner, Joel, ' "In Tangled Mazes Wrought": Hypertext and Teaching Romantic Women Poets', in Stephen C. Behrendt and Harriet Kramer Linkin (eds.), *Approaches to Teaching British Women Poets of the Romantic Period* (New York: Modern Language Association of America, 1997), pp. 45–50. To focus study, Haefner shows how a complex hypertext project based on one poem can be carried out by groups of students.

Hockey, Susan, *Electronic Texts in the Humanities: Principles and Practice* (Oxford: Oxford University Press, 2000). One of the first scholars to develop text analysis methods and programs, Hockey here provides a critical survey of the field and an overview of the main methods of analysis.

Landow, George, and Delany, Paul (eds) *The Digital Word: Text-Based Computing in the Humanities* (Cambridge, Mass. MIT Press, 1993). A collection of essays on literary texts and the computer by leading scholars in the field; now a little dated, but still a good overview of some of the major issues.

McGann, Jerome, *Radiant Textuality: Literature After the World Wide Web* (New York: Palgrave, 2001). In this seminal collection of essays McGann reflects on the implications of the electronic environment for presenting, elaborating, and studying literary texts and graphic images, and describes his experience of creating the hypertext Rossetti archive.

Miall, David S., 'The Library versus the Internet: Literary Studies Under Siege?', *PMLA* 116 (2001), 1405–14. An account of the pressures faced by publishers and libraries to produce digital editions and journals, and the implications of this change for readers and students of literature.

Tetreault, Ronald, 'New Models for Electronic Publishing', *Literary and Linguistic Computing*, 16 (2001), 189–98. An account of publishing a literary edition on the Internet (Wordsworth's *Lyrical Ballads*) by one of the pioneers in this field.

WEB LINKS

Blake Archive, ed. Morris Eaves, Robert Essick, and Joseph Viscomi.

http://www.blakearchive.org/

Provides copies of multiple editions of Blake's illustrated books, including transcriptions of the text and annotations of images.

British Women Romantic Poets, 1789–1832. Shields Library, University of California, Davis.

http:dRwww.lib.ucdavis.edu/English/BWRP/index.htm

About fifty books of poetry are available, many never published since the Romantic period; texts are encoded by SGML but can also be read onscreen in HTML format.

Canon and the Web: Reconfiguring Romanticism in the Information Age (A Special Session, Modern Language Association Convention, December 1996).

http://www.english.ucsb.edu/faculty/ayliu/research/canonweb.html

Discussions of the way electronic resources are challenging and changing the Romantic canon and how this is impacting on teaching and research. The site includes both the original papers and a guide to relevant resources, such as course syllabi.

Concordance. R. J. C. Watt, University of Dundee.

http://www.dundee.ac.uk/english/wics/wics.htm

A Windows-based program for text analysis, enabling distributions of words and collocations of words to be studied; the program is available for download, and is best used with a lightly encoded electronic text.

Dreamweaver MX. Macromedia.

http:dRwww.macromedia.com/software/dreamweaver/

One of the standard programs for authoring web pages; easy to start using to create a basic page with a few graphics or a table (the tutorial should be avoided at first).

HyperPo. Stéfan Sinclair, University of Alberta.

http://huco.ualberta.ca/HyperPo/

An Internet-based text analysis program, still in development (watch out for hang-ups and bugs); can be used with any text whether on the Internet or on one's local hard drive.

Internet Public Library.

http://www.ipl.org/

Provides an extensive listing of links to online electronic texts, including Romantic writers (see Books under Reading Room).

Literary Resources—Romantic, ed. Jack Lynch.

http://andromeda.rutgers.edu/~jlynch/Lit/romantic.html

A comprehensive and up-to-date listing of Romantic resources on the Internet, including general sites and sites listed by author from Austen to Wordsworth.

Lyrical Ballads, ed. Ronald Tetreault and Bruce Graver. Romantic Circles and Cambridge University Press.

http://www.rc.umd.edu/editions/LB/

An important scholarly edition of *Lyrical Ballads*, providing an Internet facility for studying the four main editions of the book. All versions of a given poem can be viewed simultaneously.

Poems (1793) by Anna Laetitia Aikin, A Hypertext Edition, ed. Lisa Vargo and Allison Muri. Romantic Circles.

http://www.rc.umd.edu/editions/contemps/barbauld/poems1773/

An Internet edition that provides both facscimiles of each page and a transcription; includes some notes, annotations, and additional links.

Project Gutenberg.

http://promo.net/pg/

The project started in 1971 with the aim of providing plain (not encoded) electronic versions of important texts. The archive currently contains over 6,000 titles, including files for a number of Romantic writings that can be downloaded free.

Romantic Circles, ed. Neil Fraistat, Steven E. Jones, and Carl Stahmer.

http://www.rc.umd.edu/

Resources primarily for the study of the later Romantic writers edited to a high standard: includes several digital editions, collections of essays on significant topics, notices of recent publications, and a facility for high school study of Romantic literature.

Romanticism Chronology.

http://english.ucsb.edu:591/rchrono/

A rich if slightly erratic guide to people, events, and movements from the pre-Romantic period up to 1851. Especially helpful for studying the historical context of Romantic writing.

Romanticism On the Net.

http://www.ron.umontreal.ca/

The standard electronic journal for Romantic scholarship, published online (and only online) since 1996; includes both full-length original articles and reviews and organized sets of links to Internet resources.

Romanticism: The CD-ROM, ed. David S. Miall and Duncan Wu.

http://www.ualberta.ca/~dmiall/romcdinf.htm

Currently published with Duncan Wu's *Romanticism: An Anthology* (Oxford: Blackwell 1997), it provides an extensive collection of additional texts from the Romantic period in history, education, travel, the Gothic, etc., and a large archive of prints and photographs.

Rossetti, Dante Gabriel: The Complete Writings and Pictures.

http://www.iath.virginia.edu/rossetti/index.html

While Rossetti is not a Romantic writer, this site provides a significant example of the use of the Internet to represent the text and graphic work of a major author.

TAPoR. University of Alberta.

http://huco.ualberta.ca/Tapor/

The introductory website for a major Canadian project that will provide materials and programmes for working with electronic text on the Internet.

Voice of the Shuttle: Romantics.

http://vos.ucsb.edu/browse.asp?id=2750

A comprehensive and usually up-to-date listing of resources for Romanticism on the Internet.

Women of the Romantic Period.

http://www.cwrl.utexas.edu/~worp/

Based on a full transcription of Richard Polwhele's poem *The Unsex'd Females* (1798), the edition provides information about the women writers criticized by Polwhele.

Wordsmith. Mike Smith, University of Liverpool.

http://www.lexically.net/wordsmith/

A Windows-based program for text analysis, including word frequencies, collocations and clusters, and some descriptive statistics; the program can be downloaded for free in a slightly crippled version from the website.

NOTES

1. Richard Coyne, *Technoromanticism: Digital Narrative, Holism, and the Romance of the Real* (Cambridge, Mass: MIT Press, 1999), p. 47.
2. Jane Austen, *Emma* (Oxford: Oxford University Press, 1990), p. 139.
3. Ibid. 18.
4. Ibid. 1.
5. Ibid. 20.
6. Karl Kroeber, 'Perils of Quantification. The Exemplary Case of Jane Austen's *Emma*', in Lubomir Dolozel and Richard Bailey (eds.), *Statistics and Style* (New York: American Elsevier, 1969), pp. 197–213: 201.
7. J. F. Burrows, *Computation into Criticism: A Study of Jane Austen's Novels and an Experiment in Method* (Oxford: Clarendon Press, 1987), 31.
8. Mary DeForest and Eric Johnson, 'The Density of Latinate Words in the Speeches of Jane Austen's Characters', *Literary and Linguistic Computing*, 16 (2001), 389–401: 393.
9. Ibid. 394.
10. Nancy Ide, 'Meaning and Method: Computer-Assisted Analysis of Blake', in Rosanne G. Potter (ed.), *Literary Computing and Literary Criticism: Theoretical and Practical Essays on Theme and Rhetoric* (Philadelphia: University of Pennsylvania Press, 1989), pp. 123–41; Thomas Rommel, ' "So soft, so sweet, so delicately clear": A Computer-assisted Analysis of Accumulated Words and Phrases in Lord Byron's Epic Poem *Don Juan*', *Literary and Linguistic Computing*, 9 (1994), 7–12.
11. Lisa Vargo, 'The Anna Letitia Barbauld Web Page: 1773 meets 2000', *Romanticism on the Net*, 19 (Aug. 2000) at http://www.erudit.org/revue/ron/2000/v/n19/005940ar.html
12. Ronald Tetrault and Bruce Graver (eds.), *Lyrical Ballads*. Romantic Circles and Cambridge University Press at http://www.rc.umd.edu/editions/LB/
13. Jerome J. McGann, 'Prologue: Compu[e]ting Editorial Fu[ea]tures', in Elizabeth Bergmann Loizeaux and Neil Fraistat (eds.), *Reimagining Textuality: Textual Studies in the Late Age of Print* (Madison: University of Wisconsin Press, 2002), pp. 17–27: 21–2.

Index

Note: Page numbers in *italics* refer to illustrations.

Hemans, Felicia (*cont'd.*)
  Siege of Valencia, The 187
  Welsh Melodies 115
Hemmings, David 638
Henley, Samuel 142
Herbert, George 294
Herd, David 115
Herder, J. G. 40, 680
heroism 63, 643–4
Herschel, Caroline 688, 691
Herschel, William 44, 98, 686, 688, 691, 692
Hicks, William 633
Hill, Julia Butterfly 702
Hindu culture 141–2
historical context 15–26
historical criticism 38, 39–41
'historical' novel 385, 463
historicism 10, 165–81, 575
Hitler, Adolf 680, 701
Hobhouse, John Cam 563
Hockey, Susan 716
Hodges, William 139
Hoffmann, E. T. A. 129, 130
Hofkosh, Sonia 238
Hogan, Charles Beecher 417
Hogg, James 118, 430, 431, 489
  Confessions of a Justified Sinner 58, 118, 226,
    374, 379–80, 620
Holcroft, Thomas 78, 86, 411, 441
Hölderlin, Friedrich 130
Holford, Margaret 192
holism 699
Holland, Tom 672
Home, John 121
Homer 35, 39, 40, 41, 333, 335, 468
homosexuality, in ancient Greece 43
Hone, William 81, 86, 392, 396–7
  Clerical Magistrate, The 396
  'Don John' or 'Don Juan' Unmasked 405
  Political House that Jack Built, The 72, 78–9, 80,
    397, 405
Hood, Thomas 431
Hook, James 73
Hope, Alexander Augustus *see* Hatfield, John
Hopkins, Gerard Manley 599
Horace 34
Horne, Richard Henry [or Hengist] 644
Horner, Francis 432
Hoyle, Fred 691, 692
Hubble, Edwin 692
Huggan, Graham 240
Hughes, Ted 612, 671–2
Hugo, Victor 131, 132, 153
Hulme, T. E. 172, 594, 598, 666, 669

humanitarianism 53, 241
Humboldt, Alexander von 151, 697
Hume, David 51–2, 103, 104, 108, 118, 339, 657
Hunt, Isaac 2
Hunt, John 81, 404, 428–9
Hunt, Leigh 3–4, 5, 6, 8, 9, 11, 35, 86, 263, 395,
    474, 538, 539, 543, 584
  autobiographical writings 445, 446
  and *The Examiner* 358, 428–9, 474, 478
  Italian influences 357–8, 362
  and Keats 307, 345, 478
  on pantomime 393, 394, 404
  and satire 33, 34
  'Nile, The' 302
  'On a Lock of Milton's Hair' 306–7
  'On the Realities of Imagination' 550–3
  Story of Rimini, The 275, 357–8, 362, 478
  Ultra-Crepidarius 33
Hunt, Marianne 72
Hunter, James 693
Hunter, John 91, 96, 97, 693
Hurd, Richard 35, 467, 468, 483
Hurley, Elizabeth 637, 651
Hutchinson, Mary 114, 535
Hutchinson, Sara 535
Hutton, James 91, 686, 688, 689–90
hybrid identities 250
hymns 28, 75
hysteria 223–4

I

I Remember Nelson (film) 634
I Was a Teenage Frankenstein (film) 650
Icke, David 703
Ide, Nancy 711
Idealist thought 156
identity politics 250
illustration 65–6, 73
imagination 600–3, 643, 669, 675, 676
  Coleridge's theory of 106–8, 264
  Leigh Hunt on 550–3
Imagism 598, 666, 668
Imlay, Gilbert 459
imperialism 22–3, 138–9, 140, 143, 237–8, 556,
    561, 565, 572, 657, 680–1, 699
impersonality 600, 654, 660, 663, 665, 666
imposters 521, 524–6, 528–36
Impressionism 70
Inchbald, Elizabeth 3, 184, 642, 651
India 22, 139, 140, 146
individualism 63, 448, 699
industrial revolution 24, 99, 207–8, 209
industrial society 697–701